Instructor's Edition

Organizational Behavior

Second Edition

Robert Kreitner
Angelo Kinicki

IRWIN
Homewood, IL 60430
Boston, MA 02116

© RICHARD D. IRWIN, INC., 1992

Senior editor: Karen Johnson
Developmental editor: Elizabeth Rubenstein
Project editor: Lynne Basler
Production manager: Bette K. Ittersagen

Typeface: 10/12 Times Roman
Printer: Von Hoffmann Press, Inc.

Library of Congress Cataloging-in-Publication Data

Kreitner, Robert.
    Organizational behavior / Robert Kreitner, Angelo Kinicki.—2nd
ed.
      p.   cm.
    Includes bibliographical references.
    ISBN 0–256–08500–5 ISBN 0–256–11283–5 (Instructor's Edition)
    1. Organizational behavior I. Kinicki, Angelo.   II. Title.
HD58.7.K75 1991
658.3—dc20   91–29586

TO THE INSTRUCTOR

The purpose of this *Instructor's Edition* is to minimize the amount of time that you will need to effectively teach this course while maximizing the amount of material from which you can teach. Thus, in addition to the questions and exercises that are interspersed throughout this text, we have provided you with a wealth of additional instructional resources. We sincerely hope that you will find this *Instructor's Edition* a valuable classroom aid.

For each chapter of the *Instructor's Edition* for ORGANIZATIONAL BEHAVIOR, second edition, the instructor will find the following items:

1. *Capsule Summary*. This summary gives you a brief review of what's contained in the chapter.

2. *Lecture Outline*. A listing of all A-heads and B-heads serves as a structure for key terms, key concepts, and other important points. Complete definitions of key terms are provided in the same order as they appear in the text.

3. *Opening Case Analysis*. All discussion questions in the "Back to the Opening Case" box following each chapter are answered. Of course, many of the questions have several legitimate answers, depending on one's interpretation of the facts and the frame of reference. Our answers are intended to be guidelines for your own interpretation.

4. *End-of-Chapter Answers*. Solutions, recommendations, and teaching tips are provided for each end-of-chapter exercise in the text.

5. *Instructional Resources*. In addition to directing you to the various instructional modules in the Muto *Lecture Supplement Manual* that accompanies this instructional material, other experimental exercises are cited.

6. *Topical Resources*. Worthwhile theoretical research or application books or articles not cited in the text (or published since the text went to press) are listed. In addition to providing you with updated sources for your lectures, these references can be used by your students for any individual or team projects you might assign.

7. *Discussion/Essay Questions*. Five thought-provoking questions are provided for use in class discussion or essay exams.

Gene E. Burton
California State University, Fresno

CONTENTS

1

Managing Organizational Behavior

CAPSULE SUMMARY

Chapter 1 demonstrates how managerial and organizational success is due largely to the skill with which people are managed. The authors review managerial roles and the motivation to manage. A brief historical review traces the evolution of organizational behavior (OB) through the prescientific, classical, behavioral, and modern eras, with emphasis given to the new contingency approach. The concept of OB is developed from a framework of theory, research, and practice, and a topical model is introduced as a map that guides the reader through the entire book.

LECTURE OUTLINE

The authors outline two key thrusts for the text:

  (1) a human resource development thrust that views employees as strategically valuable resources to be nurtured and developed; and
  (2) a managerial thrust that applies the knowledge of organizational behavior (OB) to the effective management of people.

A. **People: The Key to Managerial and Organizational Success**
  1. *People and Managerial Success*
    a. In the study of derailed managers, the most common problem was found to be "insensitivity to others."
    b. In their book, *In Search of Excellence*, Peters and Waterman found one of the excellent qualities of a firm to be "productivity through people."

B. **The Manager's Job: Getting Things Done Through Others**

> KEY TERM: *Management* is the process of working with and through others to achieve organizational objectives in an efficient manner.

  1. *What Do Managers Do?*
    a. A national survey of managers revealed seven basic managerial tasks:
      (1) managing individual performance
      (2) instructing subordinates
      (3) representing one's staff
      (4) managing group performance
      (5) planning and allocating resources
      (6) coordinating interdependent groups
      (7) monitoring the business environment.
  2. *Motivation to Manage*

> KEY TERM: *Motivation to manage* is a measurement of personal traits, using Miner's psychometric test, that predicts how far and how fast people move up the managerial ladder.

    a. Motivation to manage among U.S. college students is low but no longer declining. The historical gap between male and female business students has closed.

C. **The Field of Organizational Behavior: Past and Present**

> KEY TERM: *Organizational behavior*, commonly referred to as OB, is an interdisciplinary field dedicated to better understanding and managing people at work.

  1. *The Prescientific Era*
    a. The primary locus of work moved from farms to factories during the Industrial Revolution.
  2. *The Classical Era*
    a. This era was typified by two major thrusts:
      (1) administrative theory (Fayol's universal functions and principles)
      (2) Taylor's scientific management (time and task studies, piece-rate incentives, systematic selection and training).

> KEY TERM: *Administrative theory* of the universal school of management, as proposed by Fayol, that divided the manager's job into five functions (planning, organizing, command, coordination, and control) and provided 14 universal principles of management (division of work, authority, discipline, unity of command, unity of direction, subordination, remuneration, centralization, scalar chain, order, equity, stability, initiative, and esprit de corps).

> KEY TERM: *Scientific management* conducts business or affairs by standards established by facts or truths gained through systematic observation, experiment, or reasoning.

   3. *The Behavioral Era*
     a. From 1930 to 1960, greater attention was given to the human factor, spurred by the work of Elton Mayo and the Hawthorne studies.
   4. *The Modern Era*

> KEY TERM: *Theory Y* is a modern set of positive assumptions about the nature of people and work, as authored by Douglas McGregor.

> KEY TERM: *Contingency approach* uses management techniques in a situationally appropriate manner.

     a. The complexities of the modern work environment demand managerial consideration of contingencies among individuals, groups, the organization, and its environment.

  D. **Learning about OB from Theory, Research, and Practice**
   1. *Learning from Theory*

> KEY TERM: *Theory* - a story that explains "why."

     a. A good OB theory defines key terms, constructs a conceptual framework, and provides a departure point for research and practice.
   2. *Learning from Research*
     a. The five sources of OB research insights, listed in diminishing order of practical usefulness, are:

> KEY TERM: *Meta-analysis* is a statistical pooling technique that permits behavioral scientists to draw general conclusions about certain variables from many different studies.

> KEY TERM: *Field studies* probe individual or group processes in an organizational setting.

> KEY TERM: *Laboratory studies* manipulate and measure variables in contrived situations.

> KEY TERM: *Sample surveys* of samples of people from specified populations who respond to questionnaires.

> KEY TERM: *Case studies* are in-depth analyses of an individual, group, or organization.

    b. OB research findings can be put to instrumental use (direct application), conceptual use (general enlightenment), or symbolic use (verification of beliefs).

  3. *Learning from Practice*
    a. Applied research successfully links OB research and practice when resulting techniques have descriptive and goal relevance for managers.

> KEY TERM: *Descriptive relevance* is the extent to which a research project captures phenomena which are encountered by practitioners in applied settings.

> KEY TERM: *Goal relevance* is the extent to which researchers focus on outcomes that managers see as important (e.g., performance, satisfaction, absenteeism, turnover, etc.).

E. **A Topical Model for Understanding and Managing OB**
  1. The topical model is a road map for the balance of the book that focuses on achieving greater organizational effectiveness through the understanding and managing of individual behavior, group processes, and organizational processes.

OPENING CASE SOLUTION

1. The key to Goya's success at Levi Strauss is her belief in and dedication to the firm's mission of "creating an environment for success" in which people enjoy coming to work.

2. Goya performs the following managerial tasks (Figure 1-1):
- Instructing subordinates—helping them achieve a balance between their personal and professional lives and a "walk like you talk" philosophy.
- Representing one's staff—as an employee advocate.
- Planning and allocating resources—for human resources.
- Coordinating independent groups—getting people to "share ideas, take some accountability and responsibility . . .".
- Monitoring the business environment—"everything is changing so rapidly that the way we do business has to change."

3. Goya scored as follows with respect to the motivation to manage:
- Authority figures—7 (she established open relationships with her superiors.)
- Competitive games—insufficient information (but she seems to cooperate, not compete with her husband.)
- Competitive situations—4 (she avoided the "struggle" of merchandising, but she has risen to senior vice president for personnel.)
- Assertive role—5 (she avoided merchandising conflict, but she was able to discuss her situation with superiors.)
- Imposing wishes—(her people programs are successful.)
- Standing out from the group—7 (she serves as a change agent and has been promoted for her performance.)
- Routine administrative functions—7 (she couldn't have been promoted without this attribute.)

4. The Levi Strauss/Donna Goya philosophy is closer to McGregor's Theory Y, as noted below (See Table 1-3):
   - Workers have fun—they enjoy coming to work.
   - Workers are challenged and motivated.
   - Workers are committed to company objectives.
   - Workers take accountability and responsibility.
   - Workers share ideas.

5. The Levi Strauss/Goya philosophy could be applied to other cultures that share in the believe that the individual has unique value and importance. The philosophy could be modified to better suit cultures that emphasize the importance of the group and the limited role of the individual.

END-OF-CHAPTER EXERCISE

1. Students should learn some valuable lessons about managing people from perspectives other than their own, which should strengthen their understanding of the contingency approach.

2. Students should become more sensitive to the ways by which people should NOT be managed.

3. Students can be urged to trace the field of OB from the prescientific era to the modern era.

4. Students should perceive that the management of people is moving to a flexible contingency approach that values the uniqueness of each new situation.

5. Overall, today's managers may be seen as applying too many Theory X assumptions.

6. Student teams will probably suffer from early stage dysfunctions (see Chap. 9) that should improve over time.

INSTRUCTIONAL RESOURCES

1. A 20-item survey that measures the respondent's managerial role tendencies can be found in Gene E. Burton, "Managerial Role Questionnaire (MRQ)," *Exercises in Management*, 3rd ed. (Boston: Houghton Mifflin Company, 1990), pp. 7-10.

2. A 20-item survey that measures the respondent's Theory X—Theory Y assumptions can be found in Gene E. Burton, "Theory X—Theory Y Questionnaire," *Exercises in Management*, 3rd ed. (Boston: Houghton Mifflin Company, 1990), pp. 19-22.

3. A film that explains the classical era is "Henri Fayol" (Salenger Films).

4. The qualities of excellent companies are provided in the film, "In Search of Excellence," (Public Broadcasting Services).

5. An in-depth study of the implications of the Hawthorne studies is presented in the film, "The Hawthorne Studies for Today's Managers," (Educational Media).

6. A good film on the subject of managing people is, "The People Factor: The Hawthorne Studies for Today's Managers," (Salenger Films).

7. For a good analysis of the industrial revolution, see the film, "The Industrial Revolution," (Encyclopedia Britannica Education Center).

8. Ideas on the computerization of the OB classroom are to be found in Edward Szewczak and Uma Sekaran, "Introducing Personal Computers Technology in the Teaching of Organizational Behavior Courses," *The Organizational Behavior Teaching Review*, no. 2 (1987- 1988), pp. 72-85.

9. Good ways to get your class started on the right foot are presented in Jeanne Lindholm, "First Class Ideas: Creating an Atmosphere Conducive to Active Class Participation," *The Organizational Behavior Teaching Review*, no. 3, 1987-1988, pp. 110- 112.

10. *Note* : The *Journal of Management Education* (Formerly *The Organizational Behavior Teaching Review)* is an excellent source of contemporary instructional resources.

11. See the various modules for Chapter 1 in the Muto, Kreitner, and Kinicki *Lecture Supplement Manual*.

TOPICAL RESOURCES

1. The qualities of excellent companies are described in Tom Peters and Robert Waterman, *In Search of Excellence* (New York: Harper & Row, 1982).

2. Another look at excellent companies is found in Tom Peters and Nancy Austin, *Passion for Excellence* (New York, Random House, 1986).

3. Unique new views for the management of people are presented in Tom Peters, *Thriving on Chaos* (New York: Alfred A.Knopf, 1987).

4. An excellent discussion of the history of management is found in Daniel Wren, *The Evolution of Management Thought*, 2nd ed. (New York: Wiley, 1979).

5. Another popular perspective of management thought is presented in Harold Koontz, "The Management Theory Jungle Revisited," *Academy of Management Review*, April 1980, pp. 175-187.

6. Scientific management concepts are evaluated in Edwin Locke, "The Ideas of Frederick W. Taylor: An Evaluation," *The Academy of Management Review* 7, no. 1, 1982, pp. 14-24.

7. An up-dated analysis of the Hawthorne studies is provided in, "Hawthorne Revisited: The Legend and the Legacy," *Organizational Dynamics*, Winter 1975.

8. An excellent portrayal of emerging OB models is found in Keith Davis, "Evolving Models of Organizational Behavior," *Academy of Management Journal*, March 1968, pp. 27-38.

9. For a thorough presentation of Theory X—Theory Y assumptions, see Douglas McGregor, *The Human Side of Enterprise* (New York: McGraw-Hill, 1960).

10. An analysis of the contingency approach to OB is provided by Henry Tosi, "A Contingency Model of Organizational Behavior," *Organizational Behavior and Management* (Boston: PWS-Kent, 1990), pp. 16-22.

DISCUSSION/ESSAY QUESTIONS

1. How can McGregor's Theory Y assumptions be applied to the problems of managing in a modern working environment?

2. How do the elements of motivation to manage contribute to managerial success?

3. What is meant by the concept of the "jungle" of management theory?

4. Apply the contingency approach to management to the administration of a progressive university.

5. How can the issue of ethics be incorporated into the future directions of OB?

2

Managing a Diverse Work Force

CAPSULE SUMMARY

Chapter 2 examines past, present, and future business environments in order to provide an overview of the forces that have reshaped the work force and to highlight emerging solutions for these changes. After reviewing the meaning of work, the chapter moves to:

(1) a discussion of the changing nature of work
(2) the increasing diversity in the work force
(3) the integration of home and work life
(4) emerging solutions for accommodating the new work force

LECTURE OUTLINE

A. **The Meaning of Work**
1. *Work: More Than a Stream of Income*
    a. A national survey found that 85 percent of workers would continue to work even if they had enough money to live comfortably. Thus, work must have meaning beyond its income. As depicted in Figure 2-2, work:
        (1) encourages setting general life goals
        (2) provides economic security
        (3) provides personal status and identity
        (4) enforces goal-oriented activity
        (5) facilitates social contact
        (6) provides a sense of teamwork and camaraderie
        (7) imposes a time structure.
2. *Is The Work Ethic Dead?*

    > KEY TERM: *Work ethic* reflects the extent to which an individual values work.

    a. Researchers have found that a strong work ethic is associated with greater earnings, initiative, job satisfaction, productivity, need for achievement, and conservative attitudes and beliefs.
3. *Some Encouraging Evidence*
    a. A national study found that 52 percent of workers have a strong desire to do the very best job they can.
    b. This suggests that a majority of U.S. workers have a strong work ethic, but for some reason they are not working to their potential.
4. *Stifled Work Ethic*
    a. Several experts claim that management is to blame for stifling the work ethic by failing to provide incentive pay and by designing work that is dull, repetitive, and unchallenging..
    b. Unions and society, in general, also stifle incentives to work.
5. *Implications for OB*
    a. Management must nurture the work ethic by:
        (1) providing a rewarding place in which to work
        (2) providing equitable incentive pay plans
        (3) identifying the motivators of performance.

B. **The Changing Nature of Work**
America's economy and work force are undergoing profound changes that promise to significantly alter the practice of management.
1. *Working in the New Economy*
    a. Technology will create dynamic organizational changes for the future.
    b. Ninety percent of all U.S. jobs will be affected by the technological revolution. Jobs will either be displaced, replaced, or modified.
2. *Low-Tech Jobs in a High-Tech Revolution*
    a. Occupations projected to create the most new job openings in the foreseeable future are in the relatively low-paying, low-tech service sector.

3. *More Part-Timers*

> KEY TERM: *Part-time work* is defined as "regular wage employment with hours of work substantially shorter than normal in the establishment concerned."

a. More and more companies are hiring part-time workers.
b. The total number of U.S. part-timer workers increased 21 percent from 1980 to 1990.
c. Approximately 17 percent of all U.S. workers worked part-time in 1990.

4. *Working in a Service Economy*

a. The three main sectors of U.S. employment are agriculture, goods producing, and service producing.
b. Employment in the U.S. service economy increased from 18 percent in 1850 to 74 percent in 1988.
c. Evidence indicates that the sluggish productivity growth in the U.S. is directly attributable to low productivity in the service sector.

5. *Implications for OB*

a. Service industries have the distinction of employing the most people and having the lowest productivity.
b. Because of the serious problems in the service sector and other changes in the nature of work, management must utilize OB concepts to identify and appeal to the needs, motives, and sources of satisfaction for this growing segment of the work force.

C. Increasing Diversity in the Work Force

> KEY TERM: *Work force demographics* are statistical profiles of the characteristics and composition of the adult working population that are an invaluable human resource planning aid.

1. *More Women and Minorities in the Labor Force*

a. Women represented 40 percent of the U.S. work force in 1976 and are expected to account for 47 percent by the year 2000.
b. Hispanics and other minorities also represent a growing share of the labor force.

2. *Women Will Account for the Majority of the New Entrants in the Work Force Between the Years 1988-2000*

a. Female employment is still concentrated in relatively lower-level, low-paying occupations.
b. In 1989, women were still underpaid relative to men, receiving 69 percent as much as men.
c. There are signs that this low-pay trend is slowly coming to an end.

3. *Minorities Will Account for a Third of the New Entrants into the Work Force Between the Years 1988-2000*

a. Hispanics are predicted to account for 27.5 of this increase.
b. Black females are predicted to add a greater net percent increase than black males.

4. *Educational Mismatches*

a. The education level of U.S. workers has been rising.
b. In 1988, about 26 percent of the labor force had a college degree.
c. Unfortunately, many of these more highly educated workers may be overtrained for available jobs and may find their lofty expectations shortchanged by the changing nature of work. This situation has led to underemployment.

> KEY TERM: *Underemployment* exists when a job requires less than a person's full potential as determined by his or her formal education, training, or skills.

    d.   At the other end of the education-level scale, employers of many young entry-level workers find them to be deficient in basic reading, math, and social skills.

5. *An Older Work Force*
    a.   America's population and its work force are getting older.
    b.   The median age of the work force is projected to reach 39 by the year 2000.
    c.   The number of pre-school aged children increased 11.8 percent from 1980 to 1990, demanding more day care centers and more flexible work schedules.
    d.   The number of entry-level workers aged 18-24 decreased from 1980 to 1990, and this shortage will continue through the year 2000.
    e.   The "baby-boomers" contributed a 46.5 percent increase in the number of 35-44 year-olds during 1980-1990. They will create top-heavy organizations.
    f.   The decrease in people 35-44 years of age over the years 2000-2010 may result in a shortage of middle mangers.

6. *Implications for OB*
    a.   To facilitate more women in the work force, firms need to foster programs such as day care, elder care, flexible work schedules, cafeteria benefit programs, paternal leaves, and less rigid relocation policies.
    b.   To cope with educational mismatches, employers need to redesign jobs to fit higher employee skill levels and to provide remedial education for those who lack basic skills.
    c.   As baby-boomers approach retirement, the work force will be top heavy with older employees, creating problems of career plateauing for younger employees.

> KEY TERM: *Career plateauing* is that point in a career in which future hierarchical mobility seems unlikely.

    d.   Management will have to find alternative rewards to promotion.

D. Integrating Home and Work Life

> KEY TERM: *Job satisfaction* is an affective or emotional response toward various facets of the job.

1. *Job Satisfaction and Life Satisfaction Are Reciprocally Related*
2. *Implications for OB*
    a.   Organizations are revamping many traditional approaches to human resource management to attempt to integrate home and work life.

E. Emerging Solutions for Managing a Reshaped Work Force
1. *Implement Alternative Work Schedules*, such as:

> KEY TERM: *Flextime* provides employees with greater autonomy by allowing them to choose their daily starting and finishing times.

> KEY TERM: *Compressed workweeks* allow workers to work 40 hours in less than five days.

> KEY TERM: *Job sharing* allows a job to be filled by two part-timers.

> KEY TERM: *Telecommuting* allows people to work at home through computer hook-ups.

2. *Institute New Strategies for Recruiting Employees*
3. *Increase the Amount of Both Skill-Based Training and Management Development*
4. *Implement Cafeteria Benefit Plans*

> KEY TERM: *Cafeteria benefit plans* allow employees to spend a prespecified amount of credits or dollars on benefits from a menu of choices.

5. *Create Day Care and Elder Care Programs*

OPENING CASE SOLUTION

1. Among the forces creating the need for a new management paradigm are the changing nature of work, the increasing diversity of the work force, and the integration of home and work life.
2. A new managerial paradigm is needed to meet the changes in the work force and the work place in order to reverse America's fall from business dominance.
3. The old managerial paradigm "held that numbers were all important, that professional managers can handle any enterprise, and that control can and should be held at the top. The new managerial paradigm puts people—customers and employees—at the center of the universe and replaces the rigid hierarchies of the industrial age with a network structure that emphasizes interconnectedness".
4. Levi Strauss seeks to tap the fullest potential of its people by having managers serve as coaches, exhorting a team spirit through communication that is not restricted by a hierarchy. At GE, the organization has been streamlined, and a new "productivity" culture has been introduced with a focus on people working in a "boundaryless organization."
5. It would seem that both Robert Haas and Jack Welch can be advised to continue with their new managerial paradigms, as change will continue to reshape their business environment.

END-OF-CHAPTER EXERCISE

1. Students will have an opportunity to measure their work ethic and to determine how well their work ethic scores predict their work habits.
2. Students should remember that these surveys are subject to error and should not overreact to their results. (The survey is primarily an instructional tool for stimulating thinking and discussion.)

INSTRUCTIONAL RESOURCES

1. For an insight into discrimination experienced by female and minority job applicants, use "The Application Blank Exercise," in Gene E. Burton, *Exercises in Management*, 3rd ed. (Boston: Houghton Mifflin Company, 1990), pp. 123-126.

2. To help students understand the current forces for change, try the exercise, "Forces for Change," in Gene E. Burton, *Exercises in Management*, 3rd ed. (Boston: Houghton Mifflin Company, 1990), pp. 135-138.

3. A 14-item survey, "What Do Students Want From Their Jobs?" can be found in Gene E. Burton, *Exercises in Management*, 3rd ed. (Boston: Houghton Mifflin Company, 1990), pp. 157-159.

4. An interesting exercise dealing with demographics is "Demography and the Future," in Lawrence Jauch, et al, *The Managerial Experience*, 4th ed. (Chicago: Dryden Press, 1988), pp. 274-275.

5. Educational mismatches are explored in the film, "Career Escalator: Education and Job Competition," (Learning Corporation of America).

6. Student career planning can be aided by the exercise, "Career Paths," in Marshall Sashkin and William Morris, *Experiencing Management* (Reading, MA: Addison-Wesley, 1987), p. 213.

7. The problems facing female managers are analyzed in the film, "Women in Management," (CRM/McGraw-Hill).

8. See the various modules for Chapter 2 in the Muto, Kreitner, and Kinicki *Lecture Supplement Manual*.

TOPICAL RESOURCES

1. Additional material regarding labor force trends may be found in Howard Fullerton and John Tschetter, "The 1995 Labor Force: A Second Look," *The Monthly Labor Review*, November 1983, pp. 3-10; and Robert Goddard, "Work Force 2000," *Personnel Journal*, February 1989, pp. 64-71

2. Another perspective of work life is presented by Richard Walton, "Quality of Work Life: What Is It?" *Sloan Management Review*, Fall 1973, pp. 11-21.

3. Insight into telecommuting is found in Brenton Schlender, "New Software Beginning to Unlock the Power of Personal Computing," *Wall Street Journal*, November 16, 1987, p. 33.

4. The use of company structure to improve the work ethic is developed by John Miller and Norman Smith, "Can Organizational Design Make up for Motivational Decline?" *The Wharton Magazine*, Summer 1981, pp. 29-35.

5. The use of job redesign to improve the work ethic is the focus of Richard Kopelman, "Job Redesign and Productivity: A Review of the Evidence," *National Productivity Review*, Summer 1985, p. 239.

6. Creative compensation practices are discussed in Luis R. Gomez—Mejia, David B. Backin, and George T. Mickovich, "Rethinking Rewards for Technical Employees," *Organizational Dynamics*, spring 1990, pp. 62-75

7. For good background information on Managing Diversity, see R. Roosevelt Thomas, Jr., "From Affirmative Action to Affirming Diversity," *Harvard Business Review*, March-April 1990, pp. 107-117; and Beverly Geber, "Managing Diversity," *Training*, July 1990, pp. 23-30.

DISCUSSION/ESSAY QUESTIONS

1. Discuss the avenues for correcting the nation's educational mismatches.
2. What can be done to fill the predicted shortage of managerial talent in the year 2000?
3. What can an employer do to effectively integrate work and family life for the year 1995?
4. How can the U.S. rekindle the work ethic?
5. What is the meaning of work in today's complex society?

3

Individual Differences, Values, and Ethics

CAPSULE SUMMARY

Chapter 3 attempts to provide managers of the future with an appreciation of individual differences and the influence of culture on individual characteristics. The idea of self-concept is developed within the parameters of cognitions, self-esteem, and self-efficacy. Personality traits, such as locus of control, introversion, and extroversion are examined with respect to genetic endowment and environmental influences. The linkages between attitudes and behavior are examined. Abilities, intelligence, and cognitive factors are analyzed with respect to their impact on performance. Finally, ethics is discussed as both a personal value and an organizational factor.

LECTURE OUTLINE

A. **Self-Concept**

> KEY TERM: *Self* is the core of one's conscious existence.

> KEY TERM: *Self-concept* is the concept the individual has of himself as a physical, social, and spiritual or moral being.

> KEY TERM: *Cognitions* represent any knowledge, opinion, or belief about the environment, about oneself, or about one's behavior.

1. *Self-Esteem*

> KEY TERM: *Self-esteem* is a belief about one's own worth based on an overall self-evaluation.

> KEY TERM: *Organization-based self-esteem* is the self-perceived value that individuals have of themselves as organizational members acting within an organizational context.

   a. *Practical Tips for Building On-The-Job Self Esteem*
      According to a national study, managers can build employee self-esteem in four ways:
      (1) be supportive
      (2) offer work involving variety, autonomy, and challenge that suits the individual's values, skills, and contributions
      (3) strive for management-employee cohesiveness and trust
      (4) have faith in each employee's self-management ability.

2. *Self-Efficacy*

> KEY TERM: *Self-efficacy* is a person's belief about his or her chances of successfully accomplishing a specific task.

   a. Researchers have documented a strong linkage between high self-efficacy expectations and success in many endeavors.
   b. Researchers have documented a strong linkage between low self-efficacy and a condition called learned helplessness.

> KEY TERM: *Learned helplessness* is the severely debilitating belief that one has no control over one's environment.

   c. *What Are the Mechanisms of Self-Efficacy?*
      The mechanisms of self-efficacy are contained in the model found in Figure 3-3.
   d. *Self-Efficacy Implications for Managers*
      Self-efficacy requires constructive action in each of the following managerial areas:
      (1) recruiting/selection/job assignments
      (2) job design
      (3) training and development
      (4) self-management
      (5) goal-setting
      (6) coaching
      (7) leadership

(8) rewards.

B. Personality and Organizational Behavior

> KEY TERM: *Personality* is the combination of stable physical and mental characteristics that give the individual his or her identity.

1. *Locus of Control: Self or Environment*

> KEY TERM: *Internal locus of control* is the belief that one controls the events affecting one's life.

> KEY TERM: *External locus of control* is the tendency to attribute outcomes to environmental causes such as fate or luck.

   a. Studies show that internals tend to have greater work motivation, stronger expectations, higher pay, and less anxiety than externals.

2. *Introversion-Extroversion*
   a. Introverts have a higher level of internal arousal than extroverts. As a result, introverts tend to avoid external stimulation.
   b. Extroverts tend to seek external stimulation to reduce differences between their inherent and optimal levels of arousal.

3. *Implications for Management*
   a. Managers should consider each worker's tendency toward locus of control and introversion/extroversion when staffing work groups and assigning jobs.

C. Attitudes and Behavior

1. *Attitudes Versus Values*

> KEY TERM: *Attitude*: "a learned predisposition to respond in a consistently favorable or unfavorable manner with respect to a given object."

   a. While values represent global beliefs that influence behavior across *all* situations, attitudes relate only to behavior directed toward *specific* objects, persons, or situations.

2. *Attitudes and Behavioral Intentions*
   a. According to Fishbein and Ajzen's model of behavioral intentions, behavior is a function of beliefs, attitudes, and subjective norms.
   b. Attitudes tend to have relatively greater influence than norms over behavioral intentions when the behavior is personally important or risky.

3. *Attitudinal Research and Application*
   a. Research has demonstrated the predictive power of the Fishbein and Ajzen model with regard to certain job-related behaviors, such as choosing a career, reenlisting in the National Guard, and voting in union certification elections.

D. Abilities and Performance

> KEY TERM: *Ability* represents a broad and stable characteristic responsible for a person's maximum—as opposed to typical—performance on mental and physical tasks.

> KEY TERM: *Skill* is the specific capacity to physically manipulate objects. Successful job performance depends on the right combination of effort, ability, and skill.

1. *Intelligence and Cognitive Abilities*

> KEY TERM: *Intelligence* represents an individual's capacity for constructive thinking and reasoning.

   a.   Psychologist Charles Spearman proposed that cognitive performance is determined by two types of abilities:
      (1) a general mental ability needed for *all* cognitive tasks
      (2) an ability unique to the task at hand.
   b.   The seven most frequently cited mental abilities are:
      (1) verbal comprehension
      (2) word fluency
      (3) numerical
      (4) spatial
      (5) memory
      (6) perceptual speed
      (7) inductive reasoning.

2. *Jung's Cognitive Styles Typology*

> KEY TERM: *Cognitive style* refers to the mental processes associated with how people perceive and make judgments from information.

   a.   Psychoanalyst Carl Jung found that people perceive things in two ways:
      (1) sensation
      (2) intuition.
   b.   According to Jung's model, judgments are made through thinking or feeling.
   c.   Combining these four variables, Jung identified four cognitive styles:
      (1) sensation/thinking [ST]
      (2) intuition/thinking [NT]
      (3) sensation/feeling [SF]
      (4) intuition/feeling [NF]
   d.   Characteristic behaviors have been observed for people with the various cognitive styles, as follows: ST = practical technician; NT = logical planner; SF = sympathetic teacher; and NF = enthusiastic artist.

E.   **Personal Values and Ethics**

1. *Values and Enduring Beliefs*

> KEY TERM: *Value*: an enduring belief that a specific mode of conduct or end-state of existence is personally or socially preferable to an opposite or converse mode of conduct or end- state of existence.

> KEY TERM: *Value system*: an enduring organization of beliefs concerning preferable modes of conduct or end-states along a continuum of relative importance.

2. *What Is Your Value Profile?*

> KEY TERM: *Instrumental values*: alternative behaviors or means by which we achieve desired end-states.

> KEY TERM: *Terminal values*: end-states or goals the individual would like to achieve during his or her lifetime.

3. *Value Conflicts*
   a. Intrapersonal value conflict occurs when one's own values are incompatible (e.g., valuing obedience while yearning for freedom).
   b. Interpersonal value conflict occurs when two individuals are incompatible.
   c. Individual-organizational value conflict occurs when an individual's key values are incompatible with the values embraced by the organization's culture.

4. *Ethics and Organizational Behavior*

> KEY TERM: *Ethics* involves the study of moral issues and choices. It is concerned with right versus wrong, good versus bad, and the shades of gray in supposedly black-and-white issues.

   a. *A Model of Ethical Behavior* traces such behavior through family influences, organizational influences, political/legal influences, role expectations, and individual characteristics.
   b. *How to Improve the Organization's Ethical Climate*
      Organizational ethics can be improved by the following actions:
      (1) behave ethically yourself
      (2) screen potential employees (e.g., honesty testing)
      (3) develop a meaningful code of ethics
      (4) provide ethics training
      (5) reinforce ethical behavior
      (6) create positions, units and other structural mechanisms to deal with ethics.
   c. *How to Deal with Specific Unethical Conduct*
      A contingency approach to dealing with unethical behavior is suggested.

> KEY TERM: *Whistle blowing* is the practice of reporting questionable activity to higher management, the media, or outside agencies.

OPENING CASE SOLUTION

1. Prior to his downfall, Dennis Levine had very high levels of both self-esteem and self-efficacy. As he became aware of his addiction to insider training, his self-esteem declined, but his self-efficacy led him to continue the practice.
2. Prior to his arrest, Dennis Levine reflected an internal locus of control.
3. In terms of the Fishbein and Ajzen model of behavioral intention, Dennis Levine changed his attitude toward insider training because
   (1) he discovered new outcomes for that behavior and
   (2) his beliefs about the attitudes of others changed.
4. Using the model of ethical behavior, Levine's criminal conduct was supported by his perception of ethical codes, perceived pressure for results, the reward system, the permissiveness of the political/legal system, and by his own personality, values, and history of reinforcement.

5. Levine's employer may have prevented his illegal behavior if it had instilled an ethical culture that prescribed acceptable behaviors with greater clarity. His employer's vague ethical expectations gave Levine enough rope to hang himself (and his company).

END-OF-CHAPTER EXERCISE

1. On the perceptual scale, student scores will probably lean more to a sensing style than to an intuitive style. On the decisional scale, students will probably lean more to a feeling style, although older students may lean more to a thinking style.

2. Students should learn that cognitive style is influenced by personality, values, attitudes, beliefs, culture, family, age, education, and other environmental conditions. The challenge in today's team-oriented workplace, is to be able to work productively with people who think and act very differently (e.g., Diversity).

INSTRUCTIONAL RESOURCES

1. A good measure of problem-solving style is the "Problem- Solving Questionnaire (PSSQ)" in Gene E. Burton, *Exercises in Management*, 3rd ed. (Boston: Houghton Mifflin Company, 1990), pp. 45- 48.

2. Students can learn about ethical inconsistencies from David Frizche and Helmet Becker, "Linking Management Behavior to Ethical Philosophy—An Empirical Investigation," *Academy of Management Journal*, March 1984, pp. 156-175.

3. A good outline of how NOT to make ethical decisions is found in Saul Gellerman, "Why 'Good' Managers Make Bad Ethical Choices," *Harvard Business Review*, July-August 1986, pp. 85-91.

4. An application of ethical reasoning is the student debate exercise, "Social Responsibility Versus Social Irresponsibility," in Gene E. Burton, *Exercises in Management*, 3rd ed. (Boston: Houghton Mifflin Company, 1990), pp. 283-284.

5. Students can learn to facilitate whistleblowing by studying Janet Near, "Whistleblowing: Encourage It," *Business Horizons*, January-February 1989, pp. 2-6.

6. An insightful 20-item ethics survey instrument is "The Ethics Questionnaire" in Gene E. Burton, *Exercises in Management*, 3rd ed. (Boston: Houghton Mifflin Company, 1990), pp. 285-288.

7. Ethical applications are documented in the film, "Business Ethics," (Coronet/MTI).

8. Ethical problems resulting from the information revolution are explored in the film. "Ethics in the Computer Age" (Brigham Young University).

9. Students can apply ethical reasoning in the exercise, "The New Ethics of Information Management," in Gene E. Burton, *Exercises in Management*, 3rd ed. (Boston: Houghton Mifflin Company, 1990), p. 229.

10. See the various modules for Chapter 3 in the Muto, Kreitner, and Kinicki *Lecture Supplement Manual*.

TOPICAL RESOURCES

1. For in in-depth examination of self-efficacy, see Marilyn Gist, "Self-Efficacy: Implications for Organizational Behavior and Human Resource Management," *Academy of Management Review*, July 1987, 472-485.

2. A classical look at individual differences in reasoning is presented in Elliot Aronson, "The Rationalizing Animal," *Psychology Today*, May 1973.

3. An examination of the roles of intuition and emotion in decision making is provided in Herbert Simon, "Making Management Decisions: The Role of Intuition and Emotion," *The Academy of Management Executive*, February 1987, pp. 57-64.

4. Pressures against whistleblowing are discussed in M. Cash Mathews in "Whistleblowing: Acts of Courage Are Often Discouraged," *Business and Society Review*, Fall 1987, pp. 40-44.

5. A good overview of modern business ethics is found in Larue Hoemer, *The Ethics of Management* (Homewood, IL: Irwin, 1987).

6. Illegal business practices are examined in Charles Alexander, "Crime in the Suites," *Time*, June 10, 1985, p. 56.

7. The difficulties of achieving ethical decisions are analyzed in Barbara Toffler, "Tough Choices: Managers Talk Ethics," *New Management*, Spring 1987, pp. 34-39.

8. For a good primer on business ethics, see O.C. Ferrell and John Fraedrich, *Business Ethics: Ethical Decision Making and Cases* (Boston: Houghton Mifflin, 1991).

DISCUSSION/ESSAY QUESTIONS

1. Differentiate between beliefs, values, and attitudes.

2. In what ways are attitudes rational? Irrational?

3. Discuss the applications of Carl Jung's cognitive styles typology.

4. Analyze the similarities and differences between the locus of control concept and the introversion/extroversion approach.

5. Discuss managerial ethics in the information age.

4

Perceptions and Attributions

CAPSULE SUMMARY

Chapter 4 explores the manner in which organizational behavior is influenced by the phenomena of perception and causal attributions. Since the principal focus of organizational behavior is on people, the chapter emphasizes social perception, as opposed to object perception. Accordingly, a four-stage information processing model of social perception is analyzed. The perceptual outcomes of stereotyping and the self-fulfilling prophecy (Pygmalion effect) are explored. The attribution models of Harold Kelley and Bernard Weiner are discussed along with two attributional tendencies:

(1) fundamental attribution bias

(2) self-serving bias

LECTURE OUTLINE

Organizational behavior is greatly influenced by the subtle processes of perception and causal attributions. Therefore, a better understanding of these critical processes can assist managers in effectively motivating and influencing others.

A. **A Social Information Processing Model of Perception**

> KEY TERM: *Perception* is a mental and cognitive process that enables us to interpret and understand our surroundings. Since the principal focus of organizational behavior is on people, it is more important for managers to understand *social* perception.

1. *Four-Stage Sequence and a Working Example*
   a. The four stages of the social information processing model are:
      (1) selective attention/comprehension
      (2) encoding and simplification
      (3) storage and retention
      (4) retrieval and response.
   b. The working example that gives meaning to the model uses the process by which students might select a professor for a course in personal finance.

2. *Stage 1: Selective Attention/Comprehension*

> KEY TERM: *Attention* is the process of becoming consciously aware of something or someone. Attention can be focused on information from the environment or from memory.

   a. Salient stimuli stand out and attract attention. Social salience is determined by such factors as:
      (1) being novel
      (2) being bright
      (3) being unusual for that person
      (4) being unusual for people in general; being extremely positive
      (7) being dominant in the visual field.

3. *Stage 2: Encoding and Simplification*
   a. Observed information is translated into mental representations through encoding.

> KEY TERM: *Cognitive categories* are used to store information in memory. They contain one's personal knowledge about objects which are considered to be equivalent.

> KEY TERM: *Schema* is a mental picture or summary of a particular event or type of stimulus. Table 4-2 provides an example of a restaurant schema.

4. *Stage 3: Storage and Retention*
   a. Long-term memory is comprised of three compartments containing:
      (1) event memory
      (2) semantic memory
      (3) person memory.

5. *Stage 4: Retrieval and Response*
   a. This stage of the model deals with converting mental representations into real-world judgments and decisions.

6. *Managerial Implications*
   a. Perception can have a major impact on many managerial processes, such as performance appraisal, hiring, leadership, motivation, and communication.

B. **Stereotypes: Perceptions About Groups of People**

   1. *Stereotype Formation and Maintenance*

   > KEY TERM: *Stereotypes* represent grossly oversimplified beliefs or expectations about groups of people.

   a. Stereotyping is a four-step process:
      (1) people are categorized into groups according to such criteria as gender, age, race, and occupation
      (2) it is inferred that all people within a particular category possess the same traits or characteristics
      (3) these stereotypes are used to form expectations of others and to interpret their behavior
      (4) stereotypes are maintained.
   b. Stereotypes are maintained by:
      (1) overestimating the frequency of stereotypic behaviors exhibited by others
      (2) incorrectly explaining expected and unexpected behaviors
      (3) differentiating minority individuals from ourselves.

   2. *Sex-Role Stereotypes*

   > KEY TERM: *Sex-role stereotype*: a belief that differing traits and abilities make men and women particularly well suited to different roles.

   a. Research indicates that men and women do not systematically differ in the manner suggested by traditional stereotypes.
   b. Research also suggests that sex-role stereotyping in the workplace has been reduced significantly.

   3. *Age Stereotypes*
      a. Age stereotypes depict older employees as less satisfied, not as involved with their work, less motivated, not as committed, more accident prone, and less productive than their younger co-workers.
      b. Research suggests that these stereotypes are not accurate.

   4. *Race Stereotypes*
      a. There is not a large percentage of hispanic, black, and asian managers in the United Sates.
      b. A recent study found that blacks, as compared to whites, felt less accepted by their peers, perceived lower managerial discretion on their jobs, reached career plateaus more frequently, noted lower levels of career satisfaction, and received lower performance ratings.
      c. Given the increasing number of minorities that will enter the workforce over the next ten years, employers should focus on nurturing and developing minorities as well as increasing managers' sensitivity to invalid racial stereotypes.
      d. Managers should also identify valid individual differences that differentiate successful from unsuccessful employees.
         For instance, research reveals that experience is a better predictor of performance than age and that ethical behavior varies by age.

e. Managers should also remove promotional barriers for both men and women of different racial groups.

C. **Self-Fulfilling Prophecy: The Pygmalion Effect**

> KEY TERM: *Self-fulfilling prophecy* or Pygmalion effect: the tendency for people's expectations or beliefs to determine their behavior and performance, thus serving to make their expectations come true.

1. *Research and an Explanatory Model*
   a. Research has shown that, by raising instructors' and managers' expectations for individuals performing a wide variety of tasks, higher levels of achievement/productivity can be obtained.
   b. The model of the self-fulfilling prophecy outlines how supervisory expectations affect employee performance. High supervisory expectancy produces better leadership (linkage 1), which subsequently leads employees to develop higher self-expectations (linkage 2). Higher expectations motivate workers to exert more effort (linkage 3), ultimately increasing performance (linkage 4) and supervisory expectancies (linkage 5). Successful performance also improves an employee's self-expectancy for achievement (linkage 6).

2. *Putting the Self-Fulfilling Prophecy to Work*
   a. Managers need to harness the Pygmalion effect by building a hierarchical framework that reinforces positive performance expectations throughout the organization.
   b. Managers can create positive performance expectations when they:
      (1) recognize that everyone has the potential to increase his or her performance
      (2) instill confidence in the staff
      (3) set high performance goals
      (4) positively reinforce employees for a job well done
      (5) provide constructive feedback when necessary
      (6) help employees advance through the organization
      (7) introduce new employees as if they have outstanding potential
      (8) become aware of personal prejudices and nonverbal messages that may discourage others.

D. **Causal Attributions**

> KEY TERM: *Causal attributions* are suspected or inferred causes of behavior. Managers' causal attributions of employees' performance affect how they treat employees.

1. *Kelley's Model of Attribution*

> KEY TERM: *Internal factors* are those within a person (such as ability).

> KEY TERM: *External factors* are those within the working environment (such as a difficult task).

   a. Fritz Heider, the founder of attribution theory, proposed that behavior can be attributed to either internal or external factors.
   b. Kelley's Model of Attribution hypothesizes that people make causal attributions after gathering information about three dimensions of behavior:
      (1) consensus
      (2) distinctiveness

(3) consistency
2. *Weiner's Model of Attribution*
   a. According to Weiner's Model of Attribution, attributions for success and failure influence the way individuals perceive themselves and attempts to explain achievement behavior and subsequent changes in motivation and performance.
   b. Weiner proposes that ability, effort, task difficulty, luck, and help from others are the primary causes of achievement behavior.
3. *Attribution Tendencies*

> KEY TERM: *Fundamental attribution bias* reflects one's tendency to attribute another person's behavior to his or her personal characteristics, as opposed to situational factors (e.g., the belief that poor people are lazy).

> KEY TERM: *Self-serving bias* represents one's tendency to take more personal responsibility for success than for failure.

4. *Managerial Application and Implications*
   a. Managers tend to disproportionately attribute behavior to internal causes, leading to inaccurate performance evaluations and reduced employee motivation.
   b. Attributional biases on the part of managers may lead to inappropriate managerial actions, including promotions, transfers, layoffs, and so on.

OPENING CASE SOLUTION

1. The stereotypes of military men affect U.S. servicewomen in a number of ways. There is the belief that women lack the sheer physical strength to be a fighter, but brute force is irrelevant in many forms of modern combat, such as flying a jet fighter. There is also the belief that women would disrupt the male bonding that allows warriors to perform acts of heroism under fire.

2. Saudi stereotypes victimize U.S. servicewomen, who may drive vehicles discreetly only while on duty, can use a gym on one base during limited hours only if they come and go through the back door, cannot wear shorts, jog, or even shop on military bases unless accompanied by a man.

3. The self-fulfilling prophecy affects U.S. servicewomen in several ways. First of all, since it is believed that women do not have the sheer physical strength to engage in combat, they are assigned light-weight clerical and staff duties that perpetuate this belief. Similarly, efforts to treat women the same as men in the military are blocked by legislation that prohibits women from serving in front-line combat positions.

4. Weiner's Attribution Model contends that ability, effort, task difficulty, luck, and help from others are the primary causes of achievement behavior. For the U.S. servicewomen stationed in Saudi Arabia, there is little chance of securing any of these causal factors, so they will tend to have low expectations of achievement success. Consequently, they may have a low desire for achievement, low performance goals, and feelings of depression and futility.

END-OF-CHAPTER EXERCISE

1. Once each student has completed the analysis, it is suggested that the class be divided into small teams, with each team given about fifteen minutes to reach a consensus on the causes and appropriateness of corrective actions to be taken. A team spokesperson can then present the team's findings in a class discussion.

2. The exercise may be modified to focus on the relationship between levels of performance, causal attributions, and consequences of performance. Use the same basic scenario, but describe Mary's performance as exceptional. For instance, the case information could be changed as follows:
   (1) Mary has not missed a day of work
   (2) Mary completes routine programs in 20 hours
   (3) Mary completes major problems in about 85 hours
   (4) Mary's peer reviews are generally positive
   (5) users of Mary's programs indicate that her output is useful for managerial decision making. The differences in attributions and corrective actions for high and low performance can then be analyzed.

INSTRUCTIONAL RESOURCES

1. Students can gain a better insight into the perceptual process by taking part in the "Perception of Task: A Teaching-Learning Exercise," in J. Jones and J. Pfeiffer, eds. *The 1973 Annual Handbook for Group Facilitators* (San Diego: University Associates, 1973).

2. The managerial implications of attributional tendencies are clarified in the film. "Managing Motivation," (Salenger Educational Media).

3. The impact of the perceptual process is the subject of the film, "Perception," (McGraw-Hill Films).

4. Students can learn to apply the concept of self-fulfilling prophecy in D. Eden and A. Shani, "Pygmalion Goes to Boot Camp: Expectancy, Leadership, and Trainee Performance," *Journal of Applied Psychology* 67 (1982), 194-199.

5. Making assumptions and stereotyping is the learning objective of the exercise, "Assumptions and Perceptions," in Stephen Robbins, *Organizational Behavior*, 4th ed. (Englewood Cliffs, N.J.: Prentice Hall, 1989), pp. 112-113.

6. Students can learn more about sex, age, and racial stereotyping by participating in "The Application Blank Exercise," in Gene E. Burton, *Exercises in Management*, 3rd ed. (Boston: Houghton Mifflin, 1990, pp. 123-126.

7. See the various modules for Chapter 4 in the Muto, Kreitner, and Kinicki *Lecture Supplement Manual*.

TOPICAL RESOURCES

1. A look at the practical implications of perceptions is provided in John Senger, "Seeing Eye to Eye: Practical Problems of Perception," *Personnel Journal*, October 1974, pp. 744-751.

2. An action view of attribution theory is presented in Terence Mitchell, "Attributions and Actions: A Note of Caution," *Journal of Management*, Spring 1982, pp. 65-74.

3. For a detailed study of the attributional impact of ability, effort, and support, see John Schermerhorn, "Team Development for High Performance Management," *Training & Development Journal*, November 1986, pp. 38-41.

4. The concept of impression management is explained in B. R. Schlenker, *Impression Management: The Self-Concept, Self Identity, and Interpersonal Relations* (Monterey, CA: Brooks/Cole, 1980).

5. An in-depth examination of perceptual processes is found in Jack Feldman, "Perception, Cognition, and the Organization," *Journal of Applied Psychology*, 1981, pp. 128-138.

6. An interesting look at stereotyping is presented in C. McCauley, et al, "Stereotyping: From Prejudice to Prediction," *Psychological Bulletin*, January 1980, pp. 195-208.

7. For an investigation into the relationship between causal attributions and performance, see M. Mikulincer and B. Nizan, "Causal Attribution, Cognitive Inference, and the Generalization of Learned Helplessness," *Journal of Personality and Social Psychology*, May 1988, pp. 181-192.

DISCUSSION/ESSAY QUESTIONS

1. Discuss Figure 4-1, An Overview of the Perceptual Process, with emphases on stereotypes, self-fulfilling prophecy, and attributions.

2. Apply the four-stage information processing model to the purchase of new car.

3. Examine the formulation of internal and external attributions in both Kelley's and Weiner's models.

4. Apply attribution bias and self-serving bias to an important situation in your life.

5. How can the self-fulfilling prophecy be used to motivate employee performance?

5

Motivation through Needs, Job Design, and Satisfaction

CAPSULE SUMMARY

Chapter 5 provides a definitional and conceptual foundation for the overall study of motivation. Motivation is defined within both a general model of motivation and the historical roots of modern motivation theories. Two basic need theories are discussed: Maslow's need hierarchy theory and McClelland's need theory. The historical approaches of job design and Herzberg's motivator-hygiene theory of job satisfaction are linked to the more modern job characteristics and social information-processing approaches to job design. Finally, the causes and consequences of job satisfaction are analyzed.

LECTURE OUTLINE

Effective employee motivation has long been one of management's most difficult and important duties. Success in this endeavor is becoming a more challenging task in light of the changing dynamics of organizational life.

A. **What Does Motivation Involve?**

> KEY TERM: *Motivation* represents those psychological processes that cause the arousal, direction, and persistence of voluntary actions that are goal directed. Managers need to understand these psychological processes if they are to successfully guide employees toward accomplishing organizational objectives.

1. *A Conceptual Framework of Motivation*

   A conceptual framework for understanding motivation in the workplace is presented in Figure 5-1.
   a. Employee motivation is partially determined by group, organizational, and individual characteristics.
   b. Performance is moderated by such factors as goal commitment, ability, task complexity, and situational constraints.
   c. Performance leads to
      (1) feedback regarding task, self, and others that moderates one's individual characteristics and
      (2) rewards that impact satisfaction and commitment to the organization, while moderating individual characteristics.

2. *Historical Roots of Modern Motivation Theories*

> KEY TERM: *Hedonism* is a principle which states that people are motivated to consciously seek pleasure and avoid pain.

   a. Hedonism has proven to be unsatisfactory as a separate and self-contained theory of human motivation.
   b. Four ways of explaining motivation have evolved—needs, reinforcement, cognitions, and job characteristics.

3. *Needs*
   a. Need theories are based on the premise that people are motivated by unsatisfied needs.

4. *Reinforcement*
   a. Reinforcement theories are based on the premise that people are controlled by the consequences of behavior.

5. *Cognitions*
   a. Cognitive theories are based on the premise that people behave in accordance with their beliefs, values, attitudes, and other mental cognitions.

6. *Job Characteristics*
   a. Job characteristics theories are based on the premise that task motivation is a function of the task itself.

7. *A Motivational Puzzle*
   a. Motivation theory presents managers with a psychological puzzle composed of alternate explanations and recommendations.

8. *Motivation Is Only One Factor in the Performance Equation.*
   Performance is seen as a function of both ability and motivation, as indicated by the formula:

   Performance = (Ability X Motivation)

B. **Need Theories of Motivation**

> KEY TERM: *Needs* are physiological or psychological deficiencies that arouse behavior.

1. *Maslow's Need Hierarchy Theory*
   a. Maslow's need hierarchy perceives needs to be comprised of five fundamental needs—physiological, safety, love, esteem, and self-actualization.
   b. These five needs are arranged in a prepotent hierarchy, and the lowest need that is not well gratified will tend to dominate behavior.
   c. Different cultures have different need hierarchies.
   d. Maslow's theories are not well supported by research.
   e. *Managerial Implications of Maslow's Theory.*
      A satisfied need loses its motivational potential, so managers are encouraged to motivate employees by designing programs or practices aimed at satisfying emerging or unmet needs.

2. *McClelland's Need Theory*
   a. The Thematic Apperception Test (TAT) is used to measure an individual's motivation to satisfy various needs.
   b. The Need for Achievement.

> KEY TERM: *Need for achievement* is the need to accomplish something difficult in a rapid and independent fashion.
> Achievement oriented people share three common characteristics:
>   (1) preference for tasks of moderate difficulty
>   (2) situations in which performance is due to their own efforts
>   (3) a desire for more performance feedback.

   c. The Need for Affiliation.

> KEY TERM: *Need for affiliation* is the need for maintaining social relationships, joining groups, and wanting to be loved.

   d. Need for Power.

> KEY TERM: *Need for power* is the need to influence and control others.

C. **Historical Approaches to Job Design**

> KEY TERM: *Job design*, or job redesign, refers to any set of activities that involve the alteration of specific jobs or interdependent systems of jobs with the intent of improving the quality of employee job experience and their on-the-job productivity.

1. *Scientific Management*
   a. Developed by Frederick Taylor, scientific management relied on research and experimentation to determine the most efficient way to perform jobs.

b. Scientifically designed jobs are often repetitive, boring, and dissatisfying—conditions that may be relieved through job enlargement, job rotation, and job enrichment.

> KEY TERM: *Job enlargement* involves putting more variety into a worker's job by combining specialized tasks of comparable difficulty.

> KEY TERM: *Job rotation* calls for moving employees from one specialized job to another. In addition to employee rotation, some firms have implemented executive rotation.

> KEY TERM: *Job enrichment* is the practical application of Frederick Herzberg's motivator-hygiene theory of job satisfaction and involves using vertical loading to give workers more responsibility.

a. The Legacy of Herzberg's Motivator-Hygiene Theory.

> KEY TERM: *Motivators* consist of factors such as achievement, recognition, responsibility, and advancement that are related to outcomes associated with the nature of the work itself. Motivators cause a person to move from a state of no satisfaction to satisfaction.

> KEY TERM: *Hygiene factors* consist of factors such as company policy and administration, technical supervision, salary, and working conditions. Hygiene factors are not motivational.

D. **Job Characteristics and Social Information-Processing Approaches to Job Design**
  1. *Overview of the Job Characteristics Model*

> KEY TERM: *Internal motivation* occurs when an individual is motivated by positive internal feelings associated with doing well, rather than on external factors such as incentive pay.

a. The psychological states of experienced meaningfulness, experienced responsibility, and knowledge of results generate internal work motivation.

> KEY TERM: *Experienced meaningfulness* is the extent to which an individual believes his or her job is worthwhile or valuable to others.

> KEY TERM: *Experienced responsibility* is the extent to which an individual is accountable for the outcome of his or her efforts.

> KEY TERM: *Knowledge of results* is the extent to which an individual receives regular feedback about work performance.

> KEY TERM: *Core job dimensions* are common characteristics found to a varying degree in all jobs.

b. The psychological state of experienced meaningfulness is determined by the core job characteristics of skill variety, task identity, and task significance.
c. The psychological state of experienced responsibility is determined by the core job characteristic of autonomy.
d. The psychological state of knowledge of results is determined by the core job characteristic of feedback.

> KEY TERM: *Motivating potential score (MPS)* is a summary index that represents the extent to which job characteristics foster internal work motivation.

    e. People respond positively to jobs with a high MPS score when:
       (1) they have the knowledge and skills necessary to do the job
       (2) they have high growth needs
       (3) they are satisfied with various aspects of the work context.

  2. *The Social Information-Processing Model*

> KEY TERM: *Social information-processing model of job design* proposes that social cues provided by co-workers and managers have a greater impact on perceptions of job characteristics than do actual/objective job characteristics.

    a. There is only moderate research support for the theory.
    b. Managers are encouraged to consider the role of relevant social factors when redesigning a job.

E. **Unraveling the Controversy Surrounding Job Satisfaction**
  1. *The Causes of Job Satisfaction*
    a. Job satisfaction is an affective or emotional response toward various facets of one's job.
    b. The five dominant models of job satisfaction are:
       (1) need fulfillment
       (2) discrepancies
       (3) value attainment
       (4) equity
       (5) genetic components.

  2. *The Consequences of Job Satisfaction*
    a. There is a weak relationship between job satisfaction and absenteeism, a moderate relationship between job satisfaction and lower turnover, heart disease, stress, pro-union voting, and higher life satisfaction and mental health, and a positive relationship between job satisfaction and organizational citizenship behavior and organizational commitment.

OPENING CASE SOLUTION

1. The Thorneburg motivational program covers virtually every facet of the text's conceptual framework of motivation. It deals with group characteristics (such as supervisory support and teamwork), organizational characteristics (such as leadership and a quality culture), and individual characteristics (such as the need for achievement and an internal locus of control).

2. Someone who continues to work for Thorneburg will probably develop a need structure dominated by the higher order needs of esteem and self-actualization.

3. Thorneburg applied a number of job enrichment principles. He created a management system in which each employee becomes accountable for his or her work, increasing personal responsibility, achievement, and recognition. Quality circles were also used to increase these same factors. By giving employees information that had been limited to su-

pervisors, Thorneburg fostered internal recognition. Individual growth and development was increased by giving workers new and more challenging tasks.

4. Job redesign resulted in increased work motivation and job satisfaction. Participative management was established through quality circles, creating an atmosphere of trust and openness, goal-setting, information-sharing, teamwork, and self-development. The physical environment was improved by a modern plant. There is also a plan to share ownership with the employees.

END-OF-CHAPTER EXERCISE

1. Students who work should find it interesting to assess the MPS of their current or former job(s).
2. The greatest learning potential from this exercise comes when the students determine which job characteristics should be changed and how their jobs might be redesigned.

INSTRUCTIONAL RESOURCES

1. Students can determine their own Maslow's need structure by completing the "Motivation Feedback Opinionnaire," in J. Pfeiffer and J. Jones, Eds. *The 1973 Annual Handbook for Group Facilitators* (San Diego: University Associates, 1973).
2. Students can analyze a classic job redesign in the exercise, "Redesigning Assembly-Line Jobs: Hovey and Beard Company," by G. Strauss and A. Bavelas, in William Whyte, Ed. *Money and Motivation* (New York: Harper & Row, 1955).
3. Pay as an incentive is explored in the exercise, "Money Motivation Debate," in R. Lewicki, et al, *Experiences in Management and Organizational Behavior*, 3rd ed. (New York: Wiley, 1988).
4. Students have the opportunity to redesign jobs in the exercise, "Redesigning Jobs," in J. Gibson and R. Hodgetts, *Readings and Exercises in Organizational Behavior* (Orlando: Academic Press, 1985).
5. An in-depth look at job enrichment is found in the film, "Job Enrichment: Managerial Milestone or Myth?" (Salenger).
6. A study of individual/group needs is presented in the film, "Individuality and Teamwork," (BNA Communications, Inc.).
7. Experiencing the difficulty of designing a motivational program is the focus of the exercise," The Problem at Bluefield," in Gene E. Burton, *Exercises in Management*, 3rd ed. (Boston: Houghton Mifflin Company, 1990), pp. 127-129.
8. Current motivational programs are previewed in the film, "A New Look at Motivation," (CRM/McGraw-Hill).
9. An analysis of achievement motivation is presented in the film, "The Self-Motivated Achiever," (BNA Communications, Inc.).
10. See the various modules for chapter 5 in the Muto, Kreitner, and Kinicki *Lecture Supplement Manual*.

TOPICAL RESOURCES

1. An excellent comparison of job enlargement and job enrichment is found in K. Chung and M. Ross, "Differences in Motivational Properties Between Job Enlargement and Job Enrichment," *Academy of Management Review*, January 1977, pp. 113-122.

2. The whole motivational issue is addressed in the classic, "One More Time—How Do You Motivate People?" by Frederick Herzberg, *Harvard Business Review*, February 1968, pp. 53-62.

3. Every student should read Frederick Herzberg's *Work and the Nature of Man* (New York: World, 1971).

4. Maslow's theory is developed in Abraham Maslow, *Motivation and Personality*, 2nd ed. (New York: Harper & Row, 1970).

5. McClelland's motivation concepts are presented in David M. McClelland, *Human Motivation* (Glenview, IL: Scott, Foresman, 1985).

6. A thorough review of the development of motivational theory is found in R. Katzell and D. Thompson, "Work Motivation: Theory and Practice," *American Psychologist*, February 1990, pp. 144-153.

7. For an in-depth analysis of the relationships between ability and performance, see W. Coward and P. Sackett, "Linearity of Ability- Performance Relationships: A Reconfirmation," *Journal of Applied Psychology*, June 1990, pp. 297-300.

8. A recent job redesign study is reported in Ricky W. Griffin, "Effects of Work Redesign on Employee Perceptions, Attitudes, and Behaviors: A Long-Term Investigation," *Academy or Management Journal*, June 1991, pp. 425-435.

DISCUSSION/ESSAY QUESTIONS

1. Trace the evolution of modern motivation theory.
2. Compare the need approaches of Maslow and Herzberg.
3. Compare the significance of motivators and hygiene factors.
4. Discuss the importance of McClelland's needs.
5. Discuss the job satisfaction controversy

6

Motivation through Equity, Expectancy, and Goal Setting

CAPSULE SUMMARY

Chapter 6 continues the analysis of motivation by exploring three major process theories of motivation. First, Adam's equity theory of motivation is discussed. Following an introduction to the expectancy concept of motivation, Vroom's expectancy theory is analyzed. Then the goal-setting approach is covered, with emphasis on the definition of goals, the motivational mechanisms of goal setting, and a summary of the research. A three-stage procedure for applying goal setting to motivation is provided. Finally, an overall model of motivation management is presented.

LECTURE OUTLINE

Cognitive process theories explain how people are motivated by examining the manner in which they perceive and consciously respond to the environment around them.

A. Adam's Equity Theory of Motivation

> KEY TERM: *Equity theory* is a model of motivation that explains how people strive for *fairness* and *justice* in social exchanges or give-and-take relationships. Equity theory is based on cognitive dissonance theory, which proposes that people are motivated to maintain consistency between their cognitive beliefs and their behavior.

1. *The Individual-Organizational Exchange Relationship*
    a. Employee inputs (e.g., education, experience, skills, effort) and outcomes (e.g., pay, job security, status symbols) are the two primary components in the employee-employer exchange.
    b. Equity perceptions are formulated on the basis of recognizable and relevant inputs and outcomes.

2. *Negative and Positive Inequity*
    a. On the job, feelings of inequity revolve around a person's evaluation of whether he or she receives adequate rewards to compensate for his or her contributive inputs.
    b. People perform these evaluations by comparing the perceived fairness of their employment exchange to that of relevant others.
    c. There are three categories of relevant others:
        (1) *other*—including others inside or outside the organization, in same or similar jobs
        (2) *self*—self-comparisons over time and against one's ideal ratio
        (3) *system*—based on individual-organizational exchanges.

> KEY TERM: *Negative inequity* stems from a situation in which a person has a lower outcome/input ratio than a relevant comparison other and believes that he or she is receiving less than is rightfully deserved..

> KEY TERM: *Positive inequity* stems from a situation in which a person has a greater outcome/input ratio than a relevant other and believes that he or she is receiving more than is rightfully earned.

3. *Dynamics of Perceived Inequity*
    a. Negative inequity is less tolerable that positive inequity.
    b. People attempt to maximize the amount of positive outcomes.
    c. People resist increasing inputs when it requires substantial effort or costs.
    d. People resist behavioral or cognitive changes in inputs important to their self-concept or self-esteem.
    e. Rather than change cognitions about oneself, an individual is more likely to change cognitions about the comparison other's inputs and outcomes.
    f. Quitting is chosen only when severe inequity cannot be resolved through other methods.
    g. A person tends to reduce perceived inequities in eight ways:
        (1) increase inputs
        (2) decrease inputs
        (3) attempt to increase outcomes
        (4) decrease outcomes
        (5) leave the field

        (6) psychologically distort his or her inputs and outcomes

        (7) psychologically distort the inputs and outcomes of comparison other

        (8) change comparison other.

  4. *Equity Research Findings*

    a. Overall, the research supports equity theory.

  5. *Practical Lessons from Equity Theory*

    a. Equity theory provides managers with another explanation of how beliefs and attitudes affect job performance.

    b. Equity theory emphasizes the need for managers to pay attention to employee equity perceptions.

    c. Managers benefit by allowing employees to participate in making decisions about important work outcomes.

    d. Employees should be given the opportunity to appeal decisions about their welfare.

    e. Perceptions of fair treatment promote job satisfaction, organizational commitment, and help to reduce absenteeism and turnover.

B. Expectancy Theory of Motivation

> **KEY TERM:** *Expectancy theory* holds that people are motivated to behave in ways that produce desired combinations of desired outcomes. Expectancy theory is founded on the principle of hedonism, by which people strive to maximize pleasure and minimize pain.

  1. *Vroom's Expectancy Theory*

    a. Motivation is perceived to be based on a decision of how much effort to exert in a specific work situation, a decision based on a two-step sequence of expectations:

      (1) effort—performance

      (2) performance—outcome.

> **KEY TERM:** *Expectancy* is an individual's belief that a particular degree of effort will be followed by a particular level of performance.

> **KEY TERM:** *Instrumentality* is a performance—outcome perception representing the individual's belief that a particular outcome is contingent upon accomplishing a particular level of performance.

> **KEY TERM:** *Valence* refers to the positive or negative value people place on outcomes.

    b. According to Vroom, motivation is dependent upon three factors:

      (1) the effort—performance expectancy must be greater than zero

      (2) the performance—outcome instrumentality must be greater than zero

      (3) the outcome must have a positive valence.

  2. *Porter and Lawler's Extension*

    a. Porter and Lawler have developed an expectancy model that is an extension of Vroom's model.

    b. Effort is viewed as a function of the perceived value of a reward (outcome valence) and the perceived effort—reward probability (expectancy).

    c. Performance is determined by effort, abilities, and traits.

    d. Rewards are perceived to be intrinsic (e.g., achievement and a sense of accomplishment) or extrinsic (e.g., pay and working conditions).

    3. *Research on Expectancy Theory and Managerial Implications*
       a. A summary of 16 studies revealed that expectancy theory correctly predicted occupational or organizational choice 63.4 percent of the time.
       b. Expectancy theory accurately predicted job satisfaction, decisions to retire (80 percent accuracy), voting behavior in union elections (over 75 percent accuracy), reenlistment in the National Guard (66 percent accuracy), and the frequency of drinking alcohol.
       c. Expectancy theory is difficult to test, and the measures used to assess expectancy, instrumentality, and valence have questionable validity.

  C. **Motivation Through Goal Setting**
    1. *Successful People Are Goal Directed*
    2. Goals: Definition and Background

> KEY TERM: *Goals* are objects or aims of action, representing end-points people are trying to achieve.

       a. The founder of scientific management, Frederick Taylor, was one of the first to advocate goal setting.
    3. *How Does Goal Setting Work?*
       a. Goals provide four motivational mechanisms:
         (1) goals direct attention
         (2) goals regulate effort
         (3) goals increase persistence
         (4) goals foster strategies and action plans.

> KEY TERM: *Persistence* is the amount of effort an individual expends on a task over an extended period of time.

    4. *Insights from Goal-Setting Research*
       a. Research consistently supports goal setting as a motivational technique.
       b. Difficult goals can lead to higher performance.

> KEY TERM: *Goal difficulty* reflects the amount of effort required to achieve a goal.

       c. Specific, difficult goals may or may not lead to higher performance.

> KEY TERM: *Goal specificity* pertains to the quantifiability of a goal.

       d. Feedback enhances the effect of specific, difficult goals.
       e. Participative goals, assigned goals, and self-set goals are equally effective.
    5. *Practical Application of Goal Setting*
       a. There are three general steps to follow when implementing a goal-setting program:
         (1) establish the goal
         (2) foster goal commitment
         (3) provide employees with support and feedback.

  D. **Putting Motivational Theories to Work**
    1. Successfully designing and implementing motivational programs is not easy.
    2. Managers must gauge the extent to which motivation significantly affects performance.
    3. Managers must be sensitive to individual differences.

4. Managers should make rewards contingent on performance.

5. Mangers need to apply a contingency approach to the design and implementation of goal-setting programs.

OPENING CASE SOLUTION

1. Cypress Semiconductor Corporation treats its employees equitably through a computer-based management system that monitors every facet of operations and allocates rewards on the basis of performance. Company watchwords— "discipline, accountability, and relentless attention to detail" —provide the framework within which each employee establishes specific short- and long-range goals that are objectively monitored constantly. Reward outcomes are dependent upon the manner in which each person achieves specific goals that he or she establishes.

2. The Cypress computerized management system is compatible with expectancy theory in that the effort—performance expectancy, the performance—outcome instrumentality, and outcome valences can be electronically monitored by each employee. Since most goals and activities are self-imposed, individuals can adjust inputs, outputs, processes, and so on to satisfy personal expectancies.

3. Each week, Cypress employees set their own goals, commit to achieving them by a specific date, enter them in the system database, and report whether or not they completed prior goals. Managers work with their people to anticipate overload and conflicting goals, to sort out priorities, to organize work, and to make mutual commitments about what's going to get done. People receive instantaneous feedback regarding progress, a completed goal triggers a performance minireview, and rewards are pegged against performance.

4. The Cypress management system appears to be following the more positive aspects of all four of the insights from goal-setting research:
   (1) difficult goals lead to higher performance
   (2) specific, difficult goals *may* or may not lead to higher performance
   (3) feedback enhances the effect of specific, difficult goals
   (4) participative goals, assigned goals, and self-set goals are equally effective.

END-OF-CHAPTER EXERCISE

1. Students must understand that worker attitudes vary significantly, so discrepancies with the national survey results should not surprise participants. Furthermore, many students have had little or no work experience upon which to base responses.

2. The greatest learning value should come when the student applies the expectancy theory factors of effort—performance expectancy, performance—outcome instrumentality, and valence.

3. Students tend to reflect stronger intrinsic work values than older workers. This factor needs to be considered as part of the individual characteristics reflected in the Model of Performance Motivation presented in Figure 6-8.

4. Students should note that it would be a mistake to generalize the survey results to all non-managerial employees. Such a generalization would not give adequate attention to expected variances in group characteristics, organizational characteristics, cross cultural differences, individual characteristics, moderators (goal commitment, ability, task complexity, and situational constraints), feedback, rewards, and so on.

INSTRUCTIONAL RESOURCES

1. As an alternative to the chapter-ending exercise dealing with what workers want from their jobs, students might relate better to the exercise, "What Do Students Want from Their Jobs," in Gene E. Burton, *Exercises in Management*, 3rd ed. (Boston: Houghton Mifflin Company, 1990), pp. 157-159.

2. Another student work need survey is "What Motivates You?" in John Schermerhorn, Jr., *Management for Productivity*, 3rd ed. (New York: Wiley, 1989), pp. 378-379.

3. A real-world application of motivation theory is found in "Designing a Motivational Program," in Gene E. Burton, *Exercises in Management*, 3rd ed. (Houghton Mifflin Company, 1990), pp. 151-155.

4. Goal-setting techniques are delineated by Edwin Locke and Gary Latham in *Goal Setting: A Motivational Technique That Works* (New York: Harper & Row, 1970).

5. Students can experience the difficulty of goal setting in the exercise, "Goal Setting," in Gene E. Burton, *Exercises in Management*, 3rd ed. (Houghton Mifflin Company, 1990), pp. 49-52.

6. A 20-item survey that measures goal-setting tendencies is the "Goal-Setting Questionnaire," provided in Gene E. Burton, *Exercises in Management*, 3rd ed. (Houghton Mifflin Company, 1990), pp. 61-64.

7. A review of modern motivational approaches is contained in the film," A New Look at Motivation," (CRM/McGraw-Hill).

8. An overview of motivation theories is presented in the film, "Understanding Motivation," (BNA Communications, Inc.).

9. An action approach to motivation is shown in the film, "Motivation: Making It Happen," (Stephen Bosustow Productions).

10. See the various modules for chapter 6 in the Muto, Kreitner, and Kinicki, *Lecture Supplement Manual*.

TOPICAL RESOURCES

1. For an in-depth look at equity concepts, see Stacy Adams, "Toward an Understanding of Equity," *Journal of Abnormal Psychology*, November 1963, pp. 422-436.

2. Expectancy theory is discussed at length in Victor Vroom, *Work and Motivation* (New York: Wiley, 1965).

3. An interesting analysis of worker motivation is found in Frederick Herzberg, "Worker Needs: The Same Around the World," *Industry Week*, September 21, 1987, pp. 29-32.

4. The relationships between attitudes and performance is explored in Lyman Porter and Edward Lawler, III, *Managerial Attitudes and Performance* (New York: Knopf, 1971).

5. An interesting application of motivation concepts is found in Kelly Kerin and Charles Waldo, "NFL Coaches and Motivation Theory," *MSU Business Topics*, Autumn 1978, pp. 15-18.

6. Every student should read the classic, "On the Folly of Rewarding A, While Hoping for B," by Steven Kerr in *The Academy of Management Journal*, 1975, pp. 769-783.

7. An international perspective of motivation is provided by Geert Hofstede, "Motivation, Leadership, and Organization: Do American Theories Apply Abroad?" *Organization Dynamics*, Summer 1980, pp. 42-63.

8. An introduction to self-motivation is presented in Charles Manz, "Self-Leadership: Toward an Expanded Theory of Self-Influence Processes in Organizations," *Academy of Management Review*, July 1986, pp. 585-600.

9. A look at the impact of environmental factors on motivation is provided in Keith Davis, "Low Productivity? Try Improving the Social Environment," *Business Horizons*, June 1980, pp. 27-29.

10. Goal setting in a computer simulation is examined in Amelia A. Chesney and Edwin A. Locks, "Relationships Among Goal Difficulty, Business Strategies, and Performance on a Complex Managment Simulation Task," *Academy of Management Journal*, June 1991, pp. 400-424.

11. Relative to equity theory, mine aspects of *fairness* and a "Fairness Climate Questionnaire" can be found in Marshall Sashkin and Richard L. Williams, "Does Fairness Make a Difference?" *Organizational Dynamics*, autumn 1990, pp. 56-71.

DISCUSSION/ESSAY QUESTIONS

1. Discuss the relationships between an equitable situation, positive inequity, and negative inequity.

2. Explain worker motivation in terms of Vroom's expectancy theory.

3. How can expectancy theory be applied to managerial problems in today's complex organizations?

4. How could you, as a management trainee, be motivated by a goal-setting program?

5. How did Porter and Lawler extend the theories of Adams and Vroom?

7

Behavior Modification and Self-Management

CAPSULE SUMMARY

Chapter 7 serves as an overall introduction to modern behaviorism. First, the principles of behavior modification are detailed with a focus on Antecedent—Behavior—Consequence (A—B—C) contingencies. The concepts of positive and negative reinforcement and punishment are described. Continuous and intermittent schedules of reinforcement are compared. A four-stage model of job behavior modification is presented along with a review of behavior modification research. Finally, behavioral self-management, an outgrowth of social learning theory, is explained.

Chapter 7

LECTURE OUTLINE

A. **The Evolution of Modern Behaviorism**

> KEY TERM: *Behavioral learning theory* strives to explain how behavior is acquired and changed through person-environment interaction. Three key behavioral learning models are:
> (1) Watson's stimulus-response behaviorism
> (2) Thorndike's law of effect, and
> (3) Skinner's operant conditioning model.

1. *Watson's Stimulus-Response Behaviorism*

> KEY TERM: *Classical conditioning*: through repeated pairings between a specific stimulus and response, people learn to exhibit the response in the mere presence of the specific stimulus.

> KEY TERM: *Behaviorism* is a philosophy of human learning that rejects notions of mental processes and self-control when explaining human behavior.

2. *Thorndike's Law of Effect*

> KEY TERM: *Law of effect*: behavior with favorable consequences tends to be repeated, while behavior with unfavorable consequences tends to disappear.

3. *Skinner's Operant Conditioning Model*
   a. Skinner contends that behavior is a function of its consequences, as opposed to prior causal stimulation or self-determination.

> KEY TERM: *Respondent behavior*: unlearned reflexes or stimulus-response connections.

> KEY TERM: *Operant behavior*: behavior learned when one operates on the environment to produce desired consequences.

B. **Principles of Behavior Modification**

> KEY TERM: *Behavior modification* involves making specific behavior occur more or less often by systematically managing antecedent cues and contingent consequences.

1. *A—B—C Contingencies*

> KEY TERM: *Behavioral contingencies*: the Antecedent—Behavior—Consequences (A—B—C) model of person-environment interaction.

> KEY TERM: *Functional analysis*: the process of reducing person-environment interaction to A—B—C terms.

   a. Antecedents cue rather than cause behavior.
   b. Behavior modification requires managers to focus on observable instead of unobservable inner states.

2. *Contingent Consequences*

> **KEY TERM:** *Positive reinforcement*: the process of strengthening a behavior by contingently presenting something pleasing.

> **KEY TERM:** *Negative reinforcement*: the process of strengthening a behavior by contingently withdrawing something displeasing.

> **KEY TERM:** *Punishment*: the process of weakening behavior through either the contingent presentation of something displeasing or the contingent withdrawal of something pleasing. The latter is called response cost punishment.

> **KEY TERM:** *Extinction*: the weakening of a behavior by ignoring it or making sure it is not reinforced.

3. *Schedules of Reinforcement*

> **KEY TERM:** *Continuous reinforcement*: reinforcing every instance of a target behavior.

> **KEY TERM:** *Intermittent reinforcement*: reinforcing some but not all instances of a target behavior.

   a. *Ratio* schedules of reinforcement are tied to the number of responses emitted.
   b. *Interval* schedules of reinforcement are tied to the passage of time.
   c. Four types of intermittent reinforcement are:
       (1) fixed ratio [e.g., piece-rate pay]
       (2) variable ratio [e.g., slot machines]
       (3) fixed interval [e.g., hourly pay]
       (4) variable interval [e.g., random supervisory praise].

4. *Shaping*
   a. Shaping is the process of reinforcing closer and closer approximations to a target behavior.

C. *A Model for Modifying Job Behavior*
   1. *Step 1: Identify Target Behavior*
      a. Target desirable behavior that occurs too seldom or undesirable behavior that occurs too often.
      b. In modern complex organizations, behavior modifiers must sometimes settle for the results of behavior rather than observing actual behavior first hand.
   2. *Step 2: Functionally Analyze the Situation*
      a. Managers need to pinpoint existent A—B—C relationships prior to rearranging them.
   3. *Step 3: Arrange Antecedents and Provide Consequences*
      a. Antecedents can be managed by removing obstacles and/or providing opportunities.
      b. Six guidelines for managing consequences are:
          (1) reinforce improvement, not just final results
          (2) fit the consequences to the behavior
          (3) emphasize natural rewards over contrived rewards

> **KEY TERM:** *Natural rewards* are potentially reinforcing consequences derived from day-to-day social and administrative interactions.

(4) provide individuals with objective feedback whenever possible

(5) emphasize positive reinforcement; deemphasize punishment

(6) schedule reinforcement appropriately.

4. *Step 4: Evaluate Results*

> KEY TERM: *Baseline data*: preintervention behavioral data collected without the target person's knowledge.

> KEY TERM: *Behavior chart*: a B. Mod. program evaluation tool that includes both preintervention baseline data and postintervention data.

5.

a. Although some see B. Mod. as manipulative and demeaning, it is virtually impossible to manage job behavior without systematically managing antecedents and consequences.

b. B. Mod replaces the usual haphazard approach with a systematic approach complete with formal program evaluation.

D. Behavioral Self-Management

In the process of self-management, people need more than advice about willpower, self-discipline, resisting temptation, or seeking divine guidance. They need proven social learning theory techniques.

1. *Bandura's Social Learning Theory*

a. The social learning theory extends Skinner's operant model by emphasizing that cognitive or mental processes affect how one responds to surroundings.

b. Reciprocal determinism implies that people control their environment as mush as it controls them.

> KEY TERM: *Social learning*: the process of acquiring behavior through the reciprocal interaction of the person's cognitions, behavior, and environment.

2. *A Managerial Context for Behavioral Self-Management*

> KEY TERM: *Behavioral self-management* (BSM) is the process of modifying one's own behavior by systematically managing cues, cognitive processes, and contingent consequences.

3. *Social Learning Model of Self-Management*

a. Social learning theorists such as Albert Bandura say, behavior is a function of the reciprocal interaction among
    (1) cognitive processes,
    (2) cues and consequences, and
    (3) the behavior itself.

b. Self-control involves the dilemma of doing unappealing (in the short run) but necessary (in the long run) things.

c. Situational cues for self-control are reminders and attention focusers, self-observation data, avoidance of negative cues, seeking positive cues, personal goal setting, and self-contracts.

d. Three important cognitive supports in behavioral self-management are
    (1) visual and verbal symbolic coding,
    (2) mental or actual rehearsal, and
    (3) self-talk.

     e.   Self-reinforcement encourages repetition of desired behavior.

4. *Research and Managerial Implications*
    a.   Preliminary evidence suggests that BSM works, but much more complete research is needed.

OPENING CASE SOLUTION

1. Owner James W. Parsons should be rated an expert at modifying behavior. He instigated a consequence system that clearly identified productive and safe job behavior. He focused on specific behavior rather than on attitudes. All of Parsons' consequences were contingent upon appropriate behavior and maximized their motivational influence. He functionally analyzed the trade-off between well pay and retro pay, and clearly explained the long-term consequences of reporting to work sick.

2. The following antecedent management was identified:
    a.   The plans for well pay, retro pay, and profit-sharing were the administrative antecedents to desired job behavior.
    b.   The explanation of the trade-off between short-term well pay and long-term retro pay served as an antecedent designed to preclude workers from coming to work sick simply to collect well pay.
    c.   Films and safety programs were antecedents for safe working behavior.
    d.   The display pyramid of 250 rat traps served as a strong cue to remind workers that they can help control overhead expenses.
    e.   Parsons' comment after the Christmas luncheon that it cost the company $3,000 to let employees take the rest of the day off served as a cue to encourage workers to vote to keep working.

3. Each student will have an opportunity to apply his or her own interpretation to the A—B—C behavioral contingencies. The focus of this learning experience is to carefully explain the case in A—B—C terms.

4. Two possible problems could have developed from the retro plan. First of all, the premium that was paid to the state accident insurance fund was pegged to the company's accident rate for the prior year, and a lower accident rate meant a lower premium. So employees could be penalized with smaller future refunds for working safer. Also, the retro plan might have encouraged employees not to report accidents, and small traceable workplace injuries could have become large medical bills and lost time if not treated by medical personnel. With respect to the profit-sharing plan, what happens if the firm has a losing year? Employee morale could rise and fall with the firm's profit picture.

END-OF-CHAPTER EXERCISE

1. This exercise provides the students with the opportunity to learn the principles of behavior modification by applying them to personally relevant problems. Students who prefer not to work on someone else can be challenged to select and improve one of their own behaviors through BSM.

2. Each student may be encouraged to write a short proposal outlining his/her BSM or B. Mod. project for review by the instructor.

3. The use of behavior charts is encouraged.

4. Classroom presentations and/or formal written summaries may be used to add closure to the exercise.

INSTRUCTIONAL RESOURCES

1. Techniques for the use of positive reinforcement are presented in Barbara Carlson and Jo-anne Collins, "Motivating Managers with Positive Reinforcement," *Management Accounting*, March 1986, pp. 48- 51.

2. Students can explore reinforcement problems by analyzing the case, "Reinforcing the Wrong Behavior," in Michael Albert, *Effective Management: Readings, Cases, and Experiences*, 3rd ed. (New York: Harper & Row, 1990), p. 135.

3. An excellent B. Mod. exercise is, "Application of Behavior Modification," in John Samaras, *Management Applications: Exercises, Cases, and Readings* (Englewood Cliffs, N.J.: Prentice Hall, 1989), p. 121.

4. Another B. Mod. exercise is, "Behavior Modification," in Keith Davis and John Newstrom, *Organizational Behavior: Readings and Exercises*, 7th ed. (New York: McGraw-Hill, 1985), 517-518.

5. Alternatives to punishment are addressed in the film, "Discipline Without Punishment," (CRM/McGraw-Hill).

6. Human relations problems in OB Mod. are analyzed in the film, "The Human Problems of Management: Approaches to Organizational Behavior Modification," (University of Illinois).

7. Positive reinforcement is the theme of the film, "The Power of Positive Reinforcement," (CRM/McGraw-Hill).

8. See the various modules for Chapter 7 in Muto, Kreitner, and Kinicki, *Lecture Supplement Manual*.

TOPICAL RESOURCES

1. For a thorough analysis of social learning theory, read A. Bandura, *Social Learning Theory* (Englewood Cliffs, N.J.: Prentice Hall, 1977).

2. All students should read B. F. Skinner, *Beyond Freedom and Dignity* (New York: Knopf, 1971).

3. Behavior modification through positive reinforcement is the thrust of W. Clay Hammer and Ellen Hammer, "Behavior Modification on the Bottom Line," *Organizational Dynamics*, Spring 1976.

4. An introduction to self-management is presented by Charles Manz, "Self-Leadership: Toward an Expanded Theory of Self-Influence Processes in Organizations," *Academy of Management Review*, July 1986, pp. 585-600.

5. An application of behavior shaping is provided in John Bruening, "Shaping Workers' Attitudes Toward Safety,"*Occupational Hazards*, March 1990, pp. 49-51.

6. Research evidence on feedback seeking and self-management is presented in Susan J. Ashford and Anne S. Tsui, "Self-Regulation for Managerial Effectiveness: The Role of Active Feedback Seeking, " *Academy of Management Journal*, June 1991, pp. 251-280.

7. Regarding better self-management, all students should read Stephen R. Covey, *The Seven Habits of Highly Effective People* (New York: Simon & Schuster, 1989).

DISCUSSION/ESSAY QUESTIONS

1. Discuss the application of Watson's stimulus-response behaviorism to selected performance problems?

2. Compare Bandura's social learning theory with Skinner's operant model.

3. How can management apply the A—B—C model to selected performance problems.

4. Analyze the differences between positive reinforcement, negative reinforcement, and punishment.

5. Compare B. Mod. with behavioral self-management.

8

Socialization, Mentoring, and Careers

CAPSULE SUMMARY

Chapter 8 presents some foundation material for the study of group processes in today's complex organizations and introduces the student to the concept of career management. The chapter offers assistance in understanding the myriad of social interrelationships that people experience in day-to-day living. First, the chapter presents the foundations of organizational socialization as the process used by organizations to encourage employees to exhibit desired behaviors. The discussion covers four socialization techniques that are often used by organizations—psychological contracts, realistic job previews, behavior modeling, and mentoring. Organizational roles and norms are analyzed. Finally, the chapter offers an overview of career management, with special attention to career transitions and career anchors.

LECTURE OUTLINE

Figure 8-1 provides an overview of the process that guides the chapter material. Organizations rely on organizational socialization to encourage employees to exhibit desired behaviors. This is accomplished through a variety of socialization techniques that reinforce and support organizational roles and norms. At the individual level, employees use career management to facilitate a match between their needs and organizational requirements.

A. **The Organizational Socialization Process**

> KEY TERM: *Organizational socialization*: the process by which a person learns the values, norms, and required behaviors which permit him or her to participate as a member of an organization.

1. *A Three-Phase Model of Organizational Socialization*
   Feldman's model of organizational socialization consists of three phases by which outsiders are transformed into productive and involved insiders.
   a. *Phase 1: Anticipatory Socialization*—occurs before the individual joins the organization.
   b. *Phase 2: Encounter*—a time following the employment contract for surprise and sense making.

   > KEY TERM: *Reality shock*: a situation on which an organizational newcomer's world is turned upside down.

   c. *Phase 3: Change and Acquisition*—important tasks are mastered and role conflicts are resolved.

2. *Practical Application of Socialization Research*
   a. Managers should avoid a haphazard, sink-or-swim approach to organizational socialization.
   b. The encounter phase of socialization is particularly correlated with later performance.
   c. Females derive fewer benefits from socialization than do males.
   d. Research indicates that the different stages of socialization do occur, but they are not identical in order, length, or content for all people or jobs.

B. **Socialization Techniques**

1. *Psychological Contracts*

   > KEY TERM: *Psychological contract*: the sum total of all written and unwritten, spoken and unspoken, expectations of the employer and the employee.

   a. Frank and open discussion of psychological contracts can bring unrealistic expectations into line and thus enhance individual-organization fit.

2. *Realistic Job Previews*

   > KEY TERM: *Realistic job preview* (RJP): involves giving recruits a realistic idea of what lies ahead by presenting both positive and negative aspects of the job.

   a. RJPs can lower a recruit's unrealistically high expectations.
   b. RJPs can increase job satisfaction and decrease turnover.
   c. RJPs are more effective for complex, higher-paying jobs.

3. *Behavior Modeling*

> KEY TERM: *Behavior modeling*: a learning process by which one observes and imitates the behavior of relevant others.

   a. Behavior modeling is a "vicarious process" of sharing the experience of relevant others.
   b. Bandura's observational learning model contains four subprocesses:
      (1) attention
      (2) retention
      (3) reproduction
      (4) motivation.
   c. Sorcher's successful training protocol, called Applied Learning, contains four steps:
      (1) modeling
      (2) role-playing
      (3) social reinforcement
      (4) transfer of training.

4. *Mentoring*

> KEY TERM: *Mentoring*: the process of forming and maintaining an intensive and lasting developmental relationship between a senior person and a junior person.

   a. Kram's research found that mentors performed career and psychosocial functions for junior members.
   b. Mentoring is perceived as a process of four steps:
      (1) initiation
      (2) cultivation
      (3) separation
      (4) redefinition.
   c. Research finds that mentoring increases career mobility, pay, and job satisfaction.
   d. Research finds that mentoring enhances the effectiveness of organizational communication.
   e. Mentoring can be an informal, spontaneous process or a formally structured one.
   f. Mentoring has been zealously oversold, so managers should apply it cautiously.

C. **Organizational Roles and Norms**

  1. Organizational roles and norms exercise a subtle but powerful influence over organizational behavior.

> KEY TERM: *Roles*: sets of behaviors that persons expect of occupants of a specific position.

   a. A role episode consists of a role sender and a focal person.

> KEY TERM: *Role overload* occurs when the sum total of what role senders expect of the focal person far exceeds what he or she is able to do.

> KEY TERM: *Role conflict* is experienced when different members of the role set expect different things of the focal person or when job demands conflict with personal demands.

> KEY TERM: *Role ambiguity* occurs when the focal person has too little or ambiguous information about the job.

2. *Norms*

> KEY TERM: *Norm*: an attitude, opinion, feeling, or action—shared by two or more people—that guides behavior.

> KEY TERM: *Ostracism*: when a nonconformist is rejected by the group.

   a. Usually, norms develop from a combination of the following:
       (1) explicit statements by supervisors or co-workers
       (2) critical events in the group's history
       (3) primacy, or the early patterns of group behavior
       (4) carryover behavior from past situations.
   b. Norms are enforced by the group when they:
       (1) help the group or organization survive
       (2) clarify or simplify behavioral expectations
       (3) help individuals avoid embarrassing situations
       (4) clarify the group's or organization's central values and/or unique identity.
   c. Role conflict and role ambiguity have been found to be associated with job dissatisfaction, tension, anxiety, lack of organizational commitment, intentions to quit, and job performance.
   d. Managers can use feedback, formal rules and procedures, directive leadership, setting specific, hard goals, and participation to relieve the problems of role conflict and role ambiguity.

D. Career Management
   1. Failing to manage one's career may lead to professional plateauing, poor work attitudes, stress, and ultimately a lower quality of life.
   2. Unfortunately, career management appears to be a problem with a large number of people.
   3. *Career Management Model*

> KEY TERM: *Career*: the pattern of work-related experiences that span the course of one's life.

> KEY TERM: *Career Management*: a problem-solving/decision-making process aimed at optimizing the match between an individual's needs and values and his or her work-related experiences.

   a. The model of career management shown in Figure 8-8 consists of eight phases:
       (1) career exploration
       (2) awareness of self and environment
       (3) goal setting
       (4) strategy development
       (5) strategy implementation
       (6) progress toward goal
       (7) career appraisal
       (8) feedback: work, nonwork.
   b. The two key phases in the career management model are career planning and career appraisal.

    c.   *Career Planning* consists of steps one through four of the career management model.

> KEY TERM: *Career exploration* entails gathering career-related information about oneself and the environment.

    d.   *Career Appraisal*

> KEY TERM: *Career Appraisal* consists of obtaining and using career-related feed-back from both work and nonwork sources.

E. Career Transitions

    1. Careers, like life in general, involve change.

    2. Needs, career aspirations, and job skills change over time.

> KEY TERM: *Career Stages* represent common work experiences that occur at similar points in individuals' careers and are independent of occupation or organization.

    3. Careers are affected by one's career anchor.

> KEY TERM: *Career anchor*: the self-image that a person develops around his or her career, which both guides and constrains career decisions.

    4. *Professional Career Stages*
       a. Professional careers evolve over four successive stages:
          (1) apprentice
          (2) colleague
          (3) mentor
          (4) sponsor.
       b. Different career stages involve different tasks, primary relationships, and psychological issues to be resolved.
       c. Managers can use the four-stage model when discussing performance and career issues with subordinates.

    5. *Making The Transition from Student to Professional*
       a. The successful transition from student to professional apprentice requires the resolution of frequent problems.
       b. Successful problem resolutions include:
          (1) acquiring technical competence
          (2) learning as much as possible about the organization
          (3) demonstrating independence in solving organizational problems.

    6. *Career Anchors*
       a. Career anchors represent that part of the self-concept that relates to one's career image and reflects one's important career-related values and needs.
       b. A well developed career anchor provides answers to the following questions:
          (1) What are my talents, skills, areas of competence?
          (2) What are my main motives, drives, goals in life? and
          (3) What are my values?

OPENING CASE SOLUTION

1. The organizational socialization process, or "people process," is used by Goldman Sachs to help employees learn the values, norms, and required behaviors necessary to participate successfully within the company. Goldman Sachs "socializes" employees to become committed to the goal of partner. The partner-selection process culminates in a two-month-long competition that is a closely held secret. After weeks of informal lobbying and quiet investigation, the management committee meets in a more formal phase to select the successful new partners.

2. Norms are those attitudes, opinions, feelings and actions that guide behavior in social environments. At Goldman Sachs, the desired norms are total commitment to the firm, a willingness to give up their entire lives for the firm, to become team players and "culture carriers" who are willing to fit into the firm's tradition.

3. Mentoring is the process of forming and maintaining an intensive and lasting developmental relationship between a senior person and a junior person. The partner-selection process involves written nominations, a cross-examination of candidates' qualifications, and an 11th-hour "town meeting" of all partners. The process is kept secret, but the decision is made by partners. A junior employee must have one or more supportive mentors in order to attain partnership approval.

4. A career anchor is defined as that part of the self concept that relates to one's career. A career anchor reflects one's talents, values, motives, and life goals. Robin Illgen probably has an "autonomy/independence" career anchor (see Table 8-7), featuring autonomous contract or project work with skill-based pay and benefits and portable recognition.

END-OF-CHAPTER EXERCISE

1. This is a good opportunity for students to apply their knowledge of socialization techniques to real-world examples.

2. Unfortunately, many students do not have any meaningful work experience on which to base this exercise. Those who are weak in this regard are encouraged to interview a manager or professional in order to apply his or her insights to this exercise.

3. A good closure technique might be a class discussion of findings along with a discussion of such issues as the trade-off between a high degree of socialization and the limits to individuality and freedom.

INSTRUCTIONAL RESOURCES

1. Role definition is explored in the exercise, "The Role Evaluation Exercise," in Peter Dawson, *Fundamentals of Organizational Behavior: An Experiential Approach* (Englewood Cliffs, N.J.: Prentice Hall, 1985), pp. 447-448.

2. An analysis of norms and conformity is provided in the film, "Conformity and Independence," (University of Illinois Film Center).

3. An overall view of career planning is provided in the film, "Career Development: A Plan for All Seasons," (CRM Films).

4. A guide to successful job-hunting is outlined in Les Dlabay and John Slocum, Jr., *How to Pack Your Career Parachute* (Reading, MA: Addison-Wesley, 1989).

5. A survey providing life-goal insights is the "Life-Style Questionnaire" by R. Driscoll and D. Eckstein in *Instrumentation Kit* (San Diego: University Associates, 1987).

6. Students will learn by doing "Exercise: Personal Career Planning," in John Schermerhorn, et el, *Managing Organizational Behavior*, 3rd ed. (New York: Wiley, 1988), pp. 570-571.

7. The unique problems involved with international careers are addressed in the exercise, "Overseas Management Issues," in Gene E. Burton, *Exercises in Management*, 3rd ed. (Boston: Houghton Mifflin Company, 1990), pp. 277-281.

8. See the various modules for Chapter 8 in Muto, Kreitner, and Kinicki *Lecture Supplement Manual*.

TOPICAL RESOURCES

1. An in-depth study of norms is found in Daniel Feldman, "The Development and Enforcement of Group Norms," *Academy of Management Review*, January 1984, pp. 47-53.

2. The two-career couple is the subject of Eugene Hall and Douglas Hall, *The Two-Career Couple* (Reading, MA: Addison-Wesley, 1983).

3. The importance of international experience in career planning is addressed by Amanda Bennett, "Going Global: Chief Executives in the Year 2000 Will Be Experienced Abroad," *Wall Street Journal*, January 27, 1989, A1, A9.

4. The unique career problems of mothers are discussed in Elizabeth Erlich, "The Mommy Track: Juggling Kids and Careers in Corporate America Takes a Controversial Turn," *Business Week*, March 20, 1989, pp. 126-134.

5. For recent research on mentoring and managerial careers, see William Whitely, et al., "Relationship of Career Mentoring and Socioconomic Origin to Managers' and Professionals' Early Career Progress," *Academy of Management Journal*, June 1991, pp. 331-351.

DISCUSSION/ESSAY QUESTIONS

1. Discuss the socialization process from the basis of Feldman's model.

2. How are organizational roles developed, and how are they enforced?

3. What are the advantages and disadvantages of realistic job previews?

4. Analyze the role of modeling with respect to Sorcher's Applied Learning.

5. Discuss the problems that students typically have when they make the transition from student to professional apprentice.

9

Group and Intergroup Dynamics

CAPSULE SUMMARY

Chapter 9 explores the critical dimensions of people working in groups. The chapter opens with an introduction to the concept of social facilitation and a sociological definition of a group. Group types and functions are viewed from both individual and organizational perspectives. The nature of group formation, structure and composition, and task and maintenance roles are analyzed in view of current group research. The unique problems of male-female work groups are examined in light of the changes in the workforce. Finally, the chapter investigates threats to group effectiveness and the techniques for minimizing those threats.

LECTURE OUTLINE

A. **Social Interaction in the Workplace**

When two people interact at work or elsewhere, the net result is synergy—something greater than the sum of what the two individuals bring to the situation.

> KEY TERM: *Synergy*: a situation where the whole is greater than the sum of its parts.

1. *Social Facilitation*

> KEY TERM: *Social facilitation*: positive or negative influences on performance caused by the mere presence of others.

   a. Research finds that the mere presence of others has a small impact (3 percent or less) on performance.
   b. The presence of others tends to aid the performance of simple tasks and hamper the performance of complex tasks.
   c. Managing the effects of social facilitation involves paying attention to general training, computer familiarization, and office design.

2. *Groups*

> KEY TERM: Group: two or more freely interacting individuals who share collective norms and goals and have a common identity.

B. **Group Types, Functions, and Development**

It is helpful to classify groups by their type, functions, and stages of development.

1. *Formal and Informal Groups*

> KEY TERM: *Formal group*: a group charged with helping the organization accomplish its objectives.

> KEY TERM: *Informal group*: a group whose overriding purpose is getting together in friendship.

2. *Functions of Formal Groups*
   a. Formal groups fulfill both organizational and individual functions (see Table 9-1).

3. *Stages of the Group Development Process*
   a. During the first three stages of the six-stage development process, uncertainty over authority and power is an overriding obstacle. The focus shifts to coping with uncertainty over interpersonal relations during the last three stages.
   b. *Stage 1: Orientation* - the ice-breaking stage when trust is low and either a formal or an emergent leader takes charge.
   c. *Stage 2: Conflict and Challenge* - the testing period during which subgroups emerge and subtle rebellion occurs.
   d. *Stage 3: Cohesion* - a time when someone other than the leader urges the group to resolve power struggles and get something accomplished.
   e. *Stage 4: Delusion* - a period of good feelings and active participation.
   f. *Stage 5: Disillusion* - a time when an unrealistic sense of harmony gives way to conflict between subgroups that has a negative impact on cohesiveness and commitment.
   g. *Stage 6: Acceptance* - finally, an influential member of the group challenges everyone to do some reality testing and sharing of mutual expectations, thus bringing the group to productive maturity.

4. *Group Development: Research and Practical Implications*
   a. *Feedback*
      One study of feedback found that:
      (1) interpersonal feedback increases as the group develops through successive stages
      (2) as the group develops, positive feedback increases and negative feedback decreases
      (3) interpersonal feedback becomes more specific as the group develops
      (4) the credibility of peer feedback increases as the group develops.
   b. *Deadlines*
      Deadlines can have both positive and negative impacts on group performance. When group members accurately perceive important deadlines, the pacing of work and the timing of interdependent tasks tends to be more efficient.
   c. *Leadership Styles*
      Different leadership styles are needed as groups develop. In the early stages of group development, the best leadership is active, aggressive, directive, structured, and task-oriented. In later stages of group development, the best leadership is supportive, democratic, decentralized, and participative.

C. *Group Structure and Composition*
   1. *Functional Roles Performed by Group Members*

      > KEY TERM: *Task roles* enable the work group to define, clarify, and pursue a common purpose (see Table 9-2).

      > KEY TERM: *Maintenance roles* foster supportive and constructive interpersonal relationships (see Table 9-2).

   2. *Technology-Structure Fit*

      > KEY TERM: *Vertical differentiation* involves the number of hierarchical levels represented in the group.

      > KEY TERM: *Horizontal differentiation* involves the number of different job categories represented in the group.

      a. Vertical differentiation is best for complex problems.
      b. Horizontal differentiation is best when the types of problems cannot be reliably predicted.
   3. *Group Size*
      a. Mathematical modeling has not provided a concise answer to the question of how many members should there be in a group.
      b. Lab simulations suggest that five members is about optimum for good decision quality.
      c. A contingency approach recommends three to five members if decision quality is the main objective. If creativity, participation, socialization of new members, or the communication of policy are the objectives, then more than five members is appropriate.
   4. *Women Face an Uphill Battle in Mixed-Gender Task Groups*
      a. Recent research indicates that women still face inequality in mixed-gender groups.
      b. Managers are faced with the challenge of countering discriminatory tendencies in group dynamics.
   5. *Individual Ability and Group Effectiveness*

a.   Research of Israeli three-man tank crews found that uniformly high-ability crews far outperformed mixed-ability and low-ability groups.
b.   The study suggests a contingency approach to staffing groups according to members' abilities by spreading high-ability individuals around to all groups, if the objective is to improve the performance of all groups or to train novices.

D. **Threats to Group Effectiveness**
The Asch effect, groupthink, and social loafing are found to be threats to group effectiveness.
1. *The Asch Effect*

> KEY TERM: *The Asch effect*: named after the social psychologists Solomon Asch's famous "minority of one study," it is the distortion of individual judgment by a unanimous but incorrect opposition.

2. *Groupthink*

> KEY TERM: *Groupthink* is a mode of thinking that people engage in when they are deeply involved in a cohesive in-group, when members' strivings for unanimity override their motivation to realistically appraise alternative courses of action. Groupthink is a term coined by Irving Janis.

a.   The eight symptoms of groupthink are:
(1) invulnerability
(2) inherent morality
(3) rationalization
(4) stereotyped views of opposition
(5) self-censorship
(6) illusions of unanimity
(7) peer pressure
(8) mindguards, or self-appointed protectors against adverse information.
b.   Research indicates that highly cohesive groups victimized by groupthink tend to make poor decisions, despite confidence in their decisions.
c.   Janis suggests the following as groupthink prevention techniques:
(1) each member should be assigned the role of critical evaluator
(2) executives should not use policy committees to rubber-stamp decisions that have already been made
(3) different groups with different leaders should explore the same policy questions
(4) subgroup debates and outside experts should be used to introduce new perspectives
(5) someone should play the role of devil's advocate when discussing major alternatives
(6) once a consensus has been reached, everyone should be encouraged to rethink their position to check for flaws.
3. *Social Loafing*

> KEY TERM: *Social loafing*: the tendency for individual effort to decline as group size increases.

a.   Possible explanations for social loafing are:
(1) equity of effort
(2) loss of personal accountability

(3) motivational loss due to sharing of rewards
(4) coordination loss as more people perform the task.
b. In laboratory studies, social loafing occurred when:
(1) the task was viewed as unimportant
(2) contributors thought their individual output was unidentifiable
(3) people expected their co-workers to loaf.
c. Social loafing can be defused by challenging tasks, personal accountability, and positive expectations of hard work.

E. **Social Networks: Toward Understanding Intergroup Interactions**

> KEY TERM: *Social network analysis*: the process of graphically mapping and categorizing social transactions to identify meaningful patterns.

1. *Social Network Functions*
   a. Five social network functions are:
   (1) star
   (2) liaison
   (3) bridge
   (4) gatekeeper
   (5) isolate.
2. *Prescribed and Emergent Clusters*
   a. Prescribed clusters are task teams or formal committees carrying out assigned jobs.
   b. Emergent clusters are informal, unofficial groupings of network members.

> KEY TERM: *Clique*: an emergent cluster based on lasting friendships.

3. *The Practical Value of a Social Network Perspective*
   a. Network analysis is a handy diagnostic tool for interpersonal problems.
   b. Gatekeepers can serve as the organization's eyes and ears of the world.
   c. Network isolates may require special managerial support.

OPENING CASE SOLUTION

1. Janet Long's Wilderness Lab group satisfied the criteria of a sociological group. It was small enough, and the activities were structured to facilitate free and open interaction. There were collective norms imposed both by the group and by the trainers. The trust ladder and "the wall" served as collective goals. Lastly, the trainees felt a common identity throughout the training.

2. The trust ladder played a key role in helping the group move from the orientation stage to the conflict and challenge stage. The trust ladder helped the group members achieve a feeling of mutual trust and dependency that is necessary before the group can attempt challenging tasks such as "the wall."

3. During the climbing of "the wall," there was no social loafing because everyone had an essential and visible role to fulfill. If one person failed, the whole group failed, so there was total commitment to accomplishing the group task.

END-OF-CHAPTER EXERCISE

1. This is an interesting hands-on learning tool by which students may become more familiar with organizational socialization techniques.

2. It is preferred that students refer to present work organizations as their reference base. However, for students who do not have such an experiential base, interviewing a manager should provide some meaningful insight into the issue.

3. Closure may be achieved by a follow-up class discussion on the trade-off between a high degree of socialization and the protection of individual freedom.

INSTRUCTIONAL RESOURCES

1. A classic experiential lesson dealing with the types of problems that are best for groups is "Discussion Methods and Problem Solving," in Norman Maier, *Psychology in Industrial Organizations*, 4th ed. (Boston: Houghton Mifflin, 1973), pp. 326-328.

2. The differences between formal and informal groups is the focus of the exercise, "Formal and Informal Organizations," in Keith Davis and John Newstrom, *Organizational Behavior: Readings and Exercises*, 7th ed. (New York: McGraw-Hill, 1985), pp. 530-534.

3. For a better understanding of group roles, try "The Role Evaluation Exercise," in Peter Dawson, *Organizational Behavior: An Experiential Approach* (Englewood Cliffs, N.J.: Prentice Hall, 1985), pp. 447-448.

4. Students can learn how roles are developed through the exercise, "Role Negotiation," in Douglas Hall, et al, *Experiences in Management and Organizational Behavior* (Chicago: St. Clair Press, 1988), 296-297.

5. The construction of sociograms is the thrust of the exercise, "Sociogram," in Douglas Hall, et al, *Experiences in Management and Organizational Behavior* (Chicago: St. Clair Press, 1988), pp. 215- 216.

6. For an interesting look at groupthink, see the film, "Group Dynamics: Groupthink," (CRM/McGraw-Hill).

7. See the various modules for Chapter 9 in the Muto, Kreitner, and Kinicki *Lecture Supplement Manual*.

TOPICAL RESOURCES

1. For a classic exploration of functional roles, read Kenneth Benne and Paul Sheats, "Function Roles of Group Members," *Journal of Social Issues,* no. 2, 1948, pp. 43-54.

2. An excellent approach to the enforcement of group norms is presented by Daniel Feldman, "The Development and Enforcement of Group Norms," *Academy of Management Review*, January 1984, pp. 47-53.

3. Every student should read *Victims of Groupthink*, 2nd ed. by Irving Janis (Boston: Houghton Mifflin, 1982).

4. The student of sociometry should read J.L. Moreno, *Foundations of Sociometry Monographs*, no. 4 (Boston: Beacon, 1943).

5. In-group loyalty is the focus of Gene E. Burton "The Measurement of Distortion Tendencies Induced by the Win-Lose Nature of In-Group Loyalty," *Small Group Research*, February 1990, pp. 128- 141.

DISCUSSION/ESSAY QUESTIONS

1. Discuss the influence of social facilitation on the development of group roles.
2. Analyze the key issues to be addressed at each stage of the group development process.
3. How does a manager decide the optimum size of a work group?
4. What is the value of spreading the best people throughout a firm's work groups?
5. Discuss the practical application of the five social network functions.

10

Power, Politics, and Conflict

CAPSULE SUMMARY

Chapter 10 deals with the important issues surrounding interpersonal influence. At the very heart of interpersonal dealings in today's work organizations is a constant struggle between individual and collective interests. A foundation for the material is found in the presentation of eight generic influence tactics that demonstrate how people try to get their own way in the work place. Social power is defined and contrasted with the organizational concept of authority. Socialized power is compared with personalized power. There is a discussion of French and Raven's five bases of power. Organizational politics is addressed through the issues of political action and political tactics. Conflict is analyzed in terms of functional versus dysfunctional conflict, antecedents of conflict, and conflict-handling styles. Finally, the chapter offers a contingency approach for the management of conflict.

LECTURE OUTLINE

Preoccupation with self-interests is understandable. After all, each of us was born, not as a cooperating organizational member, but as an individual with instincts of self-preservation. Figure 10-1 graphically portrays the constant tug-of-war between employees' self interests and the organization's need for mutuality of interests.

> KEY TERM: *Mutuality of interest* involves win-win situations in which one's self interests are served by cooperating actively and creatively with potential adversaries.

A. **Organizational Influence Tactics: Getting One's Way at Work**
   A large measure of interpersonal interaction involves *social influence* - attempts to influence others.
   1. *Eight Generic Influence Tactics*
      a. Research by David Kipnis and others found eight generic influence tactics in use in organizations.
      b. The eight tactics in diminishing order of use by managers for *downward* influence were:
         (1) consultation
         (2) rational persuasion
         (3) inspirational appeals
         (4) ingratiating tactics
         (5) coalition tactics
         (6) pressure tactics
         (7) upward appeals
         (8) exchange tactics
   2. *Other Research Insights*
      a. No difference has been found between the influence tactics used by or with men and women.
      b. Upward influence tactics have been found to vary to suit the leadership style of the boss. Upward appeals and ingratiating tactics tended to be used most often to influence authoritarian managers. Rational persuasion was used to influence participative managers.
   3. *How to Extend Your Influence by Forming Strategic Alliances*
      a. Influence can be extended through alliances, which are win-win relationships based on complementary strengths.
      b. Research by Cohen and Bradford found that influence can be extended through the use of:
         (1) mutual respect
         (2) openness
         (3) trust
         (4) mutual benefit.
      c. Although these tactics involve some personal risks, the effectiveness of interpersonal strategic alliances is anchored to the concept of reciprocity.

> KEY TERM: *Reciprocity*: the almost universal belief that people should be paid back for what they do—that one good (or bad) turn deserves another.

B. Social Power and Power Sharing

> KEY TERM: *Social power*: the ability to marshal the human, informational, and material resources to get something done.

1. *Dimensions of Power*
   a. Power may or may not overlap with one's authority.

   > KEY TERM: *Authority*: the right or the obligation to seek compliance. In contrast, power is the demonstrated ability to achieve compliance.

2. *Two Types of Power*
   a. Recent research has drawn a distinction between socialized power and personalized power.

   > KEY TERM: *Socialized power*: plans, self-doubts, mixed outcomes, and concern for others, as measured on the Thematic Apperception Test (TAT).

   > KEY TERM: *Personalized power*: expressions of power for the sake of personal aggrandizement are paramount.

3. Five Bases of Power
   a. French and Raven have proposed that power arises from five different power bases:
      (1) reward power
      (2) coercive power
      (3) legitimate power
      (4) expert power
      (5) referent power.

   > KEY TERM: *Reward power*: the extent to which one obtains compliance by promising or granting rewards.

   > KEY TERM: *Coercive power*: the extent to which one obtains compliance by threatened or actual punishment.

   > KEY TERM: *Legitimate power*: possessed by those who gain compliance by virtue of their formal authority to make decisions.

   > KEY TERM: *Expert power*: compliance is gained by virtue of one's knowledge and information.

   > KEY TERM: *Referent power*: one's personality is the reason for compliance.

4. *Research Insights About Social Power*
   a. Males and females have been found to have similar needs for power and personalized power, but females have a higher need for socialized power.
   b. Expert, referent, reward, and legitimate power were found to have a positive impact on job performance, job satisfaction, and turnover, while coercive power had a slightly negative impact.

5. *Responsible Management of Power*
   a. Responsible managers strive for socialized power while avoiding personalized power.

  b. *From Compliance to Internalization*
   Reward, coercive, and negative legitimate power tend to produce only compliance,
   but positive legitimate, expert, and referent power tend to foster internalization (intrinsic motivation).
  c. *From Power Sharing to Power Distribution*
   Figure 10-3 contains a graphic representation of the evolution of power from domination to delegation.

> KEY TERM: *Delegation*: the process of granting decision-making authority to subor-
> dinates.

 C. *Organizational Politics*
  Organizational politics may or may not involve dirty dealing; but it is an ever-present feature
  of modern organizational life.
   1. *Definition and Domain of Organizational Politics*

> KEY TERM: *Organizational politics*: involves intentional acts of influence to en-
> hance or protect the self-interest of individuals or groups.

    a. Political maneuvering is triggered by uncertainty as a result of :
     (1) unclear objectives
     (2) vague performance measures
     (3) ill-defined decision processes
     (4) strong individual or group competition
     (5) any type of change.
    b. The three levels of political action are:
     (1) network level
     (2) coalition level
     (3) individual level.

> KEY TERM: *Coalition*: an informal group bound together by the active pursuit of a
> single issue.

   2. *Political Tactics*
    a. One study identified eight political tactics, which are, in descending order of occur-
     rence:
     (1) attacking or blaming others
     (2) using information as a political tool
     (3) creating a favorable image
     (4) developing a base of support
     (5) praising others, or ingratiation
     (6) forming power coalitions with strong allies
     (7) associating with influential people
     (8) creating obligations, or reciprocity
   3. *Research Evidence on Organizational Politics*
    a. Political activity is found to be common, associated with larger organizations, trig-
     gered by ambiguity and conflict, associated with higher levels of management and
     staff positions, and a self-perpetuating cycle.
   4. *Managing Organizational Politics*
    a. Organizational politics cannot be eliminated, but they can be managed.

b.   The best line of defense against destructive politics is measurable objectives.

D. **Managing Interpersonal and Intergroup Conflict**

> KEY TERM: *Conflict*: all kinds of opposition or antagonistic interaction based on scarcity of power, resources or social position, and differing value systems.

1. *A Conflict Continuum*
   a.   Recognizing that both too little or too much conflict can be counterproductive, a middle ground is recommended.

2. *Functional Versus Dysfunctional Conflict*

> KEY TERM: *Functional conflict*: serves the organization's interests by keeping people open to change and promoting creativity.

> KEY TERM: *Dysfunctional conflict*: hinders organizational performance.

3. *Antecedents of Conflict*
   a.   Proactive managers are good at reading the early warning signs of conflict and taking corrective action.

4. *Stimulating Functional Conflict*

> KEY TERM: *Programmed conflict*: raises different opinions regardless of the personal feelings of the managers. Two proven types of programmed conflict are devil's advocacy and the dialectic method.

> KEY TERM: *Devil's advocacy*: assigning someone the role of critic.

> KEY TERM: *Dialectic method*: a structured debate of opposing views prior to making a decision.

5. *Alternative Styles of Handling Conflict*
   a.   Conflict can be handled through:
       (1) ingratiating, or problem solving
       (2) obliging, or smoothing
       (3) dominating, or forcing
       (4) avoiding
       (5) compromising.

6. *Conflict Research Evidence*
   a.   Personality characteristics affect how people handle conflict.
   b.   How one disagrees may be more important that what the disagreement is about.
   c.   Aggression breeds aggression.
   d.   Conflict and group satisfaction are negatively related.

7. *Conflict Management: A Contingency Approach*
   a.   Conflict needs to be stimulated if there is too little of it.
   b.   Dysfunctional conflict requires the appropriate conflict handling style.

OPENING CASE SOLUTION

1. At General Motors, HulKi Aldikacti seemed to be operating from a power base of expert power from his perceived consultative expertise. Since people seemed unwilling to challenge him, he may also have wielded some coercive power.

2. The organizational power struggle between the Pontiac and Chevrolet divisions is at the forefront of this case. Individuals were reluctant to challenge Aldikacti, because it meant challenging the political power of the entire Pontiac division.

3. The conflict proved to be dysfunctional, as the Fiero never achieved the success that was planned for it. Functional conflict might have spurred creative solutions to the car's problems.

4. One major antecedent in this case is the impression that "the Chevy people always seemed to get everything." Thus, the Pontiac people felt that past inequities gave their effort some moral basis.

5. It would seem that an integrating or problem-solving approach should have been used in the Fiero situation. Interested parties could confront the issues and cooperatively identify problems and generate and evaluate alternative solutions.

END-OF-CHAPTER EXERCISE

1. This role-playing exercise is designed to show students the practical value of alternative conflict handing techniques. This exercise can create a learning environment in which students can experiment with a conflict handling style with which they may not be familiar.

2. The exercise can be modified by assigning a third person to each team as a neutral observer.

3. Observers and/or participants can report their findings and feelings as part of a culminating class discussion.

INSTRUCTIONAL RESOURCES

1. Students can learn first-hand about power bases in the exercise, "Occupational Power Bases," in Gene E,. Burton, *Exercises in Management*, 3rd ed. (Boston: Houghton Mifflin Company, 1990), pp. 171-177.

2. A supervisor-subordinate conflict is the focus of the exercise, "Analyzing the Case of the Storm Windows," in Norman Maier, *Psychology in Industrial Organizations*, 4th ed. (Boston: Houghton Mifflin Company, 1973), pp. 352-356.

3. Conflict management is experienced in the exercise, "Conflict Management Styles," in J. Jones and J. Pfeiffer, *The 1977 Handbook for Group Facilitators* (San Diego: University Associates, 1977).

4. Corporate conflict is the focus of the exercise, "Corporate Conflict," in J. Gibson and R. Hodgettes, *Readings and Exercises in Organizational Behavior* (Orlando: Academic Press, 1985), pp. 258-260.

5. A case of group conflict is found in the exercise, "Identify the Conflict," in John Samaras, *Management Applications: Exercises, Cases, and Readings* (Englewood Cliffs, N.J.: Prentice Hall, 1989), p. 85.

6. Causes and resolution of conflict are the focus of the film, "Conflict: Causes and Resolutions," (CRM Productions).

7. Conflict in a production environment is analyzed in the film, "Conflict on the Line: A Case Study," (CRM Productions).

8. See the various modules for chapter 10 in the Muto, Kreitner, and Kinicki *Lecture Supplement Manual*.

TOPICAL RESOURCES

1. The proper use of managerial power is the thrust of "The Effective Use of Managerial Power," by G. Yukl and T. Taber in *Personnel*, March-April 1983.

2. For a look at management of agreement, see "The Abilene Paradox: The Management of Agreement," *Organizational Dynamics*, Summer 1974.

3. A contingency model of power is presented in G. Salancik and J. Pfeffer, "Who Gets Power—and How They Hold on to It: A Strategic Contingency Model of Power," *Organizational Dynamics*, Winter 1977.

4. A review of managerial influence is found in David Kipnis, et al, "Patterns of Managerial Influence: Shotgun Managers, Tacticians, and Bystanders," *Organizational Dynamics*, Winter 1984.

5. Interpersonal conflict is the subject of "What to Do When an Employee Is Talented—and a Pain in the Neck," by Larry Rubenstein, *Wall Street Journal*, August 8, 1986.

5. For an analysis of conflict management, read, Rahim Afzalur, "A Strategy for Managing Conflict in Complex Organizations," *Human Relations*, no. 1, 1985, pp. 81-89.

6. An interesting insight into organizational politics is provided in Stanley Young, "Politicking: The Unsung Managerial Skill," *Personnel*, June 1987.

7. Additional research on influence tactics can be found in Chester A. Schriesheim and Timothy R. Hinkin, "Influence Tactics Used by Subordinates," *Journal of Applied Psychology*, June 1990, pp. 246-257.

8. A good update on conflict theory and management is Dean Tjosvold, *The Conflict–Positive Organization* (Reading, Mass.: Addison–Wesley, 1991).

9. A practical guide to organizational politics is Andrew DuBrin, *Winning Office Politics: DuBrin's Guide for the '90s* (Englewood Cliffs, N.J.: Prentice–Hall, 1990).

DISCUSSION/ESSAY QUESTIONS

1. Discuss the constant tug-of-war between self-interests and mutuality of interest in organizations.

2. Analyze the eight generic influence tactics as they can be applied to managerial situations.

3. Explore the managerial implications in the distinction between socialized power and personalized power.

4. How do the five bases of power, as established by French and Raven, impact our daily lifes?

5. Discuss the application of the contingency approach to handing conflict.

11

Effective Teamwork

CAPSULE SUMMARY

Chapter 11 completes the coverage of group and intergroup dynamics by closely examining work teams. Teams and teamwork are popular terms in management circles these days, as the team approach to managing organizations is having diverse and substantial impacts. The chapter begins by identifying four different types of work teams—advice teams, production teams, project teams, and action teams. A model of team effectiveness is introduced, with emphasis on the criteria of performance and viability. A discussion of team effectiveness finds cooperation, trust, and cohesiveness to be important. Quality circles and self-managed teams, the two most popular team concepts, are reviewed. Finally, the chapter explores recent team building techniques.

LECTURE OUTLINE

A. **Work Teams: Definitions, Types, and Effectiveness**

> KEY TERM: *Team*: an officially sanctioned collection of individuals who have been charged with completing a mission by an organization and who must depend upon one another for successful completion of that work.

1. *Eight Attributes of High-Performance Teams*
   a. *Participative Leadership* - creating an interdependency by empowering, freeing up, and serving others.
   b. *Shared Responsibility* - establishing an environment in which all team members feel as responsible as the manager for the performance of the work unit.
   c. *Aligned on Purpose* - having a sense of common purpose about why the team exists and the function it serves.
   d. *High Communication* - creating a climate of trust and open, honest communication.
   e. *Future Focused* - seeing change as an opportunity for growth.
   f. *Focused on Task* - keeping meetings focused on results.
   g. *Creative Talents* - applying individual talents and creativity.
   h. *Rapid Response* - identifying and acting on opportunities.

2. *A General Typology of Work Teams*
   a. Four general types of work teams are shown in Table 11-1:
      (1) advice
      (2) production
      (3) project
      (4) action.
   b. The four key variables in the typology deal with:
      (1) technical specialization
      (2) coordination
      (3) work cycles
      (4) outputs.
   c. *Advice Teams* - created to broaden the information base for managerial decisions,
   d. *Production Teams* - responsible for performing day-to-day operations.
   e. *Project Teams* - require creative problem solving, often involving the application of specialized knowledge.
   f. *Action Teams* - combine high specialization with high coordination for performance "on demand."

3. *Work Team Effectiveness: An Ecological Model*

> KEY TERM: *Performance*: means acceptability of output to customers within and outside the organization who receive team products, services, information, decisions, or performance events.

> KEY TERM: *Team viability*: team member satisfaction and continued willingness to contribute.

B. Effective Teamwork Through Cooperation, Trust, and Cohesiveness

   1. *Cooperation*

> KEY TERM: *Collaboration*: occurs when group members share responsibility for certain outcomes.

> KEY TERM: *Coordination*: involves arranging subtasks sequentially.

      a. Both expert opinion and research support cooperation rather than competition as the best way to bring out the best in people.

      b. Cooperation can be fostered by setting cooperative goals and creating functional conflict.

      c. *TIT For TAT* cooperative game strategy offers management four suggestions:

         (1) Demonstrate the group's or individual's fundamental desire for cooperation, not competition.

         (2) Demand that others not take advantages of oneself or one's group, and make them realize that one can and will reciprocate if they do.

         (3) Make others realize that they are not considered enemies or opponents, but are invited to become allies if they want a working relationship.

         (4) Demonstrate trust and openness by modeling the type of behavior one wishes others to enact.

   2. *Trust*

      a. Trust seems to be a key determinant of success for Japanese companies with production facilities in the U.S.

> KEY TERM: *Trust*: the reciprocal faith in others' intentions and behavior.

      b. Trust requires a "cognitive leap' beyond the expectations that reason and experience alone would warrant.

      c. According to Zand's model, trust evolves from a cycle of vulnerability, information disclosure, participation, and self-control.

      d. *How to Build Trust*

      Fernando Bartolome offers the following six guidelines for building and maintaining trust:

         (1) *Communication* - Keep team members and subordinates informed by explaining policies and decisions and by providing accurate feedback.

         (2) *Support* - Be available and approachable.

         (3) *Respect* - Delegation, in the form of real decision-making authority, is the most important expression of managerial respect.

         (4) *Fairness* - Be quick to give credit and recognition to those who deserve it.

         (5) *Predictability* - Be consistent and predictable in your daily affairs.

         (6) *Competence* - Enhance your credibility by demonstrating good business sense, technical ability, and professionalism.

   3. *Cohesiveness*

> KEY TERM: *Cohesiveness*: a process whereby a sense of we-ness emerges to transcend individual differences and motives.

> KEY TERM: *Socio-emotional cohesiveness*: a sense of togetherness that develops when individuals derive satisfaction from group participation.

> KEY TERM: *Instrumental cohesiveness*: a sense of togetherness that develops when group members are mutually dependent on one another because they believe they could not achieve the group's goal by acting separately.

    a.   Research has found a positive relationship between cohesiveness and group member satisfaction, group effectiveness, and interpersonal communication.

C. Teams in Action: From Quality Circles to Self-Managed Teams
This section strives to bring the team approach to life by exploring two different team formats found in today's work place:
        (1) quality circles
        (2) self-managed teams.

1. *Quality Circles*

> KEY TERM: *Quality circles*: small groups of people from the same work area who voluntarily get together to identify, analyze, and recommend solutions for problems related to quality, productivity, and cost reduction.

    a.   With an ideal size of 10 to 12 members, quality circles typically meet for about an hour on a regular basis.
    b.   Management facilitates the quality circle program through skills training and listening to periodic presentations and recommendations.

2. *The Quality Circle Movement*
    a.   American quality control experts helped introduce the basic idea of quality circles to Japan soon after World War II.
    b.   The idea eventually returned to the U.S. and reached fad proportions during the 1970s and 1980s.
    c.   The dramatic growth of quality circles in the U.S. has been attributed to:
        (1) a desire to replicate Japan's industrial success
        (2) America's penchant for business fads
        (3) the relative ease of installing quality circles without restructuring the organization.

3. *A Life-Cycle Perspective of Quality Circle Programs*
    a.   The six phases of the quality circle life cycle are:
        (1) start-up
        (2) initial problem solving
        (3) presentation/ approval of suggestions
        (4) implementation
        (5) expansion
        (6) decline.

4. *Insights from Field Research on Quality Circles*
    a.   Quality circles have failure rates of more than 60 percent.
    b.   Poor implementation is probably the root cause of most failures.
    c.   Research found a positive relationship between quality circle participation and the desire to continue working for the organization.
    d.   A longitudinal study found that quality circles had only a marginal impact on employee attitudes, but had a positive impact on productivity.
    e.   Another study found that quality circle participants received better job performance ratings and more frequent promotions.

      f.   Overall, quality circles appear to be a promising participation tool, if they are careful-ly implemented and supported by all levels of management during the first five phases of the program life cycle.

   5. *Self-Managed Teams*

> KEY TERM: *Self-managed teams*: groups of workers who are given administrative oversight for their task domains.

      a.   Administrative oversight involves delegated activities such as planing, scheduling, monitoring, and staffing.
      b.   Self-managed teams are variously referred to as semiautonomous work teams, autonomous work teams, and superteams.
      c.   A common feature of self-managed teams is cross-functionalism.

> KEY TERM: *Cross-functionalism*: placing of specialists from different areas on the same team.

   6. *Are Self-Managed Teams Effective? Research Evidence*
      a.   A review of three recent studies led to the finding that self-managed teams have:
          (1) a positive impact on productivity
          (2) a positive impact on specific attitudes relating to self-management (e.g., respon-sibility and control)
          (3) no significant impact on general attitudes (e.g., job satisfaction and organization-al commitment)
          (4) no significant impact on absenteeism or turnover.

D. Team Building

> KEY TERM: *Team building*: a catchall term for a whole host of techniques aimed at improving the internal functioning of work groups.

   1. Richard Beckhard identified four purposes of team building:
          (1) to set goals and/or priorities
          (2) to analyze or allocate the way work is performed
          (3) to examine the way a group is working
          (4) to examine relationships among the people doing the work.
   2. Willaim Dyer recommends the following six-phase team-building cycle:
          (1) recognition of a current problem
          (2) data gathering
          (3) data evaluation
          (4) problem solving and planning
          (5) implementation
          (6) evaluation.
   3. *Developing Team Members' Self-Management Skills*

> KEY TERM: *Self-management leadership*: the process of leading others to lead themselves.

      a.   A field study identified the following six self-management leadership behaviors:
          (1) encourages self-reinforcement
          (2) encourages self-observation/evaluation

(3) encourages self- expectation
(4) encourages self-goal-setting
(5) encourages rehearsal
(6) encourages self-criticism.

OPENING CASE SOLUTION

1. The teams at AT&T Credit Corporation (ATTCC) may be perceived as only partially effective. According to the Ecological Model of Work Team Effectiveness, there are two major criteria for measuring team effectiveness—performance and viability. With respect to bottom-line performance figures, the teams are considered to be most effective. However, the teams fail the criterion of viability, as employee satisfaction with the teams is waning and turnover is high, primarily due to a lack of promotion opportunities.

2. Trust is defined as reciprocal faith in others' intentions and behavior. Trust is one of the foundations of the ATTCC team concept, as the teams work with virtually no supervision.

3. Perhaps the most critical drawback in the ATTCC team concept is the absence of a perceived career ladder. Team members who are achievement oriented see too few opportunities for promotion. Secondly, there is also an intense perceived pressure on co-workers to produce. These two drawbacks probably account for the high rate of turnover at ATTCC.

END-OF-CHAPTER EXERCISE

1. This is an excellent opportunity for students to learn, first-hand, the components of teamwork as well as a technique for diagnosing teamwork effectiveness.

2. Students will find this diagnostic tool to be most versatile if they apply it to work groups, class project groups, committees, project teams, clubs, fraternities, sororities, or athletic teams.

INSTRUCTIONAL RESOURCES

1. An excellent audio-tape/workbook learning tool is found in "Effective Team Building," distributed by the American Management Associates.

2. An interesting approach to teams is presented in the film, "Team Building," (CRM/Mc-Graw-Hill).

3. A 20-item survey by which students can measure their aptitude for delegation is the "Delegation Aptitude Survey," in Gene E. Burton, *Exercises in Management*, 3rd ed. (Boston: Houghton Mifflin Company, 1990), pp. 103-106.

4. A "how-to" manual for the serious student of quality circles is Roger James and A. Elkins, *How to Train and Lead a Quality Circle* (San Diego: University Associates, 1983).

5. The role of trust in teamwork is the focus of the film, " Trust Your Team," (Films Incorporated).

6. See the various modules for Chapter 11 in the Muto, Kreitner, and Kinicki *Lecture Supplement Manual*.

TOPICAL RESOURCES

1. An in-depth look at team development is found in Connie Gersuh, "Time and Transition in Work Teams: Toward a New Model Development," *Academy of Management Journal*, March 1988, pp. 9-41.

2. The proper design of work teams is the thrust of Richard Hackman, "The Design of Work Teams," in Jay Lorsch, ed. *Handbook of Organizational Behavior* (Englewood Cliffs, N.J.: Prentice Hall, 1987), pp. 343-357.

3. A look at some quality circle limitations is the subject of Edward Lawler and Susan Mohrman, "Quality Circles: After the Honeymoon," *Organizational Dynamics*, Spring 1987, pp. 42-54.

4. A study of hospital quality circles is reported in Gene E. Burton, "Quality Circles in a Hospital Environment: A Longitudinal Analysis of Withdrawal Precursers and Behavior," *Hospital Topics*, November-december 1986, pp. 11-17.

5. An in-depth examination of group effectiveness is provided in Gregory Shea and Richard Guzzo, "Group Effectiveness: What Really Matters?" *Sloan Management Review*, Spring 1987, p. 25.

6. For more on self-managed teams, see Charles C. Manz, David E. Keating, and Anne Donnellson, "Preparing for an Organizational Change to Employee Self-Management: The Managerial Transition," *Organizational Dynamics*, autumn 1990, pp. 15-26.

7. Self-managed teams and leadership are covered in David Barry, "Managing the Bossless Team: Lessons from Distributed Leadership," *Organizational Dynamics*, summer 1991, pp. 31-47.

8. A good overview of teams is Richard S. Wellins, William C. Byham, and Jeanne M. Wilson, *Empowered Teams* (San Francisco: Jossey-Bass, 1991)

DISCUSSION/ESSAY QUESTIONS

1. Explain and compare the four general types of work teams.
2. Apply the Ecological Model of Work Team Effectiveness to a real-world work situation.
3. Analyze and evaluate Zand's model of trust.
4. What can managers do to increase the levels of cooperation, trust, and cohesiveness?
5. Contrast and compare the application of quality circles and self-managed teams in the U.S.

12

Organizational Communication Processes

CAPSULE SUMMARY

Every managerial function and activity involves some form of direct or indirect communication. Whether planning and organizing, or directing and leading, managers find themselves communicating with and through others. Managerial decisions and organizational policies are ineffective unless they are understood by those responsible for enacting them. Chapter 12 will help future managers to both improve their communication skills and design more effective communication programs. The chapter discusses the basic dimensions of the communication process, focusing on a perceptual process model and a contingency approach to selecting media. The dynamics of interpersonal and organizational communication are explored. Finally, the barriers to effective communication are analyzed.

LECTURE OUTLINE

A. **Basic Dimensions of the Communication Process**

> KEY TERM: *Communication*: the exchange of information between a sender and a receiver, and the inference of meaning between the individuals involved.

1. *A Perceptual Process Model of Communication*
    a. Historically, the communication process was described in terms of a conduit model, but this approach has been criticized for being based on unrealistic assumptions.
    b. Researchers in communication now describe communication as a form of social information processing.

    > KEY TERM: *Perceptual Model of Communication*: depicts communication as a process in which receivers create meaning in their own minds.

    c. *Sender*
        The sender is the individual, group, or organization that desires to communicate with a particular receiver, which may be an individual, group, or organization.
    d. *Encoding*
        Encoding is the process, performed by the sender, of translating thoughts into a code or language that can be understood by others.
    e. *The Message*
        The output of encoding is a message. Messages may contain hidden agendas as well as trigger affective or emotional reactions. Messages must also match the medium used to transmit them.
    f. *Decoding*
        Decoding is the process, performed by the receiver, of translating verbal, oral, or visual aspects of a message into a form that can be interpreted, so that meaning can be created in the mind of the receiver.
    g. *Feedback*
        The receiver's response to the message is transmitted to the sender in the form of feedback.
    h. *Noise*

    > KEY TERM: *Noise*: represents anything that interferes with the transmission and understanding of a message.

2. *Choosing Media: A Contingency Perspective*
    a. Media selection is based on the interaction between information richness and the complexity of the problem/situation at hand.

    > KEY TERM: *Information richness*: the extent to which an item of data provides new understanding.

    b. Information richness is determined by four factors:
        (1) feedback
        (2) channel
        (3) type of communication
        (4) language source.

       c.   Effective communication occurs when the richness of the medium is matched appropriately with the complexity of the problem.

B. Interpersonal Communication

> KEY TERM: *Communication competence*: a performance-based index of how well an individual communicates.

1. *Assertiveness, Aggressiveness, and Nonassertiveness*
   a. Research indicates an assertive communication style is more effective than either an aggressive or nonassertive style.

> KEY TERM: *Assertive style*: expressive and self-enhancing and based on the ethical notion that one should not violate another individual's basic human rights.

> KEY TERM: *Aggressive style*: expressive and self-enhancing and strives to take unfair advantage of others.

> KEY TERM: *Nonassertive style*: characterized by timid and self-denying behavior.

   b. Managers can improve their communication competence by trying to be more assertive and less aggressive and nonassertive.

2. *Interaction Involvement*

> KEY TERM: *Interaction involvement*: the extent to which an individual participates in or is consciously involved in an ongoing conversation.

   a. An individual's interaction involvement is composed of responsiveness, perceptiveness, and attentiveness.
   b. Research supports the notion that interaction involvement is an important component of communication competence.
   c. Assessment, awareness, and self-control are key aspects of enhancing one's interaction involvement.

3. *Sources of Nonverbal Communication*

> KEY TERM: *Nonverbal communication*: any message sent or received independent of the written or spoken word

   a. *Physical Features*
      An individual's physical features, such as body type, skin color, and physical handicaps, are important sources of nonverbal communication.
   b. *Body Movements and Gestures*
      Body movements, such as leaning forward or backward, and gestures, such as pointing, provide additional nonverbal information.
   c. *Touch*
      Touching is another powerful nonverbal cue. In many cultures, touch can signal compassion, warmth, attraction, and friendliness.
   d. *Facial Expressions*
      Facial expressions, such as smiling, convey a wealth of information.
   e. *Eye Contact*
      Eye contact is a strong nonverbal cue that serves a number of communication functions.

    f. *Interpersonal Distance Zones*
Interpersonal interactions are influenced by cultural perceptions of intimate distance, personal distance, social distance, and public distance.

4. *Active Listening*

    a. Research suggests that managers spend about 45 percent of their working day listening.

> KEY TERM: *Listening*: the process of decoding and interpreting verbal messages. Listening requires cognitive attention and information processing.

    b. Listener comprehension is a function of listener characteristics, speaker characteristics, message characteristics, and environmental characteristics.

    c. Experts have identified three unique types of listening styles:

        (1) results-style

        (2) reasons-style

        (3) process-style.

> KEY TERM: *Results-style*: listeners are quick to get to the bottom line and ask questions.

> KEY TERM: *Reasons-style*: listeners want to know the rationale for what someone is saying or proposing.

> KEY TERM: *Process-style*: listeners want to discuss issues in detail.

    d. Table 12-2 presents 10 keys to effective listening.

C. **Organizational Communication Patterns**

  1. *Hierarchical Communication*

> KEY TERM: *Hierarchical communication*: those exchanges of information and influence between employees, at least one of whom has formal authority to direct and evaluate the activities of other organizational members.

  2. *The Grapevine*

> KEY TERM: *Grapevine*: the unofficial communication system of the informal organization.

    a. Communication along the grapevine follows predictable patterns (see Figure 12-6).

> KEY TERM: *Liaison individuals*: people who consistently pass along grapevine information to others.

    b. Research has found the grapevine to be fast, accurate, selective in terms of transmitting information, and relied upon when employees feel insecure.

    c. Effective managers must monitor and influence the grapevine.

D. **Barriers to Effective Communication**

> KEY TERM: *Barriers to Communication*: personal and environmental characteristics that interfere with the accurate transmission or reception of a message.

1. *Personal Barriers to Effective Communication*
   a. According to Carl Rogers, two personal influences in communication are:
      (1) the natural tendency to evaluate or judge a sender's message and
      (2) listening with understanding.

   > KEY TERM: *Listening with understanding*: occurs when a receiver can see the expressed idea and attitude from the other person's point of view.

2. *Communication Distortion Between Managers and Employees*

   > KEY TERM: *Communication distortion*: occurs when an employee purposely modifies the content of a message, thereby reducing the accuracy of communication between managers and employees.

   a. Four antecedents of distortion in upward communication are:
      (1) the supervisor's upward influence
      (2) the supervisor's power
      (3) the subordinate's aspiration for upward mobility
      (4) the subordinate's trust in the supervisor.

OPENING CASE SOLUTION

1. In the communication process, noise represents anything that interferes with the communication and understanding of a message. Electronic meetings can reduce such common noise as speech impairment, poor telephone connections, illegible handwriting, and poor hearing.
2. Effective communication occurs when the richness, or the potential information-carrying capacity of the medium is matched appropriately with the complexity of the problem or situation. The contingency model for selecting communication media suggests that this match is best accomplished with face-to-face communication. Electronic meetings would seem to be a fairly-close facsimile to face-to-face meetings.
3. For electronic meetings, the best communication style would probably be an assertive style which is expressive and based on the ethical notion that it is wrong to violate our own or other's basic human rights.
4. Communication distortion occurs when an employee purposely modifies the content of a message, thereby reducing the accuracy of communication between the employee and management. Because electronic meetings provide anonymity, there is no reason for such distortion behavior.

END-OF-CHAPTER EXERCISE

1. The role-playing exercise is designed to help students learn to communicate with more assertiveness. The questions at the end of the exercise can direct student attention to a greater awareness of assertive, aggressive, and nonaggressive communication styles.

2. The exercise can be modified by holding a role-play in front of the entire class before allowing them to do their own small-group role-plays. In this manner, the students would have a model to follow and to reinforce a positive environment for providing feedback.

INSTRUCTIONAL RESOURCES

1. Students can experience the phenomena of one-way and two-way communication in "Comparing One-Way and Two-Way Communication," in Gene Burton, *Exercises in Management*, 3rd ed. (Boston: Houghton Mifflin Company, 1990), pp. 193-197.

2. Active listening is the object of the exercise, "Active Listening," in Marshall Sashkin and William Morris, *Experiencing Management* (Reading, MA: Addison-Wesley, 1987), pp. 143-144.

3. An 18-item survey of communication skills is found in "A Communications Skill Survey," in Gene E. Burton, *Exercises in Management*, 3rd ed. (Boston: Houghton Mifflin Company, 1990, pp. 199- 202.

4. Communication feedback is learned experientially in "Feedback," in Douglas Hall, et al, *Experiences in Management and Organizational Behavior* (Chicago: St. Clair Press, 1975), pp. 139- 142.

5. Students can learn an appreciation for the distortion caused by technical jargon in "The Letter of Justification," in Gene E. Burton, *Exercises in Management*, 3rd ed. (Boston: Houghton Mifflin Company, 1990), pp. 191-192.

6. Nonverbal communication is the focus of the film, "Communication: The Nonverbal Agenda," (CRM/McGraw-Hill).

7. Depersonalizing communication is addressed in the film, "Communicating Non-Defensively: Don't Take it Personally," (CRM/McGraw-Hill).

8. See the various modules for Chapter 12 in the Muto, Kreitner, and Kinicki *Lecture Supplement Manual*.

TOPICAL RESOURCES

1. A classic book on communication is William Haney, *Communication and Organizational Behavior: Text and Cases* (Homewood, IL: Richard Irwin, 1973).

2. Issues surrounding media richness are presented in Richard Daft and Robert Lengel, "Organizational Information Requirements, Media Richness and Structural Design," *Management Science*, March 1986, pp. 554-572.

3. For a practical update on media richness, see Robert H. Lengel and Richard L. Daft, "The Selection of Communication Media as an Executive Skill," *Academy of Management Executive*, August 1988, pp. 225-232.

4. An outcome of *distortion* in group processes is explained in Gene E. Burton," The Measurement of Distortion Tendencies Induced by the Win-Lose Nature of In-Group Loyalty," *Small Group Research*, February 1990, pp. 128-141.

5. An interesting exploration into the grapevine is found in Alan Zaremba, "Working with the Organizational Grapevine," *Personnel Journal*, July 1988,

6. An in-depth analysis of active listening is presented in Carl Rogers and Richard Farson, *Active Listening* (Chicago: University of Chicago, 1955).

7. Nonverbal communication is the focus of James Kouzes and Barry Posner, "In the Eye of the Beholder," *Vision/Action*, March 1986, pp. 1-4.

DISCUSSION/ESSAY QUESTIONS

1. Discuss the elements of the communication process within the context of the perceptual process model of communication.

2. Describe the application of the contingency approach to the selection of media.

3. Contrast and compare the assertiveness, aggressiveness, and nonassertiveness styles of communication.

4. Analyze the problem of managing nonverbal communication in the workplace.

5. Provide a real-world example that demonstrates the antecedents of communication distortion.

13

Performance Appraisal, Feedback, and Rewards

CAPSULE SUMMARY

Chapter 13 presents an integrated perspective dealing with instructive performance appraisals, supportive feedback, and desired rewards. Performance appraisals are presented as processes that can create functional results as well as dysfunctional dissatisfaction. Three major appraisal approaches are discussed - trait, behavioral, and results - along with a contingency model for maximizing their use. Objective feedback is analyzed as both a generic control technique and as a cognitive process. Extrinsic and intrinsic rewards are compared and contrasted as a foundation for exploring alternative organizational reward norms, distribution criteria, and desired outcomes of the reward process. Finally, the controversial relationships between pay and performance are examined.

LECTURE OUTLINE

A. **Performance Appraisal: Definition and Components**

> KEY TERM: *Performance appraisal*: involves the judgmental evaluation of a jobholder's traits, behavior, or accomplishments as a basis for making important personnel decisions.

1. *Components of the Performance Appraisal Process*
   a. Performance appraisals are almost universal, but they generate a great deal of dissatisfaction among both appraisers and appraisees.
   b. The four major elements of the appraisal process are:
      (1) the appraiser
      (2) the appraisee
      (3) the appraisal method
      (4) the outcomes.
   c. Research generally supports charges that appraisers are often guilty of racism, sexism, and perceptual distortion.
   d. Employees play a characteristically passive listening and watching role when their performance is being evaluated. The experience can be demeaning and often threatening, so employees are encouraged to take one of four proactive roles in their evaluation process:
      (1) analyzer
      (2) influencer
      (3) planner or
      (4) protege.
   e. The three basic approaches to the appraisal of job performance involve traits, behaviors, or results. Managers are advised to apply a contingency approach.

2. *Performance Appraisal Research Insights*
   a. Studies find that appraisers typically rate same-race appraisees higher.
   b. Although a great deal of effort has been devoted to creating more precise rating formats, only 4 to 8 percent of the variance in appraisals is accounted for by the appraisal format.
   c. Performance appraisers are found to give poor performers significantly higher ratings when they have to give the appraisees face-to-face feedback, as opposed to anonymous written feedback or no feedback.
   d. More experienced appraisers tend to render higher-quality appraisals.

B. **Practical Issues and Answers in Performance Appraisal**

1. *How Can Managers Resolve the Evaluation-Versus-Development Dilemma?*
   a. When appraising performance, managers face two conflicting objectives:
      (1) the need to evaluate *past* performance
      (2) the need to develop *future* performance.
   b. The criticism and stress of a face-to-face performance review do little to set the proper tone for a constructive discussion of future improvement. Thus, a two-meeting approach is suggested.

2. *Who Should Evaluate Performance?*
   a. Traditionally, one's immediate supervisor is involved in the evaluation process.
   b. Interest is growing in nontraditional appraisals by subordinates, peers, and self.

3. *How Can the Behavioral Focus of Appraisals Be Sharpened?*

      a. Behavior-based appraisals are more legally defensible than commonly-used trait appraisals.

      c. Two techniques can help managers increase the behavioral orientation of performance appraisals:

         (1) critical incidents

         (2) behaviorally anchored rating scales (BARS).

> KEY TERM: *Critical incidents*: notable examples of good or bad performance that are written down soon after they occur.

> KEY TERM: *Behaviorally anchored rating scales (BARS)*: graphic rating scales with behavioral descriptions attached to specific points as determined by a consensus of those familiar with the job in question.

C. **Feedback**

> KEY TERM: *Feedback*: objective information about the adequacy of one's own job performance. Feedback serves two functions for those who receive it:

         (1) instructional

         (2) motivational.

  1. *Feedback Is a Control Mechanism*

      a. The modern concept of feedback traces to cybernetic theory, involving mechanical systems.

      b. Any basic feedback control system, such as a thermostat, monitors the system's output for deviations from a preset standard and makes appropriate adjustments.

  2. *A Conceptual Model of the Feedback Process*

      a. Three sources of feedback on job performance are others, task, and self.

      b. A recipient's openness to feedback depends in part on two perceptual variables:

         (1) his/her desire for objective feedback

         (2) the sign and content of the feedback message. People tend to resist negative or threatening feedback.

      c. Feedback is cognitively evaluated in terms of its accuracy, credibility of the source, fairness of the system, the individual's expectancies, and relevant behavioral standards.

      d. Four behavioral outcomes of feedback are direction, effort, persistence, and resistance.

  3. *Practical Lessons from Feedback Research*

      a. The acceptance of feedback should not be treated as a given. It is often misperceived or rejected, especially in intercultural situations.

      b. Managers can enhance their credibility as sources of feedback by developing their expertise and creating a climate of trust.

      c. Negative feedback is typically misperceived or rejected.

      d. Feedback must be tailored to the recipient.

      e. Destructive criticism tends to cause conflict and reduce motivation.

D. **Organizational Reward Systems**

The concept of organizational rewards goes far beyond the traditional paycheck. A model of organizational rewards is composed of four components:

         (1) types of rewards:

            (2) reward norms
            (3) distribution criteria
            (4) desired outcomes.

1. *Types of Rewards*

> KEY TERM: *Extrinsic rewards*, such as financial, material, and social rewards, come from the environment.

> KEY TERM: *Intrinsic rewards* are psychic rewards that are self-granted.

2. *Organizational Reward Norms*
   a.   Four reward norms are:
       (1) profit maximization
       (2) equity
       (3) equality
       (4) need.

> KEY TERM: *Reward equity norm*: rewards are allocated proportionate to contributions.

> KEY TERM: *Reward equality norm*: all parties are rewarded equally, regardless of their comparative contributions.

3. *Reward Distribution Criteria*
   a.   Three reward distribution criteria are:
       (1) performance/results
       (2) performance/actions and behaviors
       (3) nonperformance considerations.

4. *Desired Outcomes of the Reward System*
   a.   A good reward system should attract, motivate, develop, satisfy, and retain productive individuals.

E. **Pay for Performance**

1. *Putting Pay for Performance in Perspective*

> KEY TERM: *Pay for performance*: the popular term for monetary incentives linking at least some portion of the paycheck directly to results or accomplishments.

   a.   The most blatant form of pay for performance is the traditional piece rate plan.
   b.   U.S. employers are spending an estimated $125 billion annually on incentive compensation.
   c.   Research finds little relationship between incentive payment plans and corporate performance.

2. *Incentive Bonuses and Motivation: A Double-Impact Model*
   a.   Figure 13-9 presents the model, "The Double-Impact of Incentive Bonuses on Employee Motivation and Performance." Both promised and granted bonuses have motivational power.
   b.   Promised bonuses are perceived to lead to employee participation in developing, implementing, and updating the performance-reward standards.

3. *Profit Sharing Versus Gainsharing*

> KEY TERM: *Profit sharing* occurs when individual employees or work groups are granted a specified portion of any profits earned by the business as a whole.

> KEY TERM: *Gainsharing* involves a measurement of productivity combined with the calculation of a bonus designed to offer employees a mutual share of any increases in total organizational productivity.

    a. *How Do Profit Sharing and Gainsharing Measure up?*
        Available research evidence suggests that gainsharing is superior to profit sharing.

4. *Making Pay for Performance Work*
    a. Make pay for performance an integral part of the organization's basic strategy.
    b. Base incentive determinations on objective performance criteria.
    c. Have all employees actively participate in the development, implementation, and revision of the performance-pay formulas.
    d. Encourage two-way communication so problems with the pay for performance plan will be detected early.
    e. Build the pay for performance plan around participative structures such as suggestion systems or quality circles.
    f. Reward teamwork and cooperation whenever possible.
    g. Actively sell the plan to supervisors and middle managers.
    h. Remember that money motivates when it comes in significant amounts, not occasional nickels and dimes.

OPENING CASE SOLUTION

1. The PepsiCo performance evaluation process is a unique two-step procedure. The first step, called the annual performance review, serves to weed out the weak managers and to identify the strong. The second step, dubbed Human Resource Planning (HRP), involves the establishment of new challenges for the coming year and big rewards for the stars. The first step in the evaluation process is based on the objective feedback approach to performance appraisal and is successful in clearly identifying appropriate bottom-line outcomes. The second step involves both intrinsic and extrinsic rewards that successfully motivate the "eagles to fly in formation." That is, the reward process provides the opportunities for the independent, creative, and aggressive actions that high-achievers crave, while holding them "in formation" by requiring that they meet carefully established organizational performance goals.

2. The main drawback to the PepsiCo performance evaluation process is that the stars are promoted so fast and moved so often and with such little notice that the company loses a lot in terms of continuity. It also may cause relocation and other stress-related problems for the stars and their families.

3. In terms of Figure 13-7, the PepsiCo performance evaluation process may be evaluated on the basis of sources, the recipient, and the behavioral outcomes. Objective feedback is based on bottom-line measurements of goals that are clearly established each year. The recipients with high expectancies (the eagles) perceive the organizational goals and contingent rewards to be clear, objective, and desirable. Outcome behaviors are monitored in terms of direction, effort, persistence, and resistance.

4. PepsiCo's organizational rewards are distributed according to a reward equity norm that allocates rewards commensurate with contributions. The distribution seems to be
   - (1) performance, as measured by tangible organizational results, and
   - (2) performance, as measured by actions and behaviors, such as risk-taking and team-work. As long as the eagles continue to fly in formation, the appraisal process is perceived to be a success.

END-OF-CHAPTER EXERCISE

1. This exercise provides students with a good opportunity to experience the various issues involved in the feedback process. This exercise is probably especially meaningful to students who have a substantial work history.

2. Students without appropriate work experience may wish to apply the exercise to some nonwork situation, such as some social group or the class.

3. Students will find considerable differences in student perceptions of the nature of desirable feedback. For instance, creative people tend to rely more on self and task feedback than on feedback from others.

INSTRUCTIONAL RESOURCES

1. Students can apply their performance appraisal knowledge to a real-world situation in the exercise, "Performance Appraisal," in Gene E. Burton, *Exercises in Management*, 3rd ed. (Boston: Houghton Mifflin Company, 1990), pp. 127-129.

2. The allocation of pay is the subject of "Exercise: Annual Pay Raises," in John Schermerhorn, Jr., et al, *Managing Organizational Behavior*, 4th ed. (New York: Wiley, 1991), pp. 183-184.

3. Students can experience using graphic rating scales in the exercise, "Using Graphic Rating Scales," in Gene E. Burton, *Exercises in Management*, 3rd ed. (Boston: Houghton Mifflin Company, 1990), pp. 117 121.

4. Money as a motivator is the focus of "Motivation through Compensation: A Learning Exercise," in Roy Lewicki, et al, *Experiences in Management and Organizational Behavior*, 3rd ed. (New York, Wiley, 1988), pp. 49-51.

5. The performance-pay issue can be experienced in "Money Motivation Debate," in Roy Lewicki, et al, *Experiences in Management and Organizational Behavior*, 3rd ed. (New York: Wiley, 1988), pp. 20-22.

6. The motivational power of money is investigated in the film, "More Than Money," (Films Incorporated).

7. Intrinsic rewards are examined in the film, "It's a Matter of Pride," (Salenger).

8. See the various modules for Chapter 13 in the Muto, Kreitner, and Kinicki *Lecture Supplement Manual*.

TOPICAL RESOURCES

1. An excellent treatment of the concept of inequity is found in Stacy Adams, "Toward an Understanding of Inequity," *Journal of Abnormal Psychology*, November 1963, pp. 422-436.

2. For an international look at performance and rewards, see Frederick Herzberg, "Worker's Needs: The Same Around the World," *Industry Week*, September 21, 1987, pp. 29-32.

3. The inherent problem of hidden agenda in performance evaluation is the theme of Beverly Geber, "The Hidden Agenda of Performance Appraisals," *Training*, June 1988.

4. An innovative performance appraisal program is revealed in Saul Gellerman and William Hodgson "Cyanamid's New Take on Performance Appraisal," *Harvard Business Review*, May/June 1988.

5. The impact of politics on performance appraisal is discussed in Clinton Longenecker, et al, "Behind the Mask: The Politics of Employee Appraisal," *Academy of Management Executive*, August 1987, pp. 183-193.

6. Research of the dynamics or top executive pay is presented in Charles W. L. Hill and Philip Phan, "CEO Tenure as a Determinant of CEO Pay," *Academy Of Management Journal*, September 1991, pp. 707-717.

DISCUSSION/ESSAY QUESTIONS

1. Discuss the pitfalls and problems found in the trait approach to performance appraisal.

2. Would you prefer for your academic performance to be evaluated in terms of traits, behavior, or results? Why?

3. Discuss the advantages and disadvantages of behaviorally anchored rating scales (BARS).

4. Develop your own model of an organizational reward system.

5. Discuss the motivational potential of pay.

14

Leadership

CAPSULE SUMMARY

Chapter 14 opens with a formal and definitional examination of leadership. The history of leadership is traced from the earliest inquiry to the evolution of modern leadership theory. Basically, leadership theory has evolved from trait theory, to behavioral styles theory, to situational theory. The chapter examines alternative contingency theories such as Fiedler's contingency model, House's path-goal theory, and the Hersey and Blanchard situational theory. Green's role-making model and attribution theory are explored. Finally, the distinction between transactional and transformational leadership is investigated.

LECTURE OUTLINE

A. **What Does Leadership Involve?**

> KEY TERM: *Leadership*: a social process by which an individual seeks the voluntary participation of others in an effort to accomplish organizational objectives.

1. Leadership involves more than wielding power and exercising authority.
2. Leadership theory has evolved from trait theory, behavioral styles theory, and situational theory.

B. **Trait and Behavioral Theories of Leadership**

1. *Trait Theory*

> KEY TERM: *Leader trait*: a physical or personality characteristic that can be used to differentiate leaders from followers.

   a. Although the prevailing belief at the turn of the 20th century was that leaders were born with certain traits, subsequent research summarized by Ralph Stogdill (1948) and Richard Mann (1959) caused the trait theory to fall into disfavor.
   b. Contemporary research finds that past research was incorrectly analyzed and further finds that leader behavior can be attributed to stable underlying traits.
   c. Research by Warren Bennis identified four key leadership traits:
      (1) management of attention
      (2) management of meaning
      (3) management of trust
      (4) management of self.

2. *Behavioral Styles Theory*
   a. This phase of leadership research began during World War II and was an outgrowth of:
      (1) the inability of trait theory to explain leadership
      (2) the human relations movement.
   b. The behavioral styles approach was guided by the belief that leader behavior directly affects group effectiveness.
   c. Researchers at Ohio State University found two independent dimensions of leader behavior:
      (1) consideration
      (2) initiating structure.

> KEY TERM: *Consideration*: involves leader behavior associated with creating mutual respect or trust and focuses on a concern for group members' needs and desires.

> KEY TERM: *Initiating structure*: leader behavior that organizes and defines what group members should be doing to maximize output.

   d. Research did not support the contention that a high structure, high consideration style was the one best style of leadership.
   e. Researchers at the University of Michigan similarly identified two important styles of leadership:
      (1) employee-centered
      (2) job-centered.

f. Blake and Mouton devised the Managerial Grid (Renamed the Leadership Grid) for the purpose of studying leadership behavior.

> KEY TERM: *Leadership Grid*: a matrix formed by the intersection of the leader behavior dimensions of "concern for people" and "concern for production."

g. Using the Leadership Grid, Blake and colleagues proposed that the one best leadership style consisted of a high concern for both people and production.

h. Behavioral styles theories fail to consider powerful situational determinants of leader effectiveness.

C. Situational Theories

Situational theories of leadership grew out of an attempt to explain inconsistent findings regarding traits and styles.

> KEY TERM: *Situational theories*: propose that the effectiveness of a particular leadership behavior depends on the situation.

1. *Fiedler's Contingency Model*

   The model is based on the premise that leader effectiveness is contingent upon an appropriate match between the leader's style and the degree to which the leader controls the situation.

   a. *The Leader's Style: Task-Oriented or Relationship-Oriented*

      (1) A leader's style is measured by an instrument called the "Least Preferred Co-worker (LPC) Scale."

   > KEY TERM: *Task-oriented style*: a person who describes his or her least preferred co-worker in negative terms, and is thought to be task-oriented.

   > KEY TERM: *Relationship-oriented style*: a person who describes his or her least preferred co-worker in positive terms, and is thought to be relationship oriented.

   b. Middle-LPC leaders exhibit characteristics of both high- and low-LPC styles and score between 65 and 72 on the LPC.

   c. *Situational Control*

      (1) Situational control is the control and influence the leader has in his or her immediate work environment, ranges from high to low, and is comprised of leader- member relations, task structure, and position power.

   > KEY TERM: *Leader-member relations*: reflects the extent to which the leader has the support, loyalty, and trust of the work group.

   > KEY TERM *Task structure*: the amount of structure contained within tasks performed by the work group.

   > KEY TERM: *Position power*: the degree to which the leader has formal power to reward, punish, or otherwise obtain compliance from employees.

   d. *Linking Leadership Style and Situational Control*

      (1) Fiedler's contingency model (Figure 14-4) contains eight separate control situations.

(2) Task-oriented leaders are predicted to be more effective than relationship-oriented leaders under conditions of both high and low situational control.

(3) Relationship-oriented leaders are predicted to be more effective than task-oriented leaders under conditions of moderate control.

e. *Research and Managerial Implications*

(1) The validity of the LPC scale is questionable, so there is need for further research.

(2) Field studies provide complete and partial support for three and five control situations, respectively.

(3) Subordinates of in-match leaders had higher job satisfaction, and in-match leaders displayed less stress and absenteeism.

f. *Leader Match Training*

Leader match training teaches managers to manage the situational control within the leadership environment.

2. *Path-Goal Theory*

a. Developed by Robert House, this theory is based on expectancy theory.

b. House believes leaders can exhibit a number of leadership styles, such as directive, supportive, participative, and achievement-oriented leadership.

> KEY TERM: *Contingency factors*: situational variables that cause one style of leadership to be more effective than another.

c. Contingency variables identified by House include employee characteristics (e.g., locus of control, task ability) and environmental factors (e.g., employee's task, authority system, work group).

d. This theory has not been widely tested, but research supports the prediction that supportive leader behavior promoted job satisfaction when individuals are performing structured tasks.

e. A major managerial implication is that leaders possess and use more than one leadership style.

3. *Hersey and Blanchard's Situational Leadership Theory*

a. According to Situational Leadership Theory (SLT), effective leader behavior depends on the readiness level of a leader's followers.

> KEY TERM: *Readiness*: the extent to which a follower possesses the ability and willingness to complete a task.

b. The SLT model matches follower readiness with one of four leadership styles:

(1) telling
(2) selling
(3) participating
(4) delegating.

c. As follower readiness increases, managers are advised to move from a telling, to a selling, to a participating, and eventually to a delegating style.

d. SLT is widely used as a training tool, but it is not strongly supported by research.

D. **Role-Making and Attribution Theories**

1. *Green's Role-Making (VDL) Model of Leadership*

> KEY TERM: *Vertical dyad linkage (VDL) model*: based on the assumption that leaders develop unique one-to-one relationships with each of the people reporting to them, resulting in one of two distinct leader-member relationships:

  (1) ingroup exchange
  (2) outgroup exchange.

> KEY TERM: *Ingroup exchange*: a leader-member exchange in which leaders and followers develop a partnership characterized by reciprocal influence, mutual trust, respect and liking, and a sense of common fates.

> KEY TERM: *Outgroup exchange*: a leader-member exchange in which leaders are characterized as overseers who fail to create a sense of mutual trust, respect, or common fate.

    a. Research supports a significant relationship between the type of leader-member exchange and job-related outcomes.
    b. The VDL model underscores the need to train managers to improve leader-member relations.

  2. *An Attribution Model*
    a. The attribution model is based on the idea that leaders form cause-effect attributions from information about employee behavior which, in turn, affect the way leaders respond to an employee's performance.
    b. The attribution model is found in Figure 14-8.
    c. Research has examined components of the model rather than the entire attribution process.
    d. Results indicate managers tend to see poor employee performance as internally caused, while employees see it as externally caused.

E. **From Transactional to Transformational Leadership**
  1. *What Is the Difference Between Transactional and Transformational Leadership?*

> KEY TERM: *Transactional leadership*: focuses on the interpersonal transactions between managers and employees.

There are two underlying characteristics of transactional leadership:
    (1) leaders use contingent rewards to motivate employees
    (2) leaders exert corrective action only when subordinates fail to obtain performance goals.

> KEY TERM: *Transformational leadership*: occurs when leaders create the vision and environment that motivates employees to elevate the good of the group or organization above their own self-interests.

  2. *How Do Leaders Transform Followers?*
    a. According to research, the characteristics of charismatic or transformational leaders can be categorized in three ways:
      (1) Transformational leaders do not accept the status quo, but recognize the need to revitalize organizations.
      (2) Transformational leaders create new corporate visions and mobilize employee commitment to those visions.

(3) Transformational leaders institutionalize organizational change by modeling appropriate behaviors, by intellectually stimulating employees, and by giving personal attention to employees.

3. *Research Highlights the Need for Both Transactional and Transformational Leadership*
   a. Transformational leadership can make the difference between success and failure.
   b. Neither transactional or transformational leadership alone is enough to ensure maximum effectiveness.

OPENING CASE SOLUTION

1. Microsoft's CEO, Bill Gates demonstrates a number of leadership traits. He exhibits all the traits shown in Figure 14-1—need for achievement (wants Microsoft on every desk and in every home), need for power (he will probably never step down - "The company is my life."), cognitive ability (brainstorming ability), interpersonal skills (joins brainstorming sessions, drops in to chat, responds to electronic mail), and self-confidence (freely delegates).

2. On the Blake and Mouton Leadership Grid, Bill Gates is probably a 9,9—high concern for production and high concern for people. According to the Grid, Gates uses the Team Management approach, in which work is accomplished by committed people, interdependence is based on a "common stake" in organization purpose that leads to relationships of trust and respect.

3. Bill Gates fulfills all the requirements of path-goal theory by:
   (1) reducing roadblocks that interfere with goal accomplishment
   (2) providing the guidance and support needed by employees
   (3) tying meaningful rewards to goal accomplishment. Of the four leadership styles identified by House—directive, supportive, participative, and achievement-oriented—Gates most closely follows achievement-oriented leadership.

4. Bill Gates is both a transactional and a transformational leader. With respect to transactional leadership, he uses contingent rewards to motivate employees and exerts corrective action only when subordinates fail to obtain performance goals. As a transformational leader, Gates creates the vision and environment that motivates employees to elevate the good of the group (the BUMS) or organization above their self-interests.

5. Employee commitment is largely mobilized by transformational leadership through the provision of the vision and environmental conditions necessary to foster employee loyalty.

END-OF-CHAPTER EXERCISE

1. This is an excellent opportunity for students to learn by doing. Completing the LPC scale will give each student valuable insight into his or her leadership style.

2. Students should remember that one style is not better than the other, but has different application potential.

3. In the "Leadership Vignette," the student faces low situational control, so task-oriented leadership should be the more effective style.

INSTRUCTIONAL RESOURCES

1. One of the classic leadership instruments is the 35-item "T-P Leadership Questionnaire: An Assessment of Style," by Sergiovanni, Metzcus, and Burden and modified by J. Pfeiffer and J. Jones, Eds. *A Handbook for Human Relations Training, Vol. 1* (San Diego: University Associates, 1974).

2. Students can apply their knowledge of leadership traits in the exercise, "Identifying Leadership Traits," in Gene E. Burton, *Exercises in Management*, 3rd ed. (Boston: Houghton Mifflin Company, 1990), pp. 167-169.

3. Students can experience the practical application of leadership styles in "Role Playing: The Case of the Storm Windows," in Norman Maier, *Psychology in Industrial Organizations*, 4th ed. (Boston: Houghton Mifflin Company, 1973), pp. 352-356.

4. Leadership styles are the focus of the exercise, "Choosing an Influence Style," in Michael Albert, *Effective Management: Readings, Cases, and Experiences* (New York: Harper Row, 1988), pp. 183-184.

5. Students are encouraged to see the film, "Machiavelli," (BARR Films).

6. Determinants of leadership style are examined in the film, "Leadership: Style or Circumstance?" (CRM/McGraw-Hill).

7. See the various modules for Chapter 14 in the Muto, Kreitner, and Kinicki *Lecture Supplement Module*.

TOPICAL RESOURCES

1. The Hersey-Blanchard model of leadership is discussed in Paul Hersey and Kenneth H. Blanchard, *Management of Organizational Behavior: Utilizing Human Resources* 5th ed. (Englewood Cliffs, N.J.: Prentice Hall, 1988).

2. Fiedler's contingency approach is introduced in Fred Fiedler, *A Theory of Leadership Effectiveness* (New York: McGraw-Hill, 1967).

3. The Vroom-Yago leadership model is presented in Victor Vroom and Arthur Yago, *The New Leadership: Managing Participation in Organizations* (Englewood Cliffs, N.J.: Prentice Hall, 1988).

4. Public leadership is examined in Irving Janis, *Crucial Decisions: Leadership in Policymaking and Crises Management* (New York: Free Press, 1989).

5. Contemporary leadership is addressed in Warren Bennis, *On Becoming a Leader* (Reading, MA: Addison Wesley, 1989).

6. An in-depth examination of transformational leadership is provided in Bernard Bass, et al, "Biography and the Assessment of Transformational Leadership at the World Class Level," *Journal of Management*, Spring 1987, pp. 7-19.

7. An excellent overview of leadership is Gary A Yukl, *Leadership in Organizations*, 2nd ed. (Englewood Cliffs, N.J.: Prentice-Hall, 1989).

8. Transformational leadership is discussed in James M. Kouzes and Barry Z. Posner, *The Leadership Challenge* (San Francisco, Jossey-Bass, 1987).

9. Leadership abuses are covered in Jay A. Conger, "The Dark Side of Leadership," *Organizational Dynamics*, autumn 1990, pp. 44-55.

DISCUSSION/ESSAY QUESTIONS

1. Trace the evolutionary development of contemporary leadership theory.
2. Debate the pros and cons of the contention that there is one best way to lead.
3. Analyze contingency leadership as determined by Fred Fiedler's contingency model.
4. Discuss the application of the attribution theory to the leadership of a student organization on campus.
5. Compare transactional and transformational leadership.

15

Individual and Group Decision Making

CAPSULE SUMMARY

Chapter 15 focuses on the fact that decision making is one of the most essential ingredients of managerial and organizational success. First, the types of decisions are examined, with emphases on programmed and nonprogrammed decisions. Models of decision making are analyzed, with the rational, normative and garbage can models being compared and contrasted. The dynamics of decision making are reviewed, and a contingency model is outlined for selecting solutions. Group versus individual decision making is explored,with emphasis on participative management. Finally, the concept of creativity is examined.

LECTURE OUTLINE

Decision making is one of the primary responsibilities of being a manager.

> KEY TERM: *Decision making*: is a means to an end. It entails identifying and choosing alternative solutions that lead to a desired state of affairs.

A. **Types of Managerial Decisions**

It is important to distinguish between two different types of managerial decisions because different techniques are used to solve them.

1. *Programmed Decisions*

> KEY TERM: *Programmed decisions*: tend to be repetitive and routine.

   a. Habit and standard operating procedures are the most frequently used techniques for making programmed decisions.

2. *Nonprogrammed Decisions*

> KEY TERM: *Nonprogrammed decisions*: are novel and unstructured and tend to have important consequences.

   a. Managers resolve nonprogrammed decisions by using judgment, intuition, creativity, and where possible, computer simulations.

B. **Models of Decision Making**

There are several models of decision making. This discussion will focus on three models:
   (1) the Rational Model
   (2) Simon's Normative Model
   (3) the Garbage Can Model.

1. *The Rational Model*

> KEY TERM: *Rational model*: used by managers to make rational decisions in a four-step process:

   (1) identifying the problem
   (2) generating alternative solutions
   (3) selecting a solution
   (4) implementing and evaluating the solution.

   a. *Identifying the Problem*
      (1) A problem exists when the actual situation and the desired situation differ. Managers use past experience, historical cues, planning, and other peoples' perceptions to identify problems.

> KEY TERM: *Scenario technique*: a speculative, conjectural forecasting tool used to identify future states, given a certain set of environmental conditions.

   b. *Generating Solutions*
      (1) Alternatives are readily available from programmed decisions.
      (2) For nonprogrammed decisions, generating alternatives is the creative part of problem solving.
   c. *Selecting a Solution*
      (1) Optimally, decision makers want to choose the alternative with the greatest value.

(2) Assigning values to alternatives is complicated and prone to error.
  d. *Implementing and Evaluating the Solution*
    Three managerial tendencies reduce the effectiveness of implementation:
    (1) the tendency not to ensure that people understand what needs to be done
    (2) the tendency not to ensure the acceptance or motivation for what needs to be done
    (3) the tendency not to provide appropriate resources for what needs to be done.
  e. *Summarizing the Rational Model*
    The rational model is based on the following assumptions:
    (1) managers optimize their decisions
    (2) managers have knowledge of all possible alternatives
    (3) managers have complete knowledge about the consequences that follow each alternative
    (4) managers have a well-organized and stable set of preferences for these consequences
    (5) managers have the computational ability to compare consequences and to determine which one is preferred.

KEY TERM: *Optimizing*: involves solving problems by producing the best possible solution.

2. *Simon's Normative Model*
  a. Herbert Simon developed the normative model to identify the process managers actually use when making decisions.
  b. The normative model is based on the concept of bounded rationality.

KEY TERM: *Bounded rationality*: the notion that decision makers are "bounded" or restricted by a variety of constraints when making decisions.

  c. As opposed to the rational model, the normative model suggests that decision making is characterized by:
    (1) limited information processing
    (2) the use of rules of thumb or shortcuts
    (3) and satisficing.

KEY TERM: *Satisficing*: choosing a solution that meets some minimum qualifications, one that is "good enough."

3. *The Garbage Can Model*
  a. The garbage can model assumes that decision making does not follow an orderly series of steps.

KEY TERM: *Garbage can model*: decisions result from a complex interaction between four streams of events:

    (1) problems
    (2) solutions
    (3) participants
    (4) choice opportunities.
  b. Because the four streams of events interact in a random fashion, the garbage can model assumes decision making is more a function of random chance than a rational process.

  c. The garbage can model has four management implications:

    (1) many decisions will be made by oversight or the presence of salient opportunity

    (2) political motives frequently guide the process by which participants make decisions

    (3) the process is sensitive to load

    (4) important problems are more likely to be solved than unimportant problems because they are more salient to organizational participants.

C. Dynamics of Decision Making

 1. *Selecting Solutions: A Contingency Perspective*

  a. To evaluate the cost and benefits of alternate decisions, decision makers use one of three approaches:

    (1) aided- analytic:

    (2) unaided-analytic

    (3) nonanalytic.

> KEY TERM: *Aided-analytic*: decision makers systematically use tools such as mathematical equations, calculators, or computers to analyze and evaluate alternatives.

> KEY TERM: *Unaided-analytic*: decision makers systematically compare alternatives, but the analysis is limited to evaluating information that can be directly processed in the decision-maker's mind.

> KEY TERM: *Nonanalytic*: making decisions by using simple preformulated rules.

 2. *Escalation of Commitment*

> KEY TERM: *Escalation of commitment*: the tendency to stick to an ineffective course of action when it is unlikely that the bad situation can be reversed.

  a. Barry Staw and Jerry Ross identified four reasons for escalation of commitment:

    (1) project characteristics

    (2) psychological determinants

    (3) social forces

    (4) organizational determinants.

  b. Escalation of commitment can be reduced by:

    (1) having different individuals make the initial and subsequent decisions about a project

    (2) encouraging decision makers to become less ego-involved with a project

    (3) providing more frequent feedback about project completion and costs

    (4) reducing the risk or penalties of failure

    (5) making decision makers aware of the costs of persistence.

D. Group Decision-Making

 1. *Advantages and Disadvantages of Group-Aided Decision Making*

  a. On the positive side, groups:

    (1) contain a greater pool of knowledge

    (2) provide more varied perspectives

    (3) create greater comprehension of decisions

    (4) increase decision acceptance

    (5) create a training ground for inexperienced employees.

  b. On the negative side, groups tend to foster:

         (1) social pressure to conform
         (2) minority domination
         (3) logrolling
         (4) goal displacement
         (5) "Groupthink"

    c. Group performance is found to be generally qualitatively and quantitatively superior to that of the average individual.

    d. Given time constraints, let the most competent individual, not the group, make the decision.

  2. *Participative Management*

> KEY TERM: *Participative management*: the process whereby employees play a direct role in:

         (1) setting goals
         (2) making decisions
         (3) solving problems
         (4) making changes in the organization.

    a. *A Model of Participative Management*
       Participative management is predicted to increase employee motivation because it helps fulfill three basic needs:
       (1) autonomy
       (2) meaningfulness of work
       (3) interpersonal contact.

    b. Figure 15-5 presents a model of participative management that focuses on three major components:
       (1) individual contingency factors:
       (2) organizational contingency factors
       (3) environmental contingency factors.

    c. Research finds that participative management has significantly increased employee creativity and lowered role conflict and ambiguity.

    d. Two studies found that participation had a moderately strong impact on job satisfaction.

  3. *When to Use Groups in Decision-Making*

    a. Victor Vroom and Philip Yetton developed a model to help managers determine the extent to which they should include groups in decision making.

    b. The expanded Vroom-Jago model is represented as a decision tree in Figure 15-6. The manager's task is to move from left to right along the branches of the tree.

    c. Depending on the situation at hand, a manager can choose one of five distinct decision-making styles.

    d. Because it is so new, very little research has tested the accuracy of the model.

E. **Group Problem-Solving Techniques**

  1. Using groups to make decisions requires that they reach consensus.

> KEY TERM: *Consensus*: is reached when all members of a group can say that they either agree with the decision or have had their "day in court" and were unable to convince the others of their viewpoint.

  2. *Brainstorming*

     a.   Brainstorming was developed by A. F. Osborn to increase creativity.

> KEY TERM: *Brainstorming*: used to help groups generate multiple ideas and alterna-
> tives for solving problems.

     b.   When brainstorming, a group is convened and the problem is revealed. Individual members offer ideas that are written on a board or flip chart.
        (1) Freewheeling is encouraged.
        (2) Criticism is discouraged.
        (3) Quantity of ideas isare encouraged.
        (4) Combination and improvement of ideas is pursued.

   3. *The Nominal Grouping Technique*
     a.   Nominal grouping is used to generate ideas, but in a more structured atmosphere.
     b.   The process begins with each individual preparing his or her list of ideas that is later shared with the group in round-robin fashion.
     c.   Voting then occurs.

   4. *The Delphi Technique*
     a.   The delphi process anonymously generates ideas or judgments from physically dispersed experts.
     b.   Results of the initial survey are summarized and returned to participants for further analysis. The cycle repeats itself until the delphi manager has sufficient information.

F. **Creativity**

   1. *Definition and Stages*

> KEY TERM: *Creativity*: is the creation of something new.

     a.   Creativity takes place in a five-stage process:
        (1) preparation
        (2) concentration
        (3) incubation
        (4) illumination
        (5) verification.

   2. *Characteristics of Creative People*
     a.   Creative people seem to march to a different drummer. Table 15-7 presents a summary of the characteristics of creative people.

   3. *Managing Creative People*
     a.   Managers must establish work environments that are hospitable to creative people and the creative process.
     b.   Table 15-8 contains a list of suggestions for improving employee creativity.

OPENING CASE SOLUTION

1. The rational decision-making model uses a rational, four-step sequence for the making of decisions. The garbage can model, on the other hand, suggests that decisions are made through a complex interaction of four independent streams of events:
     (1) problems

(2) solutions
(3) participants
(4) opportunities.

The garbage can model is more realistic and best represents the process at Disney.

2. Escalation of commitment is the tendency to stick to an ineffective course of action when it is unlikely that the bad situation can be reversed. Michael Eisner tries to prevent escalation of commitment so that bad decisions are not pursued after it becomes apparent that the decision was a bad one.

3. Eisner holds regular meetings, called charrettes, with all the major participants in a project. This is in keeping with a national trend toward increased participation.

4. The participative charrette project meetings represent one creative technique employed at Disney. Eisner also uses deadlines as a motivational tool.

END-OF-CHAPTER EXERCISE

1. After the students have assessed their levels of creativity, the group might discuss the accuracy of the assessment. Students might be asked if they agree with the overall categorization and whether they are comfortable with their level of creativity.

2. Next, the students might consider which of Roger von Oech's 10 mental locks impair their creativity. This should make for a lively discussion.

INSTRUCTIONAL RESOURCES

1. Students can experience Japan's favorite group problem-solving technique in the exercise, "The Fishbone," in Gene E. Burton, *Exercises in Management*, 3rd ed. (Boston: Houghton Mifflin Company, 1990), pp. 243-246.

2. For an experiential comparison of individual versus group decision-making processes, have students participate in "Discussion Methods and Problem Solving," in Norman Maier, *Psychology of Industrial Organizations*, 4th ed. (Boston: Houghton Mifflin Company, 1973), pp. 326-328.

3. Another creativity exercise is "Mind-Scaping: An Exercise in Innovative Thought," in David Holt, *Management Principles and Practices*, 2nd ed. (Englewood Cliffs, N.J.: Prentice Hall, 1990), pp. 705-706.

4. A 20-item survey designed to determine one's problem-solving style is "Problem-Solving Questionnaire," in Gene E. Burton, *Exercises in Management*, 3rd ed. (Boston: Houghton Mifflin Company, 1990), pp. 45-48.

5. Creative problem-solving techniques are provided in the film, "Creative Problem Solving: How to Get Better Ideas," (CRM/McGraw- Hill).

6. Students should have a chance to view the classic film, "Twelve Angry Men," (MGM).

7. See the various modules for Chapter 15 in the Muto, Kreitner, and Kinicki *Lecture Supplement Manual*.

TOPICAL RESOURCES

1. A thorough review of the nominal group technique is presented in Gene E. Burton, "The Clustering Effect: An Idea- Generation Phenomenon During Nominal Grouping," *Small Group Behavior*, May 1987, pp. 224-238.

2. An overview of the U.S. innovation crises is contained in "Innovation in America," *Business Week*, Special Edition, June 1989.

3. Intuition is analyzed in Weston Agor, "The Logic of Intuition: How Top Executives Make Important Decisions," *Organizational Dynamics*, 1986, pp. 5-18.

4. An excellent review of group decision making processes is contained in Andre Delbecq, et al, *Group Techniques for Program Planning* (Philadelphia: Franklin Institute, 1981).

5. The difficulties in achieving group consensus are thoroughly discussed in Dean Tjosvold and Richard Field, "Effects of Social Context on Consensus and Majority Vote Decision Making," *Academy of Management Journal*, September 1983, pp. 500-506.

6. For recent research evidence on decision making speed, see William Q. Judge and Alex Miller, " Antecedents and Outcomes of Decision Speed in Different Environmental Contexts," *Academy of Management Journal*, June 1991, pp. 449-463.

DISCUSSION/ESSAY QUESTIONS

1. Discuss the differences between problem solving and decision making.

2. Contrast the rational model, the normative model, and the garbage can model of decision making.

3. Compare the decision making potential of individuals versus groups.

4. Why is the nominal group technique often found to be a better idea-generation technique than brainstorming.

5. Discuss the advantages of participative management in the modern working environment.

16

Managing Occupational Stress

CAPSULE SUMMARY

Chapter 16 explains the importance of effectively managing occupational stress. The foundations of stress are reviewed by defining stress and discussing an instructive model. An important category of stressors—stressful life events—and the stress outcomes of burnout and substance abuse are considered. The analysis then turns to three moderators of occupational stress—social support, coping, and hardiness. Finally, the chapter examines stress-reduction techniques, including muscle relaxation, biofeedback, meditation, cognitive restructuring, and a holistic wellness model.

LECTURE OUTLINE

In the working environment, stress has been linked to low productivity, substance abuse, absenteeism, and intention to quit. These negative organizational outcomes can be reduced by effectively managing occupational stress.

A. **Foundations of Stress**

> KEY TERM: *Fight-or-flight response*: an automatic response to stress that consists of either actively fighting the stressful situation or passively leaving or accepting the situation.

    1. *Defining Stress*

> KEY TERM: *Stress*: an adaptive response, influenced by individual differences, resulting from any environmental action or situation that places special physical and/or psychological demands upon a person.

        a. Hans Seyle pioneered the distinction between stressors and the stress response.

    2. *A Model of Occupational Stress*

        a. Stressors lead to stress, which in turn produces a variety of outcomes.

> KEY TERM: *Stressors*: environmental factors that produce stress.

        b. There are four major types of stressors:
            (1) individual level
            (2) group level
            (3) organizational level
            (4) extraorganizational level.

        c. Researchers have only recently begun to examine the relationship between stress and work-related behavior and cognitive outcomes.

        d. Although laboratory studies supported the inverted U-shaped relationship between stress and performance, three field tests did not.

    3. *Economic Costs and Legal Liabilities of Stress*

        a. Managers need to understand the causes and consequences of stress for four reasons:
            (1) workers are more satisfied when they have a safe and comfortable work environment
            (2) a moral imperative suggests that stress should be reduced because it leads to negative outcomes
            (3) stress-related illnesses cost U.S. businesses between $50 and $70 billion a year
            (4) employees are increasingly suing their employers for worker compensation benefits resulting from stress-related problems.

B. **Important Stressors and Stress Outcomes**

    1. *Stressful Life Events*

> KEY TERM: *Stressful life event*: nonwork-related changes that disrupt an individual's lifestyle and social relationships.

        a. The Schedule of Recent Experiences (SRE) is the dominant method for assessing an individual's cumulative stressful life events.

        b. Suggest that the students complete the SRE, which is found in the OB Exercise.

    c.   Studies discover that employee illness and job performance are adversely affected by negative and uncontrollable extraorganizational stressors.

  2. *Burnout*

> KEY TERM: *Burnout*: a condition that occurs over time and is characterized by emotional exhaustion and a combination of negative attitudes.

    a.   Ten attitudinal characteristics of burnout are presented in Table 16-2.
    b.   Burnout is caused by a combination of traditional and unique stressors.
    c.   Removing stressors that cause burnout is the most straight-forward way to prevent it.

> KEY TERM: *Buffers*: resources or administrative changes that alleviate symptoms of burnout.

  3. *Substance Abuse*

> KEY TERM: *Employee substance abuse*: occurs when the use of alcohol or drugs hurts one's job performance.

    a.   U.S. government experts estimate that 10 to 23 percent of the American work force uses dangerous drugs at work.
    b.   Although no single symptom is indicative of substance abuse, behavioral changes such as increased absenteeism, radical mood swings, sleeping at work, or working in frantic, spasmodic bursts are suggestive of substance abuse.
    c.   Companies have attacked substance abuse with sting operations, drug testing, and employee assistance programs.

> KEY TERM: *Employee assistance programs*: provide treatment for employees' problems that interfere with their work performance.

C. **Moderators of Occupational Stress**

Moderators are variables that cause the relationships between stressors, stress, and outcomes to be weaker for some people and stronger for others. The major moderators are social support, coping, and hardiness.

  1. Social Support

> KEY TERM: *Social support*: the amount of perceived helpfulness derived from social relationships.

    a.   People receive social support from culture, social institutions, groups, and individuals.
    b.   There are four types of support provided by sources of social support:
        (1) esteem support
        (2) informational support
        (3) social companionship
        (4) instrumental support.

> KEY TERM: *Global social support*: the total amount of support available from the four sources. It is applicable to any situation at any time.

> KEY TERM: *Functional social support*: buffers the effects of stressors or stress in specific situations.

    c. Research supports the positive benefits of social support.

2. *Coping*

> KEY TERM: *Coping*: the process of managing both external and internal demands that are appraised as taxing or exceeding an individual's resources.

    a. The coping process has three major components:
        (1) situational and personal factors
        (2) cognitive appraisal of the stressor
        (3) coping strategies.
    b. People cope with stressors and stress by using a control strategy, an escape strategy, and/or a symptom management strategy.
    c. A control coping strategy is more likely to produce positive outcomes.

3. *Hardiness*

> KEY TERM: *Hardiness*: a collection of personal characteristics that neutralizes occupational stress.

    a. The personality characteristics of hardiness are composed of commitment, internal locus of control, and challenge.

D. Stress-Reduction Techniques

1. *Muscle Relaxation*
    a. The common denominators of muscle relaxation techniques are slow and deep breathing, a conscious effort to relieve muscle tension, and an altered state of consciousness.

2. *Biofeedback*
    a. A biofeedback machine is used to train people to detect and control stress-related symptoms such as tense muscles and elevated blood pressure.

3. *Meditation*
    a. Meditation activates a relaxation response by redirecting one's thoughts away from oneself.

> KEY TERM: *Relaxation response*: the physiological and psychological opposite of the fight-or-flight stress response.

    b. The four steps for meditation are:
        (1) find a quiet environment
        (2) use a mental device to shift the mind from externally oriented thoughts
        (3) disregard distracting thoughts by relying on a passive attitude (most important step)
        (4) assume a comfortable position.

4. *Cognitive Restructuring*
    a. A two-step procedure of identifying and replacing irrational thoughts is followed.

5. *Effectiveness of Stress-Reduction Techniques*
    a. Muscle relaxation, biofeedback, meditation, and cognitive restructuring were found to help employees cope with occupational stress.
    b. The positive effects of stress-reduction programs do not last for a long period of time.

6. *A Holistic Wellness Model*

KEY TERM: *Holistic wellness model*: goes beyond stress reduction by advocating that individuals strive for a balance between physical, mental, and social well-being by accepting one's personal responsibility for following a health-related program.

a. The five dimensions of a holistic wellness program are:
    (1) self-responsibility
    (2) nutritional awareness
    (3) stress reduction and relaxation
    (4) physical fitness
    (5) environmental sensitivity.

OPENING CASE SOLUTION

1. The nature of the job exposes paramedics to many stressors. They experience the individual-level stressors of role ambiguity and responsibility for people. Role ambiguity is caused by the high rate of false alarms and the uncertainty associated with determining the cause of an individual's problem. The fact that paramedics must quickly deal with life and death situations is another source of stress. Status incongruencies between paramedics and both police officers and fire fighters is a group-level stressor. At the organizational level, meager benefits and pay and a lack of an attractive career path are all sources of stress. Ambulance sirens are another organizational-level stressor. Patients that curse and throw things at paramedics are extraorganizational sources of stress.

2. Paramedics experience the behavioral outcomes of job dissatisfaction and turnover. Negative attitudes associated with burnout are also stress outcomes encountered by paramedics. Frustration associated with false alarms and not being able to find people who called for help are common stress outcomes. Physiologically, ambulance sirens are hard on hearing, and the tension of emergencies raises blood pressure.

3. Paramedics experience all three of the unique stressors that cause burnout. They experience unfulfilled expectations in that they can not always help those in need. Paramedics are highly affected by high-pressure working conditions associated with having to deal with life and death situations in a timely fashion. Finally, although paramedics experience a great "high" by saving lives, they also encounter poor benefits and pay and a lack of a career ladder.

4. A control coping strategy consists of using behaviors and cognitions to directly anticipate or solve problems. Paramedics may use a variety of behaviors and cognitions to reduce stress. For example, paramedics can get together with other paramedics or supervisors to discuss potential solutions to alleviate typically encountered stressors. They can also tell themselves they are winners and important to society even though they do not receive pay comparable to police officers and firefighters. With respect to dealing with angry patients, paramedics can devise standard procedures for resolving such situations. Paramedics can also try to resolve the poor benefits and pay by becoming more involved with the union, which would also enhance their sense of control. Stress associated with ambulance sirens can be reduced by wearing ear plugs.

END-OF-CHAPTER EXERCISE

1. This exercise provides a good vehicle for students to assess their level of burnout.

2. To facilitate student awareness of the relationship between burnout and outcomes, the class may be divided into groups of low, moderate, and high burnout. Each group may then be asked to summarize its standing on the burnout outcomes. Students should be encouraged to include additional outcomes beyond those in the exercise.

3. Groups may then be asked to give class reports. The chalkboard may be used to summarize each group's standing on the outcomes.

INSTRUCTIONAL RESOURCES

1. A stress-coping experience is provided by "Coping with Work Stress," in Keith Davis and John Newstrom, *Organizational Behavior: Readings and Exercises*, 6th ed. (New York: McGraw-Hill, 1985), pp. 544-548.

2. Another stress measurement is "Stress: Down or up?" in David Holt, *Management Principles and Practices*, 2nd ed. (Englewood Cliffs, N.J.: Prentice-Hall, 1990), pp. 644-645.

3. Life stressors are determined by "Life Stress Inventory," in Marshall Sashkin and William Morris, *Experiencing Management* (Reading, MA: Addison-Wesley, 1987), pp. 145-181.

4. Burnout is explored in the film, "Burnout," (University Film & Video).

5. Stress coping is explored in the film, "Coping with Stress," (Professional Research, Inc.).

6. Living with day-to-day stress is addressed in the film, "Learn to Live with Stress," (Document Associates).

7. Relaxation techniques are shown in the film, "Progressive Relaxation Training," (Research Press Company).

8. See the various modules for Chapter 16 in the Muto, Kreitner, and Kinicki *Lecture Supplement Manual*.

TOPICAL RESOURCES

1. An excellent overall presentation of job stress is found in Alan McLean, *Work Stress* (Reading, MA: Addison-Wesley, 1979).

2. For insight into the emerging stress problems arising from personal computers, read "Relax, DP Stress Isn't All It's Cracked up to Be," by Gene E. Burton in *Data Management*, June 1985.

3. A complete analysis of the stress implications of Type A behavior is presented in Meyer Friedman and Roy H. Rosenman, *Type A Behavior and Your Heart* (New York: Knopf, 1974).

4. The subject of social support for stress management is the subject of Douglas Hall, *Work Stress and Social Support* (Reading, MA: Addison-Wesley, 1983).

5. An in-depth examination of the problems generated by burnout is provided by Michael Lauderdale, *Burnout: Strategies for Personal and Organizational Life Speculations on Evolving Paradigms* (Austin, TX: Learning Concepts, 1982).

6. Stress management techniques are discussed in Leon Warshaw, *Managing Stress* (Reading, MA: Addison-Wesley, 1984).

DISCUSSION/ESSAY QUESTIONS

1. Identify and discuss the stressors in your life, their sources, and sources of support.
2. What types of stressors are most apt to affect college graduates on their entry-level job?
3. Discuss the limitations to the various coping strategies.
4. What sort of burnout problems are most common among college students? Why?
5. Outline the key ingredients in a holistic wellness program.

17

Organizations: Structure and Effectiveness

CAPSULE SUMMARY

Chapter 17 examines the complex but vital relationships between
organizational structure and effectiveness. First, the four characteristics of all
organizations are explained. Then the discussion turns to structural concepts
such as organization charts, hierarchy of authority, division of labor, span of
control, and line versus staff positions. The evolution of organizational
metaphors is traced from military/mechanical bureaucracies to biological
systems to cognitive systems. The discussion then turns to the radical reshaping
of today's organizations. Finally, the chapter introduces the important matter of
organizational effectiveness.

LECTURE OUTLINE

Present and future managers need a working knowledge of modern organizations to improve their chances of making the right moves when managing people at work.

A. **Defining and Charting Organizations**

   1. *What Is an Organization?*

> KEY TERM: *Organization*: a system of consciously coordinated activities or forces of two or more persons.

      a. The four common denominators found in all organizations are:
        (1) coordination of effort
        (2) a common goal
        (3) division of labor
        (4) a hierarchy of authority.

> KEY TERM: *Unity of command principle*: specifies that each employee should report only to one manager, thus avoiding inefficiency and lack of personal accountability.

   2. *Organization Charts*

> KEY TERM: *Organization chart*: a graphic representation of formal authority and division of labor relationships.

      a. Organization charts reveal four basic dimensions of organizational structure:
        (1) hierarchy of authority
        (2) division of labor
        (3) spans of control
        (4) line and staff distinctions.

> KEY TERM: *Span of control*: the number of people reporting directly to a given manager.

> KEY TERM: *Staff personnel*: do background research and provide technical advice and recommendations to their line managers.

> KEY TERM: *Line managers*: have the authority to make decisions.

B. **The Evolution of Organizational Metaphors**

Metaphors serve to help understand complex and hard-to-describe phenomena such as organizations. Organizations have been characterized as military/mechanical bureaucracies, biological systems, and cognitive systems.

   1. *Closed versus Open Systems*

> KEY TERM: *Closed system*: a self-sufficient entity.

> KEY TERM: *Open system*: an entity that depends on constant interaction with the environment for survival.

   2. *Organizations as Military/Mechanical Bureaucracies*

> KEY TERM: *Bureaucracy*: Max Weber's concept for the most rationally efficient
> form of organization, patterned after the Prussian army.

   a. The four factors that supposedly made Weberian bureaucracies the epitome of efficiency were:
     (1) division of labor
     (2) a hierarchy of authority
     (3) a framework of rules
     (4) administrative impersonality.
   b. Bureaucracies have become the symbol of inefficiency because the foregoing characteristics have been taken to extreme.

3. *Organizations as Biological Systems*
   a. According to this perspective, organization-environment interaction is of foremost importance.
   b. Kast and Rosenzweig portray organizations in terms of inputs, outputs, and four overlapping and interdependent organizational subsystems:
     (1) goals and values subsystem
     (2) technical subsystem
     (3) structural subsystem
     (4) psychosocial subsystem.

4. *Organizations as Cognitive Systems*
   a. Daft and Weick have characterized organizations as interpretation systems that foster organizational learning and adaptation.

5. *Organizational Metaphors in Perspective*
   a. It is useful to integrate the biological and cognitive metaphors so that the resulting organizational metaphor has both a "body" and a "head."

C. **The Radical Reshaping of Today's Organizations**
  1. The reorganization revolution that began in the 1980s and continues today is nothing less than a frontal assault on the once-unquestioned notion of *hierarchy*.
  2. The so-called chain of command concept, as discussed earlier as an element common to all organizations, will never be the same.
  3. Whether carried out in the name of downsizing, delayering, retrenching, cost-cutting, restructuring, or competitiveness, the desired result is the same—flatter, more decentralized, less costly, and more responsive organizations.
  4. Today's leaner organizations rely more extensively on cross-functional teamwork and have pushed decision making down to where output is actually created.
  5. *How Necessary is Hierarchy?*
   a. Management's reliance on hierarchical control is subject to debate.
   b. Elliott Jaques and Edward Lawler, III agree that hierarchy is a necessary feature of organizations, but Lawler argues that less hierarchy is better.
  6. *Substitutes for Hierarchy: A Contingency Approach*
   a. Lawler's contingency model of substitutes (see Table 17-2) lists 12 supervisory functions that must be performed along with eight substitutes for hierarchy that facilitate their functioning.

> KEY TERM: *Substitutes for hierarchy*: may be used situationally to reduce or eliminate the need for organizational hierarchy.

    b.   The eight substitutes for Hierarchy are:
       (1) work design
       (2) information systems technology
       (3) financial data
       (4) reward system practices
       (5) supplier/customer contact
       (6) training
       (7) vision/values
       (8) emergent leadership.
    c.   There is no perfect substitute for hierarchy.
    d.   Substitutes for hierarchy should be used in a situationally-appropriate manner.

D. Assessing Organizational Effectiveness
    1. *Fortune* applies the following organizational effectiveness criteria:
       (1) quality of management
       (2) quality of products/services
       (3) innovativeness
       (4) long-term investment value
       (5) financial soundness
       (6) ability to attract, develop, and keep talented people
       (7) community/environmental responsibility
       (8) use of corporate assets.
    2. *Generic Organizational Effectiveness Criteria*
      a.   There is no single best effectiveness criterion for organizations.
      b.   Four generic organizational effectiveness criteria are:
       (1) goal accomplishment
       (2) resource acquisition
       (3) internal processes
       (4) strategic constituencies satisfaction.

> KEY TERM: *Stakeholder audit*: identifies all parties significantly impacted by the organization's performance.

    3. *Multiple Effectiveness Criteria: Some Practical Guidelines*
      a.   Experts recommend a multidimensional approach to assessing the effectiveness of modern organizations.
      b.   In well-run organizations, effectiveness criteria are mixed and matched.
      c.   The *goal accomplishment* approach is appropriate when goals are clear, consensual, time-bounded, and measurable.
      d.   The *resource acquisition* approach is appropriate when inputs have a traceable impact on results or outputs.
      e.   The *internal process* approach is appropriate when organizational performance is strongly influenced by specific processes (e.g., cross-functional teamwork).
      f.   The *strategic constituencies* approach is appropriate when powerful stakeholders can significantly benefit or harm the organization.

OPENING CASE SOLUTION

1. The General Electric plant in Salisbury is best described by the cognitive systems metaphor. This approach perceives the organization as more than a transformation process or control system. To survive, organizations must have mechanisms to interpret ambiguous events and to provide meaning and direction for participants. The interpretation process, carried out at the strategic level, leads to organizational learning and adaptation. The flow of events in the cognitive model is: environmental ambiguity — interpretation — strategy — structure —organizational performance.

2. The goal at the Salisbury GE plant was to get rid of all line supervisors and quality inspectors. This was done by employing such substitutes for hierarchy as work design, informations systems technology, customer contact, reward system practices, and emergent leadership. The case indicates that workers have, to some degree, taken over such supervisory functions as motivating, recordkeeping, coordinating, assigning work, making some personnel decisions, setting goals, planning, and controlling.

3. The most appropriate criterion for evaluating the Salisbury plant is probably the goal accomplishment approach. This is the most widely used effectiveness criterion. Key results or outputs are compared with previously stated goals or objectives. Deviations then require corrective action. The goal accomplishment approach is considered to be most appropriate when goals are clear, consensual, time-bounded, and measurable.

4. Using Figure 17-6 as a guide, a stakeholder audit would probably identify the following stakeholders: people in the local community, financial community, press, competitors, customers, consumer activists, suppliers, employees, unions, environmentalists, government regulators, executive branch, congress, federal government, and state and local government.

END-OF-CHAPTER EXERCISE

1. This exercise is a rare opportunity for students to apply practical methodology, not emotional or opportunistic rhetoric, to a ppopular and complex issue—the environment.

2. Students might explore the differences that will arise with respect to the effectiveness criteria selected for the evaluation of the Corp during the next three to five years.

3. Additional awareness will be gained during the stakeholder audit and the identification of potentially troublesome strategic constituencies.

4. A class discussion of this exercise might be facilitated and organized by using transparencies of Figure 17-5 and Figure 17-6.

INSTRUCTIONAL RESOURCES

1. Students can have hands-on experience in analyzing and revising an organization chart in "Analyzing the Organization Chart," in Gene E. Burton, *Exercises in Management*, 3rd ed. (Boston: Houghton Mifflin Company, 1990), pp. 93-97.

2. Determining the key characteristics needed for organizational effectiveness is the thrust of the exercise, "Organizational Characteristics," in Keith Davis and John Newstrom,

Organizational Behavior: Readings and Exercises, 7th ed. (New York: McGraw Hill, 1985), pp. 527-529.

3. Designing the organization to satisfy meet its primary stakeholders is the focus of the exercise, "Designed to Fit," in Marshall Sashkin and William Morris, *Experiencing Management* (Reading, MA: Addison-Wesley, 1987), pp. 95-100.

4. Contingency organizational design is the theme of the film, "Changing Organizations: Designing for People and Purpose," (Document Associates).

5. Applying contingency organization design concepts is the subject of the film, "Organizing for Successful Project Management," (Britannica).

6. Students can learn how to analyze an organization's strengths, weaknesses, opportunities, and threats in "The SWOT Analysis," in Gene E. Burton, *Exercises in Management*, 3rd ed. (Boston: Houghton Mifflin Company, 1990), pp. 65-68.

7. See the various modules for Chapter 17 in the Muto, Kreitner, and Kinicki *Lecture Supplement Manual*.

TOPICAL RESOURCES

1. The revolution in organizational design is discussed by Peter Drucker in "The Coming of the New Organization," *Harvard Business Review*, January-February 1988, pp. 45-53.

2. The information processing model is applied to organization design by Jay Galbraith in "Organization Design: An Information Process Model," *Interfaces*, May 1974.

3. The impact of new organization designs on middle management is addressed in Rosabeth Kanter, "The Reshaping of Middle Management," *Management Review*, January 1986, pp. 19-20.

4. One of the early arguments for a new look at organizational structure was the article, "Structure Is Not Organization," by Robert Waterman, Jr., et al, *Business Horizons*, June 1980, pp. 14-26.

5. An in-depth review of organizational metaphors is presented in Sonja Sackmann, "The Role of Metaphors in Organization Transformation," *Human Relations*, June 1989, pp. 463-485.

6. An interesting comparison of line and staff positions is provided in Meni Koslowsky, "Staff/Line Distinctions in Job and Organizational Commitment," *Journal of Occupational Psychology*, June 1990, pp. 167-173.

7. An excellent discussion of substitutes for hierarchy is developed in Edward Lawler III, "Substitutes for Hierarchy," *Organizational Dynamics*, Summer 1988, p. 13.

DISCUSSION/ESSAY QUESTIONS

1. Contrast and compare closed and open systems.

2. Compare, contrast, and integrate the biological and cognitive metaphors for organizations.

3. Discuss the significance of Lawler's substitutes for hierarchy.

4. Discuss the likely shape of tomorrow's organizations.

5. Discuss the contingency approach to the use of organizational effectiveness criteria.

18

Organizational Life Cycles and Design

CAPSULE SUMMARY

Chapter 18 introduces the student to the concepts of organizational life cycles and alternative organizational design approaches. Organizations are seen to evolve through the stages of inception, high-growth, maturity, and decline. Next, the authors explore a number of contingency approaches to organization design, including differentiation/integration and mechanistic/organic. The impact on organization design of technology, size, and strategic choice are examined. Finally, Mintzberg's typology of organization design is explored.

LECTURE OUTLINE

A. **Organizational Life Cycles**

   1. *Organizational Life Cycle Stages*

      a. The three stages to the organizational life cycle are:

          (1) inception

          (2) high-growth

          (3) maturity.

      b. Although not actually a stage in the organizational life cycle, organizational decline is an ever-present threat that needs to be managed by monitoring and responding to the following early warning signs:

          (1) excess personnel

          (2) tolerance of incompetence

          (3) cumbersome administrative procedures

          (4) disproportionate staff power

          (5) replacement of substance with form

          (6) scarcity of clear goals and decision benchmarks

          (7) fear of embarrassment and conflict

          (8) loss of effective communication

          (9) outdated organizational structure

          (10) increased scapegoating by leaders

          (11) resistance to change

          (12) low morale

          (13) special interest groups are more vocal

          (14) decreased motivation

B. **The Contingency Approach to Organization Design**

> KEY TERM: *Contingency Approach to Organization Design*: the view that organizations tend to be more effective when they are structured to fit the demands of the situation.

   1. *Assessing Environmental Uncertainty*

      a. Environmental uncertainty can range from low to high, according to Duncan's four-way classification of organizational environments, based on

          (1) a simple — complex dimension

          (2) a static —dynamic dimension.

   2. *Differentiation and Integration: The Lawrence and Lorsch Study*

> KEY TERM: *Differentiation*: occurs through division of labor and technical specialization. It tends to fragment or split apart the organization.

> KEY TERM: *Integration*: occurs when specialists cooperate to achieve a common goal. It tends to coordinate or bind the organization together.

      a. Lawrence and Lorsch's research conclusion was that, as environmental complexity increased, successful organizations exhibited higher degrees of both differentiation and integration.

   3. *Mechanistic versus Organic Organizations*

      a. This distinction is from the classic contingency design study by British behavioral scientists Tom Burns and G.M. Stalker.

> KEY TERM: *Mechanistic organizations*: rigid bureaucracies with strict rules, narrowly defined tasks, and top-down communication. They are characterized by centralized decision making.

> KEY TERM: *Organic organizations*: flexible networks of multitalented individuals who perform a variety of tasks. They are characterized by decentralized decision making.

> KEY TERM: *Centralized decision making*: occurs when key decisions are made by top management.

> KEY TERM: *Decentralized decision making*: occurs when key decisions are made by middle- or lower-level managers.

    b.   Burns and Stalker found mechanistic structure appropriate in stable and certain environmental conditions and organic structure better for unstable and uncertain situations. Each has its appropriate place.

C. Three Important Contingency Variables: Technology, Size, and Strategic Choice
Although Lawrence and Lorsch and Burns and Stalker proposed an "environmental imperative" for organizational structure, others have placed relatively more weight on variables such as core technology, organization and subunit size, and corporate strategy.

  1. *The Impact of Technology on Structure*
    a.   Joan Woodward proposed a technical imperative when she found systematic variations in structure among effective organizations relying on low-, medium-. or high-complexity technology.

  2. *Organizational Size and Performance*
    a.   Controversy about appropriate organizational size has erupted between the "bigger is better" (economies of scale) school of thought and those who believe that "small is beautiful" (diminishing returns).
    b.   Research suggests that bigger is not necessarily better and small is not necessarily beautiful. Today's managers are challenged to create structural smallness within large organizations.

  3. *Strategic Choice and Organizational Structure*
    a.   This perspective advises us to consider how key decision-maker's personal beliefs, attitudes, and values shape organizational strategy which, in turn, shapes structure.

D. Alternative Organizational Design Configurations: Mintzberg's Typology
Henry Mintzberg believes that organizations fall into five natural structure-situation configurations:

        (1) simple structure
        (2) machine bureaucracy:
        (3) professional bureaucracy
        (4) divisionalized form
        (5) adhocracy.

  1. *Simple Structure*
    a.   Typically found in small entrepreneurial companies; organic in design due to a lack of formality.

  2. *Machine Bureaucracy*

     a. Most prevalent configuration built around narrowly-defined, repetitive, and low-skill jobs; mechanistic in design.

3. *Professional Bureaucracy*
   a. Unlike machine bureaucracies, this variation achieves coordination and control by relying on highly trained professionals to exercise self-control. Appropriate in static or stable environments.

4. *Divisionalized Form*
   a. A structure based on semiautonomous market-based subunits. Typically a loose collection of machine bureaucracies.

5. *Adhocracy*

> KEY TERM: *Adhocracy*: a term Mintzberg borrowed from Alvin Toffler to describe highly-organic structures based on temporary project teams.

> KEY TERM: *Matrix organization*: a project-oriented approach to organization design that combines vertical and horizontal authority.

   a. Matrix design has been found by researchers to be associated with a greater quantity (but lower quality) of communication. Negative impacts on work attitudes and coordination have also been observed.

OPENING CASE SOLUTION

1. An organic organization is defined as a flexible network of multitalented people who perform a variety of tasks. The organization at W.L. Gore certainly meets the conditions of that definition. In fact, the Gore structure is described as a free-form management structure, with leaders—not bosses—who head teams who take shape like amoebas. Its "lattice" system replaces the typical hierarchy and allows staffers to communicate with anyone at the firm. In organic environments, this sort of organic structure should give Gore the decentralization necessary to improve their market responsiveness, create low-cost shared resources, improve communications, maximize problem solutions, and achieve greater teamwork and worker accountability.

2. Most students would probably like to work at W.L. Gore, and this question should spark a good discussion and a disclosure into what students really want from their jobs (But those who do not show initiative and prefer to be told what to do might be very frustrated with the ambiguity at Gore.)

3. The "lattice" system of organization at W.L. Gore may cause some communication overload for key individuals. It could also result in some unnecessary controversy and status incongruencies. Accountability may weaken if people see others encroaching on their turf. If a really severe controversy arose, it's not clear how this structure would deal with it without increased political activities that could prove to be dysfunctional.

4. As W.L. Gore increases in size, its strategy for remaining small seems to be quite successful. By breaking-up plants, when they become too large, Gore is pursuing the belief that "small is beautiful." "The trick is to create smallness within bigness." This ploy may have its practical limitations, when and if the firm reaches the point when it has too many small units to hold together effectively.

END-OF-CHAPTER EXERCISE

1. The Chapter 17 exercise is an excellent way for students to gain additional insights into the mechanistic-organic distinction in a real-word situation.

2. If a field survey is deemed inappropriate, ask the students to complete the survey based on their most recent work experience.

3. Figure 18-3 might serve as a good focal piece to structure an overall class discussion of the findings.

4. The instructor might, whenever possible, reinforce the perception of the conceptual linkage between organization structure and environmental uncertainty.

INSTRUCTIONAL RESOURCES

1. A 20-item survey to clarify the mechanistic/organic structure issue is found in "The Mechanistic/Organic Organization Survey," in Gene E. Burton, *Exercises in Management*, 3rd ed. (Boston: Houghton Mifflin Company, 1990), pp. 107-111.

2. Span of control and delegation/decentralization issues come to live in the exercise, "Increasing Employee Self-Control," by Barron Harvey in *Instrumentation Kit* (San Diego, CA: University Associates, 1987).

3. A survey that deals with ambiguity-coping is "Coping with Ambiguity: The Managerial Attitude Questionnaire," by Rick Roskin, *Instrumentation Kit* (San Diego, CA: University Associates, 1987).

4. The concept of organic networks is the focus of the exercise, "Intertwine," in Marshall Sashkin and William Morris, *Experiencing Management* (Reading, MA: Addison-Wesley, 1987), pp. 93- 94.

5. Students have the opportunity to apply their organizational design knowledge to the redesign of jobs in the exercise, "Redesigning Jobs," Jane Gibson and Richard Hodgetts, *Readings and Exercises in Organizational Behavior* (Orlando: Academic Press, 1985), pp. 184-185.

6. High-tech/high touch is the organization design thrust of the film, "To Humanize the Assembly Line," (Hobel-Leiterman/Cinema Guild).

7. The impact of modern technology on organization design is the subject of the film, "Nails: The Impact of Technological Change on One Industry," (Salenger).

8. The creation of organic networks and work teams is the focus of the film, "Team Building," (University of California).

9. Achieving a task-organization fit is the theme of the film, "Changing Organizations: Designing for People and Purpose," (Hobel- Leiterman Productions).

10. Students have the opportunity to apply all their organizational structure understanding to an institution with which they should all have some familiarity in Gene E. Burton, "Organizing the Business School," *Exercises in Management*, 3rd ed. (Boston: Houghton Mifflin Company, 1990), pp. 99-102.

11. See the various modules for Chapter 18 in the Muto, Kreitner, and Kinicki *Lecture Supplement Manual.*

TOPICAL RESOURCES

1. Problems of uncertainty are highlighted in "Nine Forces Reshaping America," *The Futurist*, July-August 1990, pp. 9-16.

2. An overall analysis of organizational design trends is presented in Keith Davis, "Trends in Organizational Design," in Keith Davis and John Newstrom, *Organizational Behavior: Readings and Exercises* (New York: McGraw Hill, 1985), pp. 284-291.

3. An interesting peek at the future is offered by John Eckhouse, "Computerized Factory—The Future Is Now," *San Francisco Chronicle*, November 4, 1985, pp. 22,-33.

4. The organizational design imperatives of quality and productivity are analyzed in Glenn Hayes, "Quality and Productivity: Challenges for Management," *Quality Progress*, October 1985, pp. 42- 46.

5. A critical look at the effectiveness of new organizational designs is presented in Richard Kopelman, "Job Redesign and Productivity: A Review of the Evidence," *National Productivity Review*, Summer 1985, p. 239.

6. Students are advised to read Tom Burns and G. M. Stalker "Organic and Mechanistic Organizations," in Henry Tosi, ed. *Organizational Behavior and Management* (Boston: PWS-Kent, 1990), pp. 248-254.

7. The impact of human personality on organization structure is explored in Henry Tosi, "Personality and Organization Structure," *Organizational Behavior and Management* (Boston: PWS-Kent, 1990), pp. 255-273.

8. An examination of strategy's influence on structure is one of the key issues addressed in Raymond Miles, et al, "Organizational Strategy, Structure, and Process," *Academy of Management Review*, no. 3 (1978), pp. 346-362.

DISCUSSION/ESSAY QUESTIONS

1. Analyze the three stages of the organizational life cycle in view of modern business trends.

2. How could the notion of organizational decline be incorporated into the organizational life cycle?

3. Apply the contingency approach to organization design to the growth, development, and future states for Apple Computer.

4. Discuss the balance/imbalance relationship between differentiation and integration.

5. Apply the Burns and Stalker findings regarding mechanistic and organic organizations to the design of the ideal university.

19

International OB and Organizational Cultures

CAPSULE SUMMARY

Chapter 20 is designed to help the student take that important first step into exploring the impact of culture on work behavior in today's increasingly internationalized organizations. The chapter begins with a coverage of both societal and organizational culture, because they have a common conceptual heritage-cultural anthropology. A model is presented that shows how societal culture and organizational culture combine to influence work behavior. The key dimensions of international OB are investigated with the goal of enhancing cross-cultural awareness. Finally, attention turns to understanding and managing organizational cultures. Special attention is focused on the functions of organizational cultures and on practical tips for developing an organization's culture.

LECTURE OUTLINE

A. **Culture and Organizational Behavior**

    1. In today's culturally-mixed work environment, a manager cannot attribute behavior to personalities alone.

    2. When dealing with people from other cultures, a manager who attributes behavior to cultural differences has a better chance of making valid interpretations.

B. **Culture Defined**

> **KEY TERM:** *Culture*: a pattern of basic assumptions—invented, discovered, or developed by a given group as it learns to cope with its problems of external adaptation and internal integration—that has worked well enough to be considered valid and, therefore, to be taught to new members as the correct way to perceive, think, and feel in relation to those problems.

    1. Most cultural lessons are learned by observing and imitating role models as they go about their daily affairs or as observed in the media.

    2. *Culture Is a Subtle but Pervasive Force*

        a. Culture generally remains below the threshold of conscious awareness because it involves *taken-for-granted assumptions* about how one should perceive, think, act, and feel.

        b. It has been said that "You are your culture, and your culture is you."

    2. *A Model of Societal and Organizational Cultures*

        a. As shown in Figure 19-1, culture influences organizational behavior in two ways:

            (1) employees bring their societal culture to work with them; and

            (2) once at work, the employees are further affected by the organization's culture.

    3. *High-Context and Low-Context Societal Cultures*

> **KEY TERM:** *High-context cultures*: rely heavily on situational cues for meaning when perceiving and communicating with another person. Nonverbal cues, such as one's official position or status, convey meanings more powerfully than do spoken words. Japanese culture is relatively high-context.

> **KEY TERM:** *Low-context cultures*: written and spoken words carry the burden of shared meaning. German culture is low-context, as is the U.S.

        a. High- and low-context cultural differences can be found in countries with heterogeneous populations (e.g., U.S., Australia, Canada).

C. **Toward Greater Cross-Cultural Awareness**

    Aside from being high- or low-context, cultures also tend to differ with respect to:

        (1) time;

        (2) interpersonal space;

        (3) language; and

        (4) religion.

    1. *Cultural Perceptions of Time*

> KEY TERM: *Monochronic time*: ordered, precise, schedule-driven, use of public time that typifies and even caricatures efficient Northern Europeans and North Americans.

> KEY TERM: *Polychronic time*: multiple and cyclical activities and concurrent involvement with different people in Mediterranean, Latin America, and especially Arab cultures. Time viewed as flexible and fluid.

   a. Managers need to reset their mental clocks when doing business across cultures.

2. *Interpersonal Space*

   a. People from high-context cultures tend to stand close when talking to someone. Business conversations in Latin American and Asian cultures typically take place within one foot of space.

   b. People from low-context cultures tend to need a greater amount of interpersonal space. North American business conversations normally are conducted at about a 3 to 4 foot range.

> KEY TERM: *Proxemics*: the study of cultural expectations about interpersonal space.

3. *Language*

   a. More than 3,000 different languages are spoken worldwide.

   b. *Relativists* claim each language fosters unique perceptions.

   c. *Universalists* claim that all languages share common elements and thus foster common thought processes and perceptions.

   d. For Americans who claim that English has become the universal language of business, there is still need for cross-cultural familiarity.

4. *Religion*

   a. Religious beliefs and practices have a profound effect on cross-cultural relations.

   b. The following list gives the most important work-related value for each of the five major religious affiliations:

      (1) *Catholic* - Consideration (for the employee)

      (2) *Protestant* - Employer effectiveness

      (3) *Buddhist* - Social responsibility

      (4) *Muslim* - Continuity

      (5) *No religious preference* - Professional challenge

   c. Thus, researchers found virtually no agreement across cultures about the primary work value.

D. **Practical Insights From Cross-Cultural Management Research**

> KEY TERM: *Cross-cultural management*: studies the behavior of people in organizations around the world and trains people to work in organizations with employees and client populations of several cultures.

1. *The Hofstede-Bond Stream of Research*

   a. Table 19-1 shows the key cultural dimensions in the Hofstede-Bond stream of research:

      (1) *Power Distance* - How much do people expect inequality in social institutions?

      (2) *Individualism-Collectivism* - How loose or tight is the bond between individuals and societal groups?

(3) *Masculinity-femininity* - To what extent do people embrace competitive masculine traits or nurturing feminine traits?

(4) *Uncertainty Avoidance* - To what extent do people seek to avoid unstructured situations through laws, rules, and procedures?

(5) *Confucian Dynamism* - To what extent do people perceive the importance of the values of persistence, status, thrift, and feeling shame and the unimportance of the values of personal stability, face saving, respect for tradition, and reciprocation of favors and gifts?

  b. The U.S. scored the highest in individualism, moderate in power distance, masculinity, and uncertainty avoidance, and low in Confucian dynamism.

  c. *Practical Lessons From the Studies*

    (1) Due to varying cultural values, management theories and practices need to be adapted to the local culture.

    (2) High Confucian dynamism was the only one of the five cultural dimensions to correlate positively with national economic growth.

    (3) Industrious cultural values are a necessary but insufficient condition for economic growth.

    (4) Cultural arrogance is a luxury individuals and nations can no longer afford in a global economy.

2. *A Contingency Model for Cross-Cultural Leadership*

  a. Table 19-3 presents a useful contingency model for cross-cultural leadership.

  b. The model matches four path-goal leadership styles (directive, supportive, participative, and achievement) with variations of three of Hofstede's cultural dimensions (power distance, individualism-collectivism, and uncertainty avoidance).

  c. The participative style is the most broadly applicable.

3. *Interpersonal Conflict Handling Styles*

  a. In a cross-cultural study, the collaborative (problem solving) style of handling conflict emerged as the preferred option in three diverse cultures (Jordanian, Turkish, and U.S.).

E. **Understanding Organizational Cultures**

1. *What Is Organizational Culture?*

> KEY TERM: *Organizational culture*: the social glue that binds members of the organization together through shared values, symbolic devices, and social ideals,

2. *Manifestations of Organizational Culture*

  a. The model in 19-4 shows four manifestations of organizational culture:

    (1) objects - shared things;

    (2) talk - shared sayings;

    (3) behavior - shared doings; and

    (4) emotion - shared feelings.

  b. Organizational culture is a deep phenomenon with many other manifestations (see Table 19-4), such as values and organizational heros.

3. *Four Functions of Organizational Culture*

  a. Organizational cultures:

    (1) provide an organizational identity;

    (2) facilitate collective commitment;

    (3) promote social system stability; and

    (4) help employees make sense of their surroundings.

4. *Research on Organizational Cultures*

    a. Anecdotal evidence from best-selling books on the subject points to strong cultures as a key to organizational success.

    b. Ouchi formulated his Theory Z model after studying American organizations with Japanese-like qualities such as participative, consensual decision making. He called these successful Theory Z organizations *clans*.

F. **Developing Organizational Cultures**

1. *Organizational Culture as a Competitive Advantage*

    a. An organization's culture can give it a sustained competitive advantage if it is valuable, rare, and impossible to imitate.

2. *A Practical Model for Developing an Organization's Culture*

    a. Although cultural imitation may be a waste of time, cultural adaptation can be productive.

    b. One model for developing an organization's culture is based on the acronym HOME: History, Oneness, Membership, and Exchange (see Figure 19-7).

OPENING CASE SOLUTION

1. Students will probably agree that Mazda's Japanese managers should better understand that American workers are:

    (1) from a relatively low-context culture;

    (2) prone to a monochronic time perspective;

    (3) high on individualism;

    (4) moderately high in power distance, masculinity, and uncertainty avoidance:

    (5) low in Confucian dynamism;

    (6) low on directive leadership; and

    (7) prone to short-term employment, rapid evaluation and promotion, specialized career paths, explicit control, individual decision making, personal responsibility, and concern for the person's role in the organization.

2. On the other hand, American workers should better understand that Japanese managers are:

    (1) from a high-context culture;

    (2) prone to a more polychronic time perspective;

    (3) high on collectivism and Confucian dynamism;

    (4) very high on masculinity and uncertainty avoidance;

    (5) high on directive leadership; and

    (7) prone to lifetime employment, rigorous evaluation, slow promotion, nonspecialized career paths, implicit control, collective decision making, collective responsibility, and concern for a person's whole life.

3. Japanese managers believe in the concept of *kaizen*, or continuous improvement, while American workers perceive it as a threat. This is not surprising, as *kaizen* appears to be compatible with Japanese culture (as noted in answer 2, above) and incompatible with American culture (as noted in answer 1, above). In order to correct this major misconception, students could develop a cultural-shaping process based on the specific manifestations of organizational culture as shown in Table 19-4.

4. Mazda could improve the organizational culture at its Flat Rock, Michigan, facility by applying the process portrayed in Figure 19-7, How to Develop an Organization's Culture. The process is based on four major interventions identified by the acronym HOME:

   (1) develop a sense of *H*istory;
   (2) create a sense of *O*penness;
   (3) promote a sense of *M*embership; and
   (4) increase *E*xchange among members.

END-OF-CHAPTER EXERCISE

1. This exercise offers a great opportunity for students to increase their cross-cultural awareness and to see how their own work goals compare on an international scope.

2. Perhaps the greatest potential for learning in this exercise would result if students were asked to explain differences in the test scores across cultures with the unique characteristics of the different cultures as addressed in this chapter.

INSTRUCTIONAL RESOURCES

1. Students can experience adapting a product or service offering to a cross-cultural market in Gene E. Burton, "Planning the Overseas Venture," *Exercises in Management*, 3rd ed. (Boston: Houghton Mifflin Company, 1990), pp. 269-272.

2. The key functions of organizational culture are examined in the exercise, "Cultural Functions Questionnaire," Marshall Sashkin and William Morris, *Experiencing Management* (Reading, MA: Addison- Wesley, 1987), pp. 165-168.

4. The major training needs of U.S. expatriates are explored in the exercise, "Training U.S. Expatriates," in Gene E. Burton, *Exercises in Management*, 3rd ed. (Boston: Houghton Mifflin Company, 1990), pp. 277-281.

5. The cultural characteristics of excellent U.S. firms are portrayed in the film, "In Search of Excellence," (Tom Peters Group, Inc.).

6. An overview of organizational culture is provided in the film, "Organizational Culture," (CRM/McGraw-Hill).

7. See the various modules for Chapter 19 in the Muto, Kreitner, and Kinicki *Lecture Supplement Manual*.

TOPICAL RESOURCES

1. A comparison of U.S. and Japanese cultural and business environments that may account for performance differences is presented in Gene E. Burton, "Japan vs. USA: A Comparison of Corporate Environments and Characteristics," *Human Systems Management* 8, no. 2, 1989, pp. 167-173.

2. Culture as a competitive advantage is the thrust of J. B. Barney, "Organizational Culture: Can It Be a Source of Sustained Competitive Advantage?" *Academy of Management Review*, July 1986, pp. 656-665.

3. Cultural change through myth making is discussed in David Boje, et el, "Myth Making: A Qualitative Step in OD Interventions," *The Journal of Applied Behavioral Science*, no. 1, 1982, pp. 17-28.

4. Techniques for the management of organizational culture are provided in Thomas Fitzgerald, "Can Change in Organizational Culture Really Be Managed?" *Organizational Dynamics*, Autumn 1988, pp. 4-15.

5. An analysis of excellent U.S. organizational cultures is the theme of Thomas Peters and Robert Waterman, *In Search of Excellence: Lessons from America's Best-Run Companies* (New York: Harper & Row, 1982).

DISCUSSION/ESSAY QUESTIONS

1. Compare and contrast the concepts of societal culture and organizational culture.
2. Contrast the differences between a low-context culture and a high-context culture with respect to implications for management.
3. What U.S. cultural characteristics would make it difficult for an Arabic manager?
4. Pick a company of your choice and explain how its organizational culture gives it a competitive advantage in the marketplace.
5. Explain how the HOME model could be used to improve the culture of a typical American company, as defined by Ouchi.

20

Changing and Developing Organizations

CAPSULE SUMMARY

Chapter 20 explores the complex process of organizational change and how it can be managed through a collection of techniques called organization development. The chapter discusses the forces that create a need for organizational change, resistance to change, models of planned change, and organization development. The chapter ends with a review of a model of organization development that can be used to help managers facilitate and manage planned change.

LECTURE OUTLINE

A. **Forces for Change**
   1. Organizational survival depends on the ability to effectively respond to change.
   2. Organizations encounter many different forces for change. These forces come from both external and internal sources.
   3. *External Forces*

   > KEY TERM: *External forces for change*: originate outside the organization. There are four key external forces for change:

       (1) demographic characteristics
       (2) technological advancements
       (3) market changes
       (4) social and political pressures.
     a. *Demographic Characteristics*
       The demographic changes in the workplace were outlined in Chapter 2.
     b. *Technological Advancements*
       There is a marked trend toward new technology, such as robotics, computerized numeric control (CNC), computer-aided design (CAD), computer-aided manufacturing (CAM), and office automation.

   > KEY TERM: *Office automation*: a host of computerized technologies that are used to obtain, store, analyze, retrieve, and communicate information.

     c. *Market Changes*
       Many market changes have been escalated by the creation of a global economy and the required restructuring for global competition.
     d. *Social and Political Pressures*
       Managers must adapt to new societal values and political/legal pressures.
   3. *Internal Forces*

   > KEY TERM: *Internal forces for change*: come from inside the organization as the result of

       (1) human resource problems and
       (2) managerial behavior/decisions.
     a. *Human Resource Problems*
       These problems stem from employee perceptions about how they are treated and the match between organizational needs and desires.
     b. *Managerial Behavior/Decisions*
       Inappropriate management behaviors, such as inadequate direction and support, may result in the human resource problems mentioned above.

B. **Understanding and Managing Resistance to Change**
   1. We are all creatures of habit, so it is difficult for us to try new things.
   2. *Why People Resist Changes in the Workplace*

> **KEY TERM:** *Resistance to change*: an emotional/behavioral response to real or imagined threats to an established work routine. The eight leading reasons for resistance to change are: (1) *Surprise and Fear of the Unknown;* (2) *Climate of Mistrust;* (3) *Fear of Failure;* (4) *Loss of Status and/or Job Security;* (5) *Peer Pressure;* (6) *Disruption of Cultural Traditions and/or Group Relationships;* (7) *Personality Conflicts;* (8) *Lack of Tact and/or Poor Timing;*

3. *Research on Resistance to Change.*
   a. In Coch and French's classic study, participation turned out to be a good tactic to combat resistance to change in a factory setting.
   b. More recent research involving computers and advanced technology indicates the value of hands-on experience and indoctrination about the benefits of adopting new technology.

4. *Alternative Strategies for Overcoming Resistance to Change*
   a. Organizational change is less successful when top management fails to keep employees informed about the process of change.
   b. Employees' perceptions or interpretations of a change significantly affect resistance.
   c. Managers are advised to:
      (1) provide as much information as possible to employees about the change
      (2) inform employees about the reasons/rationale for the change
      (3) conduct meetings to clarify employees' questions regarding the change
      (4) provide employees the opportunity to discuss how the proposed change might affect them.
   d. Employee participation in the change process is another generic approach for reducing resistance to change.

C. **Models and Dynamics of Planned Change**
   1. *Types of Change*
      a. Three types of change are:
         (1) adaptive change—reintroducing a familiar practice
         (2) innovative change—introducing a practice new to the organization
         (3) radically innovative change—introducing a practice new to the industry.
   2. *Lewin's Change Model*
      a. Lewin developed a three-stage model of planned change and explained how to initiate, manage, and stabilize the change process.
      b. The three stages are:
         (1) unfreezing
         (2) changing
         (3) refreezing.
      c. The model is based on five basic assumptions:
         (1) the change process involves learning something new
         (2) change will not occur unless there is motivation to change
         (3) people are the hub of all organizational change
         (4) resistance to change is found even when the goals of change are highly desirable
         (5) effective change requires reinforcing new behaviors, attitudes, and organizational practices.

3. *A Systems Model of Change*
   a. A systems model of change takes a "big picture" perspective of organizational change. It is based on the notion that any change, no matter how large or small, has a cascading impact throughout the organization.
   b. The three main components of a systems model of change are:
      (1) inputs
      (2) target elements of change
      (3) outputs.

   > KEY TERM: *Mission statement*: describes an organization's ultimate purpose.

   > KEY TERM: *Strategic plan*: outlines an organization's long-term direction and actions necessary to achieve planned results.

4. *A Transactional Model of Planned Change*
   a. Nutt's transactional model of planned change is realistic because it shows the dynamic relationships between the manager and team members.
   b. In Nutt's model, the manager is in the decision mode and the team members are in the developmental mode.
   c. The five transactions with the developmental mode are:
      (1) formulation
      (2) concept development
      (3) detailing
      (4) evaluation
      (5) installation.

5. *Implementation Tactics: Research Insights*
   a. Four basic implementation tactics are:
      (1) intervention
      (2) participation
      (3) persuasion
      (4) edict.
   b. Research found that intervention and participation were the least frequently used, but the most effective, tactics.

D. Organization Development

   > KEY TERM: *Organization development*: concerned with helping managers plan change in organizing and managing people that will develop requisite commitment, coordination, and competence. Its purpose is to enhance both the effectiveness of organizations and the well-being of their members through planned interventions on the organization's human processes, structures, and systems, using knowledge of behavioral science and its intervention methods.

1. *History of Organization Development*
   a. Organization development (OD) is a branch of applied behavioral science that has a short but colorful history.
   b. Its roots trace back to the mid-1940s and such practices as laboratory training, T-groups, sensitivity training, and survey feedback.
   c. The field of OD has continued to grow since these mixed beginnings, and there are now some 375 separate OD techniques.

2. *Identifying Characteristics of Organization Development*
   a. A better understanding of OD can be achieved by considering its four identifying characteristics:
      (1) OD involves profound change
      (2) OD is value-loaded
      (3) OD is a diagnosis/prescription cycle
      (4) OD is process-oriented.

E. A Model of Organization Development
   Figure 20-5 reveals that OD is a three-step process:
      (1) organizational diagnosis
      (2) prescribe and implement the intervention
      (3) monitor progress and take correct action.

1. *Organizational Diagnosis*
   a. There are two purposes for an organizational diagnosis:
      (1) to proactively identify future changes that are needed
      (2) to identify past or current organizational problems that inhibit effectiveness.

   > KEY TERM: *Needs analysis*: figuring out the type of skills or competencies that employees must possess in order for the organization to accomplish its goals.

   b. The needs analysis should probe six organizational areas:
      (1) purpose
      (2) structure
      (3) rewards
      (4) support systems
      (5) relationships
      (6) leadership.

2. *Prescribe and Implement an Intervention*
   a. There are two dominant strategies for implementing OD:
      (1) the human-process approach
      (2) the technostructural approach.
   b. Four frequently used interventions are:
      (1) role analysis
      (2) survey research and feedback
      (3) team building
      (4) work restructuring.

   > KEY TERM: *Role analysis*: strives to enhance cooperation among work group members by getting them to discuss their mutual expectations.

   > KEY TERM: *Survey research and feedback*: a stimulus for improvement through surveying employees and then feeding back the results of the survey.

   > KEY TERM: *Team building*: a host of techniques aimed at improving the functioning of work groups.

   > KEY TERM: *Work restructuring*: job design based on the notion that employee motivation is increased by giving employees meaningful work, responsibility for work outcomes, and feedback.

3. *Monitor Progress and Take Corrective Action*
   Evaluation and feedback is the final step of the OD process.

4. *OD Research and Practical Implications*
   a. Multifaceted interventions, using more than one OD technique, are more effective than single interventions in changing job satisfaction and work attitudes.
   b. Team building was the most effective technique for modifying job satisfaction and work attitudes.
   c. OD had a greater effect on work attitudes than it did on job satisfaction.

OPENING CASE SOLUTION

1. There were a number of forces for change at the Will-Burt Company. The major external forces for change were the liability lawsuits. Internal forces for change included poor profits, poor quality (which may have had something to do with the lawsuits), and low employee morale.

2. When Harry Featherstone introduced radical change at Will-Burt, it was opposed because of employee resistance to change. The reasons for the resistance to change included surprise and fear of the unknown, a climate of mistrust, loss of job security, peer pressure, disruption of cultural traditions, a lack of tack, and poor timing.

3. Using the Framework for Diagnosing Organizational Problems (Figure 20-6), the problem at Will-Burt begins with "purpose," or a lack of direction from the top, a reward system that does not motivate quality performance, poor support systems, and a lack of leadership.

4. The worst things that Mr. Featherstone did were to establish an employee stock ownership plan without properly preparing and involving the employees in the process. Another mistake might have been the unexplained change in product line that required the lay-off of 80 people. On the positive side, he eventually did some correct things, such as explaining the ESOP, establishing the zero defects program, implementing a training program, improving the compensation/benefits program, and having the courage to radically change the organization instead of giving up on it.

END-OF-CHAPTER EXERCISE

1. This exercise provides a good opportunity for students to gain first-hand experience with the process of organizational diagnosis. Students are advised to conduct the needs audit with an increased sensitivity for organizational strengths and weaknesses.

2. It is important for the students to recognize that the diagnosis has two major purposes:
   (1) to proactively identify future changes that are needed to help the company meet its strategic goals
   (2) to identify past or current problems that inhibit organizational effectiveness.

INSTRUCTIONAL RESOURCES

1. Students can apply Lewin's force-field analysis in the exercise, "Forces for Change," in Gene E. Burton, *Exercises in Management*, 3rd ed. (Boston: Houghton Mifflin Company, 1990), pp. 135-138.

2. Students investigate change in work processes in the exercise, "Change of Work Procedures," developed by N.R.F. Maier and adapted in D.T. Hall in *Experiences in Management and Organizational Behavior*, 3rd ed., by Roy Lewicki et al. (New York: John Wiley, 1988), pp. 242- 245.

3. Students can deal with resistance to change in the exercise, "Resist the Resistance to Change," from John Samaras, *Management Applications: Exercises, Cases, and Readings* (Englewood Cliffs, N.J.: Prentice Hall, 1989), p. 83.

4. The application of change processes to the university is the focus of the exercise, "Change at the State University," in Gene E. Burton, *Exercises in Management*, 3rd ed. (Boston: Houghton Mifflin Company, 1990), pp. 1349-144.

5. Change management techniques are the subject of the film, "All Change (The Management of Change)," (Films Incorporated).

6. A look at the ten major changes in society are examined in the film, "Megatrends," (Purdue Film Library).

7. See the various modules for Chapter 20 in the Muto, Kreitner, and Kinicki *Lecture Supplement Manual*.

TOPICAL RESOURCES

1. Current changes in society are investigated in Joe Cappo, *Futurescope: Success Strategies for the 1990s and Beyond* (Chicago: Longman Financial Services, 1990).

2. For a comprehensive examination of change and those who create it, see Rosabeth Kanter, *The Change Masters* (New York: Simon and Schuster, 1983).

3. A thorough study of OD techniques is presented in Robert Blake and Jane Mouton, *Consultation: A Handbook for Individual and Organization Development*, 2nd ed. (Reading, MA: Addison-Wesley, 1983).

4. An in-depth examination of OD is contained in Wendell French et al, *Organization Development: Theory, Practice, and Research* (Plano, TX: BPI, 1983).

5. OD techniques for strategic change are explored in P. Buller, "For Successful Strategic Change: Blend OD Practices with Strategic Management," *Organizational Dynamics*, Winter 1988, pp. 42-55.

6. The challenge of turning around mature organizations is covered in Richard W. Beatty and David O. Ulrich, "Re-energizing the Mature Organization," *Organizational Dynamics*, summer 1991, pp. 16-30.

DISCUSSION/ESSAY QUESTIONS

1. Discuss the forces for change for an American University.
2. Analyze the forces for change that have impacted the U.S. auto industry over the past twenty years.
3. Why is employee participation in the change process probably the best way to mediate resistance to change?
4. Apply Nutt's transformational model of planned change to the reorganization of your school of business.
5. Apply the organizational diagnosis model to the analysis of your employing institution or a student organization.

ORGANIZATIONAL
BEHAVIOR

ORGANIZATIONAL BEHAVIOR

Second Edition

ROBERT KREITNER
ANGELO KINICKI
both of Arizona State University

IRWIN

Homewood, IL 60430
Boston, MA 02116

© RICHARD D. IRWIN, INC., 1989 and 1992

Sponsoring editor:	Karen Johnson
Developmental editor:	Elizabeth Rubenstein
Project editor:	Lynne Basler
Production manager:	Bette K. Ittersagen
Designer:	Tara L. Bazata
Artist:	Arcata Graphics/Kingsport
Compositor:	Better Graphics, Inc.
Typeface:	10/12 Times Roman
Printer:	Von Hoffmann Press

Library of Congress Cataloging-in-Publication Data

Kreitner, Robert.
   Organizational behavior / Robert Kreitner, Angelo Kinicki.—2nd
ed.
    p.   cm.
   Includes bibliographical references.
   ISBN 0–256–08500–5 ISBN 0–256–11394–7 (Int'l. ed.)
    1. Organizational behavior I. Kinicki, Angelo.   II. Title.
HD58.7.K75 1991
658.3—dc20   91–29586

Printed in the United States of America
1 2 3 4 5 6 7 8 9 0 VH 8 7 6 5 4 3 2 1

Preface

A s the competitive pressures of a global economy continue to intensify, the skillful management of *people* is more important than ever. No matter how sophisticated an organization's strategy and technology, the *human factor* inevitably is the key to success. Thus, the central purpose of this textbook is to help present and future managers better understand and manage people at work. The second edition of *Organizational Bahavior* is intended for use in similarly named courses at the undergraduate level. This text is the culmination of our 30 years of teaching and researching organizational behavior, combined with detailed feedback on the first edition from students, instructors, and practicing managers. Many changes have been made in this edition, reflecting new research evidence, new management techniques, and the fruits of our own learning process.

Because this text is *user driven* (as a result of listening carefully to our readers), we believe we have achieved important balances in this second edition. Among them are balances between theory and practice, between solid content and interesting coverage, and between instructive presentation and readability. Students and instructors say they want an up-to-date, relevant, and interesting textbook that actively involves the reader in the learning process. Our efforts toward this end are evidenced by scores of new topics and real-life examples, a stimulating art program, thought-provoking cases and boxed inserts, end-of-chapter experiential exercises, and self-assessment exercises integrated into the text. We realize that reading a comprehensive textbook is hard work, but we also firmly believe that the process should be interesting (and sometimes fun).

• Structural Changes in the Second Edition

Like the first edition, this edition flows from micro (individuals) to macro (groups and organizations) topics. However, in response to feedback, coverage of macro topics has been expanded to achieve an even balance between micro and macro. As a guide for users of the first edition, these major structural changes need to be noted:

- Managing cultural diversity woven throughout Chapter 2.
- New coverage of ethics in Chapter 3.
- Learning theory consolidated with behavior modification and self-management in Chapter 7.
- Job design moved forward to Chapter 5.
- Performance appraisal, feedback, and rewards moved from Part II to Part IV.
- Topical integration of socialization, mentoring, and careers in Chapter 8.
- A whole new chapter on teamwork (Chapter 11) that features the topic of trust.
- A completely reworked chapter on individual and group decision making (Chapter 15) that encompasses participative management.
- An expanded and reworked Part V on organizations, featuring new coverage of international organizational behavior (Chapter 19). A completely revamped chapter on organizational change and development (Chapter 20) that focuses on the forces creating change, models of organizational change, and organizational diagnosis.
- Whereas the first edition had 18 chapters, this edition has 20.

• New Topical Coverage

In keeping with the AACSB's call for greater attention to business *ethics* and broader *global and cross-cultural awareness*, we made the following changes:

- Ethics is given up-front treatment in Chapter 3. Additionally, 23 boxed features titled "A Matter of Ethics" can be found throughout the text. This integrated coverage of ethics in the workplace makes it clear that ethical considerations need to be a forethought, rather than an afterthought, when managing people at work.
- Seventy-five percent of Chapter 19 is devoted to international perspectives, including a unique contingency model for cross-cultural leadership. International themes are weaved into the entire text via 28 boxed features titled "International OB." Among the different nations and regions featured are Australia, Canada, Europe, Japan, Soviet Union, People's Republic of China, Poland, Asia, Thailand, Sweden, Germany, Korea, Iraq, and Great Britain.

Supplementing our comprehensive coverage of ethical and international topics are the following timely thrusts:

- *Teams* have become the organizational unit of choice in recent years. This reality prompted us to break with tradition and write a completely new and separate chapter on teams and teamwork. Team effectiveness, trust, quality circles, self-managed teams, and cross-functional teams are explored in an integrated fashion in Chapter 11.

- Increased cultural, gender, and ethnic *diversity* in the work force has made "managing diversity" a high priority area for today's and tomorrow's managers. Consequently, Chapter 2 has been completely updated and reworked under a new title, "Managing a Diverse Work Force."

Among the other many new topics in this second edition are self-concept, self-efficacy, ethics training, racial stereotypes, Porter/Lawler expectancy model, a new model for putting motivation theories to work, career plateauing, women in mixed-gender groups, sexual harassment, genetic components of job satisfaction, interpersonal strategic alliances, interpersonal reciprocity, power sharing versus power distribution, delegation, stimulating conflict with devil's advocacy and the dialectic method, attributes of high-performance teams, six ways to build trust, developing team members' self-management skills, active listening, listening styles, barriers to effective communication, nontraditional performance appraisals (by subordinates, peers, and self), making pay for performance work, profit sharing versus gainsharing, Hersey/Blanchard Situational Leadership Theory, transformational leadership, escalation of commitment dilemma in decision making, the Vroom/Jago decision-making model, group decision-making techniques (including brainstorming, nominal group, and delphi), a new creativity model, employee substance abuse, radical reshaping of today's organizations, substitutes for hierarchy, stakeholder audits, complacency and organizational decline, culture and organizational behavior, cross-cultural research insights, forces for organizational change, Lewin's model of organizational change, organizational diagnosis, expanded treatment of organization development, and cautions about personality testing.

• Pedagogical Features

The second edition of *Organizational Behavior* is designed to be a complete teaching/learning tool that captures the reader's interest and imparts useful knowledge. Some of the most significant pedagogical features are as follows:

- Classic and modern topics are given balanced treatment in terms of the latest and best available theoretical models, research evidence, and practical applications. Complete coverage of traditional topics such as motivation, group dynamics, communication, leadership, and organization structure/design is complemented by discussion of emerging topics. Among these modern topics are self-concept, social information processing, social learning theory, behavioral self-management, information richness, communication competence, transformational leadership, the garbage can model of decision making, social support and hardiness as moderators of stress, coping with stress, self-managed teams, organizational life cycles and effectiveness, and organizational cultures.

- Several concise learning objectives open each chapter to: (1) focus the reader's attention, and (2) serve as a comprehension check.
- Every chapter begins with a real-name, real-world case study to provide a context for the material at hand. Each case is followed by a warm-up question to promote learning readiness. A "Back to the Opening Case" feature following each chapter offers questions to underscore the practical implications of what was just read.
- Most chapters begin with an overview model that serves as a conceptual roadmap for what lies ahead. This way, topics are encountered as part of an integrated whole, not as unrelated bits and pieces.
- A colorful and lively art program includes 45 captioned photographs, 147 figures, and more than 100 boxed features.
- Hundreds of real-world examples involving 319 large and small organizations have been integrated into the textual material to make this edition up-to-date, interesting, and relevant. Fifty-five boxed features titled "OB in Action" throughout the text also serve to link the reader and text material with the real world.
- Women play a prominent role throughout this text, as befitting their large and growing presence in the workplace. Lots of women role models are included. Special effort has been devoted to uncovering research insights about relevant and important gender-related differences.
- Key terms are emphasized in bold print where they are first defined and listed at the end of each chapter for review purposes. A glossary of key terms is located at the end of the text.
- A "Summary of Key Concepts" feature following each chapter concisely refamiliarizes the reader with the material just covered.
- Twenty-two "OB Exercises" are distributed throughout the book to foster personal involvement and greater self-awareness. Readers will gain experiential insights about their motivation to manage, self-esteem, personal values, perception, motives, sense of fairness, roles, power, tendency toward office politics, conflict handling style, interpersonal trust, work group autonomy, decision-making style, and stress.
- Ten discussion questions at the end of every chapter challenge the reader to explore the personal and practical implications of what has just been covered.
- Hand-on exercises at the end of each chapter foster experiential learning. Although some of the exercises are best done in classroom groups, facilitated by the instructor, the vast majority can be completed by readers studying alone. Discussion questions for each exercise facilitate students' learning.

Also available with this edition is a computerized version of the test bank, teletest, and instructional videos to accompany the text. These videos are organized by topic area, such as leadership and motivation. Additionally, there are over 75 color acetates.

• Words of Appreciation

This textbook, as with any book, represents the collective fruit of many people's labor. Our colleagues at Arizona State University have been very supportive of both editions. Our students at Arizona State University and the American Graduate School of International Management (Thunderbird) have been enthusiastic and candid academic "customers." We are grateful for their feedback and we hope we have done it justice in this new edition. Sincere appreciation goes to Gene E. Burton, California State, Fresno, and Maria Muto, Arizona State University, for their dedicated, skillful, and timely work on the Instructor's Manual/Test Bank and Lecture Supplement Manual, respectively. Our thanks for a job well done go to Robin Beltramini for her excellent work on the permissions and glossary. Both of us truly appreciate sage managerial advice from Ed Hargroves, Chief Executive Officer of Credit Card Software, Inc., and the always wise counsel of our friend and colleague Keith Davis.

To the following reviewers of all or portions of the first and second edition manuscripts go our gratitude and thanks. Their feedback was thoughtful, rigorous, constructive, and above all, essential to our goal of *Kaizen* (continuous improvement):

Gene E. Burton, California State University, Fresno; Gene Bocialetti, University of New Hampshire; Edward J. Conlon, University of Iowa; Bruce Drake, University of Portland; John A. Drexler, Jr., Oregon State University; Jan English, George Mason University; Joseph R. Foerst, Georgia State University; Ronald H. Gorman, American University; Peter Hom, Arizona State University; Avis L. Johnson, University of Akron; David G. Kuhn, Florida State University; Daniel McAllister, University of Nevada–Las Vegas; Steven Meisel, LaSalle University; Tony Mento, Loyola College, Maryland; Sandra Morgan, University of Hartford; Pamela Morrow, Iowa State University; Gene Murkison, Georgia Southern College; Margaret Neale, Northwestern University; Arnon Reichers, Ohio State University; Robert Roth, City University, Bellevue, Washington; Chester A. Schriesheim, University of Miami; Lewis A. Taylor III, University of Miami; Linda Travino, Penn State University; Don Warrick, University of Colorado; Pamela Wolfmeyer, Winona State University; and Peter Yeager, Richmond, Virginia.

Finally, we would like to thank our wives, Margaret and Joyce, for being understanding, patient, and helpful "book widows." Thanks in large measure to their love and moral support, this project has strengthened rather than strained a very valuable possession—our friendship.

We hope you enjoy this textbook. Best wishes for success and happiness!

Robert Kreitner
Angelo Kinicki

Contents in Brief

                   PROBLEMS   471

          13   Performance Appraisal, Feedback, and Rewards   473

          14   Leadership   513

          15   Individual and Group Decision Making   549

          16   Managing Occupational Stress   593

● PART V   UNDERSTANDING AND MANAGING THE EVOLVING ORGANIZATION   631

          17   Organizations: Structure and Effectiveness   633

          18   Organizational Life Cycles and Design   659

          19   International OB and Organizational Cultures   689

          20   Changing and Developing Organizations   723

          Advanced Learning Module A   762

          Advanced Learning Module B   771

          Glossary   775
          Name Index   783
          Subject Index   795

Contents

PART II
UNDERSTANDING AND MANAGING
INDIVIDUAL BEHAVIOR 77

> **PART III**
> **UNDERSTANDING AND MANAGING GROUP AND SOCIAL PROCESSES   273**

PART IV
UNDERSTANDING AND MANAGING ORGANIZATIONAL PROCESSES AND PROBLEMS 471

PART V
UNDERSTANDING AND MANAGING THE EVOLVING ORGANIZATION 631

ORGANIZATIONAL
BEHAVIOR

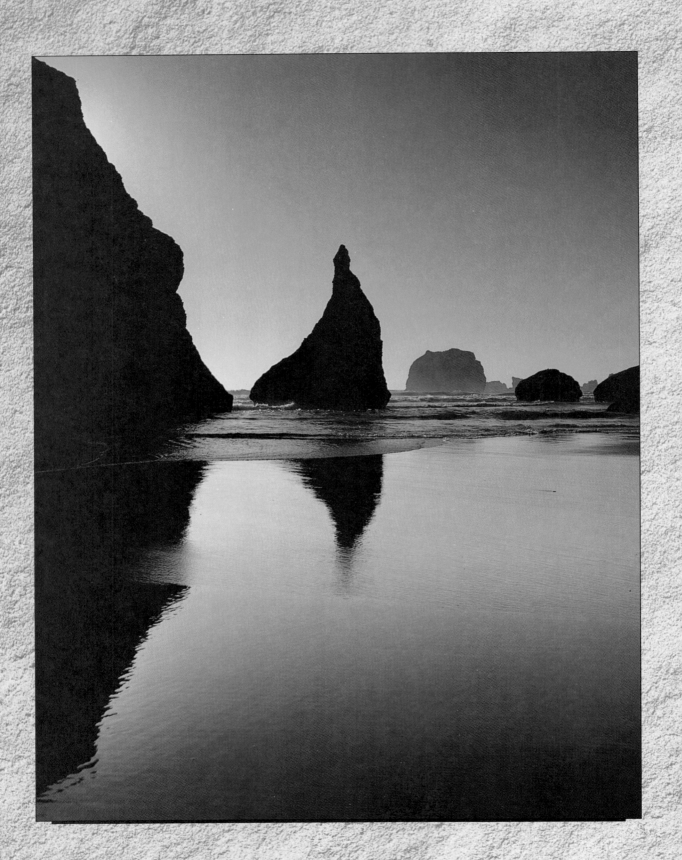

ORGANIZATIONAL BEHAVIOR: DEFINITION, BACKGROUND, AND CONTEXT

Managing
Organizational Behavior

When you finish studying the material in this chapter, you should be able to:

- Explain how people can make or break both managers and organizations.
- Define the term *management*.
- Explain what managers do and how their role is evolving.
- Identify the seven characteristics associated with motivation to manage.

- Summarize the research evidence about motivation to manage among college students.
- Define the term *organizational behavior* (OB) and explain why OB is a "horizontal" discipline.
- Review the historical development of managing people at work.

- Contrast McGregor's Theory X and Theory Y assumptions about employees.
- Explain how the contingency approach has influenced modern management thinking.
- Identify and briefly explain five sources and three uses of organizational behavior research.

OPENING CASE 1

Fun = Success for Donna Goya at Levi Strauss

Sharon Hoogstraten

It is 10 A.M. and employees at the headquarters of Levi Strauss and Co. are confused. Throughout the morning, short bursts of music have been piping through the loud speaker, all of which have magic as their theme. Employees are hearing phrases like, "You've got to believe you are magic, nothing can stand in your way." The receptionist is calling various departments trying to find out what is happening, but no one seems to know.

As the wonderment continues, Donna Goya, senior vice presi-

dent for personnel, and the brainchild behind the event, is peeking out of her office, obviously delighted with the growing interest among employees. At 11 A.M. Levi Strauss employees all over the world are called away from their work. Each one receives a certificate replicating a pair of the company's trademark, 501 bluejeans. Across the top of the certificate are the words, "You are a Miracle Worker" and tucked in the back pocket is a check for $501. Afterwards, there are celebrations in the individual departments, all ending at noon since it is a Friday and during the summer, the company closes at 12 o'clock.

"We started the year with horrible sales projections," said Goya. "It has totally turned around so we are handing out checks to say thank you for helping make history at Levi Strauss." That day, after the event is over— a spectacular success judging by the reaction of the employees— Goya is greeted by a beaming CEO, Bob Haas.

Goya's ability to sit comfortably on both sides of the fence— as an employee advocate and also as someone responsible for the business health of the company— may have something to do with her career beginnings. At Berkeley, she majored in business with an emphasis in marketing. When she approached Levi Strauss, she was looking for a position in merchandising.

"Isn't it interesting how careers are made?" said Goya. "Timing is most of it. After I got married in 1970 my husband started law school here in the city. A man at the executive search firm where I was working said if you're going to move to San Francisco, you'd better work for Levi Strauss, they are the best company around. At the time, there were no openings in merchandising. So, I asked what was open and there was an opening in personnel. I intended to switch over after a year," said Goya.

"The personnel function was growing rapidly. After I had been here a couple of years, I spoke to

S omeone once said the best place to begin is at the end. This practice holds true for the topic of managing people because management is a goal-oriented, or ends-oriented, endeavor. As we will see in the content of this book, a worthy goal for future managers is to develop a progressive philosophy of managing our most important resource, *people*. Consider, for example, the enlightened philosophy expressed recently by Walter B. Wriston, former chairman of Citicorp, the largest banking company in the United States.

> Talent is the number one commodity in short supply. You can't have enough good people in your organization. Because the terrible truth is that good people can make bad systems work. And bad people can ruin even the best system. So the job of the manager today is very simple and very difficult: To find the best people you can, motivate them to do the job, and allow them to do it their own way.

OPENING CASE 1

(continued)

some of the division presidents about making the shift into merchandising. I learned that it would be more difficult to balance my personal and professional life by going in that direction. Our merchandisers travel 25 percent to 30 percent of the time—some of them more. I had planned to have children, so I had a good, open discussion with the presidents and they said I needed to consider that.

"Then I talked to some of the people who were struggling, traveling, trying to take care of small children, and I basically made a change in my career path to stay in personnel," said Goya. "I was enjoying it; this is a fun company in which to be in human resources. Not only is it liberal—we can try new and different things—but the company really and truly cares about its employees. That's why I stayed in personnel," said Goya. . . .

Levi Strauss functions in a distinct environment. As a personnel executive, Goya sees her job as creating that environment, or, as she puts it, "creating an environment for success." Goya brings her own blend of good human resource practices to the company. A strong emphasis on employee relations, a commitment to helping employees achieve a balance between their personal and professional lives and a "walk-like-you-talk" philosophy. . . .

"Everything is changing so rapidly that the way we do business has to change. I don't think a senior management team can even pretend to know how to address all the issues that are coming," said Goya. "People have to be able to share ideas, take some accountability and responsibility to help get us where we need to go. We just can't do it on our own. . . .

Put all together, our mission is to create an environment that makes employees effective."

"When you do that, it benefits employees because they enjoy coming to work, they have fun, they feel challenged and motivated, and the company benefits. That's what drives me. The way we do business is not just so people can have fun, it's to ensure commercial success." . . .

For most of its history, Levi Strauss has been a family-run company. The company is trying to change from its paternalistic roots so that employees are empowered, encouraged to take risks, given greater authority and more accountability.

Goya is a staunch advocate of these changing values, all of which are outlined in Levi Strauss' Aspiration Statement, a policy she had a hand in composing. In fact, she has tried to apply some of the values to raising her 14-year-old daughter.

For Discussion

Do you agree or disagree with Donna Goya's philosophy of managing people? Explain.

• Additional discussion questions linking this case with the following material appear at the end of this chapter.

Source: Excerpted from Holly Rawlinson, "Homegrown for HRM," *Personnel Administrator*, August 1989, pp. 49–53.

Interestingly, it's this description of the manager's job that is at the heart of the age we are entering, the Age of Restructuring. Whether it's the threat of global competition, the threat of the takeover, the threat of Europe 1992, or just the fact that every so many years, industry, to survive, must restructure itself—U.S. managers no longer accept a business that is a loser, even if the balance sheet can hide the loss by rounding out the numbers. Managers are both listening more carefully to their people and asking them tougher questions. They are looking at their businesses and asking, "How can we create more value?" Answering that question will make companies lean and mean, run faster and be more agile, achieve world-class success—all the words that describe the new world of the business leader.[1]

Aside from being an admirable goal for present and future managers, this philosophy pinpoints two key thrusts of this book. They are:

• The staggering death toll during construction of the Panama Canal is a vivid illustration of the danger inherent in viewing workers as expendable commodities.   *(North Wind Picture Archives)*

1. *A human resource development thrust.* Are employees a commodity to be hired and discarded depending on the short-run whims of the organization? Or are they a valuable resource to be nurtured and developed? Historically, the first assumption was the rule. A stark illustration of the use of labor as an expendable commodity is the digging of the Panama Canal, called by historians the most dangerous construction project in American history. "When it was finished at last in 1914, the estimated cost in lives of the French and American projects was about 25,000—or 500 dead for every one of the canal's 51 miles."[2] Fortunately, modern society will not tolerate such inhumane treatment of employees. Thanks in part to stiff foreign competition and a more demanding work force at home, the human resource perspective of employees has blossomed. Joseph Duffey, Chancellor of the University of Massachusetts at Amherst and member of the National Council on Competitiveness, has framed the human resource perspective as follows:

> We must recognize that human capital is our greatest competitive potential. The talents of inventors, engineers, managers, and skilled workers will remain our best hope for economic achievement. Our ability to compete hinges on the ability to take advantage of a creative, well-trained labor force. Business and government should see workers as an asset, and not simply as a cost of production. Part of the secret of enhanced productivity lies in making people feel as though they are valued members of the economic community.[3]

A MATTER OF ETHICS

Experts Say Ethical Behavior Can Be Managed

Ethical behavior in business organizations is a complex, multi-faceted problem with significant individual and situational dimensions. Effective management of ethical behavior requires that organizations espouse ethics, expect ethical behavior from managers, screen potential applicants effectively, provide meaningful ethical training for employees, create ethics units, measure ethics, report ethics, reward ethics and make the tough decisions when none of this works. Developing systems with these characteristics requires sound leadership and support from the organizational culture and authority. Managers must often be willing to take risks in effectively implementing such a system. Yes, managing ethical behavior in business organization is possible, but it is no easy task.

Source: W. Edward Stead, Dan L. Worrell, and Jean Garner Stead, "An Integrative Model for Understanding and Managing Ethical Behavior in Business Organizations," *Journal of Business Ethics*, March 1990, p. 241.

This progressive view is in keeping with the call for a more ethical approach to management (see A Matter of Ethics). Accordingly, this book firmly embraces the idea that people are valuable human resources requiring systematic nurturing and development.

2. *A managerial thrust.* Few would argue with the claim that we all should know more about why people behave as they do. After all, by better understanding others, we gain greater understanding of ourselves. But from a managerial standpoint, simply acquiring knowledge about organizational behavior is not enough. That knowledge needs to be put to work to get something accomplished. Hence, this book strives to help you both understand and manage organizational behavior by blending theory, research, and practical techniques.

The purpose of this chapter is to discuss people as the key to managerial and organizational success, explore the manager's job, define organizational behavior, and consider how we can learn more about organizational behavior. A topical model for the balance of the book also is introduced.

• PEOPLE: THE KEY TO MANAGERIAL AND ORGANIZATIONAL SUCCESS

Given the high degree of complexity and rapid change managers face today, personal and organizational success can be elusive. Unforeseen economic, political, social, or technological changes can render even the best laid plans useless. More often than not, the success of individual managers and organizations pivots on such human factors as commitment, motivation, communication, leadership, and trust. Those who fail to appreciate the vital role *people* play in managerial and organizational success are destined to finish behind those who do.

People and Managerial Success

Why do some managers steadily move up through the ranks while others, who are similarly qualified, prematurely derail? A study conducted by researchers at the Center for Creative Leadership provides a revealing answer to this question. Interviewers asked top-level managers in several Fortune 500 companies to relate stories about two types of managers: (1) those who made it to top management positions and (2) those who did not. Stories about 20 successful managers were then compared with stories about 21 derailed managers.

All 41 managers possessed significant strengths. However, "insensitivity to others was cited as a reason for derailment more often than any other flaw."[4] Managers in this study were considered to be insensitive if they intimidated co-workers with an abrasive and bullying style. In addition, managers who failed to make it to the top were perceived as more aloof and arrogant than their successful counterparts.

 OB IN ACTION

Wal-Mart's Secret to Success? 250,000 Entrepreneurs!

In the sluggish retailing industry, Wal-Mart stores stands out as one of the few players with any adrenaline. Its first stadium-size store opened in the Arkansas boondocks just 27 years ago. Today Wal-Mart's profits as a percent of sales are already higher than those of its largest competitors, Sears and K mart. Revenues, which topped $25 billion in 1989, may well outstrip both by 1995. . . .

But don't give billionaire Sam Walton, Wal-Mart's charismatic founder, all the credit. That lofty ranking is also a tribute to the man he designated as his successor two years ago, David Glass, 55.

As a manager, Glass, like Walton, relies on the 1980s mantra, participation. "We have no superstars at Wal-Mart," he says. "We have average people operating in an environment that encourages everyone to perform way above average."

To stay in touch with employees—or "associates," as they're known in Wal-Martese—Glass and his lieutenants at the company's out-of-the-way headquarters in Bentonville, Arkansas, rely on a communications network worthy of the Pentagon. It includes everything from a six-channel satellite system to a private air force of 11 planes, mostly turboprops. Says Glass: "We believe nothing constructive happens in Bentonville. Our grass-roots philosophy is that the best ideas come from people on the firing line." Glass himself spends several days a week visiting the stores.

To heighen associates' sense of mission, the new boss hands them plenty of responsibility. Glass, who pushed Walton to install computers in every store in the mid-1970s, expects managers for each of the 34 departments within a typical Wal-Mart to run their operations as if they were running their own businesses. The managers are supported with detailed financial statements that show costs and profit margins. Says Glass: "Instead of having one entrepreneur who founded the business, we have got 250,000 entrepreneurs out there running their part of the business."

Source: Sarah Smith, "Quality of Management," *Fortune*, January 29, 1990, p. 46.

These research findings reinforce what enlightened managers have known all along. For instance, a General Electric Company executive told *Business Week:* "People don't fail due to lack of technical skills and energy. . . . They are most often derailed because of people problems."[5] Managers need to be able to work effectively with others if they are to make it to the top of the organizational pyramid.

People and Organizational Success

In recent years, many executives have said something along the lines of, "We're a good company because we have good people" (see OB in Action). Critics generally view this type of statement as a hollow cliché or a public relations ploy. But there is mounting evidence that *successful* organizations treat *all* their employees with care and respect. Evidence of this connection between a "people orientation" and organizational success was uncovered by Peters and Waterman, the authors of the best-selling book *In Search of Excellence*.

After studying 43 consistently successful businesses, including IBM, Procter & Gamble, McDonald's, and Delta Air Lines, Inc., Peters and Waterman identified eight attributes of excellence. Important among those attributes is "productivity through people." Regarding this key contributor

• A key to Wal-Mart stores' profitability is its treatment of all employees as valuable resources. *(Courtesy of Wal-Mart Stores, Inc.)*

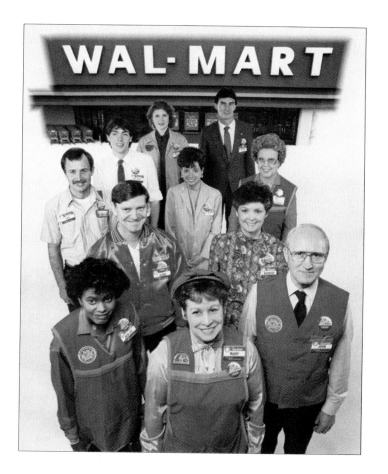

to corporate excellence, Peters and Waterman concluded that truly excellent organizations:

> Treat people as adults. Treat them as partners; treat them with dignity; treat them with respect. Treat *them*—not capital spending and automation—as the primary source of productivity gains. These are fundamental lessons from the excellent companies research. In other words, if you want productivity and the financial reward that goes with it, you must treat your workers as your most important asset.[6]

Although Peters and Waterman's research methodology has been criticized for not being rigorous enough,[7] their conclusion that a genuine concern for people and organizational success go hand in hand is a convincing one. As an intuitive test of this proposition, can you think of an organization that treats its people with contempt, yet still has enjoyed long-term success? Probably not.

• THE MANAGER'S JOB: GETTING THINGS DONE THROUGH OTHERS

For better or for worse, managers touch our lives in many ways. Schools, hospitals, government agencies, and large and small businesses all require systematic management. Formally defined, **management** is the process of working with and through others to achieve organizational objectives in an efficient manner. From the standpoint of organizational behavior, the central feature of this definition is "working with and through others." Managers play a constantly evolving role (see International OB for indications of where the evolution is headed). Today's successful managers are no longer the I've-got-everything-under-control order givers of yesteryear. Rather, they need to creatively envision and actively sell bold new directions in an ethical and sensitive manner. Effective managers are team players empowered by the willing and active support of others who are driven by conflicting self-interests. Each of us has a huge stake in how well managers carry out their evolving role. Henry Mintzberg, a respected management scholar, observed: "No job is more vital to our society than that of the manager. It is the manager who determines whether our social institutions serve us well or whether they squander our talents and resources."[8]

Extending our managerial thrust, let us take a closer look at the tasks managers perform and the psychological orientation that compels some people to become managers.

What Do Managers Do?

Observational studies by Mintzberg and others have found the typical manager's day to be a fragmented collection of brief episodes.[9] Interruptions are commonplace, large blocks of time for planning and reflective thinking are not. In one particular study, four top-level managers spent 63 percent of their time on activities lasting less than nine minutes each. Only 5 percent of the managers' time was devoted to activities lasting more than a hour.[10] But what specific tasks do managers perform during their hectic and fragmented workdays? Recent research evidence gives us some instructive and interesting answers.

INTERNATIONAL OB

Australian Study of the Changing Role of Management Shows People Skills to Be More Critical to Success than Ever

A study of 50 Australian chief executive officers (CEOs) by David C. Limerick and his colleagues uncovered what they call the *new managerial role*:

- *Skills in empathy.* The CEOs stressed that managers should be empathetic, warm, and able to supervise autonomous individuals. The capacity to communicate, often symbolically, also was important.
- *Skills in transformation.* The rapid pace of change requires skills in changing systems and values. Thus managers require transformational leadership skills; they have to be strong and able to both mold and change their organizations.
- *Proactivity.* Using such phrases as "self-driven," "doers," "bias for action," and "ambitious," the CEOs stressed the need for an ability to get things done. Pragmatic common sense, reflected in such phrases as "smell for the dollar," "common business sense," and "good knowledge of what the business is about," also is required.
- *Political skills.* Managers have to be able to understand the political climate and deal with the political environment.
- *Networking skills.* Managers need the capacity to network between the elements of the broader organizational picture, interpreting for them the mission and identity of the organization.
- *Intuitive, creative thinking.* The CEOs stressed creativity, intuition, imagination, innovation, lateral thinking, and the ability to ask "what if" questions rather than linear logical abilities.
- *Personal maturity.* The task of networking throughout very different autonomous systems makes enormous demands on the maturity of the individual, who is no longer able to cling to a specific role within a coherent structure for a sense of identity. Thus managers need both self-understanding and a commitment to the values of the larger system. They must understand their strengths and weaknesses, continue learning by self-evaluation, and have the capacity to cope with stress. They also must be mature, professional, loyal, and ethical in business practice.

Source: David C. Limerick, "Managers of Meaning: From Bob Geldof's Band to Australian CEOs," *Organizational Dynamics*, Spring 1990, pp. 31–32.

In a survey, researchers asked 1,412 managers (658 first-line supervisors; 553 middle managers; 201 executives) to rank the relative importance of 57 different managerial duties. Statistical analysis of the results revealed seven basic managerial tasks:

1. Managing individual performance.
2. Instructing subordinates.
3. Representing one's staff.
4. Managing group performance.
5. Planning and allocating resources.
6. Coordinating interdependent groups.
7. Monitoring the business environment.[11]

The second phase of the analysis produced task profiles for the three different levels of management (see Figure 1–1). Significantly, this level-by-level comparison overcame a limitation of Mintzberg's observational study that included only five chief executive officers.

Careful examination of the data in Figure 1–1 leads us to the following conclusions:

• There are basic managerial tasks common to all levels of management.

• The perceived importance of those tasks changes as one moves up the managerial ladder. As depicted by the percentages shown in Figure 1–1, tasks 1 and 2 are paramount for first-line supervisors, tasks 3, 4, and 5 for middle managers, and tasks 6 and 7 for executives.

• People-oriented tasks (numbers 1, 2, 3, 4, and 6) comprise the vast bulk of the manager's job.

Summarizing, managers at different levels perform the same basic tasks but with different emphasis. The common denominator of management, however, remains the management of people. A solid background in organiza-

---

• **FIGURE 1–1**   Different Levels of Management Have Different Task Profiles*

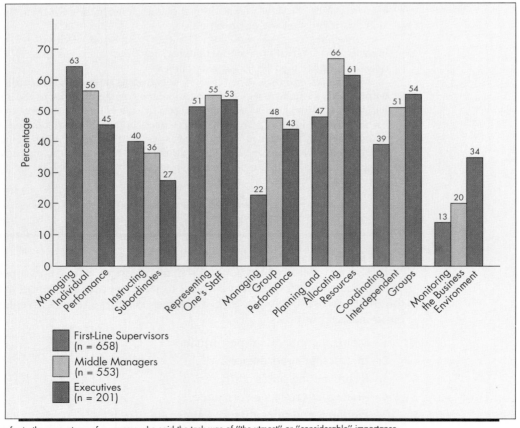

* Numbers refer to the percentage of managers who said the task was of "the utmost" or "considerable" importance.

Source: Data adapted from Allen I. Kraut, Patricia R. Pedigo, D. Douglas McKenna, and Marvin D. Dunnette, "The Role of the Manager: What's Really Important in Different Management Jobs," *Academy of Management Executive*, November 1989, pp. 286–93.

tional behavior can help managers efficiently get things done with and through others.

Motivation to Manage

Is there a formula for managerial success? Experience tells us it takes a combination of ability, desire, and opportunity. Of course, to some degree, luck—such as being in the right place at the right time—plays a role in managerial success. Desire deserves special attention here because it often enables aspiring managers to translate ability, opportunities, and luck into success. Take Frederick W. Smith, founder of Federal Express, for example. He built his successful billion-dollar airfreight company from an idea he formulated in an economics term paper while studying at Yale University. Ironically, Smith's professor told him it was an ill-conceived idea and gave him a C.[12] Someone with less desire than Smith might have become discouraged and given up. But Smith, like many successful managers, forged ahead despite setbacks. Research on motivation to manage during the last couple of decades has advanced our understanding of desire and other contributors to managerial success.

By identifying personal traits positively correlated with both rapid movement up the career ladder and managerial effectiveness, John B. Miner developed a psychometric test for measuring **motivation to manage.** The questionnaire assesses the strength of seven factors (see OB Exercise). Although the complete questionnaire is not presented in the exercise, we have added scales so you can gauge the strength of your motivation to manage. (Arbitrary norms for comparison purposes are: Total score of 7–21 = Relatively low motivation to manage; 22–34 = Moderate; 35–49 = Relatively high.) How do you measure up? Remember, though, high motivation to manage is only part of the formula for managerial success. The right combination of ability and opportunity is also necessary.

Longitudinal research by Miner and others shows that the steady decline in motivation to manage among college students during the 1960s and 1970s has stopped. Scores still remain comparatively low, however, and there is concern that this foreshadows a future shortage of managerial talent. On the positive side, the gap between males and females has closed. Historically, female business students scored lower in motivation to manage than did their male counterparts. In a more recent study, researchers found that MBA students with higher motivation-to-manage scores tended to earn more money after graduation. But students with higher motivation to manage did not earn better grades or complete their degree program sooner than those with lower motivation to manage.[13]

• THE FIELD OF ORGANIZATIONAL BEHAVIOR: PAST AND PRESENT

Organizational behavior, commonly referred to as OB, is an interdisciplinary field dedicated to better understanding and managing people at work. By definition, organizational behavior is both research- and application-oriented. Three basic levels of analysis in OB are individual, group, and organizational. OB draws upon a diverse array of disciplines, including psychology, management, sociology, organization theory, social psychology, statistics, anthropology, general systems theory, economics, informa-

• OB EXERCISE

How Strong Is Your Motivation to Manage?
(Circle one number for each factor)

Factor	Description	Scale
1. Authority figures	A desire to meet managerial role requirements in terms of positive relationships with superiors	Weak 1–2–3–4–5–6–7 Strong
2. Competitive games	A desire to engage in competition with peers involving games or sports and thus meet managerial role requirements in this regard	Weak 1–2–3–4–5–6–7 Strong
3. Competitive situations	A desire to engage in competition with peers involving occupational or work-related activities and thus meet managerial role requirements in this regard	Weak 1–2–3–4–5–6–7 Strong
4. Assertive role	A desire to behave in an active and assertive manner involving activities that in this society are often viewed as predominantly masculine and thus to meet managerial role requirements	Weak 1–2–3–4–5–6–7 Strong
5. Imposing wishes	A desire to tell others what to do and to utilize sanctions in influencing others, thus indicating a capacity to fulfill managerial role requirements in relationships with subordinates	Weak 1–2–3–4–5–6–7 Strong
6. Standing out from group	A desire to assume a distinctive position of a unique and highly visible nature in a manner that is role-congruent for managerial jobs	Weak 1–2–3–4–5–6–7 Strong
7. Routine administrative functions	A desire to meet managerial role requirements regarding activities often associated with managerial work that are of a day-to-day administrative nature	Weak 1–2–3–4–5–6–7 Strong
		Total = _____

Source: Adapted from John B. Miner and Norman R. Smith, "Decline and Stabilization of Managerial Motivation Over a 20-Year Period," *Journal of Applied Psychology*, June 1982, p. 298.

• **FIGURE 1-2**   Organizational Behavior (OB) Is a Horizontal Discipline

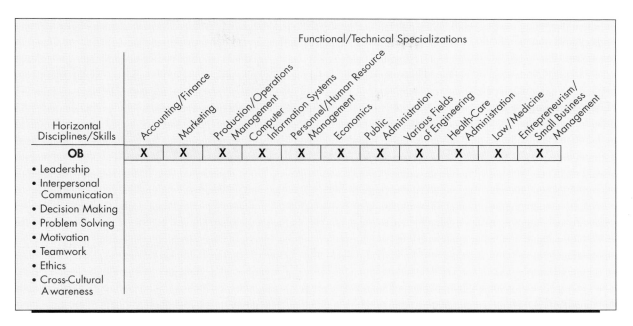

tion technology, political science, vocational counseling, human stress management, psychometrics, ergonomics, decision theory, and ethics. This rich heritage has spawned many competing perspectives and theories about human work behavior. By the mid-1980s, one researcher had identified 110 distinct theories about behavior within the field of OB.[14]

Organizational behavior is an academic designation. With the exception of teaching/research positions, OB is not an everyday job category such as accounting, marketing, or finance. Students of OB typically do not get jobs in organizational behavior, per se. This reality in no way demeans OB or lessens its importance in effective organizational management. Indeed, as graphically depicted in Figure 1–2, OB is a *horizontal* discipline that cuts across virtually every job category, business function, and professional specialty. Each of the other horizontal disciplines/skills listed in the left-hand side of Figure 1–2 is covered in this text as an integral part of OB. Anyone who plans to make a living in a large or small, public or private, organization needs to study organizational behavior.

A historical perspective of the study of people at work helps in studying organizational behavior. According to a management history expert, this is important because:

> Historical perspective is the study of a subject in light of its earliest phases and subsequent evolution. Historical perspective differs from history in that the object of historical perspective is to sharpen one's vision of the present, not the past.[15]

In other words, we can better understand where the field of OB is today and where it appears to be headed by appreciating where it has been. A general historical perspective relating to the field of OB is displayed in Table 1–1.

• TABLE 1-1   Assumptions about People at Work Have Changed Dramatically through the Years

Period	Pre-1800–1880	1880–1930	1930–1960	1960–Today
General theory of management	Prescientific	Classical	Behavioral	Modern
Nature of society	Agrarian	Industrial		Postindustrial
Locus of work	Farm/home	Factory		Office/home
Assumptions about human nature	Economic person		Social and self-actualizing person	Complex person
Role of management		Control employee behavior	Maintain employee social systems	Facilitate employee development

Source: Adapted from James L. Bowditch and Anthony F. Buono, *A Primer on Organizational Behavior* (New York: John Wiley & Sons, copyright © 1985). Reprinted by permission of John Wiley & Sons, Inc.

Four significant eras—prescientific, classical, behavioral, and modern—have paved the way for the field of OB.

The Prescientific Era

The practice of management can be traced to earliest recorded history. Abundant archaeological evidence, such as the great pyramids, stands in silent tribute to the talents of bygone managers. Illiterate workers (or slaves), miserable working conditions, primitive agrarian economies, and crude tools made the task of managers in ancient civilizations extremely difficult. Moreover, even though managers during the prescientific era did not have formal education and training in proven management methods, they accomplished amazing things.

As time passed, exploitation of natural resources and technological advances led to the Industrial Revolution. This changed the nature of society and the location of work. People left their farms and went to work in urban factories. Money economies replaced barter economies, thus expediting the payment of wages. Another outcome of the Industrial Revolution was an interest in rationalizing the managerial process. Haphazard and unsystematic management practices proved to be inadequate for large-scale factory operations. The classical management era was born out of this interest.

The Classical Era

The classical management era lasted from about 1880 to 1930, and during this time the first general theories of management began to evolve. Two major thrusts were administrative theory and scientific management. Interestingly, both theories were proposed by engineers.

Administrative Theory   Also called the universal process school of management, the administrative theory approach can be traced to Henri Fayol, a

• **TABLE 1-2**   Fayol's Universal Principles of Management

1. **Division of work.** Specialization of labor is necessary for organizational success.
2. **Authority.** The right to give orders must accompany responsibility.
3. **Discipline.** Obedience and respect help an organization run smoothly.
4. **Unity of command.** Each employee should receive orders from only one superior.
5. **Unity of direction.** The efforts of everyone in the organization should be coordinated and focused in the same direction.
6. **Subordination of individual interests to the general interest.** Resolving the tug of war between personal and organizational interests in favor of the organization is one of management's greatest difficulties.
7. **Remuneration.** Employees should be paid fairly in accordance with their contribution.
8. **Centralization.** The relationship between centralization and decentralization is a matter of proportion; the optimum balance must be found for each organization.
9. **Scalar chain.** Subordinates should observe the formal chain of command unless expressly authorized by their respective superiors to communicate with each other.
10. **Order.** Both material things and people should be in their proper places.
11. **Equity.** Fairness that results from a combination of kindliness and justice will lead to devoted and loyal service.
12. **Stability and tenure of personnel.** People need time to get to know their jobs.
13. **Initiative.** One of the greatest satisfactions is formulating and carrying out a plan.
14. **Espirit de corps.** Harmonious effort among individuals is the key to organizational success.

Source: Robert Kreitner, *Management*, 4th ed. (Boston: Houghton Mifflin, 1989), p. 58, as adapted from Henri Fayol, *General and Industrial Management*, trans. Constance Storrs (London: Isaac Pitman & Sons, 1949).

French industrialist. In his 1916 classic, *Administration Industrielle et Generale,* Fayol divided the manager's job into five functions: planning, organizing, command, coordination, and control. He then recommended 14 universal principles of management (see Table 1–2). Three-quarters of a century later, most of Fayol's universal principles are still relevant. His calls for matching authority and responsibility, equitable treatment, initiative, and espirit de corps remain pillars of good management. On the other hand, some modern observers regard Fayol's emphasis on discipline, obedience, the hierarchical chain of command, order, and stability as archaic and out of touch with today's fast-changing organizational circumstances. On balance, Fayol gave us an invaluable foundation for the systematic study of organized effort.

Scientific Management   According to a time-honored definition, **scientific management** "is that kind of management which conducts a business or affairs by standards established by facts or truths gained through systematic observation, experiment, or reasoning."[16] Frederick Taylor, credited with being the father of scientific management, published *The Principles of Scientific Management* in 1911. Because Taylor conducted much of his early experimentation in the steel industry, he focused on shop floor and factory operations.

Through time and task study, standardization of tools and procedures, development of piece-rate incentive schemes, and systematic selection and training, Taylor dramatically improved output. Scientific management replaced haphazard rules of thumb with systematic, experimentally derived techniques. Regarding employees, Taylor's goal was to make work behavior as stable and predictable as possible so increasingly sophisticated machines and factories would achieve maximum efficiency. He relied heavily on monetary incentives because he saw workers as basically lazy beings motivated primarily by money. Although Taylor has been roundly criticized for encouraging managers to treat employees like mindless machines, many fruits of his pioneering work are still evident.[17]

The Behavioral Era

A unique combination of factors fostered the emergence of the behavioral era during the 1930s. First, following legalization of union-management collective bargaining in the United States in 1935, management began looking for new ways of handling employees. Second, behavioral scientists conducting on-the-job research started calling for more attention to the "human" factor. Managers who had lost the battle to keep unions out of their factories heeded the call for better human relations and improved working conditions. One such study, conducted at Western Electric's Hawthorne plant, was a prime stimulus for the *human relations movement.* Ironically, many of the Hawthorne findings have turned out to be more myth than fact.

The Hawthorne Legacy   Recent interviews with three subjects of the Hawthorne studies and re-analysis of the original data with modern statistical techniques do not support initial conclusions about the positive effect of supportive supervision. Specifically, money, fear of unemployment during the Great Depression, managerial discipline, and high-quality raw materials—not supportive supervision—turned out to be responsible for high output in the relay assembly test room experiments.[18] Nonetheless, the human relations movement gathered momentum through the 1950s, as academics and managers alike made stirring claims about the powerful impact that individual needs, supportive supervision, and group dynamics apparently had on job performance.

The Writings of Mayo and Follett   Essential to the human relations movement were the writings of Elton Mayo and Mary Parker Follett. Australian-born Mayo, who headed the Harvard researchers at Hawthorne, advised managers to attend to employees' emotional needs in his 1933 classic, *The Human Problems of an Industrial Civilization.* Follett was a true pioneer, not only as a woman management consultant in a male-dominated industrial world of the 1920s, but also as a writer who saw employees as complex combinations of attitudes, beliefs, and needs. Mary Parker Follett was way ahead of her time in telling managers to motivate job performance instead of merely demanding it, a "pull" rather than "push" strategy. She also built a logical bridge between political democracy and a cooperative spirit in the workplace.[19]

New Assumptions about Human Nature   Unfortunately, unsophisticated behavioral research methods caused the human relationists to embrace some naive and misleading conclusions. For example, human relationists believed in the axiom, "A satisfied employee is a hardworking employee." Subsequent research, as discussed later in this book, shows the satisfaction-performance linkage to be more complex than originally thought.

Despite its shortcomings, the behavioral era opened the door to more progressive thinking about human nature. Rather than continuing to view employees as passive economic beings, managers began to see them as active social beings and took steps to create more humane work environments.

The Modern Era

In 1960, Douglas McGregor wrote a book titled *The Human Side of Enterprise*, which has become an important philosophical base for the modern view of people at work.[20] Drawing upon his experience as a management consultant, McGregor formulated two sharply contrasting sets of assumptions about human nature (see Table 1–3). His Theory X assumptions were pessimistic and negative and, according to McGregor's interpretation, typical of how managers traditionally perceived employees. To help managers break with this negative tradition, McGregor formulated his **Theory Y,** a modern and positive set of assumptions about people. McGregor believed managers could accomplish more through others by viewing them as self-energized, committed, responsible, and creative beings.

McGregor's Theory Y challenges theorists and practicing managers to adopt a *developmental* approach to employees. Many modern managers endorse McGregor's progressive Theory Y philosophy. For example, here's what Mark Suwyn, a group vice president at Du Pont, recently had to say about his firm's manufacturing employees: "These people manage their lives well outside the factory. They sit on school boards or coach Little League. We have to create a culture where we can bring that creative energy into the work force."[21] Linda Honold, Director of Member Development at Johnsonville Foods in Wisconsin, put it this way: "U.S. companies need to change their beliefs about the ability of average employees. We must expect

• **TABLE 1-3** McGregor's Theory X and Theory Y

Outdated (Theory X) Assumptions about People at Work	Modern (Theory Y) Assumptions about People at Work
1. Most people dislike work; they avoid it when they can.	1. Work is a natural activity, like play or rest.
2. Most people must be coerced and threatened with punishment before they will work. People require close direction when they are working.	2. People are capable of self-direction and self-control if they are committed to objectives.
3. Most people actually prefer to be directed. They tend to avoid responsibility and exhibit little ambition. They are interested only in security.	3. People generally become committed to organizational objectives if they are rewarded for doing so.
	4. The typical employee can learn to accept and seek responsibility.
	5. The typical member of the general population has imagination, ingenuity, and creativity.

Source: Adapted from Douglas McGregor, *The Human Side of Enterprise* (New York: McGraw-Hill, 1960), chap. 4.

them to be involved in every aspect of their job. When we do, we will start realizing a dramatic increase in productivity and quality."[22]

Given society's rapid change and increased complexity in recent years, McGregor's Theory Y now qualifies as an inspiring beginning rather than an adequate end. Reflecting increased complexity in the workplace, management and OB theories have become more complex and abstract. Consider, for example, the modern contingency approach to management.

A Contingency Approach   Management scholars responded to increased complexity by formulating a **contingency approach** that calls for using management techniques in a situationally appropriate manner, instead of trying to rely on "one best way." According to a pair of contingency theorists:

> [Contingency theories] developed and their acceptance grew largely because they responded to criticisms that the classical theories advocated "one best way" of organizing and managing. Contingency theories, on the other hand, proposed that the appropriate organizational structure and management style were dependent upon a set of "contingency" factors, usually the uncertainty and instability of the environment.[23]

The contingency approach encourages managers to view organizational behavior within a situational context. According to this modern perspective, evolving situations, not hard-and-fast rules, determine when and where various management techniques are appropriate. For example, as discussed in Chapter 14, contingency researchers have determined that there is no single best style of leadership. Organizational behavior specialists embrace the contingency approach because it helps them realistically interrelate individuals, groups, and organizations. Moreover, the contingency approach sends a clear message to managers: Carefully read the situation and then be flexible enough to adapt.

No Simple Answers Anymore   As an interesting example, consider the growing problem of workplace gambling (e.g., football and baseball pools). Managers complain that work remains undone when employees devote time to making and collecting bets. How would experts from earlier management eras interpret this problem? Fayol would probably say the employees were out of control because authority and the chain of command had broken down. Taylor would claim the culprits had fallen into a natural pattern of laziness because they were being paid by the hour and not by units of work completed. No doubt Taylor would allude to the economic incentive of betting. As for the human relationists, they would explain the situation in terms of the satisfaction of natural social needs and peer pressure. Here is a modern interpretation:

> Money is but one of the lures of office pools. They are social equalizers, in which junior flunkies can outwit senior executives. They are boredom antidotes, in which spread-sheets can be set aside for point-spread sheets. And, for the lucky winners, they are status-builders in which the envious congratulations of co-workers come with a stack of crumpled bills.[24]

By examining the problem closely, an apparently simple situation turns out to be extremely complex. The path to a workable solution will be equally complex. Fortunately, the field of OB and the contingency approach to management can light the way.

In summary, each management era has enabled us to accomplish more through organized endeavor. Modern OB, which considers the contingencies among individuals, groups, the organization, and the external environment, promises to help us better understand and manage people at work. Now that we have reviewed OB's historical context, we need to address how we learn about OB through a combination of theory, research, and practice.

• LEARNING ABOUT OB FROM THEORY, RESEARCH, AND PRACTICE

As a human being, with years of interpersonal experience to draw upon, you already know a good deal about people at work. But more systematic and comprehensive understanding is possible and desirable. A working knowledge of current OB theory, research, and practice can help you develop a tightly integrated understanding of why organizational contributors think and act as they do. In order for this to happen, however, prepare yourself for some intellectual surprises from theoretical models, research results, or techniques that may run counter to your current thinking. For instance, conventional wisdom says that physically active employees perform better than their out-of-shape co-workers. But in a recent study of 522 factory employees (half of whom exercised each workday for 15 minutes before lunch and half of whom did not), both groups did the same amount of work despite the perception among the exercisers that they had accomplished more with less fatigue. So regular exercise, while still a good idea for general health and lifestyle purposes, is not a quick fix for productivity improvement.[25] Recognizing that surprises are what makes learning fun, let us examine the dynamic relationship between OB theory, research, and practice and the value of each.

Figure 1–3 illustrates how theory, research, and practice are related. Throughout the balance of this book, we focus primarily on the central portion, where all three areas overlap. Knowledge of why people behave as they do and what managers can do to improve performance is greatest within this area of maximum overlap. For each major topic, we build a foundation for understanding with generally accepted theory. This theoretical foundation is then tested and expanded by reviewing the latest relevant research findings. After interpreting the research, we discuss the nature and effectiveness of related practical applications.

Sometimes, depending on the subject matter, it is necessary to venture into the large areas outside the central portion of Figure 1–3. For example, an insightful theory supported by convincing research evidence might suggest an untried or different way of managing. In other instances, an innovative management technique might call for an explanatory theoretical model and exploratory research. Each area—theory, research, and practice—supports and in turn is supported by the other two. Each area makes a valuable contribution to our understanding of, and ability to, manage organizational behavior.

• **Figure 1-3**   Learning about OB through a Combination of Theory, Research, and Practice

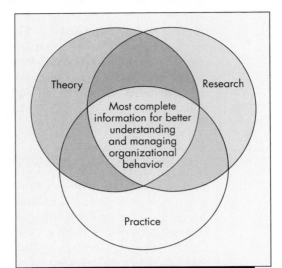

Learning from Theory

A respected behavioral scientist, Kurt Lewin, once said there is nothing as practical as a good theory. According to one management researcher, a **theory** is a story that explains "why."[26] Another calls well-constructed theories "disciplined imagination."[27] A good OB theory, then, is a story that effectively explains why individuals and groups behave as they do. Moreover, a good theoretical model:

1. *Defines* key terms.
2. Constructs a *conceptual framework* that explains how important factors are interrelated. (Graphic models are often used to achieve this end.)
3. Provides a *departure point* for research and practical application.

Indeed, good theories are a fundamental contributor to improved understanding and management of organizational behavior.

Learning from Research

Because of unfamiliar jargon and complicated statistical procedures, many present and future managers are put off by behavioral research. This is unfortunate because many practical lessons can be learned as OB researchers steadily push back the frontier of knowledge. Let us examine the various sources and uses of OB research evidence.

Five Sources of OB Research Insights   To enhance the instructional value of our coverage of major topics, we systematically cite "hard" evidence from five different categories. Worthwhile evidence was obtained by drawing upon the following *priority* of research methodologies:

- *Meta-analyses.* A **meta-analysis** is a statistical pooling technique that permits behavioral scientists to draw general conclusions about certain variables from many different studies.[28] It typically encompasses a vast number of subjects, often reaching the thousands. Meta-analyses are instructive because they focus on general patterns of research evidence, not fragmented bits and pieces or isolated studies.
- *Field studies.* In OB, a **field study** probes individual or group processes in an organizational setting. Because field studies involve real-life situations, their results often have immediate and practical relevance for managers.
- *Laboratory studies.* In a **laboratory study,** variables are manipulated and measured in contrived situations. College students are commonly used as subjects. The highly controlled nature of laboratory studies enhances research precision. But generalizing the results to organizational management requires caution.[29]
- *Sample surveys.* In a **sample survey,** samples of people from specified populations respond to questionnaires. The researchers then draw conclusions about the relevant population. Generalizability of the results depends on the quality of the sampling and questioning techniques.
- *Case studies.* A **case study** is an in-depth analysis of a single individual, group, or organization. Because of their limited scope, case studies yield realistic but not very generalizable results.[30]

Three Uses of OB Research Findings   Organizational scholars point out that managers can put relevant research findings to use in three different ways:[31]

1. *Instrumental use.* This involves directly applying research findings to practical problems. For example, a manager experiencing high stress tries a relaxation technique after reading a research report about its effectiveness.
2. *Conceptual use.* Research is put to conceptual use when managers derive general enlightenment from its findings. The impact here is less specific and more indirect than with instrumental use. For example, after reading a recently reported meta-analysis showing a negative correlation between absenteeism and age,[32] a manager might develop a more positive attitude toward hiring older people.
3. *Symbolic use.* Symbolic use occurs when research results are relied on to verify or legitimize already held positions. Negative forms of symbolic use involve self-serving bias, prejudice, selective perception, and distortion. For example, tobacco industry spokespersons routinely deny any link between smoking and lung cancer because researchers are largely, but not 100 percent, in agreement about the negative effects of smoking. A positive example would be managers maintaining their confidence in setting performance goals after reading a research report about the favorable impact of goal setting on job performance.

By systematically reviewing and interpreting research relevant to key topics, this book provides instructive insights about OB. (The mechanics of the scientific method and OB research are discussed in detail in Advanced Learning Module A at the end of this text.)

Learning from Practice

Relative to learning more about how to effectively manage people at work, one might be tempted to ask, "Why bother with theory and research; let's get right down to *how to do it*." Our answer lies in the contingency approach, discussed earlier. The effectiveness of specific theoretical models or management techniques is contingent on the situations in which they are applied. For example, one cross-cultural study of a large multinational corporation's employees working in 50 countries led the researcher to conclude that most made-in-America management theories and techniques are inappropriate in other cultures.[33] Many otherwise well-intentioned performance-improvement programs based on American cultural values have failed in other cultures because of naive assumptions about transferability. (International cultures are discussed in Chapter 19.) Fortunately, systematic research is available that tests our "common sense" assumptions about what works where. Management "cookbooks" that provide only how-to-do-it advice with no underlying theoretical models or supporting research practically guarantee misapplication. As mentioned earlier, theory, research, and practice mutually reinforce one another.

A particularly fruitful link between research and practice comes from what has been called *applied research*. The type of applied OB research we are interested in here involves the systematic study of on-the- job processes and techniques that have descriptive and goal relevance for managers. "**Descriptive relevance** refers to the extent to which a research project captures phenomena which are encountered by practitioners in applied settings."[34] In contrast, **goal relevance** is said to exist when researchers focus on outcomes that managers see as important (e.g., performance, absenteeism, turnover, commitment, satisfaction). Whenever available, the results of applied OB research with descriptive and goal relevance are discussed in this text so as to test situational appropriateness.

The theory→research→practice sequence discussed in this section will help you better understand each major topic addressed later in this book. Attention now turns to a topical model that sets the stage for what lies ahead.

• A TOPICAL MODEL FOR UNDERSTANDING AND MANAGING OB

Figure 1–4 is a topical road map for our journey through this book. Our destination is organizational effectiveness. Four different criteria for determining whether or not an organization is effective are discussed in Chapter 17. The study of OB can be a wandering and pointless trip if we overlook the need to translate OB lessons into effective and efficient organized endeavor.

• FIGURE 1-4   A Topical Model for What Lies Ahead

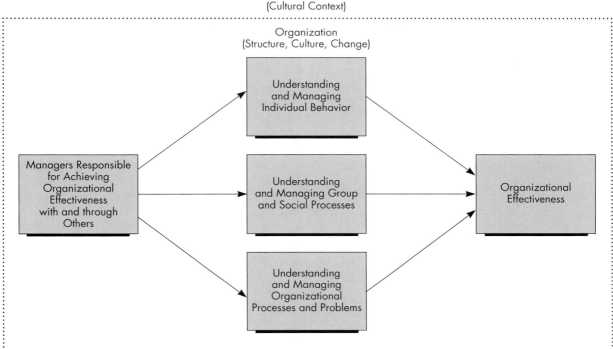

At the far left side of our topical road map are managers, those who are responsible for accomplishing organizational goals with and through others. The three boxes at the center of our road map correspond to Parts II, III, and IV of this text. Logically, the flow of topical coverage in this book goes from individuals, to group processes, to organizational processes and problems, to organizations. Around the core of our topical road map in Figure 1-4 is the organization. Accordingly, we end our journey with organization-related material in Part V. Organizational structure and design are covered there in Chapters 17 and 18 to establish and develop the *organizational* context of organizational behavior. Rounding out our organizational context are discussions of organizational cultures in Chapter 19 and organizational change in Chapter 20.

The broken line represents a permeable boundary between the organization and its environment. Energy and influence flow both ways across this permeable boundary. Truly, no organization is an island in today's highly interactive and interdependent world. Relative to the *external* environment, international cultures are explored in Chapter 19. Organization–environment contingencies are examined in Chaper 18.

Chapter 2 examines the OB implications of significant demographic and social trends and Chapter 3 explores important ethical considerations. These discussions provide a realistic context for studying and managing people at work.

Bon voyage! Enjoy your trip through the challenging, interesting, and often surprising world of OB.

• SUMMARY OF KEY CONCEPTS

A. This book has two key thrusts. The first underscores that people are valuable human resources needing systematic nurturing and development. A managerial thrust reminds us the purpose of learning about organizational behavior is to accomplish organizational goals.

B. Successful people are essential to managerial and organizational success. One study contrasting successful managers with derailed managers found the latter to be insensitive, abrasive, and bullying. Peters and Waterman, authors of the best-seller *In Search of Excellence,* found that truly excellent companies treat their people as adults and as the primary source of productivity gains.

C. Management is defined as the process of working with and through others to achieve organizational objectives in an efficient manner. Observational studies by Mintzberg and others found the typical manager's day to be a hectic stream of fragmented activities with lots of interruptions. According to a recent survey of 50 Australian CEOs, the traditional portrayal of managers as everything-under-control order givers has given way to more sensitive and ethical team players who must actively sell their creative ideas to others with conflicting self-interests.

D. Recent research identified seven basic managerial tasks, dealing primarily with the management of people. The three different levels of management were found to place different emphasis on these seven basic tasks.

E. Miner's motivation-to-manage questionnaire measures seven personal characteristics that predict managerial effectiveness. Of course, ability and opportunity round out the formula for managerial success. The steady decline in college students' motivation to manage in recent decades has stopped, and the male-female gap has closed. Still, Miner is worried that we face a shortage of managerial talent.

F. Organizational behavior (OB) is an interdisciplinary field dedicated to better understanding and managing people at work. It is both research- and application-oriented. Except for teaching/research positions, one does not normally get a job in OB. Rather, because OB is a horizontal discipline, OB concepts and lessons are applicable to virtually every job category, business function, and professional specialty.

G. A historical perspective of OB shows how it has evolved from four eras: prescientific, classical, behavioral, and modern. Not until the behavioral era (and McGregor's Theory Y) were employees viewed as active and creative beings seeking personal growth and social recognition. In response to growing complexity, a modern contingency (or situational) approach to management is recommended. ''One best way'' is no longer adequate; situational realities need to be considered when applying OB theory and techniques.

H. Much can be learned about OB by studying the overlap of relevant theory, research, and practice. Theories, defined as stories that explain ''why,'' helpfully provide definitions, conceptual frameworks, and departure points for research and application. Five sources of OB research evidence are meta-analyses, field studies, laboratory studies, sample surveys, and case studies. OB research can be put to instrumental, conceptual, or symbolic use by managers. Applied OB research, particularly when it has descriptive and goal relevance for managers, effectively links research and practice.

I. A topical model providing a road map for what lies ahead reminds us the manager's job is to achieve organizational effectiveness. This is accomplished only by adequately understanding and successfully managing individual behavior, group processes, and organizational processes and problems. Situational factors to be considered when managing organizational behavior include organizational structure, cultures, and change. General ethical and cultural influences play increasingly important roles.

• KEY TERMS

management	meta-analysis
motivation to manage	field study
organizational behavior	laboratory study
scientific management	sample survey
Theory Y	case study
contingency approach	descriptive relevance
theory	goal relevance

• DISCUSSION QUESTIONS

1. Why view the typical employee as a human resource?
2. How would you respond to a fellow student who says "I have a hard time getting along with other people, but I think I could be a good manager"?
3. Based on either personal experience as a manager or on your observation of managers at work, are the seven managerial tasks in Figure 1–1 a realistic portrayal of what managers do?
4. Examining Figure 1–1, which of the three levels of management has the most difficult job? Why?
5. Referring to the OB Exercise, what is your motivation to manage? Do you believe our adaptation of Miner's scale accurately assessed your potential as a manager? Explain.
6. Why was the behavioral era essential to development of the field of OB?
7. Do you use a contingency approach in your daily affairs? Explain.
8. What "practical" theories have you formulated to achieve the things you want in life (e.g., graduating, keeping fit, getting a good job, meeting that special someone)?

9. From a manager's standpoint, which use of research is better: instrumental or conceptual? Explain your rationale.
10. What are the instructional benefits of examining OB topics through a consistent theory→research→practice format? Why not dispense with the theory and research and simply review the "three easy steps" to managing people?

BACK TO THE OPENING CASE

Now that you have read Chapter 1, you should be able to answer the following questions about the Donna Goya/Levi Strauss case:

1. What is the key to Goya's success at Levi Strauss?
2. Citing specific evidence, which of the managerial tasks in Figure 1–1 does Goya perform during her regular duties at Levi Strauss?
3. Making reasonable inferences from the facts of the case, how would you assess Goya's motivation to manage relative to each of the seven characteristics listed in the OB Exercise?
4. Is the Levi Strauss/Goya philosophy of managing people closer to McGregor's Theory X or Theory Y? Explain with evidence from the case.
5. Would the Levi Strauss/Goya philosophy of management apply equally well in other cultures around the world? Explain. (Feel free to draw upon your knowledge of various cultures.)

• EXERCISE 1

Objectives

1. To get to know some of your fellow students.
2. To put the management of people into a lively and interesting historical context.
3. To begin to develop your teamwork skills.

Introduction

This exercise is titled "Timeless Advice." Your creative energy, willingness to see familiar things in unfamiliar ways, and ability to have fun while learning are keys to the success of this warm-up exercise. A 20-minute, small group session will be followed by brief oral presentations and a general class discussion. Total time required is approximately 40–45 minutes.

Instructions

Your instructor will divide your class randomly into groups of four to six people each. Acting as a team, with everyone offering ideas and one person serving as official recorder, each group will be responsible for writing a one-page memo to your present class. Subject matter of your group's memo will be "My advice for managing people today is. . . ." The fun part of this exercise (and its creative element) involves writing the memo from the viewpoint of the person assigned to your group by your instructor.

Among the memo viewpoints your instructor may assign are:

- An ancient Egyptian slave master (building the great pyramids).
- Henri Fayol (refer to The Classical Era in this Chapter).
- Frederick Taylor (refer to The Classical Era).
- Mary Parker Follett (refer to The Behavioral Era).
- Douglas McGregor (refer to The Modern Era).
- A Theory X supervisor of a construction crew (see McGregor's Theories X and Y in Table 1–3).
- A contingency management theorist (The Modern Era).
- A Japanese auto company executive.
- The chief executive officer of IBM in the year 2030.
- Commander of the Starship Enterprise II in the year 3001.
- Others, as assigned by your instructor.

Use your imagination, make sure everyone participates, and try to be true to any historical facts you've encountered. Attempt to be as specific and realistic as possible. Remember, the idea is to provide advice about managing people from another point in time (or from a particular point of view at the present time).

Make sure you manage your 20-minute time limit carefully. A recommended approach is to spend 2 to 3 minutes putting the exercise into proper perspective. Next, take about 10 to 12 minutes brainstorming ideas for your memo, with your recorder jotting down key ideas and phrases. Have your recorder use the remaining time to write your group's one-page memo, with constructive comments and help from the others. Pick a spokesperson to read your group's memo to the class.

Questions for Consideration/Class Discussion

1. What valuable lessons about managing people have you heard?
2. What have you learned about how NOT to manage people?
3. From the distant past to today, what significant shifts in the management of people seem to have taken place?
4. Where does the management of people appear to be headed?
5. All things considered, what mistakes are today's managers typically making when managing people?
6. How well did your group function as a "team"?

• NOTES

[1] Walter B. Wriston, "The State of American Management," *Harvard Business Review,* January–February 1990, p. 80.

[2] Pete Hamill, "Rites of Passage," *Travel Holiday,* April 1990, p. 132.

[3] Joseph Duffey, "Competitiveness and Human Resources," *California Management Review,* Spring 1988, p. 93.

4 Morgan W. McCall, Jr., and Michael M. Lombardo, "What Makes a Top Executive?" *Psychology Today,* February 1983, pp. 26, 28.

5 Teresa Carson, "Fast-Track Kids," *Business Week,* November 10, 1986, p. 92.

6 Thomas J. Peters and Robert H. Waterman, Jr., *In Search of Excellence* (New York: Harper & Row, 1982), p. 238.

7 Critical reviews of *In Search of Excellence* may be found in Daniel T. Carroll, "A Disappointing Search for Excellence," *Harvard Business Review,* November–December 1983, pp. 78–88; "Who's Excellent Now?" *Business Week,* November 5, 1984, pp. 76–78; and Michael A. Hitt and R. Duane Ireland, "Peters and Waterman Revisited: The Unended Quest for Excellence," *Academy of Management Executive,* May 1987, pp. 91–98.

8 Henry Mintzberg, "The Manager's Job: Folklore and Fact," *Harvard Business Review,* July–August 1975, p. 61.

9 See, for example, Henry Mintzberg, "Managerial Work: Analysis from Observation," *Management Science,* October 1971, pp. B97–B110; and Fred Luthans, "Successful vs. Effective Real Managers," *Academy of Management Executive,* May 1988, pp. 127–32. For an instructive critique of the structured observation method, see Mark J. Martinko and William L. Gardner, "Beyond Structured Observation: Methodological Issues and New Directions," *Academy of Management Review,* October 1985, pp. 676–95.

10 See Lance B. Kurke and Howard E. Aldrich, "Mintzberg Was Right!: A Replication and Extension of *The Nature of Managerial Work,*" *Management Science,* August 1983, pp. 975–84.

11 Adapted from Allen I. Kraut, Patricia R. Pedigo, D. Douglas McKenna, and Marvin D. Dunnette, "The Role of the Manager: What's Really Important in Different Management Jobs," *Academy of Management Executive,* November 1989, pp. 286–93.

12 See Eugene Linden, "Frederick W. Smith of Federal Express: He Didn't Get There Overnight." *Inc.,* April 1984, p. 89.

13 These research results are discussed in detail in John B. Miner and Norman R. Smith, "Decline and Stabilization of Managerial Motivation Over a 20-Year Period," *Journal of Applied Psychology,* June 1982, pp. 297–305; and Kathryn M. Bartol and David C. Martin, "Managerial Motivation among MBA Students: A Longitudinal Assessment," *Journal of Occupational Psychology,* March 1987, pp. 1–12.

14 See John B. Miner, "The Validity and Usefulness of Theories in an Emerging Organizational Science," *Academy of Management Review,* April 1984, pp. 296–306.

15 Barbara S. Lawrence, "Historical Perspective: Using the Past to Study the Present," *Academy of Management Review,* April 1984, p. 307.

16 George D. Babcock, *The Taylor System in Franklin Management,* 2nd ed. (New York: Engineering Magazine Company, 1917), p. 31.

17 For an interesting critique of Taylor's work, see Edwin A. Locke, "The Ideas of Frederick W. Taylor: An Evaluation," *Academy of Management Review,* January 1982, pp. 14–24.

18 Evidence indicating that the original conclusions of the famous Hawthorne studies were unjustified may be found in Ronald G. Greenwood, Alfred A. Bolton, and Regina A. Greenwood, "Hawthorne a Half Century Later: Relay Assembly Participants Remember," *Journal of Management,* Fall–Winter 1983, pp. 217–31; and Richard H. Franke and James D. Kaul, "The Hawthorne Experiments: First Statistical Interpretation," *American Sociological Review,* October 1978, pp. 623–43. For a positive interpretation of the Hawthorne studies, see Jeffrey A. Sonnenfeld, "Shedding Light on the Hawthorne Studies," *Journal of Occupational Behaviour,* April 1985, pp. 111–30.

[19] See Mary Parker Follett, *Freedom and Coordination* (London: Management Publications Trust, 1949).

[20] See Douglas McGregor, *The Human Side of Enterprise* (New York: McGraw-Hill, 1960).

[21] Brian Dumaine, "Creating a New Company Culture," *Fortune*, January 15, 1990, p. 130.

[22] Linda Honold, "Letters to Fortune," *Fortune,* June 4, 1990, p. 290.

[23] Henry L. Tosi, Jr., and John W. Slocum, Jr., "Contingency Theory: Some Suggested Directions," *Journal of Management,* Spring 1984, p. 9.

[24] Jeffrey Zaslow, "Everyone in the Pool! Almost Everyone Is on This Super Friday," *The Wall Street Journal,* January 18, 1985, p. 1.

[25] Data from Oded Rosenfeld, Gershon Tenenbaum, Hillel Ruskin, and Siman-Tov Halfon, "The Effect of Physical Training on Objective and Subjective Measures of Productivity and Efficiency," *Ergonomics,* August 1989, pp. 1019–28.

[26] See Richard L. Daft, "Learning the Craft of Organizational Research," *Academy of Management Review,* October 1983, pp. 539–46.

[27] See Karl E. Weick, "Theory Construction as Disciplined Imagination," *Academy of Management Review,* October 1989, pp. 516–31. Also see David A. Whetten's article in the same issue, pp. 490–95.

[28] Complete discussion of this technique can be found in John E. Hunter, Frank L. Schmidt, and Gregg B. Jackson, *Meta-Analysis: Cumulating Research Findings across Studies* (Beverly Hills, Calif.: Sage Publications, 1982) and John E. Hunter and Frank L. Schmidt, *Methods of Meta-Analysis: Correcting Error and Bias In Research Findings* (Newbury Park, Calif.: Sage Publications, 1990).

[29] For an interesting debate about the use of students as subjects, see Jerald Greenberg, "The College Sophomore as Guinea Pig: Setting the Record Straight," *Academy of Management Review,* January 1987, pp. 157–59; and Michael E. Gordon, L. Allen Slade, and Neal Schmitt, "Student Guinea Pigs: Porcine Predictors and Particularistic Phenomena," *Academy of Management Review,* January 1987, pp. 160–63.

[30] Good discussions of case studies can be found in Allen S. Lee, "Case Studies as Natural Experiments," *Human Relations,* February 1989, pp. 117–37; and Kathleen M. Eisenhardt, "Building Theories from Case Study Research," *Academy of Management Review,* October 1989, pp. 532–50.

[31] Based on discussion found in Janice M. Beyer and Harrison M. Trice, "The Utilization Process: A Conceptual Framework and Synthesis of Empirical Findings," *Administrative Science Quarterly,* December 1982, pp. 591–622.

[32] See Joseph J. Martocchio, "Age-Related Differences in Employee Absenteeism: A Meta-Analysis," *Psychology & Aging,* December 1989, pp. 409–14.

[33] For complete details, see Geert Hofstede, "The Cultural Relativity of Organizational Practices and Theories," *Journal of International Business Studies,* Fall 1983, pp. 75–89.

[34] Stephen Strasser and Thomas S. Bateman, "What We Should Study, Problems We Should Solve: Perspectives of Two Constituencies," *Personnel Psychology,* Spring 1984, p. 78.

Managing a Diverse Work Force

LEARNING OBJECTIVES

When you finish the material in this chapter, you should be able to:

- Identify the forces that reshaped the work force.
- List at least five reasons why people work.
- Explain why the work ethic is not dead among American employees.

- Describe at least three major characteristics of the changing nature of work.
- Discuss the demographic changes responsible for increased diversity in the work force.
- Explain how job and life satisfaction interact.

- Demonstrate your familiarity with four popular alternative work schedules.
- Discuss five key solutions for managing a reshaped work force.

OPENING CASE 2

Visionary Leaders and Thinkers Recommend Adopting a New Managerial Paradigm

Sharon Hoogstraten

Now companies like AT&T, Procter & Gamble, and DuPont are offering employees personal-growth experiences of their own, hoping to spur creativity, encourage learning, and promote "ownership" of the company's results. A handful of visionary leaders—General Electric Chairman Jack Welch chief among them—are going beyond training seminars to a fundamental reordering of managerial priorities. Meanwhile, a small network of consultants, thinkers, and academics are working to transform business. Propelled by a belief that the world is undergoing major change, they call for a new paradigm—a whole new framework for seeing and understanding business—that will carry humankind beyond the industrial age.

The result is a curious convergence; executives seeking ways to reverse America's fall from dominance sharing common ground with freethinkers drawn to business as the most powerful institution in a global society. . . .

The new paradigm might be described as New Age without the glazed eyes. The word "paradigm" comes from the Greek for "pattern," and the new paradigm is just that: a new pattern of behavior that stems from a new way of looking at the world. The old world view—Newtonian, mechanistic, analytical—is present in everything from the Constitution, with its clockwork system of checks and balances, to the rectilinear street plans of Washington, D.C., and San Francisco, to the assembly lines devised by Henry Ford. The new paradigm takes ideas from quantum physics, cybernetics, chaos theory, cognitive science, and Eastern and Western spiritual traditions to form a world view in which everything is interconnected, in which reality is not absolute but a by-product of human consciousness. Nobody is promising universal enlightenment next week, however. "What we're talking about here is not a search for nirvana," says Michael Ray, 51, holder of the BancOne chair in creativity at the Stanford business school. "It's an attempt to deal with a very difficult time."

So far, what has emerged is a host of management theories and practices befitting an age of global enterprise, instantaneous communication, and ecological limits. Some are familiar: hierarchical organizations being replaced by more flexible networks; workers being "empowered" to make decisions on their own; organizations developing a capacity for group learning instead of waiting for wisdom from above; national horizons giving way to global thinking. Others may still seem a little far-out; creativity and intuition joining numerical analysis as aids to decision-making; love and caring being recognized as motivators in the workplace; even the primacy of the profit motive being questioned by those who argue that the real goal of enterprise is the mental and spiritual enrichment of those who take part in it.

Individually, each of these developments is just one manifestation of progressive management thought. Together, they suggest the possibility of a fundamental shift. Applied to business, the old paradigm held that numbers are all-important, that professional managers can handle any enterprise, that control can and should be held at the top. The new paradigm puts people—customers and employees—at the center of the universe and replaces the rigid hierarchies of the industrial age with a network structure that emphasizes interconnectedness.

Why would companies want to embrace a new paradigm? "Because the old paradigm isn't working," says Ray. He argues that the decline of American business from its postwar apogee is like a scientific anomaly—a situation

OPENING CASE 2

(concluded)

the old theories fail to explain. Just as a new paradigm emerges in science when old theories stop working, the new paradigm in business began to take form when the old-by-the-numbers school of management started to founder during the Seventies. The surprise success of *In Search of Excellence*, with its explicit attack on the old model, signaled the beginnings of a new perspective.

Several factors since have encouraged the trend. Perhaps the most visible is the faltering performance that has fed the vogue for Japanese management techniques and the quest for "excellence." But the driving force is the need for speed: The spread of computers and telecommunications and the rise of global markets have rendered bureaucracies hopelessly unwieldy. At the same time, a series of wrenching changes—deregulation, corporate takeovers, the demise of the Soviet bloc—has made the extraordinary seem commonplace. The sudden backlash against the money mania of the Eighties—combined, some say, with the gradual rise to power of the Sixties generation—has put idealism back on the agenda. The result is a vague but growing sense that business has to be conducted differently. . . .

In a recent speech before San Francisco's Commonwealth Club, Levi Strauss Chairman Robert Haas, 48, sketched his idea of the corporation of the future: a global

enterprise relying on employees who "are able to tap their fullest potential" and managers who act not as authority figures but as "coaches, facilitators, and role models." Levi Strauss is striving to transform itself along those lines because it needs creative thinking and rapid response to satisfy a fashion-conscious public. "This company isn't turning into a group of Moonies for some Platonic management good," observes chief counsel Tom Bauch, 47. "It's a way of promoting our own success."

Presumably Levi Strauss won't be turning into a bunch of Moonies at all. The point of the new paradigm is not to get people to om out in front of some guru but to encourage them to think for themselves. Ideally, this yields an organization that functions like a rugby team. "Rugby is a flow sport," says Noel Tichy of the University of Michigan business school. "It looks chaotic, but it requires tremendous communication, continuous adjustment to an uncertain environment, and problem solving without using a hierarchy." American business has been conducted more like football, with every play a call from the sidelines.

One man who's ready to play rugby is Jack Welch of GE. Having streamlined GE organizationally with a flurry of sales, acquisitions, and plant closings, Welch has now turned to the culture. "Productivity is the

key," says GE's head of management development, James Baughman, a former Harvard business school professor charged with effecting much of the change. "You can only get so much more productivity out of reorganization and automation. Where you really get productivity leaps is in the minds and hearts of people." . . .

But GE's moves bear the twin hallmarks of new-paradigm thinking: the systems view—seeing everything as interconnected—and the focus on people. Welch's goal is fast turnaround, and to get it he intends to create what he calls the "boundaryless organization"—no hierarchical boundaries vertically, no functional boundaries horizontally. . . .

So what's the alternative? Business as a spiritual pursuit? Don't laugh. Jack Welch recently remarked that he wants people at GE to feel rewarded "in both the pocketbook and the soul." This is the lesson of the new paradigm: If people are your greatest resource and creativity the key to success, then business results cannot be divorced from personal fulfillment.

For Discussion

How would you describe the new managerial paradigm?

• Additional discussion questions linking this case with the following material appear at the end of this chapter.

Source: Excerpted from Frank Rose, "A New Age For Business?" *Fortune*, October 8, 1990, pp. 156–64.

S uppose some friends called and asked if you would be interested in going on a 10-day hiking and camping trip. First, you would want to know where they planned to go. A trip to the seashore would require different clothing and gear than a trip to the mountains. Primitive trails without water and facilities would require more planning than established hiking trails. Next, you would be wise to ask your friends if they had checked the weather forecast. Late spring snowstorms can prove fatal for campers in the mountains, and a few days of heavy rain can break the spirits of even the hardiest lowland hikers. In short, forehand knowledge of terrain and weather conditions are crucial to a safe and enjoyable camping trip. Intelligent preparation for any endeavor requires relevant contextual knowledge. So, too, if you are to get full benefit from the study of organizational behavior, you first need to explore its relevant context.

This chapter provides a context for the study and management of organizational behavior. To understand it, you need to consider what reshaped the U.S. work force over the last 20 years. Figure 2–1 indicates the American work force was dramatically reshaped by the changing nature of work, increasing diversity among workers, the integration of home and work life, the growth in internationl competition, and a renewed social agenda.[1] In turn, the values and needs of employees correspondingly changed. This produced a 1990s work force that is quite different from that in the previous two decades. Because "traditional" managerial approaches are somewhat inconsistent with the values and needs of the current work force, successful managers are using new managerial practices, and organizations are testing the effectiveness of new organizational structures.

This chapter will provide an overview of three of the forces that reshaped the work force and highlight the emerging solutions to these changes. After first reviewing the meaning of work, we discuss (1) the changing nature of

---

• **FIGURE 2-1**   A Reshaped Work Force Underscores the Need for New Managerial Practices and Organizational Structures

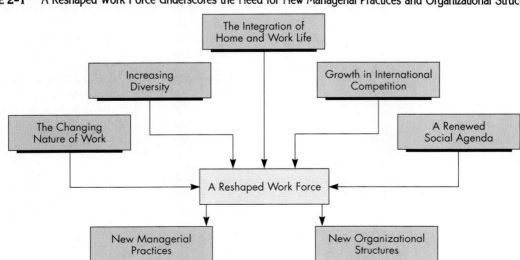

work, (2) the increasing diversity in the work force, and (3) the integration of home and work life. The emerging solutions for accommodating the new work force are indicated along with references to further coverage in later chapters.

• THE MEANING OF WORK

Do you like to work all the time? Would you skip a vacation in order to complete a special project? If you answered yes, your job probably turns you on. While some top executives love their jobs (see those featured in International OB), others are equally excited about going home and forgetting about work. Work means different things to different people, and it plays varied roles in our lives. Additional insights into the meaning and functions of work can be obtained by interviewing the unemployed, by discovering why people work, and by considering the new work ethic. We conclude this section by discussing the implications of the meaning of work for organizational behavior.

Work: Looking in from the Outside

As the saying goes, "You never know how good something is until you've lost it." This section examines the meaning of work from the perspective of the unemployed. After reviewing and analyzing the unemployment experiences of many people, researchers identified several basic functions of work.[2] As depicted in Figure 2–2, work:

- Encourages setting general life goals (such as owning a new home).
- Provides economic security (paying the bills).

INTERNATIONAL OB

Canadian CEOs Love Their Work

To Jim Gray of Canadian Hunter Exploration Ltd., the very idea of a workaholic is a misnomer. "If you're working 12 to 14 hours a day at something you love to do, it's almost therapeutic."

Izzy Asper, chairman of Winnipeg's CanWest Capital Group Inc., shares the sentiment: "My family claims there's only been one time I haven't gone away on a holiday with a briefcase. My work turns me on so much that I can't leave it. I really enjoy it." If you think Izzy's a head case, consider his Winnipeg colleague, Federal Industries Ltd. President and CEO Jack Fraser. Every weekend he heads off to his Lake of the Woods cabin with briefcases. "I don't feel sorry for myself," says Fraser. "I enjoy my work and I love working at the lake. It's relaxing."

Source: Robert Collison, "Work Habits of the Rich and Famous," *Canadian Business*, August 1990, p. 37.

• **FIGURE 2-2**   Functions of Work Identified by Unemployed Workers

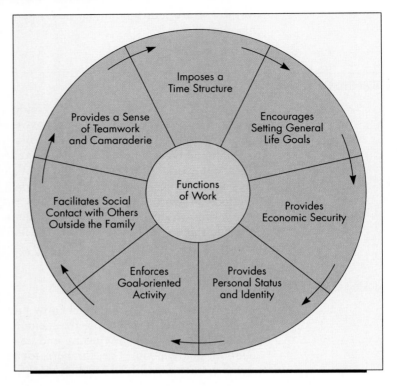

Source: Adapted in part from Stephen Fineman, "Work Meanings, Non-Work, and the Taken-for-Granted," *Journal of Management Studies*, April 1983, pp. 143–57.

- Provides personal status and identity (doctors have higher status than security guards).
- Enforces goal-oriented activity (such as getting out of bed and going to a job instead of hiding under the covers).
- Facilitates social contact with others outside the family.
- Provides a sense of teamwork and camaraderie. (For example, at Apple Computer, the team that designed the successful Macintosh computer raised a pirate flag above its building as a competitive challenge to the rest of the company[3].)
- Imposes a time structure (such as attending scheduled meetings).

The list above underscores that work means different things to different people. A research study that examined the impact of joblessness on 100 managers and professionals provides further insights into the meaning of work. One fifth of those sampled believed they had lost a very significant part of their lives. They were devastated over losing their jobs. Surprisingly, one third of those interviewed were very happy about being unemployed. These professionals were happy because their former jobs made them feel alienated, stressed, and trapped.[4] A job truly is a many-sided experience.

Work: More than a Stream of Income

Behavioral scientists have long been interested in why people work. The National Opinion Research Center (NORC) conducted a longitudinal investigation of people's motives for working. NORC asked national samples of 11,000 people from 1972 to 1982, 6,000 during 1983–87, and 1,000 in 1988 the question: "If you were to get enough money to live as comfortably as you like for the rest of your life, would you continue to work or would you stop working?"

Among the respondents during 1972–82, 70 percent indicated they would continue working. The figure jumped to 74 percent during the period 1983–87. Eighty-five percent of the 1988 sample stated they would continue working. These results suggest the commitment to work is strong and growing.[5] Other researchers similarly examined the meaning of work across different age groups and different countries.[6]

For example, an international study of the meaning of work across eight countries—Holland, Belgium, West Germany, England, Israel, Yugoslavia, United States, and Japan—revealed that work played a much more central role in the lives of Japanese. Further, older Japanese men placed more importance on work than did males under 30 years of age.[7] This trend was supported in a recent study of 4,567 American and 3,735 Japanese employees. Results indicated that older men were more committed to work than younger men in both countries. However, although this pattern was true for American women, there were no age differences in the commitment to work among Japanese women.[8]

Why does work constitute such a central life interest to the Japanese? A respected Japanese researcher traced this work orientation to the fact that the Japanese historically made a living from farming. Because farming the rocky terrain of Japan required long and hard work, a strong work orientation simply became a matter of survival over time.[9]

Is the Work Ethic Dead?

The **work ethic** reflects the extent to which an individual values work. A strong work ethic involves the belief that hard work is the key to success and happiness. Researchers have found that a strong work ethic is associated with greater earnings, initiative, job satisfaction, productivity, need for achievement, and conservative attitudes and beliefs.[10] In recent years, there has been widespread concern that the work ethic is dead or dying. This worry is based on findings from observational studies and employee attitude surveys.

For instance, according to an observational study of employee behavior over a two-year period, employees spent only 51 percent of the typical workday actually working. The remaining 49 percent was taken up by unproductive activities such as drinking coffee, chatting with co-workers, and arriving late and leaving early.[11] Employee attitude surveys have uncovered similar evidence. For example, in a national survey of 845 American employees conducted by the Public Agenda Foundation, 23 percent indicated they were not working to their full potential. In addition, 44 percent said they did not put more effort into their jobs than was required. Finally,

62 percent agreed with the belief that people do not work as hard as they used to. Other evidence, however, suggests that these findings portray an unrealistically negative picture.

Some Encouraging Evidence   Fifty-two percent of the Public Agenda Foundation sample mentioned above indicated they had a strong desire to do the very best job they could.[12] This suggests a majority of American workers possess a strong work ethic, but for some reason this majority is not working to its potential.

Stifled Work Ethic   How then can it be claimed that workers who work halfheartedly have a strong work ethic? According to several experts, management is to blame. Rather than bringing out the work ethic, management too often thwarts it by taking actions that cripple the incentive to work hard.[13] For example, paying people by the hour gives them an incentive to show up for work but not necessarily to be fully productive. Moreover, a dull, repetitive, and unchallenging job makes it more desirable to loaf than to work hard. In contrast, another management researcher believes society at large is the culprit.

> In our society, mechanisms for reducing the frustrations, anxieties, disappointments, and losses of personal pride and property resulting from failure are on the increase. . . . Alternative jobs exist in relative abundance, making it possible for those who fail at one job to be retrained for another, or find employment in another company. Legislation now makes it difficult to release employees for failure to perform. Psychologists have convinced managers not to use various disciplinary procedures and penalties for poor performance. Finally, unions have negotiated freedom from penalty for numerous types of nonperformance. The evidence is clear: penalties for lack of success are fast becoming extinct.[14]

In conclusion, the work ethic appears to be alive and well, but managerial and societal forces sometimes encourage employees to exert less effort.

Implications for OB

Work means different things to different people. This suggests that each of us is an individual who is satisfied and motivated by different types of rewards. Chapter 3 discusses the foundation of important individual differences. Chapters 5 and 6 go one step further by applying individual differences to several models of motivation.

Most people still want to work even when they do not need the money. This suggests that people work for more than economic reasons. For example, people satisfy social and self-esteem needs through their work. Employee motivation may thus be increased by offering employees a variety of rewards that satisfy both financial and nonfinancial needs.

Although employees generally have a positive work ethic, boring jobs and haphazard managerial practices too often encourage them to put minimum effort into their work. This likely will lead managers to believe workers do not care about their jobs. If such is the case, managers may come to view subordinates as lazy, thus prompting the use of punishment and an authoritarian or heavy-handed leadership style. Given the importance of the work ethic, management needs to attempt to nurture it. This can be done in a variety of ways. For one, organizations can provide employees a rewarding place in which to work. At a minimum, employees desire to be treated with dignity and respect. Nothing kills employees' work ethic more than the belief that the organization does not care about their well-being.[15] Second, organizations can try to equitably reward performance by using a variety of incentive programs (discussed in Chapter 13). Consider how Harman Management Corp., Kentucky Fried Chicken's first and currently largest franchisee, has followed both of these recommendations (see OB in Action). A third approach is to identify what *motivates,* as opposed to *satisfies,* an individual. A two-factor theory that explains the interaction between motivation and satisfaction is presented in Chapter 5. Finally, organizational structures need to be reexamined (see Chapter 17). This reexamination will help identify whether organizational policies and practices are inhibiting the work ethic.

OB IN ACTION

Harman Management Corporation Creates Employee Loyalty and Commitment

Harman Management spends the equivalent of more than 1.5 percent of its annual sales of $178 million on people-oriented management practices. Putting people first has clearly paid off.

The company's units enjoy average sales that are about 20 percent higher than the chicken segment's average of roughly $600,000. . . .

Insiders say that the Harman Management culture is competitive and demands excellence, yet it also has a caring family side. Harman and his wife, Arline, who worked alongside him at the start, share a mutually warm relationship with the employees that transcends business. It's a telling sign that lithographs of the founding couple are one of the company awards for management success.

There are many other manifestations of family feeling. Each summer, picnics for employees, spouses, and children take place. The company publishes an annual yearbook with portraits of every family in the system. The company family itself is a diverse mix that well represents genders and minority groups, including recent immigrants. . . .

Moreover, the family ethic is apparent in Harman Management's unique ownership sharing arrangement for managers. Each store is organized as a separate corporation. Husband-and-wife teams that have successfully managed a store for a nine-month period are eligible to purchase up to 40 percent of its stock.

Single managers may purchase up to 30 percent of stock. In addition, managers in Harman's distribution company, which is a separate corporation, and home-office employees with tenure can qualify to buy company stock. Managers who save their money and invest in their stores by buying stock realize earnings much higher than the industry norm. Top producers may take home in excess of $100,000 per year.

Source: James Scarpa, "Harman Management Corporation: Company of the Year," *Restaurant Business,* October 10, 1990, pp. 110–11.

• THE CHANGING NATURE OF WORK

America's economy and work force are undergoing profound changes that promise to significantly alter the practice of management. As one respected observer predicted:

> Tomorrow's work force will probably be older, more diverse in terms of gender and race, marked by intense competition for jobs and promotions, less unionized, and better educated.
>
> . . . social values developed during the 1960s and 1970s will create a high priority for work environment reforms, such as participative decision making, pleasant work conditions, considerate management, and such supportive facilities as day-care centers.[16]

Because the work force is increasingly diverse, some managerial practices that worked well in the past are no longer appropriate. For example, unlike the obedient "organization man" of the 1950s who strived to blend in, many of today's aspiring managers and technical specialists are risk takers who are not afraid to rock the boat to make their own contribution. Progressive companies are learning how to encourage and reward rather than stifle creative risk takers.

To help you get a better understanding of this important context for organizationl behavior, we will now explore work patterns in the current economy and discuss work in the dominant service sector.

Working in the New Economy

Technological advances, which are discussed in Chapter 20, have created a new economy. According to one management expert, technology will create dramatic organizational changes over the next decade:

> If the past forty years are any indication, the workplace of the future will undergo tremendous changes due primarily to the technological choices being made by managers and workers today. Witness the tremendous inroads made in recent decades by computerized systems in both the office and the factory, the automation of many mechanical functions in the blue-collar sector, and the emergence of the personal computer in the home. The acceleration of these and other technological trends in coming decades will create important qualitative changes in almost every dimension of work.[17]

Experts estimate that 90 percent of all jobs in the United States will be affected by this technological revolution. Jobs will either be displaced, replaced, or modified.[18] Nonetheless, while high-tech occupations will grow rapidly during the next decade, they will account for a comparatively small proportion of new job opportunities.

Low-Tech Jobs in a High-Tech Revolution   Occupations projected to create the most new job openings in the foreseeable future are in the relatively low-paying, low-tech service sector. Table 2–1 shows those occupations which are predicted to generate the largest number of new jobs between the years 1988–2000. Contrary to the impression created by popular media accounts of the high-tech revolution, salespersons will be the big gainers. Next in line for

• TABLE 2-1   Jobs with the Largest Increase in Job Opportunities, 1988–2000

	Number of New Jobs (in thousands) 1988–2000*	Percent Change
1. Salespersons	730	19%
2. Registered nurses	613	39
3. Janitors and cleaners	555	19
4. Waiters and waitresses	551	31
5. General managers and top executives	479	16
6. General office clerks	455	18
7. Secretaries, except legal and medical	385	13
8. Nurses' aides, orderlies, and attendants	378	32
9. Truck drivers, light and heavy	369	15
10. Receptionists and information clerks	331	40
11. Cashiers	304	13
12. Guards	255	32
13. Computer programmers	250	48
14. Food counter, fountain, and related workers	240	15
15. Food preparation workers	233	23
16. Licensed practical nurses	229	37
17. Teachers, secondary schools	224	19
18. Computer systems analyst	214	53
19. Accountants and auditors	211	22
20. Teachers, kindergarten and elementary	208	15

* Changes are based on moderate growth estimates.

Source: U.S. Bureau of the Census, *Statistical Abstract of the United States: 1990* (110th ed.), Washington, D.C., Table no. 646, p. 392.

vigorous job opportunity growth will be registered nurses, a trend consistent with an aging American population, janitors and cleaners, and waiters and waitresses. Some lofty expectations are bound to be dashed on the rocks of this reality. Although technical jobs will not create the largest number of actual employment opportunities, Table 2–1 indicates that computer systems analysts and computer programmers will experience the largest *percentage* increase in new jobs.

More Part-Timers   More and more companies are hiring people to work part-time. **Part-time work** is defined as "regular wage employment with hours of work substantially shorter than normal in the establishment concerned."[19] The total number of part-timers grew 21 percent from 1980 to 1990. Approximately 17 percent of all workers in the United States worked part-time in 1990. While women currently represent the majority of these workers, retirees are becoming the fastest-growing segment of the part-time work force.[20] This trend is likely to continue as more organizations recruit retirees to fill vacant positions caused by a shortage of entry-level workers (discussed in the next section of this chapter). Not only does hiring part-timers reduce an organization's labor costs, but it also accommodates the flexibility desired by a growing segment of the labor force.

Working in a Service Economy

As depicted in Figure 2–3, employment has shifted dramatically in the U.S. economy's three main sectors: agriculture, goods producing, and service producing. Sixty-four percent of the work force was employed in agriculture in 1850, as opposed to 3 percent in 1988, and a 2.5 percent projection for the year 2000. In contrast, employment in the service sector increased from 18 percent in 1850 to 74 percent in 1988. The U.S. government predicts that 77 percent of the U.S. work force will be employed in the service sector by the year 2000.

After analyzing these employment shifts, one economist noted:

> Suggested explanations for the faster growth of services employment include changes in the demand for goods and services as a result of rising income and relative price movements, slower productivity growth in services, the increasing participation of women in the labor force since World War II, and the growing importance of the public and nonprofit sector in general.[21]

• **FIGURE 2-3**   Distribution of U.S. Employment by Major Sectors

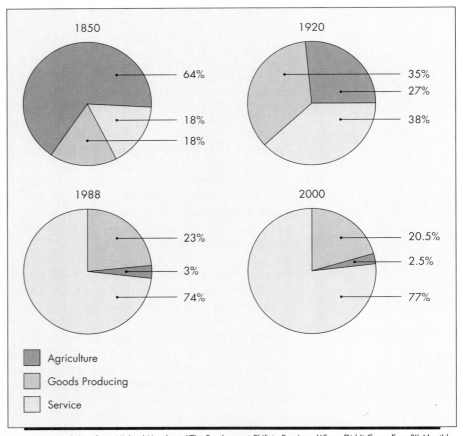

Source: Historical data from Michael Urquhart, "The Employment Shift to Services: Where Did It Come From?" *Monthly Labor Review*, April 1984, p. 16; 1988 and projection data for 2000 are from U.S. Bureau of the Census, *Statistical Abstract of the United States: 1990* (110th ed.), Washington, D.C., Table no. 651, p. 395.

This economic scenario presents management with a significant challenge. Specifically, the service sector, the largest source of employment in the United States, has the lowest productivity.

Evidence indicates that sluggish productivity growth in the United States is directly attributable to low productivity in the service sector. During the early 1980s, service-sector productivity began to lag behind manufacturing productivity (see Figure 2–4). The gap has continued to grow. Prior to 1985, however, the productivity gap between manufacturing and service sectors was partially due to increased investment in technology by the manufacturing sector. Unfortunately, service sector productivity has not increased significantly since 1985 despite massive investment in information technology.[22] One should not automatically conclude that inept management and workers are totally responsible for this problem. Part of the problem is due to the difficulty in measuring productivity within service industries.

It is not easy for a service company to define and measure the most appropriate index of service productivity. For example, how would you measure the productivity of a computer programmer? Is it lines of code completed per day? Is it the number of programming errors or the seriousness of each error? Is it the length of time to complete a program? As you can see, choosing a productivity index for service jobs is not a clear-cut issue. Because of this problem, researchers are investigating various methods of assessing services productivity.[23] These measures must be tailor made to fit the business at hand, or the service being provided. For example, Olsten Corp., an employment services company, Avis, and Philadelphia's Rosenbluth Travel, use customer satisfaction surveys as a measure of productivity. Quality Inns monitors minutes to clean a room and meals served per hour.[24]

• **FIGURE 2–4**   Although on the Upswing, U.S. Service-Sector Productivity Still Lags

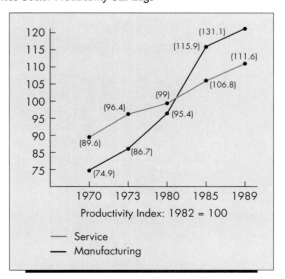

Source: Data were obtained from "Annual Indexes of Productivity, Hourly Compensation, Unit Costs, and Prices, Selected Years," Table 46, *Monthly Labor Review*, December 1990, p. 103.

Implications for OB

Part-timers, who now number more than ever before, have a greater tendency to quit than full-time employees.[25] This trend is probably due to the fact that part-time wages are less than full-time wages. A recent study found a difference of just under 8 percent less for women and 6 percent for men. Further, among part-timers, only 30–50 percent are as likely as full-time workers to receive health insurance or pension coverage.[26] Observers say there is a risk of creating a growing underclass of employees (generally called the "working poor"). Consequently, management needs to identify and appeal to the unique needs, motives, and sources of satisfaction for this growing segment of the work force. Companies such as Aetna Life & Casualty, Arthur Andersen, Corning, Kaiser Permanente, and US Sprint are following this recommendation (see OB in Action). Each of these companies used progressive compensation and benefit packages to attract and retain good part-time workers.

Service industries have the distinction of employing the most people and having the lowest productivity. This highlights the need to identify causes and develop solutions for the service-sector productivity problem. For instance, one management expert predicted "a massive restructuring of the service sector, as companies concentrate on using information technology to cut labor costs and improve productivity among the far larger ranks of technical, sales, clerical, and other support personnel."[27] Chapter 20 discusses a variety of techniques that can be used to diagnose organizational problems.

In response to growing service-sector employment and automation, unions are stepping up recruitment of service employees. This suggests management needs to pay better attention to the wants and desires of this segment of the work force.

• INCREASING DIVERSITY IN THE WORK FORCE

Work-force demographics, which are statistical profiles of the characteristics and composition of the adult working population, are an invaluable human-resource planning aid. They enable managers to anticipate and adjust for surpluses or shortages of appropriately skilled individuals. For example, the U.S. work force is expected to grow about 1.2 percent between 1988 and 2000.[28] However, the number of new jobs created in the United States is projected to exceed this growth. These demographics reveal that organizations need to devise strategies to manage the mismatch in labor supply and demand.

Hiring immigrants is one solution to this problem. The House Judiciary Committee, for instance, recently approved a bill that would allow 840,000 immigrants to enter the United States in 1991 and 1992, up from 540,000 in 1990, and then level off at 775,000.[29] This trend has important implications for organizational behavior because immigrants tend to possess different educational and occupational backgrounds from people in the United States.

Moreover, general population demographics give managers a preview of the values and motives of future employees. Demographic changes in the U.S. work force during the last two or three decades have immense implica-

OB IN ACTION

Corporate Examples of the Progressive Treatment of Part-Time Workers

Aetna Life & Casualty

Hartford, Conn. (43,000 employees nationwide). To cut training costs and help recruit trained certified public accountants, bond raters, auditors and specialized lawyers, Aetna offers an attractive part-time package. Salaries and all types of paid leave are prorated, and employees working at least 15 hours a week are entitled to full medical, dental and life insurance benefits.

Arthur Andersen

Chicago (25,000 employees nationwide). Forty-five percent of the new hires at this traditionally male accounting and management-consulting firm are women. So the company has initiated a program allowing employees to return to work part-time after the birth or adoption of a child. All benefits are prorated; employees help pay for life, medical, dental and long-term disability insurance plans based on the number of hours worked.

Corning

Corning, N.Y. (20,000 employees nationwide). To help attract and keep skilled professional women, the company asks managers and supervisors to try to accommodate full-time employees who need to switch to part-time work. Employees putting in at least 30 hours a week qualify for full benefits; those working 20 to 30 hours get prorated days off, short-term disability coverage and basic medical and life insurance.

Kaiser Permanente

Northern California region (25,000 employees). About 28 percent of staff members work part-time in this region of Kaiser, the nation's largest group-practice health maintenance organization. Employees who work 20 or more hours a week get full benefits. Part-time hours are popular among nurses, pharmacists, technicians, and nursing assistants, but most supervisors and managers must work full-time to maintain continuity. Northern California Kaiser is developing a pilot program to allow job-sharing among its physicians.

US Sprint

Kansas City, Mo. (16,000 employees nationwide). Managers are encouraged to explore every option for making a job part-time if an employee needs such an arrangement. Part-time work is most feasible in customer service, field sales, telemarketing and technical positions; job-sharing is an alternative for company attorneys. All benefits are prorated, and part-time salaries are commensurate with pay for equivalent full-time work.

Source: Nancy Henderson and Sherri Buri, "Tactics That Win Good Part-Time Jobs," *Changing Times,* May 1990, p. 66.

tions for organizational behavior. Imagine the ripple effect of changes associated with a 58 percent increase in the number of workers from 1960 to 1982, largely due to the baby-boom generation's entry into the job market. This section examines four demographic trends that are creating an increasingly diverse work force: women continue to enter the work force in increasing numbers; minorities represent a growing share of the labor force;

there is a critical mismatch between workers' educational attainment and occupational requirements; and the work force is aging.

More Women and Minorities in the Work Force

Women have been entering the labor force in increasing numbers. Women represented 40 percent of the work force in 1976; their numbers are estimated to grow to be 47 percent in the year 2000. Hispanics and other minorities also represent a growing share of the labor force. Figure 2–5 shows the percentages of projected entrants, leavers, and net change in the work force by gender and race from 1988 to 2000.

Women Will Account for the Majority of the New Entrants in the Work Force between the Years 1988–2000   Figure 2–5 shows that females are expected to contribute 51.5 percent of the *new entrants* while also accounting for 42.3

• **FIGURE 2-5**   Projected Entrants, Leavers, and Net Change in the Work Force from 1988 to 2000

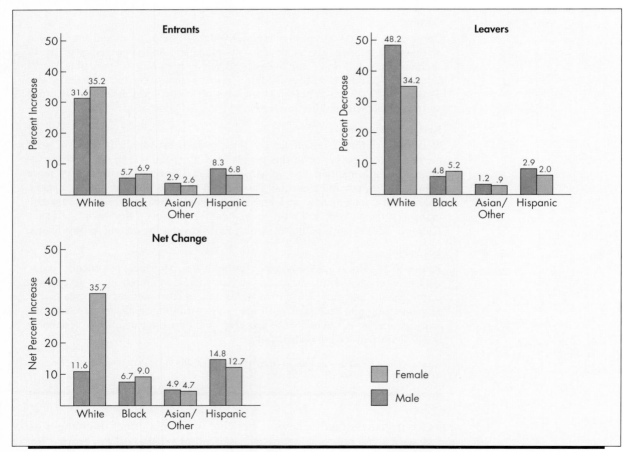

Source: Data were obtained from Howard N. Fullerton, Jr., "New Labor Force Projections, Spanning 1988–2000," *Monthly Labor Review*, November 1989, pp. 3–12.

percent of the *leavers*. (These percentages were calculated by adding across all female groups in each of the categories of entrants and leavers.) In aggregate, females are predicted to contribute 62.1 percent of the *net* increase in the work force between 1988 and 2000. Figure 2–5 indicates white females will contribute the single largest net increase (35.7 percent).[30] This contrasts with an 11.6 percent net increase in the work force from white males over the same time period.

A majority of the increase in the number of women entering the labor force comes from participation by women with children. For example, 53 percent of the married women with children aged one or under were working in 1987. In 1989, 71 percent of the mothers with children under 18 were working.[31]

Female employment is still concentrated in relatively lower-level, low-paying occupations. In 1989 women were still underpaid relative to men: women received 69 percent as much as men. Nonetheless, there are signs that this trend may be changing. Women are beginning to obtain employment in professional jobs traditionally held by men. For instance, women working in executive, administrative, or managerial positions increased from 18 percent in 1970 to roughly 40 percent in 1990.[32] This demographic shift has created a unique set of dynamics between young female managers and their male and female subordinates (see OB in Action).

Despite the increase in women managers, women still have not broken into the highest echelon of corporate America. Consider the results from a study conducted by *Fortune* in 1990. It was uncovered that only 19 women—less than one half of 1 percent—were the highest-paid executive officers and directors of the 1,000 largest U.S. industrial and service companies. Negative stereotypes (discussed in Chapter 4) and the lack of mentors have been identified as two key barriers to women reaching the top.[33]

Minorities Will Account for a Third of the New Entrants into the Work Force between the Years 1988 and 2000   Minorities are projected to add 33.2 percent of the new entrants in the work force from 1988–2000 (see Figure 2–5). Since fewer minorities will leave the work force than whites between 1988–2000, minorities account for an even greater *net* percentage increase in new workers. Figure 2–5 indicates that male and female minorities are expected to provide a net increase of about 53 percent. Hispanics are predicted to account for 27.5 percent of this net increase. Black females are predicted to add a greater net percent increase than black males.

It also is worth noting that minorities tend to be concentrated in certain geographic areas. For example, the populations of Mississippi, South Carolina, and Louisiana are more than 30 percent black. With respect to Asians, approximately 32 percent of all Asians living in the United States reside in California. Further, more than half of all Hispanics in the United States live in California or Texas. Thirty-eight percent of the population of New Mexico is Hispanic.[34] These trends are important because minority groups possess different cultural backgrounds from the white majority. As such, organizations located in areas heavily populated by minorities need to make a more concerted effort at managing diversity in the work force.

OB in Action

Demographic Shifts Can Cause Conflict and Problems

After 20 years of cooking, cleaning, and kids, a middle-aged woman gets a job and finds herself working for a woman 10 or more years her junior. How does she feel?

"It's a double whammy," says 45-year-old Joanna Henderson, who helped organize a seminar at Boston's Simmons College on the subject after she was hired by a younger woman. "The stigma is more intense if your boss is both younger and a woman."

The phenomenon of older women working for younger women is the latest of a series of social upheavals unsettling corporate psyches. While older women long have accepted the inevitability of working for younger men in a largely male domain, and even older men know that aggressive younger men may surpass them, other pairings meet greater resistance. Many white workers still resent taking orders from blacks and many men chafe at working for women.

But experts say the conflict between older women and their younger-women bosses can be especially intense.

The older woman generally has entered the work force late after raising a family, or has been stuck for years in a dead-end, traditionally female job—secretary, nurse, or teacher. So she often resents younger managers, who have advantages she generally was denied—a business-school education, special-ized training, and fewer barriers to the corporate fast track.

Meanwhile, the younger women managers harbor their own resentments toward their older colleagues. And because this situation was once so rare, younger women managers have few role models who have handled such conflicts.

Today more than 1.3 million women under age 35 hold managerial or administrative posts, up from only 322,000 a dozen years ago. Meanwhile, more than half the women over age 45 also work. "Your first reaction" to having a younger woman boss, says Eileen Bergquist, a 39–year-old Wheaton College career counselor, "is what the heck does this kid know?" . . .

Older women workers admit that they are sometimes deferential with col-leagues and maternal with superiors. "I freaked out when I started working for younger people," says a 46-year-old software specialist at Data General Corp. "You sort of want to pick up after them and wipe their noses."

But such an attitude infuriates younger women managers, raised on the feminism of the 1970s. "I don't respond to a mother, because I've got one and that was plenty," says Lori King, a Boston University career counselor, who supervises women 10 and 20 years older.

Educational Mismatches

The education level of American workers has been rising. As of 1988, approximately 26 percent of the labor force had a college degree. This represented a 12 percent increase from 1970. By 1988, 18.7 percent of all male workers had one to three years of college and 28.8 percent had four or more years. The corresponding figures for females in 1988 were 21.3 and 23.7 percent (see Figure 2–6). Unfortunately, many of these more highly educated workers may find their lofty expectations shortchanged by the changing nature of work (discussed earlier in this chapter). According to a pair of labor economists:

> From a national standpoint, a better-trained work force is highly desirable. However, with respect to the college educated, the growth in the number of adult workers with degrees carries with it the possibility of an uncertain future for many young college graduates. This is because the greatest increase in the number of jobs over the decade to come is projected for such occupations as janitors, salesclerks, secretaries, and so forth. Thus, the potential exists for a growing mismatch between actual educational levels and those required for occupations with the greatest anticipated growth. In other words, many college graduates—perhaps 20 percent—will not be able to get jobs requiring a college degree, continuing the situation that has prevailed in recent years. Such mismatches could seriously affect the lives of many young workers and their families for years to come.[35]

This situation has created *under*employment.

Underemployment exists when a job requires less than a person's full potential as determined by his or her higher formal education, training, or skills. Underemployment is associated with higher arrest rates for young adults and job dissatisfaction within the work force.[36] Unfortunately, underemployment is expected to grow due to an increase in low-level jobs within the service sector and a surplus of college graduates.[37] Consider, for example, the competition for jobs, given a surplus of 4 million college graduates by 1980 coupled with an expected surplus of 2 million to 3 million from 1983 to 1993.[38] Managers thus need to devise strategies for coping with underemployment and its associated expectations gap as the proportion of college graduates in the labor force continues to increase.

There are even more serious problems at the other end of the educational spectrum in the United States. Buried in the average increase in educational attainment statistic is a worsening public high school dropout problem.

> These days, almost 29 percent of each entering class doesn't make it to graduation, says Pat Choate, a [former] vice President at TRW's public policy office in Arlington, Virginia, and the author of a 1986 book titled *The High-Flex Society:* "The top third of America's young people is the best educated in the world, but the middle third is slipping into mediocrity, and the bottom third is at Third World standards."[39]

Increasingly, employers of young entry-level workers are finding them to be deficient in basic reading, math, and social skills.

Educational Testing Service conducted a survey of 3,600 21 to 25-year-olds in 1988 to determine the extent of this problem. Results indicated that only 34 percent of whites, 20 percent of Hispanics, and 8 percent of blacks were able to figure out the tip and change for a two-item restaurant bill.

• **FIGURE 2-6**   Educational Profile of the U.S. Work Force

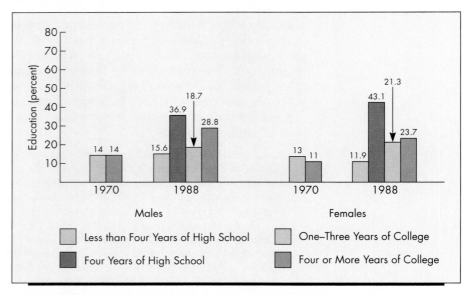

Source: Adapted from "Educational Attainment of the Civilian Labor Force by Sex, Race, and Hispanic Origin, March, Selected Years, 1959–1984," *Handbook of Labor Statistics, Bulletin 2217,* June 1985, p. 164; and Table no. 648, U.S. Bureau of the Census, *Statistical Abstract of the United States: 1990* (110th ed.), Washington, D.C., Table no. 648.

Moreover, only 25 percent of whites, 7 percent of Hispanics, and 3 percent of blacks could interpret a complicated bus schedule.[40]

This lack of basic educational skills is not restricted to 21–25-year-olds. There are an estimated 27 million adult Americans who are functionally illiterate. This amounts to almost one out of five adult Americans.[41] In summary, there is a critical mismatch between educational attainment and occupational requirements. But this time, directly opposite to the problem of underemployment, many job applicants are not up to the challenge.

An Older Work Force

America's population and its work force are getting older. The median age in the United States climbed from just under 28 in 1970 to 30 at the outset of the 1980s. The median age of the work force is projected to reach 39 by the year 2000. By 2030, almost 22 percent of the U.S. population is expected to be over 65.[42] Table 2–2 shows the changes in age distributions of the U.S. population from 1980 thru 2010. There are five interesting trends worth noting.

First, the number of preschool-aged children increased 11.8 percent during the period 1980–90. These children, who were in need of day care during this time, will become students in 1990–2000. This trend suggests that flexible work schedules may become more important than day care between 1990 and the turn of the century. Second, the percentage of entry-level workers aged 18 to 24 decreased between 1980 and 1990. Table 2–2 indicates that this shortage will continue during the years 1990 to 2000. These results, coupled with the increasing number of entry-level job openings, suggest that

• TABLE 2-2   Age Distribution Changes of U.S. Population: 1980–2010*

Population Age	Percent Change		
	1980–90	1990–2000	2000–2010
0–4	11.8%	− 8.2%	.05%
5–17	− 3.4	7.0	− 6.3
18–24	−13.9	− 3.5	7.6
25–34	16.7	−15.4	1.1
35–44	46.5	15.9	−15.3
45–64	5.2	31.0	28.1
65 and over	3.9	10.5	12.8

* Given in terms of percentage of net change.

Source: U.S. Bureau of the Census, *Statistical Abstract of the United States: 1990* (110th ed.), Washington, D.C., Table nos. 13 and 18, pp. 13 and 16.

organizations will need to adjust the way they recruit and retain younger workers. Third, the "baby-boomers" contributed a 46.5 percent increase in the number of 35–44-year-olds during 1980–90. Following this group of individuals throughout Table 2–2 indicates that they will ultimately create top-heavy organizations around the turn of the century. Finally, the decrease in people 35–44 years of age over the years 2000–2010 may result in a shortage of middle-level managers. If willing, the aging baby boomers may fill this void. The next section considers the implications of a demographically changed work force.

Implications for OB

Women now account for nearly half of the U.S. labor force. A wide variety of interpersonal, group, and organizational processes have been affected. Consequently, this book contains numerous discussions of gender-related topics. For example, interpersonal dynamics between men and women have a significant impact on communication processes. While at work, males and females must strive to communicate in a professional manner free from sexual connotations. A solid grounding in organizational behavior and basic communication processes, as discussed in Chapter 12, can help.

Additionally, women will be in high demand, given future labor shortages. To attract the best workers, companies need to adopt policies and programs that meet the needs of women. Programs such as day care, elder care, flexible work schedules, cafeteria benefit programs, paternal leaves, and less rigid relocation policies are likely to become more common. At Merck & Co., for instance, instituting these types of programs led to increased employee satisfaction, positive public relations, and an abundance of good job applicants (see OB in Action). Some of these programs are discussed in the last section of this chapter.

Mismatches between the amount of education needed to perform current jobs and the amount of education possessed by members of the work force are growing. Underemployment among college graduates threatens to erode job satisfaction and work motivation. As well-educated workers begin to

OB IN ACTION

Companies Receive Accolades for Instituting Programs That Meet the Needs of Women

Merck & Co., named the nation's most admired company by *Fortune* magazine and one of the 10 best companies for working mothers by *Working Mother* magazine, says the accolades are a definite assist. "Let's face it, Merck is not a household name," a spokesman allows. Being *Fortune*'s most admired for three years, he says, has helped draw in "over 100,000 applications for jobs from New Jersey alone."

Syntex Corp. brags about its *Working Mother* listing in recruiting and its annual report. **PepsiCo Inc.** boasts of its *Fortune* seventh-most-admired ranking in employee publications. **Hoffman-La Roche Inc.** cites its *Working Mother* mention to job candidates.

Source: "Labor Letter: A Special News Report on People and Their Jobs in Offices, Fields, and Factories," *The Wall Street Journal*, October 10, 1989, p. A1.

look for jobs commensurate with their qualifications and expectations, absenteeism and turnover likely will increase. This problem underscores the need for job redesign (see the discussion in Chapter 5). In addition, organizations will need to consider interventions, such as realistic job previews and positive reinforcement programs, to reduce absenteeism and turnover. On-the-job remedial skills training will be necessary to help the growing number of dropouts cope with job demands.

Moreover, organizations will continue to be asked to help resolve the educational problems in the United States. Supporting education is good for business and society at large. A better education system not only contributes to the United States's ability to compete internationally, but it facilitates a better quality of life for all its population. Some organizations view this assistance as one form of social responsibility (see A Matter of Ethics).

With labor force size not expected to increase significantly during the 1990s, a shortage of qualified entry-level workers and late career managers is predicted. However, as the baby-boom generation reaches retirement age after the turn of the century, the work force will be top heavy with older employees, creating the problem of career plateauing for younger workers. **Career plateauing** is defined "as that point in a career which future hierarchical mobility seems unlikely."[43] Because employees frequently view career plateauing as career failure, career plateauing is associated with stress and dissatisfaction.[44] Managers thus will need to find alternatives besides promotions to help employees satisfy their needs and to feel successful. Career management is discussed in Chapter 8. In addition, organizations may need to devise more flexible and creative retirement plans. If managers are to be more responsive to older workers, they also need to be aware of how aging affects one's values and attitudes. Employee values and attitudes are discussed in Chapter 3.

• Organizations such as Coors are demonstrating their concern about education by donating funds to fight illiteracy. *(Courtesy of Coors Foundation for Family Literacy)*

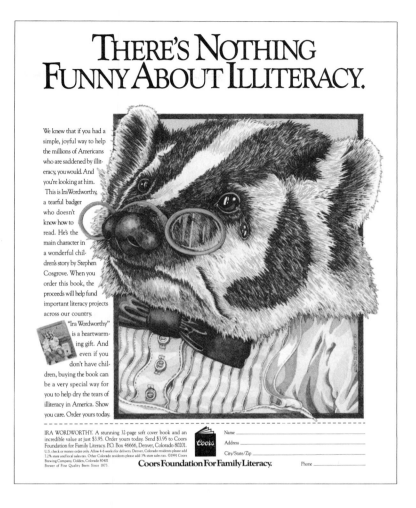

A MATTER OF ETHICS

Companies Make Large Financial Contributions in Support of Public Education

IBM alone spent more than $20 million on K–12 projects in 1989 and has committed at least $52 million over the next five years. A 1990 *Fortune* magazine poll of the nation's 1,000 largest industrial and service companies found that 98 percent of respondents are giving at least some money to public education. Twenty-eight percent donate more than $100,000 a year and 18 percent more than $1 million. Exxon, Coca Cola, Procter & Gamble, General Electric, AT&T, Du Pont, 3M, Shell Oil, Ford, Eastman Kodak, Boeing—the list of big donors reads like a "Who's Who" of American business.

Source: Jack Gordon, "Can Business Save the Schools?" *Training,* August 1990, p. 20.

• INTEGRATION OF HOME AND WORK LIFE

The relationship between job satisfaction and life satisfaction is more important in light of the demographic trends just discussed. For example, the increased number of women in the work force (particularly those with children), the increased percentage of preschool children between the years 1980–90, the growth in dual-career couples, and an aging population are pressuring employees to more effectively balance family and work life issues. In order to gain an appreciation for why the balance is important, let us begin by discussing job satisfaction.

Job satisfaction is an affective or emotional response toward various facets of one's job. In other words, job satisfaction involves a person's positive (or negative) feelings about his or her job. The popular press generally contends that the American work force is in the midst of a job-satisfaction crisis. But recent evidence suggests these claims probably are overstated. Internationally, the U.S. labor force seems to be faring quite well. For example, one study contrasted the average job satisfaction and organizational commitment of 8,302 employees working in 106 factories located in the United States and Japan. Results indicated that the American workers were significantly more satisfied and committed than their Japanese counterparts.[45] In addition, the National Opinion Research Center's 1988

• A scene like this one, with a working father taking time off for child care, is increasingly necessary in our dual-career couple world. *(Bruce Byers/FPG International)*

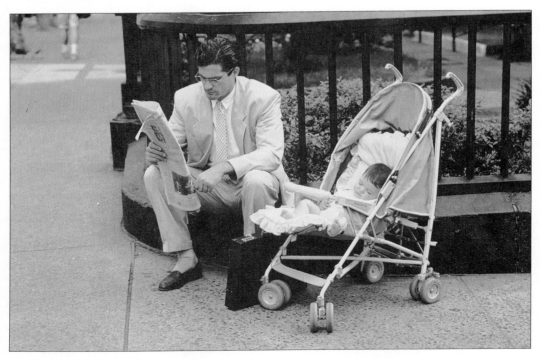

• **FIGURE 2-7** Impact of Work and Nonwork Factors on Quality of Life

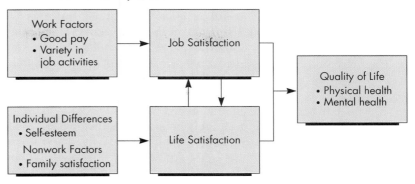

survey of 1,000 employees indicated that 87 percent were satisfied with their jobs. Researchers also found that job satisfaction tends to be greater among people in higher occupational levels, among those who grew up in smaller communities (2,500 to 10,000 persons), and among individuals with higher socioeconomic status and income.[46] Work organizations are not completely responsible for the current level of job satisfaction among U.S. employees, however. As illustrated in Figure 2–7, job satisfaction also is influenced by nonwork factors.

Job Satisfaction and Life Satisfaction Are Reciprocally Related

Have you ever done poorly on a test you were really prepared for because you had an argument with a friend the night before? If you have, you know your personal life can influence your work and vice versa. As exemplified by Lulu Wang, senior vice president of the Equitable Capital Management Group, the same goes for job and life satisfaction.

> Wang . . . refuses to separate business from home life, because trying to do so increases stress. At the age of 12, Wang's son could read the stock pages of *The Wall Street Journal* and join in a lively discussion about a merger at the dinner table. Why not? As a pension fund portfolio manager, his mom controls over $1 billion in assets.
>
> "I've always made it a point to integrate my professional and family lives," says Wang. Keeping the two lives separate produces stress and anxiety. "Your family sees your job as something which strings you out and competes with them for your time." But if you let them share in your highs and lows, "they can't help but be supportive partners," she says.[47]

As Lulu Wang probably knows, it is difficult to balance family and work responsibilities.

For example, a researcher at Boston University surveyed 1,600 employees from two different organizations about family and work issues. Thirty-six percent of the fathers and 37 percent of the mothers reported feeling "a lot of stress" in balancing their home and work lives. A sample of 1,200 employees from a Minneapolis company further indicated that 60 percent of the men were having problems managing home and family conflicts. In turn, these conflicts negatively affected the respondent's job performance and career progression. On average, however, women experienced more stress than men from home/work conflicts because they had more responsibility for domestic chores.[48] Results from a study of 4,000 Du Pont employees uncovered similar results.[49] Behavioral scientists have proposed three rival hypotheses to explain the dynamic interaction between job and life satisfaction.

The first, called the *compensation effect*, suggests job and life satisfaction are negatively related. In other words, we compensate for low job or life satisfaction by seeking satisfying activities in other domains. A recent meta-analysis of 34 studies covering 19,811 people failed to support this prediction. Results revealed a significant and positive correlation between job and life satisfaction.[50] On the other hand, the *segmentation model* proposes that job satisfaction and life satisfaction are independent—one supposedly does not influence the other. Research also did not support this model. Recent research supports the third model, which is called the *spillover model*.[51]

The **spillover model** hypothesizes that job satisfaction or dissatisfaction spills over into one's life and vice versa. In other words, each affects the other both positively and negatively on an ongoing basis. For example, one study of 48 men examined the relationship between stressful work events and wife abuse. Consistent with the spillover model, the frequency and negativity of stressful work events were significantly related to wife abuse.[52] Research also has shown that the relationship between job and life satisfaction is stronger for people who value work in their lives, and people with more education and higher income levels.[53] Ultimately, as illustrated in Figure 2–7, the reciprocal interaction between job and life satisfaction affects the individual's overall quality of life and physical and mental health. More is said about the nature and causes of job satisfaction in Chapter 5.

Implications for OB

Since job satisfaction and life satisfaction affect the quality of our lives, managers need to keep abreast of employee attitudes and problems. Many organizations have responded to this need by creating human resource departments. These departments concentrate on solving employee problems before they erupt into a crisis. Other organizations—such as Leaseway Transportation Corp. and Hartmarx Corp.—use attitude surveys to keep their finger on the pulse of employee sentiments (see OB in Action). Attitude surveys are increasingly being used to diagnose organizational problems and to improve relations between management and employees. For example, unionized firms conducting attitude surveys were less likely to have experienced a labor strike within the previous six years.[54]

Organizations also are revamping many traditional approaches to human resource management in an attempt to integrate home and work life.[55] As discussed in the next section, programs such as flexible work schedules, cafeteria benefit plans, and child-care and elder-care programs are becoming more popular. Finally, employee assistance programs are becoming the dominant method of helping individuals solve personal and work-related problems such as alcohol and drug abuse (see Chapter 16).

OB IN ACTION

Attitude Surveys Produce Positive Results for Leaseway Transportation Corp. and Hartmarx Corp.

Truck drivers for Leaseway Transportation Corp. were asked earlier this year in an anonymous company survey how they felt about their bosses. Their response appalled the company's management.

"They said the supervisors didn't encourage ideas from them, they weren't receptive to them, they were curt to them," recalls Charles T. Deeble, the company's training and development manager. "It was, 'You're a truck driver, here are the keys, go down the road.' They were treating them like children."

Soon after Cleveland-based Leaseway began offering management-training courses. . . .

Hartmarx began surveying its 25,000 employees last year, a process the company plans to repeat every three years. After the results were compiled by computer, workers met with personnel staffers in small groups, where they were encouraged to expand on their responses.

The company has already taken several steps on issues raised.

Source: Excerpted from Larry Reibstein "A Finger on the Pulse: Companies Expand Use of Employee Surveys," *The Wall Street Journal*, October 27, 1986, p. 27.

• EMERGING SOLUTIONS FOR MANAGING A RESHAPED WORK FORCE

This chapter reviewed a variety of demographic trends in the work force. We would like you to consider one more statistical profile:

> Every eight seconds of the school day, an American student drops out, according to the Children's Defense Fund. Every 67 seconds, a teenager has a baby. Every seven minutes a child is arrested for drugs. Every year the U.S. school system graduates 700,000 young people who cannot read their diplomas.[56]

What are the managerial implications of these trends? As suggested in the Chapter Opening Case, it is time for a new managerial paradigm, a new way of managing employees. Table 2–3 contains a list of potential solutions to managing a reshaped work force. The purpose of this final section is to provide more detail on five of the more popular solutions: implement alternative work schedules, institute new strategies for recruiting employees, increase the amount of both skill-based training and management development, implement cafeteria benefit plans, and create day-care and elder-care programs.

Implement Alternative Work Schedules

Alternative work schedules permit employees more flexibility in managing conflicts between home and work demands. Flextime, compressed workweeks, job sharing, and telecommuting are four of the most popular alternative work schedules. Let us briefly consider each approach.

• TABLE 2-3   Potential Solutions for Managing a Reshaped Work Force

1. Implement alternative work schedules.
2. Institute new strategies for recruiting employees.
3. Increase the amount of both skill-based training and management development.
4. Implement cafeteria benefit plans.
5. Create day-care and elder-care programs.
6. Try to identify and reduce stereotypes (see Chapter 4).
7. Use job design to create intrinsically motivating work environments (see Chapter 5).
8. Develop motivational programs geared toward a diverse work force (see Chapters 5 and 6).
9. Develop mentoring programs (see Chapter 8).
10. Address career plateauing (see Chapter 8).
11. Use realistic job previews when hiring employees (see Chapter 8).
12. Restructure the organization around teams (see Chapter 11).
13. Institute programs to reduce language barriers (communication is discussed in Chapter 12).
14. Include the management of diversity as a measure of managerial performance; reward this behavior accordingly (see Chapter 13).
15. Exhibit leadership that increases the appreciation of employee diversity (leadership is discussed in Chapter 14).
16. Increase the amount of participative management (see Chapter 15).
17. Decentralize decision making (see Chapters 15 and 17).
18. Implement employee assistance programs (see Chapter 16).

Flextime   **Flextime** provides employees with greater autonomy by allowing them to choose their daily starting and finishing times within a given period called a bandwidth (see Figure 2–8). The only other stipulation is that all employees must be present during a *core period* of time. According to recent estimates, more than 9 million workers in the United States are using flextime. Managers and professionals use flextime more than other employee groups.[57] Although very little research has empirically investigated the benefits of flextime, research suggests that flextime helps employees manage home/work conflicts and sometimes improves productivity. The mixed effect on productivity implies that flextime is not appropriate for all types of jobs.[58]

Compressed Workweek   Under a **compressed workweek** plan, employees work approximatley 40 hours in less than five days. The two typical patterns are to work 40 hours in four days (4/40) or 38 in three (3/38). Research on compressed schedules indicates inconsistent effects on productivity, absenteeism, turnover, and job satisfaction.[59] Although some people prefer this schedule, additional high-quality research is needed before we can conclusively evaluate its effectiveness.

Job Sharing   **Job sharing** entails reconstructing a full-time position so that it is performed by two employees, each working part-time. In this arrangement, the job gets completed by each person working two and a half days a

• **FIGURE 2-8**   A Flextime Program

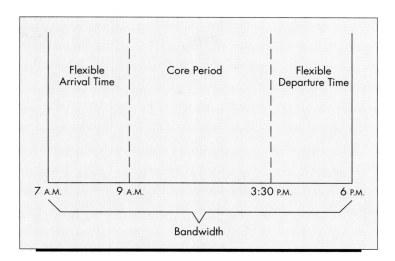

week. Job sharing is more common for professional positions in banking, insurance, teaching, and libraries. There is not adequate research to draw any firm conclusions about the effectiveness of job sharing.[60]

Telecommuting   **Telecommuting** involves receiving and sending work from home by using a modem to link a home computer to an office computer. Full-time telecommuters generally work two days at home and three at the office. Telecommuting is more common in "information jobs" that require analysis, research, writing, typing, or computer programming. An estimated 3.4 million workers from over 350 organizations were involved with formal telecommuting programs in 1990.[61] Proposed benefits of telecommuting include:

1. Increased flexibility and autonomy for workers.
2. Ability to retain qualified and trained personnel who are either unwilling or unable to work in an office.
3. Ability to recruit from a larger geographic area.
4. Lower office expenses.
5. Ability to tap nontraditional labor pools (such as prison inmates and home-bound disabled persons).

Although telecommuting represents an attempt to accommodate employee needs and desires, it requires adjustments and is not for everybody. According to John Naisbitt, the futurist who wrote the best-selling *Megatrends,* "not very many of us will be willing to work at home. People want to be with people; people want to go to the office."[62] It thus appears that the growth of telecommuting will depend more on behavioral than technical limitations. Given the prevalence of dual-career couples and working mothers, it is likely that more organizations will experiment with telecommuting.

Institute New Strategies for Recruiting Employees

Organizations are changing the way they recruit and select employees. Rather than sit back and wait for qualified applicants, successful organizations are proactively trying to recruit the best possible employees. This entails placing more importance on recruiting minorities, disabled people (see OB in Action), older workers, retirees, and part-timers.[63] Additionally, companies are learning that proactive recruitment entails evaluating and possibly changing the employee benefit package. In addition to higher starting salaries for hard-to-fill positions, organizations are beginning to devise benefits that satisfy the diverse needs of a heterogeneous work force. Consider the case of Herbert Schervish.

> The turnover rate had reached 179 percent at the Burger King in downtown Detroit's Renaissance Center three years ago. Operations were disrupted as each position had to be filled twice every 13 months, owner Herbert Schervish recalls. And he estimates that it cost $1,500 in training expenses and lost productivity each time he had to recruit a new worker.
>
> Schervish had tried to remedy the problem by raising wages and improving working conditions, but those efforts didn't reduce turnover. Then he took another approach—offering to pay the cost of tuition and books for employees attending either of two local community colleges. That strategy succeeded.[64]

Mr. Schervish's approach to recruitment produced a drop in turnover from 179 percent to 39 percent while also resulting in a 3 percent increase in productivity.

Increase the Amount of Both Skill-Based Training and Management Development

This solution is hard to ignore, given the educational mismatches previously discussed. Unfortunately, U.S. companies have not firmly grabbed the bull

---

 OB IN ACTION

Companies Increasingly Target the Recruitment of Disabled Individuals

Holiday Inns—prompted by a growing labor shortage and a "recognition of increasing cultural diversity"—makes hiring the handicapped a "major focus." At one recently opened unit in New York City, one in 10 employees is hearing impaired or has a learning difficulty. For another hotel, Holiday Inns interviews 150 handicapped workers. Lighted phones, vibrating beepers and sign-language training for supervisors help the hearing-impaired do their jobs.

Wyse Technology Corp. signals its interest in handicapped workers in every ad. Each month it also lists itself with a California agency that helps handicapped workers. Equifax Inc. works with the Epilepsy Foundation and other groups. Domino's Pizza Inc. recruits emotionally and physically handicapped workers through community health organizations. Weyerhaeuser Co. tries to make its headquarters more accessible to the handicapped.

Source: "Labor Letter: A Special News Report on People and Their Jobs in Offices, Fields, and Factories," *The Wall Street Journal*, October 3, 1989, p. A1.

by the horns. For instance, the Department of Labor estimated that U.S. companies spent $30 billion on employee training in 1989. Although this sounds like a lot of money, it only represented 1.5 percent of the private sector payroll. Moreover, experts discovered that nearly 90 percent of this training was targeted for managers and professionals and not for employees in the trenches who need it the most. This trend persists today. Finally, a 1989 survey conducted by the American Society for Training and Development discovered that less than half of the 500 largest corporations in the United States conducted any training programs at all.[65]

On the positive side, companies are beginning to offer basic skill and literacy training. The charge is being led by the likes of Motorola, General Electric, Polaroid, the Big Three automakers, Planters Peanuts, Stouffer Foods, and Square D. In addition to basic skill training, companies such as Motorola, General Motors, Ford, IBM, and Xerox implemented training programs to help employees more effectively use advanced technology. This type of training will become increasingly important as organizations adopt a host of manufacturing technology and office automation in the future (these technologies are discussed in Chapter 20).[66]

In summary, a commitment to training is a prerequisite for making the workplace more competitive and profitable. How large is this commitment? The American Society for Training and Development estimated that over 50 million current workers in the United States will need new or expanded training between the years 1990–2000.[67]

Implement Cafeteria Benefit Plans

Cafeteria benefit plans, also referred to as *flexible benefits*, allow employees to spend a predetermined amount of credits or dollars on benefits from a menu of choices: Some plans allow people to select cash in lieu of benefits. As such, these plans allow employees to select a package of benefits that meets their personal needs. The typical menu of benefits includes health and life insurance, dental, vision, sick leave, vacation, disability, dependent care assistance, and tuition reimbursement.[68] For example, an employee with children in need of braces may select increased dental coverage as an additional benefit instead of receiving elder care.

A 1990 study by Hewitt Associates revealed that 55 percent of the nation's largest companies implemented cafeteria benefit plans. A large-scale study of the use of cafeteria plans by the Conference Board in 1989 indicated that 15–20 percent of all U.S. companies have cafeteria plans.[69] These plans are well suited to managing diversity in the work force and are expected to grow in popularity in the future.

Create Day-Care and Elder-Care Programs

The growth in day-care and elder-care programs as an employee benefit was fueled by the combination of more dual-career couples, more women and minorities in the work force, and an aging population. Research reveals that employees' work performance is adversely affected by child-care and elder-care concerns.[70] These programs thus are aimed at helping employees integrate family and work responsibilities in order to positively affect productivity and employee well-being. Stride Rite Corp., for example, is noted for

• Day care is a necessity in today's workplace. Stride-Rite, with its Intergenerational Care Center, has extended the concept to include both senior citizens and children. *(Courtesy of Stride Rite Intergenerational Center.)*

having implemented an intergenerational day-care center that provides both day care and elder care (see OB in Action).

The Conference Board's Work and Family Information Center estimated that the number of companies offering some form of child-care assistance doubled from 2,500 in 1986 to 5,400 in 1990. Child-care assistance is typically given in the form of information and referral, direct financial assistance, and on or near-site child care. Direct financial assistance is the dominant form of child care. Elder care provides employees with benefits to take care of older relatives. The Conference Board identified 300 companies that offered this benefit in 1990, up from practically none in 1986.[71] Practical experience at many different companies suggests that the benefits of providing these forms of employee assistance exceeds the costs.[72]

• SUMMARY OF KEY CONCEPTS

A. Surveys of unemployed people have revealed seven basic functions of work. They center around life goals, economic security, status and identity, goal-oriented activity, nonfamily social contact, teamwork and camaraderie, and time structure.

B. Some claim the work ethic, which reflects the extent to which an individual values work, is dead in America. However, survey evidence indicates that most employees have a strong desire to do their very best. Both management and societal forces have been blamed for stifling an otherwise strong work ethic among employees in the United States.

C. Technology will create dramatic organizational changes over the next decade. Nonetheless, a comparative few will end up with high-paying,

OB IN ACTION

Stride Rite Corp. Implements an Intergenerational Day-Care Center

The shoe manufacturer—generally credited with launching the nation's first corporate facility for workers' children in Roxbury, Mass., in 1971—turns now to looking after elders, as well. The company has opened a center at its Cambridge, Mass., headquarters that eventually will provide 10 hours of care for 55 youngsters and 24 elders who need assistance. The first 50 of the children entered last week; the adults are expected to start arriving before month end.

"People caring for elder relatives lose as many days of work, four or five a year, as people with young children," says Karen Leibold, the program director, in explaining the commitment to the center that cost the company and its charitable foundation more than $700,000 to establish. Company and government subsidies will pay half the . . . [$8,000-a-year] operating tab; clients from the company and community will pay the rest, based on financial ability.

Source: "Labor Letter: A Special News Report on People and Their Jobs in Offices, Fields, and Factories," *The Wall Street Journal*, February 2, 1990, p. A1.

---

high-tech jobs, while many will find themselves occupying lower-paying service jobs. More Americans are working part-time. The service sector of the economy is the biggest in employment and the lowest in productivity.

D. The U.S. work force has become more diverse. Demographically, women are predicted to represent 47 percent of the work force in the year 2000. Despite the increase of women in the work force, women are still overrepresented in lower-paying, lower-level occupations. Minorities are predicted to account for a third of all *new* entrants in the work force between 1988 and 2000. Hispanics are predicted to account for the largest *net* increase in minority employment.

E. As the educational level of the work force continues to increase, the problem of underemployment will worsen. A growing army of inadequately skilled high-school dropouts poses another serious threat to the economy. As the baby-boom generation grows older, the average age of the work force will rise steadily (39 by the year 2000). Many baby-boomers will face the problem of career plateauing.

F. Job satisfaction involves one's positive or negative feelings about his or her job. Compared to their Japanese counterparts, American workers generally are more satisfied with their jobs. Job satisfaction tends to increase as education and income increase.

G. Research points toward a reciprocal relationship between job and life satisfaction in which each affects the other on an ongoing basis. One's physical and mental health are affected by this reciprocal relationship. Employee relations departments, attitude surveys, and employee assistance programs for such problems as alcohol and drug abuse are modern organizational attempts to enhance the job and life satisfaction connection.

H. There are many different solutions for managing a reshaped work force. Five popular solutions are to implement alternative work schedules, institute new strategies for recruiting employees, increase the amount of both skill-based training and management development, implement cafeteria benefit plans, and create day-care and elder-care programs. Flextime, compressed workweeks, job sharing, and telecommuting are the most popular alternative work schedules.

• KEY TERMS

work ethic	spillover model
part-time work	flextime
work force demographics	compressed workweek
underemployment	job sharing
career plateauing	telecommuting
job satisfaction	cafeteria benefit plans

• DISCUSSION QUESTIONS

1. From your standpoint, which of the seven functions of work in Figure 2–2 is most important? Explain your reasoning.

2. Have you ever worked for an organization that stifled your work ethic? Describe the circumstances. What should have been done to correct the situation?

3. Were you surprised to see which jobs will have the most job opportunities between the years 1988 and 2000? What does this trend suggest for managing your own career?

4. What do you think is the primary cause of low productivity in the service sector? What might be done to improve this national problem? Explain.

5. Have you experienced any conflict in the workplace that might be attributed to the increase of women in the managerial ranks? From an OB standpoint, what could management have done to prevent this conflict?

6. What is the most critical organizational challenge associated with the increase of minorities in the work force? What can be done to facilitate the career success of minorities? Explain your rationale.

7. Why is underemployment a serious human resource management problem? If you have ever been underemployed, what were your feelings about it?

8. How is the graying of America likely to affect organizational life?

9. Do you think organizations are making an honest attempt at helping

employees to integrate home and work life? What examples have you observed?

10. As you look forward to working in a reshaped work force, what are your concerns?

BACK TO THE OPENING CASE

Now that you have read Chapter 2, you should be able to answer the following questions about the chapter opening case:

1. What are the forces creating the need for a new managerial paradigm?

2. Do you think we need a new managerial paradigm? Explain your rationale.

3. Contrast the old and new managerial paradigms. Do you think American businesses will embrace a new approach to management?

4. Which of the solutions for managing a reshaped work force are Robert Haas, Chairman of Levi Strauss, and GE's Jack Welch using? Provide examples.

5. Based on what you have read about the reshaped work force, what advice would you offer Robert Haas and Jack Welch?

• EXERCISE 2

Objectives

1. To measure your work ethic.
2. To determine how well your work ethic score predicts your work habits.

Introduction

People differ in terms of how much they believe in the work ethic. These differences influence a variety of behavioral outcomes. What better way to gain insight into the work ethic than by measuring your own work ethic and seeing how well it predicts your everyday work habits?

Instructions

To assess your work ethic, complete the eight-item instrument developed by a respected behavioral scientist.[73] Being honest with yourself, circle your responses on the rating scales following each of the eight items. There are no right or wrong answers. Add up your total score for the eight items and record it in the space provided. *The higher your total score, the stronger your work ethic.*

Following the work ethic scale is a short personal-work-habits questionnaire. Your responses to this questionnaire will help you determine whether your work ethic score is a good predictor of your work habits.

Work Ethic Scale

1. When the workday is finished, people should forget their jobs and enjoy themselves.
   Agree completely   1—2—3—4—5   Disagree completely

2. Hard work does not make an individual a better person.
   Agree completely   1—2—3—4—5   Disagree completely

3. The principal purpose of a job is to provide a person with the means for enjoying his or her free time.
   Agree completely   1—2—3—4—5   Disagree completely

4. Wasting time is not as bad as wasting money.
   Agree completely   1—2—3—4—5   Disagree completely

5. Whenever possible, a person should relax and accept life as it is, rather than always striving for unreachable goals.
   Agree completely   1—2—3—4—5   Disagree completely

6. A person's worth should not be based on how well he or she performs a job.
   Agree completely   1—2—3—4—5   Disagree completely

7. People who do things the easy way are the smart ones.
   Agree completely   1—2—3—4—5   Disagree completely

8. If all other things are equal, it is better to have a job with little responsibility than one with a lot of responsibility.
   Agree completely   1—2—3—4—5   Disagree completely
   Total = _____

Personal Work Habits Questionnaire

1. How many unexcused absences from classes did you have last semester or quarter?
   _____ absences

2. How many credit hours are you taking this semester or quarter?
   _____ hours

3. What is your overall grade point average?
   _____ GPA

4. What percentage of your school expenses are you earning through full- or part-time employment?
   _____ percent

5. In terms of percent, how much effort do you typically put forth at school and/or work?
   School = _____%   Work = _____%

Questions for Consideration/Class Discussion

1. How strong is your work ethic?
   Weak = 8–18   Moderate = 19–29   Strong = 30–40

2. How would you rate your work habits/results?
   Below average_____   Average_____   Above average _____

3. How well does your work ethic score predict your work habits or work results?
   Poorly_____   Moderately well_____   Very well_____

• NOTES

[1] A thorough discussion of the forces that reshaped the work force can be found in Joseph F. Coates, Jennifer Jarratt, and John B. Mahaffie, *Future Work: Seven Critical Forces Reshaping Work and the Work Force in North America* (San Francisco, Calif.: Jossey-Bass, 1990).

[2] Adapted in part from Judith A. Brook and Richard J. Brook, "Exploring the Meaning of Work and Nonwork," *Journal of Organizational Behavior,* April 1989, pp. 169–78; and Stephen Fineman, "Work Meanings, Non-Work, and the Taken-For-Granted," *Journal of Management Studies,* April 1983, pp. 143–57.

[3] See Michael Moritz, "Apple Launches a Mac Attack," *Time,* January 30, 1984, pp. 68–69.

[4] See Fineman, "Work Meanings, Non-Work, and the Taken-For-Granted."

[5] Results from this study are reported in Seymor Martin Lipset, "The Work Ethic—Then and Now," *The Public Interest,* Winter 1990, pp. 61–69.

[6] Representative studies can be found in Liana Giorgi and Catherine Marsh, "The Protestant Work Ethic as a Cultural Phenomenon," *European Journal of Social Psychology,* November–December 1990, pp. 499–517; and Vishwanath V. Baba, "Central Life Interests and Job Involvement: An Exploratory Study in the Developing World," *International Journal of Comparative Sociology,* September–December 1989, pp. 181–94.

[7] See Jyuji Misumi, "The Japanese Meaning of Work and Small Group Activities in Japanese Industrial Organizations," *International Journal of Psychology,* 1990, pp. 819–32.

[8] Results can be found in Karyn A. Loscocco and Arne L. Kalleberg, "Age and the Meaning of Work in the United States and Japan," *Social Forces,* December 1988, pp. 337–56.

[9] A history of the Japanese work ethic is discussed by Misumi, "The Japanese Meaning of Work and Small Group Activities."

[10] This research is reviewed by Adrian Furnham and Eva Koritsas, "The Protestant Work Ethic and Vocational Preference," *Journal of Organizational Behavior,* January 1990, pp. 43–55; and Patrick C. L. Heaven, "Suggestions for Reducing Unemployment: A Study of Protestant Work Ethic and Economic Locus of Control Beliefs," *British Journal of Social Psychology,* March 1990, pp. 55–65.

[11] From Marc Miller, "The 'Wild Card' of Business: How to Manage the Work Ethic in the Automated Workplace," *Management Review,* September 1983, pp. 8–12.

[12] Ibid.

[13] See discussions by Jack Gordon, "Who Killed Corporate Loyalty?" *Training,* March 1990, pp. 25–32; and J. D. Grable, "Low Productivity and Low Morale," *Supervision,* March 1990, pp. 3–6.

[14] Phillip C. Grant, "Why Employee Motivation Has Declined in America," *Personnel Journal,* December 1982, p. 907.

[15] See Robert Eisenberger, Peter Fasolo, and Valerie Davis-LaMastro, "Perceived Organizational Support and Employee Diligence, Commitment, and Innovation," *Journal of Applied Psychology,* February 1990, pp. 51–59; and Lois A. James and Lawrence R. James, "Integrating Work Environment Perceptions: Explorations into the Measurement of Meaning," *Journal of Applied Psychology,* October 1989, pp. 739–51.

[16] Fred Best, "The Nature of Working in a Changing Society," *Personnel Journal,* January 1985, pp. 40–41.

[17] Michael Wallace, "Brave New Workplace: Technology and Work in the New Economy," *Work and Occupations,* November 1989, pp. 363–92.

[18] The impact of technology on jobs is discussed by David Herold, "Using Technology to Improve Our Management of Labour Market Trends," *Journal of Organizational Change Management*, vol. 3, 1990, pp. 44–57; and William B. Johnston and Arnold H. Packer, *Workforce 2000: Work and Workers For the 21st Century* (Indianapolis, Ind.: Hudson Institute, 1987).

[19] Joseph E. Thurman and Gabriele Trah, "Part-Time Work in International Perspective," *International Labour Review*, January–February 1990, p. 23.

[20] See Nancy Henderson and Sherri Buri, "Tactics That Win Good Part-Time Jobs," *Changing Times*, May 1990, pp. 61, 62, 66; and "Labor Letter: A Special News Report on People and Their Jobs in Offices, Fields, and Factories," *The Wall Street Journal*, March 7, 1989, p. A1.

[21] Michael Urquhart, "The Employment Shift to Services: Where Did It Come From?" *Monthly Labor Review*, April 1984, p. 15.

[22] The relationship between productivity and investment in technology is discussed by Tim R. V. Davis, "Information Technology and White-Collar Productivity," *The Academy of Management Executive*, February 1991, pp. 55–67; Laurence C. Seifert and Alfred D. Zeisler, "A National Manufacturing Policy: An Industry Perspective on Promoting Sustained Improvement in U.S. Global Competitiveness," *Technological Forecasting and Social Change*, March 1989, pp. 1–11; and Stephen S. Roach, "Technology and the Services Sector: The Hidden Competitive Challenge," *Technological Forecasting and Social Change*, December 1988, pp. 387–403.

[23] See Jan van Dalen, Johan Koerts, and A. Roy Thurik, "The Measurement of Labour Productivity in Wholesaling," *International Journal of Research in Marketing*, August 1990, pp. 21–34; William J. Baumol, "Quality Changes and Productivity Measurement: Hedonics and an Alternative," *Journal of Accounting, Auditing and Finance*, Winter 1990, pp. 105–17; and Charles R. White and Jeffrey S. Austin, "Productivity Measurement: Untangling White-Collar Web," *Journal of Management in Engineering*, October 1989, pp. 371–78.

[24] These examples were discussed in "Labor Letter: A Special News Report on People and Their Jobs in Offices, Fields, and Factories," *The Wall Street Journal*, April 10, 1990, p. A1.

[25] Supporting evidence is found in Ellen F. Jackofsky and Lawrence H. Peters, "Part-Time versus Full-Time Employment Status Differences: A Replication and Extension," *Journal of Occupational Behavior*, January 1987, pp. 1–9.

[26] For details of this study, see Alan L. Otten, "People Patterns: Part-Time Work is Fine, If It's What You Want," *The Wall Street Journal*, April 23, 1990, p. B1.

[27] Gene Koretz, "No Service Sector Pain, No Productivity Gain," *Business Week*, January 21, 1991, p. 20.

[28] Data are contained in "Tomorrow's Jobs," in *Occupational Outlook Handbook* (Washington, D.C.: U.S. Department of Labor, April 1990).

[29] See "Labor Letter: A Special News Report on People and Their Jobs in Offices, Fields, and Factories, *The Wall Street Journal*, August 14, 1990, p. A1.

[30] A complete description of this data can be found in Howard N. Fullerton, Jr., "New Labor Force Projections, Spanning 1988 to 2000," *Monthly Labor Review*, November 1989, pp. 3–12.

[31] See Lynn R. Offermann and Marilyn K. Gowing, "Organizations of the Future: Changes and Challenges," *American Psychologist*, February 1990, pp. 95–108.

[32] Data were obtained from Jaclyn Fierman, "Why Women Still Don't Hit The Top," *Fortune*, July 30, 1990, pp. 40–60.

[33] Ibid.

[34] Data are contained in William Dunn, "Minorities A Larger Part of Population," *USA Today*, June 21, 1989, p. 1.

[35] Anne McDougall Young and Howard Hayghe, "More U.S. Workers Are College Graduates," *Monthly Labor Review*, March 1984, p. 48.

[36] See Emile Andersen Allan and Darrell J. Steffensmeier, "Youth, Underemployment, and Property Crime: Differential Effects of Job Availability and Job Quality on Juvenile and Young Adult Arrest Rates," *American Sociological Review*, February 1989, pp. 107–23.

[37] The future status of underemployment is discussed by Leann M. Tigges and Deborah M. Tootle, "Labor Supply, Labor Demand, and Men's Underemployment in Rural and Urban Labor Markets," *Rural Sociology,* Fall 1990, pp. 328–56; and Stephen Nord, "The Relationships among Labor-Force Participation, Service-Sector Employment, and Underemployment," *Journal of Regional Science*, August 1989, pp. 407–21.

[38] See Samuel M. Enrenhalt, "What Lies Ahead for College Graduates?" *American Demographics,* September 1983, pp. 29–33.

[39] Louis S. Richman, "Tomorrow's Jobs: Plentiful, But . . . ," *Fortune,* April 11, 1988, p. 48.

[40] Results from the study are discussed by Offermann and Gowing, in "Organizations of the Future: Changes and Challenges."

[41] See "Business and Education: The Demand for Partnership," *Business Week,* Special Advertising Section, May 2, 1988, pp. 124–35.

[42] Data are from Louis S. Richman, "The Coming World Labor Shortage," *Fortune,* April 9, 1990, pp. 70–77.

[43] Priscilla M. Elsass and David A. Ralston, "Individual Responses to the Stress of Career Plateauing," *Journal of Management,* Spring 1989, p. 35.

[44] Ibid, pp. 35–47; Mary Ann Archer, "Planning: Canada Housing and Mortgage Surmounts Plateauing," *Personnel Journal,* April 1990, pp. 141–42; and Debra L. Nelson, James Campbell Quick, Michael A. Hitt, and Doug Moesel, "Politics, Lack of Career Progress, and Work/Home Conflict: Stress and Strain for Working Women," *Sex Roles,* August 1990, pp. 169–85.

[45] Details of this study can be found in James R. Lincoln, "Employee Work Attitudes and Management Practice in the United States and Japan: Evidence from a Large Comparative Study," *California Management Review,* Fall 1989, pp. 89–106.

[46] See Lipset, "The Work Ethic—Then and Now;" for evidence of satisfaction by segments of the work force, see Oscar B. Martinson and E. A. Wilkening, "Rural-Urban Differences in Job Satisfaction: Further Evidence," *Academy of Management Journal,* March 1984, pp. 199–206; and Garnett Stokes Shaffer, "Patterns of Work and Nonwork Satisfaction," *Journal of Applied Psychology,* February 1987, pp. 115–24.

[47] Sharon Nelton and Karen Berney, "Women: The Second Wave," *Nation's Business,* May 1987, pp. 20, 22.

[48] Results from these studies are discussed in Cathy Trost, "Men, Too, Wrestle with Career-Family Stress: Few Firms Offer Working Fathers Much Support," *The Wall Street Journal,* November 1, 1988, p. B1.

[49] Results from these studies can be found in Douglas T. Hall, "Promoting Work/Family Balance: An Organization-Change Approach," *Organizational Dynamics,* Winter 1990, pp. 5–18.

[50] The meta-analysis was conducted by Marianne Tait, Margaret Youtz Padgett, and Timothy T. Baldwin, "Job and Life Satisfaction: A Reevaluation of the Strength of the Relationship and Gender Effects as a Function of the Date of the Study," *Journal of Applied Psychology,* June 1989, pp. 502–07.

[51] See, for example, Kuo-Tsai Liou, Ronald D. Sylvia, and Gregory Brunk, "Non-

Work Factors and Job Satisfaction Revisited,'' *Human Relations,* January 1990, pp. 77–86.

52 Results are presented in Julian Barling and Alan Rosenbaum, ''Work Stressors and Wife Abuse,'' *Journal of Applied Psychology,* May 1986, pp. 346–48.

53 See Dirk D. Steiner and Donald M. Truxillo, ''An Improved Test of the Disaggregration Hypothesis of Job and Life Satisfaction,'' *Journal of Occupational Psychology,* March 1989, pp. 33–39; and Richard E. Kopelman, Jeffrey H. Greenhaus, and Thomas G. Connolly, ''A Model of Work, Family, and Interrole Conflict: A Construct Validation Study,'' *Organizational Behavior and Human Performance,* October 1983, pp. 198–215.

54 For complete details, see Robert J. Aiello, ''Employee Attitude Surveys: Impact on Corporate Decisions,'' *Public Relations Journal,* March 1983, p. 21.

55 Thorough discussion of these changes is provided by Frances J. Milliken, Jane E. Dutton, and Janice M. Beyer, ''Understanding Organizational Adaptation to Change: The Case of Work–Family Issues,'' *Human Resource Planning,* vol. 13, 1990, pp. 91–107; and Randall S. Schuler, ''Scanning the Environment: Planning for Human Resource Management and Organizational Change,'' *Human Resource Planning,* vol. 12, 1989, pp. 257–76.

56 Ann M. Morrison, ''Saving Our Schools,'' *Fortune,* Spring 1990, p. 8.

57 Statistics on the use of flextime can be found in Robert N. Lussier, ''Should Your Organization Use Flextime?'' *Supervision,* September 1990, pp. 14–16; and Table no. 643 in the U.S. Bureau of Labor Statistics, USDL News Release, *Annual Pay Levels in Metropolitan Areas,* 1988, p. 388.

58 See Nancy A. Mason, Wendy R. Perry, and Michael L. Ryan, ''Alternative Work Schedules for Female Pharmacists,'' *American Journal of Hospital Pharmacy,* January 1991, pp. 85–91; and Kathleen E. Christensen and Graham L. Staines, ''Flextime: A Viable Solution to Work/Family Conflict?'' *Journal of Family Issues,* December 1990, pp. 455–76.

59 The effectiveness of compressed workweeks was examined by Lisa Fischel-Wolovick, Connie Cotter, Ilene Masser, Emily Kelman-Bravo, Ronnie Sue Jaffe, Gary Rosenberg, and Beth Wittenberg, ''Alternative Work Scheduling for Professional Social Workers,'' *Administration in Social Work,* Winter 1988, pp. 93–102; and Randall B. Dunham, Jon L. Pierce, and Maria B. Castaneda, ''Alternative Work Schedules: Two Field Quasi-Experiments,'' *Personnel Psychology,* Summer 1987, pp. 215–42.

60 See Julie A. Cohen, ''Managing Tomorrow's Workforce Today,'' *Management Review,* January 1991, pp. 17–21; and Rober N. Lussier, ''Should Your Organization Use Job Sharing?'' *Supervision,* April 1990, pp. 9–11.

61 For a description of telecommuting programs, see Jonathan N. Goodrich, ''Telecommuting in America,'' *Business Horizons,* July–August 1990, pp. 31–37; and Michael Alexander, ''Travel-Free Commuting,'' *Nation's Business,* December 1990, pp. 33–37.

62 John Naisbitt, *Megatrends: Ten New Directions Transforming Our Lives* (New York: Warner Books, 1982), p. 36.

63 See Daniel C. Feldman, ''Risky Business: The Socialisation of Managers in the 21st Century,'' *Journal of Organizational Change Management,* vol. 3, 1990, pp. 16–29; and Gilbert Fuchsberg, ''Many Businesses Responding Too Slowly To Rapid Work Force Shifts, Study Says,'' *The Wall Street Journal,* July 20, 1990, p. B1.

64 Sal D. Rinella and Robert J. Kopecky, ''Tuition Payments Cut Job Turnover,'' *Nation's Business,* August 1989, p. 25.

65 For an interesting discussion of training patterns within the United States, see Jack

Gordon, "Where the Training Goes," *Training*, October 1990, pp. 51–69; and Geoffrey M. Smith, "Coping with the Coming Labor Shortage," *Vital Speeches of the Day*, August 15, 1989, pp. 669–71.

[66] See Irwin L. Goldstein and Harold W. Goldstein, "Training as an Approach for Organisations to the Challenge of Human Resource Issues in the Year 2000," *Journal of Organizational Change Management*, vol. 3, 1990, pp. 30–41; "Labor Month in Review," *Monthly Labor Review*, December 1990, p. 2.

[67] Results from the survey are discussed in "Labor Month in Review," *Monthly Labor Review*, December 1990, p. 2.

[68] Descriptions of cafeteria benefit plans can be found in Sandy Grogan Dresser, "Employee Benefits: À La Carte," *Association Management*, April 1989, pp. 73–81.

[69] See "Labor Letter: A Special News Report on People and Their Jobs in Offices, Fields, and Factories," *The Wall Street Journal*, March 3, 1990, p. A1.; and Stanley D. Nollen, "The Work-Family Dilemma: How HR Managers Can Help," *Personnel*, May 1989, pp. 25–30.

[70] See Fairlee E. Winfield, *The Work & Family Sourcebook* (Greenvale, NY: Panel Publishers, 1988).

[71] The Conference Board study is discussed in Miriam Basch Scott, "Dependent Care: How Companies Help with Family Care," *Employee Benefit Plan Review*, May 1990, pp. 12–14.

[72] See Stephen E. Ewing, "Nourish Thy Children: Investing in Child Care to Nourish Corporate Productivity," *Vital Speeches of the Day*, June 12, 1990, pp. 517–19; and "Labor Letter: A Special News Report on People and Their Jobs in Offices, Fields, and Factories," *The Wall Street Journal*, September 26, 1990, p. A1.

[73] Adapted from Milton R. Blood, "Work Values and Job Satisfaction," *Journal of Applied Psychology*, December 1969, pp. 456–59.

PART

II

UNDERSTANDING AND MANAGING INDIVIDUAL BEHAVIOR

Individual Differences, Values, and Ethics

When you finish studying the material in this chapter, you should be able to:

- Distinguish between self-esteem and self-efficacy.
- Discuss how an internal locus of control differs from an external locus of control.
- Explain the role of arousal in introversion–extroversion.

- Explain how attitudes influence behavior in terms of the Fishbein and Ajzen model of behavioral intentions.
- Explain Carl Jung's cognitive styles typology.
- Distinguish between instrumental and terminal values.

- Identify and explain at least four steps for improving an organization's ethical climate.
- Discuss the contingency model for taking action against specific unethical practices.

OPENING CASE 3

The Inside Story of an Inside Trader

Sharon Hoogstraten

Dennis Levine made history. The disclosure of his misdeeds exposed those of Ivan Boesky, his illicit partner, and Boesky in turn led the government to Michael Milken and Drexel Burnham Lambert. The stocks Levine bought and sold through offshore bank accounts were mainly of target companies in soon-to-be-announced mergers. According to

the Securities and Exchange Commission, he made his largest single insider-trading profit on securities of Nabisco Brands. The SEC alleges that he bought 150,000 Nabisco shares some three weeks before the company announced merger talks with R.J. Reynolds in 1985. When the stock's price rose, Levine sold for a $2.7 million profit.

Here, for the first time, Levine tells his inside story, a personal odyssey to the heights of Wall Street and then down to its criminal depths. Boesky and others involved in these felonies differ with some aspects of Levine's story, but they are not telling their tales. A notable success as an investment banker on Wall Street, Levine was undone by ambition so intense it drove him over the line. Thereafter he found himself in a quagmire of deceit and betrayal.

Waking early in my Park Avenue apartment on May 12, 1986, I

read the morning papers, checked on the European securities markets, and ate breakfast with my wife, Laurie, then six weeks pregnant, and my son, Adam, who was 4. By 8 A.M. I was in downtown Manhattan, meeting with my staff at Drexel Burnham Lambert. At 33, I was a leading merger specialist and a partner in one of the most powerful investment banks on Wall Street. Among the many appointments on my calendar that day were meetings with two CEOs, including Revlon's Ronald Perelman, to discuss multibillion-dollar takeovers. I was a happy man.

In midafternoon two strangers, one tall and one short, came looking for me at Drexel. They didn't identify themselves, but the receptionist said they weren't dressed like clients. For ten months, I knew, the Securities and Exchange Commission had been investigating the Bahamian

---

What makes you *you*? What characteristics do you share with others? Which ones set you apart? Perhaps you have a dynamic personality and dress and act accordingly, while a low-key friend dresses conservatively and avoids crowds. Maybe your values, attitudes, and beliefs vary. Someone is politically active, someone else is not. Another person likes ear-splitting heavy metal music while still another prefers soft classical music. Some computer buffs would rather program than eat; other people suffer from computer phobia. Some employees pad their expense accounts without a second thought; others call the practice unethical and refrain. Thanks to a vast array of individual differences such as these, modern organizations have a rich and interesting human texture. On the other hand, individual differences make the manager's job endlessly challenging. (See OB in Action on p. 84 for a humorous look at individual differences.)

Growing work force diversity, as discussed in Chapter 2, compels manag-

OPENING CASE 3

(continued)

subsidiary of Bank Leu, the Swiss bank that had executed insider stock trades for me since 1980. That very morning I had spoken on the phone with one of the bank's employees, who reassured me that everything was under control. Still, I knew something was wrong, and I fled. While the authorities searched for me, I drove around New York in my BMW, making anxious calls on the car phone to my wife, my father, my boss. Before leaving the car, I hired a legal team headed by superstar lawyer Arthur Liman, who went on to serve as chief Senate counsel in the Iran-contra investigation and is now representing Michael Milken.

By the time I had hired Liman, my darkest secret was being broadcast by TV stations across the country. Early in the evening, I drove alone to the U.S. Attorney's office in lower Manhattan, expecting only to be served

with a subpoena. The federal officers read me my rights instead. At the nearby Metropolitan Correctional Center, they locked me up with a bunch of drug dealers in a cell whose odor I won't soon forget. It was like an out-of-body experience. As I ate cornflakes at the prison cafeteria the next morning, I watched the story of my arrest on a TV wake-up show. My carefully orchestrated career, years of planning and sacrifice, thousands of hours of work that had lifted me from Bayside, Queens, to the pinnacle of Wall Street—all reduced to nothing. Just like that.

I have had four years to reflect on the events leading up to my arrest. Part of that time—15 months and two days—I spent in Lewisburg federal prison camp in Pennsylvania. Getting your comeuppance is painful, and I have tried to take it on the chin. Unfortunately, my family also had to

endure the trauma of humiliation, disgrace, and loss of privacy—and they did nothing to deserve it.

I will regret my mistakes forever. I blame only myself for my actions and accept full responsibility for what I have done. No one led me down the garden path. I've gained an abiding respect for the fairness of our system of justice: For the hard work and creativity I brought to my investment banking career, I was well rewarded. When I broke the law, I was punished. The system works.

People always ask, *Why would somebody who's making over $1 million a year start trading on inside information?* That's the wrong question. Here's what I thought at the time, misguided as I was: When I started trading on nonpublic information in 1978, I wasn't making a million. I was a 25-year-old trainee at Citibank with a $19,000 annual salary. I was wet behind the ears, impa-

ers to view individual differences in a fresh new way. The case for this new perspective was recently outlined in Britain's *Journal of Managerial Psychology*:

For many years America's businesses sought homogeneity—a work force that believed in, supported, and presented a particular image. The notion of the company man dressed for success in the banker's blue or corporation's grey flannel suit was *de rigueur*. Those able to move into leadership positions succeeded to the extent they behaved and dressed according to a rather narrowly defined standard.

To compete today, and in preparation for the work force of tomorrow, successful businesses and organisations are adapting to both internal and external changes. New operational styles, language, customs, values, and even dress, are a real part of this adaptation. We now hear leaders talking about "valuing differences," and learning to "manage diversity."[1]

tient, burning with ambition. In those days people didn't think about insider trading the way they do now: You'd call it "a hot stock tip." The first U.S. criminal prosecution for insider trading wasn't until around that time, and it was not highly publicized. In the early years I regarded the practice as just a way to make some fast money. Of course I soon realized what I was doing was wrong, but I rationalized it as harmless. I told myself that the frequent run-ups in target-company stock prices before merger announcements proved others were doing it too.

Eventually insider trading became an addiction for me. It was just so easy. In seven years I built $39,750 into $11.5 million, and all it took was a 20-second phone call to my offshore bank a couple of times a month—maybe 200 calls total. My account was growing at 125 percent a year, compounded. Believe me, I felt a rush when I would check the price of one of my stocks on the office Quotron and learn I'd just made several hundred thousand dollars. I was confident that the elaborate veils of secrecy I had created—plus overseas bank-privacy laws— would protect me.

And Wall Street was crazy in those days. These were the 1980s, remember, the decade of excess, greed, and materialism. I became a go-go guy, consumed by the high-pressure, ultracompetitive world of investment banking. I was helping my clients make tens and even hundreds of millions of dollars. I served as the lead banker on Perelman's nearly $2 billion takeover of Revlon, four months of work that enabled Drexel to earn $60 million in fees. The daily exposure to such deals, the pursuit of larger and larger transactions, and the numbing effect of 60- to 100-hour workweeks helped erode my values and distort my judgment. In this unbelievable world of billions and billions of dollars, the millions I made by trading on nonpublic information seemed almost insignificant.

At the root of my compulsive trading was an inability to set limits. Perhaps it's worth noting that my legitimate success stemmed from the same root. My ambition was so strong it went beyond rationality, and I gradually lost sight of what constitutes ethical behavior. At each new level of success I set higher goals, imprisoning myself in a cycle from which I saw no escape. When I became a senior vice president, I wanted to be a managing director, and when I became a managing director, I wanted to be a client. If I was making $100,000 a year, I thought, *I can make $200,000.* And if I made $1 million, *I can make $3 million.* And so it went.

Competitive jealousy is normal

So rather than limiting diversity, as in the past, today's managers need to better understand and accommodate employee diversity and individual differences.

This chapter explores the following important dimensions of individual differences: (1) self-concept, (2) personality traits, (3) attitudes, (4) abilities, and (5) personal values and ethics. Figure 3–1 is a conceptual model showing the relationship between self-concept (how you view yourself), personality (how you appear to others), and key forms of self-expression. Considered as an integrated package, these factors provide a foundation for better understanding each organizational contributor as a unique and special individual.

• SELF-CONCEPT: THE I AND ME IN OB

Self is the core of one's conscious existence. Awareness of self is referred to as one's self-concept. Sociologist Viktor Gecas defines **self-concept** as "the concept the individual has of himself as a physical, social, and spiritual or

---

OPENING CASE 3

(concluded)

in business. Everybody wants to make more than the guy down the hall. It is the same in investment banking, but the numbers have more zeroes. Only a small percentage of the people these firms hire at the entry level of associate go on to make partner, and as the pyramid narrows, the competition grows ever more intense. By the time I made partner at Drexel, I was out of control.

My parents always encouraged me to play straight. I come from a strong, old-fashioned family; I was the youngest of three boys. My mother, Selma, was short-changed by life: She died of a stroke at 53, when I was 23. I'm still very close to my brothers, Larry and Robert, and my father, Philip; we talk often and meet for dinner and backyard barbecues.

Until he retired in 1983, my father worked long hours running his own business. His home-remodeling company finished basements, installed siding, added dormers, and so on. He taught me to work hard, believe in myself, and persevere. Off and on, from my early teens, he hired me to canvass door to door for new customers. Those cold calls were hard, but they showed me how to sell. I tried to overcome objections, never taking no for an answer.

As a kid I always worked. I would be shoveling snow or delivering newspapers. My folks gave me piano lessons from the time I was 7, and during my early teens I started making money as a musician, playing keyboards at parties and dances. By the end of high school I was in a band that sometimes opened local concerts by touring rock groups, including the Association and the Turtles. I wasn't a particularly dedicated student in those days, but I had a *lot* of friends.

I began studying the stock market when I was 13, reading books and investing part of my earnings—a few hundred dollars at first—in over-the-counter securities. In eighth grade I became a regular reader of *The Wall Street Journal*. By the time I enrolled at City University of New York's Bernard M. Baruch College in Manhattan, I was heading for a career in finance. Soon I narrowed my focus to investment banking, which seemed a great way to make money.

For Discussion

Why did Dennis Levine wind up on the wrong side of the law?

• Additional discussion questions linking this case with the following material appear at the end of this chapter.

Source: Excerpted from Dennis B. Levine, "The Inside Story of an Inside Trader," *Fortune*, May 21, 1990, pp. 80, 82.

---

moral being."[2] In other words, if you have a self-concept, you recognize yourself as a distinct human being. A self-concept would be impossible without the capacity to think. This brings us to the role of cognitions. **Cognitions** represent "any knowledge, opinion, or belief about the environment, about oneself, or about one's behavior."[3] Among many different types of cognitions, those involving anticipation, planning, goal setting, evaluating, and setting personal standards are particularly relevant to OB. Several cognition-based topics are discussed in later chapters. Differing cognitive styles are introduced in this chapter. Cognitions play a central role in social perception, as will be discussed in Chapter 4. Also, as we will see in Chapters 5 and 6, modern motivation theories and techniques are powered by cognitions. Successful self-management, covered in Chapter 7 requires cognitive support.

Importantly, ideas of self and self-concept vary from one historical era to another, from one socioeconomic class to another, and from culture to culture.[4] How well one detects and adjusts to different cultural notions of self can spell the difference between success and failure in international

OB IN ACTION

So Who's Normal?

It takes all kinds of people to make a world. Indeed, the longer I am around the stranger other people seem. And although it is with some modesty and reluctance, I have come to the conclusion I am one of the very few normal people left in my circle of friends.

I am not trying to make a case that normality has totally left the human race; but why can't other people stick to standard behavior the way I do?

For example, I have a friend who dotes on cheesecake. At a restaurant he asks for the dessert menu. He looks it over for five minutes—and always decides on cheesecake. He considers himself an outstanding authority on cheesecake.

Once, driving through Iowa, we stopped at a diner and asked for cheesecake, which they didn't have. The owner, being a public-minded citizen, recommended a restaurant in a town 40 miles back which was world famous for its cheesecake. So, at the insistence of my friend, we drove the 40 miles only to find the owner was all sold out. To say this put a strain on our relationship is one of the great understatements of the year.

Equally weird is my friend who always expects to find a valuable coin with a rare date. He takes 15 minutes after paying his dinner check to examine his change.

He will often try trading some of the coins back for other coins. This is really tiresome because even if he isn't the one paying the check he will look over your shoulder and poke the pennies around.

Not all peculiar people are men. We have a female friend who has a very maddening habit. If one admires her dress, she says, "Yes, I got this at Lord and Taylor, May 26, the day I had lunch with Cousin Etta at the Spanish restaurant."

Once I tried to recall a picnic when we first met. "Oh, that was June 15," she said. "The day it rained in the afternoon, and two days after Sara Potts got engaged to the airline captain, and three days before we bought the new car."

She even remembers the day she had her car's oil changed.

I don't have any hang-ups on cheesecake. I never examine the dates on coins. I certainly don't remember the day I had the oil changed, or, for that matter, the date I proposed to my wife. That's why I lay claim to the fact I am among the few normal people left in the world.

Of course I avoid stepping on the cracks in the sidewalk, but I don't think that counts.

Source: Guernsey Le Pelley, "Normal People," *The Christian Science Monitor*, October 12, 1989, p. 19.

dealings. For example, as detailed in International OB, page 86, Japanese–U.S. communication and understanding is often hindered by significantly different degrees of self-disclosure. With a comparatively large public self, Americans pride themselves in being open, honest, candid, and to the point. Meanwhile, Japanese, who culturally discourage self-disclosure, typically

• **FIGURE 3-1**   A Conceptual Model for the Study of Individual Differences in OB

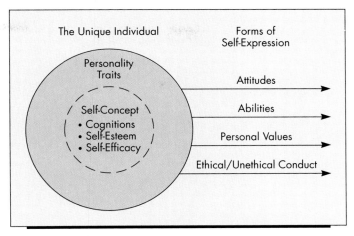

view Americans as blunt, prying, and insensitive to formalities. For their part, Americans tend to see Japanese as distant, cold, and evasive.[5] One culture is not right and the other wrong. They are just different, and a key difference involves culturally rooted conceptions of self and self-disclosure.

Keeping this cultural qualification in mind, let us explore two topics invariably mentioned when behavioral scientists discuss self-concept. They are self-esteem and self-efficacy. Each deserves a closer look by those who want to better understand and effectively manage people at work.

Self-Esteem

Self-esteem is a belief about one's own worth based on an overall self-evaluation.[6] Those with low self-esteem tend to view themselves in negative terms. They do not feel good about themselves, tend to have trouble dealing effectively with others, and are hampered by self-doubts. High self-esteem individuals, in contrast, see themselves as worthwhile, capable, and acceptable. Although high self-esteem generally is considered a good thing because it is associated with better performance and greater satisfaction, recent research uncovered a flaw among those with high self-esteem. Specifically, high self-esteem subjects tended to become egotistical and boastful when faced with pressure situations.[7] So self- esteem, like many other good things in life, appears to be best in moderation.

Feelings of self-esteem are shaped by our circumstances and how others treat us. Researchers who tracked 654 young adults (192 male; 462 female) for eight years found higher self-esteem among those in school or working full-time than among those with part-time jobs or unemployed.[8] Skillful parental attention during one's developmental years also is critical. Consider, for example, the following bit of advice to busy managers who want to be good parents:

INTERNATIONAL OB

Culture Dictates the Degree of Self-Disclosure in Japan and the United States

Japanese Public and Private Self

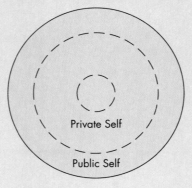

American Public and Private Self

Private Self (the self not revealed to others)
Public Self (the self made accessible to others)

Survey research in Japan and the United States uncovered the following *distinct contrasts* in Japanese versus American self-disclosure:

* Americans disclosed nearly as much to strangers as the Japanese did to their own fathers.

* Americans reported two to three times greater physical contact with parents and twice greater contact with friends than the Japanese.

* The Japanese may be frightened at the prospect of being communicatively invaded (because of the unexpected spontaneity and bluntness of the American); the American is annoyed at the prospect of endless formalities and tangential replies.

* American emphasis on self-assertion and talkativeness cultivates a communicator who is highly self-oriented and expressive; the Japanese emphasis on "reserve" and "sensitivity" cultivates a communicator who is other-oriented and receptive.

Source: Adapted from Dean C. Barnlund, "Public and Private Self in Communicating with Japan," *Business Horizons*, March–April 1989, pp. 32–40.

The most important thing a parent can do for a child is to encourage a high sense of self-esteem. Easier said than done, of course. The tricky part is helping children set appropriate, satisfying goals and then providing an environment that lets them reach the goals on their own. Building your child's self-esteem is an inconvenient, time-consuming, and maddeningly imprecise occupation, and don't be amazed if you mess up. . . . But kids who have a sense of self-worth flourish.[9]

Accordingly, a job-related laboratory study found high self-esteem individuals more willing to accept the challenge of difficult goals than did low self-esteem individuals.[10] Goal setting, as we will see in Chapter 6, is a well-documented motivational technique for improving job performance. Moreover, a study of computer-manufacturing employees found successful work teams to have significantly higher average self-esteem scores than unsuccessful teams.[11] Thus, both individual and group job performance tend to improve as self-esteem increases.

Organization-Based Self-Esteem   The self-esteem referred to above is a global belief about oneself. But what about self-esteem in organizations, a more restricted context of greater importance to managers? A model of organization-based self-esteem was recently developed and validated with seven studies involving 2,444 teachers, students, managers, and employees. The researchers defined **organization-based self-esteem (OBSE)** as ''the self-perceived value that individuals have of themselves as organization members acting within an organizational context.''[12] Those scoring high on OBSE tend to view themselves as important, worthwhile, effectual, and meaningful within the context of their employing organization. Take a moment to complete the brief OBSE questionnaire in the OB Exercise. This exercise will help you better understand the concept of organization-based self-esteem, as well as assessing the supportiveness of your work setting. (Arbitrary norms for comparison purposes are: Low OBSE = 10–20; Moderate OBSE = 21–39; High OBSE = 40–50.)

A basic model of OBSE is displayed in Figure 3–2. On the left-hand side of the model are three primary determinants of organization-based self-esteem. OBSE tends to increase when employees believe their supervisors

---

OB EXERCISE

How Strong Is Your Organization-Based Self-Esteem (OBSE)?

Instructions:
Relative to your present (or last) job, how strongly do you agree or disagree with each of the following statements?

	Strongly Disagree				Strongly Agree
1. I count around here.	1—2—3—4—5				
2. I am taken seriously around here.	1—2—3—4—5				
3. I am important around here.	1—2—3—4—5				
4. I am trusted around here.	1—2—3—4—5				
5. There is faith in me around here.	1—2—3—4—5				
6. I can make a difference around here.	1—2—3—4—5				
7. I am valuable around here.	1—2—3—4—5				
8. I am helpful around here.	1—2—3—4—5				
9. I am efficient around here.	1—2—3—4—5				
10. I am cooperative around here.	1—2—3—4—5				

Total score = _____

Source: Adapted from discussion in Jon L. Pierce, Donald G. Gardner, Larry L. Cummings, and Randall B. Dunham, ''Organization-Based Self-Esteem: Construct Definition, Measurement, and Validation,'' *Academy of Management Journal*, September 1989, pp. 622–48.

• **FIGURE 3–2**   The Determinants and Consequences of Organization-Based Self-Esteem (OBSE)

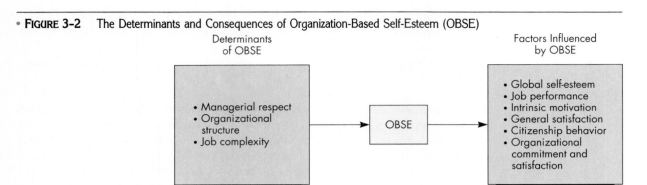

Source: Adapted from discussion in Jon L. Pierce, Donald G. Gardner, Larry L. Cummings, and Randall B. Dunham, "Organization-Based Self-Esteem: Construct Definition, Measurement, and Validation," *Academy of Management Journal*, September 1989, pp. 622–48.

have a genuine concern for employees' welfare. Flexible, organic organization structures generate higher OBSE than do mechanistic (rigid bureaucratic) structures (the organic-mechanistic distinction is discussed in Chapter 18). Complex and challenging jobs foster higher OBSE than do simple, repetitive, and boring jobs. Significantly, these same factors also are associated with greater task motivation.

Factors positively influenced by high OBSE and negatively impacted by low OBSE are listed in the right-hand side of Figure 3–2. Intrinsic motivation refers to personal feelings of accomplishment. Citizenship behavior involves doing things beneficial for the organization itself. The other consequences of OBSE are self-explanatory. In sum, active enhancement of organization-based self-esteem promises to build a very important cognitive bridge to greater productivity and satisfaction.

Practical Tips for Building on-the-Job Self-Esteem   According to a study by the American Society for Personnel Administration (now the Society for Human Resource Management), managers can build employee self-esteem in four ways:

1. Be supportive by showing concern for personal problems, interests, status, and contributions.
2. Offer work involving variety, autonomy, and challenges that suit the individual's values, skills, and abilities.
3. Strive for management-employee cohesiveness and build trust. (Trust, an important teamwork element, is discussed in Chapter 11.)
4. Have faith in each employee's self-management ability (see Chapter 7). Reward successes.[13]

Self-Efficacy

Have you noticed how those who are confident about their ability tend to succeed, while those who are preoccupied with failing tend to fail? Perhaps that explains the comparative golfing performance of your authors! One consistently stays in the fairways and hits the greens. The other spends the day thrashing through the underbrush, wading in water hazards, and blasting out of sand traps. At the heart of this performance dilemma is a specific

• People achieve self-efficacy more readily—and in spite of adversity—when they *believe* they will be successful and thus work harder toward that end.
(Charles Gupton/Stock Boston)

dimension of self-esteem called self-efficacy. **Self-efficacy** is a person's belief about his or her chances of successfully accomplishing a specific task. According to one OB writer, "self-efficacy arises from the gradual acquisition of complex cognitive, social, linguistic, and/or physical skills through experience."[14] Researchers have documented a strong linkage between high self-efficacy expectations and success in widely varied physical and mental tasks, anxiety reduction, addiction control, pain tolerance, and illness recovery.[15] Oppositely, those with low self-efficacy expectations tend to have low success rates. Chronically low self-efficacy is associated with a condition called **learned helplessness,** the severely debilitating belief that one has no control over one's environment.[16] Although self-efficacy sounds like some sort of mental magic, it operates in a very straightforward manner, as a model will show.

What Are the Mechanisms of Self-Efficacy?   A basic model of self-efficacy is displayed in Figure 3–3. It draws upon the work of Stanford psychologist Albert Bandura. Let us explore this model with a simple illustrative task. Imagine you have been told to prepare and deliver a 10-minute talk to an OB class of 50 students on the workings of the self-efficacy model in Figure 3–3. Your self-efficacy calculation would involve cognitive appraisal of the interaction between your perceived capability and situational opportunities and obstacles.

As you begin to prepare for your presentation, the four sources of self-efficacy beliefs would come into play. Because prior experience is the most potent source, according to Bandura, it is listed first and connected to self-efficacy beliefs with a solid line. Past success in public speaking would boost your self-efficacy. But bad experiences with delivering speeches would foster low self-efficacy. Regarding behavior models as a source of self-efficacy beliefs, you would be influenced by the success or failure of your classmates in delivering similar talks. Their successes would tend to bolster you (or perhaps their failure would if you were very competitive and had

• **FIGURE 3-3**   A Model of How Self-Efficacy Beliefs Can Pave the Way for Success or Failure

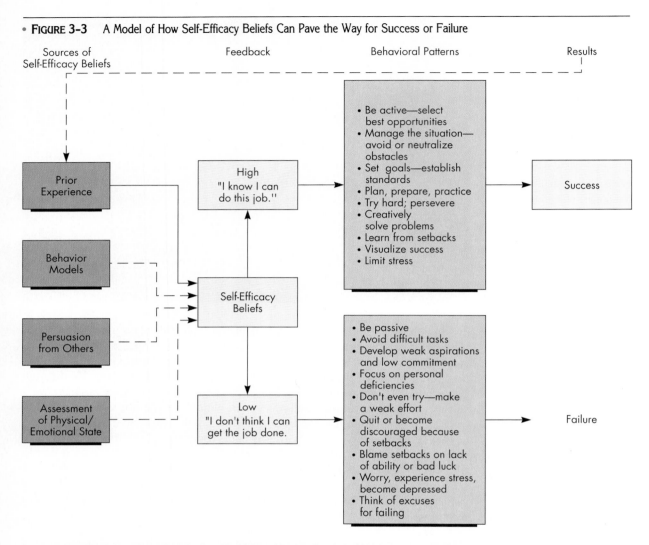

Sources: Adapted from discussion in Albert Bandura, "Regulation of Cognitive Processes through Perceived Self-Efficacy," *Developmental Psychology*, September 1989, pp. 729–35, and Robert Wood and Albert Bandura, "Social Cognitive Theory of Organizational Management," *Academy of Management Review*, July 1989, pp. 361–84.

high self-esteem). Likewise, any supportive persuasion from your class-mates that you will do a good job could enhance your self-efficacy. Physical and emotional factors also might impact your self-confidence. A sudden case of laryngitis or a bout of stage fright could cause your self-efficacy expecta-tions to plunge. Your cognitive evaluation of the situation then would yield a self-efficacy belief—ranging from high to low expectations for success. Importantly, self-efficacy beliefs are not merely boastful statements based on bravado; they are deep convictions supported by experience.

Moving to the *behavioral patterns* portion of Figure 3–3, we see how self-efficacy beliefs are acted out. In short, if you have high self-efficacy about giving your 10-minute speech you will work harder, more creatively, and longer when preparing for your talk than will your low-self-efficacy class-mates. The results would then take shape accordingly. People program themselves for success or failure by enacting their self-efficacy expectations. Positive or negative results subsequently become feedback for one's base of personal experience.

Self-Efficacy Implications for Managers   On-the-job research evidence encourages managers to nurture self-efficacy, both in themselves and in others. In one study, for example, the sales performance of life insurance agents was much better among those with high self-efficacy.[17] Self-efficacy requires constructive action in each of the following managerial areas:

1. **Recruiting/selection/job assignments**—Interview questions can be designed to probe job applicants' general self-efficacy as a basis for determining orientation and training needs. Pencil-and-paper tests for self-efficacy are not in an advanced stage of development and validation. Care needs to be taken not to hire solely on the basis of self-efficacy because studies have detected below-average self-esteem and self-efficacy among women and protected minorities.[18]

2. **Job design**—Complex, challenging, and autonomous jobs tend to enhance perceived self-efficacy. Boring, tedious jobs generally do the opposite.

OB IN ACTION

How the New Head of Wang Laboratories Unleashed a Middle Manager's Self-Efficacy

When he arrived at Wang . . . [in mid-1989 as the new chief executive officer, Richard Miller] found he had plenty of leadership talent already aboard. "To find the stars," he says, "all you have to do is provide the vision to let the good ideas and bright people surface." He believes that examining a manager's past performance does little good—you have to go by instinct. In most cases, he says, you can pick out a company's real leaders in the first 60 days of a turnaround.

 Putting them to work may entail breaking with old habits, in ways that genuinely do empower people. Miller called a middle manager to his office (something that would not have happened under the prior regime) and gave him the biggest assignment of his career: analyzing Wang's computer pricing worldwide. In just three weeks the manager surveyed pricing for the company and its competitors on six continents. He not only found where the problems were, but also suggested how to fix them. In the process the man happened to hear some complaints about service, so he suggested that with some of the computers Wang sells, it should give away a fax machine and a number for a fax installed on Miller's desk. If a customer had a complaint he could fax the CEO directly. Miller promptly bought the idea. He claims that so far he has received only compliments, and he likes feeling more in touch with customers. The larger point, he says, is that the middle manager took the initiative, acted fast, and came up with creative solutions: "In my book, that's leadership."

Source: Excerpted from Brian Dumaine, "The New Turnaround Champs," *Fortune*, July 16, 1990, pp. 39–40.

3. **Training and development**—Employees' self-efficacy expectations for key tasks can be improved through guided experience, mentoring, and role modeling (see Chapters 7 and 8).

4. **Self-management**—Systematic self-management training, as discussed in Chapter 7, involves enhancement of self-efficacy expectations.

5. **Goal setting**—Goal difficulty needs to match the individual's perceived self-efficacy. As self-efficacy and performance improve, goals can be made more challenging.

6. **Coaching**—Those with low self-efficacy and employees victimized by learned helplessness need lots of constructive pointers and positive feedback.

7. **Leadership**—Needed leadership talent surfaces when top management gives high self-efficacy managers a chance to prove themselves under pressure (see, for example, OB in Action on p. 91).

8. **Rewards**—Small successes need to be rewarded as stepping-stones to a stronger self-image and greater achievements.

Now that we have a better understanding of self-image, our attention turns to how others see us as unique individuals.

• PERSONALITY AND ORGANIZATIONAL BEHAVIOR

Individuals have their own way of thinking and acting, their own unique style or *personality*. **Personality** is defined as the combination of stable physical and mental characteristics that give the individual his or her identity. These characteristics or traits, including how you look, think, act, and feel,[19] are the product of interacting genetic and environmental influences (see Figure 3–4).

• **FIGURE 3-4**   How One's Personality Takes Shape

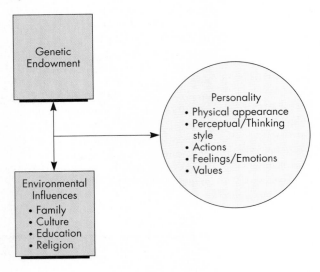

Over the years, vigorous debate has surrounded the issue of whether nature (genetic endowment) or nurture (environmental influences) primarily determines personality. As discussed in OB in Action on page 94, the researchers' best answer can be expressed in the following general formula: 50 percent Nature + 50 percent Nurture = Personality. These are average proportions across all characteristics. However, certain characteristics, as pointed out in OB in Action, deviate from a 50–50 split.

In this section, we examine two key personality traits. They are: locus of control and introversion–extroversion. Our rationale for selecting these two particular traits is twofold. First, they can be readily inferred from everyday behavior, without the aid of sophisticated personality testing. (For words of caution about personality testing, see Advanced Learning Module B at the back of this book.) Second, they can significantly affect organizational and interpersonal effectiveness.

Locus of Control: Self or Environment?

Individuals vary in terms of how much personal responsibility they take for their behavior and its consequences. Julian Rotter, a personality researcher, identified a dimension of personality he labeled *locus of control* to explain these differences. He proposed that people tend to attribute the causes of their behavior primarily to either themselves or environmental factors.[20] This personality trait produces distinctly different behavior patterns.

• Although they were raised apart, when they met, the Springer twins found that they had an uncanny number of common qualities: both have dogs named Toy; both chain-smoke the same brand of cigarette. The question: Nature or nurture? Which plays a greater part?
(*Enrico Ferorelli*)

OB in Action

Are We the Product of Nature or Nurture?

Like many identical twins reared apart, Jim Lewis and Jim Springer found they had been leading eerily similar lives. Separated four weeks after birth in 1940, the Jim twins grew up 45 miles apart in Ohio and were reunited in 1979. Eventually they discovered that both drove the same model blue Chevrolet, chain-smoked Salems, chewed their fingernails and owned dogs named Toy. Each had spent a good deal of time vacationing at the same three-block strip of beach in Florida. More important, when tested for such personality traits as flexibility, self-control and sociability, the twins responded almost exactly alike.

The two Jims were the first of 348 pairs of twins studied at the University of Minnesota, home of the Minnesota Center for Twin and Adoption Research. Much of the investigation concerns the obvious question raised by siblings like Springer and Lewis: How much of an individual's personality is due to heredity? The center's answer: about half.

The project, summed up in a scholarly paper that has been submitted to the *Journal of Personality and Social Psychology,* is considered the most comprehensive of its kind. The Minnesota researchers report the results of six-day tests of their subjects, including 44 pairs of identical twins who were brought up apart. Well-being, alienation, aggression and the shunning of risk or danger were found to owe as much or more to nature as to nurture. Of eleven key traits or clusters of traits analyzed in the study, researchers estimated that a high of 61 percent of what they call "social potency" (a tendency toward leadership or dominance) is inherited, while "social closeness" (the need for intimacy, comfort and help) was lowest, at 33 percent.

The study finds that even a penchant for conservatism seems to have a genetic base. One of the eleven traits, traditionalism (respect for authority, rules, standards and high morals), was discovered to be 60% inherited. Among other traits listed at more than 50% were vulnerability or resistance to stress, dedication to hard work and achievement and the capacity for being caught up in imaginative experiences.

The director of the study, Thomas Bouchard, cautions that the numbers so far may not be strictly accurate. "In general," he says, "the degree of genetic influence tends to be around 50%."

Source: John Leo, "Exploring the Traits of Twins," *Time*, January 12, 1987, p. 63. Copyright 1987 Time Inc. All rights reserved. Reprinted by permission from *Time*.

People who believe they control the events and consequences that affect their lives are said to possess an **internal locus of control.** For example, such a person tends to attribute positive outcomes, like getting a passing grade on an exam, to his or her own abilities. Similarly, an "internal" tends to blame negative events, like failing an exam, on personal shortcomings—not studying hard enough, perhaps. Many entrepreneurs eventually succeed because their *internal* locus of control helps them overcome setbacks and disappointments. They see themselves as masters of their own fate.

On the other side of this personality dimension are those who believe their performance is the product of circumstances beyond their immediate control. These individuals are said to possess an **external locus of control** and

---

OB EXERCISE

Where Is Your Locus of Control?

Circle one letter for each pair of items, in accordance with your beliefs:

1. A. Many of the unhappy things in people's lives are partly due to bad luck.
   B. People's misfortunes result from the mistakes they make.
2. A. Unfortunately, an individual's worth often passes unrecognized no matter how hard he tries.
   B. In the long run, people get the respect they deserve.
3. A. Without the right breaks one cannot be an effective leader.
   B. Capable people who fail to become leaders have not taken advantage of their opportunities.
4. A. I have often found that what is going to happen will happen.
   B. Trusting to fate has never turned out as well for me as making a decision to take a definite course of action.
5. A. Most people don't realize the extent to which their lives are controlled by accidental happenings.
   B. There really is no such thing as "luck."
6. A. In the long run, the bad things that happen to us are balanced by the good ones.
   B. Most misfortunes are the result of lack of ability, ignorance, laziness, or all three.
7. A. Many times I feel I have little influence over the things that happen to me.
   B. It is impossible for me to believe that chance or luck plays an important role in my life.

Note: In determining your score, A = 0 and B = 1.

Source: Excerpted from Julian B. Rotter, "Generalized Expectancies for Internal versus External Control of Reinforcement," *Psychological Monographs*, vol. 80 (Whole no. 609, 1966), pp. 11–12.

---

tend to attribute outcomes to environmental causes, such as luck or fate. Unlike someone with an internal locus of control, an "external" would attribute a passing grade on an exam to something external (an easy test or a good day) and attribute a failing grade to an unfair test or problems at home. A shortened version of an instrument Rotter developed to measure one's locus of control is presented in the OB Exercise. (Arbitrary norms for this shortened version are: 1–3 = External locus of control; 4 = Balanced internal and external locus of control; 5–7 = Internal locus of control.) Where is your locus of control: internal, external, or a combination?

Research Findings on Locus of Control Researchers have found significant and important behavioral differences between internals and externals:

- Internals display greater work motivation.
- Internals have stronger expectations that effort leads to performance.
- Internals exhibit higher performance on tasks involving learning or problem solving, when performance leads to valued rewards.
- There is a stronger relationship between job satisfaction and performance for internals than externals.
- Internals obtain higher salaries and greater salary increases than externals.
- Externals tend to be more anxious than internals.[21]

Implications of Locus of Control Differences for Managers   The above summary of research findings on locus of control has important implications for managing people at work. Let us examine two of them.

First, since internals have a tendency to believe they control the work environment through their behavior, they will attempt to exert control over the work setting. This can be done by trying to influence work procedures, working conditions, task assignments, or relationships with peers and supervisors. As these possibilities imply, internals may resist a manager's attempts to closely supervise their work. Therefore, management may want to place internals in jobs requiring high initiative and low compliance. Externals, on the other hand, might be more amenable to highly structured jobs requiring greater compliance. Direct participation also can bolster the attitudes and performance of externals. This conclusion comes from a recent field study of 85 computer system users in a wide variety of business and government organizations. Externals who had been significantly involved in designing their organization's computer information system had more favorable attitudes toward the system than their external-locus co-workers who had not participated.[22]

Second, locus of control has implications for reward systems. Given that internals have a greater belief that their effort leads to performance, internals likely would prefer and respond more productively to incentives such as merit pay or sales commissions.[23]

Introversion-Extroversion

Picture two friends at a large party; one is introverted and the other is extroverted. Why is it the introvert probably will retreat to a quiet corner while the extrovert might end up being the life of the party? H. J. Eysenck, an esteemed psychologist, proposed a theory of personality that answers this question.

Arousal Is the Key   Eysenck's theory centers on the concept of arousal. Arousal refers to an individual's level of activation, alertness, or vigor. A combination of both internal (physiological) and external stimulation determines the level of arousal. Greater stimulation means greater arousal. Eysenck's theory is based on three key ideas supported by many years of research. First, introverts and extroverts inherently are different in terms of their level of arousal. On the average, introverts have a higher level of internal arousal than extroverts. Second, there is an optimal level of arousal. Finally, individuals will try to alleviate the difference between their inherent and optimal levels of arousal. By considering these ideas simultaneously, we can better understand the systematic differences in behavior exhibited by introverts and extroverts.

A personality expert noted:

> Extroverts and introverts, in learning to adapt to their environments, adopt different strategies for resolving the conflict between inherent level of arousal and optimum level of arousal. The extrovert must work to raise his level of arousal to the optimum. Therefore he seeks stimulation: interaction with others, novel experiences, stimuli of greater complexity, variety and intensity. Stimuli, if repeated often, lose their arousing quality. Much of the extrovert's behavior can be

• TABLE 3-1   Introverts and Extroverts Exhibit Different Patterns of Behavior

Behavioral Characteristics	
Introverts	**Extroverts**
Are more highly aroused in the morning	Are more highly aroused in the afternoon
Like to work with ideas	Like to work with people or things
Have a hard time expressing ideas in a clear fashion	More expressive with words
Work best when they are not bothered by competing stimuli (interruptions)	Work best when they are stimulated by competing stimuli (noise)
Do better on tasks requiring vigilance	Do not perform well on unstimulating tasks
Tend to be cautious and careful	Tend to be talkative and outgoing

Source: Adapted from D. W. J. Corcoran, "Introversion–Extroversion, Stress, and Arousal," in *Dimensions of Personality: Papers in Honour of H J Eysenck,* ed. Richard Lynn (New York: Pergamon Press, 1981).

seen in terms of this constant quest for stimulation. . . . Introverts, on the other hand, must work to reduce incoming stimulation: they prefer their own company, or the company of well-established companions, they follow well-worn and predictable paths, they shun excessive sensory input.[24]

Important behavioral differences between introverts and extroverts are highlighted in Table 3–1.

Implications for Management   Eysenck's theory and supporting research provide guidance for understanding and appropriately managing introverts and extroverts.[25] For example, a person's level of arousal should be considered when providing feedback about performance. Feedback, as an important source of external stimulation, would increase arousal. Because extroverts actively seek outside stimulation to compensate for their lower internal stimulation, they can be expected to respond more favorably than introverts to supervisory coaching and feedback. Likewise, extroverts feel more comfortable serving on committees and participating in problem-solving teams than do introverts. Considering the contrasting characteristics in Table 3–1, introverts and extroverts require different motivational approaches and job assignments.

Attention now turns to the important connection between attitudes and behavior.

• ATTITUDES AND BEHAVIOR

Hardly a day goes by without the popular media reporting the results of another attitude survey. The idea is to take the pulse of public opinion. What do we think about candidate X, the war on drugs, gun control, or abortion? In the workplace, meanwhile, managers conduct attitude surveys to monitor such things as job and pay satisfaction. All this attention to attitudes is based on the assumption that attitudes somehow influence behavior such as voting for someone, working hard, or quitting one's job. In this section, we will examine the connection between attitudes and behavior.

• Corporations recognize that their responsibilities go beyond their fiscal well-being.   *(Courtesy of PFIZER Inc.)*

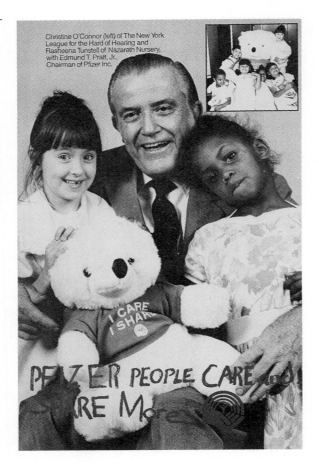

Christine O'Connor (left) of The New York League for the Hard of Hearing and Rasheena Tunstell of Nazareth Nursery, with Edmund T. Pratt, Jr., Chairman of Pfizer Inc.

Attitudes versus Values

An **attitude** is defined as "a learned predisposition to respond in a consistently favorable or unfavorable manner with respect to a given object."[26] Regarding the matter of consistency, researchers found the *job* attitudes of 5,000 middle-aged male employees to be very stable over a five-year period.[27] Employees with positive attitudes toward the job tended to maintain their positive attitudes. Negative-attitude employees tended to remain negative. Even those who changed jobs or occupations tended to maintain their prior job attitudes. Thus, attitudes tend to be consistent over time *and* across related situations.

Attitudes affect behavior at a different level than do values, a topic discussed later in this chapter. While values represent global beliefs that influence behavior across *all* situations, attitudes relate only to behavior directed toward *specific* objects, persons, or situations.[28] Values and attitudes generally, but not always, are in harmony. A manager who strongly values helpful behavior may have a negative attitude toward helping an unethical co-worker.

Because our cultural backgrounds and experiences vary, our attitudes and behavior vary. Attitudes are translated into behavior via behavioral intentions. Let us examine an established model of this important process.

• **FIGURE 3-5**   A Model of Behavioral Intention

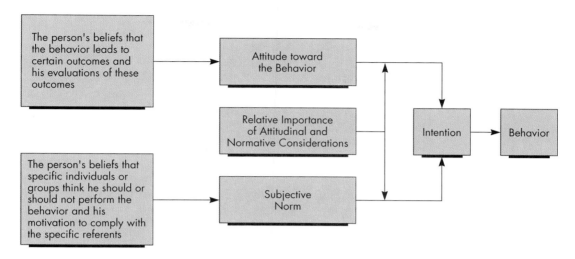

Note: Arrows indicate the direction of influence.

Source: Icek Ajzen and Martin Fishbein, *Understanding Attitudes and Predicting Social Behavior,* © 1980, p. 8. Reprinted by permission of Prentice Hall, Englewood Cliffs, New Jersey.

Attitudes and Behavioral Intentions

Behavioral scientists Martin Fishbein and Icek Ajzen developed a comprehensive model of behavioral intentions used widely to explain attitude—behavior relationships.[29] As depicted in Figure 3–5, an individual's intention to engage in a given behavior is the best predictor of that behavior. For example, the quickest and possibly most accurate way of determining whether an individual will quit his or her job is to have an objective third party ask if he or she intends to quit. A meta-analysis of 34 studies of employee turnover involving more than 83,000 employees, validated this direct approach. The researchers found stated behavioral intentions to be a better predictor of employee turnover than job satisfaction, satisfaction with the work itself, or organizational commitment.[30]

Although asking about intentions enables one to predict who will quit, it does not help explain *why* an individual would want to quit. Thus, to better understand why employees exhibit certain behaviors, such as quitting their jobs, one needs to consider their relevant attitudes. As shown in Figure 3–5, behavioral intentions are influenced both by one's attitude toward the behavior and by perceived norms about exhibiting the behavior. In turn, attitudes and subjective norms are determined by personal beliefs.

Beliefs Influence Attitudes   A person's belief system is a mental representation of his or her relevant surroundings, complete with probable cause-and-effect relationships. Beliefs are the result of direct observation and inferences from previously learned relationships. For example, we tend to infer that a laughing co-worker is happy. In terms of the strength of the relationship between beliefs and attitudes, beliefs do not have equal impacts on attitudes. Research indicates that attitudes are based on salient or important beliefs that may change as relevant information is received. For example, your beliefs about the quality of a particular automobile may change after hearing the car has been recalled for defective brakes.

In Figure 3–5, you can see that an individual will have positive attitudes toward performing a behavior when he or she believes the behavior is associated with positive outcomes. An individual is more likely to quit a job when he or she believes quitting will result in a better position and a reduction in job stress. In contrast, negative attitudes toward quitting will be formed when a person believes quitting leads to negative outcomes, such as the loss of money and status.

Beliefs Influence Subjective Norms   Subjective norms refer to perceived social pressure to perform a specific behavior. As noted by Ajzen and Fishbein, "Subjective norms are also a function of beliefs, but beliefs of a different kind, namely the person's beliefs that specific individuals or groups think he should or should not perform the behavior."[31] Subjective norms can exert a powerful influence on the behavioral intentions of those who are sensitive to the opinions of respected role models. This effect was observed in a recent laboratory study of students' intentions to apply for a job at companies that reportedly tested employees for drugs. The students generally had a negative attitude about companies that tested for drugs. But positive statements from influential persons about the need for drug testing tended to strengthen intentions to apply at companies engaged in drug testing.[32]

Thus, as diagrammed in Figure 3–5, both attitudes and subjective norms shape behavioral intentions.

Attitudinal Research and Application

Research has demonstrated that Fishbein and Ajzen's model accurately predicted intentions to buy consumer products, have children, and choose a career versus becoming a homemaker. Weight loss intentions and behavior, voting for political candidates, attending on-the-job training sessions, and reenlisting in the National Guard also have been predicted successfully by the model.[33] In fact, the model correctly identified 82 percent of the 225 National Guard personnel in the study who actually reenlisted.[34]

From a practical management standpoint, the behavioral intention model we have just reviewed has important implications. First, managers need to appreciate the dynamic relationships between beliefs, attitudes, subjective norms, and behavioral intentions when attempting to foster productive behavior. Although attitudes often are resistant to change, meaningful training experiences can have a favorable impact.[35] Redirection of subjective norms through clear and credible communication and organizational culture values is both possible and desirable. Finally, regular employee-attitude surveys can let managers know if their ideas and changes go with or against the grain of popular sentiment.

• ABILITIES AND PERFORMANCE

Individual differences in abilities and accompanying skills are a central concern for managers because nothing can be accomplished without appropriately skilled personnel. An **ability** represents a broad and stable characteristic responsible for a person's maximum—as opposed to typical—performance on mental and physical tasks. A **skill,** on the other hand, is the specific capacity to physically manipulate objects. Consider this difference as you imagine yourself being the only passenger on a small commuter airplane in which the pilot has just passed out. As the plane nose-dives, your effort and abilities will not be enough to save yourself and the pilot if you do not possess flying skills. As shown in Figure 3–6, successful performance (be it landing an airplane or performing any other job) depends on the right combination of effort, ability, and skill.

Abilities can profoundly affect an organization's bottom line. Selecting employees who have the ability to perform assigned jobs can significantly affect the organization's labor costs. A pair of personnel selection experts noted:

> The use of cognitive ability tests for selection in hiring can produce large labor cost savings, ranging from $18 million per year for small employers such as the Philadelphia police department . . . to $16 billion per year for large employers such as the federal government.[36]

Importantly, the cautions about personality testing and employment-related decisions in Advanced Learning Module B, apply equally to cognitive ability and intelligence testing.

This section explores important cognitive abilities and cognitive styles related to job performance.

Intelligence and Cognitive Abilities

Although experts do not agree on a specific definition, **intelligence** represents an individual's capacity for constructive thinking, reasoning, and problem solving. Historically, intelligence was believed to be an innate capacity,

• **FIGURE 3–6**   Performance Depends on the Right Combination of Effort, Ability, and Skill

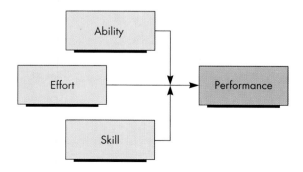

passed genetically from one generation to the next. Research since has shown, however, that intelligence (like personality) also is a function of environmental influences.[37] Organic factors have more recently been added to the formula as a result of mounting evidence of the connection between alcohol and drug abuse by pregnant women and intellectual development problems in their children.[38]

Two Types of Abilities   Human intelligence has been studied predominantly through the empirical approach. By examining the relationships between measures of mental abilities and behavior, researchers have statistically isolated major components of intelligence. Using this empirical procedure, pioneering psychologist Charles Spearman proposed in 1927 that all cognitive performance is determined by two types of abilities. The first can be characterized as a general mental ability needed for *all* cognitive tasks. The second is unique to the task at hand. For example, an individual's ability to complete crossword puzzles is a function of his or her broad mental abilities as well as the specific ability to perceive patterns in partially completed words.

Seven Major Mental Abilities   Through the years, much research has been devoted to developing and expanding Spearman's ideas on the relationship between cognitive abilities and intelligence. One research psychologist listed 120 distinct mental abilities. Table 3–2 contains definitions of the seven most frequently cited mental abilities. Of the seven abilities, personnel selection researchers have found verbal ability, numerical ability, spatial ability, and

---

• **TABLE 3-2**   Mental Abilities Underlying Performance

Ability	Description
1. Verbal comprehension	The ability to understand what words mean and to readily comprehend what is read
2. Word fluency	The ability to produce isolated words that fulfill specific symbolic or structural requirements (such as all words that begin with the letter *b* and have two vowels)
3. Numerical	The ability to make quick and accurate arithmetic computations such as adding and subtracting
4. Spatial	Being able to perceive spatial patterns and to visualize how geometric shapes would look if transformed in shape or position
5. Memory	Having good rote memory for paired words, symbols, lists of numbers, or other associated items
6. Perceptual speed	The ability to perceive figures, identify similarities and differences, and carry out tasks involving visual perception.
7. Inductive reasoning	The ability to reason from specifics to general conclusions

Source: Adapted from Marvin D. Dunnette, "Aptitudes, Abilities, and Skills," in *Handbook of Industrial and Organizational Psychology*, ed. Marvin D. Dunnette (Skokie, Ill.: Rand McNally, 1976), pp. 478–83.

inductive reasoning to be valid predictors of job performance for both minority and majority applicants.[38]

Jung's Cognitive Styles Topology

Within the context of Jung's theory, the term **cognitive style** refers to mental processes associated with how people perceive and make judgments from information. Although the landmark work on cognitive styles was completed in the 1920s by the noted Swiss psychoanalyst Carl Jung, his ideas did not catch on in the United States until the 1970s, when a complete English translation became available.[40]

Four Different Cognitive Styles   According to Jung, two dimensions influence perception and two others affect individual judgment. Perception is based on either *sensation,* using one's physical senses to interpret situations, or *intuition,* relying on past experience. In turn, judgments are made by either *thinking* or *feeling*. Finally, Jung proposed that an individual's cognitive style is determined by the pairing of one's perception and judgment tendencies. The resulting four cognitive styles are:

- Sensation/thinking (ST).
- Intuition/thinking (NT).
- Sensation/feeling (SF).
- Intuition/feeling (NF).

Characteristics of each style are presented in Figure 3–7.[41] (The exercise at the end of this chapter will help you determine your cognitive style.)

An individual with an ST style uses senses for perception and rational thinking for judgment. The ST-style person uses facts and impersonal analysis, and develops greater abilities in technical areas involving facts and objects. A successful engineer could be expected to exhibit this cognitive style. In contrast, a person with an NT style focuses on possibilities rather than facts and displays abilities in areas involving theoretical or technical development. This style would enhance the performance of a research scientist. Although an SF person likely is interested in gathering facts, he or she tends to treat others with personal warmth, sympathy, and friendliness. Successful counselors or teachers probably use this style. Finally, an individual with an NF style tends to exhibit artistic flair while relying heavily on personal insights rather than objective facts (see Figure 3–7).

Practical Research Findings   If Jung's cognitive styles typology is valid, then individuals with different cognitive styles should seek different kinds of information when making a decision. A study of 50 master-of-business-administration students found that those with different cognitive styles did in fact use qualitatively different information while working on a strategic planning problem.[42] Research also has shown that people with different cognitive styles prefer different careers. For example, people who rely on intuition prefer careers in psychology, advertising, teaching, and the arts.

Findings have further shown that individuals who make judgments based

• **FIGURE 3-7**   People Have Different Cognitive Styles and Corresponding Characteristics

	Decision Style			
	ST ⚡ Sensation/Thinking	**NT** △ Intuition/Thinking	**SF** ⬭ Sensation/Feeling	**NF** ⬭ Intuition/Feeling
Focus of Attention	Facts	Possibilities	Facts	Possibilities
Method of Handling Things	Impersonal Analysis	Impersonal Analysis	Personal Warmth	Personal Warmth
Tendency to Become	Practical and Matter-of-Fact	Logical and Ingenious	Sympathetic and Friendly	Enthusiastic and Insightful
Expression of Abilities	Technical Skills with Facts and Objects	Theoretical and Technical Developments	Practical Help and Services for People	Understanding and Communicating with People
	Technician	Planner	Teacher	Artist
Representative Occupation	Manager			

Source: William Taggart and Daniel Robey, "Minds and Managers: On the Dual Nature of Human Information Processing and Management," *Academy of Management Review,* April 1981, p. 190. Used with permission.

on the "thinking" approach have higher work motivation and quality of work life than those who take a "feeling" approach. In addition, individuals with a sensation mode of perception have higher job satisfaction than those relying on intuition.[43] Small business owner/managers with a "thinking" style made more money than their "feeling" counterparts. But no correlation was found between the four Jungian styles and small business owner/manager success.[44] On balance, Jung's cognitive styles typology is useful for training and development purposes but inadequate as a basis for personnel decisions.

• PERSONAL VALUES AND ETHICS

The 1990s have been called the "three E decade," with the three E's standing for Economy, Environment, and Ethics.[45] Inclusion of ethics in this lofty set of priorities is a clear sign of the times. A growing chorus of calls for greater attention to values and ethics has been heard recently from government, business, and academic leaders alike (see, for example, A Matter of Ethics). They are simply reacting to daily headlines about defense contract scandals, the S&L mess, campaign financing abuses, corporate misconduct, and the jailing of Wall Street's elite. This final section examines personal values and ethics, a pair of intertwined OB topics.

A MATTER OF ETHICS

Calls for Improvement

Fortune magazine's vision for the 1990s:

Perhaps America's richest gift to the rest of the world now would be to show that racial and ethnic harmony can work, that the relatively affluent 85 percent of society can help lift the 15 percent who remain poor, often despondently so. This will require a deeper sense of community, more Americans working together with values that are inclusive, nurturing, and caring, as opposed to competitive, individualistic, and selfish.

Kenneth R. Andrews, professor emeritus, Harvard Business School:

In summary, my ideas are quite simple. Perhaps the most important is that management's total loyalty to the maximization of profit is the principal obstacle to achieving higher standards of ethical practice. Defining the purpose of the corporation as exclusively economic is a deadly oversimplification, which allows overemphasis on self-interest at the expense of consideration of others.

The practice of management requires a prolonged play of judgment. Executives must find in their own will, experience, and intelligence the principles they apply in balancing conflicting claims. Wise men and women will submit their views to others, for open discussion of problems reveals unsuspected ethical dimensions and develops alternative viewpoints that should be taken into account.

Sources: The Staff of Fortune, "An American Vision for the 1990s," *Fortune*, March 26, 1990, p. 16, and Kenneth R. Andrews, "Ethics in Practice," *Harvard Business Review*, September–October 1989, p. 104.

Values Are Enduring Beliefs

According to Milton Rokeach, a leading researcher of values, a **value** is "an enduring belief that a specific mode of conduct or end-state of existence is personally or socially preferable to an opposite or converse mode of conduct or end-state of existence."[46] An individual's **value system** is defined by Rokeach as an "enduring organization of beliefs concerning preferable modes of conduct or end-states of existence along a continuum of relative importance."[47] Extensive research supports Rokeach's contention that different value systems go a long way toward explaining individual differences in behavior. Value→behavior connections have been documented for a wide variety of behaviors, ranging from weight loss, to shopping selections, to political party affiliation, to religious involvement, to choice of college major.[48]

What Is Your Value Profile?

Lifelong behavior patterns are dictated by values that are fairly well set by the time an individual is in his or her early teens. For example, consider how early experiences shaped the values of the young founder of Lotus

Development Corp., producer of the highly successful 1–2–3® personal computer spreadsheet program.

> In the 1960s, Mitchell D. Kapor revered the Beatles, grew his hair long, and joined protest marches against the Vietnam War. . . .
>
> While he now describes much of the turmoil of the 1960s as "no more than standard, adolescent growth pains," he says the period imparted a sense of social obligation that he has carried into corporate life. "Many people who came of age in the 60s share a common set of experiences and values," Kapor says. "It's possible to make money and at the same time to have a company where people are proud to work and can be happy."[49]

Although values tend to jell early in life, significant life events—such as having a child, business failure, or surviving a serious accident—can reshape one's value system during adulthood (see OB in Action).

In line with Rokeach's distinction between modes of conduct and end-states of existence, he developed a value survey instrument based on what he calls instrumental and terminal values. Take the time now to complete the brief value survey in the OB Exercise. Rokeach contends that his value survey can be used to assess the value systems of individuals or groups.

Instrumental Values   The instrumental values in Rokeach's value survey involve different categories of behavior. **Instrumental values** are alternative behaviors or means by which we achieve desired ends (terminal values). Someone who ranks the instrumental value "honest" high is likely to be honest more often than someone who ranks it low. Thus, instrumental values are a fairly good, but not perfect, predictor of actual behavior. What is your most important instrumental value? In a study of 83 female and 107 male college students, "loving" turned out to be the most highly rated instrumental value.[50]

Terminal Values   Highly ranked **terminal values,** such as wisdom or salvation, are end-states or goals the individual would like to achieve during his or her lifetime. Some would say terminal values are what life is all about. History is full of examples of people who were persecuted or put to death for their passionately held terminal values. Which of the 5 terminal values in the OB exercise did you rank the highest? In the survey of 190 college students mentioned above, "happiness" was the highest-ranked terminal value.[51]

Contrary to the impression created by the social turbulence of the 1960s and 1970s, a comparison of national samples conducted in 1968, 1971, 1974, and 1981 revealed relative stability in terminal values among Americans. Six terminal values consistently ranked in the top one-third were family security, a world at peace, freedom, self-respect, happiness, and wisdom.[52]

Value Conflicts

Managers need to be aware of three types of value conflict, both in themselves and in their co-workers. These are intrapersonal, interpersonal, and individual–organization value conflict.

OB IN ACTION

Have Tough Times Made Ted Turner a Kinder, Gentler Man?

Then: Spurned in his hostile raid on CBS Inc., in 1986 the founder and chairman of Turner Broadcasting flew to Hollywood to pay a pricey—some say laughable—$1.4 billion for MGM Entertainment Co.'s library of 3,300 vintage movies. Suddenly, the flamboyant cable pioneer found himself awash in debt and perilously close to losing his company.

Now: Of course, Turner got the last laugh. CNN's 1989 operating profits totaled an astounding $134 million. . . . And Turner Broadcasting's other holdings are strong. The purchase of MGM's storehouse of old movies, ridiculed as a bad deal at the time, has turned out to be a gold mine. . . .

[Turner's] ideological journey has been a long one. ''I dreamed about fighting when I was younger. I thought it was exciting,'' he told *Newsweek*. ''My heroes were Alexander the Great and General Patton, and now they're Gandhi and Martin Luther King. I don't want to hurt anybody.''

Sources: Scott Ticer, ''Captain Comeback,'' *Business Week*, July 17, 1989, p. 98; and Jonathan Alter, ''Ted's Global Village,'' *Newsweek*, June 11, 1990, p. 50.

• OB EXERCISE

Abbreviated Version of the Rokeach Value Survey*
Instructions:

Rank the five values in each of the two categories from 1 (most important to you) to 5 (least important to you):

Instrumental Values	Terminal Values
Rank	Rank
_____ Ambitious (hardworking, aspiring)	_____ A sense of accomplishment (lasting contribution)
_____ Honest (sincere, truthful)	_____ Happiness (contentedness)
_____ Independent (self-sufficient)	_____ Pleasure (an enjoyable, leisurely life)
_____ Loving (affectionate, tender)	_____ Salvation (saved, eternal life)
_____ Obedient (dutiful, respectful)	_____ Wisdom (a mature understanding of life)

*The complete copyrighted version lists 18 values in each category.

Source: Adapted from Milton Rokeach, *Beliefs, Attitudes, and Values* (San Francisco: Jossey-Bass, 1968).

Intrapersonal Value Conflict   Inner conflict and resultant stress typically are experienced when highly ranked instrumental or terminal values pull the individual in different directions. For example, in the category of instrumental values, ''honest'' can be pushed aside by ''ambitious'' and ''obedient'' in hard-driving managers. Former President Nixon's assistant, John Dean, discussed being victimized by this particular value conflict in his biography,

Blind Ambition. Similarly, intrapersonal conflicts between terminal values such as "pleasure" and "a sense of accomplishment" can be a problem. Otherwise serious students who have been tempted away from their homework by partying friends are well aware of this conflict of terminal values.

Yet another type of intrapersonal value conflict occurs when highly ranked instrumental and terminal values clash. For example, someone who assigns a high ranking to the instrumental value "independent" may be too aloof to achieve the terminal value "true friendship." Regarding your own value system, as measured by the Rokeach value survey, it is instructive to ask yourself if your top-ranked instrumental values will enable you to achieve your top-ranked terminal values.

Interpersonal Value Conflict   This problem generally is at the core of so-called personality clashes common at work and elsewhere. According to Rokeach and a colleague:

> Interpersonal value conflicts usually exist whenever a person is encountering difficulties in interpersonal relations with, say, spouse, parent, boss, employee, or group with which one identifies.[53]

Managers need to consider value differences when attempting to resolve interpersonal conflicts. (Conflict resolution techniques are discussed in Chapter 10.)

Individual–Organization Value Conflict   As discussed in Chapter 19, every organization has a distinct culture complete with its own prevailing value system. Not surprisingly, individual employees often find themselves at odds with their employing organization's value system. Generally, the individual's only options are to join the system, leave the system, or fight the system. In sum, managers need to consider each *individual's* unique value system when making judgments and decisions about people at work.

Ethics and Organizational Behavior

Among the individual differences discussed in this chapter, none is receiving greater attention today than the distinction between ethical and unethical managerial conduct. For instance, fraud is said to have played a role in 60 percent of the savings and loan failures that could eventually cost U.S. taxpayers $500 billion ($5,000 per household).[54] OB is an excellent vantage point for better understanding and improving workplace ethics. If OB can provide insights about managing human work behavior, then it can teach us something about avoiding *misbehavior*.

Ethics involves the study of moral issues and choices. It is concerned with right versus wrong, good versus bad, and the many shades of gray in supposedly black-and-white issues. Relative to the workplace, the terms *business ethics* and *management ethics* often are heard. But, according to James K. Baker, chairman of the U.S. Chamber of Commerce and head of a Fortune 500 company, "There is no such thing as business ethics. . . . There's only ethics. What you do over *here* is no different from what you do over *there*."[55] Moral implications spring from virtually every decision, both on and off the job. Managers are challenged to have moral imagination and the courage to do the right thing. To meet that challenge, present and future managers need a conceptual framework for ethical/unethical behavior.

In this section, we will discuss a general model of ethical behavior and two approaches to improving workplace ethics. The first approach is organizational in scope and preventive in nature. The second is personal and reactive.

A Model of Ethical Behavior   Ethical and unethical conduct is the product of a complex combination of influences (see Figure 3–8). Let us examine key aspects of this model.

At the center of the model in Figure 3–8 is the individual decision maker. He or she has a unique combination of personality characteristics and values leaning toward or away from ethical behavior. Personal experience with being rewarded or reinforced for certain behaviors and punished for others also shapes the individual's tendency to act ethically or unethically.

Next, we see in Figure 3–8 three major sources of influence on one's role expectations. People play many roles in life, including those of employee or manager. One's expectations for how those roles should be played are shaped by cultural, organizational, and general environmental factors. Focusing on one particular source of organizational influence, for example, many studies have found a tendency among middle- and lower-level managers to act unethically in the face of perceived pressure for results.[56] This helps explain the common situation in which top managers truthfully say ''I didn't tell anyone to do anything illegal or unethical'' when confronted with

---

• **FIGURE 3-8**   A Model of Ethical Behavior in the Workplace

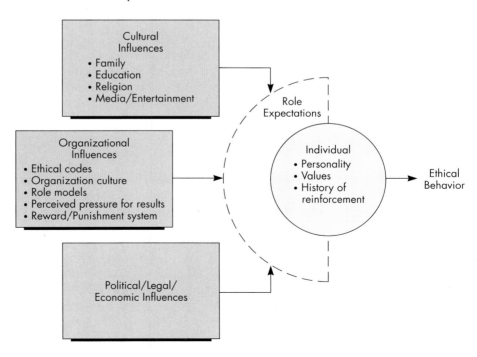

the unethical deeds of their employees. By fostering a pressure-cooker atmosphere for results, managers can unwittingly set the stage for unethical shortcuts by employees who seek to please and to be loyal to the company.

So, as can be seen in Figure 3–8, ethical or unethical behavior is the result of person–situation interaction. Workplace ethics can be improved by systematically managing toward ethical choices for as many factors in Figure 3–8 as possible.

How to Improve the Organization's Ethical Climate   A team of management researchers recently recommended the following actions for improving on-the-job ethics:[57]

• *Behave ethically yourself.* Managers are potent role models whose habits and actual behavior send clear signals about the importance of ethical conduct. Ethical behavior is a top-to-bottom proposition. For those who are not sure where to begin, Stanford engineering professor Ronald Howard, a frequent consultant to top management, offers the following basic rules: "don't lie, don't steal, and don't hurt."[58] Good advice!

• *Screen potential employees.* Surprisingly, employers are generally lax when it comes to checking references, credentials, transcripts, and other information on applicant résumés. More diligent action in this area can screen out those given to fraud and misrepresentation. *Honesty testing,* an increasingly popular screening technique involving pencil-and-paper integrity tests, has fair validity but is not a panacea.[59] In the United States, the Employee Polygraph Protection Act of 1988 severely restricted the use of so-called lie detectors in the private business sector.[60] Questionable validity and rampant abuses prompted passage of this legislation.

• *Develop a meaningful code of ethics.* Codes of ethics can have a positive impact if they satisfy these four criteria: (1) they are *distributed* to every employee; (2) they are firmly *supported* by top management; (3) they refer to *specific* practices and ethical dilemmas likely to be encountered by target employees (e.g., salespersons paying kickbacks, purchasing agents receiving payoffs, laboratory scientists doctoring data, or accountants "cooking the books"), and (4) they are evenly *enforced* with rewards for compliance and strict penalties for noncompliance.

• *Provide ethics training.* Employees can be trained to identify and deal with ethical issues during orientation and through seminar and video training sessions.

• *Reinforce ethical behavior.* As discussed later in Chapter 7, behavior that is reinforced tends to be repeated, whereas behavior that is not reinforced tends to disappear. Sadly, as illustrated in A Matter of Ethics, ethical conduct too often is punished while unethical behavior is rewarded.

• *Create positions, units and other structural mechanisms to deal with ethics.* Ethics needs to be an everyday affair, not a one-time announcement of a new ethical code that gets filed away and forgotten. Xerox monitors company ethics with an internal audit committee. General Dynamics has a full-time corporate ethics director and an ethics hot line that logged 3,646 calls in a single year.[61]

A MATTER OF ETHICS

Mixed Signals for Ethical Behavior

Virtue may be its own reward, but it seems to stop there, or so two Columbia University business school professors discovered in surveying 25 years of alumni experience, seeking to demonstrate the value of ethics training.

Of the 1,070 alumni responding from the classes of 1953 through 1987, 40 percent said they had been implicitly or explicitly rewarded for taking some action they considered to be ethically troubling—twice as many as were rewarded in some way for refusing to do something ethically wrong.

What's more, 31 percent of those who refused to take some ethically troubling action said that they had been penalized for their choice. The penalties ranged from outright punishment to a vague sense that the person's status within the company had been diminished.

One marketing manager for a new product that could contain toxins recommended that the project be scrapped. The manager was ordered to proceed, but was laid off three months later. Another person, a consultant, refused to recommend that a hospital expand after a feasibility study showed the hospital would go bankrupt. The consultant gave in to pressure to alter the study, but later left the firm.

"I was really surprised to see these results," says John Thomas Delaney, an associate business professor at University of Iowa and at Columbia, and one of the study's authors. Despite a flood of interest in ethics education and in corporate value statements, Mr. Delaney says the survey demonstrates that "there are cases where people get rewarded for doing these things, and companies don't want to acknowledge it."

Source: Amanda Bennett, "Managing: Doing the 'Right' Thing Has Its Repercussions," *The Wall Street Journal*, January 25, 1990, p. B1.

How to Deal with Specific Unethical Conduct   Employees and managers who fight unethical behavior on the job typically wage an uphill battle. Success depends on courage, patience, support, and some luck. Careful documentation of one's claim also is critical. A contingency model for taking action against perceived unethical practices is presented in Figure 3–9.

The key contingency variable is the degree of situational support. Someone with plenty of time to act, good leadership skills, and a feeling of trust in power holders can exercise leadership to build a coalition of supporters. This collective option is facilitated by an organizational culture that condones dissent and a win-win issue in which all parties can come out ahead. When most or all of these situational factors are low or absent, the individual must act alone. Make no mistake about it, this solo option can prove fatal to one's career. But justifiable moral outrage can overcome the greatest obstacles.

Whistle blowing, the practice of reporting questionable activity to higher

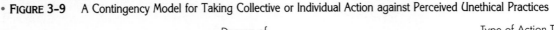

• FIGURE 3-9   A Contingency Model for Taking Collective or Individual Action against Perceived Unethical Practices

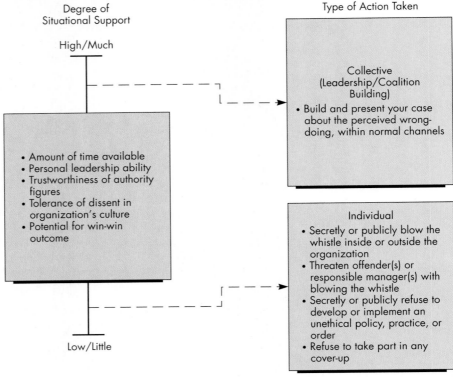

Source: Adapted from discussion in Richard P. Nielsen, "Changing Unethical Organizational Behavior," *The Academy of Management Executive,* May 1989, pp. 123–30.

management, the media, or outside agencies, is a serious threat to managerial authority. Who tends to blow the whistle? In a survey of 8,587 federal employees, whistle blowers, compared with nonwhistle blowers, tended to be nonsupervisors with greater seniority and higher pay but less education.[62]

• SUMMARY OF KEY CONCEPTS

A. Individual differences, formerly viewed as a threat to organizational homogeneity, now need to be understood and accommodated by managers because of increased diversity in the work force. Self-concept is made possible by cognitions, defined as any knowledge, opinion, or belief about oneself and one's circumstances. Two important dimensions of self-concept are self-esteem and self-efficacy.

B. Self-esteem is one's overall evaluation of oneself. Those high in self-esteem feel good about themselves and what they are capable of doing. Organization-based self-esteem (OBSE) has been found to be a strong predictor of positive individual outcomes such as job performance, satisfaction, and commitment to the organization.

C. Self-efficacy involves one's belief about his/her ability to accomplish specific tasks. Those extremely low in self-efficacy suffer from learned helplessness. Four sources of self-efficacy beliefs are prior experience, behavior models, persuasion from others, and assessment of one's physical and emotional states. High self-efficacy beliefs foster constructive and goal-oriented action whereas low self-efficacy fosters passive, failure-prone activities and emotions. Managers can enhance employees' self-efficacy expectations through job design, training, goal setting, leadership, and rewards, among others.

D. Physical and mental characteristics combine to form the individual's personality. Personality and intelligence are said to be the result of both genetic and environmental influences. Two organizationally important personality traits are locus of control and introversion–extroversion characteristics. People with an *internal* locus of control, such as entrepreneurs, believe they are masters of their own fate. Those with an *external* locus of control attribute their behavior and its results to situational forces. Researchers tell us that introverts avoid external stimulation such as social contacts with strangers because of their innate, optimal level of internal arousal. Extroverts, in contrast, achieve their optimum level of arousal through exposure to external stimulation.

E. Attitudes are another popular way of explaining individual differences in behavior. Whereas values are global in scope, attitudes involve predispositions to behave favorably or unfavorably toward specific objects or persons. According to Fishbein and Ajzen's model, beliefs influence attitudes and subjective norms. Depending on their relative importance, attitudes and norms together foster a behavioral intention, the best predictor of actual behavior. The Fishbein and Ajzen behavioral intention model has stood up well under research.

F. Organizations require individuals with appropriate abilities and skills. Abilities relate to one's maximum physical and mental potential, while skills involve one's capacity to actually manipulate objects. Successful performance depends on the right combination of effort, ability, and skill. Human intelligence is said to be based on seven mental abilities. By combining two dimensions of perception (sensation and intuition) with two dimensions of judgment (thinking and feeling), Carl Jung identified four cognitive styles. Each style has its own distinct pattern of characteristics and abilities.

G. Highly publicized accounts of illegal and unethical managerial behavior have generated renewed interest in values and ethics. Some cognitive psychologists contend that instrumental and terminal values, defined as enduring beliefs in modes of conduct and desired end-states of existence, determine much of our behavior. Organizational members can experience intrapersonal, interpersonal, and individual–organization value conflicts.

H. Ethics involves the study of moral issues and choices. On-the-job ethical/unethical conduct is the net result of a complex interaction of factors, including personality and role expectations shaped by cultural, organizational, and general environmental influences.

Specific steps can and must be taken to improve the organization's ethical climate. A contingency approach, involving either collective or individual action, is required to combat specific instances of unethical conduct.

• KEY TERMS

self-concept
cognitions
self-esteem
organization-based self-esteem (OBSE)
self-efficacy
learned helplessness
personality
internal locus of control
external locus of control

attitude
ability
skill
intelligence
cognitive style
value
value system
instrumental values
terminal values
ethics
whistle blowing

• DISCUSSION QUESTIONS

1. How should the reality of a more diverse work force affect management's approach to dealing with individual differences?
2. What is your personal experience with organization-based self-esteem?
3. How is someone you know with low self-efficacy, relative to a specified task, "programming themselves for failure?" What could be done to help that individual develop high self-efficacy?
4. How would you respond to the following statement? "Whenever possible, managers should hire people with an external locus of control."
5. Why is it crucial to consider the concept of optimal level of arousal when discussing introversion-extroversion?
6. Which factor—your attitudes or your subjective norms—presently has a greater impact on your performance in school (or at work)? How do you know?
7. According to Jung's typology, which cognitive style do you exhibit? How can you tell? Is it an advantage or a disadvantage?
8. Do your top-ranked instrumental and terminal values, according to the Rokeach value survey in the OB Exercise, accurately predict your behavior? Explain pro or con.

9. How would you respond to the following statement by a manager? ''This whole ethics thing has been blown all out of reasonable proportion.''

10. What is your experience with unethical conduct on the job? What could management and/or you do to prevent or correct specified instances of unethical conduct?

BACK TO THE OPENING CASE

Now that you have read Chapter 3, you should be able to answer the following questions about the Dennis Levine case:

1. How would you rate Levine's self-esteem and self-efficacy prior to his downfall? On balance, were they positive or negative factors? Explain.

2. Prior to his arrest, did Dennis Levine have an internal or external locus of control? Was it a positive or negative influence in his life?

3. Using Fishbein and Ajzen's model of behavioral intentions as a guide, how and why did Levine's attitudes toward insider trading change?

4. Which factors, relative to the model of ethical behavior in Figure 3–8, were primarily responsible for Levine's criminal conduct? Explain your rationale.

5. What, if anything, could Levine's employer, Drexel Burnham Lambert, have done to prevent him from engaging in illegal insider trading?

• EXERCISE 3

Objectives

1. To identify your cognitive style, according to Carl Jung's typology.[63]
2. To consider the managerial implications of your cognitive style.

Instructions

Please respond to the 16 items below. There are no right or wrong answers. After you have completed all the items, refer to the scoring key and follow its directions.

Questionnaire

Part I. Circle the response that comes closest to how you usually feel or act.

1. Are you more careful about:
   A. People's feelings
   B. Their rights

2. Do you usually get along better with:
   A. Imaginative people
   B. Realistic people
3. Which of these two is the higher compliment:
   A. A person has real feeling
   B. A person is consistently reasonable
4. In doing something with many other people, does it appeal more to you:
   A. To do it in the accepted way
   B. To invent a way of your own
5. Do you get more annoyed at:
   A. Fancy theories
   B. People who don't like theories
6. It is higher praise to call someone:
   A. A person of vision
   B. A person of common sense
7. Do you more often let:
   A. Your heart rule your head
   B. Your head rule your heart
8. Do you think it is worse:
   A. To show too much warmth
   B. To be unsympathetic
9. If you were a teacher, would you rather teach:
   A. Courses involving theory
   B. Fact courses

Part II. Which word in each of the following pairs appeals to you more? Circle A or B.

10. A. Compassion
    B. Foresight
11. A. Justice
    B. Mercy
12. A. Production
    B. Design
13. A. Gentle
    B. Firm
14. A. Uncritical
    B. Critical
15. A. Literal
    B. Figurative
16. A. Imaginative
    B. Matter of fact

Scoring Key

To categorize your responses to the questionnaire, count one point for each response on the following four scales and total the number of points recorded in each column. Instructions for classifying your scores are indicated below.

Sensation	Intuition	Thinking	Feeling
2 B _____	2 A _____	1 B _____	1 A _____
4 A _____	4 B _____	3 B _____	3 A _____
5 A _____	5 B _____	7 B _____	7 A _____
6 B _____	6 A _____	8 A _____	8 B _____
9 B _____	9 A _____	10 B _____	10 A _____
12 A _____	12 B _____	11 A _____	11 B _____
15 A _____	15 B _____	13 B _____	13 A _____
16 B _____	16 A _____	14 B _____	14 A _____
Totals = _____	_____	_____	_____

Classifying Total Scores

Write *intuitive* if your intuition score is equal to or greater than sensation score.

Write *sensation* if sensation is greater than intuition.

Write *feeling* if feeling is greater than thinking.

Write *thinking* if thinking is greater than feeling.

When *thinking* equals feeling, you should write feeling if a male and thinking if a female.

Questions for Consideration/Class Discussion

1. What is your cognitive style?
   Sensation/thinking (ST) _____
   Intuition/thinking (NT) _____
   Sensation/feeling (SF) _____
   Intuition/feeling (NF) _____
2. Do you agree with this assessment? Why or why not?
3. Will your cognitive style, as determined in this exercise, help you achieve your career goal(s)?
4. Would your style be an asset or liability for a managerial position involving getting things done through others?

• NOTES

[1] Sandra I. Cheldelin and Louis A. Foritano, "Psychometrics: Their Use in Organisation Development," *Journal of Managerial Psychology*, no. 4, 1989, p. 21.

[2] Viktor Gecas, "The Self-Concept," in *Annual Review of Sociology*, eds. Ralph H. Turner and James F. Short, Jr. (Palo Alto, Calif.: Annual Reviews Inc., 1982), vol. 8, p. 3. Also see Arthur P. Brief and Ramon J. Aldag, "The 'Self' in Work Organizations: A Conceptual Review," *Academy of Management Review*, January 1981, pp. 75–88; and Jerry J. Sullivan, "Self Theories and Employee Motivation," *Journal of Management*, June 1989, pp. 345–63.

[3] Leon Festinger, *A Theory of Cognitive Dissonance* (Stanford, Calif.: Stanford University Press, 1957), p. 3.

[4] For contrasting perspectives of self, see Philip Cushman, "Why the Self Is Empty," *American Psychologist*, May 1990, pp. 599–611.

5 See Dean C. Barnlund, "Public and Private Self in Communicating with Japan," *Business Horizons*, March–April 1989, pp. 32–40.

6 Based in part on a definition found in Gecas, "The Self Concept."

7 Details may be found in Barry R. Schlenker, Michael F. Weigold, and John R. Hallam, "Self-Serving Attributions in Social Context: Effects of Self-Esteem and Social Pressure," *Journal of Personality and Social Psychology*, May 1990, pp. 855–63.

8 See Judith A. Stein, Michael D. Newcomb, and P. M. Bentler, "The Relative Influence on Vocational Behavior and Family Involvement on Self-Esteem: Longitudinal Analyses of Young Adult Women and Men," *Journal of Vocational Behavior*, June 1990, pp. 320–38.

9 Brian O'Reilly, "Why Grade 'A' Execs Get an 'F' as Parents," *Fortune*, January 1, 1990, pp. 36–37.

10 See John R. Hollenbeck and Arthur P. Brief, "The Effects of Individual Differences and Goal Origin on Goal Setting and Performance," *Organizational Behavior and Human Decision Processes*, December 1987, pp. 392–414.

11 Details may be found in Joel Brockner and Ted Hess, "Self-Esteem and Task Performance in Quality Circles," *Academy of Management Journal*, September 1986, pp. 617–23.

12 Jon L. Pierce, Donald G. Gardner, Larry L. Cummings, and Randall B. Dunham, "Organization-Based Self-Esteem: Construct Definition, Measurement, and Validation," *Academy of Management Journal*, September 1989, p. 625.

13 Adapted from discussion in J. Kenneth Matejka and Richard J. Dunsing, "Great Expectations," *Management World*, January 1987, pp. 16–17.

14 Marilyn E. Gist, "Self-Efficacy: Implications for Organizational Behavior and Human Resource Management," *Academy of Management Review*, July 1987, p. 472. Also see Albert Bandura, "Self-Efficacy: Toward a Unifying Theory of Behavioral Change," *Psychological Review*, March 1977, pp. 191–215.

15 See, for example, Viktor Gecas, "The Social Psychology of Self-Efficacy," in *Annual Review of Sociology*, eds. W. Richard Scott and Judith Blake (Palo Alto, Calif.: Annual Reviews, Inc., 1989), vol. 15, pp. 291–316.

16 For more on learned helplessness, see Gecas, "The Social Psychology of Self-Efficacy," and Mark J. Martinko and William L. Gardner, "Learned Helplessness: An Alternative Explanation for Performance Deficits," *Academy of Management Review*, April 1982, pp. 195–204.

17 For details, see Julian Barling and Russell Beattie, "Self-Efficacy Beliefs and Sales Performance," *Journal of Organizational Behavior Management*, Spring 1983, pp. 41–51.

18 Based in part on discussion in Gecas, "The Social Psychology of Self-Efficacy."

19 Adapted from discussion in Joseph R. Royce, "Personality Integration: A Synthesis of the Parts and Wholes of Individuality Theory," *Journal of Personality*, December 1983, pp. 683–706.

20 For an instructive update, see Julian B. Rotter, "Internal versus External Control of Reinforcement: A Case History of a Variable," *American Psychologist*, April 1990, pp. 489–93.

21 For an overall review of research on locus of control, see Paul E. Spector, "Behavior in Organizations as a Function of Employee's Locus of Control," *Psychological Bulletin*, May 1982, pp. 482–97; the relationship between locus of control and performance and satisfaction is examined in Dwight R. Norris and Robert E. Niebuhr, "Attributional Influences on the Job Performance–Job Satisfaction Relationship," *Academy of Management Journal*, June 1984, pp. 424–31; salary differences between internals and externals were examined by Paul C. Nystrom,

"Managers' Salaries and Their Beliefs about Reinforcement Control," *The Journal of Social Psychology*, August 1983, pp. 291–92.

[22] See Stephen R. Hawk, "Locus of Control and Computer Attitude: The Effect of User Involvement," *Computers in Human Behavior*, no. 3, 1989, pp. 199–206.

[23] These recommendations are from Spector, "Behavior in Organizations as a Function of Employee's Locus of Control."

[24] Anthony Gale, "EEG Studies of Extraversion–Introversion: What's the Next Step?" in *Dimensions of Personality: Papers in Honour of H J Eysenck,* ed. Richard Lynn (New York: Pergamon Press, 1981), p. 184.

[25] For a review of research on the relationship between introversion–extroversion, motivation, and performance, see Michael S. Humphreys and William Revelle, "Personality, Motivation, and Performance: A Theory of the Relationship between Individual Differences and Information Processing," *Psychological Review*, April 1984, pp. 153–84.

[26] Martin Fishbein and Icek Ajzen, *Belief, Attitude, Intention and Behavior: An Introduction to Theory and Research* (Reading, Mass.: Addison-Wesley Publishing, 1975), p. 6.

[27] See Barry M. Staw and Jerry Ross, "Stability in the Midst of Change: A Dispositional Approach to Job Attitudes," *Journal of Applied Psychology*, August 1985, pp. 469–80.

[28] For a discussion of the difference between values and attitudes, see Boris W. Becker and Patrick E. Connor, "Changing American Values—Debunking the Myth," *Business*, January–March 1985, pp. 56–59.

[29] For a brief overview and update of the model, see Martin Fishbein and Mark Stasson, "The Role of Desires, Self-Predictions, and Perceived Control in the Prediction of Training Session Attendance," *Journal of Applied Social Psychology*, February 1990, pp. 173–98.

[30] See Robert P. Steel and Nestor K. Ovalle II, "A Review and Meta-Analysis of Research on the Relationship between Behavioral Intentions and Employee Turnover," *Journal of Applied Psychology*, November 1984, pp. 673–86.

[31] Icek Ajzen and Martin Fishbein, *Understanding Attitudes and Predicting Social Behavior* (Englewood Cliffs, N.J.: Prentice-Hall, 1980), p. 7.

[32] Drawn from J. Michael Grant and Thomas S. Bateman, "An Experimental Test of the Impact of Drug-Testing Programs on Potential Job Applicants' Attitudes and Intentions," *Journal of Applied Psychology*, April 1990, pp. 127–31.

[33] For an overall review of attitude formation research, see Ajzen and Fishbein, *Understanding Attitudes and Predicting Social Behavior.* Also see Shelly Chaiken and Charles Stangor, "Attitudes and Attitude Change," in *Annual Review of Psychology*, ed. Mark R. Rosenzweig and Lyman W. Porter (Palo Alto, Calif.: Annual Reviews, 1987), pp. 575–630; and Fishbein and Stasson, "The Role of Desires, Self-Predictions, and Perceived Control in the Prediction of Training Session Attendance."

[34] See Peter W. Hom and Charles L. Hulin, "A Competitive Test of the Prediction of Reenlistment by Several Models," *Journal of Applied Psychology*, February 1981, pp. 23–39. Also see Paul R. Warshaw, Roger Calantone, and Mary Joyce, "A Field Study Application of the Fishbein and Ajzen Intention Model," *The Journal of Social Psychology*, February 1986, pp. 135–365.

[35] See, for example, Deborah A. Byrnes and Gary Kiger, "The Effect of a Prejudice-Reduction Simulation on Attitude Change," *Journal of Applied Social Psychology*, March 1990, pp. 341–56.

[36] Frank L. Schmidt and John E. Hunter, "Employment Testing: Old Theories and New Research Findings," *American Psychologist*, October 1981, p. 1128.

[37] For an excellent update on intelligence, including definitional distinctions and a historical perspective of the IQ controversy, see Richard A. Weinberg, "Intelligence and IQ," *American Psychologist,* February 1989, pp. 98–104.

[38] Ibid.

[39] See Schmidt and Hunter, "Employment Testing: Old Theories and New Research Findings." For evidence of the economic impact of using cognitive ability tests to select employees, see John E. Hunter and Frank L. Schmidt, "Quantifying the Effects of Psychological Interventions on Employee Job Performance and Work-Force Productivity," *American Psychologist,* April 1983, pp. 473–78.

[40] See John L. Bledsoe, "Your Four Communicating Styles," *Training*, March 1976, pp. 18–21.

[41] For a complete discussion of each cognitive style, see John W. Slocum, Jr., and Don Hellriegel, "A Look at How Managers' Minds Work," *Business Horizons*, July–August 1983, pp. 58–68; and William Taggart and Daniel Robey, "Minds and Managers: On the Dual Nature of Human Information Processing and Management," *Academy of Management Review*, April 1981, pp. 187–95.

[42] See Bruce K. Blaylock and Loren P. Rees, "Cognitive Style and the Usefulness of Information," *Decision Sciences,* Winter 1984, pp. 74–91.

[43] Additional material on cognitive styles may be found in Ferdinand A. Gul, "The Joint and Moderating Role of Personality and Cognitive Style on Decision Making," *The Accounting Review*, April 1984, pp. 264–77; Brian H. Kleiner, "The Interrelationship of Jungian Modes of Mental Functioning with Organizational Factors: Implications for Management Development," *Human Relations*, November 1983, pp. 997–1012; and James L. McKenney and Peter G. W. Keen, "How Managers' Minds Work," *Harvard Business Review*, May–June 1974, pp. 79–90.

[44] See George H. Rice, Jr., and David P. Lindecamp, "Personality Types and Business Success of Small Retailers," *Journal of Occupational Psychology*, June 1989, pp. 177–82.

[45] Taken from Rushworth M. Kidder, "The Three E's of the 1990s," *The Christian Science Monitor*, March 19, 1990, p. 12.

[46] Milton Rokeach, *The Nature of Human Values* (New York: Free Press, 1973), p. 5.

[47] Ibid.

[48] See Shalom H. Schwartz and Wolfgang Bilsky, "Toward a Theory of the Universal Content and Structure of Values: Extensions and Cross-Cultural Replications," *Journal of Personality and Social Psychology*, May 1990, pp. 878–91.

[49] "A Bit of the '60s Lives on at Lotus," *Business Week*, July 2, 1984, p. 59.

[50] See Anthony J. DeVito, Janet F. Carlson, and Joanne Kraus, "Values in Relation to Career Orientation, Gender, and Each Other," *Counseling and Values*, July 1984, pp. 202–6.

[51] Ibid.

[52] Data from Milton Rokeach and Sandra J. Ball-Rokeach, "Stability and Change in American Value Priorities, 1968–1981," *American Psychologist*, May 1989, pp. 775–84.

[53] Milton Rokeach and John F. Reagan, "The Role of Values in the Counseling Situation," *Personnel and Guidance Journal*, May 1980, p. 578.

[54] Based on David E. Rosenbaum, "All Roads Lead to Washington and Politics in S&L Calamity," *The Arizona Republic*, June 10, 1990, pp. F1, F3–F5.

[55] Rushworth M. Kidder, "A Yardstick for Business Ethics," *The Christian Science Monitor*, February 26, 1990, p. 14.

[56] For a review of this research, see Phillip V. Lewis, "Defining 'Business Ethics': Like Nailing Jello to the Wall," *Journal of Business Ethics*, October 1985, pp. 377–83.

[57] Adapted from W. Edward Stead, Dan L. Worrell, and Jean Garner Stead, "An Integrative Model for Understanding and Managing Ethical Behavior in Business Organizations," *Journal of Business Ethics*, March 1990, pp. 233–42.

[58] Rushworth M. Kidder, "He Calls Ethics Crucial to Survival," *The Christian Science Monitor*, June 19, 1989, p. 14.

[59] See, for example, Paul R. Sackett, Laura R. Burris, and Christine Callahan, "Integrity Testing for Personnel Selection: An Update," *Personnel Psychology*, Autumn 1989, pp. 491–529.

[60] See James G. Frierson, "New Polygraph Test Limits," *Personnel Journal*, December 1988, pp. 84–92.

[61] Data from William H. Wagel, "A New Focus on Business Ethics at General Dynamics," *Personnel*, August 1987, pp. 4–8.

[62] For details, see Marcia Parmerlee Miceli and Janet P. Near, "The Relationships among Beliefs, Organizational Position, and Whistle-Blowing Status: A Discriminant Analysis," *Academy of Management Journal*, December 1984, pp. 687–705.

[63] The questionnaire and scoring key excerpted from John W. Slocum, Jr., and Don Hellriegel, "A Look at How Managers' Minds Work," *Business Horizons*, July–August 1983, pp. 58–68.

Perception and Attributions

LEARNING OBJECTIVES

When you finish studying the material in this chapter, you should be able to:

- Describe perception in terms of social information processing.
- Discuss the process of stereotype formation and maintenance.
- Summarize the managerial implications of sex-role, age, and race stereotypes.

- Discuss how individual and organizational self-fulfilling prophecies are created.
- Explain, according to Kelley's model, how external and internal causal attributions are formulated.

- Review Weiner's model of attribution.
- Contrast fundamental attribution bias and self-serving bias.

OPENING CASE 4

U.S. Servicewomen Encounter Stereotypes

Sharon Hoogstraten

Women have taken part in every American military crisis since the Revolutionary War. But never before have they served on such a large scale or in such a wide variety of jobs. As the massive deployment in the Persian Gulf continues [fall of 1990], women pilots from the 101st Airborne Division are ferrying supplies and personnel in Huey helicopters. Female mechanics from the 24th Mechanized Division are maintaining tanks, handling petroleum, and coordinating water supply. Throughout the region, women are working as truck drivers, cargo handlers, intelligence specialists, paratroopers, flight controllers, shipboard navigators, communications experts, and

ground-crew chiefs. Their precise number in Operation Desert Shield is classified, but one Army personnel expert says women will soon match their overall proportion in the services: roughly 11 percent of the 2 million-member armed forces.

Women are still not permitted to serve in combat positions—by law in the Navy, Air Force and Marines and by policy in the Army. [Congress voted to broaden the combat role of women in mid-1991.] But ever since the Pentagon began recruiting women in large numbers in the 1970s, the services have defined "combat" ever more narrowly, giving women increasingly critical roles. . . .

For now, the U.S. servicewomen in Saudi Arabia are doing just what the men are doing: setting up vast military installations in the desert, fortifying supply lines and waiting. If the shooting begins, there are no plans to withdraw the women from the theater—and few illusions that they might not be among the casualties. [Women ended up being both casualties and prisoners of war]. "Just because you're not in a combat unit doesn't mean you won't be in combat," says Lawrence Korb, former assistant sec-

retary of Defense for manpower. "When they start lobbing SCUDS with chemical weapons, they'll be aiming at everybody." To that end, female troops in Saudi Arabia have been issued protective gear, and are required to carry it at all times, just like the men. They also carry arms and are trained to use them should they come under attack. . . .

Given the desert realities, some servicewomen are lobbying the military to lift the combat restrictions. "I can fly that F-15 just as well as a man," insists 25-year old Lt. Stephanie Shaw, who controls flight missions for a tactical air wing in the gulf. "I volunteered for the Army, not the Girl Scouts," echoes Capt. Leola Davis, commander of a heavy-maintenance company that fixes everything from tanks to HUMV jeeps at the Army's First Cavalry Division at Fort Hood, Texas. But the objections to women on the front lines are deeply entrenched, as [Congresswoman Patricia] Schroeder found this year when she proposed legislation calling for a four-year Army test of women in combat posts. . . .

One of the chief arguments against women on the fighting lines is sheer physical strength. Within the tough, tattooed all-

As human beings, we constantly strive to make sense of the world around us. The resulting knowledge influences our behavior and helps us navigate our way through life. Think of the perceptual process that occurs when meeting someone for the first time. Your attention is drawn to the individual's physical appearance, mannerisms, actions, and reactions to what you say and do. You ultimately arrive at conclusions based on your

OPENING CASE 4

(concluded)

male tanker brigades at Fort Hood, for example, it's an article of faith that women don't have the upper-body strength needed to load 60-pound shells into guns. But brute force is irrelevant in many of the combat jobs from which women are excluded. "On a ship, war is high tech," says one former Navy submariner. "Men aren't any better at video games than women."

Male Bonding

Many military men firmly believe the presence of women on the front lines would disrupt what they call "unit cohesion"—the male bonding that theoretically allows warriors to perform acts of heroism under fire. "I want people on my right and on my left who will take the pressure when the shooting starts," says Brig. Gen. Ed Scholes, who commands the 18th Airborne Corps in Saudi Arabia. "Men simply cannot treat women like other men. And it's silly to think that a few months' training can make them into some kind of sexless soldiers," says Brian Mitchell, a former Army captain and author of a 1989 book, "Weak Link: The Feminization of the American Military." But historian Linda Grant De Pauw, founder of the Minerva Center,

which studies women in the military, counters that such objections are mired in old stereotypes of women as victims. "It's like the image they used to have of blacks before they served with them— that they were too cowardly, too stupid or would break their weapons," she argues. . . .

The U.S. women in Saudi Arabia face a more immediate problem—the clash of cultures with their Muslim hosts. In a country where women can't drive, show their faces or venture out alone, Saudi troops don't know what to make of female GIs wearing fatigues and issuing orders. American women are similarly stunned by the Saudis. Two female paratroopers, interviewed in Dhahran last week, couldn't help but stare as a Muslim woman in a black veil walked by. "Tragic," said First Lt. Jennifer Ann Wood, who quoted a maxim from her West Point days: "That's a tradition unhampered by progress."

The Saudis have made some cultural concessions. U.S. servicewomen can now discreetly drive vehicles while on duty, and at one air base, they can use a gym during limited hours, though they must enter through the back door. Still, they are not permitted to wear shorts, jog or even shop on

military bases unless accompanied by a man. Some American women take the restrictions in stride: "This is their culture. We shouldn't impose our ways on them," said Capt. Susan Beausoleil, a paratrooper with the 18th Airborne Corps. Others aren't so complacent. The Saudis "look at you like a dog—they don't want American women here," griped one Army staff sergeant. That kind of treatment incenses Schroeder, as does the U.S. military's tolerance. "Can you imagine if we sent black soldiers to South Africa and told them to go along with the apartheid rules?" she asks.

For Discussion

Should women be given combat assignments?

• Additional discussion questions linking this case with the following material appears at the end of this chapter.

Source: Excerpted from Melinda Beck, Ray Wilkinson, Bill Turque, and Clara Bingham, "Our Women in the Desert," *Newsweek*, September 10, pp. 22–24. Copyright 1990, Newsweek, Inc. All rights reserved. Reprinted by permission.

perceptions of this social interaction. The brown-haired, green-eyed individual turns out to be friendly and fond of outdoor activities. You further conclude that you like this person and then ask him or her to go to a concert.

This reciprocal process of perception, interpretation, and behavioral response also applies at work. A recent field study illustrates this relationship. Researchers wanted to know whether employee's perceptions of how much an organization valued them affected their behavior and attitudes. The researchers asked samples of high school teachers, brokerage-firm clerks, manufacturing workers, insurance representatives, and police officers to indicate their perception of the extent to which their organization valued their contributions and their well-being. Employees who perceived that their organization cared about them reciprocated with reduced absenteeism, increased performance, innovation, and positive work attitudes.[1] As another example, consider the case of Glenn Davis:

> Glenn Davis of Houston, a chain-smoking former executive of Oceaneering International, Inc., was called into his boss's office last year for a frank talk. "The boss said, 'Glenn, you look like hell,'" Mr. Davis recalls.
>
> He had to agree. Heredity and years of job stress had left a pair of fleshy bags draped like funeral bunting under Mr. Davis's eyes. "Have you ever thought of going to a plastic surgeon?" the boss asked, and before long a surgeon was snipping the fatty deposits from Mr. Davis's eyes.
>
> . . . [Davis's] new, younger-looking face invigorated him with such a surge of entrepreneurial spirit that he started a new company, replaced his wardrobe, and splurged on a turbo-charged, jet-black sports car.[2]

Mr. Davis acquired new behavior patterns because of his boss's perception and his altered self-perception. This chapter explores these perceptual processes.

To guide our discussion, Figure 4–1 provides an overview of the perception process. As shown, the perceptual process is instigated by the presence of environmental stimuli. These stimuli are selectively perceived and interpreted. In turn, there are perceptual outcomes of stereotypes, self-fulfilling prophecies, and attributions formed, and reinforced, by interpretations of environmental stimuli. Finally, perceptual outcomes directly affect attitudes, motivation, and behavior.

In this chapter we focus on: (1) a social information processing model of perception, (2) stereotypes, (3) the self-fulfilling prophecy, and (4) how causal attributions are used to interpret behavior.

• A SOCIAL INFORMATION PROCESSING MODEL OF PERCEPTION

Perception is a mental and cognitive process that enables us to interpret and understand our surroundings. Recognition of objects is one of this process's major functions. For example, both people and animals recognize familiar objects in their environments. You would recognize a picture of your best

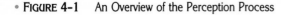

• **FIGURE 4-1**   An Overview of the Perception Process

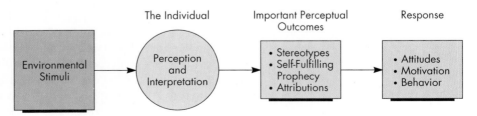

friend; dogs and cats can recognize their food dishes or a favorite toy. Reading involves recognition of visual patterns representing letters in the alphabet. People must recognize objects to meaningfully interact with their environment. But since OB's principal focus is on people, the following discussion emphasizes *social* perception rather than object perception.

The study of how people perceive one another has been labeled *social cognition* and *social information processing*. In contrast to the perception of objects:

> Social cognition is the study of how people make sense of other people and themselves. It focuses on how ordinary people think about people and how they think they think about people. . . .
>
> Research on social cognition also goes beyond naive psychology. The study of social cognition entails a fine-grained analysis of how people think about themselves and others, and it leans heavily on the theory and methods of cognitive psychology.[3]

Although the cognitive or mental processes guiding object perception also can be used to describe aspects of social perception, fundamental differences exist (see Table 4–1). Moreover, while general theories of perception date back many years, the study of social perception is relatively new, having originated about 1976.[4]

• TABLE 4–1   Important Differences between Person and Object Perception

- People intentionally influence the environment; they attempt to control it for their own purposes. Objects, of course, are not intentional causal agents.
- People perceive back; as you are busy forming impressions of them, they are doing the same to you. Social cognition is mutual cognition.
- A social stimulus may change upon being the target of cognition. People worry about how they come across and may adjust their appearance or behavior accordingly; coffee cups obviously do not.
- People's traits are nonobservable attributes that are vital to thinking about them. An object's nonobservable attributes are somewhat less crucial. Both a person and a cup can be fragile, but the inferred characteristics is both less important and more directly seen in the cup.
- People change over time and circumstances more than objects typically do. This can make cognitions rapidly obsolete or unreliable.
- The accuracy of one's cognitions about people is harder to check than the accuracy of one's cognitions about objects. Even psychologists have a hard time agreeing on whether a given person is extroverted, sensitive, or honest, but most ordinary people easily could test whether a given cup is heat resistant, fragile, or leaky.
- People are unavoidably complex. One cannot study cognitions about people without making numerous choices to simplify. The researcher has to simplify in object cognition, too, but it is less of a distortion. One cannot simplify a social stimulus without eliminating much of the inherent richness of the target.
- Because people are so complex, and because they have traits and intents hidden from view, and because they affect us in ways objects do not, social cognition automatically involves social explanation. It is more important for an ordinary person to explain why a person is fragile than to explain why a cup is.

Source: Susan T. Fiske and Shelley E. Taylor, *Social Cognition* (Reading, Mass.: Addison-Wesley Publishing, 1984), pp. 16–17. Copyright © 1984 by Newbery Award Records, Inc., and Random House, Inc.

• **FIGURE 4-2**   Social Perception: A Social Information Processing Model

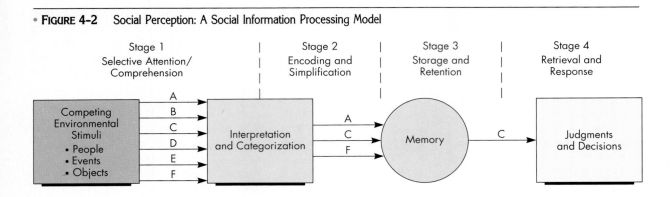

Four-Stage Sequence and a Working Example

Social perception involves a four-stage information processing sequence (hence, the label "social information processing"). Figure 4–2 illustrates a basic social information processing model. Three of the stages in this model—selective attention/comprehension, encoding and simplification, and storage and retention—describe how specific social information is observed and stored in memory. The fourth and final stage, retrieval and response, involves turning mental representations into real-world judgments and decisions.

Keep the following everyday example in mind as we look at the four stages of social perception. Suppose you were thinking of taking a course in, say, personal finance. Three professors teach the same course, using different types of instruction and testing procedures. Through personal experience, you have come to prefer good professors who rely on the case method of instruction and essay tests. According to social perception theory, you would likely arrive at a decision regarding which professor to take as follows:

Stage 1: Selective Attention/Comprehension

People are constantly bombarded by physical and social stimuli in the environment. Since they do not have the mental capacity to fully comprehend all this information, they selectively perceive subsets of environmental stimuli. This is where attention plays a role. **Attention** is the process of becoming consciously aware of something or someone. Attention can be focused on information either from the environment or from memory. Regarding the latter situation, if you sometimes find yourself thinking about totally unrelated events or people while reading a textbook, your memory is the focus of your attention. Research has shown that people tend to pay attention to salient stimuli.

Salient Stimuli   Something is *salient* when it stands out from its context. For example, a 250-pound man would certainly be salient in a women's aerobics class but not at a meeting of the National Football League Players' Association. Social salience is determined by several factors, including:

- Being novel (the only person in a group of that race, gender, hair color, or age).
- Being bright (wearing a yellow shirt).
- Being unusual for that person (behaving in an unexpected way, like a person with a fear of heights climbing a steep mountain).
- Being unusual for a person's social category (like a company president driving a motorcycle to work).
- Being unusual for people in general (driving 20 miles per hour in a 55-mph speed zone).
- Being extremely positive (a noted celebrity) or negative (the victim of a bad traffic accident).
- Being dominant in the visual field (sitting at the head of the table).[5]

One's needs and goals often dictate which stimuli are salient. For a driver whose gas gauge is on empty, an Exxon or Mobil sign is more salient than a McDonald's or Burger King sign. The reverse would be true for a hungry driver with a full gas tank.

Back to Our Example You begin your search for the "right" personal finance professor by asking friends who have taken classes from the three professors. Because you are concerned about the method of instruction and testing procedures, information in those areas is particularly salient to you. Perhaps you even interview the professors to gather still more relevant information. Meanwhile, thousands of competing stimuli fail to get your attention.

Stage 2: Encoding and Simplification

Observed information is not stored in memory in its original form. Encoding is required; raw information is interpreted or translated into mental representations. To accomplish this, perceivers assign pieces of information to **cognitive categories**. "By *category* we mean a number of objects that are considered equivalent. Categories are generally designated by names, e.g., *dog, animal*."[6] People, events, and objects are interpreted and categorized by comparing their characteristics with *schemata* (or *schema* in singular form).

Schemata According to social information processing theory, a **schema** represents a person's mental picture or summary of a particular event or type of stimulus.[7] For example, your restaurant schema probably is quite similar to the description provided in Table 4–2.

Cognitive-category labels are needed to make schemata meaningful. For example, read the passage in the OB Exercise *now* and determine how comprehensive it is by using the scale at the bottom of the table. Having done this, find the label for this schema in reference note 8.[8] Read the passage again and rate it for comprehensiveness. Your comprehension improved because the cognitive-category label bridged the gap between the description and the laundry schema in your memory.

• **TABLE 4-2**   Restaurant Schema

Schema: Restaurant.
Characters: Customers, hostess, waiter, chef, cashier.

Scene 1: Entering.
  Customer goes into restaurant.
  Customer finds a place to sit.
    He may find it himself.
    He may be seated by a hostess.
      He asks the hostess for a table.
      She gives him permission to go to the table.

Scene 2: Ordering.
  Customer receives a menu.
  Customer reads it.
  Customer decides what to order.
  Waiter takes the order.
    Waiter sees the customer.
    Waiter goes to the customer.
    Customer orders what he wants.
  Chef cooks the meal.

Scene 3: Eating.
  After some time the waiter brings the meal from the chef.
  Customer eats the meal.

Scene 4: Exiting.
  Customer asks the waiter for the check.
  Waiter gives the check to the customer.
  Customer leaves a tip.
    The size of the tip depends on the goodness of the service.
  Customer pays the cashier.
  Customer leaves the restaurant.

Source: From *Memory, Thought and Behavior* by Robert W. Weisberg. Copyright © 1980 by Oxford University Press, Inc. Reprinted by permission.

Back to Our Example   Having collected relevant information about the three personal finance professors and their approaches, your mind creates a mental picture of each by drawing upon your relevant schemata (see Figure 4–3). Thus, by selectively attending to environmental and mental information, you have created simplified mental representations of what it would be like to take a class from each of the three professors. This enables you to render a good decision, as opposed to your life being dictated by random chance.

Stage 3: Storage and Retention

This phase involves storage of information in long-term memory. Long-term memory is like an apartment complex consisting of separate units connected to one another. Although different people live in each apartment, they sometimes interact. In addition, large apartment complexes have different wings (like A, B, and C). Long-term memory similarly consists of separate but related categories. Like the individual apartments inhabited by unique residents, the connected categories contain different types of information.

• **OB EXERCISE**

How Comprehensive Is This Passage?

The procedure is actually quite simple. First you arrange things into different groups. Of course, one pile may be sufficient depending on how much there is to do. If you have to go somewhere else due to lack of facilities that is the next step, otherwise you are pretty well set. It is important not to overdo things. That is, it is better to do too few things at once than too many. In the short run this may not seem important but complications can easily arise. A mistake can be expensive as well. At first the whole procedure will seem complicated. Soon, however, it will become just another facet of life. It is difficult to foresee any end to the necessity for this task in the immediate future, but then one never can tell. After the procedure is completed one arranges the materials into different groups again. Then they can be put into their appropriate places. Eventually they will be used once more and the whole cycle will then have to be repeated. However, that is part of life.

		Comprehensiveness Scale				
Very **uncomprehensive**	1	2	**Neither** 3	4	5	**Very** **comprehensive**

Source: John D. Bransford and Marcia K. Johnson, "Contextual Prerequisite for Understanding: Some Investigations of Comprehension and Recall," *Journal of Verbal Learning and Verbal Behavior*, December 1972, p. 722. Used with permission.

• **FIGURE 4-3**   Examples of Mental Schemata in Social Perception

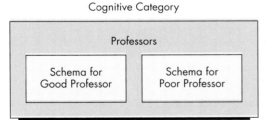

Cognitive Category

Professors

Schema for Good Professor

Schema for Poor Professor

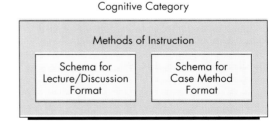

Cognitive Category

Methods of Instruction

Schema for Lecture/Discussion Format

Schema for Case Method Format

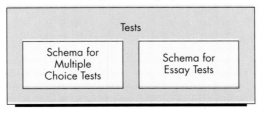

Cognitive Category

Tests

Schema for Multiple Choice Tests

Schema for Essay Tests

• **FIGURE 4-4**   The Structure of Memory

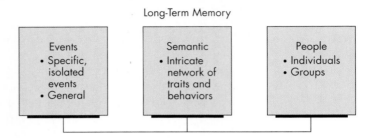

Long-Term Memory

Information also passes among these categories. Finally, long-term memory is made up of three compartments (or wings) containing categories of information about events, semantic materials, and people (see Figure 4–4).[9]

Event Memory   This compartment is composed of categories containing information about both specific and general events. Information in these categories is stored chronologically (or relative to time). Thus, for example, your memory of your last vacation would flow from beginning to end.

Semantic Memory   Semantic memory functions as a mental dictionary of concepts. Each concept contains a definition (a good leader, for example) and associated traits (outgoing), emotional states (happy), physical characteristics (tall), and behaviors (works hard). Just as there are schemata for general events, concepts in semantic memory are stored as schemata.

Person Memory   Categories within this compartment contain information about a single individual (your supervisor) or groups of people (managers).

Back to Our Example   As the time draws near for you to decide which personal finance professor to take, your schemata of them are stored in the three categories of long-term memory. These schemata are available for immediate comparison and/or retrieval.

Stage 4: Retrieval and Response

Concluding our example, it is registration day and you have to choose which professor to take for personal finance. After retrieving from memory your schemata-based impressions of the three professors, you select a good one who uses the case method and gives essay tests.

Managerial Implications

Social cognition is the window through which we all observe, interpret, and prepare our responses to people and events. A wide variety of managerial activities, organizational processes, and quality-of-life issues (see OB in Action) are thus affected by perception. Consider, for example, the following implications.

OB IN ACTION

Artificial Windows Enhance Patients' Recuperation

This month Stanford became the first U.S. medical facility to install a comput-erized "window" that simulates the progress of daily light changes—and the passage of time—from sunrise to sunset.

The artificial window, which measures 4 feet by 5 feet, was developed by California nature photographer Joey Fischer, who saw a need when his father had a heart attack and spent hours counting holes in the hospital ceiling tiles because there was nothing else to look at. The Stanford window is actually a computer-controlled light box behind a blowup of a 35-mm slide. The scene depicts a peaceful pasture with billowing clouds in the background. An elec-tronic digital timer produces 650 separate light changes every 24 hours, starting with the pale pink hues of sunrise and ending—on the opposite side of the window—with deeper shades of coral fading into dusk. An updated version will include a moon and twinkling stars. . . .

Source: Excerpted from Jean Seligman and Linda Buckley, "A Sickroom with a View: A New Artificial Window Brightens Patients' Days," *Newsweek*, March 26, p. 61. Copyright 1990, News-week, Inc. All rights reserved. Reprinted by permission.

Performance Appraisal   Faulty schemata about what constitutes good versus poor performance can lead to inaccurate performance appraisals, which erode work motivation, commitment, and loyalty. Therefore, it is important for managers to accurately identify the behavioral characteristics and results indicative of good performance at the beginning of a performance review cycle. These characteristics then can serve as the benchmarks for evaluating employee performance. Furthermore, because memory for specific in-stances of employee performance deteriorates over time, managers need a mechanism for accurately recalling employee behavior. Research reveals that managers can improve their performance-rating accuracy by recording employee performance in performance diaries.[10]

Hiring   Interviewers make hiring decisions based on their impression of how an applicant fits the perceived requirements of a job. Inaccurate impressions in either direction produce poor hiring decisions. Moreover, interviewers with racist or sexist schemata can undermine the accuracy and legality of hiring decisions. Those invalid schemata need to be confronted and im-proved through coaching and training.[11]

Leadership   Research demonstrates that employees' evaluations of leader effectiveness are influenced strongly by their schemata of good and poor leaders. A leader will have a difficult time influencing employees when he or she exhibits behaviors contained in employees' schemata of poor leaders.

Motivation   Perceptions of pay inequity reduce employee motivation and increase employee turnover. Chapter 6 provides a thorough discussion of how equity perceptions affect employee motivation.

• A computer generates the images seen through this "window," thus fostering the perception of being in a more positive and stimulating environment. Experts believe a positive outlook aids the healing process. Rick Browne/ Photoreporters

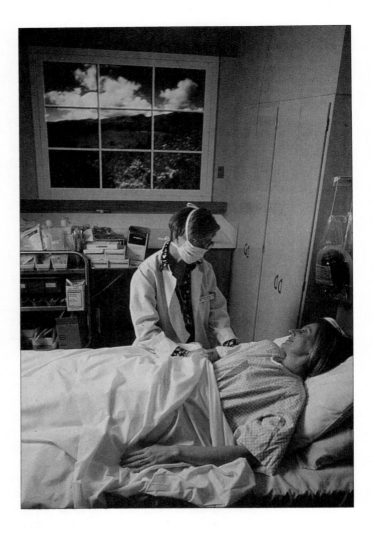

Communication   Managers need to remember that social perception is a screening process that can distort communication, both coming and going. Messages are interpreted and categorized according to schemata developed through past experiences and influenced by one's age, gender, and ethnic, geographic, and cultural orientations. Effective communicators try to tailor their messages to the receiver's perceptual schemata.[12] This requires well-developed listening and observation skills and cross-cultural sensitivity.

• STEREOTYPES: PERCEPTIONS ABOUT GROUPS OF PEOPLE

While it is often true that beauty is in the eye of the beholder, perception does result in some predictable outcomes. Managers aware of the perception process and its outcomes enjoy a competitive edge. The Walt Disney Com-

• TABLE 4-3   Commonly Found Perceptual Errors

Perceptual Error	Description	Example
Halo	A rater forms an overall impression about an object and then uses that impression to bias ratings about the object.	Rating a professor high on the teaching dimensions of ability to motivate students, knowledge, and communication because we like him or her.
Leniency	A personal characteristic that leads an individual to consistently evaluate other people or objects in an extremely positive fashion.	Rating a professor high on all dimensions of performance regardless of his or her actual performance. The rater who hates to say negative things about others.
Central tendency	The tendency to avoid all extreme judgments and rate people and objects as average or neutral.	Rating a professor average on all dimensions of performance regardless of his or her actual performance.
Recency effects	The tendency to remember recent information. If the recent information is negative, the person or object is evaluated negatively.	Although a professor has given good lectures for 12 of 15 weeks, he or she is evaluated negatively because lectures over the last three weeks were done poorly.
Contrast effects	The tendency to evaluate people or objects by comparing them to characteristics of recently observed people or objects.	Rating a good professor as average because you compared his or her performance to three of the best professors you have ever had in college. You are currently taking courses from the three excellent professors.

pany, for instance, takes full advantage of perceptual tendencies to influence customers' reactions to waiting in long lines at its theme parks:

> In order to make the experience less psychologically wearing, the waiting times posted by each attraction are generously overestimated, so that one comes away mysteriously grateful for having hung around 20 minutes for a 58-second twirl in the Alice in Wonderland teacups. ("I used the same trick when I was trying to sell sitcoms to the networks," says [Chairman and CEO Michael D.] Eisner. "I showed them a 23-minute 'Happy Days' pilot and told them it was a half hour. They thought it was the fastest-paced show they'd ever seen.")
>
> The lines, moreover, are always moving, even if what looks like the end is actually the start of a second set of switchbacks leading to—oh, no!—a pre-ride waiting area. Those little tricks of the theme park mean a lot.[13]

Likewise, managers can use knowledge of perceptual outcomes to help them interact more effectively with employees. For example, Table 4–3 describes five common perceptual errors. Since these perceptual errors often distort the evaluation of job applicants and of employee performance, managers need to guard against them. This section examines one of the most important and potentially harmful perceptual outcomes associated with person perception: stereotypes. After exploring the process of stereotype formation and maintenance, we discuss sex-role stereotypes, age stereotypes, race stereotypes, and the managerial challenge to avoid stereotypical biases.

Stereotype Formation and Maintenance

Stereotypes represent grossly oversimplified beliefs or expectations about groups of people. "Stereotyping is said to occur when a perceiver makes inferences about a person because of the person's membership in some group."[14] Consider walking into a business meeting with 10 people situated around a conference table. You notice a male at the head of the table and a woman seated immediately to his right, taking periodic notes. Due to ingrained stereotypes, you are likely to assume that the man is the top-ranking person in the room and the woman, his secretary.

This example highlights how people use stereotypes to help reduce information-processing demands and to base predictions of behavior on group membership.[15] Unfortunately, stereotypes can lead to poor decisions and can create barriers for minority advancement. For example, statistics in Figure 4–5 suggest minorities are not obtaining their fair share of managerial jobs. Although it is difficult to determine cause and effect relationships among these statistics, it seems reasonable to conclude that stereotypes are significant contributors.

Stereotyping is a four-step process. It begins by categorizing people into groups according to various criteria, such as gender, age, race, and occupation. Next, we infer that all people within a particular category possess the same traits or characteristics (for instance, all women are nurturing; older people have more job-related accidents; all blacks are good athletes; all

---

• **FIGURE 4–5**   Percentages of Management Jobs Held by Different Groups of Employees, 1988 Data*

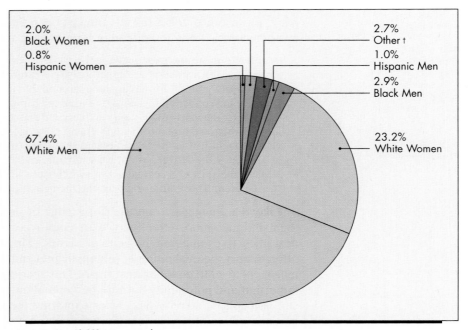

* At companies with 100 or more employees.
† Includes Asian-American and Native-American men and women.
Source: Keith L. Alexander, "Both Racism and Sexism Block the Path to Management for Minority Women," *The Wall Street Journal*, July 25, 1990, p. B1.

professors are absentminded). Then, we form expectations of others and interpret their behavior according to our stereotypes. Finally, stereotypes are maintained by the process shown in Figure 4–6. Specifically, stereotypes are maintained by (1) overestimating the frequency of stereotypic behaviors exhibited by others, (2) incorrectly explaining expected and unexpected behaviors, and (3) differentiating minority individuals from oneself. Let us now take a look at different types of stereotypes.

Sex-Role Stereotypes

A **sex-role stereotype** is the belief that differing traits and abilities make men and women particularly well suited to different roles (see OB in Action). This perceptual tendency was documented in a classic 1972 study. After administering a sex-role questionnaire to 383 women and 599 men, the researchers drew the following conclusion: ''Our research demonstrates the

• **FIGURE 4-6** The Process of Maintaining Stereotypes

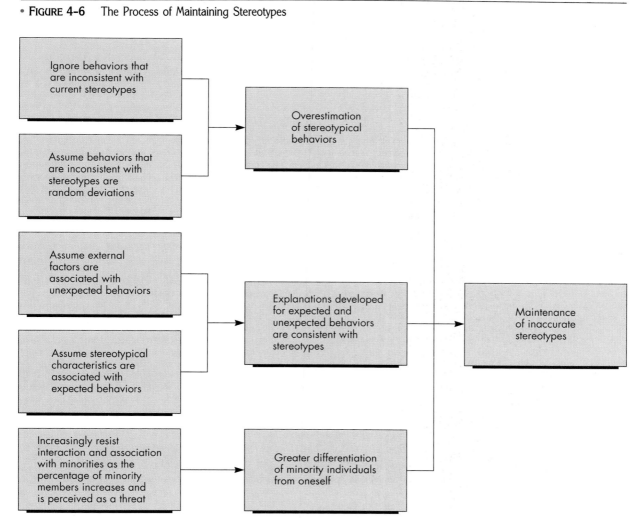

Source: Adapted from Loren Falkenberg, ''Improving the Accuracy of Stereotypes within the Workplace,'' *Journal of Management*, March 1990, p. 110.

OB IN ACTION

A Sex-Role Stereotype Is Debunked

Biologists, psychologists, anthropologists and sociologists have been seeking the origin of gender differences for more than a century, debating the possibilities with increasing rancor ever since researchers were forced to question their favorite theory back in 1902. At that time many scientists believed that intelligence was a function of brain size and that males uniformly had larger brains than women—a fact that would nicely explain men's pre-eminence in art, science and letters. This treasured hypothesis began to disintegrate when a woman graduate student compared the cranial capacities of a group of male scientists with those of female college students; several women came out ahead of the men, and one of the smallest skulls belonged to a famous male anthropologist.

Source: Laura Shapiro, "Guns and Dolls," *Newsweek*, May 28, p. 56. Copyright 1990, Newsweek, Inc. All rights reserved. Reprinted by permission.

contemporary existence of clearly defined sex-role stereotypes for men and women contrary to the phenomenon of 'unisex' currently touted in the media."[16] They further explained:

> Women are·perceived as relatively less competent, less independent, less objective, and less logical than men; men are perceived as lacking interpersonal sensitivity, warmth, and expressiveness in comparison to women. Moreover, stereotypically masculine traits are more often perceived to be desirable than are stereotypically feminine characteristics. Most importantly, both men and women incorporate both the positive and negative traits of the appropriate stereotype into their self-concepts. Since more feminine traits are negatively valued than are masculine traits, women tend to have more negative self-concepts than do men.[17]

More recent research indicates that men and women do not systematically differ in the manner suggested by traditional stereotypes.[18] Sex-role stereotypes are indeed gross oversimplifications of reality. Women and men need to be judged as individuals, when making personnel decisions, not as members of supposedly homogeneous groups. (The same holds true for racial and ethnic minorities.) Findings from laboratory research suggest that managers may be following this recommendation.

A recent meta-analysis of 24 experimental studies revealed that men and women received similar performance ratings for the same level of task performance. Stated differently, there was no pro-male bias. Further, a second meta-analysis of 19 studies found no significant relationship between applicant gender and hiring recommendations.[19] These results are encouraging. They are also consistent with recent evaluations of employees' attitudes toward female executives. Alma Baron, an expert on women in management, tracked managers' attitudes toward female executives from 1981 to 1988. She compared a 1981 national sample of 1,800 managers (all men) with a sample of 1,700 managers (13 percent women) in 1988. Results presented in Table 4–4 indicate a trend toward increasing acceptance of women in management.

• Since the 1950s, when women were expected to be model homemakers, much has changed. H. Richmor/ FPG International

• **TABLE 4–4**   National Surveys Reveal Increasing Acceptance of Women in Management

Statement	1981	1988	
1. In time women executives will become commonplace.	81.9%	87.5%	Agree
2. Typical women's characteristics make them less capable for management positions than men.	60.1	77.5	Disagree
3. Female executives cause male subordinates to overreact to criticism.	28.5	17.9	Agree
4. Generally, women become top executives by using sexual favors.	87.3	93.2	Disagree
5. Male subordinates feel inferior when their superiors are female.	25.9	21.9	Agree
6. Generally women are not as career-oriented as men.	51.5	29.3	Agree
7. Women are reluctant to work for females.	49.2	28.9	Agree
8. Male subordiantes are equally productive under male or female superiors.	53.3	64.0	Agree
9. A man is better suited for handling executive responsibilities than a woman is.	59.5	76.2	Disagree
10. Women make good executives.	50.5	69.0	Agree

Source: Alma S. Baron, "What Men Are Saying about Women in Business: A Decade Later," *Business Horizons,* July–August 1989, p. 52.

OB EXERCISE

What Are Your Attitudes toward Women Executives?

Read each question and mark your answer by circling whether you:

1 = Strongly disagree
2 = Disagree
3 = Neither disagree nor agree
4 = Agree
5 = Strongly agree

Females have the capabilities for responsible managerial positions.	1 2 3 4 5
A female executive merits the same trust and respect as a male executive.	1 2 3 4 5
Women in responsible managerial positions must have the capabilities for their positions and therefore men should honor their decisions.	1 2 3 4 5
It's about time we had some women executives in organizations.	1 2 3 4 5
Women executives are not ignorant when it comes to highly technical subjects.	1 2 3 4 5
It is unfair to say women became top executives by using sexual favors.	1 2 3 4 5
A man is not better suited for handling executive responsibility than a woman is.	1 2 3 4 5
There are no problems with a male working for a female executive if both are dedicated, competent, and learned workers.	1 2 3 4 5
Women are not taking men's positions nowadays.	1 2 3 4 5

Total score = _____

Source: Based on Peter Dubno, John Costas, Hugh Cannon, Charles Wankel, and Hussein Emin, "An Empirically Keyed Scale for Measuring Managerial Attitudes toward Women Executives," *Psychology of Women Quarterly*, Summer 1979, pp. 360–61. (Copyrighted by and reprinted with the permission of Cambridge University Press.)

What are your attitudes toward women executives? To find out, complete the survey in the OB Exercise. Compute your score by adding your nine responses. (Revised norms for comparison purposes are: Total score of 9–20 = Unfavorable attitude toward female executives; 21–33 = Middle of the road; 34–45 = Favorable.) What are the organizational and career implications of your attitudes toward women executives?

Age Stereotypes

Age stereotypes reinforce age discrimination (see International OB) because of their negative orientation. For example, long-standing age stereotypes depict older workers as less satisfied, not as involved with their work, less motivated, not as committed, less productive than their younger co-workers, and more apt to be absent from work. Older employees are also perceived as being more accident prone.[20] As with sex-role stereotypes, these age stereotypes are more fiction than fact.

OB researcher Susan Rhodes sought to determine whether age stereotypes were supported by data from 185 different studies. She discovered

INTERNATIONAL OB

Europeans Strive to Reduce Age Bias

Rampant job bias against older Europeans is just starting to decline, thanks to a scarcity of young people and the spread of U.S.-style advocacy groups. Unlike America, Europe lacks tough laws broadly barring age discrimination. Employers routinely run advertisements seeking workers under 40, force staffers as young as 55 to retire and fire people simply for being too old.

Source: Joann S. Lublin, "Graying Europeans Battling Age Bias," *The Wall Street Journal*, August 14, 1990, p. B1.

that as age increases so do employees' job satisfaction, job involvement, internal work motivation, and organizational commitment. Moreover, older workers were not more accident prone.[21]

Regarding job performance, a recent meta-analysis of 96 studies representing 38,983 people and a cross section of jobs revealed that age and job performance were unrelated.[22] In spite of these meta-analytic results, some executives still believe that older workers make better service employees. Jim Hodkinson, chief executive officer of B&Q PLC, Britain's biggest home-improvement chain, concluded that the company exceeded its 1990 sales goal by 40 percent partly because of its age profile: Consumers preferred to work with older salespeople. Hodkinson planned on opening two new outlets in 1990 staffed solely with people over 50.[23]

What about absenteeism? Do older employees miss more days of work? A recent meta-analysis of 34 studies encompassing 7,772 workers indicated that age was inversely related to both voluntary (a day at the beach) and involuntary (sick day) absenteeism.[24] Contrary to stereotypes, older workers are ready and able to meet their job requirements. Moreover, results from the meta-analysis suggest managers should focus more attention on absenteeism among younger workers than among older workers.

Race Stereotypes

There is not a large percentage of Hispanic, black, and Asian managers in the United States (refer back to Figure 4–5). Negative racial stereotypes are one of several potential explanations for this state of affairs. Consider women of color. There appears to be a stereotype that minority women are frequently hired in order to fulfill equal employment opportunity requirements. "Personnel executives sometimes call them 'twofers' because they fulfill two equal opportunity obligations, and that label undercuts their credibility on the job."[25] This is precisely what happened to 40-year-old Charleyse Pratt.

> As an assistant personnel director at a Midwest electronics company, she gave seminars to senior executives on sexual and racial harassment. One day, after a four-hour presentation to 20 white male senior managers, one of the men, whose last name was pronounced "coon," stood up and said, "Do you mean the coons can't stick together?" All the men, including her boss, broke into laughter. . . .

More recently, at a Midwestern manufacturer, she was told outright that she was hired to meet affirmative action goals. And not long ago, she found herself teaching her job to a white man who had been promoted over her. "He told me, 'You're going to have to learn to subordinate yourself to me,'" says Mrs. Pratt.[26]

A recent field study reinforces Mrs. Pratt's experience. A team of researchers examined the relationship of race to employee attitudes across samples of 814 black managers and 814 white managers. Results demonstrated that blacks, compared to whites, felt less accepted by their peers, perceived lower managerial discretion on their jobs, reached career plateaus more frequently, noted lower levels of career satisfaction, and received lower performance ratings.[27] In contrast, another recent study was more optimistic about the impact of race stereotypes. Based on 39,537 rater–ratee pairs of black and white employees, results revealed that performance ratings were not systematically affected by rater bias.[28] Given the increasing number of minorities that will enter the work force over the next 10 years (recall our discussion in Chapter 2), employers should focus on nurturing and developing minorities as well as increasing managers' sensitivities to invalid racial stereotypes.

Managerial Challenges and Recommendations

As noted by Ralph Ablon, chairman of Ogden Corp., number 74 on the Fortune list of the 100 largest diversified service companies in the United States, discrimination is still a problem in the workplace (see OB in Action). The key managerial challenge is to make decisions that are blind to gender, age, and race. Training managers to be aware of and avoid both invalid stereotypes and the perceptual errors listed in Table 4–3 (page 135) is one recommendation for accomplishing this objective.

 OB IN ACTION

The CEO of Ogden Corporation Tries to Reduce Discrimination

According to Ralph Ablon, CEO of Ogden Corp., "Sure there's discrimination. It's stupid to say there's not. Despite our intellectual efforts to deny it, prejudices exist and will exist until a new generation comes along that doesn't have them." . . . At age 73, Ablon seems an unlikely harbinger of new thinking. But three years ago he appointed Maria Monet, now 40, as his company's chief financial officer, and he pays her more than $730,000 a year, making her one of the top-earning women in corporate America. Enlightenment, Ablon concedes, has come only with age and a lot of contemplation: "When I became CEO 29 years ago, I don't believe I could have been as liberal. And I couldn't have gotten away with appointing a woman as CFO. Today I could."

Source: Jaclyn Fierman, "Why Women Still Don't Hit the Top." *Fortune*, July 30, 1990, p. 42.

Another recommendation is for managers to identify valid individual differences (discussed in Chapter 3) that differentiate successful from unsuccessful performers. For example, research reveals that experience is a better predictor of performance than age and that ethical behavior varies by age.[29] Let us consider the case of ethical behavior.

Are younger employees more permissive in terms of perceived ethical behavior than older workers? Before reading further, we would like you to answer the questions in A Matter of Ethics. How acceptable did you find these activities? A team of researchers sent out 10,000 questionnaires (2,156 were returned) to managerial and professional employees of all ages to determine an answer. Respondents were asked to evaluate the acceptability of 16 hypothetical vignettes (including the two you read). Younger (ages 21 to 40) respondents had an average score of 3.37 for the first vignette shown in A Matter of Ethics, whereas the average score for older respondents (ages 51 to 70) was 2.71. For the second vignette involving misleading financial reporting, 25.5 percent of the older group indicated that the behavior was never acceptable as compared to 10.9 percent of the younger group. Overall, younger respondents were consistently more permissive in their views than were older respondents across all 16 vignettes. These results suggest that employees' ethical orientation varies by age. At a minimum, senior-level

 A MATTER OF ETHICS

What Is Your Ethical Orientation?

Below are two managerial vignettes. Based on your personal values, evaluate the acceptability of the behavior described in each vignette. Use the scale shown below to record your evaluation.

1	2	3	4	5	6	7
Never Acceptable			Sometimes Acceptable			Always Acceptable

A company president recognized that sending expensive Christmas gifts to purchasing agents might compromise their positions. However, he continued the policy since it was common practice and changing it might result in loss of business.

Your rating _____

A comptroller selected a legal method of financial reporting that concealed some embarrassing financial facts that would otherwise have become public knowledge.

Your rating _____

Source: Vignettes were taken from Justin G. Longenecker, Joseph A. McKinney, and Carlos W. Moore, "The Generation Gap in Business Ethics," *Business Horizons*, September–October 1989, p. 10.

managers should not assume that younger managers share their ethical views.

A third recommendation is to remove promotional barriers for both men and women and for people of different racial groups. This can be accomplished by minimizing the differences in job experience across groups of people. Similar experience, coupled with the accurate evaluation of performance, helps managers to make gender, age, and racially blind decisions.

Finally, hiring older workers is a good solution for reducing turnover, providing role models for younger employees, and coping with the current shortage of qualified entry-level workers. Results from both a meta-analysis and actual corporate experience support this recommendation.[30] Days Inn of America represents a good example.

> Now one-third of the staff at the reservation centers, which had a 100 percent turnover rate, is made up of older workers. The turnover rate among seniors is a mere 1 percent. "We recruited older workers as a solution to a problem and found they were more successful—wonderful, dependable, patient—than we dreamed," says Days Inn spokeswoman Shira Miller.[31]

• SELF-FULFILLING PROPHECY: THE PYGMALION EFFECT

Historical roots of the self-fulfilling prophecy are found in Greek mythology. According to mythology, Pygmalion was a sculptor who hated women, yet fell in love with an ivory statue he carved of a beautiful woman. He became so infatuated with the statue that he prayed to the goddess Aphrodite to bring her to life. The goddess heard his prayer, granted his wish, and Pygmalion's statue came to life. The essence of the **self-fulfilling prophecy,** or Pygmalion effect, is that people's expectations or beliefs determine their behavior and performance, thus serving to make their expectations come true. In other words, we strive to validate our *perceptions* of reality, no matter how faulty they may be. Thus, the self-fulfilling prophecy is an important perceptual outcome we need to better understand.

The following self-fulfilling prophecy dramatically affected an entire company:

> The folks who run Epoch Group, Inc., say that if you "create your own reality," you may be much more successful in business than you ever thought you could be.
>
> Michael D. Topf, president of the management consulting firm, . . . once challenged the head of a formal wear retail chain who said that he had had a great spring season but that now the company was "gearing down" for the summer.
>
> The firm and its employees had been operating under the mindset that spring, with its proms and weddings, was the busy season and that summer was slow, says Topf. So when summer came, they would relax. And sure enough, summer turned out to be slow.
>
> Topf got the retailer to make a declaration to his people: "We're going to have the busiest summer we've ever had." At first, there was disbelief, but the retailer, with Epoch's support, was insistent that it was going to be a busy season. So his marketing and promotion people began to come up with some strategies, pushing

more formal weddings in the summer, promoting formal parties, and looking at other items, such as jewelry, that the stores could sell.

And of course you know the ending to the story. The chain had the busiest summer of all its 50 years.[32]

Research and an Explanatory Model

The self-fulfilling prophecy was first demonstrated in an academic environment. After giving a bogus test of academic potential to students from grades 1 to 6, researchers informed teachers that certain students had high potential for achievement. In reality, students were randomly assigned to the "high potential" and "control" (normal potential) groups. Results showed that children designated as having high potential obtained significantly greater increases in both IQ scores and reading ability than did the control students.[33] The teachers of the supposedly high potential group got better results because their high expectations caused them to give harder assignments, more feedback, and more recognition of achievement. Students in the normal potential group did not excel because their teachers did not expect outstanding results.

Research similarly has shown that by raising instructors' and managers' expectations for individuals performing a wide variety of tasks, higher levels of achievement/productivity can be obtained.[34] Subjects in these field studies included airmen at the United States Air Force Academy Preparatory School, disadvantaged people in job-training programs, electronics assemblers, trainees in a military command course, and U.S. naval personnel.

Figure 4–7 presents a model of the self-fulfilling prophecy that helps explain these results. This model attempts to outline how supervisory expectations affect employee performance. As indicated, high supervisory expectancy produces better leadership (linkage 1), which subsequently leads employees to develop higher self-expectations (linkage 2). Higher expectations motivate workers to exert more effort (linkage 3), ultimately increasing performance (linkage 4) and supervisory expectancies (linkage 5). Successful performance also improves an employee's self-expectancy for achievement (linkage 6).

Putting the Self-Fulfilling Prophecy to Work

Largely due to the Pygmalion effect, managerial expectations powerfully influence employee behavior and performance. Consequently, managers need to harness the Pygmalion effect by building a hierarchical framework that reinforces positive performance expectations throughout the organization.

As shown in Figure 4–8, employees' self-expectations are the foundation of this framework. In turn, positive self-expectations improve interpersonal expectations by encouraging people to work toward common goals. This cooperation enhances group-level productivity and promotes positive performance expectations within the work group. At Microsoft Corporation, for example, employees routinely put in 75-hour weeks, especially when work

• **FIGURE 4-7**   A Model of the Self-Fulfilling Prophecy

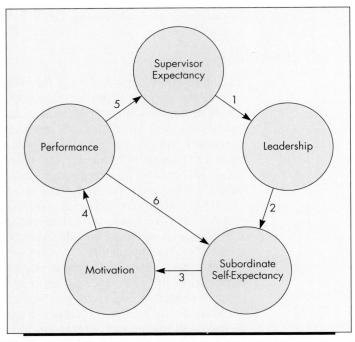

Source: Dov Eden, "Self-Fulfilling Prophecy as a Management Tool: Harnessing Pygmalion," *Academy of Management Review*, January 1984, p. 67. Used with permission.

• **FIGURE 4-8**   Building an Organizational Pygmalion Effect

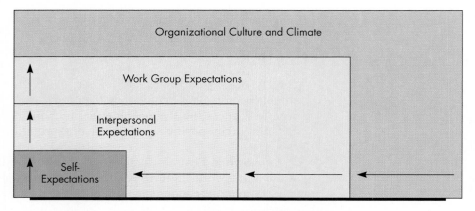

Source: Adapted from Richard H. G. Field and David A. Van Seters, "Management by Expectations (MBE): The Power of Positive Prophecy," *Journal of General Management*, Winter 1988, p. 30.

groups are trying to meet shipment deadlines for new products. Because Microsoft is known for meeting its deadlines, positive group-level expectations help create and reinforce an organizational culture of high expectancy for success. This process then excites people about working for the organization, thereby reducing turnover. Microsoft's turnover is well below industry standards, even for highly marketable computer programmers.[35]

Because positive self-expectations are the foundation for creating an organization-wide Pygmalion effect, let us consider how managers can create positive performance expectations. This task may be accomplished by using various combinations of the following:

1. Recognize that everyone has the potential to increase his or her performance.
2. Instill confidence in your staff.
3. Set high performance goals.
4. Positively reinforce employees for a job well done.
5. Provide constructive feedback when necessary.
6. Help employees advance through the organization.
7. Introduce new employees as if they have outstanding potential.
8. Become aware of your personal prejudices and nonverbal messages that may discourage others.[36]

• CAUSAL ATTRIBUTIONS

Attribution theory is based on the premise that people attempt to infer causes for observed behavior. Rightly or wrongly, we constantly formulate cause-and-effect explanations for our own and others' behavior. Attributional statements such as the following are common: "Joe drinks too much because he has no willpower; but I need a couple of drinks after work because I'm under a lot of pressure." Formally defined, **causal attributions** are suspected or inferred causes of behavior. Even though our causal attributions tend to be self-serving and are often invalid, it is important to understand how people formulate attributions because they profoundly affect organizational behavior. For example, a supervisor who attributes an employee's poor performance to a lack of effort might reprimand that individual. However, training might be deemed necessary if the supervisor attributes the poor performance to a lack of ability.

Generally speaking, people formulate causal attributions by considering the events preceding an observed behavior (see Figure 4–9). This section

---

• **FIGURE 4-9** A General Model of Attribution

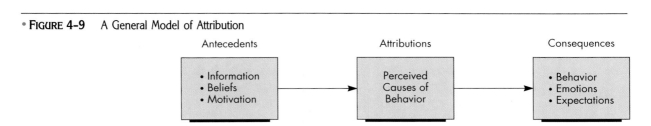

introduces and explores two different widely cited attribution models proposed by Harold Kelley and Bernard Weiner. Attributional tendencies, research, and related managerial implications also are discussed.

Kelley's Model of Attribution

Current models of attribution, such as Kelley's, are based on the pioneering work of the late Fritz Heider. Heider, the founder of attribution theory, proposed that behavior can be attributed either to **internal factors** within a person (such as ability) or to **external factors** within the environment (such as a difficult task). This line of thought parallels the idea of an internal versus external locus of control, as discussed in Chapter 3. Building on Heider's work, Kelley attempted to pinpoint major antecedents of internal and external attributions. Kelley hypothesized that people make causal attributions after gathering information about three dimensions of behavior: consensus, distinctiveness, and consistency.[37] These dimensions vary independently, thus forming various combinations and leading to differing attributions.

One needs a working knowledge of all three dimensions if Kelley's model is to be understood and applied.

• *Consensus* involves comparison of an individual's behavior with that of his or her peers. There is high consensus when one acts like the rest of the group and low consensus when one acts differently.
• *Distinctiveness* is determined by comparing a person's behavior on one task with his or her behavior on other tasks. High distinctiveness means the individual has performed the task in question differently than other tasks. Low distinctiveness means stable performance or quality from one task to another.
• *Consistency* is determined by judging if the individual's performance on a given task is consistent over time. High consistency means one performs a certain task the same, time after time. Unstable performance of a given task over time would mean low consistency.

Figure 4–10 presents performance charts showing low versus high consensus, distinctiveness, and consistency. It is instructive to remember that consensus relates to other *people*, distinctiveness relates to other *tasks*, and consistency relates to *time*. The question now is: How does information about these three dimensions of behavior lead to internal or external attributions?

Kelley hypothesized that people attribute behavior to *external* causes (environmental factors) when they perceive high consensus, high distinctiveness, and low consistency. *Internal* attributions (personal factors) tend to be made when observed behavior is characterized by low consensus, low distinctiveness, and high consistency. So, for example, when all employees are performing poorly (high consensus), when the poor performance occurs on only one of several tasks (high distinctiveness), and the poor performance occurs during only one time period (low consistency), a supervisor will probably attribute an employee's poor performance to an external source such as peer pressure or an overly difficult task. In contrast, perform-

• **FIGURE 4-10**   Performance Charts Showing Low and High Consensus, Distinctiveness, and Consistency Information

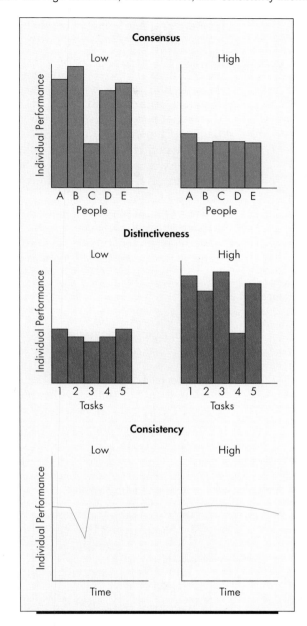

Source: Karen A. Brown, "Explaining Group Poor Performance: An Attributional Analysis," *Academy of Management Review,* January 1984, p. 56. Used with permission.

ance will be attributed to an employee's personal characteristics (an internal attribution) when only the individual in question is performing poorly (low consensus), when the inferior performance is found across several tasks (low distinctiveness), and when the low performance has persisted over time (high consistency).

Weiner's Model of Attribution

Bernard Weiner, a noted motivation theorist, developed an attribution model to explain achievement behavior and to predict subsequent changes in motivation and performance. In his model, Weiner proposes that ability, effort, task difficulty, luck, and help from others are the primary causes of achievement behavior (see Figure 4–11). In turn, these attributions for success and failure influence how individuals feel about themselves. For instance, a meta-analysis of 104 studies involving almost 15,000 subjects found that people who attributed failure to their lack of ability (as opposed to bad luck) experienced psychological depression. The exact opposite attributions (to good luck rather than to high ability) tended to trigger depression in people experiencing positive events. In short, perceived bad luck took the sting out of a negative outcome, but perceived good luck reduced the joy associated with success.[38]

In further support of Weiner's model, research shows that when individuals attribute their success to internal rather than external factors, they (1) have higher expectations for future success, (2) report a greater desire for achievement, and (3) set higher performance goals.[39]

Attributional Tendencies

Researchers have uncovered two attributional tendencies that distort one's interpretation of observed behavior—*fundamental attribution bias* and *self-serving bias*.

Fundamental Attribution Bias   The **fundamental attribution bias** reflects one's tendency to attribute another person's behavior to his or her personal characteristics, as opposed to situational factors. This bias causes perceivers to ignore important environmental forces that often significantly

---

• **FIGURE 4–11**   A Modified Version of Weiner's Attribution Model

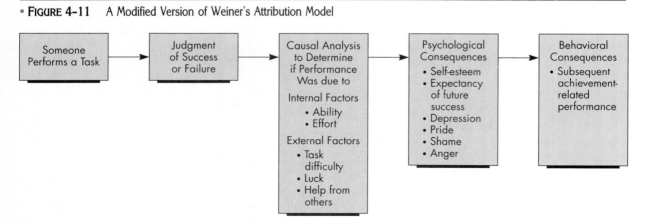

Source: Based in part on Bernard Weiner, "An Attributional Theory of Achievement Motivation and Emotion," *Psychological Review*, October 1985, pp. 548–73.

affect behavior. For example, there is a "popular tendency to view emotional disorders as failures of character rather than manifestations of mental illness, especially when they result in harm to others."[40]

Self-Serving Bias   The **self-serving bias** represents one's tendency to take more personal responsibility for success than for failure. Referring again to Figure 4–11, employees tend to attribute their successes to internal factors (high ability and/or hard work) and their failures to uncontrollable external factors (tough job, bad luck, unproductive co-workers, or an unsympathetic boss). This self-serving bias is evident in how students typically analyze their performance on exams. "A" students are likely to attribute their grade to high ability or hard work. "D" students, meanwhile, tend to pin the blame on factors like an unfair test, bad luck, or unclear lectures. Because of self-serving bias, it is very difficult to pin down personal responsibility for mistakes in today's complex organizations.

Managerial Application and Implications

Attribution models can be used to explain how managers handle poorly performing employees. One study revealed that corrective action was more punitive when managers attributed poor performance to low effort. A second study indicated that managers tended to transfer employees whose poor performance was attributed to a lack of ability. These same managers also decided to take no immediate action when poor performance was attributed to external factors beyond an individual's control.[41]

The above situations have several important implications for managers. First, managers tend to disproportionately attribute behavior to *internal* causes. This can result in inaccurate evaluations of performance, leading to reduced employee motivation. No one likes to be blamed because of factors they perceive to be beyond their control. Further, since managers' responses to employee performance vary according to their attributions, attributional biases may lead to inappropriate managerial actions, including promotions, transfers, layoffs, and so forth. This can dampen motivation and performance. Attributional training sessions for managers are in order. Basic attributional processes can be explained, and managers can be taught to detect and avoid attributional biases. Finally, an employee's attributions for his or her own performance have dramatic effects on subsequent motivation, performance, and personal attitudes such as self-esteem. For instance, people tend to give up, develop lower expectations for future success, and experience decreased self-esteem when they attribute failure to a lack of ability. Fortunately, attributional retraining can improve both motivation and performance. Research shows that employees can be taught to attribute their failures to a lack of effort rather than to a lack of ability.[42] This attributional realignment paves the way for improved motivation and performance.

In summary, managers need to keep a finger on the pulse of employee attributions if they are to make full use of the motivation concepts in the next two chapters.

• Summary of Key Concepts

A. Perception is a mental and cognitive process that enables us to interpret and understand our surroundings. Social perception, also known as social cognition and social information processing, is a four-stage process. The four stages are selective attention/comprehension, encoding and simplification, storage and retention, and retrieval and response. During social cognition, salient stimuli are matched with schemata, assigned to cognitive categories, and stored in long-term memory for events, semantic materials, or people.

B. Stereotypes represent grossly oversimplified beliefs or expectations about groups of people. Stereotypes are maintained by (1) over-estimating the frequency of stereotypical behaviors exhibited by others, (2) incorrectly explaining expected and unexpected behaviors, and (3) differentiating minority individuals from oneself. Managers need to be particularly aware of sex-role, age, and race stereotypes because they can adversely affect personnel decisions.

C. The self-fulfilling prophecy, also known as the Pygmalion effect, describes how people behave so their expectations come true. High managerial expectations foster high employee self-expectations. These in turn lead to greater effort and better performance, and yet higher expectations. Conversely, a downward spiral of expectations-performance may occur. Managers are encouraged to harness the Pygmalion effect by building a hierarchical framework that reinforces positive performance expectations throughout the organization.

D. Attribution theory attempts to describe how people infer causes for observed behavior. According to Kelley's model of causal attribution, external attributions tend to be made when consensus and distinctiveness are high and consistency is low. Internal (personal responsibility) attributions tend to be made when consensus and distinctiveness are low and consistency is high.

E. Weiner's model of attribution predicts achievement behavior in terms of causal attributions. Attributions of ability, effort, task difficulty, luck, and help from others affect how individuals feel about themselves. In turn, these feelings directly influence subsequent achievement-related performance.

F. Fundamental attribution bias involves emphasizing personal factors more than situational factors while formulating causal attributions for the behavior of others. Self-serving bias involves personalizing the causes of one's successes and externalizing the causes of one's failures.

• Key Terms

perception	self-fulfilling prophecy
attention	causal attributions
cognitive categories	internal factors
schema	external factors

stereotypes   fundamental attribution bias
sex-role stereotypes   self-serving bias

• DISCUSSION QUESTIONS

1. Why is it important for managers to have a working knowledge of perception and attribution?
2. When you are sitting in class, what stimuli are salient? What is your schema for classroom activity?
3. Have you ever been the victim of a sex-role stereotype? Discuss.
4. Which type of stereotype (sex-role, age, or race) is more pervasive and negative in organizations? Why?
5. What evidence of self-fulfilling prophecies have you seen lately?
6. How might the model of building an organizational Pygmalion effect (Figure 4–8) be applied in this class?
7. How would you formulate an attribution, according to Kelley's model, for the behavior of a classmate who starts arguing in class with your professor?
8. In what situations do you tend to attribute your successes/failures to luck? How well does Weiner's attributional model in Figure 4–11 explain your answers? Explain.
9. Are poor people victimized by a fundamental attribution bias? Explain.
10. What evidence of the self-serving bias have you observed lately?

BACK TO THE OPENING CASE

Now that you have read Chapter 4, you should be able to answer the following questions about the U.S. Servicewomen case:

1. How do military men's stereotypes affect U.S. servicewomen?
2. How did Saudi Arabian stereotypes victimize U.S. servicewomen?
3. What role does the self-fulfilling prophecy play in this case?
4. Using Weiner's attributional model as a framework for analyses (see Figure 4–11), what were the likely behavioral consequences associated with U.S. servicewomen's involvement in Saudi Arabia during the gulf war?

• EXERCISE 4

Objectives

1. To gain experience determining the causes of performance.
2. To decide on corrective action for employee performance.

Introduction

Attributions are typically made to internal and external factors. Perceivers arrive at their assessments by using various informational cues or antecedents. To determine the types of antecedents people use, we have developed a case containing various informational cues about an individual's performance. You will be asked to read the case and make attributions about the causes of performance. To assess the impact of attributions on managerial behavior, you will also be asked to recommend corrective action.

Instructions

Presented below is a case that depicts the performance of Mary Martin, a computer programmer. Please read the case and then identify the causes of her behavior by answering the questions following the case. After completing this task, decide on the appropriateness of various forms of corrective action. A list of potential recommendations has been developed. The list is divided into four categories. Read each action and evaluate its appropriateness by using the scale provided. Next, compute a total score for each of the four categories.

The Case of Mary Martin

> Mary Martin, 30, received her baccalaureate degree in computer science from a reputable state school in the Midwest. She also graduated with above-average grades. Mary is currently working in the computer support/analysis department as a programmer for a nationally based firm. During the past year, Mary has missed 10 days of work. She seems unmotivated and rarely has her assignments completed on time. Mary is usually given the harder programs to work on.
>
> Past records indicate Mary, on the average, completes programs classified as "routine" in about 45 hours. Her co-workers, on the other hand, complete "routine" programs in an average time of 32 hours. Further, Mary finishes programs considered "major problems," on the average, in about 115 hours. Her co-workers, however, finish these same "major problem" assignments, on the average, in about 100 hours. When Mary has worked in programming teams, her peer performance reviews are generally average to negative. Her male peers have noted she is not creative in attacking problems and she is difficult to work with.
>
> The computer department recently sent a questionnaire to all users of its services to evaluate the usefulness and accuracy of data received. The results indicate many departments are not using computer output because they cannot understand the reports. It was also determined that the users of output generated from Mary's programs found the output chaotic and not useful for managerial decision making.[43]

Causes of Performance

> To what extent was each of the following a cause of Mary's performance? Use the following scale:
>
> Very little   Very much
> 1————————2————————3————————4————————5
>
> | | | |
> |---|---|---|
> | a. High ability | 1 2 3 4 5 |
> | b. Low ability | 1 2 3 4 5 |
> | c. Low effort | 1 2 3 4 5 |
> | d. Difficult job | 1 2 3 4 5 |
> | e. Unproductive co-workers | 1 2 3 4 5 |
> | f. Bad luck | 1 2 3 4 5 |

Appropriateness of Corrective Action

Evaluate the following courses of action by using the scale below:

Very inappropriate				Very appropriate
1—————	2—————	3—————	4—————	5

Coercive actions
a. Reprimand Mary for her performance   1 2 3 4 5
b. Threaten to fire Mary if her performance does not improve   1 2 3 4 5
Change job
c. Transfer Mary to another job   1 2 3 4 5
d. Demote Mary to a less demanding job   1 2 3 4 5
Nonpunitive actions
e. Work with Mary to help her do her job better   1 2 3 4 5
f. Offer Mary encouragement to help her improve   1 2 3 4 5
No immediate action
g. Do nothing   1 2 3 4 5
h. Promise Mary a pay raise if she improves   1 2 3 4 5

Compute a score for the four categories:[44]

Coercive actions = a + b =
Change job = c + d =
Nonpunitive actions = e + f =
No immediate actions = g + h =

Questions for Consideration/Class Discussion

1. How would you evaluate Mary's performance in terms of consensus, distinctiveness, and consistency?
2. Is Mary's performance due to internal or external causes?
3. What did you identify as the top two causes of Mary's performance? Are your choices consistent with Weiner's classification of internal and external factors? Explain.
4. Which of the four types of corrective action do you think is most appropriate? Explain. Can you identify any negative consequences of this choice?

• NOTES

[1] Details may be found in Robert Eisenberger, Peter Fasolo, and Valerie Davis-LaMastro, "Perceived Organizational Support and Employee Diligence, Commitment, and Innovation," *Journal of Applied Psychology,* February 1990, pp. 51–59.

[2] Dianna Solis, "Plastic Surgery Wooing Patients Hoping to Move Up Career Ladder," *The Wall Street Journal,* September 6, 1985, p. 31.

[3] Susan T. Fiske and Shelley E. Taylor, *Social Cognition* (Reading, Mass.: Addison-Wesley Publishing, 1984), pp. 1–2.

[4] For a review of the history of social cognition, see Robert G. Lord and Karen J. Maher, "Alternative Information Processing Models and Their Implications for Theory, Research, and Practice," *Academy of Management Review,* January 1990, pp. 9–28.

5 Adapted from discussion in Fiske and Taylor, *Social Cognition,* pp. 186–87.

6 Eleanor Rosch, Carolyn B. Mervis, Wayne D. Gray, David M. Johnson, and Penny Boyes-Braem, "Basic Objects in Natural Categories," *Cognitive Psychology*, July 1976, p. 383.

7 A thorough discussion of schema and their role in information processing is presented by Susan T. Fiske and Steven L. Neuberg, "A Continuum of Impression Formation, from Category-Based to Individuating Processes: Influences of Information and Motivation on Attention and Interpretation," in *Advances in Experimental Social Psychology*, ed. Mark P. Zanna (New York: Academic Press, 1990), vol. 23, pp. 1–74.

8 Washing clothes.

9 The discussion of these three compartments is based on material in Robert S. Wyer, Jr., and Thomas K. Srull, "The Processing of Social Stimulus Information: A Conceptual Integration," in *Person Memory: The Cognitive Basis of Social Perception,* eds. Reid Hastie, Thomas M. Ostrom, Ebbe B. Ebbesen, Robert S. Wyer, Jr., David L. Hamilton, and Donal E. Carlston (Hillsdale, N.J.: Lawrence Erlbaum, 1980). Research examining the relationships among categories in memory is presented by Peter Borkenau, "Traits as Ideal-Based and Goal-Derived Social Categories," *Journal of Personality and Social Psychology*, March 1990, pp. 381–96.

10 Results of an empirical study can be found in Angelo S. DeNisi, Tina Robbins, and Thomas P. Cafferty, "Organization of Information Used for Performance Appraisals: Role of Diary-Keeping," *Journal of Applied Psychology*, February 1989, pp. 124–29.

11 A social information processing model of the interview was developed and tested by Amanda Peek Phillips and Robert L. Dipboye, "Correlational Tests of Predictions from a Process Model of the Interview," *Journal of Applied Psychology*, February 1989, pp. 41–52.

12 A social information processing approach for studying communication is presented and tested by Constantine Sedikides, "Effects of Fortuitously Activated Constructs versus Activated Communication Goals on Person Impressions," *Journal of Personality and Social Psychology*, March 1990, pp. 397–408.

13 Charles Leerhsen, "How Disney Does It," *Newsweek*, April 3, 1989, p. 52.

14 David L. Hamilton, "A Cognitive-Attributional Analysis of Stereotyping," in *Advances in Experimental Social Psychology*, ed. L. Berkowitz (New York: Academic Press, 1979), vol. 12, pp. 53–84.

15 A detailed discussion of stereotype formation and maintenance can be found in Loren Falkenberg, "Improving the Accuracy of Stereotypes within the Workplace," *Journal of Management*, March 1990, pp. 107–18.

16 Inge K. Broverman, Susan Raymond Vogel, Donald M. Broverman, Frank E. Clarkson, and Paul S. Rosenkrantz, "Sex-Role Stereotypes: A Current Appraisal," *Journal of Social Issues* 28, no. 2 (1972), p. 75.

17 Ibid.

18 A practical discussion of this research is contained in Laura Shapiro, "Guns and Dolls," *Newsweek*, May 28, 1990, pp. 56–69, 61–62, 65.

19 Results from the meta-analyses are discussed in Kenneth P. Carson, Cynthia L. Sutton, and Patricia D. Corner, "Gender Bias in Performance Appraisals: A Meta-Analysis," paper presented at the 49th Annual Academy of Management Meeting, Washington, D.C.: 1989; and Judy D. Olian, Donald P. Schwab, and Yitchak Haberfeld, "The Impact of Applicant Gender Compared to Qualifications on Hiring Recommendations: A Meta-Analysis of Experimental Studies," *Organizational Behavior and Human Decision Processes,* April 1988, pp. 180–95.

[20] A thorough discussion of the theoretical basis of age stereotypes is contained in Bruce J. Avolio, David A. Waldman, and Michael A. McDaniel, ''Age and Work Performance in Nonmanagerial Jobs: The Effects of Experience and Occupational Type,'' *Academy of Management Journal*, June 1990, pp. 407–22.

[21] For a complete review, see Susan R. Rhodes, ''Age-Related Differences in Work Attitudes and Behavior: A Review and Conceptual Analysis,'' *Psychological Bulletin,* March 1983, pp. 38–367.

[22] See Glenn M. McEvoy, ''Cumulative Evidence of the Relationship between Employee Age and Job Performance,'' *Journal of Applied Psychology*, February 1989, pp. 11–17.

[23] See Joann S. Lublin, ''Graying Europeans Battling Age Bias,'' *The Wall Street Journal*, August 14, 1990, p. B1.

[24] This study was conducted by Joseph J. Martocchio, ''Age-Related Differences in Employee Absenteeism: A Meta-Analysis,'' *Psychology and Aging*, December 1989, pp. 409–14.

[25] Keith L. Alexander, ''Both Racism and Sexism Block the Path to Management for Minority Women,'' *The Wall Street Journal,* July 25, 1990, p. B1.

[26] Ibid.

[27] Details of this study may be found in Jeffrey H. Greenhaus, Saroj Parasuraman, Wayne M. Wormley, ''Effects of Race on Organizational Experiences, Job Performance Evaluations, and Career Outcomes,'' *Academy of Management Journal*, March 1990, pp. 64–86.

[28] See Elaine D. Pulakos, Leonard A. White, Scott H. Oppler, and Walter C. Borman, ''Examination of Race and Sex Effects on Performance Ratings,'' *Journal of Applied Psychology*, October 1989, pp. 770–80.

[29] The relationship between age, experience, and performance was examined by Avolio, Waldman, and McDaniel, ''Age and Work Performance in Nonmanagerial Jobs.'' Complete discussion of the ethics study may be found in Justin G. Longenecker, Joseph A. McKinney, and Carlos W. Moore, ''The Generation Gap in Business Ethics'', *Business Horizons*, September–October 1989, pp. 9–14.

[30] Results from the meta-analysis may be found in John L. Cotton and Jeffrey M. Tuttle, ''Employee Turnover: A Meta-Analysis and Review with Implications for Research,'' *Academy of Management Review,* January 1986, pp. 55–70.

[31] Lucia Mouat, ''Demographics Prompt Labor Shift,'' *The Christian Science Monitor*, March 21, 1990, p. 8.

[32] ''Break the Tie that Binds,'' *Nation's Business,* November 1985, p. 66. Reprinted by permission from *Nation's Business,* November 1985, Copyright 1985, U.S. Chamber of Commerce.

[33] The background and results for this study are presented in Robert Rosenthal and Lenore Jacobson, *Pygmalion in the Classroom: Teacher Expectation and Pupils' Intellectual Development* (New York: Holt, Rinehart & Winston, 1968).

[34] Research on the Pygmalion effect is summarized in Dov Eden, *Pygmalion in Management: Productivity as a Self-Fulfilling Prophecy* (Lexington, Mass.: Lexington Books, 1990), chapter 2.

[35] See Brenton Schlender, ''How Bill Gates Keeps the Magic Going,'' *Fortune*, June 18, 1990, pp. 82–89.

[36] These recommendations were adapted from Robert W. Goddard, ''The Pygmalion Effect,'' *Personnel Journal*, June 1985, p. 10.

[37] Kelley's model is discussed in detail in Harold H. Kelley, ''The Processes of Causal Attribution,'' *American Psychologist,* February 1973, pp. 107–28.

[38] See Paul D. Sweeney, Karen Anderson, and Scott Bailey, "Attributional Style in Depression: A Meta-Analytic Review," *Journal of Personality and Social Psychology*, May 1986, pp. 974–91.

[39] Results can be found in Neal M. Ashkanasy, "Causal Attribution and Supervisors' Response to Subordinate Performance: The Green and Mitchell Model Revisited," *Journal of Applied Social Psychology*, March 1989, pp. 309–30; and Thomas I. Chacko and James C. McElroy, "The Cognitive Component in Locke's Theory of Goal Setting: Suggestive Evidence for a Causal Attribution Interpretation," *Academy of Management Journal*, March 1983, pp. 104–18.

[40] David Gelman, "Was It Illness or Immorality?," *Newsweek*, June 11, 1990, p. 55.

[41] Details may be found in Kathleen Watson Dugan, "Ability and Effort Attributions: Do They Affect How Managers Communicate Performance Feedback Information?" *Academy of Management Journal,* March 1989, pp. 87–114; and Earl C. Pence, William C. Pendelton, Greg H. Dobbins, and Joseph A. Sgro, "Effects of Causal Explanations and Sex Variables on Recommendations for Corrective Actions Following Employee Failure," *Organizational Behavior and Human Performance*, April 1982, pp. 227–40.

[42] For a review of attributional retraining, see Friedrich Forsterling, "Attributional Retraining: A Review," *Psychological Bulletin*, November 1985, pp. 496–512.

[43] Adapted from Angelo J. Kinicki and Rodger W. Griffeth, "The Impact of Sex-Role Stereotypes on Performance Ratings and Causal Attributions of Performance," *Journal of Vocational Behavior*, April 1985, pp. 155–70.

[44] Based on Pence, Pendleton, Dobbins, and Sgro, "Effects of Causal Explanations and Sex Variables on Recommendations for Corrective Actions Following Employee Failure," pp. 227–40.

Motivation through Needs, Job Design, and Satisfaction

LEARNING OBJECTIVES

When you finish studying the material in this chapter, you should be able to:

- Define the term *motivation*.
- Discuss the conceptual model of motivation.
- Highlight the evolution of modern motivation theory.
- Contrast Maslow's and McClelland's need theories.

- Demonstrate your familiarity with scientific management, job enlargement, job rotation, and job enrichment.
- Explain the practical significance of Herzberg's distinction between motivators and hygiene factors.

- Describe how internal work motivation is increased by using the job characteristics model.
- Discuss the social information processing model of job design.
- Put the job satisfaction controversy into proper perspective.

Thorneburg Hosiery Implements a Corporate Motivational Program

Sharon Hoogstraten

Just before Christmas in 1982, Jim Thorneburg called the first company-wide meeting in Thorneburg Hosiery Company's history and issued an ultimatum: Every employee had to be operating under what he called the "new system" in two years. He would go broke, if he had to, to bring about the change, but if they could not make it work, he would sell the company.

The problem was that things were going too well for the Statesville, N.C., firm. When it started manufacturing an innovative line of sports socks in 1980, sales jumped from $800,000 to $2.7 million in one year. As sales soared to more than $5 million the following year, Thorneburg realized that the little company his parents had founded nearly three decades before "was growing faster than was healthy."

Thorneburg had invented the new line. Called Thor-Lo PADDS Foot Equipment, it consists of eight types of socks, each engineered for a different sport. Averaging $6 a pair, they are the most expensive athletic socks made.

With the Thor-Lo line, Thorneburg believed his company could become a $50 million company. Except for the fact that it was not ready to take on that kind of growth. He was concerned about whether his employees would care enough to produce socks of the quality and quantity he knew were needed.

Thorneburg, 48, decided to revamp the corporate culture. "We've got every reason to believe that we can go to a $100 million or a $200 million company,"

he said at a meeting. He wanted to build "a great company for people to work in." And down the road, he said he envisioned sharing ownership of the company with its 140 employees.

But to make these things happen, he said, everybody—including himself—had to change. Under the new system, each employee would be held accountable for the quality and quantity of his own work. Thorneburg recalls saying, "The person that you work for is no longer responsible for your work. You are. Not your supervisor."

He predicted that the new system would be hardest on the company's 15 or so supervisors. In the past, they had been rewarded for exerting control and given credit when their subordinates were productive. Now he wanted them—and management—to become "servants to the worker."

"You are to teach, you are to coordinate, you are to move information to and from, you are to be a friend and counselor," he instructed them. "And when you do those things well, your people will

---

E ffective employee motivation has long been one of management's most difficult and important duties. Success in this endeavor is becoming a more difficult challenge in light of managing a diverse work force, as discussed in Chapter 2. Unfortunately, anecdotal reports suggest managers are not adequately meeting this challenge. Consider an incident that occurred at General Motors Corporation.

> GM managers allowed workers to leave once they finished banging out the day's quota of parts. The move sparked a startling jump in productivity: Employees, many on the job for more than 20 years, suddenly found ways to do a full day's work before lunch.

OPENING CASE 5

(continued)

produce." He said he would fire any supervisors who tried to make subordinates perform.

He offered $500 "exit bonuses" to employees who felt they would be unhappy with the changes (there were two takers). He threatened to sell if the new system did not work, because if it did not, he no longer wanted to run the company.

In the months that followed the Christmas meeting, quality circles were formed—not for the purpose of improving productivity or solving problems, Thorneburg says, but as a safe environment in which his employees, largely unskilled, could express their ideas without fear of ridicule and learn to cooperate with and trust one another. In addition, the quality circles were to be educational tools, involving employees in decisions about their work and helping them develop judgment.

Supervisors, too, went through an educational process. Instead of ordering subordinates to do something . . . they learned to ask, and to offer an explanation of why a certain job had to be done. That

way, the subordinate would understand and become more knowledgeable.

In handling discipline problems, supervisors began to take more time counseling and coaching an employee, rather than jumping quickly to punitive solutions. The immediate supervisors still conduct performance reviews, but they do not set goals— the quality circles do that.

Early last year [1984], Thorneburg moved the company into a new $1.8 million plant, aimed at increasing productivity and improving working conditions.

He saw some signs of change. Employees began to pay more attention to how they looked when they came to work. The mill was kept cleaner. Some workers with drug problems began coming forward and asking for help. And some employees went back to get high school diplomas on their own time so they could participate more effectively in the quality circles.

Thorneburg's two years were up last December [1984]. He still owns the company, and he hasn't

gone broke. Has the experiment met his expectations?

"Absolutely!" he responds. Sales have continued upward, reaching $7.5 million last year [1984]. . . .

His all-important knitters group has achieved 99.3 percent "first quality" production (meaning goods of high enough quality to be sent on to the retailers), against an industry average of about 90 percent.

For Discussion

What motivates the people at Thorneburg Hosiery?

• Additional discussion questions linking this case with the following material appear at the end of this chapter.

Source: Sharon Nelton, "Socking It to the Old Style." Reprinted by permission from *Nation's Business*, May 1985, p. 63. Copyright 1985, U.S. Chamber of Commerce.

But management, dismayed at paying a full day's wage for a half day's work, unilaterally increased the quotas to the point that workers have to put in eight hours even at the higher production levels they had achieved when they had the incentive to finish early.[1]

Initially, the GM workers were not motivated since they were capable of completing a quota for eight hours of work in just four hours time. Further, management's response to the increased productivity provided the catalyst for once again demotivating employees. In the end, mutual mistrust was created and employees threatened a local strike. Why were employees demotivated in the first place? What could management have done to create long-term employee motivation? The purpose of this chapter, as well as the next, is to provide you with insight needed to answer these types of motivational questions.

Specifically, this chapter provides a definitional and theoretical foundation for the topic of motivation so a rich variety of motivation theories and techniques can be introduced and discussed. Coverage of employee motivation extends to Chapter 6. After providing a conceptual model for understanding motivation, this chapter focuses on: (1) need theories of motivation, (2) an overview of job design methods used to motivate employees, (3) job characteristics and social information processing approaches to job design, and (4) causes and consequences of job satisfaction. In the next chapter attention turns to equity, expectancy, and goal-setting theory, research, and practice.

• WHAT DOES MOTIVATION INVOLVE?

The term *motivation* derives from the Latin word *movere* meaning "to move." In the present context, **motivation** represents "those psychological processes that cause the arousal, direction, and persistence of voluntary actions that are goal directed."[2] Managers need to understand these psychological processes if they are to successfully guide employees toward accomplishing organizational objectives. After considering a conceptual framework for understanding motivation, this section examines the historical roots of motivational concepts and the relationship between motivation and performance.

A Job Performance Model of Motivation

A conceptual model for understanding motivation (Figure 5–1) was created by integrating elements from several of the theories we discuss in this book. The foundation of the model is based on systems theory and reinforcement theory. Systems theory suggests that good performance results from a process of combining effort and technology to transform inputs into desired outputs. Systems theory further implies that people do not perform in isolation. Rather, employees frequently work on interdependent tasks and rely on each other's output as their input. Reinforcement theory, the other component of the model, is discussed in Chapter 7. Reinforcement theory involves making performance stronger with feedback and contingent consequences. Now let us take a closer look at Figure 5–1.

Figure 5–1 shows four types of inputs that affect employee effort and performance: individual differences and needs, supervisory support and coaching, performance goals, and job characteristics. As you may recall from Chapter 3, individual differences are the self-concepts, ethics, skills, abilities, personality characteristics, values, and needs that vary among people. These differences can significantly affect employee performance. Need theories of motivation are discussed in the next section of this chapter.

Managers use support and coaching as input to employee performance. Support entails supplying employees with adequate resources to get the job done. In addition, coaching involves providing employees with direction,

• **FIGURE 5-1**   A Job Performance Motivation System

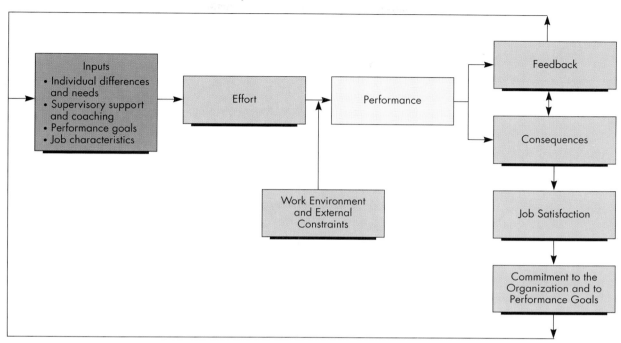

advice, and guidance. These behaviors include effective listening (discussed in Chapter 12), furnishing employees with successful role models, showing employees how to complete complex tasks, and helping them maintain high self-efficacy and self-esteem (recall the discussion in Chapter 3).

Because behavior is geared toward accomplishing end results, performance goals are a critical input to employee performance. Goals and action plans provide employees with direction and guidance about how to spend their time on specific tasks. Chapter 6 reviews how challenging goals lead to higher performance. Job characteristics, the final input variable, represent the types of tasks completed by employees. The role of job characteristics in employee motivation is discussed later in this chapter.

Returning to Figure 5–1, you can see that the relationship between employee effort and performance is affected by work environment and external constraints. These constraints, which include such things as defective raw materials, broken equipment, poor management, and economic considerations, can impair employees' ability to transform their inputs into desired performance outcomes. It is management's responsibility to manage and remove such performance roadblocks.[3] In addition, managers dramatically affect employee effort and performance by providing feedback and by reinforcing employee behavior with consequences.

For example, an individual's self-esteem, self-efficacy, and achievement orientation are enhanced by positive performance feedback. Moreover, managers can increase employee motivation by administering appropriate rewards, such as praise or a pay raise. These processes are thoroughly discussed in Chapters 7 and 13. Job satisfaction is affected by how positively employees evaluate the rewards they receive for a given level of performance. In general, people are more satisfied and committed to the organization and its goals when they receive equitable rewards that they value. Satisfied employees are less likely to quit, join unions, engage in substance abuse or theft, or put forth less effort.[4]

Historical Roots of Modern Motivation Theories

Most contemporary theories of motivation are rooted partially in the principle of **hedonism,** which states that people are motivated to consciously seek pleasure and avoid pain. Hedonism dates to the Greek philosophers. As a separate and self-contained theory of human motivation, hedonism proved unsatisfactory for two reasons: First, hedonism failed to adequately reconcile the relationship between short-term and long-term consequences. For example, hedonism cannot explain why some people choose to become professional football players who willingly risk their health during bruising Sunday afternoon games. Obviously, the football players are sustaining short-term pain in order to attain longer-term rewards such as recognition and lucrative contracts. Second, due to the rich variation among people, hedonists could not neatly categorize hundreds of different activities and consequences into distinct pleasure and pain categories. Writing, for example, may be a pleasure for professional writers, but it is definitely a pain for many college students. Let us now examine the historical development of subsequent theories of motivation.[5]

Four ways of explaining behavior—needs, reinforcement, cognition, and job characteristics—underlie the evolution of modern theories of human motivation. As we proceed through this review, remember the objective of each alternative motivation theory is to explain and predict purposeful or goal-directed behavior. As will become apparent, the differences between theoretical perspectives lie in the causal mechanisms used to explain behavior.

Needs   Need theories are based on the premise that individuals are motivated by unsatisfied needs. Dissatisfaction with your social life, for example, should motivate you to participate in more social activities. Henry Murray, a 1930s psychologist, was the first behavioral scientist to propose a list of needs thought to underlie goal-directed behavior (see Table 5–1). From Murray's work sprang a wide variety of need theories, some of which remain influential today. Recognized need theories of motivation are explored in the next section of this chapter.

Reinforcement   Reinforcement theorists, such as Edward L. Thorndike and B. F. Skinner, proposed that behavior is controlled by its consequences, not by the result of hypothetical internal states such as instincts, drives, or needs. This proposition is based on research data demonstrating that people repeat behaviors followed by favorable consequences and avoid behaviors resulting in unfavorable consequences. Few would argue with the statement that organizational rewards have a motivational impact on job behavior. However, behaviorists and cognitive theorists do disagree over the role of internal states and processes in motivation.

165

• **TABLE 5-1**   Murray's Taxonomy of Needs

Needs	Characteristics
Abasement	Complying with and giving in to others
Achievement	Overcoming obstacles and succeeding at challenging tasks
Affiliation	Establishing meaningful social relationships, joining groups, and wanting to be loved
Aggression	Physically or psychologically injuring another person
Autonomy	Resisting the influence of others and striving for independence
Counteraction	Defending one's honor and proudly using retaliation to overcome defeat
Deference	Serving others by following direction and guidance
Defendance	Defending oneself by offering explanations, causes, and excuses
Dominance	Directing, leading, or controlling others
Exhibition	Drawing attention to oneself
Harm avoidance	Avoiding activities or situations that may be dangerous
Infavoidance	Attempting to avoid failure, shame, humiliation, or ridicule
Nurturance	Aiding or helping someone in need
Order	Being tidy, organized, and extremely precise
Play	Relaxing, joking, being entertained, or just having fun
Rejection	Ignoring or excluding others from activities
Sentience	Desiring sensuous gratifications, particularly by having objects contact the body
Sex	Desiring an erotic relationship or engaging in sexual intercourse
Succorance	Seeking help or sympathy from others
Understanding	Defining relationships and abstract ideas and concepts

Source: Adapted from Henry A. Murray, *Explorations in Personality* (New York: John Wiley & Sons, 1938), pp. 77–83.

Cognitions   Uncomfortable with the idea that behavior is shaped completely by environmental consequences, cognitive motivation theorists contend that behavior is a function of beliefs, expectations, values, and other mental cognitions. Behavior is therefore viewed as the result of rational and conscious choices among alternative courses of action. In Chapter 6, we discuss cognitive motivation theories involving equity, expectancies, and goal setting.

Job Characteristics   According to this most recent addition to the evolution of motivation theory, the task itself is said to be the key to employee motivation. Specifically, a boring and monotonous job stifles motivation to perform well, whereas a challenging job enhances motivation. Three ingredients of a more challenging job are variety, autonomy, and decision authority. Two popular ways of adding variety and challenge to routine jobs are job enrichment (or job redesign) and job rotation. These techniques are discussed later in this chapter.

A Motivational Puzzle   Motivation theory presents managers with a psychological puzzle composed of alternative explanations and recommendations. Nonetheless, managers can learn important lessons about employee behavior from each motivation theory. Within a contingency management framework, managers need to pick and choose motivational techniques best suited to the people and situation involved. The matrix in Figure 5–2 was created to help managers make these decisions.

• **FIGURE 5–2**   Motivation Theories and Workplace Outcomes: A Contingency Approach

Outcome of Interest	Motivation Theories					
	Need	Reinforcement	Equity	Expectancy	Goal Setting	Job Characteristics
• Choice to Pursue a Course of Action				X		
• Effort	X	X	X	X	X	X
• Performance		X	X		X	X
• Satisfaction	X		X			X
• Absenteeism		X	X			X
• Turnover		X	X	X		X

Source: Adapted and extended from Frank J. Landy and Wendy S. Becker, "Motivation Theory Reconsidered," in L. L. Cummings and Barry M. Staw (eds.), *Research in Organizational Behavior* (Greenwich, Conn.: JAI Press, 1987), vol. 9, p. 33.

The matrix crosses managerial outcomes of interest with major theories of motivation. Entries in the matrix indicate which theories are best suited for explaining each outcome. For instance, each motivation theory can help managers determine how to increase employee effort. In contrast, need, equity, and job characteristics theory are most helpful in developing programs aimed at increasing employees' job satisfaction. Managers faced with high turnover are advised to use reinforcement, equity, expectancy, or job characteristics theory to correct the problem.

Motivation Is Only One Factor in the Performance Equation

All too often, motivation and performance are assumed to be one and the same. This faulty assumption can lead to poor managerial decisions. The following formula for performance helps put motivation into proper perspective:

$$\text{Performance} = (\text{Ability} \times \text{Motivation})$$

Thus, we see motivation is a necessary but insufficient contributor to job performance. The multiplication sign is used to emphasize how a weakness in one factor can negate the other. Drawing a distinction between performance and motivation has its advantages. According to one motivation expert:

> The implication is that there probably are some jobs for which trying to influence motivation will be irrelevant for performance. These circumstances can occur in a variety of ways. There may be situations in which ability factors or role expectation factors are simply more important than motivation. For example, the best predictor of high school grades typically is intellectual endowment, not hours spent studying. . . .
>
> Another circumstance may occur in which performance is controlled by technological factors. For example, on an assembly line, given that minimally competent and attentive people are there to do the job, performance may not vary from individual to individual. Exerting effort may be irrelevant for performance.[6]

Managers are better able to identify and correct performance problems when they recognize that poor performance is not due solely to inadequate motivation. This awareness can foster better interpersonal relations in the workplace.

• NEED THEORIES OF MOTIVATION

Need theories attempt to pinpoint internal factors that energize behavior. **Needs** are physiological or psychological deficiencies that arouse behavior. They can be strong or weak and are influenced by environmental factors. Thus, human needs vary over time and place. Two popular need theories are discussed in this section: Maslow's need hierarchy theory and McClelland's need theory.

Maslow's Need Hierarchy Theory

In 1943, psychologist Abraham Maslow published his now-famous need hierarchy theory of motivation. Although the theory was based on his clinical observation of a few neurotic individuals, it has subsequently been used to explain the entire spectrum of human behavior. Relying on Murray's taxonomy of needs as a starting point, Maslow proposed that motivation is a function of five basic needs—physiological, safety, love, esteem, and self-actualization (see Figure 5–3).

Maslow said these five need categories are arranged in a prepotent hierarchy. In other words, he believed human needs generally emerge in a predictable stair-step fashion. Accordingly, when one's physiological needs are relatively satisfied, one's safety needs emerge, and so on up the need hierarchy, one step at a time. Once a need is satisfied it activates the next higher need in the hierarchy. This process continues until the need for self-actualization is activated.[7] Unfortunately, many people living in the Soviet Union are not enjoying the satisfaction of higher order needs. They are stuck at lower levels on the need hierarchy (see International OB: Living Low on the Need Hierarchy in the Soviet Union).

Cultural Translation Required   It is important to note, from an international management perspective, that different cultures yield different need hierarchies. Because Maslow's five-level hierarchy is rooted in American culture, it does not necessarily fit significantly different cultures (see International OB: Need Hierarchies Vary). In fact, cultural translation is required for all "made in America" motivation theories.

Research Findings on Maslow's Theory   Research does not clearly support this theory because results from studies testing the need hierarchy are difficult to interpret. A well-known motivation scholar summarized the research evidence as follows:

> In balance, Maslow's theory remains very popular among managers and students of organizational behavior, although there are still very few studies that can legitimately confirm (or refute) it. . . . It may be that the dynamics implied by

• **FIGURE 5-3**   Maslow's Need Hierarchy

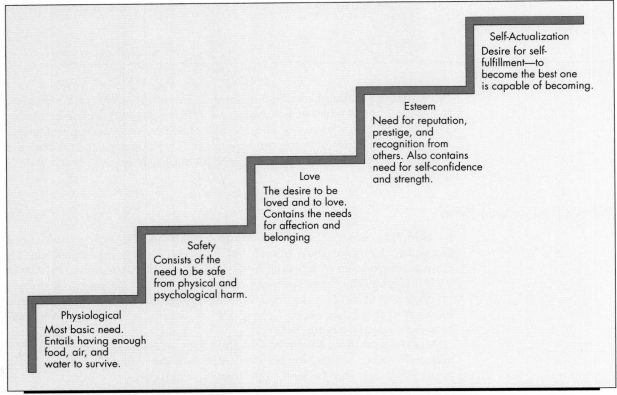

Self-Actualization
Desire for self-
fulfillment—to
become the best one
is capable of becoming.

Esteem
Need for reputation,
prestige, and
recognition from
others. Also contains
need for self-confidence
and strength.

Love
The desire to be
loved and to love.
Contains the needs
for affection and
belonging

Safety
Consists of the
need to be safe
from physical and
psychological harm.

Physiological
Most basic need.
Entails having enough
food, air, and
water to survive.

Source: Adapted from descriptions provided by Abraham H. Maslow, "A Theory of Human Motivation," *Psychological Review*, July 1943, pp. 370–96.

Maslow's theory of needs are too complex to be operationalized and confirmed by scientific research. If this is the case, we may never be able to determine how valid the theory is, or—more precisely—which aspects of the theory are valid and which are not.[8]

Managerial Implications of Maslow's Theory   A satisfied need may lose its motivational potential. Therefore, managers are advised to motivate employees by devising programs or practices aimed at satisfying emerging or unmet needs. For example, in the face of technological displacement and mass layoffs (U.S. employers dismissed 30,000 people per month during the first eight months of 1990), employers can boost motivation by giving workers a job-security pledge.[9] Corporations such as IBM, Honeywell, and Advanced Micro Devices followed this recommendation by writing "no layoff" policies or by using part-timers and subcontractors to protect full-time workers during recessionary periods. Once employees feel secure in their jobs, management might attempt to satisfy esteem needs. This can be done using status symbols, participative management, and positive performance feed-

INTERNATIONAL OB

Living Low on the Need Hierarchy in the Soviet Union

. . . Soviet poverty more broadly defined reaches well beyond the broke and the lost. It is a state of being for tens of millions of people and is reflected less in salary levels than in daily, unending shortages of meat and apartments, medicines and vegetables, soap and shoes.

On Nikolai Ostrovsky Lane, the airy pre-revolutionary apartments of merchants and artists were long ago divided up into communal flats. Five or six families, most of them with regular salaries or pensions, share a toilet and a kitchen and take turns complaining to blank-eyed local officials about the rusted pipes, the cascade of plaster. Evenings after work, they stand endlessly in lines, hunting for milk, oatmeal, toilet paper, whatever can be found.

Beyond Moscow, miners in Vorkuta in the polar north don't have enough soap to wash the coal dust from their faces; mothers on the Far Eastern island of Sakhalin give birth in rented rooms for lack of a maternity hospital there; Byelorussian villagers scavenge scrap metal, rags or even pig fat to pay for shoes, and the staff at a huge hospital in the Siberian city of Krasnoyarsk reuses needles after, as one doctor admits, ''We sharpen them up, straighten them out and scrape off the rust.'' Such stories, and countless others, are not printed in official papers that once told only of the triumphs of the Soviet system. . . .

''How can we feed ourselves and live decent lives? That is what it's all about,'' says Tatyana Zaslavskaya, a sociologist who has long been a keen intellectual influence on Gorbachev. ''Everything revolves around that.''

Source: David Remnick, ''A Vast Landscape of Want: In the Soviet Union, Poverty Is a Way of Life,'' *The Washington Post National Weekly Edition*, May 28–June 3, 1990, p. 6.

back. When employees' esteem needs are satisfied, management can enhance motivation by redesigning jobs to provide more autonomy and responsibility.

McClelland's Need Theory

David McClelland, a well-known psychologist, has been studying the relationship between needs and behavior since the late 1940s. Although he is most recognized for his research on the need for achievement, he also investigated the needs for affiliation and power. Before discussing each of these needs, let us consider the typical approach used to measure the strength of an individual's needs.

Measuring Need Strength   The Thematic Apperception Test (TAT) is frequently used to measure an individual's motivation to satisfy various needs.[10] In completing the TAT, people are asked to write stories about ambiguous pictures. These descriptions are then scored for the extent to which they contain achievement, power, and affiliation imagery. At this

INTERNATIONAL OB

Need Hierarchies Vary from Culture to Culture: An Example from the People's Republic of China

After conducting research in the People's Republic of China, Edwin C. Nevis concluded that the Chinese hierarchy of needs is arranged differently and has fewer levels than Maslow's American hierarchy. These differences owe primarily to the Chinese cultural emphasis on service and loyalty to society and the American cultural emphasis on self-determination and individualism. Nevis's Chinese hierarchy of needs is arranged as follows:

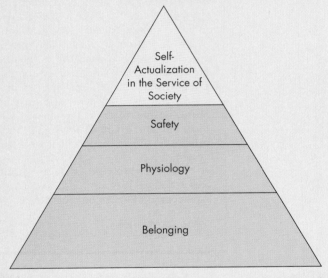

Source: Reprinted with permission from NTL Institute, "Using an American Perspective in Understanding Another Culture: Toward a Hierarchy of Needs for the People's Republic of China," by Edwin C. Nevis, p. 256, *The Journal of Applied Behavioral Science*, vol. 19, no. 3; copyright 1983.

time, we would like you to examine the picture in OB Exercise and then write a brief description of what you think is happening to the people in the picture and what you think will happen to them in the future. Use the scoring guide to determine your need strength. What is your most important need?

The Need for Achievement   Achievement theories propose that motivation and performance vary according to the strength of one's need for achievement. For example, a recent field study of 222 life insurance brokers found a positive correlation between the number of policies sold and the brokers' need for achievement.[11] Henry Murray, the psychologist who proposed the list of needs presented in Table 5–1, was the first to call attention to the **need for achievement.** He defined this need as the desire:

> to accomplish something difficult. To master, manipulate or organize physical objects, human beings, or ideas. To do this as rapidly and as independently as

OB EXERCISE

Assess Your Need Strength with a Thematic Apperception Test (TAT)

What is happening in this picture?

	Low	Moderate	High
• Achievement motivation	1 —— 2 —— 3 —— 4 —— 5		
• Power motivation	1 —— 2 —— 3 —— 4 —— 5		
• Affiliation motivation	1 —— 2 —— 3 —— 4 —— 5		

Score *achievement* motivation high if:

- A goal, objective, or standard of excellence is mentioned.
- Words such as good, better, or best are used to evaluate performance.
- Someone in your story is striving for a unique accomplishment.
- Reference is made to career status or being a success in life.

Score *power* motivation high if:

- There is emotional concern for influencing someone else.
- Someone is actively striving to gain or keep control over others by ordering, arguing, demanding, convincing, threatening, or punishing.
- Clear reference is made to a superior-subordinate relationship and the superior is taking steps to gain or keep control over the subordinate.

Score *affiliation* motivation high if:

- Someone is concerned about establishing or maintaining a friendly relationship with another.
- Someone expresses the desire to be liked by someone else.
- There are references to family ties, friendly discussions, visits, reunions, parties, or informal get-togethers.

possible. To overcome obstacles and attain a high standard. To excel one's self. To rival and surpass others. To increase self-regard by the successful exercise of talent.[12]

This definition reveals that the need for achievement overlaps Maslow's higher order needs of esteem and self-actualization. Let us now consider the characteristics of high achievers.

Characteristics of High Achievers   Achievement-motivated people share three common characteristics. One is a preference for working on tasks of *moderate* difficulty. For example, when high achievers are asked to stand wherever they like while tossing rings at a peg on the floor, they tend to stand about 10 to 20 feet from the peg. This distance presents the ring tosser with a challenging but not impossible task. People with a low need for achievement, in contrast, tend to either walk up to the peg and drop the rings on or gamble on a lucky shot from far away. The high achiever's preference for moderately difficult tasks reinforces achievement behavior by reducing the frequency of failure and increasing the satisfaction associated with successfully completing challenging tasks.

Achievers also like situations in which their performance is due to their own efforts rather than to other factors, such as luck. A third identifying characteristic of high achievers is that they desire more feedback on their successes and failures than do low achievers. Given these characteristics, McClelland proposed that high achievers are more likely to be successful entrepreneurs. A recent study supported this proposition. Data obtained from 118 entrepreneurs indicated that the growth of their firms was positively related to their achievement orientation.[13] Interestingly, research documented a positive correlation between achievement motivation and the economic development of entire societies.[14]

The Need for Affiliation   People with a high **need for affiliation** prefer to spend more time maintaining social relationships, joining groups, and wanting to be loved. Individuals high in this need are not the most effective managers or leaders because they have a hard time making difficult decisions without worrying about being disliked.[15]

The Need for Power   The **need for power** reflects an individual's desire to influence and control others. There is a positive and negative side to this need. The negative face of power is characterized by an "if I win, you lose" mentality (see A Matter of Ethics). In contrast, people with a positive orientation to power focus on accomplishing group goals and helping employees obtain the feeling of competence. More is said about the two faces of power in Chapter 10.

McClelland now believes that individuals with high achievement motivation are *not* best suited for top management positions. Because effective managers must positively influence others, McClelland proposes that top managers should have a high need for power coupled with a low need for affiliation. Several studies support these propositions.[16]

A MATTER OF ETHICS

The Negative Face of Power Can Hurt Workers and the General Public

John Borowski, owner of a small defense contractor here [Burlington, Mass.], never seemed to worry much about how to dispose of the toxic wastes his plant produced. He had developed a simple, cheap method.

Using buckets, his workers would scoop fuming nitric acid and nickel wastes out of vats and pour them down a sink. When workers questioned the practice, Mr. Borowski told them not to worry because it wouldn't hurt anyone, former employees say. He knew the dumping was illegal but considered it ''like not counting tips for income tax,'' says Peter Kruczynski, a former manager at Mr. Borowski's Borjohn Optical Technology Inc. . . .

Thousands of gallons of wastes went down Mr. Borowski's sink over the past decade, from there finding their way into Boston Harbor. Some of the workers in his bucket brigade developed rashes and other ailments, but Mr. Borowski attributed the problems to drinking or laziness, former employees testified at his trial. ''If I had to follow every rule on the books, I'd be out of business,'' one worker testified Mr. Borowski told him.

Source: David Stipp, ''Toxic Turpitude: Environmental Crime Can Land Executives in Prison These Days,'' *The Wall Street Journal*, September 10, 1990.

Managerial Implications   Given that adults can be trained to increase their achievement motivation,[17] organizations should consider the benefits of providing achievement training for employees. Moreover, achievement, affiliation, and power needs can be considered during the selection process, for better placement. For example, recruiters might want to look for high power motivation when hiring top-level executives. On the other hand, a high need for achievement would be a good staffing prerequisite for lower- and middle-level managers. Finally, managers should create challenging task assignments or goals because challenge arouses the need for achievement.[18] Fred Carr, chairman of First Executive Corporation, endorsed this recommendation when interviewed by *The Wall Street Journal*. Mr. Carr concluded: '' 'If you can motivate people to be happy, that's great. But I don't think you can do it all the time.' He believes 'continuous challenge' is how you get the most from workers.''[19] Challenge can be created by setting difficult goals, providing a more autonomous work environment, and delegating.

• HISTORICAL APPROACHES TO JOB DESIGN

Job design, also referred to as job redesign, ''refers to any set of activities that involve the alteration of specific jobs or interdependent systems of jobs with the intent of improving the quality of employee job experience and their on-the-job productivity.''[20] There are two very different routes, one traditional and one modern, that can be taken when deciding how to design jobs. Each is based on a different assumption about people.

The first route entails *fitting people to jobs*. It is based on the assumption that people will gradually adjust and adapt to any work situation. Thus, employee attitudes toward the job are ignored, and jobs are designed to produce maximum economic and technological efficiency. This approach uses the principles of scientific management and work simplification (recall our discussion in Chapter 1). In contrast, the second route involves *fitting jobs to people*. It assumes that people are underutilized at work and that they desire more challenge and responsibility. Thus, employee attitudes play an important part in determining how jobs should be designed. Techniques such as job enlargement, job rotation, job enrichment, and job characteristics are used when designing jobs according to this second alternative.

The remainder of this section discusses the first four methods of job design to be widely used in industry (see Figure 5–4). They are scientific management, job enlargement, job rotation, and job enrichment. The next section explores the job characteristics and social information processing approaches to job design.

Scientific Management

Developed by Frederick Taylor, scientific management relied on research and experimentation to determine the most efficient way to perform jobs (recall our discussion in Chapter 1). As shown in Figure 5–4, jobs are highly specialized and standardized when they are designed according to the principles of scientific management. This technique was the impetus for the development of assembly line technology and currently is used in many manufacturing and production-oriented firms throughout the United States.

• **FIGURE 5–4**   Historical Development of Job Design

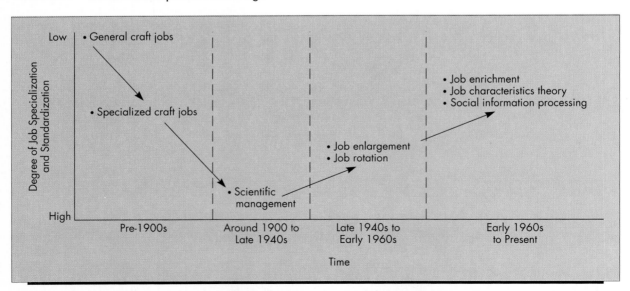

Source: Adapted from *Task Design: An Integrative Approach* by Ricky W. Griffin. Copyright © 1982 by Scott, Foresman and Company. Reprinted by permission. After A. Filley, R. House, & S. Kerr. *Managerial Process and Organizational Behavior*, 2/E, 1976.

Designing jobs according to the principles of scientific management has both positive and negative consequences. Positively, employee efficiency and productivity are increased. On the other hand, research reveals that simplified, repetitive jobs also lead to job dissatisfaction, poor mental health, and low sense of accomplishment and personal growth.[21] These negative consequences paved the way for the development of other job designs. Newer approaches attempt to design intrinsically satisfying jobs.

Job Enlargement

This technique was first used in the late 1940s in response to complaints about tedious and overspecialized jobs. **Job enlargement** involves putting more variety into a worker's job by combining specialized tasks of comparable difficulty. Some call this *horizontally loading* the job. For instance, the job of installing television picture tubes could be enlarged to include installation of the circuit boards.

Proponents of job enlargement claim it can improve employee satisfaction, motivation, and quality of production. Unfortunately, research reveals that job enlargement, by itself, does not have a significant and lasting positive impact on job performance.[22]

Job Rotation

As with job enlargement, job rotation's purpose is to give employees greater variety in their work. **Job rotation** calls for moving employees from one specialized job to another. Rather than performing only one job, workers are trained and given the opportunity to perform two or more separate jobs on a rotating basis. By rotating employees from job to job, managers believe they

• Hyatt President Thomas J. Pritzker takes part in job rotation by working behind the front desk. *(Courtesy of Hyatt Hotels Corporation)*

OB IN ACTION

Job Rotation Is Used in a Variety of Companies

Executive Rotation

At Xerox Corporation, executives spend one day a month taking complaints from customers about machines, bills, and service. At Hyatt hotels, senior executives—including President Pritzker—put in time as bellhops.

Employee Rotation

Polaroid Corp. paid factory workers at a camera plant to demonstrate the SX-70 instant camera in Boston-area stores during Christmas. It says the move boosted sales.

Tony Lama Co., the El Paso, Texas, bootmaker, each year sends six workers in its customer-complaint department to work in a store. Also, its salespeople work a week a year in the shipping department. Every employee in his first year at Church's Fried Chicken is required to work at one of its fast-food outlets for two weeks, cutting chicken, scrubbing floors and frying food.

Sources: Stephen Phillips, Amy Dunkin, James B. Treece, and Keith H. Hammonds, "King Customer: At Companies that Listen Hard and Respond Fast, Bottom Lines Thrive," *Business Week*, March 12, 1990, p. 91. "Labor Letter: A Special News Report on People and Their Jobs in Offices, Fields, and Factories," *The Wall Street Journal*, March 12, 1985, p. 1.

can stimulate interest and motivation, while providing employees with a broader perspective of the organization. An interesting variety of job rotation programs can be found in today's workplace (see OB in Action).

Other proposed advantages of job rotation include increased worker flexibility and easier scheduling because employees are cross-trained to perform different jobs. Unfortunately, the promised benefits associated with job rotation programs have not been adequately researched. Thus, it is impossible to draw any empirical conclusions about their effectiveness.[23]

Job Enrichment

Job enrichment is the practical application of Frederick Herzberg's motivator–hygiene theory of job satisfaction.[24] After reviewing the foundation of Herzberg's theory, we will discuss its application through job enrichment.

The Legacy of Herzberg's Motivator-Hygiene Theory   Herzberg's theory is based on a landmark study in which he interviewed 203 accountants and engineers. These interviews sought to determine the factors responsible for job satisfaction and dissatisfaction. Herzberg found separate and distinct clusters of factors associated with job satisfaction and dissatisfaction. Job satisfaction was more frequently associated with achievement, recognition, characteristics of the work, responsibility, and advancement. These factors were all related to outcomes associated with the *content* of the task being performed. Herzberg labeled these factors **motivators** because each was associated with strong effort and good performance. He hypothesized that

• **Figure 5-5**   Herzberg's Motivator–Hygiene Model

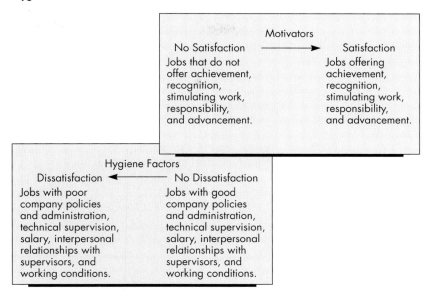

Source: Adapted in part from David A. Whitsett and Erik K. Winslow, "An Analysis of Studies Critical of the Motivator–Hygiene Theory," *Personnel Psychology*, Winter 1967, pp. 391–415.

motivators cause a person to move from a state of no satisfaction to satisfaction (see Figure 5–5). Therefore, Herzberg's theory predicts managers can motivate individuals by incorporating "motivators" into an individual's job.

Herzberg found job *dissatisfaction* to be associated primarily with factors in the work *context* or environment. Specifically, company policy and administration, technical supervision, salary, interpersonal relations with one's supervisor, and working conditions were most frequently mentioned by employees expressing job dissatisfaction. Herzberg labeled this second cluster of factors **hygiene factors.** He further proposed that they were not motivational. At best, according to Herzberg's interpretation, an individual will experience no job dissatisfaction when he or she has no grievances about hygiene factors (refer to Figure 5–5).[25]

A Zero Midpoint   The key to adequately understanding Herzberg's motivator–hygiene theory is recognizing that he does not place dissatisfaction and satisfaction on opposite ends of a single, unbroken continuum. Instead, he believes there is a zero midpoint between dissatisfaction and satisfaction. Conceivably, an organization member who has good supervision, pay, and working conditions but a tedious and unchallenging task with little chance of advancement would be at the zero midpoint. That person would have no dissatisfaction (because of good hygiene factors) and no satisfaction (because of a lack of motivators). Consequently, Herzberg warns managers that it takes more than good pay and good working conditions to motivate today's employees. It takes an "enriched job" that offers the individual opportunity for achievement and recognition, stimulation, responsibility, and advancement (see OB in Action).

OB IN ACTION

Motivators and Hygiene Factors à la Disney World's "Goofy"

Goofy said it all comes down to money and job security. He said the Kids of the Kingdom, who dance and mime songs, are paid more [than the costumed characters], but did not take anywhere near the risks taken by the characters who wear cumbersome costumes and dance on floats.

To boot, he said, Disney has gone to a two-year contract with the characters, after which they audition and then their contract is renewed for another year, or they are transferred to another department or they are dismissed.

"It's rotten," said Goofy, "but I love it. You can be around little kids, . . . [handicapped people,] old people, and just to make them smile, believe me, it's an incredible turn-on."

Source: Excerpted from Gregory Jaynes, "Goofy and Pluto Gripe about Disney Policies," *The Arizona Republic*, October 4, 1981, p. E3.

Research on the Motivator–Hygiene Theory   Herzberg's theory generated a great deal of research and controversy. The controversy revolved around whether studies supporting the theory were flawed, and thus invalid.[26] A motivation scholar attempted to sort out the controversy by concluding:

> In balance, when we combine all of the evidence with all of the allegations that the theory has been misinterpreted, and that its major concepts have not been assessed properly, one is left, more than twenty years later, not really knowing whether to take the theory seriously, let alone whether it should be put into practice in organizational settings. . . . There is support for many of the implications the theory has for enriching jobs to make them more motivating. But the two-factor aspect of the theory—the feature that makes it unique—is not really a necessary element in the use of the theory for designing jobs, per se.[27]

Applying Herzberg's Model through Vertical Loading   Herzberg proposed that people are motivated by "motivators"—achievement, recognition, stimulating work, responsibility, and advancement—in their jobs. These characteristics are incorporated into a job through vertical loading.

Rather than giving employees additional tasks of similar difficulty (horizontal loading), *vertical loading* consists of giving workers more responsibility. In other words, employees take on chores normally performed by their supervisors. Managers are advised to follow seven principles when vertically loading jobs (see Table 5–2). As an example, consider how Montgomery Ward is using vertical loading. "Montgomery Ward Chairman Bernard F. Brennan has authorized 7,700 salespeople to approve checks and handle merchandise-return problems—functions that once were reserved for store managers."[28]

• **TABLE 5-2**   Principles of Vertically Loading a Job

Principle	Motivators Involved
A. Removing some controls while retaining accountability	Responsibility and personal achievement
B. Increasing the accountability of individuals for their own work	Responsibility and recognition
C. Giving a person a complete natural unit of work (module, division, area, and so on)	Responsibility, achievement, and recognition
D. Granting additional authority to an employee in his activity; job freedom	Responsibility, achievement, and recognition
E. Making periodic reports directly available to the worker himself rather than to the supervisor	Internal recognition
F. Introducing new and more difficult tasks not previously handled	Growth and learning
G. Assigning individuals specific or specialized tasks, enabling them to become experts	Responsibility, growth, and advancement

Source: Reprinted by permission of the *Harvard Business Review*. An exhibit from "One More Time: How Do You Motivate Employees?" by Frederick Herzberg (January/February 1968). Copyright © 1968 by the President and Fellows of Harvard College; all rights reserved.

• JOB CHARACTERISTICS AND SOCIAL INFORMATION PROCESSING APPROACHES TO JOB DESIGN

The job characteristics model and social information-processing model (SIPM) are the most recent approaches to job design. Each is based on a different point of view. The job characteristics approach (an outgrowth of job enrichment) attempts to pinpoint those situations and those individuals for which job design is most effective. In this regard, the job characteristics model represents a contingency approach.

In contrast, the SIPM is based on the premise that employee perceptions affect attitudes and behaviors (recall our discussion in Chapter 4). Accordingly, this method focuses on the process by which employees form perceptions about both the type and the amount of job characteristics contained in their jobs, and how these perceptions affect work attitudes and behaviors. We now explore each of these approaches to job design.

Overview of the Job Characteristics Model

Two OB researchers, J. Richard Hackman and Greg Oldham, played a central role in developing the job characteristics approach. These researchers tried to determine how work can be structured so that employees are internally (or intrinsically) motivated. **Internal motivation** occurs when an individual is "turned on to one's work because of the positive internal feelings that are generated by doing well, rather than being dependent on external factors (such as incentive pay or compliments from the boss) for the motivation to work effectively."[29] These positive feelings power a self-perpetuating cycle of motivation. As shown in Figure 5–6, internal work motivation is determined by three psychological states. In turn, these psy-

• FIGURE 5-6   The Job Characteristics Model

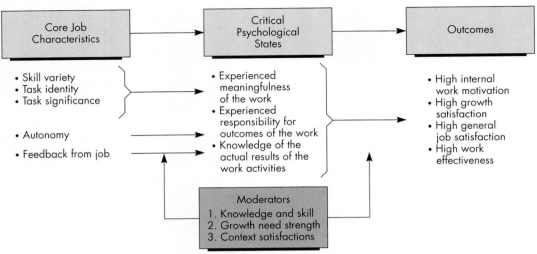

Source: J. Richard Hackman and Greg R. Oldham, *Work Redesign,* © 1980, Addison-Wesley Publishing Co., Reading, Mass., p. 90. Reprinted with permission.

chological states are fostered by the presence of five core job dimensions.[30] As you can see in Figure 5–6, the object of this approach is to promote high internal motivation by designing jobs that possess the five core job characteristics. Let us examine the major components of this model to see how it works.

Critical Psychological States   A group of management experts described the conditions under which individuals experienced the three critical psychological states. They are:

1. **Experienced meaningfulness:** The individual must perceive his work as worthwhile or important by some system of values he accepts.
2. **Experienced responsibility:** He must believe that he personally is accountable for the outcomes of his efforts.
3. **Knowledge of results:** He must be able to determine, on some fairly regular basis, whether or not the outcomes of his work are satisfactory.[31]

These psychological states generate internal work motivation. Moreover, they encourage job satisfaction and perseverance because they are self-reinforcing. Consider, for example, the important role the three psychological states no doubt played in Angela Azzaretti's decision to pass up two lucrative promotions in favor of her present job that offered more responsibility and challenge (see OB in Action).

If one of the three psychological states is shortchanged, motivation diminishes. For example, if an individual is completely responsible for outcomes associated with a meaningful job, but receives no feedback (knowledge of results) about performance, he or she will not experience the positive feelings that create internal motivation.

OB IN ACTION

Responsibility and Challenge Are More Important than Money to Angela Azzaretti

Angela Azzaretti, 25, the daughter of Italian immigrants, was graduated from the University of Illinois and took a job at Caterpillar's headquarters in Peoria during the summer of 1987.

Angela was the first generation of her Chicago family to go to college, and she was first to work for a *Fortune* 500 company. Caterpillar trained her for a year, with jobs in marketing and manufacturing, and then assigned her to the heavy-duty engine plant in Mossville, Illinois, as the "plant communicator." She wrote speeches for the division's top executives, published the plant newsletter, and produced videotapes viewed by 5,200 workers and managers at monthly meetings.

Her work played well in Mossville, near Peoria, and soon she was offered a promotion to Caterpillar's headquarters staff. Angela turned it down. Then she was offered another promotion, entailing a move to a different plant. Once again she said no.

"Job satisfaction is the most important thing to me," says Angela. "In those other jobs, I would have had less responsibility, less of a challenge. The only benefit was more money. I know it sounds crazy, but I evaluated the situation."

Source: Alan Deutschman, "What 25-Year-Olds Want," *Fortune*, August 27, 1990, p. 42.

Core Job Dimensions   In general terms, **core job dimensions** are common characteristics found to a varying degree in all jobs. Once again, five core job characteristics elicit the three psychological states (see Figure 5–6). Three of those job characteristics combine to determine experienced meaningfulness of work. They are:

- *Skill variety:* The extent to which the job requires an individual to perform a variety of tasks that require him or her to use different skills and abilities.
- *Task identity:* The extent to which the job requires an individual to perform a whole or completely identifiable piece of work. In other words, task identity is high when a person works on a product or project from beginning to end and sees a tangible result.
- *Task significance:* The extent to which the job affects the lives of other people within or outside the organization.

Experienced responsibility is elicited by the job characteristic of autonomy, defined as follows:

- *Autonomy:* The extent to which the job enables an individual to experience freedom, independence, and discretion in both scheduling and determining the procedures used in completing the job.

Finally, knowledge of results is fostered by the job characteristic of feedback, defined as follows:

• Job satisfaction was all-important to Angela Azzaretti, which is why she turned down two promotions at Caterpillar, both of which would have significantly increased her salary. *(Alen MacWeeney)*

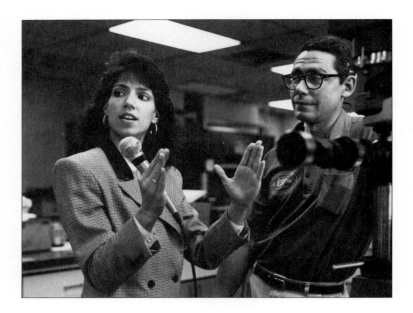

• *Feedback:* The extent to which an individual receives direct and clear information about how effectively he or she is performing the job.[32]

Motivating Potential of a Job   Hackman and Oldham devised a self-report instrument to assess the extent to which a specific job possesses the five core job characteristics. With this instrument, which is discussed in the next section, it is possible to calculate a motivating potential score for a job. The **motivating potential score** (MPS) is a summary index that represents the extent to which the job characteristics foster internal work motivation. Low scores indicate that an individual will not experience high internal work motivation from the job. Such a job is a prime candidate for job redesign. High scores reveal that the job is capable of stimulating internal motivation. The MPS is computed as follows:

$$\text{MPS} = \frac{\dfrac{\text{Skill}}{\text{variety}} + \dfrac{\text{Task}}{\text{identity}} + \dfrac{\text{Task}}{\text{significance}}}{3} \times \text{Autonomy} \times \text{Feedback}$$

Judging from this equation, which core job characteristic do you think is relatively more important in determining the motivational potential of a job? Since MPS equals zero when autonomy or feedback are zero, you are correct if you said both experienced autonomy and feedback.

The Theory Does Not Work for Everyone   As previously discussed, not all people want enriched work. Hackman and Oldham incorporated this conclusion into their model by identifying three attributes that affect how individuals respond to jobs with a high MPS. These attributes are concerned with the individual's knowledge and skill, growth need strength (representing the desire to grow and develop as an individual), and context satisfactions (see Figure 5–6). Context satisfactions represent the extent to which employees are satisfied with various aspects of their job, such as satisfaction with pay, co-workers, or supervision. Recalling Herzberg's motivator–hygiene theory, managers should not attempt to motivate employees through the job characteristics approach unless those employees are satisfied with the hygiene factors.

As was shown in Figure 5–6, people respond positively to jobs with a high MPS when (1) they have the knowledge and skills necessary to do the job, (2) they have high growth needs, and (3) they are satisfied with various aspects of the work context, such as pay and co-workers. On the other hand, employees who score low on these attributes will be stretched by a job with a high MPS. Ultimately, these individuals will experience weaker psychological states and poorer work outcomes. For example, consider the response of an employee who has the necessary knowledge and skills and a strong desire to grow, but feels underpaid and does not get along with co-workers. Do you think this person would respond positively to having his or her job made more complex through enriched work? This dissatisfied employee would probably resent any attempts to make him or her work harder.

Applying the Job Characteristics Model   There are three major steps to follow when applying Hackman and Oldham's model. Since the model seeks to increase employee motivation and satisfaction, the first step consists of diagnosing the work environment to determine if a problem exists. Hackman and Oldham developed a self-report instrument for managers to use called the *Job Diagnostic Survey* (JDS).

Diagnosis begins by determining if motivation and satisfaction are lower than desired. If they are, a manager then assesses the MPS of the jobs being examined. National norms are used to determine whether the MPS is low or high.[33] If the MPS is low, an attempt is made to determine which of the core job characteristics is causing the problem. If the MPS is high, managers need to look for other factors eroding motivation and satisfaction. (You can calculate your own MPS in the exercise at the end of this chapter.) Potential factors may be identified by considering other motivation theories discussed in this book.

Step two consists of determining whether job redesign is appropriate for a given group of employees. Job redesign is most likely to work for employees who have high knowledge and skills, strong growth needs, and context satisfactions.[34]

In the third step, managers need to consider how to redesign the job. Hackman and Oldham suggest five implementing concepts. Each one, as shown in Figure 5–7, represents a specific action step aimed at bolstering one or more of the core job characteristics.

Some Practical Implications   Since a meta-analysis covering 15,542 people indicated a moderately strong relationship between job characteristics and job satisfaction, managers may want to use this model to increase employee satisfaction.[35] Unfortunately, job redesign appears to reduce the quantity of output just as often as it has a positive impact. Caution and situational appropriateness are advised. For example, a recent study demonstrated that job redesign works better in less complex organizations (small plants or companies).[36] Nonetheless, managers are likely to find noticeable increases

• **FIGURE 5-7**   Implementing Principles That Affect Core Job Characteristics

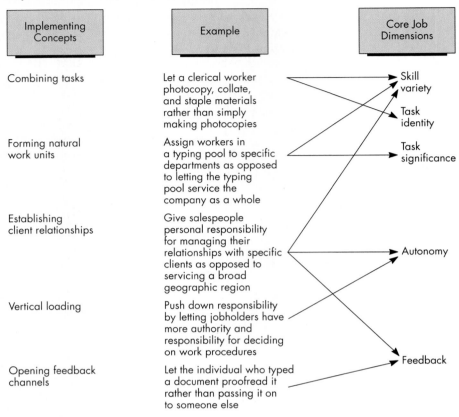

Source: Modified from J. Richard Hackman, Greg Oldham, Robert Janson, and Kenneth Purdy, "A New Strategy for Job Enrichment," *California Management Review,* Summer 1975.

in the quality of performance after a job redesign program. Results from 21 experimental studies revealed that job redesign resulted in a median increase of 28 percent in the quality of performance.[37]

Moreover, two separate meta-analyses support the practice of using the job characteristics model to help managers reduce absenteeism and turnover.[38] In conclusion, managers need to realize that job redesign is not a panacea for all their employee satisfaction and motivation problems. To enhance their chances of success with this approach, managers need to remember that a change in one job or department can create problems of perceived inequity in related areas or systems within the organization. Managers need to take an open systems perspective when implementing job redesign, as was suggested by Hackman and Oldham. They wrote:

> Our observations of work redesign programs suggest that attempts to change jobs frequently run into—and sometimes get run over by—other organizational systems and practices, leading to a diminution (or even a reversal) of anticipated outcomes. . . .
>
>   The "small change" effect, for example, often develops as managers begin to realize that radical changes in work design will necessitate major changes in other organizational systems as well.[39]

• **FIGURE 5-8**   A Social Information Processing Approach to Job Design

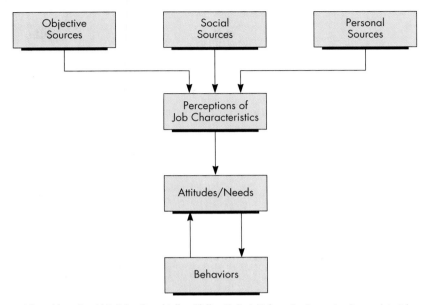

Source: Adapted from Gerald R. Salancik and Jeffrey Pfeffer, "A Social Information Processing Approach to Job Attitudes and Task Design," *Administrative Science Quarterly*, June 1978, p. 227.

The Social Information Processing Model

The social information processing model (SIPM) proposes that employees' perceptions of their work environments are more important than actual job characteristics in explaining attitudes and behavior. If true, "changing a job to improve employee attitudes may be fruitless if the employees' perceptions of the job are based on social information that remains unchanged."[40]

Three sources of information influence perceptions about job characteristics according to this model (see Figure 5–8). Objective sources include the physical working environment, the task itself, and formal policies and procedures. Social sources include other people in both the immediate work environment—such as co-workers and managers—and external to the organization, such as family and friends.[41] Past experience and background are sources of personal information. According to the **social information processing model of job design,** social cues provided by co-workers and managers may have the strongest impact on perceptions of job characteristics. For example, an ambulance driver may believe he or she has a lot of skill variety, autonomy, and independence until sharing work experiences with a doctor. This comparison is likely to reveal that the doctor's job exhibits a richer variety of the core job characteristics. As this example illustrates, employees' perceptions of their own job characteristics may be more a function of *subjective social cues* than of objective information.

Jeffrey Pfeffer, a respected OB researcher, summarized four major propositions that represent the basic philosophy of the SIPM.

First, the individual's social environment may provide cues as to which dimensions might be used to characterize the work environment. . . . Second, the social environment may provide information concerning how the individual should weight the various dimensions—whether autonomy is more or less important than variety of skill, whether pay is more or less important than variety of skill, whether pay is more or less important than social usefulness or worth. Third, the social context provides cues concerning how others have come to evaluate the work environment on each of the selected dimensions. Whether a given job situation provides or does not provide autonomy, variety, or high pay is as much a matter of social perception as it is a function of the specific job. And fourth, it is possible that the social context provides direct evaluation of the work setting along positive or negative dimensions, leaving it to the individual to construct a rationale to make sense of the generally shared affective reactions.[42]

Let us turn to the relevant research and managerial implications of this model.

Research Findings   A meta-analysis covering 10 studies and 1,698 individuals provided moderate support for the proposition that social cues affect perceptions of job characteristics and satisfaction. Nonetheless, this meta-analysis failed to uncover a consistent relationship between social cues and performance.[43] Finally, contrary to predictions made by the SIPM, objective information had a stronger impact on perceptions of job characteristics than social cues.[44]

Managerial Implications   When implementing a job design program, social factors inevitably will come into play. Thus, it is important that managers not overlook the role of relevant social factors when redesigning jobs. Managers are encouraged to openly discuss and explain the rationale behind job design changes. Moreover, employee involvement in job design is likely to reduce the amount of inaccurate information from social sources as well as build employee commitment to the job redesign process.

These suggestions mesh well with the idea of participative management discussed in Chapter 15.

UNRAVELING THE CONTROVERSY SURROUNDING JOB SATISFACTION

Job satisfaction is one of the most frequently studied variables in OB. One researcher estimated there were 3,350 articles written on the subject between 1957 and 1976.[45] Hundreds more have appeared since. A good measure of this preoccupation with job satisfaction stems from Herzberg's motivator–hygiene theory. As just discussed, Herzberg's theory assumes there is a causal linkage from job satisfaction to motivation, and ultimately to job performance. This suggests that the best way to increase performance is to improve job satisfaction. Unfortunately, subsequent research has found the job satisfaction → performance relationship to be less than clear-cut. Consequently, we need to sort out the various causes and consequences of job satisfaction.

The Causes of Job Satisfaction

Job satisfaction was defined in Chapter 2 as an affective or emotional response toward various facets of one's job. This definition means job satisfaction is not a unitary concept. Rather, a person can be relatively satisfied with one aspect of his or her job and dissatisfied with one or more other aspects. For example, researchers at Cornell University developed the Job Descriptive Index (JDI) to assess one's satisfaction with the following job dimensions: work, pay, promotions, co-workers, and supervision.[46] Taking a more analytical approach, researchers at the University of Minnesota concluded there are 20 different dimensions underlying job satisfaction. Selected Minnesota Satisfaction Questionnaire (MSQ) items measuring satisfaction with recognition and compensation are listed in the OB Exercise. Please take a moment now to determine how satisfied you are with these two aspects of your present or most recent job. (Comparative norms for each dimension of job satisfaction are: total score of 5–10 = Low job satisfaction; 11–19 = Moderate satisfaction; 20 and above = High satisfaction.)[47] How do you feel about your job?

Five predominant models of job satisfaction specify its causes. They are need fulfillment, discrepancy, value attainment, equity, and genetic components. A brief review of these models will provide insight into the complexity of this seemingly simple concept.

Need Fulfillment   These models propose that satisfaction is determined by the extent to which the characteristics of a job allow an individual to fulfill his or her needs. Although these models have intuitive appeal, they have been sharply criticized. As two management experts noted:

• OB EXERCISE

How Satisfied Are You with Your Present Job?

1. The way I am noticed when I do a good job	Very dissatisfied 1 2 3 4 5 Very satisfied	
2. The way I get full credit for the work I do	Very dissatisfied 1 2 3 4 5 Very satisfied	
3. The recognition I get for the work I do	Very dissatisfied 1 2 3 4 5 Very satisfied	
4. The way they usually tell me when I do my job well	Very dissatisfied 1 2 3 4 5 Very satisfied	
5. The praise I get for doing a good job	Very dissatisfied 1 2 3 4 5 Very satisfied	
6. The amount of pay for the work I do	Very dissatisfied 1 2 3 4 5 Very satisfied	
7. The chance to make as much money as my friends	Very dissatisfied 1 2 3 4 5 Very satisfied	
8. How my pay compares with that for similar jobs in other companies	Very dissatisfied 1 2 3 4 5 Very satisfied	
9. My pay and the amount of work I do	Very dissatisfied 1 2 3 4 5 Very satisfied	
10. How my pay compares with that of other workers	Very dissatisfied 1 2 3 4 5 Very satisfied	

Total score for satisfaction with recognition (add questions 1–5) and compensation (add questions 6–10).

Source: Adapted from David J. Weiss, Rene V. Dawis, George W. England, and Lloyd H. Lofquist, *Manual for the Minnesota Satisfaction Questionnaire* (Minneapolis: Industrial Relations Center, University of Minnesota, 1967). Used with permission.

The need-satisfaction model must be seriously reexamined, and does not warrant the unquestioning acceptance it has attained in organizational psychology literature. . . . The principal concepts of the model—needs and job characteristics— are both open to serious questioning and to alternative interpretations. The calculus relating needs to job satisfaction, through the mechanism of job characteristics, has not been well specified.[48]

Discrepancies   These models propose that satisfaction is a result of met expectations. **Met expectations** represent the difference between what an individual expects to receive from a job, like good pay and promotional opportunities, and what he or she actually receives. When expectations are greater than what is received, a person will be dissatisfied. In contrast, this model predicts the individual will be satisfied when he or she attains outcomes above and beyond expectations. A recent study of 78 employed college students provided support for the discrepancy model. Exceeded expectations were positively related to job satisfaction.[49]

Value Attainment   The idea underlying **value attainment** is that satisfaction results from the perception that a job allows for fulfillment of an individual's important work values.[50] In general, research consistently supports the prediction that value fulfillment is positively related to job satisfaction. However, results from one study indicate that fulfillment of important values leads to satisfaction only in certain situations.[51] Therefore, managers do not have to concentrate solely on satisfying an employee's most important values. Gains in satisfaction can be obtained by providing workers with outcomes of lesser value.

Equity   In this model, satisfaction is a function of how "fairly" an individual is treated at work. Satisfaction results from one's perception that work outcomes, relative to inputs, compares favorably with a significant other's outcomes/inputs. A recent study examined this model across four different samples of employees. In support of the equity model, dissatisfaction with pay and income was consistently related to the extent to which respondents felt they were underpaid relative to similar others.[52] Chapter 6 explores this promising model in detail.

Genetic Components   Have you ever noticed that some of your co-workers or friends appear to be satisfied across a variety of job circumstances, whereas others always seem dissatisfied? This model of satisfaction attempts to explain this pattern. Specifically, the genetic model is based on the belief that job satisfaction is partially a function of genetic factors. As such, this model implies that stable individual differences are just as important in explaining job satisfaction as are characteristics of the work environment. Although very little research has tested these propositions, a recent study of 34 monozygotic twin pairs (these identical twins share the same genetic structure) reared apart supported the genetic model. Genetic factors significantly predicted both general job satisfaction and intrinsic satisfaction. Moreover, the twins tended to hold similar jobs.[53] Additional research is needed to test this new model of job satisfaction.

• **TABLE 5-3**   Correlates of Job Satisfaction

Variables Related with Satisfaction	Direction of Relationship	Strength of Relationship
Absenteeism	Negative	Weak
Tardiness	Negative	Weak
Turnover	Negative	Moderate
Heart disease	Negative	Moderate
Stress	Negative	Moderate
Pro-union voting	Negative	Moderate
Organizational citizenship behavior	Positive	Moderate
Organizational commitment	Positive	Moderate
Job performance	Positive	Weak
Life satisfaction	Positive	Moderate
Mental health	Positive	Moderate

The Consequences of Job Satisfaction

This area has significant managerial implications. As previously mentioned, thousands of studies have examined the relationship between job satisfaction and other organizational variables. Since it is impossible to examine them all, we will consider a subset of the more important variables, from the standpoint of managerial relevance (see Table 5–3).

Absenteeism   Absenteeism is costly and managers are constantly on the lookout for ways to reduce it. One recommendation has been to increase job satisfaction. If this is a valid recommendation, there should be a strong negative relationship (or negative correlation) between satisfaction and absenteeism. In other words, as satisfaction increases, absenteeism should decrease. A researcher recently tracked this prediction by synthesizing three separate meta-analyses containing a total of 74 studies. Results revealed a weak negative relationship between satisfaction and absenteeism.[54] It is unlikely, therefore, that managers will realize any significant decrease in absenteeism by increasing job satisfaction.

Turnover   Turnover is important to managers because it both disrupts organizational continuity and is very costly. For example, a 1977 study of bank tellers indicated turnover cost the bank $23,404.44 per month, or $208,853.28 per year.[55] These costs would be higher today. A meta-analysis of 28 studies demonstrated a moderate negative relationship between satisfaction and turnover.[56] (See Table 5–3.) Given the strength of this relationship, managers would be well advised to try to reduce turnover by increasing employee job satisfaction.

Organizational Citizenship Behavior   Organizational citizenship behaviors consist of employee behaviors that are beyond the call of duty. Examples include "such gestures as constructive statements about the department, expression of personal interest in the work of others, suggestions for improvement, training new people, respect for the spirit as well as the letter of housekeeping rules, care for organizational property, and punctuality and attendance well beyond standard or enforceable levels."[57] Managers certainly would like employees to exhibit these behaviors. Because organizational citizenship behaviors are moderately related to job satisfaction, managers can increase the frequency of such behaviors by increasing employee job satisfaction.[58]

Organizational Commitment   Organizational commitment reflects the extent to which an individual identifies with an organization and is committed to its goals. A recent meta-analysis indicated that both job satisfaction and performance are significantly correlated with organizational commitment.[59] Managers are advised to increase job satisfaction in order to elicit higher levels of commitment. In turn, higher commitment can facilitate higher productivity (recall Figure 5–1).

Job Performance   One of the biggest controversies within organizational research centers on the relationship between satisfaction and job performance. Some, such as Herzberg, argue that satisfaction leads to higher performance, while others contend that high performance leads to satisfaction. In an attempt to resolve this controversy, a meta-analysis accumulated results from 74 studies. Overall, the relationship between job satisfaction and job performance was examined for 12,192 people. It was discovered that satisfaction and performance were only slightly related.[60] This suggests managers are unlikely to enjoy substantial increases in job performance as a result of enhancing job satisfaction.

Pro-Union Voting   Results from 11 studies revealed a significant negative correlation between job satisfaction and pro-union voting.[61] In other words, people tend to vote for unions when they are dissatisfied with their jobs. Union organizers have taken advantage of this reality for decades. This suggests organizations may want to monitor employee satisfaction if they desire to maintain a nonunionized status.

Broader Implications   In a general sense, job satisfaction has important implications because it affects an individual's quality of work life. The term *quality of work life* refers to the overall quality of an individual's experiences at work. As suggested by research results listed in Table 5–3, job dissatisfaction is associated with increased heart disease, increased stress, and poor mental health.[62] It is hoped enlightened managers will develop an interest in reducing these negative work-related outcomes by improving job satisfaction.

• SUMMARY OF KEY CONCEPTS

A. Motivation is defined as those psychological processes that cause the arousal, direction, and persistence of voluntary, goal-oriented actions. Four types of inputs affect employee effort and performance: individual differences and needs, supervisory support and coaching, performance goals, and job characteristics. It is management's responsibility to manage and remove performance roadblocks.

B. Historically, motivation theory has evolved from hedonism to needs, reinforcement, cognitions, and job characteristics. Some theories of motivation focus on internal energizers of behavior such as needs and satisfaction. Other motivation theories, which deal in terms of reinforcement, cognitions, and job characteristics, focus on more complex person-environment interactions.

C. There is no single, universally accepted theory of motivation. Each alternative theory holds important managerial lessons. Managers need to pick and choose ideas from the various motivation theories as the situation dictates. When attempting to understand and manage job performance, motivation is a necessary but insufficient factor.

D. Two well-known need theories of motivation are Maslow's need hierarchy and McClelland's need theory. Maslow's notion of a prepotent or stair-step hierarchy of five levels of needs has not stood up well under research. McClelland believes that motivation and performance vary according to the strength of an individual's need for achievement. High achievers prefer moderate risks and situations where they can control their own destiny. Top managers should have a high need for power coupled with a low need for affiliation.

E. Job design is one possible solution for the mismatch between jobs that people perform and the needs, expectations, and values of the work force. Job design involves altering jobs with the intent of increasing both employee job satisfaction and productivity.

F. Scientific management designs jobs by using research and experimentation to identify the most efficient way to perform tasks. Jobs are horizontally loaded in job enlargement by giving workers more than one specialized task to complete. Job rotation increases workplace variety by moving employees from one specialized job to another. Job enrichment vertically loads jobs by giving employees administrative duties normally performed by their superiors.

G. Herzberg believes job satisfaction motivates better job performance. His *hygiene* factors, such as policies, supervision, and salary, erase sources of dissatisfaction. On the other hand, his *motivators,* such as achievement, responsibility, and recognition, foster job satisfaction. Although Herzberg's motivator–hygiene theory of job satisfaction has been criticized on methodological grounds, it has practical significance for job enrichment.

H. The psychological states of experienced meaningfulness, experienced responsibility, and knowledge of results produce internal work motivation. These psychological states are fostered by the presence of five core job characteristics. People respond positively to jobs containing these core job characteristics when they have the knowledge and skills necessary to perform the job, high growth needs, and high context satisfactions. According to the social information processing model, social and situational cues play an importrant role in determining employee perceptions about job characteristics.

I. Owing to Herzberg's work, the satisfaction-performance relationship has stirred much controversy in OB circles. Actually, job satisfaction has a complex web of causes and consequences. The correlation between job satisfaction and turnover, heart disease, stress, and pro-union voting is moderately negative. A moderately positive relationship has been found between job satisfaction and organizational citizenship, behavior, organizational commitment, life satisfaction, and mental health.

• KEY TERMS

motivation

hedonism

needs

need for achievement

need for affiliation

need for power

job design

job enlargement

job rotation

motivators

hygiene factors

internal motivation

experienced meaningfulness

experienced responsibility

knowledge of results

core job dimensions

motivating potential score

social information processing
  model of job design

met expectations

value attainment

• DISCUSSION QUESTIONS

1. Why should the average manager be well versed in the various motivation theories?

2. From a practical standpoint, what is a major drawback of theories of motivation based on internal factors such as needs and satisfaction?

3. Are you a high achiever? How can you tell? How will this help or hinder your path to top management?

4. If you were redesigning a job, would you use one or more of the methods of job design we discussed? Explain your rationale.

5. How have hygiene factors and motivators affected your job satisfaction and performance?

6. How might the implementing concepts of the job characteristics model be used to increase your internal motivation to study?

7. Do you know anyone who would not respond positively to an enriched job? Describe this person.

8. Have social cues ever influenced your choice of what professor to take for a course? Describe how these cues affected your decision.

9. Do you think job satisfaction leads directly to better job performance? Explain.

10. What are the three most valuable lessons about employee motivation that you have learned from this chapter?

BACK TO THE OPENING CASE

Now that you have read Chapter 5, you should be able to answer the following questions about the Thorneburg Hosiery case:

1. Using the conceptual framework for motivation in Figure 5–1, why do you think Thorneburg's motivational program is working?
2. Using Maslow's need hierarchy theory, what is likely to happen to the motivation of someone who continues to work at Thorneburg?
3. How did Jim Thorneburg use the principles of job enrichment?
4. Which of the implementing concepts for the job characteristics approach were used by the company?

• EXERCISE 5

Objectives

1. To assess the motivating potential score (MPS) of your current or former job.
2. To determine which core job characteristics need to be changed.
3. To explore how you might redesign the job.

Introduction

The first step in calculating the MPS of a job is to complete the job diagnostic survey (JDS). Since the JDS is a long questionnaire, we would like you to complete a subset of the instrument. This will enable you to calculate the MPS, identify deficient job characteristics, and begin thinking about redesigning the job.

Instructions

Indicate whether each of the following statements in the JDS is an accurate or inaccurate description of your present or most recent job. Please select one number from the following scale for each statement. After completing the instrument, use the scoring key to compute a total score for each of the core job characteristics.

1 = Very inaccurate	5 = Slightly accurate
2 = Mostly inaccurate	6 = Mostly accurate
3 = Slightly inaccurate	7 = Very accurate
4 = Uncertain	

_____ 1. Supervisors often let me know how well they think I am performing the job.
_____ 2. The job requires me to use a number of complex or high-level skills.
_____ 3. The job is arranged so that I have the chance to do an entire piece of work from beginning to end.
_____ 4. Just doing the work required by the job provides many chances for me to figure out how well I am doing.

_____ 5. The job is not simple and repetitive.

_____ 6. This job is one where a lot of other people can be affected by how well the work gets done.

_____ 7. The job does not deny me the chance to use my personal initiative or judgment in carrying out the work.

_____ 8. The job provides me the chance to completely finish the pieces of work I begin.

_____ 9. The job itself provides plenty of clues about whether or not I am performing well.

_____ 10. The job gives me considerable opportunity for independence and freedom in how I do the work.

_____ 11. The job itself is very significant or important in the broader scheme of things.

_____ 12. The supervisors and co-workers on this job almost always give me "feedback" about how well I am doing in my work.

Scoring Key   Compute the **average** of the two items that measure each job characteristic.

Skill variety (#2 and #5)	_____
Task identity (#3 and #8)	_____
Task significance (#6 and #11)	_____
Autonomy (#7 and #10)	_____
Feedback from job itself (#4 and #9)	_____
Feedback from others (#1 and #12)	_____

Now you are ready to calculate the MPS. First, you need to compute a total score for the feedback job characteristic. This is done by computing the average of the job characteristics entitled "feedback from job itself" and "feedback from others." Second, use the MPS formula presented earlier in this chapter. Finally, norms are provided below to help you interpret the relative status of the MPS and each individual job characteristic.[63]

Norms

	Type Of Job			
	Professional/ Technical	Clerical	Sales	Service
Skill variety	5.4	4.0	4.8	5.0
Task identity	5.1	4.7	4.4	4.7
Task significance	5.6	5.3	5.5	5.7
Autonomy	5.4	4.5	4.8	5.0
Feedback from job itself	5.1	4.6	5.4	5.1
Feedback from others	4.2	4.0	3.6	3.8
MPS	154	106	146	152

Questions for Consideration/Class Discussion

1. What is the MPS of your job? Is it high, average, or low?

2. Using the norms, which job characteristics are high, average, or low?

3. Which job characteristics would you change? Why?

4. How might you use the implementing concepts to redesign your job?

• NOTES

[1] Gregory A. Patterson, "Credibility Gap: UAW and Big Three Face Mutual Mistrust as Auto Talks Heat Up," *The Wall Street Journal,* August 29, 1990, p. A1.

[2] Terence R. Mitchell, "Motivation: New Direction for Theory, Research, and Practice," *Academy of Management Review,* January 1982, p. 81.

[3] For a detailed discussion of management's role in managing performance roadblocks, see Mary Walton, *The Deming Management Method* (New York, NY: Perigee Books, 1986).

[4] See Edwin A. Locke and Gary P. Latham, "Work Motivation and Satisfaction: Light at the End of the Tunnel," *Psychological Science,* July 1990, pp. 240–46.

[5] For a thorough discussion of the historical development of motivation theories, see Raymond Katzell and Donna E. Thompson, "Work Motivation: Theory and Practice," *American Psychologist,* February 1990, pp. 144–53.

[6] Mitchell, "Motivation: New Direction for Theory, Research, and Practice," p. 83. A recent meta-analysis of the relationship between ability and performance was conducted by W. Mark Coward and Paul R. Sackett, "Linearity of Ability-Performance Relationships: A Reconfirmation," *Journal of Applied Psychology,* June 1990, pp. 297–300.

[7] For a complete description of Maslow's theory, see Abraham H. Maslow, "A Theory of Human Motivation," *Psychological Review,* July 1943, pp. 370–96.

[8] Craig C. Pinder, *Work Motivation: Theory, Issues, and Applications* (Glenview, Ill.: Scott, Foresman, 1984), p. 52.

[9] Layoff statistics are discussed in Amanda Bennett, "A White-Collar Guide to Job Security," *The Wall Street Journal,* September 11, 1990, pp. B1 and B12. Corporate examples of job security pledges are contained in "Labor Letter: A Special News Report on People and Their Jobs in Offices, Fields, and Factories," *The Wall Street Journal,* May 14, 1985, p. 1.

[10] Alternative techniques for measuring achievement needs can be found in Aharon Tziner and Dov Elizur, "Achievement Motive: A Reconceptualization and New Instrument," *Journal of Occupational Behavior,* July 1985, pp. 209–28; and Michael J. Stahl and Adrian M. Harrell, "Evolution and Validation of a Behavioral Decision Theory Measurement Approach to Achievement, Power, and Affiliation," *Journal of Applied Psychology,* December 1982, pp. 744–51.

[11] Results can be found in Stephen D. Bluen, Julian Barling, and Warren Burns, "Predicting Sales Performance, Job Satisfaction, and Depression by Using the Achievement Strivings and Impatience–Irritability Dimensions of Type A Behavior," *Journal of Applied Psychology,* April 1990, pp. 212–16.

[12] Henry A. Murray, *Explorations in Personality* (New York: John Wiley & Sons, 1938), p. 164.

[13] Results are presented in John B. Miner, Norman R. Smith, and Jeffrey S. Bracker, "Role of Entrepreneurial Task Motivation in the Growth of Technologically Innovative Firms, *Journal of Applied Psychology,* August 1989, pp. 554–60.

[14] See David C. McClelland, *The Achieving Society* (New York: Free Press, 1961).

[15] See David C. McClelland, *Power: The Inner Experience* (New York: John Wiley & Sons, 1975).

[16] See the following series of research reports: Adrian M. Harrell and Michael J. Stahl, "A Behavioral Decision Theory Approach for Measuring McClelland's Trichotomy of Needs," *Journal of Applied Psychology,* April 1981, pp. 242–47; Michael J. Stahl and Adrian M. Harrell, "Evolution and Validation of a Behavioral Decision Theory Measurement Approach to Achievement, Power, and Affiliation," *Journal of Applied Psychology,* December 1982, pp. 744–51; and Michael J. Stahl, "Achievement, Power and Managerial Motivation: Selecting Managerial Talent with the Job Choice Exercise," *Personnel Psychology,* Winter 1983, pp. 775–89.

[17] For a review of the foundation of achievement motivation training, see David C. McClelland, "Toward a Theory of Motive Acquisition," *American Psychologist,* May 1965, pp. 321–33. Evidence for the validity of motivation training can be found in Heinz Heckhausen and Siegbert Krug, "Motive Modification," in *Motivation and Society,* ed. Abigail J. Stewart (San Francisco: Jossey-Bass, 1982).

[18] Supporting evidence is contained in Sharon Rae Jenkins, "Need for Achievement and Women's Careers Over 14 Years: Evidence for Occupational Structure Effects," *Journal of Personality and Social Psychology,* November 1987, pp. 922–32; and Robert J. House and Jitendra V. Singh, "Organizational Behavior: Some New Directions for I/O Psychology," in *Annual Review of Psychology,* ed. Mark Rosenzweig and Lyman W. Porter (Palo Alto, Calif.: Annual Reviews, 1987).

[19] "Labor Letter: A Special News Report on People and Their Jobs in Offices, Fields, and Factories," *The Wall Street Journal,* December 29, 1987, p. 1.

[20] James L. Bowditch and Anthony F. Buono, *A Primer on Organizational Behavior* (New York: John Wiley & Sons, 1985), p. 210.

[21] Research on scientific management is reviewed by Toby D. Wall and Robin Martin, "Job and Work Design," in *International Review of Industrial and Organizational Psychology,* ed. Cary L. Cooper and Ivan T. Robertson (New York: John Wiley & Sons, 1987), pp. 61–91.

[22] Research on job enlargement was summarized by Ricky W. Griffin, *Task Design: An Integrative Approach* (Glenview, Ill.: Scott, Foresman, 1982).

[23] Research on job rotation is reviewed in Griffin, *Task Design: An Integrative Approach.*

[24] See Frederick Herzberg, Bernard Mausner, and Barbara B. Snyderman, *The Motivation to Work* (New York: John Wiley & Sons, 1959).

[25] Ibid.

[26] Both sides of the Herzberg controversy are discussed by Nathan King, "Clarification and Evaluation of the Two-Factor Theory of Job Satisfaction," *Psychological Bulletin,* July 1970, pp. 18–31; and Ben Grigaliunas and Yoash Weiner, "Has the Research Challenge to Motivation–Hygiene Theory Been Conclusive? An Analysis of Critical Studies," *Human Relations,* December 1974, pp. 839–71.

[27] Pinder, *Work Motivation: Theory, Issues, and Applications,* p. 28.

[28] Stephen Phillips, Amy Dunkin, James B. Treece, and Keith H. Hammonds, "King Customer: At Companies That Listen Hard and Respond Fast, Bottom Lines Thrive," *Business Week,* March 12, 1990, p. 91.

[29] J. Richard Hackman, Greg R. Oldham, Robert Janson, and Kenneth Purdy, "A New Strategy for Job Enrichment," *California Management Review,* Summer 1975, p. 58.

[30] For an expanded discussion of this approach, see J. Richard Hackman and Greg R. Oldham, *Work Redesign* (Reading, Mass.: Addison-Wesley Publishing, 1980).

[31] Hackman, Oldham, Janson, and Purdy, "A New Strategy for Job Enrichment," p. 58. (Emphasis added.)

[32] Definitions of the job characteristics were adapted from J. Richard Hackman and Greg R. Oldham, ''Motivation through the Design of Work: Test of a Theory,'' *Organizational Behavior and Human Performance,* August 1976, pp. 250–79.

[33] The complete JDS and norms for the MPS are presented in Hackman and Oldham, *Work Redesign.* Studies that revised the JDS were conducted by Jacqueline R. Idaszak and Fritz Drasgow, ''A Revision of the Job Diagnostic Survey: Elimination of a Measurement Artifact,'' *Journal of Applied Psychology,* February 1987, pp. 69–74; and Yitzhak Fried and Gerald R. Ferris, ''The Dimensionality of Job Characteristics: Some Neglected Issues, ''*Journal of Applied Psychology,* August 1986, pp. 419–26.

[34] For research on moderators of job design effectiveness, see Michael A. Campion, ''Ability Requirement Implications of Job Design: An Interdisciplinary Perspective,'' *Personnel Psychology,* Spring 1989, pp. 1–24; John W. Medcof, ''The Effect of Use of Information Technology and Job of the User upon Task Characteristics,'' *Human Relations,* January 1989, pp. 23–41; and Brian T. Loher, Raymond A. Noe, Nancy L. Moeller, and Michael P. Fitzgerald, ''A Meta-Analysis of the Relation of Job Characteristics to Job Satisfaction,'' *Journal of Applied Psychology,* May 1985, pp. 280–89.

[35] See Loher, Noe, Moeller, and Fitzgerald, ''A Meta-Analysis of the Relation of Job Characteristics to Job Satisfaction.''

[36] Results can be found in Maryellen R. Kelley, New Process Technology, Job Design, and Work Organization: A Contingency Model,'' *American Sociological Review,* April 1990, pp. 191–208.

[37] Productivity studies are reviewed in Richard E. Kopelman, *Managing Productivity in Organizations* (New York: McGraw-Hill, 1986).

[38] Absenteeism results are discussed in Yitzhak Fried and Gerald R. Ferris, ''The Validity of the Job Characteristics Model: A Review and Meta-Analysis,'' *Personnel Psychology,* Summer 1987, pp. 287–322. The turnover meta-analysis was conducted by Glen M. McEvoy and Wayne F. Cascio, ''Strategies for Reducing Turnover: A Meta-Analysis,'' *Journal of Applied Psychology,* May 1985, pp. 342–53.

[39] Greg R. Oldham and J. Richard Hackman, ''Work Design in the Organizational Context,'' in *Research in Organizational Behavior,* ed. Barry M. Staw and Larry L. Cummings (Greenwich, Conn.: JAI Press, 1980), pp. 248–49.

[40] Joe G. Thomas and Ricky W. Griffin, ''The Power of Social Information in the Workplace,'' *Organizational Dynamics,* Autumn 1989, p. 63.

[41] See Joe G. Thomas, ''Sources of Social Information: A Longitudinal Analysis,'' *Human Relations,* September 1986, pp. 855–70.

[42] Jeffrey Pfeffer, ''Management as Symbolic Action: The Creation and Maintenance of Organizational Paradigms,'' in *Research in Organizational Behavior,* ed. Larry L. Cummings and Barry M. Staw (Greenwich, Conn.: JAI Press, 1981), p. 10.

[43] See Joe Thomas and Ricky Griffin, ''The Social Information Processing Model of Task Design: A Review of the Literature,'' *Academy of Management Review,* October 1983, pp. 672–82.

[44] Results are found in Gary J. Blau, ''Source-Related Determinants of Perceived Job Scope,'' *Human Communication Research,* Summer 1985, pp. 536–53.

[45] See Edwin A. Locke, ''The Nature and Causes of Job Satisfaction,'' in *Handbook of Industrial and Organizational Psychology,* ed. Marvin D. Dunnette (Skokie, Ill.: Rand McNally, 1976).

[46] For a review of the development of the JDI, see Patricia C. Smith, L. M. Kendall, and Charles L. Hulin, *The Measurement of Satisfaction in Work and Retirement* (Skokie, Ill.: Rand McNally, 1969).

[47] For norms on the MSQ, see David J. Weiss, Rene V. Dawis, George W. England,

and Lloyd H. Lofquist, *Manual for the Minnesota Satisfaction Questionnaire* (Minneapolis: Industrial Relations Center, University of Minnesota, 1967).

[48] Gerald R. Salancik and Jeffrey Pfeffer, "An Examination of Need-Satisfaction Models of Job Attitudes," *Administrative Science Quarterly,* September 1977, p. 453.

[49] Results can be found in Robert W. Rice, Dean B. McFarlin, and Debbie E. Bennett, "Standards of Comparison and Job Satisfaction," *Journal of Applied Psychology,* August 1989, pp. 591–98.

[50] A complete description of this model is provided by E. A. Locke, "Job Satisfaction," in *Social Psychology and Organizational Behavior,* ed. Michael Gruneberg and Toby Wall (New York: John Wiley & Sons, 1984).

[51] For a test of the value fulfillment model, see John K. Butler, Jr., "Value Importance as a Moderator of the Value Fulfillment—Job Satisfaction Relationship: Group Differences," *Journal of Applied Psychology,* August 1983, pp. 420–28. For a review of earlier research, see Locke, "The Nature and Causes of Job Satisfaction."

[52] See Paul D. Sweeney, Dean B. McFarlin, and Edward J. Inderrieden, "Using Relative Deprivation Theory to Explain Satisfaction with Income and Pay Level: A Multistudy Examination," *Academy of Management Journal,* June 1990, pp. 423–36.

[53] This interesting study was conducted by Richard D. Arvey, Thomas J. Bouchard, Jr., Nancy L. Segal, and Lauren M. Abraham, "Job Satisfaction: Environmental and Genetic Components," *Journal of Applied Psychology,* April 1989, pp. 187–92.

[54] See Rick D. Hackett, "Work Attitudes and Employee Absenteeism: A Synthesis of the Literature," *Journal of Occupational Psychology,* 1989, pp. 235–48.

[55] The costs of turnover were assessed by Philip H. Mirvis and Edward E. Lawler III, "Measuring the Financial Impact of Employee Attitudes," *Journal of Applied Psychology,* February 1977, pp. 1–8.

[56] Results are presented in John L. Cotton and Jeffrey M. Tuttle, "Employee Turnover: A Meta-Analysis and Review with Implications for Research," *Academy of Management Review,* January 1986, pp. 55–70.

[57] Dennis W. Organ, "The Motivational Basis of Organizational Citizenship Behavior," in *Research in Organizational Behavior,* ed. Barry M. Staw and Larry L. Cummings (Greenwich, Conn.: JAI Press, 1990), p. 46.

[58] A field study of organizational citizenship behaviors was conducted by Dennis W. Organ and Mary Konovsky, "Cognitive versus Affective Determinants of Organizational Citizenship Behavior," *Journal of Applied Psychology,* February 1989, pp. 157–64.

[59] See John E. Mathieu and Dennis Zajac, "A Review and Meta-analysis of the Antecedents, Correlates, and Consequences of Organizational Commitment," *Psychological Bulletin,"* September 1990, pp. 171–94.

[60] The relationship between performance and satisfaction was reviewed by Michelle T. Iaffaldano and Paul M. Muchinsky, "Job Satisfaction and Job Performance: A Meta-Analysis," *Psychological Bulletin,* March 1985, pp. 251–73.

[61] For an overall review of the satisfaction–pro-union voting relationship, see Herbert G. Heneman III and Marcus H. Sandver, "Predicting the Outcome of Union Certification Elections: A Review of the Literature," *Industrial and Labor Relations Review,* July 1983, pp. 537–59. Two recent studies were conducted by Steven Mellor, "The Relationship between Membership Decline and Union Commitment: A Field Study of Local Unions in Crisis," *Journal of Applied Psychology,* June 1990, pp. 258–67; and Bert Klandermans, "Union Commitment: Replications and Tests in the Dutch Context," *Journal of Applied Psychology,* December 1989, pp. 869–75.

[62] See John M. Ivancevich and Michael T. Matteson, *Stress and Work: A Managerial Perspective* (Glenview, Ill.: Scott, Foresman, 1980). For a review of the causes of heart disease, see C. David Jenkins, ''Psychologic and Social Precursors of Coronary Disease,'' *The New England Journal of Medicine,* February 1971, pp. 307–16.

[63] The JDS and its norms were adapted from J. Richard Hackman and Greg R. Oldham, *Work Redesign* (Reading, Mass.: Addison-Wesley Publishing, 1980), pp. 280–81, 317.

CHAPTER

6

Motivation through Equity, Expectancy, and Goal Setting

LEARNING OBJECTIVES

When you finish studying the material in this chapter, you should be able to:

- Discuss the role of perceived inequity in employee motivation.
- Distinguish between positive and negative inequity.

- Define Vroom's concepts of expectancy, instrumentality, and valence.
- Discuss Porter and Lawler's expectancy theory of motivation.
- Describe the practical implications of expectancy theory of motivation.
- Explain how goal setting motivates an individual.

- Identify four practical lessons from goal-setting research.
- Specify issues that should be addressed before implementing a motivational program.

Opening Case 6

Cypress Semiconductor Corporation Uses a Computerized Management System to Monitor and Motivate Employees

Sharon Hoogstraten

T. J. Rodgers, CEO, says: "Most companies don't fail for lack of talent or strategic vision. They fail for lack of execution—the mundane blocking and tackling that the great companies consistently do well and strive to do better.

At Cypress, our management systems track corporate, departmental, and individual performance so regularly and in such

detail that no manager, including me, can plausibly claim to be in the dark about critical problems. Our systems give managers the capacity to monitor what's happening at all levels of the organization, to anticipate problems or conflicts, to intervene when appropriate, and to identify best practices—without creating layers of bureaucracy that bog down decisions and sap morale.

Lots of companies espouse a 'no surprises' philosophy. At Cypress, 'no surprises' is a way of life. We operate in a treacherous and unforgiving business. An integrated circuit is the end result of a thousand multidisciplinary tasks; doing 999 of them right guarantees failure, not success. Last year, we shipped 159 different chips (56 of which were new in 1989) in 7 distinct product categories using 26 different process-technology variations. This year, we plan to add

another 50 products to our portfolio. Our watchwords are discipline, accountability, and relentless attention to detail—at every level of the organization.

How do we measure success at Cypress? By doing what we say we are going to do. We meet sales projections within a percentage point or two every quarter. We don't go over budget—ever. Our silicon wafer manufacturing plant in Round Rock, Texas, which now accounts for 70 percent of our sales, shipped its first revenue wafer eight months after ground breaking. That performance tied the industry record, which had been set in 1984 by our manufacturing facility in San Jose. . . .

All of Cypress's 1,400 employees have goals, which, in theory, makes them no different from employees at most other companies. What does make our people different is that every week they set their own goals, commit to achiev-

---

T his chapter explores three cognitive process theories of work motivation: equity, expectancy, and goal-setting. Each theory is based on the premise that employees' cognitions are the key to understanding their motivation. To help you apply what you have learned, we conclude the chapter by highlighting the prerequisites of successful motivational programs.

• Adams' Equity Theory of Motivation

Defined generally, **equity theory** is a model of motivation that explains how people strive for *fairness* and *justice* in social exchanges or give-and-take relationships. Equity theory is based on cognitive dissonance theory, developed by social psychologist Leon Festinger in the 1950s.[1]

OPENING CASE 6

(continued)

ing them by a specific date, enter them into a database, and report whether or not they completed prior goals. Cypress's computerized goal system is an important part of our managerial infrastructure. It is a detailed guide to the future and an objective record of the past. In any given week, some 6,000 goals in the database come due. Our ability to meet those goals ultimately determines our success or failure.

Most of the work in our company is organized by project rather than along strict functional lines. Members of a project team may be (and usually are) from different parts of the organization. Project managers need not be (and often aren't) the highest ranking member of the group. Likewise, the goal system is organized by project and function. In Monday project meetings, employees set short-term goals and rank them in priority order. Short-term goals

take from one to six weeks to complete, and different employees have different numbers of goals. At the beginning of a typical week, for example, a member of our production-control staff initiated seven new goals in connection with three different projects. He said he would, among other things, report on progress with certain minicomputer problems (two weeks), monitor and report on quality rejection rates for certain products (three weeks), update killer software for the assembly department (two weeks), and assist a marketing executive with a forecasting software enhancement (four weeks).

On Monday night, the project goals are fed back into a central computer. On Tuesday mornings, functional managers receive a printout of their direct reports' new and pending project goals. These printouts are the basis of Tuesday afternoon meetings in

which managers work with their people to anticipate overload and conflicting goals, sort out priorities, organize work, and make mutual commitments about what's going to get done. This is a critical step. The failure mode in our company (and I suspect in most growing companies) is that people overcommit themselves rather than establish unchallenging goals. By 5 P.M. Tuesday, the revised schedule is fed back into the central database.

This 'two pass' system generates the work program that coordinates the mostly self-imposed activities of every Cypress employee. It allows the organization to be project driven, which helps us emphasize speed and agility, as well as functionally accurate, which works against burnout and failure to execute. On Wednesday morning, our eight vice presidents receive goal printouts for their people and the people below

According to Festinger's theory, people are motivated to maintain consistency between their cognitive beliefs and their behavior. Perceived inconsistencies create cognitive dissonance (or psychological discomfort), which in turn motivates corrective action. For example, a cigarette smoker who sees a heavy-smoking relative die of lung cancer probably would be motivated to quit smoking if he or she attributes the death to smoking. Accordingly, when victimized by unfair social exchanges, our resulting cognitive dissonance prompts us to correct the situation. Corrective action may range from a slight change in attitude or behavior to the extreme case of trying to harm someone (see A Matter of Ethics).

Psychologist J. Stacy Adams pioneered application of the equity principle to the workplace. Central to understanding Adams' equity theory of motivation is an awareness of key components of the individual–organization exchange relationship. This relationship is pivotal in the formation of employees' perceptions of equity and inequity.

OPENING CASE 6

(continued)

them—another conflict-resolution mechanism. . . .

On Wednesday afternoons at my weekly staff meeting, I review various database reports with my vice presidents. We talk about what's going wrong and how to help managers who are running into problems. The following reports typically serve as the basis for discussion: progress with goals on critical projects; percentage of delinquent goals sorted by managers (their goals plus those of their subordinates); percentage of delinquent goals sorted by vice president (the percentage of pending goals that are delinquent for all people reporting up the chain of command to each vice president); all employees without goals (something I do not tolerate); all goals five or more weeks delinquent; and all employees with two or more delinquent goals, sorted by manager.

As we've refined the goal system and used it more extensively, I've developed some general principles. First, people are going to have goals they don't achieve on time; the key is to sense when a vice president or a manager is losing control of the operation. My rule of thumb is that vice presidents should not have delinquency rates above 20 percent, and managers should not let more than 30 percent of their goals become delinquent. When managers do have a delinquency problem, I usually intervene with a short note: 'Your delinquency rate is running at 35 percent, what can I do to help?' I often get back requests for specific assistance. Part of my role is to hold people accountable. But it is also to identify problems before they become crises and to provide help in getting them fixed.

Second, people need positive feedback. Every month we issue a Completed Goal Report for every person in the company. The report lists all goals completed over the past four weeks as well as those that have yet to come due. 'Individual Monthly Goal Report,' an excerpt from a monthly report for a production-control staffer, lists all goals completed in workweek 45 of last year. The entire report consists of 49 goals, 28 of which were completed on time, 4 of which were completed late, and 17 of which were pending—an outstanding record.

The completed goal report is also a valuable tool for performance evaluation. . . . At Cypress, the completed goal report triggers a performance minireview; each month managers read through their people's printouts and prepare brief, factual evaluations. At year end, managers have a dozen such objective reviews to

A MATTER OF ETHICS

An Employee Seeks Revenge after Perceived Inequity

People look to exact revenge when they believe they have been slighted and feel the need to repair the perceived damage done to them, says Ronald S. Ebert, a psychologist at the Levinson Institute in Belmont, Mass. "While to an objective observer, the slight may appear to be of small consequence, to the individual who feels harmed, it's significant." . . .

Revenge takes many forms, from the subtle to the shocking. Mr. Ebert cites one of his patients who, demoted to a menial job after years with a Boston-area high-tech company, was found with a loaded gun in the company parking lot. He blamed his supervisor for the demotion and was waiting for the supervisor to arrive at work to retaliate violently.

Source: L. A. Winokur, "Sweet Revenge is Souring the Office," *The Wall Street Journal*, September 9, 1990, p. B1.

OPENING CASE 6

(concluded)

refresh their memories and fight the proximity effect.

Managers shouldn't expect outstanding performance unless they're prepared to reward outstanding performers. Yet evaluation and reward systems remain an organizational black hole for three reasons.

First, managers aren't very scientific about rating their people. They may be able to identify the real stars and the worst laggards, but the vast majority of people (who must still be ranked) get lost somewhere in the middle. Second, even if they evaluate people correctly, managers like to spread raises around evenly to keep the troops happy. This is a deadly policy that saps the morale of standouts who deserve more and sends the wrong signal to weak performers. Third, managers are totally incapable of distinguishing between 'merit' and 'equity' when

awarding increases. Merit refers to that portion of a raise awarded for the quality of past performance. Equity refers to adjustments in that raise to more closely align salaries of equally ranked peers. Merit and equity both have a place in the incentive mix, but confusing the two makes for mushy logic, counterproductive results, and dissatisfied people. . . .

As with all our resource-allocation systems, the focal-review system starts with policies at the top and forces middle management decisions to be consistent with that thinking. Senior management and the board of directors review our annual revenue forecasts, survey compensation trends among our competitors, and settle on a total corporate allowance for raises. The 'raise budget' is not negotiable, and it drives raises throughout the company. If the corporate budget is 8 percent,

then every department must meet a weighted-average salary increase of 8 percent. It's up to managers to distribute the 8 percent pool, which is where the focal-review system comes in. . . .

Only after they have awarded percentage increases based strictly on merit can managers make adjustments for salary inequities created by personal circumstances and historical accidents.''

For Discussion

Why is Cypress so successful in meeting its goals?

• Additional discussion questions linking this case with the following material appear at the end of this chapter.

Source: Excerpted from T. J. Rodgers, "No Excuses Management," *Harvard Business Review*, July–August 1990, pp. 84–98.

The Individual–Organization Exchange Relationship

Adams points out that two primary components are involved in the employee–employer exchange, *inputs* and *outcomes*. An employee's inputs, for which he or she expects a just return, include education, experience, skills, and effort. On the outcome side of the exchange, the organization provides such things as pay, fringe benefits, and recognition. These outcomes vary widely, depending on one's organization and rank. For example, a recent survey conducted by Hewitt Associates indicated that the most popular corporate perks for top executives included the use of a company car and plane, country-club memberships, financial counseling, first-class air travel, income-tax preparation, and annual physical exams.[2] In contrast, European executives receive outcomes such as company-subsidized yachts, country estates, gardeners, chauffeurs, home entertainment, and payment of personal phone bills.[3] More typical on-the-job inputs and outcomes are listed in Table 6–1.

• **TABLE 6-1**   Factors Considered When Making Equity Comparisons

Inputs	Outcomes
Time	Pay/bonuses
Education/training	Fringe benefits
Experience	Challenging assignments
Skills	Job security
Creativity	Career advancement/promotions
Seniority	Status symbols
Loyalty to organization	Pleasant/safe working environment
Age	Opportunity for personal growth/development
Personality traits	Supportive supervision
Effort expended	Recognition
Personal appearance	Participation in important decisions

Source: Based in part on J. Stacy Adams, "Toward an Understanding of Inequity," *Journal of Abnormal and Social Psychology*, November 1963, pp. 422–36.

Negative and Positive Inequity

On the job, feelings of inequity revolve around a person's evaluation of whether he or she receives adequate rewards to compensate for his or her contributive inputs. As shown in Figure 6–1, people perform these evaluations by comparing the perceived fairness of their employment exchange to that of relevant others. This comparative process, which is based on an equity norm, was found to generalize across countries.[4] OB scholar Robert Vecchio identified three major categories of relevant others that people use when making equity comparisons:

(1) *Other* (including referent others inside and outside the organization, and referent others in similar or different jobs), (2) *self* (self-comparisons over time and against one's ideal ratio), and (3) *system* (based on exchanges between an individual and the organization). In addition to these categorizations, it should be noted that a group or even multiple groups can serve as referents.[5]

People tend to compare themselves to similar others—such as people performing the same job, or individuals of the same gender or educational level—rather than dissimilar others.[6]

Three different equity relationships are illustrated in Figure 6–2; equity, negative inequity, and positive inequity. Assume the two people in each of the equity relationships in Figure 6–2 have equivalent backgrounds (equal education, seniority, and so forth) and perform identical tasks. Only their hourly pay rates differ. Equity exists for an individual when his or her ratio of perceived outcomes to inputs is equal to the ratio of outcomes to inputs for a relevant co-worker (see part A in Figure 6–2). Since equity is based on comparing *ratios* of outcomes to inputs, inequity will not necessarily be perceived just because someone else receives greater rewards. If the other person's additional outcomes are due to his or her greater inputs, a sense of equity may still exist. However, if the comparison person enjoys greater outcomes for similar inputs, **negative inequity** will be perceived (see Part B in Figure 6–2). On the other hand, a person will experience **positive inequity**

• **FIGURE 6-1**   A Basic Model of Equity Theory

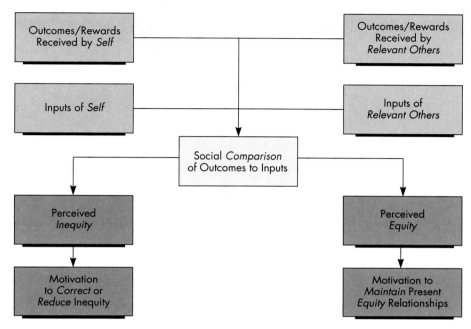

when his or her outcome to input ratio is greater than that of a relevant co-worker (see part C in Figure 6–2).

Dynamics of Perceived Inequity

Managers can derive practical benefits from Adams' equity theory by recognizing: (1) negative inequity is less tolerable than positive inequity, and (2) inequity can be reduced in a variety of ways.

Thresholds of Inequity   People have a lower tolerance for negative inequity than they do for positive inequity. Those who are shortchanged are more powerfully motivated to correct the situation than those who are excessively rewarded. For example, if you have ever been overworked and underpaid, you know how negative inequity can erode your job satisfaction and performance. Perhaps you quit the job to escape the negative inequity. Hence, it takes much more positive than negative inequity to produce the same degree of motivation. Moreover, research indicates that males respond more strongly to negative inequity than do females.[7] Males thus are more likely to complain or reduce their inputs when faced with negative inequity.

Reducing Inequity   Table 6–2 lists eight possible ways to reduce inequity. It is important to note that equity can be restored by altering one's equity ratios behaviorally and/or cognitively.[8] Equity theorists propose that the many possible combinations of behavioral and cognitive adjustments are influenced by the following tendencies:

• **FIGURE 6-2**   Negative and Positive Inequity

A. An Equitable Situation

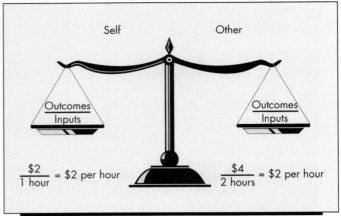

$$\frac{\$2}{1\ hour} = \$2\ per\ hour \qquad \frac{\$4}{2\ hours} = \$2\ per\ hour$$

B. Negative Inequity

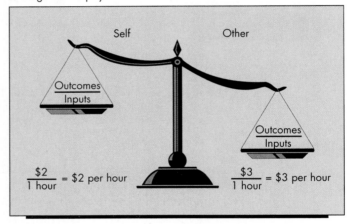

$$\frac{\$2}{1\ hour} = \$2\ per\ hour \qquad \frac{\$3}{1\ hour} = \$3\ per\ hour$$

C. Positive Inequity

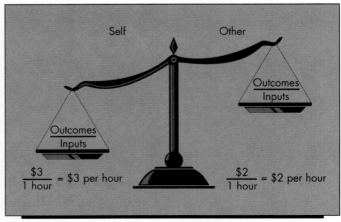

$$\frac{\$3}{1\ hour} = \$3\ per\ hour \qquad \frac{\$2}{1\ hour} = \$2\ per\ hour$$

• **TABLE 6-2**   Eight Ways to Reduce Inequity

Methods	Examples
1. Person can increase his or her inputs.	Work harder; attend school or a specialized training program.
2. Person can decrease his or her inputs.	Don't work as hard; take longer breaks.
3. Person can attempt to increase his or her outcomes.	Ask for a raise; ask for a new title; seek outside intervention.
4. Person can decrease his or her outcomes.	Ask for less pay.
5. Leave the field.	Absenteeism and turnover.
6. Person can psychologically distort his or her inputs and outcomes.	Convince self that certain inputs are not important; convince self that he or she has a boring and monotonous job.
7. Person can psychologically distort the inputs or outcomes of comparison other.	Conclude that other has more experience or works harder; conclude that other has a more important title.
8. Change comparison other.	Pick a new comparison person; compare self to previous job.

Source: Adapted from J. Stacy Adams, "Toward an Understanding of Inequity," *Journal of Abnormal and Social Psychology*, November 1963, pp. 422–36.

1. An individual will attempt to maximize the amount of positive outcomes he or she receives.
2. People resist increasing inputs when it requires substantial effort or costs.
3. People resist behavioral or cognitive changes in inputs important to their self-concept or self-esteem.
4. Rather than change cognitions about oneself, an individual is more likely to change cognitions about the comparison other's inputs and outcomes.
5. Leaving the field (quitting) is chosen only when severe inequity cannot be resolved through other methods.[9]

Equity Research Findings

Different managerial insights have been gained from laboratory and field studies.

Insights from Laboratory Studies   The basic approach used in laboratory studies is to pay an experimental subject more (overpayment) or less (underpayment) than the standard rate for completing a task. People are paid on either an hourly or piece-rate basis. Research findings supported equity theory. Overpaid subjects on a piece-rate system lowered the quantity of their performance and increased the quality of their performance. In contrast, underpaid subjects increased the quantity and decreased the quality of their performance.[10]

Insights from Field Studies   Employees reported greater levels of job satisfaction, organizational commitment, and trust in their supervisors when they perceived that compensation decisions were fair or equitable. It thus is beneficial for managers to equitably distribute monetary rewards.[11] Further, employee absenteeism and turnover were positively related to perceptions of inequity.[12] Treating employees equitably is a useful managerial practice to reduce absenteeism and turnover.

Practical Lessons from Equity Theory

Equity theory has at least five important practical implications. First, equity theory provides managers with yet another explanation of how beliefs and attitudes affect job performance (recall the discussion of attitudes and values in Chapter 3). According to this line of thinking, the best way to manage job behavior is to adequately understand underlying cognitive processes. Indeed, we are motivated powerfully to correct the situation when our ideas of fairness and justice are offended. Consider the case of a longtime Walt Disney Co. employee who felt inequity after being passed over for a promotion she thought she deserved.

> Knowing that her new boss faced pressure to vastly improve the work he supervised, the woman began taking much longer than usual to complete projects. When he wrote a negative job evaluation, without even talking to her, and placed it in her employment file, she responded with a lengthy memo—and sent copies to the division's top brass. She also made nasty comments about his actions to a few colleagues behind his back.
>
> "This was vengeful, and I did it purposely," she admits. "But I felt totally justified. I knew it would really hurt my boss and destroy his credibility." And it did. "All hell broke loose," she recounts. Within months her boss was fired—and she got his job.[13]

Second, research on equity theory emphasizes the need for managers to pay attention to employees' perceptions of what is fair and equitable. No matter how fair management thinks the organization's policies, procedures, and reward system are, each employee's *perceptions* of the equity of those factors are what count. For example, as described in International OB, an American employee may interpret the word *fair* to mean equitable treatment, whereas a Japanese employee thinks it means *equal* treatment. Cross-cultural training can help managers be more sensitive to equity perceptions in multinational situations.

Third, managers benefit by allowing employees to participate in making decisions about important work outcomes. For example, research reveals that employees are more likely to perceive pay plans as fair when they provide input in developing the plan.[14] Fourth, employees should be given the opportunity to appeal decisions that effect their welfare. Being able to appeal a decision promotes the belief that management treats employees fairly.[15] In turn, perceptions of fair treatment promote job satisfaction and organizational commitment, and help to reduce absenteeism and turnover.

Equity perceptions can be monitored through informal conversations, interviews, or attitude surveys. Please take a moment now to complete the brief equity/fairness questionnaire in the OB Exercise. If you perceive your work organization as unfair, you probably are dissatisfied and have contemplated quitting. In contrast, your organizational loyalty and attachment likely are greater if you believe you are treated fairly at work.

Finally, treating employees inequitably can lead to litigation and costly court settlements. Employees denied justice at work are turning increasingly

INTERNATIONAL OB

Equity Perceptions Vary from Culture to Culture

The American manager who promised to be fair thought he was telling his Japanese staff that their hard work would be rewarded; but when some workers received higher salary increases than others, there were complaints. "You told us you'd be fair, and you lied to us," accused one salesman. "It took me a year and a half," sighed the American, "to realize that 'fair,' to my staff, meant being treated equally."

Source: Excerpted from Michael Berger, "Building Bridges over the Cultural Rivers," *International Management*, July–August 1987, p. 61.

• OB EXERCISE

Measuring Perceived Organizational Equity/Fairness

Instructions:
Evaluate your present (or most recent) job according to the following five dimensions.

Dimensions	Item	Score
		False 　　　　　True
1. Pay rules	The rules for granting pay raises in my organization are fair.	1—2—3—4—5—6—7
2. Pay administration	My supervisor rates everyone fairly when considering them for promotion.	1—2—3—4—5—6—7
3. Pay level	My employer pays me more for my work than I would receive from other organizations in this area.	1—2—3—4—5—6—7
4. Work pace	My supervisor makes everyone meet their performance standards.	1—2—3—4—5—6—7
5. Rule administration	My supervisor makes everyone come to work on time and adhere to the same rules of conduct.	1—2—3—4—5—6—7

Total score = _____

Norms

Very fair organization = 26–35
Moderately fair organization = 15–25
Unfair organization = 5–14

Source: Adapted in part from John E. Dittrich and Michael R. Carrell, "Organizational Equity Perceptions, Employee Job Satisfaction, and Departmental Absence and Turnover Rates," *Organizational Behavior and Human Performance*, August 1979, pp. 29–40.

to arbitration and the courts. Managers knowledgeable about equity theory can keep things from getting that far out of hand.

• Expectancy Theory of Motivation

Expectancy theory holds that people are motivated to behave in ways that produce desired combinations of expected outcomes. Perception plays a central role in expectancy theory because it emphasizes cognitive ability to anticipate likely consequences of behavior. Embedded in expectancy theory is the principle of hedonism. As mentioned in Chapter 5, hedonistic people strive to maximize their pleasure and minimize their pain. Generally, expectancy theory can be used to predict behavior in any situation in which a choice between two or more alternatives must be made. For example, it can be used to predict whether to quit or stay at a job, whether to exert substantial or minimal effort at a task, and whether to major in management, computer science, accounting, or finance.

This section introduces and explores two expectancy theories of motivation: Vroom's expectancy theory and Porter and Lawler's expectancy theory. Understanding these cognitive process theories can help managers develop organizational policies and practices that enhance rather than inhibit employee motivation.

Vroom's Expectancy Theory

Victor Vroom formulated a mathematical model of expectancy theory in his 1964 book *Work and Motivation*.[16] Vroom's theory has been summarized as follows:

> The strength of a tendency to act in a certain way depends on the strength of an expectancy that the act will be followed by a given consequence (or outcome) and on the value or attractiveness of that consequence (or outcome) to the actor.[17]

A general model of Vroom's theory is presented in Figure 6–3. It outlines the variables that influence an individual's level of motivation. Motivation, according to Vroom, boils down to the decision of how much effort to exert in a specific task situation. This choice is based on a two-stage sequence of expectations (effort→performance and performance→outcome). First, motivation is affected by an individual's expectation that a certain level of effort will produce the intended performance goal. For example, if you do not believe increasing the amount of time you spend studying will significantly raise your grade on an exam, you probably will not study any harder than usual. Motivation also is influenced by the employee's perceived chances of getting various outcomes as a result of accomplishing his or her performance goal. Finally, individuals are motivated to the extent that they value the outcomes received. The U.S. Justice Department, for example, recently instituted a plan to encourage employees' motivation to expose unethical managerial practices (see A Matter of Ethics).

Vroom used a mathematical equation to integrate these concepts into a predictive model of motivational force or strength. For our purposes, how-

• **FIGURE 6-3**   A General Model of Vroom's Expectancy Theory

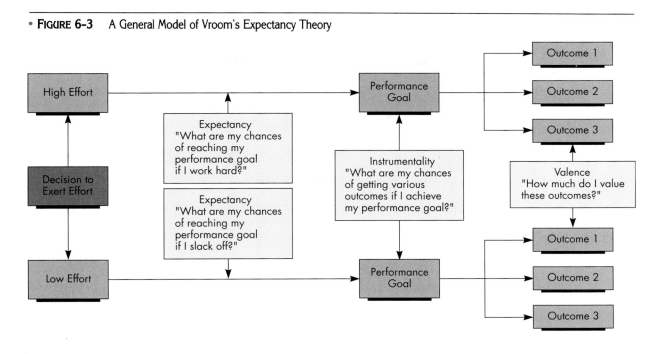

ever, it is sufficient to define and explain the three key concepts within Vroom's model—*expectancy, instrumentality,* and *valence.*

Expectancy   An **expectancy,** according to Vroom's terminology, represents an individual's belief that a particular degree of effort will be followed by a particular level of performance. In other words, it is an effort→performance expectation. Expectancies take the form of subjective probabilities. As you may recall from a course in statistics, probabilities range from zero to one. An expectancy of zero indicates effort has no anticipated impact on performance.

For example, suppose you do not know how to use a typewriter. No matter how much effort you exert, your perceived probability of typing 30 error-free words per minute likely would be zero. An expectancy of one suggests that performance is totally dependent on effort. If you decided to take a typing course as well as practice a couple of hours a day for a few weeks (high effort), you should be able to type 30 words per minute without any errors. In contrast, if you do not take a typing course and only practice an hour or two per week (low effort), there is a very low probability (say, a 20 percent chance) of being able to type 30 words per minute without any errors.

The following factors influence an employee's expectancy perceptions:

- Self-esteem.
- Previous success at the task.
- Help received from a supervisor and subordinates.
- Information necessary to complete the task.
- Good materials and equipment to work with.[18]

A MATTER OF ETHICS

**U.S. Justice Department Motivates Employees to Expose
Unethical Management Practices**

Textron Inc. agreed to pay the government $17.9 million to settle civil charges
that the company fraudulently sold the U.S. Coast Guard faulty helicopter
engines.

A former procurement official with another company involved in the helicopter contract charged in May 1988 that the engines broke down and required
extensive repairs far more quickly than Textron had promised they would. The
whistleblower, Robert Ballew, will receive 15 percent of the settlement, or $2.7
million, under a federal law that provides incentives for individuals to report
fraud against the government. The Justice Department said the settlement was
the largest-ever in a whistleblower lawsuit.

Source: Paul M. Barrett, "Textron to Settle Whistleblower Suit, Pay $17.9 Million," *The Wall
Street Journal,* July 11, 1990, p. A6.

Instrumentality   An **instrumentality** is a performance→outcome perception.
As shown in Figure 6–3, it represents a person's belief that a particular
outcome is contingent on accomplishing a specific level of performance.
Performance is instrumental when it leads to something else. For example,
passing exams is instrumental to graduating from college.

Instrumentalities range from −1.0 to 1.0. An instrumentality of 1.0 indicates attainment of a particular outcome is totally dependent on task performance. For instance, consider an audio equipment salesperson being paid
on commission. The amount of pay received depends solely on the number
of units sold. An instrumentality of zero indicates there is no relationship
between performance and outcome. For example, most companies link the
number of vacation days to seniority, not job performance. Finally, an
instrumentality of −1.0 reveals that high performance reduces the chance of
obtaining an outcome while low performance increases the chance. For
example, the more time you spend studying to get an A (high performance)
on an exam, the less time you will have for enjoying leisure activities.
Similarly, as you lower the amount of time spent studying (low performance), you increase the amount of time that may be devoted to leisure
activities.

Valence   As Vroom used the term, **valence** refers to the positive or negative
value people place on outcomes. Valence mirrors our personal preferences.[19] For example, most employees have a positive valence for receiving
additional money or recognition. In contrast, job stress and being laid off
would likely be negatively valent for most individuals. In Vroom's expectancy model, *outcomes* refer to different consequences that are contingent
on performance, such as pay, promotions, or recognition. An outcome's
valence depends on an individual's needs and can be measured for research
purposes with scales ranging from a negative value to a positive value. For

• Because there are monetary incentives for people who report fraud against the government, a former Textron employee was handsomely rewarded for speaking up about faulty engines in a batch of U.S. Coast Guard helicopters. *(U.S. Coast Guard Photography/Video)*

example, an individual's valence toward more recognition can be assessed on a scale ranging from -2 (very undesirable) to 0 (neutral) to $+2$ (very desirable).

Vroom's Expectancy Theory in Action   Vroom's expectancy model of motivation can be used to analyze a real-life motivation program (see OB in Action). The general expectancy model in Figure 6–3 can be our explanatory road map. Federal Express did a good job of motivating its college-age cargo handlers to switch from the low-effort portion of Figure 6–3 to the high-effort portion. According to Vroom's model, the student workers originally exerted low effort because they were paid on the basis of time, not output. It was in their best interest to work slowly and accumulate as many hours as possible. By offering to let the student workers *go home early if and when they completed their assigned duties,* Federal Express prompted high effort. This new arrangement created two positively valued outcomes: guaranteed pay plus the opportunity to leave early. The motivation to exert high effort became greater than the motivation to exert low effort.

Judging from the impressive results, the student workers had both high effort→performance expectancies and positive performance→outcome instrumentalities. Moreover, the guaranteed pay and early departure opportunity evidently had strongly positive valences for the student workers.

Porter and Lawler's Extension

Two OB researchers, Lyman Porter and Edward Lawler III, developed an expectancy model of motivation that extended Vroom's work. This model attempted to (1) identify the source of people's valences and expectancies and (2) link effort with performance and job satisfaction. The model is presented in Figure 6–4.[20]

OB IN ACTION

Federal Express Tells Its Cargo Handlers: "Get Done Early and You Can Leave with Full Pay"

Here is an excerpt from an interview between *Inc.* magazine and Frederick W. Smith, founder and chief executive officer of Federal Express Corp., the successful overnight delivery company:

> **Inc.:** Can you give an example of an innovation that solved people-related problems?
>
> **Smith:** There's one from our cargo terminal here in Memphis. It was several years ago, when we were having a helluva problem keeping things running on time. The airplanes would come in, and everything would get backed up. We tried every kind of control mechanism that you could think of, and none of them worked. Finally, it became obvious that the underlying problem was that it was in the interest of the employees at the cargo terminal—they were college kids, mostly—to run late, because it meant that they made more money. So what we did was give them all a minimum guarantee and say, "Look, if you get through before a certain time, just go home, and you will have beat the system." Well, it was unbelievable. I mean, in the space of about 45 days, the place was way ahead of schedule. And I don't even think it was a conscious thing on their part.

Source: Excerpted from "Federal Express's Fred Smith," p. 38. Reprinted with permission, *Inc.* magazine, October 1986. Copyright © 1986 by Goldhirsh Group, Inc., 38 Commercial Wharf, Boston, MA 02110.

Predictors of Effort   Effort is viewed as a function of the perceived value of a reward (the reward's valence) and the perceived effort→reward probability (an expectancy). Employees should exhibit more effort when they believe they will receive valued rewards for task accomplishment.

Predictors of Performance   Performance is determined by more than effort. Figure 6–4 indicates that the relationship between effort and performance is moderated by an employee's abilities and traits and role perceptions. That is, employees with higher abilities attain higher performance for a given level of effort than employees with less ability.[21] Similarly, effort results in higher performance when employees clearly understand and are comfortable with their roles. This occurs because effort is channeled into the most important job activities or tasks. For example, stage fright can render an otherwise well prepared actor or speaker ineffective.

Predictors of Satisfaction   Employees receive both intrinsic and extrinsic rewards for performance. Intrinsic rewards are self-granted and consist of intangibles such as a sense of accomplishment and achievement. Extrinsic rewards are tangible outcomes such as pay and public recognition. In turn, job satisfaction is determined by employees' perceptions of the equity of the rewards received. Employees are more satisfied when they feel

• **FIGURE 6-4**   Porter and Lawler's Expectancy Model

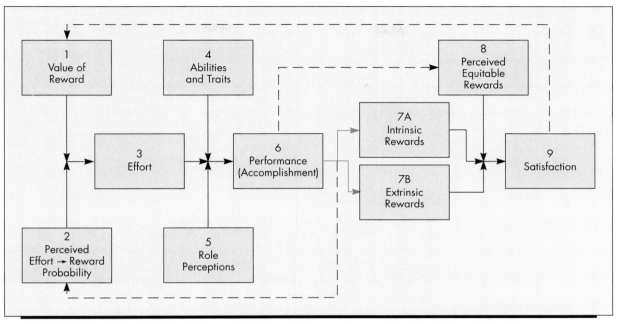

Source: Lyman W. Porter and Edward E. Lawler III, *Managerial Attitudes and Performance* (Homewood, III.: Richard D. Irwin, 1968), p. 165.

equitably rewarded.[22] Figure 6–4 further shows that job satisfaction affects employees' subsequent valence of rewards. Finally, employees' future effort→reward probabilities are influenced by past experience with performance and rewards.

Research on Expectancy Theory and Managerial Implications

Many researchers have tested expectancy theory. A summary of 16 studies revealed that expectancy theory correctly predicted occupational or organizational choice 63.4 percent of the time: This was significantly better than chance predictions.[23] Further, expectancy theory accurately predicted job satisfaction, decisions to retire (80 percent accuracy), voting behavior in union representation elections (over 75 percent accuracy), reenlistment in the National Guard (66 percent accuracy), and the frequency of drinking alcohol.[24]

Nonetheless, expectancy theory has been criticized for a variety of reasons. For example, the theory is difficult to test and the measures used to assess expectancy, instrumentality, and valence have questionable validity.[25] In the final analysis, however, expectancy theory has important practical implications for individual managers and organizations as a whole (see Table 6–3).

Managers are advised to enhance effort→performance expectancies by helping employees accomplish their performance goals. Managers can do this by serving as role models, providing adequate resources, and increasing

• Table 6-3   Managerial and Organizational Implications of Expectancy Theory

Implications for Managers	Implications for Organizations
Determine the outcomes employees value.	Reward people for desired performance and do not keep pay decisions secret.
Identify good performance so appropriate behaviors can be rewarded.	Design challenging jobs.
Make sure employees can achieve targeted performance levels.	Tie some rewards to group accomplishments to build teamwork and encourage cooperation.
Link desired outcomes to targeted levels of performance.	Reward managers for creating, monitoring, and maintaining expectancies, instrumentalities, and outcomes that lead to high effort and goal attainment.
Make sure changes in outcomes are large enough to motivate high effort.	Monitor employee motivation through interviews or anonymous questionnaires.
Monitor the reward system for inequities.	Accommodate individual differences by building flexibility into the motivation program.

employees' self-efficacy by using the methods suggested in Chapter 3. It also is important for managers to influence employees' instrumentalities and to monitor valences for various rewards.

With respect to instrumentalities and valences, managers should attempt to link employee performance and valued rewards. There are four ways to accomplish this recommendation. *First,* managers need to develop and communicate performance standards to employees. Increased motivation will not result in higher performance unless employees know how and where to direct their efforts. Consider how GTE Telephone Operations in Irving, Texas, focused employees on the goal of improved customer service. The company boosted the weight given to customer-service in performance evaluations from 15 percent of total performance in 1987 to 35 percent in 1990.[26]

Second, managers need valid and accurate performance ratings with which to compare employees.[27] Inaccurate ratings create perceptions of inequity and thereby erode motivation. *Third,* managers should use the performance ratings to differentially allocate rewards among employees. That is, it is critical that managers allocate significantly different amounts of rewards for various levels of performance. Unfortunately, this is not always the case. A 1989 survey of 459 industrial firms indicated that average performers received a 4.7 percent salary increase, while outstanding workers obtained a 7.7 percent raise. This amounted to a $17-a-week after-tax difference between average and outstanding performers.[28] Would you be motivated to work extra hard for $17-a-week? *Fourth,* managers need to identify the rewards valued by employees. Employee attitude surveys or interviews and careful listening can be used to obtain this information.

• Motivation Through Goal Setting

Regardless of the nature of their specific achievements, successful people tend to have one thing in common. Their lives are goal-oriented. This is as true for politicians seeking votes as it is for rocket scientists probing outerspace. In Lewis Carroll's delightful tale of *Alice's Adventures in Wonderland,* the smiling Cheshire cat advised the bewildered Alice, "If you

• Without a firm goal of reaching the top of the mountain, these people might have called it quits when the going got tough, and missed the elation of success. *(Gilles Guittard/The Image Bank)*

don't know where you're going, any road will take you there.'' Goal-oriented managers tend to find the right road because they know where they are going. Within the context of employee motivation, this section explores the theory, research, and practice of goal setting.

Goals: Definition and Background

Edwin Locke, a leading authority on goal setting, and his colleagues define a **goal** as ''what an individual is trying to accomplish; it is the object or aim of an action.''[29] Expanding this definition, they add:

> The concept is similar in meaning to the concepts of purpose and intent. . . . Other frequently used concepts that are also similar in meaning to that of goal include performance standard (a measuring rod for evaluating performance), quota (a minimum amount of work or production), work norm (a standard of acceptable behavior defined by a work group), task (a piece of work to be accomplished), objective (the ultimate aim of an action or series of actions), deadline (a time limit for completing a task), and budget (a spending goal or limit).[39]

The motivational impact of performance goals and goal-based reward plans has been recognized for a long time. At the turn of the century, Frederick Taylor attempted to scientifically establish how much work of a specified quality an individual should be assigned each day. He proposed that bonuses be based on accomplishing those output standards. More recently, goal setting has been promoted through a widely used management technique called management by objectives (MBO). Along similar lines, merit pay plans anchored to measurable goals are growing in popularity at both profit-making and nonprofit-making organizations.[31] At Planned Parenthood, for example, ''all employees must set personal objectives every year. Each goal is assigned a percentage weight to determine its importance. Managers evaluate progress against each goal, grading from 1 for unsatisfactory to 5 for superior performance.''[32] Pay hikes then are based on an employee's level of goal accomplishment.

How Does Goal Setting Work?

Despite abundant goal-setting research and practice, goal-setting theories are surprisingly scarce. An instructive model was formulated by Locke and his associates (see Figure 6–5). According to Locke's model, goal setting has four motivational mechanisms.[33]

Goals Direct Attention   Goals that are personally meaningful tend to focus one's attention on what is relevant and important. If, for example, you have a term project due in a few days, your thoughts tend to revolve around completing that project. Similarly, the members of a home appliance sales force who are told they can win a trip to Hawaii for selling the most refrigerators will tend to steer customers toward the refrigerator display.

Goals Regulate Effort   Not only do goals make us selectively perceptive, they also motivate us to act. The instructor's deadline for turning in your term project would prompt you to complete it, as opposed to going out with friends, watching television, or studying for another course. Generally, the level of effort expended is proportionate to the difficulty of the goal.

Goals Increase Persistence   Within the context of goal setting, **persistence** represents the effort expended on a task over an extended period of time. It takes effort to run 100 meters; it takes persistence to run a 26-mile marathon. Persistent people tend to see obstacles as challenges to be overcome rather than as reasons to fail. A difficult goal that is important to the individual is a constant reminder to keep exerting effort in the appropriate direction.

Goals Foster Strategies and Action Plans   If you are here and your goal is out there somewhere, you face the problem of getting from here to there. For example, the person who has resolved to lose 20 pounds must develop a plan for getting from ''here'' (his or her present weight) to ''there'' (20 pounds lighter). Goals can help because they encourage people to develop strategies and action plans that enable them to achieve their goals.[34] By virtue of setting a weight-reduction goal, the dieter may choose a strategy of exercising more, eating less, or some combination of the two. For a work-related example, consider the case of Marriott Corporation.

• **FIGURE 6-5** Locke's Model of Goal Setting

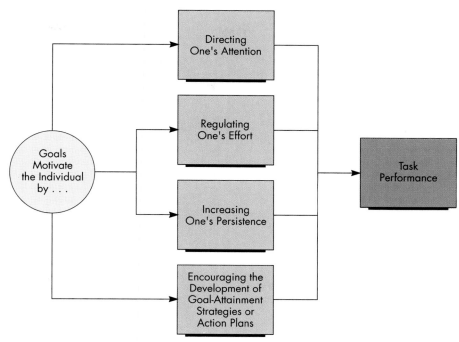

Source: Adapted from discussion in Edwin A. Locke and Gary P. Latham, *A Theory of Goal Setting & Task Performance* (Englewood Cliffs, N.J.: Prentice-Hall, 1990). Reprinted by permission of Prentice Hall, Inc.

For years, Marriott's room-service business didn't live up to its potential. But after initiating a 15-minute-delivery guarantee for breakfast in 1985, Marriott's breakfast business—the biggest portion of its room-service revenue—jumped 25 percent. Marriott got employees to devise better ways to deliver the meals on time, including having deliverers carry walkie-talkies so they could receive instructions more quickly.[15]

Insights from Goal-Setting Research

Research consistently has supported goal setting as a motivational technique. Setting performance goals increases individual, group, and organizational performance. Further, the positive effects of goal setting were found in six other countries or regions: Australia, Canada, the Caribbean, England, West Germany, and Japan.[36] Goal setting works in different cultures. Reviews of the many goal-setting studies conducted over the last couple of decades have given managers four practical insights:

1. *Difficult Goals Lead to Higher Performance.* **Goal difficulty** reflects the amount of effort required to meet a goal. It is more difficult to sell nine cars a month than it is to sell three cars a month. An extensive review of goal-setting studies by Locke and his associates led them to conclude that performance tends to increase as goals become more difficult, but only to a point. As illustrated in Figure 6–6, the positive relationship between goal difficulty and performance breaks down when goals are perceived to be impossible. Of 57 research studies, 48 demonstrated that performance goes

• **FIGURE 6-6**   Relationship between Goal Difficulty and Performance

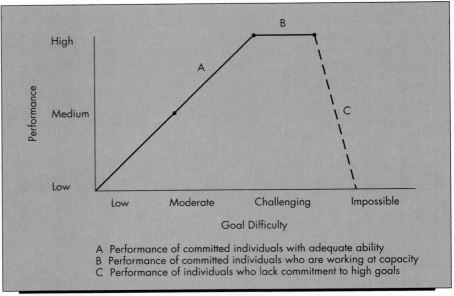

A Performance of committed individuals with adequate ability
B Performance of committed individuals who are working at capacity
C Performance of individuals who lack commitment to high goals

Source: Edwin A. Locke and Gary P. Latham, *Goal Setting: A Motivational Technique That Works!* © 1984, p. 22. Reprinted by permission of Prentice Hall, Inc., Englewood Cliffs, New Jersey.

up when employees are given hard goals as opposed to easy or moderate goals (section A of Figure 6–6).[37] However, as the difficulty of a goal increases, performance plateaus (section B) and eventually decreases when the goal becomes impossible (section C).

A meta-analysis of 70 goal-setting studies conducted between 1966 and 1984, involving 7,407 subjects, led the researchers to the following conclusion: "Clearly, difficult goals have a dramatic effect on performance outcomes."[38]

2. *Specific, Difficult Goals May or May Not Lead to Higher Performance.* **Goal specificity** pertains to the quantifiability of a goal. For example, a goal of selling nine cars a month is more specific than telling a salesperson to do his or her best. In the Locke review of goal-setting research, 99 out of 110 studies (90 percent) found that specific, hard goals led to better performance than did easy, medium, do-your-best, or no goals.[39] This result was confirmed in the 1966–1984 meta-analysis.

In contrast to these positive effects, several recent studies demonstrated that setting specific, difficult goals leads to poorer performance under certain circumstances. For example, a meta-analysis of 125 studies indicated that goal-setting effects were strongest for easy tasks and weakest for complex tasks.[40] Positive effects of goal setting also were reduced when people worked on novel decision-making tasks and interdependent tasks.[41] These results suggest that managers should use a contingency approach when setting performance goals.

3. *Feedback Enhances the Effect of Specific, Difficult Goals.* The 1966–1984 meta-analysis of goal-setting studies led the researchers to conclude

"the presence of feedback had a considerable impact on performance when used in conjunction with difficult specific goals."[42] Feedback lets people know if they are headed toward their goals or if they are off-course and need to redirect their efforts. Goals plus feedback is the recommended approach. Goals inform people about performance standards and expectations so that they can channel their energies accordingly. In turn, feedback provides the information needed to adjust direction, effort, and strategies for goal accomplishment.

4. *Participative Goals, Assigned Goals, and Self-Set Goals Are Equally Effective*. Both managers and researchers are interested in identifying the best way to set goals. Should goals be participatively set, assigned, or set by the employee himself or herself? A recent summary of goal-setting research indicated that no single approach was consistently more effective than others in increasing performance.[43] Managers thus are advised to use a contingency approach by picking a method that seems best suited for the individual and situation at hand. For example, employees' preferences for participation should be considered. Some employees desire to participate in the process of setting goals whereas others do not.

Practical Application of Goal Setting

There are three general steps to follow when implementing a goal-setting program (see Figure 6–7). Serious deficiencies in one step cannot make up for strength in the other two. The three steps need to be implemented in a systematic fashion.

Step 1: Goal Setting   A number of sources can be used as input during this goal-setting stage.[44] Time and motion studies are one source. Goals also may be based on the average past performance of job holders. Third, the employee and his or her manager may set the goal participatively, through give-and-take negotiation. Fourth, goal setting often is constrained by external factors. For example, the production schedule of a firm with a government contract may be dictated largely by the terms of that agreement. Finally, the overall strategy of a company (e.g., become the lowest-cost producer) may affect the goals set by employees at various levels in the organization.

In accordance with available research evidence, goals should be specific and difficult, yet attainable through persistent effort. For complex tasks however, managers should set slightly less difficult goals because difficult goals lead to lower performance than do easier goals. Specificity can be achieved by stating goals in quantitative terms (e.g., units of output, dollars, or percent of desired increase or decrease). With respect to measuring performance, it is important to achieve a workable balance between quantity and quality. Well-conceived goals also have a built-in time limit or deadline. Priorities need to be established in multiple-goal situations.

Finally, because of individual differences in skills and abilities, it may be necessary to establish different goals for employees performing the same job. For example, a recent study revealed that more difficult goals were set by individuals with high rather than low task abilities. Moreover, a second study uncovered a positive goal difficulty→performance relationship for individuals with high as opposed to low self-esteem.[45] If an employee has

• **FIGURE 6-7**   Three Key Steps in Implementing a Goal-Setting Program

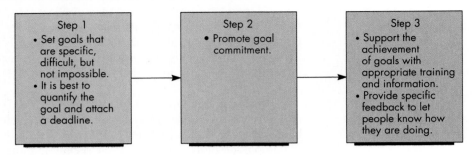

low self-esteem or lacks the ability to perform the job, then progressively harder developmental goals may be in order. But this practice may create feelings of inequity among co-workers, necessitating other alternatives. For example, inability to perform at the standard may suggest a training deficiency or the need to transfer the individual to another job. In any event, managers need to keep in mind that motivation diminishes when people continually fail to meet their goals.

Step 2: Goal Commitment   **Goal commitment** is the extent to which an individual is committed personally to achieving an organizational goal. This step is important because employees will not be motivated to pursue goals they view as unreasonable, unobtainable, or unfair. Goal commitment may be increased by using one or more of the following techniques:

1. Provide instructions and an explanation for implementing the program.
2. Be supportive and do not use goals to threaten employees.
3. Encourage employees to participate in the goal-setting process.
4. Train managers in how to conduct goal-setting sessions.
5. Use selection procedures that identify applicants who have the ability to accomplish the typical goal.
6. Provide monetary incentives or other rewards for accomplishing goals.[46]

Step 3: Support and Feedback   Step 3 calls for providing employees with the necessary support elements or resources to get the job done. This includes ensuring that each employee has the necessary abilities and information to reach his or her goals. As a pair of goal-setting experts succinctly stated: "Motivation without knowledge is useless."[47] Training often is required to help employees achieve difficult goals. Moreover, managers should pay attention to employees' perceptions of effort→performance expectancies, self-efficacy, and valence of rewards. A recent study demonstrated that all three of these cognitions significantly affected employees' performance on multiple goals.[48] Finally, as discussed in detail in Chapter 13, employees

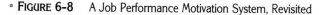

• **FIGURE 6-8**   A Job Performance Motivation System, Revisited

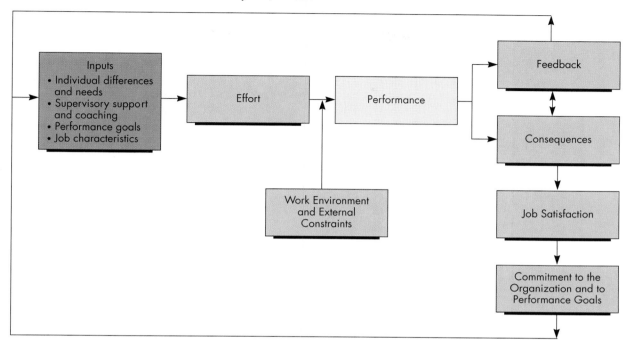

should be provided with timely, specific feedback (knowledge of results) on how they are doing.

• PUTTING MOTIVATIONAL THEORIES TO WORK

Successfully designing and implementing motivational programs is not easy. Managers cannot simply take one of the theories discussed in this book and apply it word for word. Dynamics within organizations interfere with applying motivation theories in ''pure'' form. According to management scholar Terence Mitchell:

> There are situations and settings that make it exceptionally difficult for a motivational system to work. These circumstances may involve the kinds of jobs or people present, the technology, the presence of a union, and so on. The factors that hinder the application of motivational theory have not been articulated either frequently or systematically.[49]

With Mitchell's cautionary statement in mind, this section uses the conceptual model of motivation introduced in Chapter 5, which is shown once again in Figure 6–8, to raise issues that need to be addressed before implementing a motivational program. Our intent here is not to discuss all relevant considerations, but rather to highlight a few important ones.

Assuming a motivational program is being considered to improve productivity, the first issue revolves around the difference between motivation and performance. As pointed out in Chapter 5, motivation and performance are not one and the same. Motivation is only one of several factors that influence performance. For example, poor performance may be more a function of a lack of ability, poor supervisory support and coaching, not having goals to direct one's efforts, or a variety of job and work environment characteristics. Job characteristics, discussed in Chapter 5 (autonomy and responsibility), work environment characteristics (teamwork and conflict), organizational characteristics (reward systems and organizational structure), and external environmental characteristics (technological advances and economic cycles) similarly affect job performance. Motivation cannot make up for deficient individual characteristics or negative supervisory and job/work environment characteristics. Managers, therefore, need to gauge the degree to which motivation significantly affects performance.

Importantly, managers should not ignore the individual differences discussed in Chapter 3. Figure 6–8 clearly indicates that individual differences and needs influence performance. Therefore managers should develop and nurture positive employee characteristics, such as self-esteem, self-efficacy, and need for achievement.

Because motivation is goal directed, the process of developing and setting goals should be consistent with our previous discussion. Moreover, the method used to evaluate performance also needs to be considered. Without a valid performance appraisal system, it is difficult, if not impossible, to accurately distinguish good and poor performers. Managers need to keep in mind that both equity and expectancy theory suggest that employee motivation is squelched by inaccurate performance ratings. Inaccurate ratings also make it difficult to evaluate the effectiveness of any motivational program, so it is beneficial for managers to assess the accuracy and validity of their appraisal systems.

Consistent with expectancy theory and the principles of behavior modification discussed in Chapter 7, managers should make rewards contingent on performance. In doing so, it is important that managers consider the accuracy and fairness of the reward system. As discussed under expectancy theory, the promise of increased rewards will not prompt higher effort and good performance unless those rewards clearly are tied to performance. Moreover, equity theory tells us that motivation is influenced by employee perceptions about the fairness of reward allocations. Motivation is decreased when employees believe rewards are inequitably allocated. Rewards also need to be integrated appropriately into the appraisal system. If performance is measured at the individual level, individual achievements need to be rewarded. On the other hand, when performance is the result of group effort, rewards should be allocated to the group.

Figure 6–8 indicates that feedback also should be linked with performance. Feedback provides the information and direction needed to keep employees focused on relevant tasks, activities, and goals. Managers should strive to provide specific, timely, and accurate feedback to employees. Chapter 13 provides a thorough discussion of feedback.

Finally, managers need to use a contingency approach when developing motivational programs. Recalling our discussion in Chapter 5, theories of motivation selectively explain various organizational outcomes (see Figure 5–2). Managers need to use motivation techniques that are best suited to the individuals and situation at hand.

• SUMMARY OF KEY CONCEPTS

A. Unlike the subconscious theories of motivation presented in Chapter 5, the three theories discussed in this chapter deal in terms of perception and conscious decision making. Equity, expectancy, and goal-setting theories involve different cognitive processes that affect one's motivation.

B. Adams' equity theory focuses on the perceived fairness of social exchanges. It is based on Festinger's cognitive dissonance theory. People perform equity evaluations by comparing their ratio of outcomes to inputs with those of relevant others.

C. Negative inequity occurs when someone is underrewarded. Positive inequity occurs when someone is overrewarded. People tend to have a lower tolerance for negative inequity than for positive inequity. We reduce perceived inequity through various combinations of behavioral and cognitive adjustments. Managers need to monitor employees' equity perceptions.

D. Expectancy theory assumes motivation is determined by one's perceived chances of achieving valued outcomes. Vroom's expectancy model of motivation reveals how effort→performance expectancies and performance→outcome instrumentalities influence the degree of effort expended to achieve desired (positively valent) outcomes.

E. Porter and Lawler developed a model of expectancy that expanded upon the theory proposed by Vroom. This model specifies (1) the source of people's valences and expectancies and (2) the relationship between performance and satisfaction.

F. Four motivational mechanisms of goal setting are: (1) goals direct one's attention, (2) goals regulate effort, (3) goals increase one's persistence, and (4) goals encourage development of goal-attainment strategies and action plans.

G. Goal-setting research recommends difficult, quantified goals that are followed by specific feedback on performance.

H. Well-conceived goals include a deadline. Participative goals, assigned goals, and self-set goals are equally effective. Managers can use a variety of techniques to increase employees' goal commitment.

I. When implementing a motivational program, managers should consider the key determinants of performance, the desired goals to be achieved, and the validity of the performance appraisal system. Also requiring careful consideration are the performance-reward linkages, the equity of rewards allocated, and the adequacy of feedback. Managers should use motivation techniques that are best suited to the individuals and situation at hand.

• KEY TERMS

equity theory	valence
negative inequity	goal
positive inequity	persistence

expectancy theory   goal difficulty
expectancy   goal specificity
instrumentality   goal commitment

• DISCUSSION QUESTIONS

1. Have you experienced positive or negative inequity at work? Describe the circumstances in terms of the inputs and outcomes of the comparison person and yourself.

2. Could a manager's attempt to treat his or her employees equally lead to perceptions of inequity? Explain.

3. What work outcomes (refer to Table 6–1) are most important to you? Do you think different age groups value different outcomes? What are the implications for managers who seek to be equitable?

4. Relative to Table 6–2, what techniques have you relied on recently to reduce either positive or negative inequity?

5. What is your definition of studying hard? What is your expectancy for earning an A on the next exam in this course? What is the basis of this expectancy?

6. If someone who reported to you at work had a low expectancy for successful performance, what could you do to increase this person's expectancy?

7. Do goals play an important role in your life? Explain.

8. How would you respond to a manager who said, "Goals must be participatively set."

9. Goal-setting research suggests that people should be given difficult goals. How does this prescription mesh with expectancy theory? Explain.

10. How could a professor use equity, expectancy, and goal-setting theory to motivate students?

BACK TO THE OPENING CASE

Now that you have read Chapter 6, you should be able to answer the following questions about the Cypress Case:

1. Does Cypress treat its employees equitably?

2. To what extent is Cypress's management system consistent with expectancy theory?

3. How does Cypress use goal setting to motivate employees?

4. Which of the four insights from goal-setting research is Cypress following?

• EXERCISE 6

Objectives

1. To determine how accurately you perceive the outcomes that motivate nonmanagerial employees.
2. To examine the managerial implications of inaccurately assessing employee motivators.

Introduction

One thousand employees were given a list of 10 outcomes people want from their work. They were asked to rank these items from most important to least important.[50] We are going to have you estimate how you think these workers ranked the various outcomes. This will enable you to compare your perceptions with the average rankings documented by a researcher. Since the results are presented at the end of this exercise, please do not read them until indicated.

Instructions

Below is a list of 10 outcomes people want from their work. Read the list and then rank each item according to how you think the typical nonmanagerial employee would rank them. Rank the outcomes from 1 to 10, 1 = Most important and 10 = Least important. (Please do this now before reading the rest of these instructions.) After you have completed your ranking, calculate the discrepancy between your perceptions and the actual results. Take the absolute value of the difference between your ranking and the actual ranking for each item and then add them to get a total discrepancy score. For example, if you gave job security of ranking of 1, your discrepancy score would be 3, because the actual ranking was 4. The lower your discrepancy score, the more accurate your perception of the typical employee's needs. The actual rankings are shown below under the heading *Survey Results*.

How do you believe the typical nonmanagerial employee would rank these outcomes?

_____ Full appreciation of work done
_____ Job security
_____ Good working conditions
_____ Feeling of being in on things
_____ Good wages
_____ Tactful discipline
_____ Personal loyalty to employees
_____ Interesting work
_____ Sympathetic help with personal problems
_____ Promotion and growth in the organization

Questions for Consideration/Class Discussion

1. Were your perceptions accurate? Why or why not?
2. What would expectancy theory suggest you should do?
3. Based on the size of your discrepancy, what does the job perfor-

mance motivation System in Figure 6–8 suggest will happen to satisfaction and commitment?

4. Would you generalize the actual survey results to all nonmanagerial employees? Why or why not?

Survey Results—Employee Ranking

1. Interesting work
2. Full appreciation of work done
3. Feeling of being in on things
4. Job security
5. Good wages
6. Promotion and growth in the organization
7. Good working conditions
8. Personal loyalty to employees
9. Tactful discipline
10. Sympathetic help with personal problems

• NOTES

[1] See Leon Festinger, *A Theory of Cognitive Dissonance* (Stanford, Calif.: Stanford University Press, 1957).

[2] Results can be found in "Popular Perks," *The Wall Street Journal, Special Supplement on Executive Pay,* April 18, 1990, p. R25.

[3] A good discussion of international differences in executive pay and perks can be found in Joann S. Lublin, "The Continental Divide: The Gap between Executive Pay in the U.S. and in Europe is Narrowing, but It May Never Close," *The Wall Street Journal, Special Supplement on Executive Pay*, April 18, 1990, pp. R28–29.

[4] The generalizability of the equity norm was examined by Ken I. Kim, Hun-Joon Park, and Nori Suzuki, "Reward Allocations in the United States, Japan, and Korea: A Comparison of Individualistic and Collectivistic Cultures," *Academy of Management Journal,* March 1990, pp. 188–98.

[5] Robert P. Vecchio, "Models of Psychological Inequity, *Organizational Behavior and Human Performance,* October 1984, p. 268. (Emphasis added.)

[6] The choice of a comparison person is discussed by Jerald Greenberg and Claire L. McCarty, "Comparable Worth: A Matter of Justice," in *Research in Personnel and Human Resources Management,* eds. Gerald R. Ferris and Kendrith M. Rowland, (Greenwich, Conn.: JAI Press, Inc., 1990), vol. 8, pp. 265–303; and Joanne V. Wood, "Theory and Research Concerning Social Comparisons of Personal Attributes," *Psychological Bulletin,* September 1989, pp. 231–48.

[7] See Greenberg and McCarty, "Comparable Worth: A Matter of Justice."

[8] For a field study example of how people cognitively reevaluated outcomes following felt inequity, see Jerald Greenberg, "Cognitive Reevaluation of Outcomes in Response to Underpayment Inequity," *Academy of Management Journal,* March 1989, pp. 174–84.

[9] Adapted from a discussion in Robert L. Opsahl and Marvin D. Dunnette, "The Role of Financial Compensation in Industrial Motivation," *Psychological Bulletin,* August 1966, pp. 94–118.

[10] Results can be found in Rodger W. Griffeth, Robert P. Vecchio, and James W. Logan, Jr., "Equity Theory and Interpersonal Attraction," *Journal of Applied Psychology,* June 1989, pp. 394–401; and Robert P. Vecchio, "Predicting Worker Performance in Inequitable Settings," *Academy of Management Review,* January 1982, pp. 103–10.

[11] See Paul D. Sweeney, Dean B. McFarlin, and Edward J. Inderrieden, "Using Relative Deprivation Theory to Explain Satisfaction with Income and Pay Level: A Multistudy Examination," *Academy of Management Journal,* June 1990, pp. 423–36; and Robert Folger and Mary Konovsky, "Effects of Procedural and Distributive Justice on Reactions to Pay Raise Decisions," *Academy of Management Journal,* March 1989, pp. 115–30.

[12] The relationship between equity and absenteeism and turnover was examined by John E. Dittrich and Michael R. Carrell, "Organizational Equity Perceptions, Employee Job Satisfaction, and Departmental Absence and Turnover Rates, *Organizational Behavior and Human Performance,* August 1979, pp. 29–40; and Peter W. Hom, Rodger W. Griffeth, and C. Louise Sellaro, "The Validity of Mobley's (1977) Model of Turnover," *Organizational Behavior and Human Performance,* October 1984, pp. 141–74.

[13] L. A. Winokur, "Sweet Revenge Is Souring the Office," *The Wall Street Journal,* September 9, 1990, p. B1.

[14] See Greenberg and McCarty, "Comparable Worth: A Matter of Justice."

[15] Managerial techniques for promoting perceptions of fairness are discussed by Jerald Greenberg, "Looking Fair vs. Being Fair: Managing Impressions of Organizational Justice," in *Research in Organizational Behavior,* eds. Barry M. Staw and Larry L. Cummings (Greenwich, Conn.: JAI Press, Inc., 1990), vol. 12, pp. 111–58.

[16] For a complete discussion of Vroom's theory, see Victor H. Vroom, *Work and Motivation* (New York: John Wiley & Sons, 1964).

[17] Edward E. Lawler III, *Motivation in Work Organizations* (Belmont, Calif.: Wadsworth, 1973), p. 45.

[18] See Craig C. Pinder, *Work Motivation* (Glenview, Ill.: Scott, Foresman, 1984), chap. 7.

[19] For a discussion of the definition and measurement of valence, see Anthony Pecotich and Gilbert A. Churchill, Jr., "An Examination of the Anticipated-Satisfaction Importance Valence Controversy," *Organizational Behavior and Human Performance,* April 1981, pp. 213–26.

[20] For a thorough discussion of the model, see Lyman W. Porter and Edward E. Lawler III, *Managerial Attitudes and Performance* (Homewood, Ill.: Richard D. Irwin, 1968).

[21] The relationship between ability and performance was examined by W. Mark Coward and Paul R. Sackett, "Linearity of Ability–Performance Relationships: A Reconfirmation," *Journal of Applied Psychology,* June 1990, pp. 297–300.

[22] See Robert W. Rice, Suzanne M. Phillips, and Dean B. McFarlin, "Multiple Discrepancies and Pay Satisfaction," *Journal of Applied Psychology,* August 1990, pp. 386–93.

[23] See John P. Wanous, Thomas L. Keon, and Janina C. Latack, "Expectancy Theory and Occupational/Organizational Choices: A Review and Test," *Organizational Behavior and Human Performance,* August 1983, pp. 66–86.

[24] These results are based on the following studies: Elaine D. Pulakos and Neal Schmitt, "A Longitudinal Study of a Valence Model Approach for the Prediction of Job Satisfaction of New Employees," *Journal of Applied Psychology,* May 1983, pp. 307–12; Angelo J. Kinicki, "Predicting Occupational Role Choices for Involuntary Job Loss," *Journal of Vocational Behavior,* October 1989, pp. 204–218; Thomas A.

DeCotiis and Jean-Yves LeLouarn, ''A Predictive Study of Voting Behavior in a Representation Election Using Union Instrumentality and Work Perceptions,'' *Organizational Behavior and Human Performance,* February 1981, pp. 103–18; Peter W. Hom, ''Expectancy Prediction of Reenlistment in the National Guard,'' *Journal of Vocational Behavior,* April 1980, pp. 235–48; and Donald F. Parker and Lee Dyer, ''Expectancy Theory as a Within-Person Behavioral Choice Model: An Empirical Test of Some Conceptual and Methodological Refinements,'' *Organizational Behavior and Human Performance,* October 1976, pp. 97–117; Alan W. Stacy, Keith F. Widaman, and G. Alan Marlatt, ''Expectancy Models of Alcohol Use,'' *Journal of Personality and Social Psychology,* May 1990, pp. 918–28.

25 For reviews of the criticisms of expectancy theory, see Frank J. Landy and Wendy S. Becker, ''Motivation Theory Reconsidered,'' in *Research In Organizational Behavior,* Vol. 9, eds. L. L. Cummings and Barry M. Staw (Greenwich, Conn.: JAI Press, 1987). pp.1–38; and Terence R. Mitchell, ''Expectancy Models of Job Satisfaction, Occupational Preference and Effort: A Theoretical, Methodological, and Empirical Appraisal, *Psychological Bulletin,* December 1974, pp. 1053–77.

26 A description of GTE's approach is discussed in Stephen Phillips, Amy Dunkin, James B. Treece, and Keith H. Hammonds, ''King Customer: At Companies That Listen Hard and Respond Fast, Bottom Lines Thrive,'' *Business Week,* March 12, 1990, pp. 88–91, 94.

27 The relationship between performance appraisal systems and organizational pay is thoroughly discussed by Edward E. Lawler III, *Strategic Pay* (San Francisco: Jossey-Bass, 1990).

28 Results from this survey are presented by Amanda Bennett, ''Caught in the Middle: Managers Don't Mind that the CEO Makes a Lot of Money, but They Raise Questions about Fairness,'' *The Wall Street Journal, Special Supplement on Executive Pay,* April 18, 1990, p. R9.

29 Edwin A. Locke, Karyll N. Shaw, Lise M. Saari, and Gary P. Latham, ''Goal Setting and Task Performance: 1969–1980,'' *Psychological Bulletin,* July 1981, p. 126.

30 Ibid.

31 An instructive overview of merit pay may be found in Frederick S. Hills, Robert M. Madigan, K. Dow Scott, and Steven E. Markham, ''Tracking the Merit of Merit Pay,'' *Personnel Administrator,* March 1987, pp. 50–57.

32 ''A Little Publicity Can't Hurt,'' *Business Week,* March 26, 1990, p. 69.

33 A complete review of goal setting theory and research is presented by Edwin A. Locke and Gary P. Latham, *A Theory of Goal Setting & Task Performance* (Englewood Cliffs, N.J.: Prentice-Hall, 1990).

34 Recent research evidence may be found in Terence R. Mitchell and William S. Silver, ''Individual and Group Goals When Workers Are Interdependent: Effects on Task Strategies and Performance,'' *Journal of Applied Psychology,* April 1990, pp. 185–93.

35 Phillips, Dunkin, Treece, and Hammonds, ''King customer: At Companies that Listen Hard and Respond Fast, Bottom Lines Thrive,'' p. 91.

36 See Locke and Latham, *A Theory of Goal Setting & Task Performance.*

37 Drawn from Locke, Shaw, Saari, and Latham, ''Goal Setting and Task Performance: 1969–1980.''

38 Anthony J. Mento, Robert P. Steel, and Ronald J. Karren, ''A Meta-Analytic Study of the Effects of Goal Setting on Task Performance: 1966–1984,'' *Organizational Behavior and Human Decision Processes,* February 1987, p. 69.

39 See Locke, Shaw, Saari, and Latham, ''Goal Setting and Task Performance: 1969–1980.''

[40] Results from the meta-analysis can be found in Robert E. Wood, Anthony J. Mento, and Edwin A. Locke, ''Task Complexity as a Moderator of Goal Effects: A Meta-Analysis,'' *Journal of Applied Psychology,* August 1987, pp. 416–25. The impact of task complexity on goal-setting also was examined by Barry M. Staw and Richard D. Boettger, ''Task Revision: A Neglected Form of Work Performance,'' *Academy of Management Journal,* September 1990, pp. 534–59.

[41] See P. Christopher Earley, Terry Connolly, and Goran Ekegren, ''Goals, Strategy Development, and Task Performance: Some Limits on the Efficacy of Goal Setting,'' *Journal of Applied Psychology,* February 1989, pp. 24–33; and Mitchell and Silver ''Individual and Group Goals When Workers Are Interdependent: Effects on Task Strategies and Performance.''

[42] See Locke and Latham, *A Theory of Goal Setting & Task Performance.*

[43] Ibid.

[44] These recommendations are taken from Gary P. Latham and Edwin A. Locke, ''Goal Setting—A Motivational Technique That Works!'' *Organizational Dynamics,* Autumn 1979, pp. 68–80.

[45] The relationship between goal difficulty and ability was examined by Robert J. Vance and Adrienne Colella, ''Effects of Two Types of Feedback on Goal Acceptance and Personal Goals,'' *Journal of Applied Psychology,* February 1990, pp. 68–76. Self-esteem and goal setting was investigated by John R. Hollenbeck and Arthur P. Brief, ''The Effects of Individual Differences and Goal Origin on Goal Setting and Performance,'' *Organizational Behavior and Human Decision Processes,* December 1987, pp. 392–414.

[46] These recommendations are adapted from Edwin A. Locke and Gary P. Latham, *Goal Setting: A Motivational Technique That Works!* (Englewood Cliffs, N.J.: Prentice-Hall, 1984).

[47] Ibid., p. 79.

[48] Results are shown in Mary C. Kernan and Robert G. Lord, ''Effects of Valence, Expectancies, and Goal-Performance Discrepancies in Single and Multiple Goal Environments,'' *Journal of Applied Psychology,* April 1990, pp. 194–203.

[49] Terence R. Mitchell, ''Motivation: New Directions for Theory, Research, and Practice,'' *Academy of Management Review,* January 1982, p. 81.

[50] Results from this study are reported in Kenneth A. Kovach, ''What Motivates Employees? Workers and Supervisors Give Different Answers,'' *Business Horizons,* September–October 1987, pp. 58–65.

Behavior Modification and Self-Management

LEARNING OBJECTIVES

When you finish studying the material in this chapter, you should be able to:

- Explain Skinner's distinction between respondent and operant behavior.
- Define the term *behavior modification* and explain the A→B→C model.
- Differentiate the following consequence management strategies: positive reinforcement, negative reinforcement, punishment, and extinction.

- Explain why the scheduling of reinforcement is so important in B. Mod.
- Define and give your own example of behavior shaping.
- Identify and briefly explain each step in the four-step B. Mod. process.

- Specify the six guidelines for managing consequences during B. Mod.
- Explain how behavioral self-management differs from B. Mod.
- Demonstrate your familiarity with the four major components of the social learning model of self-management.

OPENING CASE 7

How to Earn "Well Pay"

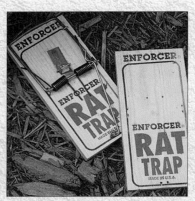

Sharon Hoogstraten

The woman in blue jeans and a logger's shirt looks up from the production line and says grimly: "I can't miss work today. It's almost the end of the month, and I'm going to earn that 'well pay' if it kills me."

At Parsons Pine Products Inc. in Ashland, Ore., "well pay" is the opposite of sick pay. It is an extra eight hours' wages that the company gives workers who are neither absent nor late for a full month. It is also one of four incentives that owner James W. Parsons has built into a "positive reinforcement plan" for workers: well pay, retro pay, safety pay, and profit-sharing pay.

Beating the Tax Man

The formula, Parsons says, enables him and his wife to beat the combination of federal and state income taxes that leaves them only 14 percent of any increase in earnings; it allows them to pass along much of the potential tax money to the workers. Under the Parsons system, an employee earning $10,000 a year can add as much as $3,500 to his income by helping the plant operate economically.

Parsons Pine employs some 100 workers to cut lumber into specialty items—primarily louver slats for shutters, bifold doors, and blinds, and bases for rat traps. It is reportedly the U.S.'s biggest producer of these items, with sales last year [1977] of $2.5 million.

The company began handing out "well pay" in January 1977. "We had a problem with lateness," Parsons explains. "Just before the 7 A.M. starting time, the foreman in a department would take a head count and assign three people to this machine and six over there. Then a few minutes later someone else comes in and he has to recalculate and reshuffle. Or he may be so short as to leave a machine idle."

"Well pay" brought lateness down to almost zero and cut absenteeism more than Parsons wanted it reduced, because some workers came to work even when they were sick. He dealt with this awkwardness by reminding them of "retro pay." Says Parsons: "I'd say, 'By being here while not feeling well, you may have a costly accident, and that will not only cause you pain and suffering, but it will also affect the retro plan, which could cost you a lot more than one day's 'well pay.'"

Reducing Accidents

The retro pay plan offers a bonus based on any reductions in premiums received from the state's industrial accident insurance fund. Before the retro plan went into effect in 1976, Parsons Pine had a high accident rate, 86 percent above the statewide base, and paid the fund accordingly. Parsons told his workers that if the plant cut its accident rate, the retroactive refund would be distributed to them. The upshot was a 1977 accident bill of $2,500 compared to a 1976 bill of $28,500. After deducting administrative expenses, the state will return $89,000 of a $100,000 premium, some $900 per employee.

I magine you are the general manager of the public transportation authority in a large city, and one of your main duties is overseeing the city's bus system. During the past several years, you have noted with growing concern the increasing number and severity of bus accidents. In the face of mounting public and administrative pressure, it is clear that a workable accident-prevention program must be enacted. Large pay raises for the bus drivers and other expensive options are impossible because of a tight city

OPENING CASE 7

(concluded)

The retro plan did not improve the accident rate unaided, Parsons concedes. "We showed films and introduced every safety program the state has," he says. "But no matter what you do, it doesn't really make a dent until the people themselves see that they are going to lose a dollar by not being safe. When management puts on the pressure, they say, 'He's just trying to make a buck for himself,' but when fellow workers say, 'Let's work safe,' that means a lot."

The "Little Hurts"

Employees can also earn safety pay—two hours' wages—by remaining accident-free for a month. "Six hours a quarter isn't such a great incentive," says Parsons, "but it helps. When it didn't cost them anything, workers would go to the doctor for every little thing. Now they take care of the little hurts themselves."

As its most substantial incentive, the company offers a profit-sharing bonus—everything the business earns over 4 percent after taxes, which is Parsons' idea of a fair profit. Each supervisor rates his employees in four categories of excellence, with a worker's bonus figured as a per-

centage of his wages multiplied by his category. Top-ranked employees generally receive bonuses of 8 percent to 10 percent. One year they got 16½ percent. Two-thirds of the bonus is paid in cash and the rest goes into the retirement fund.

To illustrate how workers can contribute to profits, and profit-sharing bonuses, Parsons presents a dramatic display that has a modest fame in Ashland. Inviting the work force to lunch, he sets up a pyramid of 250 rat trap bases, each representing $10,000 in sales. Then he knocks 100 onto the floor, saying: "That's for raw materials. See why it is important not to waste?" Then he pushes over 100 more, adding: "That's for wages." And pointing to the 50 left, he says: "Out of this little pile we have to do all the other things—maintenance, repairs, supplies, taxes. With so many blocks gone, that doesn't leave much for either you or me."

A Vote for Work

The lunch guests apparently find the display persuasive. Says one nine-year veteran: "We get the most we can out of every piece of wood after seeing that. When new

employees come, we work with them to cut down waste."

The message also lingered at the last Christmas luncheon, when, after distribution of checks, someone said: "Hey, how about the afternoon off?" Parsons replied: "OK, our production is on schedule and the customers won't be hurt. But you know where the cost comes from." Parsons recalls that someone asked him, "How much?" and he replied that the loss would be about $3,000.

"There was a bit of chatter and we took a vote," he says. "Only two hands were raised for the afternoon off. That was because they knew it was not just my money. It was their money, too."

For Discussion

What makes James Parsons a good manager?

• Additional discussion questions linking this case with the following material appear at the end of this chapter.

Source: "How to Earn 'Well Pay.'" Reprinted from June 12, 1978, issue of *Business Week* by special permission, © 1978 by McGraw-Hill, Inc. pp. 143, 146.

budget. Based on what you have read about motivation, what remedial action do you propose? (Please take a moment now to jot down some ideas.)

Since these facts have been drawn from a real-life field study, we can see what happened.[1] Management tried to curb the accident rate with some typical programs, including yearly safety awards, stiffer enforcement of a disciplinary code, complimentary coffee and doughnuts for drivers who had a day without an accident, and a comprehensive training program. Despite these remedial actions, the accident rate kept climbing. Finally, management agreed to a behavior modification experiment that directly attacked unsafe driver behavior.

One hundred of the city's 425 drivers were randomly divided into four experimental teams of 25 each. The remaining drivers served as a control group. During an 18-week period, the drivers received daily feedback on their safety performance on a chart posted in their lunchroom. An accident-free day was noted on the chart with a green dot, while a driver involved in an accident found a red dot posted next to his or her name. At two-week intervals, members of the team with the best competitive safety record received their choice of incentives averaging $5 in value (e.g., cash, free gas, free bus passes). Teams that went an entire two-week period without an accident received double incentives.

Unlike previous interventions, the behavior modification program reduced the accident rate. Compared to the control group, the experimental group recorded a 25 percent lower accident rate. During an 18-week period following termination of the incentive program, the experimental group's accident rate remained a respectable 16 percent better than the control group's. This indicated a positive, long-term effect. Moreover, the program was cost-effective. The incentives cost the organization $2,033.18, while it realized a savings of $9,416.25 in accident settlement expenses (a 1 to 4.6 cost/benefit ratio).

Why did this particular program work, while earlier attempts failed? It worked because a specific behavior (safe driving) was modified through *systematic* management of the drivers' work environment. If the posted feedback, team competition, and rewards had been implemented in traditional piecemeal fashion, they probably would have failed to reduce the accident rate. However, when combined in a coordinated and systematic fashion, these common techniques produced favorable results.

This chapter introduces two systematic ways to manage job *behavior:* behavior modification and behavioral self-management. Both areas have a common theoretical heritage, modern behaviorism.

• THE EVOLUTION OF MODERN BEHAVIORISM

Before getting into the details of behavior modification and self-management, we need to trace the historical development of behavioral learning theory (or simply, *behaviorism*). **Behavioral learning theory** strives to explain how behavior is acquired and changed through person–environment interaction. Three key behavioral learning models are: Watson's stimulus–response behaviorism, Thorndike's law of effect, and Skinner's operant conditioning model. Figure 7–1 illustrates the contributions each of these perspectives made to the evolution of modern behaviorism.

Watson's Stimulus–Response Behaviorism

This most primitive interpretation of learning is traced to 19th century Russian physiologists such as Ivan Pavlov. Pavlov trained dogs to salivate at the sound of a bell by initially pairing a ringing bell with the presentation of food. The animals reflexively salivated at the sight and smell of the food.

• **FIGURE 7-1**   The Evolution of Modern Behavioral Learning Theory

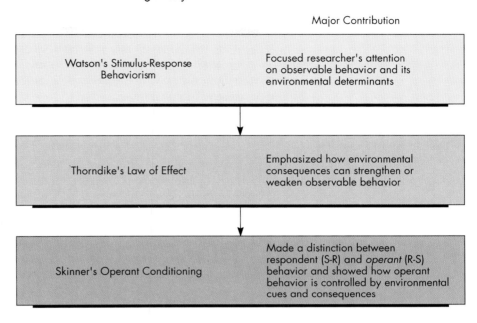

Major Contribution

| Watson's Stimulus-Response Behaviorism | Focused researcher's attention on observable behavior and its environmental determinants |

| Thorndike's Law of Effect | Emphasized how environmental consequences can strengthen or weaken observable behavior |

| Skinner's Operant Conditioning | Made a distinction between respondent (S-R) and *operant* (R-S) behavior and showed how operant behavior is controlled by environmental cues and consequences |

However, several pairings later, Pavlov's dogs salivated when the bell was rung but the food was withheld. This conditioned reflex amounted to a rudimentary form of learning, called **classical conditioning.** Through repeated exposure to bell-food pairings, Pavlov's dogs *learned* to associate the sound of the bell with eating. Interestingly, movie producers take full advantage of classical conditioning in thrillers such as *Jaws* and *Jaws II*. By getting viewers to associate a thumping music score with a man-eating white shark, stomachs in the audience soon tighten merely upon hearing the music.

He Caused Psychology to Lose Its Mind   Classical conditioning was brought into the mainstream of American psychology by a researcher named John B. Watson. Before he left academe to become a successful advertising executive, Watson stood the young field of psychology on its ear during the early 1900s by rejecting the then-popular instinct theory. In its stead, he proposed a stimulus–response (S–R) approach that focused on observable behavior rather than mental processes. In 1929, Watson wrote:

> Why don't we make what we can observe the real field of psychology? Let us limit ourselves to things that can be observed, and formulate laws concerning only the observed things. Now what can we observe? Well, we can observe behavior— what the organism does or says.[2]

Thus, Watson launched a philosophy of human learning known as **behaviorism.** As a behaviorist, Watson rejected notions of mental processes and self-control when explaining human behavior. Critics chided Watson for causing American psychology to lose its mind!

Finding the Right Stimulus   Watson made the conceptual leap from reflex physiology to psychology by claiming virtually all human behavior was elicited by specific prior stimulation. In other words, he viewed all human behavior in S–R terms. According to Watson's S–R model of learning, the key to getting someone to learn a new behavior was to find the causal stimulus for that response. From that point on, as Watson saw it, the individual would reflexively engage in the target behavior when exposed to the appropriate stimulus.

Thorndike's Law of Effect

Also during the early 1900s, Edward L. Thorndike observed in his psychology laboratory that a cat would behave randomly and wildly when placed in a small box with a secret trip lever that opened a door. However, once the cat accidentally tripped the lever and escaped, the animal would go straight to the lever when placed back in the box. Hence, Thorndike formulated his **law of effect,** which said *behavior with favorable consequences tends to be repeated, while behavior with unfavorable consequences tends to disappear*.[3] Although Thorndike adhered to Watson's notion of S–R pairings, his belief that behaviors also are controlled by their consequences caused him to subsequently be labeled a reinforcement theorist.

Skinner's Operant Conditioning Model

After an initial wave of support for Watson's S–R model, many psychologists rejected it in favor of more mentalistic and cognitive interpretations that centered on variables such as needs, drives, attitudes, and perception. However, a soon-to-be famous psychologist named B. F. Skinner adopted and refined behaviorism. Skinner agreed with Watson that *behavior* should be the primary unit of analysis. But rather than explaining all behavior in S–R terms, Skinner contended that most human behavior is controlled primarily by its *consequences*. According to Skinner, behavior is a function of its consequences, as opposed to prior causal stimulation or self-determination. Hence, Skinner endorsed and refined Thorndike's law of effect. By merging Watson's and Thorndike's ideas, Skinner qualified as a combination behaviorist and reinforcement theorist.

Respondent versus Operant Behavior   In his 1938 classic, *The Behavior of Organisms,* Skinner drew an important distinction between two types of behavior: respondent behavior and operant behavior.[4] He labeled unlearned reflexes or (S–R) connections **respondent behavior.** This category of behavior was said to describe a very small proportion of adult human behavior. Examples of respondent behavior would include crying while peeling onions and withdrawing one's hand from a hot stove. Skinner attached the label **operant behavior** to behavior that is learned when one "operates on" the environment to produce desired consequences. Some call this a response–stimulus (R–S) model. Years of controlled experiments with pigeons in "Skinner boxes" helped Skinner develop a sophisticated technology of

• B. F. Skinner, 1904 to 1990. *(R. Epstein)*

operant conditioning. For example, he taught pigeons how to pace figure eights and how to bowl by reinforcing them with food whenever they more closely approximated target behaviors. Skinner's work has significant implications for OB because the vast majority of organizational behavior falls into the operant category.

Behavior Modification   The systematic application of Skinner's operant conditioning techniques to everyday behavior is called behavior modification. More precisely, **behavior modification** (or B. Mod.) involves making specific behavior occur more or less often by systematically managing antecedent cues and contingent consequences.[5] On-the-job behavior modification has been alternatively labeled *organizational behavior modification, organizational behavior management,* and *performance management.* To avoid unnecessary confusion, we use the generic term *behavior modification* throughout this chapter.

• PRINCIPLES OF BEHAVIOR MODIFICATION

Although B. Mod. interventions in the workplace often involve widely used techniques such as goal setting, feedback, and rewards, B. Mod. is unique in its adherence to Skinner's operant model of learning. To review, operant theorists assume it is more productive to deal with observable behavior and its environmental determinants than with personality traits, perception, or inferred internal causes of behavior such as needs or cognitions. The purpose of this section is to introduce important concepts and terminology associated with B. Mod. Subsequent sections explore B. Mod. application and research and some issues, pro and con.

• **FIGURE 7-2**   Productive Job Behavior Requires Supportive Antecedents and Consequences

Antecedent→	Behavior→	Consequence	Behavior outcome
Manager: "I suppose you haven't finished the payroll report yet."	*Payroll clerk:* "No way! I'm behind schedule because the supervisors didn't submit their payroll cards on time."	*Manager:* "I'm sure everyone will enjoy getting their paychecks late again!"	The payroll clerk continues to make excuses while missing important deadlines because of the manager's negative antecedents and sarcastic consequences.
Manager: "How are you coming along on this week's payroll report?"	*Payroll clerk:* "I'm a little behind schedule. But if I work during my lunch hour, I'll have it in on time."	*Manager:* "I appreciate the extra effort! How would you like to spend tomorrow working on that bonus-pay project you suggested last week?"	The payroll clerk continues to meet important deadlines because of the manager's non-threatening antecedents and rewarding consequences.

A→B→C Contingencies

To adequately understand the operant learning process, one needs a working knowledge of **behavioral contingencies,** as characterized by the A→B→C model. The initials stand for Antecedent→Behavior→Consequence. When person–environment interaction is reduced to A→B→C terms (as in Figure 7-2), a **functional analysis** has taken place.[6]

Within the context of B. Mod., *contingency* means the antecedent, behavior, and consequence in a given A→B→C relationship are connected in "if-then" fashion. If the antecedent is present, then the behavior is more likely to be displayed. If the behavior is displayed, then the consequence is experienced. Furthermore, as learned from Thorndike's law of effect, if the consequence is pleasing, the behavior will be strengthened (meaning it will occur more often). According to a pair of writers, one a clinical psychologist and the other a manager:

> Some contingencies occur automatically; others we set up by linking our behavior with the behavior of others in an attempt to design an environment that will best serve our purposes. Setting up a contingency involves designating behaviors and assigning consequences to follow. We design contingencies for children fairly simply ("If you finish your homework, I'll let you watch television"), but influencing the behavior of people in the work force is more difficult.
>
> As a result, managers often fail to use contingencies to their full advantage.[7]

Let us look more closely at antecedents, behavior, and consequences to fully understand A→B→C contingencies.

The Role of Antecedents   Unlike the S in the reflexive stimulus–response (S–R) model, antecedents *cue* rather than cause behavior. For example, in classic S–R fashion, a blistering hot piece of pizza *causes* you to quickly withdraw it from your mouth. In contrast, a yellow traffic light *cues* rather than causes you to step on the brake. Because many motorists step on the gas when green traffic signals change to yellow, traffic signals have probable rather than absolute control over driving behavior. Antecedents get the power to cue certain behaviors from associated consequences. For instance,

OB IN ACTION

Behaviorists Explain How Managers Should Describe Job Behavior: A Brief Case Study

The Wrong Way: **Subjective appraisal of the *person*, rather than objective information about *performance*.**

Phil Oaks, the department manager, describes his subordinate, Joe Scott, as follows:

> Well, Joe is just not easy to get along with. He's so disagreeable and negative all the time. He's very aggressive and disruptive. When he's unhappy he just sulks a lot, and he daydreams. He's also insubordinate and doesn't follow the rules. I don't know if he's immature, not intelligent, or irrational. Overall, his motivation is very low. He lacks drive and is generally hostile. I suspect that there may be a home problem also.

The Right Way: **Objective information about *observable performance behaviors*, rather than subjective appraisal of the person.**

In contrast, if Phil had training in pinpointing behaviors, he might describe Joe as follows:

> Well, whenever Joe is given some direction, he responds by immediately *telling you why it can't be done.* He frequently *threatens* other employees and has even been in one or two *fights.* He *leaves his own work area to tell jokes* to other workers. Sometimes he just *sits in a corner, or stares out the window* for several minutes.
>
> He has violated several company rules such as *smoking in a non-smoking zone, working without safety goggles,* and *parking in a fire lane.* He can't seem to *tell right-handed prints from left-handed prints.* Also, he *arrived late for work* ten times in the last month, and *returned from his break late* on twelve occasions.

Source: Performance descriptions excerpted from Charles C. Manz and Henry P. Sims, Jr., *SuperLeadership: Leading Others to Lead Themselves* (New York: Prentice-Hall, 1989), pp. 66–67.

if you have just received a ticket for running a red light, you will probably step on the brake when encountering the next few yellow traffic signals.

Focusing on Behavior   True to Watsonian and Skinnerian behaviorism, B. Mod. proponents emphasize the practical value of focusing on *behavior*. They caution against references to unobservable psychological states and general personality traits when explaining job performance (for example, see OB in Action). Phil's behavioral descriptions (the italicized portions in the bottom half of OB in Action) give him a solid foundation for modifying Joe's behavioral performance problems.

When managers focus exclusively on behavior, without regard for personality traits or cognitive processes, their approach qualifies as radical behaviorism.[8] As one might suspect, this extreme perspective has stirred debate and controversy, complete with philosophical and ethical implications.

Contingent Consequences

Contingent consequences, according to Skinner's operant theory, control behavior in four ways: positive reinforcement, negative reinforcement, punishment, and extinction.[9] These contingent consequences are managed systematically in B. Mod. programs. To avoid the all-too-common mislabeling of these consequences, let us review some formal definitions.

Positive Reinforcement Strengthens Behavior　**Positive reinforcement** is the process of strengthening a behavior by contingently presenting something pleasing. (Remember that a behavior is strengthened when it increases in frequency and weakened when it decreases in frequency.) A young design engineer who works overtime because of praise and recognition from the boss is responding to positive reinforcement. Similarly, people tend to return to restaurants where they are positively reinforced with good food and friendly service.

Negative Reinforcement Also Strengthens Behavior　**Negative reinforcement** is the process of strengthening a behavior by contingently withdrawing something displeasing. For example, an army sergeant who stops yelling when a recruit jumps out of bed has negatively reinforced that particular behavior. Similarly, the behavior of clamping our hands over our ears when watching a jumbo jet take off is negatively reinforced by relief from the noise. Negative reinforcement is often confused with punishment. But the two strategies have opposite effects on behavior. Negative reinforcement, as the word *reinforcement* indicates, strengthens a behavior because it provides relief from an unpleasant situation.

Punishment Weakens Behavior　**Punishment** is the process of weakening behavior through either the contingent presentation of something displeasing (see International OB) or the contingent withdrawal of something positive. A manager assigning a tardy employee to a dirty job exemplifies the first type of punishment. Docking a tardy employee's pay is an example of the second type of punishment, called "response cost" punishment. Legal fines involve response cost punishment. Salespeople who must make up any cash register shortages out of their own pockets are being managed through response cost punishment.

Extinction Also Weakens Behavior　**Extinction** is the weakening of a behavior by ignoring it or making sure it is not reinforced. Getting rid of an old boyfriend or girlfriend by refusing to answer their phone calls is an extinction strategy. A good analogy for extinction is to imagine what would happen to your houseplants if you stopped watering them. Like a plant without water, a behavior without occasional reinforcement eventually dies. Although very different processes, both punishment and extinction have the same weakening effect on behavior.

How to Properly Categorize Contingent Consequences　In B. Mod., consequences are defined in terms of their demonstrated impact on behavior (see Figure 7–3), not subjectively or by their intended impact. For example,

INTERNATIONAL OB

Canadians Modify Behavior with Classical Music!

Music can do magical things, especially in Canada. First there was the 7-Eleven store in British Columbia that piped Muzak into the parking lot to keep teenagers from loitering. Out blasted the Mantovani and the kids scattered, leaving only a wake of Slurpee cups. Now downtown businesses in Edmonton, Alberta, are playing Bach and Mozart in a city park to drive away drug dealers and their clients. Police say drug activity in the park has dropped dramatically since Johann and Wolfgang arrived.

Source: "Let's Split!," *Newsweek,* August 20, 1990, p. 2.

• **FIGURE 7-3**   Contingent Consequences in Behavior Modification

		Nature of Consequence	
		Positive or Pleasing	Negative or Displeasing
Behavior-Consequence Relationship	Contingent Presentation	Positive Reinforcement *Behavioral Outcome* Target behavior occurs *more* often	Punishment *Behavioral Outcome* Target behavior occurs *less* often
	Contingent Withdrawal	Punishment (Response Cost) *Behavioral Outcome* Target behavior occurs *less* often	Negative Reinforcement *Behavioral Outcome* Target behavior occurs *more* often

(no contingent consequence)

Extinction

Behavioral Outcome

Target behavior occurs *less* often

---

notice how one expert in the field distinguishes between reinforcement and rewards:

> Reinforcement is distinguished from reward in that a reward is something that is perceived to be desirable and is delivered to an individual after performance. An increase in pay, a promotion, and a comment on good work performance may all be rewards. But rewards are not necessarily reinforcers. Reinforcers are defined by the increase in the rate of behavior.[10]

A promotion is both a reward and a positive reinforcer if the individual's performance subsequently improves. On the other hand, apparent rewards may turn out to be the opposite. For example, consider Tampa Electric

OB in Action

"You've Been Misbehaving, Take a Day Off with Pay!"

Tampa Electric Company's "positive discipline" program:

It works like this: Employees who come in late, do a sloppy job, or mistreat a colleague first get an oral "reminder" rather than a "reprimand." Next comes a written reminder, then the paid day off—called a "decision-making leave day."

After a pensive day on the beach, naughty employees must agree in writing—or orally, at some union shops—that they will be on their best behavior for the next year. The paid day off is a one-shot chance at reform. If the employee doesn't shape up, it's curtains. The process is documented, so employees often have little legal recourse.

Source: Laurie Baum, "Punishing Workers with a Day Off," *Business Week,* June 16, 1986, p. 80.

Co.'s successful "positive discipline" program, which gives misbehaving employees *a paid day off* (see OB in Action).

Contingent consequences are always categorized "after the fact" by answering the following two questions: (1) Was something contingently presented or withdrawn? and (2) Did the target behavior subsequently occur more or less often? Using these two diagnostic questions, can you figure out why Tampa Electric's apparent reward turned out to be punishment for employees? Referring to the upper-right-hand quadrant in Figure 7–3, something was contingently presented and the target behavior (tardiness, sloppy work, etc.) was weakened. Hence, it was a punishment contingency.

Schedules of Reinforcement

As just illustrated, contingent consequences are an important determinant of future behavior. The *timing* of behavioral consequences can be even more important. Based on years of tedious laboratory experiments with pigeons in highly controlled environments, Skinner and his colleagues discovered distinct patterns of responding for various schedules of reinforcement.[11] Although some of their conclusions can be generalized to negative reinforcement, punishment, and extinction, it is best to think only of positive reinforcement when discussing schedules.

Continuous Reinforcement   As indicated in Table 7–1, every instance of a target behavior is reinforced when a **continuous reinforcement** (CRF) schedule is in effect. For instance, when your television set is operating properly, you are reinforced with a picture every time you turn it on (a CRF schedule). But, as with any CRF schedule of reinforcement, the behavior of turning on the television will undergo rapid extinction if the set breaks.

• **TABLE 7-1**   Schedules of Reinforcement

Schedule	Description	Probable Effects on Responding
Continuous (CRF)	Reinforcer follows every response.	Steady high rate of performance as long as reinforcement continues to follow every response.
		High frequency of reinforcement may lead to early satiation.
		Behavior weakens rapidly (undergoes extinction) when reinforcers are withheld.
		Appropriate for newly emitted, unstable, or low-frequency responses.
Intermittent	Reinforcer does not follow every response.	Capable of producing high frequencies of responding.
		Low frequency of reinforcement precludes early satiation.
		Appropriate for stable or high-frequency responses.
Fixed ratio (FR)	A fixed number of responses must be emitted before reinforcement occurs.	A fixed ratio of 1:1 (reinforcement occurs after every response) is the same as a continuous schedule.
		Tends to produce a high rate of response which is vigorous and steady.
Variable ratio (VR)	A varying or random number of responses must be emitted before reinforcement occurs.	Capable of producing a high rate of response which is vigorous, steady, and resistant to extinction.
Fixed interval (FI)	The first response after a specific period of time has elapsed is reinforced.	Produces an uneven response pattern varying from a very slow, unenergetic response immediately following reinforcement to a very fast, vigorous response immediately preceding reinforcement.
Variable interval (VI)	The first response after varying or random periods of time have elapsed is reinforced.	Tends to produce a high rate of response which is vigorous, steady, and resistant to extinction.

Source: Fred Luthans and Robert Kreitner, *Organizational Behavior Modification and Beyond: An Operant and Social Learning Approach* (Glenview, Ill.: Scott, Foresman, 1985), p. 58. Used with permission.

Intermittent Reinforcement   Unlike CRF schedules, **intermittent reinforcement** involves reinforcement of some but not all instances of a target behavior. Four subcategories of intermittent schedules, described in Table 7–1, are fixed and variable ratio schedules and fixed and variable interval schedules. Reinforcement in *ratio* schedules is contingent on the number of responses emitted. *Interval* reinforcement is tied to the passage of time. Some common examples of the four types of intermittent reinforcement are:

- *Fixed ratio* (piece-rate pay; bonuses tied to the sale of a fixed number of units).
- *Variable ratio* (slot machines that pay off after a variable number of lever pulls; lotteries that pay off after the purchase of a variable number of tickets).
- *Fixed interval* (hourly pay; annual salary paid on a regular basis).
- *Variable interval* (random supervisory praise and pats on the back for employees who have been doing a good job). (See OB Exercise.)

• OB EXERCISE

A Test of How Well You Know the Schedules of Reinforcement

Company: Drakenfeld Colors, Ciba-Geigy Corp., Washington, Pennsylvania.
Target behavior: Absenteeism
Instructions: Read the following case incident, select one of the answers listed below, and then check the interpretation in footnote 12 at the end of this chapter.

Drakenfeld had a population of about 250 employees with an absenteeism rate of only 0.89 percent. In fact, a full 44 percent of its employees had perfect attendance records in 1987. . . .

Because of the significant population of perfect attendees, it was decided to capitalize upon the strengths and to not only reward these people but to showcase them to the organization-at-large. This included a monetary bonus of $50 at six months and again at 12, with an additional $25 bonus for a full-calendar year of perfect attendance. Such an incentive alone may not sound as though it would induce someone to crawl out of bed on a day he or she might not otherwise do so, but the majority of the work force already had a strong work ethic and that root behavior was still dominant.

In order to make the program visible and exciting, employees with perfect attendance were entered into a sweepstakes drawing to take place at a special awards banquet with employees, spouses and management. The winner would receive an all-expenses paid trip for two to a resort location. The cost/benefit ratio of this incentive is obvious. . . .

Response to . . . [this] aspect of the program was extremely well received, with perfect attendance increasing from an already impressive 44 percent to a new high of 62 percent in the first year (1988).

Which schedules of reinforcement were used in this case?

a. Fixed interval plus variable interval.
b. Variable ratio plus variable interval.
c. Fixed ratio plus fixed interval.
d. Variable interval plus fixed ratio.
e. Fixed ratio plus variable ratio.

Source: Case incident excerpted from John Putzier and Frank T. Nowak, "Attendance Management and Control," *Personnel Administrator*, August 1989, pp. 59–60.

Scheduling Is Critical The schedule of reinforcement can more powerfully influence behavior than the magnitude of reinforcement. Although this proposition grew out of experiments with pigeons, subsequent on-the-job research confirmed it. Consider, for example, a field study of 12 unionized beaver trappers employed by a lumber company to keep the large rodents from eating newly planted tree seedlings.[13]

The beaver trappers were randomly divided into two groups that alternated weekly between two different bonus plans. Under the first schedule, each trapper earned his regular $7 per hour wage plus $1 for each beaver

• Using behavior shaping, which involves the reinforcement of progressively more difficult behavior, this trainer teaches a dolphin tricks.   *(Peter Pearson/Tony Stone Worldwide)*

caught. Technically, this bonus was paid on a continuous reinforcement (CRF) schedule. The second bonus plan involved the regular $7 per hour wage plus a one-in-four chance (as determined by rolling the dice) of receiving $4 for each beaver trapped. This second bonus plan qualified as a variable ratio (VR-4) schedule. In the long run, both incentive schemes averaged out to a $1-per-beaver bonus. Surprisingly, however, when the trappers were under the VR-4 schedule, they were 58 percent more productive than under the CRF schedule, despite the fact that the net amount of pay averaged out the same for the two groups during the 12-week trapping season.

Organizations Rely on the Weakest Schedule   Generally, variable ratio and variable interval schedules of reinforcement produce the strongest behavior that is most resistant to extinction. As gamblers will attest, variable schedules hold the promise of reinforcement after the next target response. Time-based pay schemes such as hourly pay and salaries that have become predominant in today's service economy are the weakest schedule of reinforcement (fixed interval).

Behavior Shaping

Have you ever wondered how trainers at aquarium parks manage to get bottle-nosed dolphins to do flips, killer whales to carry people on their backs, and seals to juggle balls? The results are seemingly magical. Actually, a mundane learning process called shaping is responsible for the animals' antics.

Two-ton killer whales, for example, have a big appetite and they find buckets of fish very reinforcing. So if the trainer wants to ride a killer whale, he or she reinforces very basic behaviors that will eventually lead to the

• **TABLE 7-2**   Ten Practical Tips for Shaping Job Behavior

> 1. *Accommodate the process of behavioral change.* Behaviors change in gradual stages, not in broad, sweeping motions.
> 2. *Define new behavior patterns specifically.* State what you wish to accomplish in explicit terms and in small amounts that can be easily grasped.
> 3. *Give individuals feedback on their performance.* A once-a-year performance appraisal is not sufficient.
> 4. *Reinforce behavior as quickly as possible.*
> 5. *Use powerful reinforcements.* In order to be effective, rewards must be important to the employee—not to the manager.
> 6. *Use a continuous reinforcement schedule.* New behaviors should be reinforced *every time* they occur. This reinforcement should continue until these behaviors become habitual.
> 7. *Use a variable reinforcement schedule for maintenance.* Even after behavior has become habitual, it still needs to be rewarded, though not necessarily every time it occurs.
> 8. *Reward teamwork—not competition.* Group goals and group rewards are one way to encourage cooperation in situations in which jobs and performance are interdependent.
> 9. *Make all rewards contingent on performance.*
> 10. *Never take good performance for granted.* Even superior performance, if left unrewarded, will eventually deteriorate.

Source: Adapted from A. T. Hollingsworth and Denise Tanquay Hoyer, "How Supervisors Can Shape Behavior," *Personnel Journal,* May 1985, pp. 86, 88.

whale being ridden. The killer whale is contingently reinforced with a few fish for coming near the trainer, then for being touched, then for putting its nose in a harness, then for being straddled, and eventually for swimming with the trainer on its back. In effect, the trainer systematically raises the behavioral requirement for reinforcement. Thus, **shaping** is defined as the process of reinforcing closer and closer approximations to a target behavior.

Shaping works very well with people, too. Praise, recognition, and instructive and credible feedback cost managers little more than moments of their time. Yet, when used in conjunction with a behavior-shaping program, these consequences can efficiently foster significant improvements in job performance.[14] The key to successful behavior shaping lies in reducing a complex target behavior to easily learned steps and then faithfully (and patiently) reinforcing any improvement. Table 7–2 lists practical tips on shaping.

• A MODEL FOR MODIFYING JOB BEHAVIOR

Someone once observed that children and pets are the world's best behavior modifiers. In fact, one of your authors responds obediently to his cats, while the other jumps to satisfy contingencies arranged by his dogs! Despite their ignorance of operant theory, children and pets are good behavior modifiers because they (1) know precisely what behavior they want to elicit, (2) provide clear antecedents, and (3) wield situationally appropriate and powerful contingent consequences. Let us learn from these ''masters'' of behavior modification and examine a four-step B. Mod. process for manag-

• **FIGURE 7–4**   Modifying On-the-Job Behavior

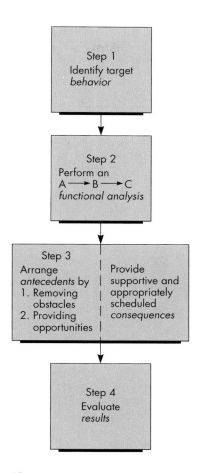

ing on-the-job behavior[15] (see Figure 7–4). A review of practical implications follows.

Step 1: Identify Target Behavior

Managers who strictly follow the operant principle of focusing on observable behavior rather than on inferred internal states, have two alternatives in Step 1. They can pinpoint a *desirable* behavior that occurs too *seldom* (e.g., contributing creative ideas at staff meetings), or they can focus on an *undesirable* behavior that occurs too *often* (e.g., making disruptive comments at staff meetings). Organizational behavior modification proponents prefer the first alternative because it requires managers to see things in a positive, growth-oriented manner instead of in a negative, punitive manner. As a case in point, researchers have documented the benefits of "well pay" versus the costs of traditional sick pay.[16] In short, every undesirable behavior has a desirable opposite. Just a few of many possible examples are: being absent/being on time, having an accident/working safely, remaining aloof/participating actively, procrastinating/completing assignments on time, competing destructively/being a team player.

Pointers for Identifying Behavior   According to the former editor of the *Journal of Organizational Behavior Management,* a journal devoted to the study of B. Mod. in the workplace, too many B. Mod. programs focus on process (rule following) rather than on accomplishments. Thus, he offers the following three pointers for identifying target behaviors:

1. The primary focus should be on accomplishments or outcomes. These accomplishments should have *significant* organizational impact.
2. The targeting of process behaviors (rule adherence, etc.) should only occur when that behavior can be functionally related to a significant organizational accomplishment.
3. There should be broad participation in the development of behavioral targets.[17]

These pointers are intended to prevent managers from falling victim to charges of unethical manipulation.

A Word of Caution about Shifting the Focus from Behavior to Results   In laboratory settings or highly controlled situations such as classrooms or machine shops, it is possible to directly observe and record the frequency of specific behaviors. Asking a question in class, arriving late at work, and handing in an error-free report are all observable behavioral events. However, in today's complex organizations, it is not always possible (or desirable) to observe and record work behaviors firsthand. For example, top-level managers and technical specialists often spend time alone in closed offices. When work behavior cannot be monitored firsthand, the next best alternative is to track results. Examples include number of units sold, number of customer complaints, degree of goal attainment, and percent of projects completed. Managers who build contingencies around results need to keep in mind that those contingencies will be less precise than ones anchored to observable behavioral events. For instance, the wrong person could be reinforced because organizational politicians sometimes take credit for others' results.

Step 2: Functionally Analyze the Situation

Any behaviors occurring on a regular basis necessarily have their own supportive cues and consequences. Thus, it is important for managers to identify existing A→B→C contingencies before trying to rearrange things. For example, it is important to know that a recently uncooperative employee is being pressured by co-workers to vote yes in an upcoming union certification election.

Step 3: Arrange Antecedents and Provide Consequences

In this step, analysis gives way to action. An instructive way to discuss step 3 is to explore separately antecedent management and consequence management. In practice, antecedent and consequence management are closely intertwined.

• **TABLE 7–3**   Paving the Way for Good Job Performance with Helpful Antecedents

Remove Obstacles	Provide Opportunities
Eliminate unrealistic plans, schedules, and deadlines	Formulate difficult but attainable goals
Identify and remedy skill deficiencies through training	Provide clear instructions
Eliminate confusing or contradictory rules	Give friendly reminders, constructive suggestions, and helpful tips
Avoid conflicting orders and priorities	Ask nonthreatening questions about progress
Remove distracting co-workers	Display posters with helpful advice
	Rely on easy-to-use forms
	Build enthusiasm and commitment through participation and challenging work assignments
	Promote personal growth and development through training

Managing Antecedents   As specified in Step 3 of Figure 7–4, antecedent management involves two basic strategies: (1) removing obstacles and/or (2) providing opportunities. Some practical suggestions are listed in Table 7–3. Based on the discussion of goal setting in Chapter 6, challenging objectives that specify what and when something is to be accomplished are probably the most potent antecedent management tool. For instance, supervisors in one study handed in their weekly reports more promptly when they were given specific target dates.[18]

By rearranging apparently insignificant antecedents, significant results can be achieved. Importantly, these must be *contingent* antecedents, as identified through an A→B→C functional analysis. For example, a telephone company was losing an estimated $250,000 annually because its telephone installers were not reporting the installation of "ceiling drops." A ceiling drop involves installing extra wiring to compensate for a lowered ceiling. Despite comprehensive training on how to install and report ceiling drops, a large percentage of ceiling drops remained unreported and thus unbilled by the company. The following turn of events then took place.

> A specialist in training design was called in to find out why the training had failed. She noted a curious thing. The form that the installers were required to fill out was extremely complicated and the part dealing with ceiling drops was even more complicated. . . .
>
> One small change was made by adding a box where the installer could merely check "ceiling drop installed." Now the installer no longer had to fill out an extensive explanation of what took place in the house. Within one week after the change in the form, the number of ceiling drops reported and charged back to the customers had increased dramatically, far above what it was immediately after the training sessions.[19]

Summarizing, from a B. Mod. perspective the telephone installers did not have an attitude or motivation problem. Nor did they have a knowledge deficiency requiring more training. They simply did not report ceiling drops because it was too complicated to do so. The streamlined reporting form presented the installers with an opportunity to behave properly, whereas the old form was an obstacle to good performance. In A→B→C terms, the streamlined reporting form became an antecedent that efficiently cued the desired behavior.

Managing Consequences   Step 3 in Figure 7–4 calls for providing supportive and appropriately scheduled consequences. Six guidelines for successfully managing consequences during B. Mod. are:

1. *Reinforce improvement, not just final results.* Proper shaping cannot occur if the behavioral requirement for reinforcement is too demanding. Behavior undergoes extinction when it is not shaped in achievable step-by-step increments.

2. *Fit the consequences to the behavior.* A pair of B. Mod. scholars interpreted this guideline as follows:

> Overrewarding a worker may make him feel guilty and certainly reinforces his current performance level. If the performance level is lower than that of others who get the same reward, he has no reason to increase his output. When a worker is underrewarded, he becomes angry with the system. His behavior is being extinguished and the company may be forcing the good employee (under-rewarded) to seek employment elsewhere while encouraging the poor employee (overrewarded) to stay on.[20]

Note how this recommendation is consistent with the discussion of equity theory in Chapter 6.

3. *Emphasize natural rewards over contrived rewards.* **Natural rewards** are potentially reinforcing consequences derived from day-to-day social and administrative interactions (see A Matter of Ethics). Typical natural rewards include supervisory praise, assignment to favored tasks, early time off with pay, flexible work schedules, and extended breaks. Contrived rewards include money and other tangible rewards. Regarding this distinction, it has been pointed out that:

A MATTER OF ETHICS

Japanese Employers Emphasize Natural Rewards

If there is a single element of the Japanese approach to labor relations that has not received substantial attention in this country, despite its potential for success, it is the Japanese desire to find ways to make work easier for employees. It is an understatement to say that the work ethic is alive and well in Japan, but Japanese manufacturing plants are by no means sweatshops. On the contrary, major Japanese employers believe it is essential not to overburden their workers, not only because of a moral commitment to the people who work for them, but also because they have found that overburdening results in inefficiency, product defects, and safety problems.

Source: Excerpted from Stanley J. Brown, "The Japanese Approach to Labor Relations: Can it Work in America?" *Personnel,* April 1987, p. 26.

Natural social rewards are potentially the most powerful and universally applicable reinforcers. In contrast to contrived rewards, they do not generally lead to satiation (people seldom get tired of compliments, attention, or recognition) and can be administered on a very contingent basis.[21]

4. *Provide individuals with objective feedback whenever possible.* As discussed in Chapter 13, objective feedback can have a positive impact on future behavior. This is particularly true when people have the opportunity to keep track of their own performance, as was the case at Emery Air Freight[22] (see OB in Action). The three-way marriage of goal setting, objective feedback, and positive reinforcement for improvement can be fruitful indeed. For example, a field study of college hockey players demonstrated that a B. Mod. intervention of goal setting, feedback, and praise increased the team's winning percentage by almost 100 percent for two consecutive years.[23]

 OB IN ACTION

Emery Air Freight's Successful Behavior Modification Program

According to the manager primarily responsible for developing the B. Mod. program that reportedly saved Emery Air Freight over $3 million, this is what took place:

The firm used large containers to forward small packages in order to cut handling and delivery times to airlines, and since usage of these containers had been promulgated by management, it and dock workers assumed that the containers were being used 90 percent of the time when possible. But an on-the-job analysis found the figure closer to 45 percent. Since most of the workers knew how and when to use the containers, it was reasoned that an educational program would have little impact.

Management concluded that the answer was to tell the workers how much they were falling short of the 90 percent utilization rate and how profits would be increased if the containers were used at an optimum level.

To start, management developed a checklist on which the dock worker would indicate each time he or she used a container. At the end of each shift, the worker totaled his or her own results to see whether the 90 percent goal had been reached. Supervisors and regional managers were encouraged to provide positive reinforcement by praising any improvement in employee performance. If a worker's improvement was minimal, he or she was not criticized. Instead, he or she was lauded for keeping an honest record of container usage.

The results were impressive. In 80 percent of the offices where the technique was tried, the use of containers rose from 45 percent to 95 percent. The increase was matched throughout the company and meant a saving of nearly $650,000 a year.

5. *Emphasize positive reinforcement; de-emphasize punishment.* Proponents of B. Mod. in the workplace, as mentioned earlier, recommend building up good behavior with positive reinforcement instead of tearing down bad behavior with punishment. For instance, the authors of the best-seller, *The One Minute Manager,* told their readers to "catch them doing something right!"[24] In other words, managers who focus on what's right with job performance unavoidably end up emphasizing positive reinforcement.

Regarding the use of punishment, operant researchers found it tends to suppress undesirable behavior only temporarily while prompting emotional side effects. For example, a computer programmer who is reprimanded publicly for failing to "debug" an important program may get even with the boss by skillfully sabotaging another program. Moreover, those punished come to fear and dislike the person administering the punishment.[25] Thus, it is unlikely that punitive managers can build the climate of trust so necessary for success in modern organizations. For example, the "giant retailer W. T. Grant, which went bankrupt in 1975, made it a practice to cut the tie of any sales manager who did not meet his quota."[26]

6. *Schedule reinforcement appropriately.* Once again, immature behavior requires the nurture of continuous reinforcement. Established or habitual behavior, in contrast, can be maintained with fixed or variable schedules of intermittent reinforcement.

Step 4: Evaluate Results

B. Mod. intervention is effective if (1) a desirable target behavior occurs more often or (2) an undesirable target behavior occurs less often. Since *more* or *less* are relative terms, managers need a measurement tool that provides an objective basis for comparing preintervention with postintervention data. This is where baseline data and behavior charting can make a valuable contribution.

Baseline data are preintervention behavioral data collected without the target person's knowledge. This "before" measure later provides a basis for assessing an intervention's effectiveness.

A **behavior chart** is a B. Mod. program evaluation tool that includes both preintervention baseline data and postintervention data. The vertical axis of a behavior chart can be expressed in terms of behavior frequency, percent, or results attained. A time dimension is typically found on the horizontal axis of a behavior chart. When a goal is included, as shown in Figure 7–5, a behavior chart quickly tells the individual where his or her performance has been, is, and should be. As the successful bus driver safety program discussed at the opening of this chapter illustrates, posted feedback can be a very effective management tool. Moreover, a behavior chart provides an ongoing evaluation of a B. Mod. program.

Some Practical Implications

Some believe B. Mod. does not belong in the workplace.[27] They see it as blatantly manipulative and demeaning. Although even the severest critics admit it works, they rightly point out that on-the-job applications of B. Mod. have focused on superficial rule-following behavior such as getting to work

• **FIGURE 7-5**   Behavior Charts Help Evaluate B. Mod. Programs and Provide Feedback

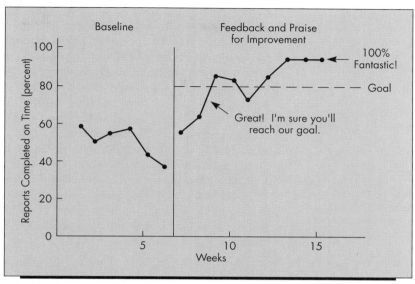

Source: Reprinted, by permission of the publisher, from "Graphing Employee Performance: An Effective Feedback Technique," Rodney R. Nordstrom and R. Vance Hall, *Supervisory Management*, December 1985, p. 4, © (1985) American Management Association, New York. All rights reserved.

on time. Indeed, B. Mod. is still in early transition from highly controlled and simple laboratory and clinical settings to loosely controlled and complex organizational settings. Despite the need for more B. Mod. research and application in complex organizations, some practical lessons already have been learned.

First, it is very difficult and maybe impossible to change organizational behavior without systematically managing antecedents and contingent consequences. Second, even the best-intentioned reward system will fail if it does not include clear behavior-consequence contingencies. Third, behavior shaping is a valuable developmental technique. Fourth, goal setting, objective feedback, and positive reinforcement for improvement, when combined in systematic A→B→C fashion, are a powerful management tool. Finally, because formal program evaluation is fundamental to B. Mod., those who use it on the job can be held accountable.

• BEHAVIORAL SELF-MANAGEMENT

Judging from the number of diet books appearing on best-seller lists each year, self-control seems to be in rather short supply. Historically, when someone sought to wage the war of self-control, he or she was told to exercise willpower, be self-disciplined, resist temptation, or seek divine guidance. Although well-intentioned, this advice gives the individual very little to go on relative to actually changing behavior. Fortunately, behavioral scientists formulated step-by-step self-management models that have helped individuals conquer serious behavioral problems. Typical among those problems are alcohol and drug abuse, overeating, cigarette smoking, phobias, and antisocial behavior. True to its interdisciplinary nature, the field of OB has recently translated self-management theory and techniques from the clinic to the workplace.

Formally defined, **behavioral self-management** (BSM) is the process of modifying one's own behavior by systematically managing cues, cognitive processes, and contingent consequences. The term *behavioral* signifies that BSM focuses primarily on modifying behavior, rather than on changing values, attitudes, or personalities. At first glance, BSM appears to be little more than self-imposed B. Mod. But BSM differs from B. Mod. in that cognitive processes are considered in BSM, while ignored in B. Mod. This adjustment reflects the influence of Albert Bandura's extension of operant theory into social learning theory.

In this section, we discuss Bandura's social learning theory, from which BSM has evolved. Next, a brief overview of the managerial context for BSM is presented. A social learning model of self-management is then introduced and explored, followed by some practical implications of relevant research findings.

Bandura's Social Learning Theory

Albert Bandura built on Skinner's work by initially demonstrating how people acquire new behavior by imitating role models (called vicarious learning) and later exploring the cognitive processing of cues and consequences. (Recall our discussion of the Stanford psychologist's ideas about self-efficacy in Chapter 3.) Like Skinner's operant model, Bandura's approach makes observable behavior the primary unit of analysis. Bandura also goes along with Skinner's contention that behavior is controlled by environmental cues and consequences. However, Bandura has extended Skinner's operant model by emphasizing that cognitive or mental processes affect how one responds to surroundings. In short, Bandura considers factors *inside* the individual, whereas the operant model stays outside the person. This extension is called social learning theory.

Reciprocal Determinism   According to Bandura:

> Social learning theory approaches the explanation of human behavior in terms of a continuous reciprocal interaction between cognitive, behavioral, and environmental determinants. Within the process of reciprocal determinism lies the opportunity for people to influence their destiny as well as the limits of self-direction. This conception of human functioning then neither casts people into the role of powerless objects controlled by environmental forces nor free agents who can become whatever they choose. Both people and their environments are reciprocal determinants of each other.[29]

Social Learning Defined   Working from Bandura's comments, we define **social learning** as the process of acquiring behavior through the *reciprocal* interaction of the person's cognitions, behavior, and environment. The concept of reciprocal determination means we control our environment (e.g., dropping a boring class) as much as it controls us (e.g., buying a new product after seeing it advertised on television). As indicated in Figure 7–6, symbolic

• **FIGURE 7-6**   A Basic Model of Social Learning, with Emphasis on Self-Control

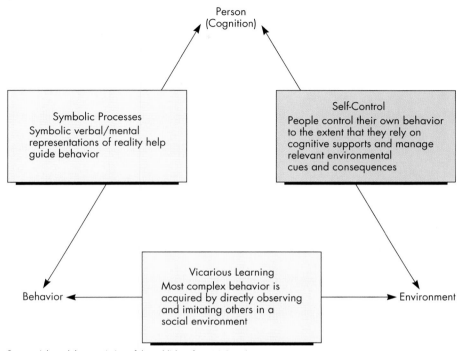

Source: Adapted, by permission of the publisher, from "A Social Learning Approach to Behavioral Management: Radical Behaviorists 'Mellowing Out,'" Robert Kreitner and Fred Luthans, *Organizational Dynamics*, Autumn 1984, p. 56, © 1984 American Management Association, New York. All rights reserved.

processes, vicarious learning, and *self-control* facilitate this reciprocal relationship in which each point of the triangle influences the other two points. An example of a symbolic process is relying on the mental picture of an angel to remember the name Angelo.

Keep Bandura's reciprocal model in mind because it is the conceptual foundation for the behavioral self-management process.

A Managerial Context for Behavioral Self-Management

In 1979, OB scholars Fred Luthans and Tim Davis developed the managerial context for BSM as follows:

> Research and writing in the management field have given a great deal of attention to managing societies, organizations, groups, and individuals. Strangely, almost no one has paid any attention to managing oneself more effectively. . . . Self-management seems to be a basic prerequisite for effective management of other people, groups, organizations, and societies.[30]

Moreover, some have wrapped BSM in ethical terms: "Proponents of self-control contend that it is more ethically defensible than externally imposed behavior control techniques when used for job enrichment, behavior modification, management by objectives, or organization development."[31] Still others have placed self-management within a managerial context by discuss-

• **FIGURE 7-7**   A Social Learning Model of Self-Management

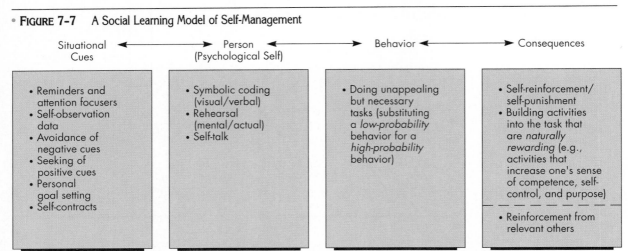

Source: Adapted in part from material found in Charles C. Manz, *The Art of Self-Leadership* (Englewood Cliffs, N.J.: Prentice Hall, 1983), chap. 3; and Fred Luthans and Robert Kreitner, *Organizational Behavior Modification and Beyond: An Operant and Social Learning Approach* (Glenview, Ill.: Scott, Foresman, 1985), p. 163.

ing it as a substitute for hierarchical leadership.[32] BSM is an important first step toward effectively managing others.

Social Learning Model of Self-Management

Bandura has put self-management into a social learning context by noting:

> [A] distinguishing feature of social learning theory is the prominent role it assigns to self-regulatory capacities. By arranging environmental inducements, generating cognitive supports, and producing consequences for their own actions people are able to exercise some measure of control over their own behavior.[33]

In other words, to the extent that you can control your environment and your cognitive representations of your environment, you are the master of your own behavior. The practical BSM model displayed in Figure 7–7 is derived from social learning theory; hence, the two-headed arrows indicating reciprocal interaction. (Note how the triangular social learning model in Figure 7–6 has been translated into a four-component model in Figure 7–7 by breaking the environment into two parts: situational cues and consequences.) Each of the four major components of this BSM model requires a closer look. Since this is a *behavioral* model, let us begin our examination with the behavior component.

Behavioral Dilemmas   Any form of self-control is difficult because it involves engaging in behaviors that are unappealing in the short run but beneficial or necessary in the long run. All too often, people engage in behaviors that are appealing in the short run but damaging to health, career, and friendships in the long run. For example, an overweight junk-food connoisseur would find it unappealing to pass up a hot fudge sundae. Yet his or her health and happiness may eventually depend on doing just that, and doing it over and over. Table 7–4 lists several unappealing but necessary managerial tasks.

• **TABLE 7–4**   Doing Unappealing but Necessary Managerial Tasks: A Challenge for Better Self-Management

Substituting Low-Probability Behavior for	High-Probability Behavior
Sticking to schedules and deadlines	Procrastinating
Preparing for and accepting changes in the workplace	Prejudicially resisting changes in the workplace
Catching people doing things *right*	Managing strictly by exception
Doing paperwork	Putting off paperwork
Delegating	Doing everything oneself
Positively reinforcing performance improvement	Taking performance improvement for granted and ignoring it
Giving corrective feedback during performance review meetings	Conducting "good news only" performance review meetings
Planning and scheduling activities	Doing everything at the last moment
Addressing ethical questions and dilemmas	Avoiding ethical issues
Anticipating and preventing problems	Reacting to existing problems ("fire fighting")
Getting ahead through competence and hard work	Getting ahead through political maneuvering
Confronting personality conflicts	Running away from personality conflicts
Conveying bad news to one's superiors	Falsely telling one's superiors that "everything's fine"
Assertively pursuing one's desires	Passively giving in to others
Listening	Communicating without listening

Notice how the challenge of self-management pivots around the substitution of a low-probability behavior for its high-probability counterpart. For instance, a manager who does not delegate (low-probability behavior) tends to perform all tasks himself or herself (high-probability behavior). Managers need BSM to tackle the behavioral dilemmas in Table 7–4 that might be keeping them from reaching their full potential.

As a procedural note, behavior charts can be used in BSM to evaluate progress toward one's goals, but baseline data ideally should be collected by someone else to ensure objectivity.

Managing Situational Cues   When people try to give up a nagging habit like smoking, the cards are stacked against them. Many people (friends who smoke) and situations (after dinner, when under stress at work, or when relaxing) serve as subtle yet powerful cues telling the individual to light up. If the behavior is to be changed, the cues need to be rearranged so as to trigger the alternative behavior. Six techniques for managing situational cues are listed in the left-hand column of Figure 7–7.

Reminders and attention focusers do just that. For example, many students and managers cue themselves about deadlines and appointments with yellow Post-it™ notes stuck all over their work areas, refrigerators, and dashboards. Self-observation data, when compared against a goal or standard, can be a potent cue for improvement. Those who keep a weight chart near their bathroom scale will attest to the value of this tactic (see OB in

OB IN ACTION

A Best-Selling Novelist Shares His Self-Management Secret

Here is how Irving Wallace, author of such best-sellers as *The Prize* (later a movie starring Paul Newman) and *The Man,* got himself to sit down and complete his manuscripts on time:

> I kept a work chart when I wrote my first book—which remains unpublished—at the age of 19. I maintained work charts while writing my first four published books. These charts showed the date I started each chapter, the date I finished it, and the number of pages written in that period. With my fifth book, I started keeping a more detailed chart, which also showed how many pages I had written by the end of every working day. . . . I am not sure why I started keeping such records. I suspect that it was because, as a freelance writer, entirely on my own, without employer or deadline, I wanted to create disciplines for myself, ones that were guilt-making when ignored. A chart on the wall served as such a discipline, its figures scolding me or encouraging me.

Source: Irving Wallace, *The Writing of One Novel* (Richmond Hill, Ontario: Simon & Schuster of Canada, 1971), as found in Irving Wallace, "Self-Control Techniques of Famous Novelists," *Journal of Applied Behavior Analysis,* Fall 1977, p. 516.

Action). Successful self-management calls for avoiding negative cues while seeking positive cues. Managers in Northwestern Mutual Life Insurance Company's new business department appreciate the value of avoiding negative cues: "On Wednesdays, the department shuts off all incoming calls, allowing workers to speed processing of new policies. On those days, the unit averages 23 percent more policies than on other days."[34]

Goals, as repeatedly mentioned in this text, are the touchstone of good management. So it is with challenging yet attainable personal goals and effective self-management. Goals simultaneously provide a target and a measuring stick of progress.[35] Finally, a self-contract act is an "if-then" agreement with oneself. For example, if you can define all the key terms at the end of this chapter, then treat yourself to something special.

Arranging Cognitive Supports   This component makes BSM distinctly different from conventional behavior modification. Referring to the *person* portion of the self-management model in Figure 7–7 three cognitive supports for behavior change are symbolic coding, rehearsal, and self-talk. These amount to psychological, as opposed to environmental, cues. Yet they prompt appropriate behavior in the same manner. Each requires brief explanation:

- *Symbolic coding:* From a social learning theory perspective, the human brain stores information in visual and verbal codes. For example, a sales manager could use the visual picture of a man chopping down a huge tree to remember Woodman, the name of a promising new client. In contrast, people commonly rely on acronyms to recall names, rules for behavior, and other information. An acronym (or verbal code) that is often heard in managerial circles is the KISS principle, standing for "Keep It Simple, Stupid."

• *Rehearsal:* While it is true that practice often makes perfect, mental rehearsal of challenging tasks also can increase one's chances of success. Importantly, experts draw a clear distinction between systematic visualization of how one should proceed and daydreaming about success.

> The big difference between daydreaming and visualizing is that "visualizing is much more specific and detailed," says Philadelphia consultant Judith Schuster. "A daydream typically has gaps in it—we jump immediately to where we want to wind up. In visualization, we use building blocks and, step-by-step, construct the result we want."[36]

Managers stand to learn a great deal about mental rehearsal and visualization from successful athletes. Mary Lou Retton, 1984 Olympic gold medal gymnast, is an inspiring example:

> "Before I dropped off to sleep inside the Olympic Village, I did what I always do before a major competition—mind-scripted it completely. I mentally ran through each routine, every move, imagining everything done perfectly," recalls Retton.[37]

Job-finding seminars are very popular on college campuses today because they typically involve mental and actual rehearsal of tough job interviews. This sort of manufactured experience can build the confidence and self-efficacy necessary for real-world success.

• *Self-talk:* According to an expert on the subject, "**self-talk** is the set of evaluating thoughts that you give yourself about facts and events that happen to you."[38] Personal experience tells us that self-talk tends to be a self-fulfilling prophecy (recall the discussion in Chapter 4). Negative self-talk tends to pave the way for failure, whereas positive self-talk often facilitates success. Replacing negative self-talk ("I'll never get a raise") with positive self- talk ("I deserve a raise and I'm going to get it") is fundamental to better self-management.

Self-Reinforcement The satisfaction of self-contracts and other personal achievements calls for self-reinforcement. According to Bandura, three criteria must be satisfied before self-reinforcement can occur:

1. The individual must have *control over desired reinforcers.*
2. Reinforcers must be *self-administered on a conditional basis.* Failure to meet the performance requirement must lead to self-denial.
3. *Performance standards must be adopted* to establish the quantity and quality of target behavior required for self-reinforcement.[39]

In view of the following realities, self-reinforcement strategies need to be resourceful and creative:

> Self-granted rewards can lead to self-improvement. But as failed dieters and smokers can attest, there are short-run as well as long-run influences on self-reinforcement. For the overeater, the immediate gratification of eating has more influence than the promise of a new wardrobe. The same sort of dilemma plagues

procrastinators. Consequently, one needs to weave a powerful web of cues, cognitive supports, and internal and external consequences to win the tug-of-war with status-quo payoffs. Primarily because it is so easy to avoid, self-punishment tends to be ineffectual. As with managing the behavior of others, positive instead of negative consequences are recommended for effective self-management.[40]

In addition, it helps to solicit positive reinforcement for self-improvement from supportive friends and relatives.

Research and Managerial Implications

There is ample evidence that behavioral self-management works. For example, in one controlled study of 20 college students, 17 were able to successfully modify their own behavior problems involving smoking, lack of assertiveness, poor study habits, overeating, sloppy housekeeping, lack of exercise, and moodiness.[41] But because BSM has only recently been transplanted from clinical and classroom applications to the workplace, on-the-job research evidence is limited. One pair of researchers reported successful BSM interventions with managerial problems, including overdependence on the boss, ignoring paperwork, leaving the office without notifying anyone, and failing to fill out expense reports.[42] Also, absenteeism of unionized state government employees was significantly reduced with BSM training.[32] A survey of 36 organization development consultants found positive applications of mental imagery and visualization for organizational problem solving.[44] These preliminary studies need to be supplemented by research of how, why, and under what conditions BSM does or does not work. In the meantime, present and future managers can fine-tune their own behavior by taking lessons from proven self-management techniques.

• SUMMARY OF KEY CONCEPTS

A. Modern behaviorism evolved from the works of Watson, Thorndike, and Skinner. Skinner formulated his operant conditioning model by combining Watson's emphasis on observable *behavior* and Thorndike's emphasis on *consequences*.

B. *Behavior modification* (B. Mod.) is defined as the process of making specific behavior occur more or less often by systematically managing (1) antecedent cues and (2) contingent consequences.

C. B. Mod. involves managing person–environment interactions that can be functionally analyzed into antecedent→behavior→consequence (A→B→C) relationships. Antecedents cue rather than cause subsequent behavior. Contingent consequences, in turn, either strengthen or weaken that behavior.

D. Positive and negative reinforcement are consequence management strategies that strengthen behavior, whereas punishment and extinction weaken behavior. These strategies need to be defined objectively in terms of their actual impact on behavior frequency, not subjectively on the basis of intended impact.

E. Every instance of a behavior is reinforced with a continuous reinforcement (CRF) schedule. Under intermittent reinforcement schedules—fixed and variable ratio or fixed and variable interval— some, rather than all, instances of a target behavior are reinforced. Variable schedules produce the most extinction-resistant behavior. Behavior shaping occurs when closer approximations of a target behavior are contingently reinforced.

F. On-the-job behavior can be modified with the following four-step model: (1) Identify target behavior, (2) functionally analyze the situation, (3) arrange antecedents and provide consequences, and (4) evaluate results. Improvement should be reinforced equitably and with natural rewards whenever possible. New behavior requires continuous reinforcement. Intermittent reinforcement can maintain established behavior. Behavior charts, with baseline data for before-and-after comparison, are a practical way of evaluating the effectiveness of a B. Mod. program.

G. *Behavioral self-management* (BSM) is the process of modifying one's own behavior by systematically managing cues, cognitive processes, and contingent consequences. Because BSM is based on Bandura's social learning theory, rather than on pure operant theory (radical behaviorism), it deals with cognitive processes such as visual and verbal symbolic coding, mental rehearsal, and self-talk.

H. A social learning model of self-management holds that one's behavior results from the reciprocal interaction among four components: (1) situational cues, (2) the person's psychological self, (3) the behavior itself, and (4) consequences. Self-management represents a dilemma because it involves replacing high-probability (appealing but unnecessary) behavior with low-probability (unappealing but necessary) behavior.

• KEY TERMS

behavioral learning theory	punishment
classical conditioning	extinction
behaviorism	continuous reinforcement
law of effect	intermittent reinforcement
respondent behavior	shaping
operant behavior	natural rewards
behavior modification	baseline data
behavioral contingencies	behavior chart
functional analysis	behavioral self-management
positive reinforcement	social learning
negative reinforcement	self-talk

• Discussion Questions

1. What would an A→B→C functional analysis of your departing your residence *on time* for school or work look like? How about a functional analysis of your leaving late?

2. Why is the term *contingency* central to understanding the basics of B. Mod.?

3. What real-life examples of positive reinforcement, negative reinforcement, both forms of punishment, and extinction can you draw from your recent experience? Were these strategies appropriately or inappropriately used?

4. From a schedules of reinforcement perspective, why do people find gambling so addictive?

5. What sort of behavior shaping have you engaged in lately? Explain your success or failure.

6. Regarding the six guidelines for successfully managing consequences, which do you think ranks as the most important? Explain your rationale.

7. Why is valid baseline data essential in a B. Mod. program?

8. What sort of luck have you had with self-management recently? Which of the self-management techniques discussed in this chapter would help you do better?

9. Do you agree with the assumption that managers need to do a good job with self-management before they can effectively manage others? Explain.

10. What importance would you attach to self-talk in self-management? Explain.

BACK TO THE OPENING CASE

Now that you have read Chapter 7, you should be able to answer the following questions about the Parsons Pine Products case:

1. How would you rate James W. Parsons, the owner, as a behavior modifier? Explain in technical B. Mod. terms.

2. What sort of antecedent management has taken place in this case?

3. In A→B→C terms, which of Parsons' plans—well pay, retro pay, safety pay, and profit-sharing pay—probably has the most powerful influence on the target behavior?

4. Could any of Parsons' elaborate reinforcement schemes backfire? Explain potential problems and offer suggestions.

• Exercise 7

Objectives

1. To better understand the principles of behavior modification through firsthand experience.
2. To improve your own or someone else's behavior by putting to use what you have learned in this chapter.

Introduction

Because the areas of B. Mod. and BSM are application oriented, they need to be put to practical use if they are to be fully appreciated. In a general sense, everyone is a behavior modifier. Unfortunately, those without a working knowledge of behavioral principles tend to manage their own and others' behavior rather haphazardly. They tend to unwittingly reinforce undesirable behavior, put desirable behavior on extinction, and rely too heavily on punishment and negative reinforcement. This exercise is designed to help you become a more systematic manager of behavior.

Instructions

Selecting the target behavior of your choice, put the four-step behavior modification model in Figure 7–4 into practice. The target may be your own behavior (e.g., studying more, smoking fewer cigarettes, eating less or eating more nutritionally, or one of the managerial BSM problems in Table 7–4) or someone else's (e.g., improving a roommate's housekeeping behavior). Be sure to construct a behavior chart (as in Figure 7–5) with the frequency of the target behavior on the vertical axis and time on the horizontal axis. It is best to focus on a behavior that occurs daily so a three- or four-day baseline period can be followed by a one- to two-week intervention period. Make sure you follow as many of the six consequence management guidelines as possible.

You will find it useful to perform an A→B→C functional analysis of the target behavior to identify its supporting (or hindering) cues and consequences. Then you will be in a position to set a reasonable goal and design an intervention strategy involving antecedent and consequence management. When planning a self-management intervention, give careful thought to how you can use cognitive supports. Make sure you use appropriate schedules of reinforcement.

Questions for Consideration/Class Discussion

1. Did you target a specific behavior (e.g., eating) or an outcome (e.g., pounds lost)? What was the advantage or disadvantage of tracking that particular target?
2. How did your B. Mod. or BSM program turn out? What did you do wrong? What did you do right?
3. How has this exercise increased your working knowledge of B. Mod. and/or BSM?

• NOTES

[1] Complete details of this field study may be found in Robert S. Haynes, Randall C. Pine, and H. Gordon Fitch, "Reducing Accident Rates with Organizational Behavior Modification," *Academy of Management Journal,* June 1982, pp. 407–16.

[2] J. B. Watson and W. MacDougall, *The Battle of Behaviorism* (New York: W. W. Norton, 1929), p. 18.

[3] See Edward L. Thorndike, *Educational Psychology: The Psychology of Learning, Vol. II* (New York: Columbia University Teachers College, 1913).

[4] See B. F. Skinner, *The Behavior of Organisms* (New York: Appleton-Century-Crofts, 1938).

[5] Based on a similar definition in Robert Kreitner, "The Feedforward and Feedback Control of Job Performance through Organizational Behavior Management (OBM)," *Journal of Organizational Behavior Management,* no. 3, 1982, pp. 3–20. Three excellent resources, relative to B. Mod. in the workplace, are Lee W. Frederiksen, ed., *Handbook of Organizational Behavior Management* (New York: John Wiley & Sons, 1982); Frank Andrasik, "Organizational Behavior Modification in Business Settings: A Methodological and Content Review," *Journal of Organizational Behavior Management,* no. 1, 1989, pp. 59–77; and Gerald A. Merwi, Jr., John A. Thomason, and Eleanor E. Sanford, "A Methodology and Content Review of Organizational Behavior Management in the Private Sector: 1978–1986," *Journal of Organizational Behavior Management,* no. 1, 1989, pp. 39–57.

[6] Complete discussion of the A→B→C model may be found in Fred Luthans and Robert Kreitner, *Organizational Behavior Modification and Beyond: An Operant and Social Learning Approach* (Glenview, Ill.: Scott, Foresman, 1985), pp. 46–49.

[7] Douglas H. Ruben and Marilyn J. Ruben, "Behavioral Principles on the Job: Control or Manipulation?" *Personnel,* May 1985, p. 61.

[8] See P. A. Lamal, "The Continuing Mischaracterization of Radical Behaviorism," *American Psychologist,* January 1990, p. 71.

[9] See Luthans and Kreitner, *Organizational Behavior Modification and Beyond,* pp. 49–56.

[10] Lawrence M. Miller, *Behavior Management: The New Science of Managing People at Work* (New York: John Wiley & Sons, 1978), p. 106.

[11] See C. B. Ferster and B. F. Skinner, *Schedules of Reinforcement* (New York: Appleton-Century-Crofts, 1957).

[12] Our choice is *e*. Of course, the correct answer to this challenging exercise is a matter of interpretation. There is plenty of room for honest disagreement. Our interpretation is based on the belief that the passage of time is *not* the primary criterion for granting reinforcement. The first reinforcement schedule, involving cash bonuses at the end of 6-month and 12-month periods for perfect attendance, is anchored to a specific number of complete work days. Every employee, regardless of his or her attendance record, does not automatically receive the cash bonuses at 6- and 12-month intervals (as would be the case with a fixed interval schedule). Hence, it is a fixed ratio schedule.

The second reinforcement schedule is anchored to whether or not one is eligible to enter the drawing. Again, the criterion is a specific set of behaviors, not the passage of time. This second reinforcement schedule qualifies as variable ratio, because a random number of perfect attendance days must pass before a given employee wins the all-expenses paid trip. Maintaining perfect attendance to qualify for the drawing each year is just like playing a slot machine. Together, these two schedules of reinforcement are a good incentive for perfect attendance.

[13] See Lise M. Saari and Gary P. Latham, "Employee Reactions to Continuous and

Variable Ratio Reinforcement Schedules Involving a Monetary Incentive," *Journal of Applied Psychology,* August 1982, pp. 506–8.

[14] See, for example, John C. Bruening, "Shaping Workers' Attitudes toward Safety," *Occupational Hazards,* March 1990, pp. 49–51.

[15] An alternative five-step model—Pinpoint, Record, Involve, Coach, Evaluate—may be found in Kenneth Blanchard and Robert Lorber, *Putting the One Minute Manager to Work* (New York: Berkley Books, 1984), p. 58.

[16] For example, see Barron H. Harvey, Judy A. Schultze, and Jerome F. Rogers, "Rewarding Employees for Not Using Sick Leave," *Personnel Administrator,* May 1983, pp. 55–59.

[17] Lee W. Frederiksen, "The Selection of Targets for Organizational Interventions," *Journal of Organizational Behavior Management,* no. 4, 1981–1982, p. 4.

[18] See James Conrin, "A Comparison of Two Types of Antecedent Control over Supervisory Behavior," *Journal of Organizational Behavior Management,* Fall–Winter 1982, pp. 37–47. For a report of the positive impact of antecedents on consumer behavior, see Mark J. Martinko, J. Dennis White, and Barbara Hassell, "An Operant Analysis of Prompting in a Sales Environment," *Journal of Organizational Behavior Management,* no. 1, 1989, pp. 93–107.

[19] Thomas K. Connellan, *How to Improve Human Performance: Behaviorism in Business and Industry* (New York: Harper & Row, 1978), p. 27.

[20] W. Clay Hamner and Ellen P. Hamner, "Behavior Modification on the Bottom Line," *Organizational Dynamics,* Spring 1976, p. 8.

[21] Luthans and Kreitner, *Organizational Behavior Modification and Beyond,* p. 128. Also see Charles C. Manz and Henry P. Sims, Jr., *SuperLeadership: Leading Others to Lead Themselves* (New York: Prentice-Hall, 1989), pp. 28–34, 139–43.

[22] For details, see "At Emery Air Freight: Positive Reinforcement Boosts Performance," *Organizational Dynamics,* Winter 1973, pp. 41–50.

[23] See D. Chris Anderson, Charles R. Crowell, Mark Doman, and George S. Howard, "Performance Posting, Goal Setting, and Activity-Contingent Praise as Applied to a University Hockey Team," *Journal of Applied Psychology,* February 1988, pp. 87–95.

[24] Kenneth Blanchard and Spencer Johnson, *The One Minute Manager* (New York: Berkley Books, 1982), p. 39. Interestingly, managers were given this identical bit of advice, "Catch them doing something right!" five years earlier by Robert Kreitner, "People Are Systems, Too: Filling the Feedback Vacuum," *Business Horizons,* November 1977, pp. 54–58.

[25] For a review of this research, see Luthans and Kreitner, *Organizational Behavior Modification and Beyond,* pp. 139–44. An alternative view of the benefits of punishment is discussed by Richard D. Arvey and John M. Ivancevich, "Punishment in Organizations: A Review, Propositions, and Research Suggestions," *Academy of Management Review,* January 1980, pp. 123–32.

[26] Susan Narod, "Off-Beat Company Customs," *Dun's Business Month,* November 1984, p. 66.

[27] For example, see Fred L. Fry, "Operant Conditioning in Organizational Settings: Of Mice or Men?" *Personnel,* July–August 1974, pp. 17–24, and Edwin A. Locke, "The Myths of Behavior Mod in Organizations," *Academy of Management Review,* 1977, pp. 543–53.

[28] Evidence of constructive applications of B. Mod. in the workplace can be found in Kirk O'Hara, C. Merle Johnson, and Terry A. Beehr, "Organizational Behavior Management in the Private Sector: A Review of Empirical Research and Recommendations for Further Investigation," *Academy of Management Review,* October 1985, pp. 848–64. Also see recent issues of *Journal of Organizational Behavior Manage-*

ment, particularly the special issue: "Promoting Excellence through Performance Management," *Journal of Organizational Behavior Management,* no. 1, 1990.

29 Albert Bandura, *Social Learning Theory* (Englewood Cliffs, N.J.: Prentice-Hall, 1977), p. vii.

30 Fred Luthans and Tim R. V. Davis, "Behavioral Self-Management—The Missing Link in Managerial Effectiveness," *Organizational Dynamics,* Summer 1979, p. 43.

31 Luthans and Kreitner, *Organizational Behavior Modification and Beyond,* p. 158.

32 See, for example, Charles C. Manz and Henry P. Sims, Jr., "Self-Management as a Substitute for Leadership: A Social Learning Theory Perspective," *Academy of Management Review,* July 1980, pp. 361–67; Charles C. Manz, *The Art of Self-Leadership* (Englewood Cliffs, N.J.: Prentice-Hall, 1983); Charles C. Manz, "Self-Leadership: Toward an Expanded Theory of Self-Influence Processes in Organizations," *Academy of Management Review,* July 1986, pp. 585–600; and Charles C. Manz and Henry P. Sims, Jr., *SuperLeadership: Leading Others to Lead Themselves* (New York: Prentice-Hall, 1989).

33 Bandura, *Social Learning Theory,* p. 13.

34 "Labor Letter: A Special News Report on People and their Jobs in Offices, Fields, and Factories," *The Wall Street Journal,* October 15, 1985, p. 1.

35 Helpful instructions on formulating career goals may be found in Dorothy Heide and Elliot N. Kushell, "I Can Improve My Management Skills by: _____," *Personnel Journal,* June 1984, pp. 52–54.

36 Robert McGarvey, "Rehearsing for Success," *Executive Female,* January/February 1990, p. 36.

37 Ibid.

38 Charles Zastrow, *Talk to Yourself: Using the Power of Self-Talk* (Englewood Cliffs, N.J.: Prentice-Hall, 1979), p. 60. Also see Manz and Sims, *SuperLeadership* pp. 41–43; and Charles C. Manz and Chris P. Neck, "Inner Leadership: Creating Productive Thought Patterns," *Academy of Management Executive,* August 1991, pp. 87–95.

39 Drawn from discussion in Albert Bandura, "Self-Reinforcement: Theoretical and Methodological Considerations," *Behaviorism,* Fall 1976, pp. 135–55.

40 Robert Kreitner and Fred Luthans, "A Social Learning Approach to Behavioral Management: Radical Behaviorists 'Mellowing Out,'" *Organizational Dynamics,* Autumn 1984, p. 63.

41 See Richard F. Rakos and Mark V. Grodek, "An Empirical Evaluation of a Behavioral Self-Management Course in a College Setting," *Teaching of Psychology,* October 1984, pp. 157–62.

42 Luthans and Davis, "Behavioral Self-Management—The Missing Link in Managerial Effectiveness," pp. 52–59.

43 Results are presented in Colette A. Frayne and Gary P. Latham, "Application of Social Learning Theory to Employee Self-Management of Attendance," *Journal of Applied Psychology,* August 1987, pp. 387–92. Follow-up data are presented in Gary P. Latham and Colette A. Frayne, "Self-Management Training for Increasing Job Attendance: A Follow-Up and a Replication," *Journal of Applied Psychology,* June 1989, pp. 411–16.

44 See Maurice A. Howe, "Using Imagery to Facilitate Organizational Development and Change," *Group & Organization Studies,* March 1989, pp. 70–82.

UNDERSTANDING AND MANAGING GROUP AND SOCIAL PROCESSES

Socialization, Mentoring, and Careers

LEARNING OBJECTIVES

When you finish studying the material in this chapter, you should be able to:

- Briefly describe the three phases in Feldman's model of organizational socialization.
- Explain how psychological contracts and realistic job previews (RJPs) can be used to socialize employees.

- Discuss the appropriate role of behavior modeling in employee training.
- Describe the two basic functions of mentoring.
- Distinguish between role conflict and role ambiguity.
- Specify four reasons why norms are enforced in organizations.

- Discuss the steps in the model of career management.
- Explain the stages of a professional career.
- Identify the characteristics of the different career anchors.

OPENING CASE 8

Sweating It Out at Goldman Sachs

Sharon Hoogstraten

On the nerve-racking Monday before the fateful Tuesday, Robin Illgen felt her life was "suspended in Jell-O." Vinod Ahooja played five hours of tennis "to make sure I didn't come in and sock someone on the jaw." Richard Witten thought about chilling a bottle of champagne but, superstitious, decided not to tempt the Fates. And at Goldman, Sachs & Co., the phones rang on.

Ms. Illgen and Messrs. Ahooja and Witten knew they were "in the zone"—three of the select few who might be named the next day to a partnership at Goldman.

Every two years, Goldman, the last of Wall Street's major private partnerships, picks a small number of new partners from among its hundreds of young executives. On the one hand, the promotion might seem a somewhat dubious prize. Goldman partners toil notoriously long hours. The firm is known as a fraternal but tough place to work and it has had an abysmal record of promoting women and blacks.

On the other hand, partners typically retire as multimillionaires after only a decade or so. That's a significant other hand. Winners are set for life. And while losers don't exactly get a one-way ticket to Palookaville, they're often devastated. Some lock themselves in their offices for hours. Others miss days of work.

They console themselves with their $500,000 salaries and dreams of better luck next time.

Goldman is enjoying fat profits—perhaps a record $650 million this year [1990]—even as much of Wall Street is mired in a deep slump. That makes partnerships bigger trophies than ever: Besides an annual salary of a tax-free $150,000, partners share in those profits. . . .

Before the most recent appointments, Goldman could count just one woman partner out of 128—embarrassing even on male-dominated Wall Street. Besides this, the partners knew they would drive away some good people who didn't get the nod.

David Elfrig, a top futures salesman, bolted Goldman in July after he saw his path blocked. He says he knew he couldn't beat out two managers in his department with far more experience than his four years. "I was looking at eight years out," says Mr. Elfrig, now

---

This chapter launches our study of OB in a new direction. Whereas we drew heavily upon the field of psychology in Part II, we now gather ideas from the fields of sociology and social psychology. Our primary focus shifts from the individual to interpersonal and intergroup behavior. Once again, OB is an interdisciplinary field with roots in all the behavioral sciences and beyond.

This chapter explores how organizations and individuals try to match their respective needs and desires. Figure 8–1 depicts the steps in this process as a guide for our discussion. Organizations rely on organizational socialization to encourage employees to exhibit desired behaviors. This is accomplished through a variety of socialization techniques that reinforce and support organizational roles and norms. At the individual level, employees use career management to facilitate the match between their needs and values and organizational requirements. Ultimately, one's work attitudes and stress are partly determined by the effectiveness of career management.

OPENING CASE 8

(continued)

at Chase Manhattan Bank. "It didn't make sense."

Exactly what goes on behind the scenes of the two-month-long competition is a closely held secret. Current partners paint it, of course, as a rigorous but fair process in which politics is unimportant. ("I think the partnership process is one of the best things we do," incoming co-chairman Stephen Friedman says. "And we're trying to do it better.") Losing candidates don't want to talk about it for fear of hurting their chances next time around. And most people who leave Goldman just don't want to talk about it at all. . . .

It started with winnowing down the worldwide work force of 6,600 to a list of 50 to 60 serious candidates. After a complicated procedure involving written nominations, a cross-examination of candidates' qualifications and an 11th-hour "town meeting" of all partners, Goldman named 32 new

members to its exclusive club, now numbering 148. It added three women; now there are four. There is still one black.

The first step is for current partners to nominate new partners. What are they looking for? Not toadies, they insist. People at Goldman snipe about one would-be partner a couple of years ago who joined the same health club as many of the partners, played basketball with one and bought another's home. He still hasn't been named a partner, though.

And Goldman denies that it is looking for automatons willing to give up their entire lives for the firm. That isn't how some people see it. "They brainwash you," says Mr. Elfrig. Claims a former trader who never made partner: "They want you to think, feel and dream about the place. They want your life."

Instead, Goldman says it is simply looking for what it calls "culture carriers," people willing

to fit into a rich tradition dating back to the 1860s, when Marcus Goldman began hawking commercial paper on the streets of New York. Because of the partnership, Goldman has had smoother leadership transitions than other Wall Street firms.

Goldman says there is no "checklist" for what makes partnership material. But it does say it is looking for team players. "If you can't sublimate your ego or work with others, you have a problem," says Geoffrey Boisi, a top partner.

Candidates face enormous pressure to conform to Goldman's conservative style. . . .

At Goldman, the hot tempers and irreverent sense of humor seen frequently at other Wall Street firms are taboo. A few years ago, a Goldman partner was talking with one talented candidate about his abilities, pointing out that the firm boasted several

---

This chapter describes those important components of the individual/organization interface: (1) organizational socialization, (2) socialization techniques, (3) organizational roles and norms, (4) career management, and (5) career transitions.

• THE ORGANIZATIONAL SOCIALIZATION PROCESS

Joining the military, going to college, pledging a sorority or fraternity, taking a full-time job, and getting transferred have more in common than initially meets the eye. In each case, the individual experiences the shaping process called organizational socialization. As shown in Figure 8–2, this process involves many sources of influence, some of which are beyond management's direct control. One authority on the subject refers to **organizational socialization** as "people processing" and defines it as "the process by which a person learns the values, norms, and required behaviors which permit him

OPENING CASE 8

(continued)

top athletes and a chess champion. The candidate shot back: "I can pick up girls in singles bars." The Goldman executive wasn't amused. "I'd like you to change your humor," he responded. The candidate has since left Goldman. . . .

Goldman also demands total commitment. Partners are expected to cheerfully answer 2 A.M. phone calls from work and fly off on recruiting trips at a moment's notice. Veteran stock trader Robert Mnuchin, who announced his retirement a few weeks ago, says he loved his 33-year Goldman career, but "I'd like to have breakfast with my wife for once." . . .

More than 100 people were nominated, and Ms. Illgen, the real-estate specialist, knew she was one of the 50 or 60 serious candidates. Since joining Goldman in 1982 as a junior investment banker, she had thrown herself into her job, with little time for much else. That meant at least 12-hour work days, plus six hours on Sundays, helping blue-chip clients

buy and sell commercial real estate. She rested only on Saturday, to observe the Jewish Sabbath.

Ms. Illgen, 36, had increasing trouble reading or even thinking as decision day drew closer. Mr. Ahooja dealt with the pressure by leaving work aside Monday to play tennis. The 39-year-old India native and Harvard M.B.A. took a major gamble on his career a few years ago by moving from the then-booming investment banking department to the unglamorous operations division, which runs computers and processes securities trades.

Mr. Witten, 36, had reason to be superstitious. Two years ago, the Harvard-educated lawyer missed making partner after seven years at the firm. His division head pulled him aside shortly before the new partners were announced and assured him he was a valued employee who shouldn't "get the wrong message."

John McNulty, a 37-year-old capital-markets executive, calmed himself by remembering advice he had heard: After 3,000 working

days before being considered for partner, there wasn't much he could do to change things in the last 30 days.

Mr. McNulty, a Wharton M.B.A., coordinated the marketing for Goldman's successful $750 million Water Street Recovery Fund, which will invest in financially distressed companies. The son of an Irish immigrant gardener, Mr. McNulty grew up in a working-class neighborhood in Philadelphia and never dreamed of becoming an investment banker. "I thought if I made $100 a week, I'd be happy," he says.

A Goldman partner does considerably better than that. A typical candidate at Goldman in his or her mid-30s already makes half a million or more a year. The first reward for making partner is to take maybe a two-thirds reduction in salary. But on paper, new partners immediately become wealthy. They are entitled to a cut of Goldman's future profits, which averaged $5 million a partner last year, before taxes.

A partner's cut typically starts

to participate as a member of the organization."[1] In short, organizational socialization turns outsiders into fully functioning insiders. Consider how Lincoln Electric, a well-run manufacturing company located in Cleveland, Ohio, begins the socialization process.

> When this spring's crop of MBA types arrive, including four from Harvard, they will be rolling up their French cuffs for four to ten weeks of real hands-on training—at the company's welding school. Lincoln makes electric arc-welding equipment; management reasons that everyone in a position of responsibility should know how the gear works. From there, recruits proceed through as much as a year of on-the-job training in a specialty.[2]

The socialization process is an anxiety-producing time because newcomers—called recruits, new hires, rookies, pledges, trainees, or appren-

OPENING CASE 8

(concluded)

at $1 million, but within a few years can balloon to well over $10 million a year. . . .

The departures of retired partners made room for more partners, but didn't make the process much easier. After weeks of informal lobbying and quiet investigation, the management committee moved into a more formal phase. This year, recognizing that Goldman isn't the close-knit place it once was and not everybody knows everybody, the management committee established a process it called "crossruffing," a term from the game of bridge. Members of the management committee who weren't in a certain candidate's division were assigned to grill department heads and other partners about the nominee's qualifications, then report back. . . .

On Monday, all of the partners gathered in a spartan second-floor conference room at Goldman for the traditional "town meeting." As always, the room was quiet and filled with anticipation. Mr. Weinberg talked about tradition

and ethics—and finally presented the list. . . .

Telling the winners on Tuesday is the easy part. Breaking bad news is another matter. Goldman wants to let people down easy, both to keep them from being personally devastated and also to keep them at the firm. Goldman partners lapse into sports metaphors to convince young executives that it's worth staying. The "team" has a "great bench" but only several "starting slots," the losers are often told. And they are reminded that Goldman isn't a law firm, where it's "up or out." There's always next time.

Of the 32 people who got good news, the average age is 36, and they tell a lot about the firm's strategy for the '90s. Although 20 percent of the firm's operations are overseas, until this year only 10 percent of partners were based abroad. Goldman named eight new partners from its European and Tokyo operations, areas that had hardly any partners despite their growing importance.

Ms. Illgen, the real-estate in-

vestment banker, walked into the office Tuesday at 8:40 A.M. There was an 8:33 phone message from Mr. Weinberg. "Do you want to become a partner at Goldman Sachs?" he asked.

Mr. Ahooja, the operations executive, and Mr. McNulty, the capital-markets executive, got good news, too. And so did the superstitious Mr. Witten.

Fortunately, his wife had quietly hidden a bottle of champagne in the refrigerator.

For Discussion

Would you be willing to make the sacrifices necessary to become a partner at Goldman Sachs?

• Additional discussion questions linking this case with the following material appear at the end of this chapter.

Source: Excerpted from William Power and Michael Siconolfi, "Who Will Be Rich?" How Goldman Sachs Chooses New Partners: with a Lot of Angst." *The Wall Street Journal*, October 19, 1990, pp. A1, A8. Reprinted by permission of *The Wall Street Journal*, © 1990 Dow Jones & Company, Inc. All rights reserved Worldwide.

tices—must adapt or fall by the wayside. This section introduces a three-phase model of organizational socialization and examines the practical application of socialization research.

Present and future managers need to have a working knowledge of organizational socialization for at least four reasons. *First,* such understanding can enhance one's chances of successfully clearing the career hurdles into and through the organized world of work. *Second,* human resource management specialists report there is a turnover epidemic among recent college graduates. Moreover, management experts estimate that this problem will become more severe in response to organizational restructuring.[3] Organizations can counter this costly trend by skillfully managing the socialization process. *Third,* because socialization helps people transition into productive employees, effective socialization can increase both job satisfaction and productiv-

• **FIGURE 8-1**   Facilitating the Individual/Organizational Match

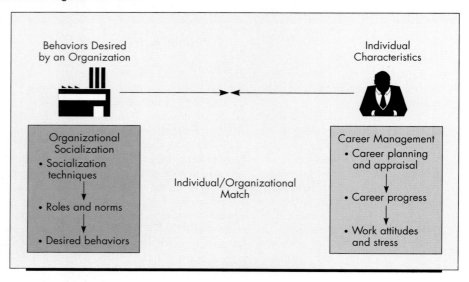

• **FIGURE 8-2**   Newcomers Receive Information from a Variety of Sources during the Socialization Process

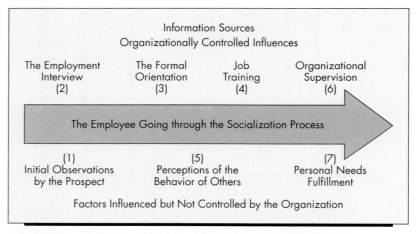

Source: Reprinted, by permission of the publisher, from "First Impressions: How They Affect Long-Term Performance," R. Thomas George, *Supervisory Management*, March 1986, p. 6, © (1986) American Management Association, New York. All rights reserved.

ity. *Fourth,* more effective socialization programs help enhance an organization's continuity and chances of survival in an increasingly competitive world.

A Three-Phase Model of Organizational Socialization

One's first year in a complex organization can be confusing. There is a constant swirl of new faces, strange jargon, conflicting expectations, and apparently unrelated events. Some organizations treat new members in a

• Through organizational socialization, the U.S. Marine Corps. attracts recruits, then takes them through the hurdles that shapes them into productive members of the Corps. *(U.S. Marine Corps)*

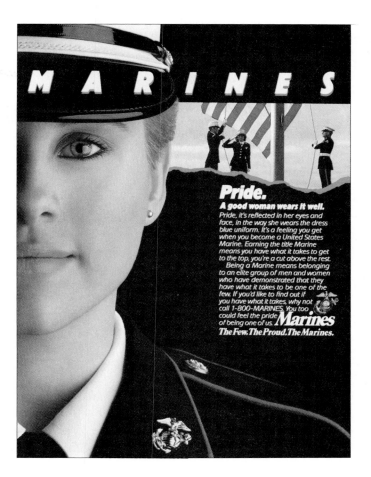

rather haphazard, sink-or-swim manner. More typically, though, the socialization process is characterized by a sequence of identifiable steps.[4]

Organizational behavior researcher Daniel Feldman has proposed a three-phase model of organizational socialization that promotes deeper understanding of this important process. As illustrated in Figure 8–3, the three phases are: (1) anticipatory socialization, (2) encounter, and (3) change and acquisition. Each phase has its associated perceptual and social processes. Feldman's model also specifies behavioral and affective outcomes that can be used to judge how well the individual has been socialized. The entire three-phase sequence may take from a few weeks to a year to complete, depending on individual differences and the complexity of the situation.

Phase 1: Anticipatory Socialization   Organizational socialization begins *before* the individual actually joins the organization. Anticipatory socialization information comes from many sources. U.S. Marine recruiting ads, for example, prepare future recruits for a rough-and-tumble experience. Widely circulated stories about IBM being the "white shirt" company probably deter from applying those who would prefer working in jeans. And a manager at Steelcase, a Michigan-based maker of office systems, told the editor of *Management Review:* "We have many second- and third-generation employees, who are loyal workers before they even join the company."[5]

• FIGURE 8-3   A Model of Organizational Socialization

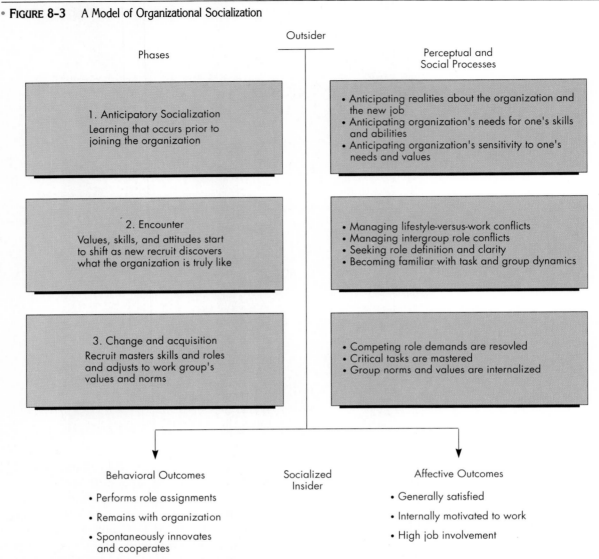

Source: Adapted from material in Daniel C. Feldman, "The Multiple Socialization of Organization Members," *Academy of Management Review*, April 1981, pp. 309–18.

All of this information—whether formal or informal, accurate or inaccurate—helps the individual anticipate organizational realities. Unrealistic expectations about the nature of the work, pay, and promotions are often formulated during phase 1. Fortunately, management can curb unrealistic expectations by relying on the psychological contracting and realistic job preview techniques discussed later in this chapter.

Phase 2: Encounter   This second phase begins when the employment contract has been signed. It is a time for surprise and making sense as the newcomer enters unfamiliar territory. Behavioral scientists warn that **reality shock** can occur during the encounter phase.

> Becoming a member of an organization will upset the everyday order of even the most well-informed newcomer. Matters concerning such aspects as friendships, time, purpose, demeanor, competence, and the expectations the person holds of the immediate and distant future are suddenly made problematic. The newcomer's most pressing task is to build a set of guidelines and interpretations to explain and make meaningful the myriad of activities observed as going on in the organization.[6]

During the encounter phase, the individual is challenged to resolve any conflicts between the job and outside interests. If the hours prove too long, for example, family duties may require the individual to quit and find a more suitable work schedule. Also, as indicated in Figure 8–3, role conflict stemming from competing demands of different groups needs to be confronted and resolved.

Phase 3: Change and Acquisition   Mastery of important tasks and resolution of role conflict signals the beginning of this final phase of the socialization process. Those who do not make the transition to phase 3 leave voluntarily or involuntarily or become network isolates.

Practical Application of Socialization Research

Although credible research results in this area have begun to appear only recently, findings suggest four practical guidelines for managing organizational socialization:

1. Managers should avoid a haphazard, sink-or-swim approach to organizational socialization. Socialization needs to be managed systematically so newcomers get a clear idea of what is expected of them.[7]

2. The encounter phase of socialization is particularly important. Studies of newly hired managers at AT&T demonstrated that early job challenge was positively correlated with later performance.[8] It appears that employees develop higher work standards when they are challenged from day one. Managers thus are encouraged to challenge new hires, rather than overextend or bore them.

3. There are gender-based differences regarding the perceived helpfulness of socialization activities. A study of 134 males and 83 females indicated that women derived fewer benefits from socialization than did their male counterparts.[9] These results suggest that managers should be attentive to differential needs and expectations between men and women.

4. Support for stage models is mixed. Although there are different stages of socialization, they are not identical in order, length, or content for all people or jobs.[10] Managers are advised to use a contingency approach toward organizational socialization. In other words, different techniques, discussed in the next section, are appropriate for different people at different times.

• SOCIALIZATION TECHNIQUES

Returning to Figure 8–1, note that socialization techniques are used to reinforce organizational roles and norms that support desirable organizational behavior. This section discusses four frequently used techniques; psychological contracts, realistic job previews, behavior modeling, and mentoring.

Psychological Contracts

Although not readily apparent, new employees have two overlapping contracts with their employers. First, and most widely recognized, is the employment contract. This typically is a legal document specifying such things as compensation, hours, and conditions of employment. In addition, there is a *psychological* contract that encompasses and goes beyond the employment contract. According to a personnel research psychologist, "The **psychological contract** is the sum total of all written and unwritten, spoken and unspoken, expectations of the employer and employee."[11] Employees have implicit expectations about pay raises, promotions, and job security. Meanwhile, employers have their own expectations about the individual's loyalty, willingness to learn, and creativity.[12] Problems arise when these unwritten and unspoken expectations turn out to be unrealistic.

Unmet Expectations   Individuals begin to formulate their side of the psychological contract before they join the organization. Subsequent to the signing of an employment contract, the psychological contract evolves and shifts as employee and employer modify their expectations for each other. Problems can and do arise when either party in the psychological contract feels cheated. Anyone who has not gotten an expected promotion can attest to the dampening effect unmet expectations can have on job satisfaction and performance. Likewise, managers feel cheated when their expectations for an employee's performance go unmet. Conflict between students and teachers over course requirements and grades generally can be traced to psychological contracts and mistaken assumptions about mutual expectations.

Surfacing the Psychological Contract   Employers and employees alike are urged to openly discuss the terms of their psychological contracts. The idea is to improve individual-organization fit by bringing unrealistic expectations into line with reality. This psychological contracting can be done before, during, and/or after actual hiring. Personnel specialists claim free discussion of mutual expectations will enhance satisfaction and performance while reducing turnover. As a practical example, the U.S. Navy is attempting to improve enlistment rates, job performance, morale, and reenlistment rates by having its recruiters discuss psychological contracts more openly and skillfully (see OB in Action).

Although very little research has examined the effectiveness of psychological contracts in work settings, counselors and psychologists view this technique as a prerequisite for achieving any type of behavioral change.[13]

OB IN ACTION

How the U.S. Navy Is Doing a Better Job of Handling Psychological Contracts

The Navy's enlistment program has been improved in the following ways:

1. A general increase in the amount of information delivered by the recruiter or classifier regarding Navy lifestyle, recruit training, and so on.
2. More comprehensive, factual and detailed presentation of Navy career opportunities, rating and assignment possibility in a consistent and unbiased fashion.
3. More extensive exploration of applicant job values, educational aspirations, desired working conditions, aptitudes, interests, motivations, and career goals before enlistment.
4. Improvement of the fit between Navy requirements and policies and individual aptitudes and interests.

Source: Excerpted from Herbert George Baker, ''The Unwritten Contract: Job Perceptions,'' *Personnel Journal*, July 1985, p. 40.

Realistic Job Previews

During the recruiting process, newcomers typically are told about the good things they can expect from the organization. For example, they may hear about the paid holidays, the recreational facilities, and the new family dental insurance plan. Unfortunately, these good-news-only job previews tell the individual very little about what he or she will be doing each day. Too often the result is the same. The person's unrealistically high expectations come crashing down after a few weeks on the job and he or she quits. Take the case of Lynda McDermott, for example:

> To Lynda McDermott, the job offer sounded ideal. So she left her position at an accounting firm and became executive vice president of a fledgling management consulting company in New York, a job that her new boss said would allow her to play a major role in landing new business. . . .
>
> Eleven months later she quit. Her boss, she says, had immediately relegated her to administrative duties, a far cry from the role she had expected. . . .
>
> As Ms. McDermott sees it, she was a victim of a job bait-and-switch. Promised the world as an applicant, the new employee eventually realizes that the job is something quite different, leading to disgruntlement, stalled careers and costly turnover.[14]

A **realistic job preview (RJP)** involves giving recruits such as Lynda McDermott a realistic idea of what lies ahead by presenting both positive and negative aspects of the job. RJPs may be verbal, in booklet form, audiovisual, or hands-on.

The Psychology of RJPs   There are two major outcomes associated with using RJPs (see Figure 8–4). First, a frank presentation of the job's positive and

• FIGURE 8-4   The Desired Psychological Outcomes of Realistic Job Previews

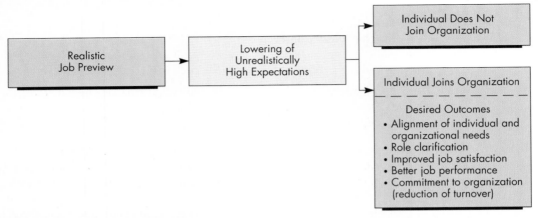

Source: Adapted from John P. Wanous, "Realistic Job Previews: Can a Procedure to Reduce Turnover Also Influence the Relationship between Abilities and Performance?" *Personnel Psychology,* Summer 1978, p. 251.

negative aspects may convince recruits with unrealistic expectations to seek employment elsewhere. This increases the possibility of avoiding some early turnover. Second, recruits, whose unrealistically high expectations are lowered by an RJP, may decide to join the organization. These individuals are more likely to experience subsequent job satisfaction and decreased turnover because of a better match between individual and organization needs.[15] Let us now consider the managerial application of RJP research.[16]

Managerial Application of RJP Research   RJPs produce favorable results. Their most significant contribution is to lower a recruit's unrealistically high expectations. RJPs thus appear to be particularly suited for hiring new employees with high career expectations. Moreover, a meta-analysis of 21 RJP experiments that included 9,166 subjects demonstrated that RJPs increased job satisfaction and decreased turnover.[17] These results suggest that managers can use RJPs to positively affect satisfaction and turnover. Finally, RJPs are more effective for complex, higher-paying jobs than for routine jobs that pay comparatively less.[18]

Behavior Modeling

Also known as observational learning or vicarious learning, **behavior modeling** is a learning process by which one observes and imitates the behavior of relevant others. According to social learning theorist Albert Bandura, "One of the fundamental means by which new modes of behavior are acquired and existing patterns are modified entails modeling and vicarious processes."[19] A pair of OB experts more recently added:

> The fundamental characteristic of modeling is that learning takes place, *not* through actual experience, but through observation or imitation of another individual's experience. Modeling is a "vicarious process," which implies sharing in the experience of another person through imagination or sympathetic participation.[20]

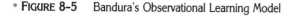

• **FIGURE 8-5**   Bandura's Observational Learning Model

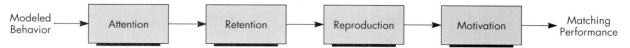

Sports fans who wildly celebrate when their favorite team wins the championship are engaging in a vicarious process. Organizational newcomers, who are especially hungry for sense-making information regarding what to do, whom to trust, and so forth, acquire a great deal of adaptive behavior through behavior modeling.

From an organizational perspective, people learn both productive and counter-productive behavior by watching and imitating others. For example, a new employee in a furniture factory might observe that old-timers can turn out work faster by removing the safety guards from their power saws. Of course, the supervisor should discourage this behavior because it could lead to a painful and costly accident.

Let us examine the underlying process by which people learn from behavior modeling.

Bandura's Observational Learning Model   According to Bandura, successful behavior modeling depends on the four subprocesses illustrated in Figure 8–5. Note the similarities between this model and the model of perception discussed in Chapter 4. Before someone else's behavior can be imitated, it must be attended to and retained. Then it must be attempted (or reproduced) and achieve adequate motivational support if it is to endure (see International OB). Relative to organizational socialization, training programs make extensive use of behavior models today via films and videotaped role playing.

Modeling: Practical Research Insights   The primary research thrust in this area has centered on the use of behavior models in industrial training programs.[21] A supervisory training program developed during the 1970s by Melvin Sorcher, an industrial psychologist at General Electric, is the most widely used approach. Called ''Applied Learning,'' Sorcher's training program is based on the following four steps:

1. *Modeling,* in which small groups of supervisor–trainees watch filmed supervisor and employee models interact in effective ways in a problem situation.
2. *Role-playing,* in which the trainees take part in extensive practice and rehearsal of the specific behaviors demonstrated by the models. As their role-play behaviors become more and more similar to the models:
3. *Social reinforcement* (praise, reward, constructive feedback) is provided by both the trainers and other trainees. These three procedures are implemented in such a way that:
4. *Transfer of training* from classroom to job setting is encouraged.[22]

Marriott Uses Behavior Modeling to Train New Polish Managers

Modeling was central to the approach that Marriott adopted to meet a remarkable challenge in opening the Warsaw Marriott, Poland's first Western-owned hotel. In late 1987, two years before it opened, the company recruited 20 Polish managers, none with lodging-industry background. Says Haile Aguilar, a 17-year Marriott veteran who is now the Warsaw Marriott's general manager: "A sense of hospitality is not characteristic of hotels in Poland. We wanted people with no experience and a willingness to learn from us."

The Poles flew to Boston, where Marriott managers led classroom discussions in matters such as running a smooth room-service operation and taking accurate messages for guests. Says Dorota Kowalska, the Warsaw hotel's director of human resources: "Role-playing helped more than three hours of lectures because it made the trainees think like customers."

When the trainees returned home, they hired and instructed a staff of 1,000. Quickly they proved that bosses don't have to be behind-closed-door dictators. Says Kowalska, 32, the daughter of a Polish diplomat and previously a teacher of English, French, and Arabic in Warsaw: "Seeing the executive director of food and beverage actually clear tables in the breakfast room was something our people had never experienced before." Now her compatriots are passing up lunch breaks and working extra-long hours, for the sake of caring for the guests. And the Warsaw Marriott, which attracts mostly Westerners, has been earning even higher customer satisfaction ratings than Marriott's U.S. hotels.

On-the-job research demonstrates the practical value of Sorcher's modeling program. In one carefully controlled experiment, 20 supervisors were encouraged to imitate filmed behavior models successfully handling common interpersonal problems. Among those problems were giving orientations and recognition, improving poor work habits, and overcoming resistance to change. One year after the training, the trainees' job performance was rated as significantly better than that for a matched control group of 20 supervisors.[23] Thanks to this sort of practical research, experts have offered some instructive modeling tips for managers (see Table 8–1).

Mentoring

Mentoring is defined as the process of forming and maintaining an intensive and lasting developmental relationship between a senior person (the mentor) and a junior person (the protégé, if male; or protégée, if female). The modern word *mentor* derives from Mentor, the name of a wise and trusted counselor in Greek mythology. Terms typically used in connection with mentoring are *teacher, coach, godfather,* and *sponsor*. Although mentoring often occurs

• **Table 8-1**   Using Behavior Models Effectively in Employee Training Programs

	Observational Learning
Subprocess	**Practical Tips**
Attention	1. Behavior models tend to attract more attention when: a. They have high status and/or credibility in the trainees' eyes. b. The complexity of the modeled behavior is appropriate to the trainees' capabilities. c. The modeled behavior is repeated two or more times. d. The modeled behavior is presented in an appealing, detailed, and vivid manner.
Retention	2. Modeled behavior tends to be retained when trainees rehearse and practice it both mentally and behaviorally.
Reproduction/motivation	3. Modeled behavior tends to be imitated when trainees are appropriately reinforced or rewarded for doing so.

Source: Adapted from Henry P. Sims, Jr., and Charles C. Manz, "Modeling Influences on Employee Behavior," *Personnel Journal,* January 1982, p. 62.

• Mentoring, which influenced the development of Alexander the Great (356–323 B.C.), continues to play a major role in enhancing people's careers.   *(Steve Leonard/Tony Stone Worldwide)*

naturally, it sometimes is actively managed as part of career development or management succession programs. Consider the mentoring programs at Johnson & Johnson, Pacific Bell, and Bell Laboratories, for example:

> A Johnson & Johnson Co. unit, Ortho Pharmaceutical Corp., assigns mentors to the college graduates it hires. . . . At Pacific Bell, a unit of Pacific Telesis Group, the firm's 75 summer management interns, hired after their junior year in college, get mentors; the mentors later help decide whether the interns will be offered permanent jobs. The system is credited with drawing better-quality new hires.
>
> AT&T Bell Laboratories gives new employees "technical mentors" to help them learn their jobs, and assigns advisors to women and minority hires.[24]

Functions of Mentoring Kathy Kram, a Boston University researcher, conducted in-depth interviews with both members of 18 pairs of senior and junior managers. Each pair exhibited a significant developmental relationship. All the subjects worked for a large public utility in the northeastern United States. While there were seven female protégées, only one of the mentors was a woman.[25] As a by-product of this study, Kram identified two general functions—career and psychosocial—of the mentoring process (see Figure 8–6). Five *career functions* that enhanced career development were sponsorship, exposure-and-visibility, coaching, protection, and challenging assignments. Four *psychosocial functions* were role modeling, acceptance-and-confirmation, counseling, and friendship. The psychosocial functions clarified the participants' identities and enhanced their feelings of competence.

Both members of the mentoring relationship can benefit from these career and psychosocial functions. Mentoring is not strictly a top-down proposition, as many mistakenly believe. According to a team of mentoring experts:

• **FIGURE 8-6** The Career and Psychosocial Functions of Mentoring

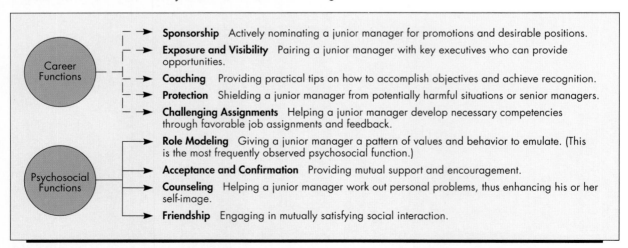

Source: Adapted from discussion in Kathy E. Kram, *Mentoring at Work: Developmental Relationships in Organizational Life* (Glenview, Ill.: Scott, Foresman, 1985), pp. 22–39.

The mentor is also doing something for himself. The mentor is making productive use of his own knowledge and skill . . . and is learning in ways that would otherwise not be possible for him. Thus the mentoring relationship is one of mutual benefit.[26]

Phases of Mentoring   In addition to identifying the functions of mentoring, Kram's research revealed four phases of the mentoring process: (1) initiation, (2) cultivation, (3) separation, and (4) redefinition. As indicated in Table 8–2, the phases involve *variable* rather than fixed time periods. Tell-

• **TABLE 8–2**   Phases of the Mentor Relationship

Phase	Definition	Turning Points*
Initiation	A period of six months to a year during which time the relationship gets started and begins to have importance for both managers.	Fantasies become concrete expectations. Expectations are met; senior manager provides coaching, challenging work, visibility; junior manager provides technical assistance, respect, and desire to be coached. There are opportunities for interaction around work tasks.
Cultivation	A period of two to five years during which time the range of career and psychosocial functions provided expand to a maximum.	Both individuals continue to benefit from the relationship. Opportunities for meaningful and more frequent interaction increase. Emotional bond deepens and intimacy increases.
Separation	A period of six months to two years after a significant change in the structural role relationship and/or in the emotional experience of the relationship.	Junior manager no longer wants guidance but rather the opportunity to work more autonomously. Senior manager faces midlife crisis and is less available to provide mentoring functions. Job rotation or promotion limits opportunities for continued interaction; career and psychosocial functions can no longer be provided. Blocked opportunity creates resentment and hostility that disrupts positive interaction.
Redefinition	An indefinite period after the separation phase, during which time the relationship is ended or takes on significantly different characteristics, making it a more peerlike friendship.	Stresses of separation diminish, and new relationships are formed. The mentor relationship is no longer needed in its previous form. Resentment and anger diminish; gratitude and appreciation increase. Peer status is achieved.

*Examples of the most frequently observed psychological and organizational factors that cause movement into the current relationship phase.

Source: Kathy E. Kram, "Phases of the Mentor Relationship," *Academy of Management Journal*, December 1983, p. 622. Used with permission.

tale turning points signal the evolution from one phase to the next. For example, when a junior manager begins to resist guidance and strives to work more autonomously, the separation phase begins. The mentoring relationships in Kram's sample lasted an average of five years.

Research Evidence on Mentoring   Research findings uncovered both individual and organizational benefits of mentoring programs. Individual benefits include career mobility and increased pay and job satisfaction. For example, a recent study of 147 women and 173 men indicated that individuals who were extensively mentored received more promotions, had higher incomes, and were more satisfied with their jobs than individuals who experienced little mentoring.[27] Research also investigated the dynamics of cross-gender mentoring.

Because of the underrepresentation of women in executive-level positions, the most common cross-gender mentor relationship is a male mentor and female protégée. Relationships of this type have long been considered problematic due to the potential for romantic involvement. Results of 32 mentor–protégée pairings (14 male–female; 18 female–female) suggest that male–female mentor relationships are more beneficial than harmful. According to the researcher:

> It would appear that the most productive mentoring functions occur *after* the initial attraction of identification has mellowed. From a practical perspective, it may be that we should stop advising young women to avoid or maintain their distance with male mentors despite the acknowledged possibility that sexual entanglements can emerge. If, as was found in this sample, male mentors are at least as likely (if not more so) to provide psychosocial functions for female protégées, young women may find cross-sex mentoring uniquely valuable.[28]

Research also supports the organizational benefits of mentoring. In addition to the obvious benefit of employee development, mentoring enhances the effectiveness of organizational communication. Specifically, mentoring increases the amount of vertical communication both up and down an organization and it provides a mechanism for modifying or reinforcing organizational culture.[29]

Getting the Most Out of Mentoring   Mentoring can be an informal, spontaneous process or a formally structured one. As examples of the latter approach, both Schering-Plough, a pharmaceutical company, and J. Walter Thompson Advertising Agency assign new employees to carefully screened mentors.[30] Regardless of the approach taken, it is important to realize that mentoring has been zealously oversold in recent years. Some managers do not want to be a mentor or a protégé. If managers are forced into such roles by a formal mentoring program, resistance and resentment could damage relationships and careers.

A workable alternative involves establishing a career development program that fosters the performance of mentoring functions and behaviors without forcing artificial relationships. This organizational climate encourages emergence of informal and trusting relationships that are essential to successful mentoring.

• ORGANIZATIONAL ROLES AND NORMS

Employees need to behave with a fairly high degree of predictability if organizations are to accomplish their objectives. Imagine what it would be like if a teller at your local bank stopped in the middle of your transaction and said it was time to go shopping! Formal policies, rules, regulations, and socialization techniques foster predictable job behavior. But other, more subtle forces are at work as well. In this section, the subtle yet powerful social forces behavioral scientists call *roles* and *norms* are examined.

Roles

Nearly four centuries have passed since William Shakespeare had his character Jaques speak the following memorable lines in Act II of *As You Like It:* "All the world's a stage, And all the men and women merely players; They have their exits and their entrances; And one man in his time plays many parts. . . ." This intriguing notion of all people as actors in a universal play was not lost on 20th-century sociologists who developed a complex theory of human interaction based on roles. According to an OB scholar, "**roles** are sets of behaviors that persons expect of occupants of a position."[31] Role theory attempts to explain how these social expectations influence employee behavior. This section explores role theory by analyzing a role episode and defining the terms *role overload, role conflict,* and *role ambiguity.*

Role Episodes A role episode, as illustrated in Figure 8–7, consists of a snapshot of the ongoing interaction between two people. In any given role episode, there is a role sender and a focal person who is expected to act out the role. Within a broader context, one may be simultaneously a role sender and a focal person. For the sake of social analysis, however, it is instructive to deal with separate role episodes.

Role episodes begin with the role sender's perception of the relevant organization's or group's behavioral requirements. Those requirements serve as a standard for formulating expectations for the focal person's behavior. The role sender then cognitively evaluates the focal person's

---

 **FIGURE 8-7**   A Role Episode

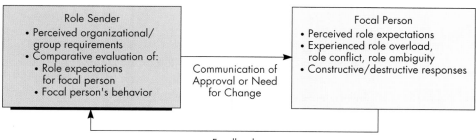

Source: Adapted in part from Robert L. Kahn, Donald M. Wolfe, Robert P. Quinn, and J. Diedrick Snoek, *Organizational Stress: Studies in Role Conflict and Ambiguity,* 1981 edition (Malabar, Fla.: Robert E. Krieger Publishing Co., 1964), p. 26.

actual behavior against those expectations. Appropriate verbal and nonverbal messages are then sent to the focal person to pressure him or her into behaving as expected. Consider how Westinghouse used a carrot-and-stick approach to communicate role expectations.

> The carrot is a plan, that since 1984, has rewarded 134 managers with options to buy 764,000 shares of stock for boosting the company's financial performance.
>
> The stick is quarterly meetings that are used to rank managers by how much their operations contribute to earnings per share. The soft-spoken . . . [chairman of the board] doesn't scold. He just charts in green the results of the sectors that have met their goals and charts the laggards in red. Peer pressure does the rest. Shame "is a powerful tool," says one executive.[32]

On the receiving end of the role episode, the focal person accurately or inaccurately perceives the communicated role expectations. Various combinations of role overload, role conflict, and role ambiguity are then experienced. (These three outcomes are defined and discussed in the following sections.) The focal person then responds constructively by engaging in problem solving, for example, or destructively because of undue tension, stress, and strain.[33] Stress is discussed in detail in Chapter 16.

Role Overload   According to organizational psychologist Edgar Schein, **role overload** occurs when "the sum total of what role senders expect of the focal person far exceeds what he or she is able to do."[34] Students who attempt to handle a full course load and maintain a decent social life while working 30 or more hours a week know full well the consequences of role overload. As the individual tries to do more and more in less and less time, stress mounts and personal effectiveness slips.

Role Conflict   Have you ever felt like you were being torn apart by the conflicting demands of those around you? If so, you were a victim of role conflict. **Role conflict** is experienced when "different members of the role set expect different things of the focal person."[35] Managers often face conflicting demands between work and family, for example. Interestingly, however, women experience greater role conflict between work and family than men because women perform the majority of the household duties and child care responsibilities (see International OB).[36]

Role conflict also may be experienced when internalized values, ethics, or personal standards collide with others' expectations. For instance, an otherwise ethical production supervisor may be told by a superior to "fudge a little" on the quality control reports so an important deadline will be met. The resulting role conflict forces the supervisor to choose between being loyal but unethical or ethical but disloyal. Tough ethical choices such as this mean personal turmoil, interpersonal conflict, and even resignation. Consequently, experts say business schools should do a better job of weaving ethics training into their course requirements.

Role Ambiguity   Those who experience role conflict may have trouble complying with role demands, but they at least know what is expected of them. Such is not the case with **role ambiguity,** which occurs when "members of the role set fail to communicate to the focal person expectations they have or

INTERNATIONAL OB

Women in China and in the United States Both Experience Role Conflict between Work and Family Responsibilities

How to cope with the "Superwoman Syndrome" emerged as a major topic of discussion among more than 500 Chinese and American experts at a conference on women's issues. . . .

One central theme of the meeting, which covered women's career advancement, education and training, well-being, and child care, was how Chinese and American women combine family and work. Women from both countries say they feel under pressure to play multiple roles, performing the duties of a traditional wife and mother while achieving professionally.

"Chinese professional women face a great burden of work and family," says Wang Xingjuan, President of the Women's Research Center in Beijing.

"If they don't have a job, they have no social standing, no voice in the family—they have to 'eat the husband's rice,'" says Ms. Wang. "So they want to leave the home. But when they return, they have two to four hours of housework to do." . . .

Women in America walk a tightrope of wanting to do it all; of being nurturing and contributing in their families and at work, and at the same time being relaxed and at peace with their results," says Professor Eberhart [a professor at Palomar College in California].

Source: Excerpted from Ann Scott Tyson, "Women in China, US See Common Problems, Goals," *The Christian Science Monitor*, July 6, 1990, p. 5. © 1990 The Christian Science Publishing Society. All rights reserved.

information needed to perform the role, either because they do not have the information or because they deliberately withhold it."[37] In short, people experience role ambiguity when they do not know what is expected of them. Organizational newcomers often complain about unclear job descriptions and vague promotion criteria. According to role theory, prolonged role ambiguity can foster job dissatisfaction, erode self-confidence, and hamper job performance.

Take a moment now to complete the self-assessment exercise in the OB Exercise. See if you can distinguish between sources of role conflict and sources of role ambiguity, as they affect your working life.

Norms

Norms are more encompassing than roles. While roles involve behavioral expectations for specific positions, norms help organizational members determine right from wrong and good from bad. According to one respected team of management consultants: "A **norm** is an attitude, opinion, feeling, or action—shared by two or more people—that guides their behavior."[39] Although norms are typically unwritten and seldom discussed openly, they have a powerful influence on group and organizational behavior. PepsiCo Inc., for instance, has evolved a norm that equates corporate competitiveness with physical fitness. According to observers:

• OB EXERCISE

Measuring Role Conflict and Role Ambiguity

Instructions:

Step 1: While thinking of your present (or last) job, circle one response for each of the following statements. Please consider each statement carefully because some are worded positively and some negatively.

Step 2: In the space in the far right column, label each statement with either a "C" for role conflict or an "A" for role ambiguity. (See note 38 for a correct categorization.)

Step 3: Calculate separate totals for role conflict and role ambiguity and compare them with these arbitrary norms: 5–14 = low; 15–25 = moderate; 26–35 = high.

		Very False	Very True	
1.	I feel certain about how much authority I have.	7—6—5—4—3—2—1		_____
2.	I have to do things that should be done differently.	1—2—3—4—5—6—7		_____
3.	I know that I have divided my time properly.	7—6—5—4—3—2—1		_____
4.	I know what my responsibilities are.	7—6—5—4—3—2—1		_____
5.	I have to buck a rule or policy in order to carry out an assignment.	1—2—3—4—5—6—7		_____
6.	I feel certain how I will be evaluated for a raise or promotion.	7—6—5—4—3—2—1		_____
7.	I work with two or more groups who operate quite differently.	1—2—3—4—5—6—7		_____
8.	I know exactly what is expected of me.	7—6—5—4—3—2—1		_____
9.	I do things that are apt to be accepted by one person and not accepted by others.	1—2—3—4—5—6—7		_____
10.	I work on unnecessary things.	1—2—3—4—5—6—7		_____

Role conflict score   = _____
Role ambiguity score = _____

Source: Adapted from John R. Rizzo, Robert J. House, and Sidney I. Lirtzman, "Role Conflict and Ambiguity in Complex Organizations," *Administrative Science Quarterly*, June 1970, p. 156.

Leanness and nimbleness are qualities that pervade the company. When Pepsi's brash young managers take a few minutes away from the office, they often head straight for the company's physical fitness center or for a jog around the museum-quality sculptures outside of PepsiCo's Purchase, New York, headquarters.[40]

At PepsiCo and elsewhere, group members positively reinforce those who adhere to current norms with friendship and acceptance. On the other hand, nonconformists experience criticism and even *ostracism,* or rejection by group members. Anyone who has experienced the "silent treatment" from a group of friends knows what a potent social weapon ostracism can be. Norms can be put into proper perspective by understanding how they develop and why they are enforced.

How Norms Are Developed   Experts say norms evolve in an informal manner as the group or organization determines what it takes to be effective. Generally speaking, norms develop in various combinations of the following four ways:

1. *Explicit statements by supervisors or co-workers . . .* For instance, a group leader might explicitly set norms about not drinking at lunch. . . .

2. *Critical events in the group's history.* At times there is a critical event in the group's history that established an important precedent. [For example, a key recruit may have decided to work elsewhere because a group member said too many negative things about the organization. Hence, a norm against such "sour grapes" behavior might evolve.]

3. *Primacy.* The first behavior pattern that emerges in a group often sets group expectations. If the first group meeting is marked by very formal interaction between supervisors and subordinates, then the group often expects future meetings to be conducted in the same way. . . .

4. *Carryover behaviors from past situations.* . . . Such carryover of individual behaviors from past situations can increase the predictability of group members' behaviors in new settings and facilitate task accomplishment. For instance, students and professors carry fairly constant sets of expectations from class to class.[41]

We would like you to take a few moments and think about the norms that are currently in effect in your classroom. List the norms on a sheet of paper. Do these norms help or hinder your ability to learn? Norms can affect performance either positively or negatively.

Why Norms Are Enforced   Norms tend to be enforced by group members when they:

- Help the group or organization survive.
- Clarify or simplify behavioral expectations.
- Help individuals avoid embarrassing situations.
- Clarify the group's or organization's central values and/or unique identity.[42]

Working examples of each of these four situations are presented in Table 8–3.

Relevant Research Insights and Managerial Implications

Although instruments used to measure role conflict and role ambiguity have questionable validity,[43] two separate meta-analyses indicated that role conflict and role ambiguity negatively affected employees. Specifically, role conflict and role ambiguity were associated with job dissatisfaction, tension and anxiety, lack of organizational commitment, intentions to quit, and, to a lesser extent, poor job performance.[44]

• **Table 8-3**   Four Reasons Why Norms Are Enforced

Norm	Reason for Enforcement	Example
"Make our department look good in top management's eyes."	Group/organization survival	After vigorously defending the vital role played by the Human Resources Management Department at a divisional meeting, a staff specialist is complimented by her boss.
"Success comes to those who work hard and don't make waves."	Clarification of behavioral expectations	A senior manager takes a young associate aside and cautions him to be a bit more patient with co-workers who see things differently.
"Be a team player, not a star."	Avoidance of embarrassment	A project team member is ridiculed by her peers for dominating the discussion during a progress report to top management.
"Customer service is our top priority."	Clarification of central values/unique identity	Two sales representatives are given a surprise Friday afternoon party for having received prestigious best-in-the-industry customer service awards from an industry association.

The meta-analyses results hold few surprises for managers. Generally, because of the negative association reported, it pays management to reduce both role conflict and role ambiguity. In this endeavor, managers can use feedback, formal rules and procedures, directive leadership, setting of specific (difficult) goals, and participation. Managers also can use the socialization techniques discussed in the previous section of this chapter to reduce role conflict and ambiguity.

• Career Management

Some people are spectators who prefer to passively watch life go by, while others are active participants. The same is true of career management. Individuals can leave their fates in the hands of others or can influence their careers by taking charge. Skillful career management is important because people are happier and more satisfied when their personal and work lives are compatible. Moreover, failing to manage one's career may lead to professional plateauing, poor work attitudes, stress, and ultimately a lower quality of life.[45]

Unfortunately, poor career management appears to be a common problem. A recent national survey of 1,350 people by the Gallup Organization indicated that only 41 percent held jobs that they desired or had planned.[46] The next two sections of this chapter are based on the premise that you can enhance your personal and professional success by proactively managing your career. This material also helps present and future managers to address employees' career needs and aspirations.

In the first section, we present a model of career management; in the second, we discuss career stages and we offer tips for successfully making the transition from student to professional. Finally, we discuss career anchors.

Career Management Model

People today change careers on the average of four to six times during their working lifetime.[47] A **career** is "the pattern of work-related experiences that span the course of a person's life."[48] Work-related experiences include "objective events or situations such as a series of job positions, job duties or activities, and work-related decisions, and subjective interpretations of work-related events (past, present, or future) such as work aspirations, expectations, values, needs, and feelings about particular work experiences."[49] In turn, **career management** is a problem-solving/decision-making process aimed at optimizing the match between an individual's needs and values and his or her work-related experiences. Figure 8–8 presents a model of career management.

Career management is an ongoing process of gathering information, being aware of self and environment, setting career goals and action plans, obtaining feedback, and assessing career progress and satisfaction (see Figure 8–8). Although this process may appear to be unrealistically rational, research indicates students can be taught to follow its guidelines. There are two key phases within the eight-step process in Figure 8–8: career planning and career appraisal.

• **FIGURE 8-8**   A Model of Career Management

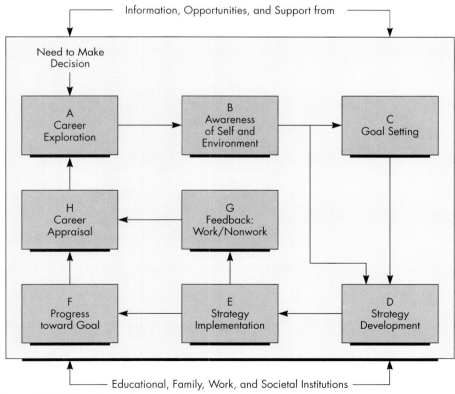

Source: Exhibit 2.1 from *Career Management,* by Jeffrey H. Greenhaus, copyright © 1987 by the Dryden Press, a division of Holt, Rinehart and Winston, Inc., reprinted by permission of the publisher.

Career Planning   From an employee's point of view, career planning helps an individual to determine career goals. It also assists an individual in balancing the demands of family, friends, leisure, and work.[50] This phase consists of steps A through D in Figure 8–8. **Career exploration** entails gathering career-related information about oneself and the environment. Self-exploration focuses on identifying one's values, needs, aspirations, abilities, and skills. In so doing, individuals are better able to match their values and ethical views with their careers (see A Matter of Ethics). Environmental exploration, on the other hand, is occupationally focused. That is, individuals seek information about specific job requirements, job duties, and job opportunities. Although awareness of self and environment (step B) is the primary benefit of career exploration, extensive career exploration was found to generate more job interviews, job offers, and higher organizational commitment.[51]

Awareness is the extent to which one has an accurate perception of her or his personal qualities and environmental characteristics. High awareness enables individuals to set realistic career goals (step C) and career strategies (step D). This is what happened to Barrie Christman as she advanced from a management trainee in 1974 to chief executive of Mellon Bank in Maryland ($220 million in assets).

> Christman got where she is by demonstrating unusual drive and initiative. After joining Mellon with a degree in math and economics, she found that her peers had MBAs. Soon she was hitting the books at night at the University of Pittsburgh's Graduate School of Business, earning an MBA in three years. ''I don't like operating at a disadvantage,'' she says.[52]

A MATTER OF ETHICS

Career Exploration Involves Ethical Choices

Working for nonprofit organizations has been the traditional way for graduates to reconcile their values with their careers. This approach allows students to be part of the solution to endemic problems, albeit at a relatively low salary. The difference today is that graduates who choose corporate careers also are making ethical decisions about the companies and industries they'll work for, say placement officials.

''I'm an extreme animal-rights activist, and I'm also very environmentally aware,'' says Jennifer Lovin, a senior business and psychology major at Southern Methodist University in Dallas. ''There's no way I would work for a company that doesn't take these values into account in some way.''

A recent survey of M.B.A.s by the Katz School of Business confirms the trend. When asked what firms they would shun during their job searches, 61 percent of the M.B.A.s cited tobacco producers, 39 percent mentioned investment banks and 35 percent listed defense contractors.

Source: Perri Capell, ''Let Ethics Guide Your Job Search,'' *The Wall Street Journal: Managing Your Career*, Fall 1990, p. 7.

• **TABLE 8-4**   Common Career Strategies

Strategy	Description
Competence in current job	Trying to perform effectively in one's current job.
Extended work involvement	Devoting more time and effort to one's job.
Skill development	Enhancing one's work-related skills and abilities through training or work experience.
Opportunity development	Promoting one's interests and aspirations to others and identifying job opportunities consistent with these interests and aspirations.
Development of mentor relationships	Trying to establish a key relationship with someone who will provide needed work-related information, career guidance, and professional support.
Image building	Promoting one's self image by communicating the appearance of potential, acceptability, and success.
Organizational politics	Obtaining career outcomes by using political behaviors to influence others.

Source: Adapted from Jeffrey H. Greenhaus, *Career Management* (Hinsdale, Ill.: The Dryden Press, 1987), p. 27. Copyright © 1987 by The Dryden Press. Reprinted by permission of the publisher.

As demonstrated by Christman's experience, *career goals* are motivational because they help individuals direct their effort and attention to specific career-related outcomes such as a promotion. Moreover, career goals foster development of career strategies (recall the discussion of goal strategies in Chapter 6). *Career strategies* are action plans that provide the direction or guidance for accomplishing career goals. Table 8–4 presents seven commonly used career strategies.

Career Appraisal   **Career appraisal** consists of obtaining and using career-related feedback from both work and nonwork sources (steps E through H in Figure 8–8 on page 299). Common work sources include performance appraisals, supervisors or managers, co-workers, and people working within the organizational function of personnel/human resource management. Family members, friends, and professional acquaintances are good nonwork sources of career feedback.

Feedback is a critical component of career management because it enables one to evaluate and monitor progress toward career goals. For instance, working long hours may lead to praise from a boss and criticism from a spouse. Interpreting career feedback, however, is dependent on one's original career goals. Returning to the example, working long hours may be consistent with a career goal of promotion, but inconsistent with a personal lifestyle goal of a happy family. Thus, depending on the career goal, feedback may reinforce or require modification of the goal.

Ultimately, career appraisal becomes a valuable piece of information used during career exploration (see Figure 8–8). It represents a feedback loop that perpetuates the process of career management. Progressive companies such as Coca-Cola have recognized this fact by formally linking the performance appraisal process with a career development system that includes annual career development reviews.

• CAREER TRANSITIONS

Careers, like life in general, involve change. Needs, career aspirations, and job skills change over time. Nevertheless, researchers found that people encountered common work experiences at similar points in their careers. These commonalities are called **career stages** and are independent of occupation or organization. In this section we examine the four stages of a professionally oriented career. This is followed by an overview of the issues you will encounter when making the transition from student to professional. This discussion helps you to manage your own professional career and provides managers with a framework for facilitating the career development of others.

Furthermore, careers are affected by one's career anchor. Edgar Schein, a well-known career researcher, defined a **career anchor** as "the self-image that a person develops around his or her career, which both guides and constrains career decisions."[53] It is important to understand different types of career anchors because they strongly influence career-related choices such as integrating work, family, and personal priorities. Career anchors also are discussed in this section.

Professional Career Stages

Professional careers evolve over four successive stages: apprentice, colleague, mentor, and sponsor. The length of each stage varies by individual and occupation, but is not necessarily related to age. Each stage involves different tasks, different primary relationships, and different psychological issues needing to be resolved.[54] The following discussion of career stages focuses on these differences (see Table 8–5).

Stage I: Apprentice   New professionals generally lack experience and thus work under close supervision. Central activities during this stage involve

• TABLE 8-5   Four Stages of Professional Careers

	Stage I	Stage II	Stage III	Stage IV
Central activity	Helping Learning Following directions	Independent contributor	Training Interfacing	Shaping the direction of the organization
Primary relationship	Apprentice	Colleague	Mentor	Sponsor
Major psychological issues	Dependence	Independence	Assuming responsibility for others	Exercising power

helping others, learning which elements of work are important and/or of greatest priority, and following directions. Such activities tend to be routine. The primary relationship entails being subordinate to someone else and necessitates a willingness to accept supervision and direction. This type of relationship creates dependence, the key psychological issue to be resolved.

Stage II: Colleague Independence is the key theme underlying this stage. It is acquired by demonstrating a high level of technical competence. Once competence is established, by developing a specialty in one content area, for example, peer relationships become more important. Consequently, supervisors are less frequently relied on for guidance as one develops his or her own resources to solve organizational problems. Coping with the responsibilities associated with independence is the critical psychological issue to be resolved during stage II. To successfully cope, an individual must develop her or his own performance standards. Organizational norms, peers, and professional associations are commonly used in this pursuit.

Stage III: Mentor Key activities involve training, guiding, influencing, or directing others. Individuals begin to work in more than one area and strive for greater breadth of technical competence. These activities create a drastic shift in the primary relationship. Individuals now must take care of others while also assuming responsibility for their work. Self-confidence, good interpersonal skills, and learning to derive satisfaction from the success of others are necessary for successfully surviving the career transition during this third stage.

Stage IV: Sponsor Shaping and influencing an organization's business strategy or direction is the key activity during the final career stage. This activity requires an individual to assume the roles of manager, idea innovator, and entrepreneur. One must learn to use one's power to be an effective sponsor.

Practical Implications Although the stage model has not been tested thoroughly, it does provide a useful device for managers when discussing performance and career issues with employees. Linking back to Figure 8–8, career stages can be used as career goals. Managers can use performance feedback to help employees develop career strategies aimed at moving to successive career stages.

Moreover, stage models suggest that managers and human resource specialists should not promise employees a career path. Career stages are achieved through performance and preparation, not promises. Individuals must meet performance expectations, make career choices, develop appropriate relationships, and take the chances necessary to advance along the continuum of career stages.

Making the Transition from Student to Professional

Career researchers have uncovered problem areas interfering with the successful transition from student to professional apprentice.[55] Table 8–6 identifies the six most frequent transitional problems and provides recommendations for overcoming them. For example, new college graduates often

• TABLE 8-6   Career Transitions from Student to Professional

Transitional Problem	Solution
1. Loss of hard-earned status	Be prepared to start as an "organizational" freshman who must prove oneself.
2. Impatience with close supervision and performance of routine tasks	Acquire technical competence; learn as much as possible about the organization; and demonstrate independence in solving organizational problems.
3. Changing from a competitive academic environment to a cooperative/collaborative environment	Learn to work with others—this requires good social and interpersonal skills; and demonstrate the willingness to be a team player.
4. Identifying what constitutes competent performance	Clarify expectations with one's supervisor; demonstrate technical accuracy in completing job assignments; try to adopt the boss's broader managerial perspective; and demonstrate disciplined performance by completing tasks on time and by not avoiding difficult assignments.
5. Being resourceful and innovative	Learn when to ask for assistance and when not to. Do not be afaiad to do more than is "formally" required of the position.
6. Longer feedback loops	Seek feedback at appropriate times—this necessitates learning how much feedback to ask for without becoming a nuisance.

Source: Based in part on discussion in Paul H. Thompson and Gene W. Dalton, "Balancing Your Expectations," *Business Week Careers*, February–March 1987, pp. 32–35.

are impatient with being closely supervised and with performing routine tasks. You need to find ways to adjust to this problem because it is inherent to the apprentice stage of career development (see Table 8–5). Possible solutions are: (1) acquiring technical competence, (2) learning as much as possible about the organization, and (3) demonstrating independence in solving organizational problems.

Longer feedback loops are another career transition problem. As students, you receive frequent feedback in the form of test scores and grades on assignments. This feedback can be very intensive. In contrast, organizational feedback loops are much longer. Managers typically provide formal performance feedback during annual performance appraisal review sessions. Annual feedback is inadequate for changing behavior, particularly for less experienced employees. Your challenge is to obtain the necessary feedback to help you meet your performance goals without becoming a nuisance to your boss.

How do you successfully survive the transition from student to professional? First off, don't overcommit. New college graduates have a tendency to take on too much too soon in order to impress their managers. This may lead to poor performance, and create an overwhelming feeling of self-perceived incompetence.[56] Second, be prepared for painful adjustments, shattered expectations, and most importantly, take charge of your career. By combining self-awareness, planning, career goals and strategies, and self-monitored feedback, you stand a much greater chance of success.

Career Anchors

A career anchor was previously defined as the part of the self-concept relating to one's career image. Through experience, a well-developed career anchor provides answers to the following questions.

1. What are my talents, skills, areas of competence? What are my strengths and what are my weaknesses?
2. What are my main motives, drives, goals in life? What am I after?
3. What are my values, the main criteria by which I judge what I am doing? Am I in the right kind of organization or job? How good do I feel about what I am doing?[57]

As suggested by these questions, career anchors reflect an individual's important career-related values and needs. Returning to the model of career management in Figure 8–8 on page 299, identifying one's career anchor is an important component of self-exploration (step A), strongly affecting one's level of self-awareness (step B).

In an extensive study of career anchors, Schein identified eight distinct types. His results further revealed that people with various career anchors preferred different types of work, different types of pay and promotion systems, and different types of recognition (see Table 8–7). Consider the case of Spencer Clements, an MBA student at Rice University in Houston:

> "I know I won't fit into a typical corporation, where they pat me on the back after six months or a year and give me an 8 percent raise, then repeat that process every year or so until I retire and get a gold watch at 60," says Clements, 25. "Marathon Oil was very structured, and I didn't enjoy it. I want to get into real estate where it's deal- or project-oriented, and I can make it or lose it on my own."
>
> "I want a company where they give me all the responsibility I can handle and then some, and maybe even a piece of the deal. If I don't perform, I'm out. That's okay with me," he adds. "I'm motivated by challenge and money."[58]

Using Table 8–7 as a point of reference, it appears Clements has autonomy/independence and managerial career anchors. He likes challenging work that is "deal- or project-oriented," and prefers pay and promotion systems that are merit-based.

Consistent with Spencer Clements's self-observations, empirical research revealed that satisfaction with one's career was related to the match between a career anchor and the specific type of job being performed.[59] Thus, for example, if you have an autonomy career anchor, you will be dissatisfied with jobs in which you are closely supervised or receive pay raises based on seniority or cost of living. It is important for you to gain awareness of your career anchor in order to optimize the match between personal values and

• TABLE 8-7   Characteristics of Career Anchors

Career Anchor	Preferred Type of Work	Preferred Pay and Benefits	Preferred Type of Promotion System	Preferred Type of Recognition
Security/stability	Stable and predict-able, more concerned about context than con-tent of work	Steady increments based on length of service; likes insurance and retirement programs	Seniority-based	Loyalty and steady performance
Autonomy/independence	Contract or project work within areas of exper-tise; low supervision and clearly defined goals	Merit pay for performance; portable benefits and cafeteria style choice of benefits	Merit-based that leads to more autonomy	Portable (medals, prizes, awards, testimonials, etc.)
Technical/functional competence	Challenging work that is intrinsi-cally interesting; low supervision and clearly defined goals; administrative or managerial work is not desirable	Skill-based defined by work experi-ence and education; exter-nal equity is important; porta-ble benefits and cafeteria style choice of benefits	Professional pro-motional ladder that parallels the typical manage-rial ladder	Opportunities for self-development in specialty; peer recognition more important than awards from members of management
Managerial	High levels of responsibility; challenging, varied, and inte-grative in nature; prefers lead-ership opportunities	Internal equity is important; short-run bonuses and good retirement programs	Merit-based	Promotions and monetary recognition
Entrepreneurial	High need to create; easily bored and re-quires a constant new challenge	Ownership is key; wants wealth as a way of showing personal success	Total flexibility; wants to do whatever one wants at any point in time	Building a fortune; high personal visibility and public recognition
Sense of service	Work that enables one to satisfy critical values—helping people; prefers autonomy	Fair pay and por-table benefits; money not a critical concern	Merit-based	Support from pro-fessional peers and superiors
Pure challenge	Any work that enables one to compete with others; seeks tougher and tougher challenges	Pay that rewards winning	Merit-based	Praise for winning
Lifestyle	Any work that en-ables one to balance personal and professional life; flexibility is essential	Options that permit one to integrate personal, family, and professional concerns	Flexible	Respect for per-sonal and family considerations

Source: Based in part on Edgar H. Schein, "Individuals and Careers," in *Handbook of Organizational Behavior*, ed. Jay W. Lorsch (Englewood Cliffs, N.J.: Prentice-Hall, 1987), pp. 155–71.

needs and the characteristics of a particular job. Keep in mind, however, your career anchor is largely determined by work-related experience and thus is subject to modification.[60] We wish you good fortune and the best of luck in your chosen career!

• SUMMARY OF KEY CONCEPTS

A. Organizational outsiders are shaped into fully functioning insiders through organizational socialization. The three phases of Feldman's organizational socialization model are anticipatory socialization, encounter, and change and acquisition. Researchers have found that formalized socialization processes (e.g., orientation and training) are more effective than informal processes.

B. Psychological contracts encompass the mutual expectations employees and employers have for each other. The contracts may be written or unwritten, spoken or unspoken. Both parties are urged to openly discuss their perceptions of the psychological contract.

C. Proponents of realistic job previews (RJPs) recommend that managers give recruits an honest appraisal about the positive and negative aspects of the job so as to curb unrealistic expectations and reduce costly turnover. RJP research documented that managers can use RJPs to positively affect satisfaction and turnover.

D. Behavior modeling is a learning process involving imitating others' behavior. The four subprocesses in Bandura's observational learning model are attention, retention, reproduction, and motivation. Researchers documented the effectiveness of employee training programs that involve the imitation of behavior models.

E. Mentoring is a socialization process whereby junior managers form intensive and lasting developmental relationships with senior managers. Mentors fulfill both career and psychosocial functions. Four phases of the mentoring process are initiation, cultivation, separation, and redefinition. Managers reportedly prefer informal mentoring over formal programs.

F. Organizational *roles* are sets of behaviors persons expect of occupants of a position. One may experience role overload (too much to do in too little time), role conflict (conflicting role expectations), or role ambiguity (unclear role expectations).

G. While roles are specific to the person's position, norms are shared attitudes that differentiate appropriate from inappropriate behavior in a variety of situations. Norms evolve informally and are enforced because they help the group or organization survive, clarify behavioral expectations, help people avoid embarrassing situations, and clarify the group's or organization's central values.

H. Career management is a problem-solving/decision-making process aimed at optimizing the match between an individual's needs and values and his or her work-related experiences. Career planning and career appraisal are the two key phases within the eight-step process of career management.

I. There are four stages within a professional career: apprentice, colleague, mentor, and sponsor. New college graduates experience common problems when transitioning from a student to a professional.

J. Career anchors reflect an individual's important career-related values and needs. Research identified eight distinct types of career anchors. It is important for an individual to gain awareness of his or her career anchors in order to optimize the match between personal values and needs and the characteristics of a particular job.

• KEY TERMS

organizational socialization
reality shock
psychological contract
realistic job preview (RJP)
behavior modeling
mentoring
roles
role overload
role conflict

role ambiguity
norm
career
career management
career exploration
career appraisal
career stages
career anchor

• DISCUSSION QUESTIONS

1. Why is socialization essential to organizational success?
2. What sort of anticipatory socialization did you undergo at your present school or job?
3. What are the terms of the various psychological contracts you have with people in positions of authority (e.g., bosses, teachers, and so on)?
4. How would you respond to a manager who asked you if realistic job previews are worthwhile?
5. Can you think of any behaviors you have acquired recently through behavior modeling? Explain.
6. Have you ever had a mentor? Explain how things turned out.
7. Considering your present lifestyle, how many different roles are you playing? What sorts of role conflict and role ambiguity are you experiencing?
8. What norms do college students usually enforce in class?
9. What are your career goals? How do you plan to achieve them?
10. What is your career anchor?

BACK TO THE OPENING CASE

Now that you have read Chapter 8, you should be able to answer the following questions about the Goldman Sachs case:

1. How does Goldman Sachs practice organizational socialization? Explain.
2. What are the norms for becoming a partner?
3. What role does mentoring play in becoming a partner? Explain.
4. Judging from the available evidence, what is Robin Illgen's career anchor? Is her career anchor consistent with the job requirements at Goldman Sachs? Discuss your rationale.

• EXERCISE 8

Objectives

1. To promote deeper understanding of organizational socialization processes.
2. To provide you with a useful tool for analyzing and comparing organizations.

Introduction

Employees are socialized in many different ways in today's organizations. Some organizations, such as IBM, have made an exact science out of organizational socialization. Others leave things to chance in hopes that collective goals will somehow be achieved. The questionnaire[61] in this exercise is designed to help you gauge how widespread and systematic the socialization process is in a particular organization.

Instructions

If you are presently employed and have a good working knowledge of your organization, you can complete this questionnaire yourself. If not, identify a manager or professional (e.g., corporate lawyer, engineer, nurse) and have that individual complete the questionnaire for his or her organization.

Respond to the items below as they apply to the handling of professional employees (including managers). Upon completion, compute the total score by adding up your responses. For comparison, scores for a number of strong, intermediate, and weak culture firms are provided.

	Not true of this company				Very true of this company
1. Recruiters receive at least one week of intensive training.	1	2	3	4	5
2. Recruitment forms identify several key traits deemed crucial to the firm's success, traits are defined in concrete terms and interviewer records specific evidence of each trait.	1	2	3	4	5
3. Recruits are subjected to at least four in-depth interviews.	1	2	3	4	5
4. Company actively facilitates de-selection during the recruiting process by revealing minuses as well as pluses.	1	2	3	4	5
5. New hires work long hours, are exposed to intensive training of considerable difficulty, and/or perform relatively menial tasks in the first months.	1	2	3	4	5
6. The intensity of entry-level experience builds cohesiveness among peers in each entering class.	1	2	3	4	5
7. All professional employees in a particular discipline begin in entry-level positions regardless of experience or advanced degrees.	1	2	3	4	5
8. Reward systems and promotion criteria require mastery of a core discipline as a precondition of advancement.	1	2	3	4	5
9. The career path for professional employees is relatively consistent over the first 6 to 10 years with the company.	1	2	3	4	5
10. Reward systems, performance incentives, promotion criteria and other primary measures of success reflect a high degree of congruence.	1	2	3	4	5
11. Virtually all professional employees can identify and articulate the firm's shared values (i.e., the purpose or mission that ties the firm to society, the customer, or its employees).	1	2	3	4	5
12. There are very few instances when actions of management appear to violate the firm's espoused values.	1	2	3	4	5
13. Employees frequently make personal sacrifices for the firm out of commitment to the firm's shared values.	1	2	3	4	5
14. When confronted with trade-offs between systems measuring short-term results and doing what's best for the company in the long term, the firm usually decides in favor of the long term.	1	2	3	4	5
15. This organization fosters mentor-protégé relationships.	1	2	3	4	5
16. There is considerable similarity among high potential candidates in each particular discipline.	1	2	3	4	5

Total score = _____

For comparative purposes:

	Scores:	
Strongly socialized firms	65–80	IBM, P&G, Morgan Guaranty
	55–64	AT&T, Morgan Stanley, Delta Airlines
	45–54	United Airlines, Coca Cola
	35–44	General Foods, PepsiCo
	25–34	United Technologies, ITT
Weakly socialized firms	Below 25	Atari

Questions for Consideration/Class Discussion

1. How strongly socialized is the organization in question? What implications does this degree of socialization have for satisfaction, commitment, and turnover?

2. In examining the 16 items in the above questionnaire, what evidence of realistic job previews and behavior modeling can you find? Explain.

3. What does this questionnaire say about how organizational norms are established and enforced? Frame your answer in terms of specific items in the questionnaire.

4. Using this questionnaire as a gauge, would you rather work for a strongly, moderately, or weakly socialized organization?

• NOTES

1 John Van Maanen, "Breaking In: Socialization to Work," in *Handbook of Work, Organization, and Society,* ed. R. Dubin (Chicago: Rand-McNally, 1976), p. 67.

2 Walter Kiechel III, "Love, Don't Lose, the Newly Hired," *Fortune,* June 16, 1988, p. 271.

3 See David Kirkpatrick, "Is Your Career on Track?," *Fortune* July 2, 1990, pp. 38–48.

4 For an instructive capsule summary of the five different organizational socialization models, see John P. Wanous, Arnon E. Reichers, and S. D. Malik, "Organizational Socialization and Group Development: Toward an Integrative Perspective," *Academy of Management Review,* October 1984, pp. 670–83, table 1. Also see Daniel C. Feldman, *Managing Careers in Organizations* (Glenview, Ill.: Scott, Foresman, 1988), chap. 5.

5 Anthony J. Rutigliano, "Steelcase: Nice Guys Finish First," *Management Review,* November 1985, p. 46.

6 John Van Maanen, "People Processing: Strategies of Organizational Socialization," *Organizational Dynamics,* Summer 1978, p. 21.

7 See Gareth R. Jones, "Socialization Tactics, Self-Efficacy, and Newcomers' Adjustments to Organizations," *Academy of Management Journal,* June 1986, pp. 262–79.

8 Results can be found in Douglas W. Bray, Richard J. Campbell, and Donald L. Grant, *Formative Years In Business: A Long-Term AT&T Study of Managerial Lives* (New York: John Wiley, 1974); and David E. Berlew and Douglas T. Hall, "The Socialization of Managers: Effects of Expectations on Performance, *Administrative Science Quarterly,* September 1966, pp. 207–23.

9 Results can be found in Barry Z. Posner and Gary N. Powell, "Female and Male Socialization Experiences: An Initial Investigation," *Journal of Occupational Psychology,* March 1985, pp. 81–85.

10 A summary of socialization research is provided by John P. Wanous and Adrienne Colella, "Organizational Entry Research: Current Status and Future Directions," in *Research in Personnel and Human Resources Management,* eds. Gerald R. Ferris and Kendrith M. Rowland (Greenwich, Conn.: JAI Press, 1989), pp. 59–120; and Cynthia D. Fisher, "Organizational Socialization: An Integrative Review," in *Research in Personnel and Human Resources Management,* ed. Kendrith M. Rowland and Gerald R. Ferris (Greenwich, Conn.: JAI Press, 1986), pp. 101–45.

[11] Herbert George Baker, "The Unwritten Contract: Job Perceptions," *Personnel Journal,* July 1985, p. 37. (Emphasis added.)

[12] An expanded discussion of the two types of employment contracts may be found in Denise M. Rousseau, "Psychological and Implied Contracts in Organizations." *Employee Responsibilities and Rights Journal,* June 1989, pp. 121–39.

[13] The application of psychological contracts within counseling settings is discussed by Luis H. Zayas and Michael Katch, "Contracting with Adolescents: An Ego-Psychological Approach," *Social Casework,* January 1989, pp. 3–9.

[14] Larry Reibstein, "Crushed Hopes: When a New Job Proves to Be Something Different," *The Wall Street Journal,* June 10, 1987, p. 21.

[15] This matching process is discussed and tested by Robert J. Vandenberg and Vida Scarpello, "The Matching Model: An Examination of the Processes Underlying Realistic Job Previews," *Journal of Applied Psychology,* February 1990, pp. 60–67.

[16] The managerial application of RJPs is thoroughly discussed by John P. Wanous, "Installing a Realistic Job Preview: Ten Tough Choices," *Personnel Psychology,* Spring 1989, pp. 117–34.

[17] See Steven L. Premack and John P. Wanous, "A Meta-Analysis of Realistic Job Preview Experiments," *Journal of Applied Psychology,* November 1985, pp. 706–19.

[18] A review of RJP research can be found in Wanous and Colella, "Organizational Entry Research: Current Status and Future Directions."

[19] Albert Bandura, *Principles of Behavior Modification* (New York: Holt, Rinehart & Winston, 1969), p. 118. For an instructive update on alternative observational learning theories, see Gina Green and J. Grayson Osborne, "Does Vicarious Instigation Provide Support for Observational Learning Theories? A Critical Review," *Psychological Bulletin,* January 1985, pp. 3–17. Also see Dennis A. Gioia and Charles C. Manz, "Linking Cognition and Behavior: A Script Processing Interpretation of Vicarious Learning," *Academy of Management Review,* July 1985, pp. 527–39.

[20] Henry P. Sims and Charles C. Manz, "Modeling Influences on Employee Behavior," *Personnel Journal,* January 1982, p. 58.

[21] For a review of the application of behavior modeling within industrial training, see William M. Fox, "Getting the Most from Behavior Modeling Training," *National Productivity Review,* Summer 1988, pp. 238–45.

[22] Arnold P. Goldstein and Melvin Sorcher, *Changing Supervisor Behavior* (New York: Pergamon Press, 1974), p. ix.

[23] See Gary P. Latham and Lise M. Saari, "Application of Social-Learning Theory to Training Supervisors through Behavioral Modeling," *Journal of Applied Psychology,* June 1979, pp. 239–46. Additional insightful research may be found in Steven J. Mayer and James S. Russell, "Behavior Modeling Training in Organizations: Concerns and Conclusions," *Journal of Management,* Spring 1987, pp. 21–40.

[24] "Labor Letter: A Special News Report on People and Their Jobs in Offices, Fields, and Factories," *The Wall Street Journal,* February 23, 1988, p. 1.

[25] See Kathy E. Kram, "Phases of the Mentor Relationship," *Academy of Management Journal,* December 1983, pp. 608–25.

[26] R. J. Burke and C. A. McKeen, "Mentoring in Organizations: Implications for Women," *Journal of Business Ethics,* April/May 1990, p. 322.

[27] Results can be found in George F. Dreher and Ronald A. Ash, "A Comparative Study of Mentoring among Men and Women in Managerial, Professional, and Technical Positions," *Journal of Applied Psychology,* October 1990, pp. 539–46.

28 Donald D. Bowen, "The Role of Identification in Mentoring Female Protégées," *Group & Organization Studies,* March–June 1986, p. 72. Also see James G. Clawson and Kathy E. Kram, "Managing Cross-Gender Mentoring," *Business Horizons,* May–June 1984, pp. 22–32; and Selwyn Feinstein, "Women and Minority Workers in Business Find a Mentor Can Be a Rare Commodity," *The Wall Street Journal,* November 11, 1987, p. 37.

29 The organizational benefits of mentoring are thoroughly discussed by James A. Wilson and Nancy S. Elman, "Organizational Benefits of Mentoring," *Academy of Management Executive,* November 1990, pp. 88–94.

30 These mentoring programs are discussed by Kiechel, "Love, Don't Lose, the Newly hired." Additional practical advice may be found in John Lawrie, "How to Establish a Mentoring Program," *Training and Development Journal,* March 1987, pp. 25–27; and Daniel C. Feldman, *Managing Careers in Organizations* (Glenview, Ill.: Scott, Foresman, 1988), chap. 7.

31 George Graen, "Role-Making Processes within Complex Organizations," in *Handbook of Industrial and Organizational Psychology,* ed. Marvin D. Dunnette (Chicago: Rand McNally, 1976), p. 1201.

32 Excerpted from Gregory L. Miles, "Doug Danforth's Plan to Put Westinghouse in the 'Winner's circle,'" *Business Week,* July 28, 1986, p. 75.

33 For a review of research on the role episode model, see Lynda A. King and Daniel W. King, "Role Conflict and Role Ambiguity: A Critical Assessment of Construct Validity," *Psychological Bulletin,* January 1990, pp. 48–64.

34 Edgar H. Schein, *Organizational Psychology,* 3rd ed. (Englewood Cliffs, N.J.: Prentice-Hall, 1980), p. 198.

35 Ibid.

36 See Alan L. Otten, "People Patterns: Wives May Not benefit When Men Do Chores," *The Wall Street Journal,* October 30, 1989, p. B1.

37 Schein, *Organizational Psychology,* p. 198.

38 1 = A; 2 = C; 3 = A; 4 = A; 5 = C; 6 = A; 7 = C; 8 = A; 9 = C; 10 = C.

39 Robert R. Blake and Jane Srygley Mouton, "Don't Let Group Norms Stifle Creativity," *Personnel,* August 1985, p. 28.

40 Amy Dunkin, "Pepsi's Marketing Magic: Why Nobody Does It Better," *Business Week,* February 10, 1986, p. 52.

41 Daniel C. Feldman, "The Development and Enforcement of Group Norms," *Academy of Management Review,* January 1984, pp. 50–52.

42 Ibid.

43 See Richard G. Netemeyer, Mark W. Johnston, and Scot Burton, "Analysis of Role Conflict and Role Ambiguity in a Structural Equations Framework," *Journal of Applied Psychology,* April 1990, pp. 148–157; and Gail W. McGee, Carl E. Ferguson, Jr., and Anson Seers, "Role Conflict and Role Ambiguity: Do the Scales Measure These Two Constructs?," *Journal of Applied Psychology,* October 1989, pp. 815–18.

44 See Susan E. Jackson and Randall S. Schuler, "A Meta-Analysis and Conceptual Critique of Research on Role Ambiguity and Role Conflict in Work Settings," *Organizational Behavior and Human Decision Processes,* August 1985, pp. 16–78. Also see King and King, "Role Conflict and Role Ambiguity: A Critical Assessment of Construct Validity."

45 See Lawson K. Savery, "Comparing Plateaued and Nonplateaued Employees," *Journal of Managerial Psychology,* 1989, pp. 12–15; Suzanne K. Stout, John W. Slocum, Jr., and William L. Cron, "Dynamics of the Career Plateauing Process,"

Journal of Vocational Behavior, February 1988, pp. 74–91; and Daniel C. Feldman and Barton A. Weitz, "Career Plateaus Reconsidered," *Journal of Management,* March 1988, pp. 69–80.

[46] Results were reported in Karen Ball, "Majority Surveyed Not in Job of Choice," *The Arizona Republic,* January 12, 1990, p. 1.

[47] See Jack Falvey, "Career Navigation: Learn to Plot Your Own Destiny Rather Than Let It Drift," *Training and Development Journal,* February 1988, pp. 32–36.

[48] Jeffrey H. Greenhaus, *Career Management* (Hinsdale, Ill.: The Dryden Press, 1987), p. 6.

[49] Ibid., pp. 6–7.

[50] Career Planning is thoroughly discussed by Daniel C. Feldman, "Central Issues in Career Planning," in *The 1990 Annual: Developing Human Resources,* ed. J. William Pfeiffer (San Diego, Calif.: University Associates, Inc., 1990), pp. 271–79.

[51] See Brian D. Steffy and Jack W. Jones, "The Impact of Family and Career Planning Variables on the Organizational, Career, and Community Commitment of Professional Women," *Journal of Vocational Behavior,* April 1988, pp. 196–212; and Stephen A. Stumpf, Elizabeth J. Austin, and Karen Hartman, "The Impact of Career Exploration and Interview Readiness on Interview Performance and Outcomes," *Journal of Vocational Behavior,* April 1984, pp. 221–35.

[52] Matt Rothman, "Breathing New Life into a Failed S&L," *Business Week,* November 10, 1986, p. 93.

[53] Edgar H. Schein, "Individuals and Careers," in *Handbook of Organizational Behavior,* ed. Jay W. Lorsch (Englewood Cliffs, N.J.: Prentice-Hall, 1987), p. 155.

[54] Thorough discussions of career stage models can be found in Gene W. Dalton, "Developmental Views of Careers in Organizations," in *Handbook of Career Theory,* eds. Michael B. Arthur, Douglas T. Hall, and Barbara S. Lawrence (New York: Cambridge University Press, 1989), pp. 89–109; and Douglas T. Hall, *Careers in Organizations* (Pacific Palisades, Calif.: Goodyear, 1976).

[55] See Paul H. Thompson and Gene W. Dalton, "Balancing Your Expectations," *Business Week Careers,* February–March 1987, pp. 32–35; and Jack Falvey, "Career Navigation," pp. 32–36.

[56] Solutions to this problem are discussed by Michael F. Kastre, How Not to Get in Over Your Head," *The Wall Street Journal: Managing Your Career,* Spring 1990, pp. 18–21; and Kenneth Oldfield, "Survival of the Newest," *Personnel Journal,* March 1989, pp. 53–59.

[57] Schein, "Individuals and Careers," p. 157.

[58] Greg Thompson, "Corporate Cultures Compared: Which Climate Suits Your Personality?," *The Wall Street Journal: Managing Your Career,* Spring 1990, p. 13.

[59] Schein, "Individuals and Careers," pp. 155–71.

[60] The stability of career anchors is discussed by Daniel C. Feldman, "Careers in Organizations: Recent Trends and Future Directions," *Journal of Management,* June 1989, pp. 135–56.

[61] This exercise has been adapted from Richard Pascale, "The Paradox of 'Corporate Culture:' Reconciling Ourselves to Socialization," pp. 26–41. © 1985 by the Regents of the University of California. Reprinted/Condensed from the *California Management Review,* vol. XXVII, no 2. By permission of The Regents.

Group and Intergroup Dynamics

LEARNING OBJECTIVES

When you finish studying the material in this chapter, you should be able to:

- Explain why the social facilitation effect is not necessarily a bad thing.
- Identify the four criteria of a group, from a sociological perspective.
- Describe the six stages of group development.

- Distinguish between task and maintenance functions in groups.
- Summarize the practical contingency management lessons learned from research on technology–structure fit, group size, and group member ability.
- Discuss why managers need to carefully handle mixed-gender task groups.

- Describe groupthink and identify at least four of its symptoms.
- Explain what managers can do to reduce social loafing.
- Identify and describe the five social network functions and the two social network clusters.

OPENING CASE 9

The Wilderness Lab (Janet W. Long)

Sharon Hoogstraten

I found myself on a bus . . . winding into the Rockies west of Denver toward the base camp used by the Corporate Development Program of the Colorado Outward Bound School. There were 18 other refugees from the white-collar world, all headed for five days of management development in the woods. Outward Bound offers "Reaching Your Management Potential" in conjunction with the University of Denver Center for Management Development. . . .

Our bus carried a diverse group into the mountains. We represented organizations from Washington State to Washington, D.C. . . . from one-person consulting firms to multinational corporations. The participants included wise, understated, seasoned managers as well as bright young travelers on the corporate ladder whose rough edges were softened by the positive energy in their eyes. There were managers whose natural interests in people and leadership ability had taken them up the ranks, and highly skilled technicians, used to being independent contributors, who had recently found themselves in the uncomfortable position of needing to manage others. Ages ranged from 24 to 44, and disciplines included law, engineering, architecture, marketing and education, among others. Some participants were veterans of many training programs; others were fairly new to the realm of management development.

Most of us wanted to be there. Some had learned of the program themselves and lobbied to go. Others had been sent by their organizations to learn to work more effectively in groups—either because they were normally reticent in groups, or because they tended to dominate and compete. The outdoor medium had been selected by some because it is a more comfortable setting than the traditional classroom. Others had chosen it because it is a substantial step *beyond* the familiar corporate comfort zone and as such is a ripe environment for testing the ways we plan, solve problems, and work with others.

Most of us were a little scared. Our fears ranged from making fools of ourselves to falling off a cliff. It was hard to determine which of those fears was more serious. . . .

At the top of the hill we found a "trust ladder" nailed to one of the many pines surrounding us. There appeared to be a little more risk here than looking silly. Eric [the course director] explained that we would need to rely on one another under many circumstances in the coming week, and that the object of this exercise was to climb the ladder and fall off backwards into the arms of the group. He showed us how to line up and join hands to catch our falling teammate, and he headed for the ladder before we could ponder the matter too thoroughly. I was afraid that I wouldn't be able to hold him . . . and, of course, I couldn't have alone. One by one we climbed the ladder and thumped down into the waiting arms.

This was the first activity that we analyzed. We talked about risk taking, trusting one's support system, communicating needs and checking to be sure that the support system is ready before relying on it . . . and a little about what's involved in supporting someone effectively.

Our most physical group challenge was a 13-foot wall the entire group had to scale. It was sheer and smooth, with a platform behind it on which one could stand at about waist level with the top of the wall. This platform could be occupied by two people (once we got them up and over) to help haul up the rest of the group. A ladder was provided on the back for

OPENING CASE 9

(concluded)

climbing down to earth. Thirteen feet had never seemed so imposing. We were given a few safety restrictions, and the stopwatch began ticking. Group planning and problem solving were again germane, with special attention to the first and last people over the wall.

We decided that we needed to boost some strong people up first to help pull the rest up, and keep some powerful boosters on the ground. The middle group would be relatively straightforward, with help from above and below. The final climb appeared to require two key players: someone strong enough to act as a "human rope," facing the wall and hanging with his shoulders looped over the top; and someone light and strong enough to scramble up the wall, using the human rope until he could get a hand from the pullers.

The roles clear, we began to assess our resources. I was proud of the group as we offered up both our strengths *and* limitations. We had walked past THE WALL several times over the previous two days, and it was the culmination of our group challenges. We were hungry to do it well, and the chance to play a key role was tantalizing. But the group interdependence in this exercise took on a more serious note. Despite good safety precautions (such as helmets and "spotters" whose job it would be to break anyone's fall) we really did have one another's safety in our hands. It would not

do to play the hero here and be unable to come through. Some of our most athletic team members owned up to prohibitive injuries that would keep them in the middle of the progression. Others stepped forward to fill the void, each assessing his or her own capabilities with a balance of commitment and responsibility. Soon we all knew our roles, and the adrenaline began to flow.

The scene that followed was an organized frenzy of push, pull, scramble, encourage, and keep those hands in the air in case someone fell. No one spent a moment uninvolved in the process. We all ached for our last two teammates as they completed the grueling climb. It was a tired and happy group that sat in a circle beneath the wall to talk not only about planning and problem solving but also the dynamics of sensible group risk taking, and the strength of being part of a multi-talented, interdependent and mutually supportive team.

As I leaned back against the wall and watched all this with an analytical trainer's eye, I became aware of the powerful lesson I was experiencing at gut level. [Whitewater canoeing had] . . . left me with a shoulder that chronically dislocates, which not only put me in the center of the progression up the wall, but made me feel like a liability to the group. As I stepped up for my boost, I told the pullers what to expect. "All right,

Wayne, you can pull for all you're worth. But Mike, I can't extend this right arm very high, and if I call your name, let go in a hurry." I could feel the spotters move in around me, but I was up and over in a moment with no trouble.

During the debriefing I asked what effect my limitation had on the group, especially Wayne and Mike. "None at all," said Wayne. "None," echoed Mike, "because you told us what your needs were. I could lean down the wall further and put myself into a more vulnerable position with more leverage because I knew you wouldn't be pulling very hard with that arm." I've never been good at making my needs known, but in this situation I felt a responsibility to the group. I thought back to the office and wondered how many projects I had avoided or contributed less than I could have because I didn't give someone the chance to fill in my weak spots.

For Discussion

Why might the wilderness lab be a better learning environment than the classroom?

• Additional discussion questions linking this case with the following material appear at the end of this chapter.

Source: Excerpted from Janet W. Long, "The Wilderness Lab," *Training and Development Journal*, May 1984, pp. 58–69. Used with permission.

I f you were a waitress in a restaurant and you wanted to maximize your tips while serving male–female couples, which of the following approaches would you use?

a. Touch the male lightly and briefly on the shoulder while asking if everything was all right.

b. Do not touch either person while asking if everything was all right.

c. Touch the female lightly and briefly on the shoulder while asking if everything was all right.

Think briefly about why you have selected that answer before reading further.

According to the results of a social psychology field study in a Greensboro, North Carolina, restaurant, the last approach would be your most profitable alternative. This approach produced an average tip of 15 percent, whereas the first and second tactics yielded average tips of 13 percent and 11 percent, respectively.[1] Of course, different results could be expected in cultures where public physical contact is discouraged. The outcome for a male waiter might be different, too. Nonetheless, this little multiple-choice quiz illustrates the curious twists behavior can take when individuals interact. Because the management of organizational behavior is above all else a

---

FIGURE 9-1   Group and Intergroup Dynamics Have a Major Impact on Organizational Effectiveness

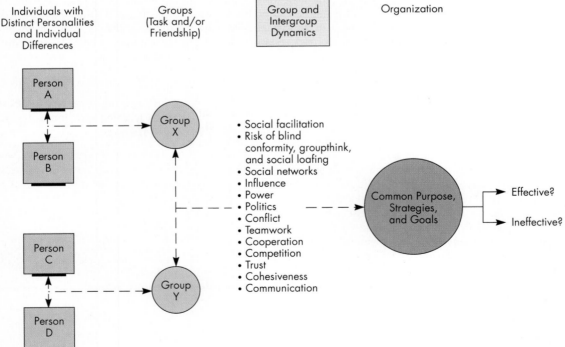

social endeavor, managers need a working knowledge of *interpersonal* behavior.

Our road map for the remaining chapters in this section is Figure 9–1. Notice how groups, whether based on assigned tasks or friendship, serve as a gateway to the achievement of organizational goals. Depending on the precise nature of group and intergroup dynamics, the gate may be open or closed. Group and intergroup dynamics can be constructive or destructive. Some surprises are in store in this chapter and the others in Part III. For instance, power and conflict are not necessarily bad. Indeed, to a certain extent, each is essential to organizational effectiveness.

Let us begin by examining the most basic form of on-the-job interaction, the mere presence of another person. We will then define the term *group* as a prelude to examining types of groups, functions of group members, and the group development process. Impacts of group structure and member characteristics on group outcomes are then explored. Three serious threats to group effectiveness are discussed. Finally, a social-network-analysis approach to intergroup dynamics is considered.

• SOCIAL INTERACTION IN THE WORKPLACE

When two people interact at work or elsewhere, the net result is greater than the sum of what the two individuals bring to the situation. In effect, something extra enters the picture. Technically, the term *synergy* relates to the whole being greater than the sum of its parts. Some call **synergy** the 1 + 1 = 3 effect. For example, consuming alcohol along with certain drugs can lead to devastating consequences. Because interpersonal behavior is synergistic, we need to explore what happens when ''I'' becomes ''We'' (see OB in Action). A good starting point is to understand social facilitation and how sociologists define the term *group*.

OB IN ACTION

How Ford Engineer Linda Persico Plans to Balance the ''I'' and ''We'' Aspects of Her Life

She grew up in the Detroit suburbs and studied mechanical engineering at Michigan State. In 1987 she signed on at Ford Motor Co., where her father has worked as an engineer for 30 years. . . .

''Maybe a career isn't all it's cracked up to be. It's still important to me, but it's not the no. 1 thing in my life. I have outside interests. Now that I'm engaged [she plans to wed a fellow Ford engineer next year], I'm more concerned about the time I spend with my fiancé and what it's going to be like after we're married. If it came down to career or relationship, I would have to think that the relationship comes first.''

Source: Excerpted from Alan Deutschman, ''What 25-Year-Olds Want,'' *Fortune,* August 27, 1990, pp. 43–44.

Social Facilitation

In task situations, does the mere presence of others help or hinder one's performance? This question, centering on what social scientists call **social facilitation,** has intrigued researchers for nearly a century. Not surprisingly, findings and recommendations have varied through the years. In the early 1900s, Frederick Taylor claimed that workers would loaf or engage in what he called "systematic soldiering" if allowed to mingle during work hours.[2] During the bank wiring room portion of the famous Hawthorne studies, researchers did observe workers conspiring to restrict output.[3] On the other hand, an early 1950s experiment showed that self-selected teams of construction workers had lower production costs, lower turnover, and greater satisfaction than workers in assigned teams.[4]

Research Insights   Thanks to a meta-analysis of 241 studies encompassing almost 24,000 subjects, decades of conflicting findings on social facilitation can be boiled down to the following conclusions:

1. The mere presence of others has a relatively small (3 percent or less) impact on the performance of individuals.
2. Performance of simple tasks tends to be speeded up and made more accurate by the presence of others.
3. Performance of complex tasks tends to be slowed and made less accurate by the presence of others.[5]

Unfortunately, the exact causes of these social facilitation effects have not been pinned down. One theory is that the presence of others motivates one to try harder. This would explain the positive impact in simple-task situations. Other theories attempt to explain the negative effect in complex-task situations. These theories focus on performance anxiety and fear of

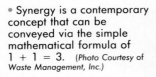

• Synergy is a contemporary concept that can be conveyed via the simple mathematical formula of 1 + 1 = 3.   (*Photo Courtesy of Waste Management, Inc.*)

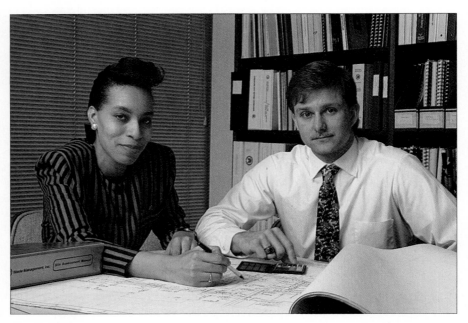

criticism. Regardless of the exact cause of negative social facilitation effects, managers cannot afford to ignore any possible erosion of job performance. In today's competitive environment, two or three percentage points can mean the difference between success and failure.

Managing the Negative Effects of Social Facilitation Three areas deserving managerial attention are general training, computer familiarization, and office design. The research evidence reviewed above leads to this conclusion about general employee training: Training for simple tasks can be done in groups, whereas training for complex tasks needs to include private practice sessions. High on the list of complex tasks is computer competence. Computer novices, according to a recent study, are particularly prone to the social facilitation effect.[6] Inexperienced computer users tended to become discouraged when practicing in the presence of others. Managers in today's increasingly computerized offices and factories need to combat this source of computer resistance with systematic self-efficacy training. (Recall the self-efficacy model in Chapter 3.) Step-by-step computer familiarization, first in private and then in front of others, is the recommended course.

Another stream of social facilitation research reveals practical implications for office design. Open offices, those without the visual and auditory privacy of a closed office, had both positive and negative effects on the performance of selected senior managers.[7] Those responsible for office layout and design need to take individual reactions to the presence of others into consideration, rather than force fitting everyone into either open or closed offices.

Groups

Groups are an inescapable aspect of modern life. College students are often teamed with their peers for class projects. Parents serve on community advisory boards at their local high school. Managers find themselves on product planning committees and productivity task forces. Productive organizations simply cannot function without groups.[8] But, as personal experience shows, group effort can bring out both the best and the worst in people. A marketing department meeting, where several people excitedly brainstorm and refine a creative new advertising campaign, can yield results beyond the capabilities of individual contributors. Conversely, committees have become the butt of jokes (e.g., a committee is a place where they take minutes and waste hours; a camel is a horse designed by a committee) because they all too often are plagued by lack of direction and by conflict. Modern managers need a solid understanding of groups and group processes so as to both avoid their pitfalls and tap their vast potential.

For example, the fate of the General Motors newly opened multibillion dollar Saturn project will be determined to a great extent by the company's revolutionary use of groups. The Saturn project's objective is to manufacture automobiles in the United States that will be cost-competitive with the Japanese.

The basic groups in Saturn plants will be work units of 6 to 15 UAW [United Auto Workers Union] members who will elect a "counselor" from their own ranks. The team will decide who does which job. It will also maintain equipment, order

• FIGURE 9-2   Four Sociological Criteria of a Group

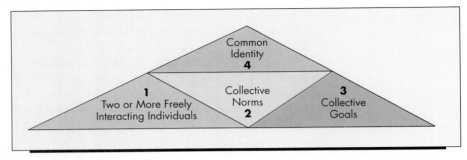

supplies, and set the relief and vacation schedules of its members. Each group will have a personal computer for keeping tabs on business data, ranging from production schedules to freight pickups and deliveries.[9]

This approach, discussed under the heading of teams in Chapter 11, will require unprecedented degrees of cooperation and mutual trust between management and labor. But General Motors obviously believes in the power and potential of teamwork because the Saturn project's success hinges on *group* performance.

Although other definitions of groups exist, we draw from the field of sociology and define a **group** as two or more freely interacting individuals who share collective norms and goals and have a common identity.[10] Figure 9-2 illustrates how the four criteria in this definition combine to form a conceptual whole. Organizational psychologist Edgar Schein shed additional light on this concept by drawing instructive distinctions between a group, a crowd, and an organization:

> The size of a group is thus limited by the possibilities of mutual interaction and mutual awareness. Mere aggregates of people do not fit this definition because they do not interact and do not perceive themselves to be a group even if they are aware of each other as, for instance, a crowd on a street corner watching some event. A total department, a union, or a whole organization would not be a group in spite of thinking of themselves as "we," because they generally do not all interact and are not all aware of each other. However, work teams, committees, subparts of departments, cliques, and various other informal associations among organizational members would fit this definition of a group.[11]

Take a moment now to think of various groups of which you are a member. Does each of your "groups" satisfy the four criteria in Figure 9-2?

• GROUP TYPES, FUNCTIONS, AND DEVELOPMENT

Research-oriented disciplines each have classification systems that serve as a departure point for deeper understanding. Group dynamics is no exception. Three insightful ways of classifying groups are by *type,* the *functions* they perform, and their developmental *stages.*

• TABLE 9-1   Formal Groups Fulfill Organizational and Individual Functions

Organizational Functions	Individual Functions
1. Accomplish *complex, interdependent tasks* that are beyond the capabilities of individuals. 2. Generate *new or creative ideas* and *solutions.* 3. Coordinate interdepartmental *efforts.* 4. Provide a *problem-solving mechanism* for *complex problems* requiring varied information and assessments. 5. *Implement* complex *decisions.* 6. *Socialize* and *train* newcomers.	1. Satisfy the individual's *need for affiliation.* 2. Develop, enhance, and confirm the individual's *self-esteem* and sense of *identity.* 3. Give individuals an opportunity to *test* and *share* their perceptions of *social reality.* 4. *Reduce* the individual's *anxieties* and feelings of *insecurity* and *powerlessness.* 5. Provide a *problem-solving mechanism* for *personal* and *interpersonal problems.*

Source: Adapted from Edgar H. Schein, *Organizational Psychology*, 3rd ed. (Englewood Cliffs, N.J.: Prentice Hall, 1980), pp. 149–51.

Formal and Informal Groups

Individuals join groups, or are assigned to groups, to accomplish various purposes. If the group is formed by a manager to help the organization accomplish its goals, then it qualifies as a **formal group.** Formal groups typically wear such labels as work group, team, committee, quality circle, or task force. An **informal group** exists when the members' overriding purpose of getting together is friendship. Although formal and informal groups often overlap, such as a team of corporate auditors heading for the tennis courts after work, some employees are not friends with their co-workers. The desirability of overlapping formal and informal groups is problematic. Some managers firmly believe personal friendship fosters productive teamwork on the job while others view workplace "bull sessions" as a serious threat to productivity. Both situations are common, and it is the manager's job to strike a workable balance, based on the maturity and goals of the people involved.

Functions of Formal Groups

Researchers point out that formal groups fulfill two basic functions: *organizational* and *individual.*[12] The various functions are listed in Table 9–1. Complex combinations of these functions can be found in formal groups at any given time.

For example, consider what Mazda's new American employees experienced when they spent a month working in Japan before the opening of the firm's Flat Rock, Michigan, plant in 1987.

> After a month of training in Mazda's factory methods, whipping their new Japanese buddies at softball and sampling local watering holes, the Americans were fired up. . . . [A maintenance manager] even faintly praised the Japanese practice of holding group calisthenics at the start of each working day: "I didn't think I'd like doing exercises every morning, but I kind of like it."[13]

While Mazda pursued the organizational functions it wanted—interdependent teamwork, creativity, coordination, problem solving, and training—the American workers benefited from the individual functions of formal groups.

Among those benefits were affiliation with new friends, enhanced self-esteem, exposure to the Japanese social reality, and reduction of anxieties about working for a foreign-owned company. In short, Mazda created a workable blend of organizational and individual group functions by training its newly hired American employees in Japan.

• STAGES OF THE GROUP DEVELOPMENT PROCESS

Chapter 8 detailed how the organizational socialization process can be reduced to a sequence of identifiable phases. So it is with the group development process. This implies groups go through a predictable maturation process, such as one would find in any life-cycle situation (e.g., humans, organizations, products). However, while there is general agreement among theorists that the group development process occurs in identifiable stages, they disagree about the exact number, sequence, length, and nature of those stages.[14] An instructive model of group development is depicted in Figure 9–3. Notice how *uncertainty over authority and power* is an overriding obstacle during the first three phases. During the last three phases, *uncertainty over interpersonal relations* becomes the major obstacle.

Let us briefly examine each of the six stages.[15] You can make this process come to life by relating the various stages to your own experiences with work groups, committees, athletic teams, social or religious groups, or class project teams. Some group happenings that surprised you when they occured may now make sense or strike you as inevitable when seen as part of a developmental process.

Stage 1: Orientation   During this "ice-breaking" stage, group members tend to be uncertain and anxious about such things as their roles, who is in

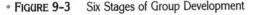

• **FIGURE 9-3**   Six Stages of Group Development

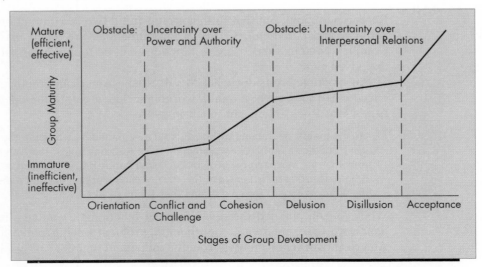

Source: Adapted from Linda N. Jewell and H. Joseph Reitz, *Group Effectiveness in Organizations* (Glenview, Ill.: Scott Foresman, 1981), p. 20.

charge, and the group's goals. Mutual trust is low and there is a good deal of holding back to see who takes charge and how. If the formal leader (e.g., a supervisor) does not assert his or her authority, an emergent leader will eventually step in to fulfill the group's need for leadership and direction. Leaders typically mistake this honeymoon period as a mandate for permanent control. But later problems may force a leadership change.

Stage 2: Conflict and Challenge   This is a time of testing. Individuals test the leader's policies and assumptions as they try to determine how they fit into the power structure. Subgroups take shape, and subtle forms of rebellion, such as procrastination, occur. Many groups stall in stage 2 because power politics erupts into open rebellion.

Stage 3: Cohesion   Groups that make it through stage 2 generally do so because a respected member, other than the leader, challenges the group to resolve its power struggles so something can be accomplished. Questions about authority and power are resolved rather quickly through unemotional, matter-of-fact group discussion. A renewed feeling of team spirit is experienced because members believe they have found their proper roles.

Stage 4: Delusion   Having resolved major disputes over power and authority, the group's members feel a sense of relief over having been ''through the worst of it.'' Unfortunately, pressures build up as the quest for harmony and goodwill causes individuals to stifle their complaints. Participation is very active during this stage.

Stage 5: Disillusion   The unrealistic sense of harmony in stage 4 begins to fray around the edges as some members point out that the group is not fulfilling its potential. Conflict between subgroups may arise over whether or not individuals should reveal their relative strengths and weaknesses. A drop in group cohesiveness is evidenced by increased absenteeism, withheld commitment, and critical remarks.

Stage 6: Acceptance   The hurdle between stages 4 and 5 is much like that between stages 2 and 3. Consequently, it once again falls on an influential member of the group, typically not the leader, to challenge his or her peers to do some reality testing. This exercise promotes greater understanding about the members' expectations for each other and for the group as a whole.

> As a result of overcoming this final obstacle, the group structure can become flexible and adjust to fit the requirements of the situation without causing problems for the members. Influence can shift depending on who has the particular expertise or skills required for the group task or activity. Subgroups can work on special problems or subproblems without posing threats to the authority or cohesiveness of the rest of the group.[16]

These characteristics combine to signal that the group has matured. B. F. Goodrich Co.'s team-oriented participative management program is a good example. The success of that program depends on mature groups that have survived the ups and downs of the group development process (see OB in Action).

OB IN ACTION

**The Systematic Development of Group Maturity Keeps
B. F. Goodrich's Participative Management Program
on Track**

The B. F. Goodrich Tire Group is using work teams in its controller's organization to involve employees in problem solving and departmental planning.
[These voluntary eight- to twelve-member teams meet weekly.] The purpose of
this form of participative management—called the Employee Involvement
Network (EIN)—is to encourage employees to use their skills and ideas in
order to improve productivity. Specific objectives of EIN are:

To enlist employees' and their managers' support in identifying and solving
  problems by more effective two-way communication within a group or
  department.

To develop a sense of corporate "ownership" among employees, and create
  the necessary environment to improve group or department performance.

To recognize the group or department's achievements in order to encourage
  and stimulate employee participation. . . .

   During the early stages of the work team, the group tends to center on
improving the work environment. In some cases, team members test management's commitment to the employee involvement network. Management's
willingness to listen and implement new ideas is very important to continued
group development. Not receiving clear and full explanations, or having ideas,
requests or suggestions rejected outright without good reason can be harmful
to a team's development. How well the work team performs also depends upon
the degree of employee involvement at the meetings and if team members use
the proper problem solving techniques. Team members also should critique
their own meetings.

   A fully functioning work team is characterized by stable participation and
steady leadership. Generally, the meetings are productive and there is ongoing
problem solving. It could take up to a year for a work group to develop into a
cohesive and productive team. The team at this stage focuses on improving the
department's work, reviewing productivity gains, controlling costs, or making
other improvements.

   . . . a monitoring of the Billing Department's operations reveals the contribution EIN has made to the controller's organization. In the first year we have
been able to increase the number of billing documents processed each work
day by 21 percent, and the number of billing documents processed per em-
ployee-hour by 15 percent. We have been able to reduce the cost for each hour
employed by 9.4 percent, the cost of each bill produced by 11 percent, and total
department expense by 2.2 percent. The average number of days absent per
employee went down by 40 percent.

Source: Excerpted from material in Gene L. Smith, "Improving Productivity in the Controller's
Organization," *Management Accounting*, January 1986, pp. 49–51. Used with permission.

Group Development: Research and Practical Implications

A growing body of group development research provides managers with
some practical insights.

Feedback One fruitful study was carried out by a pair of Dutch social psychologists. They hypothesized that interpersonal feedback would vary systematically during the group development process. "The unit of feedback measured was a verbal message directed from one participant to another in which some aspect of behavior was addressed."[17] After collecting and categorizing 1,600 instances of feedback from four different eight-person groups, they concluded:

- Interpersonal feedback increases as the group develops through successive stages.
- As the group develops, positive feedback increases and negative feedback decreases.
- Interpersonal feedback becomes more specific as the group develops.
- The credibility of peer feedback increases as the group develops.[18]

These findings hold important lessons for managers. The content and delivery of interpersonal feedback among work group or committee members can be used as a gauge of whether the group is developing properly. For example, the onset of stages 2 (conflict and challenge) and 5 (disillusion) will be signaled by a noticeable increase in *negative* feedback. Effort can then be directed at generating specific, positive feedback among the members so the group's development will not stall. The feedback model discussed in Chapter 13 is helpful in this regard.

Deadlines Recent field and laboratory studies found uncertainty about deadlines to be a major disruptive force in both group development and intergroup relations. The practical implications of this finding were summed up by the researcher as follows:

> Uncertain or shifting deadlines are a fact of life in many organizations. Interdependent organizational units and groups may keep each other waiting, may suddenly move deadlines forward or back, or may create deadlines that are known to be earlier than is necessary in efforts to control erratic workflows. The current research suggests that the consequences of such uncertainty may involve more than stress, wasted time, overtime work, and intergroup conflicts. Synchrony in group members' expectations about deadlines may be critical to groups' abilities to accomplish successful transitions in their work.[19]

Thus, effective group management involves clarifying not only tasks and goals, but deadlines as well. When group members accurately perceive important deadlines, the pacing of work and timing of interdependent tasks tends to be more efficient.

Leadership Styles Along a somewhat different line, experts in the area of leadership contend that different leadership styles are needed as work groups develop.

> In general, it has been documented that leadership behavior that is active, aggressive, directive, structured, and task-oriented seems to have favorable results early in the group's history. However, when those behaviors are maintained throughout the life of the group, they seem to have a negative impact on cohesiveness and quality of work. Conversely, leadership behavior that is supportive, democratic, decentralized, and participative seems to be related to poorer functioning in the early group development stages. However, when these behav-

iors are maintained throughout the life of the group, more productivity, satisfaction, and creativity result.[20]

The practical punch line here is that managers are advised to shift from a directive and structured leadership style to a participative and supportive style as the group develops. (Leadership is discussed in detail in Chapter 14.)

• GROUP STRUCTURE AND COMPOSITION

Work groups of varying size are made up of individuals with varying ability and motivation. Moreover, those individuals perform different roles, on either an assigned or voluntary basis. No wonder some work groups are more productive than others. No wonder some committees are tightly knit while others wallow in conflict. In this section, we examine five important dimensions of group structure and composition: (1) functional roles of group members, (2) technology–structure fit, (3) group size, (4) gender composition, and (5) group member ability. Each of these dimensions alternatively can enhance or hinder group effectiveness, depending on how it is managed.

Functional Roles Performed by Group Members

In Chapter 8, we introduced and discussed the sociological concept of *roles*. Here we extend that concept by considering two categories of functional roles that individuals fulfill while working in groups. Specifically, task and maintenance roles (see Table 9–2) need to be performed if a given work group is to get anything accomplished.

Task versus Maintenance Roles   **Task roles** enable the work group to define, clarify, and pursue a common purpose. Meanwhile, **maintenance roles** foster supportive and constructive interpersonal relationships. In short, task roles keep the group *on track* while maintenance roles keep the group *together*. A fraternity or sorority member is performing a task function when he or she stands at a business meeting and says: "What is the real issue here? We don't seem to be getting anywhere." Another individual who says, "Let's hear from those who oppose this plan," is performing a maintenance function. Importantly, each of the various task and maintenance roles may be played in varying combinations and sequences by either the group's leader or any of its members.

Checklist for Managers   The task and maintenance roles listed in Table 9–2 can serve as a handy checklist for managers and group leaders who wish to ensure proper group development. Roles that are not always performed when needed, such as those of coordinator, evaluator, and gatekeeper, can be performed in a timely manner by the formal leader or assigned to other members.

International managers need to be sensitive to cultural differences regarding the relative importance of task and maintenance roles. In Japan, for example, cultural tradition calls for more emphasis on maintenance roles (see International OB).

• **TABLE 9–2** Functional Roles Performed by Group Members

Task Roles	Description
Initiator:	Suggests new goals or ideas.
Information seeker/giver:	Clarifies key issues.
Opinion seeker/giver:	Clarifies pertinent values.
Elaborator:	Promotes greater understanding through examples or exploration of implications.
Coordinator:	Pulls together ideas and suggestions.
Orienter:	Keeps group headed toward its stated goal(s).
Evaluator:	Tests group's accomplishments with various criteria such as logic and practicality.
Energizer:	Prods group to move along or to accomplish more.
Procedural technician:	Performs routine duties (e.g., handing out materials or rearranging seats).
Recorder:	Performs a "group memory" function by documenting discussion and outcomes.

Maintenance Roles	Description
Encourager:	Fosters group solidarity by accepting and praising various points of view.
Harmonizer:	Mediates conflict through reconciliation or humor.
Compromiser:	Helps resolve conflict by meeting others "half way."
Gatekeeper:	Encourages all group members to participate.
Standard setter:	Evaluates the quality of group processes.
Commentator:	Records and comments on group processes/dynamics.
Follower:	Serves as a passive audience.

Source: Adapted from discussion in Kenneth D. Benne and Paul Sheats, "Functionl Roles of Group Members," *Journal of Social Issues,* Spring 1948; pp. 41–49.

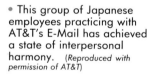

• This group of Japanese employees practicing with AT&T's E-Mail has achieved a state of interpersonal harmony. *(Reproduced with permission of AT&T)*

INTERNATIONAL OB

What It Takes to Be a Good Group Member in Japan

In every kind of group, one quality is desired above all—interpersonal harmony. Much of members' behavior is directed toward creating a pleasant state in their unit. They are gracious, courteous, and gentle; they smile often, bow low and long to friends and to strangers they respect, avoid acts of rivalry, offer help to those in need, show agreement by repeatedly saying "yes" while a companion is speaking, and are shy with superiors. In informal gatherings participants eschew behaviors that might ruffle the composure of those assembled. They do not match wits, engage in sparkling repartee, or display hostile jocularity.

Courtesy requires that members not be conspicuous or disputatious in a meeting or classroom. If two or more members discover that their views differ—a fact that is tactfully taken to be unfortunate—they adjourn to find more information and to work toward a stance that all can accept. They do not press their personal opinions through strong arguments, neat logic, or rewards and threats. And they do not hesitate to shift their beliefs if doing so will preserve smooth interpersonal relations. (To lose is to win.)

A meeting is a joint effort to find a mutually agreeable solution; it is not a debate. Promotions within a company, moreover, are based in large part on an employee's capacity to work well with others.

Source: Alvin Zander, "The Value of Belonging to a Group in Japan," *Small Group Behavior*, vol. 14 (February 1983), pp. 7–8. Copyright © 1983 by Sage Publications, Inc. Reprinted by permission of Sage Publications, Inc.

Technology–Structure Fit

In Chapter 18, we will discuss the contingency approach to organization design. According to this established perspective, effective organizations are those structured to fit the demands of the situation. An inappropriately structured organization causes problems, akin to someone wearing the wrong size shoes. A recent field study of 221 bank managers who worked in 10 departments extended this contingency concept of situational fit to the work group level.[22] Technology and structure variables were measured and correlated with group performance.

Technology was defined in terms of the type of problem solving required to handle bank managers' daily duties. Problems were categorized as simple or complex and predictable or unpredictable. Among the structural variables measured were vertical and horizontal differentiation. **Vertical differentiation** involved the number of hierarchical levels represented in the work group. In contrast, **horizontal differentiation** involved the number of different job categories represented in the work group. When the researchers related these situational variables to group performance, two contingencies became apparent (see Figure 9–4).

When complex problems were the norm, work groups with high vertical differentiation tended to be the most effective. However, when the bank managers could not reliably predict the types of problems they would encounter on a given day, groups with high horizontal differentiation tended to

• FIGURE 9-4   A Partial Contingency Model for Work Group Effectiveness

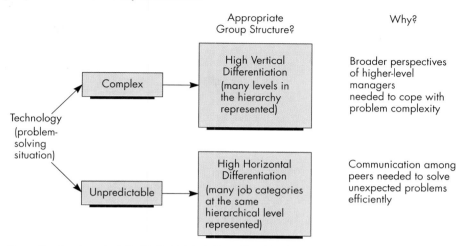

Source: Based on discussion in Fred R. David, John A. Pearce II, and W. Alan Randolph, "Linking Technology and Structure to Enhance Group Performance," *Journal of Applied Psychology*, April 1989, pp. 233–41.

perform the best. Practical reasons for these two linkages are listed in the right-hand side of Figure 9–4.

These findings are a good start. But more research is needed to pinpoint other group-level contingencies for various types of problems. In the meantime, managers are advised to carefully consider the type of problems encountered when staffing task groups. The contingencies in Figure 9–4 are a useful guide.

Group Size

How many group members is too many? The answer to this deceptively simple question has intrigued managers and academics for years. Folk wisdom says "two heads are better than one" but that "too many cooks spoil the broth." So where should a manager draw the line when staffing a committee? At 3? At 5 or 6? At 10 or more? Researchers have taken two different approaches to pinpointing optimum group size: mathematical modeling and laboratory simulations. Let us briefly review recent findings from these two approaches.

The Mathematical Modeling Approach   This approach involves building a mathematical model around certain desired outcomes of group action such as decision quality. Due to differing assumptions and statistical techniques, the results of this research are inconclusive. Statistical estimates of optimum group size have ranged from 3 to 13.[23]

The Laboratory Simulation Approach   This stream of research is based on the assumption that group behavior needs to be observed firsthand in controlled laboratory settings. A laboratory study by respected Australian researcher Philip Yetton and his colleague, Preston Bottger, provides useful insights about group size and performance.[24]

Five hundred fifty-five subjects (330 managers and 225 graduate management students, of whom 20 percent were female) were assigned to task teams ranging in size from 2 to 6. The teams worked on the National Aeronautics and Space Administration moon survival exercise. (This exercise involves the rank ordering of 15 pieces of equipment that would enable a spaceship crew on the moon to survive a 200-mile trip between a crash-landing site and home base.)[25] After analyzing the relationships between group size and group performance, Yetton and Bottger concluded:

> It would be difficult, at least with respect to decision quality, to justify groups larger than five members. . . . Of course, to meet needs other than high decision quality, organizations may employ groups significantly larger than four or five.[26]

Managerial Implications   Within a contingency management framework, there is no hard-and-fast rule about group size. It depends on the manager's objective for the group. If a high-quality decision is the main objective, then a three-to five-member group would be appropriate. However, if the objective is to generate creative ideas, encourage participation, socialize new members, engage in training, or communicate policies, then groups much larger than five could be justified. But managers need to be aware of *qualitative* changes that occur when group size increases. A recent meta-analysis of eight studies found the following relationships: as group size increased, group leaders tended to become more directive and group member satisfaction tended to decline slightly.[27]

Odd-numbered groups (e.g., three, five, seven members, etc.), are recommended if the issue is to be settled by a majority vote. Voting deadlocks (e.g., 2–2, 3–3) too often hamper effectiveness of even-numbered groups. A majority decision rule is not necessarily a good idea. A recent study found that better group outcomes were obtained by negotiation groups that used a unanimous as opposed to majority decision rule. Individuals' self-interests were more effectively integrated when groups used a unanimous decision criterion.[28]

Effects of Men and Women Working Together in Groups

As pointed out in Chapter 2, the female portion of the U.S. labor force has grown significantly in recent years. This demographic shift brought an increase in the number of organizational committees and teams composed of both men and women. Some profound effects on group dynamics might be expected. Let us see what researchers have found in the way of group gender composition effects and what managers can do about them.

Women Face an Uphill Battle in Mixed-Gender Task Groups   Recent laboratory and field studies paint a picture of inequality for women working in mixed-gender groups. Both women and men need to be aware of these often subtle but powerful group dynamics so corrective steps can be taken.

In a laboratory study of six-person task groups, a clear pattern of gender inequality was found in the way group members interrupted each other. Men interrupted women significantly more often than they did other men. Women, who tended to interrupt less frequently and less successfully than men, interrupted men and women equally.[29]

A field study of mixed-gender police and nursing teams in the Netherlands found another group dynamics disadvantage for women. These two particular professions—police work and nursing—were fruitful research areas because men dominate the former while women dominate the latter. As women move into male-dominated police forces and men gain employment opportunities in the female-dominated world of nursing, who faces the greatest resistance? The answer from this study was the women police officers. As the representation of the minority gender (either female police officers or male nurses) increased in the work groups, the following changes in attitude were observed:

> The attitude of the male majority changes from neutral to resistant, whereas the attitude of the female majority changes from favorable to neutral. In other words, men increasingly want to keep their domain for themselves, while women remain willing to share their domain with men.[30]

Again, managers are faced with the challenge of countering discriminatory tendencies in group dynamics.

Social-sexual behavior was the focus of a random survey of 1,232 working men (n = 405) and women (n = 827) in the Los Angeles area.[31] Both harassing and nonharassing sexual conduct were investigated. One third of the female employees and one fourth of the male employees reported being sexually harassed in their present job. Nonharassing sexual behavior was much more common, with 80 percent of the total sample reporting experience with such behavior. Indeed, according to the researchers, increased social contact between men and women in work groups and organizations had led to increased sexualization of the workplace. (To assess the extent of sexualization in your present or former workplace, take a moment to complete the OB Exercise. What are the practical implications of your score?)

Constructive Managerial Action   Male and female employees can and often do work well together in groups. A survey of 387 male U.S. government employees sought to determine how they were affected by the growing number of female co-workers. The researchers concluded, ''Under many circumstances, including intergender interaction in work groups, frequent contact leads to cooperative and supportive social relations.''[32] Still, managers need to take affirmative steps to ensure that the documented sexualization of work environments does not erode into sexual harassment. Whether perpetrated against women or men, sexual harassment is demeaning and appropriately called ''work environment pollution.'' Moreover, the U.S. Equal Employment Opportunity Commission holds employers legally accountable for behavior it considers sexually harassing (see Table 9–3 for specifics).

Beyond avoiding lawsuits by establishing and enforcing anti-discrimination and sexual harassment policies, managers need to take additional steps. Work force diversity training is a popular approach today. Gender-issue workshops are another option. ''Du Pont Co., for example, holds monthly workshops to make managers aware of gender-related attitudes.''[33] Phyllis B. Davis, a senior vice president at Avon Corp., has framed the goal of such efforts by saying: ''It's a question of consciously creating an environment where everyone has an equal shot at contributing, participating, and most of all advancing.''[34] (See OB in Action.)

> ## • OB EXERCISE
>
> ### What Is the Degree of Sexualization in Your Work Environment?
>
> **Instructions:**
> Describe the work environment at your present (or last) job by selecting one number along the following scale for each question.
>
>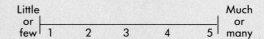
>
> ```
>  Little
>   or   |————————————————————————————|
>  few    1      2      3      4      5
> ```
> Little or few — Much or many
>
> _____ 1. How much joking or talking about sexual matters do you hear?
> _____ 2. How much social pressure are women under to flirt with men?
> _____ 3. How much social pressure are men under to flirt with women?
> _____ 4. How much of a problem is sexual harassment in your workplace?
> _____ 5. How many women dress in a sexually attractive way to men?
> _____ 6. How many men dress in a sexually attractive way to women?
> _____ 7. How many women act in sexually seductive ways toward men?
> _____ 8. How many men act in sexually seductive ways toward women?
>
> _____ = Total score
>
> *Norms*
>
> Low degree of sexualization: 8–16
> Moderate degree of sexualization: 17–31
> High degree of sexualization: 32–40
>
> Source: Adapted from Barbara A. Gutek, Aaron Groff Cohen, and Alison M. Konrad, "Predicting Social-Sexual Behavior at Work: A Contact Hypothesis," *Academy of Management Journal*, September 1990, p. 577.

• TABLE 9–3   Sexual Harassment: Behavioral and Legal Aspects

> What exactly is sexual harassment? The Equal Employment Opportunity Commission (EEOC) says that unwelcome sexual advances, requests for sexual favors, and other verbal or physical conduct of a sexual nature constitute sexual harassment when submission to such conduct is made a condition of employment; when submission to or rejection of sexual advances is used as a basis for employment decisions; or when such conduct creates an intimidating, hostile, or offensive work environment. These EEOC guidelines interpreting Title VII of the Civil Rights Act of 1964 further state that employers are responsible for the actions of their supervisors and agents and that employers are responsible for the actions of other employees if the employer knows or should have known about the sexual harassment.

Source: Adapted from B. Terry Thornton, "Sexual Harassment, 1: Discouraging It in the Work Place," *Personnel*, April 1986, p. 18

Individual Ability and Group Effectiveness

Imagine that you are a department manager charged with making an important staffing decision amid the following circumstances. You need to form eight 3-person task teams from a pool of 24 employees. Based on each of the employee's prior work records and their scores on ability tests, you know

OB IN ACTION

Corning's Gender-Awareness Workshops Make a Difference

During a gender-awareness workshop at Corning in Corning, N.Y., women executives complained that their male colleagues never invited them [to informal gatherings]. Not that lunch per se was important. But the women felt they were missing out on useful gossip. That could include news of someone being transferred, which would mean that a job had opened. . . .

For Corning men, realizing that they were cutting out women was just the first step. Now, coed executive groups can be seen frequenting Corning's favorite lunch haunts or having drinks after work.

Source: Adapted from Walecia Konrad, "Welcome to the Woman-Friendly Company," *Business Week,* August 6, 1990, p. 53.

that 12 have high ability and 12 have low ability. The crux of your problem is how to assign the 12 high-ability employees. Should you spread your best talent around by making sure there are both high- and low-ability employees on each team? Then again, you may want to concentrate your best talent by forming four high-ability teams and four low-ability teams. Or should you attempt to find a compromise between these two extremes? What is your decision? Why? A recent field experiment provided an instructive and interesting answer.

The Israeli Tank-Crew Study   Aharon Tziner and Dov Eden, researchers from Tel Aviv University, systematically manipulated the composition of 208 three-man tank crews. All possible combinations of high- and low-ability personnel were studied (high-high-high; high-high-low; high-low-low; and low-low-low). Ability was a composite measure of (1) overall intelligence, (2) amount of formal education, (3) proficiency in Hebrew, and (4) interview ratings. Successful operation of the tanks required the three-man crews to perform with a high degree of synchronized interdependence.[35] Tank-crew effectiveness was determined by commanding officers during military maneuvers for the Israel Defense Forces.

As expected, the high-high-high ability tank crews performed the best and the low-low-low the worst. But the researchers discovered an important *interaction effect:*

> Each member's ability influenced crew performance effectiveness differently depending on the ability levels of the other two members. A high-ability member appears to achieve more in combination with other uniformly high-ability members than in combination with low-ability members.[36]

The tank crews composed of three high-ability personnel far outperformed all other ability combinations. The interaction effect also worked in a negative direction because the low-low-low ability crews performed far below expected levels. Moreover, as illustrated in Figure 9–5, significantly greater performance gains were achieved by creating high-high-high ability crews than by upgrading low-low-low ability crews with one or two high-ability members.

• **FIGURE 9-5**   Ability of Israeli Tank-Crew Members and Improvement in Effectiveness

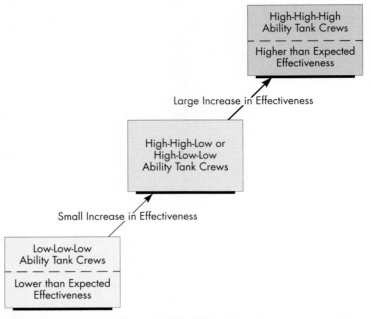

Source: Based on discussion in Aharon Tziner and Dov Eden, "Effects of Crew Composition on Crew Performance: Does the Whole Equal the Sum of Its Parts?" *Journal of Applied Psychology*, February 1985, pp. 85–93.

• **FIGURE 9-6**   A Contingency Model for Staffing Work Groups: Effective Use of Available Talent

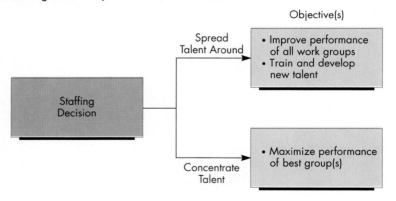

This returns us to the staffing problem at the beginning of this section. Tziner and Eden recommended the following solution:

> Our experimental results suggest that the most productive solution would be to allocate six highs and all 12 lows to six teams of high-low-low ability and to assign the six remaining highs to two teams of high-high-high ability. This avoids the disproportionately low productivity of the low-low-low ability combination, while leaving some of the highs for high-high-high ability teams where they are most productive. . . . Our results show that talent is used more effectively when concentrated than when spread around.[37]

A Managerial Interpretation   While the real-life aspect of the tank-crew study makes its results fairly generalizable, a qualification is in order. Specifically, modern complex organizations demand a more flexible contingency approach. Figure 9–6 shows two basic contingencies. If management seeks to *improve* the performance of *all* groups or train novices, high-ability personnel can be spread around. This option would be appropriate in a high-volume production operation. But if the desired outcome is to *maximize* performance of the *best* group(s), then high-ability personnel should be concentrated. This second option would be advisable in research and development departments, for example, where technological breakthroughs need to be achieved. Extraordinary achievements require clusters of extraordinary talent.

• THREATS TO GROUP EFFECTIVENESS

Even when managers carefully staff and organize task groups, group dynamics can still go haywire. Forehand knowledge of three major threats to group effectiveness—the Asch effect, groupthink, and social loafing—can help managers take necessary preventive steps. Because the first two problems relate to blind conformity, some brief background work is in order.

Very little would be accomplished in task groups and organizations without conformity to norms, role expectations, policies, and rules and regulations. After all, deadlines, commitments, and product/service quality standards have to be established and adhered to if the organization is to survive. But, as pointed out by management consultants Robert Blake and Jane Srygley Mouton, conformity is a two-edged sword:

> Social forces powerful enough to influence members to conform may influence them to perform at a very high level of quality and productivity. All too often, however, the pressure to conform stifles creativity, influencing members to cling to attitudes that may be out of touch with organizational needs and even out of kilter with the times.[38]

Moreover, excessive or blind conformity can stifle critical thinking, the last line of defense against unethical conduct. Almost daily accounts in the popular media of insider trading scandals, illegal dumping of hazardous wastes, and other unethical practices make it imperative that future managers understand the mechanics of blind conformity.

The Asch Effect

Forty years ago, social psychologist Solomon Asch conducted a series of laboratory experiments that revealed a negative side of group dynamics.[39] Under the guise of a "perception test," Asch had groups of seven to nine volunteer college students look at 12 pairs of cards such as the ones in Figure 9–7. The object was to identify the line that was the same length as the standard line. Each individual was told to announce his or her choice to the group. Since the differences among the comparison lines were obvious, there should have been unanimous agreement during each of the 12 rounds. But that was not the case.

• **FIGURE 9-7**   The Asch Experiment

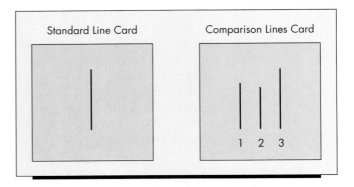

A Minority of One   All but one member of each group were Asch's confederates who agreed to systematically select the wrong line during seven of the rounds (the other five rounds were control rounds for comparison purposes). The remaining individual was the naive subject who was being tricked. Group pressure was created by having the naive subject in each group be among the last to announce his or her choice. Thirty-one subjects were tested. Asch's research question was: "How often would the naive subjects conform to a majority opinion that was obviously wrong?"

Only 20 percent of Asch's subjects remained entirely independent; 80 percent yielded to the pressures of group opinion at least once! Fifty-eight percent knuckled under to the "immoral majority" at least twice. Hence, the **Asch effect,** the distortion of individual judgment by a unanimous but incorrect opposition, was documented. (Do you ever turn your back on your better judgment by giving in to group pressure?)

A Managerial Perspective   Asch's experiment has been widely replicated with mixed results. Both high and low degrees of blind conformity have been observed with various situations and subjects. Recent replications in Japan and Kuwait have demonstrated that the Asch effect is not unique to the United States.[40] But the point is not precisely how great the Asch effect is in a given situation or culture, but rather, managers committed to ethical conduct need to be concerned that the Asch effect exists. Even isolated instances of blind, unthinking conformity seriously threaten the effectiveness and integrity of work groups and organizations. (For example, put yourself in Evelyn's place in A Matter of Ethics. How would you handle her ethical dilemma with the Asch effect?) Functional conflict and assertiveness, discussed in Chapters 10 and 12, can help employees respond appropriately when they find themselves facing an immoral majority. Ethical codes mentioning specific practices also can provide support and guidance.

Groupthink

Why did President Lyndon B. Johnson and his group of highly intelligent White House advisers make some very *unintelligent* decisions that escalated the Vietnam War? Those fateful decisions were made despite obvious warn-

A MATTER OF ETHICS

What Should Evelyn Do?

Evelyn worked for an automotive steel casting company. She was part of a small group asked to investigate the cause of an operating problem that had developed in the wheel castings of a new luxury automobile and to make recommendations for its improvement. The problem did not directly create an unsafe condition, but it did lead to irritating sounds. The Vice President of Engineering told the group that he was certain that the problem was due to tensile stress in the castings.

Evelyn and a lab technician conducted tests and found conclusive evidence that the problem was not tensile stress. As Evelyn began work on other possible explanations of the problem, she was told that the problem had been solved. A report prepared by Evelyn's boss strongly supported the tensile stress hypothesis. All of the data points from Evelyn's experiments have been changed to fit the curves, and some of the points which were far from where the theory would predict have been omitted. The report "proved" that tensile stress was responsible for the problem.

Should Evelyn contradict her boss's report? . . . Is it important that people do everything they can to have the truth known? . . . Suppose the problem with the brake involved more than irritating sounds. Would it make a difference if the brake problem caused uneven brake applications and skids? . . . The data in the boss's report are false. Does it make it morally wrong if Evelyn fails to contradict the report?

Note: It might help to refer back to the ethics discussion in Chapter 3 when identifying and weighing options.

Source: James Weber, "Managers' Moral Reasoning: Assessing Their Responses to Three Moral Dilemmas," *Human Relations,* July 1990, pp. 699–700.

ing signals, including stronger than expected resistance from the North Vietnamese and withering support at home and abroad. Systematic analysis of the decision-making processes underlying the war in Vietnam and other U.S. foreign policy fiascoes prompted Yale University's Irving Janis to coin the term *groupthink*.[41] Modern managers can all too easily become victims of groupthink, just like President Johnson's staff, if they passively ignore the danger.

Definition and Symptoms of Groupthink   Janis defines **groupthink** as "a mode of thinking that people engage in when they are deeply involved in a cohesive in-group, when members' strivings for unanimity override their motivation to realistically appraise alternative courses of action."[42] He adds, "Groupthink refers to a deterioration of mental efficiency, reality testing, and moral judgment that results from in-group pressures."[43] Unlike Asch's subjects, who were strangers to each other, members of groups victimized by groupthink are friendly, tightly knit, and cohesive.

The symptoms of groupthink listed in Figure 9–8 thrive in the sort of climate outlined in the following critique of corporate directors in the United States:

• **Figure 9-8**   Symptoms of Groupthink Lead to Defective Decision Making

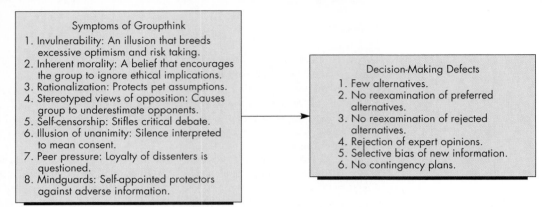

Sources: Symptoms adapted from Irving L. Janis, *Groupthink*, 2nd ed. (Boston: Houghton Mifflin, 1982), pp. 174–75. Defects excerpted from Gregory Moorhead, "Groupthink: Hypothesis in Need of Testing," *Group & Organization Studies*, December 1982, p. 434.

Many directors simply don't rock the boat. "No one likes to be the skunk at the garden party," says [management consultant] Victor H. Palmieri. . . . "One does not make friends and influence people in the boardroom or elsewhere by raising hard questions that create embarrassment or discomfort for management."[44]

In short, policy- and decision-making groups can become so cohesive that strong-willed executives are able to gain unanimous support for poor decisions. (See OB in Action.)

Groupthink Research and Prevention   Laboratory studies using college students as subjects validate portions of Janis's groupthink concept. Specifically, it has been found that:

- Groups with a moderate amount of cohesiveness produce better decisions than low- or high-cohesive groups.
- Highly cohesive groups victimized by groupthink make the poorest decisions, despite high confidence in those decisions.[45]

Janis believes prevention is better than cure when dealing with groupthink. He recommends the following preventive measures:

1. Each member of the group should be assigned the role of critical evaluator. This role involves actively voicing objections and doubts.
2. Top-level executives should not use policy committees to rubberstamp decisions that have already been made.
3. Different groups with different leaders should explore the same policy questions.
4. Subgroup debates and outside experts should be used to introduce fresh perspectives.
5. Someone should be given the role of devil's advocate when discussing major alternatives. This person tries to uncover every conceivable negative factor.

OB IN ACTION

What Is the Potential for Groupthink in the Bush White House?

George Bush's is a high-energy, do-it-yourself presidency driven by a zest for problem solving—or as he put it in his acceptance speech at the Republican National Convention, "missions defined, missions completed." He understands the mechanics of government, and he loves to pull the levers. While he respects the bureaucracy, he often circumvents it, going out of channels for information. He dives into the nitty-gritty of policymaking. . . .

The President's emphasis on teamwork has its occasional downside. Says one aide: "Sometimes controversial ideas and issues get swept under the rug." Adds former Bush chief of staff Craig Fuller: "People tend to watch where Secretary of State James Baker and [Budget Director Richard] Darman are coming down on an issue, then fall into line." . . .

At the White House, Bush's past is prologue. Outraged by the internal warfare that characterized the Reagan Administration, Bush put a high priority on team play. While Reagan turned to a headhunter to fill most Cabinet and White House posts, Bush personally chose loyal and seasoned friends. Sitting around the pool at Camp David, First Lady Barbara Bush told Environmental Protection Agency Administrator William Reilly, the only newcomer to Bush's inner circle, "I said to George: 'You know, almost your entire Cabinet are our friends.' He said: 'Well, what would you expect?'" . . .

He invites strongly argued points of view and takes his time deciding. But once he's spoken, he expects his troops to fall in line. Bush told a packed Republican fund-raiser on his 66th birthday in June: "I thank my lucky stars that we can fight like cats and dogs in Cabinet meetings but once I make a decision, move on as a team." He also likes to point out: "Loyalty is not a character flaw."

Source: Excerpted from Ann Reilly Dowd, "How Bush Manages the Presidency," *Fortune*, August 27, 1990, pp. 68–70. Copyright 1990 The Time Inc. Magazine Company.

---

6. Once a consensus has been reached, everyone should be encouraged to rethink their position to check for flaws.[46]

These anti-groupthink measures can help cohesive groups produce sound recommendations and decisions.

Social Loafing

Is group performance less than, equal to, or greater than the sum of its parts? Can three people, for example, working together accomplish less than, the same as, or more than they would working separately? An interesting study conducted more than a half century ago by a French agricultural engineer named Ringelmann found the answer to be "less than."[47] In a rope-pulling exercise, Ringlemann reportedly found that three people pulling together could achieve only two and a half times the average individual rate. Eight pullers achieved less than four times the individual rate. This tendency for individual effort to decline as group size increases has come to be called **social loafing.** Let us briefly analyze this threat to group effectiveness and synergy with an eye toward avoiding it.

Social Loafing Theory and Research   Among the theoretical explanations for the social loafing effect are: (1) equity of effort ("Everyone else is goofing off, so why shouldn't I?"), (2) loss of personal accountability ("I'm lost in the crowd, so who cares?"), (3) motivational loss due to the sharing of rewards ("Why should I work harder than the others when everyone gets the same reward?"), and (4) coordination loss as more people perform the task ("We're getting in each other's way.").

Laboratory studies refined these theories by identifying situational factors that moderated the social loafing effect. Social loafing occurred when:

- The task was perceived to be unimportant or simple.[48]
- Group members thought their individual output was not identifiable.[49]
- Group members expected their co-workers to loaf.[50]

But social loafing did *not* occur when group members in two recent laboratory studies expected to be evaluated.[51]

Practical Implications   These findings demonstrate that social loafing is not an inevitable part of group effort. Management can curb this threat to group effectiveness by making sure the task is challenging and perceived as important. Additionally, it is a good idea to hold group members personally accountable for identifiable portions of the group's task. (Recall the discussion of goal setting in Chapter 6.) Finally, positive expectations that everyone in the group will be working hard need to be fostered via trust and supportive leadership. Trust is covered in Chapter 11 and leadership is discussed in Chapter 14.

• SOCIAL NETWORKS: TOWARD UNDERSTANDING INTERGROUP INTERACTIONS

Social network analysis is defined as the process of graphically mapping and categorizing social transactions to identify meaningful patterns. Although this sociological technique, in one form or another, has been around for many years, it was not proposed as an OB tool until 1979. According to those responsible for extending the social network perspective to the field of OB:

> In network analysis, an organization is conceived of as clusters of people joined by a variety of links which transmit goods and services, information, influence, and affect [feelings]. These clusters of people are both formal (prescribed), such as departments or work groups, and informal (emergent), such as coalitions and cliques.[52]

The social network perspective is presented here as an instructive analytical tool, which will help you better understand social processes such as socialization, group formation, power, politics, conflict, communication, and organizational cultures. Social network analysis is instructive for managers because it:

- Is a generic tool that can be used to better understand both interpersonal and intergroup interaction.
- Realistically characterizes organizations as complex, changing, and dynamic rather than simple and static.
- Treats formal and informal interactions as equally important. (Informal interactions too often are underemphasized or ignored.)
- Sorts out the complex web of multiple relationships among organizational members and groups.
- Shows the relative importance of network members (including but not limited to their formal authority and status).
- Identifies the different functions performed by network members.

The following sections explore the social network perspective by considering five functions of network members, network clusters, recent research, and managerial implications.

Social Network Functions

Depending on the number and nature of their social transactions with others, individuals fulfill different network functions. They may function as stars, liaisons, bridges, gatekeepers, or isolates. Each social network function is defined as follows:

- *Star*—an individual with the most linkages in the network.
- *Liaison*—an individual who links two or more clusters without belonging to a cluster.
- *Bridge*—an individual who serves as a linking pin by belonging to two or more clusters.
- *Gatekeeper*—an individual who links his or her network to outside domains such as suppliers, clients, government agencies, and so on.
- *Isolate*—an individual who is no longer connected to the network.[53]

Figure 9–9 portrays an idealized social network to illustrate each of these five functions. Note that individuals 1 and 4 are both stars because each has five network linkages or connections. But 4 is labeled a gatekeeper because of his or her outside connection. Importantly, three of the network functions—liaison, bridge, and gatekeeper—deal with intergroup activity.

Prescribed and Emergent Clusters

Two types of clusters also appear in Figure 9–9. They are equivalent to the formal and informal groups discussed earlier. *Prescribed clusters* are task teams or formal committees carrying out assigned jobs. The *emergent cluster* is an informal, unofficial grouping of network members. The star ① obviously is the central figure in this emergent cluster. This cluster is a *coalition* if it is a temporary alliance with a specific purpose. For example, a group of factory employees who band together to complain to management

• **FIGURE 9-9**   Social Network Functions and Key Intergroup Dynamics

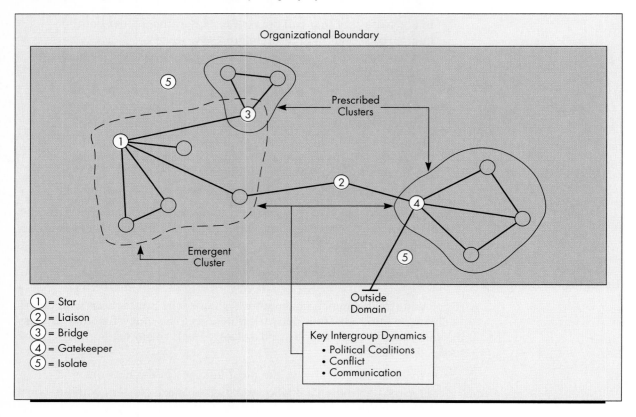

about toxic fumes in the work area is a coalition. If this emergent cluster is based on lasting friendships, then it is a **clique.**[54]

Political coalitions, conflict, and communication—the key intergroup dynamics included in Figure 9–9—are discussed in detail in subsequent chapters.

Field Research Insights

Organizational research of social networks is still somewhat sparse because of its relatively recent introduction to the field of OB. A pioneering 1984 study conducted at a newspaper publishing company found that central (nonsupervisory) members of the various networks were promoted to supervisory positions more often than noncentral members. Central network members were those who had the greatest control over their co-workers' access to resources and information. This outcome prompted the researchers to conclude that, regarding promotions, it pays to be in the "right place" in organizational networks.[55]

Another study examined the relationship between social networks and turnover for employees in three fast-food restaurants. Findings indicated that turnover was clustered by social networks. That is, employees who perceived themselves as belonging to certain networks either stayed together or quit together.[56]

A recent social network analysis of 580 work group members employed by 20 diverse organizations found that strong interpersonal and intergroup relationships were associated with less intergroup conflict. Relationship strength was measured in terms of frequency of contact. Thus, familiarity tends to breed intergroup harmony.[57]

The Practical Value of a Social Network Perspective

Managers who view their work units and organizations as social networks of individuals and groups have a handy early detection system for interpersonal problems and opportunities. Keeping track of those who fulfill key network functions, for example, is a good idea. A star of an emergent cluster might be a good candidate for a managerial position. Liaisons are in a good position to be objective observers and communication monitors because they link clusters without belonging to them. Those who serve as bridges may be able to help management resolve intergroup conflicts because of their familiarity with the parties involved.

Gatekeepers, meanwhile, can keep an organization properly tuned to its environment. PepsiCo's emphasis on the gatekeeper function prompted the head of the firm to tell *Business Week:* "You hear a lot of conversations around Pepsi about what's going on with the consumer, what's going on at the supermarket, what the competition is doing."[58] Thus, it is no accident that PepsiCo is widely admired for its ability to read and quickly respond to shifting markets.

From an intergroup perspective, cross-functional project teams that bring together specialists from many areas have the potential to reduce intergroup conflict. This sort of interaction serves to broaden one's focus and foster empathy for others' situations and problems. Tandem Computers, Inc., greases the social wheels at its Cupertino, California, headquarters by sponsoring a "popcorn party" every Friday at 4 P.M. Employees from all levels and specialties enjoy free refreshments and popcorn while exchanging ideas in an informal atmosphere with invited customers and others. Who says group and intergroup dynamics can't be fun?

• SUMMARY OF KEY CONCEPTS

A. Synergy, the concept of the whole being greater than the sum of its parts (or the 1 + 1 = 3 effect), instructively describes what happens when two individuals or groups interact. The social facilitation effect, caused by the mere presence of another person, tends to enhance the performance of simple tasks but hampers those working on complex tasks.

B. Sociologically, a *group* is defined as two or more freely interacting individuals who share collective norms and goals and have a common identity. There are formal (task-oriented) groups and informal (friendship-oriented) groups. Formal groups fulfill both organizational and individual functions. Groups mature through six stages of development: orientation, conflict and challenge, cohesion, delusion, disillusion, and acceptance. Interpersonal feedback increases and becomes more positive, specific, and credible as the group matures.

     Uncertainty about deadlines can disrupt the group development process. Leaders need to become more supportive as the group develops.

C. Members of formal groups need to perform both task (goal-oriented) and maintenance (relationship-oriented) roles if anything is to be accomplished. Two contingency management insights have emerged from field research of group technology–structure fit: (1) groups facing complex problems need to be staffed with people from different levels; (2) groups facing unpredictable problems need to be staffed with varied specialists.

D. Laboratory simulation studies suggest decision-making groups should be limited to five or fewer members. Larger groups are appropriate when creativity, participation, or socialization are the main objectives. If majority votes are to be taken, odd-numbered groups are recommended, to avoid deadlocks.

E. Women face special group dynamics challenges in mixed-gender task groups. Steps need to be taken to make sure increased sexualization of work environments does not erode into illegal sexual harassment. Results of the Israeli tank-crew study prompted researchers to conclude that it is better to concentrate high-ability personnel in separate groups. Within a contingency management perspective, however, there are situations in which it is advisable to spread high-ability people around.

F. Three threats to group effectiveness are the Asch effect, groupthink, and social loafing. The first two involve blind conformity. The Asch effect occurs when a minority of one goes along with an incorrect majority. Groupthink plagues cohesive in-groups that shortchange moral judgment while putting too much emphasis on unanimity. Critical evaluators, outside expertise, and devil's advocates are among the preventive measures recommended by Irving Janis, who coined the term *groupthink*. Social loafing involves the tendency for individual effort to decrease as group size increases. This problem can be contained if the task is challenging and important, individuals are held accountable for results, and group members expect everyone to work hard.

G. Social network analysis examines organizations in terms of formal (prescribed) and informal (emergent) clusters of individuals that link to transmit goods and services, information, influence, and feelings. Various individuals perform the following social network functions: star, liaison, bridge, gatekeeper, and isolate. Three key intergroup dynamics affecting social networks are political coalitions, conflict, and communication.

● **Key Terms**

synergy	group
social facilitation	formal group

informal group   Asch effect
task roles   groupthink
maintenance roles   social loafing
vertical differentiation   social network analysis
horizontal differentiation   clique

• DISCUSSION QUESTIONS

1. In what situations is your performance helped or hindered by the presence of others (the social facilitation effect)?
2. Which of the following would qualify as a sociological group? A crowd watching a baseball game? One of the baseball teams? Explain.
3. What is your opinion about employees being friends with their co-workers (overlapping formal and informal groups)?
4. What is your personal experience with groups that failed to achieve the sixth stage of group development? At which stage did they stall?
5. Which roles do you prefer to play in work groups: task or maintenance? How could you do a better job in this regard?
6. Are women typically at a disadvantage in mixed-gender work groups? Give your rationale.
7. When forming class project teams, would it be better for the instructor to concentrate the high-ability students or to spread them around evenly among all the teams? Give your rationale.
8. Have you ever been a victim of either the Asch effect or groupthink? Explain the circumstances.
9. Have you observed any social loafing recently? What were the circumstances and what could be done to correct the problem?
10. From a social network perspective, what prescribed and emergent clusters do you belong to? Which of the five social network functions do you fulfill? Explain the circumstances.

BACK TO THE OPENING CASE

Now that you have read Chapter 9, you should be able to answer the following questions about Janet Long's Wilderness Lab experience:

1. Did Janet Long's group satisfy the criteria of a sociological group?
2. The trust ladder played a key role relative to which stage of the group development process?
3. Why was social loafing probably not a problem during the wall-climbing exercise?

• EXERCISE 9

Objectives

1. To give you firsthand experience with work group dynamics through a role-playing exercise.[59]
2. To develop your ability to evaluate group effectiveness.

Introduction

Please read the following case before going on:

The Johnny Rocco Case

Johnny has a grim personal background. He is the third child in a family of seven. He has not seen his father for several years and his recollection is that his father used to come home drunk and beat up every member of the family; everyone ran when his father came staggering home.

His mother, according to Johnny, wasn't much better. She was irritable and unhappy and she always predicted that Johnny would come to no good end. Yet she worked when her health allowed her to do so in order to keep the family in food and clothing. She always decried the fact that she was not able to be the kind of mother she would like to be.

Johnny quit school in the seventh grade. He had great difficulty conforming to the school routine—he misbehaved often, was truant frequently, and fought with schoolmates. On several occasions he was picked up by the police and, along with members of his group, questioned during several investigations into cases of both petty and grand larceny. The police regarded him as "probably a bad one."

The juvenile officer of the court saw in Johnny some good qualities that no one else seemed to sense. Mr. O'Brien took it on himself to act as a "big brother" to Johnny. He had several long conversations with Johnny, during which he managed to penetrate to some degree Johnny's defensive shell. He represented to Johnny the first semblance of personal interest in his life. Through Mr. O'Brien's efforts, Johnny returned to school and obtained a high school diploma. Afterwards, Mr. O'Brien helped him obtain a job.

Now 20, Johnny is a stockroom clerk in one of the laboratories where you are employed. On the whole Johnny's performance has been acceptable, but there have been glaring exceptions. One involved a clear act of insubordination on a fairly unimportant matter. In another, Johnny was accused, on circumstantial grounds, of destroying some expensive equipment. Though the investigation is still open, it now appears the destruction was accidental.

Johnny's supervisor wants to keep him on for at least a trial period, but he wants "outside" advice as to the best way of helping Johnny grow into greater responsibility. Of course, much depends on how Johnny behaves in the next few months. Naturally, his supervisor must follow personnel policies that are accepted in the company as a whole. It is important to note that Johnny is not an attractive young man. He is rather weak and sickly, and he shows unmistakable signs of long years of social deprivation.

A committee is formed to decide the fate of Johnny Rocco. The chairperson of the meeting is Johnny's supervisor and should begin by assigning roles to the group members. These roles (shop steward [representing the union], head of production, Johnny's co-worker, director of personnel, and social worker who helped Johnny in the past) represent points of view the chairperson believes should be included in this meeting. (Johnny is not to be included.) Two observers should also be assigned. Thus, each group will have eight members.

Instructions

After roles have been assigned, each role player should complete the personal preference part of the work sheet, ranking from 1 to 11 the alternatives according to their appropriateness from the vantage point of his or her role.

Once the individual preferences have been determined, the chairperson should call the meeting to order. The following rules govern the meeting: (1) the group must reach a consensus ranking of the alternatives; (2) the group cannot use a statistical aggregation, or majority vote, decision-making process; (3) members should stay "in character" throughout the discussion. Treat this as a committee meeting consisting of members with different backgrounds, orientation, and interests who share a problem.

After the group has completed the assignment, the observers should conduct a discussion of the group process, using the Group Effectiveness Questions here as a guide. Group members should not look at these questions until after the group task has been completed.

Worksheet

Personal Preference	Group Decision	
_____	_____	Warn Johnny that at the next sign of trouble he will be fired.
_____	_____	Do nothing, as it is unclear if Johnny did anything wrong.
_____	_____	Create strict controls (do's and don'ts) for Johnny with immediate strong punishment for any misbehavior.
_____	_____	Give Johnny a great deal of warmth and personal attention and affection (overlooking his present behavior) so he can learn to depend on others.
_____	_____	Fire him. It's not worth the time and effort spent for such a low-level position.
_____	_____	Talk over the problem with Johnny in an understanding way so he can learn to ask others for help in solving his problems.
_____	_____	Give Johnny a well-structured schedule of daily activities with immediate and unpleasant consequences for not adhering to the schedule.
_____	_____	Do nothing now, but watch him carefully and provide immediate punishment for any future behavior.
_____	_____	Treat Johnny the same as everyone else, but provide an orderly routine so he can learn to stand on his own two feet.
_____	_____	Call Johnny in and logically discuss the problem with him and ask what you can do to help him.
_____	_____	Do nothing now, but watch him so you can reward him the next time he does something good.

Group Effectiveness Questions

A. Referring to Table 9–2, what task roles were performed? By whom?

B. What maintenance roles were performed? By whom?

C. Were any important task or maintenance roles ignored? Which?

D. Was there any evidence of the Asch effect, groupthink, or social loafing? Explain.

Questions for Consideration/Class Discussion

1. Did your committee do a good job? Explain.

2. What, if anything, should have been done differently?

3. How much similarity in rankings is there among the different groups in your class? What group dynamics apparently were responsible for any variations in rankings?

• NOTES

[1] See Renee Stephen and Richard L. Zweigenhaft, "The Effect on Tipping of a Waitress's Touching Male and Female Customers," *The Journal of Social Psychology,* February 1986, pp. 141–42.

[2] Details may be found in Frederick W. Taylor, *The Principles of Scientific Management* (New York: Harper & Row, 1911).

[3] See F. J. Roethlisberger and William J. Dickson, *Management and the Worker* (Cambridge, Mass.: Harvard University Press, 1939); and Henry A. Landsberger, *Hawthorne Revisited* (Ithaca, N.Y.: Cornell University, 1958).

[4] For details of this study, see Raymond H. Van Zelst, "Sociometrically Selected Work Teams Increase Production," *Personnel Psychology,* Autumn 1952, pp. 175–85.

[5] Research conclusions drawn from Charles F. Bond, Jr., and Linda J. Titus, "Social Facilitation: A Meta-Analysis of 241 Studies," *Psychological Bulletin,* September 1983, pp. 265–92. Also see Bernard Guerin, "Social Inhibition of Behavior," *The Journal of Social Psychology,* April 1989, pp. 225–33.

[6] See Kris Robinson-Staveley and Joel Cooper, "Mere Presence, Gender, and Reactions to Computers: Studying Human–Computer Interaction in the Social Context," *Journal of Experimental Social Psychology,* March 1990, pp. 168–83.

[7] Details may be found in Andrew Crouch and Umar Nimran, "Office Design and the Behavior of Senior Managers," *Human Relations,* February 1989, pp. 139–55.

[8] For an instructive overview of recent research on groups, see John M. Levine and Richard L. Moreland, "Progress in Small-Group Research," in *Annual Review of Psychology,* vol. 41, eds. Mark R. Rosenzweig and Lyman W. Porter (Palo Alto, Calif.: Annual Reviews Inc., 1990), pp. 585–634.

[9] Maralyn Edid, "How Power Will be Balanced on Saturn's Shop Floor," *Business Week,* August 5, 1985, p. 65.

[10] This definition is based in part on one found in David Horton Smith, "A Parsimonious Definition of 'Group': Toward Conceptual Clarity and Scientific Utility," *Sociological Inquiry,* Spring 1967, pp. 141–67.

[11] Edgar H. Schein, *Organizational Psychology,* 3rd ed. (Englewood Cliffs, N.J.: Prentice-Hall, 1980), p. 145

[12] Ibid., pp. 149–53.

[13] Janice Castro, ''Mazda U.,'' *Time*, October 20, 1986, p. 65.

[14] For an instructive overview of five different theories of group development, see John P. Wanous, Arnon E. Reichers, and S. D. Malik, ''Organizational Socialization and Group Development: Toward an Integrative Perspective,'' *Academy of Management Review*, October 1984, pp. 670–83.

[15] Adapted from discussion in Linda N. Jewell and H. Joseph Reitz, *Group Effectiveness in Organizations* (Glenview, Ill.: Scott, Foresman, 1981), pp. 15–20.

[16] Ibid., p. 19.

[17] Don Davies and Bart C. Kuypers, ''Group Development and Interpersonal Feedback,'' *Group & Organization Studies*, June 1985, p. 194.

[18] Ibid., pp. 184–208.

[19] Connie J. G. Gersick, ''Marking Time: Predictable Transitions in Task Groups,'' *Academy of Management Journal*, June 1989, pp. 274–309.

[20] Donald K. Carew, Eunice Parisi-Carew, and Kenneth H. Blanchard, ''Group Development and Situational Leadership: A Model for Managing Groups,'' *Training and Development Journal*, June 1986, pp. 48–49. For evidence linking leadership and group effectiveness, see Gervase R. Bushe and A. Lea Johnson, ''Contextual and Internal Variables Affecting Task Group Outcomes in Organizations,'' *Group & Organization Studies*, December 1989, pp. 462–82.

[21] See Kenneth D. Benne and Paul Sheats, ''Functional Roles of Group Members,'' *Journal of Social Issues*, Spring 1948, pp. 41–49.

[22] For complete details, see Fred R. David, John A. Pearce II, and W. Alan Randolph, ''Linking Technology and Structure to Enhance Group Performance,'' *Journal of Applied Psychology*, April 1989, pp. 233–41.

[23] For example, see Bernard Grofman, Scott L. Feld, and Guillermo Owen, ''Group Size and the Performance of a Composite Group Majority: Statistical Truths and Empirical Results,'' *Organizational Behavior and Human Performance*, June 1984, pp. 350–59.

[24] See Philip Yetton and Preston Bottger, ''The Relationships among Group Size, Member Ability, Social Decision Schemes, and Performance,'' *Organizational Behavior and Human Performance*, October 1983, pp. 145–59.

[25] This copyrighted exercise may be found in Jay Hall, ''Decisions, Decisions, Decisions,'' *Psychology Today*, November 1971, pp. 51–54, 86, 88.

[26] Yetton and Bottger, ''The Relationships among Group Size, Member Ability, Social Decision Schemes, and Performance,'' p. 158.

[27] Drawn from Brian Mullen, Cynthia Symons, Li-Tze Hu, and Eduardo Salas, ''Group Size, Leadership Behavior, and Subordinate Satisfaction,'' *The Journal of General Psychology*, April 1989, pp. 155–69. Also see Pamela Oliver and Gerald Marwell, ''The Paradox of Group Size in Collective Action: A Theory of the Critical Mass. II.,'' *American Sociological Review*, February 1988, pp. 1–8.

[28] Details of this study are presented in Leigh L. Thompson, Elizabeth A. Mannix, and Max H. Bazerman, ''Group Negotiation: Effects of Decision Rule, Agenda, and Aspiration,'' *Journal of Personality and Social Psychology*, January 1988, pp. 86–95.

[29] See Lynn Smith-Lovin and Charles Brody, ''Interruptions in Group Discussions: The Effects of Gender and Group Composition,'' *American Sociological Review*, June 1989, pp. 424–35.

[30] E. Marlies Ott, ''Effects of the Male–Female Ratio at Work,'' *Psychology of Women Quarterly*, March 1989, p. 53.

[31] Data from Barbara A. Gutek, Aaron Groff Cohen, and Alison M. Konrad, ''Predicting Social-Sexual Behavior at Work: A Contact Hypothesis,'' *Academy of Management Journal*, September 1990, pp. 560–77.

[32] Scott J. South, Charles M. Bonjean, William T. Markham, and Judy Corder, "Female Labor Force Participation and the Organizational Experiences of Male Workers," *The Sociological Quarterly,* Summer 1983, p. 378.

[33] Irene Pave, "A Woman's Place Is at GE, Federal Express, P&G . . . ," *Business Week,* June 23, 1986, p. 78.

[34] Walecia Konrad, "Welcome to the Woman-Friendly Company," *Business Week,* August 6, 1990, p. 50.

[35] A former Israeli tank commander's first-hand account of tank warfare in the desert can be found in Avigdor Kahalani, "Advice from a Desert Warrior," *Newsweek,* September 3, 1990, p. 32.

[36] Aharon Tziner and Dov Eden, "Effects of Crew Composition on Crew Performance: Does the Whole Equal the Sum of Its Parts?" *Journal of Applied Psychology,* February 1985, p. 91.

[37] Ibid.

[38] Robert R. Blake and Jane Srygley Mouton, "Don't Let Group Norms Stifle Creativity," *Personnel,* August 1985, p. 29.

[39] For additional information, see Solomon E. Asch, *Social Psychology* (Englewood Cliffs, N.J.: Prentice-Hall, 1952), chap. 16.

[40] See Timothy P. Williams and Shunya Sogon, "Group Composition and Conforming Behavior in Japanese Students," *Japanese Psychological Research,* no. 4, 1984, pp. 231–34; and Taha Amir, "The Asch Conformity Effect: A Study in Kuwait," *Social Behavior and Personality,* no. 2, 1984, pp. 187–90

[41] For an interesting analysis of the presence or absence of groupthink in selected U.S. foreign policy decisions, see Clark McCauley, "The Nature of Social Influence in Groupthink: Compliance and Internalization," *Journal of Personality and Social Psychology,* August 1989, pp. 250–60. Also see Glen Whyte, "Groupthink Reconsidered," *Academy of Management Review,* January 1989, pp. 40–56.

[42] Irving L. Janis, *Groupthink,* 2nd ed. (Boston: Houghton Mifflin, 1982), p. 9.

[43] Ibid.

[44] Laurie Baum, "The Job Nobody Wants," *Business Week,* September 8, 1986, p. 60.

[45] Details of this study may be found in Michael R. Callaway and James K. Esser, "Groupthink: Effects of Cohesiveness and Problem-Solving Procedures on Group Decision Making," *Social Behavior and Personality,* no. 2, 1984, pp. 157–64. Also see Carrie R. Leana, "A Partial Test of Janis's Groupthink Model: Effects of Group Cohesiveness and Leader Behavior on Defective Decision Making," *Journal of Management,* Spring 1985, pp. 5–17; and Gregory Moorhead and John R. Montanari, "An Empirical Investigation of the Groupthink Phenomenon," *Human Relations,* May 1986, pp. 399–410.

[46] Adapted from discussion in Janis, *Groupthink,* chap. 11.

[47] Based on discussion in Bibb Latane, Kipling Williams, and Stephen Harkins, "Many Hands Make Light the Work: The Causes and Consequences of Social Loafing," *Journal of Personality and Social Psychology,* June 1979, pp. 822–32; and David A. Kravitz and Barbara Martin, "Ringelmann Rediscovered: The Original Article," *Journal of Personality and Social Psychology,* May 1986, pp. 936–41.

[48] See Stephen J. Zaccaro, "Social Loafing: The Role of Task Attractiveness," *Personality and Social Psychology Bulletin,* March 1984, pp. 99–106; and Jeffrey M. Jackson and Kipling D. Williams, "Social Loafing on Difficult Tasks: Working Collectively Can Improve Performance," *Journal of Personality and Social Psychology,* October 1985, pp. 937–42.

[49] For complete details, see Kipling Williams, Stephen Harkins, and Bibb Latane, "Identifiability as a Deterrent to Social Loafing: Two Cheering Experiments," *Journal of Personality and Social Psychology,* February 1981, pp. 303–11.

[50] See Jeffrey M. Jackson and Stephen G. Harkins, "Equity in Effort: An Explanation of the Social Loafing Effect," *Journal of Personality and Social Psychology,* November 1985, pp. 1199–1206.

[51] Both studies are reported in Stephen G. Harkins and Kate Szymanski, "Social Loafing and Group Evaluation," *Journal of Personality and Social Psychology,* June 1989, pp. 934–41.

[52] Noel Tichy and Charles Fombrun, "Network Analysis in Organizational Settings," *Human Relations,* November 1979, pp. 925–26. Also see Robert R. Blake and Anne Adams McCanse, "The Rediscovery of Sociometry," *Journal of Group Psychotherapy, Psychodrama, and Sociometry,* Fall 1989, pp. 148–65.

[53] These definitions are adapted from discussion in Noel M. Tichy, Michael L. Tushman, and Charles Fombrun, "Social Network Analysis for Organizations," *Academy of Management Review,* October 1979, pp. 507–19. An alternative typology of network functions, focusing on intergroup transactions, is presented and discussed in Deborah Gladstein Ancona and David F. Caldwell, "Beyond Task and Maintenance: Defining External Functions in Groups," *Group & Organizational Studies,* December 1988, pp. 468–94.

[54] Adapted from material in Tichy and Fombrun, "Network Analysis in Organizational Settings," p. 929.

[55] For details, see Daniel J. Brass, "Being in the Right Place: A Structural Analysis of Individual Influence in an Organization," *Administrative Science Quarterly,* December 1984, pp. 518–39.

[56] See David Krackhardt and Lyman W. Porter, "The Snowball Effect: Turnover Embedded in Communication Networks," *Journal of Applied Psychology,* February 1986, pp. 50–55.

[57] Data from Reed E. Nelson, "The Strength of Strong Ties: Social Networks and Intergroup Conflict in Organizations," *Academy of Management Journal,* June 1989, pp. 377–401.

[58] Amy Dunkin, "Pepsi's Marketing Magic: Why Nobody Does It Better," *Business Week*, February 10, 1986, p. 53.

[59] The case and instructions portions of this exercise excerpted from *Developing Management Skills* by David A. Whetten and Kim S. Cameron. Copyright © 1984 by Scott, Foresman and Company. Reprinted by permission of HarperCollins Publishers.

CHAPTER

10

Power, Politics, and Conflict

LEARNING OBJECTIVES

When you finish studying the material in this chapter, you should be able to:

- Identify and describe the three most common influence tactics in organizations.
- Distinguish between authority and power.
- Identify and briefly describe French and Raven's five bases of power.

- Explain the difference between power sharing and power distribution.
- Define organizational politics and explain what triggers it.
- Explain the role of coalitions in organizational politics.

- Draw a distinction between functional and dysfunctional conflict.
- Explain how managers can stimulate functional conflict.
- Describe five conflict-handling styles and explain why a contingency approach to managing conflict is in order.

OPENING CASE 10

How General Motors' Fiero Turned into a Fiasco

Sharon Hoogstraten

The Pontiac Fiero could have been one of Roger Smith's dream cars. On the computer design screen, the little two-seater seemed to capture the changes that Smith sought to impose on General Motors Corp. during his decade as its chief.

Bright and daring, it was out of keeping with an image of dullness and look-alike predictability that would steadily envelop the giant automaker in the 1980s. Encased in lightweight, high-strength plastic, the Fiero proclaimed GM's technological prowess. Its $7,999 price tag left it within range of younger car buyers who were deserting GM in favor of its foreign rivals.

But the Fiero failed.

Now, a few weeks after Smith's departure as GM's chairman, the Fiero is a fast-receding memory. Its memorial is a deserted steel and concrete auto plant on the northwest border of this small industrial town, the Fiero assembly line that opened with banners and bands in 1983 and closed with recrimination and excuses five years later. . . .

The Pontiac sports car, introduced in 1983, could not escape the gravitational hold of GM's bureaucracy, which imposed a series of compromises on its design and construction that hurt the car badly with customers and demanded profits the car could not produce.

"The problem is the system," says Dennis Virag, a Michigan automotive industry analyst. "It's not Roger Smith or any one individual. It is just a system that has grown up over the decades that is difficult to govern."

Pontiac executives saw the Fiero as a way to revive the division's sagging public image.

"It was not just a little red car. It was an opportunity," says Hulki Aldikacti, the advance design engineer and Pontiac project manager who guided the Fiero into production.

The Fiero would be the first American mid-engine two-seater ever sold to the general public and the first to use new lightweight, high-strength plastic body panels. It also would mark the first time that GM successfully experimented with simultaneous design and manufacturing—developing the car and its production system at the same time in a bid to turn out the product quickly, cheaply and with relatively few defects.

Opposition to the program was based on economics and politics, says James Wangers, a Detroit auto-marketing consultant who helped to develop the Fiero's early advertising campaigns. Some top GM executives reasoned that GM already had a two-seater, the Corvette. GM officials couldn't see why Pontiac should

A   t the very heart of interpersonal dealings in today's work organizations is a constant struggle between individual and collective interests. For example, Sid wants a raise but his company doesn't make enough money to both grant raises and pay minimum stockholder dividends. Preoccupation with self-interest is understandable. After all, each of us was born, not as a cooperating organization member, but as an individual with instincts for self-preservation. It took socialization in family, school, religious, sports, recreation, and employment settings to introduce us to the notion of mutuality of interest. Basically, **mutuality of interest** involves win-win situations in which one's self-interest is served by cooperating actively and creatively with

OPENING CASE 10

(concluded)

do battle with Chevrolet, he says. For years, the powerful Chevrolet Motor Division opposed the Fiero inside GM's Product Policy Group and executive committee, the key decision-making bodies on new vehicles.

"You've got to realize that the Fiero had as many haters as it did lovers," the Pontiac official says. "You had two camps—the Pontiac people who were upset because they felt they never got what they wanted from the corporation and who wanted a car exclusively all their own, and the Chevy people who always seemed to get everything.

"The Fiero was the first car Pontiac got that it didn't have to share with any other division, and they partly got it by implying that what they really were going to build was a two-seat version of the ordinary econobox."

Still, championed by several Pontiac executives, including Robert C. Stempel, now GM's new chairman, the Fiero had obtained tentative production approval from the Product Planning Group by the time Smith took

charge. But orders to stop work on the Fiero went out twice under the aegis of Smith's budget people. Curiously, those orders never reached the people who were doing the work, and therein lies a tale of how a giant corporate bureaucracy can be circumvented.

"I had excellent protection," recalls Aldikacti, now a consultant to GM's Saturn Corp. Aldikacti says he kept working on the Fiero and didn't go to any meetings where I thought that they were going to discuss something that I had already made a decision on." Pontiac division manager William E. Hoglund, or one of Aldikacti's other Pontiac bosses, went to the meetings instead.

"I told them that if anybody had a question for me, 'Here's my telephone number and addresses. They can come and see me or call me and discuss their concerns. But they had also better have an answer for my concerns. Otherwise, I'm not going to waste their time or my time.'" Aldikacti says.

The strategy was aimed at getting Fiero critics "one-on-one, on

my ground, where they did not have a forum," Aldikacti says. It worked perfectly in a corporate environment where direct personal confrontation is strenuously avoided.

"Bill [Hoglund] would tell them, 'Talk to Hulki about that,' but no one ever came," Aldikacti says. And because no one ever came to personally order him to stop working, "I kept going," Aldikacti says.

In 1982, Smith's lieutenants, with his blessing, gave the go-ahead for fall 1983 production of the Fiero as a 1984 model.

For Discussion

What do you think about Hulki Aldikacti's conduct in this case?

• Additional discussion questions linking this case with the following material appears at the end of this chapter.

Source: Excerpted from Warren Brown, "The Little Car that Couldn't," *The Washington Post National Weekly Edition*, August 20–26, 1990, pp. 11–12. Copyright 1990, *The Washington Post*. Reprinted with permission.

potential adversaries. A pair of organization development consultants recently offered this managerial perspective of mutuality of interest:

> Nothing is more important than this sense of mutuality to the effectiveness and quality of an organization's products and services. Management must strive to stimulate a strong sense of shared ownership in every employee, because otherwise an organization cannot do its best in the long run. Employees who identify their own personal self-interest with the quality of their organization's output understand mutuality and strive to maintain it in their jobs and work relations.[1]

Figure 10–1 graphically portrays the constant tug-of-war between employees' self-interest and the organization's need for mutuality of interest. It also serves as an overview model for this chapter, dealing with social

• FIGURE 10-1   The Constant Tug-of-War between Self-Interest and Mutuality of Interest Requires Managerial Action

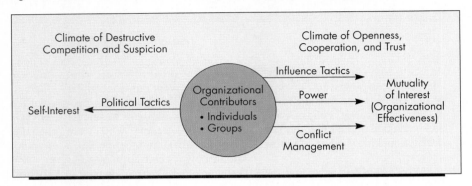

influence tactics, social power, organizational politics, and conflict management. Notice how political tactics, motivated by self-interest, tend to pull individuals and groups away from mutual self-interest (organizational effectiveness). Oppositely, managers have three counteracting interpersonal tools at their disposal: influence tactics, power, and conflict management techniques. At stake in this tug-of-war between individual and collective interests is no less than the ultimate survival of the organization.

• ORGANIZATIONAL INFLUENCE TACTICS: GETTING ONE'S WAY AT WORK

How do you get others to carry out your wishes? Do you simply tell them what to do? Or do you prefer a less direct approach, such as promising to return the favor? Whatever approach you use, the crux of the issue is *social influence*. A large measure of interpersonal interaction involves attempts to influence others, including parents, bosses, co-workers, spouses, teachers, friends, and children. Consider how the power of persuasion and a car phone got results in this curious example: "Doug Dusenberg, a Houston businessman, dialed his Jeep Cherokee when he discovered it missing from a parking lot and talked the two young joyriders into returning it; he let them keep the $20 in the glove compartment."[2] Even if managers do not expect to get such dramatic results, they need to sharpen their influence skills. A good starting point is familiarity with the following research insights.

Eight Generic Influence Tactics

A particularly fruitful stream of research, initiated by David Kipnis and his colleagues in 1980, reveals how people influence each other in organizations. The Kipnis methodology involved asking employees how they managed to get either their bosses, co-workers, or subordinates to do what they wanted them to do.[3] Statistical refinements and replications by other researchers over a 10-year period eventually yielded the eight influence tactics listed and defined in Table 10-1. The eight tactics, in diminishing order of use by managers for *downward* influence are:

• **TABLE 10-1**   Eight Generic Influence Tactics: Documented Frequency of Use

Tactic	Definition	Rank Order of *Downward* Use	Rank Order of *Lateral* Use	Rank Order of *Upward* Use
Consultation	The person seeks your participation in making a decision or planning how to implement a proposed policy, strategy, or change.	1	1	2
Rational persuasion	The person uses logical arguments and factual evidence to persuade you that a proposal or request is viable and likely to result in the attainment of task objectives.	2	2	1
Inspirational appeals	The person makes an emotional request or proposal that arouses enthusiasm by appealing to your values and ideals, or by increasing your confidence that you can do it.	3	3	3
Ingratiating tactics	The person seeks to get you in a good mood or to think favorably of him or her before asking you to do something.	4	4	5
Coalition tactics	The person seeks the aid of others to persuade you to do something or uses the support of others as an argument for you to agree also.	5	5	4
Pressure tactics	The person uses demands, threats, or intimidation to convince you to comply with a request or to support a proposal.	6	7	7
Upward appeals	The person seeks to persuade you that the request is approved by higher management, or appeals to higher management for assistance in gaining your compliance with the request.	7	6	6
Exchange tactics	The person makes an explicit or implicit promise that you will receive rewards or tangible benefits if you comply with a request or support a proposal, or reminds you of a prior favor to be reciprocated.	8	8	8

Source: Adapted from Gary Yukl and Cecilia M. Falbe, "Influence Tactics and Objectives in Upward, Downward, and Lateral Influence Attempts," *Journal of Applied Psychology*, April 1990, pp. 132–40, Tables 1 and 7.

- Consultation
- Rational persuasion
- Inspirational appeals
- Ingratiating tactics
- Coalition tactics
- Pressure tactics
- Upward appeals
- Exchange tactics[4]

These approaches can be considered generic influence tactics because they characterize social influence in all directions. Notice in Table 10–1 how the rankings remained nearly the same regardless of whether the direction of influence was downward, lateral, or upward. Consultation, rational persuasion, and inspirational appeals were the tactics of choice. Pressure tactics, upward appeal, and exchange tactics consistently were the least preferred. Ingratiating and coalition tactics were used to a moderate extent.

• Consulting with subordinates, as opposed to using
pressure tactics, is the
preferred management
technique in most situations.
(Courtesy of Clarcor)

Other Research Insights

Notably, no gender effect has been found to date. In other words, no
significant difference has been found between the influence tactics used
either by or with men and women.[5] A study of 125 male and 59 female
middle-level managers in Israel similarly demonstrated that men and women
used the same influence tactics.[6] Regarding *upward* influence, employees in
another study varied their influence tactics to suit the leadership style of
their boss. Upward appeals and ingratiating tactics tended to be used most
often to influence authoritarian managers. Rational persuasion was used to
influence participative managers.[7] These last results suggest a contingency
approach to interpersonal influence. More research is needed, however, to
discover which tactics are effective (or appropriate) in which situations. In
the meantime, the following practical tips can help.

How to Extend Your Influence by Forming Strategic Alliances

In their recent book, *Influence without Authority,* Allan R. Cohen and David
L. Bradford extended the concept of corporate strategic alliances to interpersonal influence. Hardly a day goes by without another mention in the
business press of a new strategic alliance between two global companies
intent on staying competitive. These win-win relationships are based on
complementary strengths. According to Cohen and Bradford, managers
need to follow suit by forming some strategic alliances of their own with
anyone who has a stake in their area. This is particularly true given today's
rapid change, cross-functional work teams, and diminished reliance on traditional authority structures.

While admitting the task is not an easy one, Cohen and Bradford recommend the following tips for dealing with potential allies:

1. *Mutual respect.* Assume they are competent and smart.

INTERNATIONAL OB

The Meaning of Reciprocity in Thailand (S. E. Asia)

The relationship between employer and employee is unequal but there is a subtle balance within it, designed to respect the dignity of both parties.

To the Western mind, one of the most difficult points to accept is that an unequal relationship can be equitable despite the absence of any specification of the rights of the subordinate. Thais view acceptability and fairness not so much in terms of measurable rights but in terms of feelings and ambience. . . .

The essence of the subtlety of interrelationships is what reciprocity means in Thai thinking. It is not simply unquestioning obligation. Loyalty and deference to authority depends upon whether the superior is judged to remain worthy of loyalty and deference and that there is genuine reciprocity. . . . the manager will be shown the utmost deference, but unless the Thais believe that their deference is being reciprocated with genuine concern for individuals, staff may become uncooperative and quietly obstructionist.

Source: Excerpted from Allan G. Thompson, "Cross-Cultural Management of Labour in a Thai Environment," *Asia Pacific Journal of Management*, April 1989, pp. 323–38.

2. *Openness*. Talk straight to them. It isn't possible for any one person to know everything, so give them the information they need to know to help you better.

3. *Trust*. Assume that no one will take any action that is purposely intended to hurt another, so hold back no information that the other could use, even if it doesn't help your immediate position.

4. *Mutual benefit*. Plan every strategy so that both parties win. If that doesn't happen over time, the alliance will break up. When dissolving a partnership becomes necessary as a last resort, try to do it in a clean way that minimizes residual anger. Some day, you may want a new alliance with that person.[8]

True, these tactics involve taking some personal risks. But the effectiveness of interpersonal strategic alliances is anchored to the concept of reciprocity. **"Reciprocity** is the almost universal belief that people should be paid back for what they do—that one good (or bad) turn deserves another." (See International OB.) In short, people tend to get what they give when attempting to influence others.

By demonstrating the rich texture of social influence, the foregoing research evidence and practical advice whet our appetite for learning more about how today's managers can and do reconcile individual and organizational interests. Let us focus on social power.

• SOCIAL POWER AND POWER SHARING

The term *power* evokes mixed and often passionate reactions. Citing recent instances of government corruption and corporate misconduct, many observers view power as a sinister force. To these critics, Lord Acton's time-honored statement that "power corrupts and absolute power corrupts absolutely" is as true as ever. However, OB specialists remind us that, like it or not, power is a fact of life in modern organizations. According to one management writer:

> Power must be used because managers must influence those they depend on. Power also is crucial in the development of managers' self-confidence and willingness to support subordinates. From this perspective, power should be accepted as a natural part of any organization. Managers should recognize and develop their own power to coordinate and support the work of subordinates; it is powerlessness, not power, that undermines organizational effectiveness.[10]

Thus, power is a necessary and generally positive force in organizations. As the term is used here, **social power** is defined as ''the ability to marshal the human, informational, and material resources to get something done.''[11]

Dimensions of Power

While power may be an elusive concept to the casual observer, social scientists view power as having reasonably clear dimensions. Three dimensions of power that deserve our attention are: (1) the distinction between power and authority, (2) socialized versus personalized power, and (3) the five bases of power.

Power and Authority   In our definition of power, emphasis must be placed on the word *ability* because it sets power apart from the concept of authority. **Authority** is the ''right'' or the ''obligation'' to seek compliance; power is the ''demonstrated ability'' to achieve compliance. As illustrated in Figure 10–2, three classic situations can arise because power and authority often do not overlap. Effective managers are able to back up their authority with power (the middle portion of Figure 10–2).

• FIGURE 10-2   Power and Authority Are Not Necessarily the Same Thing

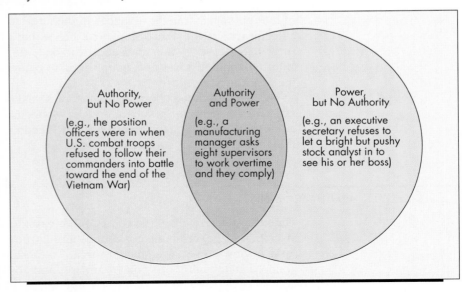

This distinction between power and authority may appear to be a simple one, but those who fail to appreciate the difference can unwittingly commit career suicide. For instance, nonmanagerial employees who have no official authority may wield a great deal of power because of who or what they know. Staff assistants, who have no real authority in the formal chain of command, often are very powerful. For example:

> At Intel Corp., Jean C. Jones, executive secretary to Chairman Gordon E. Moore, is curator of Intel's high-tech museum. But most of her influence—as well as the power most executive assistants wield—derives from many of those old-fashioned secretarial duties. Each week, she decides how much of the 30-in. stack of mail her boss will see and how many of the 125 telephone calls will gain his ear. Jones deflects 80 percent of those calls, weeding out the insurance salesmen and the stockbrokers. By scheduling Moore's calendar, she helps determine who gets to see the boss in person.[12]

Part of the organizational socialization process discussed in Chapter 8 involves teaching newcomers where the real power lies.

Two Types of Power   Behavioral scientists such as David McClelland contend that one of the basic human needs is the need for power (n Pwr). Because this need is learned and not innate, the need for power has been extensively studied. Historically, need for power was scored when subjects interpreted TAT pictures in terms of one person attempting to influence, convince, persuade, or control another as discussed in Chapter 5. More recently, however, researchers have drawn a distinction between **socialized power** and **personalized power.**

> There are two subscales or "faces" in n Pwr. One face is termed "socialized" (s Pwr) and is scored in the Thematic Apperception Test (TAT) as "plans, self-doubts, mixed outcomes and concerns for others, . . ." while the second face is "personalized" power (p Pwr), in which expressions of power for the sake of personal aggrandizement become paramount.[13]

This distinction between socialized and personalized power helps explain why power has a negative connotation for many people. Managers and others who pursue personalized power for their own selfish ends give power a bad name. But managers like Dorothy Terrell, one of the most successful black female managers in America, exercise power effectively and ethically (see A Matter of Ethics). She does so by emphasizing socialized power and de-emphasizing personalized power.

Five Bases of Power   A popular classification scheme for social power traces back more than 30 years to the work of John French and Bertram Raven. They proposed that power arises from five different bases: reward power, coercive power, legitimate power, expert power, and referent power.[14] Each involves a different approach to influencing others.

- *Reward power:* A manager has **reward power** to the extent that he or she obtains compliance by promising or granting rewards. On-the-job behavior modification, for example, relies heavily on reward power.
- *Coercive power:* Threats of punishment and actual punishment give an individual **coercive power.** A sales manager who threatens to fire

A MATTER OF ETHICS

**Digital's Dorothy Terrell Knows How to Handle Power
as a Plant Manager with 375 Employees
and a $35 Million Budget**

"I have profit-loss responsibility for this plant. We produce a quality keyboard at competitive cost. But I have to decide what it will take to produce that keyboard in terms of money, people, space and materials. That's a major responsibility that could easily impact on the corporation's revenues."

The staff who must report to her includes the plant comptroller, personnel manager, operations manager, engineering and technology manager and the information systems and new products manager.

"How powerful am I? I'm very powerful. But power is a word that took me a little time to get comfortable with. I always thought of power as being negative, something other people had and used to oppress others. I've since understood that's not necessarily the case. You can be powerful and share what makes you powerful. I can make things happen and *that* for me is powerful," she says.

Dorothy Terrell uses that power on the plant floor, where she encourages her employees to manufacture the best product they can.

"I like people. I value them to the extent that I'll push them to do things that stretch them. I really believe in having employees use their brains as well as their hands," says Terrell, who regularly puts in 12-hour days at the plant.

Terrell also asks staff members and plant employees for their input. She favors a style of management that encourges participation and says she has no problem admitting she doesn't know everything.

"It's important for me to hear what people have to say. It's not important, however, for me to agree with what people have to say," explains Terrell, who describes herself as a tough but fair manager.

Source: Excerpted from Lloyd Gite, "Dorothy Terrell," *Black Enterprise*, April 1987, pp. 46–48. Copyright The Earl G. Graves Publishing Co., Inc. 130 Fifth Ave., New York, NY 10011. All rights reserved.

any salesperson who uses a company car for family vacations is relying on coercive power.

- *Legitimate power:* This base of power is anchored to one's formal position or authority. Thus, individuals who obtain compliance primarily because of their formal authority to make decisions have **legitimate power.** Legitimate power may express itself in either a positive or negative manner in managing people. Positive legitimate power focuses constructively on job performance. Negative legitimate power tends to be threatening and demeaning to those being influenced. Its main purpose is to build the power holder's ego.

- *Expert power:* Valued knowledge or information gives an individual **expert power** over those who need such knowledge or information. The power of supervisors is enhanced because they know about work schedules and assignments before their subordinates do.

- *Referent power:* Also called charisma, **referent power** comes into play when one's personality becomes the reason for compliance. Role

---

• OB EXERCISE

What Is Your Self-Perceived Power?

Instructions:
Score your various bases of power for your present (or former) job, using the following scale:

1 = Strongly disagree   4 = Agree
2 = Disagree   5 = Strongly agree
3 = Slightly agree

Reward power score = _____
1. I can reward persons at lower levels. _____
2. My review actions affect the rewards gained at lower levels. _____
3. Based on my decisions, lower level personnel may receive a bonus. _____

Coercive power score = _____
1. I can punish employees at lower levels. _____
2. My work is a check on lower-level employees. _____
3. My diligence reduces error. _____

Legitimate power score = _____
1. My position gives me a great deal of authority. _____
2. The decisions made at my level are of critical importance. _____
3. Employees look to me for guidance. _____

Expert power score = _____
1. I am an expert in this job. _____
2. My ability gives me an advantage in this job. _____
3. Given some time, I could improve the methods used on this job. _____

Referent power score = _____
1. I attempt to set a good example for other employees. _____
2. My personality allows me to work well in this job. _____
3. My fellow employees look to me as their informal leader. _____

Source: Adapted and excerpted in part from Duncan L. Dieterly and Benjamin Schneider, "The Effect of Organizational Environment on Perceived Power and Climate: A Laboratory Study," *Organizational Behavior and Human Performance*, June 1974, pp. 316–37.

---

models have referent power over those who identify closely with them.

To further your understanding of these five bases of power and to assess your self-perceived power, please take a moment to complete the questionnaire in the OB Exercise. Think of your present job or your most recent job when responding to the various items. Arbitrary norms for each of the five bases of power are: 3–6 = Weak power base; 7–11 = Moderate power base; 12–15 = Strong power base. How is your power profile?

Research Insights about Social Power

In one study, a sample of 94 male and 84 female nonmanagerial and professional employees in Denver, Colorado, completed TAT tests. The researchers found that the male and female employees had similar needs for power (n Pwr) and personalized power (p Pwr). But the women had a significantly higher need for socialized power (s Pwr) than did their male counterparts.[15] This bodes well for today's work organizations where women are playing an ever greater administrative role.

A 1985 reanalysis of 18 field studies that measured French and Raven's five bases of power uncovered "severe methodological shortcomings."[16] After correcting for these problems, the researchers identified the following relationships between power bases and work outcomes such as job performance, job satisfaction, and turnover:

- Expert and referent power had a generally positive impact.
- Reward and legitimate power had a slightly positive impact.
- Coercive power had a slightly negative impact.

The same researcher, in a 1990 follow-up study involving 251 employed business seniors, looked at the relationship between influence styles and bases of power. This was a bottom-up study. In other words, subordinate perceptions of managerial influence and power were examined. Rational persuasion was found to be a highly acceptable managerial influence tactic. Why? Because subordinates perceived it to be associated with the three bases of power they viewed positively: legitimate, expert, and referent.[17]

In summary, expert and referent power appear to get the best *combination* of results and favorable subordinate reactions.

Responsible Management of Power

If managers are to use their various bases of power effectively and ethically, they need to understand the differences between compliance and internalization and power sharing and power distribution.

From Compliance to Internalization   Responsible managers strive for socialized power while avoiding personalized power. This, in addition to being aware of the relative strengths of their bases of power, can help managers use their power effectively. It is important to recognize, however, that the various power bases tend to produce two very different modes of behavior change. Reward, coercive, and negative legitimate power tend to produce *compliance*. On the other hand, positive legitimate, expert, and referent power tend to foster *internalization*. Internalization is superior to compliance because it is driven by internal or intrinsic motivation. Employees who merely comply require frequent "jolts" of power from the boss to keep them headed in a productive direction. Those who internalize the task at hand tend to become self-starters who do not require close supervision.

According to the research cited above, expert and referent power have the greatest potential for improving job performance and satisfaction and reducing turnover. Formal education, training, and self-development can build a manager's expert power. At the same time, one's referent power base can be strengthened by forming and developing the strategic alliances discussed earlier under the heading of influence tactics.

Empowerment: from Power Sharing to Power Distribution   Before leaving the topic of social power, we need to briefly highlight a very exciting trend in

• **FIGURE 10-3**   The Evolution of Power: From Domination to Delegation

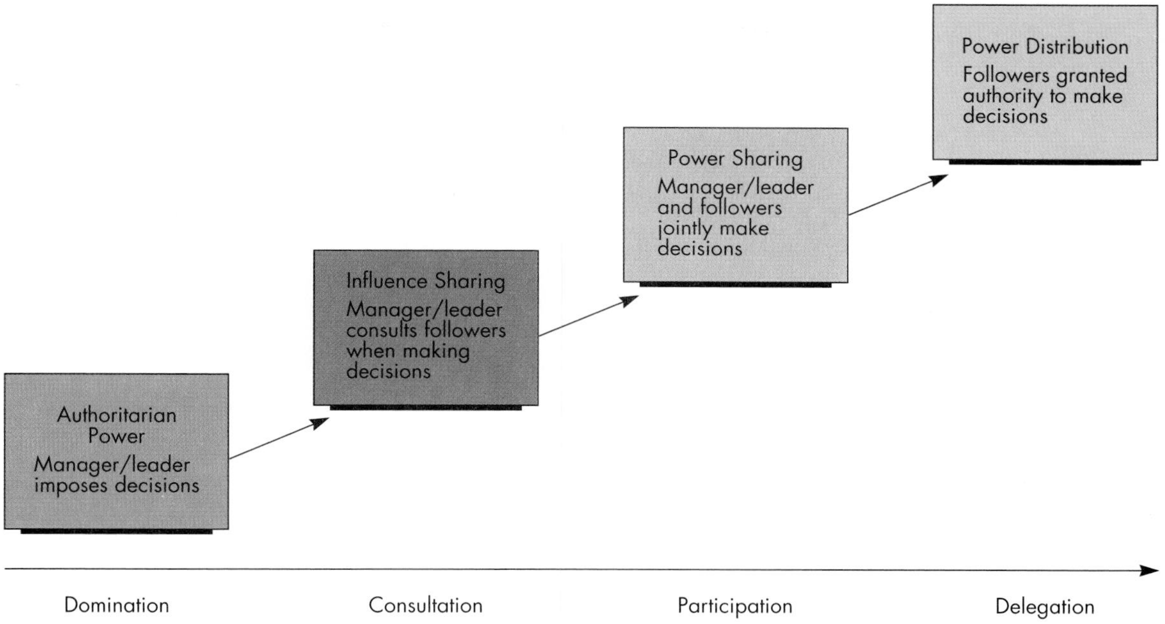

Power Distribution
Followers granted
authority to make
decisions

Power Sharing
Manager/leader
and followers
jointly make
decisions

Influence Sharing
Manager/leader
consults followers
when making
decisions

Authoritarian
Power
Manager/leader
imposes decisions

Domination   Consultation   Participation   Delegation

today's organizations. Some call it empowerment or power sharing. Others use traditional labels such as participative management, participative decision making, and delegation. Regardless of the term one prefers, the underlying process is the same. Namely, the decentralization of power. Where power once resided solely in the hands of managers, it now is being shifted to the hands of nonmanagers (see Figure 10–3). The overriding goal is to increase productivity and competitiveness in leaner organizations. Each step in this evolution increases the power of organizational contributors who traditionally had little or no legitimate power. Participative decision making and leadership are discussed in later chapters. So here we will describe the highest degree of power evolution—delegation—as a foundation concept for later chapters.

Delegation is the process of granting decision-making authority to subordinates. Importantly, delegation gives nonmanagerial employees more than simply a voice in decisions. It empowers them to make their own decisions (see International OB). Delegation has long been the recommended way to lighten the busy manager's load while at the same time developing subordinates' abilities. Unfortunately, research support for testimonial claims[18] stemming from the human relations movement was slow in coming. But, according to Carrie Leana's pioneering field study of 26 insurance claims supervisors, subordinates who enjoyed a greater degree of delegation processed more insurance claims at lower cost.[19] Power distribution via delegation does indeed seem to work.

The promising area of power distribution is explored further in the next chapter under the heading of autonomous (self-managed) work teams.

INTERNATIONAL OB

Sweden's Volvo Car Corp. Says No to Assembly Lines and Yes to Delegation at Its Uddevalla Plant

It is divided into six assembly plants, each of which has eight teams. The teams largely manage themselves, handling scheduling, quality control, hiring, and other duties normally performed by supervisors. Indeed, there are no first-line foremen and only two tiers of managers. Each team has a spokesperson/ombudsman, who reports to one of six plant managers, who in turn report to Leif Karlberg, president of the entire complex.

Morale seems high at Uddevalla. Absenteeism is only 8 percent.

Source: Jonathan Kapstein, "Volvo's Radical New Plant: 'The Death of the Assembly Line'?" *Business Week,* August 28, 1989, pp. 92–93.

• ORGANIZATIONAL POLITICS

Most students of OB find the study of organizational politics intriguing. Perhaps this topic owes its appeal to the antics of Hollywood characters, such as "Dallas's" J. R. Ewing, who get their way by stepping on anyone and everyone. As we will see, however, organizational politics includes, but is not limited to, dirty dealing. Organizational politics is an ever-present and often positive force in modern work organizations. Roberta Bhasin, a district manager for Mountain Bell Telephone Company, put organizational politics into perspective by observing:

> Most of us would like to believe that organizations are rationally structured, based on reasonable divisions of labor, a clear hierarchical communication flow, and well-defined lines of authority aimed at meeting universally understood goals and objectives.
>
> But organizations are made up of *people* with personal agendas designed to win power and influence. The agenda—the game—is called corporate politics. It is played by avoiding the rational structure, manipulating the communications hierarchy, and ignoring established lines of authority. The rules are never written down and seldom discussed.
>
> For some, corporate politics are second nature. They instinctively know the unspoken rules of the game. Others must learn. Managers who don't understand the politics of their organizations are at a disadvantage, not only in winning raises and promotions, but even in getting things *done.*[20]

We explore this important and interesting area by: (1) defining the term *organizational politics,* (2) identifying three levels of political action, (3) discussing eight specific political tactics, and (4) examining relevant research and practical implications.

Definition and Domain of Organizational Politics

"Organizational politics involves intentional acts of influence to enhance or protect the self-interest of individuals or groups."[21] An emphasis on *self-interest* distinguishes this form of social influence. Managers are endlessly

OB IN ACTION

Positive and Negative Faces of Organizational Politics

A Positive Face

One of the best ways to move up is by doing something patently political—proposing a new job only you can fill. . . .

For example: An engineering firm had always had trouble with basic administration because a large number of secretaries and word-processing people were needed, but the turnover was high. One engineer, Duncan R., tired of his straight engineering job, developed a scheme that allowed coverage of both the telephones and the word-processing equipment with 20 percent fewer people. This involved a pool approach and incorporated some part-timers and home-based workers at peak times. He wrote a job description for the person who would manage the new system, including the purchase of microcomputers and a new job title, director of staff service. . . .

It worked, as did his new organizational scheme. His boss's only comment was, "Why didn't you propose this job sooner?"

A Negative Face

"Some people have a compulsion to be considered in the same light as upper-level executives—and that can have dire consequences," says [a management consultant]. . . .

Such an obsession ruined one middle manager who found out on the sly that top executives would be monitoring a seminar he was attending. While other attendees were dressed casually—as suggested—he showed up in a three-piece suit, equipped with pointer, pocket calculator, and Cross pen. Until the top executives departed, that is. During the first break he quickly changed into slacks and sweater. The display created animosity and he was subsequently undermined by his own staff.

Sources: Excerpted from Marilyn Moats Kennedy, "Corporate Politics 101," *Canadian Business*, August 1985, pp. 62–63; and Charles R. Day, Jr., "The Politics Game," *Industry Week*, March 31, 1986, p. 80.

challenged to achieve a workable balance between employees' self-interests and organizational interests. As demonstrated by the first example in OB in Action, the pursuit of self-interest may serve the organization's interests. Political behavior becomes a negative force when self-interests erode or defeat organizational interests. For example, researchers recently documented the political tactic of filtering and distorting information flowing up to the boss. This self-serving practice put the reporting employees in the best possible light.[22] (More is said about communication distortion in Chapter 12.)

Uncertainty Triggers Political Behavior   Political maneuvering is triggered primarily by *uncertainty*. Five common sources of uncertainty within organizations are:

1. Unclear objectives.
2. Vague performance measures.
3. Ill-defined decision processes.

4. Strong individual or group competition.[23]

5. Any type of change.

Regarding this last source of uncertainty, organization development specialist Anthony Raia noted "Whatever we attempt to change, the political subsystem becomes active. Vested interests are almost always at stake and the distribution of power is challenged."[24]

Thus, we would expect a field sales representative, striving to achieve an assigned quota, to be less political than a management trainee working on a variety of projects. While some management trainees stake their career success on hard work, competence, and a bit of luck, many do not. These people attempt to gain a competitive edge through some combination of the political tactics discussed below. Meanwhile, the salesperson's performance is measured in actual sales, not in terms of being friends with the boss or taking credit for others' work. Thus, the management trainee would tend to be more political than the field salesperson because of greater uncertainty about management's expectations.

Because employees generally experience greater uncertainty during the earlier stages of their careers, are junior employees more political than more senior ones? The answer is yes, according to a survey of 243 employed adults in upstate New York. In fact, one senior employee nearing retirement told the researcher: "I used to play political games when I was younger. Now I just do my job."[25]

Three Levels of Political Action   Although much political maneuvering occurs at the individual level, it also can involve group or collective action. Figure 10–4 illustrates three different levels of political action: the individual level, the coalition level, and the network level.[26] Each level has its distinguishing characteristics. At the individual level, personal self-interests are pursued by the individual. The political aspects of coalitions and networks are not so obvious, however.

People with a common interest can become a political coalition by fitting the following definition. In an organizational context, a **coalition** is an informal group bound together by the *active* pursuit of a *single* issue. Coalitions

• **Figure 10–4**   Levels of Political Action in Organizations

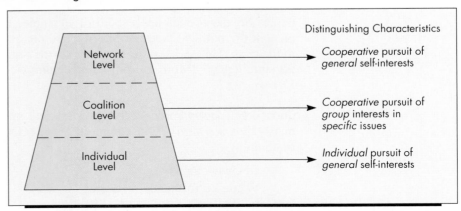

may or may not coincide with formal group membership. When the target issue is resolved (a sexually harrassing supervisor is fired, for example), the coalition disbands. Experts note that political coalitions have "fuzzy boundaries," meaning they are fluid in membership, flexible in structure, and temporary in duration.[27]

Coalitions are a potent political force in organizations. Consider the situation Charles J. Bradshaw faced in a finance committee meeting at Transworld Corp. in 1986: Bradshaw, president of the company, opposed the chairman's plan to acquire a $93 million nursing home company.

> [The senior vice president for finance] kicked off the meeting with a battery of facts and figures in support of the deal. "Within two or three minutes, I knew I had lost," Bradshaw concedes. "No one was talking directly to me, but all statements addressed my opposition. I could tell there was a general agreement around the board table." . . .
> Then the vote was taken. Five hands went up. Only Bradshaw voted "no."[28]

After the meeting, Bradshaw resigned his $530,000-a-year position, without as much as a handshake or good-bye from the chairman. In Bradshaw's case, the finance committee was a formal group that temporarily became a political coalition aimed at sealing his fate at Transworld.

A third level of political action involves networks. Unlike coalitions, which pivot on specific issues, networks are loose associations of individuals seeking social support for their general self-interests. Politically, networks are people-oriented, while coalitions are issue-oriented. Networks have broader and longer-term agendas than do coalitions For instance, Avon's Hispanic employees have built a network to enhance the members' career opportunities.

Political Tactics

Anyone who has worked in an organization has firsthand knowledge of blatant politicking. Blaming someone else for your mistake is an obvious political ploy. But other political tactics are more subtle. Researchers have identified a range of political behavior.

One landmark study, involving in-depth interviews with 87 managers from 30 electronics companies in Southern California, identified eight political tactics. Top-, middle-, and lower-level managers were represented about equally in the sample. According to the researchers: "Respondents were asked to describe organizational political tactics and personal characteristics of effective political actors based upon their accumulated experience in *all* organizations in which they had worked."[29] Listed in descending order of occurrence, the eight political tactics that emerged were:

1. Attacking or blaming others.
2. Using information as a political tool.
3. Creating a favorable image.
4. Developing a base of support.
5. Praising others (ingratiation).
6. Forming power coalitions with strong allies.
7. Associating with influential people.
8. Creating obligations (reciprocity).

• **TABLE 10-2**   Eight Common Political Tactics in Organizations

Political Tactic	Percent of Managers Mentioning Tactic	Brief Description of Tactic
1. Attacking or blaming others	54%	Used to avoid or minimize association with failure. Reactive when scapegoating is involved. Proactive when goal is to reduce competition for limited resources.
2. Using information as a political tool	54	Involves the purposeful withholding or distortion of information. Obscuring an unfavorable situation by overwhelming superiors with information.
3. Creating a favorable image	53	Dressing/grooming for success. Adhering to organizational norms and drawing attention to one's successes and influence. Taking credit for others' accomplishments.
4. Developing a base of support	37	Getting prior support for a decision. Building others' commitment to a decision through participation.
5. Praising others (ingratiation)	25	Making influential people feel good ("apple polishing").
6. Forming power coalitions with strong allies	25	Teaming up with powerful people who can get results.
7. Associating with influential people	24	Building a support network both inside and outside the organization.
8. Creating obligations (reciprocity)	13	Creating social debts ("I did you a favor, so you owe me a favor").

Source: Adapted from Robert W. Allen, Dan L. Madison, Lyman W. Porter, Patrcia A. Renwick, and Bronston T. Mayes, "Organizational Politics: Tactics and Characteristics of Its Actors," *California Management Review*, Fall 1979, pp. 77–83.

Table 10–2 describes these political tactics and indicates how often each reportedly was used by the interviewed managers.

The researchers distinguished between reactive and proactive political tactics. Some of the tactics, such as scapegoating, were *reactive* because the intent was to *defend* one's self-interest. Other tactics, such as developing a base of support, were *proactive* because they sought to *promote* the individual's self-interest.

Find out how political you are with the questionnaire in the OB Exercise. After responding to all 10 items, determine your political tendencies by using the scoring system recommended by the author of this quiz:

A confirmed organizational politician will answer "true" to all 10 questions. Organizational politicians with fundamental ethical standards will answer "false" to Questions 5 and 6, which deal with deliberate lies and uncharitable behavior. Individuals who regard manipulation, incomplete disclosure, and self-serving behavior as unacceptable will answer "false" to all or almost all of the questions.[30]

Research Evidence on Organizational Politics

Field research evidence in the area of organizational politics is slowly accumulating. Three particularly insightful studies are discussed in this

---

• OB EXERCISE

How Political Are You? A Self-Quiz

The Political Behavior Inventory

To determine your political appreciation and tendencies, please answer the following questions. Select the answer that best represents your behavior or belief, even if that particular behavior or belief is not present all the time.

1. You should make others feel important through an open appreciation of their ideas and work. _____ True _____ False
2. Because people tend to judge you when they first meet you, always try to make a good first impression. _____ True _____ False
3. Try to let others do most of the talking, be sympathetic to their problems, and resist telling people that they are totally wrong. _____ True _____ False
4. Praise the good traits of the people you meet and always give people an opportunity to save face if they are wrong or make a mistake. _____ True _____ False
5. Spreading false rumors, planting misleading information, and backstabbing are necessary, if somewhat unpleasant, methods to deal with your enemies. _____ True _____ False
6. Sometimes it is necessary to make promises that you know you will not or cannot keep. _____ True _____ False
7. It is important to get along with everybody, even with those who are generally recognized as windbags, abrasive, or constant complainers. _____ True _____ False
8. It is vital to do favors for others so that you can call in these IOUs at times when they will do you the most good. _____ True _____ False
9. Be willing to compromise, particularly on issues that are minor to you, but important to others. _____ True _____ False
10. On controversial issues, it is important to delay or avoid your involvement if possible. _____ True _____ False

Source: Joseph F. Byrnes, "Connecting Organizational Politics and Conflict Resolution," *Personnel Administrator*, June 1986, p. 49. Used with author's permission.

---

section. Two are based on self-report questionnaires, the third on direct observation of managers in action.

A follow-up research report on the sample of Southern California electronics industry managers, discussed earlier, provided the following insights:

- Sixty percent of the managers reported organizational politics was a frequent occurrence.
- The larger the organization, the greater the perceived political activity.
- Ambiguous roles and goals and increased conflict were associated with increased political activity.
- Marketing staffs and members of corporate boards of directors were rated as the most political, while production, accounting, and finance personnel were viewed as the least political.
- Reorganizations and personnel changes prompted the most political activity.[31]

Another study analyzed 330 brief reports written by 90 middle managers from a variety of industries. Those reports dealt with how the managers had "taken a position on a decision" or "resisted a decision." The researchers concluded that middle managers, often acting in coalitions, are a formidable barrier to implementing strategic plans they consider contrary to their self-interests.[32]

A more recent observational study of 248 managers, employed by a variety of organizations, found a curious relationship between the amount of time spent networking and career success and managerial effectiveness. The University of Nebraska research team, directed by Fred Luthans, defined networking as socializing, interacting with outsiders, and politicking. Career success was determined by how fast the individual has been promoted up the managerial ladder. Managerial effectiveness was assessed in terms of sub-unit performance and subordinates' satisfaction and commitment. It turned out that only 10 percent of the managers were both successful and effective. Among the other 90 percent, those who enjoyed career success devoted the largest share of their time to networking. In contrast, the effective managers devoted the *least* amount of their time to networking. This evidence prompted Luthans to ask:

> Could this finding explain some of the performance problems facing American organizations today? Could it be that the successful managers, the politically savvy ones who are being rapidly promoted into responsible positions, may not be the effective managers, the ones with satisfied, committed subordinates turning out quantity and quality performance in their units?[33]

Luthans then called for a concerted effort to create more *balanced* managers who are *both successful and effective*. One likely approach is to teach effective managers career management and networking skills.

Managing Organizational Politics

Organizational politics cannot be eliminated. A manager would be naive to expect such an outcome. But political maneuvering can and should be managed to keep it constructive and within reasonable bounds. Harvard's Abraham Zaleznik put the issue this way: "People can focus their attention on only so many things. The more it lands on politics, the less energy—emotional and intellectual—is available to attend to the problems that fall under the heading of real work"[34] Perhaps this explains why only 10 percent of the Luthans' sample managed to be promoted rapidly, while at the same time, doing a good job. The successful, but not effective, managers evidently spent too much of their emotional and intellectual energy on politicking. An appropriate middle ground needs to be achieved.

An individual's degree of politicalness is a matter of personal values, ethics, and temperament. People who are either strictly nonpolitical or highly political generally pay a price for their behavior. The former may experience slow promotions and feel left out, while the latter may run the risk of being called self-serving and lose their credibility. People at both ends of the political spectrum may be considered poor team players. A moderate amount of prudent political behavior generally is considered a survival tool in complex organizations.

• TABLE 10-3   Some Practical Advice on Managing Organizational Politics

To Reduce System Uncertainty:
Make clear what are the bases and processes for evaluation.
Differentiate rewards among high and low performers.
Make sure the rewards are as immediately and directly related to performance as possible.

To Reduce Competition:
Try to minimize resource competition among managers.
Replace resource competition with externally oriented goals and objectives.

To Break Existing Political Fiefdoms:
Where highly cohesive political empires exist, break them apart by removing or splitting the most dysfunctional subgroups.
If you are an executive, be keenly sensitive to managers whose mode of operation is the personalization of political patronage. First, approach these persons with a directive to "stop the political maneuvering." If it continues, remove them from the positions and, preferably, the company.

To Prevent Future Fiefdoms:
Make one of the most important criteria for promotion an apolitical attitude that puts organizational ends ahead of personal power ends.

Source: Don R. Beeman and Thomas W. Sharkey, "The Use and Abuse of Corporate Politics," *Business Horizons,* March-April 1987, p. 30.

With this perspective in mind, the practical steps in Table 10–3 are recommended. Notice the importance of reducing uncertainty through standardized performance evaluations and clear performance-reward linkages.[35] Measurable objectives are management's first line of defense against negative expressions of organizational politics. To resolve the conflict between middle managers' self-interests and strategy implementation, top managers need to build commitment to strategic plans through participative strategic goal setting.

• MANAGING INTERPERSONAL AND INTERGROUP CONFLICT

Mention the term *conflict* and most people envision fights, riots, or war. But these extreme situations represent only the most overt and combative expressions of conflict. During the typical workday, managers encounter more subtle and nonviolent types of opposition such as arguments, criticism, and disagreement. Conflict, like power and organizational politics, is an inevitable and sometimes positive force in modern work organizations. For example, a sincere dissenting opinion by a member of an executive planning committee might prevent the group from falling victim to groupthink. OB scholar Stephen Robbins defines **conflict** as "all kinds of opposition or antagonistic interaction. It is based on scarcity of power, resources or social position, and differing value systems."[36] Research reveals that managers spend about 21 percent of their time dealing with conflict,[37] so they need to be well grounded in conflict theory, research, and practice.

Conflict occurs at two levels within organizations: interpersonal and intergroup. This section addresses both levels of conflict by (1) distinguishing between functional and dysfunctional conflict, (2) identifying antecedents of conflict, (3) explaining how to promote functional conflict, (4) examining alternative styles of handling conflict, (5) reviewing recent research evidence, and (6) discussing a contingency approach to managing conflict.

A Conflict Continuum

Ideas about managing conflict have undergone an interesting evolution during this century. Initially, scientific management experts such as Frederick W. Taylor believed all conflict ultimately threatened management's authority and thus had to be avoided or quickly resolved. Later, human relationists recognized the inevitability of conflict and advised managers to learn to live with it. Emphasis remained on resolving conflict whenever possible, however. Beginning in the 1970s, OB specialists realized conflict had both positive and negative outcomes, depending on its nature and intensity. This perspective introduced the revolutionary idea that organizations could suffer from *too little* conflict. Figure 10–5 illustrates the relationship between conflict intensity and outcomes.

Work groups, departments, or organizations that experience too little conflict tend to be plagued by apathy, lack of creativity, indecision, and missed deadlines. Excessive conflict, on the other hand, can erode organizational performance because of political infighting, dissatisfaction, lack of teamwork, and turnover. Appropriate types and levels of conflict energize people in constructive directions.

Functional versus Dysfunctional Conflict

The distinction between **functional conflict** and **dysfunctional conflict** pivots on whether or not the organization's interests are served. According to Robbins:

• **FIGURE 10-5**   The Relationship between Conflict Intensity and Outcomes

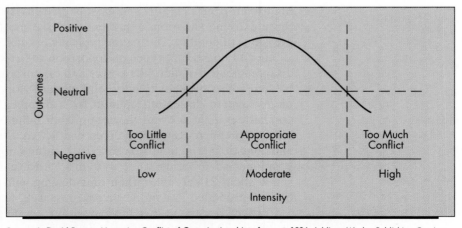

Source: L. David Brown, *Managing Conflict of Organizational Interfaces,* © 1986, Addison-Wesley Publishing Co., Inc., Reading, Massachusetts. Figure 1.1 on page 8. Reprinted with permission.

Some [types of conflict] support the goals of the organization and improve performance; these are functional, constructive forms of conflict. They benefit or support the main purposes of the organization. Additionally, there are those types of conflict that hinder organizational performance; these are dysfunctional or destructive forms. They are undesirable and the manager should seek their eradication.[38]

Functional conflict is commonly referred to in management circles as constructive conflict, or constructive confrontation.[39] Executives such as Finis F. Conner, head of the fast-growing maker of computer disk drives bearing his name, rely on functional conflict to keep themselves open to new ideas and to keep the operation headed in a productive direction (see OB in Action). In contrast, managers such as Fred Ackman, former chairman of Superior Oil Corp., foster dysfunctional conflict by dealing with personalities rather than with issues. Not surprisingly, of 13 top executives at Superior Oil, nine left within one year after Ackman joined the company.

Antecedents of Conflict

Certain situations produce more conflict than others. By knowing the antecedents of conflict, managers are better able to anticipate conflict and take steps to resolve it if it becomes dysfunctional. Among the situations that tend to produce either functional or dysfunctional conflict are:

 OB IN ACTION

Functional and Dysfunctional Conflict

Functional Conflict

Finis F. Conner, Chairman, Conner Peripherals

Now that he is boss of a major disk drive business at long last, Conner has discovered he must curb his tendency to want everything his own way. The company's vice president of finance, Albert Pimentel, recalls a meeting in which a disagreement about cost allocation deteriorated into a shouting match, with Conner bullying Pimentel in front of subordinates. After the meeting Conner sought him out and said apologetically, "Don't give in to me, because it's important that I do the right thing."

Dysfunctional Conflict

Fred Ackman, former chairman, Superior Oil

Familiarity bred contempt. Employees say Ackman proved thoroughly autocratic, refusing even to discuss staff suggestions. He tended to treat disagreement as disloyalty. Many were put off by Ackman's abusive temper, which together with his stature (5 feet 8½ inches) and red hair earned him the nickname "Little Red Fred." Says a former subordinate, "He couldn't stand it when somebody disagreed with him, even in private. He'd eat you up alive, calling you a dumb S.O.B. or asking if you had your head up your ass. It happened all the time."

Sources: Andrew Kupfer, "America's Fastest Growing Company," *Fortune*, August 13, 1990, p. 54, and Steven Flax, "The Toughest Bosses in America," *Fortune*, August 6, 1984, p. 21.

- Incompatible personalities or value systems.
- Overlapping or unclear job boundaries.
- Competition for limited resources.
- Inadequate communication.
- Interdependent tasks (for example, one person cannot complete his or her assignment until others have completed their work).
- Organizational complexity (conflict tends to increase as the number of hierarchical layers and specialized tasks increase).
- Unreasonable or unclear policies, standards, or rules.
- Unreasonable deadlines or extreme time pressure.
- Collective decision making (the greater the number of people participating in a decision, the greater the potential for conflict).
- Decision making by consensus (100 percent agreement often is impossible to achieve without much arguing).
- Unmet expectations (employees who have unrealistic expectations about job assignments, pay, or promotions are more prone to conflict).
- Unresolved or suppressed conflicts.[40]

Proactive managers carefully read these early warnings and take appropriate action. For example, group conflict can be reduced by making decisions on the basis of a majority vote rather than seeking a consensus.

Stimulating Functional Conflict

Sometimes committees and decision-making groups become so bogged down in details and procedures that nothing substantive is accomplished. Carefully monitored functional conflict can help get the creative juices flowing once again. Managers basically have two options. They can fan the fires of naturally occurring conflict—but this approach can be unreliable and slow. Alternatively, managers can resort to programmed conflict. Experts in the field define **programmed conflict** as "conflict that raises different opinions *regardless of the personal feelings of the managers.*"[41] The trick is to get contributors to either defend or criticize ideas based on relevant facts, rather than on the basis of personal preference or political interests. This requires disciplined role playing. Two programmed conflict techniques with proven track records are devil's advocacy and the dialectic method. Let us explore these two ways of stimulating functional conflict.

Devil's Advocacy   This technique gets its name from a traditional practice within the Roman Catholic Church. When someone's name came before the College of Cardinals for elevation to sainthood, it was absolutely essential to ensure that he or she had a spotless record. Consequently, one individual was assigned the role of *devil's advocate* to uncover and air all possible objections to the person's canonization. In accordance with this practice, **devil's advocacy** in today's organizations involves assigning someone the role of critic. Recall from the last chapter, Irving Janis recommended the devil's advocate role for preventing groupthink.

• **FIGURE 10-6** Techniques for Stimulating Functional Conflict: Devil's Advocacy and the Dialectic Method

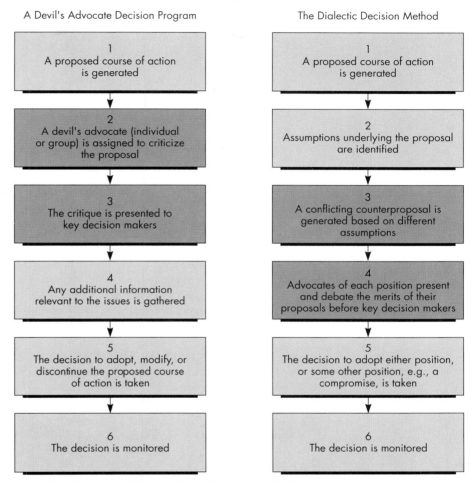

Source: Richard A. Cosier and Charles R. Schwenk, "Agreement and Thinking Alike: Ingredients for Poor Decisions," *Academy of Management Executive*, February 1990, pp. 72–73.

In the left half of Figure 10–6 note how devil's advocacy alters the usual decision-making process in steps 2 and 3. This approach to programmed conflict is intended to generate critical thinking and reality testing.[42] It is a good idea to rotate the job of devil's advocate so no one person or group develops a strictly negative reputation. Moreover, periodic devil's advocacy role-playing is good training for developing analytical and communicative skills.

The Dialectic Method   Like devil's advocacy, the dialectic method is a time-honored practice. This particular approach to programmed conflict traces back to the dialectic school of philosophy in ancient Greece. Plato and his followers attempted to synthesize truths by exploring opposite positions (called thesis and antithesis). Court systems in the United States and else-where rely on directly opposing points of view for determining guilt or

• When the dialectic method emerged from the School of Athens, the ancient Greeks had no way of knowing that their technique would be embraced centuries later by businesspeople seeking to resolve a conflict to make a profitable decision.   *(North Wind Picture Archives)*

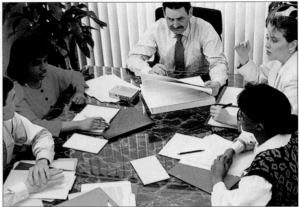

innocence. Accordingly, today's **dialectic method** calls for managers to foster a structured debate of opposing viewpoints prior to making a decision. Steps 3 and 4 in the right half of Figure 10–6 set the dialectic approach apart from the normal decision-making process. A practice of Andrew Grove, Intel's chief executive officer, exemplifies the dialectic method. According to Grove: "I get a much better understanding of an issue with which I am not familiar by listening to two people with opposing views discuss it than I do by listening to one side only."[43] (See OB in Action.)

A major drawback of the dialectic method is that "winning the debate" may overshadow the issue at hand. Also, the dialectic method requires more skill training than does devil's advocacy. Regarding the comparative effectiveness of these two approaches to stimulating functional conflict, how-

   OB IN ACTION

Anheuser-Busch's Policy Committee Relies on the Dialectic Method

When the policy committee . . . considers a major move—getting into or out of a business, or making a big capital expenditure—it sometimes assigns teams to make the case for each side of the question. There may be two teams or even three. Each is knowledgeable about the subject; each has access to the same information. Occasionally someone in favor of the project is chosen to lead the dissent, and an opponent to argue for it. Pat Stokes, who heads the company's beer empire, describes the result: "We end up with decisions and alternatives we hadn't thought of previously," sometimes representing a synthesis of the opposing views. "You become a lot more anticipatory, better able to see what might happen, because you have thought through the process."

Source: Walter Kiechel III, "How to Escape the Echo Chamber," *Fortune*, June 18, 1990, p. 130.

• **FIGURE 10–7**   Five Conflict-Handling Styles

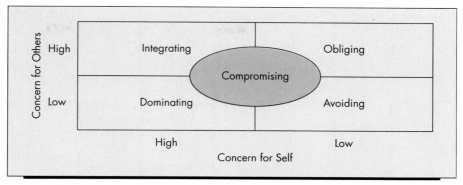

Source: M. Afzalur Rahim, "A Strategy for Managing Conflict in Complex Organizations, *Human Relations*, January 1985, p. 84. Used with author's permission.

ever, a recent laboratory study ended in a tie. Compared with groups that strived to reach a consensus, decision-making groups using either devil's advocacy or the dialectic method yielded equally higher quality decisions.[44] In light of this evidence, managers have some latitude in using either devil's advocacy or the dialectic method for pumping creative life back into stalled deliberations. Personal preference and the role players' experience may well be the deciding factors in choosing one approach over the other. The important thing is to actively stimulate functional conflict when necessary (such as when the risk of blind conformity or groupthink is high).

Alternative Styles for Handling Dysfunctional Conflict

People tend to handle negative conflict in patterned ways referred to as *styles*. Several conflict styles have been categorized over the years. According to conflict specialist Afzalur Rahim's model, five different conflict-handling styles can be plotted on a 2 × 2 grid. High to low concern for *self* is found on the horizontal axis of the grid while low to high concern for *others* forms the vertical axis (see Figure 10–7). Various combinations of these variables produce the five different conflict-handling styles: integrating, obliging, dominating, avoiding, and compromising. There is no single best style; each has strengths and limitations and is subject to situational constraints.

Integrating (Problem Solving)   In this style, interested parties confront the issue and cooperatively identify the problem, generate and weigh alternative solutions, and select a solution. Integrating is appropriate for complex issues plagued by misunderstanding. However, it is inappropriate for resolving conflicts rooted in opposing value systems. Its primary strength is its longer-lasting impact because it deals with the underlying problem rather than merely with symptoms. The primary weakness of this style is that it's very time-consuming.

Obliging (Smoothing)   "An obliging person neglects his or her own concern to satisfy the concern of the other party."[45] This style, often called smoothing, involves playing down differences while emphasizing commonalities.

OB IN ACTION

A Heavy Hand Gets Things Moving at Xerox

It took a newly hired outsider, former IBM man William C. Lowe, executive vice president for development, to finally address Xerox's problem: Product development and marketing just weren't talking. At O'Hare, he gathered 18 top engineers, scientists, and marketing pros to hash out ways to focus research better and move the results more quickly to market. Some old Xerox hands balked, but as Lowe dryly notes: "Some of those people aren't with us now."

Source: Excerpted from Todd Vogel, "At Xerox, They're Shouting 'Once More into the Breach,'" *Business Week,* July 23, 1990, p. 62.

Obliging may be an appropriate conflict-handling strategy when it is possible to eventually get something in return. But it is inappropriate for complex or worsening problems. Its primary strength is that it encourages cooperation. Its main weakness is that it's a temporary fix that fails to confront the underlying problem.

Dominating (Forcing)   High concern for self and low concern for others encourages "I win, you lose" tactics. The other party's needs are largely ignored. This style is often called forcing, because it relies on formal authority to force compliance. Dominating is appropriate when an unpopular solution must be implemented, the issue is minor, or a deadline is near (see OB in Action). It is inappropriate in an open and participative climate. Speed is its primary strength. The primary weakness of this domineering style is that it often breeds resentment.

Avoiding   This tactic may involve either passive withdrawal from the problem or active suppression of the issue. Avoidance is appropriate for trivial issues or when the costs of confrontation outweigh the benefits of resolving the conflict. It is inappropriate for difficult and worsening problems. The main strength of this style is that it buys time in unfolding or ambiguous situations. The primary weakness is that the tactic provides a temporary fix that sidesteps the underlying problem.

Compromising   This is a give-and-take approach involving moderate concern for both self and others. "Each party is required to give up something of value. Includes external or third party interventions, negotiation, and voting."[46] Compromise is appropriate when parties have opposite goals or possess equal power (such as labor-management contract negotiations).[47] But compromise is inappropriate when overuse would lead to inconclusive action (e.g., failure to meet production deadlines). The primary strength of this tactic is that the democratic process has no losers, but it's a temporary fix that can stifle creative problem solving.

To reinforce your knowledge of these conflict styles and learn more about yourself, take a few moments to complete the self-quiz in the OB Exercise. The instrument from which this quiz was drawn was validated through a

• OB EXERCISE

What Is Your Primary Conflict-Handling Style?

Instructions:

For each of the 15 items, indicate how often you rely on that tactic by circling the appropriate number. After you have responded to all 15 items, complete the scoring key below.

Conflict–Handling Tatics	Rarely Always
1. I argue my case with my co-workers to show the merits of my position.	1—2—3—4—5
2. I negotiate with my co-workers so that a compromise can be reached.	1—2—3—4—5
3. I try to satisfy the expectations of my co-workers.	1—2—3—4—5
4. I try to investigate an issue with my co-workers to find a solution acceptable to us.	1—2—3—4—5
5. I am firm in pursuing my side of the issue.	1—2—3—4—5
6. I attempt to avoid being "put on the spot" and try to keep my conflict with my co-workers to myself.	1—2—3—4—5
7. I hold on to my solution to a problem.	1—2—3—4—5
8. I use "give and take" so that a compromise can be made.	1—2—3—4—5
9. I exchange accurate information with my co-workers to solve a problem together.	1—2—3—4—5
10. I avoid open discussion of my differences with my co-workers.	1—2—3—4—5
11. I accommodate the wishes of my co-workers.	1—2—3—4—5
12. I try to bring all our concerns out in the open so that the issues can be resolved in the best possible way.	1—2—3—4—5
13. I propose a middle ground for breaking deadlocks.	1—2—3—4—5
14. I go along with the suggestions of my co-workers.	1—2—3—4—5
15. I try to keep my disagreements with my co-workers to myself in order to avoid hard feelings.	1—2—3—4—5

Scoring Key:

Integrating		**Obliging**		**Dominating**	
Item	Score	Item	Score	Item	Score
4.	_____	3.	_____	1.	_____
9.	_____	11.	_____	5.	_____
12.	_____	14.	_____	7.	_____
Total = _____		Total = _____		Total = _____	

Avoiding		**Compromising**	
Item	Score	Item	Score
6.	_____	2.	_____
10.	_____	8.	_____
15.	_____	13.	_____
Total = _____		Total = _____	

Your primary conflict-handling style is: _____
  (The category with the highest total.)

Your backup conflict-handling style is: _____
  (The category with the second highest total.)

Source: Adapted and excerpted in part from M. Afzalur Rahim, "A Measure of Styles of Handling Interpersonal Conflict," *Academy of Management Journal*, June 1983, pp. 368–76.

factor analysis of responses from 1,219 managers from across the United States.[48] Are the results what you expected or are they a surprise?

With the antecedents of conflict, the stimulation of functional conflict, and the five conflict-handling styles in mind, let us probe the relevant research for instructive insights.

Conflict Research Evidence

Laboratory studies, relying on college students as subjects, uncovered the following insights about organizational conflict:

- People with a high need for affiliation tended to rely on a smoothing (obliging) style while avoiding a forcing (dominating) style.[49] Thus, personality traits affect how people handle conflict.
- Disagreement expressed in an arrogant and demeaning manner produced significantly more negative effects than the same sort of disagreement expressed in a reasonable manner.[50] In other words, *how* you disagree with someone is very important in conflict situations.
- Threats and punishment, by one party in a disagreement, tended to produce intensifying threats and punishment from the other party.[51] In short, aggression breeds aggression.
- As conflict increased, group satisfaction decreased. An integrative style of handling conflict led to higher group satisfaction than did an avoidance style.[52]

Field studies involving managers and real organizations have given us the following insights:

- Both intradepartmental and interdepartmental conflict decreased as goal difficulty and goal clarity increased. Thus, as was the case with politics, challenging and clear goals can defuse conflict.
- Higher levels of conflict tended to erode job satisfaction and internal work motivation.[53]
- Men and women at the same managerial level tended to handle conflict similarly. In short, there was no gender effect.[54]
- Conflict tended to move around the organization in a case study of a public school system.[55] Thus, managers need to be alerted to the fact that conflict often originates in one area or level and becomes evident somewhere else. Conflict needs to be traced back to its source if there is to be lasting improvement.

Conflict Management: A Contingency Approach

Three realities dictate how organizational conflict should be managed. First, conflict is inevitable because it is triggered by a wide variety of antecedents. Second, too little conflict may be as counterproductive as too much. Third, there is no single best way of resolving conflict. Consequently, conflict specialists recommend a contingency approach to managing conflict. Antecedents of conflict and actual conflict need to be monitored. If signs of too little conflict such as apathy or lack of creativity appear, then functional conflict needs to be stimulated. This can be done by nurturing appropriate antecedents of conflict and/or programming conflict with techniques such as

OB IN ACTION

A Skillful Conflict Manager

Suzan Couch has been both a target and an arbiter of jealousy on the job. As vice president of marketing services at Warner Amex Cable Communications in New York, she sensed overt jealousy from a male executive apparently resentful of her success. He criticized her performance to colleagues as "not serious," she says, and spread snide remarks about her personal life. She retaliated, not with fire, but with friendliness. "Every time I saw him, I gave him another compliment," she says. "I was so sweet that he finally gave up his campaign."

In her role as manager, she faced a potentially explosive rivalry between two subordinates, both "very talented, high-powered women," who were vying for the same promotion. She worried that the loser, in her bitterness, would undermine projects and poison office camaraderie. "With a lot of deadlines to meet, I couldn't afford that," says Ms. Couch, who now heads her own marketing firm, CB Communication Inc. in New York.

Her approach, after tapping her choice, was to make sure the other employee accepted the situation graciously but still felt part of the winner's circle. Ms. Couch held out the hope of a future promotion and also arranged for the two rivals to share a "no hard feelings" champagne lunch. "They're still friends," she notes.

Source: Excerpted from Carol Hymowitz and Timothy D. Schellhardt, "Thy Neighbor's Job: As Insecurities Grow, Office Jealousy Flourishes." Reprinted by permission of *The Wall Street Journal*, Dow Jones & Company, Inc., July 17, 1986. All rights reserved.

devil's advocacy and the dialectic method. On the other hand, when conflict becomes dysfunctional, the appropriate conflict-handling style needs to be enacted. Realistic training involving role playing can prepare managers to try alternative conflict styles.

Managers can keep from getting too deeply embroiled in conflict by applying three lessons from recent research: (1) establish challenging and clear goals, (2) disagree in a constructive and reasonable manner, and (3) refuse to get caught in the aggression-breeds-aggression spiral (see OB in Action).

• SUMMARY OF KEY CONCEPTS

A. Managers are constantly challenged to foster mutuality of interest (a win–win situation) between individual and organizational interests. A decade of research has identified eight generic influence tactics: consultation, rational persuasion, inspirational appeals, ingratiating tactics, coalition tactics, pressure tactics, upward appeals, and exchange tactics. Managers can build their influence and enjoy positive reciprocity by forming strategic alliances with co-workers.

B. Social power is the *ability* to get things done, whereas authority is the *right* to seek compliance. Socialized power embraces a concern for the welfare of others. Personalized power is rooted in self-interest.

French and Raven's five bases of power are reward power, coercive power, legitimate power, expert power, and referent power.

C. An exciting and promising trend in today's organizations is the decentralization of power. In short, power is shifting to nonmanagerial employees as a way of boosting productivity and competitiveness. The highest evolution of power is delegation. Delegation gives employees more than a participatory role in decision making. It allows them to make their own work-related decisions.

D. Organizational politics is defined as intentional acts of influence to enhance or protect the self-interests of individuals or groups. Uncertainty triggers most politicking in organizations. Political action occurs at individual, coalition, and network levels. Coalitions are informal, temporary, and single-issue alliances.

E. Researchers find political maneuvering associated with larger organizations, ambiguous roles and goals, conflict, reorganizations, and personnel changes. Organizational politics can be managed but never eliminated.

F. Conflict is defined as all kinds of opposition or antagonistic interaction. It is inevitable and not necessarily destructive. Too little conflict, as evidenced by apathy or lack of creativity, can be as great a problem as too much conflict. Functional conflict enhances organizational interests while dysfunctional conflict is counterproductive.

G. There are many antecedents of conflict—including incompatible personalities, competition for limited resources, and unrealized expectations—that need to be monitored. Functional conflict can be stimulated by permitting selected antecedents of conflict to persist and/or programming conflict during decision making with devil's advocates or the dialectic method.

H. Five alternative conflict-handling styles are integrating (problem solving), obliging (smoothing), dominating (forcing), avoiding, and compromising. There is no single best style. Conflict research demonstrates a link between personality and conflict style and that aggression breeds aggression. Challenging and measurable goals are an effective tool for containing both political behavior and conflict.

• KEY TERMS

mutuality of interest	referent power
reciprocity	delegation
social power	organizational politics
authority	coalition
socialized power	conflict
personalized power	functional conflict
reward power	dysfunctional conflict
coercive power	programmed conflict
legitimate power	devil's advocacy
expert power	dialectic method

● DISCUSSION QUESTIONS

1. Of the eight generic influence tactics, which do you use the most when dealing with friends, parents, your boss, or your professors? Would other tactics be more effective?

2. Before reading this chapter, did the term *power* have a negative connotation for you? Do you view it differently now? Explain.

3. What base(s) of power do you rely on in your daily affairs? (Use the OB Exercise to assess your power bases at work.) Do you handle power effectively and responsibly?

4. What are the main advantages and drawbacks of the trend toward increased delegation?

5. Why do you think organizational politics is triggered primarily by uncertainty?

6. What personal experiences have you had with coalitions? Explain any positive or negative outcomes.

7. How political are you prepared to be at work? (Use the self-quiz in the OB Exercise as an assessment tool.) What are the career implications of your behavior?

8. What examples of functional and dysfunctional conflict have you encountered?

9. What has been your experience with playing the devil's advocate role?

10. According to the OB Exercise, what is your primary conflict-handling style? Would this help or hinder your effectiveness as a manager?

BACK TO THE OPENING CASE

Now that you have read Chapter 10, you should be able to answer the following questions about the GM Fiero case:

1. What was Hulki Aldikacti's primary base of power? Did he use it effectively? Explain.
2. What evidence of organizational politics can you find in this case? Did coalitions enter the picture in any significant way? Explain.
3. Was the conflict in this case largely functional or dysfunctional? Explain.
4. What antecedents of conflict can you pinpoint in this case?
5. How should the conflict between the Pontiac Division and the Chevrolet Motor Division have been handled?

● EXERCISE 10

Objectives

1. To further your knowledge of interpersonal conflict and conflict-handling styles.

2. To give you a firsthand opportunity to try the various styles of handling conflict.

Introduction

This is a role-playing exercise intended to develop your ability to handle conflict. There is no single best way to resolve the conflict in this exercise. One style might work for one person, while another gets the job done for someone else.

Instructions

Read the following short case, "Can Larry Fit In?" Pair up with someone else and decide which of you will play the role of Larry and which will play the manager. Pick up the action from where the case leaves off. Try to be realistic and true to the characters in the case. The manager is primarily responsible for resolving this conflict situation. Whoever plays Larry should resist any unreasonable requests or demands and cooperate with any personally workable solution. *Note:* To conserve time, try to resolve this situation in less than 15 minutes.

Case: "Can Larry Fit In?" [56]

You are the manager of an auditing team for a major accounting firm. You are sitting in your office reading some complicated new reporting procedures that have just arrived from the home office. Your concentration is suddenly interrupted by a loud knock on your door. Without waiting for an invitation to enter, Larry, one of your auditors, bursts into your office. He is obviously very upset, and it is not difficult for you to surmise why he is in such a nasty mood. You have just posted the audit assignments for the next month, and you scheduled Larry for a job you knew he wouldn't like. Larry is one of your senior auditors, and the company norm is that they get the better assignments. This particular job will require him to spend two weeks away from home, in a remote town, working with a company whose records are notorious for being a mess.

Unfortunately, you have had to assign several of these less desirable audits to Larry recently because you are short of personnel. But that's not the only reason. You have received several complaints from the junior staff members recently about Larry's treating them in an obnoxious manner. They feel he is always looking for an opportunity to boss them around, as if he were their supervisor instead of a member of the audit team. As a result, your whole operation works smoothly when you can send Larry out of town on a solo project for several days. It keeps him from coming into your office telling you how to do your job, and the morale of the rest of the auditing staff is significantly higher.

Larry slams the door and proceeds to express his anger over this assignment. He says you are deliberately trying to undermine his status in the group by giving him all the dirty assignments. He accuses you of being insensitive to his feelings and says that if things don't change, he is going to register a formal complaint with your boss.

Questions for Consideration/Class Discussion

1. What antecedents of conflict appear to be present in this situation? What can be done about them?

2. Having heard how others handled this conflict, did one particular style seem to work better than the others?

3. Did influence tactics, power, and politics enter into your deliberations? Explain.

• NOTES

1 Henry Malcolm and Claire Sokoloff, "Values, Human Relations, and Organization Development," in *The Emerging Practice of Organization Development,* eds. Walter Sikes, Allan Drexler, and Jack Gant (San Diego: University Associates, 1989), p. 64.

2 "Push-Button Age," *Newsweek,* July 9, 1990, p. 57.

3 See David Kipnis, Stuart M. Schmidt, and Ian Wilkinson, "Intraorganizational Influence Tactics: Explorations in Getting One's Way," *Journal of Applied Psychology,* August 1980, pp. 440–52. Also see Chester A. Schriesheim and Timothy R. Hinkin, "Influence Tactics Used by Subordinates: A Theoretical and Empirical Analysis and Refinement of the Kipnis, Schmidt, and Wilkinson Subscales," *Journal of Applied Psychology,* June 1990, pp. 246–57.

4 Based on Gary Yukl and Cecilia M. Falbe, "Influence Tactics and Objectives in Upward, Downward, and Lateral Influence Attempts," *Journal of Applied Psychology,* April 1990, pp. 132–40.

5 See, for example, George F. Dreher, Thomas W. Dougherty, and William Whitely, "Influence Tactics and Salary Attainment: A Gender-Specific Analysis," *Sex Roles,* May 1989, pp. 535–50.

6 See Dafna N. Izraeli, "Sex Effects in the Evaluation of Influence Tactics," *Journal of Occupational Behaviour,* January 1987, pp. 79–86.

7 Details of this study are provided in Mahfooz A. Ansari and Alka Kapoor, "Organizational Context and Upward Influence Tactics," *Organizational Behavior and Human Decision Processes,* August 1987, pp. 39–49.

8 Allan R. Cohen and David L. Bradford, *Influence Without Authority* (New York: John Wiley & Sons, 1990), pp. 23–24.

9 Ibid., p. 28. Another excellent source on this subject is Robert B. Cialdini, *Influence* (New York: William Morrow, 1984).

10 Dean Tjosvold, "The Dynamics of Positive Power," *Training and Development Journal,* June 1984, p. 72.

11 Morgan W. McCall, Jr., *Power, Influence, and Authority: The Hazards of Carrying a Sword,* Technical Report No. 10 (Greensboro, N.C.: Center for Creative Leadership, 1978), p. 5. For an excellent update on power, see Edwin P. Hollander and Lynn R. Offermann, "Power and Leadership in Organizations," *American Psychologist,* February 1990, pp. 179–89.

12 Laurie Baum and John A. Byrne, "Executive Secretary: A New Rung on the Corporate Ladder," *Business Week,* April 21, 1986, p. 74.

13 Leonard H. Chusmir, "Personalized vs. Socialized Power Needs among Working Women and Men," *Human Relations,* February 1986, p. 149.

14 See John R. P. French and Bertram Raven, "The Bases of Social Power," in *Studies in Social Power,* ed. Dorwin Cartwright (Ann Arbor: University of Michigan Press, 1959), pp. 150–67.

[15] Details may be found in Chusmir, "Personalized vs. Socialized Power Needs among Working Women and Men," pp. 149–59. For a review of research on individual differences in the need for power, see Robert J. House, "Power and Personality in Complex Organizations," in *Research in Organizational Behavior,* ed. Barry M. Staw and L. L. Cummings (Greenwich, Conn.: JAI Press, 1988), pp. 305–57.

[16] Philip M. Podsakoff and Chester A. Schriesheim, "Field Studies of French and Raven's Bases of Power: Critique, Reanalysis, and Suggestions for Future Research," *Psychological Bulletin,* May 1985, p. 388. Also see M. Afzalur Rahim and Gabriel F. Buntzman, "Supervisory Power Bases, Styles of Handling Conflict with Subordinates, and Subordinate Compliance and Satisfaction," *Journal of Psychology,* March 1989, pp. 195–210; and Dean Tjosvold, "Power and Social Context in Superior-Subordinate Interaction," *Organizational Behavior and Human Decision Processes,* June 1985, pp. 281–93.

[17] See Timothy R. Hinkin and Chester A. Schriesheim, "Relationships between Subordinate Perceptions and Supervisor Influence Tactics and Attributed Bases of Supervisory Power," *Human Relations,* March 1990, pp. 221–37.

[18] For example, see Laurie Baum, "Delegating Your Way to Job Survival," *Business Week,* November 2, 1987, p. 206.

[19] For complete details, see Carrie R. Leana, "Power Relinquishment versus Power Sharing: Theoretical Clarification and Empirical Comparison of Delegation and Participation," *Journal of Applied Psychology,* May 1987, pp. 228–33.

[20] Roberta Bhasin, "On Playing Corporate Politics," *Pulp & Paper,* October 1985, p. 175.

[21] Robert W. Allen, Dan L. Madison, Lyman W. Porter, Patricia A. Renwick, and Bronston T. Mayes, "Organizational Politics: Tactics and Characteristics of Its Actors," *California Management Review,* Fall 1979, p. 77.

[22] See Patricia M. Fandt and Gerald R. Ferris, "The Management of Information and Impressions: When Employees Behave Opportunistically," *Organizational Behavior and Human Decision Processes,* February 1990, pp. 140–58.

[23] First four based on discussion in Don R. Beeman and Thomas W. Sharkey, "The Use and Abuse of Corporate Politics," *Business Horizons,* March–April 1987, pp. 26–30.

[24] Anthony Raia, "Power, Politics, and the Human Resource Professional," *Human Resource Planning*, no. 4, 1985, p. 203.

[25] Andrew J. DuBrin, "Career Maturity, Organizational Rank, and Political Behavioral Tendencies: A Correlational Analysis of Organizational Politics and Career Experience," *Psychological Reports,* October 1988, p. 535.

[26] This three-level distinction comes from Anthony T. Cobb, "Political Diagnosis: Applications in Organizational Development," *Academy of Management Review,* July 1986, pp. 482–96.

[27] An excellent historical and theoretical perspective of coalitions can be found in William B. Stevenson, Jone L. Pearce, and Lyman W. Porter, "The Concept of 'Coalition' in Organization Theory and Research," *Academy of Management Review,* April 1985, pp. 256–68.

[28] Laurie Baum, "The Day Charlie Bradshaw Kissed Off Transworld," *Business Week,* September 29, 1986, p. 68.

[29] Allen, Madison, Porter, Renwick, and Mayes, "Organizational Politics: Tactics and Characteristics of Its Actors," p. 77.

[30] Joseph F. Byrnes, "Connecting Organizational Politics and Conflict Resolution," *Personnel Administrator,* June 1986, pp. 49–50. An alternative 50-item questionnaire may be found in Andrew J. DuBrin, "Winning at Office Politics," *Success,* September 1981, pp. 26–28, 46.

[31] See Dan L. Madison, Robert W. Allen, Lyman W. Porter, Patricia A. Renwick, and Bronston T. Mayes, "Organizational Politics: An Exploration of Managers' Perceptions," *Human Relations,* February 1980, pp. 79–100.

[32] For additional details, see William D. Guth and Ian C. Macmillan, "Strategy Implementation versus Middle Management Self-Interest," *Strategic Management Journal,* July–August 1986, pp. 313–27.

[33] Fred Luthans, "Successful vs. Effective Real Managers," *Academy of Management Executive,* May 1988, p. 127.

[34] Abraham Zaleznik, "Real Work," *Harvard Business Review,* January–February 1989, p. 60.

[35] The management of organizational politics also is discussed in Stephen L. Payne and Bernard F. Pettingill, "Coping with Organizational Politics," *Supervisory Management,* April 1986, pp. 28–31; Clinton O. Longenecker, "Truth or Consequences: Politics and Performance Appraisals," *Business Horizons,* November–December 1989, pp. 76–82; and Jerry B. Harvey, "Some Thoughts about Organizational Backstabbing: Or, How Come Every Time I Get Stabbed in the Back My Fingerprints Are on the Knife?" *Academy of Management Executive,* November 1989, pp. 271–77.

[36] Stephen P. Robbins, *Managing Organizational Conflict: A Nontraditional Approach* (Englewood Cliffs, N.J.: Prentice-Hall, 1974), p. 23.

[37] See Kenneth W. Thomas and Warren H. Schmidt, "A Survey of Managerial Interests with Respect to Conflict," *Academy of Management Journal,* June 1976, pp. 315–18.

[38] Stephen P. Robbins, " 'Conflict Management' and 'Conflict Resolution' Are Not Synonymous Terms," *California Management Review,* Winter 1978, p. 70.

[39] See Andrew S. Grove, "How to Make Confrontation Work for You," *Fortune,* July 23, 1984, pp. 73–75; and M. Michael Markowich and JoAnna Farber, "Managing Your Achilles' Heel," *Personnel Administrator,* June 1987, pp. 137–49.

[40] Adapted in part from discussion in Alan C. Filley, *Interpersonal Conflict Resolution* (Glenview, Ill.: Scott, Foresman, 1975), pp. 9–12.

[41] Richard A. Cosier and Charles R. Schwenk, "Agreement and Thinking Alike: Ingredients for Poor Decisions," *Academy of Management Executive,* February 1990, p. 71.

[42] Good background reading on devil's advocacy can be found in Charles R. Schwenk, "Devil's Advocacy in Managerial Decision Making," *Journal of Management Studies,* April 1984, pp. 153–68.

[43] Andrew S. Grove, *High Output Management* (New York: Random House, 1983), p. 79.

[44] See David M. Schweiger, William R. Sandberg, and Paula L. Rechner, "Experiential Effects of Dialectical Inquiry, Devil's Advocacy, and Consensus Approaches to Strategic Decision Making," *Academy of Management Journal,* December 1989, pp. 745–72.

[45] M. Afzalur Rahim, "A Strategy for Managing Conflict in Complex Organizations," *Human Relations,* January 1985, p. 84.

[46] Robbins, " 'Conflict Management' and 'Conflict Resolution' Are Not Synonymous Terms," p. 73.

[47] An empirically derived list of 43 third-party mediation tactics can be found in Rodney G. Lim and Peter J. D. Carnevale, "Contingencies in the Mediation of Disputes," *Journal of Personality and Social Psychology,* February 1990, pp. 259–72.

[48] The complete instrument may be found in M. Afzalur Rahim, "A Measure of Styles of Handling Interpersonal Conflict," *Academy of Management Journal,* June

1983, pp. 368–76. A Validation study of Rahim's instrument may be found in Evert Van De Vliert and Boris Kabanoff, "Toward Theory-Based Measures of Conflict Management," *Academy of Management Journal,* March 1990, pp. 199–209.

[49] See Robert E. Jones and Bonita H. Melcher, "Personality and the Preference for Modes of Conflict Resolution," *Human Relations,* August 1982, pp. 649–58.

[50] See Robert A. Baron, "Reducing Organizational Conflict: An Incompatible Response Approach," *Journal of Applied Psychology,* May 1984, pp. 272–79.

[51] See George A. Youngs, Jr., "Patterns of Threat and Punishment Reciprocity in a Conflict Setting," *Journal of Personality and Social Psychology,* September 1986, pp. 541–46.

[52] For more details, see Victor D. Wall, Jr., and Linda L. Nolan, "Small Group Conflict: A Look at Equity, Satisfaction, and Styles of Conflict Management," *Small Group Behavior,* May 1987, pp. 188–211.

[53] See Mel E. Schnake and Daniel S. Cochran, "Effect of Two Goal-Setting Dimensions on Perceived Intraorganizational Conflict," *Group & Organization Studies,* June 1985, pp. 168–83.

[54] Drawn from Leonard H. Chusmir and Joan Mills, "Gender Differences in Conflict Resolution Styles of Managers: At Work and at Home," *Sex Roles,* February 1989, pp. 149–63.

[55] See Kenwyn K. Smith, "The Movement of Conflict in Organizations: The Joint Dynamics of Splitting and Triangulation," *Administrative Science Quarterly,* March 1989, pp. 1–20.

[56] This case is quoted from *Developing Management Skills* by David A. Whetten and Kim S. Cameron. Copyright © 1984 by Scott, Foresman and Company. Reprinted by permission.

Effective Teamwork

LEARNING OBJECTIVES

When you finish studying the material in this chapter, you should be able to:

- Identify and give examples of the four general types of work teams.
- Explain the ecological model of work team effectiveness.
- Discuss how managers can foster cooperation.
- Explain the mechanics of Zand's model of trust.

- List at least three things managers can do to build trust.
- Distinguish two different types of cohesiveness.
- Contrast quality circles and self-managed teams.
- Identify at least four problems typically encountered during the life cycle of a quality circle program.

- Discuss what must be done to set the stage for self-managed teams.
- Explain the role of self-management leadership behaviors in team building.

OPENING CASE 11

Teamwork Gets Results at AT&T Credit Corp.

Sharon Hoogstraten

It's not only Rust Belt America that needs to overhaul the way work is organized. Millions of clerical employees toil in the back offices of financial companies, processing applications, claims, and customer accounts on what amount to electronic assembly lines. The jobs are dull and re-petitive and efficiency gains min-uscule—when they come at all.

That was the case with *AT&T* Credit Corp. (ATTCC) when it opened shop in 1985 as a newly created subsidiary of American Telephone & Telegraph Co. Based in Morristown, N.J., ATTCC provides financing for customers who lease equipment from AT&T and other companies. A bank initially retained by ATTCC to process lease applications couldn't keep up with the volume of new business.

ATTCC President Thomas C. Wajnert saw that the fault lay in the bank's method of dividing labor into narrow tasks and orga-nizing work by function. One department handled applications and checked the customer's credit standing, a second drew up con-tracts, and a third collected pay-ments. So no one person or group had responsibility for providing full service to a customer. "The employees had no sense of how their jobs contributed to the fi-nal solution for the customer," Wajnert says.

Unexpected Bonus

Wajnert decided to hire his own employees and give them "ownership and accountability." His first concern was to increase efficiency, not to provide more re-warding jobs. But in the end, he did both.

In 1986, ATTCC set up 11 teams of 10 to 15 newly hired workers in a high-volume division serving small businesses. The three major lease-processing func-tions were combined in each team. No longer were calls from customers shunted from depart-ment to department. The com-pany also divided its national staff of field agents into seven regions and assigned two or three teams to

Teams and *teamwork* are popular terms in management circles these days. A cynic might dismiss teamwork as just another management fad or quick-fix gimmick. But a close look reveals that much more than catchy buzz words are involved here. The team approach to managing organiza-tions is having diverse and substantial impacts. Teams promise to be a cornerstone of progressive management for the foreseeable future. Accord-ing to management expert Peter Drucker, tomorrow's organization's will be flatter, information-based, and organized around teams. Drucker envisions the following:

> Today's typical organization in which knowledge tends to be concentrated in service staffs, perched rather insecurely between top management and the operat-ing people, will likely be labeled a phase, an attempt to infuse knowledge from the top rather than obtain information from below. . . .
>
> A good deal of work will be done differently in the information-based organiza-tion. Traditional departments will serve as guardians of standards, as centers for

OPENING CASE 11

(concluded)

handle business from each region. That way, the same teams always worked with the same sales staff, establishing a personal relationship with them and their customers. Above all, team members took responsibility for solving customers' problems. ATTCC's new slogan: "Whoever gets the call owns the problem."

The teams largely manage themselves. Members make most decisions on how to deal with customers, schedule their own time off, reassign work when people are absent, and interview prospective new employees. The only supervisors are seven regional managers who advise the team members, rather than give orders. The result: The teams process up to 800 lease applications a day vs. 400 under the old system. Instead of taking several days to give a final yes or no, the teams do it in 24 to 48 hours. As a result,

ATTCC is growing at a 40 percent-to-50 percent compound annual rate, Wajnert says.

Extra Cash

The teams also have economic incentives for providing good service. A bonus plan tied to each team's costs and profits can produce extra cash. The employees, most of whom are young college graduates, can add $1,500 a year to average salaries of $28,000, and pay rises as employees learn new skills. "It's a phenomenal learning opportunity," says 24-year-old team member Michael LoCastro.

But LoCastro and others complain that promotions are rare because there are few managerial positions. And everyone comes under intense pressure from co-workers to produce more. The annual turnover rate is high: some 20 percent of ATTCC employees either quit or transfer to other parts

of AT&T. Still, the team experiment has been so successful that ATTCC is involving employees in planning to extend the concept throughout the company. "They will probably come up with as good an organizational design as management could," Wajnert says, "and it will work a lot better because the employees will take ownership for it."

For Discussion

Why is ATTCC's team approach effective?

• Additional discussion questions linking this case with the following material appear at the end of this chapter.

Source: John Hoerr, "Benefits for the Back Office, Too," *Business Week,* July 10, 1989, p. 59. Copyright 1989 by McGraw Hill, Inc.

training and the assignment of specialists; they won't be where the work gets done. That will happen largely in task-focused teams.[1]

Examples of this trend abound.

Hospitals, for example, are installing health-care teams to control runaway costs and improve quality of care. Team policing is a growing practice in public safety departments. Commercial airline pilots are attending team-building seminars to improve cockpit communication and coordination skills. Swedish carmaker Volvo, as mentioned in the last chapter, has replaced some of its assembly lines with self-managed teams. Industrial giants such as Boeing have adopted cross-functional teams to speed product design and delivery by better coordinating the work of technical specialists. This is how the world's largest airplane manufacturer plans to get its next-generation Boeing 777 jetliner to market by 1995.

In a major departure, it has handed the 777 over to Japanese-style design-build teams. The idea: Bunch marketing, engineering, manufacturing, finance, and service representatives on teams so that each department knows what the other is

• Teamwork is essential both on the playing field and in the office.

John P. Kelly/The Image Bank

Dave Hoffman

doing. Boeing also plans to arm the teams with "digital preassembly" design technology so that the 777 can be conceived, engineered, and "assembled" in three-dimensional computer models. Before a single piece of metal is cut, Boeing people in all disciplines will know if each phase of the design is feasible.[2]

Like General Motors and its Saturn project, Boeing is staking its future competitiveness on the team approach.

This chapter rounds out our coverage of group and intergroup dynamics by closely examining work teams. Emphasis in this chapter is on tapping the full and promising potential of work groups. We will (1) identify different types of work teams, (2) introduce a model of team effectiveness, (3) discuss keys to effective teamwork—such as trust, (4) explore applications of the team concept, and (5) review team-building techniques.

• WORK TEAMS: DEFINITION, TYPES, AND EFFECTIVENESS

OB writers often use the terms *group* and *team* interchangeably. Notice how the following definition is a general restatement of the one given for the term *group* in Chapter 9: "a **team** is an officially sanctioned collection of individuals who have been charged with completing a mission by an organization and who must depend upon one another for successful completion of that work."[3] Managers, on the other hand, seem to expect more from a "team" than they do from ordinary work groups. A nationwide survey of team members, from many organizations, by Wilson Learning Corp. provides a glimpse of what managers expect of teams.

The researchers' question was simply: "What is a high-performance team?"[4] The respondents were asked to describe their peak experiences in work teams. Analysis of the survey results yielded the following eight attributues of high-performance teams:

> *Participative leadership*—creating an interdependency by empowering, freeing up, and serving others.

Shared responsibility—establishing an environment in which all team members feel as responsible as the manager for the performance of the work unit.

Aligned on purpose—having a sense of common purpose about why the team exists and the function it serves.

High communication—creating a climate of trust and open, honest communication.

Future focused—seeing change as an opportunity for growth.

Focused on task—keeping meetings focused on results.

Creative talents—applying individual talents and creativity.

Rapid response—identifying and acting on opportunities.[5]

No wonder managers seem to expect a lot from teams! These eight attributes effectively combine many of today's most progressive ideas on management. Among them being participation, empowerment, service ethic, individual responsibility and development, self-management, trust, active listening, and envisioning. So managers expect a team to be much more than simply a collection of employees with a common identity and purpose. But patience and diligence are required. According to a manager familiar with work teams, "high-performance teams may take three to five years to build."[6] Let us keep this inspiring model of high-performance teams in mind as we develop the concept of work teams.

A General Typology of Work Teams

Work teams are created for various purposes and thus face different challenges. Managers can deal more effectively with those challenges when they understand how teams differ. A helpful way of sorting things out is to consider a typology of work teams developed by Eric Sundstrom and his colleagues.[7] Four general types of work teams listed in Table 11–1 are (1) advice, (2) production, (3) project, and (4) action. Each of these labels identifies a basic *purpose*. For instance, advice teams generally make recommendations for managerial decisions. Less commonly do they actually make final decisions. In contrast, production and action teams carry out management's decisions.

Four key variables in Table 11–1 deal with technical specialization, coordination, work cycles, and outputs. Technical specialization is low when the team draws upon members' general experience and problem-solving ability. It is high when team members are required to apply technical skills acquired through higher education and/or extensive training. The degree of coordination with other work units is determined by the team's relative independence (low coordination) or interdependence (high coordination). Work cycles are the amount of time teams need to discharge their missions. The various outputs listed in Table 11–1 are intended to illustrate real-life impacts. A closer look at each type of work team is in order.

Advice Teams   As their name implies, advice teams are created to broaden the information base for managerial decisions. Quality circles, discussed later, are a prime example because they facilitate suggestions for improve-

• **TABLE 11-1**   Four General Types of Work Teams and Their Outputs

Types and Examples	Degree of Technical Specialization	Degree of Coordination with Other Work Units	Work Cycles	Typical Outputs
Advice Committees Review panels, boards Quality circles Employee involvement groups Advisory councils	Low	Low	Work-cycles can be brief or long; one cycle can be team life span.	Decisions Selections Suggestions Proposals Recommendations
Production Assembly teams Manufacturing crews Mining teams Flight attendant crews Data processing groups Maintenance crews	Low	High	Work-cycles typically repeated or continuous process; cycles often briefer than team life span.	Food, chemicals Components Assemblies Retail sales Customer service Equipment repairs
Project Research groups Planning teams Architect teams Engineering teams Development teams Task forces	High	Low (for traditional units) or High (for cross-functional units)	Work-cycles typically differ for each new project; one cycle can be team life span.	Plans, designs Investigations Presentations Prototypes Reports, findings
Action Sports teams Entertainment groups Expeditions Negotiating teams Surgery teams Cockpit crews Military platoons and squads	High	High	Brief performance events, often repeated under new conditions, requiring extended training and/or preparation.	Combat missions Expeditions Contracts, lawsuits Concerts Surgical operations Competitive events

Source: Excerpted and adapted from Eric Sundstrom, Kenneth P. De Meuse, and David Futrell, "Work Teams," *American Psychologist*, February 1990, p. 125.

ment from volunteer production or service workers. Advice teams tend to have a low degree of technical specialization. Coordination also is low because advice teams work pretty much on their own. Ad hoc committees (e.g., the annual picnic committee) have shorter life cycles than standing committees (e.g., the grievance committee).

Production Teams   This second type of team is responsible for performing day-to-day operations. Minimal training for routine tasks accounts for the low degree of technical specialization. But coordination typically is high because work flows from one team to another. For example, railroad maintenance crews require fresh information about needed repairs from train crews.

OB IN ACTION

The Team Approach at General Foods Gets Its Just Desserts

About five years ago the company launched a line of ready-to-eat desserts by setting up a team of nine people with the freedom to operate like entrepreneurs starting their own business. The team even had to oversee construction of a factory with the technology required to manufacture their product.

Historically, it's taken companies five to seven years to go from concept to shipping. But this high-performance team had Jell-O Pudding Snacks desserts in grocery stores nationwide within three years—fast enough to establish a dominant market position. General Foods' ready-to-eat desserts sales now exceed $100 million.

Since that rousing start, the team concept is expanding throughout the company. Once used primarily in the planning sessions of division managers and in development, teams now are used even on the factory floor, where employee productivity teams work to lower costs and improve working conditions.

Source: Pamela King, "What Makes Teamwork Work?" *Psychology Today*, December 1989, p. 16.

Project Teams Projects require creative problem solving, often involving the application of specialized knowledge. The Boeing 777 team discussed earlier, for example, has a high degree of technical specialization. It also requires a high degree of coordination among organizational subunits because it is cross-functional. A pharmaceutical research team of biochemists, on the other hand, would interact less with other work units because it is relatively self-contained.

Action Teams This last type of team is best exemplified by a Major League baseball club. High specialization is combined with high coordination. Nine highly trained athletes play specialized defensive positions. But good defensive play is not enough because effective hitting is necessary. Moreover, coordination between the manager, base runners, base coaches, and the bull pen needs to be precise. So it is with airline cockpit crews, hospital surgery teams, mountain-climbing expeditions, rock music groups, labor contract negotiating teams, and police SWAT teams, among others. A unique challenge for action teams is to exhibit peak performance on demand.

This four-way typology of work teams is dynamic and changing, not static. Some teams evolve from one type to another. For example, notice in OB in Action how the General Foods team started out as a project team and then became an action team. During its project stage, the team planned the new product line and necessary production facilities. Later, acting as an action team, it got the facility up and running. Significantly, this successful team effort served as a role model for *production* teams on the factory floor.

• **FIGURE 11-1**   An Ecological Model of Work Team Effectiveness

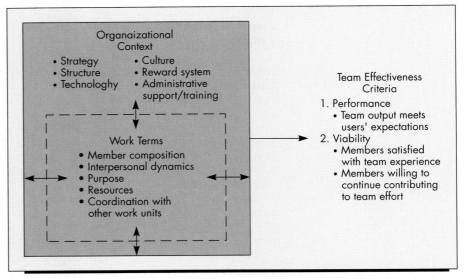

Source: Adapted in part from Eric Sundstrom, Kenneth P. De Meuse, and David Futrell, "Work Teams," *American Psychologist*, February 1990, pp. 120–33.

Work Team Effectiveness: An Ecological Model

The effectiveness of athletic teams is a straightforward matter of wins and losses. Things become more complicated, however, when the focus shifts to work teams in today's organizations.[8] Figure 11–1 lists two effectiveness criteria for work teams: performance and viability. According to Sundstrom and his colleagues: "*Performance* means acceptability of output to customers within or outside the organization who receive team products, services, information, decisions, or performance events (such as presentations or competitions)."[9] While the foregoing relates to satisfying the needs and expectations of outsiders such as clients, customers, and fans, another team-effectiveness criterion arises. Namely, **team viability,** defined as team member satisfaction and continued willingness to contribute. Are the team members better or worse off for having contributed to the team effort? A work team is not truly effective if it gets the job done but self-destructs in the process.

Figure 11–1 is an *ecological* model because it portrays work teams within their organizational environment. In keeping with the true meaning of the word *ecology*—the study of interactions between organisms and their environments—this model emphasizes that work teams need an organizational life-support system. Six critical organizational context variables are listed in Figure 11–1. Work teams have a much greater chance of being effective if they are nurtured and facilitated by the organization. The team's purpose needs to be in concert with the organization's strategy. Similarly, team participation and autonomy require an organizational culture that values those processes. Team members also need appropriate technological tools and training. Teamwork needs to be reinforced by the organizational reward system. Such is not the case when pay and bonuses are tied solely to individual output. Phillips–Van Heusen, the clothing manufacturer, is a striking example of a company that rewards teamwork. The firm's founder, Lawrence S. Phillips, offered each of the top 11 executives the chance to earn a $1 million bonus over a four-year period. *Fortune* explained the deal as follows: "The first $500,000 can be earned incrementally by meeting earnings-per-share goals for each year. If the company makes the combined target in the fourth year, each of the 11 receives the second $500,000 as a kicker."[10] Thus, each executive has a strong *personal* incentive to help reach *collective* goals.

Regarding the internal processes of work teams, five important factors are listed in Figure 11–1. Chapters 9 and 10 provided a good background for dealing with these factors. Additional insights lie ahead as we turn our attention to cooperation, trust, and cohesiveness.

• EFFECTIVE TEAMWORK THROUGH COOPERATION, TRUST, AND COHESIVENESS

As competitive pressures intensify, organizational success increasingly will depend on teamwork rather than individual stars. Compaq Computer Corp., the fastest-growing company in American business history, has become the world's second-largest maker of personal computers through effective teamwork. According to *Inc.* magazine:

> "I'm not a superstar with all the vision, just a guy who moderates the consensus among a pretty bright bunch of people," explains president Rod Canion in his austere office amidst the pine forests of suburban Houston. "Our way has been to work as a team to find out the market needs and execute our product. If people say, 'Ho hum' and that we need more pizzazz, I think they miss the point."
>
> Canion's point is that entrepreneurial success is far less dependent these days on the brilliant insights and force of personality of hard-charging chief executive officers. A growing number of companies are organizing themselves around a "smart team" of experienced, savvy managers who substitute collegialty for hierarchy and keep their focus on a single goal: building a company that's going to last.[11]

If this sort of testimonial to teamwork has a familiar ring, it is because World Series baseball and Super Bowl football champions are often heard saying virtually the same thing. Whether in the athletic arena or the world of organizational behavior, three components of teamwork that turn up repeatedly are cooperation, trust, and cohesiveness. Let us carefully examine the contributions each can make to effective teamwork.

Cooperation

Individuals are said to be cooperating when their efforts are systematically *integrated* to achieve a collective objective. The greater the integration, the greater the degree of cooperation. In work teams and organizations made up of interdependent task groups, integration can be achieved in two ways: collaboration and coordination (see Figure 11–2).[12]

Collaboration versus Coordination   **Collaboration** occurs when group members share joint responsibility for certain outcomes. For instance, team members

• **Figure 11-2**   Two Dimensions of Cooperation

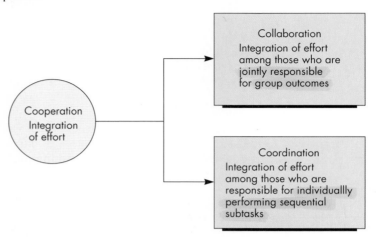

in a tug-of-war contest must collaborate if they are to succeed. Similarly, the members of a hospital's cost-containment committee must collaborate if they are to develop good recommendations. **Coordination,** on the other hand, involves arranging subtasks sequentially. Assembly lines, for example, require a high degree of coordination because task A must be completed before task B, which must be completed before task C. Because collaboration requires a mature group characterized by effective communication, mutual trust, and cohesiveness, it is administratively more difficult to achieve than coordination. Managers who desire to build teamwork in today's complex organizations need to work on both dimensions of cooperation.

Cooperation versus Competition   A widely held assumption among American managers is that "competition brings out the best in people." From an economic standpoint, business survival depends on staying ahead of the competition. But from an interpersonal standpoint, critics contend competition has been overemphasized, primarily at the expense of cooperation. According to Alfie Kohn, a strong advocate of greater emphasis on cooperation in our classrooms, offices, and factories:

> My review of the evidence has convinced me that there are two . . . important reasons for competition's failure. First, success often depends on sharing resources efficiently, and this is nearly impossible when people have to work against one another. Cooperation takes advantage of all the skills represented in a group as well as the mysterious process by which that group becomes more than the sum of its parts. By contrast, competition makes people suspicious and hostile toward one another and actively discourages this process. . . .
>
> Second, competition generally does not promote excellence because trying to do well and trying to beat others simply are two different things. Consider a child in class, waving his arm wildly to attract the teacher's attention, crying, "Oooh! Oooh! Pick me!" When he is finally recognized, he seems befuddled. "Um, what was the question again?" he finally asks. His mind is focused on beating his classmates, not on the subject matter.[13]

Research Support for Cooperation   After conducting a meta-analysis of 122 studies encompassing a wide variety of subjects and settings, one team of researchers concluded:

1. Cooperation is superior to competition in promoting achievement and productivity.
2. Cooperation is superior to individualistic efforts in promoting achievement and productivity.
3. Cooperation without intergroup competition promotes higher achievement and productivity than cooperation with intergroup competition.[14]

Given the size and diversity of the research base, these findings strongly endorse cooperation in modern organizations. Cooperation can be encouraged by reward systems that reinforce teamwork as well as individual achievement.

Another study involving 84 male U.S. Air Force trainees uncovered an encouraging link between cooperation and favorable race relations. After observing the subjects interact in three-man teams during a management game, the researchers concluded: [Helpful]"teammates, both black and white, attract greater respect and liking than do teammates who have not helped. This is particularly true when the helping occurs voluntarily."[15] These findings suggest that managers can enhance equal employment opportunity and diversity programs by encouraging *voluntary* helping behavior in interracial work teams. Accordingly, it is reasonable to conclude that voluntary helping behavior could build cooperation in mixed-gender teams and groups as well.

A recent study involving 72 health-care professionals in a U.S. Veterans Affairs Medical Center found a negative correlation between cooperation and team size. In other words, cooperation diminished as the health-care team became larger.[16] Managers thus need to restrict the size of work teams if they desire to facilitate cooperation.

How to Foster Cooperation   In addition to limiting the size of work teams, management can take other positive steps to generate cooperation. One recommendation comes from a recent survey of 35 airline pilots, first and second officers, and flight attendants. These flight personnel were asked to describe hazardous situations that were handled either effectively or poorly. A total of 60 critical incidents were described. *Cooperative goals* and *functional conflict* were found to be keys to resolving safety hazards. (Recall our discussions of goals and conflict in Chapters 6 and 10.) According to the researcher:

> Cooperative goals, especially when supplemented with constructive controversy in which people express their views open-mindedly, consider opposing opinions, feel accepted, and exchange resources, were strongly correlated with crew members' coping with hazards. They worked efficiently, used safe procedures, and were confident that they could collaborate successfully in the future when they had cooperative goals. . . .
>
> In addition to suggesting the value of cooperative goals, evidence also suggests how crew members develop them. A sense of shared purpose, understanding that

they have a common task, and recognition that their roles are complementary were found to be important reasons for cooperative goals.[17]

Additional practical suggestions for fostering cooperation come from an unexpected source. Computer gaming theorists developed a simple program for encouraging cooperation and discouraging competition. Called TIT FOR TAT, this gaming strategy is totally unlike the combative Nintendo or video game strategies one typically encounters. The TIT FOR TAT strategy was subsequently translated by organization development specialists into these four pointers for managers and team leaders:

1. Demonstrate the group's (or individual's) fundamental desire for cooperation, not competition.
2. Demand that others not take advantage of oneself or one's group, and make them realize that one can and will reciprocate if they do so.
3. Make others realize that they are not considered enemies or opponents, but are invited to become allies if they want a working relationship.

 A MATTER OF ETHICS

The Wrong Chemistry at Kellogg

In September 1989, William E. LaMothe, Kellogg's Chairman and Chief Executive Officer, summarily fired Horst W. Schroeder after [serving] only nine months as President of the company.

    Mr. LaMothe, in an interview cites a failure of management "chemistry." He says he erred seriously in choosing an executive whose background and style so strikingly departed, he sees in retrospect, from the Kellogg norm. . . .

    Others say Mr. Schroeder ignored their input and seemed intolerant of dissent, in stark contrast to Mr. LaMothe, who they say favors teamwork by individuals strong enough to confront him. "He wanted to be challenged and questioned," while Mr. Schroeder "seemed more inclined to manage without being questioned," says John Melangton, the company's recently retired investor relations director. "That's not Kellogg's style." . . .

    Mr. Schroeder enjoyed some successes, and there is speculation that these may have confirmed him in his autocratic style. Despite intense internal opposition, Mr. Schroeder persuaded Mr. LaMothe that Mueslix, a Kellogg fruit, flake and nut cereal popular in Europe, would score well with American yuppies. It became one of the country's 10 best sellers.

    But at Kellogg, success is normally shared, and others say Mr. Schroeder took all the credit. As for this and other criticism, Mr. Schroeder will say only, "It's one word against the other. This is not the time to talk." . . .

    At a meeting last year, . . . [union official J. R.] Munoz says, "every time the vice presidents tried to say something, Horst would abruptly cut them off." He was known for deriding any unimpressive presentation as a "CE"—career ending—"performance." So when Mr. Schroeder himself needed the support of vice presidents and other managers, it wasn't there.

4. Demonstrate trust and openness by modeling the type of behavior one wishes others to enact.[18]

This TIT FOR TAT strategy effectively models and reinforces ''win–win'' cooperation between potential adversaries. Meanwhile, ''win–lose'' competition is discouraged. Parents, teachers, managers, and team leaders can balance effectiveness and intergroup harmony by consistently using the TIT FOR TAT strategy. Notice how trust, our next topic, plays a key role in the TIT FOR TAT strategy. Managers who ignore or defy the TIT FOR TAT strategy may run afoul of accepted ethical standards and suffer the consequences (see A Matter of Ethics).

Trust

American managers have been intrigued and somewhat embarrassed in recent years as Japanese companies have come to the United States and dramatically reversed the fortunes of one losing operation after another. According to a special report in *Business Week,* the Japanese success story hinges on *trust*:

> A key element of the Japanese transplants' success is their adroit handling of American workers. The Japanese approach to production, emphasizing flexible teams, just-in-time deliveries, and attention to quality, demands extremely high employee loyalty, which is a sharp departure from the traditional adversary relationship in most U.S. factories. Workers given responsibility for running the production line will care about and catch mistakes, but only if they trust management. The trust must be mutual, too, because the just-in-time delivery system, which depends on a steady stream of components, is easy to sabotage.[19]

Clearly, U.S. managers need to do a much better job of building labor-management trust. Trust is important off the job, too. Many friendships, budding romances, and marriages have been ruined by betrayed trust.[20] We now turn our attention to exploring the concept of trust and discussing a research-based model of trust that has important managerial implications. Six practical guidelines follow.

A Cognitive Leap   **Trust** is defined as reciprocal faith in others' intentions and behavior. Experts on the subject explain the reciprocal (give-and-take) aspect of trust as follows:

> When we see others acting in ways that imply that they trust us, we become more disposed to reciprocate by trusting in them more. Conversely, we come to distrust those whose actions appear to violate our trust or to distrust us.[21]

In short, we tend to give what we get: trust begets trust; distrust begets distrust. (Take a few moments now to complete the OB Exercise.)

Trust involves ''a cognitive 'leap' beyond the expectations that reason and experience alone would warrant''[22] (see Figure 11–3). For example, suppose a member of a newly formed class project team works hard, based on the assumption that her teammates also are working hard. That assumption, on which her trust is based, is a cognitive leap that goes beyond her actual experience with her teammates. When you trust someone, you have *faith* in their good intentions. The act of trusting someone, however, carries

---

• OB EXERCISE

Measuring Interpersonal Trust

Instructions:

Think of a specific individual who plays an important role in your present life (e.g., present or future spouse, friend, supervisor, co-worker, team member, etc.) and rate his/her trustworthiness for each statement according to the following scale.

Strongly Disagree   **Strongly Agree**

1—2—3—4—5—6—7—8—9—10

Score

Overall trust:
1. I can expect this person to play fair.   _____
2. I can confide in this person and know she or he desires to listen.   _____
3. I can expect this person to tell me the truth.   _____

Emotional trust:
4. This person would never intentionally misrepresent my point of view to other people.   _____
5. I can confide in this person and know that he or she will not discuss it with others.   _____

Reliableness:
6. If this person promised to do me a favor, she or he would carry out that promise.   _____
7. If I had an appointment with this person, I could count on him or her showing up.   _____
8. I could lend this person money and count on getting it back as soon as possible.   _____

Total score = _____

Trustworthiness Scale

65–80 = High (Trust is a precious thing.)

24–64 = Moderate (Be careful; get a rearview mirror.)

8–23 = Low (Lock up your valuables!)

Source: Adapted from Cynthia Johnson-George and Walter C. Swap, "Measurement of Specific Interpersonal Trust: Construction and Validation of a Scale to Assess Trust in a Specific Other," *Journal of Personality and Social Psychology*, December 1982, pp. 1306–17.

---

with it the inherent risk of betrayal. Progressive managers believe that the benefits of interpersonal trust far outweigh any risks of betrayed trust.

Zand's Model of Trust   Dale Zand's model explains how trust evolves in problem-solving groups such as committees and task teams. It shows the interaction among three variables: information, influence, and control. As illustrated in Figure 11–4, formal and informal leaders can initiate trusting relationships by becoming more vulnerable through admitting one's limitations, claiming responsibility for one's mistakes, sharing important information, and encouraging meaningful participation and self-control. In response to this trusting posture, group members tend to share useful task-oriented information and be more open to influence by others. These factors, when

• **FIGURE 11-3** Interpersonal Trust Involves a Cognitive Leap

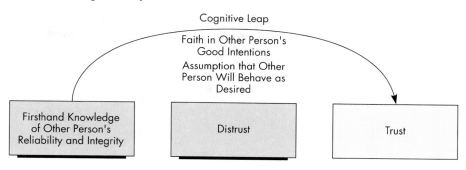

• **FIGURE 11-4** Zand's Model of Trust

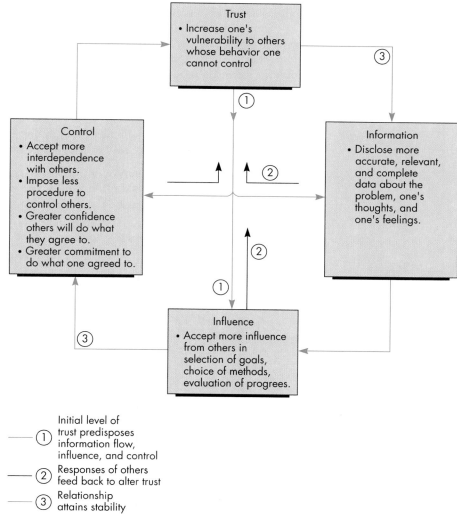

Source: Reprinted from "Trust and Managerial Problem Solving" by Dale E. Zand, published in *Administrative Science Quarterly* (June 1972) by permission of *Administrative Science Quarterly*. © 1972 by Cornell University.

combined with an emphasis on *self-control* rather than procedural control, tend to strengthen the cycle of trust. Oppositely, distrust prevails if leaders try to be invulnerable, relevant information is not shared, influence is resisted, and rules and regulations stifle self-control. In support of this contention, a recent study of 278 government managers in India found a negative relationship between trust and organizational politics. The greater the trust, the lesser the politicking.[23]

Zand tested his model of trust with 64 middle managers working in eight-person managerial problem-solving teams. Half of the teams were told to expect high trust, while the other half were told to expect low trust. As hypothesized, the high-trust groups significantly outperformed the low-trust groups. Zand concluded:

> The results indicate that it is useful to conceptualize trust as behavior that conveys appropriate information, permits mutuality of influence, encourages self-control, and avoids abuse of the vulnerability of others.[24]

Thus, Zand has given managers a behaviorally specific definition of trust.

From a practical standpoint, actions speak louder than words when it comes to trust. According to well-known management scholar George Odiorne: "The people we trust are the people whose behavior is predictable."[25] Zand's model tells managers exactly which behavior needs to be predictable if trust and teamwork are to prevail.

How to Build Trust Management professor/consultant Fernando Bartolomé offers the following six guidelines for building and maintaining trust. As a whole, they effectively bring Zand's cycle of trust to life:

1. *Communication*—Keep team members and subordinates informed by explaining policies and decisions and providing accurate feedback. Be candid about one's own problems and limitations.
2. *Support*—Be available and approachable. Provide help, advice, coaching, and support for team members' ideas.
3. *Respect*—Delegation, in the form of real decision-making authority, is the most important expression of managerial respect. Actively listening to the ideas of others is a close second.
4. *Fairness*—Be quick to give credit and recognition to those who deserve it. Make sure all performance appraisals and evaluations are objective and impartial.
5. *Predictability*—As mentioned above, be consistent and predictable in your daily affairs. Keep both expressed and implied promises.
6. *Competence*—Enhance your credibility by demonstrating good business sense, technical ability, and professionalism.[26]

Trust needs to be earned; it cannot be demanded.[27]

Cohesiveness

Cohesiveness is a process whereby "a sense of 'we-ness' emerges to transcend individual differences and motives."[28] Members of a cohesive group stick together. They are reluctant to leave the group. Cohesive group members stick together for one or both of the following reasons: (1) because they enjoy each others' company, or (2) because they need each other to accomplish a common goal. Accordingly, two types of group cohesiveness, identified by sociologists, are socio-emotional cohesiveness and instrumental cohesiveness.[29]

Socio-Emotional and Instrumental Cohesivess

Socio-emotional cohesiveness is a sense of togetherness that develops when individuals derive emotional satisfaction from group participation. Most general discussions of group cohesiveness are limited to this type. However, from the standpoint of getting things accomplished in task groups and teams, we cannot afford to ignore instrumental cohesiveness. **Instrumental cohesiveness** is a sense of togetherness that develops when group members are mutually dependent on one another because they believe they could not achieve the group's goal by acting separately. A feeling of "we-ness" is *instrumental* in achieving the common goal. Both types of cohesiveness are essential to productive teamwork.

Lessons from Group Cohesiveness Research

After reviewing the relevant research literature, a Texas A&M University scholar concluded:

- Highly cohesive groups have greater member satisfaction than groups with low cohesiveness.
- High-cohesion groups are more effective than low-cohesion groups.
- Members of highly cohesive groups communicate more frequently and more positively than members of low-cohesion groups.[30]

In a second study of 125 groups with interaction problems, trained observers found lack of cohesiveness to be the number one problem. Leadership was the next greatest problem.[31]

The relationship between cohesiveness and performance remains ambiguous. Studies have found a mixture of positive, negative, and neutral relationships. This unexpected trend is partially due to researchers using inconsistent measures of cohesiveness.[32]

Putting Cohesiveness to Work

Because cohesiveness has proved to be an important component of effective teamwork, managers need to take constructive steps to foster both types (see Table 11–2). A good example is Westinghouse's highly automated military radar electronics plant in College Station, Texas. Compared to their counterparts at a traditional factory in Baltimore, each of the Texas plant's 500 employees produces eight times more, at half the per-unit cost.

> The key, says Westinghouse, is not the robots but the people. Employees work in teams of 8 to 12. Members devise their own solutions to problems. Teams measure daily how each person's performance compares with that of other members and how the team's performance compares with the plant's. Joseph L. Johnson, 28, a robotics technician, says that is a big change from a previous hourly factory job where he cared only about "picking up my paycheck." Here, peer pressure "makes sure you get the job done."[33]

Self-selected work teams (in which people pick their own teammates) and off-the-job social events can stimulate socio-emotional cohesiveness. The fostering of socio-emotional cohesiveness needs to be balanced with instru-

• TABLE 11-2   Steps Managers Can Take to Enhance the Two Types of Group Cohesiveness

Socio-Emotional Cohesiveness:
Keep the group relatively small.
Strive for a favorable public image to increase the status and prestige of belonging.
Encourage interaction and cooperation.
Emphasize members' common characteristics and interests.
Point out environmental threats (e.g., competitors' achievements) to rally the group.

Instrumental Cohesiveness:
Regularly update and clarify the group's goal(s).
Give every group member a vital "piece of the action."
Channel each group member's special talents toward the common goal(s).
Recognize and equitably reinforce every member's contributions.
Frequently remind group members they need each other to get the job done.

mental cohesiveness. The latter can be encouraged by making sure everyone in the group recognizes and appreciates each member's vital contribution to the group goal. While balancing the two types of cohesiveness, managers need to remember that groupthink theory and research, discussed in Chapter 9, cautions against too much cohesiveness.

• TEAMS IN ACTION: FROM QUALITY CIRCLES TO SELF-MANAGED TEAMS

This section strives to bring the team approach to life for present and future managers. It does so by exploring two different team formats found in the workplace today: quality circles and self-managed teams. We have chosen these two particular applications of teamwork, out of a growing variety, for three reasons: First, they are sharply contrasting approaches to teamwork. Managers can gain valuable insights about work teams by understanding their basic differences. Second, each is established enough to be generally recognizable. Third, both approaches have been evaluated by OB researchers.

Table 11–3 provides a conceptual foundation for this section by highlighting important distinctions between quality circles and self-managed teams. Quality circles involve limited empowerment in the form of consultation (recall our discussion in Chapter 10). Thus, they qualify as *advice* teams (as described in Table 11–1). Self-managed teams, in contrast, enjoy a high degree of empowerment through delegation. Production, project, and/or action teams may be self-managed because decision authority can be delegated to teams in virtually any part of the organization. Regarding membership, quality circles rely on volunteers while employees are assigned to self-managed teams or selected by the team itself. Another vital distinction involves the team's relationship to the organization's structure and hierarchy. Quality circles are called parallel structures[34] because they exist outside normal channels of authority and communication. Self-managed teams, on the other hand, are integrated into the basic organizational structure. Quality circles make recommendations to management which retains all decision-making authority. Self-managed teams, meanwhile, make and

• TABLE 11-3   Some Basic Distinctions between Quality Circles and Self-Managed Teams

	Quality Circles	**Self-Managed Teams**
Type of team (see Table 11–1)	Advice	Production, project, or action
Type of empowerment (see Figure 10–3)	Consultation	Delegation
Basis of membership	Voluntary	Assigned
Relationship to organization structure	Parallel	Integrated
Focus of influence	Lower-level operations	Possibly all organizational levels and functions, depending upon make-up of team

implement their own decisions. Finally, quality circles primarily influence production and service operations at the lowest levels. Self-managed teams tend to have much broader influence because of greater reliance on technical and staff specialists throughout the organization.

Keeping these conceptual distinctions in mind, let us examine quality circles and self-managed teams more closely.

Quality Circles

Quality circles are small groups of people from the same work area who voluntarily get together to identify, analyze, and recommend solutions for problems related to quality, productivity, and cost reduction. Some prefer the term *quality control circles*. With an ideal size of 10 to 12 members, they typically meet for about 60 to 90 minutes on a regular basis. Some companies allow meetings during work hours, others encourage quality circles to meet after work on employees' time. Once a week or twice a month are common schedules. Management facilitates the quality circle program through skills training and listening to periodic presentations of recommendations. Monetary rewards for suggestions tend to be the exception rather than the rule. Intrinsic motivation, derived from learning new skills and meaningful participation, is the primary payoff for quality circle volunteers.

The Quality Circle Movement   American quality control experts helped introduce the basic idea of quality circles to Japanese industry soon after World War II. The idea eventually returned to the United States and reached fad proportions during the 1970s and 1980s. Proponents made zealous claims about how quality circles were the key to higher productivity, lower costs, employee development, and improved job attitudes. At its zenith during the mid-1980s, the quality circle movement claimed millions of employee participants around the world. Hundreds of U.S. companies and government agencies adopted the idea under a variety of labels.[35] Dramatic growth of quality circles in the United States has been attributed to: (1) a desire to replicate Japan's industrial success; (2) America's penchant for business fads; and (3) the relative ease of installing quality circles without restructuring the organization.[36] All too often, however, early enthusiasm gave way to disappointment, apathy, and abandonment.[37]

But quality circles, if properly administered and supported by management, can be much more than a management fad seemingly past its prime. According to USC researchers Edward E. Lawler and Susan A. Mohrman, "quality circles can be an important first step toward organizational effectiveness through employee involvement."[38] As we will see later, quality circles can be a steppingstone to self-managed teams.

A life cycle perspective of quality circles helps us better appreciate their promises and pitfalls.

A Life Cycle Perspective of Quality Circle Programs   The six-phase life cycle model in Figure 11–5 makes two important contributions to management's thinking. First, it portrays an organization's quality circle program as a step-by-step evolution rather than a one-shot deal. Second, it warns of potentially

• **FIGURE 11-5**   A Life Cycle Model of Quality Circle Programs

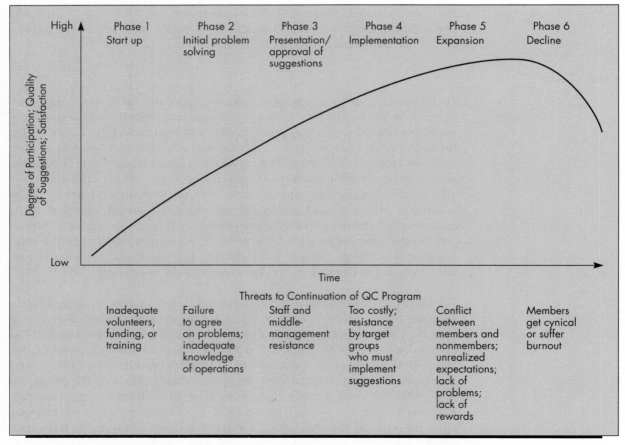

Source: Adapted from Gerald E. Ledford, Jr., Edward E. Lawler III, and Susan A. Mohrman, "The Quality Circle and Its Variations," in *Productivity in Organizations*, eds. John P. Campbell, Richard J. Campbell and Associates (San Francisco: Jossey-Bass, 1988), pp. 255–94.

fatal problems during each phase. By systematically anticipating and addressing each set of problems along the bottom of Figure 11–5, managers can reach and prolong Phase 5 (the expansion phase).

Management's first significant hurdle is to sell the idea to suspicious and possibly mistrusting employees. Remember, *volunteers* are the lifeblood of quality circles. This can be a particularly hard sell with militant union members. Imagine yourself as a manager at Scott Paper Company in Chester, Pennsylvania, trying to win over John Brodie, the President of United Paperworkers Local 448. *Business Week* quoted Brodie as saying:

> What the company wants is for us to work like the Japanese. Everybody go out and do jumping jacks in the morning and kiss each other when they go home at night. You work as a team, rat on each other, and lose control of your destiny. That's not going to work in this country.[39]

This sort of opposition to quality circles or any other form of teamwork needs to be overcome with care, honesty, and patience. Monetary rewards can help, too. Beyond overcoming resistance, quality circle members need to be adequately trained in problem solving and presentation skills. A good working knowledge of company operations also is a must. Otherwise, unrealistic recommendations will be made. Resistance from supervisors and middle managers, who sometimes view employee participation as a threat to their authority, needs to be neutralized. This can be accomplished through their personal involvement and recognition of benefits for management.

Another problem, encountered in Phase 4, relates to quality circles being outside the normal hierarchy. Just because one group of managers has endorsed a proposal made during a quality circle presentation, prompt implementation by other managers does not automatically follow. The parallel or ad hoc structure of quality circles makes implementation very problematic. In Phase 5, a whole host of problems can arise. Not the least being that the quality circle can work itself out of business by running out of problems. If the threats to success during Phases 1 through 5 are allowed to accumulate, then cynicism and burnout will eventually kill the program.

Insights from Field Research on Quality Circles A body of objective field research on quality circles is growing. Still, much of what we know comes from testimonials and case histories from managers and consultants who have a vested interest in demonstrating the technique's success. Although documented failures are scarce, one expert concluded that quality circles have failure rates of more than 60 percent.[40] Poor implementation is probably more at fault than the quality circle concept itself. Consider, for example, what happened when General Motors tried to implement quality circles at its Adrian, Michigan, plant (see OB in Action).

To date, field research on quality circles has been inconclusive. Lack of standardized variables is the main problem, as it typically is when comparing the results of field studies. Team participation programs of all sizes and shapes have been called quality circles. Here's what we have learned to date. A case study of military and civilian personnel at a U.S. Air Force base found a positive relationship between quality circle participation and desire to continue working for the organization. The observed effect on job performance was slight. A longitudinal study spanning 24 months revealed that

OB IN ACTION

GM Takes Three Strikes at Implementing Quality Circles

Many American companies are discovering that, unlike a new piece of machinery, quality circles cannot simply be acquired, installed, and left to run on their own. This lesson was brought home repeatedly to managers and workers at General Motors' Chevrolet plant in Adrian, Michigan, southwest of Detroit, where they're now trying to make quality circles work for the third time. The factory supplies GM with plastic parts such as fan shrouds and dashboards.

GM first attempted to introduce quality circles at Adrian in 1977. In the process management broke most of the rules for how to get employees behind such a program. For starters, it failed to enlist the support of the local chapter of the United Auto Workers. It also neglected to train both workers and supervisors in how the circles were supposed to work. According to Charles Sower, president of the union local, workers soon quit the circles in disgust.

A second attempt to get the circles running began somewhat more auspiciously in 1979, with meetings for all employees at the local Holiday Inn. Meals and, on the last night, an open bar were inducements to a good turnout. However, this time management focused the circles on what might, to dignify them, be called human resources issues. Union official Sower describes the problem: "You might understand why your foreman was in a bad temper, but what were you supposed to do about it?" The circle meetings, to quote Sower, became "bitch sessions that discussed garbage like how far it was to walk to the parking lot." Predictably, this round of circles petered out too.

It wasn't until 1981 that management and the UAW jointly presented a well-planned program with solid training for managers and workers in how to make employee participation groups, as they are known throughout GM, achieve practical results. Circle members were taught how to raise issues, how to discuss them amicably, and how to implement their ideas. Sower admits that he initially "thought it was a bunch of crap," and the new plant manager, Fred Meissinger, says he was more comfortable with the old-style, more adversarial approach, but both men decided to give this try a chance. Instead of complaining about parking, workers sat down to discuss things like how to improve a troublesome conveyor belt. Two years later many of the original groups are still talking productively.

The only problem now is that the union is split over whether the circles should continue. While Sower wholeheartedly backs the experiment, two of the five members of the union's shop committee won office recently on a platform of old-style hostility to management. Sower now says he feels reluctant to show his face in the union office. The future of quality circles at the Adrian plant is by no means guaranteed.

Source: Jeremy Main, "The Trouble with Managing Japanese-Style," *Fortune*, April 2, 1984, pp. 50–51. Used with permission.

quality circles had only a marginal impact on employee attitudes, but had a positive impact on productivity. In a more recent study, utility company employees who participated in quality circles received significantly better job performance ratings and were promoted more frequently than nonparticipants. This suggests that quality circles live up to their billing as a good employee development technique.[41]

Overall, quality circles appear to be a promising participative management tool, *if they are carefully implemented and supported by all levels of management during the first five phases of the program life cycle.*

Strengthening Quality Circles   In addition to doing a better job of implementing and supporting quality circles during later phases of the life cycle, management can take other constructive steps as well. Lawler and Mohrman recommend the following changes:

> The most important of the changes is probably the development of a gainsharing formula that will let everyone participate in the benefits of performance improvement. Other possible approaches include improved information and education for circle members and the use of training, appraisal, and rewards to develop participative supervision. The suggested reward, information, and education system changes involve changing the work organization in some important ways. In essence, they call for making it a more active organization for lower-level participants by giving them new kinds of knowledge, information, supervision, and rewards. This reinforces the fact that an organization that wants to sustain a participative parallel structure must become more participative in its day-to-day business.[42]

The call for a linkage between quality circles and gainsharing strikes an important cultural cord. American workers, more so than their Japanese counterparts, expect to share directly in the fruits of their suggestions and recommendations.

Self-Managed Teams

Have you ever thought you could do a better job than your boss? Well, if the trend toward self-managed work teams continues to grow as predicted, you just may get your chance. Entrepreneurs and artisans often boast of not having a supervisor. The same generally cannot be said for employees working in organizational offices and factories. But things are changing. For example, consider the following situation:

> At a General Mills cereal plant in Lodi, California, teams . . . schedule, operate, and maintain machinery so effectively that the factory runs with no managers present during the night shift.[43]

General Mills has found that, when it comes to management, less can mean more. In this case, some of the firm's self-managed teams set higher productivity goals for themselves than management does. This section explores self-managed work teams by looking at their past, present, and future.

What Are Self-Managed Teams?   Something much more complex is involved than this apparently simple label suggests. The term *self-managed* does not mean simply turning workers loose to do their own thing. Indeed, as we will see, an organization embracing self-managed teams should be prepared to undergo revolutionary changes in management philosophy, structure, staffing and training practices, and reward systems. Moreover, the traditional notions of managerial authority and control are turned on their heads. Not surprisingly, many managers strongly resist giving up the reins of power to people they view as subordinates.

• This self-managed work team at General Mills carries out traditional managerial duties such as planning, scheduling, and evaluating performance. The Lodi, California, plant operates the night shift without a single manager being present. *(Copyright 1990 Doug Menuez)*

Self-managed teams are defined as groups of workers who are given administrative oversight for their task domains. Administrative oversight involves delegated activities such as planning, scheduling, monitoring, and staffing. These are chores normally performed by managers. In short, employees in these unique work groups act as their own supervisor. Self-managed teams are variously referred to as semiautonomous work groups, autonomous work groups, and superteams. A common feature of self-managed teams, particularly among those above the shop-floor or clerical level, is **cross-functionalism.** In other words, specialists from different areas are put on the same team. On the Boeing 777 design team, discussed earlier, marketing, engineering, manufacturing, and finance specialists rub shoulders on the same team. Creative problem solving is more productive and faster as a result of this cross-functional mix (see OB in Action).

To date, in the United States, self-managed teams are barely past the experimental stage. According to a recent survey, only 7 percent of a sample of 476 of the 1,000 largest industrial companies in America are using self-managed work teams. Importantly, half of the responding firms planned to rely significantly more on the technique in coming years.[44] Most of today's self-managed teams remain bunched at the shop-floor level in factory settings. Experts predict growth of the practice in the managerial ranks and in service operations.[45]

Historical and Conceptual Roots of Self-Managed Teams

Self-managed teams are an outgrowth of a blend of behavioral science and management practice.[46] Group dynamics research of variables such as cohesiveness initially paved the way. A later stimulus was the socio-technical systems approach in which first British, and then American researchers, tried to harmonize social and technical factors. Their goal was to simultaneously increase productivity and employees' quality of work life. More recently, the idea of self-managed

OB IN ACTION

Cross-Functional Teamwork Gets Results for Rubbermaid

In 1987, Rubbermaid began to develop a so-called auto office, a plastic, portable device that straps onto a car seat; it holds files, pens, and other articles and provides a writing surface. The company assembled a cross-functional team composed of, among others, engineers, designers, and marketers, who together went into the field to ask customers what features they wanted. Says Rubbermaid vice president Lud Huck: "A designer, an engineer, and a marketer all approach research from a different point of view."

Huck explains that while a marketer might ask potential customers about price, he'd never think to ask important design questions. With contributions from several different functions, Rubbermaid brought the new product to market . . . [in 1989]. Sales are running 50 percent above projections.

Source: Brian Dumaine, "Who Needs a Boss?" *Fortune*, May 7, 1990, p. 54.

---

teams has gotten a strong boost from job design and participative management advocates. Recall our discussion of Hackman and Oldham's job characteristics model in Chapter 5. According to their model, internal motivation, satisfaction, and performance can be enhanced through five core job characteristics. Of those five core factors, increased *autonomy* is a major benefit for members of self-managed teams. Three types of autonomy are method, scheduling, and criteria autonomy (see OB Exercise). Members of self-managed teams score high on group autonomy. Autonomy empowers those who are ready and able to handle added responsibility. How did you score? Finally, the social learning theory of self-management, as discussed in Chapter 7, has helped strengthen the case for self-managed teams.

The net result of this confluence is the continuum in Figure 11–6. The traditional clear-cut distinction between manager and managed is being blurred as subordinates are delegated greater authority and granted increased autonomy. Importantly, self-managed teams do not eliminate the need for all managerial control (see the upper right-hand corner of Figure 11–6). Semiautonomous work teams represent a balance between managerial and group control.

Are Self-Managed Teams Effective? Research Evidence   As with quality circles, much of what we know about self-managed teams comes from testimonials and case studies. Fortunately, a body of higher-quality field research is slowly developing. A relatively recent review of three meta-analyses covering 70 individual studies concluded that self-managed teams had:

- A positive impact on productivity.
- A positive impact on specific attitudes relating to self-management (e.g., responsibility and control).
- No significant impact on general attitudes (e.g., job satisfaction and organizational commitment).
- No significant impact on absenteeism or turnover.[47]

• OB Exercise

Measuring Work Group Autonomy

Instructions:
Think of your present (or past) job and work group. Characterize the group's situation by circling one number on the following scale for each statement. Add your responses for a total score.

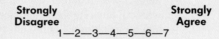

Strongly   Strongly
Disagree   Agree
1—2—3—4—5—6—7

Work Method Autonomy
1. My work group decides how to get the job done.   _____
2. My work group determines what procedures to use.   _____
3. My work group is free to choose its own methods when carrying out its work.   _____

Work Scheduling Autonomy
4. My work group controls the scheduling of its work.   _____
5. My work group determines how its work is sequenced.   _____
6. My work group decides when to do certain activities.   _____

Work Criteria Autonomy
7. My work group is allowed to modify the normal way it is evaluated so some of our activities are emphasized and some deemphasized.   _____
8. My work group is able to modify its objectives (what it is supposed to accomplish).   _____
9. My work group has some control over what it is supposed to accomplish.   _____

Total Score = _____

Norms

9–26 = Low autonomy
27–45 = Moderate autonomy
46–63 = High autonomy

Source: Adapted from an individual autonomy scale in James A. Breaugh, "The Work Autonomy Scales: Additional Validity Evidence," *Human Relations*, November 1989, pp. 1033–56.

• Figure 11-6   The Evolution of Self-Managed Work Teams

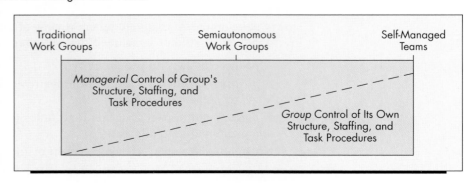

Although encouraging, these results do not qualify as a sweeping endorsement of self-managed teams. Nonetheless, experts say the trend toward self-managed work teams will continue upward in the United States because of a strong cultural bias in favor of direct participation. Managers need to be prepared for the resulting shift in organizational administration.

Setting the Stage for Self-Managed Teams   Experience shows that it is better to build a new production or service facility around self-managed teams than to attempt to convert an existing one. The former approach involves so-called "green field sites." General Foods, for example, pioneered the use of autonomous work teams in the United States in 1971 by literally building its Topeka, Kansas, Gravy Train pet food plant around them.[48] Green field sites give management the advantage of selecting appropriate technology and carefully screening job applicants.

But the fact is, most organizations are not afforded green field opportunities. They must settle for introducing self-managed teams into an existing organization structure. This is where Lawler and Mohrman's transitional model is helpful (see Figure 11–7). Even though their model builds a bridge specifically from quality circles to team organization, their recommendations apply to transition from any sort of organization structure to teams. As mentioned earlier, quality circles are a good stepping-stone from a nonparticipative organization to one driven by self-managed teams. A brief overview of each transition program is in order.

• **Figure 11-7**   Making the Transition between Quality Circles and Self-Managed Teams

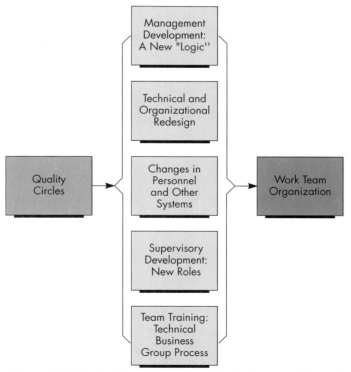

Source: Edward E. Lawler III and Susan A. Mohrman, "Quality Circles: After the Honeymoon," *Organizational Dynamics,* Spring 1987, p. 50.

Making the Transition to Self-Managed Teams   Extensive *management training and socialization* are required to deeply embed Theory Y and participative management values in the organization's culture. This new logic necessarily has to start with top management and filter down. Otherwise, resistance among middle- and lower-level managers will block the transition to teams. Some turnover can be expected among managers who refuse to adjust to broader empowerment. Both *technical and organizational redesign* are necessary. Self-managed teams may require special technology. Volvo's team-based auto assembly plant, for example, relies on portable assembly platforms rather than traditional assembly lines. Structural redesign of the organization must take place because self-managed teams are an integral part of the organization, not patched onto it as in the case of quality circles. For example, in one of Texas Instruments' computer chip factories a hierarchy of teams operates within the traditional structure. Four levels of teams

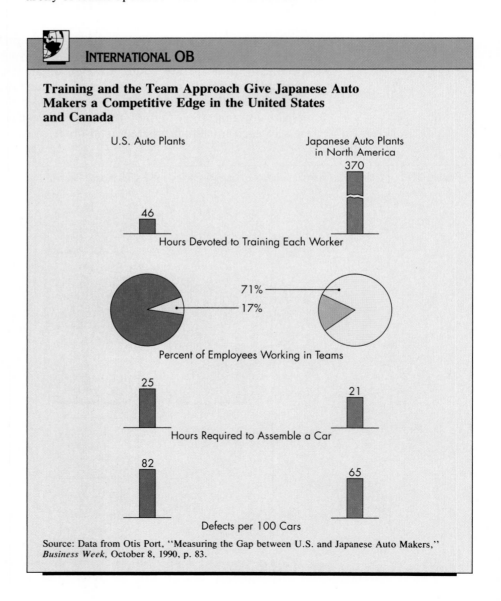

INTERNATIONAL OB

Training and the Team Approach Give Japanese Auto Makers a Competitive Edge in the United States and Canada

U.S. Auto Plants   Japanese Auto Plants in North America

370

46

Hours Devoted to Training Each Worker

71%

17%

Percent of Employees Working in Teams

25   21

Hours Required to Assemble a Car

82   65

Defects per 100 Cars

Source: Data from Otis Port, ''Measuring the Gap between U.S. and Japanese Auto Makers,'' *Business Week,* October 8, 1990, p. 83.

are responsible for different domains. Reporting to the steering team that deals with strategic issues are quality-improvement, corrective-action, and effectiveness teams. TI's quality-improvement and corrective-action teams are cross-functional teams made up of middle managers and functional specialists such as accountants and engineers. Production workers make up the effectiveness teams. The corrective-action teams are unique because they are formed to deal with short-term problems and are disbanded when a solution is found. All the other teams are long-term assignments.[49]

In turn, *personnel and reward systems* need to be adapted to encourage teamwork. Staffing decisions may shift from management to team members who hire their own co-workers. Individual bonuses must give way to team bonuses. *Supervisory development workshops* are needed to teach managers to be facilitators rather than order givers.[50] Finally, extensive *team training* is required to help team members learn more about technical details, the business as a whole, and how to be team players (see International OB). This is where team building enters the picture.

• TEAM BUILDING

Team building is a catchall term for a whole host of techniques aimed at improving the internal functioning of work groups. Whether conducted by company trainers or outside consultants, team building workshops strive for greater cooperation, better communication, and less dysfunctional conflict. Experiential learning techniques such as interpersonal trust exercises and conflict-handling role play sessions are common. Rote memorization and lecture/discussion are discouraged by team-building experts who prefer *active* versus passive learning. Greater emphasis is placed on *how* work groups get the job done than on the job itself. Team building generally is carried out in the name of organization development (OD). (Chapter 20 fully explores the field of OD.) The extensive use of team building appears to be justified. In a survey of human resource development managers from 179 Fortune 500 companies, team building reportedly was the most successful management technique.[51]

Complete coverage of the many team-building techniques would require a separate book. Consequently, the scope of our present discussion is limited to the purposes of team building, the team-building cycle, and the day-to-day development of self-management skills. This foundation is intended to give you a basis for selecting appropriate team-building techniques from the many you are likely to encounter in the years ahead.

The Purpose of Team Building

According to Richard Beckhard, a respected authority on organization development, the four purposes of team building are:

1. To set goals and/or priorities.
2. To analyze or allocate the way work is performed.
3. To examine the way a group is working, its processes (such as norms, decision making, and communication).
4. To examine relationships among the people doing the work.[52]

INTERNATIONAL OB

Team Building for the Cockpit Crews of Australian Airlines

Australian Airlines was alarmed by aviation statistics that indicate that no matter how technically sophisticated airplanes become, they will still be vulnerable to human error, causing incidents and accidents. The airline invited us to work with aircrews and design a management development initiative that would help them improve cockpit team work. The airline began by conducting a survey in various countries to see what was being done to help aircrew members manage their cockpit and flight operations effectively. Surprisingly it was found that very little had been done, particularly in the area of team management.

We conducted various interviews with captains, first officers, and flight engineers and with union representatives, senior managers, and check pilots and engineers who are accountable for examining their colleagues and licensing them to fly. Initially the aircrews expressed skepticism about the relevance of management principles to their work. They emphasized the high technical requirements of their jobs.

We listened carefully to the issues outlined by the members of the aircrews. We asked them what they felt were the major issues that they had to confront when they were flying. Interestingly, after voicing little interest in managerial matters, they went on to relate, chapter and verse, a number of incidents which indicated major management problems. . . .

Developing the Program

It became clear that pilots and flight engineers *did* recognize management problems in the cockpit but could not see how these could be rectified other than through a technical approach. We agreed to work with them to produce a prototype management development workshop focusing on team management.

This was proposed not as a cure-all but as one way in which crew members could assess their own skills and examine a wider context within which they did their technical work. This led to the formation of a steering group involving members of our own team, management, and union representatives of the

Trainers achieve these objectives by allowing team members to wrestle with simulated or real-life problems. Outcomes are then analyzed by the group to determine what group processes need improvement. Learning stems from recognizing and addressing faulty group dynamics. Perhaps one subgroup withheld key information from another, thereby hampering group progress. Organizations such as Australian Airlines have effectively used team-building workshops to foster needed teamwork (see International OB).

The Team-Building Cycle

Team-building specialist William G. Dyer recommends a six-phase cycle: (1) recognition of a current *problem;* (2) *data gathering* via interviews and/or discussions sessions; (3) *data evaluation* by the team members; (4) *problem solving and planning;* (5) *implementation;* and (6) *evaluation.*[53] Most of the work is completed by team members themselves with needed structure and support provided by the facilitator/trainer. Notice how the flow of events in

(concluded)

airline, which outlined policies and principles. Then technical advisory groups were formed consisting of pilots and flight engineers. These groups collaborated to produce the detailed materials required for the team management intervention. We acted as designers.

Over the next year we produced a wide range of resources. We were able to create a learning design covering key aspects of the management of flight operations. The program uses a variety of techniques, including the following:

Videos illustrating incidents and examples cited by the aircrews.
Role plays simulating specific incidents that the crews had to manage.
Group decision-making exercises forcing aircrews to reach decisions under pressure and learn the principles involved.
Group discussion relating key managerial principles and ideas to the technical aspects of flying.
A team management index adapted for the airline that allows aircrews to gather personal feedback on their own team management style.

The result has been the production of an intensive cockpit management development workshop under the name Aircrew Team Management. During the workshop the pilots and flight engineers deal with issues common to normal management courses: group decision making, planning and priority setting, delegation, communication, and a variety of other similar topics. However, the nature of the program concentrates specifically on the high-tech aspects of these managerial functions in the cockpit.

Source: Adapted from Charles Margerison, Rod Davies, and Dick McCann, "High-Flying Management Development," *Training and Development Journal,* February 1987, pp. 40–41. Copyright 1987, *Training and Development Journal,* American Society for Training and Development. Reprinted with permission. All rights reserved.

the Australian Airlines example followed this team-building cycle. Full participation by the cockpit crews throughout the team-building process gave them "ownership" of both the problems and solutions.

Developing Team Members' Self-Management Skills

A promising dimension of team building has emerged in recent years. It is an extension of the behavioral self-management approach discussed in Chapter 7. Proponents call it **self-management leadership,** defined as the process of leading others to lead themselves. An underlying assumption is that self-managed teams likely will fail if team members are not expressly taught to engage in self-management behaviors. This makes sense because it is unreasonable to expect employees who are accustomed to being managed and led to suddenly manage and lead themselves. Transition training is required, as discussed in the prior section. A key transition to self-management involves *current managers* engaging in self-management leadership behaviors. This is team building in the fullest meaning of the term.

Six self-management leadership behaviors were isolated in a field study of a manufacturing company organized around self-managed teams. The observed behaviors were:

1. *Encourages self-reinforcement* (e.g., getting team members to praise each other for good work and results).
2. *Encourages self-observation/evaluation* (e.g., teaching team members to judge how well they are doing).
3. *Encourages self-expectation* (e.g., encouraging team members to expect high performance from themselves and the team).
4. *Encourages self-goal-setting* (e.g., having the team set its own performance goals).
5. *Encourages rehearsal* (e.g., getting team members to think about and practice new tasks).
6. *Encourages self-criticism* (e.g., encouraging team members to be critical of their own poor performance).[54]

According to the researchers, Charles Manz and Henry Sims, this type of leadership is a dramatic departure from traditional practices such as giving orders and/or making sure everyone gets along. Empowerment, not domination, is the overriding goal.

• SUMMARY OF KEY CONCEPTS

A. Although some may be tempted to dismiss teams as a passing fad, Peter Drucker envisions them as a key feature of tomorrow's flatter, information-based organizations. When asked to describe high-performance teams, managers mention factors such as participative leadership, shared responsibility, high communication, and rapid response, among others. Four general types of work teams are advice, production, project, and action teams. Each type has its characteristic degrees of specialization and coordination, work cycle, and outputs.

B. According to the ecological model, two effectiveness criteria for work teams are performance and viability. The performance criterion is met if the group satisfies its clients/customers. A work group is viable if its members are satisfied and continue contributing. An ecological perspective is appropriate because work groups require an organizational life-support system. For instance, group participation is enhanced by an organizational culture that values employee empowerment.

C. Three key components of teamwork are cooperation, trust, and cohesiveness. Cooperative integration of effort can be achieved via collaboration or coordination. Research demonstrates the value of cooperation versus competition. Cooperative goals and functional conflict were found in field research to be keys to effective airline crew performance. From computer gaming theorists comes a practical model for encouraging cooperation and discouraging destructive competition. It is called the TIT FOR TAT strategy and it calls for systematically modeling and reinforcing cooperation while discouraging competition.

D. *Trust,* defined as reciprocal faith in others' intentions and behavior, requires a cognitive leap when we do not have firsthand knowledge of someone's reliability and integrity. Zand's research-based model of trust pivots on the interaction of information disclosure, reciprocal influence, and self-control. Six recommended ways to build trust are through communication, support, respect (especially delegation), fairness, predictability, and competence.

E. Cohesive groups have a shared sense of togetherness or a "we" feeling. Socio-emotional cohesiveness involves emotional satisfaction. Instrumental cohesiveness involves goal-directed togetherness. Despite methodological inconsistencies, research is generally supportive of cohesiveness.

F. Quality circles are groups of volunteers, usually at the lowest operating levels, who meet periodically to identify and solve quality and productivity problems. Based on Japan's success with quality circles, the practice grew to fad proportions in the United States during the 1970s and 1980s. Sloppy implementation too often led to unrealized expectations and disappointment. Managers can keep quality circle programs on track by adopting a life cycle perspective. Each of the six phases of the life cycle has its own set of threats that can derail the program if not addressed and overcome.

G. Self-managed teams, barely beyond the experimentation stage, hold great promise for tapping the full potential of today's employees by increasing their autonomy. They call for nonmanagerial employees to take over traditional managerial duties such as planning, scheduling, and even hiring. Research shows modest support for self-managed teams. Complex organizational transition programs need to be undertaken to set the stage for self-managed teams.

H. Team building strives to improve the internal functioning of work groups through experiential learning. A six-phase team-building cycle enables groups to identify real or simulated problems, gather and evaluate data, and create, implement, and evaluate solutions. A promising new dimension of team building is *self-management leadership,* defined as leading others to lead themselves. Nonmanagerial employees need to develop self-management skills if they are to help self-managed teams live up to their promise. The best way to acquire those skills is through effective leadership on the part of current management.

• KEY TERMS

team

team viability

collaboration

coordination

trust

cohesiveness

socio-emotional cohesiveness

instrumental cohesiveness

quality circles

self-managed teams

cross-functionalism

team building

self-management leadership

• DISCUSSION QUESTIONS

1. Do you agree or disagree with the vision of more team-oriented organizations? Explain your assumptions and reasoning.
2. Have you ever been a member of a high-performing team? If so, explain the circumstances and success factors.
3. Why bother taking an ecological perspective of work team effectiveness?
4. Why would collaboration generally be harder to achieve than coordination?
5. In your personal friendships, how do you come to trust someone? How fragile is that trust? Explain.
6. In your opinion, what is the single most important factor in Zand's model of trust? Explain.
7. Why should a group leader strive for both socio-emotional and instrumental cohesiveness?
8. Which threats during the life cycle of the quality circle program deserve management's closest attention? Explain.
9. Would you like to work on a self-managed team? Explain.
10. How would you respond to a manager who said, ''Why should I teach my people to manage themselves and work myself out of a job?''

BACK TO THE OPENING CASE

Now that you have read Chapter 11, you should be able to answer the following questions about the AT&T Credit Corp. case:
1. Do the ATTCC teams qualify as effective, according to the ecological model in this chapter? Explain.
2. How important is trust in this case? Explain.
3. What drawbacks in the self-managed team approach surfaced in this case? What can be done about them?

• EXERCISE 11

Objectives

1. To help you better understand the components of teamwork.
2. To give you a practical diagnostic tool to assess the need for team building.

Introduction

Teamwork is essential in modern organizations. Virtually all administrative activity is group-oriented. The more present and future managers know about effective teamwork the better.

Instructions

If you currently have a full-time or part-time job, think of your immediate work group and circle an appropriate response for each of the following five questions. If you are not currently employed, think of your work group in your last job. Alternatively, you might want to evaluate a class project team, sorority, fraternity, or club to which you belong. Compute a total score and use the scoring key for interpretation.

Questionnaire[55]

1. To what extent do I feel "under wraps," that is, have private thoughts, unspoken reservations, or unexpressed feelings and opinions that I have not felt comfortable bringing out into the open?

1	2	3	4	5
Almost completely under wraps	Under wraps many times	Slightly more free and expressive than under wraps	Quite free and expressive much of the time	Almost completely free and expressive

2. How effective are we, in our team, in getting out and using the ideas, opinions, and information of all team members in making decisions?

1	2	3	4	5
We don't really encourage everyone to share their ideas, opinions, and information with the team in making decisions.	Only the ideas, opinions, and information of a few members are really known and used in making decisions.	Sometimes we hear the views of most members before making decisions and sometimes we disregard most members.	A few are sometimes hesitant about sharing their opinions, but we generally have good participation in making decisions.	Everyone feels his or her ideas, opinions, and information are given a fair hearing before decisions are made.

3. How well does the team work at its tasks?

1	2	3	4	5
Coasts, loafs, makes no progress	Makes a little progress; most members loaf	Progress is slow, spurts of effective work	Above average in progress and pace of work	Works well; achieves definite progress

4. How are differences or conflicts handled in our team?

1	2	3	4	5
Differences or conflicts are denied, suppressed, or avoided at all cost.	Differences or conflicts are recognized, but remain unresolved mostly.	Differences or conflicts are recognized and some attempts are made to work them through by some members, often outside the team meetings.	Differences and conflicts are recognized and some attempts are made to deal with them in our team.	Differences and conflicts are recognized and the team usually is working them through satisfactorily.

5. How do people relate to the team leader, chairman, or "boss"?

1	2	3	4	5
The leader dominates the team and people are often fearful or passive.	The leader tends to control the team, although people generally agree with the leader's direction.	There is some give and take between the leader and the team members.	Team members relate easily to the leader and usually are able to influence leader decisions.	Team members respect the leader, but they work together as a unified team with everyone participating and no one dominant.

Total score = _____

Scoring Key

5–9   "Get out the boxing gloves!"
10–14 "You call this a team?"
15–19 "Almost there; Go team, go!"
20–25 "A real team! Line up for a team picture!"

Questions for Consideration/Class Discussion

1. Having analyzed your work group, is it a stronger or weaker team than you originally thought? Explain.

2. Which factor is your work group's biggest barrier to cooperative and productive teamwork?

3. What needs to be done to prepare your team for self-management?

• NOTES

[1] Peter F. Drucker, "The Coming of the New Organization," *Harvard Business Review,* January–February 1988, p. 47.

[2] Dori Jones Yang and Michael Oneal, "How Boeing Does It," *Business Week,* July 9, 1990, p. 49.

[3] Clayton P. Alderfer, "An Intergroup Perspective on Group Dynamics," in *Handbook of Organizational Behavior,* ed. Jay W. Lorsch (Englewood Cliffs, N.J.: Prentice-Hall, 1987), p. 211. (Emphasis added.)

[4] Steve Buchholz and Thomas Roth, *Creating the High-Performance Team* (New York: John Wiley & Sons, 1987), p. xi.

[5] Ibid., p. 14.

[6] Pamela King, "What Makes Teamwork Work?" *Psychology Today,* December 1989, p. 17.

[7] See Eric Sundstrom, Kenneth P. De Meuse, and David Futrell, "Work Teams," *American Psychologist,* February 1990, pp. 120–33.

[8] An instructive overview of group effectiveness models can be found in Paul S. Goodman, Elizabeth Ravlin, and Marshall Schminke, "Understanding Groups in Organizations," in *Research in Organizational Behavior,* eds. L. L. Cummings and Barry M. Staw (Greenwich, Conn.: JAI Press, 1987), vol. 9, pp. 121–73.

[9] Sundstrom et al., "Work Teams," p. 122.

[10] Christopher Knowlton, "11 Men's Million-Dollar Motivator," *Fortune,* April 9, 1990, p. 65.

[11] Joel Kotkin, "The 'Smart Team' at Compaq Computer," *Inc.*, February 1986, p. 48.

[12] This distinction is drawn from Gordon O'Brien, "The Measurement of Cooperation," *Organizationl Behavior and Human Performance*, November 1968, pp. 427–39.

[13] Alfie Kohn, "How to Succeed without Even Vying," *Psychology Today*, September 1986, pp. 27–28.

[14] David W. Johnson, Geoffrey Maruyama, Roger Johnson, Deborah Nelson, and Linda Skon, "Effects of Cooperative, Competitive, and Individualistic Goal Structures on Achievement: A Meta-Analysis," *Psychological Bulletin*, January 1981, pp. 56–57. An alternative interpretation of the foregoing study that emphasizes the influence of situational factors can be found in John L. Cotton and Michael S. Cook, "Meta-Analysis and the Effects of Various Reward Systems: Some Different Conclusions from Johnson et al.," *Psychological Bulletin*, July 1982, pp. 176–83.

[15] Stuart W. Cook and Michael Pelfrey, "Reactions to Being Helped in Cooperating Interracial Groups: A Context Effect," *Journal of Personality and Social Psychology*, November 1985, p. 1243.

[16] See Anthony J. Stahelski and Ruth Ann Tsukuda, "Predictors of Cooperation in Health Care Teams," *Small Group Research*, May 1990, pp. 220–33.

[17] Dean Tjosvold, "Flight Crew Collaboration to Manage Safety Risks," *Group & Organization Studies*, June 1990, pp. 186–88.

[18] Henry Malcolm and Claire Sokoloff, "Values, Human Relations, and Organization Development," in *The Emerging Practice of Organization Development*, eds. Walter Sikes, Allan Drexler, and Jack Gant (San Diego, Calif.: University Associates, 1989), p. 66.

[19] Aaron Bernstein, "The Difference Japanese Management Makes," *Business Week*, July 14, 1986, p. 48.

[20] For interesting reading on close personal trust, see John K. Rempel and John G. Holmes, "How Do I Trust Thee?" *Psychology Today*, February 1986, pp. 28–34.

[21] J. David Lewis and Andrew Weigert, "Trust as a Social Reality," *Social Forces*, June 1985, p. 971.

[22] Ibid., p. 970.

[23] See Pramod Kumar and Rehana Ghadially, "Organizational Politics and Its Effects on Members of Organizations," *Human Relations*, April 1989, pp. 305–14.

[24] Dale E. Zand, "Trust and Managerial Problem Solving," *Administrative Science Quarterly*, June 1972, p. 238.

[25] George S. Odiorne, "The Managerial Bait-and-Switch Game," *Personnel*, March 1986, p. 32. Also see Louis B. Barnes, "Managing the Paradox of Organizational Trust," *Harvard Business Review*, March–April 1981, pp. 107–16.

[26] Adapted from Fernando Bartolomé, "Nobody Trusts the Boss Completely—Now What?" *Harvard Business Review*, March–April 1989, pp. 135–42.

[27] Personal and social consequences of trust are discussed in Julian B. Rotter, "Interpersonal Trust, Trustworthiness, and Gullibility," *American Psychologist*, January 1980, pp. 1–7.

[28] William Foster Owen, "Metaphor Analysis of Cohesiveness in Small Discussion Groups," *Small Group Behavior*, August 1985, p. 416. Also see Joann Keyton and Jeff Springston, "Redefining Cohesiveness in Groups," *Small Group Research*, May 1990, pp. 234–54.

[29] This distinction is based on discussion in Aharon Tziner, "Differential Effects of Group Cohesiveness Types: A Clarifying Overview," *Social Behavior and Personality*, no. 2, 1982, pp. 227–39.

[30] See Owen, "Metaphor Analysis of Cohesiveness in Small Discussion Groups."

[31] Details may be found in Sanford B. Weinberg, Susan H. Rovinski, Laurie Weiman, and Michael Beitman, "Common Group Problems: A Field Study," *Small Group Behavior,* February 1981, pp. 81–92.

[32] For a summary of cohesiveness research, see Goodman, Ravlin, and Schminke, "Understanding Groups in Organizations," in *Research in Organizational Behavior.* See also Peter E. Mudrack, "Group Cohesiveness and Productivity: A Closer Look," *Human Relations,* September 1989, pp. 771–85.

[33] Gregory L. Miles, "The Plant of Tomorrow Is in Texas Today," *Business Week,* July 28, 1986, p. 76.

[34] Based on discussion in Edward E. Lawler III and Susan A. Mohrman, "Quality Circles: After the Honeymoon," *Organizational Dynamics,* Spring 1987, pp. 42–54.

[35] The historical development of quality circles is discussed by Cynthia Stohl, "Bridging the Parallel Organization: A Study of Quality Circle Effectiveness," in *Organizational Communication,* ed. Margaret L. McLaughlin (Beverly Hills, Calif.: Sage Publications, 1987), pp. 416–30; and Thomas Li-Ping Tang, Peggy Smith Tollison, and Harold D. Whiteside, "The Effect of Quality Circle Initiation on Motivation to Attend Quality Circle Meetings and on Task Performance," *Personnel Psychology,* Winter 1987, pp. 799–814.

[36] Based on discussion in Kimberly Buch and Raymond Spangler, "The Effects of Quality Circles on Performance and Promotions," *Human Relations,* June 1990, pp. 573–82.

[37] See Gerald R. Ferris and John A. Wagner III, "Quality Circles in the United States: A Conceptual Reevaluation," *The Journal of Applied Behavioral Science,* no. 2, 1985, pp. 155–67.

[38] Lawler and Mohrman, "Quality Circles: After the Honeymoon," p. 43.

[39] John Hoerr, "The Payoff from Teamwork," *Business Week,* July 10, 1989, p. 56.

[40] See Mitchell L. Marks, "The Question of Quality Circles," *Psychology Today,* March 1986, pp. 36–38, 42, 44, 46.

[41] See Robert P. Steel and Russell F. Lloyd, "Cognitive, Affective, and Behavioral Outcomes of Participation in Quality Circles: Conceptual and Empirical Findings," *The Journal of Applied Behavioral Science,* no. 1, 1988, pp. 1–17; Mitchell L. Marks, Philip H. Mirvis, Edward J. Hackett, and James F. Grady, Jr., "Employee Participation in a Quality Circle Program: Impact on Quality of Work Life, Productivity, and Absenteeism," *Journal of Applied Psychology,* February 1986, pp. 61–69; and Buch and Spangler, "The Effects of Quality Circles on Performance and Promotions."

[42] Lawler and Mohrman, "Quality Circles: After the Honeymoon," p. 52.

[43] Brian Dumaine, "Who Needs a Boss?" *Fortune,* May 7, 1990, p. 52.

[44] Ibid., pp. 52–55, 58, 60.

[45] See Paul S. Goodman, Rukmini Devadas, and Terri L. Griffith Hughson, "Groups and Productivity: Analyzing the Effectiveness of Self-Managing Teams," in *Productivity in Organizations,* eds. John P. Campbell, Richard J. Campbell and Associates (San Francisco: Jossey-Bass, 1988), pp. 295–327.

[46] Good background discussions can be found in work cited in note 45 and in Chris Lee, "Beyond Teamwork," *Training,* June 1990, pp. 25–32.

[47] Drawn from Goodman, Devadas, and Hughson, "Groups and Productivity: Analyzing the Effectiveness of Self-Managing Teams."

[48] See Richard E. Walton, "Work Innovations at Topeka: After Six Years," *The Journal of Applied Behavioral Science,* 1977, pp. 422–33.

[49] See Dumaine, "Who Needs a Boss?", pp. 55, 58.

[50] For an instructive case study on this topic, see Charles C. Manz, David E. Keating, and Anne Donnellon, "Preparing for an Organizational Change to Em-

ployee Self-Management: The Managerial Transition," *Organizational Dynamics,* Autumn 1990, pp. 15–26.

[51] Data from Eric Stephan, Gordon E. Mills, R. Wayne Pace, and Lenny Ralphs, "HRD in the Fortune 500: A Survey," *Training and Development Journal,* January 1988, pp. 26–32.

[52] Richard Beckhard, "Optimizing Team-Building Efforts," *Journal of Contemporary Business,* Summer 1972, p. 24.

[53] Complete discussion can be found in William G. Dyer, *Team Building: Issues and Alternatives,* 2nd ed. (Reading, Mass.: Addison-Wesley Publishing, 1987).

[54] Adapted from Charles C. Manz and Henry P. Sims, Jr., "Leading Workers to Lead Themselves: The External Leadership of Self-Managing Work Teams," *Administrative Science Quarterly,* March 1987, pp. 106–29. Also see Charles C. Manz, "Beyond Self-Managing Work Teams: Toward Self-Leading Teams in the Workplace," in *Research in Organizational Change and Development,* Vol. 4, eds. Richard W. Woodman and William A. Pasmore (Greenwich, Conn.: JAI Press, 1990), pp. 273–99.

[55] Excerpted from Dyer, *Team Building,* pp. 69–71.

CHAPTER

12

Organizational Communication Processes

LEARNING OBJECTIVES

When you finish studying the material in this chapter, you should be able to:

- Describe the perceptual process model of communication.
- Explain the contingency approach to media selection.
- Contrast the communication styles of assertiveness, aggressiveness, and nonassertiveness, and explain interaction involvement.

- Discuss the primary sources of both nonverbal communication and listener comprehension.
- Identify and give examples of the three different listening styles.
- Review the ten keys to effective listening.
- Discuss patterns of hierarchical communication.

- Describe the grapevine and its identifiable patterns.
- Explain how the two personal barriers to interpersonal communication distort the communication process.
- Demonstrate your familiarity with four antecedents of communication distortion between managers and employees.

OPENING CASE 12

At These Shouting Matches, No One Says A Word

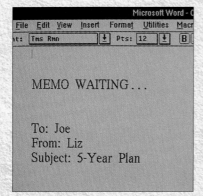

Sharon Hoogstraten

There's a bloody meeting going on. "This company has no leader—and no vision," says one frustrated participant. "Why are you being so defensive?" asks another. Someone snaps: "I've had enough—I'm looking for another job." Rough stuff—if these people were talking face-to-face. But they're not. They're sitting side-by-side in silence in front of personal computers, typing anonymous messages that flash on a projection screen at the head of the room.

Electronic encounter groups like this could soon be the meeting place of Corporate America if some key high-tech companies

and researchers have their way. Most enticing is what happens during so-called electronic meetings; People become brutally honest. The anonymity of talking through computers "turns even shy people powerful," says Alethea O. Caldwell, president of Ancilla Systems Inc., an Elk Grove (Ill.) health care company that used an electronic meeting to hammer out its five-year plan.

Timesaver

The delivery may be bruising, but the honest answers offer valuable, unfiltered information. Samuel L. Eichenfield, president of Greyhound Financial, a division of Greyhound Dial Corp., asked 20 staffers at a recent electronic meeting to rate their bosses. The results? "One manager enrolled in a management-improvement session, and another took a strategic-planning course," says Eichenfield.

Outwardly, electronic meetings are simple: Up to 50 people sit around a horseshoe-shaped table, empty except for a series of PCs. A complex local-area network tracks and sorts by topic and order of response every sentence typed in by participants. It then

displays them on the projection screen. When attendees want to vote on an issue, the computers tally the results and display them. At the end of the meeting, everybody gets a printed synopsis.

IBM is one of the biggest boosters of electronic meetings. In 1986, it gave the University of Arizona $2 million to perfect the concept and since then has built 18 electronic-meeting rooms at IBM sites and plans 2 more. Eighty employees at IBM's Federal Sector Div. are pitching the concept to such customers as Procter & Gamble Co. and General Motors Corp. and to other IBM units. So far, 7,000 IBMers, including Chairman John F. Akers, have taken part. These sessions, says IBM project manager Christopher J. McGoff, have "brought people together" who have traditionally skirmished, such as employees from product development and marketing.

Even managers who wince when electronic meetings make peers out of subordinates give the format high marks for efficiency. Chitchat is eliminated, and discussions don't digress. A study by IBM and the University of Arizona claims that electronic meetings

E very managerial function and activity involves some form of direct or indirect communication. Whether planning and organizing, or directing and leading, managers find themselves communicating with and through others. Managerial decisions and organizational policies are ineffective unless they are *understood* by those responsible for enacting them. Effective communication is a cornerstone of ethical organizational behavior (see A Matter of Ethics) and ultimately of both managerial and organizational success. In fact, the authors of the best-selling book *The 100 Best Companies to Work*

OPENING CASE 12

(concluded)

are as much as 55 percent faster than traditional ones. Phelps Dodge Mining Co. in Phoenix has proof. Last year, it held its planning meeting electronically. Usually, says Robert E. Johnson, Phelps Dodge's director of research and business development, this session takes days. This time, it lasted 12 hours. A big plus: "A lot of people were able to talk at once without stepping on toes," he says.

IBM won't have the electronic-meeting market to itself for long. Andersen Consulting is building two electronic-meeting rooms that will accommodate long-distance

sessions as well. And the University of Arizona has spawned a startup, Ventana Corp. Ventana plans to run electronic meetings for customers and sell a software package for those who want to lead their own sessions.

'It's Sad'

Electronic meetings attract diverse groups: Last year, Arizona's Democratic state legislators and Southwest Gas Corp. were among dozens of companies using them. But they do have some key drawbacks. While anonymity prevents bloody noses, it makes it impossible for people to

get credit for a good idea, says Ventana CEO J. F. Nunamaker. Also, computer-shy participants may have trouble keeping up with those who can pound out messages rapidly. And even though a crude computer shorthand can mimic human touches such as some facial expressions [see insert] many participants find the process unnatural.

Critics say these problems prove there's no substitute for oral communication. Notes one participant in a recent electronic meeting: "It's sad that we can't talk without sitting at terminals." Maybe. But similar sentiments have been heard before. In the 1890s, people said the bane of human communications would be a new invention, the telephone.

For Discussion

How would you like to attend an electronic meeting?

• Additional discussion questions linking this case with the following material appear at the end of this chapter.

Source: Jim Bartimo, "At These Shouting Matches, No One Says a Word," *Business Week*, June 11, 1990, p. 78. Reprinted from June 11, 1990 issue of *Business Week* by special permission, copyright © 1990 by McGraw-Hill, Inc.

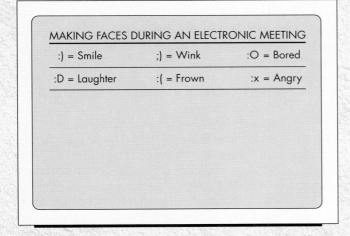

MAKING FACES DURING AN ELECTRONIC MEETING		
:) = Smile	;) = Wink	:O = Bored
:D = Laughter	:(= Frown	:x = Angry

for in America emphasized communication when listing the 12 characteristics of the "ideal" company.

> Each company is unique, but there were certain themes we heard over and over again, and the urge to draw a kind of composite picture of the ideal company is irresistible. Beyond good pay and strong benefits, such a company would: . . . Encourage open communication, informing its people of new developments and encouraging them to offer suggestions and complaints.[1]

Empirical research studies lend additional support to this observation.

A MATTER OF ETHICS

Communication Is the Cornerstone of Ethical Organizational Behavior

Communication by top executives keeps the firm on its ethical course, and top executives must ensure that the ethical climate is consistent with the company's overall objectives. Communication is important in providing guidance for ethical standards and activities that provide integration between the functional areas of the business. A vice president of marketing, for example, must communicate and work with regional sales managers and other marketing employees to make sure that all agree on what constitutes certain unethical activities such as bribery, price collusion, and deceptive sales techniques. Top corporate executives must also communicate with managers at the operations level (in production, sales, and finance, for example) and enforce overall ethical standards within the organization.

Source: O. C. Ferrell and John Fraedrich, *Business Ethics: Ethical Decision Making and Cases* (Boston: Houghton Mifflin, 1991), p. 143.

A study involving 130 vocational rehabilitation counselors revealed that employee satisfaction with organizational communication was positively and significantly correlated with both job satisfaction and performance.[2] Two additional studies demonstrated that the quality of managerial communication was directly related to organizational innovation and overall organizational performance.[3] The importance of these findings is underscored by the fact that managers reportedly spend between 70 and 87 percent of their time communicating.[4]

Even though managers spend the majority of their time communicating, they are not necessarily effective communicators. Robert Levinson, a banking industry executive, summed up the state of managerial communication by describing the typical manager as follows: "He talks too much, expresses himself poorly, and has an uncanny ability for evading the point." Levinson further concluded that most managers cannot "write a coherent letter, make a compelling presentation, dictate a concise memo, or put together a speech that doesn't have half his audience looking at their watches."[5] While some might call this appraisal too harsh, it highlights the need for better managerial communication.

This chapter will help you better understand how managers can both improve their communication skills and design more effective communication programs. We discuss (1) basic dimensions of the communication process, focusing on a perceptual process model and a contingency approach to selecting media; (2) interpersonal communication; (3) organizational communication patterns; and (4) barriers to effective communication.

• BASIC DIMENSIONS OF THE COMMUNICATION PROCESS

Communication is defined as "the exchange of information between a sender and a receiver, and the inference (perception) of meaning between the individuals involved."[6] Analysis of this exchange reveals that communica-

• FIGURE 12-1   A Perceptual Model of Communication

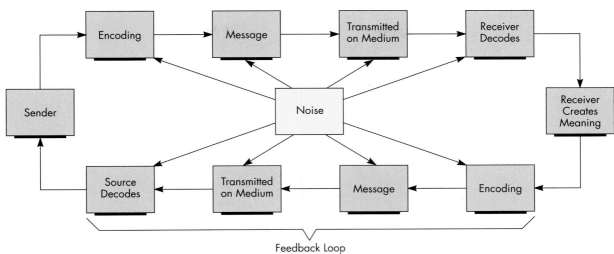

Feedback Loop

tion is a two-way process consisting of consecutively linked elements (see Figure 12–1). Managers who understand this process can analyze their own communication patterns as well as design communication programs that fit organizational needs. This section reviews a perceptual process model of communication and discusses a contingency approach to choosing communication media.

A Perceptual Process Model of Communication

The communication process historically has been described in terms of a *conduit* model. This traditional model depicts communication as a pipeline in which information and meaning are transferred from person to person. Recently, however, communication scholars have criticized the conduit model for being based on unrealistic assumptions. For example, the conduit model assumes communication transfers *intended meanings* from person to person.[7] If this assumption was true, miscommunication would not exist and there would be no need to worry about being misunderstood. We could simply say or write what we want and assume the listener or reader accurately understands our intended meaning.

As we all know, communicating is not that simple or clear-cut. Communication is fraught with miscommunication. In recognition of this, researchers have begun to examine communication as a form of social information processing (recall the discussion in Chapter 4) in which receivers interpret messages by cognitively processing information. This view led to development of a **perceptual model of communication** that depicts communication as a process in which receivers create meaning in their own minds. Let us briefly examine the elements of the perceptual process model shown in Figure 12–1.

Sender   The sender is an individual, group, or organization that desires to communicate with a particular receiver. Receivers may be individuals, groups, or organizations.

• In the perceptual model of communication, senders and receivers encode and decode messages.
(Janeart Ltd./The Image Bank)

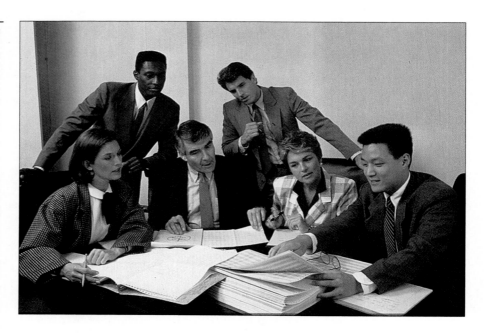

Encoding   Communication begins when a sender encodes an idea or thought. Encoding translates mental thoughts into a code or language that can be understood by others. Managers typically encode using words, numbers, gestures, nonverbal cues such as facial expressions, or pictures. Moreover, different methods of encoding can be used to portray similar ideas. The following short exercise highlights this point.

On a piece of paper, draw a picture of the area currently surrounding you. Now, write a verbal description of the same area. Does the pictorial encoding portray the same basic message as the verbal description? Which mode was harder to use and which more effective? Interestingly, a growing number of management consultants recommend using visual communication, such as drawings, to analyze and improve group interaction and problem solving and to reduce stress.[8]

The Message   The output of encoding is a message. There are two important points to keep in mind about messages. First, they contain more than meets the eye. Messages may contain hidden agendas as well as trigger affective or emotional reactions. The second point to consider about messages is that they need to match the medium used to transmit them. For example, a routine memo is a poor way to announce an emotional issue such as a large layoff.

Selecting a Medium   Managers can communicate through a variety of media. Potential media include face-to-face conversations, telephone calls, written memos or letters, photographs or drawings, meetings, bulletin boards, computer output, and charts or graphs. Choosing the appropriate media depends on many factors, including the nature of the message, its intended purpose, the type of audience, proximity to the audience, time horizon for disseminating the message, and personal preferences (see OB in Action).

OB IN ACTION

Organizations Use Different Media to Communicate about Poor Economic Conditions

Alaska Air Group workers are "mad at the world" over slumping business and Mideast events, the carrier says. At meals, the workers hit the chairman with hard questions about wasteful spending. Keeping employees informed by fax has become crucial, says BankEast, which is in bankruptcy court; the campaign instills a "rallying around" feeling.

Layoffs and other woes make morale a "significant problem," says Bolt Beranek & Newman. It, along with Western Capital Investment; J.C. Penney; Southwest Airlines; Outboard Marine; and Al's Formal Wear Inc., in Fort Worth, Texas, use means such as an electronic bulletin board, personal meetings, an open door and visits to the field, for a dialogue.

All media have advantages and disadvantages. Face-to-face conversations, for instance, are useful for communicating about sensitive or important issues and those requiring feedback and intensive interaction. Telephones are convenient, fast, and private, but lack nonverbal information. Although writing memos or letters is time-consuming, it is a good medium when it is difficult to meet with the other person, when formality and a written record are important, and when face-to-face interaction is not necessary to enhance understanding. More is said later in this chapter about choosing media.

Decoding   Decoding is the receiver's version of encoding. Decoding consists of translating verbal, oral, or visual aspects of a message into a form that can be interpreted. Receivers rely on social information processing to determine the meaning of a message during decoding. With respect to gender differences in encoding and decoding, a study of 34 males and 47 females revealed that females were both better encoders and decoders of emotional messages.[9]

Creating Meaning   In contrast to the conduit model's assumption that meaning is directly transferred from sender to receiver, the perceptual model is based on the belief that a receiver creates the meaning of a message in his or her mind. A receiver's interpretation of a message often will differ from that intended by the sender. In turn, receivers act according to their own interpretations, not the communicator's. A communication expert concluded the following after considering this element of the communication process.

> Miscommunication and unintentional communication are to be expected, for they are the norm. Organizationl communicators who take these ideas seriously would realize just how difficult successful communication truly is. Presumably, they would be conscious of the constant effort needed to communicate in ways most

closely approximating their intentions. . . . Communication is fraught with unintentionality and, thereby, great difficulty for communicators.[10]

Managers are encouraged to rely on *redundancy* of communication to reduce this unintentionality. This can be done by transmitting the message over multiple media. For example, a production manager might follow up a phone conversation about a critical schedule change with a memo.

Feedback   The receiver's response to a message is the crux of the feedback loop. At this point in the communication process, the receiver becomes a sender. Specifically, the receiver encodes a response and then transmits it to the original sender. This new message is then decoded and interpreted. As you can see from this discussion, feedback is used as a comprehension check. It gives senders an idea of how accurately their message is understood.

Noise   Noise represents anything that interferes with the transmission and understanding of a message. It affects all linkages of the communication process. Noise includes factors such as a speech impairment, poor telephone connections, illegible handwriting, inaccurate statistics in a memo or report, poor hearing and eyesight, and physical distance between sender and receiver. Managers can improve communication accuracy by reducing noise. Consider, for example, the approach used by Northrop Corp. to improve communication and productivity by reducing the physical barriers between engineers and production workers.

> At the company's new building in Hawthorne, Calif., where it makes the Tigershark fighter plane, engineers work right on the line so problems can be ironed out swiftly. "You can make changes on the plane together rather than sending memos," says Welko E. Gasich, senior vice-president for advanced projects. The result: The second Tigershark was made in 30 percent fewer work hours than the first. And the third plane "had zero defects on the fuselage, which is unheard of," Gasich says.[11]

Choosing Media: A Contingency Perspective

Managers need to determine which media to use for both obtaining and disseminating information. If an inappropriate medium is used, managerial decisions may be based on inaccurate information and/or important messages may not reach the intended audience (see International OB). Media selection therefore is a key component of communication effectiveness. This section explores a contingency model designed to help managers select communication media in a systematic and effective manner. Media selection in this model is based on the interaction between information richness and complexity of the problem/situation at hand.

Information Richness   Respected organizational theorists Richard Daft and Robert Lengel define **information richness** in the following manner:

> Richness is defined as the potential information-carrying capacity of data. If the communication of an item of data, such as a wink, provides substantial new understanding, it would be considered rich. If the datum provides little understanding, it would be low in richness.[12]

INTERNATIONAL OB

The Chinese Language Limits the Choice of a Medium

A major problem in the transmission and storage of information is the Chinese language which consists of 30,000–40,000 separate ideograms. The traditional Chinese typewriter is a complex and cumbersome machine, while electronic video display/printers and duplicators have not yet arrived.

Written information in day-to-day management is scarce, and consists of handwritten notes for which no copy exists. Perforce, decisions are by consensus discussion, with perhaps a shorthand summary on file, but that is all. Information may simply be forgotten or misunderstood. Credit for a good idea or censure for a disastrous decision may be hard to pin down. This, it might be argued, applies equally to the Japanese enterprise although with their thorough sharing of information and seeking of consensus, they probably do not incur the same problems as the Chinese.

A key tool in information dissemination in the factory is a blackboard and chalk. Normally to add new information it is necessary to wipe out the old and unless that information is readily retrievable, it may be lost.

Electronic reproduction of Chinese characters combined with word processors and computers in the next few years are likely to transform Chinese management in quite unforeseeable ways.

Source: J. M. Livingstone, "Chinese Management in Flux," *Euro-Asia Business Review*, April 1987, p. 19. Copyright © 1987. Reprinted by permission of John Wiley & Sons, Ltd.

• **FIGURE 12-2** Characteristics of Information Richness for Different Media

Information Richness	Medium	Feedback	Channel	Type of Communication	Language Source
High	Face-to-face	Immediate	Visual, audio	Personal	Body, natural
↑	Telephone	Fast	Audio	Personal	Natural
	Personal written	Slow	Limited visual	Personal	Natural
	Formal written	Very slow	Limited visual	Impersonal	Natural
Low	Formal numeric	Very slow	Limited visual	Impersonal	Numeric

Source: Adapted from Richard Daft and Robert H. Lengel, "Information Richness: A New Approach to Managerial Behavior and Organization Design," in *Research in Organizational Behavior*, ed. Barry M. Staw and Larry L. Cummings (Greenwich, Conn.: JAI Press, 1984), p. 197.

As this definition implies, alternative media possess levels of information richness that vary from high to low.

Information richness is determined by four factors: (1) feedback (ranging from immediate to very slow), (2) channel (ranging from a combined visual and audio to limited visual), (3) type of communication (personal versus impersonal), and (4) language source (body, natural, or numeric). In Figure 12–2, the information richness of five different media is categorized in terms of these four factors.

Face-to-face is the richest form of communication. It provides immediate feedback, which serves as a comprehension check. Moreover, it allows for the observation of multiple language cues, such as body language and tone of voice, over more than one channel. Although high in richness, the telephone is not as informative as the face-to-face medium. Formal numeric media such as quantitative computer printouts or video displays possess the lowest richness. Feedback is very slow, the channel involves only limited visual information, and the numeric information is impersonal.

Complexity of the Managerial Problem/Situation   Managers face problems and situations that range from low to high in complexity. Low-complexity situations are routine, predictable, and managed by using objective or standard procedures. Calculating an employee's paycheck is an example of low complexity. Highly complex situations, like a corporate reorganization, are ambiguous, unpredictable, hard to analyze, and often emotionally laden. Managers spend considerably more time analyzing these situations because they rely on more sources of information during their deliberations. There are no set solutions to complex problems or situations.

Contingency Recommendations   The contingency model for selecting media is graphically depicted in Figure 12–3. As shown, there are three zones of communication effectiveness. Effective communication occurs when the richness of the medium is matched appropriately with the complexity of the problem or situation. Media low in richness—formal numeric or formal written—are better suited for simple problems, while media high in richness—telephone or face-to-face—are appropriate for complex problems or situations. For example, an effective strategy would be for district sales managers to communicate monthly sales reports to each salesperson via formal numeric sales charts.

Conversely, ineffective communication occurs when the richness of the

---

• **FIGURE 12-3**   A Contingency Model for Selecting Communication Media

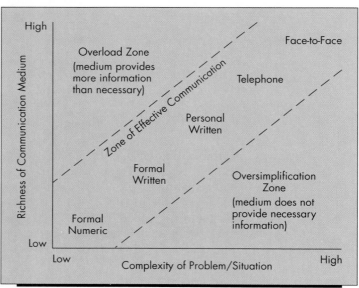

Source: Adapted from Richard L. Daft and Robert H. Lengel, "Information Richness: A New Approach to Managerial Behavior and Organization Design," in *Research in Organizational Behavior,* ed. Barry M. Staw and Larry L. Cummings (Greenwich, Conn.: JAI Press, 1984), p. 199. Used with permission.

medium is either too high or too low for the complexity of the problem or situation. Extending the above example, a district sales manager would fall into the *overload zone* if he or she communicated monthly sales reports through richer media. Conducting face-to-face meetings or telephoning each salesperson would provide excessive information and take more time than necessary to communicate monthly sales data. The oversimplification zone represents another ineffective choice of communication medium. In this situation, media with inadequate richness are used to communicate complicated problems. An example would be announcing a major reorganization via a formal memo. Effective communicators use rich media to prepare employees for reorganizations.

Research Evidence   The relationship between media richness and problem/situation complexity has not been researched extensively because the underlying theory is relatively new. Available evidence indicates that managers used richer sources when confronted with ambiguous and complicated events.[13] Moreover, a recent meta-analysis of over 40 studies revealed that media usage was significantly different across organizational levels. Upper-level executives/managers spent more time in face-to-face meetings than did lower-level managers.[14] This finding is consistent with recommendations derived from the contingency model just discussed.

• INTERPERSONAL COMMUNICATION

The quality of interpersonal communication within an organization is very important. Research demonstrated that ineffective interpersonal communication negatively affected group decision making and the individual's career progress. People with more developed communication abilities helped groups to make better decisions and were promoted more frequently than individuals with less developed abilities.[15]

Although there is no universally accepted definition of **communication competence,** it is a performance-based index of an individual's knowledge of "when and how to use language in the social context."[16] Communication competence is determined by three components: communication abilities and traits, situational factors, and the individuals involved in an interaction (see Figure 12–4). The geographic location of an organization, for example, is an important situational factor. As a case in point, contrast the communication styles used by Seinosuke Kashima, a Japanese trading-company official, while working in both New York and in Japan:

> In New York Mr. Kashima did a lot of business on the telephone. In Japan, he must personally visit people in order to conduct any important business—"so they can see my eyes." . . .
>
> Below the surface, he says, things get even more complicated. "Suppose I want to propose something new," he says. "In Japan, the first thing I should do is take a colleague from the office to a nightclub and talk around the theme—without mentioning my idea directly. Only after my office colleagues and I understand each other would I go to my superior and propose the idea. But when I first returned from the U.S., I tended to go straight ahead with my ideas. It caused problems. Now I do it the normal [Japanese] way."[17]

• FIGURE 12-4   Communication Competence Affects Upward Mobility

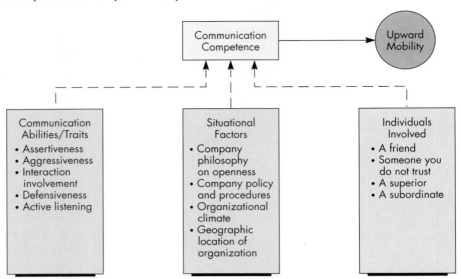

Individuals involved in an interaction also affect communication competence. For example, people are likely to withhold information and react emotionally or defensively when interacting with someone they dislike or do not trust. You can improve your communication competence through six communication styles/abilities/traits under your control: assertiveness, aggressiveness, nonassertiveness, interaction involvement, nonverbal communication, and active listening.

Assertiveness, Aggressiveness, and Nonassertiveness

The saying, "You can attract more bees with honey than with vinegar," captures the difference between using an assertive communication style and an aggressive style. Research studies indicate that assertiveness is more effective than aggressiveness in both work-related and consumer contexts.[18] An **assertive style** is expressive and self-enhancing and is based on the "ethical notion that it is not right or good to violate our own or others' basic human rights, such as the right to self-expression or the right to be treated with dignity and respect."[19] In contrast, an **aggressive style** is expressive and self-enhancing and strives to take unfair advantage of others. A **nonassertive style** is characterized by timid and self-denying behavior. Nonassertiveness is ineffective because it gives the other person an unfair advantage.

Managers may improve their communication competence by trying to be more assertive and less aggressive or nonassertive. This can be achieved by using the appropriate nonverbal and verbal behaviors listed in Table 12–1. For instance, managers should attempt to use the nonverbal behaviors of good eye contact, a strong, steady, and audible voice, and selective interruptions. They should avoid nonverbal behaviors such as glaring or little eye contact, threatening gestures, slumped posture, and a weak or whiny voice. Appropriate verbal behaviors include direct and unambiguous language and the use of "I" statements. Inappropriate behaviors consist of swear words

• TABLE 12-1   Communication Styles

Communication Style	Description	Nonverbal Behavior Pattern	Verbal Behavior Pattern
Assertive	Pushing hard without attacking; permits others to influence outcome; expressive and self-enhancing without intruding on others	Good eye contact Comfortable but firm posture Strong, steady, and audible voice Facial expressions matched to message Appropriately serious tone Selective interruptions to ensure understanding	Direct and unambiguous language No attributions or evaluations of other's behavior Use of "I" statements and cooperative "we" statements
Aggressive	Taking advantage of others; expressive and self-enhancing at other's expense	Glaring eye contact Moving or leaning too close Threatening gestures (pointed finger; clenched fist) Loud voice Frequent interruptions	Swear words and abusive language Attributions and evaluations of other's behavior Sexist or racist terms Explicit threats or putdowns
Nonassertive	Encouraging others to take advantage of us; inhibited; self-denying	Little eye contact Downward glances Slumped posture Constantly shifting weight Wringing hands Weak or whiny voice	Qualifiers ("maybe"; "kind of") Fillers ("uh," "you know," "well") Negaters ("It's not really that important"; "I'm not sure")

Source: Adapted in part from James A. Waters, "Managerial Assertiveness," *Business Horizons*, September-October 1982, pp. 24–29.

and abusive language, sexist or racist terms, and qualifiers such as "maybe."

Remember that nonverbal and verbal behaviors should complement and reinforce each other. James Waters, a communication expert, further recommends that assertiveness can be enhanced by using various combinations of the following assertiveness elements:

1. *Describe* the situation or the behavior of people to which you are reacting.
2. *Express* your feelings and/or *explain* what impact the other's behavior has on you.
3. *Empathize* with the other person's position in the situation.
4. *Specify* what changes you would like to see in the situation or in another's behavior and offer to *negotiate* those changes with the other person.
5. *Indicate*, in a nonthreatening way, the possible consequences that will follow if change does not occur.[20]

Waters offers managers the following situational advice when using the various assertiveness elements: (1) *empathize* and *negotiate* with superiors or others on whom you are dependent, (2) *specify* with friends and peers, and (3) *describe* to strangers.

Interaction Involvement

Can you recall a situation in which you were talking with someone who appeared disinterested or preoccupied? How did you feel about this interaction? Contrast these feelings with those based on an interaction with someone who was highly involved in your conversation. As suggested by these examples, **interaction involvement** represents the extent to which an individual participates in or is consciously involved in an ongoing conversation. Individuals who are psychologically and communicatively removed are said to be low in interaction involvement. Such individuals appear withdrawn, preoccupied, or distanced from the interaction. On the other hand, highly involved individuals try to integrate thoughts, feelings, and both nonverbal and verbal behaviors when responding to others. These behaviors make them more sensitive and perceptive during a conversation.

Interaction involvement is influenced by both situational factors and an individual's general orientation to communicating.[21] For example, all of us experience periods of low involvement due to situational factors such as embarrassment, preoccupation, boredom, bad mood, low energy, confusion, and contemplation.[22] These factors are a natural component of the communication process. We now consider measuring interaction involvement.

Measuring General Orientation to Interaction Involvement An individual's general orientation to interaction involvement is composed of three interrelated factors called responsiveness, perceptiveness, and attentiveness. These factors are defined by a communication expert as follows:

> *Responsiveness* is an index of an individual's certainty about how to respond in social situations. *Perceptiveness* is an individual's general sensitivity to: (1) what meanings ought to be applied to others' behavior, and (2) what meanings others have applied to one's own behavior. *Attentiveness* is the extent to which one tends to heed cues in the immediate social environment, especially one's . . . [conversation partner].[23]

Take a moment now to assess your general orientation to interaction involvement by completing the survey in the OB Exercise. Arbitrary norms for the dimensions of *responsiveness* and *attentiveness* are: 3–6 = high, 7–10 = moderate, and 11–15 = low. Norms for *perceptiveness* are: 3–7 = low, 8–11 = moderate, and 12–15 = high. What are your strongest and weakest aspects of interaction involvement?

Research-Findings and Recommendations for Improving Interaction Involvement In contrast to people with low interaction involvement, highly involved individuals are more effective at directing the flow of a conversation, speak more frequently during an ongoing social interaction, and exhibit less distracting nonverbal body movements while speaking. Highly involved individuals also possess higher self-esteem and satisfaction with communication than low-involved people.[24] Overall, research findings support the notion that interaction involvement is an important component of communication competence. Because communication competence affects an individual's career progress and the overall quality of communication in an organization, it is worthwhile to consider methods of improving interaction involvement.

• OB EXERCISE

The Interaction Involvement Scale

Instructions:

Circle your response to each item by using the following scale:

1 = Strongly disagree
2 = Disagree
3 = Neither agree or disagree
4 = Agree
5 = Strongly agree

Responsiveness:

1. Often in conversations, I'm not sure what my role is; that is, I'm not sure how I'm expected to relate to others. 1 2 3 4 5
2. Often in conversations I'm not sure what the other is really saying. 1 2 3 4 5
3. Often I feel sort of "unplugged" from the social situation of which I am part; that is, I'm uncertain of my role, others' motives, and what's happening. 1 2 3 4 5

Perceptiveness:

1. I am keenly aware of how others perceive me during my conversations. 1 2 3 4 5
2. During conversations I am sensitive to others' subtle or hidden meanings. 1 2 3 4 5
3. I am very observant during my conversations with others. 1 2 3 4 5

Attentiveness:

1. My mind wanders during conversations and I often miss parts of what is going on. 1 2 3 4 5
2. Often I will pretend to be listening to someone when in fact I'm thinking about something else. 1 2 3 4 5
3. Often I am preoccupied in my conversations and do not pay complete attention to others. 1 2 3 4 5

Source: Excerpted from Donald J. Cegala, "Affective and Cognitive Manifestations of Interaction Involvement during Unstructured and Competitive Interactions," *Communication Monographs,* December 1984, p. 322.

Assessment, awareness, and behavioral self-management are key aspects of enhancing one's interaction involvement. Your interaction involvement can be improved by consciously increasing your responsiveness, perceptiveness, and attentiveness during conversations. The self-assessment questionnaire in the OB Exercise can be used periodically to monitor your progress. If you notice that situational factors—such as fatigue or preoccupation—are lowering your involvement level, try to tactfully remove yourself from the situation. No involvement may be better than low involvement, which engenders bad feelings from others more highly involved in the conversation.

Sources of Nonverbal Communication

Nonverbal communication is "Any message, sent or received independent of the written or spoken word . . . [It] includes such factors as use of time and space, distance between persons when conversing, use of color, dress,

walking behavior, standing, positioning, seating arrangement, office locations and furnishing.''[25] Due to the prevalence of nonverbal communication
and its significant impact on organizational behavior (including, but not
limited to, perceptions of others, hiring decisions, work attitudes, and turnover),[26] it is important that managers become consciously aware of the
sources of nonverbal communication.

Physical Features   An individual's physical features are important sources of
nonverbal communication. Body type—overweight, muscular, or under-
weight—skin color, clothes, and physical handicaps affect what we infer
about what people actually say and write. Researchers have documented
that positive impressions in the United States are ascribed to those who are
thin, white-skinned, and not physically handicapped.[27] For instance, a recent study of 453 women and men indicated that obese people experienced
more frequent employment discrimination than did nonobese individuals.[28]
Although these tendencies can be criticized as unfair, racist, or sexist, they
still play a key role in communication.

Body Movements and Gestures   Body movements, such as leaning forward or
backward, and gestures, such as pointing, provide additional nonverbal
information. Open body positions such as leaning backward, communicate
immediacy, a term used to represent openness, warmth, closeness, and
availability for communication. *Defensiveness* is communicated by gestures
such as folding arms, crossing hands, and crossing one's legs.[29] Judith Hall,
a communication researcher, conducted a meta-analysis of gender differences in body movements and gestures. Results revealed that women nod-
ded their heads and moved their hands more than men. Leaning forward,
large body shifts, and foot and leg movements were exhibited more frequently by men than women.[30] Although it is both easy and fun to interpret
body movements and gestures, it is important to remember, ''There isn't a
reliable dictionary of gestures, and the meaning of gestures depends on the
context, the actor, the culture, and other factors.''[31] Managers thus need to
be careful when trying to interpret body movements. Inaccurate interpretations can create additional ''noise'' in the communication process.

Touch   Touching is another powerful nonverbal cue. In many cultures,
touch can signal compassion, warmth, attraction, and friendliness. People
tend to touch those they like. A meta-analysis of gender differences in
touching indicated that women do more touching during conversations than
men. Of particular note, however, is the fact that men and women interpret
touching differently. While women differentiate between touching for the
purposes of conveying warmth/friendship and sexual attraction, men may
not.[32] Sexual harassment claims can be reduced by keeping this perceptual
difference in mind.

Facial Expressions   Facial expressions convey a wealth of information. Smiling, for instance, typically represents warmth, happiness, or friendship;
whereas frowning conveys dissatisfaction or anger. Although puckered lips
are used for kissing, during conversations they might convey confusion or
contemplation.

Eye Contact   Eye contact is a strong nonverbal cue that serves four functions in communication. First, eye contact regulates the flow of communication by signaling the beginning and end of conversation. There is a tendency to look away from others when beginning to speak and to look at them when done. Second, gazing (as opposed to glaring) facilitates and monitors feedback because it reflects interest and attention. Third, eye contact conveys emotion. People tend to avoid eye contact when discussing bad news or providing negative feedback. Fourth, gazing relates to the type of relationship between communicators.

Interpersonal Distance Zones   Renowned anthropologist Edward Hall studied the impact of social and personal space on human communication and behavior. He identified four distance zones that regulate interpersonal interactions. These zones differ across cultures. The zones and accompanying distances for Americans are:

- *Intimate distance,* the zone for lovemaking, wrestling, comforting, and protecting, is physical contact to 18 inches.
- *Personal distance* is 1.5 to 4 feet and is used for interpersonal interactions with friends or acquaintances.
- *Social distance,* the zone used for business and casual social interactions, spans 4 to 12 feet.
- *Public distance* is used for impersonal and formal interactions and covers 12 to 25 feet.[33]

The important point to remember is that people strive to maintain a distance zone consistent with their cultural expectations and the nature of the interaction. Violating interpersonal distance zones creates discomfort, which can reduce communication effectiveness. This is particularly true in cross-cultural dealings (as discussed in Chapter 19).

Practical Tips   A communication expert offers the following advice to improve nonverbal communication skills:

Positive nonverbal actions that help to communicate include:
- Maintaining eye contact.
- Occasionally nodding the head in agreement.
- Smiling and showing animation.
- Leaning toward the speaker.
- Speaking at a moderate rate, in a quiet, assuring tone. . . .

Here are some actions . . . to avoid:
- Looking away or turning away from the speaker.
- Closing your eyes.
- Using an unpleasant voice tone.
- Speaking too quickly or too slowly.
- Yawning excessively.[34]

Practice these tips by turning the sound off while watching television, and trying to interpret emotions and interactions, and by watching yourself talk in a mirror. Honest feedback from your friends about your nonverbal communication style also may help.

Active Listening

Some communication experts contend that listening is the keystone communication skill for today's managers.[35] Estimates suggest that managers typically spend about 9 percent of a working day reading, 16 percent writing, 30 percent talking, and 45 percent listening.[35] Moreover, because listening appears to be effortless—we have the cognitive ability to process information three to four times faster than people speak—it is often neglected or taken for granted. Listening involves much more than hearing a message. Hearing is merely the physical component of listening.

Listening is the process of *actively* decoding and interpreting verbal messages. Listening requires cognitive attention and information processing; hearing does not. With these distinctions in mind, we will examine a model of listener comprehension, listening styles, and some practical advice for becoming a more effective listener.

Listener Comprehension Model   Listener comprehension represents the extent to which an individual can recall factual information and draw accurate conclusions and inferences from a verbal message. It is a function of listener, speaker, message, and environmental characteristics (see Figure 12–5). Communication researchers Kittie Watson and Larry Barker con-

• FIGURE 12-5   Listener Comprehension Model

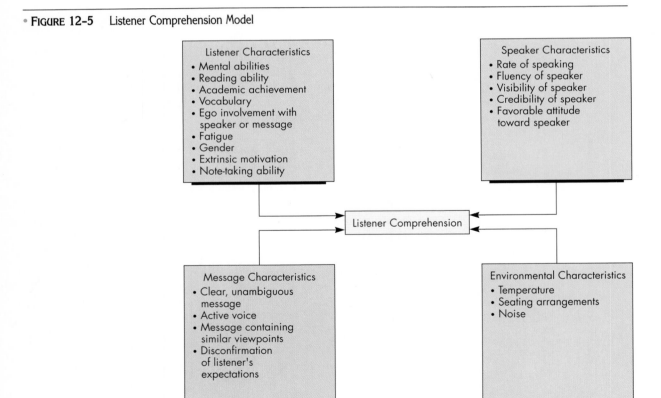

Source: Adapted from discussion in Kittie W. Watson and Larry L. Barker, "Listening Behavior: Definition and Measurement," in *Communication Yearbook 8*, ed. Robert N. Bostrom (Beverly Hills, Calif.: Sage Publications, 1984), pp. 178–97.

ducted a global review of listening behavior research and arrived at the following conclusions. Listening comprehension is positively related to high mental and reading abilities, academic achievements, a large vocabulary, being ego-involved with the speaker, having energy, being female, extrinsic motivation to pay attention, and being able to take good notes. Speakers who talk too fast or too slow, possess disturbing accents or speech patterns, are not visible to the audience, lack credibility, or are disliked have a negative impact on listening comprehension. In contrast, clear messages stated in the active voice increase listening comprehension. The same is true of messages containing viewpoints similar to the listener's or those that disconfirm expectations. Finally, comfortable environmental characteristics and compact seating arrangements enhance listening comprehension.[36]

Listening Styles   A pair of communication experts identified three different listening styles.[37] Their research indicated that people prefer to hear information that is suited to their own listening style. People also tend to speak in a style that is consistent with their own listening style. Because inconsistent styles represent a barrier to effective listening, it is important for managers to understand and respond to the different listening styles. The three listening styles are called "results," "reasons," and "process."

Results-style listeners don't like any beating around the bush. They are interested in hearing the bottom line or result of the communication message first, and then like to ask questions. These behaviors identify a results-style listener:

- They sound direct. Everything is right out front, so you never have to wonder. They may sound blunt or even rude sometimes.
- They are action-oriented.
- They are present-oriented.
- They love to problem-solve. Because of their love of fixing things and their action orientation, they are usually good crisis managers.
- Their first interest is the bottom line.[38]

Reasons-style listeners want to know the rationale for what someone is saying or proposing. They must be convinced about a point of view before accepting it. Typical behaviors exhibited by a reasons-style listener include:

- They are most concerned with whether or not a solution is practical, realistic, and reasonable for the situation.
- They weigh and balance everything. . . .
- If asked a direct question, they frequently answer, "It depends."
- They argue, out loud or internally.
- They expect people to present ideas in an organized way. They have little tolerance and no respect for a "disorderly" mind.
- Their first concern is "Why?"[39]

Process-style listeners like to discuss issues in detail. They prefer to receive background information prior to having a thorough discussion and like to know why an issue is important in the first place. You can identify process-style listeners by watching for these behaviors:

- They are people-oriented. They have a high concern for relationships, believing that people and relationships are the keys to long-term success.
- They like to know the whole story before making a decision.
- They have a high concern for quality and will hold out for a quality solution to a problem, even if it seems unrealistic to others.
- They are future-oriented. They are not only concerned about the future, but they predict what may happen in the future as a result of decisions made today.
- They have on-going conversations. They continue subjects from one conversation to the next.
- Their language and messages tend to be indirect. They imply rather than state the bottom line.
- Their primary interests are *how* and *benefits*.[40]

Managers can gain greater acceptance of their ideas and proposals by adapting the *form* and *content* of a message to fit a receiver's listening style:

1. For a results-style listener, for instance, the sender should present the bottom line at the beginning of the discussion.
2. Explain your rationale to a reasons-style listener.
3. For a process-style listener, describe the process and the benefits.

Becoming a More Effective Listener In addition to following the above recommendations, you can improve your listening skills by avoiding the 10 habits of bad listeners while cultivating the 10 good listening habits (see Table 12–2). Importantly, it takes awareness, effort, and practice to improve one's listening comprehension. Is anyone listening?

• ORGANIZATIONAL COMMUNICATION PATTERNS

Examining organizational communication patterns is a good way to identify factors contributing to effective and ineffective management. For example, research reveals that effective managers, in contrast to ineffective ones, tend to be (1) more communication-oriented and willing to speak up, (2) more receptive to employees, (3) more willing to ask or persuade than to tell, and (4) more open to explaining the "why" of things.[41] With these progressive practices in mind, this section promotes a working knowledge of two important communication patterns: hierarchical communication and the grapevine.

Hierarchical Communication

Hierarchical communication is defined as "those exchanges of information and influence between organizational members, at least one of whom has formal (as defined by official organizational sources) authority to direct and evaluate the activities of other organizational members."[42] This category of

• **TABLE 12-2**   The Keys to Effective Listening

Keys to Effective Listening	The Bad Listener	The Good Listener
1. Find areas of interest.	Tunes out dry subjects	Opportunistic: asks "What's in it for me?"
2. Judge content, not delivery.	Tunes out if delivery is poor	Judges content, skips over delivery errors
3. Hold your fire.	Tends to enter into arguments	Doesn't judge until comprehension is complete
4. Listen for ideas.	Listens for facts	Listens for central themes
5. Be flexible.	Takes intensive notes using only one system	Takes fewer notes. Uses four or five different systems, depending on speaker
5. Work at listening.	Shows no energy output; Attention is faked	Works hard, exhibits active body state
7. Resist distractions.	Is distracted easily	Fights or avoids distractions, tolerates bad habits, knows how to concentrate
8. Exercise your mind.	Resists difficult expository material; seeks light, recreational material	Uses heavier material as exercise for the mind
9. Keep your mind open.	Reacts to emotional words	Interprets color words; does not get hung up on them
10. Capitalize on the fact that *thought* is faster than speech.	Tends to daydream with slow speakers	Challenges, anticipates, mentally summarizes, weighs the evidence, listens between the lines to tone of voice

Source: Lyman K. Steil, "How Well Do You Listen?" *Executive Female*, Special Issue No. 2 (1986), p. 37. Reprinted with permission from *Executive Female*, the bimonthly publication of the National Association for Female Executives.

communication involves the information exchanges depicted in Figure 12–6. Managers provide five types of information through downward communication: job instructions, job rationale, organizational procedures and practices, feedback about performance, and indoctrination of goals. Employees, in turn, communicate information upward about themselves, co-workers and their problems, organizational practices and policies, and what needs to be done and how to do it. Timely and valid hierarchical communication can promote individual and organizational success. Consider Wal-Mart, for example, a company whose success traces in part to the communication network linking its more than 900 stores:

> To stay in touch with employees—or "associates," as they're known in Wal-Martese—CEO David Glass and his lieutenants at the company's out-of-the-way

• **Figure 12-6**   Hierarchical Communication

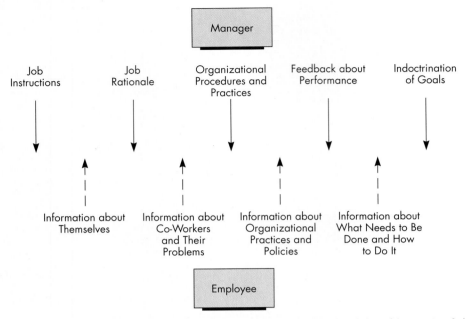

Source: Adapted from Daniel Katz and Robert L. Kahn, *The Social Psychology of Organizations*, 2nd ed. (New York: John Wiley & Sons, 1978).

headquarters in Bentonville, Arkansas, rely on a communications network worthy of the Pentagon. It includes everything from a six-channel satellite system to a private air force of 11 planes, mostly turboprops. Says Glass: "We believe nothing constructive happens in Bentonville. Our grass-roots philosophy is that the best ideas come from people on the firing line." Glass, himself, spends several days a week visiting the stores.[43]

Unfortunately, hierarchical communication systems are not always as effective or accurate as Wal-Mart's.

Research indicates that managers and employees frequently do not agree on the amount and content of information communicated downward. This incongruence is important because it negatively affects employees' job satisfaction and perceptions of intergroup and intragroup conflict.[44] To resolve the problem, organizations must first diagnose any communication "gaps." Companywide employee attitude surveys can be used for this purpose. Results from surveys then can be used to develop communication training programs and to eliminate any barriers to effective communication.[45]

The Grapevine

The term *grapevine* originated from the Civil War practice of stringing battlefield telegraph lines between trees. Today, the **grapevine** represents the unofficial communication system of the informal organization. Information traveling along the grapevine supplements official or formal channels of communication. Although the grapevine can be a source of inaccurate rumors, it functions positively as an early warning signal for organizational

• The grapevine that we speak of today is a term that originated with the stringing of telephone wires during the Civil War.   *(North Wind Picture Archives)*

changes, a medium for creating organizational culture, a mechanism for fostering group cohesiveness, and a way of informally bouncing ideas off others.[46] Evidence indicates that the grapevine is alive and well in today's workplaces.

A national survey of the readers of *Industry Week,* a professional management magazine, revealed that employees used the grapevine as their most frequent source of information.[47] Contrary to general opinion, the grapevine is not necessarily counterproductive. Plugging into the grapevine can help employees, managers, and organizations alike achieve desired results. Consider the following examples:

> Tim Scerba, a communications specialist at Teachers Insurance, heard through the grapevine that a colleague was quietly pursuing a project originally entrusted to him—in effect, an invasion of turf. Fueled with new ambition, Scerba worked harder and faster—and eventually won all the credit. . . .
>
> Ted Klein, president of a public relations firm bearing his name, learned at a casual business lunch that a Fortune 500 company might be interested in retaining his services. In calling the firm to check out the rumor, he landed the account.[48]

To enhance your understanding of the grapevine, we will explore grapevine patterns and research and managerial recommendations for monitoring this often misunderstood system of communication.

Grapevine Patterns   Communication along the grapevine follows predictable patterns (see Figure 12–7). The most frequent pattern is not a single strand or gossip chain, but the cluster pattern.[49] In this case, person A passes along a piece of information to three people, one of whom—person F—tells two others, and then one of those two—person B—tells one other. As illustrated

• **FIGURE 12-7**   Grapevine Patterns

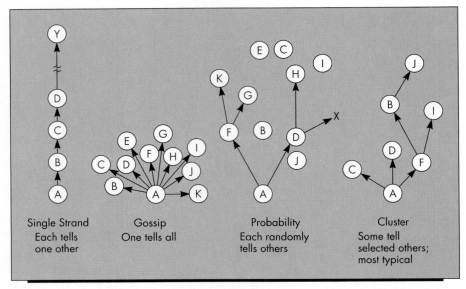

Source: Keith Davis and John W. Newstrom, *Human Behavior at Work: Organizational Behavior,* 7th ed. (New York: McGraw-Hill, 1985), p. 317. Used with permission.

in Figure 12–7, only certain individuals repeat what they hear when the cluster pattern is operating. People who consistently pass along grapevine information to others are called **liaison individuals** or "gossips."

> About 10 percent of the employees on an average grapevine will be highly active participants. They serve as liaisons with the rest of the staff members who receive information but spread it to only a few other people. Usually these liaisons are friendly, outgoing people who are in positions that allow them to cross departmental lines. For example, secretaries tend to be liaisons because they can communicate with the top executive, the janitor, and everyone in between without raising eyebrows.[50]

Effective managers monitor the pulse of work groups by regularly communicating with known liaisons.

Research and Practical Implications   Although research activity on this topic has slowed in recent years, past research about the grapevine provided the following insights; (1) it is faster than formal channels, (2) it is about 75 percent accurate, (3) people rely on it when they are insecure, threatened, or faced with organizational changes, and (4) employees use the grapevine to acquire the majority of their on-the-job information.[51]

The key managerial recommendation is to *monitor* and *influence* the grapevine rather than attempt to control it. Effective managers accomplish this by openly sharing relevant information with employees (see OB in Action). For example, managers can increase the amount of communication by both keeping in touch with liaison individuals and making sure information travels to people "isolated" from the formal communication system. Providing advance notice of departmental or organizational changes, care-

OB IN ACTION

The CEO of Square D, a Manufacturer of Electrical Equipment, Shares Important Information with Employees

At Square D, a leading manufacturer of electrical equipment, Chief Executive Jerre Stead has set up an in-house academy called Vision College. His aim is to slice through the content clutter and get everyone in the company speaking the same language. By 1991 all 19,200 employees of this Palatine, Illinois, company will have been through a two-day program of lectures and seminar that stress the primacy of quality and customer service.

Source: Ronald Henkoff, "Cost Cutting: How to Do It Right," *Fortune*, April 9, 1990, p. 48.

fully listening to employees, and selectively sending information along the grapevine are other ways to influence and monitor the grapevine.[52] Keith Davis, who has studied the grapevine for over 30 years, offers this final piece of advice:

> No administrator in his right mind would try to abolish the management grapevine. It is as permanent as humanity is. Nevertheless, many administrators have abolished the grapevine from their own minds. They think and act without giving adequate weight to it or, worse, try to ignore it. This is a mistake. The grapevine is a factor to be reckoned with in the affairs of management. The administrator should analyze it and should consciously try to influence it.[53]

• BARRIERS TO EFFECTIVE COMMUNICATION

Barriers to communication are personal and environmental characteristics that interfere with the accurate transmission or reception of a message. It is important for managers to be aware of these barriers because they reduce the accuracy of communication. We begin by highlighting personal barriers and follow with an overview of a unique type of communication distortion that occurs between managers and employees.

Personal Barriers to Effective Communication

Carl Rogers, the renowned psychologist, identified two personal characteristics that interfere with interpersonal communication.[54] They are (1) natural tendency to evaluate or judge a sender's message and (2) not listening with understanding (see Figure 12–8). To highlight the natural tendency to evaluate, consider how you might respond to the statement "I like the book you are reading." What would you say? Your likely response is to approve or disapprove with the statement. You may say, "I agree," or alternatively, "I disagree, the book is boring." The point is that we all tend to evaluate messages from our own point of view or frame of reference. The tendency to evaluate messages is greatest when one has strong feelings or emotions about the issue being discussed.

• **FIGURE 12-8**   Barriers to Effective Communication

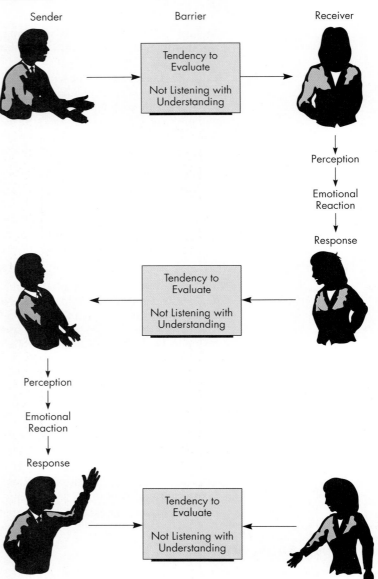

An inability to listen with understanding is the second personal barrier to effective communication. **Listening with understanding** occurs when a receiver can "see the expressed idea and attitude from the other person's point of view, to sense how it feels to him, to achieve his frame of reference in regard to the thing he is talking about."[55] Listening with understanding reduces defensiveness and improves accuracy in perceiving a message. Let us consider the example of how these personal barriers influence the communication process depicted in Figure 12–8.

• Square D's CEO instituted Vision College to improve the flow and accuracy of information throughout the company. *(Courtesy of Square D Company/© Richard Derk)*

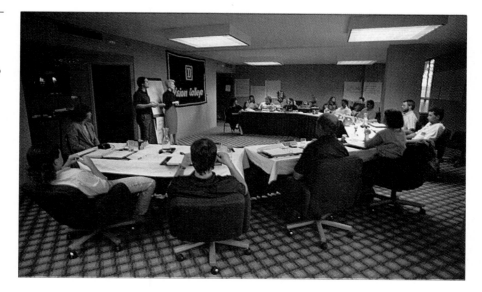

An Example of Communication Barriers The sender tells a co-worker, the receiver, that she needs to put in more hours to complete a big project they are working on jointly. The barrier of *evaluation* causes the receiver to interpret what this message "really" means. In turn, this interpretation is clouded by the barrier of *not listening with understanding*. That is, it is hard for the receiver to consider the sender's frame of reference when the receiver already is working 55 hours a week. As such, the receiver may conclude that the sender believes she is not working hard enough on the project or that her work is inferior. This perception then is likely to create a negative emotional response such as anger. Therefore, the receiver might respond defensively to the original sender by saying, "I'll put in as much effort as you do." Due to the same communication barriers, the original sender will most likely misperceive the response. He may conclude that the receiver isn't a team player or lacks commitment to the project. In the end, both communicators are talking, but neither is listening. How can these personal barriers be reduced?

Reducing the Personal Barriers Because one can not totally eliminate the natural tendency to evaluate messages, *awareness of this barrier* is a first step toward improving interpersonal communication. The second step is to have both parties to the communication be able to *come to understand* each other's point of view. This can be initiated by a third party to the exchange, or by one of the parties, independently. Exaggerated perceptions and defensive responses can be reduced by listening with understanding. Returning to our example, the receiver might not have responded defensively to the initial message if she had known that the sender was getting extreme pressure from his boss to complete the project ahead of schedule. Empathetic listening by one party to the exchange should serve as a catalyst to create further understanding.

Communication Distortion between Managers and Employees

Communication distortion occurs when an employee purposely modifies the content of a message, thereby reducing the accuracy of communication between managers and employees. Employees tend to engage in this practice because of workplace politics, a desire to manage impressions, and fear of how a manager might respond to a message.[56] Communication experts point out the organizational problems caused by distortion:

> Distortion is an important problem in organizations because modifications to messages cause misdirectives to be transmitted, nondirectives to be issued, incorrect information to be passed on, and a variety of other problems related to both the quantity and quality of information.[57]

Knowledge of the antecedents or causes of communication distortion can help managers avoid or limit these problems.

Antecedents of Distortion   Studies have identified four situational antecedents of distortion in upward communication (see Figure 12–9). Distortion tends to increase when supervisors have high upward influence and/or power. Employees also tend to modify or distort information when they aspire to move upward and when they do not trust their supervisors.[58] Because managers generally do not want to reduce their upward influence or curb their subordinates' desire for upward mobility, they can reduce distortion in several ways. First, managers can de-emphasize power differences between themselves and their subordinates. Second, they can enhance trust through a meaningful performance review process that rewards actual performance. Third, managers can encourage staff feedback by conducting smaller, more informal meetings. Fourth, they can establish performance goals that encourage employees to focus on problems rather than personalities. Finally, distortion can be limited by encouraging dialogue between those with opposing viewpoints.[59]

• **FIGURE 12-9**   Sources of Distortion in Upward Communication

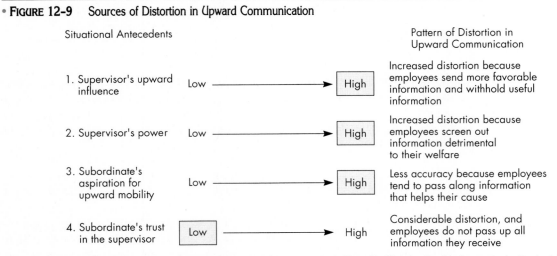

Source: Adapted in part from Janet Fulk and Sirish Mani, "Distortion of Communication in Hierarchical Relationships," in *Communication Yearbook 9*, ed. Margaret L. McLaughlin (Beverly Hills, Calif.: Sage Publications, 1986).

461

• OB EXERCISE

A Self-Assessment of Antecedents and Outcomes of Distortion in Upward Communication

Instructions:
Circle your response to each question by using the following scale:
1 = Strongly disagree
2 = Disagree
3 = Neither agree nor disagree
4 = Agree
5 = Strongly agree

Supervisor's upward influence:
In general, my immediate supervisor can have a big impact
on my career in this organization.   1   2   3   4   5

Aspiration for upward mobility:
It is very important for me to progress upward in this
organization.   1   2   3   4   5

Supervisory trust:
I feel free to discuss the problems and difficulties of my job
with my immediate supervisor without jeopardizing my
position or having it "held against" me later.   1   2   3   4   5

Withholding information:
I provide my immediate supervisor with a small amount of
the total information I receive at work.   1   2   3   4   5

Selective disclosure:
When transmitting information to my immediate supervisor,
I often emphasize those aspects that make me look good.   1   2   3   4   5

Satisfaction with communication:
In general, I am satisfied with the pattern of communication
between my supervisor and me.   1   2   3   4   5

Source: Adapted and excerpted in part from Karlene H. Roberts and Charles A. O'Reilly III, "Measuring Organizational Communication," *Journal of Applied Psychology*, June 1974, p. 323.

What Is Your Potential for Communication Distortion? To assess the communication pattern between you and your immediate supervisor, please take a moment to complete the survey in the OB Exercise. Think of your present (or last) job when responding to the various items. Do your responses to the first three statements suggest low or high potential for distortion? (Arbitrary norms for each of the first three items are: 1–2 = low, 3 = moderate, and 4–5 = high.) How does this assessment mesh with your responses to the last three statements, which measure three outcomes of distortion?

• SUMMARY OF KEY CONCEPTS

A. Managers spend the majority of their workday communicating with others. The effectiveness of this communication is significantly related to an individual's job satisfaction and performance as well as to overall organizational performance.

B. Communication is a process of consecutively linked elements. Historically, this process was described in terms of a conduit model. Criticisms of this model led to development of a perceptual process model of communication that depicts receivers as information processors who create the meaning of messages in their own mind. Because receivers' interpretations of messages often differ from those intended by senders, miscommunication is a common occurrence.

C. Selecting media is a key component of communication effectiveness. Media selection is based on the interaction between the information richness of a medium and the complexity of the problem/situation at hand. Information richness ranges from low to high and is a function of four factors: speed of feedback, characteristics of the channel, type of communication, and language source. Problems/situations range from simple to complex. Effective communication occurs when the richness of the medium matches the complexity of the problem/situation. From a contingency perspective, richer media need to be used as problems/situations become more complex.

D. Communication competence reflects the extent to which an individual is an effective communicator. It is determined by an individual's communication abilities/traits, situational factors, and the individuals involved in an interaction. An assertive communication style is more effective than either an aggressive or a nonassertive style. Effective communicators tend to exhibit high interaction involvement and active listening.

E. There are several identifiable sources of nonverbal communication that affect communication effectiveness. Physical features, body movements and gestures, touch, facial expressions, eye contact, and interpersonal distance zones are important nonverbal cues. Listening is the process of actively decoding and interpreting verbal messages. Listener characteristics, speaker characteristics, message characteristics, and environmental characteristics influence listener comprehension.

F. Communication experts identified three unique types of listening styles. A results-style listener likes to hear the bottom line or result of a communication at the beginning of a conversation. Reasons-style listeners want to know the rationale for what someone is saying or proposing. Process-style listeners like to discuss issues in detail.

G. Hierarchical communication patterns describe exchanges of information between managers and employees they supervise. Managers provide five types of downward communication: job instructions, job rationale, organizational procedures and practices, feedback about performance, and indoctrination of goals. Employees communicate information upward about themselves, co-workers and their problems, organizational practices and policies, and what needs to be done and how to do it.

H. The grapevine is the unofficial communication system of the informal organization. Communication along the grapevine follows four predictable patterns: single strand, gossip, probability, and cluster. The cluster pattern is the most common.

I. Two personal characteristics create important barriers to interpersonal communications: the natural tendency to evaluate or judge a sender's message and the inability to listen with understanding. Awareness of the evaluation tendency is the first step toward eliminating barriers. The second is attempting to empathize with the other's point of view—thus listening with understanding.

J. Communication distortion is a common problem that consists of modifying the content of a message. Employees distort upward communication when their supervisor has high upward influence and/or power. Distortion also increases when employees aspire to move upward and when they do not trust their supervisor.

• KEY TERMS

communication	listening
perceptual model of communication	results-style
noise	reasons-style
information richness	process-style
communication competence	hierarchical communication
assertive style	grapevine
aggressive style	liaison individuals
nonassertive style	barriers to communication
interaction involvement	listening with understanding
nonverbal communication	communication distortion

• DISCUSSION QUESTIONS

1. Describe a situation where you had trouble decoding a message. What caused the problem?

2. What are some sources of noise that interfere with communication during a class lecture, an encounter with a professor in his or her office, and a movie?

3. Which of the three zones of communication in Figure 12–3 (overload, effective, oversimplification) do you think is most common in today's large organizations? What is your rationale?

4. Would you describe your prevailing communication style as assertive, aggressive, or nonassertive? How can you tell? Would your style help or hinder you as a manager?

5. Are you good at reading nonverbal communication? Give some examples.

6. What is your listening style? Give behavioral examples to support your assessment.

7. What is your personal experience with the grapevine? Do you see it as a positive or negative factor in the workplace? Explain.

8. What steps do you need to take to become a better listener? Explain.

9. Which personal barrier to effective communication is more difficult to reduce? Explain.
10. Have you ever distorted upward communication? What was your reason? Was it related to one of the four antecedents of communication distortion? Explain.

BACK TO THE OPENING CASE

Now that you have read Chapter 12, you should be able to answer the following questions about the case on electronic meetings:

1. How do electronic meetings reduce noise in the communication process? Explain.
2. Are electronic meetings consistent with the contingency model for selecting media? Discuss your rationale.
3. What type of communication style is likely to be most effective during an electronic meeting? Explain.
4. Would electronic meetings lead to more or less communication distortion? Explain.

• EXERCISE 12

Objectives

1. To demonstrate the relative effectiveness of communicating assertively, aggressively, and nonassertively.
2. To give you hands-on experience with different styles of communication.

Introduction

Research shows that assertive communication is more effective than either an aggressive or nonassertive style. This *role-playing exercise* is designed to increase your ability to communicate assertively. Your task is to use different communication styles while attempting to resolve the work-related problems of a poor performer.

Instructions

Divide into groups of three and read the "Poor Performer" and "Store Manager" roles on p. 465. Then decide who will play the poor performer role, who will play the managerial role, and who will be the observer. The observer will be asked to provide feedback to the manager after each role play. When playing the managerial role, you should first attempt to resolve the problem by using an aggressive communication style. Attempt to achieve your objective by using the nonverbal and verbal behavior patterns associated with the aggressive style shown in Table 12–1. Take about four to six minutes to act out the instructions. The observer should give feedback to the manager after completing the role play. The observer should comment on how the employee responded to the aggressive behaviors displayed by the manager.

After feedback is provided on the first role play, the person playing the manager should then try to resolve the problem with a nonassertive style. Observers once again should provide feedback. Finally, the manager should confront the problem with an assertive style. Once again, rely on the relevant nonverbal and verbal behavior patterns presented in Table 12–1 and take four to six minutes to act out each scenario. Observers should try to provide detailed feedback on how effectively the manager exhibited nonverbal and verbal assertive behaviors. Be sure to provide positive and constructive feedback.

After completing these three role plays, switch roles: Manager becomes observer, observer become poor performer, and poor performer becomes the manager. When these role plays are completed, switch roles once again.

Role: Poor Performer

You sell shoes full-time for a national chain of shoe stores. During the last month you have been absent three times without giving your manager a reason. The quality of your work has been slipping. You have a lot of creative excuses when your boss tries to talk to you about your performance.

When playing this role, feel free to invent a personal problem that you may eventually want to share with your manager. However, make the manager dig for information about this problem. Otherwise, respond to your manager's comments as you normally would.

Role: Store Manager

You manage a store for a national chain of shoe stores. In the privacy of your office, you are talking to one of your salespeople who has had three unexcused absences from work during the last month. (This is excessive, according to company guidelines, and must be corrected.) The quality of his or her work has been slipping. Customers have complained that this person is rude, and co-workers have told you this individual isn't carrying his or her fair share of the work. You are fairly sure this person has some sort of personal problem. You want to identify that problem and get him or her back on the right track.

Questions for Consideration/Class Discussion

1. What drawbacks of the aggressive and nonassertive styles did you observe?
2. What were major advantages of the assertive style?
3. What were the most difficult aspects of trying to use an assertive style?
4. How important was nonverbal communication during the various role plays? Explain with examples.

• NOTES

[1] Robert Levering, Milton Moskowitz, and Michael Katz, *The 100 Best Companies to Work for in America* (Reading, Mass.: Addison-Wesley Publishing, 1984), p. *ix*.

[2] See Elmore R. Alexander, Marilyn M. Helms, and Ronnie D. Wilkins, "The Relationship between Supervisory Communication and Subordinate Performance and Satisfaction among Professionals," *Public Personnel Management*, Winter 1989, pp. 415–29.

[3] Results from the innovation study are discussed in J. David Johnson, "Effects of Communicative Factors on Participation in Innovations," *The Journal of Business Communication*, Winter 1990, pp. 7–24. For details on the second study, see Robert A. Snyder and James H. Morris, "Organizational Communication and Performance," *Journal of Applied Psychology*, August 1984, pp. 461–65.

[4] Supporting evidence can be found in William L. Gardner and Mark J. Martinko, "Impression Management: An Observational Study Linking Audience Characteristics with Verbal Self-Presentations," *Academy of Management Journal*, March 1988, pp. 42–65; and Fred Luthans and Janet K. Larsen, "How Managers Really Communicate," *Human Relations*, February 1986, pp. 161–78.

[5] Robert E. Levinson, "How's That Again?: Execs: The World's Worst Communicators," *Management World*, July–August 1986, p. 40.

[6] James L. Bowditch and Anthony F. Buono, *A Primer on Organizational Behavior* (New York: John Wiley & Sons, 1985), p. 81.

[7] For a review of these criticisms, see Stephen R. Axley, "Managerial and Organizational Communication in Terms of the Conduit Metaphor," *Academy of Management Review*, July 1984, pp. 428–37.

[8] Descriptions are provided by Robert E. Ault, "Draw on New Lines of Communication," *Personnel Journal*, September 1986, pp. 72–77.

[9] Details of this study can be found in Cynthia Gallois and Victor J. Callan, "Decoding Emotional Messages: Influence of Ethnicity, Sex, Message Type, and Channel," *Journal of Personality and Social Psychology*, October 1986, pp. 755–62.

[10] Axley, "Managerial and Organizational Communication in Terms of the Conduit Metaphor," p. 432.

[11] "The Revival of Productivity: The U.S. Is Poised for a Strong, Sustained Surge in Worker Efficiency," *Business Week*, February 13, 1984, p. 100.

[12] Richard L. Daft and Robert H. Lengel, "Information Richness: A New Approach to Managerial Behavior and Organization Design," in *Research in Organizational Behavior*, ed. Barry M. Staw and Larry L. Cummings (Greenwich, Conn.: JAI Press, 1984), p. 196.

[13] For a summary of this research, see Daft and Lengel, "Information Richness: A New Approach to Managerial Behavior and Organization Design," pp. 191–233.

[14] See Ronald E. Rice and Douglas E. Shook, "Relationships of Job Categories and Organizational Levels to Use of Communication Channels, Including Electronic Mail: A Meta-Analysis and Extension," *Journal of Management Studies*, March 1990, pp. 195–229.

[15] Results from these studies can be found in Vincent S. DiSalvo, Evelyn Nikkel, and Craig Monroe, "Theory and Practice: A Field Investigation and Identification of Group Members' Perceptions of Problems Facing Natural Work Groups," *Small Group Behavior*, November 1989, pp. 551–67; and Beverly Davenport Sypher and Theodore E. Zorn, Jr., "Communication-Related Abilities and Upward Mobility: A Longitudinal Investigation," *Human Communication Research*, Spring 1986, pp. 420–31.

16 Donald J. Cegala, "Interaction Involvement: A Cognitive Dimension of Communicative Competence," *Communication Education,* April 1981, p. 110.

17 E. S. Browning, "Unhappy Returns: After Living Abroad, Japanese Find It Hard to Adjust Back Home," *The Wall Street Journal,* May 6, 1986, p. 1.

18 Results from a work-related study are presented in Dominic A. Infante and William I. Gorden, "Superiors' Argumentativeness and Verbal Aggressiveness as Predictors of Subordinates' Satisfaction," *Human Communication Research,* Fall 1985, pp. 117–25. A consumer study was conducted by Marsha L. Richins, "An Analysis of Consumer Interaction Styles in the Marketplace," *Journal of Consumer Research,* June 1983, pp. 73–82.

19 James A. Waters, "Managerial Assertiveness," *Business Horizons,* September–October 1982, p. 25.

20 Ibid., p. 27.

21 For a discussion about the components of interaction involvement, see Donald J. Cegala, Grant T. Savage, Claire C. Brunner, and Anne B. Conrad, "An Elaboration of the Meaning of Interaction Involvement: Toward the Development of a Theoretical Concept," *Communication Monographs,* December 1982, pp. 229–48.

22 Based on discussion found in Erving Goffman, *Interaction Ritual: Essays in Face-to-Face Behavior* (Chicago: Aldine, 1967).

23 Donald J. Cegala, "Affective and Cognitive Manifestations of Interaction Involvement during Unstructured and Competitive Interactions," *Communication Monographs,* December 1984, p. 321.

24 Results are found in Cegala, Savage, Brunner, and Conrad, "An Elaboration of the Meaning of Interaction Involvement: Toward the Development of a Theoretical Concept," pp. 229–48; Cegala, "Affective and Cognitive Manifestations of Interaction Involvement during Unstructured and Competitive Interactions," pp. 320–38; and Cegala, "Interaction Involvement: A Cognitive Dimension of Communicative Competence."

25 Walter D. St. John, "You Are What You Communicate," *Personnel Journal,* October 1985, p. 40.

26 The impact of nonverbal cues on selection decisions was examined by Angelo J. Kinicki, Chris A. Lockwood, Peter W. Hom, and Rodger W. Griffeth, "Interviewer Predictions of Applicant Qualifications and Interviewer Validity: Aggregate and Individual Analyses," *Journal of Applied Psychology,* October 1990, pp. 477–86. An interesting discussion of how interviewers can use nonverbal cues to evaluate job applicants is provided by Pauline E. Henderson, "Communication: Communication without Words," *Personnel Journal,* January 1989, pp. 22–29.

27 For a summary of this research, see Karlene H. Roberts, "Communicating in Organizations," in *Modules in Management,* ed. James E. Rosenzweig and Fremont E. Kast (Chicago: Science Research Associates, 1984).

28 Results from this study can be found in Esther D. Rothblum, Pamela A. Brand, Carol T. Miller, and Helen A. Oetjen, "The Relationship between Obesity, Employment Discrimination, and Employment-Related Victimization," *Journal of Vocational Behavior,* December 1990, pp. 251–66.

29 Supporting research is presented in Peter A. Anderson, "Nonverbal Immediacy in Interpersonal Communication," in *Multichannel Integrations of Nonverbal Behavior,* ed. Aron W. Siegman and Stanley Feldstein (Hillsdale, N.J.: Lawrence Erlbaum, 1985), pp. 1–36.

30 Related research is summarized by Judith A. Hall, "Male and Female Nonverbal Behavior," in *Multichannel Integrations of Nonverbal Behavior,* ed. Aron W. Siegman and Stanley Feldstein (Hillsdale, N.J.: Lawrence Erlbaum, 1985), pp. 195–226.

[31] Roberts, "Communicating in Organizations," p. 15.

[32] Touching research is reviewed by Brenda Major, "Gender Patterns in Touching Behavior," in *Gender and Nonverbal Behavior,* ed. Nancy M. Henley (New York: Springer-Verlag, 1981). Meta-analytic results can be found in Hall, "Male and Female Nonverbal Behavior."

[33] Based on Edward T. Hall, *The Hidden Dimension* (Garden City, N.Y.: Doubleday, 1966).

[34] St. John, "You Are What You Communicate," p. 43.

[35] Estimates are provided in both Joy Hart Seibert, "Listening in the Organizational Context," in *Listening Behavior: Measurement and Application,* ed. Robert N. Bostrom (New York: The Guilford Press, 1990, pp. 119–27); and Donald W. Caudill and Regina M. Donaldson, "Effective Listening Tips for Managers," *Administrative Management,* September 1986, pp. 22–23.

[36] For a summary of supporting research, see Kittie W. Watson and Larry L. Barker, "Listening Behavior: Definition and Measurement," in *Communication Yearbook 8,* ed. Robert N. Bostrom (Beverly Hills, Calif.: Sage Publications, 1984); and Raymond W. Preiss and Lawrence R. Wheeles, "Affective Responses in Listening: A Meta-Analysis of Receiver Apprehension Outcomes," in *Listening Behavior: Measurement and Application,* ed. Robert N. Bostrom (New York: The Guilford Press, 1990, pp. 91–118).

[37] For a thorough discussion of the different listening styles, see Ruth T. Bennett and Rosemary V. Wood, "Effective Communication via Listening Styles," *Business,* April–June 1989, pp. 45–48.

[38] Bennett and Wood, "Effective Communication via Listening Styles," p. 46.

[39] Bennett and Wood, "Effective Communication via Listening Styles," p. 47.

[40] Bennett and Wood, "Effective Communication via Listening Styles," p. 46.

[41] Charles Redding, *Communication within the Organization: An Interpretive Review of Theory and Research* (New York: Industrial Communication Council, 1972).

[42] Fredric M. Jablin, "Superior-Subordinate Communication: The State of the Art," *Psychological Bulletin,* November 1979, p. 1202.

[43] Sarah Smith, "Quality of Management," *Fortune,* January 29, 1990, p. 46.

[44] See Mel E. Schnake, Michael P. Dumler, Daniel S. Cochran, and Timothy R. Barnett, "Effects of Differences in Superior and Subordinate Perceptions of Superiors' Communication Practices," *The Journal of Business Communication,* Winter 1990, pp. 37–50.

[45] A description of how to use attitude surveys for identifying communication gaps is presented by Stephen L. Guinn, "Surveys Capture Untold Story," *HRMagazine,* September 1990, pp. 64–66.

[46] Organizational benefits of the grapevine are discussed by Robert Brody, "Gossip: Pros and Cons," *USAIR Magazine,* November 1989, pp. 100–104.

[47] Results can be found in Stanley J. Modic, "Grapevine Rated Most Believable," *Industry Week,* May 15, 1989, pp. 11, 14.

[48] Robert Brody, "I Heard It through the Grapevine," *Executive Female,* September–October 1985, p. 22.

[49] See Keith Davis, "Management Communication and the Grapevine," *Harvard Business Review,* September–October 1953, pp. 43–49.

[50] Hugh B. Vickery III, "Tapping into the Employee Grapevine," *Association Management,* January 1984, pp. 59–60.

[51] Earlier research is discussed by Davis, "Management Communication and the Grapevine"; and Roy Rowan, "Where Did *That* Rumor Come From?" *Fortune,* August 13, 1979, pp. 130–31, 134, 137. More recent research is discussed in "Pruning

the Company Grapevine,'' *Supervision*, September 1986, p. 11; and Robert Half, ''Managing Your Career: 'How Can I Stop the Gossip?''' *Management Accounting*, September 1987, p. 27.

[52] For an interesting example of how the grapevine can be used to encourage employees to use an employee assistance program, see Robert Basso, ''A Consumer's Grapevine in an Employee Assistance Program,'' *Employee Assistance Quarterly*, 1989, pp. 1–10.

[53] Davis, ''Management Communication and the Grapevine,'' p. 49.

[54] For a thorough discussion of these barriers, see Carl R. Rogers and F. J. Roethlisberger, ''Barriers and Gateways to Communication,'' *Harvard Business Review*, July–August 1952, pp. 46–52.

[55] Rogers and Roethlisberger, ''Barriers and Gateways to Communication,'' p. 47.

[56] See Patricia M. Fandt and Gerald R. Ferris, ''The Management of Information and Impressions: When Employees Behave Opportunistically,'' *Organizational Behavior and Human Decision Processes*, February 1990, pp. 140–58.

[57] Janet Fulk and Sirish Mani, ''Distortion of Communication in Hierarchical Relationships,'' in *Communication Yearbook 9*, ed. Margaret L. McLaughlin (Beverly Hills, Calif.: Sage Publications, 1986), p. 483.

[58] For a review of this research, see Fulk and Mani, ''Distortion of Communication in Hierarchical Relationships,'' pp. 483–510.

[59] Based on discussion found in Walter Kiechel III, ''How to Escape the Echo Chamber,'' *Fortune*, June 18, 1990, pp. 129–30.

UNDERSTANDING AND MANAGING ORGANIZATIONAL PROCESSES AND PROBLEMS

CHAPTER

13

Performance Appraisal, Feedback, and Rewards

When you finish studying the material in this chapter, you should be able to:

- Identify four key components of the performance appraisal process.
- Explain how the trait, behavioral, and results approaches to performance appraisal vary and discuss why a contingency approach has been suggested.

- Identify two conflicting objectives of performance appraisal and explain how managers can satisfy both.
- Define the term *feedback* and identify its two main functions.
- Identify three different sources of feedback and discuss how we perceive and cognitively evaluate feedback.
- List at least three practical lessons we have learned from feedback research.
- Contrast the equity and equality reward norms.

- Discuss the impact that incentive bonuses have on employee motivation and performance.
- Explain the differences between profit sharing and gainsharing plans.
- Identify at least four ways managers can improve pay-for-performance plans.

OPENING CASE 13

PepsiCo Teaches Eagles to Fly in Formation

Sharon Hoogstraten

Grab any Wall Street analyst by the lapels and he'll tell you Pepsi-Co is a brilliant marketing company. [The $15 billion-dollar-a-year company is best known for its Pepsi-Cola and Frito-Lay products, and Taco Bell, Pizza Hut, and Kentucky Fried Chicken restaurants.] Well, sure, but then ask CEO Wayne Calloway how it got that way and he'll talk *not* about those slick ads starring Madonna and Michael Jackson, but about what he calls the three P's: "people, people, people." Ah, touchy-feely management? Anything but. Behind Calloway's alluringly alliterative slogan lies the country's most sophisticated and comprehensive system for turning bright young people into strong managers. Says he: "We take eagles and teach them to fly in formation."

Described by colleagues as "tough as nails," Calloway runs a boot camp for managers that makes Parris Island look like Coney Island. This 53-year-old CEO, who with a bald head and aquiline nose looks himself a bit like an eagle, sets back-breaking

standards and raises them methodically each year. Those who can't cut it wash out. To prove himself, each manager gets to act like an entrepreneur—risk taking is *de rigeur*, memos scarce, meetings few, and second-guessing rare. Sixty-hour weeks are typical, and managers often work Saturdays and Sundays. But teamwork counts too. If the team says move to Patagonia, you move. Although only aggressive achievers survive at PepsiCo, those who do seem to love it. Perched in Calloway's office in bucolic Purchase, New York, 30 miles north of Manhattan, is a bronze eagle, a gift from his managers, bearing the inscription "We're proud to fly in your formation."

PepsiCo takes people development more seriously than perhaps any other American corporation. Calloway spends up to two months every year personally reviewing the performance of his top 550 managers, discussing their futures with their bosses and with the personnel department. Calloway, who says he knows most of the 550 managers and spends anywhere from five to 30 minutes reviewing each one, states with conviction, "There's nothing I do that's more important." In all, he spends 40 percent of his time on people issues. He expects the people below him to do the same, so that by the end of each year every one of the company's 20,000 managers knows exactly where he or she stands.

To the winners go spoils— first-class air travel, fully loaded company cars, stock options,

bonuses that in good years can hit 90 percent of salary for top managers. Promotions come fast— every two to three years is standard. While corporate politics will always exist, PepsiCo strives to be the closest an organization of this size can come to a meritocracy. In the words of former chairman Donald Kendall, "PepsiCo is the ultimate capitalistic engine." . . .

At the heart of PepsiCo's Darwinian system are two distinctly different types of management evaluations. One is designed to weed out the weak and the other to nurture the strong. The first, called the annual performance review, requires a boss to sit down with each of his managers at least once a year and discuss performance. The focus is on what the manager actually did this year to make a big difference in the business, not whether he's a nice guy or wears the right color socks. Did he meet his sales target? Did he develop a successful new taco chip or soda commercial? Says Michael Jordan, the hard-driving CEO of Frito-Lay: "Nothing is ever good enough." If the manager met his goals, fine. His boss then typically ups the standards for next year.

But pity the manager who isn't getting results. First the boss will try to find out why and help him fix it, but after a year or two of missing the mark, the loser's a goner. Brenda Barnes, a fast-rising, 35-year-old Pepsi-Cola vice president with 700 people under her control, sums it up best when she says, "We'll never be nor should we be a warm and cuddly

OPENING CASE 13

(concluded)

environment." There is a merciful side to all this. People tend to get weeded out early in their careers rather than later, when it's much harder to find another job. . . .

This doesn't mean that the so-called "soft side" of management gets completely ignored. The company realizes that its tough style can sometimes get out of hand. Says Jordan of Frito-Lay: "We've got a lot of bright guys who piss people off." To help remedy that, PepsiCo has a feedback program in which the bosses get evaluated by their subordinates in confidential reports. Says the man who runs the PepsiCo feedback program, Robert Stringer of Sherbrooke Associates in Lexington, Massachusetts: "Managers won't get any better unless they look in the mirror occasionally."

In one case a manager at Pepsi-Cola who fits the mold of what's known around the company as Pepsi Pretty—from a good school, moving like a rocket, and thinks he walks on water—was getting great business results. But then he read his feedback reports from his underlings. They perceived him as cold, aloof, and manipulative, the kind of guy who would bark out orders at a meeting and then leave. Shocked, Mr. Pepsi Pretty tried to change his ways by sharing his ideas and spending more time with his people. Though he didn't completely change from a Mr. Hyde to a Dr. Jekyll, the manager found his feedback reports the following year to be much more positive. Yes, participative management works even at PepsiCo. . . .

As sure as geese head south at the first signs of cold, PepsiCo every winter carries out the second step of its evaluation process, dubbed human resource planning or HRP. The idea is to think seriously about the careers of PepsiCo's 20,000 managers, deciding where and how each can best help the corporation. During the two months Calloway spends discussing the performance of each of the 550 managers directly under him, he makes a point of challenging each manager's boss by asking hard questions about the person's potential.

The managers then get divided into four categories. Those at the bottom are out. In the middle, people are separated into those who need more time on the job or special training, and those who are promotable but have nowhere to go at present. The top group gets promoted. Some stars get moved to a more challenging job within the division, others get shifted to a different division or function, and still others get shipped overseas. Says Calloway: "We believe that different experiences make great managers."

One drawback to this approach: fast promotions can mean that a company loses continuity. Just when a marketing manager is putting the final touches on a Frito-Lay promotional campaign, for instance, he might be yanked off to run the Kentucky Fried Chicken division in Swaziland. . . .

Once the two-step evaluation system is up and running, it's time to start stressing values, and at PepsiCo that means a strong sense of ownership. The company encourages managers to make decisions on their own and make them fast. A few years back Roger Enrico, CEO of PepsiCo Worldwide Beverages, the company's $4.6-billion-a-year soft drink arm, decided to sign up pop star Michael Jackson for a Pepsi commercial at a record $5 million fee. He didn't telephone CEO Kendall to tell him what he was doing until a few hours before the contracts were to be signed. Enrico says blithely, "It didn't occur to me to tell him." . . .

PepsiCo deeply believes that managers who act like owners, run lean, and get big results should get big rewards. PepsiCo treats its managers extremely well. Top middle managers earn between $96,000 and $144,000 annually, not counting bonuses, stock options, and other perks. . . . How does it justify this largess? Says Roger Enrico: "Treating the people well who produce is cheaper than having a big bureaucracy following them around trying to keep down costs."

For Discussion

What do you like or dislike the most about PepsiCo's performance evaluation system?

• Additional discussion questions linking this case with the following material appear at the end of this chapter.

Source: Excerpted from Brian Dumaine, "Those Highflying PepsiCo Managers," *Fortune*, April 10, 1989, pp. 78–80, 84, 86. © 1989 The Time Inc. Magazine Company. All rights reserved.

P roductivity experts tell us that we need to work smarter, not harder. While it is true that a sound education and appropriate training are needed if one is to work smarter, the process does not end there. Today's employees need instructive performance appraisals, supportive feedback, and desired rewards if they are to translate their knowledge into improved productivity. As Figure 13–1 illustrates, constructive performance appraisals, feedback, and rewards channel effort into stable, strong job performance. These coordinated and systematic human resource management tools give life to the motivation theories presented earlier. On the other hand, a weak or uncoordinated appraisal/feedback/reward system can derail even well-intentioned effort. This chapter will help you integrate and apply concepts you have acquired about individual differences, motivation, and communication.

• PERFORMANCE APPRAISAL: DEFINITION AND COMPONENTS

In everyday life, it is hard to escape being on the receiving end of some sort of performance appraisal. There are report cards all through school, win-loss records in organized sports, and periodic meetings with one's boss. For managers, who are in the position of both giving and receiving them, performance appraisals are an especially important consideration. As used here, **performance appraisal** involves the judgmental evaluation of a jobholder's traits, behavior, or accomplishments as a basis for making important personnel decisions. A recent survey of 106 industrial psychologists identified the top 10 uses for performance appraisal data. In diminishing order of importance, they are used for:

1. Salary administration
2. Performance feedback
3. Identifying individual strengths and weaknesses
4. Documenting personnel decisions
5. Recognition of individual performance

• **FIGURE 13–1**   Performance Appraisal, Feedback, and Rewards Translate Effort into Strong Performance

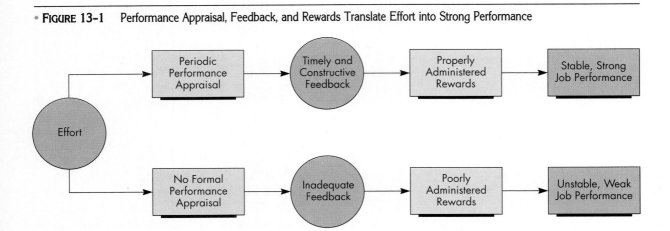

6. Identifying poor performance
7. Assisting in goal identification
8. Promotion decisions
9. Retention or termination of personnel
10. Evaluating goal achievement

Also, performance appraisal information was typically used for *multiple* purposes, rather than for a single purpose.[1] Economic efficiency and the principle of fairness dictate that these decisions be made on the basis of valid and reliable evidence, rather than as the result of prejudice and guesswork.

This section analyzes the key components of the performance appraisal process and summarizes recent research findings relative to those components. Some practical problems with performance appraisals are then addressed.

Components of the Performance Appraisal Process

Although formal performance appraisals are practically universal in the managerial ranks (91 percent according to one study),[2] few express satisfaction with them. Appraisers and appraisees alike are unhappy with the process. Much of the problem stems from the complexity of the appraisal process. One writer has captured this issue with the following example:

> If you wonder why evaluating an employee's performance can be so difficult, consider a simpler appraisal: one made by the barroom fan who concludes that his team's quarterback is a bum because several of his passes have been intercepted. An objective appraisal would raise the following questions: Were the passes really that bad or did the receivers run the wrong patterns? Did the offensive line give the quarterback adequate protection? Did he call those plays himself, or were they sent in by the coach? Was the quarterback recovering from an injury?
>
> And what about the fan? Has he ever played football himself? How good is his vision? Did he have a good view of the TV set through the barroom's smoky haze? Was he talking to his friends at the bar during the game? How many beers did he down during the game?[3]

Further complicating things are Equal Employment Opportunity laws and guidelines that constrain managers' actions during the appraisal process.[4] Let us begin to sort out the complex appraisal process by examining its key components. Four key components, as shown in Figure 13–2, are the appraiser, the appraisee, the appraisal method, and the outcomes.

The Appraiser   Managers generally express discomfort with playing the role of performance appraiser. After finding that 95 percent of the mid- to lower-level management performance appraisals at 293 U.S. companies were conducted by immediate supervisors, researchers concluded that "most supervisors dislike 'playing God' and that many try to avoid responsibility for providing subordinates with feedback of unflattering appraisal information."[5]

Charges of racism, sexism, and perceptual distortion also have been leveled at appraisers. Common perceptual errors include those discussed in Chapter 4 (halo, leniency, central tendency, recency, and contrast). In a survey of 267 corporations, 62 percent of the respondents reported that

• **FIGURE 13-2**   Components of the Performance Appraisal Process

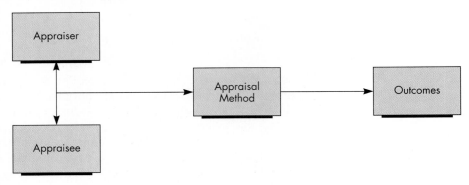

leniency error was their number one appraisal problem.[6] Everyday experience and research evidence show how stereotyping and bias can contaminate the appraisal process. For example, combined evidence from a laboratory study and a field study documented how women professors tended to get lower ratings from students with traditional stereotypes of women.[7] Another study monitored the fates of 173 unionized employees who had filed grievances against their supervisors over an eight-year period. Those who had filed grievances tended to receive lower performance ratings from their supervisors than did their co-workers who had not filed grievances. This was especially true when the grievances had been settled in favor of the employee.[8] Thus, in this study at least, supervisors were shown to use performance appraisals as a weapon to get even with disliked subordinates. The ethical implications of this practice are obvious. Moreover, because performance appraisers engage in social cognition (see Chapter 4), problems can occur in comprehending, encoding, retaining, or retrieving performance-related information.

Finally, managers typically lack the necessary performance appraisal skills. In one study, researchers concluded, "At 52 percent of the responding companies, evaluators are simply not conducting performance interviews or filling out appraisal forms correctly."[9] Experts on the subject have specified four criteria for a willing and able performance appraiser:

> The person doing the assessment must: (1) be in a position to observe the behavior and performance of the individual of interest; (2) be knowledgeable about the dimensions or features of performance; (3) have an understanding of the scale format and the instrument itself; and (4) must be motivated to do a conscientious job of rating.[10]

Managers need to ensure that all four criteria are satisfied if performance appraisals are to be conducted properly.

The Appraisee   Employees play a characteristically passive listening and watching role when their own performance is being appraised. This experience can be demeaning and often threatening. According to a pair of human resource consultants:

> Whatever method is used, performance appraisals are always manager-driven. Managers are in charge of the schedule, the agenda, and the results, and managers

• **TABLE 13-1**   Proactive Appraisee Roles during Performance Appraisal

Role	Description
Analyzer	Performs self-assessment of goal achievement. Identifies performance strengths and weaknesses. Makes suggestions for performance improvement. Takes personal responsibility for solving performance problems.
Influencer	Improves communication skills (e.g., negotiations, advocating, providing information, advising, soliciting feedback, listening). Questions old assumptions and organizational roadblocks. Strives for collaborative relationship with boss.
Planner	Develops a clear vision of why his or her job exists. Identifies quality-of-service goals relative to "customers" or "clients." Understands what his or her job contributes (or does not contribute) to the organization.
Protégé	Learns from high-performing role models without compromising personal uniqueness. Learns through personal initiative rather than by waiting for instructions from others.

Source: Adapted from Betsy Jacobson and Beverly L. Kaye, "Career Development and Performance Appraisal: It Takes Two to Tango," *Personnel*, January 1986, pp. 26–32.

are the ones that receive any training and/or rewards concerning performance appraisals. Subordinates generally are given no responsibility or particular preparation for their roles in the process beyond attending the appraisal meetings.[11]

Consequently, these consultants recommend four *proactive* roles (see Table 13–1) for appraisees. They suggest formal *appraisee* training so analyzer, influencer, planner, and protégé roles can be performed skillfully. This represents a marked departure from the usual practice of training appraisers only. The goal of this promising approach is to marry performance appraisal and career development through enhanced communication and greater personal commitment.

The Appraisal Method   Three distinct approaches to appraising job performance have emerged over the years—the trait approach, the behavioral approach, and the results approach. Figure 13–3 displays examples of these three approaches. Controversy surrounds the question of which of these three approaches (and a recently suggested contingency approach) is best.

• *Trait approach:* This approach involves rating an individual's personal traits or characteristics. Commonly assessed traits are initiative, decisiveness, and dependability. Although the trait approach is widely used by managers, it is generally considered by experts to be the weakest. Trait ratings are deficient because they are ambiguous relative to actual performance. For instance, rating someone low on initiative tells him or her nothing about how to improve job performance. Also, employees tend to react defensively to feedback about their personality (who or what they are).[12]

· **FIGURE 13-3**   Three Basic Approaches to Appraising Job Performance

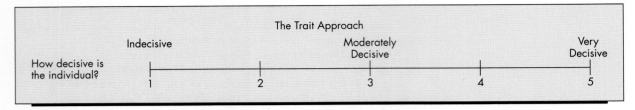

· *Behavioral approach:* How the person actually behaves, rather than his or her personality, matters in the behavioral approach. As indicated in Figure 13–4, the legal defensibility (in the United States) of performance appraisals is enhanced when performance ratings are supported with behavioral examples of performance.

· *Results approach:* Whereas the trait approach focuses on the "person" and the behavioral approach focuses on the "process," the results approach focuses on the "product" of one's efforts. In other words, what has the individual accomplished? *Management by objectives* (MBO) is the most common format for the results approach.[13]

· *Contingency approach:* A pair of performance appraisal experts has called the trait-behavioral-results controversy a "pseudo issue." They contend that each approach has its appropriate use, depending on the demands of the situation. Thus, they recommend a contingency approach (see Table 13–2). Notice how the poorly regarded trait approach is appropriate when a promotion decision needs to be made for candidates with dissimilar jobs. Although it has widespread applicability, the results approach is limited by its failure to specify why the appraisee's objectives have not been met. Overall, the behavioral approach emerges as the strongest. But it too is subject to situational limitations, such as when employees with dissimilar jobs

• **FIGURE 13-4**   Six Criteria of Legally Defensible Performance Appraisal Systems

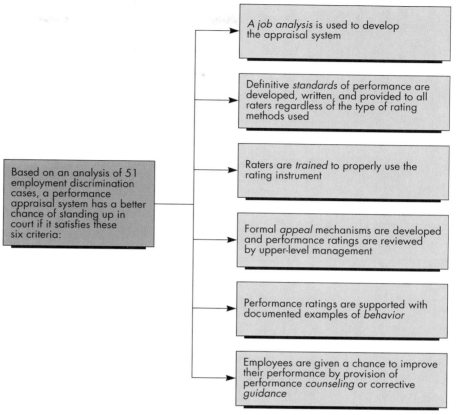

Based on an analysis of 51 employment discrimination cases, a performance appraisal system has a better chance of standing up in court if it satisfies these six criteria:

- *A job analysis* is used to develop the appraisal system
- Definitive *standards* of performance are developed, written, and provided to all raters regardless of the type of rating methods used
- Raters are *trained* to properly use the rating instrument
- Formal *appeal* mechanisms are developed and performance ratings are reviewed by upper-level management
- Performance ratings are supported with documented examples of *behavior*
- Employees are given a chance to improve their performance by provision of performance *counseling* or corrective *guidance*

Source: Adapted from Gerald V. Barrett and Mary C. Kernan, "Performance Appraisal and Terminations: A Review of Court Decisions since *Brito* v. *Zia* with Implications for Personnel Practices," *Personnel Psychology*, Autumn, 1987, pp. 489–503.

• **TABLE 13-2**   A Contingency Approach to Performance Appraisals

Function of Appraisal	Appraisal Method	Comments
Promotion decisions	Trait	Appropriate when competing appraisees have *dissimilar* jobs
	Behavioral	Appropriate when competing appraisees have *similar* jobs
	Results	Same as above
Development decisions	Trait	Tends to cause defensiveness among low self-esteem employees
	Behavioral	Pinpoints specific performance improvement needs
	Results	Identifies deficient results, but does not tell *why*
Pay decisions	Trait	Weak performance-reward linkage
	Behavioral	Enhances performance-reward linkage
	Results	Same as above
Layoff decisions	Trait	Inappropriate, potentially discriminatory
	Behavioral	Weighted combination of behaviors, results, and seniority is recommended
	Results	Same as above

Source: Adapted from Kenneth N. Wexley and Richard Klimoski, "Performance Appraisal: An Update," in *Research in Personnel and Human Resources Management*, Vol. 2, ed. Kendrith M. Rowland and Gerald R. Ferris (Greenwich, Conn.: JAI Press, 1984), pp. 35–79.

A MATTER OF ETHICS

Good Supervision or Unethical "Snoopervision?"

Place a phone order through most any catalog and chances are the clerk who answers won't be the only one on the line. Bosses have big ears these days.

Or open up an electronics magazine and peruse the ads for sneaky tape recorders and other snooping gadgets. Some would make even James Bond green with envy.

Eavesdropping—both corporate and private—is on the rise, thanks to the proliferation of surveillance technologies. And while sellers of the equipment and companies "monitoring" employees have few qualms, right-to-privacy advocates and some lawmakers are alarmed.

"New technologies are changing the way we deal with each other and the way we work," says Janlori Goldman, a staff attorney at the American Civil Liberties Union. "Our expectation of confidentiality is being eroded."

Keeping an Eye on Service

On the corporate side, companies claim that monitoring employee phone conversations is both legal and necessary to gauge productivity and ensure good service. The practice is common at catalog, insurance and phone companies, banks and telemarketers, according to trade groups and worker organizations. It's also widespread for reservations clerks in the airline, car-rental, hotel and railroad industries.

Source: Excerpted from Jill Abramson, "Mind What You Say; They're Listening," *The Wall Street Journal*, October 25, 1989, p. B1. Reprinted by permission of *The Wall Street Journal*, © 1989 Dow Jones & Company, Inc. All rights reserved worldwide.

are being evaluated for a promotion. Additionally, the growing practice of electronically monitoring job behavior has become a legitimate ethical issue in OB (see A Matter of Ethics).

Outcomes of the Appraisal   According to a researcher from the Center for Creative Leadership, there are three indicators of a useful performance appraisal. They are:

- Timely feedback on performance.
- Input for key personnel decisions.
- Individual and organizational planning tool.[14]

To this list, we would add "human resource development tool." These four appraisal outcomes cannot be left to chance. They need to be forethoughts rather than afterthoughts.

Performance Appraisal Research Insights

Researchers have probed many facets of the appraisal process. Resulting insights include:

- Appraisers typically rate same-race appraisees higher. A meta-analysis of 74 studies and 17,159 individuals revealed that white superiors tended to favor white subordinates. Similarly, black superiors tended to favor black subordinates in a meta-analysis of 14 studies and 2,248 people.[15]

• Although a great deal of effort has been devoted to creating more precise rating formats, formats account for very little difference (4 to 8 percent) in ratings.

• Performance appraisers tend to give poor performers significantly higher ratings when they have to give the appraisees face-to-face feedback, as opposed to anonymous written feedback or no feedback.

• More experienced appraisers tend to render higher-quality appraisals. This finding suggests that comprehensive appraiser training and practice can reduce rater errors.[16]

These research insights, along with evidence of rater bias discussed earlier, constitute a bad news–good news situation for management. The *bad* news: performance appraisals can be contaminated by racism, sexism, personal bias, and fear of conflict. The *good* news: managers can be trained to improve their performance appraisal skills.

Discussion now turns to specific ways to improve the effectiveness of performance appraisal.

• PRACTICAL ISSUES AND ANSWERS IN PERFORMANCE APPRAISAL

Employee performance appraisals are conducted in many different ways today. There are weighted checklists, forced distributions, graphic rating scales, and written essays, among others. Our purpose here, however, is not to discuss the relative merits of alternative appraisal formats. Not only are there far too many to adequately cover, the particular appraisal format (as indicated in our research insights above) tends to have a minor impact on appraisal results. Instead, we will address more fundamental issues that may determine the difference between effective and ineffective appraisals.

How Can Managers Resolve the Evaluation-Versus-Development Dilemma?

According to the outcomes listed earlier, managers have two conflicting objectives when appraising performance. First, they need to evaluate *past* performance. Second, they need to develop *future* performance. These two objectives generally are at odds when busy managers try to do both during a brief annual performance-review meeting with each subordinate. All too often, evaluation is emphasized to the partial or total exclusion of develop-ment.[17] Criticism and the stress of a face-to-face performance review do little to set the proper tone for a constructive discussion of future improvement.

A technique for resolving this evaluation–development dilemma is the "two-meeting" approach.[18] Performance appraisal results are discussed during the first meeting between manager and subordinate. At the second meeting, usually a week or two later, attention is focused on performance *improvement*. Goal setting, as discussed in Chapter 6, plays a central role

• TABLE 13-3   A SMART Way to Keep Job Performance on Track

> One of the toughest parts of designing a performance appraisal system is coming up with objective standards for measuring people's work.
>
> If you're going to conduct formal performance appraisals (and who isn't these days?), you've got to have some reliable yardsticks. The ones you use must be fair to both employee and employer, should provoke as little argument and interpretation as possible and must be balanced across all groups of employees. Short of calling in a federal mediator, how do you design such standards?
>
> One widely accepted way to evaluate your standards is to make sure they're smart—better make that SMART. The letters stand for Specific, Measurable, Attainable, Results-oriented and Time-related. The idea isn't new, but it's usually workable. And, according to John Reddish and George Bickley, SMART is a great way to measure the progress of employees toward just about any goal.
>
> Reddish, a West Chester, Pennsylvania, management consultant, and Bickley, president of Glenn Industries, Inc., a real estate company, define SMARTly designed performance standards as:
>
> *Specific*—that is, not defined in vague, global terms, but in precise language that leaves no doubt as to what's expected. They illustrate with an analogy about a man with two cars, two sons and two gallons of antifreeze. The father tells each son to put a gallon of antifreeze in one of the cars. One son puts it in the radiator, the other stows it in the trunk. Both are right, because the message wasn't clear enough.
>
> *Measurable*—in quantifiable terms that are meaningful, but that leave no doubt about when a performance goal has been achieved. For example, you wouldn't measure sales performance by number of calls made or sales courses attended; you'd look at the revenue the salesperson generated.
>
> *Attainable*—in that employees should be able to reach the measureable standard at least half the time. If a standard is unrealistic, people will feel they're being set up for failure.
>
> *Results-oriented*—to ensure that you're measuring output, and not the process of achieving it. Hours spent on the job, paperwork shuffled, courses logged—all become meaningless if they produce no results.
>
> *Time-related*—to the extent that the results expected have a time frame. Every job standard should have a maximum time line, and only results achieved within it should count.
>
> Standards such as these, Reddish and Bickley say, put the responsibility for performance in any job on the person doing the job, and make it difficult for marginal performers to maintain excuses such as, "You really can't measure my job."

during the developmental meeting (see Table 13–3). The cooling-off period between meetings gives the employee time to formulate realistic objectives based on the prior meeting's feedback. Two meetings enable managers to foster the necessary positive and constructive atmosphere with less risk of emotional backlash that can accompany a critical review.

Who Should Evaluate Job Performance?

Sheer force of tradition alone almost guarantees a standard answer to this question: One's immediate supervisor, of course. This answer may be the most common one, but some experts contend it is not necessarily the correct one today. Interest is growing in nontraditional appraisals by subordinates, peers, and self. How do these nontraditional approaches to performance appraisal measure up? Should managers use them?

Feedback from subordinates (generally anonymous) effectively turns the performance appraisal process on its head. According to *The Wall Street Journal:*

> Corporate managers increasingly are being put on the hot seat—by the people who work for them. The technique isn't easy to administer and makes many managers uncomfortable. But proponents contend that it can help workers feel more involved in their company. And they argue that subordinates are uniquely situated to observe and evaluate their bosses for leadership, organization, and crisis-management skills. . . .
>
> Indeed, a 1984 study found that subordinates tend to rate their supervisor tougher than the supervisor's boss. One obvious reason, suggests the author, Michael K. Mount, a University of Iowa professor, is the setting: Subordinates don't have to evaluate their boss face-to-face.[19]

Despite enthusiastic calls for bottom-up appraisal,[20] the practice is not widespread. Management resistance is strong. Moreover, the results can be readily ignored because they lack hierarchical authority. Even where it is used, subordinate feedback typically is a management development tool rather than the basis for pay and promotion decisions.

Peer- and self-appraisals also are significant affronts to tradition. The main argument in favor of both is the same one offered for subordinate appraisals. Namely, co-workers and the manager himself or herself are closer to the action. They have more opportunities to directly observe job performance. Research builds a stronger case for peer appraisals than for self-appraisals.[21]

So should management bother with subordinate, peer, and self performance appraisals? The answer is a "qualified yes." These nontraditional appraisals are an appropriate and useful *supplement* to the traditional top-down variety. They are not an adequate replacement, at least at this time and state of the art. Nontraditional feedback to managers from peers and subordinates must be anonymous. Unfortunately, this requirement destroys the rater accountability found in traditional top-down appraisals. Consequently, the best use for nontraditional performance feedback is for management training and development. General Electric's multiple-source performance evaluation system is an instructive case in point (see OB in Action).

How Can the Behavioral Focus of Appraisals Be Sharpened?

As mentioned earlier, behavior-based appraisals are more legally defensible than commonly used trait appraisals. In other words, they have a greater chance of standing up in court. This is particularly important in view of the recent upsurge in wrongful-discharge lawsuits. Two techniques can help managers increase the behavioral orientation of performance appraisals. They are: critical incidents and behaviorally anchored rating scales.

Critical incidents are notable examples of good or bad performance that are written down soon after they occur. Collections of such critical incidents can provide an objective basis for a performance appraisal. The value of critical incidents is increased when managers focus on specific behavior

OB IN ACTION

General Electric Plugs into Multiple-Source Performance Evaluations

Sales and marketing managers at General Electric Corp. are evaluated not only by the people who report to them but also by their peers as part of the company's management development program.

According to James P. Baughman, manager of corporate management development at GE, a manager's peers and subordinates are asked to fill out an evaluation questionnaire whenever the manager is scheduled for a corporate training session. The questionnaire asks about the individual's personal effectiveness in a variety of management and technical areas. The results are processed as part of the training program.

"The individual then gets feedback from the training staff in three different ways," says Baughman. "First he gets his individual results, that is, where he has done well or poorly in areas such as delegation, interpersonal relationships, and other areas. Second, he or she sees the results in comparison to other managers in that particular training class. And third, because we've built a database around these questionnaires over the years, we can see how a particular sales manager's results stack up against how other sales managers did at the same stage in their careers."

At the beginning of each day of training at the corporate center, managers get feedback on results in those areas for which they'll be receiving training. That feedback comes in the form of individual counseling on ways in which a manager can improve results and a certain amount of customizing the group training effort to address specific problem areas. "That way," Baughman says, "the individual gets what amounts to a personal plan of action for leadership development."

The important thing to note about General Electric's evaluation process, however, is that it is not part of the company's formal performance evaluation program. "We do it in a developmental context and not in an appraisal context. The results don't go to the individual's boss and don't affect performance reviews or compensation," Baughman says.

Managers can see how far they've gone in correcting their shortcomings, and how effective their training has been, by initiating the evaluation questionnaire themselves six months or a year down the road and comparing results.

And how do managers like the idea of being evaluated by their workers and peers? "They love it," Baughman says, "as long as the results stay outside the chain of command."

Source: W.P.K., "How It's Done at GE," *Sales & Marketing Management*, March 1989, p. 26. Reprinted by permission of *Sales & Marketing Management*. Copyright March 1989.

and/or results rather than on personality traits. On the negative side, busy managers often fall behind in promptly recording critical incidents.

Behaviorally anchored rating scales (BARS) are graphic rating scales with behavioral descriptions attached at specific points as determined by a consensus of those familiar with the job in question. For example, panels of students helped develop the BARS exhibited in Figure 13–5. The BARS

• **FIGURE 13-5**   A Behaviorally Anchored Rating Scale for College Professors

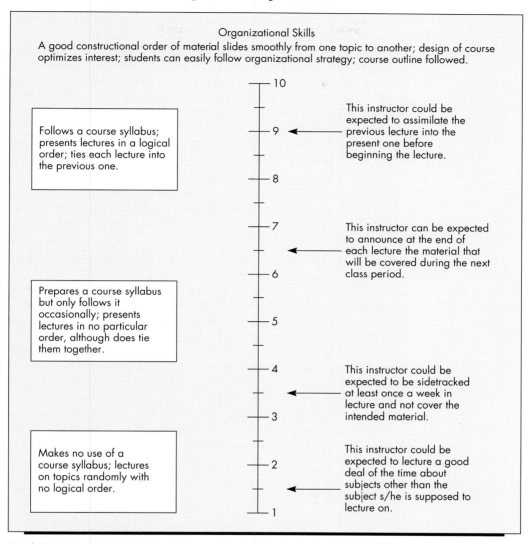

Organizational Skills
A good constructional order of material slides smoothly from one topic to another; design of course optimizes interest; students can easily follow organizational strategy; course outline followed.

Follows a course syllabus; presents lectures in a logical order; ties each lecture into the previous one.

Prepares a course syllabus but only follows it occasionally; presents lectures in no particular order, although does tie them together.

Makes no use of a course syllabus; lectures on topics randomly with no logical order.

This instructor could be expected to assimilate the previous lecture into the present one before beginning the lecture.

This instructor can be expected to announce at the end of each lecture the material that will be covered during the next class period.

This instructor could be expected to be sidetracked at least once a week in lecture and not cover the intended material.

This instructor could be expected to lecture a good deal of the time about subjects other than the subject s/he is supposed to lecture on.

Source: From H. John Bernardin and Richard W. Beatty, *Performance Appraisal: Assessing Human Behavior at Work* (Boston: Kent Publishing Company, 1984), p. 84. © by Wadsworth, Inc. Reprinted by permission of PWS-KENT Publishing Company, a division of Wadsworth, Inc., and H. John Bernardin.

technique is praised for bringing rating scales to life for the appraisers and reducing common sources of rater error (e.g., halo, leniency, and central tendency). On the negative side, three problems have emerged: (1) midscale anchors are difficult to specify; (2) BARS developed for one situation often are not applicable for other situations; and (3) development of BARS is costly. These problems led a pair of OB researchers to conclude: "The major objection to the BARS currently is whether the ratings that these scales produce are so error free that they justify the cost of scale development."[22]

• FEEDBACK

Achievement-oriented students have a hearty appetite for feedback. Following a difficult exam, for instance, students want to know two things: how they did and how their peers did. By letting students know how their work measures up to grading and competitive standards, an instructor's feedback permits the students to adjust their study habits so they can reach their goals. Likewise, managers in well-run organizations follow up goal setting with a feedback program to provide a rational basis for adjustment and improvement. Building on our example of Square D in the last chapter, consider how chief executive officer Jerre Stead has used feedback to personalize the financial goals of the company:

> [He] installed an outsize scoreboard at corporate headquarters. Up on the board are the quarterly results broken down by profit per employee, sales per employee, and return on equity for Square D and its competitors, among them Emerson Electric, General Electric, and Westinghouse. Square D workers know exactly what they're up against.[23]

Not surprisingly, Square D is an industry leader among electrical equipment manufacturers.

As the term is used here, **feedback** is objective information about the adequacy of one's own job performance. Subjective assessments such as, "You're doing a lousy job," "You're really a jerk," or "We truly appreciate your hard work" do not qualify as objective feedback. But hard data such as units sold, days absent, dollars saved, projects completed, and quality control rejects are all candidates for objective feedback programs. Because we are dealing with objective feedback here, we are focusing on a specialized subset of the interpersonal communication process presented in Chapter 12. Six advantages of objective feedback are listed in Table 13–4.

Experts say feedback serves two functions for those who receive it, one is *instructional* and the other *motivational*. Feedback instructs when it clarifies

• TABLE 13–4   Six Advantages of Objective Feedback

1. *Abundant data*—The typical organization generates a great deal of objective data through MBO [management by objectives] programs, financial and accounting procedures, and government reports that can be used in feedback programs.
2. *Small investment in time and money*—Research has shown that feedback programs that saved an average of $77,000 per year generally cost less than $1,000 to develop and implement.
3. *A natural control tool*—Straightforward presentation of objective performance data need not involve gimmicks such as lotteries or other contrived motivational techniques.
4. *Rapid results*—Immediate performance improvement is common.
5. *Suitable for most settings*—Objective feedback can be used in not-for-profit and governmental organizations that have strict limits on incentives and rewards.
6. *Complements other productivity improvement techniques*—Objective feedback is an essential part of training and management development programs and organization development (OD) interventions.

Source: Adapted from Richard E. Kopelman, *Managing Productivity in Organizations: A Practical People-Oriented Perspective* (New York: McGraw-Hill, 1986), p. 174.

roles or teaches new behavior. For example, an assistant accountant might be advised to handle a certain entry as a capital item rather than as an expense item. On the other hand, feedback motivates when it serves as a reward or promises a reward.[24] Having the boss tell you that a grueling project you worked on earlier has just been completed can be a rewarding piece of news. As documented in a recent study, the motivational function of feedback can be significantly enhanced by pairing *specific*, challenging goals with *specific* feedback about results.[25] We expand upon these two functions in this section by examining feedback as a control mechanism, analyzing a conceptual model of feedback, and reviewing the practical implications of recent feedback research.

Feedback Is a Control Mechanism

The notion of feedback has an interesting history. According to one observer: "Though not a new idea, the term *feedback* is of relatively recent vintage, owing coinage to engineer Norbert Wiener, formulator of cybernetic theory, the hot-button topic of the 1950s."[26] Wiener limited his context to mechanical systems, but behavioral scientists eagerly embraced the concept of feedback because they sought to explain how people behave as dynamic self-adjusting systems.

A Basic Feedback Control Model   Figure 13–6 illustrates how feedback, in conjunction with a standard and a mechanism for comparing actual and standard, can control virtually any system. Take the familiar home ther-

• **FIGURE 13-6**   Feedback Control

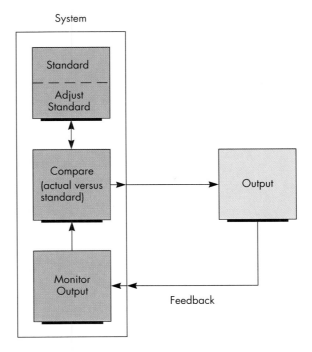

mostat, for example. If the room feels too hot, you lower the temperature setting (thus adjusting the standard). The thermostat, which constantly monitors the room temperature, turns on the cooling unit because it detects a gap between actual (feedback) and standard. When the room reaches the desired temperature, the thermostat turns off the cooling unit. Despite the imperfect analogy between mechanical and human behavioral systems, OB scholars believe feedback control is necessary and desirable in work organizations. All that is required is a set of performance standards and a mechanism for monitoring performance and providing objective feedback. Self-control is the desired end result for all feedback control systems, whether mechanical or behavioral.

A Hierarchy of Standards   The basic model in Figure 13–6 can be humanized by expanding the idea of standards. Feedback control becomes less mechanical when one realizes that employees conform to varying combinations of three types of standards. From general to specific, they are:

- *Principle standards* (conceptual or moral).
- *Program standards* (if-then decision rules).
- *Action standards* (specific behaviors).[27]

Conceptual Model of the Feedback Process

The influence of objective feedback on job behavior is a much more complex process than one might initially suspect. To begin with, as shown in Figure 13–7, feedback comes from different sources. Moreover, perceptual and cognitive hurdles must be jumped if the desired behavioral outcomes are to be achieved. Let us explore this model to better understand how feedback influences job behavior.

Sources of Feedback   It almost goes without saying that employees receive objective feedback from others such as peers, supervisors, subordinates,

• **FIGURE 13-7**   A Model of Feedback on Job Performance

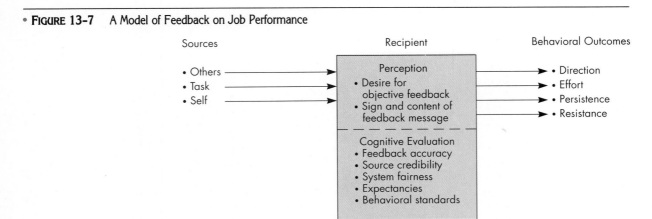

Source: Based in part on discussion in M. Susan Taylor, Cynthia D. Fisher, and Daniel R. Ilgen, "Individuals' Reactions to Performance Feedback in Organizations: A Control Theory Perspective," in *Research in Personnel and Human Resources Management*, Vol. 2, eds. Kendrith M. Rowland and Gerald R. Ferris (Greenwich, Conn.: JAI Press, 1984), pp. 81–124.

and outsiders. Perhaps less obvious is the fact that the task itself is a ready source of objective feedback. Anyone who has been "hooked into" pumping quarters into a video game such as Pac-Man® or Pole Position can appreciate the power of task-provided feedback. Similarly, skilled tasks such as computer programming or landing a jet airplane provide a steady stream of feedback about how well or poorly one is doing. A third source of feedback is oneself, but self-serving bias and other perceptual problems can contaminate this source. Those high in self-confidence tend to rely on personal feedback more than those with low self-confidence. Although circumstances vary, an employee can be bombarded by feedback from all three sources simultaneously. This is where the gatekeeping functions of perception and cognitive evaluation are needed to help sort things out.

Perception and Cognitive Evaluation of Feedback   As with other stimuli, we selectively perceive feedback. One's desire for objective feedback is an important factor here. Many people ask for objective feedback when it is the last thing they truly want. Restaurant servers who ask, "How was everything?" before presenting the bill, typically turn a deaf ear to constructive criticism. Personality characteristics, such as need for achievement, also can influence one's desire for feedback. In a laboratory study, Japanese psychology students who scored high on need for achievement responded more favorably to feedback than did their classmates who had low need for achievement. This particular relationship likely exists in Western cultures as well. Moreover, 331 employees in the marketing department of a large public utility in the United States were found to seek feedback on important issues or when faced with uncertain situations. Long-tenured employees from this sample also were less likely to seek feedback than employees with little tenure.[28] Consequently, managers need to consider each individual's readiness for objective feedback, based on relevant personality and situational variables.

The *sign* of feedback refers to whether it is positive or negative. Generally, people tend to perceive and recall positive feedback more accurately than they do negative feedback.[29] But feedback with a negative sign (e.g., being told your performance is below average) can have a *positive* motivational impact. In fact, in a recent laboratory study, those who were told they were below average on a creativity test subsequently outperformed those who were led to believe their results were above average. The subjects apparently took the negative feedback as a challenge and set and pursued higher goals. Those receiving positive feedback apparently were less motivated to do better.[30] Nonetheless, feedback with a negative sign or threatening content needs to be administered carefully to avoid creating insecurity and defensiveness.

Upon receiving feedback, people cognitively evaluate factors such as its accuracy, the credibility of the source, the fairness of the system (e.g., performance appraisal system), their performance-reward expectancies, and the reasonableness of the standards. Any feedback that fails to clear one or more of these cognitive hurdles will be rejected or downplayed. Personal experience largely dictates how these factors are weighed. For instance, you would probably discount feedback from someone who exaggerates or from someone who performed poorly on the same task you have just successfully

A MATTER OF ETHICS

Above All, We Want Our Leaders to Be Credible

Honest. Competent. Forward-looking. Inspiring. Taken singularly, these terms may not be altogether surprising descriptions of leadership attributes. But together, these characteristics comprise what communications experts refer to as "credibility."

In assessing the believability of sources of communication—people in such roles as newscasters and salespeople, as well as managers—researchers typically evaluate them on three criteria: their perceived trustworthiness, expertise, and dynamism. Those who rate more highly on these dimensions are considered to be more credible sources of information.

These three characteristics are strikingly similar to honesty, competence, and inspiration—three of the four most frequently selected items in our survey. What we found—quite unexpectedly—in our investigation of admired leadership qualities is that, more than anything, we want leaders who are credible. Above all else, we must be able to believe in our leaders. We must believe that their word can be trusted, that they will do what they say, that they have the knowledge and skill to lead, and that they are personally excited and enthusiastic about the direction in which we are headed.

Source: James M. Kouzes and Barry Z. Posner, *The Leadership Challenge* (San Francisco: Jossey-Bass, 1987), pp. 21–22. Reprinted with permission.

completed. Of course, a poor performer might be a credible source if you also have done poorly on the same task. (As indicated in A Matter of Ethics, *managerial credibility* has profound ethical implications.)

Feedback from a source who apparently shows favoritism or relies on unreasonable behavior standards would be suspect. Also, as predicted by expectancy motivation theory, feedback must foster high effort→performance expectancies and performance→reward instrumentalities if it is to motivate desired behavior. For example, many growing children have been cheated out of the rewards of athletic competition because they were told by respected adults they were too small, too short, too slow, too clumsy, and so forth. Feedback can have a profound and lasting impact on behavior.

Behavioral Outcomes of Feedback   In Chapter 6, we discussed how goal setting gives behavior direction, increases expended effort, and fosters persistence. Because feedback is intimately related to the goal-setting process, it involves the same behavioral outcomes: direction, effort, and persistence. However, while the fourth outcome of goal setting involves formulating goal-attainment strategies, the fourth possible outcome of feedback is *resistance*. Feedback schemes, that smack of manipulation or fail one or more of the perceptual and cognitive evaluation tests just discussed, breed resistance. Steve Jobs, the young cofounder of Apple Computer, left the firm amid controversy in 1985 partly because his uneven and heavy-handed feedback bred resistance.

According to several insiders, Jobs, a devout believer that new technology should supersede the old, couldn't abide the success of the venerable Apple II. Nor did he hide his feelings. He once addressed the Apple II marketing staff as members

INTERNATIONAL OB

The Meaning of Feedback Cannot Be Taken for Granted in Intercultural Situations

American versus European (performance appraisal):

> In appraisal and in training, American managers look for feedback much more often. Senior managers in many European companies would not dare to propose that they should be frequently and formally appraised or re-trained. It is seldom that a European executive will look to his boss or his subordinates for a genuine reflection of how well he is doing.

American versus Japanese (negotiation):

> In the . . . spirit of maintaining harmony, the Japanese tradition is to avoid a direct "no" at practically any cost. They may ask a counterquestion, promise an answer at some later date, change the subject and even occasionally leave the room. Another common response is no response at all, a dead silence. "This drives Americans up the wall," [says a cross-cultural negotiation researcher].

Source: Excerpted from Paul Thorne and Bill Meyer, "The Care and Feeding of Your American Management," *International Management,* October 1987, p. 114; and John Pfeiffer, "How Not to Lose the Trade Wars by Cultural Gaffes," *Smithsonian,* January 1988, pp. 150–51.

of the "dull and boring product division." As chairman and largest stockholder, with an 11.3 percent block, Jobs was a disproportionately powerful general manager. And he had disproportionate enthusiasm for the [Macintosh] staff. Says one of them: "He was so protective of us that whenever we complained about somebody outside the division, it was like unleashing a Doberman. Steve would get on the telephone and chew the guy out so fast your head would spin."[31]

Practical Lessons from Feedback Research

After reviewing dozens of laboratory and field studies of feedback, a trio of OB researchers cited the following practical implications for managers:

- The acceptance of feedback should not be treated as a given; it is often misperceived or rejected. This is especially true in intercultural situations, as indicated in International OB.
- Managers can enhance their credibility as sources of feedback by developing their expertise and creating a climate of trust.
- Negative feedback is typically misperceived or rejected.
- Although very frequent feedback may erode one's sense of personal control and initiative, feedback is too *infrequent* in most work organizations.
- Feedback needs to be tailored to the recipient.
- While average and below-average performers need extrinsic rewards for performance, high performers respond to feedback that enhances their feelings of competence and personal control.[32]

• **TABLE 13-5**   A Management Consultant's Advice on Giving Feedback

1. Verbal feedback is desired even when nonverbal feedback is positive.
2. Verbal feedback must accompany nonverbal to ensure complete clarity.
3. Immediate feedback is almost always more useful than delayed feedback.
4. Negative feedback may be better than no feedback, but positive feedback produces the best results.
5. Undeserved praise does not produce positive results.
6. People need to be primed to be more receptive to later feedback.
7. Employees tend to remember longest what they hear first and last in a message.
8. If you want a subordinate to react to your feedback, you must direct it personally—in many cases, privately—to the subordinate.
9. Low amounts of feedback cause low confidence and may result in hostility.
10. Absence of feedback also communicates approval or agreement with ideas and behaviors.

Source: Adapted from Priscilla Diffie-Couch, "How to Give Feedback," *Supervisory Management*, August 1983, pp. 27–31.

More recent research insights about feedback include:

• Computer-based performance feedback leads to greater improvements in performance when it is received directly from the computer system rather than via an immediate supervisor.[33]

• Recipients of feedback perceive it to be more accurate when they actively participate in the feedback session, versus passively receiving feedback.[34]

• Destructive criticism tends to cause conflict and reduce motivation.[35]

Managers who enact these research implications and the practical advice in Table 13–5 can be credible and effective sources of feedback.[36]

Our attention now turns to rewards, a natural follow-up to any discussion of performance appraisal and feedback.

• ORGANIZATIONAL REWARD SYSTEMS

Rewards are an ever-present feature of organizational life. Some employees see their jobs as the source of a paycheck and little else. Others derive great pleasure from their jobs and association with co-workers. Even volunteers who donate their time to charitable organizations, such as the Red Cross, walk away with rewards in the form of social recognition and pride of having given unselfishly of their time. Hence, the subject of organizational rewards includes, but goes far beyond, monetary compensation. This section examines key components of organizational reward systems to provide a conceptual background for discussing the timely topic of pay for performance.

Despite the fact that reward systems vary widely, it is possible to identify and interrelate some common components. The model in Figure 13–8 focuses on four important components: (1) types of rewards, (2) reward norms, (3) distribution criteria, and (4) desired outcomes. Let us examine these components.

• **FIGURE 13-8**   A General Model of Organizational Reward Systems

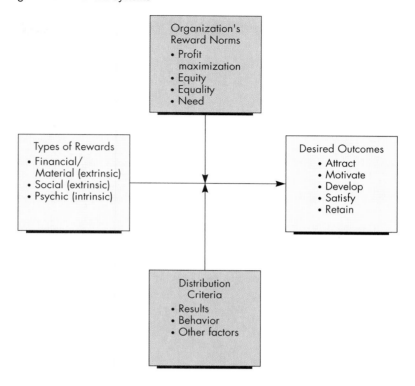

Types of Rewards

Including the usual paycheck, the variety and magnitude of organizational rewards boggles the mind (see Table 13–6). Managers generally refer to rewards in terms of pay, benefits, and employee compensation. A U.S. Bureau of Labor Statistics economist offered the following historical perspective of employee compensation:

> One of the more striking developments . . . over the past 75 years has been the growing complexity of employee compensation. Limited at the outbreak of World War I largely to straight-time pay for hours worked, compensation now includes a variety of employer-financed benefits, such as health and life insurance, retirement income, and paid time off. Although the details of each vary widely, these benefits are today standard components of the compensation package, and workers generally have come to expect them.[37]

By 1989, according to U.S. government figures, benefits accounted for over 27 percent of average hourly compensation.[38] In addition to the obvious pay and benefits, there are less obvious social and psychic rewards. Social rewards include praise and recognition from others both inside and outside the organization. Psychic rewards come from personal feelings of self-esteem, self-satisfaction, and accomplishment.

An alternative typology for organizational rewards is the distinction between extrinsic and intrinsic rewards. Financial, material, and social rewards qualify as **extrinsic rewards** because they come from the environment.

• TABLE 13-6   There Are Many Possible Rewards for Working

Consumables	Status Symbols	Monetary	Social	Opportunity
Coffee-break treats	Desk accessories	Money	Friendly greetings	Job with more
Free lunches	Personal computer	Stocks	Informal recognition	responsibility
Food baskets	Wall plaques	Stock options	Formal	Job rotation
Easter hams	Company car	Movie passes	acknowledgement	Early time off
Christmas turkeys	Watches	Discounts on	of achievement	with pay
Dinners for the	Trophies	company goods/	Feedback about	Extended breaks
family on the	Commendations	services	performance	Extended lunch
company	Rings/tie pins	Paid-up insurance	Solicitations of	period
Company picnics	Clothing	policies	suggestions	Personal time off
After-work parties	Club privileges	Dinner theater/	Solicitations of	with pay
	Office with a	sports tickets	advice	Work on personal
	window	Vacation trips	Compliment on	project on
	Piped-in music	Coupons redeem-	work progress	company time
	Redecoration of	able at local stores	Recognition in	Use of company
	work environment	Profit sharing	organizational	machinery or
	Company literature	Frequent-flier credits	publications	facilities for
	Private office	for business travel	Pat on the back	personal projects
	Popular speakers		Smile	Use of company
	or lecturers		Verbal or nonverbal	recreation facilities
	Book club		recognition or	Special assignments
	subscriptions		praise	

Source: Adapted with permission from Fred Luthans and Robert Kreitner, *Organizational Behavior Modification and Beyond: An Operant and Social Learning Approach* (Glenview, Ill.: Scott, Forseman, 1985), p. 127.

Psychic rewards, however, are **intrinsic rewards** because they are self-granted. An employee who works to obtain extrinsic rewards, such as money or praise, is said to be extrinsically motivated. One who derives pleasure from the task itself or experiences a sense of competence or self-determination is said to be intrinsically motivated.[39] The relative importance of extrinsic and intrinsic rewards is a matter of personal values and tastes.

Organizational Reward Norms

As discussed in Chapter 6 under the heading of equity theory, some OB scholars view the employer–employee linkage as an exchange relationship. Employees exchange their time and talent for rewards. Ideally, four alternative norms dictate the nature of this exchange. In pure form, each would lead to a significantly different reward distribution system. They are:

• *Profit Maximization:* The objective of each party is to maximize its net gain, regardless of how the other party fares. A profit-maximizing company would attempt to pay the least amount of wages for maximum effort. Conversely, a profit-maximizing employee would seek maximum rewards, regardless of the organization's financial well-being, and leave the organization for a better deal.

• *Equity:* According to the **reward equity norm,** rewards should be allocated proportionate to contributions. Those who contribute the most should be rewarded the most. A recent cross-cultural study of American, Japanese, and Korean college students led the researchers to the following conclusion: "Equity is probably a phenomenon

common to most cultures, but its strength will vary.''[40] Basic principles of fairness and justice, evident in most cultures, drive the equity norm.

- *Equality:* The **reward equality norm** calls for rewarding all parties equally, regardless of their comparative contributions.
- *Need:* This norm calls for distributing rewards according to employees' needs, rather than their contributions.[41]

After defining these exchange norms, a pair of researchers concluded that these contradictory norms are typically intertwined.

> We propose that employer–employee exchanges are governed by the contradictory norms of profit maximization, equity, equality, and need. These norms can coexist; what varies is the extent to which the rules for correct application of a norm are clear and the relative emphasis different managements will give to certain norms in particular allocations.[42]

Conflict often arises over the perceived fairness of reward allocations because of disagreement about reward norms (see A Matter of Ethics, for example). Stockholders might prefer a profit-maximization norm, while technical specialists would like an equity norm, and unionized hourly workers would argue for a pay system based on equality. A reward norm anchored to need might prevail in a family owned and operated business. Effective reward systems are based on clear and consensual exchange norms.

Reward Distribution Criteria

According to one expert on organizational reward systems, three general criteria for the distribution of rewards are:

A MATTER OF ETHICS

Have Top U.S. Executives Gotten Too Greedy?

The Situation

In 1988, the CEO's record $2,025,485 compensation* was 93 times an average factory worker's $21,725, 72 times a teacher's $28,008, and 44 times an engineer's $45,680. . . .

Five years ago management guru Peter F. Drucker warned that the widening gap was fomenting resentment among other professionals and managers. Drucker's concern prompted one company—innovative furniture maker Herman Miller Inc.—to impose a maximum cap on CEO pay. At Herman Miller, the CEO's total pay can't exceed a fixed multiple of 20 times the pretax income of its manufacturing employees. Not many companies followed that lead, however, and many consultants pooh-pooh the change.

*Average total compensation for chief executive officers of 354 U.S. companies.

An International Interpretation

A U.S. chief executive of a $250 million firm makes about $540,000 annually, reports the consulting firm Towers Perrin. In Japan, the head of a similar company earns about $350,000.

Is the difference justified by performance? No. But it can be explained. Our culture prizes individual opportunity. Japanese culture emphasizes the individual's responsibility to the larger group. So U.S. companies have to bribe—in effect—all their most valued and senior executives from taking their secrets and talents over to the competition. The bribes push up the whole pay scale, and naturally the guy at the top tends to get the biggest bribe. In Japan, corporate loyalty is stronger and defections are almost unthinkable. Bribes aren't needed. Here and there, it's just the way the game is played.

Sources: John A. Byrne, "Is the Boss Getting Paid Too Much?" *Business Week,* May 1, 1989, p. 48, and Robert J. Samuelson, "The Great Pay Game," *Newsweek,* February 5, 1990, p. 49.

- *Performance: Results*. Tangible outcomes such as individual, group, or organization performance; quantity and quality of performance.
- *Performance: Actions and Behaviors*. Such as teamwork, cooperation, risk-taking, creativity.
- *Nonperformance Considerations*. Customary or contractual, where the type of job, nature of the work, equity, tenure, level in hierarchy, etc., are rewarded.[43]

Well-managed organizations integrate these reward distribution criteria with the performance appraisal system. For example, a pay-for-performance system facilitates granting rewards for results, while BARS appraisals help pinpoint rewardable behavior. Nonperformance factors such as seniority are simply taken at face value.

Desired Outcomes of the Reward System

As listed in Figure 13–8, a good reward system should attract talented people and motivate and satisfy them once they have joined the organization.

Further, a good reward system should foster personal growth and development and keep talented people from leaving. A prime example is Herman Miller Inc. the profitable office-furniture maker mentioned in A Matter of Ethics. Not only does the firm maintain a much lower than average ratio between top management and shop-floor pay levels, Herman Miller shares generous productivity bonuses with its employees as well. The net results: low turnover, a strong supportive culture, and excellent employee–management working relationships.[44]

• PAY FOR PERFORMANCE

Our discussion of organizational rewards would not be complete without more closely considering the role of *money*. In the workplace, money is the most common reward. Administration of monetary rewards falls into the general category of employee compensation. A comprehensive review and analysis of the hundreds of different compensation plans in use today would require a separate textbook. Instead, let us address this important underlying OB question: How can managers increase the incentive effect of monetary compensation? Managers who adequately comprehend this issue are in a better position to make decisions about specific compensation plans.

Putting Pay for Performance in Perspective

Pay for performance is the popular term for monetary incentives linking at least some portion of the paycheck directly to results or accomplishments. The whole idea behind pay-for-performance schemes—including but not limited to merit pay, bonuses, and profit sharing—is to give employees an incentive for working harder and/or smarter. Pay for performance is something extra, compensation above and beyond basic wages and salaries. Proponents of incentive compensation say something extra is needed because hourly wages and salaries do little more than motivate one to show up at work and put in the requisite hours.[45] The most blatant form of pay for performance is the traditional piece rate plan, whereby the employee is paid a specified amount of money for each unit of work. For example, a drill press operator gets 25 cents for every gasket drilled in four places. Sales commissions, whereby a salesperson receives a specified amount of money for each unit sold, is another longstanding example of pay for performance. Today's service economy is forcing management to creatively adapt and go beyond piece rate and sales commission plans to accommodate greater emphasis on product and service quality, interdependence, and teamwork.

Employers in the United States are spending an estimated $125 billion annually on incentive compensation. Nontraditional pay plans have mushroomed and now can be found in 75 percent of U.S. companies, according to the American Productivity & Quality Center.[46] Top executives routinely are granted annual bonuses in excess of $10 million. And the U.S. Congress has tackled the issue of merit pay for federal employees. While all this activity is well-intentioned, it too often falls short of its goal of improved job performance. ''Experts say that roughly half the incentive plans they see don't work, victims of poor design and administration.''[47] Researchers have found only a weak statistical link between large executive bonuses paid out in good

OB IN ACTION

Small Businesses Are Updating Sales Commission Plans

To improve results, some companies are pegging commissions partly to company profit. At Behlen Mfg. Co., Columbus, Neb., one quarter of the commission on selling a pre-engineered building now depends on the company's profit on the deal. Until late 1988, only the actual sales price counted. Such changes have boosted profit margins, says Tony Raimondo, company president.

Other companies that once paid flat commissions are gearing pay to the work involved in making the sale. Under a new plan started last year, Seal Products Inc., an Indianapolis distributor, pays up to four times as much when a sale requires hard work as when the customer simply walks in the door. Partly because of the new plan, company sales increased 25 percent last year to $6.9 million, says Richard Chastain, president.

Source: Excerpted from Roger Ricklefs, ''Whither the Payoff on Sales Commissions,'' *The Wall Street Journal*, June 6, 1990, p. B1.

years and subsequent improvement in corporate profitability.[48] Also, in a recent survey of small business owners, more than half said their commission plans failed to motivate extra effort from their salespeople[49] (see OB in Action). Clearly, the pay-for-performance movement is in danger of stalling if constructive steps are not taken.

Incentive Bonuses and Motivation: A Double-Impact Model

A first important step toward improving pay for performance is to better understand the motivational mechanism of bonuses (see Figure 13–9). As the term is used in Figure 13–9, *bonuses* refers to all forms of incentive compensation (in other words, pay for performance). Notice how *participation* plays a central role in this model. When employees fully participate in developing, implementing, and updating the performance-reward standards, three processes are triggered. First, productivity problems are more readily identified and solved. This is particularly true when teamwork techniques, such as quality circles, discussed in Chapter 11, are in force. Second, intrinsic motivation grows as the employee finds greater personal enjoyment and challenge in her or his work. Third, increased two-way information flow between management and employees empowers the employees. In turn, each of these three processes increases one's chances of earning the promised bonus, via lower costs and/or higher productivity. Intrinsic motivation translates into increased effort. Recalling our discussion of job design in Chapter 5 and expectancy motivation theory in Chapter 6, we can appreciate the motivating potential of properly administered incentive bonuses. This model makes a significant contribution to our thinking about pay for performance by emphasizing the double impact of bonuses. They motivate both when promised and when granted! The feedback loop from bonus to participation likely bolsters the employee's self-efficacy.

• **FIGURE 13-9**   The Double Impact of Incentive Bonuses on Employee Motivation and Performance

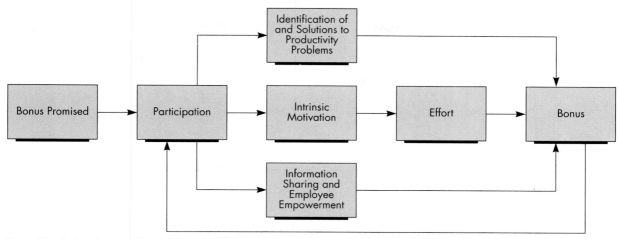

Source: Brian Graham-Moore and Timothy L. Ross, *Gainsharing* (Washington, D.C.: The Bureau of National Affairs, 1990), p. 13 as adapted from Tove Hammer, "New Developments in Profit Sharing," in *Productivity in Organizations*, ed. J. Campbell, R. Campbell, and Associates (San Francisco: Jossey-Bass, 1988). Reprinted by permission.

Keeping this model in mind as a useful conceptual framework, let us take a closer look at two distinctly different pay-for-performance practices. We then offer some practical recommendations.

Profit Sharing versus Gainsharing

The terms *profit sharing* and *gainsharing* sometimes are used interchangeably. That is not only a conceptual mistake, but a major disservice to gainsharing as well. These two general approaches to pay for performance differ significantly in both method and results.

Profit Sharing   Most of today's corporate pay-for-performance plans are profit sharing schemes. **Profit sharing** occurs when individual employees or work groups are granted a specified portion of any economic profits earned by the business as a whole. These internally distributed profits may be apportioned according to the equality or equity norms discussed earlier. Equity distributions supposedly occur when performance appraisal results are used to gauge who gets how much in the way of merit pay or profit sharing bonuses. Profit sharing bonuses may be paid in cash, deferred until retirement or death, or some combination of both (see the top section of Table 13–7).

Gainsharing   Perhaps because it tends to be used in smaller companies with 500 or fewer employees, gainsharing is not as popularly known as profit sharing. "**Gainsharing** involves a measurement of productivity combined with the calculation of a bonus designed to offer employees a mutual share of any increases in total organizational productivity. Usually all those responsible for the increase receive the bonus."[50] Gainsharing has been around for more than a half century and typically goes by one of the following names:

• **TABLE 13-7**   Profit Sharing and Gainsharing Plans

Types of Profit Sharing Plans

Deferred Plan—Credit individuals with periodic earnings, delaying actual distribution until their disability, retirement, or death.

Distribution plan—Fully distributes each period's earned benefits as soon as the profit-sharing pool can be calculated.

Combination plan—Allows employees to receive a portion of each period's earnings in cash, while the remainder awaits future distribution.

Types of Gainsharing Plans

Improshare plans—Based on employees' ability to complete assignments in less time than would be expected given the historical productivity base ratio. Work-hours saved are divided between the firm and plan participants according to a set percentage, such as 50 percent. Individuals receive a corresponding percentage increase in gross pay. Although no structural barriers exist, these plans generally do not provide formal participation in decision making.

Rucker plan—Generally limits decision-making participation to a single screening committee or the interface of a production and a screening committee. The Rucker formula assesses the relationship between the value added to produced goods as they pass through the manufacturing process and total labor costs. Unlike the typical Scanlon ratio, this formula enables workers to benefit from savings in production-related materials, supplies, and services. Bonuses result when the current ratio is better than that for the base period. A reserve pool is established to offset bad months. The reserves left over at the end of the year are paid out to employees as an additional bonus.

Scanlon plan—Uses a dual-committee system to foster companywide participation in decision making. Draws upon a historical productivity base ratio relating adjusted sales to total payroll. A bonus pool is created whenever actual output, as measured by adjusted sales, requires lower labor costs than would be expected using the base ratio. Each month, a percentage of the bonus pool is held in reserve to offset deficit months. The remaining funds are divided between the firm and employees. All of the retained funds remaining at year's end are proportionately shared by the parties.

Source: Gary W. Florkowski, "Analyzing Group Incentive Plans," *HRMagazine*, January 1990, p. 37. Reprinted with permission from HRmagazine (formerly *Personnel Administrator*) published by the Society for Human Resource Management, Alexandria, VA.

Improshare®, Rucker® plan, or Scanlon plan (see the bottom section of Table 13–7 for details). Distinguishing characteristics of gainsharing include:

- An organizational culture based on labor–management cooperation, trust, free-flowing information, and extensive participation.
- Built-in employee involvement structures such as suggestion systems or quality circles.
- Precise measurement and tracking of cost and/or productivity data for comparison purposes.
- The sharing with managerial and nonmanagerial employees of the proceeds from any productivity gains.[51]

Ideally, a self-perpetuating cycle develops. Communication and participation generate creative suggestions which foster productivity gains that yield bonuses which build motivation and trust.

How Do Profit Sharing and Gainsharing Measure Up?   Profound differences mark these two general approaches to pay for performance. Gainsharing, by definition, is anchored to hard productivity data; profit sharing typically is more loosely linked to performance appraisal results. Thus profit sharing determinations, like performance appraisals, are readily plagued by bias and misperception. Another significant problem with profit sharing is that bottom-line profits are influenced by many factors beyond the average employee's control. Those factors include strategy, pricing, competition, and fluctuating interest rates, to name just a few. Profit sharing's principal weaknesses are effectively neutralized by gainsharing's major strength, namely, a quantified performance-pay formula.

Critics of profit sharing admit it is generous to share the good times with employees, but they fear profit sharing bonuses are perceived as a reward for past performance, not as an incentive to work harder in the future. Moreover, gainsharing rewards participation and teamwork while profit sharing generally does not. On the other hand, gainsharing formulas are complex and require extensive communication and training commitments.

So, on balance, which is better? Judging by available research evidence, much of which is subjective, the vote goes to gainsharing. One study of 71 managers and professionals in a metals processing company found no significant correlation between individual performance and profit sharing bonuses.[52] Another study of 1,746 manufacturing employees, at seven firms with Scanlon plans and two control firms without Scanlon plans, found higher job satisfaction and commitment among the Scanlon employees. Additionally, participation was a significantly stronger cultural norm in the Scanlon organizations. Scanlon participants quickly passed this norm along to new employees.[53] Gainsharing seems to work best when it becomes embedded in the organization's culture.

Making Pay for Performance Work

From a practical "so what" perspective, the real issue is not profit sharing versus gainsharing. Rather, the issue is: How can managers improve the motivational impact of their present pay-for-performance plan? The fact is, most such plans are not pure types. They are hybrids. They combine features of profit sharing and gainsharing (for example, see OB in Action). One option is to hire consultants to establish one of the trademarked gainsharing plans or the Scanlon plan. A second, more broadly applicable, option is to build the best characteristics of profit sharing and gainsharing plans into the organization's pay-for-performance plan. The following practical recommendations can help in this regard:

• Make pay for performance an integral part of the organization's basic strategy (e.g., pursuit of best-in-the-industry product or service quality).
• Base incentive determinations on objective performance data.
• Have all employees actively participate in the development, implementation, and revision of the performance-pay formulas.
• Encourage two-way communication so problems with the pay-for-performance plan will be detected early.
• Build the pay-for-performance plan around participative structures such as suggestion systems or quality circles.
• Reward teamwork and cooperation whenever possible.

OB IN ACTION

Lincoln Electric's Hybrid Pay-for-Performance Plan Gets Results and Lots of Attention

Executives seeking counsel flock by the hundreds to the holy shrine of incentive pay, Lincoln Electric in Cleveland. Over the past five years more than 3,000 visitors from companies including Motorola, TRW, 3M, and McDonnell Douglas—as well as several busloads of executives and union leaders from Ford Motor and GM—have turned up at this manufacturer of industrial electric motors and welding equipment renowned for an incentive pay system that has produced spectacular productivity since 1934.

Rather than paying an hourly rate, Lincoln rewards its factory workers on a piecework basis: For each acceptable piece they produce, employees receive so many dollars. In addition, each worker receives a yearly merit rating based on his or her dependability, ideas, quality, and output, which serves as the basis for a year-end bonus. Employee bonuses average 97.6 percent of regular earnings. The payoff to Lincoln is 54 years without a losing quarter, 40 years with no layoffs, and, according to a study cited by economists William Freund and Eugene Epstein, workers who are up to three times more productive than their counterparts in similar manufacturing settings.

Source: Excerpted from Nancy J. Perry, "Here Come Richer, Riskier Pay Plans," *Fortune*, December 19, 1988, p. 51. © 1988 Time Inc. All rights reserved.

• Lincoln Electric Company's pay-for-performance system has stimulated the interest of many other companies that are looking for better incentives for their employees.   *(Courtesy of the Lincoln Electric Company, Cleveland, Ohio)*

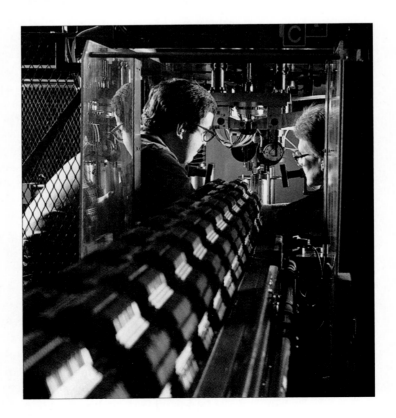

- Actively sell the plan to supervisors and middle managers who may view employee participation as a threat to their traditional notion of authority.
- If annual cash bonuses are granted, pay them in a lump sum to maximize their motivational impact.
- Remember that money motivates when it comes in significant amounts, not occasional nickels and dimes.

• SUMMARY OF KEY CONCEPTS

A. *Performance appraisal* involves the judgmental evaluation of a jobholder's traits, behavior, or accomplishments as a basis for making important personnel decisions (e.g., salary administration, performance feedback, identification of individual strengths and weaknesses).

B. Four key components of the performance appraisal process are the appraiser, the appraisee, the appraisal method, and the outcomes. Appraisers need to be wary of perceptual errors, and experts recommend a more active role for appraisees. Although the trait approach to appraisals is considered much weaker than the behavior or results approaches, each can play a role in a contingency approach.

C. Managers can resolve the performance appraisal dilemma between evaluation and development by evaluating the employee's performance in one meeting and focusing on performance improvement in a second meeting. Nontraditional approaches to performance appraisal (by subordinates, peers, or self) are a useful supplement to traditional appraisals, but an inadequate replacement. The behavioral focus of performance appraisals can be sharpened by using critical incidents and/or behaviorally anchored rating scales (BARS).

D. *Feedback* is defined as objective information about the adequacy of one's own job performance. Feedback serves both instructional and motivational functions. The idea of feedback as a control tool for systems traces back to cybernetic theory.

E. Three sources of feedback are others, the task, or oneself. If feedback is to be believed and acted upon, it must pass several perceptual and cognitive evaluation tests. Managers need to be credible sources of feedback information if they are to be effective. Four behavioral outcomes of feedback are direction, effort, persistence, and resistance. Research indicates feedback often is misperceived, needs to be tailored to the individual, and tends to be enhanced by active employee participation.

F. Organizational reward systems are based on extrinsic (financial/ material and social) and intrinsic (psychic) rewards distributed according to various reward norms and distribution criteria. A good reward system should attract, motivate, develop, satisfy, and retain talented people.

G. Pay for performance, the practice of linking pay directly to results or accomplishments, has grown dramatically in recent years despite only a 50 percent success rate. Incentive bonuses have a double impact on employee motivation and performance, because they are first promised and then delivered. Participation is a key in successful pay-for-performance plans.

H. Gainsharing tends to be more effective than profit sharing at improving performance because it requires a specific performance-pay formula, a climate of trust and participation, and employee involvement structures such as suggestions systems or quality circles. Pay-for-performance plans can work if they are strategically anchored, quantified, highly participative, and teamwork oriented.

• KEY TERMS

performance appraisal	intrinsic rewards
critical incidents	reward equity norm
behaviorally anchored rating scales (BARS)	reward equality norm
	pay for performance
feedback	profit sharing
extrinsic rewards	gainsharing

• DISCUSSION QUESTIONS

1. How could a weak link in the performance appraisal–feedback–rewards cycle damage the entire process?
2. Would you prefer to have your academic and/or work performance appraised in terms of traits, behavior, or results? Explain.
3. How would you respond to a manager who said, "The format of the performance appraisal instrument is everything?"
4. Is it unrealistic to expect performance appraisals to fill the dual purposes of evaluation and development? Explain.
5. How has feedback instructed or motivated you lately?
6. Which of the five cognitive evaluation criteria for feedback—feedback accuracy, source credibility, system fairness, expectancies, behavioral standards—do you think ranks as most important? Explain.
7. What is the most valuable lesson feedback research teaches us? Explain.
8. Which of the three organizational reward norms do you prefer? Why?
9. How would you respond to a manager who said, "Employees cannot be motivated with money"?
10. Why does gainsharing appear to have the edge over profit sharing?

BACK TO THE OPENING CASE

Now that you have read Chapter 13, you should be able to answer the following questions about the PepsiCo case:

1. What factors account for the apparent success of PepsiCo's performance evaluation process?
2. What is the main drawback of PepsiCo's performance evaluation system?
3. Using the feedback model in Figure 13–7 as a guide, how does PepsiCo keep its managers on the right track?
4. Are rewards administered effectively at PepsiCo? Explain.

• EXERCISE 13

Objectives

1. To provide actual examples of on-the-job feedback from three primary sources: organization/supervisor, co-workers, and self/task.
2. To provide a handy instrument for evaluating the comparative strength of positive feedback from these three sources.

Introduction

A pair of researchers from Georgia Tech developed and tested a 63-item feedback questionnaire to demonstrate the importance of both the sign and content of feedback messages.[54] Although their instrument contains both positive and negative feedback items, we have extracted 18 positive items for this self-awareness exercise.

Instructions

Thinking of your present job (or your most recent job), circle one number for each of the 18 items. Alternatively, you could ask one or more other employed individuals to complete the questionnaire. Once the questionnaire has been completed, calculate subtotal and total scores by adding the circled numbers. Then try to answer the discussion questions.

Instrument

How frequently do you experience each of the following outcomes in your present (or past) job?

Organizational/Supervisory Feedback

	Rarely	Occasionally	Very Frequently

1. My supervisor complimenting me on something I have done.   1——2——3——4——5
2. My supervisor increasing my responsibilities.   1——2——3——4——5
3. The company expressing pleasure with my performance.   1——2——3——4——5
4. The company giving me a raise.   1——2——3——4——5
5. My supervisor recommending me for a promotion or raise.   1——2——3——4——5
6. The company providing me with favorable data concerning my performance.   1——2——3——4——5

Subscore = _____

Co-Worker Feedback

7. My co-workers coming to me for advice.   1——2——3——4——5
8. My co-workers expressing approval of my work.   1——2——3——4——5
9. My co-workers liking to work with me.   1——2——3——4——5
10. My co-workers telling me that I am doing a good job.   1——2——3——4——5
11. My co-workers commenting favorably on something I have done.   1——2——3——4——5
12. Receiving a compliment from my co-workers.   1——2——3——4——5

Subscore = _____

Self/Task Feedback

13. Knowing that the way I go about my duties is superior to most others.   1——2——3——4——5
14. Feeling I am accomplishing more than I used to.   1——2——3——4——5
15. Knowing that I can now perform or do things which previously were difficult for me.   1——2——3——4——5
16. Finding that I am satisfying my own standards for "good work."   1——2——3——4——5
17. Knowing that what I am doing "feels right."   1——2——3——4——5
18. Feeling confident of being able to handle all aspects of my job.   1——2——3——4——5

Subscore = _____

Total score = _____

Questions for Consideration/Class Discussion

1. Which items on this questionnaire would you rate as primarily instructional in function? Are all of the remaining items primarily motivational? Explain.
2. In terms of your own feedback profile, which of the three types is the strongest (has the highest subscore)? Which is the weakest (has the lowest subscore)? How well does your feedback profile explain your job performance and/or satisfaction?
3. How does your feedback profile measure up against those of your classmates? (Arbitrary norms, for comparative purposes, are: Defi-

cient feedback = 18–42; Moderate feedback = 43–65; Abundant feedback = 66–90.)

4. Which of the three sources of feedback is most critical to your successful job performance and/or job satisfaction? Explain.

• NOTES

[1] See Jeanette N. Cleveland, Kevin R. Murphy, and Richard E. Williams, "Multiple Uses of Performance Appraisal: Prevalence and Correlates," *Journal of Applied Psychology,* February 1989, pp. 130–35.

[2] "Performance Appraisal: Current Practices and Techniques," *Personnel,* May–June 1984, p. 57.

[3] Berkeley Rice, "Performance Review: The Job Nobody Likes," *Psychology Today,* September 1986, p. 32.

[4] For a review of relevant EEO laws and guidelines, see Gerald V. Barrett and Mary C. Kernan, "Performance Appraisal and Terminations: A Review of Court Decisions Since *Brito* v. *Zia* with Implications for Personnel Practices," *Personnel Psychology,* Autumn 1987, pp. 489–503.

[5] Robert I. Lazer and Walter S. Wikstrom, *Appraising Managerial Performance: Current Practices and Future Directions,* Report 723 (New York: The Conference Board, 1977), p. 26.

[6] See "Performance Appraisals—Reappraised," *Management Review,* November 1983, p. 5. Eight common performance appraisal errors are discussed in Terry R. Lowe, "Eight Ways to Ruin a Performance Review," *Personnel Journal,* January 1986, pp. 60–62.

[7] For details, see Gregory H. Dobbins, Robert L. Cardy, and Donald M. Truxillo, "The Effects of Purpose of Appraisal and Individual Differences in Stereotypes of Women on Sex Differences in Performance Ratings: A Laboratory and Field Study," *Journal of Applied Psychology,* August 1988, pp. 551–58.

[8] Data from Brian S. Klaas and Angelo S. DeNisi, "Managerial Reactions to Employee Dissent: The Impact of Grievance Activity on Performance Ratings," *Academy of Management Journal,* December 1989, pp. 705–17.

[9] "Performance Appraisals—Reappraised," p. 5.

[10] Kenneth N. Wexley and Richard Klimoski, "Performance Appraisal: An Update," in *Research in Personnel and Human Resources Management,* Vol. 2, ed. Kendrith M. Rowland and Gerald R. Ferris (Greenwich, Conn.: JAI Press, 1984), pp. 55–56.

[11] Betsy Jacobson and Beverly L. Kaye, "Career Development and Performance Appraisal: It Takes Two to Tango," *Personnel,* January 1986, p. 27.

[12] Supporting discussion is provided by Kenneth N. Wexley, "Appraisal Interview," in *Performance Assessment,* ed. Ronald A. Berk (Baltimore, Md.: The Johns Hopkins Press Ltd., 1986).

[13] See, for example, Jan P. Muczyk and Bernard C. Reimann, "MBO as a Complement to Effective Leadership," *The Academy of Management Executive,* May 1989, pp. 131–38.

[14] See Ann M. Morrison, "Performance Appraisal: Getting from Here to There," *Human Resource Planning,* no. 2, 1984, pp. 73–77. Also see Charles Lee, "Smoothing Out Appraisal Systems," *HRMagazine,* March 1990, pp. 72–76.

15 Results are presented in Kurt Kraiger and J. Kevin Ford, "A Meta-Analysis of Ratee Race Effects in Performance Ratings," *Journal of Applied Psychology,* February 1985, pp. 56–65.

16 Research results extracted from Frank J. Landy and James L. Farr, "Performance Rating," *Psychological Bulletin,* January 1980, pp. 72–107; Wexley and Klimoski, "Performance Appraisal: An Update"; Rice, "Performance Review: The Job Nobody Likes"; Jerry W. Hedge and Michael J. Kavangh, "Improving the Accuracy of Performance Evaluations: Comparisons of Three Methods of Performance Appraiser Training," *Journal of Applied Psychology,* February 1988, pp. 68–73; and Richard Klimoski and Lawrence Inks, "Accountability Forces in Performance Appraisal," *Organizational Behavior and Human Decision Processes,* April 1990, pp. 194–208.

17 See, for example, David A. Waldman and Ron S. Kenett, "Improve Performance by Appraisal," *HRMagazine,* July 1990, pp. 66–69.

18 For example, see H. Kent Baker and Philip I. Morgan, "Two Goals in Every Performance Appraisal," *Personnel Journal,* September 1984, pp. 74–78.

19 Larry Reibstin, "Firms Ask Workers to Rate Their Bosses," *The Wall Street Journal,* June 13, 1988, p. 17.

20 For example, see Chris Lee, "Talking Back to the Boss," *Training,* April 1990, pp. 29–35.

21 See Michael M. Harris and John Schaubroeck, "A Meta-Analysis of Self-Supervisor, Self-Peer, and Peer-Supervisor Ratings," *Personnel Psychology,* Spring 1988, pp. 43–62, and John Lane and Peter Herriot, "Self-Ratings, Supervisor Ratings, Positions and Performance," *Journal of Occupational Psychology,* March 1990, pp. 77–88.

22 This critique of BARS was drawn from discusson in Landy and Farr, "Performance Rating," pp. 83–84.

23 Ronald Henkoff, "Cost Cutting: How To Do It Right," *Fortune,* April 9, 1990, p. 48.

24 Both the definition of feedback and the functions of feedback are based on discussion in Daniel R. Ilgen, Cynthia D. Fisher, and M. Susan Taylor, "Consequences of Individual Feedback on Behavior in Organizations," *Journal of Applied Psychology,* August 1979, pp. 349–71; and Richard E. Kopelman, *Managing Productivity in Organizations: A Practical People-Oriented Perspective* (New York: McGraw-Hill, 1986), p. 175.

25 See P. Christopher Earley, Gregory B. Northcraft, Cynthia Lee, and Terri R. Lituchy, "Impact of Process and Outcome Feedback on the Relation of Goal Setting to Task Performance," *Academy of Management Journal,* March 1990, pp. 87–105.

26 Ron Zemke, "Feedback Technology and the Growing Appetite for Self-Knowledge," *Training,* April 1982, p. 28.

27 Adapted from discussion in M. Susan Taylor, Cynthia D. Fisher, and Daniel R. Ilgen, "Individuals' Reactions to Performance Feedback in Organizations: A Control Theory Perspective," in *Research in Personnel and Human Resources Management,* Vol. 2, ed. Kendrith M. Rowland and Gerald R. Ferris (Greenwich, Conn.: JAI Press, 1984), pp. 81–124.

28 See Tamao Matsui, Akinori Okkada, and Takashi Kakuyama, "Influence of Achievement Need on Goal Setting, Performance, and Feedback Effectiveness," *Journal of Applied Psychology,* October 1982, pp. 645–48; and Susan J. Ashford, "Feedback-Seeking in Individual Adaptation: A Resource Perspective," *Academy of Management Journal,* September 1986, pp. 465–87.

29 See Brendan D. Bannister, "Performance Outcome Feedback and Attributional Feedback: Interactive Effects on Recipient Responses," *Journal of Applied Psychology,* May 1986, pp. 203–10.

30 For complete details, see Philip M. Podsakoff and Jiing-Lih Farh, "Effects of Feedback Sign and Credibility on Goal Setting and Task Performance," *Organizational Behavior and Human Decision Processes,* August 1989, pp. 45–67.

31 Bro Uttal, "Behind the Fall of Steve Jobs," *Fortune,* August 5, 1985, p. 22.

32 Based on discussion in Ilgen, Fisher, and Taylor, "Consequences of Individual Feedback on Behavior in Organizations," pp. 367–68.

33 See P. Christopher Earley, "Computer-Generated Performance Feedback in the Magazine-Subscription Industry," *Organizational Behavior and Human Decision Processes,* February 1988, pp. 50–64.

34 See MaryBeth De Gregorio and Cynthia D. Fisher, "Providing Performance Feedback: Reactions to Alternate Methods," *Journal of Management,* December 1988, pp. 605–16.

35 For details, see Robert A. Baron, "Countering the Effects of Destructive Criticism: The Relative Efficacy of Four Interventions," *Journal of Applied Psychology,* June 1990, pp. 235–45.

36 Practical tips for giving feedback also may be found in Robert Kreitner, "People Are Systems, Too: Filling the Feedback Vacuum," *Business Horizons,* November 1977, pp. 54–58; and Robert A. Luke, Jr., "How to Give Corrective Feedback to Employees," *Supervisory Management,* March 1990, p. 7.

37 William J. Wiatrowski, "Family-Related Benefits in the Workplace," *Monthly Labor Review,* March 1990, p. 28.

38 Data from U.S. Bureau of the Census, *Statistical Abstract of the United States: 1990* (110th edition). Washington, D.C., 1990, table No. 677, p. 413.

39 For complete discussions, see Arthur P. Brief and Ramon J. Aldag, "The Intrinsic-Extrinsic Dichotomy: Toward Conceptual Clarity," *Academy of Management Review,* July 1977, pp. 496–500; and Edward L. Deci, *Intrinsic Motivation* (New York: Plenum Press, 1975), chap. 2.

40 See Ken I. Kim, Hun-Joon Park, and Nori Suzuki, "Reward Allocations in the United States, Japan, and Korea: A Comparison of Individualistic and Collectivistic Cultures," *Academy of Management Journal,* March 1990, pp. 188–98.

41 Adapted from Jone L. Pearce and Robert H. Peters, "A Contradictory Norms View of Employer–Employee Exchange," *Journal of Management,* Spring 1985, pp. 19–30.

42 Ibid., p. 25.

43 Mary Ann Von Glinow, "Reward Strategies for Attracting, Evaluating, and Retaining Professionals," *Human Resource Management,* Summer 1985, p. 193.

44 See Kenneth Labich, "Hot Company, Warm Culture," *Fortune,* February 27, 1989, pp. 74–78.

45 Pros and cons of pay for performance are reviewed in Thomas Rollins, "Pay for Performance: Is It Worth the Trouble?" *Personnel Administrator,* May 1988, pp. 42–46; also see Jerrold R. Bratkovich and Bernadette Steele, "Compensation: Pay For Performance Boosts Productivity," *Personnel Journal,* January 1989, pp. 78–86.

46 Data from Nancy J. Perry, "Here Come Richer, Riskier Pay Plans," *Fortune,* December 19, 1988, pp. 50–58.

47 Ibid., p. 51.

48 See Michael J. Mandel, "Those Fat Bonuses Don't Seem to Boost Performance," *Business Week,* January 8, 1990, p. 26.

49 Based on discussion in Roger Ricklefs, "Whither the Payoff on Sales Commissions?" *The Wall Street Journal,* June 6, 1990, p. B1.

50 Brian Graham-Moore, "Review of the Literature," in *Gainsharing,* eds. Brian

Graham-Moore and Timothy L. Ross (Washington, D.C.: The Bureau of National Affairs, 1990), p. 20 (emphasis added).

[51] Ibid., based largely on pp. 3–4.

[52] For details, see Steven E. Markham, "Pay-for-Performance Dilemma Revisited: Empirical Example of the Importance of Group Effects," *Journal of Applied Psychology,* May 1988, pp. 172–80.

[53] Data from Katherine I. Miller, "Cultural and Role-Based Predictors of Organizational Participation and Allocation Preferences," *Communication Research,* December 1988, pp. 699–725; See also Gary W. Florkowski, "Analyzing Group Incentive Plans," *HRMagazine,* January 1990, pp. 36–38.

[54] This exercise is adapted from material in David M. Herold and Charles K. Parsons, "Assessing the Feedback Environment in Work Organizations: Development of the Job Feedback Survey," *Journal of Applied Psychology,* May 1985, pp. 290–305.

Leadership

When you finish studying the material in this chapter, you should be able to:

- Define the term *leadership* and explain the conceptual framework for understanding leadership.
- Review trait theory research.
- Discuss the idea of *one best style of leadership*, using the Ohio State studies and the Leadership Grid® as points of reference.

- Explain, according to Fiedler's contingency model, how leadership style interacts with situational control.
- Discuss House's path–goal theory and review the theory's managerial implications.
- Describe Hersey and Blanchard's situational leadership theory.

- Explain the role-making (VDL) model of leadership.
- Demonstrate your familiarity with the leader/follower attribution process.
- Define and differentiate transactional and transformational leadership.
- Discuss the characteristics of transformational leaders.

OPENING CASE 14

Microsoft's Bill Gates Is a Successful Transactional and Transformational Leader

Sharon Hoogstraten

Microsoft is no personality cult. Nor is it a corporate dictatorship. With some 5,200 employees, over $1 billion in revenues. . . [In 1990], and the broadest array of products in the personal computer software business, it is too big and too diverse to be either. From early on [Chairman William H. Gates III] has relied on a handful of strong professional managers. Despite his reputation as the consummate computer nerd, Microsoft's growth testified to his skills as manager and leader.

Microsoft—more than any other company to emerge from the personal computer revolution—is the technological, organizational, and commercial embodiment of one man's vision. Its clarity of purpose, competitiveness, tenacity, and technological self-confidence emanate from Gates. And despite his company's swelling size, he has found an effective way to keep communicating all that directly. In a business where people eat innovation for breakfast, his personal qualities have helped him keep the magic going after Microsoft's initial, spectacular success. . . .

How have Gates and his lieutenants managed to manage Microsoft so well? One key is his ability to spread himself around. While the technological strategies bear the Gates signature, he and his managers break them down into concise business goals that can be handled by small, independent "business units" of programmers and marketers. The groups are small enough so that Gates can sit around a table to chat with key members and inject his ideas personally. While he would prefer not

to be bothered with operational details, he is quick to identify both organizational weaknesses and the management talent required to repair them.

Although Gates freely delegates, his capacity for retaining business and technical details enables him to understand intimately both the forest and the trees. At meetings with his managers, he is as likely to check the math in handouts and overhead slides for errors as he is to critique fuzzy marketing strategies. He loves to join Microsoft programmers in the brainstorming sessions that give birth to new products. "It's very important to me and to the guys that work for us that Microsoft feel like a small company, even though it isn't one anymore," says Gates. "I remember how much fun it is to be small, and the business units help preserve that feeling." . . .

The key to Gates's management strategy is Microsoft's dozen business units, some of which employ as few as 30 people. Each group is in charge of a particular type of software, and each

---

Someone once observed that a leader is a person who finds out which way the parade is going, jumps in front of it, and yells "Follow me!" The plain fact is that this approach to leadership has little chance of working in today's rapidly changing world. Admired leaders, such as civil rights activist Martin Luther King, Jr., Germany's Helmut Kohl (see International OB), and General Electric's CEO Jack Welch, led people in bold new directions. They envisioned how things could be improved, rallied followers, and refused to accept failure. In short, successful leaders are those individuals who can step into a difficult situation and make a noticeable difference. But how much of a difference can leaders make in modern organizations?

OPENING CASE 14

(concluded)

knows exactly how it stacks up against its competitors by every conceivable measure, from the technical sophistication of a program to the amount of labor that went into building it. Business unit managers—known inevitably as BUMs—study the products of competitors along with any financial and productivity information their rivals make public. If the Microsoft unit doesn't outperform its competitors, the unit hears about it—often from Gates, who is known to do the same homework himself. . . .

Gates, whose father is a prominent Seattle lawyer, says the promotion and compensation plan for his programmers is similar to that of a law firm. Each programmer is rated at one of six levels between 10 and 15, with architects at 15. "When you hit 13, it's like making partner," says Gates. "We have a big ceremony and everything," including awarding the programmer more stock options. While some programmers also perform some management chores, they don't have to be managers to climb the

scale. A nifty piece of programming will do the trick.

All this inspires tremendous loyalty. The company's central role in the PC industry also helps, as does Gates's personal magnetism and accessibility. Chairman Bill encourages employees to communicate with him directly through the company's electronic mail system, and dozens do each day. He tries to respond to each message the same day he gets it. . . .

Gates insists that all the challenges only make his job more fascinating. "I'd get bored if things just stayed the same," he says. Besides, deep down he's still a technology nut. With others tackling business and organizational issues full time, he still has leisure to do what he likes best—talk techie with his architects and engineers. He tries to spend at least half his time doing that. Many evenings, long after the rest of the executive staff has left, Gates is dropping in on the business units to see what's really getting done. Says he: "When I feel good at the end of the day, it's because I find

a product group that is doing better than I expected, or because I contributed a good idea that ends up in a product."

Will Gates ever step aside? Probably not any time soon. "This company is my life," he says. Besides, Microsoft hasn't yet fulfilled the mission he and co-founder [Paul] Allen set for the company 15 years ago: "A computer on every desk and in every home, all running Microsoft software." Allen, who left the company in 1983 partly for health reasons, has just rejoined the Microsoft board. Together, he and the tenacious Gates are still chasing their ambitious goal. They may never get there, but it won't be for want of trying.

For Discussion

Is Bill Gates a good leader?

• Additional discussion questions linking this case with the following material appear at the end of this chapter.

Source: Adapted from Brenton Schlender, "How Bill Gates Keeps the Magic Going," *Fortune*, June 18, 1990, pp. 82–89. © 1990 The Time Inc. Magazine Company. All rights reserved.

OB researchers have discovered that leaders can make a *significant* difference. In one study, for example, the performance of 50 United Methodist ministers was studied over a 20-year period. After dividing the sample into effective and ineffective leaders, the researchers compared objective measures of performance for the two groups. Effective and ineffective leadership was determined by the ministers' positive or negative impact on attendance at worship services, membership in the congregation, property value, and monetary giving. Results indicated that churches with superior ministers experienced significantly greater charitable income, membership, and property value than the remaining churches.[1] Another study tracked the relationship between net profit and leadership in 167 companies from 13

INTERNATIONAL OB

Germany Is Unified through Helmut Kohl's Leadership

Mr. Kohl's list of achievements over the past 12 months is extraordinary. He unified Germany in such a way that he avoided arousing alarm abroad or nationalism at home. He kept unified Germany in the Western alliance, but he also forged closer relations with Moscow than at any time since the beginning of World War II. He made friends of Mr. Gorbachev, a man he once likened to Nazi propagandist Josef Goebbels, and he deployed his close relationship with George Bush to neutralize British and French misgivings about unification. Amid all this, he continued to press for European integration.

Many problems remain, ranging from the cost of absorbing East Germany to the challenges posed by East European and Soviet economic decline. But even many of Mr. Kohl's former critics praise him for the pitfalls he has sidestepped. Early on, he decided that missing the historical moment was a far graver risk than proceeding too quickly.

Source: Excerpted from Frederick Kempe, "German Giant: Helmut Kohl Takes Europe's Center Stage, Surprising His Critics," *The Wall Street Journal,* November 30, 1990, p. A1.

industries. It also covered a time span of 20 years. Higher net profits were earned by companies with effective leaders.[2] Leadership does make a difference in today's organizations, and that difference is worth studying because it can become a competitive advantage.

After formally defining the term *leadership,* this chapter focuses on the following areas: (1) trait and behavioral approaches to leadership, (2) alternative contingency theories of leadership, (3) role-making and attribution theories of leadership, and (4) transformational leadership.

• WHAT DOES LEADERSHIP INVOLVE

Because the topic of leadership has fascinated people for centuries, definitions abound. A common thread among these definitions is social influence. As the term is used in this chapter, **leadership** is defined as "a social influence process in which the leader seeks the voluntary participation of subordinates in an effort to reach organizational objectives."[3]

Tom Peters and Nancy Austin, authors of the best-seller, *A Passion for Excellence,* describe leadership in broader terms:

> Leadership means vision, cheerleading, enthusiasm, love, trust, verve, passion, obsession, consistency, the use of symbols, paying attention as illustrated by the content of one's calendar, out-and-out drama (and the management thereof), creating heroes at all levels, coaching, effectively wandering around, and numerous other things. Leadership must be present at all levels of the organization. It depends on a million little things done with obsession, consistency and care, but all of those million little things add up to nothing if the trust, vision and basic belief are not there.[4]

Leadership clearly entails more than wielding power and exercising authority. The label *leadership* embraces many different managerial concepts

• FIGURE 14-1   A Conceptual Framework for Understanding Leadership

Leader Characteristics/ Traits
- Need for achievement
- Need for power
- Cognitive ability
- Interpersonal skills
- Self-confidence

Managerial Behavior/ Roles
- Interpersonal roles
- Informational roles
- Decisional roles

Desired End Results
- Unit performance
- Profitability
- Goal attainment
- Job satisfaction

Situational Variables

Individual Level
- Leader's position power
- Follower motivation
- Follower role clarity
- Follower ability

Organizational Level
- Resource adequacy
- Task/technology
- Organization structure
- External environment

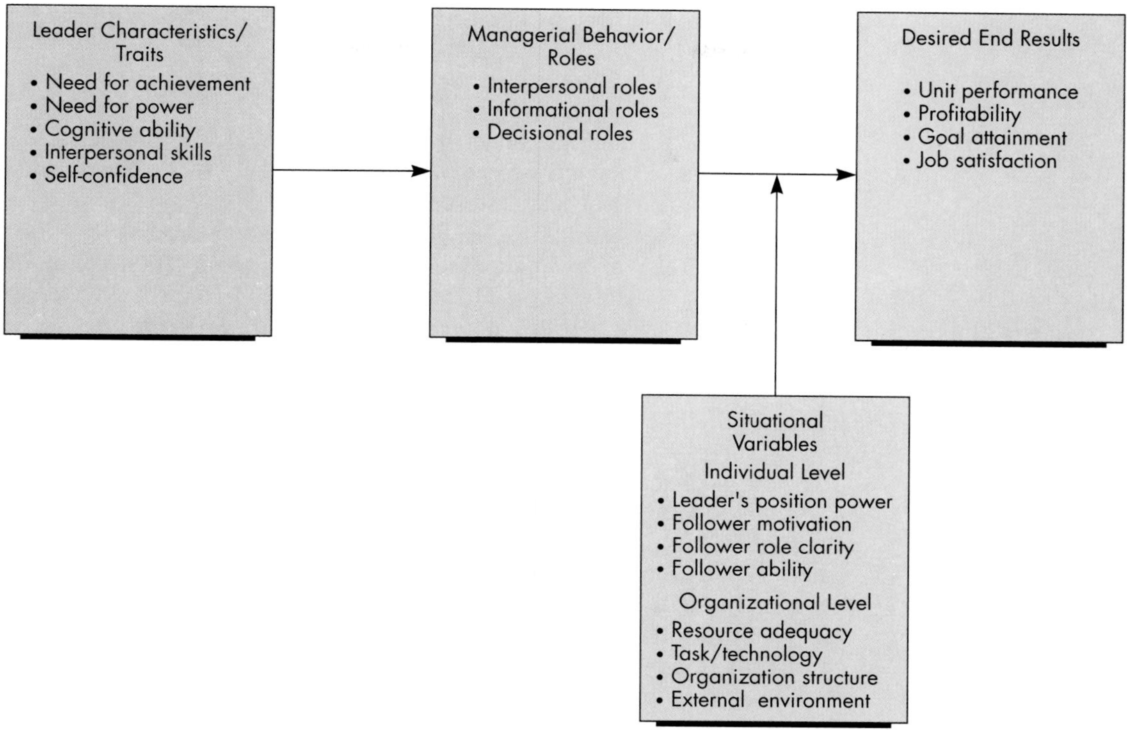

Source: Adapted in part from Gary Yukl, "Managerial Leadership: A Review of Theory and Research," *Journal of Management,* June 1989, p. 274.

already discussed, including values, perception, motivation, reinforcement, socialization, power, politics, teamwork, feedback, and communication. Figure 14–1 provides a conceptual framework for understanding leadership. It was created by integrating components of the different theories and models discussed in this chapter.

Figure 14–1 indicates that certain leader characteristics/traits are the foundation of effective leadership. (Leader traits are discussed in the next section of this chapter.) In turn, these characteristics affect an individual's ability to carry out various managerial behavior/roles. Leadership is separated from management, because each represents unique activities that are jointly needed to achieve various desired end results, such as profitability and goal attainment. One without the other leads to decreased end results.[5] Finally, research demonstrates that effective leadership depends on various situational variables. These variables are important components of the contingency leadership theories discussed later in this chapter.

• TRAIT AND BEHAVIORAL THEORIES OF LEADERSHIP

This section examines the two earliest approaches used to explain leadership. Trait theories, the old approach, focused on identifying the personal traits that differentiated leaders from followers. Behavioral theorists examined leadership from a different perspective. They tried to uncover the different kinds of leader behaviors that resulted in higher work group performance. Both approaches to leadership can teach present and future managers valuable lessons about leading.

Trait Theory

At the turn of the 20th century, the prevailing belief was that leaders were born, not made. Selected people were thought to possess inborn traits that made them successful leaders. A **leader trait** is a physical or personality characteristic that can be used to differentiate leaders from followers.

Before World War II, hundreds of studies were conducted to pinpoint the traits of successful leaders. Dozens of leadership traits were identified. During the postwar period, however, enthusiasm was replaced by widespread criticism. Studies conducted by Ralph Stogdill in 1948 and by Richard Mann in 1959, which sought to summarize the impact of traits on leadership, caused the trait approach to fall into disfavor.

Stogdill's and Mann's Findings   Based on his review, Stogdill concluded that five traits tended to differentiate leaders from average followers. They were (1) intelligence, (2) dominance, (3) self-confidence, (4) level of energy and activity, and (5) task-relevant knowledge.[6] However, these five traits did not accurately predict which individuals became leaders in organizations. People with these traits often remained followers.

Mann's review was similarly disappointing for the trait theorists. Among the seven categories of personality traits he examined, Mann found intelligence was the best predictor of leadership. However, Mann warned that all observed positive relationships between traits and leadership were weak (correlations averaged about 0.15).[7]

Together, Stogdill's and Mann's findings dealt a near deathblow to the trait approach. But now, decades later, leadership traits are once again receiving serious research attention.

Contemporary Trait Research   Two OB researchers concluded in 1983 that past trait data may have been incorrectly analyzed. By applying modern statistical techniques to an old database, they demonstrated that the majority of a leader's behavior could be attributed to stable underlying traits.[8] Unfortunately, their methodology did not single out specific traits.

A 1986 meta-analysis by Robert Lord and his associates remedied this shortcoming with the following insights: First, the Lord study criticized leadership researchers for misinterpreting Stogdill's and Mann's findings. Specifically, correlations between traits and *perceived leadership ability* were misinterpreted as linkages between traits and leader *effectiveness*. Second, a reanalysis of Mann's data and subsequent studies revealed that individuals tend to be perceived as leaders when they possess one or more of the following traits: intelligence, dominance, and masculinity. Thus, Lord and his colleagues concluded, "Personality traits are associated with leadership perceptions to a higher degree and more consistently than the popular literature indicates."[9] This conclusion was supported by results from a recent study of 122 individuals working in 28 task groups. Findings indicated that men and women became leaders more frequently when they possessed masculine as opposed to feminine characteristics.[10] It should be noted that this masculinity orientation reflects a cultural gender bias, not sexist research. Of course, equal employment opportunity laws in the United States and elsewhere prohibit basing employment decisions on gender.

Trait Theory in Perspective   We can no longer afford to ignore the implications of leadership traits. Traits play a central role in how we perceive leaders. Recalling the Chapter 4 discussion of social perception, it is important to determine the traits embodied in people's schemata (or mental pictures) for leaders. If those traits are inappropriate (i.e., foster discriminatory selection and invalid performance appraisals), they need to be corrected through training and development. Moreover, organizations may find it beneficial to consider selected leadership traits when choosing among candidates for leadership positions.

Behavioral Styles Theory

This phase of leadership research began during World War II as part of an effort to develop better military leaders. It was an outgrowth of two events: the seeming inability of trait theory to explain leadership effectiveness and the human relations movement, an outgrowth of the Hawthorne Studies. The thrust of early behavioral leadership theory was to focus on leader behavior, instead of on personality traits. It was believed that leader behavior directly affected work group effectiveness. This led researchers to identify patterns of behavior (called leadership styles) that enabled leaders to effectively influence others.

The Hawthorne Studies, discussed in Chapter 1, supposedly demonstrated that supportive supervision had a positive impact on performance. We now know this was not necessarily true. In any event, this conclusion paved the way for the belief that there is *one best style of leadership*. This view was initially reinforced by Kurt Lewin's widely cited 1939 laboratory study that documented how followers preferred leaders with a democratic style, as opposed to those with either an authoritarian or laissez-faire (hands-off) style.[11] Table 14–1 summarizes these three classic styles of leadership.

Because Lewin and his associates used young children as subjects, critics eventually pointed out the limited generalizability of the results. Consequently, teams of researchers from two universities directed their efforts to identifying the behaviors that differentiated effective and ineffective leaders.

The Ohio State Studies   Researchers at Ohio State University began by generating a list of behaviors exhibited by leaders. At one point, the list contained 1,800 statements that described nine categories of leader behavior. Ultimately, the Ohio State researchers concluded there were only two independent dimensions of leader behavior: consideration and initiating structure. **Consideration** involves leader behavior associated with creating mutual respect or trust and focuses on a concern for group members' needs and desires. **Initiating structure** is leader behavior that organizes and defines what group members should be doing to maximize output. These two dimensions of leader behavior were oriented at right angles to yield four behavioral styles of leadership (see Figure 14–2).

• **Table 14-1**   The Three Classic Styles of Leader Behavior

	Authoritarian	**Democratic**	**Laissez-faire**
Nature	Leader retains all authoriity and responsibility	Leader delegates a great deal of authority while retaining ultimate responsibility	Leader denies responsibility and abdicates authority to group
	Leader assigns people to clearly defined tasks	Work is divided and assigned on the basis of participatory decision making	Group members are told to work things out themselves and do the best they can
	Primarily a downward flow of communication	Active two-way flow of upward and downward communication	Primarily horizontal communication among peers
Primary strength	Stresses prompt, orderly, and predictable performance	Enhances personal commitment through participation	Permits self-starters to do things as they see fit without leader interference
Primary weakness	Approach tends to stifle individual initiative	Democratic process is time-consuming	Group may drift aimlessly in the absence of direction from leader

Source: Robert Kreitner, *Management*, 4th ed. (Boston: Houghton Mifflin, 1989), p. 514.

• **Figure 14-2**   Four Leadership Styles Derived from the Ohio State Studies

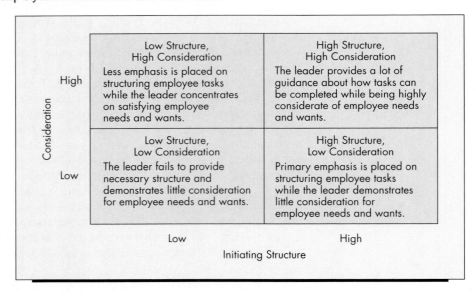

It initially was hypothesized that a high structure, high consideration style would be the one best style of leadership. Consider, for example, how Judy Lewent, Chief Financial Officer of Merck & Co., uses both structure and consideration when dealing with employees.

Known for putting in 70-hour workweeks, Lewent demands the same or greater from her staffers. If workers want to take a break, she suggests they jog at lunchtime or work out in company exercise facilities. Excruciatingly well-organized, she recently gave a colleague directions to Cooperstown, N.Y. It came complete with a list of the best rest stops along the way for the colleague's two boys.[12]

Through the years, the effectiveness of the high-high style has been tested many times. Overall, results have been mixed. Researchers thus concluded that there is not one best style of leadership.[13] Rather, it is argued that effectiveness of a given leadership style depends on situational factors.

University of Michigan Studies As in the Ohio State studies, this research sought to identify behavioral differences between effective and ineffective leaders. Researchers identified two different styles of leadership: one was employee centered, the other was job centered. These behavioral styles parallel the consideration and initiating-structure styles identified by the Ohio State group. In summarizing the results from these studies, one management expert concluded that effective leaders: (1) tend to have supportive or employee-centered relationships with employees, (2) use group rather than individual methods of supervision, and (3) set high performance goals.[14]

Blake and Mouton's Managerial/Leadership Grid® Perhaps the most widely known behavioral styles model of leadership is the Managerial Grid.® Behavioral scientists Robert Blake and Jane Srygley Mouton developed and trademarked the grid. They use it to demonstrate that there *is* one best style of leadership. Blake and Mouton's Managerial Grid® (renamed the **Leadership Grid®** in 1991) is a matrix formed by the intersection of two dimensions of leader behavior (see Figure 14–3). On the horizontal axis is "concern for production." "Concern for people" is on the vertical axis.

Blake and Mouton point out that "the variables of the Managerial Grid® are *attitudinal and conceptual,* with *behavior* descriptions derived from and connected with the thinking that lies behind action."[15] In other words, concern for production and concern for people involve attitudes and patterns of thinking, as well as specific behaviors. By scaling each axis of the grid from 1 to 9, Blake and Mouton were able to plot five leadership styles. Because it emphasizes teamwork and interdependence, the 9,9 style is considered by Blake and Mouton to be the best, regardless of the situation.

In support of the 9,9 style, Blake and Mouton cite the results of a study in which 100 experienced managers were asked to select the best way of handling 12 managerial situations. Between 72 and 90 percent of the managers selected the 9,9 style for each of the 12 situations.[16] Moreover, Blake and Mouton report, "The 9,9 orientation . . . leads to productivity, satisfaction, creativity, and health."[17] Critics point out that Blake and Mouton's research may be self-serving. At issue is the grid's extensive use as a training and consulting tool for diagnosing and correcting organizational problems.

Behavioral Styles Theory in Perspective By emphasizing leader *behavior,* something that is learned, the behavioral style approach makes it clear that leaders are made, not born. This is the opposite of the trait theorists' traditional assumption. Given what we know about behavior shaping and model-based training, leader *behaviors* can be systematically improved and developed. For example, a recent study demonstrated that managers can be taught to use positive reward behavior, reprimand behavior, and goal-setting behavior.[18]

Moreover, leadership styles appear to vary by gender. A recent meta-analysis demonstrated that women more frequently used a democratic or

• **FIGURE 14-3**   The Leadership Grid® Figure EM

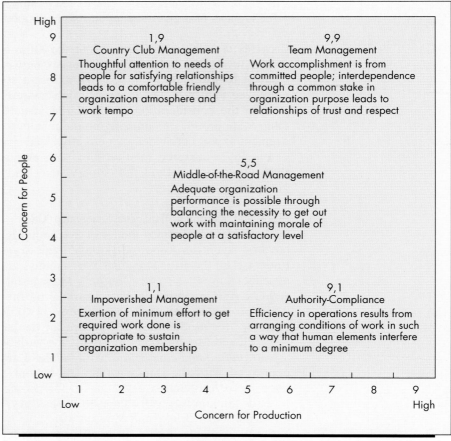

Source: From Robert R. Blake and Anne Adams McCanse (Houston: Gulf Publishing, 1991), p. 29. Copyright © 1991 by Scientific Methods, Inc. Reproduced by permission of the owners.

participative style; whereas men relied more often on an autocratic or directive style.[19] Is one of these styles better than the other? Research suggests not. The effectiveness of a particular leadership style depends on the situation at hand. For instance, employees prefer structure over consideration when faced with role ambiguity.[20] We now consider alternative situational theories of leadership.

• SITUATIONAL THEORIES

Situational leadership theories grew out of an attempt to explain the inconsistent findings about traits and styles. **Situational theories** propose that the effectiveness of a particular style of leader behavior depends on the situation. As situations change, different styles become appropriate. This directly challenges the idea of one best style of leadership. Let us closely examine three alternative situational theories of leadership that reject the notion of one best leadership style (see International OB).

INTERNATIONAL OB

In International Management There Is No One Best Style of Leadership

Business travelers carrying their *One Minute Manager,* by Kenneth Blanchard and Spencer Johnson, get a cold splash of a different reality when they plunge into business in Abu Dhabi or Bombay. . . . A one-minute praising could even bring work to a stop in Japan, where singling out an individual causes humiliation, and the authors' recommended pat on the arm will only compound the error. Never touch in Japan. . . .

Some of the concepts in the best-selling *In Search of Excellence,* by Tom Peters and Robert Waterman, travel well; others need to be discarded in the international situation. MBWA (management by walking around), for example, can permanently tarnish a boss' image in France, where proper decorum is a mark of authority and important for maintaining respect. Participative management is viewed as incompetence in Latin America and the Arab world, where bosses make decisions and good subordinates follow orders.

Source: Excerpted from Lennie Copeland, "Savoir Faire over There," *Nation's Business,* September 1986, p. 48.

Fiedler's Contingency Model

Fred Fiedler, an OB scholar, developed a situational model of leadership. It is the oldest, most widely known, and most extensively researched situational model of leadership. Fiedler's basic premise is that leader effectiveness is *contingent* upon an appropriate match between the leader's style and the degree to which he or she controls the situation. Before we examine this matching process, we need to discuss Fiedler's ideas about leadership style and situational control. After linking these variables, we conclude this section with a discussion of relevant research and a framework for applying Fiedler's model.[21]

The Leader's Style: Task-Oriented or Relationship-Oriented?
Fiedler developed the least preferred co-worker (LPC) scale to identify leadership styles. (You will be asked to complete the LPC scale when working on the exercise at the end of this chapter.) He contends that the LPC scale measures whether a leader has a **task-oriented style** or a **relationship-oriented style.** Although there has been much disagreement over the definition of these styles, they have been characterized as follows:

> Low-LPC persons, those describing their least preferred co-worker in quite negative terms, are thought to be primarily concerned with task success, i.e., they are "task-oriented." On the other hand, persons describing their least preferred co-worker in relatively positive terms (high-LPC persons) are thought to be "relationship-oriented," i.e., primarily concerned with attaining and maintaining successful interpersonal relationships.[22]

Leadership styles, according to Fiedler, are relatively stable from one situation to the next because they reflect the individual's basic motivation.

Situational Control   Situational control refers to the amount of control and influence the leader has in her or his immediate work environment. Situational control ranges from high to low. High control implies that the leader's decisions will produce predictable results because the leader has the ability to influence work outcomes. Low control implies that the leader's decisions may not influence work outcomes because the leader has very little influence. There are three dimensions of situational control: leader–member relations, task structure, and position power. These dimensions vary independently, forming eight combinations of situational control (see Figure 14–4).

The three dimensions of situational control are defined as follows:

- **Leader–member relations** reflect the extent to which the leader has the support, loyalty, and trust of the work group. This dimension is the most important component of situational control. Good leader–member relations suggest that the leader can depend on the group, thus ensuring that the work group will try to meet the leader's goals and objectives.

- **Task structure** is concerned with the amount of structure contained within tasks performed by the work group. For example, a managerial job contains less structure than that of a bank teller. Since structured tasks have guidelines for how the job should be com-

• **FIGURE 14-4**   Representation of Fiedler's Contingency Model

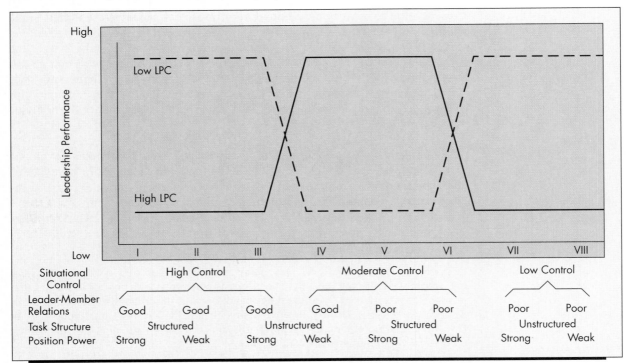

Source: Adapted from Fred E. Fiedler, "Situational Control and a Dynamic Theory of Leadership," in *Managerial Control and Organizational Democracy*, ed. Bert King, Siegfried Streufert, and Fred E. Fiedler (New York: John Wiley & Sons, 1978), p. 114. Used with permission.

pleted, the leader has more control and influence over employees performing such tasks. This dimension is the second most important component of situational control.

• **Position power** refers to the degree to which the leader has formal power to reward, punish, or otherwise obtain compliance from employees.[23]

Linking Leadership Style and Situational Control   Fiedler's complete contingency model is presented in Figure 14–4. The horizontal axis breaks out the eight control situations. Each situation represents a unique combination of leader–member relations, task structure, and position power. The vertical axis indicates the level of leader effectiveness. Plotted on the resulting quadrant are lines indicating those situations in which low-LPC (dotted line) and high-LPC (solid line) leaders are predicted to be effective.

For those situations in which the leader has high control (situations I, II, and III), task-oriented (low-LPC) leaders are hypothesized to be more effective than relationship-oriented (high-LPC) leaders. Under conditions of moderate control (situations IV, V, and VI), the interpersonal orientation of high-LPC leaders is predicted to be more effective. Finally, the task orientation of low-LPC leaders is hypothesized to be more effective under conditions of low control (situations VII and VIII). *In short, Fiedler contends that task-oriented leaders are more effective in extreme situations of either high or low control, but relationship-oriented leaders tend to be more effective in middle-of-the-road situations of moderate control.*

Research and Managerial Implications   The overall accuracy of Fiedler's contingency model was tested through a meta-analysis of 35 studies containing 137 leader style–performance relations. According to the researchers' findings: (1) the contingency theory was correctly induced from studies on which it was based; (2) for laboratory studies testing the model, the theory was supported for all leadership situations except situation II; (3) for field studies testing the model, three of the eight situations (IV, V, and VII) produced completely supportive results, while partial support was obtained for situations I, II, III, VI, and VIII.[24] This last finding suggests that Fiedler's model may need theoretical refinement. Because the LPC scale has questionable validity, this refinement might entail a reconceptualization of the meaning of a least preferred co-worker.[25]

In conclusion, except for the validity of the LPC scale, Fiedler's contingency model has considerable support. This implies that organizational effectiveness can be enhanced by appropriately matching leaders with situations. Fiedler believes it is a waste of time to try to change one's leadership style. Instead, leaders with an inappropriate style need to change their degree of situational control or be moved to a situation in which they can be effective. The following section discusses how this might be done.

Leader Match Training   Fiedler has developed a training program based on his contingency model. This program assumes that individuals are either unwilling or unable to change their leadership style. Accordingly, the training program teaches managers to manage the situational control within their leadership environment.

• **TABLE 14-2**   Techniques to Modify Situational Control

Modifying leader-member relations
Spend more or less time with your subordinates.
Organize activities that take place outside of work (e.g., picnic, bowling, etc.).
Request trusted employees that you know to work for you.
Obtain positive outcomes for your employees (e.g., special bonus, time off, etc.).
Share information with your employees.

Modifying task structure
Break the job down into smaller subtasks.
Request additional training.
Develop procedures, guidelines, or diagrams related to completing tasks.
Seek advice from others.
Seek problems to solve.
Volunteer for new tasks or assignments.
Become more of a decision maker.

Modifying position power
Exercise the powers that are inherent in your position.
Become an expert on the tasks performed by your employees.
Control the type and amount of information that your employees receive.
Delegate authority.
Incorporate the work group into planning and decision-making activities.
Do not withhold information from employees.
Avoid any trappings of demonstrating power and rank.

Source: Adapted from Fred E. Fiedler and Martin M. Chemers, *Improving Leadership Effectiveness* (New York: John Wiley & Sons, 1984), pp. 179–84. Used with permission.

Training begins by having managers assess their leadership style with the LPC. Then, diagnostic instruments are used to measure leader–member relations, task structure, and position power. After calculating the degree of situational control, managers determine whether their leadership style matches their leadership situation. Finally, managers are trained to change their leadership situations by modifying one or more of the components of situational control (see Table 14–2). For example, a high-LPC leader would not be totally effective in a high-control situation (refer back to Figure 14–4). To improve performance, this leader should modify the situation so it involves moderate control. This might be done by making the task less structured—seeking new problems to solve, for example—or lowering position power through delegation. In an evaluation of the Leader Match program, 13 studies found significant increases in leadership effectiveness following managerial training.[26]

Path–Goal Theory

Path–goal theory is based on the expectancy theory of motivation discussed in Chapter 6. Expectancy theory proposes that motivation to exert effort increases as one's effort → performance → outcome expectations improve. Path–goal theory focuses on how leaders influence followers' expectations.

Robert House originated the path–goal theory of leadership. He proposed a model that describes how expectancy perceptions are influenced by the contingent relationships between four leadership styles and various em-

• **Figure 14-5**   A General Representation of House's Path–Goal Theory

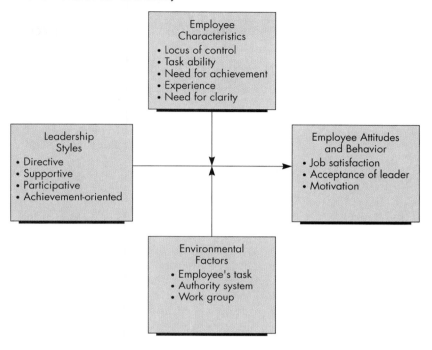

ployee attitudes and behaviors (see Figure 14–5).[27] According to the path–goal model, leader behavior is acceptable when employees view it as a source of satisfaction or as paving the way to future satisfaction. In addition, leader behavior is motivational to the extent it (1) reduces roadblocks that interfere with goal accomplishment, (2) provides the guidance and support needed by employees, and (3) ties meaningful rewards to goal accomplishment. Because the model deals with pathways to goals and rewards, it is called the path–goal theory of leadership. House sees the leader's main job as helping employees stay on the right paths to challenging goals and valued rewards.

Leadership Styles   House believes leaders can exhibit more than one leadership style. This contrasts with Fiedler, who proposes that leaders have one dominant style. The four leadership styles identified by House are:

- *Directive leadership*. Providing guidance to employees about what should be done and how to do it, scheduling work, and maintaining standards of performance.
- *Supportive leadership*. Showing concern for the well-being and needs of employees, being friendly and approachable, and treating workers as equals.
- *Participative leadership*. Consulting with employees and seriously considering their ideas when making decisions.
- *Achievement-oriented leadership*. Encouraging employees to perform at their highest level by setting challenging goals, emphasizing excellence, and demonstrating confidence in employee abilities.[28]

Research evidence supports the idea that leaders exhibit more than one leadership style.[29] Descriptions of business leaders reinforce these findings. For example, William Ziff, who built Ziff-Davis Publishing Co. into one of the largest and most profitable special-interest magazine publishers in the United States, used more than one style of leadership.

> Ziff was the epitome of the hands-on manager. He read every issue of every magazine and would often become involved in minute details, such as headlines and newsstand displays. He set up tight operational systems, such as central departments to handle circulation, promotion, and research [directive style]. But he left most lines of authority unclear, which tended to diffuse all power but his own. He avoided rule by outright fiat and often acceded to others' views [participative style]. . . .
>
> But within his circle of close friends and colleagues, he acted like "one of the guys" [supportive style].[30]

Contingency Factors   **Contingency factors** are situational variables that cause one style of leadership to be more effective than another. In the present context, these variables affect expectancy or path–goal perceptions. This model has two groups of contingency variables (see Figure 14–5). They are employee characteristics and environmental factors. Five important employee characteristics are locus of control, task ability, need for achievement, experience, and need for clarity. Three relevant environmental factors are: (1) the employee's task, (2) the authority system, and (3) the work group. All these factors have the potential for hindering or motivating employees.

Research has focused on determining whether the various contingency factors influence the effectiveness of different leadership styles. The employee characteristics of need for achievement, experience, and need for clarity affected *employees' preferences for leadership*. Specifically, a study of 298 ROTC cadets revealed that individuals with high achievement needs preferred directive leadership. People with low achievement needs wanted supportive leadership. Experienced salespeople were more satisfied when leaders granted them more autonomy and less direction, whereas inexperienced salespeople desired directive leadership.[31] Finally, employees with a high need for clarity performed better and were more satisfied with directive leadership; the opposite was true of individuals with a low need for clarity.[32]

With respect to environmental contingency factors, supportive leader behavior promoted job satisfaction when individuals performed structured tasks.[33]

Managerial Implications   There are three important managerial implications: *First,* leaders possess and use more than one style of leadership. Managers thus should not be hesitant to try new behaviors when the situation calls for them. *Second,* managers should modify their leadership style to fit employee characteristics. Employees with high achievement needs, little experience, and high need for clarity generally should receive directive leadership to increase satisfaction and performance. *Third,* the degree of task structure is a relevant contingency factor. Managers should consider using supportive supervision when the task is structured. Supportive supervision is satisfying in this context, because employees already know what they should be doing.

Hersey and Blanchard's Situational Leadership Theory

Situational leadership theory (SLT) was developed by management writers Paul Hersey and Kenneth Blanchard.[34] According to the theory, effective leader behavior depends on the readiness level of a leader's followers. **Readiness** is defined as the extent to which a follower possesses the ability and willingness to complete a task.

The SLT model is summarized in Figure 14–6. The appropriate leadership style is found by cross referencing follower readiness, which varies from low to high, with one of four leadership styles. The four leadership styles represent combinations of task and relationship-oriented leader behaviors (S_1 to S_4). Leaders are encouraged to use a "telling style" for followers with low readiness. This style combines high task-oriented leader behaviors, such as providing instructions, with low relationship-oriented behaviors, such as close supervision (see Figure 14–6). As follower readiness increases, leaders are advised to gradually move from a telling, to a selling, to a participating, and ultimately to a delegating style.

Although SLT is widely used as a training tool, it is not strongly supported by scientific research. For instance, leadership effectiveness was not due to the predicted interaction between follower readiness and leadership style in a recent study of 459 salespeople.[35] Moreover, a study of 303

• **FIGURE 14–6** Situational Leadership Theory

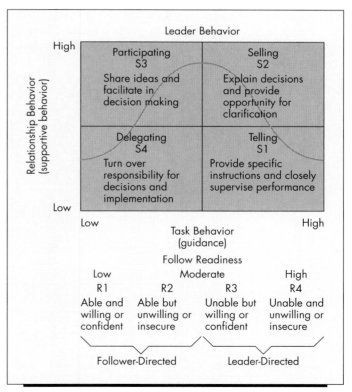

teachers indicated that SLT was accurate only for employees with low readiness. This finding is consistent with a recent survey of 57 chief nurse executives in California. These executives did not delegate in accordance with SLT.[36] Finally, researchers have concluded that the self-assessment instrument used to measure leadership style and follower readiness is inaccurate and should be used with caution.[37] In summary, managers should exercise discretion when using prescriptions from SLT..

• ROLE-MAKING AND ATTRIBUTION THEORIES

Now that we have discussed some well-established models of leadership, we will explore two comparatively new perspectives. The first examines leadership from a role-making standpoint. The second explains leadership from an attributional point of view. Although these two theories are situational, they are different from the situational models just discussed. Thus, these theories offer managers additional interesting insights about leader effectiveness.

Graen's Role-Making (VDL) Model of Leadership

George Graen, an industrial psychologist, believes popular theories of leadership are based on an incorrect assumption. Theories such as the Leadership Grid® and Fiedler's contingency model assume that leader behavior is characterized by a stable or average leadership style. In other words, these models assume a leader treats all subordinates in about the same way. This traditional approach to leadership is shown in the left side of

• FIGURE 14-7   A Role-Making (VDL) Model of Leadership

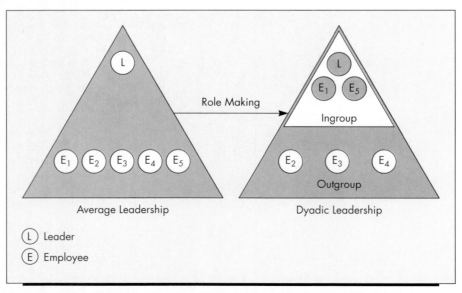

Source: Adapted from Fred Dansereau, Jr., George Graen, and William J. Haga, "A Vertical Dyad Linkage Approach to Leadership within Formal Organizations," *Organizational Behavior and Human Performance*, February 1975, p. 72.

Figure 14–7. In this case, the leader (designated by the circled L) is thought to exhibit a similar pattern of behavior toward all employees (E_1 to E_5). In contrast, Graen contends that leaders develop unique one-to-one relationships with each of the people reporting to them. Behavioral scientists call this sort of relationship a *vertical dyad*. Hence, Graen's approach is labeled the **vertical dyad linkage (VDL) model** of leadership. The forming of vertical dyads is said to be a naturally occurring process, resulting from the leader's attempt to delegate and assign work roles. As a result of this process, Graen predicts that one of two distinct types of leader–member exchange relationships will evolve.[38]

One type of leader–member exchange is called the **ingroup exchange.** In this relationship, leaders and followers develop a partnership characterized by reciprocal influence, mutual trust, respect and liking, and a sense of common fates. Figure 14–7 shows that E_1 and E_5 are members of the leader's ingroup. In the second type of exchange, referred to as an **outgroup exchange,** leaders are characterized as overseers who fail to create a sense of mutual trust, respect, or common fate.[39] E_2, E_3, and E_4 are members of the outgroup on the right side of Figure 14–7.

Research Findings If Graen's model is correct, there should be a significant relationship between the type of leader–member exchange and job-related outcomes. To date, research supports this prediction. For example, ingroup members were found to have more positive perceptions of organizational climate and higher job performance and satisfaction than did employees in the outgroup.[40] The type of leader–member exchange was found to predict not only turnover among nurses and computer analysts, but also career outcomes, such as promotability, salary level, and receipt of bonuses over a seven-year period.[41]

Managerial Implications Graen's VDL model underscores the importance of training managers to improve leader–member relations. Ideally, this should enhance the job satisfaction and performance of employees and also reduce

• Frequently, the in-group consists of the "power people"—those, for example, with access to the company jet. *(Schmid-Langsfeld/The Image Bank)*

OB IN ACTION

In or Out: What to Do about It

In truth, the best time to manage the in or out phenomenon is very early in a person's employment. If you are a new employee or if you are developing a relationship with a newly assigned boss, it is a good idea to offer your loyalty and provide expressions of cooperativeness.

If your status as an out-member is already well established, it may be difficult or impossible to break the status quo. Short of confronting the supervisor and asking for a new start, an out-group employee's only options are to:

Accept the current situation;

Try to become an in-group member by being cooperative and loyal (this is an unattractive option for many out-groupers because they may have to swallow their pride); or

Quit.

Supervisors should be mindful that in-groups and out-groups exist within their work units, and they should control potential conflict between the two divisions. Supervisors should consciously try to expand their in-groups. This means not giving up on people who may gradually be coming to see themselves as marginal members of the work unit. Supervisors who create a greater sense of in-ness among their subordinates can expect to have more effective work units.

Source: Excerpted from Robert Vecchio, "Are You *In* or *Out* with Your Boss?" *Business Horizons,* November–December 1986, p. 78. Used by permission..

turnover. A large U.S. government installation in the Midwest conducted such a training program. Results indicated a 19 percent increase on an objective measure of productivity. This improvement resulted in an estimated annual cost savings of more than $5 million.[42] VDL researcher Robert Vecchio's tips for both followers and leaders in OB in Action are a good supplement to formal training programs.

An Attributional Model

This model takes an information-processing approach to leadership. It is based on the idea that both leaders and followers form cause–effect attributions about performance. Because these attributions interact with each other, both sets of attributions ultimately affect leader behavior and employee attitudes and behaviors.[43]

Figure 14–8 presents a model of the leader/follower attribution process. The process is set in motion by the occurrence of some type of poor employee behavior (for instance, a missed deadline, errors, or absenteeism). The next step consists of the leader's interpretation or attribution for the poor performance. Chapter 4 noted that this step involves collecting information from three primary cues. These cues are related to the consensus, distinctiveness, and consistency of observed behavior. After processing these cues, the leader determines whether the behavior was due to internal

• FIGURE 14-8   Leader/Follower Attribution Process

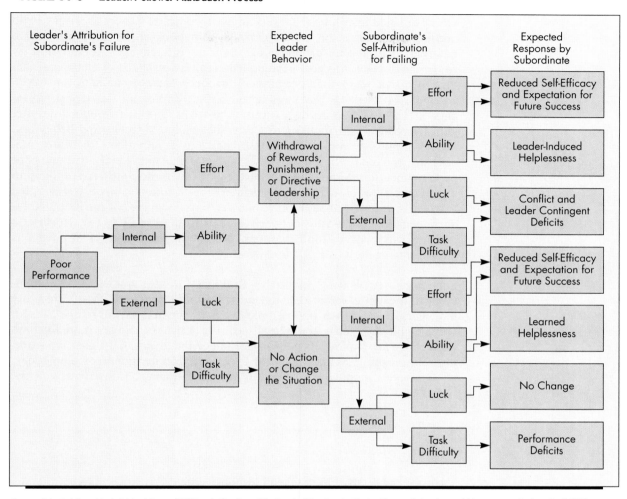

Source: Adapted from Mark J. Martinko and William L. Gardner, "The Leader/Member Attribution Process," *Academy of Management Review*, April 1987, p. 238. Used by permission.

(effort or ability) or external (luck or task difficulty) factors. For example, the leader may conclude that an employee is performing poorly because of a lack of effort. Leaders tend to make external attributions when:

(1) the subordinate has no prior history of poor performance on similar tasks, (2) the subordinate performs other tasks effectively, (3) the subordinate is doing as well as other people who are in a similar situation, (4) the effects of failures or mistakes are not serious or harmful, (5) the manager is dependent upon the subordinate for his or her own success, (6) the subordinate is perceived to have other redeeming qualities (popularity, leadership skills), (7) the subordinate has offered excuses or an apology, or (8) there is evidence indicating external causes.[44]

In turn, a leader's attribution affects his or her response to the original performance problem. Leaders tend to withdraw rewards, use punishment, or exhibit directive leadership when they believe poor performance is due to internal factors (especially low effort). Directive leadership may entail lowering the employee's goals, increasing employee ability through training, providing detailed instructions, or coaching. In contrast, leaders are prone to do nothing, or change the situation when poor performance is attributed to external factors such as bad luck. Leaders can change the situation by removing obstacles to goal accomplishment, as suggested by path–goal theory, by providing more information or resources, and by changing the task.[45]

Figure 14–8 reveals that employees' self-attribution for the poor performance is the next step in the attribution process. These attributions interact with the leader's attributions to affect subsequent attitudes and behaviors. For example, an employee's self-efficacy and expectations for future success are reduced when both the leader and the individual attribute poor performance to internal causes. Further, a leader and follower are likely to experience conflict when a leader's internal attribution is inconsistent with a follower's external attribution. Consider how inconsistent attributions undermined the relationshp between Steven Rothmeier, CEO of Northwest Airlines, and Pat Fallon, chairman of Fallon McElligott, a Minneapolis advertising agency (see OB in Action).

Summary of Attributional Leadership Research   Research examined components of the model rather than the entire attribution process. Results indicate managers tend to see poor employee performance as internally caused, while employees see it as externally caused. Leaders also are more likely to externalize an employee's poor performance the longer and closer the working relationship.[46] This may lead to inequitable treatment of employees, which erodes employee motivation and performance. Consistent with the

---

 OB IN ACTION

Inconsistent Attributions Lead to Frustration

Northwest Airlines has always liked to do things its own way—whatever the cost.

A few years ago, for instance, the company asked Fallon McElligott, a Minneapolis advertising agency, to bid for its ad business. So Pat Fallon, the agency's chairman, rode Northwest thousands of miles to get a feel for the airline.

"We found the service wasn't nearly as good as described by them," Mr. Fallon recalls. In fact, planefuls of irate passengers were already nicknaming the carrier "Northworst." But Steven G. Rothmeier, the iron-willed chairman of Northwest's parent, NWA Inc., refused to listen.

"Steve asked us to redo the work based on Northwest's perception of its own product," Mr. Fallon says. "He didn't understand that *we* weren't saying this. The *marketplace* was." Frustrated, Fallon McElligott went elsewhere—and Northwest's public image got worse.

Source: Richard Gibson, "Flying Solo: The Autocratic Style of Northwest's CEO Complicates Defense," *The Wall Street Journal*, March 1989, p. A1.

major premise of the model, leader behavior is affected by a leader's attribution for poor performance.[47]

Managerial Implications   Managers/leaders need to be aware that their behavior is influenced by their perceptions about the causes of an employee's performance. Management development programs can be used to help managers become more accurate and fair in their evaluation of employee performance. Motorola is following this recommendation. Managers also need to consider the variety of responses they can use to correct an employee's poor performance. Employees are more likely to respond positively to leader behavior that helps and coaches than to behavior that punishes. Further, it is important for managers to keep in mind that their relationship with subordinates can bias attributions. A recent study demonstrated that managers were more likely to attribute effective performance to internal factors for ingroup members than for outgroup employees.[48] Awareness and training are solutions for this problem.

Finally, managers and subordinates are likely to have inconsistent attributions for poor performance. Employees thus may misinterpret and become dissatisfied with a leader's corrective actions. Steps need to be taken to reduce these conflicting perceptions. As reviewed in Chapter 4, attributional training can help contain this problem.

• FROM TRANSACTIONAL TO TRANSFORMATIONAL LEADERSHIP

Organizations in the United States and elsewhere experienced a great deal of change and competition over the last two decades. Researchers proposed that a unique brand of leadership, referred to as transformational leadership, made the difference between survival and failure during this time period. Chrysler's Lee Iacocca and General Electric's Jack Welch were able to turn around struggling organizations during the early 1980s because they practiced transformational leadership.[49] Meanwhile, Donald Burr could not do the same at People Express because he was unable to rally the work force around his creative vision for a new airline.

This section begins by highlighting the difference between transactional and transformational leadership. We then discuss the characteristics of transformational leaders. The chapter concludes by reviewing research which suggests that organizations should foster both transactional and transformational leadership.

What Is the Difference between Transactional and Transformational Leadership?

Most of the models and theories previously discussed in this chapter represent transactional leadership. **Transactional leadership** focuses on the interpersonal transactions between managers and employees. Leaders are seen as engaging in behaviors that maintain a quality interaction between themselves and followers. The two underlying characteristics of transactional leadership are: (1) leaders use contingent rewards to motivate employees and (2) leaders exert corrective action only when subordinates fail to obtain performance goals. In contrast, **transformational leadership** occurs when leaders create the vision and environment that motivates employees to elevate the good of the group or organization above their own self-interest.[50] In other words, transformational leaders "transform" employees to pursue and achieve higher levels of performance. Researchers recommend transformational leadership because it fosters the type of organizational changes that are needed for American companies to compete in a global economy.

The following conclusion summarizes the general sentiment among many researchers about the differences between transactional and transformational leadership.

> A transactional exchange of rewards with subordinates for the services they render limits how much effort will be forthcoming from the subordinates, how satisfied the subordinates will be with the arrangements, and how effectively they will contribute to reaching the organization's goals. In contrast, the transformational leader articulates a realistic vision of the future that can be shared, stimulates subordinates intellectually, and pays attention to the differences among the subordinates.[51]

Let us now consider how leaders transform followers.

How Do Leaders Transform Followers?

The idea of transformational leadership began with German sociologist Max Weber's research on charismatic leaders. Weber believed that some people possessed charisma, a Greek word for *gift,* that enabled them to achieve extraordinary accomplishments.[52] Modern-day researchers followed up this work by trying to identify the characteristics of charismatic transformational leaders.

• **FIGURE 14-9**   Characteristics of Transformational Leaders

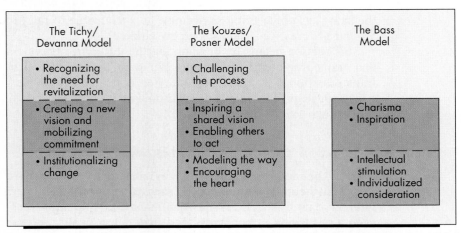

Source: Based on discussion in Noel M. Tichy and Mary Anne Devanna, *The Transformational Leader* (New York: John Wiley & Sons, 1986); James M. Kouzes and Barry Z. Posner, *The Leadership Challenge: How to Get Extraordinary Things Done in Organizations* (San Francisco: Jossey-Bass, 1990); and Bernard M. Bass, "From Transactional to Transformational Leadership: Learning to Share the Vision," *Organizational Dynamics,* Winter 1990, pp. 19–31.

Several researchers pursued this quest. Figure 14–9 summarizes those characteristics uncovered in three large-scale studies of transformational leadership. These studies were conducted by Noel Tichy and Mary Anne Devanna, James Kouzes and Barry Posner, and Bernard Bass.[53] Although each study used different terms to represent transformational characteristics, there appear to be three overlapping themes (see Figure 14–9).

Transformational leaders do not accept the status quo. They recognize the need to revitalize their organizations and challenge standard operating procedures. Transformational leaders such as 37-year-old Robin Burns, president and CEO of Estée Lauder USA cosmetics company, also create new corporate visions and mobilize employee commitment to that vision (see OB in Action). As noted by Bass, employee commitment is ignited and maintained by a leader's charisma and inspiration (see Figure 14–9). Finally, transformational leaders institutionalize organizational change by modeling appropriate behaviors, by intellectually stimulating employees, and by giving personal attention to employees.

• Transformational leaders make their marks in different ways. Napoleon epitomized the charismatic military and political leader. Robin Burns, president and CEO of Estée Lauder USA, is a modern business executive with a vision.

North Wind Picture Archives   Co Rentmeester

OB IN ACTION

Robin Burns Uses Transformational Leadership at Estée Lauder USA Cosmetics Company

Unlike the Lauders, [Robin] Burns doesn't have any celebrity friends. Although Leonard [Lauder, president of the parent company], a keen businessman, "plays his cards close to his vest, and he has 16 vests under that one," as a friend puts it, [Burns] is open and direct—if very tough indeed. The old line about "what you see is what you get" fits her perfectly. The company is now hierarchical. Says Burns: "My vision does involve a lot of change, but when I get my restructuring done . . ." Odds are there'll be a lot less structure.

It is nearly impossible to find criticism of her. To most colleagues she seems like a relief, a reminder that in the right hands, business life can be simple. No plots, no paranoia, no last-minute surprises. Instead she imparts a sense of discovery to almost everybody she works with, a feeling that anything is possible—at least for her team.

Source: Martha Duffy, "Take This Job and Love It: An Inspired Leader and a Tough Negotiator, Robin Burns May Be That Elusive Figure, the New Woman Executive," *Time,* August 6, 1990, p. 70. Copyright 1990 The Time Inc. Magazine Company. Reprinted by permission.

Research Highlights the Need for Both Transactional and Transformational Leadership

There are two key conclusions from research on transformational leadership. *First,* transformational leadership can make the difference between success and failure during times of organizational economic, or societal change. This finding suggests that organizations should hire and promote individuals possessing characteristics of transformational leaders. Standardized measuring instruments have been developed for this purpose.[54] Moreover, organizations should train managers to adopt transformational characteristics. Bernard Bass reports success with this type of training.[55]

Second, neither transactional or transformational leadership is enough to ensure maximum effectiveness. Both forms of leadership are important for organizational success.[56] Organizations need the vision, excitement, and commitment created by transformational leaders. However, organizations also need leaders who can focus on details, provide direction, clarify required behaviors, and administer rewards and punishment.[57] For example, a recent article in *Business Month* chronicled how Lee Iacocca, an acknowledged transformational leader, allowed Chrysler to once again slip back to the edge of decay because he failed to engage in a variety of instrumental leader behaviors associated with transactional leadership.[58] In conclusion, organizations are advised to cultivate both transactional and transformational leadership.

• SUMMARY OF KEY CONCEPTS

A. *Leadership* is defined as a social influence process in which the leader tries to obtain the voluntary participation of employees in an effort to reach organizational objectives. Leadership entails more than having authority and power.

B. Historically, leadership theory has evolved from traits, to behavioral styles, to situations. Although the trait approach has been roundly criticized, current research has shown that traits play an important role in perceived leader ability. The Leadership Grid® emphasizes that there is one best style of leadership (9,9). Situational theories propose that effective leadership is contingent on the situation.

C. Fiedler believes leader effectiveness depends on an appropriate match between leadership style, measured with the LPC scale, and situational control. Low-LPC leaders are task-oriented and high-LPC leaders are relationship-oriented. Situational control is composed of leader–member relations, task structure, and position power. Low-LPC leaders are effective under situations of both high and low control. High-LPC leaders are more effective when they have moderate situational control. Leader match training has produced increased leader effectiveness.

D. According to path–goal theory, leaders alternately can exhibit directive, supportive, participative, or achievement-oriented styles of leadership. The effectiveness of these styles depends on various employee characteristics and environmental factors. Path–goal theory has received limited support from research.

E. According to situational leadership theory (SLT), effective leader behavior depends on the readiness level of a leader's followers. As follower readiness increases, leaders are advised to gradually move from a telling, to a selling, to a participating, and finally to a delegating style. Research does not support SLT.

F. The role-making approach assumes leaders develop unique vertical dyad linkages (VDL) with each employee. These leader–member exchanges qualify as either ingroup or outgroup relationships. Research supports this model of leadership.

G. The attributional approach to leadership is based on the idea that both leaders and followers form cause–effect attributions about performance. A leader's attributions affect that person's behavior toward his or her employees. Ultimately, this approach suggests that employee attitudes and behaviors are a function of the consistency between leader and follower attributions.

H. There is an important difference between transactional and transformational leadership. Transactional leaders focus on the interpersonal transactions between managers and employees. Transformational leaders motivate employees to pursue the good of the group or organization above their own self-interests. Both forms of leadership are important for organizational success.

I. There are three underlying characteristics of transformational leaders. Transformational leaders (1) recognize the need for revitalization, (2) create a new vision and mobilize employee commitment, and (3) institutionalize change.

• KEY TERMS

leadership	task structure
leader trait	position power
consideration	contingency factors
initiating structure	readiness
Leadership Grid®	vertical dyad linkage (VDL) model
situational theories	ingroup exchange
task-oriented style	outgroup exchange
relationship-oriented style	transactional leadership
leader-member relations	transformational leadership

• DISCUSSION QUESTIONS

1. Are you interested in leading others? Why or why not? If yes, can you identify the source of this desire?

2. Has your college education helped you develop any of the traits that characterize leaders?

3. Do you agree with Blake and Mouton that there is one best style of leadership?

4. Does it make more sense to change a person's leadership style or the situation? How would Fred Fiedler and Robert House answer this question?

5. Based on your experience, how have managers helped clarify your path–goal perceptions?

6. Do you believe that a leader's style should be determined by employees' willingness and ability to complete a task? Explain.

7. Have you ever been a member of an ingroup or outgroup? For either situation, describe the pattern of interaction between you and your supervisor.

8. Have you ever experienced a situation in which a manager attributed your behavior to the wrong cause? Describe the situation and your reaction to the inappropriate attribution.

9. Have you ever encountered a transformational leader? Which characteristics of transformational leaders did this person possess?

10. In your view, which leadership theory has the greatest practical application? Why?

BACK TO THE OPENING CASE

Now that you have read Chapter 14, you should be able to answer the following questions about the Bill Gates case:

1. Citing examples, which different leadership traits and styles were exhibited by Bill Gates?
2. Where would you plot Gates's style of leadership on the Leadership Grid?
3. How did Bill Gates attempt to clarify path–goal relationships?
4. Is Bill Gates more of a transactional or transformational leader? Explain.
5. How does Gates mobilize commitment from Microsoft employees?

• EXERCISE 14

Objectives

1. To promote understanding of Fiedler's contingency model.
2. To assess your leadership style and gain practice at applying the model.

Introduction

According to Fiedler, leader effectiveness is contingent upon an appropriate match between the leader's style and situational control. A leader's style is either task-oriented or relationship-oriented. Fiedler developed the Least Preferred Co-Worker (LPC) Scale to measure these styles. You will complete the LPC scale as part of this exercise. You also will be given the opportunity to assess situational control and to consider which kind of leader is best suited for that situation.

Instructions

Complete the LPC scale shown below by following the directions at the top of the questionnaire. After completing your ratings, simply add the values associated with each of your 18 responses to calculate your LPC score. If your score is 73 or above, you are classified as a high-LPC person with a relationship-oriented style. A score below 64 identifies you as a low-LPC person, indicating that you have a task-oriented style. If your score is between 65 and 72, you are classified as a middle-LPC person. Middle-LPC leaders exhibit characteristics of both the high and low-LPC styles. Keep in mind that one style is not better than the other. Each is appropriate and necessary in certain situations. We next would like you to answer the questions for discussion listed directly after the LPC scale.

After answering these questions, read the leadership vignette shown after the LPC scale and answer the questions for discussion.

Least Preferred Co-Worker (LPC) Scale

Throughout your life you have worked in many groups with a wide variety of different people—on your job, in social clubs, in church organizations, in volunteer groups, on athletic teams, and in many others. You probably found working with most of your co-workers quite easy, but working with others may have been very difficult or all but impossible.

Now, think of all the people with whom you have ever worked. Next, think of the one person in your life with whom you could work least well. This individual may or may not be the person you also disliked most. It must be the one person with whom you had the most difficulty getting a job done, the one single individual with whom you would least want to work—a boss, a subordinate, or a peer. This person is called your "least preferred co-worker" (LPC).

On the scale below, describe this person by placing an "X" in the appropriate space.

	8	7	6	5	4	3	2	1		Scoring
Pleasant	8	7	6	5	4	3	2	1	Unpleasant	_____
Friendly	8	7	6	5	4	3	2	1	Unfriendly	_____
Rejecting	1	2	3	4	5	6	7	8	Accepting	_____
Tense	1	2	3	4	5	6	7	8	Relaxed	_____
Distant	1	2	3	4	5	6	7	8	Close	_____
Cold	1	2	3	4	5	6	7	8	Warm	_____
Supportive	8	7	6	5	4	3	2	1	Hostile	_____
Boring	1	2	3	4	5	6	7	8	Interesting	_____
Quarrelsome	1	2	3	4	5	6	7	8	Harmonious	_____
Gloomy	1	2	3	4	5	6	7	8	Cheerful	_____
Open	8	7	6	5	4	3	2	1	Guarded	_____
Backbiting	1	2	3	4	5	6	7	8	Loyal	_____
Untrustworthy	1	2	3	4	5	6	7	8	Trustworthy	_____
Considerate	8	7	6	5	4	3	2	1	Inconsiderate	_____
Rejecting Nasty	1	2	3	4	5	6	7	8	Nice	_____
Agreeable	8	7	6	5	4	3	2	1	Disagreeable	_____
Insincere	1	2	3	4	5	6	7	8	Sincere	_____
Kind	8	7	6	5	4	3	2	1	Unkind	_____
									Total	_____

Source: Fred E. Fiedler and Martin M. Chemers, *Improving Leadership Effectiveness* (New York: John Wiley & Sons, 1984), pp. 17–19. Used with permission.

Questions for Consideration/Class Discussion

1. What is your leadership style?
2. Do you agree with this assessment? Explain.
3. Using Figure 14–4 as a frame of reference, what type of leadership situations are you best suited for?

Leadership Vignette

You are director of a large manufacturing firm. The manager in charge of the advertising department just had a serious accident and has to be replaced, since it is doubtful that he will be able to return to work for quite some time. You need someone to fill in for him.

The situation is rather hard to define. The key people are temperamental and touchy, and there has been a great deal of infighting and conflict. The manager has had a difficult time holding the department together. Moreover, there has been a demand from other managers for more creative marketing campaigns. You need someone who can immediately take charge of this department and make it productive.[59]

Questions for Consideration/Class Discussion

1. What is the situational control in the advertising department?
2. What type of leader is best suited for this situation?
3. What would you do if you were unable to find an optimum leadership match according to Fiedler's theory?

• NOTES

[1] Results are presented in Jonathan E. Smith, Kenneth P. Carson, and Ralph A. Alexander, "Leadership: It Can Make a Difference," *Academy of Management Journal,* December 1984, pp. 765–76.

[2] See Stanley Lieberson and James F. O'Connor, "Leadership and Organizational Performance: A Study of Large Corporations," *American Sociological Review,* April 1972, pp. 117–30.

[3] Chester A. Schriesheim, James M. Tolliver, and Orlando C. Behling, "Leadership Theory: Some Implications for Managers," *MSU Business Topics,* Summer 1978, p. 35.

[4] Tom Peters and Nancy Austin, *A Passion for Excellence* (New York: Random House, 1985), pp. 5–6.

[5] For a discussion of the importance and difference between leading and managing, see James Krantz and Thomas N. Gilmore, "The Splitting of Leadership and Management as a Social Defense," *Human Relations,* February 1990, pp. 183–204; and John P. Kotter, *A Force for Change: How Leadership Differs from Management* (New York: The Free Press, 1990).

[6] For complete details, see Ralph M. Stogdill, "Personal Factors Associated with Leadership: A Survey of the Literature," *Journal of Psychology* 1948, pp. 35–71; and Ralph M. Stogdill, *Handbook of Leadership* (New York: Free Press, 1974).

[7] See Richard D. Mann, "A Review of the Relationships between Personality and Performance in Small Groups," *Psychological Bulletin,* July 1959, pp. 241–70.

[8] See David A. Kenny and Stephen J. Zaccaro, "An Estimate of Variance Due to Traits in Leadership," *Journal of Applied Psychology,* November 1983, pp. 678–85.

[9] Robert G. Lord, Christy L. De Vader, and George M. Alliger, "A Meta-Analysis of the Relation between Personality Traits and Leadership Perceptions: An Application of Validity Generalization Procedures," *Journal of Applied Psychology,* August 1986, p. 407.

[10] Results can be found in Janet R. Goktepe and Craig Eric Schneier, "Role of Sex, Gender Roles, and Attraction in Predicting Emergent Leaders," *Journal of Applied Psychology,* February 1989, pp. 165–67.

[11] Details are provided in Kurt Lewin, Ronald Lippitt, and Ralph K. White, "Patterns of Aggressive Behavior in Experimentally Created 'Social Climates,'" *Journal of Social Psychology,* May 1939, pp. 271–99.

[12] Joseph Weber, "I Am Intense, Aggressive, and Hard-Charging," *Business Week,* April 30, 1990, p. 58.

[13] This research is summarized and critiqued by Bernard M. Bass, *Bass & Stogdill's Handbook of Leadership: Theory, Research, and Managerial Applications* (New York: The Free Press, 1990), Chap. 24.

[14] See Victor H. Vroom, "Leadership," in *Handbook of Industrial and Organizational Psychology,* ed. Marvin D. Dunnette (Chicago: Rand McNally, 1976).

[15] Robert R. Blake and Jane Srygley Mouton, "A Comparative Analysis of Situationalism and 9,9 Management by Principle," *Organizationl Dynamics,* Spring 1982, p. 23.

[16] Ibid., pp. 28–29. Also see Robert R. Blake and Jane Srygley Mouton, "Management by Grid Principles or Situationalism: Which?" *Group & Organization Studies,* December 1981, pp. 439–55.

[17] Ibid., p. 21.

[18] For details, see Charles C. Manz and Henry P. Sims, Jr., "Beyond Imitation: Complex Behavioral and Affective Linkages Resulting from Exposure to Leadership Training Models," *Journal of Applied Psychology,* November 1986, pp. 571–78.

[19] Results can be found in Alice H. Eagly and Blair T. Johnson, "Gender and Leadership Styles: A Meta-Analysis," *Psychological Bulletin,* September 1990, pp. 233–56. Qualitative descriptions of gender differences are provided by Jaclyn Fierman, "Do Women Manage Differently?" *Fortune,* December 17, 1990, pp. 115–18.

[20] See Bass, *Bass & Stogdill's Handbook of Leadership: Theory, Research, and Managerial Applications,* Chaps. 20–25.

[21] For more on this theory, see Fred E. Fiedler, "A Contingency Model of Leadership Effectiveness," in *Advances in Experimental Social Psychology,* Vol. 1, ed. Leonard Berkowitz (New York: Academic Press, 1964); Fred E. Fiedler, *A Theory of Leadership Effectiveness* (New York: McGraw-Hill, 1967).

[22] Robert W. Rice and F. James Seaman, "Internal Analyses of the Least Preferred Co-Worker (LPC) Scale," *Educational and Psychological Measurement,* 1981, p. 110.

[23] Additional information on the description and calculation of situational control is contained in Fred E. Fiedler, "The Contingency Model and the Dynamics of the Leadership Process," in *Advances in Experimental Social Psychology,* Vol. 11, ed. Leonard Berkowitz (New York: Academic Press, 1978).

[24] See Lawrence H. Peters, Darrell D. Hartke, and John T. Pohlmann, "Fiedler's Contingency Theory of Leadership: An Application of the Meta-Analyses Procedures of Schmidt and Hunter," *Psychological Bulletin,* March 1985, pp. 274–85.

[25] Arguments about the validity of the LPC are contained in Chester A. Schriesheim, Brendan D. Bannister, and William H. Money, "Psychometric Properties of the LPC Scale: An Extension of Rice's Review," *Academy of Management Review,* April 1979, pp. 287–90; and Robert W. Rice, "Reliability and Validity of the LPC Scale: A Reply," *Academy of Management Review,* April 1979, pp. 291–94.

[26] For documentation, see Fred E. Fiedler and Linda Mahar, "The Effectiveness of Contingency Model Training: A Review of the Validation of Leader Match," *Personnel Psychology,* Spring 1979, pp. 45–62; Fred E. Fiedler, Cecil H. Bell, Martin M. Chemers, and Dennis Patrick, "Increasing Mine Productivity and Safety through Management Training and Organization Development: A Comparative Study," *Basic and Applied Social Psychology,* March 1984, pp. 1–18. For an alternative interpretation of the success of leader match training, see Arthur G. Jago and James W. Ragan, "The Trouble with Leader Match Is that It Doesn't Match Fiedler's Contingency Model," *Journal of Applied Psychology,* November 1986, pp. 555–59.

[27] For more detail on this theory, see Robert J. House, "A Path–Goal Theory of Leader Effectiveness," *Administrative Science Quarterly,* September 1971, pp. 321–38.

[28] Adapted from Robert J. House and Terence R. Mitchell, "Path–Goal Theory of Leadership," *Journal of Contemporary Business,* Autumn 1974, p. 83.

[29] See House, "A Path–Goal Theory of Leader Effectiveness."

[30] Chris Welles, "What's Next for the Unpredictable Bill Ziff?" *Business Week,* April 14, 1986, p. 103.

[31] The study of ROTC cadets was conducted by John E. Mathieu, "A Test of Subordinates' Achievement and Affiliation Needs as Moderators of a Leader Path–Goal Relationships," *Basic and Applied Social Psychology,* June 1990, pp. 179–89. The study of salespeople was conducted by Ajay K. Kohli, "Effects of Supervisory Behavior: The Role of Individual Differences Among Salespeople," *Journal of Marketing,* October 1989, pp. 40–50.

[32] See Robert T. Keller, "A Test of the Path–Goal Theory of Leadership with Need for Clarity as a Moderator in Research and Development Organizations," *Journal of Applied Psychology,* April 1989, pp. 208–12.

[33] For a detailed discussion of relevant research, see Chester A. Schriesheim and Angelo S. DeNisi, "Task Dimensions as Moderators of the Effects of Instrumental Leadership: A Two-Sample Replicated Test of Path–Goal Leadership Theory," *Journal of Applied Psychology,* October 1981, pp. 589–97.

[34] A thorough discussion of this theory is provided by Paul Hersey and Kenneth H. Blanchard, *Management of Organizational Behavior: Utilizing Human Resources,* 5th ed. (Englewood Cliffs, N.J.: Prentice-Hall, 1988).

[35] Results can be found in Jane R. Goodson, Gail W. McGee, and James F. Cashman, "Situational Leadership Theory," *Group & Organization Studies,* December 1989, pp. 446–61.

[36] The first study was conducted by Robert P. Vecchio, "Situational Leadership Theory: An Examination of a Prescriptive Theory," *Journal of Applied Psychology,* August 1987, pp. 444–51. Results from the study of nurse executives can be found in Carolyn Adams, "Leadership Behavior of Chief Nurse Executives," *Nursing Management,* August 1990, pp. 36–39.

[37] See Donald C. Lueder, "Don't Be Misled by LEAD," *Journal of Applied Behavioral Science,* May 1985, pp. 143–54; and Claude L. Graeff, "The Situational Leadership Theory: A Critical View," *Academy of Management Review,* April 1983, pp. 285–91.

[38] See Fred Dansereau, Jr., George Graen, and William Haga, "A Vertical Dyad Linkage Approach to Leadership within Formal Organizations," *Organizational*

Behavior and Human Performance, February 1975, pp. 46–78; and Richard M. Dienesch and Robert C. Liden, "Leader–Member Exchange Model of Leadership: A Critique and Further Development," *Academy of Management Review,* July 1986, pp. 618–34.

[39] These descriptions were taken from Dennis Duchon, Stephen G. Green, and Thomas D. Taber, "Vertical Dyad Linkage: A Longitudinal Assessment of Antecedents, Measures, and Consequences," *Journal of Applied Psychology,* February 1986, pp. 56–60.

[40] The relationship between leader–member exchange and organizational climate was investigated by Steve W. J. Kozlowski and Mary L. Doherty, "Integration of Climate and Leadership: Examination of a Neglected Issue," *Journal of Applied Psychology,* August 1989, pp. 546–53. Results pertaining to performance and satisfaction are found in Robert P. Vecchio and Bruce C. Godbel, "The Vertical Dyad Linkage Model of Leadership: Problems and Prospects," *Organizational Behavior and Human Performance,* August 1984, pp. 5–20.

[41] Turnover studies were conducted by George B. Graen, Robert C. Liden, and William Hoel, "Role of Leadership in the Employee Withdrawal Process," *Journal of Applied Psychology,* December 1982, pp. 868–72; Gerald R. Ferris, "Role of Leadership in the Employee Withdrawal Process: A Constructive Replication," *Journal of Applied Psychology,* November 1985, pp. 777–81. The career progress study was conducted by Mitsuru Wakabayashi and George B. Graen, "The Japanese Career Progress Study: A 7-Year Follow-Up," *Journal of Applied Psychology,* November 1984, pp. 603–14.

[42] See Terri A. Scandura and George B. Graen, "Moderating Effects of Initial Leader–Member Exchange Status on the Effects of a Leadership Intervention," *Journal of Applied Psychology,* August 1984, pp. 428–36.

[43] For a complete discussion of this attributional process, see Mark. J. Martinko and William L. Gardner, "The Leader/Member Attribution Process," *Academy of Management Review,* April 1987, pp. 235–49.

[44] Gary A. Yukl, *Leadership in Organizations,* 2nd ed. (Englewood Cliffs, N.J.: Prentice-Hall, 1989), p. 168.

[45] See Terence R. Mitchell, Stephen G. Green, and Robert W. Wood, "An Attributional Model of Leadership and the Poor Performing Subordinate," in *Research in Organizational Behavior,* eds. Larry L. Cummings and Barry M. Staw (Greenwich, Conn.: JAI Press, 1981).

[46] Supporting results can be found in Donald B. Fedor and Kendrith M. Rowland, "Investigating Supervisor Attributions of Subordinate Performance," *Journal of Management,* September 1989, pp. 405–16; and Robert L. Heneman, David B. Greenberger, and Chigozie Anonyuo, "Attributions and Exchanges: The Effects of Interpersonal Factors on the Diagnosis of Employee Performance," *Academy of Management Journal,* June 1989, pp. 466–76.

[47] See Gregory H. Dobbins, Joseph A. Sgro, and Elaine Smith, "The Effects of Attributions and Costs of Corrective Actions on Leaders' Implementation of Control Policy: An Extension of the Attributional Model of Leadership," *Basic and Applied Social Psychology,* March 1990, pp. 45–60; and Bass, *Bass & Stogdill's Handbook of Leadership: Theory, Research, and Managerial Applications,* Chap. 18.

[48] See Heneman, Greenberger, and Anonyuo, "Attributions and Exchanges: The Effects of Interpersonal Factors on the Diagnosis of Employee Performance," pp. 466–476.

[49] A complete discussion of the history and need for transformational leadership is found in Noel M. Tichy and Mary Anne Devanna, *The Transformational Leader* (New York: John Wiley & Sons, 1986).

[50] Detailed descriptions of both transactional and transformational leadership are provided by Ronald J. Deluga, "The Effects of Transformational, Transactional, and Laissez Faire Leadership Characteristics on Subordinate Influencing Behavior," *Basic and Applied Social Psychology,* June 1990, pp. 191–203; and Bernard M. Bass, "From Transactional to Transformational Leadership: Learning to Share the Vision," *Organizational Dynamics,* Winter 1990, pp. 19–31.

[51] Francis J. Yammarino and Bernard M. Bass, "Transformation Leadership and Multiple Levels of Analysis," *Human Relations,* 1990, p. 976.

[52] A complete discussion of charismatic leadership is presented by Jay A. Conger and Rabindra Kanungo, "Toward a Behavioral Theory of Charismatic Leadership in Organizational Settings," *Academy of Management Review,* October 1987, pp. 637–47.

[53] See Tichy and Devanna, *The Transformational Leader;* James M. Kouzes and Barry Z. Posner, *The Leadership Challenge: How to Get Extraordinary Things Done in Organizations* (San Francisco: Jossey-Bass, 1990); and Bass, "From Transactional to Transformational Leadership: Learning To Share the Vision," pp. 19–31.

[54] The measuring instrument was developed by Bernard M. Bass, *Leadership and Performance Beyond Expectations* (New York: The Free Press, 1985). Validational evidence for this instrument is contained in Bernard M. Bass and Bruce J. Avolio, "Potential Biases in Leadership Measures: How Prototypes, Leniency, and General Satisfaction Relate to Ratings and Rankings of Transformational and Transactional Leadership Constructs," *Educational and Psychological Measurement,* 1989, pp. 509–27.

[55] See Bass, "From Transactional to Transformational Leadership: Learning to Share the Vision," pp. 19–31.

[56] See David A. Nadler and Michael L. Tushman, "Beyond the Charismatic Leader: Leadership and Organizational Change," *California Management Review,* Winter 1990, pp. 77–97; and David A. Waldman, Bernard M. Bass, and Francis J. Yammarino, "Adding to Contingent-Reward Behavior: The Augmenting Effect of Charismatic Leadership," *Group & Organization Studies,* December 1990, pp. 381–94.

[57] A thorough discussion is provided by Nadler and Tushman, "Beyond the Charismatic Leader: Leadership and Organizational Change."

[58] See John B. Judis, "Myth vs. Manager: Lee Iacocca, American Hero, Has Brought Chrysler Back to the Brink of Ruin—By Shirking His Duties the Way Mere Mortals Do," *Business Month,* July 1990, pp. 24–33.

[59] This vignette is from Fred E. Fiedler and Martin M. Chemers, *Improving Leadership Effectiveness: The Leader Match Concept,* 2nd ed. (New York: John Wiley & Sons, 1984), p. 173.

Individual and Group Decision Making

When you finish studying the material in this chapter, you should be able to:

- Distinguish between programmed and nonprogrammed decisions.
- Discuss the four steps in the rational model of decision making.
- Contrast Simon's normative model and the garbage can model of decision making.

- Discuss the contingency relationship that influences the three primary strategies used to select solutions.
- Describe the model of escalation of commitment.
- Summarize the pros and cons of involving groups in the decision-making process.
- Explain how participative management affects performance.

- Review Vroom and Jago's decision-making model.
- Contrast brainstorming, the nominal group technique, and the Delphi technique.
- Describe the stages of the creative process and specify at least five characteristics of creative people.

OPENING CASE 15

Disney-Style Decision Making

Sharon Hoogstraten

An impressive turnaround, a popular CEO, a magnificent stock performance, and the potent deployment of a great brand name—no wonder Wall Street can't stop genuflecting before the Walt Disney Co. But for all the reverential reviews, Disney's most important achievement—the one that makes the others possible—has gone largely unnoticed. The company has fashioned a new way of operating its businesses that combines Hollywood's creative chutzpah and strict financial self-discipline. This dynamic fusion lets executives dream up ideas and then act on them with unusual speed and agility. The Disney team has also derived a set of tactics and precepts that it applies like a crowbar throughout its divisions to leverage their success. . . .

The product Disney sells—unique synthetic experiences—is entirely different from food and autos. The company is nevertheless a business run like many others only with more imagination. Many of the methods used at Disney have relevance for any manager eager to exploit creative ideas without letting the risks of developing them get out of hand. . . .

Disney's uniqueness stems from having a creative executive—not a finance man or lawyer—in charge. The management team believes that creative ideas provide the hydraulics for growth. That makes sense: In the film and television business, a new product line born of ideas must be manufactured from scratch every year to fill the distribution pipeline. . . .

The system of checks and balances is much more formal than [chairman and CEO Michael] Eisner makes it sound. Every creative endeavor at Disney, from making a movie to building a hotel, happens within a financial box, with reasonable risk and cost as the walls. Walt Disney Imagineering, a think-tank-cum-carpentry-shop, develops the project's design and engineering requirements. A six-man strategic planning group headed by [chief financial officer Gary] Wilson, 49, then reviews it to see if the economics make sense. They run the numbers and try to strip every idea of bogus assumptions in a rigorous process they call "truth-seeking." Together the two groups draw up a budget and schedule.

The numbers then go to [President Frank] Wells and Eisner, who make a quick decision on whether to proceed. This process explains how Disney managed to conceive and execute ideas for the new Disney-MGM movie studios theme park at Disney World in Orlando, beating MCA to the market by one year—even though MCA had the idea first.

Tight financial supervision risks stifling creativity, but Eisner has found a way around that. When the movie *Who Framed Roger Rabbit?* began to exceed its budget, Eisner immediately called his team together to reassess the project. After weighing the risks and benefits, he opted to enlarge the budgetary box. The film ultimately cost about $40 million to make but also became the highest-grossing film of 1988. . . .

D ecision making is one of the primary responsibilities of being a manager. The quality of a manager's decisions is important for two principal reasons: First, the quality of a manager's decisions directly affect his or her career opportunities, rewards, and job satisfaction.[1] Second, managerial decisions contribute to the success or failure of an organization. Consider entrepreneur Bettis Rainsford's decision to buy a textile mill (see OB in

---

OPENING CASE 15

(concluded)

Tokyo Disneyland is the only company theme park that Disney does not own and operate. It licenses the operation to a Japanese company and collects royalties, which naturally subject the company's earnings and stock to currency fluctuations. CFO Wilson did not like that and designed an imaginative hedging scheme. In May of 1988, when the yen was a strong 124 to the dollar, he sold 20 years of projected royalties from the Tokyo theme park to a group of Japanese financial institutions. The value of the payments were then discounted back to the present and converted from yen into U.S. dollars—750 million of them. By placing this hoard in U.S. government bonds, he not only hedged against a subsequent decline in the yen, which soon went from 124 to 150, he also captured a handsome interest rate spread. Long-term bonds yield 6% in Japan, so that's the rate at which the Japanese banks discounted the future royalties back to the present. But with the bonds he bought in the U.S., Wilson locked in 10% on his money, and he can get even higher yields by reinvesting this cash in Disney's own operations. . . .

Disney's three divisions cross-fertilize each other in myriad ways. The animation studio creates cartoon characters like Roger Rabbit for use in films. These characters are quickly licensed to merchandisers who turn them out as stuffed animals and print them on T-shirts and other products that can be sold in the parks, in the chain of Disney retail stores, and through the company's gift catalogues. The characters can become costumes for park cast members or the subjects of new rides or attractions. In the case of Roger, a movie sequel and a string of cartoons will continue to build the freaked-out rabbit's franchise. . . .

For Eisner and Wells, Disney is a battleship increasingly difficult to steer. "As each of the divisions becomes more successful, relationships between them are harder to manage," says Wells. One of the most difficult tasks is allocating costs to the various divisions for their role in exploiting the growing opportunities for synergy. Who, for example, pays for 100 or so brief new films that are featured in the movie studio's theme park—the filmed entertainment division or the theme parks? Instead of spending endless hours

negotiating these matters. Wells makes a call that can, if necessary, be appealed.

Similarly, to push projects along and avoid costly delays, Eisner holds a regular meeting he calls a *charrette* (French for cart), a decision-making session borrowed from the world of architecture. All the key parties in a project, say to build a new hotel, convene in one room and make decisions on everything from the architectural details to the sconces, furniture, and cutlery. Eisner is fond of using deadlines as a motivational tool, so almost every project that gets assigned comes with a demanding deadline attached. Says he: "It's kind of cruel, and it doesn't always work. And sometimes you compromise quality—but rarely, rarely."

For Discussion

What is the most important component of Disney's decision-making process?

• Additional discussion questions linking this case with the following material appear at the end of this chapter.

Source: Excerpted from Christopher Knowlton, "How Disney Keeps the Magic Going," *Fortune*, December 4, 1989, pp. 111–12, 114, 116, 120, 124, 128, 132.

Action). Rainsford's decision was personally profitable and it set the example for reviving the U.S. textile market.

Decision making is a means to an end. It entails identifying and choosing alternative solutions that lead to a desired state of affairs. The process begins with a problem and ends when a solution has been chosen. To gain an understanding of how managers can make better decisions, this chapter focuses on: (1) the types of decisions managers make, (2) models of decision

OB IN ACTION

An Entrepreneur's Decisions Make or Break a Company

Rainsford was 31 when he heard that a mill closing in his hometown of Edgefield, S.C., would put some 200 locals out of work. With textile mills shutting down across the country, no investor was interested. . . .

Critics thought Rainsford was just tilting at windmills again when, with another entrepreneur, Erwin Maddrey, he paid $1 million for the Edgefield plant. The popular wisdom was that U.S. labor costs were just too high. "I saw that in textiles only about 20 percent of the cost of goods sold is direct labor," he says. "The problem was marketing." He immediately switched to more competitive product lines, retooling the factory with cheap, used machines. When his methods worked, Rainsford's new company, Delta Woodside Industries, Inc., gobbled up one decrepit mill after another—slashing overhead, firing middle managers, automating, and setting up incentive programs for managers.

By the time Delta Woodside went public in 1987, the picture had changed for American textiles. Inspired largely by Rainsford's example, investors today are "going hog-wild" over U.S. textile companies. Delta Woodside itself grossed $569 million, with $30.3 million in profits, for fiscal 1989.

Source: "Renegades: Harassed and Scorned, They Did It Their Way—and Won," *Success*, January/February 1990, p. 31.

making, (3) the dynamics of decision making, (4) group decision making, and (5) creativity.

• TYPES OF MANAGERIAL DECISIONS

Decision theorists have identified two types of managerial decisions: programmed and nonprogrammed.[2] It is important to distinguish between these two types because different techniques are used to deal with them (see Table 15–1).

Programmed Decisions

Programmed decisions tend to be repetitive and routine. Through time and experience, organizations develop specific procedures for handling these decisions. Getting dressed in the morning or driving to school involve personal programmed decisions. Through habit, you are likely to act on a similar chain of decisions each day. Work-related examples are determining how much vacation time to give an employee, deciding when to send customers a bill, and ordering office supplies. Habit and standard operating procedures are the most frequently used techniques for making these decisions. Today, computers handle many programmed decisions.

• **TABLE 15-1**   Techniques for Dealing with Two Types of Decisions

Types of Decisions	Decision-Making Techniques	
	Traditional	**Modern**

Programmed
  Routine, repetitive decisions
  Organization develops specific
    processes for handling them
	1. Habit
	2. Clerical routine:
	    Standard operating procedures
	3. Organization structure:
	    Common expectations
	    A system of subgoals
	    Well-defined informational
	    channels
		1. Operations research
		    Mathematical analysis
		    Models
		    Computer simulation
		2. Electronic data processing

Nonprogrammed
  One-shot, ill-structured, novel,
    policy decisions
  Handled by general problem-
    solving processes
	1. Judgment, intuition, and
	    creativity
	2. Rules of thumb
	3. Selection and training of
	    executives
		Heuristic problem-solving techniques
		applied to:
		a. Training human decision
		    makers
		b. Constructing heuristic computer
		    programs

Source: Herbert A. Simon, *The New Science of Management Decision*, © 1977, p. 48. Reprinted by permission of Prentice Hall, Inc., Englewood Cliffs, New Jersey.

Nonprogrammed Decisions

Nonprogrammed decisions are novel and unstructured. Hence, there are no cut-and-dried procedures for dealing with the problem at hand. These decisions also tend to have important consequences. Consider the situation faced by Southern California Edison, an electric utility serving 3.9 million people in Southern California. After developing long-range plans for the organization, Edison experienced unforseen problems in the 1970s and 1980s

• These Southern California Edison technicians are making both programmed and nonprogrammed decisions during a difficult trouble-shooting task.
(Courtesy of Southern California Edison Company)

that all but scrapped the plans: OPEC instituted price-fixing, the U.S. government instituted new sulfur emission restrictions, and nuclear accidents occurred at Three Mile Island and Chernobyl. Edison's ultimate success depended on the organization's response to these novel and unstructured problems.[3]

To solve nonprogrammed decisions, managers tend to rely on judgment, intuition, and creativity. More and more, however, companies are forming decision-making teams—recall our discussion in Chapter 11—or using computer simulations to help solve these problems.[4] Cincinnati Milacron, for instance, created a nine-member team to develop a plastics injection molding machine to meet the challenge of foreign competition. To be competitive, the machine needed to reduce production costs 40 percent and increase machine efficiency by 40 percent. And the typical two-year development time had to be cut in half. The team succeeded.[5]

• MODELS OF DECISION MAKING

There are several models of decision making. Each is based on a different set of assumptions and offers unique insight into the decision-making process. This section reviews three key historical models of decision making. They are (1) the rational model, (2) Simon's normative model, and (3) the garbage can model. Each successive model assumes that the decision-making process is less and less rational. Let us begin with the most orderly or rational explanation of managerial decision making.

The Rational Model

The **rational model** proposes that managers use a rational, four-step sequence when making decisions: (1) identifying the problem, (2) generating alternative solutions, (3) selecting a solution, and (4) implementing and evaluating the solution (see Figure 15–1). According to this model, managers are completely objective and possess complete information to make a decision. Despite criticism for being unrealistic, the rational model is instructive because it analytically breaks down the decision-making process and serves as a conceptual anchor for newer models. Let us now consider each of these four steps.

Identifying the Problem A **problem** exists when the actual situation and the desired situation differ.[6] For example, a problem exists when you have to pay rent at the end of the month and don't have enough money. Your problem is not that you have to pay rent. Your problem is obtaining the

• **FIGURE 15–1**   The Rational Decision-Making Model

needed funds. Similarly, the problem for a sales manager who has orders for 100 personal computers, but only 80 units in stock, is the 20 units unavailable (the gap between actual and desired). One expert proposed that managers use one of three methods to identify problems: historical cues, planning, and other people's perceptions:[7]

1. Using historical cues to identify problems assumes that the recent past is the best estimate of the future. Thus, managers rely on past experience to identify discrepancies (problems) from expected trends. For example, a sales manager may conclude that a problem exists because the first-quarter sales are less than they were a year ago. This method is prone to error because it is highly subjective.

2. A planning approach is more systematic and can lead to more accurate results. This method consists of using projections or scenarios to estimate what is expected to occur in the future. A time period of one or more years is generally used. Companies are increasingly using this scenario technique as a planning tool. The **scenario technique** is a speculative, conjectural forecasting tool used to identify future states, given a certain set of environmental conditions (see OB in Action). For example, an organization might estimate future sales by using a scenario that assumes unemployment will be 10 percent. Multiple scenarios identify a range of future states by considering a variety of environmental conditions. In this case, a sales scenario might be based on projecting a 5 percent unemployment rate and an 8 percent inflation rate. An alternative scenario might use a 7 percent unemployment rate and a 10 percent inflation rate. By using scenarios, managers can discipline their intuition.

OB IN ACTION

Shell Uses Scenario Planning

Royal Dutch/Shell, which has been doing scenario planning for 19 years and is widely regarded as the master of the craft, currently has two 20-year scenarios. . . .

Group planning coordinator Peter Hadfield believes that scenario planning has helped Shell be better prepared than its competitors for external shocks. In the early Eighties, for example, while most forecasters were predicting a steadily increasing price for crude oil, Shell, in one of its scenarios, had entertained the possibility that the price would slide to $15 a barrel. As a hedge against such an eventuality, the company began looking into cost-saving exploration technologies. When the slump hit, Shell was able to sustain a higher level of drilling activity than many of its competitors. Shell realizes that its two scenarios don't encompass everything that might happen in the future, and that neither will be a perfect predictor. Says Hadfield: "They're there to condition the organization to think."

Source: Ronald Henkoff, "How to Plan for 1995," *Fortune,* December 31, 1990, p. 79.

3. A final approach to identifying problems is to rely on the perceptions of others. Professors may realize they have unrealistic grading standards when the entire class complains about the grade distribution. In other words, students' comments signal that a problem exists. Similarly, automobile manufacturers sometimes are forced to recall cars because of consumer complaints about product safety or quality.

Generating Solutions   After identifying a problem, the next logical step is generating alternative solutions. For programmed decisions, alternatives are readily available through decision rules. This is not the case for nonprogrammed decisions. For nonprogrammed decisions, this step is the creative part of problem solving. Managers can use a number of techniques to stimulate creativity. For instance, this is how Ward Hagan, the previous chief executive at Warner-Lambert, attempted to increase managerial ability to generate solutions:

> Hagan sent his top 500 managers through a program to train them to be more critical and probing, and he took care to show by promotions that he valued such behavior. The result is that his troops were able to show him how to get from here to there, so much so that stock analysts are now high on Warner-Lambert.[8]

Techniques to increase creative thinking are discussed later in this chapter.

Selecting a Solution   Optimally, decision makers want to choose the alternative with the greatest value. Decision theorists refer to this as maximizing the expected utility of an outcome. This is no easy task. First, assigning values to alternatives is complicated and prone to error. Not only are values subjective, but they also vary according to the preferences of the decision maker. Further, evaluating alternatives assumes they can be judged according to some standards or criteria. This further assumes: (1) valid criteria exist, (2) each alternative can be compared against these criteria, and (3) the decision maker actually uses the criteria. As you know from making your own key life decisions, people frequently violate these assumptions.

Implementing and Evaluating the Solution   Once a solution is chosen, it needs to be implemented. Before implementing a solution, though, managers need to do their homework. For example, three ineffective managerial tendencies have been observed frequently during the initial stages of implementation (see Table 15–2). Skillful managers try to avoid these tendencies. Table 15–2 indicates that to promote necessary understanding, acceptance, and motivation, managers should involve implementors in the choice-making step.

After the solution is implemented, the evaluation phase assesses its effectiveness. If the solution is effective, it should reduce the difference between the actual and desired states that created the problem. If the gap is not closed, the implementation was not successful and one of the following is true: Either the problem was incorrectly identified, or the solution was inappropriate. Assuming the implementation was unsuccessful, management can return to the first step, problem identification. If the problem was correctly identified, management should consider implementing one of the previously identified, but untried, solutions. This process can continue until all feasible solutions have been tried or the problem has changed.

• TABLE 15-2   Three Managerial Tendencies Reduce the Effectiveness of Implementation

Managerial Tendency	Recommended Solution
The tendency not to ensure that people understand what needs to be done.	Involve the implementors in the choice-making step. When this is not possible, a strong and explicit attempt should be made to identify any misunderstanding, perhaps by having the implementor explain what he or she thinks needs to be done and why.
The tendency not to ensure the acceptance or motivation for what needs to be done.	Once again, involve the implementors in the choice-making step. Attempts should also be made to demonstrate the payoffs for effective implementation and to show how completion of various tasks will lead to successful implementation.
The tendency not to provide appropriate resources for what needs to be done.	Many implementations are less effective than they could be because adequate resources, such as time, staff, or information, were not provided. In particular, the allocations of such resources across departments and tasks are assumed to be appropriate because they were appropriate for implementing the previous plan. These assumptions should be checked.

Source: Modified from George P. Huber, *Managerial Decision Making* (Glenview, Ill.: Scott, Foresman, 1980), p. 19.

Summarizing the Rational Model   The rational model is based on the premise that managers optimize when they make decisions. **Optimizing** involves solving problems by producing the best possible solution. This assumes that managers:

- Have knowledge of all possible alternatives.
- Have complete knowledge about the consequences that follow each alternative.
- Have a well-organized and stable set of preferences for these consequences.
- Have the computational ability to compare consequences and to determine which one is preferred.[9]

As noted by Herbert Simon, a decision theorist who in 1978 earned the Nobel Prize for his work on decision making, "The assumptions of perfect rationality are contrary to fact. It is not a question of approximation; they do not even remotely describe the processes that human beings use for making decisions in complex situations."[10] Thus, the rational model is at best an instructional tool. Since decision makers do not follow these rational procedures, Simon proposed a normative model of decision making.

Simon's Normative Model

This model attempts to identify the process that managers actually use when making decisions. The process is guided by a decision maker's bounded rationality. **Bounded rationality** represents the notion that decision makers are "bounded" or restricted by a variety of constraints when making decisions. These constraints include any personal or environmental characteristics that reduce rational decision making. Examples are the limited capacity of the human mind, problem complexity and uncertainty, amount and timeliness of information at hand, (see A Matter of Ethics), and time demands.[11] Thus, although decision makers may desire the best solution to a

A MATTER OF ETHICS

Ethics and Decision Making

Back in 1985, Syntex Corp. figured it was onto something big: a new ulcer drug that promised to relieve the misery of millions—and earn the company big profits. In its annual report Syntex showed capsules of the drug spilling forth as shining examples of research. It pictured the drug's inventor, Gabriel Garay, at work in his lab. . . .

Critics are charging that the company, after investing millions in the drug's development, played down—and even suppressed—potentially serious safety problems that could hinder its approval.

Mr. Garay says it was he who sounded alarms internally over enprostil, warning it could cause dangerous blood clots and actually prompt new ulcers. Even when an outside researcher agreed there were potential dangers, Syntex executives dismissed the findings as preliminary. Mr. Garay says Syntex then forced him out.

Source: Marilyn Chase, "A Matter of Candor: Did Syntex Withhold Data on Side Effects of a Promising Drug?" *The Wall Street Journal,* January 8, 1991, p. A1.

problem, bounded rationality precludes its identification. How then do managers make decisions?

As opposed to the rational model, Simon's normative model suggests that decision making is characterized by (1) limited information processing, (2) the use of rules of thumb or shortcuts, and (3) satisficing. Each of these characteristics is now explored.

Limited Information Processing   Managers are limited by how much information they process because of bounded rationality. This results in the tendency to acquire manageable rather than optimal amounts of information. In turn, this practice makes it difficult for managers to identify all possible alternative solutions. In the long run, the constraints of bounded rationality cause decision makers to fail to evaluate all potential alternatives.

Use of Rules of Thumb or Shortcuts   Decision makers use rules of thumb or shortcuts to reduce information-processing demands. Since these shortcuts represent knowledge gained from past experience, they help decision makers evaluate current problems. For example, recruiters may tend to hire applicants receiving degrees from the same university attended by other successful employees. In this case, the "school attended" criterion is used to facilitate complex information processing associated with employment interviews. Unfortunately, these shortcuts can result in biased decisions.[12]

Satisficing   People satisfice because they do not have time, information, or ability to handle the complexity associated with following a rational process. This is not necessarily undesirable. **Satisficing** consists of choosing a solution that meets some minimum qualifications, one that is "good enough."

According to Russell Ackoff, a managerial problem-solving expert, satisficing resolves problems by producing solutions that are satisfactory, as opposed to optimal.[13] Borrowing another student's notes may satisfice for making up a missed class, although attending class is the best way to obtain complete information.

The Garbage Can Model

As true of Simon's normative model, this approach grew from the rational model's inability to explain how decisions are actually made. It assumes that decision making does not follow an orderly series of steps. In fact, organizational decision making is said to be such a sloppy and haphazard process that the garbage can label is appropriate. This contrasts sharply with the rational model, that proposed that decision makers follow a sequential series of steps beginning with a problem and ending with a solution. According to the **garbage can model,** decisions result from a complex interaction between four independent streams of events: problems, solutions, participants, and choice opportunities.[14] The interaction of these events creates "a collection of choices looking for problems, issues and feelings looking for decision situations in which they might be aired, solutions looking for issues to which they might be the answer, and decision makers looking for work."[15] The garbage can model attempts to explain how these events interact and lead to a decision. After discussing the streams of events and how they interact, this section highlights managerial implications of the garbage can model.

Streams of Events The four streams of events—problems, solutions, participants, and choice opportunities—represent independent entities that flow into and out of organizational decision situations (see Figure 15–2). Because decisions are a function of the interaction among these independent events, the stages of problem identification and problem solution may be unrelated. For instance, a solution may be proposed for a problem that does not exist. This can be observed when students recommend that a test be curved, even though the average test score is a comparatively high 85 percent. On the other hand, some problems are never solved. Some professors, regardless of the average test score, refuse to curve exam results. Each of the four events in the garbage can model deserves a closer look.

- *Problems:* As defined earlier, problems represent a gap between an actual situation and a desired condition. But problems are independent from alternatives and solutions. The problem may or may not lead to a solution.
- *Solutions:* Solutions are answers looking for questions. They represent ideas constantly flowing through an organization. Contrary to the classical model, however, solutions are used to formulate problems rather than vice versa. This is predicted to occur because managers often do not know what they want until they have some idea of what they can get.
- *Participants:* Participants are the organizational members who come and go throughout the organization. They bring different values, at-

• FIGURE 15–2   Garbage Can Model of Organizational Decision Making

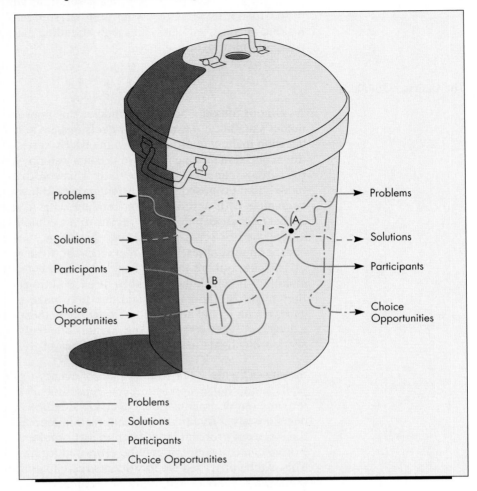

titudes, and experiences to a decision-making situation. Time pressures limit the extent to which participants are involved in decision making.

• *Choice opportunities:* Choice opportunities are occasions in which an organization is expected to make a decision. While some opportunities, such as hiring and promoting employees, occur regularly, others do not because they result from some type of crisis or unique situation. The response of the United Nations to Iraq's invasion of Kuwait in 1990 is an example of the latter situation.

Interactions among the Streams of Events   Because of the independent nature of the streams of events, they interact in a random fashion. This implies decision making is more a function of chance encounters than a rational process. Thus, the organization is characterized as a ''garbage can'' in which problems, solutions, participants, and choice opportunities are all mixed together (see Figure 15–2). Only when the four streams of events happen to connect, such as at point A in Figure 15–2, is a decision made. Since these connections randomly occur among countless combinations of streams of events, decision quality generally depends on *timing*. (Some might use the term *luck*.) In other words, good decisions are made when these streams of events interact at the proper time. This explains why problems do not necessarily relate to solutions (point B in Figure 15–2) and why solutions do not always solve problems. In support of the garbage can model, a recent study indicated that decision making in the textbook publishing industry followed a garbage can process. Moreover, knowledge of this process helped the researchers to identify a variety of best-selling textbooks.[16]

Managerial Implications   The garbage can model of organizational decision making has four practical implications.[17] First, many decisions will be made by oversight or the presence of a salient opportunity. Second, political motives frequently guide the process by which participants make decisions. Participants tend to make decisions that promise to increase their status. (Recall the discussion of organizational politics in Chapter 10.) Third, the process is sensitive to load. That is, as the number of problems increases, relative to the amount of time available to solve them, problems are less likely to be solved. Finally, important problems are more likely to be solved than unimportant ones because they are more salient to organizational participants.[18]

• DYNAMICS OF DECISION MAKING

"Decision making, like any other element of a manager's job, is partly science, partly art."[19] Accordingly, this section examines two dynamics of decision making—contingency considerations and the problem of escalation of commitment—that affect the "science" component. An understanding of these dynamics can help managers make better decisions.

Selecting Solutions: A Contingency Perspective

The previous discussion of decision-making models noted that managers typically satisfice when they select solutions. However, we did not probe how managers actually evaluate and select solutions. Let us explore the model in Figure 15–3 to better understand how individuals make decisions.

Strategies for Selecting a Solution   What procedures do decision makers use to evaluate the costs and benefits of alternative solutions? According to management experts Lee Roy Beach and Terence Mitchell, one of three approaches is used: aided-analytic, unaided-analytic, and nonanalytic.[20] Decision makers systematically use tools such as mathematical equations, calculators, or computers to analyze and evaluate alternatives within an **aided-analytic** approach. Technicians also may be commissioned to conduct a formal study. In contrast, decision makers rely on the confines of their minds when using an **unaided-analytic** strategy. In other words, the decision maker systematically compares alternatives, but the analysis is limited to

• **Figure 15-3**   A Contingency Model for Selecting a Solution

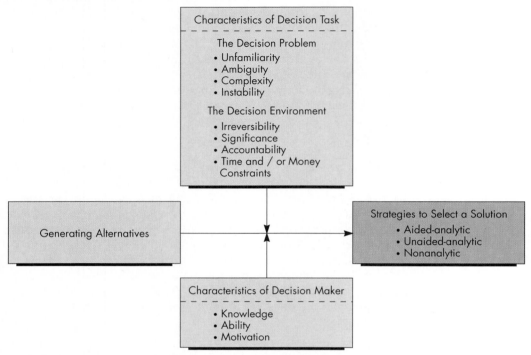

Characteristics of Decision Task

The Decision Problem
- Unfamiliarity
- Ambiguity
- Complexity
- Instability

The Decision Environment
- Irreversibility
- Significance
- Accountability
- Time and / or Money
  Constraints

Generating Alternatives

Strategies to Select a Solution
- Aided-analytic
- Unaided-analytic
- Nonanalytic

Characteristics of Decision Maker
- Knowledge
- Ability
- Motivation

Source: Based on Lee Roy Beach and Terence R. Mitchell, "A Contingency Model for the Selection of Decision Strategies," *Academy of Management Review*, July 1978, pp. 439–44.

• Chance plays a greater role when using a nonanalytic strategy to make decisions.   *(ITTC Productions/The Image Bank)*

evaluating information that can be directly processed in his or her head. Decision-making tools such as a personal computer are not used. Finally, a **nonanalytic** strategy consists of using a simple preformulated rule to make a decision. Examples are flipping a coin, habit, normal convention (''we've always done it that way''), using a conservative approach (''better safe than sorry''), or following procedures offered in instruction manuals. Both the cost and level of sophistication decrease as one moves from an aided-analytic to a nonanalytic strategy.

Determining which approach to use depends on two sets of contingency factors: characteristics of the decision task and characteristics of the decision maker (refer again to Figure 15–3).

Characteristics of the Decision Task   This set of contingency factors reflects the demands and constraints a decision maker faces. In general, the greater these demands and constraints, the higher the probability that an aided-analytic approach will be used. These characteristics are divided into two components: those pertaining to the specific problem and those related to the general decision environment. Unfamiliar, ambiguous, complex, or unstable problems are more difficult to solve and typically require more sophisticated analysis. A recent study of 162 upper-division business students demonstrated that the accuracy of a decision was inversely related to the complexity of the problem. In other words, more accurate decisions were made for easy problems and less accurate for difficult problems.[21]

The environment also restricts the type of analysis used.[22] For instance, managers experience increasing pressure to make good decisions when they are personally accountable for an irreversible decision or a significant problem. Moreover, time constraints affect selection of a solution. Poorer decisions are bound to be made in the face of severe time pressure.

Characteristics of the Decision Maker   Chapter 3 highlighted a variety of individual differences that affect employee behavior and performance. In the present context, knowledge, ability, and motivation affect the type of analytical procedure used by a decision maker. For example, a recent study of 21 financial planners revealed that experienced planners solved problems faster and better by conducting a more sophisticated analysis than did inexperienced planners.[23] In general, research supports the prediction that aided-analytic strategies are more likely to be used by competent and motivated individuals.[24]

Contingency Relationships   There are many ways in which characteristics of the decision task and decision maker can interact to influence the strategy used to select a solution.[25] In choosing a strategy, decision makers compromise between their desire to make correct decisions and the amount of time and effort they put into the decision-making process. Table 15–3 lists contingency relationships that help reconcile these competing demands.[26] As shown in this table, analytic strategies are more likely to be used when the problem is unfamiliar and irreversible. In contrast, nonanalytic methods are employed on familiar problems or problems in which the decision can be reversed.

• **TABLE 15–3**   Contingency Relationships in Decision Making

1. Analytic strategies are used when the decision problem is unfamiliar, ambiguous, complex, or unstable.
2. Nonanalytic methods are employed when the problem is familiar, straightforward, or stable.
3. Assuming there are no monetary or time constraints, analytic approaches are used when the solution is irreversible and significant, and the decision maker is accountable.
4. Nonanalytic strategies are used when the decision can be reversed and is not very significant, or the decision maker is not held accountable.
5. As the probability of making a correct decision goes down, analytic strategies are used.
6. As the probability of making a correct decision goes up, nonanalytic strategies are employed.
7. Time and money constraints automatically exclude some strategies from being used.
8. Analytic strategies are more frequently used by experienced and educated decision makers.
9. Nonanalytic approaches are used when the decision maker lacks knowledge, ability, or motivation to make a good decision.

Source: Adapted from Lee Roy Beach and Terence R. Mitchell, "A Contingency Model for the Selection of Decision Strategies," *Academy of Management Review*, July 1978, pp. 439–44.

Escalation of Commitment

Prior to reading any further, we would like you to read the scenario in the OB Exercise and answer the diagnostic question. The scenario describes an escalation situation. Escalation situations involve circumstances in which things have gone wrong, but where the situation can possibly be turned around by investing additional time, money, or effort.[27] Consider the situation faced by Lyndon Johnson during the early stages of the Vietnam war. Johnson received the following memo from George Ball, then Undersecretary of State:

> The decision you face now is crucial. Once large numbers of U.S. troops are committed to direct combat, they will begin to take heavy casualties in a war they are ill-equipped to fight in a noncooperative if not downright hostile countryside. Once we suffer large casualties, we will have started a well-nigh irreversible process. Our involvement will be so great that we cannot—without national humiliation—stop short of achieving our complete objectives. Of the two possibilities I think humiliation will be more likely than the achievement of our objectives—even after we have paid terrible costs.[28]

Unfortunately, President Johnson's increased commitment to the war helped make George Ball's prediction come true.

Let us return to the scenario in the OB Exercise. What was your answer? If you responded yes, you experienced what researchers call escalation of commitment: So did Lyndon Johnson. **Escalation of commitment** refers to the tendency to stick to an ineffective course of action when it is unlikely that the bad situation can be reversed. Personal examples include investing more money into an old or broken car, determining that one can save a disruptive interpersonal relationship, or deciding to hold a stock whose price

---

• OB EXERCISE

Making a Decision in an Escalation Situation

As the president of an airline company, you have invested 10 million dollars of the company's money into a research project. The purpose was to build a plane that would not be detected by conventional radar, in other words, a radar-blank plane. When the project is 90 percent completed, another firm begins marketing a plane that cannot be detected by radar. Also, it is apparent that their plane is much faster and far more economical than the plane your company is building. The question is: Should you invest the last 10 percent of the research funds to finish your radar-blank plane?

    Answer: Yes, invest the money.

              No, drop the project.

Source: Hal R. Arkes and Catherine Blumer, "The Psychology of Sunk Cost," *Organizational Behavior and Human Decision Processes*, February 1985, p. 129.

---

is declining. Anecdotal experience also indicates that escalation of commitment is partially responsible for some of the worst financial losses experienced by organizations. The savings and loan crisis that started in the late 1980s is a prime example.

OB researchers Barry Staw and Jerry Ross identified four reasons for escalation of commitment (see Figure 15–4). They involve characteristics of the project itself, psychological determinants, social forces, and organizational determinants. Each cause is now briefly discussed.[29]

Project Characteristics   Project characteristics involve the objective features of a project. They have the greatest impact on escalation decisions. For example, because most projects do not reap benefits until some delayed time period, decision makers are motivated to stay with the project until the end. There thus is a tendency to attribute setbacks to temporary causes that are correctable with additional expenditures.[30]

Psychological Determinants   Information-processing errors and ego-defense are the key psychological contributors to escalation of commitment. Individuals "throw good money after bad" because they tend to (1) bias facts so that they support previous decisions, (2) take more risks when a decision is stated in negative terms (to recover losses) rather than positive ones (to achieve gains), and (3) get too ego-involved with the project. Because failure threatens an individual's self-esteem or ego, people tend to ignore negative signs and push forward.

Social Forces   Social pressures can make it difficult for a manager to reverse a course of action. For instance, peer pressure makes it difficult for an individual to drop a course of action when he or she publicly supported it in the past. Further, managers may continue to support bad decisions because they don't want their mistakes exposed to others.

• **FIGURE 15-4**   A Model of Escalation of Commitment

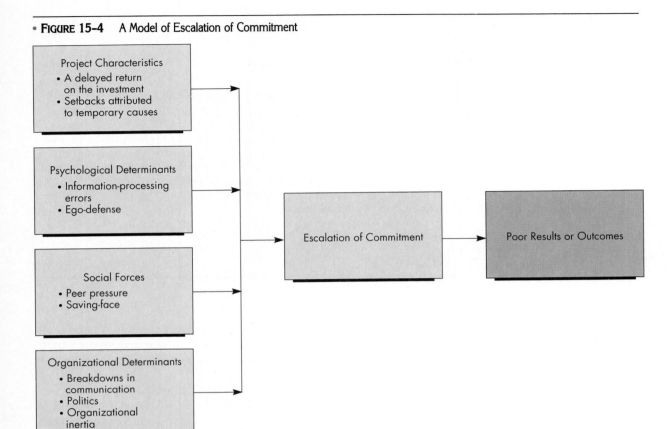

Based on discussion in Barry M. Straw and Jerry Ross, "Understanding Behavior in Escalation Situations," *Science*, October 1989, pp. 216–20.

Organizational Determinants   Breakdowns in communication, workplace politics, and organizational inertia cause organizations to maintain bad courses of action.

Reducing Escalation of Commitment   It is important to reduce escalation of commitment because it leads to poor decision making. Barry Staw and Jerry Ross, the researchers who originally identified the phenomenon of escalation, recommend several ways to reduce it:

- Have different individuals make the initial and subsequent decisions about a project.
- Encourage decision makers to become less ego-involved with a project.
- Provide more frequent feedback about project completion and costs.
- Reduce the risk or penalties of failure.
- Make decision makers aware of the costs of persistence.[31]

Although a few studies have supported some of these recommendations, additional research on the causes and reduction of escalation of commitment is needed.[32]

• GROUP DECISION MAKING

Chapter 9 examined the unique dynamics that arise when individuals work together in groups. Groups such as committees, task forces, or review panels often play a key role in the decision-making process. For example, the chapter opening case on Disney indicated that Michael Eisner, CEO of Disney, uses group decision making to manage all aspects of a project. President George Bush also uses groups to help him make key decisions. He even instituted debates to encourage group participation.

To help Bush think through an issue, White House aides stage debates, which they call "scheduled train wrecks." Aides once invited opposing sides to lobby the President separately, but quickly realized that Bush prefers—and benefits from—live skirmishes. Bush asks questions during the back and forth, takes copious notes on White House pads and often asks lower-level officials for their views. "He doesn't want filters," said a participant. "He actually wants to sit there at the table and listen to [Budget Director Richard] Darman fight with [EPA Administrator William] Reilly "Darman argued in one meeting that the clean-air proposals were too expensive for the health and safety benefits gained. "For the same amount of money," the Budget Director said, "we can buy everyone in America rubber-soled shoes, because the chance of being killed by toxic gases is about the same as being killed by lightning."[33]

Are two or more heads always better than one? Do all employees desire to have a say in the decision-making process? When and how should a manager use group decision making? This section provides the background for answering these questions, essential for gaining maximum benefits from group decision making. We discuss (1) advantages and disadvantages of group-aided decision making, (2) participative management, (3) when to use groups in decision making, and (4) group problem-solving techniques.

Advantages and Disadvantages of Group-Aided Decision Making

Including groups in the decision-making process has both pros and cons (see Table 15–4). On the positive side, groups contain a greater pool of knowledge, provide more varied perspectives, create more comprehension of decisions, increase decision acceptance, and create a training ground for inexperienced employees. These advantages must be balanced, however, with the disadvantages listed in Table 15–4. In so doing, managers need to determine the extent to which the advantages and disadvantages apply to the decision situation. The following three guidelines may then be applied to help decide whether groups should be included in the decision-making process:

1. If additional information would increase the quality of the decision, managers should involve those people who can provide the needed information.

2. If acceptance is important, managers need to involve those individuals whose acceptance and commitment are important. As chairman of Corning, James Houghton has formalized this second guideline.

Jamie has been reshaping the company with a remarkable show of consensus management, considering that the Houghtons still own 15% of Corning. His

• **TABLE 15-4**   Advantages and Disadvantages of Group-Aided Decision Making

Advantages	Disadvantages
1. **Greater pool of knowledge.** A group can bring much more information and experience to bear on a decision or problem than can an individual acting alone.	1. **Social pressure.** Unwillingness to "rock the boat" and pressure to conform may combine to stifle the creativity of individual contributors.
2. **Different perspectives.** Individuals with varied experience and interests help the group see decision situations and problems from different angles.	2. **Minority domination.** Sometimes the quality of group action is reduced when the group gives in to those who talk the loudest and longest.
3. **Greater comprehension.** Those who personally experience the give-and-take of group discussion about alternative courses of action tend to understand the rationale behind the final decision.	3. **Logrolling.** Political wheeling and dealing can displace sound thinking when an individual's pet project or vested interest is at stake.
4. **Increased acceptance.** Those who play an active role in group decision making and problem solving tend to view the outcome as "ours" rather than "theirs."	4. **Goal displacement.** Sometimes secondary considerations such as winning an argument, making a point, or getting back at a rival displace the primary task of making a sound decision or solving a problem.
5. **Training ground.** Less experienced participants in group action learn how to cope with group dynamics by actually being involved.	5. **"Groupthink."** Sometimes cohesive "in-groups" let the desire for unanimity override sound judgment when generating and evaluating alternative courses of action.

Source: Robert Kreitner, *Management*, 4th ed. (Boston: Houghton Mifflin, 1989) p. 238.

executive council of six men, which puts Corning's four operations managers atop the corporate pyramid for the first time, makes key decisions. At first, midlevel executives feared the new management by committee would stall decisions. But Houghton required the committee to respond in writing within 24 hours to middle-management presentations.[34]

3. If people can be developed through their participation, managers may want to involve those whose development is most important.[35]

Group versus Individual Performance   Before recommending that managers involve groups in decision making, it is important to examine whether groups perform better or worse than individuals. After reviewing 61 years of relevant research (see Table 15–5), a decision-making expert concluded that "Group performance was generally qualitatively and quantitatively superior to the performance of the average individual."[36] A more recent study of 222 team-learning groups supported this conclusion. Results indicated that the groups outperformed their most proficient group member 97 percent of the time. This quantitative increase was accompanied by an 8.8 percent increase in the quality of production.[37] In spite of these positive results, additional research suggests that managers should use a contingency approach when determining whether to include others in the decision-making process. Let us consider these practical contingency recommendations.

• TABLE 15-5   Summary of 61 Years of Research on Group versus Individual Performance

Variable of Interest	Conclusion
Type of task:	
Learning task	Group performance was consistently superior to the performance of an individual.
Concept mastery and creative tasks	More unshared resources by high-ability group members. Contribution of medium-ability group members was greater when they were paired with partners who had high rather than low ability.
Problem solving	Groups took longer to complete the tasks, but made more accurate decisions. On difficult problems, groups pooled and integrated their resources. On easy tasks, group performance was determined by the contribution of one competent group member.
Brainstorming	Pooling individual responses resulted in a greater number of unique ideas than did group interaction.
Complex	Groups were superior to an individual, but inferior to pooling individual responses.
Training:	
In problem solving and group dynamics	Groups benefited more than individuals.
In brainstorming	Individuals benefited more than groups.
In ability to apply new skills in work environment	Individuals took less time to apply new knowledge than did groups.
Individual differences:	High-ability individuals performed better than did groups composed of mixed ability. Higher performance was obtained by groups whose members preferred to work in a group, rather than alone.
Decision-making processes:	Groups made riskier decisions. Group members did not put forth an equal amount of effort.

Source: Conclusions were derived from Gayle W. Hill, "Group versus Individual Performance: Are N + 1 Heads Better than One?" *Psychological Bulletin*, May 1982, pp. 517–39.

Practical Contingency Recommendations   If the decision occurs frequently, such as deciding on promotions or who qualifies for a loan, use groups because they tend to produce more consistent decisions than do individuals.[38] Given time constraints, let the most competent individual, rather than a group, make the decision. In the face of environmental threats such as time pressure and potential serious impact of a decision, groups use less information and fewer communication channels. This increases the probability of a bad decision.[39] This conclusion underscores a general recommendation that managers should keep in mind: Because the quality of communication strongly affects a group's productivity, on complex tasks it is essential to devise mechanisms to enhance communication effectiveness.[40]

Participative Management

Confusion exists about the exact meaning of participative management (PM). One management expert clarified this situation by defining **participative management** as the process whereby employees play a direct role in (1) setting goals, (2) making decisions, (3) solving problems, and (4) making changes in the organization. Without question, participative management entails much more than simply asking employees for their ideas or opinions.[41]

Advocates of PM claim employee participation increases employee satisfaction, commitment, and performance. Practical experience at H. J. Heinz Company and Du Pont Company, however, produced mixed results:

> H. J. Heinz Co. figures it will generate $200 million in annual savings within four years by listening to teams of employees enlisted to boost productivity and trim waste. In one such effort at a StarKist factory in Puerto Rico, employee teams observed that tuna was being wasted because workers couldn't keep up with an accelerated processing line. Spending $4 million for additional equipment and $5 million a year for extra hands now saves the company $100 million annually, Heinz says.[42]

> But Du Pont Co. draws union flak for a program that lets some workers decide their own job responsibilities and work schedules, among other matters. . . . It's a "union-busting technique," contends Kenneth Henley, a union lawyer. He complains that the program restricts promotional opportunities, requires more work without higher pay, and causes dissension in union ranks.[43]

To get a fuller understanding of how and when participative management works, we begin by discussing a model of participative management.

A Model of Participative Management   Consistent with both Maslow's need theory and the job characteristics model of job design (see Chapter 5), participative management is predicted to increase motivation because it helps employees fulfill three basic needs: (1) autonomy, (2) meaningfulness of work, and (3) interpersonal contact. As shown in Figure 15–5, satisfaction of these needs enhances feelings of acceptance and commitment, security, challenge, and satisfaction. In turn, these positive feelings supposedly lead to increased innovation and performance.[44]

The model of participative management includes three contingency factors highlighting various situations in which PM is effective. Individual factors include employees' values, attitudes, and expectations that influence how they will respond to PM. As implied in the discussion of job enrichment, some people do not respond positively to participation.[45] They simply want to do their job and leave the decision making to managers.

The design of work and the level of trust between management and employees represent two organizational contingencies. With respect to the design of work, individual participation is counterproductive when employees are highly interdependent on each other, as on an assembly line. The problem with individual participation in this case is that interdependent employees generally do not have a broad understanding of the entire production process. Participative management also is less likely to succeed when employees do not trust management. Finally, PM is more effective when organizations face rapidly changing environmental contingencies, which include changes in technology, governmental regulations, and global competition (see International OB).

• **FIGURE 15-5**   A Model of Participative Management

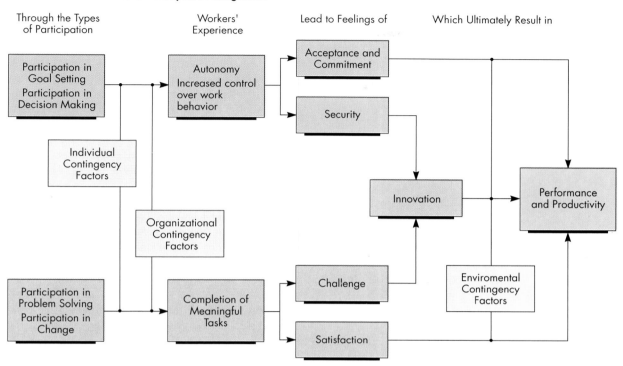

INTERNATIONAL OB

Korean-Style Participative Management

Lucky-Goldstar Group was the first large Korean company to put down U.S. roots: It opened a TV and microwave plant in Huntsville, Ala. . . .[in 1983]. Samsung followed in mid-1984. . . .

Don't confuse these immigrants with the Japanese, though. Yes, Koreans also espouse teamwork, employee participation, minimal hierarchies, and the corporation-as-family idea. But they tend to tailor their practices to the American style. "The Koreans are more flexible than we are," admits . . . [a Hitachi spokesman. According to] . . . a Samsung manager: "The Japanese are from a homogeneous society, so they are less accepting of anything that is not Japanese. Korea is a land of division, so the people are willing to listen and not get their feet stuck in concrete."

Source: Laure Baum, "Korea's Newest Export: Management Style," *Business Week*, January 19, 1987, p. 66.

Research and Practical Suggestions for Managers   Participative management significantly increased employee creativity, and it lowered employee role conflict and ambiguity.[46] Two meta-analyses further demonstrated that participation had a moderately strong impact on job satisfaction.[47] Results are not so clear cut, however, when it comes to productivity.

Some researchers interpreted the published findings as suggesting that authoritarian methods were just as effective in increasing productivity as participative management. Others disagreed; they concluded that different types of participation significantly affected productivity.[48] The issue is still unresolved and is currently being debated.[49]

So what is a manager to do? We believe that PM is not a quick-fix solution for low productivity and motivation, as some enthusiastic supporters claim. Nonetheless, since participative management is effective in certain situations, managers can increase their chances of obtaining positive results by using once again a contingency approach. For example, the effectiveness of participation depends on the type of interactions between managers and employees as they jointly solve problems.[50] Effective participation requires a constructive interaction that fosters cooperation and respect, as opposed to competition and defensiveness. Managers are advised not to use participative programs when they have destructive interpersonal interactions with their employees.

Experiences of companies implementing participative management programs suggest two additional practical recommendations. *First,* supervisors and middle managers tend to resist participative management because it reduces their power and authority. Consider the following events at Boeing:

> The case of Boeing Aerospace's manufacturing division, with 300 managers spread through four organizational levels, has been fairly typical. The division's initial thrust at participation in 1980 was to put together trouble-shooting teams of workers, engineers, and managers to smooth bumps in production. Other middle managers often perceived the teams as intruders, and the idea flopped. "The only thing that remained was a negative attitude about employee involvement," notes Carl Hicks, head of quality improvement in the division. "We're still trying to undo that damage."[51]

When implementing PM programs, it is thus important to gain the support and commitment from employees who have managerial responsibility.

Second, as concluded by Richard J. Boyle, vice president and group executive at Honeywell's Defense and Marine Systems Group, the process of implementing participative management must be managed. Honeywell's PM program almost failed because the initial implementation stages were not monitored and managed by top management.[52]

When to Have Groups Participate in Decision Making: The Vroom/Yetton/Jago Model

Victor Vroom and Philip Yetton developed a model in 1973 to help managers determine the degree of group involvement in the decision-making process. It was later expanded by Vroom and Arthur Jago.[53] The model is prescriptive in that it specifies decision-making styles that should be effective in different situations.

Vroom and Jago's model is represented as a decision tree. The manager's task is to move from left to right along the various branches of the tree. A specific decision-making style is prescribed at the end-point of each branch. Before we apply the model, however, it is necessary to consider the different decision styles managers ultimately choose from and an approach for diagnosing the problem situation.

Five Decision-Making Styles   Vroom and Yetton identified five distinct decision-making styles. In Table 15–6, each style is represented by a letter. The letter indicates the basic thrust of the style. For example, A stands for *autocratic,* C for *consultive,* and G for *group.* There are several important issues to consider as one moves from an AI style to a GII style. They are:

- The problem or decision is discussed with more people.
- Group involvement moves from merely providing data to recommending solutions.
- Group "ownership" and commitment to the solution increases.
- As group commitment increases, so does the time needed to arrive at a decision.[54]

Style choice is dependent on the type of problem situation.

Matching the Situation to Decision-Making Style   Vroom and Jago developed eight problem attributes that managers can use to diagnose a situation. They are shown at the top of the decision tree presented in Figure 15–6 and are expressed as questions. Answers to these questions lead managers along different branches, pointing the way to potentially effective decision-making styles.

• **TABLE 15–6**   Management Decision Styles

AI	You solve the problem or make the decision yourself, using information available to you at that time.
AII	You obtain the necessary information from your subordinate(s), then decide on the solution to the problem yourself. You may or may not tell your subordinates what the problem is in getting the information from them. The role played by your subordinates in making the decision is clearly one of providing the necessary information to you rather than generating or evaluating solutions.
CI	You share the problem with relevant subordinates individually, getting their ideas and suggestions without bringing them together as a group. Then you make the decision that may or may not reflect your subordinates' influence.
CII	You share the problem with your subordinates as a group, collectively obtaining their ideas and suggestions. Then you make the decision that may or may not reflect your subordinates' influence.
GII	You share a problem with your subordinates as a group. Together you generate and evaluate alternatives and attempt to reach agreement (consensus) on a solution. Your role is much like that of chairman. You do not try to influence the group to adopt "your" solution and you are willing to accept and implement any solution that has the support of the entire group.

• **FIGURE 15-6**   Vroom and Jago's Decision-Making Model

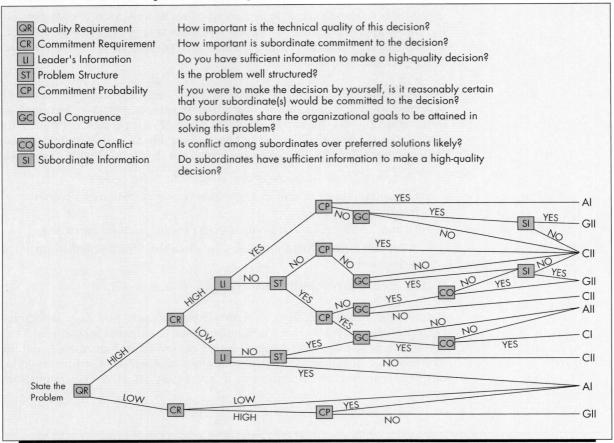

QR	Quality Requirement	How important is the technical quality of this decision?
CR	Commitment Requirement	How important is subordinate commitment to the decision?
LI	Leader's Information	Do you have sufficient information to make a high-quality decision?
ST	Problem Structure	Is the problem well structured?
CP	Commitment Probability	If you were to make the decision by yourself, is it reasonably certain that your subordinate(s) would be committed to the decision?
GC	Goal Congruence	Do subordinates share the organizational goals to be attained in solving this problem?
CO	Subordinate Conflict	Is conflict among subordinates over preferred solutions likely?
SI	Subordinate Information	Do subordinates have sufficient information to make a high-quality decision?

Source: Victor H. Vroom and Arthur G. Jago, *The New Leadership: Managing Participation in Organizations* (Englewood Cliffs, N.J.: Prentice Hall, 1988), p. 184.

Applying the Model   Because Vroom and Jago developed four decision trees, the first step is to choose one of the trees. Each tree represents a generic type of problem that managers frequently encounter. They are: (1) an individual-level problem with time constraints, (2) an individual-level problem in which the manager wants to develop an employee's decision-making abilities, (3) a group-level problem in which the manager wants to develop employees' decision-making abilities, and (4) a time-driven group problem[55] (illustrated in Figure 15–6).

To use the model in Figure 15–6, start at the left side and move toward the right by asking yourself the questions associated with each decision point (represented by a box in the figure) encountered. A decision-making style is prescribed at the end of each branch.

Let us track a simple example through Figure 15–6. Suppose you have to determine the work schedule for a group of part-time workers who report to you. The first question is "How important is the technical quality of this decision?" It seems rather low. This leads us to the second question: "How important is subordinate commitment to the decision?" Assuming acceptance is important, this takes us along the branch leading to the question about commitment probability (CP). If you were to make the decision by yourself, is it reasonably certain that your subordinate(s) would be committed to the decision? A yes answer suggests you should use an AI decision-making style (see Table 15–6) and a GII style if you answered no.

Research Insights and Managerial Implications   Because this model is relatively new, very little research has tested its prescriptive accuracy. Nonetheless, research does support the earlier model developed by Vroom and Yetton in 1973.[56] For example, a recent study of 36 departments in a large retail department store indicated that group productivity was higher when managers used decision-making styles consistent with the model.[57] Managers thus are advised to use different decision–making styles to suit situational demands.

Also, the model can help managers determine when, and to what extent, they should involve employees in decision making. By simply being aware of the eight diagnostic questions, managers can enhance their ability to structure ambiguous problems. This should ultimately enhance the quality of managerial decisions.

Group Problem-Solving Techniques

Using groups to make decisions generally requires that they reach a consensus. According to a decision-making expert, a **consensus** "is reached when all members can say they either agree with the decision or have had their 'day in court' and were unable to convince the others of their viewpoint. In the final analysis, everyone agrees to support the outcome."[58] This definition indicates that consensus does not necessarily represent unanimous agreement.

Groups can experience roadblocks when trying to arrive at a consensus decision. For one, groups may not generate all relevant alternatives to a problem because an individual dominates or intimidates other group members. This is both overt and/or subtle. For instance, group members who possess power and authority, such as a CEO, can be intimidating, regardless of interpersonal style, simply by being present in the room. Moreover, shyness inhibits the generation of alternatives. Shy individuals may withhold their input for fear of embarrassment or lack of confidence. Satisficing is another hurdle to effective group decision making. As previously noted, groups satisfice due to limited time, information, or ability to handle large amounts of information.

Decision-making experts have developed three group problem-solving techniques—brainstorming, the nominal group technique, and the Delphi technique—to reduce the above roadblocks. Knowledge of these techniques can help present and future managers to more effectively use group-aided decision making.

Brainstorming   Brainstorming was developed by A. F. Osborn, an advertising executive, to increase creativity.[59] **Brainstorming** is used to help groups generate multiple ideas and alternatives for solving problems. For example, Ford Motor Company used brainstorming to increase the productivity in its manufacturing plants (see OB in Action). This technique is effective because

OB IN ACTION

Employee Ideas Result in Increased Productivity for Ford Motor Company

When Ford asked assembly-line workers to contribute ideas, one suggested making all bolts the same size. Saving employees from sifting through bins of different-size bolts and endlessly changing wrenches makes the job go much faster. In another procedure, workers had to reach through a small hole in the car door to tighten a bolt. Employees worried that they would drop bolts inside the door, either slowing the assembly line to retrieve them or leaving behind an annoying rattle for the future owner. The straightforward solution: enlarge the hole.

Source: James B. Treece, "How to Teach Old Plants New Tricks," *Business Week*, June 16, 1989, p. 130.

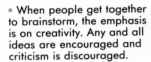

• When people get together to brainstorm, the emphasis is on creativity. Any and all ideas are encouraged and criticism is discouraged.

it helps reduce interference caused by critical and judgmental reactions to one's ideas from other group members.

When brainstorming, a group is convened and the problem at hand is reviewed. Individual members then are asked to silently generate ideas/ alternatives for solving the problem. Next, these ideas/alternatives are solicited and written on a board or flip chart. A second session is used to critique and evaluate the alternatives. Managers are advised to follow four rules when brainstorming:

1. Freewheeling is encouraged. Group members are advised to offer any and all ideas they have. The wilder, the better.

2. Criticism is discouraged. Don't criticize during the initial stage of idea generation. Phrases like "we've never done it that way," "it won't work," "it's too expensive," and "the boss will never agree" should not be used.
3. Quantity of ideas is encouraged. Managers should try to generate and write down as many ideas as possible.
4. Combination and improvement of ideas is pursued. Group members are advised to "piggyback" onto the ideas of others.

Brainstorming is an effective technique for generating new ideas/alternatives. It is not appropriate for evaluating alternatives or selecting solutions.

The Nominal Group Technique The **nominal group technique** (NGT) helps groups to generate ideas and evaluate and select solutions. NGT is more comprehensive than brainstorming. This technique primarily is used during the decision-making stage of evaluating and selecting solutions. NGT is a structured group meeting that follows this format:[60]

A group is convened to discuss a particular problem or issue. After the problem is understood, individuals silently generate ideas in writing. Each individual, in round-robin fashion, then offers one idea from his or her list. Ideas are recorded on a blackboard or flip chart; they are not discussed at this stage of the process. Once all ideas are elicited, the group discusses them. Anyone may criticize or defend any item. During this step, clarification is provided as well as general agreement or disagreement with the idea. Finally, group members anonymously vote for their top choices with a weighted voting procedure (e.g., 1st choice = 3 pts.; 2nd choice = 2 pts.; 3rd choice = 1 pt.). The group leader then adds the votes to determine the group's choice. Prior to making a final decision, the group may decide to discuss the top ranked items and conduct a second round of voting.

The nominal group technique reduces the roadblocks to group decision making by: (1) separating brainstorming from evaluation, (2) promoting balanced participation among group members, and (3) incorporating mathematical voting techniques in order to reach consensus.[61] NGT has been successfully used in many different decision-making situations.[62]

The Delphi Technique This problem-solving method was originally developed by the Rand Corporation for technological forecasting.[63] It now is used as a multipurpose planning tool. The **Delphi technique** is a group process that anonymously generates ideas or judgments from physically dispersed experts. Unlike the NGT, experts' ideas are obtained from questionnaires as opposed to face-to-face group discussions.

A manager begins the Delphi process by identifying the issue(s) he or she wants to investigate. For example, a manager might want to inquire about customer demand, customers' future preferences, or the impact of locating a plant in a certain region of the country.[64] Next, participants are identified and a questionnaire is developed. The questionnaire is sent to participants and returned to the manager. The manager then summarizes the responses and sends feedback to the participants. At this stage, participants are asked to (1) review the feedback, (2) prioritize the issues being considered, and (3) return the survey within a specified time period. This cycle repeats until the manager obtains the necessary information.

The Delphi technique is useful when face-to-face discussions are impractical, when disagreements and conflict are likely to impair communication, when certain individuals might severely dominate group discussion, and when groupthink is a probable outcome of the group process (recall our discussion in Chapter 9).[65]

● CREATIVITY

In light of today's fast-paced decisions, an organization's ability to stimulate the creativity and innovation of its employees is becoming increasingly important. As noted by two management experts, "What has become clear to many business leaders is that they and their constituents are called upon to innovate merely in order to survive. Human capital must be seen as a resource as never before."[66]

Some organizations, such as Disney and 3M, have successfully met this challenge. Others have not. For example, the decline of the U.S. steel industry is partly due to its inability to successfully innovate. To gain further insight into managing the creative process, we begin by defining creativity and highlighting stages of the creative process. This section then reviews the characteristics of creative people and discusses the management of creative individuals.

Definition and Stages

Although many definitions have been proposed, the essence of **creativity** is development of something new, something that has never existed before. It can be as simple as developing a new flavor of the month for an ice cream store or as complex as developing a pocket-size microcomputer.

Early approaches to explaining creativity were based on differences between the left and right hemispheres of the brain. Researchers thought the right side of the brain was responsible for creativity. More recently, however, researchers have questioned this explanation.

> "The left brain/right brain dichotomy is simplified and misleading," says Dr. John C. Mazziotta, a researcher at the University of California at Los Angeles School of Medicine.
>
> What scientists have found instead is that creativity is a feat of mental gymnastics engaging the conscious and subconscious parts of the brain. It draws on everything from knowledge, logic, imagination, and intuition to the ability to see connections and distinctions between ideas and things.[67]

Let us now examine a model of the creativity process.

Researchers are not absolutely certain how creativity takes place. Nonetheless, we know that creativity involves "making remote associations" between unconnected events, ideas, information stored in memory (recall our discussion in Chapter 4), or physical objects. Figure 15–7 depicts five stages underlying this process.[68]

• **FIGURE 15-7**   Stages of the Creative Process

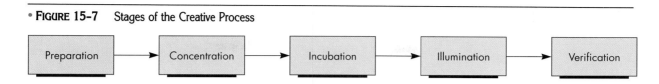

The preparation stage reflects the notion that creativity starts from a base of knowledge. Preparation includes the amount of time an individual engages in schooling, reading, on-the-job training, attending workshops, or just paying attention to one's environment. During the concentration stage, an individual focuses on the problem at hand. Consider how Dr. Yoshiro NakaMats, a Japanese inventor who created the first floppy disk, hard disk, and digital watch face, plus 2,356 additional patented ideas, accomplishes these first two stages.

> Besides reading technical reports, NakaMats induces changes in his own brain to make himself more creative. He holds his breath and dives repeatedly underwater, swimming 50 yards at a stretch, holding a waterproof pad and pencil. When inspiration hits, he writes until his lungs are ready to burst. He calls the technique, "Swim till almost die." Out of water, he thinks in a self-designed thinking chair that feeds his brain extra oxygen; he eats self-designed foods that he says contain innovation-enhancing vitamins.[69]

Incubation is done unconsciously. During this stage, people engage in daily activities while their minds simultaneously mull over information and make remote associations. These associations ultimately are generated in the illumination stage. Finally, verification entails going through the entire process in order to verify, modify, or try out the new idea.

As suggested by this model, creative ideas take time and effort. Creative people, like Dr. NakaMats, work at it. Moreover, research indicates that people can be trained to be more creative.[70]

Characteristics of Creative People

Creative people typically march to the beat of a different drummer. They are highly motivated individuals who spend many years mastering their chosen field or occupation. But contrary to stereotypes, creative people are not necessarily geniuses or introverted nerds. In addition, they are not *adaptors*. "Adaptors are those who seek to solve problems by 'doing things better.' They prefer to resolve difficulties or make decisions in such a way as to have the least impact upon the assumptions, procedures, and values of the organization. . . ."[71] In contrast, creative individuals are dissatisfied with the status quo. They look for new and exciting solutions to problems. Because of this, creative organizational members can be perceived as disruptive and hard to get along with. Further, research indicates that male and female managers do not differ in levels of creativity, and creative people are more open to experiencing new and different activities.[72] Table 15-7 presents additional characteristics of creative individuals.

Research also reveals that creativity seems to peak in early adulthood and then steadily declines. For example, Albert Einstein was 26 when he came

• **TABLE 15-7**   Characteristics of Creative People

1.	Knowledge	Creative people spend a great number of years mastering their chosen field.
2.	Education	Education does not increase creativity. Education that stresses logic tends to inhibit creativity.
3.	Intelligence	Creative people do not necessarily have high IQs. The threshold for IQ is around 130. After that, IQ does not really matter. Creative people have been found to possess the following intellectual abilities: sensitivity to problems, flexibility in forming fluid associations between objects, thinking in images rather than words, and synthesizing information.
4.	Personality	Creative people are typically risk takers who are independent, persistent, highly motivated, skeptical, open to new ideas, able to tolerate ambiguity, self-confident, and able to tolerate isolation. They also have a strong sense of humor and are hard to get along with.
5.	Childhood	Creative people have usually had a childhood marked by diversity. Experiences such as family strains, financial ups and downs, and divorces are common occurrences.
6.	Social habits	Contrary to stereotypes, creative people are not introverted nerds. Creative people tend to be outgoing and enjoy exchanging ideas with colleagues.

Source: Based in part on Robert G. Godfrey, "Tapping Employees' Creativity," *Supervisory Management*, February 1986, pp. 16–20; and "Mix Skepticism, Humor, a Rocky Childhood—and Presto! Creativity," *Business Week*, September 30, 1985, p. 81.

up with his theory of relativity and Isaac Newton figured out the laws of gravity at 24. Moreover, creativity seems to peak at different ages for people in different professions. "People who rely on pure bursts of creativity—for example physicists, theoretical mathematicians, and poets—tend to produce their most original work in their late twenties and early thirties. The output of novelists, engineers and medical researchers, on the other hand, tends to rise more slowly, peaking in the late thirties and early forties, and then falling steadily until retirement."[73] Researchers currently are trying to figure out why these patterns occur.

Managing Creative Employees

Managers are challenged by today's competitive pressures to develop an environment that supports creative behavior. This is how 3M creates such an environment.

> One way is to encourage inventive zealots like Francis Okie. The business of innovation can be a numbers game—the more tries, the more likely there will be hits. The scarcity of corporate rules at 3M leaves room for plenty of experimentation—and failure. Okie's failure is as legendary among 3Mers as his blockbuster. [His sandpaper substitute for shaving was a flop, but his waterproof sandpaper was a commercial success.] Salaries and promotions are tied to the successful shepherding of new products from inception to commercialization. One big carrot: The fanatical 3Mer who champions a new product out the door then gets the chance to manage it as if it were his or her own business.[74]

• **TABLE 15–8**   Suggestions for Improving Employee Creativity

> Develop an environment that supports creative behavior.
> Try to avoid using an autocratic style of leadership.
> Encourage employees to be more open to new ideas and experiences.
> Keep in mind that people use different strategies, like walking around or listening to music, to foster their creativity.
> Provide employees with stimulating work that creates a sense of personal growth.
> Encourage employees to view problems as opportunities.
> Don't let your decision-making style stifle those employees who have a different style.
> Guard against employees being too involved with putting out fires and dealing with urgent short-term problems.
> Make sure creative people are not bogged down with specific tasks all day long.
> Allow employees to have fun and play around.
> Encourage an open environment that is free from defensive behavior.
> Treat errors and mistakes as opportunities for learning.
> Let employees occasionally try out their pet ideas. Provide a margin of error.
> Be a catalyst instead of an obstacle.
> Avoid using a negative mind-set when an employee approaches you with a new idea.
> Encourage creative people to communicate with one another.
> Welcome diverse ideas and opinions.
> Send yourself and your employees to creativity training.
> Reward creative behavior.

Source: Adapted from discussion in Eugene Raudsepp, "101 Ways to Spark Your Employees' Creative Potential," *Office Administration and Automation*, September 1985, pp. 38, 39–43, 56.

In a similar vein, Eastman Kodak Co. set up innovation centers, and Hallmark Cards Inc. is opening a $20 million Technology & Innovation Center. At W. L. Gore & Associates, a privately held firm, employees, who are called associates, are grouped into organizational units of 150 to 200 people to encourage creativity.[75] Table 15–8 lists some specific managerial recommendations to spark employee creativity.

After a supportive environment has been created, managers may want to consider creativity training for employees. Since each of us has the potential to be creative, training gives everyone a chance to participate in the creative process. This training should help people to overcome the mental locks that stifle creativity.

Roger von Oech, a creativity consultant in Silicon Valley, identified 10 mental locks or hang-ups that interfere with creativity. They are:

1. Searching for the "right" answer.
2. Always trying to be logical.
3. Looking for solutions that "follow the rules."
4. Trying to be too practical.
5. Avoiding ambiguity.
6. Fearing failure.
7. Not playing or having fun at work.

• OB EXERCISE

Creativity Exercises

Exercise 1
In the line of letters listed below, cross out six letters so the remaining letters spell a familiar English word. You may not alter the sequence of the letters.

B S A I N X L E A T N T E A R S

Try to solve the exercise for a while before proceeding.

Exercise 2
What is this figure? Come up with as many interpretations as you can.

Source: Reprinted by permission of Warner Books/New York, from *A Whack on the Side of the Head.* Copyright © 1983 by Roger von Oech, pp. 76–78.

8. Ignoring problems outside one's specialty.
9. Not wanting to look foolish.
10. Believing you are not creative.[76]

To demonstrate how these mental locks inhibit creativity, try the two exercises in the OB Exercise. After completing these exercises, look at the solutions provided in endnote 77. (Which mental lock may have reduced your creativity?) In an organizational context, managers need to help employees identify and confront these mental locks. Finally, managers will need to modify their own behavior and attitudes (the ideas in Table 15–8 point the way).

• SUMMARY OF KEY CONCEPTS

A. There are two types of managerial decisions: programmed and nonprogrammed. Programmed decisions are repetitive and routine. Habit and standard operating procedures are most frequently used to make these decisions. Nonprogrammed decisions are novel, unstructured, and tend to have important consequences. To make these decisions, managers rely on judgment, intuition, and creativity.

B. The rational decision-making model consists of identifying the problem, generating alternative solutions, evaluating and selecting a solution, and implementing and evaluating the solution. Research indicates that decision makers do not follow the series of steps outlined in the rational model.

C. Simon's normative model is guided by a decision maker's bounded rationality. Bounded rationality means that decision makers are bounded or restricted by a variety of constraints when making decisions. The normative model suggests that decision making is characterized by (1) limited information processing, (2) the use of rules of thumb or shortcuts, and (3) satisficing.

D. The garbage can model of decision making assumes that decision making does not follow an orderly series of steps. In a garbage can process, decisions result from interaction among four independent streams of events: problems, solutions, participants, and choice opportunities.

E. Decision makers use either an aided-analytic, unaided-analytic, or nonanalytic strategy when selecting a solution. The choice of a strategy depends on the characteristics of the decision task and the characteristics of the decision maker. Several contingency relationships have been identified.

F. Escalation of commitment refers to the tendency to stick to an ineffective course of action when it is unlikely that a bad situation can be reversed. Project characteristics, psychological determinants, social forces, and organizational determinants cause managers to exhibit this decision-making error.

G. There are both pros and cons of involving groups in the decision-making process. Although research shows that groups typically outperform the average individual, managers are encouraged to use a contingency approach when determining whether to include others in the decision-making process.

H. Participative management reflects the extent to which employees participate in setting goals, making decisions, solving problems, and making changes in the organization. Research revealed that participative management does not consistently increase productivity, but does increase satisfaction.

I. Vroom, Yetton, and Jago developed a model to help managers determine the extent to which they should include groups in the decision-making process. Through the use of decision trees, the model identifies appropriate decision-making styles for various types of managerial problems. The styles range from autocratic to highly participative.

J. Group problem-solving techniques facilitate better decision making within groups. Brainstorming is used to help groups generate multiple ideas and alternatives for solving problems. The nominal group technique assists groups both to generate ideas and to evaluate and select solutions. The Delphi technique is a group process that anonymously generates ideas or judgments from physically dispersed experts.

K. Creativity is the development of something new. It is not adequately explained by differences between the left and right hemispheres of the brain. There are five stages of the creative process. They are preparation, concentration, incubation, illumination, and verification. Several characteristics differentiate creative people from average individuals. It is suggested that there are 10 mental locks that stifle an individual's creativity. Research shows that people can be trained to increase their creativity.

• KEY TERMS

decision making	aided-analytic
programmed decisions	unaided-analytic
nonprogrammed decisions	nonanalytic
rational model	escalation of commitment
problem	participative management
scenario technique	consensus
optimizing	brainstorming
bounded rationality	nominal group technique
satisficing	Delphi technique
garbage can model	creativity

• DISCUSSION QUESTIONS

1. Identify both a programmed and a nonprogrammed decision you made recently. How did you arrive at a solution for each one?

2. Do you think people are rational when they make decisions? Under what circumstances would an individual tend to follow a rational process?

3. Describe a situation in which you satisficed when making a decision. Why did you satisfice instead of optimize?

4. Do you think the garbage can model is a realistic representation of organizational decision making? Explain your rationale.

5. What is the most valuable lesson about selecting solutions through a contingency perspective? Explain.

6. Describe a situation in which you exhibited escalation of commitment. Why did you escalate a losing situation?
7. Do you prefer to solve problems in groups or by yourself? Why?
8. Given the intuitive appeal of participative management, why do you think it fails as often as it succeeds? Explain.
9. Do you think you are creative? Why or why not?
10. What advice would you offer a manager who was attempting to improve the creativity of his or her employees? Explain.

BACK TO THE OPENING CASE

Now that you have read Chapter 15, you should be able to answer the following questions about decision making at Disney:

1. Are Disney's decision-making processes more characteristic of the rational or garbage can model of decision making?
2. How does Michael Eisner try to control escalation of commitment? Explain.
3. To what extent does Disney rely on group-aided decision making? Explain.
4. What examples of creative decision making can you identify at Disney?

• EXERCISE 15

Objectives

1. To promote understanding of the Vroom, Yetton, and Jago decision-making model.
2. To develop and assess your ability to use the model.

Introduction

Vroom and Jago extended an earlier model by Vroom and Yetton to help managers determine the extent to which they should include groups in the decision-making process. In order to enhance your understanding of this model, we would like you to use it to analyze a brief case. You will be asked to read the case and use the information to determine an appropriate decision-making style. This will enable you to compare your solution with that recommended by Vroom and Jago. Since their analysis is presented at the end of this exercise, please do not read it until indicated.

Instructions

Presented below is a case depicting a situation faced by the manufacturing manager of an electronics plant.[78] Read the case and then use Vroom and

Jago's model (refer to Figure 15–6 and Table 15–6) to arrive at a solution. At this point, it might be helpful to reread the material that explains how to apply the model. Keep in mind that you move toward a solution by asking yourself the questions (at the top of Figure 15–6) associated with each relevant decision point. After completing your analysis, we would like you to compare your solution with the one offered by Vroom and Jago.

Leadership Case

You are a manufacturing manager in a large electronics plant. The company's management has recently installed new machines and put in a new simplified work system, but to the surprise of everyone, yourself included, the expected increase in productivity was not realized. In fact, production has begun to drop, quality has fallen off, and the number of employee separations has risen.

You do not believe that there is anything wrong with the machines. You have had reports from other companies that are using them and they confirm this opinion. You have also had representatives from the firm that built the machines go over them and they report that they are operating at peak efficiency.

You suspect that some parts of the new work system may be responsible for the change, but this view is not widely shared among your immediate subordinates who are four first-line supervisors, each in charge of a section, and your supply manager. The drop in production has been variously attributed to poor training of the operators, lack of an adequate system of financial incentives, and poor morale. Clearly, this is an issue about which there is considerable depth of feeling within individuals and potential disagreement among your subordinates.

This morning you received a phone call from your division manager. He had just received your production figures for the last six months and was calling to express his concern. He indicated that the problem was yours to solve in any way that you think best, but that he would like to know within a week what steps you plan to take.

You share your division manager's concern with the falling productivity and know that your [people] are also concerned. The problem is to decide what steps to take to rectify the situation.

Questions for Consideration/Class Discussion

1. What decision-making style from Table 15–6 do you recommend?
2. Did you arrive at the same solution as Vroom and Jago? If not, what do you think caused the difference?
3. Based on this experience, what problems would a manager encounter in trying to apply this model?

Vroom and Jago's Analysis and Solution

Question:
(QR: quality requirement) = Critical/High Importance
(CR: commitment requirement) = High Importance
(LI: leader's information) = Probably No

(ST: problem structure) = No
(CP: commitment probability) = Probably No
(GC: goal congruence) = Probably Yes
(CO: subordinate conflict) = Not a consideration for this problem.
(SI: subordinate information) = Maybe [but probably not]
Decision-making style = CII

• NOTES

[1] See Bernard M. Bass, *Organizational Decision Making* (Homewood, Ill.: Richard D. Irwin, 1983).

[2] A thorough discussion is provided by Herbert A. Simon, *The New Science of Management Decision* (Englewood Cliffs, N.J.: Prentice-Hall, 1977), pp. 39–81.

[3] See Ronald Henkoff, "How to Plan For 1995," *Fortune,* December 31, 1990, pp. 70–79.

[4] For examples of using computer simulations to solve nonprogrammed decisions, see Brooks Mitchell, "Interviewing Face-to-Interface," *Personnel,* January 1990, pp. 23–25; and Jolie Solomon, "Now, Simulators for Piloting Companies," *The Wall Street Journal,* July 31, 1989, p. B1.

[5] The example of Cincinnati Milacron is discussed by Peter Nulty, "The Soul of an Old Machine," *Fortune,* May 21, 1990, pp. 67–72.

[6] An interesting study of the variety of problems faced by organizations was conducted by David A. Cowan, "Developing a Classification Structure of Organizational Problems: An Empirical Investigation," *Academy of Management Journal,* June 1990, pp. 366–90.

[7] See William F. Pounds, "The Process of Problem Finding," *Industrial Management Review,* Fall 1969, pp. 1–19.

[8] Myron Magnet, "How Top Managers Make a Company's Toughest Decision," *Fortune,* March 18, 1985, p. 55.

[9] For a review of these assumptions, see Herbert A. Simon, "A Behavioral Model of Rational Choice," *The Quarterly Journal of Economics,* February 1955, pp. 99–118.

[10] Herbert A. Simon, "Rational Decision Making in Business Organizations," *The American Economic Review,* September 1979, p. 510.

[11] For a complete discussion of bounded rationality, see Herbert A. Simon, *Administrative Behavior,* 2nd ed. (New York: Free Press, 1957); and James G. March and Herbert A. Simon, *Organizations* (New York: John Wiley, 1958).

[12] Biases associated with using shortcuts in decision making are discussed by Amos Tversky and Daniel Kahneman, "Judgment under Uncertainty: Heuristics and Biases," *Science,* September 1974, pp. 1124–31.

[13] See Russell L. Ackoff, "The Art and Science of Mess Management," *Interfaces,* February 1981, pp. 20–26.

[14] The model is discussed in detail in Michael D. Cohen, James G. March, and Johan P. Olsen, "A Garbage Can Model of Organizational Choice," *Administrative Science Quarterly,* March 1971, pp. 1–25.

[15] Ibid., p. 2.

[16] Results can be found in Barbara Levitt and Clifford Nass, "The Lid on the Garbage Can: Institutional Constraints on Decision Making in the Technical Core of College-Text Publishers," *Administrative Science Quarterly,* June 1989, pp. 190–207.

[17] This discussion is based on material presented by James G. March and Roger Weissinger-Baylon, *Ambiguity and Command* (Marshfield, Mass.: Pitman Publishing, 1986), pp. 11–35.

[18] Simulated tests of the garbage can model were conducted by Michael Masuch and Perry LaPotin, "Beyond Garbage Cans: An A1 Model of Organizational Choice," *Administrative Science Quarterly,* March 1989, pp. 38–67; and Marvin B. Mandell, "The Consequences of Improving Dissemination in Garbage-Can Decision Processes," *Knowledge: Creation, Diffusion, Utilization,* March 1988, pp. 343–61.

[19] "Deciding about Decisions," *Management Review,* November 1985, p. 3.

[20] For a complete discussion, see Lee Roy Beach and Terence R. Mitchell, "A Contingency Model for the Selection of Decision Strategies," *Academy of Management Review,* July 1978, pp. 439–44.

[21] Results can be found in Thomas L. Ruble and Richard A. Cosier, "Effects of Cognitive Styles and Decision Setting on Performance," *Organizationl Behavior and Human Performance,* August 1990, pp. 283–95.

[22] See Jay J. J. Christensen-Szalanski, "A Further Examination of the Selection of Problem-Solving Strategies: The Effects of Deadlines and Analytic Aptitudes," *Organizationl Behavior and Human Performance,* February 1980, pp. 107–22.

[23] This study was conducted by Douglas A. Hershey, David A. Walsh, Stephen J. Read, and Ada S. Chulef, "The Effects of Expertise on Financial Problem Solving: Evidence for Goal-Directed, Problem-Solving Scripts," *Organizational Behavior and Human Decision Processes,* June 1990, pp. 77–101.

[24] See Robert Wood, Albert Bandura, and Trevor Bailey, "Mechanisms Governing Organizationl Performance in Complex Decision-Making Environments," *Organizational Behavior and Human Decision Processes,* August 1990, pp. 181–201; and James R. Bettman, Eric J. Johnson, and John W. Payne, "A Componential Analysis of Cognitive Effort in Choice," *Organizationl Behavior and Human Decision Processes,* February 1990, pp. 111–39.

[25] This research is summarized by Terence R. Mitchell and Lee Roy Beach, " '. . . Do I Love Thee? Let Me Count . . .' " Toward an Understanding of Intuitive and Automatic Decision Making," *Organizational Behavior and Human Decision Processes,* October 1990, pp. 1–20.

[26] For a review of related research, see John W. Payne, "Contingent Decision Behavior," *Psychological Bulletin,* September 1982, pp. 382–402.

[27] A thorough discussion of escalation situations can be found in Barry M. Staw and Jerry Ross, "Behavior in Escalation Situations: Antecedents, Prototypes, and Solutions," in *Research in Organizational Behavior,* Vol. 9, eds. L. L. Cummings and Barry M. Staw (Greenwich, Conn.: JAI Press, 1987), pp. 39–78.

[28] *The New York Times* (based on the investigative reporting of Neil Sheehan), *The Pentagon Papers* (New York: Bantam Books, 1971), p. 450.

[29] This discussion is based on Barry M. Staw and Jerry Ross, "Understanding Behavior in Escalation Situations," *Science,* October 1989, pp. 216–20.

[30] See Howard Garland, Craig A. Sandefur, and Anne C. Rogers, "De-Escalation of Commitment in Oil Exploration: When Sunk Costs and Negative Feedback Coincide," *Journal of Applied Psychology,* December 1990, pp. 721–27; and Howard Garland, "Throwing Good Money after Bad: The Effect of Sunk Costs on the Decision to Escalate Commitment to an Ongoing Project," *Journal of Applied Psychology,* December 1990, pp. 728–32.

[31] See Staw and Ross, "Behavior in Escalation Situations: Antecedents, Prototypes, and Solutions;" and William S. Silver and Terence R. Mitchell, "The Status Quo Tendency in Decision Making," *Organizational Dynamics,* Spring 1990, pp. 34–36.

[32] Staw and Ross's recommendations were investigated by Sidney L. Barton, Dennis Duchon, and Kenneth J. Dunegan, "An Empirical Test of Staw and Ross's Prescriptions for the Management of Escalation of Commitment Behavior in Organizations," *Decision Sciences,* Summer 1989, pp. 532–44.

[33] Michael Duffy, "Mr. Consensus: Cautious and Personable, George Bush Is a President Who Listens, Leans Heavily on Advisers—and Usually Comes Down the Middle," *Time,* August 21, 1989, p. 19.

[34] Barbara Buell, "Smashing the Country Club Image at Corning Glass," *Business Week,* May 5, 1986, p. 95.

[35] These guidelines were derived from George P. Huber, *Managerial Decision Making,* p. 149.

[36] Gayle W. Hill, "Group versus Individual Performance: Are N + 1 Heads Better than One?" *Psychological Bulletin,* May 1982, p. 535.

[37] Results can be found in Larry K. Michaelsen, Warren E. Watson, and Robert H. Black, "A Realistic Test of Individual Versus Group Consensus Decision Making," *Journal of Applied Psychology,* October 1989, pp. 834–39.

[38] This finding was obtained by Peter Chalos and Sue Pickard, "Information Choice and Cue Use: An Experiment in Group Information Processing," *Journal of Applied Psychology,* November 1985, pp. 634–41.

[39] See Deborah L. Gladstein and Nora P. Reilly, "Group Decision Making under Threat: The Tycoon Game," *Academy of Management Journal,* September 1985, pp. 613–27.

[40] The role of communication in group decision making is thoroughly discussed by Randy Y. Hirokawa, "The Role of Communication in Group Decision-Making Efficacy: A Task-Contingency Perspective," *Small Group Research,* May 1990, pp. 190–204.

[41] See Marshal Sashkin, "Participative Management Is an Ethical Imperative," *Organizational Dynamics,* Spring 1984, pp. 4–22. Different forms of participation are discussed by David R. Lee, "Competitive Success: Supporting Operational Level Participation," *Industrial Management,* July/August 1990, pp. 29–32.

[42] "Labor Letter: A Special News Report on People and Their Jobs in Offices, Fields, and Factories," *The Wall Street Journal,* September 18, 1990, p. A1.

[43] "Labor Letter: A Special News Report on People and Their Jobs in Offices, Fields, and Factories," *The Wall Street Journal,* May 27, 1986, p. A1.

[44] For an expanded discussion of this model, see Sashkin, "Participative Management Is an Ethical Imperative."

[45] Employee preferences for participative management are examined by Denis Collins, Ruth Ann Ross, and Timothy L. Ross, "Who Wants Participative Management?" *Group and Organization Studies,* December 1989, pp. 422–45.

[46] The relationship between PM and creativity was examined by Daniel Plunkett, "The Creative Organization: An Empirical Investigation of the Importance of Participation in Decision Making," *The Journal of Creative Behavior,* Second Quarter 1990, pp. 140–48. Results pertaining to role conflict and ambiguity can be found in Carlla S. Smith and Michael T. Brannick, "A Role and Expectancy Model of Participative Decision Making: A Replication and Theoretical Extension," *Journal of Organizational Behavior,* March 1990, pp. 91–104.

[47] See Katherine I. Miller and Peter R. Monge, "Participation, Satisfaction, and Productivity: A Meta-Analytic Review," *Academy of Management Journal,* December 1986, pp. 727–53; and John A. Wagner III and Richard Z. Gooding, "Shared Influence and Organizational Behavior: A Meta-Analysis of Situational Variables Expected to Moderate Participation–Outcome Relationships," *Academy of Management Journal,* September 1987, pp. 524–41.

[48] Opposing interpretations can be found in Edwin A. Locke, David M. Schweiger, and Gary R. Latham, "Participation in Decision Making: When Should It Be Used?" *Organizational Dynamics,* Winter 1986, pp. 65–79; and John L. Cotton, David A. Vollarth, Kirk L. Froggatt, Mark L. Lengnick-Hall, and Kenneth R. Jennings, "Employee Participation: Diverse Forms and Different Outcomes," *Academy of Management Review,* January 1988, pp. 8–22.

[49] For a thorough review of this controversy, see Carrie R. Leana, Edwin A. Locke, and David M. Schweiger, "Fact and Fiction in Analyzing Research on Participative Decision Making: A Critique of Cotton, Vollrath, Froggatt, Lengnick-Hall, and Jennings," *Academy of Management Review,* January 1990, pp. 137–46; and John L. Cotton, David A. Vollrath, Mark L. Lengnick-Hall, and Kirk L. Froggatt, "Fact: The Form of Participation Does Matter—A Rebuttal to Leana, Locke, and Schweiger," *Academy of Management Review,* January 1990, pp. 147–53.

[50] This contingency factor is thoroughly discussed by Dean Tjosvold, "Participation: A Close Look at Its Dynamics," *Journal of Management,* Winter 1987, pp. 739–50.

[51] Bill Saporito, "The Revolt against 'Working Smarter,'" *Fortune,* July 21, 1986, p. 60.

[52] Honeywell's experience is discussed in Richard J. Boyle, "Wrestling with Jellyfish," *Harvard Business Review,* January–February 1984, pp. 74–83.

[53] See Victor H. Vroom and Philip W. Yetton, *Leadership and Decision Making* (Pittsburgh, Penn.: University of Pittsburgh Press, 1973); and Victor H. Vroom and Arthur G. Jago, *The New Leadership: Managing Participation in Organizations* (Englewood Cliffs, N.J.: Prentice-Hall, 1988), p. 184.

[54] See Norman B. Wright, "Leadership Styles: Which Are Best When?" *Business Quarterly,* Winter 1984, pp. 20–23.

[55] For a complete discussion of these decision trees, see Vroom and Jago, *The New Leadership: Managing Participation in Organizations.*

[56] Supportive results can be found in Richard H. G. Field and Robert J. House, "A Test of the Vroom–Yetton Model Using Manager and Subordinate Reports," *Journal of Applied Psychology,* June 1990, pp. 362–66; and Andrew Crouch and Philip Yetton, "Manager Behavior, Leadership Style, and Subordinate Performance: An Empirical Extension of the Vroom-Yetton Conflict Rule," *Organizational Behavior and Human Decision Processes,* June 1987, pp. 384–96.

[57] See Robert J. Paul and Yar M. Ebadi, "Leadership Decision Making in a Service Organization: A Field Test of the Vroom–Yetton Model," *Journal of Occupational Psychology,* September 1989, pp. 201–11.

[58] Glenn M. Parker, *Team Players and Teamwork: The New Competitive Business Strategy* (San Francisco, Calif.: Jossey-Bass, 1990).

[59] See Alexander F. Osborn, *Applied Imagination: Principles and Procedures of Creative Thinking,* 3rd ed. (New York: Scribners, 1979).

[60] A complete description of the nominal group technique can be found in Andre L. Delbecq, Andrew H. Van de Ven, and David H. Gustafson, *Group Techniques for Program Planning: A Guide to Nominal Group and Delphi Processes* (Glenview, Ill.: Scott, Foresman, 1975).

[61] Ibid.

[62] For examples of the application of the nominal group technique, see Peter Clayton, "Nominal Group Technique and Library Management," *Library Administration and Management,* Winter 1990, pp. 24–26; and Chief Allen W. Cole, "Citizens' Advisory Committees and the Use of Nominal Group Techniques," *The Police Chief,* November 1989, pp. 71–2.

[63] See Norman C. Dalkey, Daniel L. Rourke, Ralph Lewis, and David Snyder,

Studies in the Quality of Life: Delphi and Decision Making (Lexington, Mass.: Lexington Books: D. C. Heath and Co., 1972).

64 Applications of the Delphi technique can be found in Howard Green, Colin Hunter, and Bruno Moore, "Assessing the Environmental Impact of Tourism Development: Use of the Delphi Technique," *Tourism Management,* June 1990, pp. 111–20; and Howard Green, Colin Hunter, and Bruno Moore, "Application of the Delphi Technique in Tourism," *Annals of Tourism Research,* Vol. 17, 1990, pp. 270–79.

65 Benefits of the Delphi technique are discussed by Nancy I. Whitman, "The Committee Meeting Alternative: Using the Delphi Technique," *Journal of Nursing Administration,* July/August 1990, pp. 30–36.

66 Stephen R. Grossman and Margaret J. King, "Eagles, Otters, and Unicorns: An Anatomy of Innovation," *The Journal of Creative Behavior,* Second Quarter, 1990, p. 75.

67 Emily T. Smith, "Are You Creative?" *Business Week,* September 30, 1985, pp. 81–82. For a review of research about the left and right hemispheres of the brain, see Terence Hines, "Left Brain/Right Brain Mythology and Implications for Management and Training," *Academy of Management Review,* October 1987, pp. 600–606.

68 These stages are thoroughly discussed by Edward Glassman, "Creative Problem Solving," *Supervisory Management,* January 1989, pp. 21–26.

69 "Renegades: Harassed and Scorned, They Did It Their Way—and Won," *Success,* January/February, 1990, p. 30.

70 An interesting example is contained in Roger L. Firestien, "Effects of Creative Problem-Solving Training on Communication Behaviors in Small Groups," *Small Group Research,* November 1989, pp. 507–21; and William Karl James, "Development of Creative Problem-Solving Skills," *The Technology Teacher,* February 1990, pp. 29–30.

71 Timothy A. Matherly and Ronald E. Goldsmith, "The Two Faces of Creativity," *Business Horizons,* September–October 1985, p. 9.

72 See Richard W. Woodman and Lyle F. Schoenfeldt, "An Interactionist Model of Creative Behavior," *The Journal of Creative Behavior,* First Quarter 1990, pp. 10–13; and Robert R. McCrae, "Creativity, Divergent Thinking, and Openness to Experience," *Journal of Personality and Social Psychology,* June 1987, pp. 1258–65.

73 Malcolm Gladwell, "Over the Hill at Twentysomething," *The Washington Post National Weekly Edition,* April 23–29, 1990, p. 38.

74 Russell Mitchell, "Masters of Innovations: How 3M Keeps Its New Products Coming," *Business Week,* April 10, 1989, p. 58.

75 See Smith, "Are You Creative?" pp. 80–84.

76 A detailed discussion is provided by Roger von Oech, *A Whack on the Side of Head* (New York: Warner, 1983).

77 Exercise I: One way to solve this problem is to interpret the instructions in an ambiguous fashion. Instead of crossing out six letters, you can literally cross out the S, and the I, and the X, and L, and the E, and so on until you have crossed out the words *six letters.* If you did this, you would have found the word *BANANA.* Another solution to this exercise would be to choose six different letters—say, B, S, A, I, N, and X—and cross them out every time they appear. You would end up with the word LETTER. Exercise 2: If you look at it one way, it's a bird; it could also be a question mark; if you turn it upside down, it's a seal juggling a ball on its nose.

78 Reprinted, by permission of the publisher, from "A New Look at Managerial Decision Making," Victor H. Vroom, *Organizational Dynamics,* Spring 1973, p. 72, © 1973 American Management Association, New York. All rights reserved.

Managing Occupational Stress

LEARNING OBJECTIVES

When you finish studying the material in this chapter, you should be able to:

- Define the term *stress*.
- Describe Matteson and Ivancevich's model of occupational stress.
- Discuss four reasons why it is important for managers to understand the causes and consequences of stress.

- Explain how stressful life events create stress.
- Review the model of burnout and highlight the managerial solutions to reduce it.
- Contrast how sting operations, drug testing, and employee assistance programs are used to reduce substance abuse.

- Explain the mechanisms of social support.
- Describe the coping process.
- Discuss the personality characteristic of hardiness.
- Contrast the four dominant stress-reduction techniques.

Opening Case 16

The Stressful Life of a Paramedic

Sharon Hoogstraten

New York—Certain things drive paramedics up the wall.

1:19 P.M. Richard Awe and Joseph Pessolano are cruising midtown Manhattan. "Smith's Bar & Grill, 701 Eighth Ave.," the dispatcher's voice says. "Forty-year old female going in and out of consciousness."

Sounding the siren, Mr. Awe weaves through heavy traffic to Smith's. The medical emergency is at a booth in the rear, with a half-eaten noodle dish on the table and a bulging canvas carryall on the seat beside her.

"They gave me food and then I fell on the floor," she explains. She is fairly alert. Her chief problem seems to be that she lost her room in a welfare hotel. She refuses to go to a hospital. Why—or whether—she fainted remains a mystery. The paramedics leave.

Unnecessary Calls

"I hope we get someone who is legitimately sick today," Mr. Awe says.

The fact is that most of the more than 750,000 ambulance calls handled yearly by New York City's Emergency Medical Services [EMS] are unnecessary.

More than 40 percent are false alarms. The ambulance arrives, nobody is there. "You never know if it was a real false alarm," says James Kerr, the EMS executive director. "You're all revved up to treat somebody, and you can't find them."

Maybe another third turn out to be bogus in other ways. Poor people with no doctors call the medics instead. People with minor injuries call an ambulance instead of hailing a cab. It all contributes to the paramedic's big occupational hazard, getting "fried"— burnout.

Time was, not so long ago, when ambulance drivers tended to be hot-doggers who screamed the sirens as they went for coffee and didn't have much medical training. That has changed. New York's EMS, like those in other cities, began to put the dramatic lessons of Vietnam in emergency life-saving into civilian use in the mid-1970s. . . .

Meager Benefits

Working in pairs, with radio contact to a physician if they need it, the city's medics handle everything from cardiac cases to burns and bullet wounds. They are proud of their ability to operate independently and take responsibility. But

---

Have you ever felt like you didn't fit in when attempting to work with others? If so, you were probably uncomfortable. Unfortunately, as pointed out in Part I, many employees experience a lack of fit between their needs and values and the demands of their workplace. Consider the recent wave of corporate mergers. Mergers too often result in a lack of fit between a manager's orientation and that of the acquiring company.

> After Masonite Corp. was acquired by U.S. Gypsum Co. . . [in 1985], Donald Slocum, Masonite's vice president of advanced technology, tried to adapt to his new employer's corporate practices.
>
> But in seeking support for his projects and staff, Mr. Slocum found that he had to fight through several tiers of management and thought that the parent company was wary of spending in uncharted technical areas.

OPENING CASE 16

(concluded)

the paramedic system is plagued by bureaucratic hitches, by meager benefits and pay (much lower than that of garbage collectors), and by the lack of an attractive career path.

Richard Gutwirth, 35, has been a city paramedic for six years. "I saw a show about it on TV," he recalls. "I thought, 'I'd love to do that.' It looked exciting." He did, and it was. But now he is frustrated and is active in the paramedics' union agitating for parity with police and firemen.

Turnover in the city EMS is 14 percent a year—one in seven. Many trained, experienced people simply move to the Police Department—four paramedics did that in July—or become firemen. Alexander Keuhl, the city health official who heads EMS, says, "It's very hard to develop a career ladder for paramedics unless they go into administration."

Top pay for city medics, in the mid-$20,000s, is reached in three years. Medics at voluntary hospi-

tals do a little better. Overtime adds a little. But police, firemen, and sanitation men still get maybe $8,000 more. "That's a mortgage right there," Mr. Gutwirth says.

Nevertheless, paramedics "hunger for the good job, the good save," says Richard Westphal, the director of ambulance services at St. Vincent's. But at a price. "People curse them, throw things at them," says Dr. Westphal. One patient tried to strangle Mr. Gutwirth. The nastiness comes especially from heroin addicts jolted back to reality by the drug Narcan.

Stress comes in many forms. Ambulance sirens are hard on hearing. The tension of emergencies raises blood pressure. Meals are grabbed on the run; a rush call then produces indigestion.

"You're always dealing with death," says John Clappin, paramedic instructor at St. Vincent's. Or with failure. "You work on them for an hour and then they die," he remarks. "It has to affect you."

"I love it when we save a life," says Joe Pessolano. He is 25. "We saved one man in full cardiac arrest," he recalls proudly. He also gets a charge out of delivering babies; he did that once in the bathroom of a McDonald's on 34th Street.

For Discussion

Does the stress that paramedics experience have both good and bad aspects? Explain.

• Additional discussion questions linking this case with the following material appear at the end of this chapter.

Source: Excerpted from Bowen Northrup, "A City Medic's Life: Faintings, Fatalities, Rash of False Alarms." *The Wall Street Journal,* October 31, 1986. Reprinted by permission of *The Wall Street Journal,* © 1986 Dow Jones & Company, Inc. All rights reserved Worldwide.

After nine months, he resigned. "I gave it a shot, but I felt there was a climate change," says Mr. Slocum, who now works with companies to develop new products.[1]

Imagine the personal stress experienced by Mr. Slocum as he tried to adapt to U.S. Gypsum's unfamiliar methods. Given that he eventually quit his job, the lack of fit must have been overwhelming. But such did not have to be the case. Whether due to the trauma of a merger or a variety of other situations, the stressful consequences of poor individual–organization fit are manageable problems. Hence, this chapter helps you understand and manage occupational stress.

Trying to insert a square peg into a round hole can be a frustrating and fruitless experience. Similarly, the poor fit between a progressive manager and a stodgy bureaucratic organization, as in Mr. Slocum's case, can create

• **FIGURE 16-1**   Poor Individual–Organization Fit Produces Stress

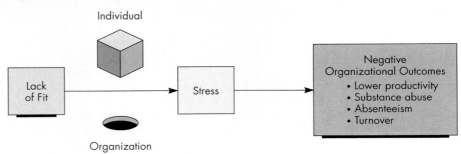

stress (see Figure 16–1). In work settings, stress has been linked to lower productivity, substance abuse, absenteeism, and intention to quit.[2] On the other hand, a good individual–organization fit can reduce stress and lead to positive work outcomes. With this end in mind, this chapter discusses the foundations of stress, examines stressors and two important outcomes of stress, highlights three moderators of occupational stress, and explores a variety of stress-reduction techniques.

• FOUNDATIONS OF STRESS

We all experience stress on a daily basis. Although stress is caused by many factors, researchers conclude that stress triggers one of two basic reactions: active fighting or passive flight (running away or acceptance). Thus, the so-called **fight-or-flight response.**[3] Physiologically, this stress response is a bio-chemical "passing gear" involving hormonal changes that mobilize the body for extraordinary demands. Imagine how our prehistoric ancestors responded to the stress associated with a charging saber-toothed tiger. To avoid being eaten, they could stand their ground and fight the beast or run away. In either case, their bodies would have been energized by an identical hormonal change, involving the release of adrenaline into the bloodstream.

In today's hectic urbanized and industrialized society, charging beasts have been replaced by problems such as deadlines, role conflict and ambiguity, financial responsibilities, traffic congestion, noise and air pollution, family problems, and work overload. As with our ancestors, our response to stress may or may not trigger negative side effects including headaches, ulcers, insomnia, heart attacks, high blood pressure, and strokes. The same stress response that helped our prehistoric ancestors survive has too often become a factor that seriously impairs our daily lives. Consider the following three examples:

> An advertising salesman treated by Bruce Yaffe, a New York internist, screamed so loudly when he argued with his boss that he punctured a lung. Another patient, an office receptionist, had such severe stress-induced vomiting that she eventually had to quit her job. And a third, a Wall Street broker treated by physician Larry Lerner for hypertension, was so certain his death was imminent that he refused to take his children to the park for fear they would be abandoned when he died.[4]

• **TABLE 16-1**   Hans Selye Defines Stress and the Stress Response

Stress is the nonspecific response of the body to any demands made upon it. To understand this definition we must first explain what we mean by nonspecific. Each demand made upon our body is in a sense unique, that is, specific. When exposed to cold, we shiver to produce more heat, and blood vessels in our skin contract to diminish the loss of heat from the body surfaces. When exposed to heat, we sweat because the evaporation of perspiration from the surface of our skin has a cooling effect. . . .

From the point of its stress-producing or stressor activity, it is immaterial whether the agent or situation we face is pleasant or unpleasant; all that counts is the intensity of the demand for readjustment or adaptation. The mother who is suddenly told that her only son died in battle suffers a terrible mental shock; if years later it turns out that the news was false and the son unexpectedly walks into her room alive and well, she experiences extreme joy. The specific results of the two events, sorrow and joy, are completely different, in fact, opposite to each other, yet their stressor effect—the nonspecific demand to readjust herself to an entirely new situation—may be the same.

Source: Hans Selye, *Stress without Distress* (New York: J.B. Lippincott Co., 1974), pp. 27–29.

Since stress and its consequences are manageable, it is important for managers to learn as much as they can about occupational stress. This section provides a conceptual foundation by defining stress, presenting a model of occupational stress, and highlighting related organizational costs.

Defining Stress

To an orchestra violinist, stress may stem from giving a solo performance before a big audience. While heat, smoke, and flames may represent stress to a firefighter, delivering a speech or presenting a lecture may be stressful for those who are shy. In short, stress means different things to different people. Managers need a working definition.

Formally defined, **stress** is "an adaptive response, mediated by individual characteristics and/or psychological processes, that is a consequence of any external action, situation, or event that places special physical and/or psychological demands upon a person."[5] This definition is not as difficult as it seems when we reduce it to three interrelated dimensions of stress: (1) environmental demands, referred to as stressors, that produce (2) an adaptive response that is influenced by (3) individual differences.

Hans Selye, considered the father of the modern concept of stress, pioneered the distinction between stressors and the stress response. Moreover, Selye emphasized that both positive and negative events can trigger an identical stress response that can be beneficial or harmful (see Table 16–1). He also noted:

- Stress is not merely nervous tension.
- Stress can have positive consequences.
- Stress is not something to be avoided.
- The complete absence of stress is death.[6]

These points make it clear that stress is inevitable. Efforts need to be directed at managing stress, not at somehow escaping it altogether.

A Model of Occupational Stress

OB researchers Michael Matteson and John Ivancevich developed an instructive model of occupational stress. As illustrated in Figure 16–2, stressors lead to stress, which in turn produces a variety of outcomes. The model also specifies several individual differences that *moderate* the stressor-stress-outcome relationship. A moderator is a variable that causes the relationship between two variables—such as stress and outcomes—to be stronger for some people and weaker for others. For example, a field study of 938 Medicare enrollees revealed that owners of pets reported less stress over one year, as evidenced by less doctor contacts, than did people without pets. Pets moderated the effects of stress. Accountability for production costs is an example of a work-related moderator. A recent study of 400 shopfloor employees indicated that stress was higher for employees who

• **FIGURE 16–2**   A Model of Occupational Stress

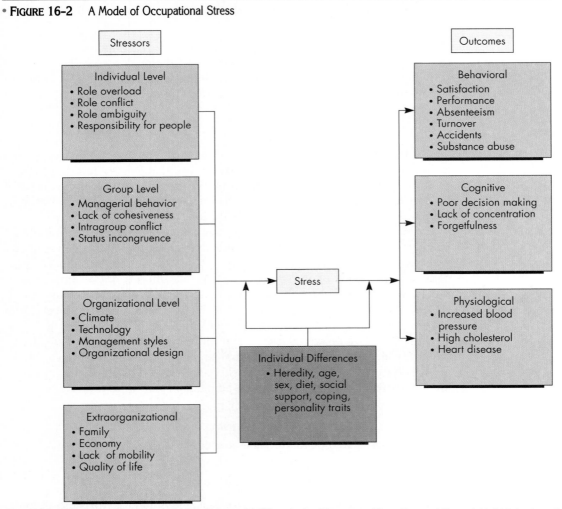

Source: Adapted from Michael T. Matteson and John M. Ivancevich, "Organizational Stressors and Heart Disease: A Research Model," *Academy of Management Review*, July 1979, p. 350. Used with permission.

were accountable for controlling costs than it was for others not held accountable.[7] Let us consider the major components of this stress model.

Stressors Stressors are environmental factors that produce stress. Stated differently, stressors are a prerequisite to experiencing the stress response. Figure 16–2 shows the four major types of stressors: individual, group, organizational, and extraorganizational. Individual-level stressors are those directly associated with a person's job duties. The most common examples are role overload, role conflict, and role ambiguity. As discussed in Chapter 8, these role characteristics create stress because they make people feel both overworked and uncertain about what they should be doing.[8] Managers can reduce these stressors by providing direction and support for their employees.

Group-level stressors are caused by group dynamics (recall our discussion in Chapter 9) and managerial behavior. Managers create stress for employees by: (1) exhibiting inconsistent behaviors, (2) failing to provide support, (3) showing lack of concern, (4) providing inadequate direction, (5) creating a high productivity environment, and (6) focusing on negatives while ignoring good performance.[9]

Organizational stressors affect large numbers of employees. Organizational climate or culture, which is discussed in Chapter 19, is a prime example. For instance, a high pressure environment, with no mechanisms for employees to release their stress, fuels the stress response. In contrast, companies such as Ben & Jerry's Homemade, a New England ice cream maker, and Odetics, a high-technology robotics firm in California, develop organizational cultures that reduce stress.

> Ben & Jerry's Homemade, for example, set up an official Joy Committee . . . Tacky Dress-Up Day, complete with plaids, paisley, and polyester, blinded the staff in Waterbury, Vermont, one day last year [1988]. Earlier, during the busiest time of the summer, the ice-cream company hired masseuses to ease the tension.
>
> At Odetics, . . . fun is part of an overall commitment to keeping employees happy and healthy. . . . Odetics has had a Fun Committee since 1982. It sponsors activities such as a 50s and 60s Day featuring Hula-Hoop contests, bubble-gum blowing competitions and telephone-booth stuffing.[10]

A participative management style also represents a potential organizational stressor. While some people dislike participation, others are pleased and happy with the opportunity to gain more control over their work environment. Research provides preliminary support for the idea that participation can reduce employee stress.[11] Finally, the office design and general office environment are important organizational-level stressors. Research demonstrates that poor lighting, loud noise, and improper placement of furniture create stress.[12] Managers are advised to monitor and eliminate these stressors.

Extraorganizational stressors are those caused by factors outside the organization. For instance, the dynamics of the changing work force discussed in Chapter 2 are becoming increasingly stressful for many people. Specifically, conflicts associated with balancing one's career and family life are difficult to manage. This stressor is likely to become more important in the future.[13]

• Companies such as Ben & Jerry's help to reduce organizational stress by ensuring that employees get involved in pleasurable events. *(Courtesy of Ben & Jerry's © 1991 Arnold Carbone.)*

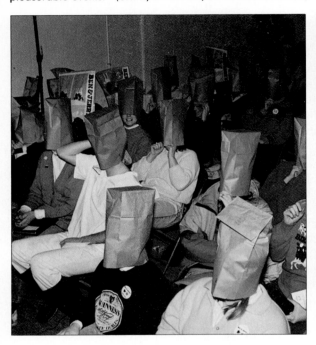

Outcomes   Theorists contend that stress has behavioral, cognitive, and physiological consequences, or outcomes. For example, International OB describes the manifestation of these stress outcomes in Saddam Hussein, President of Iraq, just prior to the war with the United Nations coalition forces in 1991. A large body of research supports the conclusion that stress produces harmful physiological outcomes.[14] But researchers have only begun to examine the relationship between stress and work-related behavioral and cognitive outcomes. Although these studies indicate a negative relationship between stress and both turnover and job satisfaction, the exact nature of the relationship between stress and performance is still open to question.[15]

Historically, researchers generally have believed there was an *inverted U-shaped relationship* between stress and performance (see dashed line in Figure 16–3). Low levels of stress were thought to lead to low performance because individuals were not "charged up" to perform. At the other extreme, high levels of stress were predicted to force an individual into an energy-sapping fight-or-flight response, thereby resulting in low performance. This hypothesized relationship proposes that optimal performance is achieved when people are subjected to moderate levels of stress.

Although several laboratory studies supported this relationship, three more recent field studies did not. For samples of 440 nurses, 227 managers, and 283 hourly workers, results demonstrated a negative relationship between stress and performance (solid line in Figure 16–3).[16] In other words, performance declined as stress increased. Despite differing evidence from laboratory and field studies, it is clear that high levels of stress diminish

INTERNATIONAL OB

Saddam Hussein Shows the Wear-and-Tear of Stress

Javier Perez de Cuellar [the United Nations Secretary-General] said Saddam Hussein appeared totally detached from the crisis at hand, uninterested in anything his visitor had to say, and even unable to focus on issues he himself has previously stressed. Instead, he seemed preoccupied with plying Mr. Perez de Cuellar with tea and coffee—a strange departure for a man who earlier visitors report had little time for pleasantries. . . .

Veteran Saddam-watchers also notice odd changes in the Iraqi president's demeanor: His speech often seems slow, his face puffy and his eyes unfocused. It would be surprising if someone in his situation didn't exhibit signs of stress. Running what is essentially a one-man regime, he has had to be on round-the-clock alert since early summer, when his plans for invading Kuwait began to take shape.

Source: Geraldine Brooks and Tony Horwitz, "Saddam Watch: Embattled Iraqi Leader Grows More Isolated Amid Signs of Stress," *The Wall Street Journal*, January 16, 1991, p. A1.

• **FIGURE 16-3**   The Relationship between Stress and Performance

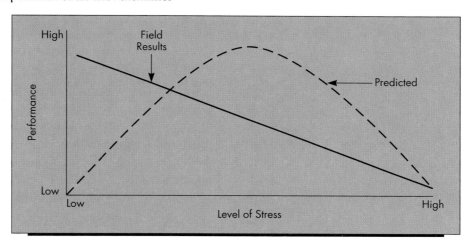

human performance. More research is needed to identify the optimum stress-performance relationship.

Individual Differences   People do not experience the same level of stress or exhibit similar outcomes for a given type of stressor. As discussed later, stressors are less apt to produce stress for people with a strong social support network and those who employ a variety of coping strategies. *Perception* of a stressor is another important moderator. If a stressor is perceived as threatening, an individual tends to experience greater stress and more negative outcomes. According to Harvard Medical School research, the type of job an individual performs is another potential moderator. Research found that employees paid by the hour had a 40 percent higher risk of developing coronary heart disease than salaried employees (after controlling for risk factors such as smoking and excess weight).[17]

Moreover, the personality trait of chronic hostility or cynicism also moderated stress. Research demonstrated that people who were chronically angry, suspicious, or mistrustful were twice as likely to have coronary artery blockages. We all can protect our hearts by learning to avoid these tendencies. Finally, a recent meta-analysis of 15 studies indicated that there were no gender differences in perceived and experienced work stress.[18] In summary, even though researchers have been able to identify several important moderators, a large gap still exists in identifying relevant individual differences.

Economic Costs and Legal Liabilities of Stress

Managers need to understand the causes and consequences of stress for at least four compelling reasons. First, from a quality-of-work-life perspective, workers are more satisfied when they have a safe and comfortable work environment. Second, a moral imperative suggests that managers should reduce occupational stress because it leads to negative outcomes. For example, mental health experts estimate that 10 percent of the work force suffers from depression or high levels of stress that may ultimately affect job performance.[19] A third reason centers on the staggering economic costs of stress. Experts estimate that stress-related illnesses cost American business between $50 and $150 billion a year.[20]

The fourth reason revolves around recent court cases where employees sued their employers for workmen's compensation for stress-related problems. A study by the National Council on Compensation Insurance, for instance, reported that 11 percent of all claims were due to mental stress.[21] Although the courts have not consistently ruled in favor of compensating people for psychological injury due to stress, the trend is in that direction. The following cases illustrate this trend:

> Helen J. Kelly, a Raytheon Co. employee with 22 years' seniority, suffered a nervous breakdown when told she would be transferred to another department. The Massachusetts Supreme Judicial Court ruled 4 to 3 that she was entitled to worker's comp benefits. . . .
> Harry A. McGarrah, an Oregon deputy sheriff, blamed his depression on the belief that his supervisor was persecuting him. . . .
> Kelly collected $40,000 and McGarrah, $20,000.[22]

In summary, managers cannot afford to ignore the many implications of occupational stress.

• IMPORTANT STRESSORS AND STRESS OUTCOMES

As we have seen, stressors trigger stress, which in turn leads to a variety of outcomes. This section explores an important category of *extraorganizational* stressors: stressful life events. Two especially troublesome stress-related outcomes—burnout and substance abuse—also are examined.

Stressful Life Events

Events such as experiencing the death of a family member, being assaulted, moving, ending an intimate relationship, being seriously ill, or taking a big test can create stress. These events are stressful because they involve significant changes that require adaptation and often social readjustment. Accordingly, **stressful life events** are defined as nonwork-related changes that disrupt an individual's lifestyle and social relationships. They have been the most extensively investigated extraorganizational stressors.

Thomas Holmes and Richard Rahe conducted pioneering research on the relationship between stressful life events and subsequent illness. During their research, they developed a widely used questionnaire to assess life stress.[23]

Assessing Stressful Life Events The *Schedule of Recent Experiences* (SRE), developed by Holmes and Rahe, is the dominant method for assessing an individual's cumulative stressful life events. As shown in the OB Exercise, the SRE consists of 43 life events. Each event has a corresponding value, called a life change unit, representing the degree of social readjustment necessary to cope with the event. The larger the value, the more stressful the event. These values were obtained from a convenience sample of 394 people who evaluated the stressfulness of each event. (Please take a moment to complete the SRE survey and calculate your total life stress score.)

Research revealed a positive relationship between the total score on the SRE and subsequent illness. For example, the odds are you will experience good health next year if you scored below 150. But there is a 50 percent chance of illness for those scoring between 150 and 300. Finally, a score above 300 suggests a 70 percent chance of illness.[24] A word of caution is in order, however. If you scored above 150, don't head for a sterile cocoon. High scores on the SRE do not guarantee you will become ill. Rather, a high score simply increases one's statistical risk of illness.

Research and Practical Implications Numerous studies have examined the relationship between life stress and both illness and job performance. Subjects with higher SRE scores had significantly more problems with chronic headaches, sudden cardiac death, pregnancy and birth complications, tuberculosis, diabetes, anxiety, depression, and a host of minor physical ailments. Meanwhile, academic and work performance declined as SRE scores increased.[25] *Negative,* as opposed to positive, personal life changes were associated with lower levels of job satisfaction and organizational commitment and greater levels of job stress, depression and anxiety.[26] Finally, life events that were *uncontrollable* (for example, death of spouse), rather than controllable (such as marriage), were more strongly associated with subsequent illness.[27]

The key implication is that employee illness and job performance are affected by extraorganizational stressors, particularly those that are negative and uncontrollable. Because employees do not leave their personal problems at the office door or factory gate, management needs to be aware of external sources of employee stress. Once identified, training programs or counseling can be used to help employees cope with these stressors. This

• OB EXERCISE

The Holmes and Rahe Schedule of Recent Experiences Survey

Instructions:
Place a check mark next to each event you experienced within the past year. Then add the life change units associated with the various events to derive your total life stress score.

Life Event	Life Change Unit
_____ Death of spouse	100
_____ Divorce	73
_____ Marital separation	65
_____ Jail term	63
_____ Death of close family member	63
_____ Personal injury or illness	53
_____ Marriage	50
_____ Fired at work	47
_____ Marital reconciliation	45
_____ Retirement	45
_____ Change in health of family member	44
_____ Pregnancy	40
_____ Sex difficulties	39
_____ Gain of new family member	39
_____ Business readjustment	39
_____ Change in financial state	38
_____ Death of close friend	37
_____ Change to different line of work	36
_____ Change in number of arguments with spouse	35
_____ Mortgage over $10,000	31
_____ Foreclosure of mortgage or loan	30
_____ Change in responsibilities at work	29
_____ Son or daughter leaving home	29
_____ Trouble with in-laws	29
_____ Outstanding personal achievement	28
_____ Wife begin or stop work	26
_____ Begin or end school	26
_____ Change in living conditions	25
_____ Revision of personal habits	24
_____ Trouble with boss	23
_____ Change in work hours or conditions	20
_____ Change in residence	20
_____ Change in schools	20
_____ Change in recreation	19
_____ Change in church activities	19
_____ Change in social activities	18
_____ Mortgage or loan less than $10,000	17
_____ Change in sleeping habits	16
_____ Change in number of family get-togethers	15
_____ Change in eating habits	15
_____ Vacation	13
_____ Christmas	12
_____ Minor violations of the law	11

Total score = _____

Source: Adapted from Thomas H. Holmes and Richard H. Rahe, ''The Social Readjustment Rating Scale,'' *Journal of Psychosomatic Research,* August 1967, p. 216. Used with permission. Copyright 1967, Pergamon Press.

not only may reduce costs associated with illnesses and absenteeism, but also may lead to positive work attitudes and better job performance. In addition, by acknowledging that work outcomes are affected by extra-organizational stressors, managers may avoid the trap of automatically attributing poor performance to low motivation or lack of ability. Such awareness is likely to engender positive reactions from employees and lead to resolution of problems, not just symptoms. For individuals with a high score on the SRE, it would be best to defer controllable stressors, such as moving or buying a new car, until things settle down.

Burnout

Burnout is a stress-induced problem common among members of "helping" professions such as teaching, social work, employee relations, nursing, and law enforcement. It does not involve a specific feeling, attitude, or physiological outcome anchored to a specific point in time. Rather, **burnout** is a condition that occurs over time and is characterized by emotional exhaustion and a combination of negative attitudes. Table 16–2 describes 10 attitudinal characteristics of burnout. Experts say a substantial number of people suffer from this problem. To promote better understanding of this important stress outcome, we turn our attention to a model of the burnout process and highlight relevant research and techniques for its prevention.

A Model of Burnout   There are two paths to burnout. As Figure 16–4 illustrates, these two paths have a cumulative effect. The first route is a direct outgrowth of the model of occupational stress we just discussed. That is, traditional work-related stressors produce stress, which leads to attitudinal and behavioral symptoms that may culminate in burnout. For example, a recent study indicated that the mental demands of a job were positively

---

• **TABLE 16-2**   Attitudinal Characteristics of Burnout

Attitude	Description
Fatalism	A feeling that you lack control over your work
Boredom	A lack of interest in doing your job
Discontent	A sense of being unhappy with your job
Cynicism	A tendency to undervalue the content of your job and the rewards received
Inadequacy	A feeling of not being able to meet your objectives
Failure	A tendency to discredit your performance and conclude that you are ineffective
Overwork	A feeling of having too much to do and not enough time to complete it
Nastiness	A tendency to be rude or unpleasant to your co-workers
Dissatisfaction	A feeling that you are not being justly rewarded for your efforts
Escape	A desire to give up and get away from it all

Source: Adapted from Donald P. Rogers, "Helping Employees Cope with Burnout," *Business*, October–December 1984, p. 4.

• **FIGURE 16–4**   A Model of Burnout

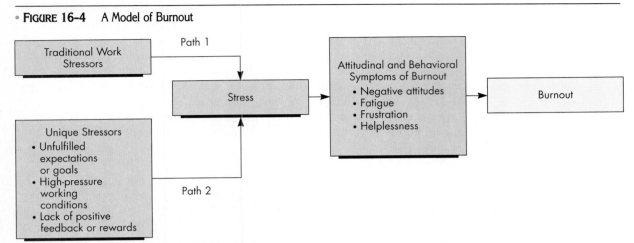

Source: Based in part on Donald P. Rogers, "Helping Employees Cope with Burnout," *Business*, October–December 1984, p. 5.

correlated with burnout for a sample of managers.[28] Burnout does not automatically occur as a result of stress and occasional symptoms of burnout. Instead, burnout develops in phases and ultimately takes place when symptoms become so severe that an individual gives up trying to perform effectively.[29] Consider the case of a teacher named Martha.

> "When I started as a teacher," says Martha, "I felt the mark I was making on every child was significant. But year in and year out, you go through the same hassles, and you begin to say to yourself, 'Nothing ever changes.' You struggle so hard with every kid, and there are so many of them every year. Eventually you realize, 'If it weren't me, somebody else would do it.' A kind of work-weariness overtakes you, like a big 'So What?'"
>
> Martha is typical of many people in the helping professions . . . who have overblown expectations. The very idealism that motivates them eventually burns them out. Anxious to make an impact, they undervalue their small successes, don't savor the struggle itself, and so never derive the satisfaction they crave.[30]

In addition to unrealistic expectations or goals (as in Martha's case), burnout is also caused by two other unique stressors (path 2 in Figure 16–4): high-pressure working conditions, and a lack of positive feedback or rewards.

Research Findings and Prevention   Burnout develops in phases and is more prevalent in the "helping" professions. Although researchers do not completely agree on the number of phases, three overall stages have been identified: from depersonalization, to feeling a lack of personal accomplishment, to emotional exhaustion.[31] Moreover, burnout is significantly associated with a lack of feedback, low job satisfaction, desire to quit one's job, impairment of interpersonal relationships with family and friends, insomnia, absenteeism, and taking more rest breaks at work.[32] This research underscores the organizational need to reduce the stress-induced problem of burnout.

Removing stressors that cause burnout is the most straightforward way to prevent it. One solution is for managers to create down-to-earth job expectations, possibly through the use of realistic job previews, discussed in Chapter 8. Managers also can reduce burnout by buffering its effects. **Buffers** are resources or administrative changes that alleviate the symptoms of burnout. Potential buffers include extra staff or equipment at peak work periods, support from top management, increased freedom to make decisions, recognition for accomplishments, time off for personal development or rest, and equitable rewards. Decreasing the quantity and increasing the *quality* of communications is another possible buffer. Finally, managers can change the content of an individual's job by adding or eliminating responsibilities, increasing the amount of participation in decision making, altering the pattern of interpersonal contacts, or assigning the person to a new position.[33]

There also are two long-term strategies for reducing burnout that are increasingly being used by companies. Apple Computer, IBM, McDonald's Corp., and Intel, for instance, use sabbaticals to replenish employees' energy and desire to work. These programs allow employees to take a designated amount of time off from work after being employed a certain number of years. McDonald's grants paid sabbaticals after 10 years of employment; for Intel, it is eight weeks off with pay after seven years for every full-time employee. An employee retreat is the second long-term strategy. Retreats entail sending employees to an offsite location for 3–5 days. While there, everyone can relax, reflect, or engage in team and relationship building activities. Hallmark Cards uses retreats to help in the fight against burnout.[34]

Substance Abuse

Employee substance abuse occurs when the use of alcohol or drugs hurts one's job performance. Although people drink alcohol and take drugs for a variety of reasons, many people reportedly rely on these mood-altering substances to relieve stress. For individuals with pressure-packed, fast-paced jobs, alcohol and barbiturates may be used to calm frayed nerves. Drugs such as cocaine or amphetamines may offer employees with monotonous or boring jobs needed stimulation. Employee substance abuse is a costly problem of epidemic proportions. It critically affects product quality and job safety.

U.S. government experts estimate that one fourth of the American work force may be substance abusers. This abuse was estimated to cost businesses $190 billion in 1986 alone. These costs are even higher today.[35] Substance abuse is found at all organizational levels. Some experts estimate the problem might be more severe in the managerial ranks, however, because managers are in a better position to hide alcohol and drug habits. Managers can close their office doors, delegate work to others, and travel more frequently. Although no single symptom is indicative of substance abuse, behavioral changes such as increased absenteeism, disappearance from the work area, sleeping at work, difficulty in concentrating, mood swings, fluctuations in work quality, failure to complete tasks, accidents, and waste of materials are suggestive of substance abuse.[36] Corporations have attacked the substance-abuse problem in three ways: sting operations, drug testing, and through employee assistance programs.

• Substance abuse is a tragic, costly, and growing problem in all walks of life. (COMSTOCK, Inc.)

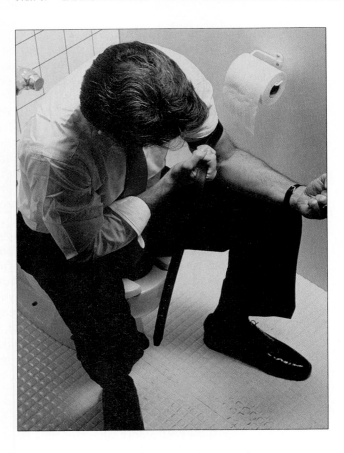

Sting Operations   Sting operations are the most controversial method of reducing substance abuse. They entail surveillance, search, and detection to identify employees involved with the sale and use of illegal drugs. Both Pennzoil and General Motors have used this approach.

Drug Testing   Drug testing—commonly through urinalysis—is typically done when screening job applicants and/or on a random basis with existing employees. Data from the Bureau of Labor Statistics revealed that 950,000 employees and 3,900,000 job applicants were tested for drug use in 1987. A more recent survey indicated that in the United States 96 percent of the largest companies screened some applicants in 1990.[37]

Drug testing is not without risks. There are both legal and technical limitations to implementing a drug-testing program.[38] Companies must be careful not to violate federal, state, or local laws (see OB in Action). For example, employees working for federal, state, or local governments possess a constitutional right to privacy. Some courts have concluded that random drug testing violates this right. Moreover, several states, including California, have included this right in their state constitutions. Drug testing should not be implemented without carefully considering the legality of the program.

OB IN ACTION

Legalities of Drug Testing

Twelve states currently have statutes and laws specifically relating to employee drug testing—Connecticut, Iowa, Kansas, Louisiana, Maryland, Minnesota, Montana, Nebraska, Rhode Island, Tennessee, Utah, and Vermont. Most regulate the drug testing process and require that certain procedures be followed.

The federal government and its agencies have mandated testing of certain governmental employees, defense contract workers, and transportation workers. Most federal contractors and grantees must comply with the Drug Free Work Place Act of 1988. This statute requires employers with federal contracts of $25,000 or more and all federal grantees to adopt specified policies, implement an employee awareness program, notify the federal agency of the conviction of an employee for a drug offense, and impose discipline or treatment on employees who violate drug statutes.

The Department of Transportation's drug testing rules became effective for employers with over 50 drivers on December 16, 1989. While portions of these regulations requiring random and post-accident testing are the subject of a federal court injunction, the remainder of the regulations are currently effective. Employers of DOT drivers must test all applicants prior to hiring and when there is "reasonable cause" to believe that the driver is under the influence of drugs or alcohol. These regulations become effective for smaller companies December 21, 1990.

Source: Steven K. Like, "Employee Drug Testing," *Small Business Reports*, December 1990, p. 50. Used by permission.

Employee Assistance Programs   Companies of all sizes have begun to implement employee assistance programs (EAPs). It is estimated that there are over 10,000 formal EAPs in existence and that nearly 80 percent of the Fortune 500 have these programs.[39] What is an EAP?

Employee assistance programs provide treatment for employees' problems that interfere with their work performance.[40] For example, just about all programs provide treatment for substance abuse. Other programs also focus on personal, marital, and financial counseling. The most all-encompassing EAPs provide treatment for all types of psychological and personal needs. There are five components of a typical EAP. They are:

1. A program policy and procedures statement which makes clear the responsibilities of the company and the employees concerning health and personal problems impacting the job.
2. Employee education of problems, which may vary from simple letters to poster campaigns to extensive training programs.
3. A supervisory training program which teaches supervisors problem recognition and performance documentation.
4. Clinical services which may be provided by a professional in-house staff or community agencies.

A MATTER OF ETHICS

Exxon Denies Reinstatement to Certain Groups of Substance Abusers

Now Exxon Corp. is flying in the face of industry practice—and its own past policy—by declaring that, even after treatment, known alcohol and drug abusers won't be allowed to return to so-called critical jobs such as piloting a ship, flying a plane or operating a refinery, although they will be given other jobs after treatment.

   Exxon declined to say exactly when the policy switch came into effect, but it follows the wreck of its oil tanker, the Exxon Valdez. The ship's captain, Joseph Hazelwood, had been treated for alcoholism and returned to work. After the accident, a blood test showed a high level of alcohol in his blood. "The reasons [for the decision] are obvious," said an Exxon spokesman. Speaking to the House Coast Guard Subcommittee, Exxon Chairman Lawrence Rawl last week said: "Even with close follow-up, there are certain things you can't have people do."

Source: Amanda Bennett, Jolie Solomon, and Allanna Sullivan, "Firms Debate Hard Line on Alcoholics: Oil Spill Spurs Exxon to Shift Job Guarantees," *The Wall Street Journal*, March 13, 1989, p. B1.

5. Follow-up monitoring to ensure real problem resolution has occurred, as opposed to the employee being more careful after referral to the EAP.[41]

Although many studies of EAP effectiveness contain methodological flaws, research suggests that EAPs are a cost-effective way to combat stress outcomes.[42]

In spite of these positive results, however, the issue of reinstatement is clouding the future success of EAPs. The issue is whether companies should reinstate an employee to his or her position after completing treatment for substance abuse through an EAP. Many experts believe that reinstatement is the hallmark of successful programs because people will not "turn-in" their co-workers unless employees are reinstated. Keep in mind that employees are most likely to know about their co-workers' problems—and long before supervisory personnel do. While the historical trend is to reinstate employees, Exxon is forging new ground by denying reinstatement to certain groups of employees (see A Matter of Ethics). Future experience and research are needed to reconcile this controversial issue. Do you support full reinstatement?

• MODERATORS OF OCCUPATIONAL STRESS

Moderators, once again, are variables that cause the relationships between stressors, stress, and outcomes to be weaker for some people and stronger for others. Managers with a working knowledge of important stress moderators can confront employee stress in the following ways.

First, awareness of moderators helps identify those most likely to experience stress and its negative outcomes. Stress reduction programs then can be formulated for high-risk employees. Second, moderators, in and of themselves, suggest possible solutions for reducing negative outcomes of occupational stress. Keeping these objectives in mind, we will examine three important moderators: social support, coping, and hardiness.

Social Support

Talking with a friend or taking part in a bull session can be comforting during times of fear, stress, or loneliness. For a variety of reasons, meaningful social relationships help people do a better job of handling stress. **Social support** is the amount of perceived helpfulness derived from social relationships. Importantly, social support is determined by both the quantity and quality of an individual's social relationships. There has been a dramatic increase in the number of support groups in the United States over the last 10 years. Experts estimated that nearly 155 million people attended at least one of 500,000 support groups over a one-week period in February 1990.[43] Figure 16–5 illustrates the mechanisms of social support.

A Model of Social Support   As Figure 16–5 shows, one's support network must be perceived before it can be used. Support networks evolve from four sources: cultural norms, social institutions, groups, or individuals. For example, there is more cultural emphasis on caring for the elderly in Japan than in America. Japanese culture is thus a strong source of social support for older Japanese people. Alternatively, individuals may fall back on social institutions such as social security or welfare, religious groups, or family and friends for support. In turn, these various sources provide four *types* of support:

- *Esteem support:* providing information that a person is accepted and respected despite any problems or inadequacies.
- *Informational support:* providing help in defining, understanding, and coping with problems.
- *Social companionship:* spending time with others in leisure and recreational activities.
- *Instrumental support:* providing financial aid, material resources, or needed services.[44]

If social support is perceived as available, an individual then decides whether or not to use it. Generally, support is used for one or both of two purposes. The first purpose is very broad in scope. **Global social support,** encompassing the total amount of support available from the four sources, is applicable to any situation at any time. The narrower **functional social support** buffers the effects of stressors or stress in specific situations. When relied on in the wrong situation, functional social support is not very helpful. For example, if you lost your job, unemployment compensation (instrumental support) would be a better buffer than sympathy from a bartender. On the other hand, social companionship would be more helpful than instrumental

• **Figure 16–5**   A Flow Model of the Mechanisms of Social Support

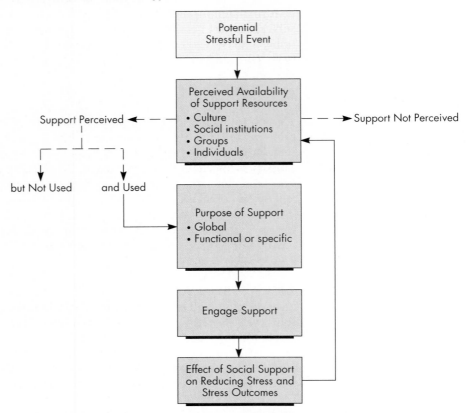

Sources: Portions adapted from Sheldon Cohen and Thomas Ashby Wills, "Stress, Social Support, and the Buffering Hypothesis," *Psychological Bulletin*, September 1985, pp. 310–57; and John G. Bruhn and Billy U. Philips, "Measuring Social Support: A Synthesis of Current Approaches," *Journal of Behavioral Medicine*, June 1984, pp. 151–69.

support in coping with loneliness. After social support is engaged for one or both of these purposes, its effectiveness can be determined. If consolation or relief is not experienced, it may be that the type of support was inappropriate. The feedback loop in Figure 16–5, from effect of social support back to perceived availability, reflects the need to fall back on other sources of support when necessary.

Research Findings and Managerial Lessons   Research shows that global social support is negatively related to mortality. In other words, people with low social support tend to die earlier than those with strong social support networks. Further, global support protects against depression, mental illness, pregnancy complications, anxiety, high blood pressure, and a variety of other ailments. In contrast, functional social support is a buffer against stress only when a match exists between the type of support and the situation.[45]

As suggested in Figure 16–5, global social support is positively related to the availability of support resources. That is, people who interact with a

• **FIGURE 16-6** A Model of the Coping Process

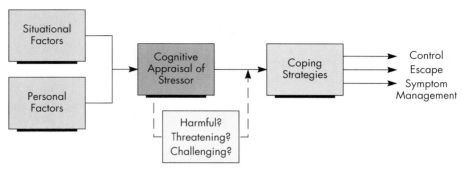

Source: Based in part on Richard S. Lazarus and Susan Folkman, "Coping and Adaptation," in *Handbook of Behavioral Medicine*, ed. W. Doyle Gentry (New York: The Guilford Press, 1984), pp. 282–325.

greater number of friends, family, or co-workers have a wider base of social support to draw upon during stressful periods.[46] Finally, gender does not influence the receipt of social support.[47]

One practical recommendation is to keep employees informed about external and internal social support systems. Internally, managers can use esteem and informational support while administering daily feedback and coaching. Further, participative management programs and company-sponsored activities that make employees feel they are an important part of an "extended family" can be rich sources of social support. Employees need time and energy to adequately maintain their social relationships. If organizational demands are excessive, employees' social relationships and support networks will suffer, resulting in stress-related illness and decreased performance. Also, the positive effects of social support are enhanced when functional support is targeted precisely.

Coping

Coping is "the process of managing demands (external or internal) that are appraised as taxing or exceeding the resources of the person."[48] Because effective coping helps reduce the impact of stressors and stress, your personal life and managerial skills can be enhanced by better understanding this process. Figure 16–6 depicts an instructive model of coping.

The coping process has three major components: (1) situational and personal factors, (2) cognitive appraisals of the stressor, and (3) coping strategies. As shown in Figure 16–6, both situational and personal factors influence appraisal of stressors. In turn, appraisal directly influences choice of coping strategy. Each of the major components of this model deserves a closer look.

Situational and Personal Factors Situational factors are environmental characteristics that affect how people interpret (appraise) stressors. For example, the ambiguity of a situation—such as walking down a dark street at night in an unfamiliar area—makes it difficult to determine whether a potentially dangerous situation exists. Ambiguity creates differences in how people appraise and subsequently cope with stressors. Other situational factors are the frequency of exposure to a stressor and social support networks.

Personal factors are personality traits and personal resources that affect the appraisal of stressors. For instance, because being tired or sick can distort the interpretation of stressors, an extremely tired individual may appraise an innocent question as a threat or challenge. Traits such as locus of control (recall the discussion in Chapter 3) and the hard-driving style characteristic of so-called Type-A individuals also were found to affect the appraisal of stressors.[49]

Cognitive Appraisal of Stressors Cognitive appraisal reflects an individual's overall evaluation of a situation or stressor. This appraisal results in a categorization of the situation as either harmful, threatening, or challenging. It is important to understand the differences among these appraisals because they influence how people cope. " 'Harm' (including loss) represents damage already done; 'threat' involves the potential for harm; and 'challenge' means the potential for significant gain under difficult odds."[50] Coping with harm usually entails undoing or reinterpreting something that occurred in the past because the damage is already done. In contrast, threatening situations engage anticipatory coping. That is, people cope with threat by preparing for harm that may occur in the future. Challenge also activates anticipatory coping. In contrast with threat, an appraisal of challenge results in coping that focuses on what can be gained rather than what may be lost.

Coping Strategies Coping strategies are characterized by the specific behaviors and cognitions used to cope with a situation. Consider, for example, how companies with hostages in Iraq during the Persian Gulf war helped stateside families cope (see International OB). People use three approaches to cope with stressors and stress (see Figure 16–6). The first, called a *control strategy,* consists of using behaviors and cognitions to directly anticipate or solve problems. A control strategy has a take-charge tone. A managerial example is to devote more time and energy to planning and scheduling. In contrast to tackling the problem head-on, an *escape strategy* amounts to running away. Behaviors and cognitions are used to avoid or escape situations. Individuals use this strategy when they passively accept stressful situations or avoid them by failing to confront the cause of stress (an obnoxious co-worker, for instance). Finally, a *symptom management strategy* consists of using methods such as relaxation, meditation, or medication to manage the symptoms of occupational stress.[51]

Research Findings and Managerial Recommendations As suggested by the model in Figure 16–6, an individual's appraisal of a stressor correlates with the choice of a coping strategy.[52] In further support of the coping model, personal factors, appraisal, and coping all significantly predicted psychological symptoms of stress. Nonetheless, research has not clearly identified which type of coping strategy—control, escape, or symptom management— is most effective. It appears that the best coping strategy depends on the situation at hand.[53] Escaping stress—by going on vacation, for example—is

INTERNATIONAL OB

Companies Help Families Cope with Hostages Taken in the Persian Gulf War

"We didn't know anything" about helping dependents, concedes T. B. O'Brien, president of O'Brien-Goins-Simpson Inc., whose OGE Drilling Inc. unit has six workers missing. . . .

Baker Hughes, Inc., too, admits being caught unawares. . . .

Companies are learning on the fly what families of hostages need. So far, everything falls into one or another of three categories: Families want a steady stream of reliable information, readily available psychological support, and assurances that salaries and benefits are sacrosanct. . . .

Many companies set up 24-hour hotlines after the Iraqi invasion. Santa Fe International Corp., a Kuwait Petroleum Corp. unit with eight oil-field workers held in Baghdad, says its human resource department provides information to families and company employees. Bechtel Group Inc., the engineering and construction giant, established a worldwide, toll-free phone network.

Source: David D. Medina and Carolyn Phillips, "Companies with Hostages in Persian Gulf Struggle to Help Stateside Families Cope," *The Wall Street Journal,* September 26, 1990, p. B1.

---

sometimes better than confronting a stressor with a control-oriented coping strategy. Researchers are currently trying to determine these contingency relationships.

The above results suggest that employees should be taught a contingency approach to coping with organizational stressors. This might begin by helping employees identify those stressors that they perceive as harmful or threatening. Training or managerial support can then be used to help employees manage and possibly eliminate the most serious stressors. The final section of this chapter describes specific techniques for that purpose.

Hardiness

Suzanne Kobasa, a behavioral scientist, identified a collection of personality characteristics that neutralize occupational stress. This collection of characteristics, referred to as **hardiness,** involves the ability to perceptually or behaviorally transform negative stressors into positive challenges. Hardiness embraces the personality dimensions of commitment, locus of control, and challenge.[54]

Personality Characteristics of Hardiness

Commitment reflects the extent to which an individual is involved in whatever he or she is doing. Committed people have a sense of purpose and do not give up under pressure because they tend to invest themselves in the situation.

As discussed in Chapter 3, individuals with an *internal locus of control* believe they can influence the events that affect their lives. People possessing this trait are more likely to foresee stressful events, thereby reducing their exposure to anxiety-producing situations. Moreover, their perception of being in control leads "internals" to use proactive coping strategies.

Challenge is represented by the belief that change is a normal part of life. Hence, change is seen as an opportunity for growth and development rather than a threat to security.

Hardiness Research and Application   A five-year study of 259 managers from a public utility revealed that hardiness—commitment, locus of control, and challenge—reduced the probability of illness following exposure to stress.[55] Hardy undergraduate students were similarly found to display lower psychological distress than their less hardy counterparts. Hardy students also were more likely to interpret stressors as positive and controllable, supporting the idea that hardy individuals perceive situations in less stressful ways. Finally, a study of 100 nurses indicated that the hardiness dimension of "commitment to work" was negatively linked with burnout.[56]

One practical offshoot of this research is organizational training and development programs that strengthen the characteristics of commitment, personal control, and challenge. Because of cost limitations, it is necessary to target key employees or those most susceptible to stress (e.g., air traffic controllers). The hardiness concept also meshes nicely with job design. Jobs can be redesigned to take fuller advantage of hardiness characteristics. As is true of orchestra conductors, for example, there appears to be a positive linkage between interesting and challenging jobs and longevity.

> Arturo Toscanini lived to be 90. Bruno Walter lived to the age of 85. Walter Damrosch lived to 88. And Leopold Stokowski married for the third time at the age of 63 to a woman 42 years younger than he was, and then went on to live to 95. One of the last things he did was sign a contract for work that he would have concluded on his 100th birthday. . . .
>
> [A professor of medicine named Donald] Atlas believed that the enviable longevity of conductors may be linked to their sense of work fulfillment. They enjoy a challenging profession in which they exercise almost complete control over their co-workers, and they often receive worldwide recognition and acclaim.[57]

A final application of the hardiness concept is as a diagnostic tool. Employees scoring low on hardiness would be good candidates for stress-reduction programs.

• STRESS-REDUCTION TECHNIQUES

Organizations are increasingly implementing a variety of stress-reduction programs to help employees cope with stress. Chase Manhattan Corp., Citicorp, and Hoffman-La Roche Inc. offer such programs.

> Chase Manhattan Corp. . . . initiated a program of lunch-time support groups, led by professional therapists, for employees feeling stress.
>
> Citicorp has also made extensive use of lunch-time stress counselors. One, Dr. Art Ulene of NBC's "Today" show, recently advised employees "to change the way you think about some of the things that drive you crazy" as one method for lowering stress. . . .

Meanwhile, at Hoffman-La Roche Inc. . . . employees receive after-hours instruction in a variety of stress management methods. They include meditation, breathing exercises, and a technique called "dot stopping." A form of biofeedback, the technique teaches employees to control their stress by recalling a wonderful moment and focusing on the feelings and sensations they had then.[58]

As these programs suggest, many stress-reduction techniques are available. The four most frequently used approaches are muscle relaxation, biofeedback, meditation, and cognitive restructuring. Each method involves somewhat different ways of coping with stress (see Table 16–3).

Muscle Relaxation

The common denominators of various muscle relaxation techniques are slow and deep breathing, a conscious effort to relieve muscle tension, and an altered state of consciousness. Among the variety of techniques available, progressive relaxation is probably most frequently used. It consists of repeatedly tensing and relaxing muscles beginning at the feet and progressing to the face. Relaxation is achieved by concentrating on the warmth and calmness associated with relaxed muscles. Take a few moments now to try this technique, as described below.

Sitting in a chair, start by taking slow, deep breaths. Inhale through your nose and exhale through your mouth. Continue until you feel calm. Begin progressive relaxation by pointing your toes toward the ceiling for 10 seconds. Concentrate on the tension within your calves and feet. Now return your toes to a normal position and focus on the relaxed state of your legs and feet. (Your goal is to experience this feeling all over your body.) Tense and relax your feet for 10 seconds one more time. Moving to your calves, and continuing all the way to the muscles in your face, tense one major muscle at a time for 10 seconds, and then let it relax. Do this twice for each muscle

• **TABLE 16–3** Stress-Reduction Techniques

Technique	Descriptions	Assessment
Muscle relaxation	Uses slow deep breathing, systematic muscle tension reduction, and an altered state of consciousness to reduce stress.	Inexpensive and easy to use. May require a trained professional to implement.
Biofeedback	A machine is used to train people to detect muscular tension. Muscle relaxation is then used to alleviate this symptom of stress.	Expensive due to costs of equipment. However, equipment can be used to evaluate effectiveness of other stress-reduction programs.
Meditation	The relaxation response is activated by redirecting one's thoughts away from oneself. A four-step procedure is used.	Least expensive, simple to implement, and can be practiced almost anywhere.
Cognitive restructuring	Irrational or maladaptive thoughts are identified and replaced with those that are rational or logical.	Expensive because it requires a trained psychologist or counselor.
Holistic wellness	A broad, interdisciplinary approach that goes beyond stress reduction by advocating that people strive for personal wellness in all aspects of their lives.	Involves inexpensive but often behaviorally-difficult lifestyle changes.

before moving to another one. You should feel totally relaxed upon completing this routine.

Biofeedback

A biofeedback machine is used to train people to detect and control stress-related symptoms such as tense muscles and elevated blood pressure. The machine translates unconscious bodily signs into a recognizable cue (flashing light or beeper). Muscle relaxation and meditative techniques are then used to alleviate the underlying stress. The person learns to recognize bodily tension without the aid of the machine. In turn, according to the advocates of biofeedback, this awareness helps the person proactively cope with stress.

Meditation

Meditation activates a relaxation response by redirecting one's thoughts away from oneself. The **relaxation response** is the physiological and psychological opposite of the fight-or-flight stress response. Importantly, however, the relaxation response must be learned and consciously activated, whereas the stress response is automatically engaged. Herbert Benson, a Harvard medical doctor, analyzed many meditation programs and derived a four-step relaxation response. The four steps are (1) find a *quiet environment,* (2) use a *mental device* such as a peaceful word or pleasant image to shift the mind from externally oriented thoughts, (3) disregard distracting thoughts by relying on a *passive attitude,* and (4) assume a *comfortable position*— preferably sitting erect—to avoid undue muscular tension or going to sleep. Benson emphasizes that the most important factor is a passive attitude. Maximum benefits supposedly are obtained by following this procedure once or twice a day for 10 to 20 minutes, preferably just before breakfast and dinner.[59]

Cognitive Restructuring

A two-step procedure is followed. First, irrational or maladaptive thought processes that create stress are identified. For example, Type-A individuals may believe they must be successful at everything they do. The second step consists of replacing these irrational thoughts with more rational or reasonable ones. Perceived failure would create stress for the Type-A person. Cognitive restructuring would alleviate stress by encouraging the person to adopt a more reasonable belief about the outcomes associated with failure. For instance, the person might be encouraged to adopt the belief that isolated failure does not mean he or she is a bad person or a loser.

Effectiveness of Stress-Reduction Techniques

A team of OB researchers recently reviewed the research on stress management interventions. Although much of the published research is methodologically weak, results offer preliminary support for the conclusion that muscle relaxation, biofeedback, meditation, and cognitive restructuring all help employees cope with occupational stress.[60]

Some researchers advise organizations not to implement these stress-reduction programs despite their positive outcomes. They rationalize that these techniques relieve *symptoms* of stress rather than eliminate stressors themselves.[61] Thus, they conclude that organizations are using a "Band-Aid" approach to stress reduction. A holistic approach has subsequently been offered as a more proactive and enduring solution.

A Holistic Wellness Model

A **holistic wellness approach** encompasses and goes beyond stress reduction by advocating that individuals strive for "a harmonious and productive balance of physical, mental, and social well-being brought about by the acceptance of one's personal responsibility for developing and adhering to a health promotion program."[62] Five dimensions of a holistic wellness approach are:

1. *Self-responsibility:* Take personal responsibility for your wellness (e.g., quit smoking, moderate your intake of alcohol, wear your seat belt, and so on). A recent study of 4,400 people revealed that continuous smoking throughout one's life reduces life expectancy by 18 years.[63]

2. *Nutritional awareness:* Because we are what we eat, try to increase your consumption of foods high in fiber, vitamins, and nutrients—such as fresh fruits and vegetables, poultry, and fish—while decreasing those high in sugar and fat.

 OB IN ACTION

Tenneco Develops a Successful Fitness Program

The two-story, 100,000-square-foot facility in Houston, where Tenneco . . . is headquartered, is open exclusively to Tenneco employees—everyone from mailroom clerk to board chairman. The center, which cost $11 million, includes indoor gardens drip-watered from above to simulate rainfall, employee and executive dining areas, four racquetball courts, dressing rooms, Nautilus exercise equipment, a sauna and whirlpool bath, and a conference and training center for 264 people. A five-mile, glass arcade jogging track belts the entire facility. There is an executive chef and a health staff that includes a doctor, nurse, physiologist and eight fitness trainers.

And there is the computer. Entering the center, a Tenneco employe inserts a metal card into a computer. When the employe finishes a workout, he reinserts the card and punches a description of what has been done. The computer prepares a "fitness profile" that includes how many calories have been burned off in exercise and how far the employe has to go in his own specially designed program. Every month the employe receives a printout of progress to date. If there is too little use of the fitness center, workout privileges may be lifted.

Source: Excerpted from Bob Getty, "How Fitness Works Out." Reprinted by permission from *Nation's Business*, July 1985. Copyright 1985, U.S. Chamber of Commerce.

• TABLE 16-4   Lifestyle Activities Leading to Personal Wellness

> Monitor your stress symptoms.
> Identify and neutralize or limit your exposure to major stressors.
> Capitalize on your strengths and work on your limitations.
> Establish and periodically review your priorities.
> Cultivate a social support network.
> Adopt a philosophical outlook to put things into proper perspective (be able to laugh at yourself).
> Build flexibility and harmony into your work and lifestyle.
> Make time for exercise and hobbies.
> Learn to relax.
> Eat nutritionally.
> Avoid alcohol and substance abuse.
> Always wear seatbelts.
> Don't smoke.

3. *Stress reduction and relaxation:* Use the techniques just discussed to relax and reduce the symptoms of stress.

4. *Physical fitness:* Exercise to maintain strength, flexibility, endurance, and a healthy body weight. More than 50,000 U.S. companies have established fitness programs for employees (see OB in Action). A recent review of employee fitness programs indicated that they were a cost-effective way to reduce medical costs, absenteeism, turnover, and occupational injuries. Fitness programs also were positively linked with job performance and job satisfaction.[64]

5. *Environmental sensitivity:* Be aware of your environment and try to identify the stressors that are causing your stress. A control coping strategy might be useful to eliminate stressors.

In conclusion, advocates say that both your personal and professional life can be enriched by adopting a holistic approach to wellness. Table 16–4 lists practical tips to get headed in the right direction.

• SUMMARY OF KEY CONCEPTS

A. Stress is an adaptive reaction to environmental demands or stressors that triggers a fight-or-flight response. This response creates hormonal changes that mobilize the body for extraordinary demands.

B. Matteson and Ivancevich's model of occupational stress indicates that stress is caused by four sets of stressors: individual level, group level, organizational level, and extraorganizational. In turn, stress has behavioral, cognitive, and physiological outcomes. Several individual differences moderate relationships between stressors, stress, and outcomes.

C. Stressful life events are changes that disrupt an individual's lifestyle and social relationships. Holmes and Rahe developed the Schedule of Recent Experiences (SRE) to assess an individual's cumulative stressful life events. A positive relationship exists between the SRE and illness. Uncontrollable events that are negative create the most stress.

D. Burnout is a stress-induced problem common among members of "helping" professions. Burnout is a process that occurs over time and is characterized by emotional exhaustion and a combination of negative attitudes.

E. Substance abuse of alcohol or drugs by employees hurts job performance. Companies have attacked the problem with sting operations, drug testing, and employee assistance programs.

F. Social support, an important moderator of relationships between stressors, stress, and outcomes, represents the amount of perceived helpfulness derived from social relationships. Cultural norms, social institutions, groups, and individuals are sources of social support. These sources provide four types of support: esteem, informational, social companionship, and instrumental.

G. Coping is the managing of stressors and stress. Coping is directly affected by the cognitive appraisal of stressors, which in turn is influenced by situational and personal factors. People cope by using control, escape, or symptom management strategies. Because research has not identified the most effective method of coping, a contingency approach to coping is recommended.

H. Hardiness is a collection of personality characteristics that neutralizes stress. It includes the characteristics of commitment, locus of control, and challenge.

I. Muscle relaxation, biofeedback, meditation, and cognitive restructuring are predominant stress-reduction techniques. Slow and deep breathing, a conscious effort to relieve muscle tension, and altered consciousness are common denominators of muscle relaxation. Biofeedback relies on a machine to train people to detect bodily signs of stress. This awareness facilitates proactive coping with stressors. Meditation activates the relaxation response by redirecting one's thoughts away from oneself. Cognitive restructuring entails identifying irrational or maladaptive thoughts and replacing them with rational or logical thoughts.

J. A holistic wellness approach to stress reduction advocates that people accept personal responsibility for their physical, mental, and social well-being.

• KEY TERMS

fight-or-flight response	social support
stress	global social support
stressors	functional social support
stressful life events	coping
burnout	hardiness
buffers	relaxation response
employee substance abuse	holistic wellness approach
employee assistance programs	

• DISCUSSION QUESTIONS

1. What are the key stressors in your life? Which ones are under your control?
2. Describe the behavioral and physiological symptoms you typically experience when under stress.
3. Why do uncontrollable events lead to more stress than controllable events? How can the SRE be used to identify uncontrollable stressors?
4. Have you ever felt burned out? Describe your feelings during this period and explain the events that culminated in this stress outcome.
5. How would you respond to a president of a small firm who asked you to recommend a method for reducing employee substance abuse?
6. From what sources do you derive social support? What type of social support do you find most useful in your role as a student?
7. Which coping strategies have you used over the last three months? How did you happen to choose one strategy over the others?
8. Do you think you have a hardy personality? Explain.
9. Do you currently follow a holistic wellness approach to stress reduction? What improvements in your lifestyle do you need to make?
10. What is the most valuable lesson you learned from this chapter about stress? Explain.

BACK TO THE OPENING CASE

Now that you have read Chapter 16, you should be able to answer the following questions about the paramedic case.

1. What individual-level, group-level, organizational-level, and extra-organizational stressors are paramedics exposed to?
2. Which types of stress outcomes do paramedics experience?
3. Which unique stressors are instrumental in causing burnout among paramedics? Explain.
4. How might a paramedic use a control coping strategy to reduce occupational stress?

• EXERCISE 16

Objectives

1. To determine the extent to which you are burned out.
2. To determine if your burnout scores are predictive of burnout outcomes.
3. To identify specific stressors that affect your level of burnout.

Introduction

An OB researcher named Christina Maslach developed a self-report scale measuring burnout. This scale assesses burnout in terms of three phases: depersonalization, personal accomplishment, and emotional exhaustion. To determine if you suffer from burnout in any of these phases, we would like you to complete an abbreviated version of this scale. Moreover, because burnout has been found to influence a variety of behavioral outcomes, we also want to determine how well burnout predicts three important outcomes.

Instructions

To assess your level of burnout, complete the following 18 statements developed by Maslach.[65] Each item probes how frequently you experience a particular feeling or attitude. If you are presently working, use your job as the frame of reference for responding to each statement. If you are a full-time student, use your role as a student as your frame of reference. After you have completed the 18 items, refer to the scoring key and follow its directions. Remember, there are no right or wrong answers. Indicate your answer for each statement by circling one number from the following scale:

1 = A few times a year
2 = Monthly
3 = A few times a month
4 = Every week
5 = A few times a week
6 = Every day

Burnout Inventory

1. I've become more callous toward people since I took this job   1 2 3 4 5 6
2. I worry that this job is hardening me emotionally   1 2 3 4 5 6
3. I don't really care what happens to some of the people who need my help   1 2 3 4 5 6
4. I feel that people who need my help blame me for some of their problems   1 2 3 4 5 6
5. I deal very effectively with the problems of those people who need my help   1 2 3 4 5 6
6. I feel I'm positively influencing other people's lives through my work   1 2 3 4 5 6
7. I feel very energetic   1 2 3 4 5 6
8. I can easily create a relaxed atmosphere with those people who need my help   1 2 3 4 5 6
9. I feel exhilarated after working closely with those who need my help   1 2 3 4 5 6
10. I have accomplished many worthwhile things in this job   1 2 3 4 5 6
11. In my work, I deal with emotional problems very calmly   1 2 3 4 5 6
12. I feel emotionally drained from my work   1 2 3 4 5 6
13. I feel used up at the end of the workday   1 2 3 4 5 6
14. I feel fatigued when I get up in the morning   1 2 3 4 5 6
15. I feel frustrated by my job   1 2 3 4 5 6
16. I feel I'm working too hard on my job   1 2 3 4 5 6
17. Working with people directly puts too much stress on me   1 2 3 4 5 6
18. I feel like I'm at the end of my rope   1 2 3 4 5 6

Scoring

Compute the average of those items measuring each phase of burnout.

Depersonalization (questions 1–4)   _____

Personal Accomplishment (questions 5–11)   _____
Emotional Exhaustion (questions 12–18)   _____

Assessing Burnout Outcomes

1. How many times were you absent from work over the last three months (indicate the number of absences from classes last semester if using the student role)?
   _____ absences
2. How satisfied are you with your job (or role as a student)? Circle one.
   Very dissatisfied   Dissatisfied   Neutral   Satisfied   Very Satisfied
3. Do you have trouble sleeping? Circle one.
   Yes   No

Questions for Consideration/Class Discussion

1. To what extent are you burned out in terms of depersonalization and emotional exhaustion?
   Low = 1–2.99   Moderate = 3–4.99   High = 5 or above

2. To what extent are you burned out in terms of personal accomplishment?
   Low = 5 or above   Moderate = 3–4.99   High = 1–2.99

3. How well do your burnout scores predict your burnout outcomes?

4. Do your burnout scores suggest that burnout follows a sequence going from depersonalization, to feeling a lack of personal accomplishment, to emotional exhaustion? Explain.

5. Which of the unique burnout stressors illustrated in Figure 16–4 are affecting your level of burnout?

• NOTES

1 Larry Reibstein, ''After a Takeover: More Managers Run, or Are Pushed, Out the Door,'' *The Wall Street Journal,* November 15, 1986, p. 29.

2 See Muhammad Jamal, ''Relationship of Job Stress and Type-A Behavior to Employees' Job Satisfaction, Organizational Commitment, Psychosomatic Health Problems, and Turnover Motivation,'' *Human Relations,* August 1990, pp. 727–38; and Mark O. Hatfield, ''Stress and the American Worker,'' *American Psychologist,* October 1990, pp. 1162–64.

3 The stress response is thoroughly discussed by Hans Selye, *Stress without Distress* (New York: J. B. Lippincott Co., 1974).

4 Thomas F. O'Boyle, ''Fear and Stress in the Office Take Toll,'' *The Wall Street Journal,* November 6, 1990, p. B1.

5 John M. Ivancevich and Michael T. Matteson, *Stress and Work: A Managerial Perspective* (Glenview, Ill.: Scott, Foresman, 1980), pp. 8–9.

6 See Selye, *Stress without Distress.*

7 Results from the Medicare study can be found in Judith M. Siegel, ''Stressful Life Events and Use of Physician Services among the Elderly: The Moderating Role of Pet Ownership,'' *Journal of Personality and Social Psychology,* June 1990, pp. 1081–86. Results from the second study are contained in Robin Martin and Toby D. Wall, ''Attentional Demand and Cost Responsibility as Stressors in Shopfloor Jobs,'' *Academy of Management Journal,* March 1989, pp. 69–86.

[8] Supporting studies were conducted by Karin E. Klenke-Hammel and John E. Mathieu, "Role Strains, Tension, and Job Satisfaction Influences on Employees' Propensity to Leave: A Multi-Sample Replication and Extension," *Human Relations,* August 1990, pp. 791–807; and Gary M. Kaufman and Terry A. Beehr, "Occupational Stressors, Individual Strains, and Social Supports among Police Officers," *Human Relations,* February 1989, pp. 185–97.

[9] See Peter Freiberg, "Surprise—Most Bosses Are Incompetent," *The APA Monitor,* January 1991, p. 23; and James D. Brodzinski, Robert F. Scherer, and Karen A. Goyer, "Workplace Stress: A Study of the Internal and External Pressures Placed upon Today's Employees," *Personnel Administrator,* July 1989, pp. 76–80.

[10] "Work Smarter Not Harder," *Psychology Today,* March 1989, p. 34.

[11] See John M. Ivancevich, Michael T. Matteson, Sara M. Freedman, and James S. Phillips, "Worksite Stress Management Interventions" *American Psychologist,* February 1990, pp. 252–61; and Susan E. Jackson, "Participation in Decision Making as a Strategy for Reducing Job-Related Strain," *Journal of Applied Psychology,* February 1983, pp. 3–19.

[12] This research is discussed by Robert F. Bettendorf, "Curing the New Ills of Technology: Proper Ergonomics Can Reduce Cumulative Trauma Disorders among Employees," *HRMagazine,* March 1990, pp. 35–36, 80; and Stephenie Overman, "Prescriptions for a Healthier Office," *HRMagazine,* February 1990, pp. 30–34.

[13] A related discussion can be found in Susan E. Jackson and Randall S. Schuller, "Human Resource Planning: Challenges for Industrial/Organizational Psychologists," *American Psychologist,* February 1990, pp. 223–39; and Marianne Frankenhaeuser, Ulf Lundberg, Mats Fredrikson, Bo Melin, Martti Tuomisto, and Anna-Lisa Myrsten, "Stress On and Off the Job as Related to Sex and Occupational Status in White-Collar Workers," *Journal of Organizational Behavior,* October 1989, pp. 321–46.

[14] A variety of evidence is presented in Robert M. Kaplan, "Behavior as the Central Outcome in Health Care," *American Psychologist,* November 1990, pp. 1211–20; and Ann O'Leary, "Stress, Emotion, and Human Immune Function," *Psychological Bulletin,* November 1990, pp. 363–82.

[15] See Jamal, "Relationship of Job Stress and Type-A Behavior to Employees' Job Satisfaction, Organizational Commitment, Psychosomatic Health Problems, and Turnover Motivation"; and Jeffrey R. Edwards, A. J. Baglioni, Jr., and Cary L. Cooper, "Stress, Type-A, Coping, and Psychological and Physical Symptoms: A Multi-Sample Test of Alternative Models," *Human Relations,* October 1990, pp. 919–56.

[16] See Muhammad Jamal, "Job Stress and Job Performance Controversy: An Empirical Assessment," *Organizational Behavior and Human Performance,* February 1984, pp. 1–21, and Muhammad Jamal, "Relationship of Job Stress to Job Performance: A Study of Managers and Blue-Collar Workers," *Human Relations,* May 1985, pp. 409–24.

[17] Research about the perception of stressors is reviewed by Philip J. Dewe, "Examining the Nature of Work Stress: Individual Evaluations of Stressful Experiences and Coping," *Human Relations,* November 1989, pp. 993–1013. Results from the Harvard study are discussed in "Labor Letter: A Special News Report on People and Their Jobs in Offices, Fields, and Factories," *The Wall Street Journal,* December 3, 1985, p. 1.

[18] Research on chronic hostility is discussed by "Healthy Lives: A New View of Stress," *University of California, Berkeley Wellness Letter,* June 1990, pp. 4–5. The meta-analysis was conducted by Joseph J. Martocchio and Anne M. O'Leary, "Sex Differences in Occupational Stress: A Meta-Analytic Review," *Journal of Applied Psychology,* June 1989, pp. 495–501.

[19] The link between stress and depression is discussed by Peter Freiberg, "Work and Well-Being: Experts Urge Changes in Work, Not the Work," *The APA Monitor,* January 1991, p. 23.

[20] See Hatfield, "Stress and the American Worker."

[21] Ibid.

[22] Resa W. King and Irene Pave, "Stress Claims Are Making Business Jumpy," *Business Week,* October 14, 1985, p. 152.

[23] This landmark study was conducted by Thomas H. Holmes and Richard H. Rahe, "The Social Readjustment Rating Scale," *Journal of Psychosomatic Research,* August 1967, pp. 213–18.

[24] Normative predictions are discussed in Orlando Behling and Arthur L. Darrow, "Managing Work-Related Stress," in *Modules in Management,* eds. James E. Rosenzweig and Fremont E. Kast (Chicago: Science Research Associates, 1984).

[25] This research is discussed by Giuseppe De Benedittis, Ariberto Lorenzetti, and Antonio Pieri, "The Role of Stressful Life Events in the Onset of Chronic Primary Headache," *Pain,* January 1990, pp. 65–75; and Rabi S. Bhagat, "Effects of Stressful Life Events on Individual Performance Effectiveness and Work Adjustment Processes within Organizational Settings: A Research Model," *Academy of Management Review,* October 1983, pp. 660–71.

[26] See Alex J. Zautra, John W. Reich, and Charles A. Guarnaccia, "Some Everyday Life Consequences of Disability and Bereavement for Older Adults," *Journal of Personality and Social Psychology,* September 1990, pp. 550–61; and Rabi S. Bhagat, Sara J. McQuaid, Hal Lindholm, and James Segovis, "Total Life Stress: A Multimethod Validation of the Construct and Its Effects on Organizationally Valued Outcomes and Withdrawal Behaviors," *Journal of Applied Psychology,* February 1985, pp. 202–14.

[27] The influence of perceived control over stressors on stress outcomes is thoroughly discussed by Peter P. Vitaliano, Deborah J. DeWolfe, Roland D. Maiuro, Joan Russo, and Wayne Katon, "Appraised Changeability of a Stressor as a Modifier of the Relationship between Coping and Depression: A Test of the Hypothesis of Fit," *Journal of Personality and Social Psychology,* September 1990, pp. 582–92; and Charles C. Benight and Angelo J. Kinicki, "Interaction of Type-A Behavior and Perceived Controllability of Stressors on Stress Outcomes," *Journal of Vocational Behavior,* August 1988, pp. 50–62.

[28] Results can be found in Anna-Maria Garden, "Burnout: The Effect of Psychological Type on Research Findings," *Journal of Occupational Psychology,* March 1989, pp. 223–34.

[29] Phase models of burnout are discussed by Robert T. Golembiewski, and R. F. Munzenrider, *The Phase Model of Burnout* (New York: Praeger, 1988); and Ronald J. Burke, "Toward a Phase Model of Burnout," *Group & Organization Studies,* March 1989, pp. 23–32.

[30] Robert Karen, "Beware of Career Burnout!" *Cosmopolitan,* May 1986, p. 120.

[31] Phases of burnout were examined by Robert T. Golembiewski, "A Note on Leiter's Study: Highlighting Two Models of Burnout," *Group & Organization Studies,* March 1989, pp. 5–13; and Michael P. Leiter, "Conceptual Implications of Two Models of Burnout," *Group & Organization Studies,* March 1989, pp. 15–22.

[32] See Adrian H. Taylor, Juri V. Daniel, Larry Leith, and Ron J. Burke, "Perceived Stress, Psychological Burnout and Paths to Turnover Intentions among Sport Officials," *Applied Sport Psychology,* March 1990, pp. 84–97; Kathleen Lahr Keller, "The Management of Stress and Prevention of Burnout in Emergency Nurses," *Journal of Emergency Nursing,* March/April 1990, pp. 90–95; and Christina Maslach

and Susan E. Jackson, "The Measurement of Experienced Burnout," *Journal of Occupational Behavior,* April 1981, pp. 99–113.

[33] These recommendations were derived from Donald P. Rogers, "Helping Employees Cope with Burnout," *Business,* October–December 1984, pp. 3–7.

[34] These examples and techniques are discussed by Lucia Landon, "Pump Up Your Employees," *HRMagazine,* May 1990, pp. 34–37.

[35] These costs are discussed in Janet Deming, "Drug-Free Workplace Is Good Business," *HRMagazine,* April 1990, pp. 61–62.

[36] See Steve Bergsman, "Addiction: Help Employees Who Help Themselves," *HRMagazine,* April 1990, pp. 46–49.

[37] See Steven K. Like, "Employee Drug Testing," *Small Business Reports,* December 1990, pp. 46–51; and "Labor Letter: A Special News Report on People and Their Jobs in Offices, Fields, and Factories," *The Wall Street Journal,* August 7, 1990, p. A1.

[38] The legal limitations of drug testing are thoroughly discussed by Arthur F. Silbergeld and Sarah Galvarro, "Private Sector Drug Testing: Legal Limitations in California," *Employee Relations,* Winter 1990/1991, pp. 347–58; and Like, "Employee Drug Testing."

[39] See Jim Castelli, "Addiction: Employer-Provided Programs Pay Off," *HRMagazine,* April 1990, pp. 55–58; and "Labor Letter: A Special News Report on People and Their Jobs in Offices, Fields, and Factories," *The Wall Street Journal,* December 12, 1990, p. A1.

[40] For a complete discussion of EAPs, see Dianne Kirrane, "EAPS: Dawning of a New Age," *HRMagazine,* January 1990, pp. 30–34; and Terry Blum and Paul M. Roman, "Employee Assistance Programs and Human Resource Management," in *Research in Personnel and Human Resources Management,* eds. Gerald R. Ferris and Kendrith M. Rowland (Greenwich, CT: JAI Press, 1989).

[41] Fred Luthans and Robert Waldersee, "What Do We Really Know about EAPs?" *Human Resource Management,* Fall 1989, pp. 386–87.

[42] See Kirrane, "EAPS: Dawning of New Age;" and Luthans and Waldersee, "What Do We Really Know about EAPs?" pp. 385–401.

[43] The status of support-groups is discussed by Charles Leerhsen, Shawn D. Lewis, Stephen Pomper, Lynn Davenport, and Margaret Nelson, "Unite and Conquer," *Newsweek,* February 5, 1990, pp. 50–55.

[44] Types of support are discussed by Sheldon Cohen and Thomas Ashby Wills, "Stress, Social Support, and the Buffering Hypothesis," *Psychological Bulletin,* September 1985, pp. 310–57.

[45] Supporting results can be found in Karen Robinson, "The Relationship between Social Skills, Social Support, Self-Esteem and Burden in Adult Caregivers," *Journal of Advanced Nursing,* July 1990, pp. 788–95; Thomas W. Kamarck, Stephen B. Manuck, and J. Richard Jennings, "Social Support Reduces Cardiovascular Reactivity to Psychological Challenge: A Laboratory Model," *Psychosomatic Medicine,* January/February 1990, pp. 42–58; and Terry A. Beehr, Lynda A. King, and Daniel W. King, "Social Support and Occupational Stress: Talking to Supervisors," *Journal of Vocational Behavior,* February 1990, pp. 61–81.

[46] For details, see Brenda Major, Catherine Cozzarelli, Anne Marie Sciacchitano, M. Lynne Cooper, Maria Testa, and Pallas M. Mueller, "Perceived Social Support, Self-Efficacy, and Adjustment to Abortion," *Journal of Personality and Social Psychology,* September 1990, pp. 452–63; and Carolyn E. Cutrona, "Objective Determinants of Perceived Social Support," *Journal of Personality and Social Psychology,* February 1986, pp. 349–55.

[47] Gender differences in social support were examined by Marcelline R. Fusilier, Daniel C. Ganster, and Bronston T. Mayes, "The Social Support and Health Relationship: Is There a Gender Difference?" *Journal of Occupational Psychology,* June 1986, pp. 145–53; and Christine Dunkel-Schetter, Susan Folkman, and Richard S. Lazarus, "Correlates of Social Support Receipt," *Journal of Personality and Social Psychology,* July 1987, pp. 71–80.

[48] Richard S. Lazarus and Susan Folkman, "Coping and Adaptation," in *Handbook of Behavioral Medicine,* ed. W. Doyle Gentry (New York: The Guilford Press, 1984), p. 283.

[49] See results and discussion in Robert Cummins, "Locus of Control and Social Support: Clarifiers of the Relationship between Job Stress and Job Satisfaction," *Journal of Applied Social Psychology,* June 1989, pp. 772–88; and T. J. Newton, "Occupational Stress and Coping with Stress: A Critique," *Human Relations,* May 1989, pp. 441–61.

[50] Lazarus and Folkman, "Coping and Adaptation," p. 289.

[51] Descriptions of coping strategies are provided by Janina C. Latack, "Coping with Job Stress: Measures and Future Directions for Scale Development," *Journal of Applied Psychology,* August 1986, pp. 377–85.

[52] Relevant results can be found in Thomas L. Patterson, Lawrence W. Smith, Igor Grant, Paul Clopton, Sharon Josepho, and Joel Yager, "Internal vs. External Determinants of Coping Responses to Stressful Life-Events in the Elderly," *British Journal of Medical Psychology,* June 1990, pp. 149–60; and Janice Robinson and Donna J. Lewis, "Coping with ICU Work-Related Stressors: A Study," *Critical Care Nurse,* May 1990, pp. 80–88.

[53] See Debra L. Nelson and Charlotte Sutton, "Chronic Work Stress and Coping: A Longitudinal Study and Suggested New Directions," *Academy of Management Journal,* December 1990, pp. 859–969; and Angelo J. Kinicki and Janina C. Latack, "Explication of the Construct of Coping with Involuntary Job Loss," *Journal of Vocational Behavior,* June 1990, pp. 339–60.

[54] This pioneering research is presented in Suzanne C. Kobasa, "Stressful Life Events, Personality, and Health: An Inquiry into Hardiness," *Journal of Personality and Social Psychology,* January 1979, pp. 1–11.

[55] See Suzanne C. Kobasa, Salvatore R. Maddi, and Stephen Kahn, "Hardiness and Health: A Prospective Study," *Journal of Personality and Social Psychology,* January 1982, pp. 168–77.

[56] Results are contained in Margaret Topf, "Personality Hardiness, Occupational Stress, and Burnout in Critical Care Nurses," *Research in Nursing & Health,* June 1989, pp. 179–86; Frederick Rhodewalt and Sjofn Agustsdottir, "On the Relationship of Hardiness to the Type-A Behavior Pattern: Perception of Life Events versus Coping with Life Events," *Journal of Research in Personality,* June 1984, pp. 212–23. A review of research on hardiness is provided by Jay G. Hull, Ronald R. Van Treuren, and Suzanne Virnelli, "Hardiness and Health: A Critique and Alternative Approach," *Journal of Personality and Social Psychology,* September 1987, pp. 518–30.

[57] "The Stokowski Advantage," *University of California, Berkeley Wellness Letter,* January 1985, p. 1.

[58] O'Boyle, "Fear and Stress in the Office Take Toll," p. B11.

[59] See Herbert Benson, *The Relaxation Response* (New York: William Morrow and Co., 1975).

[60] This research is summarized by John M. Ivancevich, Michael T. Matteson, Sara M. Freedman, and James S. Phillips, "Worksite Stress Management Interventions," *American Psychologist,* February 1990, pp. 252–61.

[61] Criticisms of stress-reduction programs are summarized by Daniel C. Ganster, Bronston T. Mayes, Wesley E. Sime, and Gerald D. Tharp, "Managing Organizational Stress: A Field Experiment," *Journal of Applied Psychology*, October 1982, pp. 533–42.

[62] Robert Kreitner, "Personal Wellness: It's Just Good Business," *Business Horizons*, May–June 1982, p. 28.

[63] Results are presented in "The 18-Year Gap," *University of California, Berkeley Wellness Letter*, January 1991, p. 2.

[64] A thorough review of this research is provided by Deborah L. Gebhardt and Carolyn E. Crump, "Employee Fitness and Wellness Programs in the Workplace," *American Psychologist*, February 1990, pp. 262–72.

[65] Adapted from Maslach and Jackson, "The Measurement of Experienced Burnout."

UNDERSTANDING AND MANAGING THE EVOLVING ORGANIZATION

CHAPTER

17

Organizations: Structure and Effectiveness

LEARNING OBJECTIVES

When you finish studying the material in this chapter, you should be able to:

- Describe the four characteristics common to all organizations.
- Distinguish between line and staff positions.
- Explain the difference between closed and open systems.

- Contrast the following organizational metaphors: military/mechanical, biological, and cognitive systems.
- Identify Lawler's substitutes for hierarchy and explain their significance for managing today's flatter organizations.

- Describe the four generic organizational effectiveness criteria.
- Explain why a multidimensional approach to organizational effectiveness is recommended.

OPENING CASE 17

This General Electric Elephant Can Dance!

Sharon Hoogstraten

Says William Sheeran, a GE general manager: "We had to speed up or die." GE's $1-billion-a-year electrical distribution and control division in Plainville, Connecticut, makes, among other things, circuit breaker boxes for commercial buildings. When threatened in the early 1980s by the market's slow growth and tough competitors like Siemens and Westinghouse, GE assembled a team of manufacturing, design, and marketing experts that focused on overhauling its manufacturing process. The goal, suitably daunting, was to cut the time between a customer's order and delivery from three weeks to three days.

Time for radical thinking. GE was producing circuit breaker boxes in six plants around the United States. Who needs six? The team decided that one plant would be more efficient, so in 1985 it consolidated its operations and focused on automating its factory in Salisbury, North Carolina.

But the team didn't want to automate operations as they were. In the old system, engineers custom-designed each box, a job

that took about a week. They chose from 28,000 unique parts to create the boxes, and setting up an automated system to handle that many parts would have been a nightmare. So the design team made most of the parts interchangeable, reducing their number to 1,275 while still leaving customers a choice of 40,000 different sizes, shapes, and configurations of boxes.

The team also devised a way to cut out the engineers, replacing them with a computer. Now when a salesman enters specifications for a circuit breaker into a computer at GE's main office in Connecticut, the order flows to a computer at Salisbury, which automatically programs the factory machines to make circuit breaker boxes with minimum waste of material.

Impressive advances, but the team still had to conquer another source of delay: solving problems and making decisions on the factory floor. The solution was to get rid of all line supervisors and quality inspectors, reducing the organizational layers between worker and plant manager from three to one. Everything those middle managers used to handle—vacation scheduling, quality, work rules—became the responsibility of the 129 workers on the floor, who are divided into teams of 15 to 20. And what do you know: The more responsibility GE gave the workers, the faster problems got solved and decisions made.

Today the Salisbury plant basically runs itself at a rapid clip. On the factory wall a giant electronic sign hung 25 feet off the ground flashes in red letters, letting work-

ers know how long it's taking them to make each circuit breaker box, how many boxes they have to make that day, and how many they've made so far. The sign lets employees pace themselves and make their own scheduling decisions. Says Dottie Barringer, an ebullient woman who has worked at the plant for the past 12½ years: "I like to be my own boss. I don't like to be told what to do. I know if I can't get it done in eight hours, I can do it in ten without getting permission for overtime. We're behind right now. No one has to tell us we have to work Saturday."

Results: The plant, which used to have a two-month backlog of orders, now works with a two-*day* backlog. Productivity has increased 20% over the past year. Manufacturing costs have dropped 30%, or $5.5 million a year, and return on investment is running at over 20%. The speed of delivery has shrunk from three weeks to three days for a higher-quality product with more features. GE is gaining share in a flat market. Says Sheeran: "We'd be out of business if we hadn't done it."

For Discussion

What is the key to G.E.'s success in this case?

• Additional discussion questions linking this case with the following material appear at the end of this chapter.

V irtually every aspect of life is affected at least indirectly by some type of organization. We look to organizations to feed, clothe, house, educate, and employ us. Organizations attend to our needs for entertainment, police and fire protection, insurance, recreation, national security, transportation, news and information, legal assistance, and health care. Many of these organizations seek a profit, others do not. Some are extremely large, others are tiny "mom-and-pop" operations. Despite this mind-boggling diversity, modern organizations have one basic thing in common. They are the primary context for *organizational* behavior. In a manner of speaking, organizations are the chessboard upon which the game of organizational behavior is played. Therefore, present and future managers need a working knowledge of modern organizations to improve their chances of making the right moves when managing people at work.

This chapter explores the structure and effectiveness of modern organizations. We begin by defining the term *organization,* discussing important dimensions of organization charts, and analyzing fundamental models of organization. Next, a way of dealing with the recent wave of corporate reorganizations is examined. We conclude this chapter with criteria for assessing the effectiveness of organizations.

• DEFINING AND CHARTING ORGANIZATIONS

As a necessary springboard for this chapter, we need to formally define the term *organization* and clarify the meaning of organization charts.

What Is an Organization?

According to Chester I. Barnard's classic definition, an **organization** is "a system of consciously coordinated activities or forces of two or more persons."[1] Embodied in the *conscious coordination* aspect of this definition are four common denominators of all organizations: coordination of effort, a common goal, division of labor, and a hierarchy of authority[2] (see Figure 17–1). Organization theorists refer to these factors as the organization's *structure*.

Coordination of effort is achieved through formulation and enforcement of policies, rules, and regulations. Division of labor occurs when the common goal is pursued by individuals performing separate but related tasks. The hierarchy of authority, also called the chain of command, is a control mechanism dedicated to making sure the right people do the right things at the right time. Historically, managers have maintained the integrity of the hierarchy of authority by adhering to the unity of command principle. The **unity of command principle** specifies that each employee should report to only one manager. Otherwise, the argument goes, inefficiency would prevail because of conflicting orders and lack of personal accountability. Managers in the hierarchy of authority also administer rewards and punishments. When the four factors in Figure 17–1 operate in concert, the dynamic entity called an organization exists.

• **FIGURE 17-1** Four Characteristics Common to All Organizations

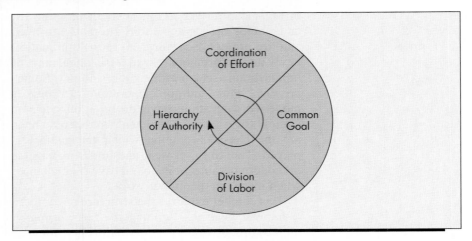

• **FIGURE 17-2** Sample Organization Chart for a Hospital (Executive and director levels only)

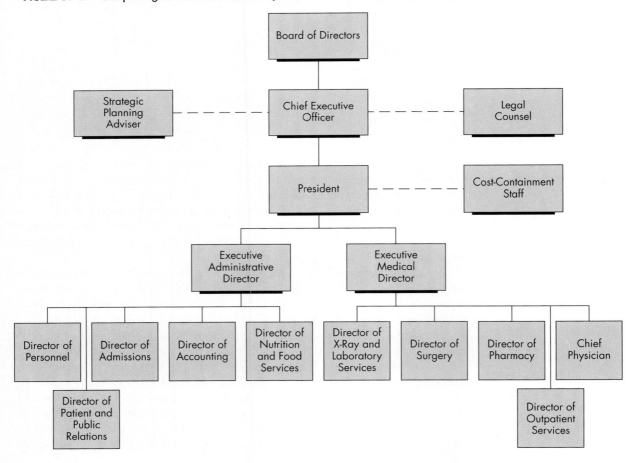

Organization Charts

An **organization chart** is a graphic representation of formal authority and division of labor relationships. To the casual observer, the term *organization chart* means the family tree-like pattern of boxes and lines posted on work place walls. Within each box one usually finds the names and titles of current position holders. To organization theorists, however, organization charts reveal much more. The partial organization chart in Figure 17–2 reveals four basic dimensions of organizationl structure: (1) hierarchy of authority (who reports to whom), (2) division of labor, (3) spans of control, and (4) line and staff positions.

Hierarchy of Authority   As Figure 17–2 illustrates, there is an unmistakable hierarchy of authority.[3] Working from bottom to top, the ten directors report to the two executive directors who report to the president who reports to the chief executive officer. Ultimately, the chief executive officer answers to the hospital's board of directors. The chart in Figure 17–2 shows strict unity of command up and down the line. A formal hierarchy of authority also delineates the official communication network.

Division of Labor   In addition to showing the chain of command, the sample organization chart indicates extensive division of labor. Immediately below the hospital's president, one executive director is responsible for general administration while another is responsible for medical affairs. Each of these two specialties is further subdivided as indicated by the next layer of positions. At each successively lower level in the organization, jobs become more specialized.

Spans of Control   The **span of control** refers to the number of people reporting directly to a given manager.[4] Spans of control can range from narrow to wide. For example, the president in Figure 17–2 has a narrow span of control of two. (Staff assistants usually are not included in a manager's span of control.) The executive administrative director in Figure 17–2 has a wider span of control of five. Spans of control exceeding 30 can be found in assembly-line operations where machine-paced and repetitive work substitutes for close supervision. Historically, spans of five to six were considered best. Despite years of debate, organization theorists have not arrived at a consensus regarding the ideal span of control.

Generally, the narrower the span of control, the closer the supervision and the higher the administrative costs due to a higher manager-to-worker ratio. Recent emphasis on leanness and administrative efficiency dictates spans of control as wide as possible but guarding against inadequate supervision and lack of coordination. Wider spans also complement the trend toward greater worker autonomy.

Line and Staff Positions   The organization chart in Figure 17–2 also distinguishes between line and staff positions. Line managers such as the president, the two executive directors, and the various directors occupy formal decision-making positions within the chain of command. Line positions generally are connected by solid lines on organization charts. Dotted lines indicate staff relationships. **Staff personnel** do background research and provide technical advice and recommendations to their **line managers** who have the authority to make decisions. For example, the cost-containment specialists in the sample organization chart merely advise the president on relevant matters. Apart from supervising the work of their own staff assistants, they have no line authority over other organizational members.

According to a recent study of 207 police officers in Israel, line personnel exhibited greater job commitment than did their staff counterparts.[5] This result was anticipated because the line managers' decision-making authority empowered them and gave them comparatively more control over their work situations.

• THE EVOLUTION OF ORGANIZATIONAL METAPHORS

The complexity of modern organizations makes them somewhat difficult to describe. Consequently, organization theorists have resorted to the use of metaphors. A metaphor is a figure of speech that characterizes one object in terms of another object. Good metaphors help us comprehend complicated things by describing them in everyday terms. For example, consider the following metaphor that envisions the modern organization as an orchestra:

> The system can be thought of as a large modern orchestra with a number of professionals playing quite different instruments and performing separate—and often very difficult—tasks. Each instrumentalist, like so many in large organizations, is indeed a specialist in a particular field whose work must be integrated with the work of others to make up the whole.
>
> The manager's job is more than what the concert-goer sees. It includes planning the performance, helping to select those numbers that the orchestra can best perform, presiding at rehearsals, and doing many of the things that are required to make the final concert notable. The manager's contribution is much more than being the one with the baton, and what the audience sees should be understood in that context.[6]

• FIGURE 17-3   Three Contrasting Organizational Metaphors

	Closed Systems	**Open Systems**	
	Military/Mechanical Model (bureaucracy)	**Biological Model (resource transformation system)**	**Cognitive Model (interpretation and meaning system)**
Metaphorical comparison:	Precision military unit/ well-oiled machine	Human body	Human mind
Assumption about organization's environment:	Predictable (controllable impacts)	Uncertain (filled with surprises)	Uncertain and ambiguous
Organization's primary goal:	Maximum economic efficiency through rigorous planning and control	Survival through adaptation to environmental constraints and opportunities	Growth and survival through environmental scanning, interpretation, and learning

OB scholar Kim Cameron sums up the value of organizational metaphors as follows: "Each time a new metaphor is used, certain aspects of organizational phenomena are uncovered that were not evident with other metaphors. In fact, the usefulness of metaphors lies in their possession of some degree of falsehood so that new images and associations emerge."[7] With the orchestra metaphor, for instance, one could come away with an exaggerated picture of harmony in large and complex organizations. On the other hand, it realistically encourages us to view managers as facilitators rather than absolute dictators.

Three organizational metaphors that have evolved over the years characterize organizations alternatively as military/mechanical systems, biological systems, and cognitive systems. These three metaphors can be plotted on a continuum ranging from simple closed systems to complex open systems (see Figure 17–3). We need to clarify the important distinction between closed and open systems before exploring the metaphors.

Closed versus Open Systems

A **closed system** is said to be a self-sufficient entity. It is "closed" to the surrounding environment. In contrast, an **open system** depends on constant interaction with the environment for survival. The distinction between closed and open systems is a matter of degree. Since every worldly system is partly closed and partly open, the key question is: How great a role does the environment play in the functioning of the system? For instance, a battery-powered clock is a relatively closed system. Once the battery is inserted, the clock performs its time-keeping function hour after hour until the battery goes dead. The human body, on the other hand, is a highly open system because it requires a constant supply of life-sustaining oxygen from the environment. Nutrients also are imported from the environment. Open systems are capable of self-correction, adaptation, and growth thanks to characteristics such as homeostasis and feedback control.

The traditional military/mechanical metaphor is a closed system model because it largely ignores environmental influences. It gives the impression that organizations are self-sufficient entities. Conversely, the biological and cognitive metaphors emphasize interaction between organizations and their environments. These newer models are based on open-system assumptions. A closer look at the three organizational metaphors reveals instructive insights about organizations and how they work. Each perspective offers something useful.

Organizations as Military/Mechanical Bureaucracies

A major by-product of the Industrial Revolution was the factory system of production. People left their farms and cottage industries to operate steam-powered machines in centralized factories. The social unit of production evolved from the family to formally managed organizations encompassing hundreds or even thousands of people. Managers sought to maximize the economic efficiency of large factories and offices by structuring them according to military principles. At the turn of the century, German sociologist, Max Weber, formulated what he termed the most rationally efficient form of organization. He patterned his ideal organization after the vaunted Prussian army and called it **bureaucracy.**

Weber's Bureaucracy   According to Weber's theory, the following four factors should make bureaucracies the epitome of efficiency:

1. Division of labor (people become proficient when they perform standardized tasks over and over again).
2. A hierarchy of authority (a formal chain of command ensures coordination and accountability).
3. A framework of rules (carefully formulated and strictly enforced rules ensure predictable behavior).
4. Administrative impersonality (personnel decisions such as hiring and promoting should be based on competence, not favoritism).[8]

How the Term *Bureaucracy* Became a Synonym for Inefficiency   All organizations possess varying degrees of these characteristics. Thus, every organization is a bureaucracy to some extent. In terms of the ideal metaphor, a bureaucracy should run like a well-oiled machine, and its members should perform with the precision of a polished military unit. But problems arise when bureaucratic characteristics become extreme or dysfunctional. For example, as explained in A Matter of Ethics, extreme expressions of specialization, rule following, and impersonality can cause a bureaucrat to treat a client as a number rather than as a person.[9]

Weber probably would be surprised and dismayed that his model of rational efficiency has become a synonym for inefficiency. Today, bureau-

A MATTER OF ETHICS

Dysfunctional Bureaucracy Can Make Employees Insensitive

The bureaucrat . . . is restricted to those actions that his work rules permit him and that fall within the scope of his jurisdiction. He, as bureaucrat, is not allowed to tune in to the subjective meanings and needs that a client of the bureaucracy is trying to convey; he must tune in only to those meanings and needs that have officially recognizable standing. For example, a welfare investigator is not officially permitted to take cognizance of the psychological stress that a mother on welfare experiences because welfare rules forbid her husband to live with her. Or a consumer advocate in a consumer protection agency cannot consider the intensity of poverty or the severity of psychic agony of a client who wishes to file a complaint but fails to produce the necessary sales receipt.

Source: Ralph P. Hummel, *The Bureaucratic Experience* (New York: St. Martin's Press, 1977), pp. 4–5.

cracy stands for being put on hold, waiting in long lines, and getting shuffled from one office to the next. This irony can be explained largely by the fact that organizations with excessive or dysfunctional bureaucratic tendencies become rigid, inflexible, and resistant to environmental demands and influences.

Organizations as Biological Systems

Drawing upon the field of general systems theory that emerged during the 1950s,[10] organization theorists suggested a more dynamic model for modern organizations. As noted in Figure 17–3, this metaphor likens organizations to the human body. Hence, it has been labeled the *biological model*. In his often-cited organization theory text, *Organizations in Action,* James D. Thompson explained the biological model of organizations in the following terms:

> Approached as a natural system, the complex organization is a set of interdependent parts which together make up a whole because each contributes something and receives something from the whole, which in turn is interdependent with some larger environment. Survival of the system is taken to be the goal, and the parts and their relationships presumably are determined through evolutionary processes. . . .
> Central to the natural-system approach is the concept of homeostasis, or self-stabilization, which spontaneously, or naturally, governs the necessary relationships among parts and activities and thereby keeps the system viable in the face of disturbances stemming from the environment.[11]

Unlike the traditional military/mechanical theorists who downplayed the environment, advocates of the biological model stress organization-environment interaction. As Figure 17–4 illustrates, the biological model characterizes the organization as an open system that transforms inputs into various outputs. The outer boundary of the organization is permeable. People, information, capital, and goods and services move back and forth across this boundary. Moreover, each of the five organizational subsystems—goals and values, technical, psychosocial, structural, and managerial—is dependent on the others. Feedback about such things as sales and customer satisfaction or dissatisfaction enables the organization to self-adjust and survive despite uncertainty and change. In effect, the organization is alive.

Organizations as Cognitive Systems

A more recent metaphor characterizes organizations in terms of mental functions. According to respected organization theorists Richard Daft and Karl Weick:

> This perspective represents a move away from mechanical and biological metaphors of organizations. Organizations are more than transformation processes or control systems. To survive, organizations must have mechanisms to interpret ambiguous events and to provide meaning and direction for participants. Organizations are meaning systems, and this distinguishes them from lower-level systems. . . .

PART V • UNDERSTANDING AND MANAGING THE EVOLVING ORGANIZATION

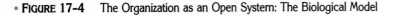

• **FIGURE 17–4**   The Organization as an Open System: The Biological Model

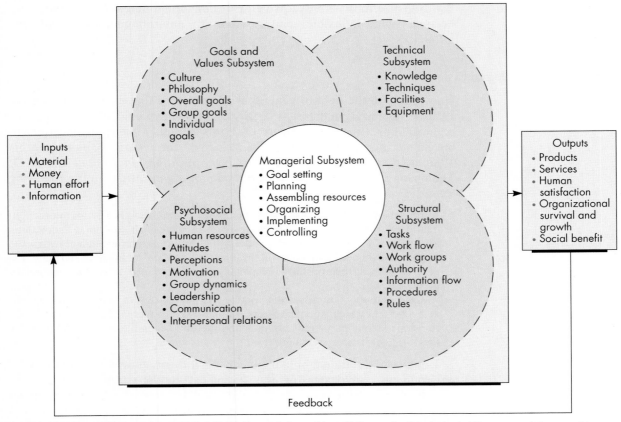

Source: This model is a combination of Figures 5–2 and 5–3 in Fremont E. Kast and James E. Rosenzweig, *Organization and Management: A Systems and Contingency Approach*, 4th ed. (New York: McGraw-Hill, 1986), pp. 112, 114. Used with permission.

> Almost all outcomes in terms of organization structure and design, whether caused by the environment, technology, or size, depend on the interpretation of problems or opportunities by key decision makers. Once interpretation occurs, the organization can formulate a response.[12]

This interpretation process, carried out at the top-management or strategic level, leads to organizational *learning* and adaptation.

U.S. tobacco companies exemplify how organizational strategists adapt to an uncertain and ambiguous environment. The cognitive processes of scanning, interpreting, and learning have led narrowly focused tobacco companies to diversify in recent years. Philip Morris's acquisition of General Foods Corp. in 1985 made sense in light of the following environmental realities:

> The business has weathered past years of bad news, from Surgeon General's reports to tax hikes. But the forces that turned tobacco into a dirty word are accelerating more and more as social, legal, and financial storm clouds gather over the industry. . . . For the survivors, cost-cutting, international expansion, and diversification are the new battle cries.[13]

Each of the five organizational subsystems at Philip Morris has changed significantly as a direct result of the company's diversification strategy.

In sum, the flow of events in the cognitive model is: environmental ambiguity → interpretation → strategy → structure → organizational performance. This sequence is expanded on in Chapter 18 under the heading of strategic choice.

Organizational Metaphors in Perspective

In newly industrialized nations with poorly educated workers, the military/mechanical approach was widely applicable. Narrowly defined jobs, military-like discipline, and strict chains of command enabled factory and office managers to control their employees and meet production quotas. As things grew more complex, however, the military/mechanical model was found lacking. Thanks to modern open-system thinking, we now see organizations as more than internally focused control mechanisms.

A useful model of modern organizations emerges when we integrate the biological and cognitive metaphors. Conceptually, the organization's *body* and *head* need to be connected. One cannot function without the other. Managers of today's productive organizations are responsible for transforming factors of production into needed goods and services (the body). Yet they can remain competitive only if they wisely *interpret* environmental opportunities and obstacles (the head). By combining the biological and cognitive models, we gain a realistic organizational context for theory and practice (see International OB).

• THE RADICAL RESHAPING OF TODAY'S ORGANIZATIONS

American businesses launched a reorganization revolution during the 1980s that continues today. Hundreds of thousands of employees were laid off, 250,000 from General Motors, Ford, and Chrysler alone.[14] Even well-paid and supposedly secure middle managers and executives in their forties and fifties found themselves looking for employment, as whole layers of organizations were eliminated. According to one estimate, 25 percent of America's middle-management jobs were eliminated during the 1980s.[15] Putting things in perspective, the reorganization revolution is nothing less than a frontal assault on the once-unquestioned notion of *hierarchy*. The so-called chain of command concept, discussed earlier as an element common to all organizations, will never be the same.

Whether carried out in the name of downsizing, delayering, retrenching, cost-cutting, restructuring, or competitiveness, the desired result is the same—flatter, more decentralized, less costly, and more responsive organizations. Indeed, many of today's larger businesses have even fewer layers of management than they had a decade ago. Motorola, for example, compressed seven layers of management at its portable-telephone factory in Schaumburg, Illinois, to four.[16] General Electric cut even deeper by reducing ten layers of management to four.[17] These leaner organizations also rely more extensively on cross-functional teamwork and have pushed decision making down to where output is actually created. Unfortunately, too many reorganizations have been haphazard and of questionable impact. Let us briefly examine this significant turn of events and explore a promising way of making today's flatter organizations work. Importantly, this approach is a

INTERNATIONAL OB

General Electric Needs to Be "Boundaryless" to Succeed in a Global Economy

John F. (Jack) Welch, Jr., Chief Executive Officer, General Electric Corp.:
Globalization is now no longer an objective but an imperative, as markets open and geographic barriers become increasingly blurred and even irrelevant. . . .

Simply doing more of what worked in the Eighties—the restructuring, the delayering, the mechanical, top-down measures that we took—will be too incremental. More than that, it will be too slow. The winners of the Nineties will be those who can develop a culture that allows them to move faster, communicate more clearly, and involve everyone in a focused effort to serve ever more demanding customers.

To move toward that winning culture we've got to create what we call a "boundaryless" company. We no longer have the time to climb over barriers between functions like engineering and marketing, or between people—hourly, salaried, management, and the like. Geographic barriers must evaporate. Our people must be as comfortable in Delhi and Seoul as they are in Louisville or Schenectady. The lines between the company and its vendors and customers must be blurred into a smooth, fluid process with no other objective than satisfying the customer and winning in the marketplace.

If we are to get the reflexes and speed we need, we've got to simplify and delegate more—simply trust more. We need to drive self-confidence deep into the organization. A company can't distribute self-confidence, but it can foster it by removing layers and giving people a chance to win. We have to undo a 100-year-old concept and convince our managers that their role is not to control people and stay "on top" of things, but rather to guide, energize, and excite.

Source: Excerpted from John F. Welch, Jr., "We've Got To Simplify and Delegate More," *Fortune*, March 26, 1990, p. 30. © 1990 The Time Inc. Magazine Company. All rights reserved.

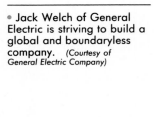

• Jack Welch of General Electric is striving to build a global and boundaryless company. *(Courtesy of General Electric Company)*

structural prerequisite for the implementation of self-managed teams (recall our discussion in Chapter 11).

How Necessary Is Hierarchy?

According to the traditional chain-of-command concept, adapted from the military, supervisors are needed to assign, monitor, motivate, and control the work of subordinates. But workers and work places have changed. Knowledge workers are better educated and hungry for responsibility. Tasks are more complex. Pressures of global competition require costs to be shaved closer than ever. And the virtue of few organizational layers has been linked with greater profitability. For example, Ford Motor Company has 17 layers of management between the chief executive and the factory floor. General Motors (GM) has 22 layers in some plants. During the 1980s, Ford captured an additional 2 percent share of the U.S. car market while GM lost a stunning 11 percent share. Interestingly, Toyota thrives with 7

• **TABLE 17-1**   Organizational Hierarchies: Pro and Con

Pro	Con
Elliot Jaques: At first glance, hierarchy may seem difficult to praise. Bureaucracy is a dirty word even among bureaucrats, and in business there is a widespread view that managerial hierarchy kills initiative, crushes creativity, and has therefore seen its day. Yet 35 years of research have convinced me that managerial hierarchy is the most efficient, the hardiest, and in fact the most natural structure ever devised for large organizations. Properly structured, hierarchy can release energy and creativity, rationalize productivity, and actually improve morale. Moreover, I think most managers know this intuitively and have only lacked a workable structure and a decent intellectual justification for what they have always known could work and work well. . . . The hierarchical kind of organization we call bureaucracy did not emerge accidentally. It is the only form of organization that can enable a company to employ large numbers of people and yet preserve unambiguous accountability for the work they do. And that is why, despite its problems, it has so doggedly persisted.	**Edward E. Lawler III:** The terms *hierarchy* and *organization* have become virtually inseparable. Most people cannot even imagine what an organization would look like without layers of management and support staff to provide counsel and, at times, direction to that hierarchy. Few, if any, business organizations in the United States lack a substantial amount of hierarchy. However, the idea of extensive and expensive hierarchies is currently under attack as never before, particularly in organizations that face intense cost competition. More and more organizations are concluding that they simply cannot afford the salary and other costs of maintaining an extensive hierarchy. . . . In a real sense, all members of the organizational hierarchy above the people who produce the organization's products or services produce nothing of value. Their only purpose is facilitating the performance of those involved in making the organization's products or delivering the organization's services. Thus they constitute an overhead expense whether they are in line or staff positions. They are worth having only if they add significant value to what is done by the people who actually produce the organization's products or services. . . . Without a thorough redesign of the organization, however, it is unlikely that a significant part of the hierarchy can be made unnecessary. Hierarchies perform some very important organizational functions that must be done in some way if coordinated, organized behavior is to take place. On the other hand, if an organization design is adopted that includes work teams, new reward systems, extensive training, and . . . various other practices . . . , organizations can operate effectively with substantially less hierarchy.

Sources: Exerpted from Elliot Jaques, "In Praise of Hierarchy," *Harvard Business Review*, January–February 1990, p. 127; and Edward E. Lawler III, "Substitutes for Hierarchy," *Organizational Dynamics*, Summer 1988, pp. 5–6, 15. Reprinted by permission of publisher. © 1988, American Management Association, New York. All rights reserved.

layers of management and Federal Express does very well with only five.[18] Consequently, management's reliance on hierarchical control is subject to debate (see Table 17–1). Both experts quoted in Table 17–1 agree that hierarchy is a necessary feature of organizations. However, Lawler's side of the argument assumes less is better. In other words, the best management may be self-management. His contingency model deserves a closer look because it is a needed tool for getting the most out of organizations with fewer layers of management.

Substitutes for Hierarchy: A Contingency Approach

Lawler's contingency model of substitutes for hierarchy is portrayed in Table 17–2. He believes the 12 supervisory functions in the left-hand column are vital and need to be performed. However, thanks to various combinations of the eight **substitutes for hierarchy** (work design, information systems technology, and so on), the need for direct supervisory control can be reduced or perhaps eliminated. For instance, the *X* in the upper-left corner indicates the motivational power of work that provides variety and challenge to the jobholder. Notice that there is *no perfect substitute for hierarchy* capable of handling all 12 supervisory functions (work design comes the closest). Brief descriptions of each substitute for hierarchy follow (with relevant chapter cross-references):

- *Work design*—Jobs are enriched to include greater variety, challenge, autonomy, and personal responsibility for results (Chap. 5).
- *Information systems technology*—This includes networked personal computers. Free access to vital information empowers employees.

• **TABLE 17-2** Substitutes for Hierarchy: Lawler's Contingency Model

Supervisory Functions	Work Design	Information Systems Technology	Financial Data	Reward System Practices	Supplier/Customer Contact	Training	Vision/Values	Emergent Leadership
Motivating	X		X	X	X	X	X	
Recordkeeping	X	X						
Coordinating	X	X	X	X	X	X	X	X
Assigning work	X							X
Making personnel decisions	X						X	X
Providing expertise		X				X		X
Setting goals	X	X	X	X	X	X	X	
Planning	X	X	X					
Linking communications	X	X	X	X			X	
Training/ Coaching	X	X		X				X
Leading	X							X
Controlling		X	X	X				

Source: Edward E. Lawler III, "Substitutes for Hierarchy," *Organizational Dynamics*, Summer 1988, p. 12.

- *Financial data*—Cost, sales, and profitability data are shared with all employees as a form of feedback (Chap. 13).
- *Reward system practices*—Skill-based pay, gainsharing, and profit sharing are powerful motivational tools (Chap. 13).
- *Supplier/Customer contact*—Direct contact with internal and external customers provides valuable feedback on performance (Chap. 13).
- *Training*—Employees can learn how to handle supervisory functions (Chaps. 7, 8, and 11).
- *Vision/Values*—Central values in the organizational culture need to emphasize personal responsibility for results (Chaps. 14 and 19).
- *Emergent leadership*—Leadership potential among nonmanagerial employees can be identified and cultivated (Chaps. 7 and 14).

Lawler emphasizes the need to rely on the substitutes for hierarchy in a situationally appropriate manner. He notes: "Technology, work interdependence, work complexity, and required knowledge clearly influence the opportunities for adopting an organizational approach that is based on minimal hierarchy and high involvement."[19] But employees must want to take greater control of their organizational lives. If they do, and the effectiveness criteria discussed next are met, today's compressed hierarchies can be both productive and satisfying.

• ASSESSING ORGANIZATIONAL EFFECTIVENESS

How effective are you? If someone asked you this apparently simple question, you would likely ask for clarification before answering. For instance, you might want to know if they were referring to your grade point average, annual income, actual accomplishments, ability to get along with others, public service, or perhaps something else entirely. So it is with modern organizations. Effectiveness criteria abound. For example, in its annual Most Admired Corporations survey, *Fortune* magazine applies the following eight effectiveness criteria:

- quality of management
- quality of products/services
- innovativeness
- long-term investment value
- financial soundness
- ability to attract, develop, and keep talented people
- community/environmental responsibility
- use of corporate assets[20]

Merck, the New Jersey–based pharmaceutical company, has dominated the top spot on *Fortune*'s Most Admired list in recent years because it does a lot of things well. But perceived organizational effectiveness can be a fleeting thing in an era of rapid-fire change. For example, Exxon plunged from the no. 6 spot on *Fortune*'s Most Admired list in 1989 to no. 110 in 1990 after the *Exxon Valdez* oil tanker spill in Alaska.[21]

Assessing organizational effectiveness is an important topic for an array of people, including managers, stockholders, government agencies, and OB specialists. The purpose of this final section is to introduce a widely applicable and useful model of organizational effectiveness.

Generic Organizational–Effectiveness Criteria

A good way to better understand this complex subject is to consider four generic approaches to assessing an organization's effectiveness (see Figure 17–5). These effectiveness criteria apply equally well to large or small and profit or not-for-profit organizations. Moreover, as denoted by the overlapping circles in Figure 17–5, the four effectiveness criteria can be used in various combinations. The key thing to remember is ''no single approach to the evaluation of effectiveness is appropriate in all circumstances or for all organization types.''[22] What do Merck and Exxon, for example, have in

• **FIGURE 17-5**   Four Ways to Assess Organizational Effectiveness

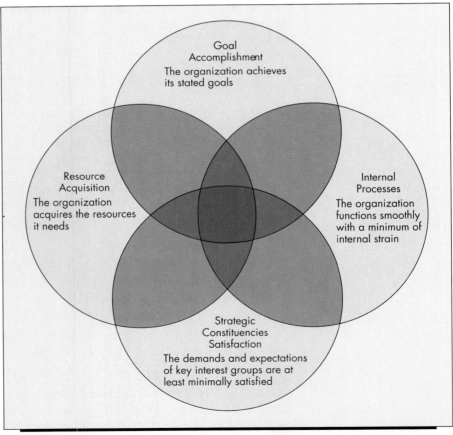

Source: Adapted from discussion in Kim Cameron, "Critical Questions in Assessing Organizational Effectiveness," *Organizational Dynamics*, Autumn 1980, pp. 66–80; and Kim S. Cameron, "Effectiveness as Paradox: Consensus and Conflict in Conceptions of Organizational Effectiveness," *Management Science*, May 1986, pp. 539–53.

common, other than being large profit-seeking corporations? Because a multidimensional approach is required, we need to look more closely at each of the four generic effectiveness criteria.

Goal Accomplishment   Goal accomplishment is the most widely used effectiveness criterion for organizations. Key organizational results or outputs are compared with previously stated goals or objectives. Deviations, either plus or minus, require corrective action. This is simply an organizational variation of the personal goal-setting process discussed in Chapter 6. Pacific Gas and Electric Company, a Northern California utility, for example, tracks its overall performance in terms of goal accomplishment:

> Out of every 10,000 hours of [service] that PGandE provides its four million customers, it is 99.96 percent reliable in terms of outages. It attempts to reach a goal of no more than 180 minutes of outage per year per customer, and in 1989 it considerably improved on this goal. In the wake of the October 17, 1989, San Francisco earthquake, the company achieved a recovery of its gas and electric system that won the praise of the community, municipal officials, and the Department of Energy.[23]

Productivity improvement, involving the relationship between inputs and outputs, is a common organization-level goal.[24] Goals also may be set for intangible organizational efforts such as minority recruiting, pollution prevention, and quality control. Given today's competitive pressures, *innovation* is a very important organizational goal worthy of measurement and monitoring (see OB in Action). Effectiveness, relative to the criterion of goal accomplishment, is gauged by how well the organization meets or exceeds its goals.

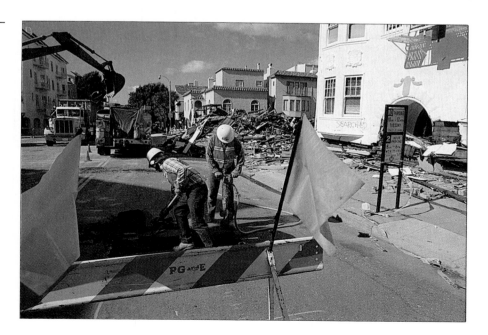

• These Pacific Gas and Electric workers were committed to working around the clock to achieve the goal of repairing the damage caused by the San Francisco earthquake.
(Courtesy of Pacific Gas & Electric Photo Department/Photograph by Judson Allen)

OB in Action

Hewlett-Packard Sets Organizational Goals for Speed and Innovation

The $12-billion-a-year maker of computers and instruments maintains a stunningly high rate of innovation: More than 50 percent of sales derive from products developed *within the past three years*. By contrast, 3M, also one of the nation's top innovators, derives 25 percent of its revenues from products developed within the past five years.

Hewlett-Packard estimates that fully 60 percent of the research conducted in its labs finds its way into product applications. The phrase drummed into every researcher's head is "time to market"—shorthand for Chief Executive John Young's conviction that products must be brought from laboratory to market quickly and be done right the first time. Under Young's leadership, H–P has devised ambitious new methods for gauging the effectiveness of R&D. The broadest and most important is what Young calls "breakeven time." It is the total elapsed time of a technology transfer, beginning with a scientific investigation and ending only when the profits from a new product offset the cost of its development. Today, on average, H–P needs three to five years to develop and launch a product, and an additional 18 to 24 months to recoup the cost of development. Young wants to cut that in half by 2000.

Source: Excerpted from Gene Bylinsky, "Turning R&D into Real Products," *Fortune*, July 2, 1990, p. 73. © 1990 The Time Inc. Magazine Company. All rights reserved.

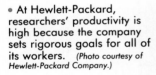

● At Hewlett-Packard, researchers' productivity is high because the company sets rigorous goals for all of its workers. *(Photo courtesy of Hewlett-Packard Company.)*

Resource Acquisition   This second criterion relates to inputs rather than outputs. An organization is deemed effective in this regard if it acquires necessary factors of production such as raw materials, labor, capital, and managerial and technical expertise. Charitable organizations such as the United Way and the Salvation Army judge their effectiveness in terms of how much money they raise from private and corporate donations.

Internal Processes   Some refer to this third effectiveness criterion as the "healthy systems" approach. An organization is said to be a healthy system if information flows smoothly, and employee loyalty, commitment, job satisfaction, and trust prevail. Goals may be set for any of these internal processes. Healthy systems, from a behavioral standpoint, tend to have a minimum of dysfunctional conflict and destructive political maneuvering.

Strategic Constituencies Satisfaction   Organizations both depend on people and affect the lives of people. Consequently, many consider the satisfaction of key interested parties to be an important criterion of organizational effectiveness.

> A **strategic constituency** is any group of individuals who have some stake in the organization—for example, resource providers, users of the organization's products or services, producers of the organization's output, groups whose cooperation is essential for the organization's survival, or those whose lives are significantly affected by the organization.[25]

Strategic constituencies (or *stakeholders*) generally have competing or conflicting interests. For instance, stock investors who want higher dividends and consumers who seek low prices would likely disagree with a union's demand for a wage increase. Strategic constituents or stakeholders can be identified systematically through a stakeholder's audit.[26] A **stakeholder audit** enables management to identify all parties significantly impacted by the organization's performance (see Figure 17–6). Conflicting interests and relative satisfaction among the listed stakeholders can then be dealt with. A never-ending challenge for management is to strike a workable balance among strategic constituencies so as to achieve at least minimal satisfaction on all fronts.

Multiple Effectiveness Criteria: Some Practical Guidelines

Experts on the subject recommend a multidimensional approach to assessing the effectiveness of modern organizations. This means no single criterion is appropriate for all stages of the organization's life cycle (the organizational life cycle concept is covered in Chapter 18). Nor will a single criterion satisfy competing stakeholders. Well-managed organizations mix and match effectiveness criteria to fit the unique requirements of the situation. Managers need to identify and seek input from strategic constituencies. This information, when merged with the organization's stated mission and philosophy, enables management to derive an appropriate *combination* of effectiveness criteria. The following guidelines are helpful in this regard:

• FIGURE 17-6   A Sample Stakeholder Audit Identifying Strategic Constituencies

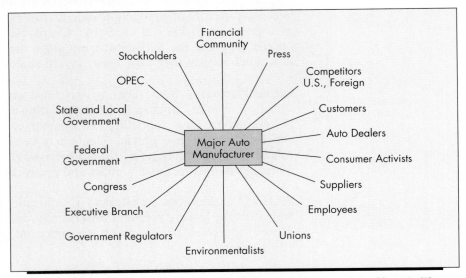

• *The goal accomplishment approach* is appropriate when "goals are clear, consensual, time-bounded, measurable."[27]

• *The resource acquisition approach* is appropriate when inputs have a traceable impact on results or output. For example, the amount of money the American Red Cross receives through donations dictates the level of services provided.

• *The internal processes approach* is appropriate when organizational performance is strongly influenced by specific processes (e.g., cross-functional teamwork).

• *The strategic constituencies approach* is appropriate when powerful stakeholders can significantly benefit or harm the organization.[28]

Keeping these basic concepts of organizational structure and effectiveness in mind, we turn our attention in Chapter 18 to the building of effective organizations.

• SUMMARY OF KEY CONCEPTS

A. An organization is a system of consciously coordinated activities or forces of two or more persons. The four common denominators of all organizations are coordination of effort, a common goal, division of labor, and a hierarchy of authority. Among other things, organization charts reveal the hierarchy of authority, division of labor, spans of control, and line–staff distinctions.

B. Three metaphors that help us to better understand complex organizations are the military/mechanical, biological, and cognitive models. While the military/mechanical model views organizations as self-sufficient closed systems, the biological and cognitive models view organizations as environment–dependent open systems.

C. Max Weber's concept of bureaucracy exemplifies the military/ mechanical model. All organizations possess some degree of bureaucracy. Extreme or dysfunctional bureaucracy has made the term synonymous with inefficiency and red tape. A combination of the biological (resource transformation) and cognitive (interpretation) metaphors paints a realistic picture of modern complex organizations.

D. Beginning in the 1980s and continuing today, a reorganization revolution has flattened large organizations. This trend has brought the traditional heavy reliance on hierarchical control into question. Some say self-management is the best form of management in a cost-conscious, competitive world. According to Lawler's contingency model, eight different substitutes for hierarchy (e.g., work design, training, and vision/values) can reduce or eliminate the need for direct supervisory control.

E. Four generic organizational–effectiveness criteria are goal accomplishment, resource acquisition, internal processes, and strategic constituencies satisfaction. Managers can employ a stakeholder's audit to identify strategic constituencies and their conflicting/competing interests. Because there is no single best effectiveness criterion, a multidimensional approach is suggested.

• KEY TERMS

organization	closed system
unity of command principle	open system
organization chart	bureaucracy
span of control	substitutes for hierarchy
staff personnel	strategic constituency
line managers	stakeholder audit

• DISCUSSION QUESTIONS

1. How many organizations directly affect your life today? List as many as you can.

2. What would an organization chart of your present (or last) place of employment look like? Does the chart you have drawn reveal the hierarchy (chain of command), division of labor, span of control, and line–staff distinctions? Does it reveal anything else? Explain.

3. Why is it appropriate to view modern organizations as open systems?

4. How would you respond to a person who said, ''All bureaucracies are useless?''

5. Why is it instructive to characterize today's complex organizations as cognitive (interpretation) systems?

6. How important is hierarchy in today's typical organization?

7. Which of Lawler's eight substitutes for hierarchy do you think has the greatest promise?

8. How would you respond to a manager who claimed the only way to measure a business's effectiveness is in terms of how much profit it makes?

9. What role can stakeholder audits play in assessing organizational effectiveness?

10. Why do you suppose goal accomplishment is the most widely used effectiveness criterion?

BACK TO THE OPENING CASE

Now that you have read Chapter 17, you should be able to answer the following questions about the General Electric case:

1. Which metaphor—military/mechanical, biological, or cognitive—best describes the organization in this case? Explain.

2. Using Table 17–2 as a guide, which substitutes for hierarchy are evident in this case? Which supervisory functions have been taken over by non-managerial employees?

3. Which criteria would be appropriate for assessing the effectiveness of the Plainville division of G.E.? Explain your reasoning.

4. What strategic constituencies would probably show up on a stakeholder audit for G.E.'s Plainville division?

• EXERCISE 17

Objectives

1. To focus your attention on the organizational level of analysis.
2. To get hands-on experience with specifying organizational effectiveness criteria.
3. To conduct a stakeholder audit and thus more fully appreciate the competing demands placed upon today's managers.

Introduction

This exercise introduces you to an organization in transition. Put yourself in the place of the head of the U.S. Army Corps of Engineers as you carry out the following instructions.

Instructions

Read the following case about the U.S. Army Corps of Engineers' changing mission and then carry out the subsequent tasks.

Case: An About-Face for the U.S. Army Corps of Engineers[29]

There is an old movie, now hidden away in the archives of the U.S. Army Corps of Engineers, that the Corps used in years past to explain its mission. In it, the Army Engineers point with pride to the bridges and other engineering achievements they built overseas to aid fighting men in all of the nation's wars.

As the film switches to scenes of flooded rivers and the music swells, the announcer explains the Corps' domestic role. "At home," he says, "the enemy is nature." To combat the enemy, the 1936 Flood Control Act gave the Corps responsibility for federal flood protection and immediately authorized some 250 projects.

Now, as the Corps begins to restyle itself as a protector of the environment, nature is no longer seen as a foe but as an opportunity for the engineers to expand their mission. Chief of Engineers General Henry Hatch has made the rounds of the Army Corps' 36 districts promoting an ambitious environmental agenda.

"Embracing and promoting our environmental ethic will change the way we do our traditional business," he says, as the agency strives to become "the environmental engineers of the future."

Dan Mauldin, who is the Army Corps of Engineers' chief of planning and director of civil works, says, "We see this as a big shift in how engineers will be used. There are a lot of environmental problems and not any of them are going to be solved without an engineer. So it is a big push on our part." In southern Florida the Corps has embraced plans to restore natural water flows to Everglades National Park, to fill in canals, and tear down levees. It is the first time that the Army Engineers have undertaken an environmental restoration project of this magnitude and the first time they have ever acknowledged that at least some of what they built caused more harm than good.

"We have messed up nature, it's no doubt," says Richard Bonner, the deputy district engineer in Jacksonville. "Now we've got to use all of our skills to put things right. Our natural environment is diminishing, and we've got to protect it."

The drainage system built by the Corps—some 1,500 miles of canals and levees—made it possible to farm what was once Everglades swamp. And the system opened the way for urban development.

But it also left Florida with a legacy of polluted and declining water supplies and a dying ecosystem in Everglades National Park. Now, having spent hundreds of millions to drain the Everglades, the Corps has enthusiastically agreed to spend hundreds of millions more to undo some of the damage. "What's good for the environment is good for us," Mauldin says.

Tasks

1. Assume you are General Henry Hatch, Chief of Engineers, and explain in detail how you will assess the Corps' organizational effectiveness during the next three to five years.

2. Making reasonable assumptions about the circumstances of this case, conduct a stakeholder audit for the Florida Everglades project. Which strategic constituents, if any, should be given a higher priority?

Questions for Consideration/Class Discussion

1. How do your effectiveness criteria measure up to those suggested by your classmates? Did you overlook any important factors? Explain.

2. Did your stakeholder audit broaden your awareness of outside interests? Explain.

3. Which strategic constituents could prove most troublesome relative to pursuing the Corps' new mission? Why? Which most helpful?

• NOTES

[1] Chester I. Barnard, *The Functions of the Executive* (Cambridge, Mass.: Harvard University Press, 1938), p. 73.

[2] Drawn from Edgar H. Schein, *Organizational Psychology,* 3rd ed. (Englewood Cliffs, N.J.: Prentice-Hall, 1980), pp. 12–15.

[3] For an interesting historical perspective of hierarchy, see Peter Miller and Ted O'Leary, "Hierarchies and American Ideals, 1900–1940," *Academy of Management Review,* April 1989, pp. 250–65.

[4] For an excellent overview of the span of control concept, see David D. Van Fleet and Arthur G. Bedeian, "A History of the Span of Management," *Academy of Management Review,* July 1977, pp. 356–72.

[5] Meni Koslowsky, "Staff/Line Distinctions in Job and Organizational Commitment," *Journal of Occupational Psychology,* June 1990, pp. 167–73.

[6] David S. Brown, "Managers' New Job Is Concert Building," *HRMagazine,* September 1990, p. 42.

[7] Kim S. Cameron, "Effectiveness as Paradox: Consensus and Conflict in Conceptions of Organizationl Effectiveness," *Management Science,* May 1986, pp. 540–41. Also see Sonja Sackmann, "The Role of Metaphors in Organization Transformation," *Human Relations,* June 1989, pp. 463–84; and Haridimos Tsoukas, "The Missing Link: A Transformational View of Metaphors in Organizational Science," *Academy of Management Review,* July 1991, pp. 566–85.

[8] Based on Max Weber, *The Theory of Social and Economic Organization,* translated by A. M. Henderson and Talcott Parsons (New York: Oxford University Press, 1947). An instructive analysis of the mistranslation of Weber's work may be found in Richard M. Weiss, "Weber on Bureaucracy: Management Consultant or Political Theorist?" *Academy of Management Review,* April 1983, pp. 242–48.

[9] For a critical appraisal of bureaucracy, see Ralph P. Hummel, *The Bureaucratic Experience,* 3rd ed. (New York: St. Martin's Press, 1987). The positive side of bureaucracy is presented in Charles T. Goodsell, *The Case for Bureaucracy: A Public Administration Polemic* (Chatham, N.J.: Chatham House Publishers, 1983).

[10] A management-oriented discussion of general systems theory—an interdisciplinary attempt to integrate the various fragmented sciences—may be found in Kenneth E. Boulding, "General Systems Theory—The Skeleton of Science," *Management Science,* April 1956, pp. 197–208.

[11] James D. Thompson, *Organizations in Action* (New York: McGraw-Hill, 1967), pp. 6–7.

[12] Richard L. Daft and Karl E. Weick, "Toward a Model of Organizations as Interpretation Systems," *Academy of Management Review,* April 1984, p. 293.

[13] Scott Ticer, "Big Tobacco's Fortunes Are Withering in the Heat," *Business Week,* July 27, 1987, p. 47.

¹⁴ Data from Frank Swoboda, "For Unions, Maybe Bitter Was Better," *The Washington Post National Weekly Edition,* May 28–June 3, 1990, p. 20.

¹⁵ Data from Joseph Weber, "Farewell, Fast Track," *Business Week,* December 10, 1990, pp. 192–200.

¹⁶ Adapted from Otis Port, "A Smarter Way to Manufacture," *Business Week,* April 30, 1990, pp. 110–17.

¹⁷ See Weber, "Farewell, Fast Track."

¹⁸ Based on discussion in James B. Treece, "Will GM Learn from Its Own Role Models?" *Business Week,* April 9, 1990, p. 62; and David Woodruff, "Ford Has a Better Idea: Let Someone Else Have the Idea," *Business Week,* April 30, 1990, pp. 116–17.

¹⁹ Edward E. Lawler III, "Substitutes for Hierarchy," *Organizational Dynamics,* Summer 1988, p. 13.

²⁰ Adapted from Sarah Smith, "America's Most Admired Corporations," *Fortune,* January 29, 1990, p. 58.

²¹ Data from *Ibid.*

²² Kim Cameron, "Critical Questions in Assessing Organizational Effectiveness," *Organizational Dynamics,* Autumn 1980, p. 70.

²³ Karlene H. Roberts, "Managing High Reliability Organizations," *California Management Review,* Summer 1990, p. 102.

²⁴ See, for example, Robert O. Brinkerhoff and Dennis E. Dressler, *Productivity Measurement: A Guide for Managers and Evaluators* (Newbury Park, Calif.: Sage Publications, 1990).

²⁵ Cameron, "Critical Questions in Assessing Organizational Effectiveness," p. 67.

²⁶ See Nancy C. Roberts and Paula J. King, "The Stakeholder Audit Goes Public," *Organizational Dynamics,* Winter 1989, pp. 63–79.

²⁷ Kim S. Cameron, "Effectiveness as Paradox: Consensus and Conflict in Conceptions of Organizational Effectiveness," *Management Science,* May 1986, p. 542.

²⁸ Alternative effectiveness criteria are discussed in Ibid.; Arthur G. Bedeian, "Organization Theory: Current Controversies, Issues, and Directions," in *International Review of Industrial and Organizational Psychology,* eds. Cary L. Cooper and Ivan T. Robertson (New York: John Wiley & Sons, 1987), pp. 1–33; and Michael Keeley, "Impartiality and Participant-Interest Theories of Organizational Effectiveness," *Administrative Science Quarterly,* March 1984, pp. 1–25.

²⁹ Excerpted from Vicki Monks, "Engineering the Everglades," *National Parks,* September/October 1990, pp. 32, 34.

Organizational Life Cycles and Design

LEARNING OBJECTIVES

When you finish studying the material in this chapter, you should be able to:

- Identify and briefly explain the three stages of the organizational life cycle.
- Discuss organizational decline relative to the organizational life cycle.
- Explain what the contingency approach to organization design involves.

- Describe the relationship between differentiation and integration in effective organizations.
- Discuss Burns and Stalker's findings regarding mechanistic and organic organizations.
- Define and briefly explain the practical significance of centralization and decentralization.

- Discuss the effective management of organizational size.
- Identify and briefly describe the five organization design configurations in Mintzberg's typology.

OPENING CASE 18

The Strange New Organizational World at W. L. Gore

Sharon Hoogstraten

When Ara E. Atkinson joined W. L. Gore & Associates Inc. eight years ago, she was a single parent with a high-school-equivalency diploma and a bit of community college. Gore hired Atkinson, who had been a hairdresser for six years, as a production-line worker soldering electronic parts at $4.50 an hour.

Atkinson, 30, is now Gore's artist-designer. Early on, a co-worker noticed her knack for drawing and knew salespeople who needed artwork for presentations. But Atkinson was a production worker, and there was no artist's job she could apply for—obstacles that would have kept her on the line at most companies.

Instead, Gore helped her create the job of illustrating sales materials and brochures. The company even paid for her commercial art training in night school at the University of Delaware. Atkinson has more than tripled her starting income.

Such stories abound at the Newark (Del.) company. The rest of Corporate America is only beginning to think about how to motivate employees now that there's a shrinking hierarchy to slot people into. But Gore, a quirky, family-held plastics company, has never had much of one: it has been experimenting with an almost free-form management structure for 32 years. As other companies look for ways to slash bureaucracy, "we can learn a great deal from companies like Gore," says Edgar S. Woolard Jr., chief executive of Du Pont Co., a major customer and supplier.

For starters, Gore isn't big on fancy titles. Each of its 5,300 employees is an "associate." Even Robert W. Gore—whose mother, Genevieve, and late father, Wilbert, founded Gore—tolerates the president's title only for legal reasons. And perks such as executive parking spots and big offices

are taboo: A personnel administrator who needs space for staff meetings has an office larger than Gore's. Instead of bosses, "leaders" head teams in plants or staff departments.

It's more than just a semantic distinction. Leaders must share the power to hire, discipline or fire associates with peer committees, personnel staffers, and "sponsors." Every employee has a sponsor, a mentor who functions as counselor and advocate. Leaders are only one part of Gore's pay-setting process, in which groups of associates meet every six months to rank peers by subjective assessment of their contributions. Committees merge the lists and set raises, ranking pay from the highest contributor on down.

Leaders also can't give orders. They can only seek commitments from associates. Take the experience of Daniel D. Johnson: Six years ago, Johnson left Du Pont after 15 years as a successful product developer to try his hand at Gore. A chemist, he experimented with using a form of Gore-Tex in printed-circuit boards for high-speed computers. Gore had no elaborate commercialization unit to help—or hinder—him.

O rganizations are much more than the familiar pattern of boxes and lines we see on organization charts. Charts may be a necessary starting point, but we need to know more if we are to adequately understand and manage organizations. Organization design scholar and consultant Robert W. Keidel recently put it this way:

> Our historical preoccupation with organization *charts*—hierarchical displays of reporting relationships—is counterproductive. Organizational design is far more a

(concluded)

And Johnson couldn't order anyone to work on his project.

First, he persuaded a few associates to help out. Intrigued, others joined, and soon the project team topped a dozen. Says Johnson: "It was like an amoeba taking shape." The new laminate, which should hit the market next year, helped earn Johnson the leadership of Gore's electronics division. "You evolve into leadership [at Gore]," he says. "You look behind you, and you've got people following you."

'Lattice' System

Gore isn't some little countercultural outfit, mind you. By turning a flexible form of Du Pont's Teflon into Gore-Tex, used in fabrics and assorted medical, electronic, and industrial products, the company has grown into a nearly $700 million-a-year outfit, with 41 plants in six countries. Although loath to reveal profits, finance associate Shanti Mehta says Gore ranks in the top 5 percent of major companies in return on assets and equity. Sales have roughly tripled since 1984, and he expects they will top $1 billion within five years.

Founder Gore was a Du Pont chemist who couldn't get his innovation—Teflon coating for electrical wires—marketed by the big company. When he left, he vowed to avoid stifling bureaucracies, so he tossed out the traditional chain of command for a "lattice" system. In it, any staffer may take an idea or complaint to any other: A machine operator can talk directly with plant leaders. Atkinson, for example, phoned Sally Gore, Robert Gore's wife and leader of human resources, to ask for help in creating the job of corporate artist.

Growth has made the fight against bureaucracy constant. The company breaks plants apart when they grow to more than 200 staffers. A few years ago, Gore noticed that a select 200 associates were seen as most important by colleagues because they attended a particular company meeting. So he opened that meeting to a broader cross section of staffers. Associates are also polled anonymously to make sure plants live up to Gore ideals. If not, task forces make changes. Vows Robert Gore, 53: "I expect to maintain the culture."

Of course, Gore's unusual culture sometimes conflicts with the more rigid ways of the outside world. Take the matter of titles: When Mehta called Wall Street investment houses for help with an employee stock-option plan a few years ago, he found he needed a fancy title to be taken seriously. At Gore's suggestion, he called himself president—and that won him the appointments he needed. Another associate came up with an even loftier-sounding solution: She once styled herself "supreme commander" on a business card. You can't expect the outside world to adopt the Gore way of doing things overnight.

For Discussion

With such a loose structure, how does anything get accomplished at Gore?

• Additional discussion questions linking this case with the following material appear at the end of this chapter.

Source: Joseph Weber, "No Bosses. And Even 'Leaders' Can't Give Orders," *Business Week*, December 10, 1990, pp. 196–97. Reprinted by special permission, copyright © 1990 by McGraw-Hill, Inc.

matter of *charting direction* and navigating among autonomy, control, and cooperation than of moving boxes around. The process is never-ending.[1]

Indeed, organizations take on a life of their own. As has been said many times, organizations are more than the sum of their parts. This chapter explores important dynamics of organizations including the life cycle perspective, with special emphasis on decline, and the contingency approach to organization design. Our underlying challenge is to learn how to build organizations capable of thriving in an environment characterized by rapid change and rugged competition.

• Organizational Life Cycles

Like the people who make up organizations, organizations themselves go through life cycles. Organizations are born and, barring early decline, eventually grow and mature. If decline is not reversed, the organization dies. Just as you will face new problems and challenges during different phases of your lifetime, so do organizations. Thus, managers need a working knowledge of organizational life cycles and the closely related topic of organizational decline. According to a pair of experts on the subject: "A consistent pattern of development seems to occur in organizations over time, and organizational activities and structures in one stage are not the same as the activities and structures present at another stage. This implies that the criteria used to evaluate an organization's success in one stage of development also may be different from criteria used to evaluate success at another stage of development."[2] This section examines stages of the organizational life cycle concept and discusses the threat of organizational decline.

Organizational Life Cycle Stages

Although the organizational life cycle concept has been around for a long time, it has enjoyed renewed interest among respected researchers in recent years. Many life cycle models have been proposed.[3] One point of agreement among the competing models is that organizations evolve in a predictable sequence of identifiable stages. Table 18–1 presents a basic organizational life cycle model. Stages 1 through 3 of the model are inception, high-growth, and maturity. Changes during these three stages can be summed up in the following rule: *As organizations mature, they tend to become larger, more formalized, and more differentiated (fragmented).* Differentiation increases

• **Table 18-1** Stages of the Organizational Life Cycle

Characteristics	Stage 1: Inception	Stage 2: High-growth	Stage 3: Maturity – – – – – – – – Decline	
Type of organizational structure	No formal structure	Centralized Formal	Decentralized Formal	Rigid, top-heavy, overly complex
Communication process and planning	Informal Face-to-face Little planning	Moderately formal Budgets	Very formal Five-year plans Rules and regulations	Communication breakdown Blind adherence to "success formula"
Method of decision making	Individual judgment Entreprenurial	Professional management Analytical tools	Professional management Bargaining	Emphasis on form rather than substance Self-serving politics
Organizational growth rate	Inconsistent but improving	Rapid positive growth	Growth slowing or declining	Declining
Organizational age and size	Young and small	Larger and older	Largest or once large and oldest	Variable age and shrinking

Source: Characteristics and first three stages excerpted from Ken G. Smith, Terence R. Mitchell, and Charles E. Summer, "Top Level Management Priorities in Different Stages of the Organizational Life Cycle," *Academy of Management Journal*, December 1985, p. 802. Organizational decline portion adapted from discussion in Peter Lorange and Robert T. Nelson, "How to Recognize–and Avoid–Organizational Decline," *Sloan Management Review*, Spring 1987, pp. 41–48.

because of added levels in the hierarchy, further division of labor, and formation of political coalitions.

Life Cycle Timing and Type of Change   Two key features of this life cycle model address the timing and type of changes experienced by the organization. Relative to timing, the duration of each phase is highly variable, depending on a host of organizational and environmental factors. This explains why there is no time frame in Table 18–1. Some organizations have short life cycles, with abbreviated or missing stages. For example, toy-maker Worlds of Wonder Inc., "with such hits as Teddy Ruxpin, reached $327 million in revenues its second year, then lost $187 million in a single quarter and plunged into bankruptcy before its third birthday."[4] The Roman Catholic Church, on the other hand, has been around for nearly two millenia.

Regarding the type of change that organizations undergo from one stage to the next, Indiana University researchers noted, "The very nature of the firm changes as a business grows in size and matures. These are not changes in degree; rather, they are fundamental changes in kind."[5] This sort of *qualitative* change helps explain the unexpected departure of founder Mitchell D. Kapor from Lotus Development Corp., maker of the highly successful 1–2–3® computer spreadsheet program. When asked by *Inc.* magazine why he walked away from it all, Kapor replied:

• Modern technology is reshaping today's organizations. In automobile assembly, robots have made the process less labor-intensive.

J. Clark/Superstock

Andrew Sacks/Tony Stone Worldwide

If you look at Lotus as it started and as it is today, I think you'll see more differences than similarities. In the beginning, it was classically entrepreneurial; a small group of people trying to break into a market with a new product around which they hoped to build a company and achieve market share for the company and financial success for themselves and their investors. Today, Lotus is a company of 1,350 people with diversified, worldwide operations, with the organizational structure and challenges of a $275 million company. And so the nature of the challenges facing the company, and facing the people in it—and, to your question, facing me—is radically different.[6]

Entrepreneurs, such as Kapor, tend to miss the inception-stage excitement and risk as their organizations move into the high-growth and maturity stages. Some entrepreneurs become liabilities because they fail to grow with their organizations. Others, Kapor included, wisely turn the reins over to professional managers who possess the ability and desire to manage large and complex organizations. Managerial skills needed during one stage of the organization's life cycle may be inappropriate or inadequate during a later stage.

The Ever-Present Threat of Decline   While decline is included in the model, it is not a distinct stage with predictable sequencing (hence the broken line between maturity and decline in Table 18–1). Organizational decline is a *potential,* rather than automatic, outcome that can occur any time during the life cycle. Stage 1 and stage 2 organizations are as readily victimized by the forces of decline as mature stage 3 organizations. Experts report 50 percent of all new businesses in the United States fail within seven years.[7] Most of the failed businesses experience decline after an extended inception stage or an abbreviated high-growth stage. While noting ''decline is almost unavoidable unless deliberate steps are taken to prevent it,''[8] specialists on the subject have alerted managers to 14 early-warning signs of organizational decline:

1. Excess personnel.
2. Tolerance of incompetence.
3. Cumbersome administrative procedures.
4. Disproportionate staff power (for example, technical staff specialists politically overpower line managers whom they view as unsophisticated and too conventional).
5. Replacement of substance with form (for example, the planning process becomes more important than the results achieved).
6. Scarcity of clear goals and decision benchmarks.
7. Fear of embarrassment and conflict (for example, formerly successful executives may resist new ideas for fear of revealing past mistakes).
8. Loss of effective communication.
9. Outdated organizational structure.[9]
10. Increased scapegoating by leaders.
11. Resistance to change.
12. Low morale.

13. Special interest groups are more vocal.

14. Decreased innovation.[10]

Managers who monitor these early warning signs of organizational decline are better able to reorganize in a timely and effective manner.[11]

Preventing Organizational Decline   The time to start doing something about organizational decline is when everything is going *right*. For it is during periods of high success that the seeds of decline are sown.[12] *Complacency* is the number one threat because it breeds overconfidence and inattentiveness. Toyota's quest for continuous improvement is an inspiring example of how to avoid organizational decline by not becoming complacent (see International OB).

Organizational Life Cycle Research and Practical Implications   The best available evidence in this area comes from the combination of a field study and a laboratory simulation. Both studies led researchers to the same conclusions. In the field study, 38 top-level electronics industry managers from 27 randomly selected companies were presented with a decision-making scenario. They then were asked to complete a questionnaire about priorities. It was

INTERNATIONAL OB

Kaizen **Helps Toyota Prevent Organizational Decline**

Of all the slogans kicked around Toyota City, the key one is *kaizen,* which means "continuous improvement" in Japanese. While many other companies strive for dramatic breakthroughs, Toyota keeps doing lots of little things better and better. . . .

One consultant calls Toyota's strategy "rapid inch-up": Take enough tiny steps and pretty soon you outdistance the competition. . . .

The company simply is tops in quality, productivity, and efficiency. From its factories pour a wide range of cars, built with unequaled precision. Toyota turns out luxury sedans with Mercedes-like quality using *one-sixth* the labor Mercedes does. The company originated just-in-time mass production and remains its leading practitioner.

In short, Toyota is the best carmaker in the world. And it keeps getting better. Says Iwao Isomura, chief of personnel: "Our current success is the best reason to change things." Extensive interviews with Toyota executives in the U.S. and Japan demonstrate the company's total dedication to continuous improvement. What is often mistaken for excessive modesty is, in fact, an expression of permanent dissatisfaction—even with exemplary performance. So the company is simultaneously restructuring its manufacturing processes, planning its global strategy for the 21st century, tinkering with its corporate culture, and even becoming a fashion leader.

• At Toyota, the emphasis is on *kaizen,* Japanese for "continuous improvement." (*Courtesy Toyota Motor Sales, USA, Inc.*)

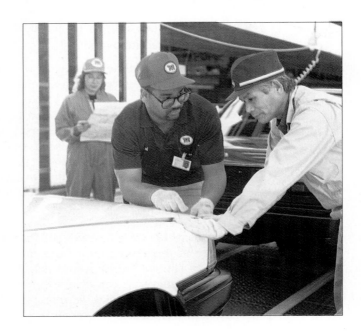

found that priorities shifted across the three life cycle stages introduced in Table 18–1. As the organization matured from stage 1 to stages 2 and 3, top management's priorities shifted as follows:

- A strong emphasis on technical efficiency grew even stronger.
- The desire for personal power and commitment from subordinates increased significantly.
- The desire for organizational integration (coordination and cooperation) decreased significantly.[13]

In a separate but related study, researchers examined the relationship between life cycle stages and effectiveness criteria. This five-year case study of a New York State mental health agency revealed that top management's effectiveness criteria changed during the organization's life cycle. Early emphasis on flexibility, resource acquisition, and employee development/satisfaction gave way to formalization as the agency matured. Formalization criteria encompassed increased attention to factors such as goal setting, information management, communication, control, productivity, and efficiency.[14]

This research reveals that different stages of the organizational life cycle are associated with distinctly different managerial responses. It must be noted, however, that management's priorities and effectiveness criteria in the foregoing studies were not necessarily the *right* ones. Much research remains to be done to identify specific contingencies. Still, the point remains that managers need to be flexible and adaptive as their organizations evolve through the various life cycle stages.[15] As learned the hard way by the U.S. banking industry during the 1980s, yesterday's formula for success can be today's formula for noncompetitiveness and decline.[16]

• THE CONTINGENCY APPROACH TO ORGANIZATION DESIGN

According to the **contingency approach to organization design,** organizations tend to be more effective when they are structured to fit the demands of the situation. A contingency approach can be put into practice by first assessing the degree of environmental uncertainty.[17] Next, the contingency model calls for using various organization design configurations to achieve an effective organization-environment fit. This section presents an environmental uncertainty model along with two classic contingency design studies.

Assessing Environmental Uncertainty

Robert Duncan proposed a two-dimensional model for classifying environmental demands on the organization (see Figure 18-1). On the horizontal axis is the simple → complex dimension. This dimension ''focuses on whether the factors in the environment considered for decision making are few in number and similar or many in number and different.''[18] On the vertical axis of Duncan's model is the static → dynamic dimension. ''The static-dynamic dimension of the environment is concerned with whether the factors of the environment remain the same over time or change.''[19] When combined, these two dimensions characterize four situations that represent increasing uncertainty for organizations. According to Duncan, the

• **FIGURE 18-1**   A Four-Way Classification of Organizational Environments

	Simple	Complex
Static	Low Perceived Uncertainty • Small number of factors and components in the environment • Factors and components are somewhat similar to one another • Factors and components remain basically the same and are not changing • Example: Soft drink industry 1	Moderately low perceived uncertainty • Large number of factors and components in the environment • Factors and components are not similar to one another • Factors and components remain basically the same • Example: Food products 2
Dynamic	Moderately High Perceived Uncertainty • Small number of factors and components in the environment • Factors and components are somewhat similar to one another • Factors and components of the environment are in continual process of change • Example: Fast-food industry 3	High Perceived Uncertainty • Large number of factors and components in the environment • Factors and components are not similar to one another • Factors and components of environment are in a continual process of change • Examples: Commercial airline industry Telephone communications (AT&T) 4

Source: Reprinted, by permission of the publisher, from ''What Is the Right Organization Structure?'' by Robert Duncan, *Organizational Dynamics*, Winter 1979, p. 63. © 1979 American Management Association, New York. All rights reserved.

complex-dynamic situation of highest uncertainty is the most common organizational environment today.

Amid these fast-paced times, nothing stands still. Not even in the simple–static quadrant. For example, during the first 94 years of Coca-Cola's history (through 1980), only one soft drink bore the company's name. Just six years later, Coke had its famous name on seven soft drinks, including Coca-Cola Classic, Coke, and Cherry Coke. Despite operating in an environment characterized as simple and static, Coca-Cola has had to become a more risk-taking, entrepreneurial company.[20] This means organizations facing moderate to high uncertainty (quadrants 3 and 4 in Figure 18–1) have to be highly flexible, responsive, and adaptive today. Contingency organization design is more important than ever because it helps managers structure their organizations to fit the key situational factors discussed next.

Differentiation and Integration: The Lawrence and Lorsch Study

In their classic text, *Organization and Environment,* Harvard researchers Paul Lawrence and Jay Lorsch explained how two structural forces simultaneously fragment the organization and bind it together. They cautioned that an imbalance between these two forces—labeled *differentiation* and *integration*—could hinder organizational effectiveness.

Differentiation Splits the Organization Apart   **Differentiation** occurs through division of labor and technical specialization. A behavioral outcome of differentiation is that technical specialists such as computer programmers tend to think and act differently than specialists in, say, accounting or marketing. Excessive differentiation can cause the organization to bog down in miscommunication, conflict, and politics. Thus, differentiation needs to be offset by an opposing structural force to ensure needed *coordination*. This is where integration enters the picture (see Figure 18–2).

Integration Binds the Organization Together   **Integration** occurs when specialists cooperate to achieve a common goal. According to the Lawrence and Lorsch model, integration can be achieved through various combinations of the following six mechanisms: (1) a formal hierarchy; (2) standardized policies, rules, and procedures; (3) departmentalization; (4) committees and cross-functional teams; (5) human relations training, and (6) individuals and groups acting as liaisons between specialists.

Achieving the Proper Balance   When Lawrence and Lorsch studied successful and unsuccessful companies in three industries, they concluded the following: *As environmental complexity increased, successful organizations exhibited higher degrees of both differentiation and integration.* In other words, an effective balance was achieved. Unsuccessful organizations, in contrast, tended to suffer from an imbalance of too much differentiation and not enough offsetting integration. This outcome was confirmed by the life cycle research discussed earlier. As the organization matured, management's desire for integration became a significantly less important priority. Managers need to fight this tendency if their growing and increasingly differentiated organizations are to be coordinated.

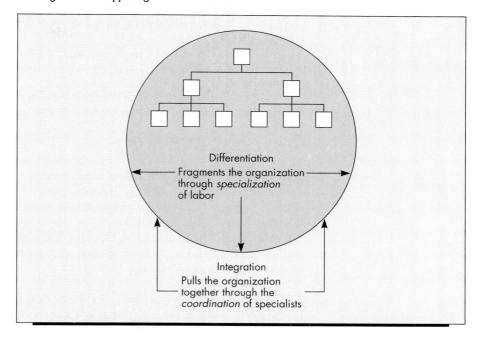

Lawrence and Lorsch also discovered that "the more differentiated an organization, the more difficult it is to achieve integration."[21] Managers of today's complex organizations need to strive constantly and creatively to achieve greater integration.[22] For example, how does 3M Company, with its dozens of autonomous divisions and over 60,000 products, successfully maintain its competitive edge in technology? Among other things, 3M makes sure its technical specialists frequently interact with one another so cross-fertilization of ideas takes place. Art Fry, credited with inventing the now ubiquitous Post-It Notes, actually owes much of his success to colleague Spencer Silver, an engineer down the hall who created an apparently useless semi-adhesive. If Fry and Silver had worked in a company without a strong commitment to integration, we probably would not have Post-It Notes. 3M does not leave this sort of cross-fertilization to chance. It organizes for integration with such things as a Technology Council that regularly convenes researchers from various divisions and an annual science fair at which 3M scientists enthusiastically hawk their new ideas, not to customers, but to each other![23]

Mechanistic versus Organic Organizations

A second classic contingency design study was reported by a pair of British behavioral scientists, Tom Burns and G. M. Stalker. In the course of their research, they drew a very instructive distinction between what they called mechanistic and organic organizations. **Mechanistic organizations** are rigid bureaucracies with strict rules, narrowly defined tasks, and top-down communication. For example, when *Business Week* correspondent Kathleen

Deveny spent a day working in a McDonald's restaurant, she found a very mechanistic organization:

> Here every job is broken down into the smallest of steps, and the whole process is automated. . . .
>
> Anyone could do this, I think. But McDonald's restaurants operate like Swiss watches, and the minute I step behind the counter I am a loose part in the works. . . .
>
> I bag French fries for a few minutes, but I'm much too slow. Worse, I can't seem to keep my station clean enough. Failing at French fries is a fluke, I tell myself. . . .
>
> I try to move faster, but my co-workers are playing at 45 rpm, and I'm stuck at 33⅓.[24]

This sort of mechanistic structure is necessary at McDonald's because of the competitive need for uniform product quality, speedy service, and cleanliness. Oppositely, **organic organizations** are flexible networks of multitalented individuals who perform a variety of tasks. W. L. Gore & Associates, as discussed in the Opening Case, is a highly organic organization because it lacks job descriptions and a formalized hierarchy and deemphasizes titles and status.

A Matter of Degree   Importantly, as illustrated in Figure 18–3, each of the mechanistic-organic characteristics is a matter of degree. Organizations tend to be *relatively* mechanistic or *relatively* organic. Pure types are rare because divisions, departments, or units in the same organization may be more or less mechanistic or organic. From an employee's standpoint, which organization structure would you prefer?

Different Approaches to Decision Making   Decision making tends to be centralized in mechanistic organizations and decentralized in organic organizations. **Centralized decision making** occurs when key decisions are made by

• **FIGURE 18–3**   Characteristics of Mechanistic and Organic Organizations

Characteristic	Mechanistic Organization	Organic Organization
1. Task definition and knowledge required	Narrow; technical	⟶ Broad; general
2. Linkage between individual's contribution and organization's purpose	Vague or indirect	⟶ Clear or direct
3. Task flexibility	Rigid; routine	⟶ Flexible; varied
4. Specification of techniques, obligations, and rights	Specific	⟶ General
5. Degree of hierarchical control	High	⟶ Low (self-control emphasized)
6. Primary communication pattern	Top-down	⟶ Lateral (between peers)
7. Primary decision-making style	Authoritarian	⟶ Democratic; participative
9. Emphasis on obedience and loyalty	High	⟶ Low

Source: Adapted from discussion in Tom Burns and G. M. Stalker, *The Management of Innovation* (London: Tavistock, 1961), pp. 119–25.

top management. **Decentralized decision making** occurs when important decisions are made by middle- and lower-level managers. Generally, centralized organizations are more tightly controlled while decentralized organizations are more adaptive to changing situations. Each has its appropriate use. For example, both Delta Air Lines and General Electric are very respected and successful companies, yet the former prefers centralization while the latter pushes decentralization (see OB in Action).

Experts on the subject warn against extremes of centralization or decentralization. The challenge is to achieve a workable balance between the two extremes. A management consultant recently put it this way:

> The modern organization in transition will recognize the pull of two polarities: a need for greater centralization to create low-cost shared resources; and, a need to improve market responsiveness with greater decentralization. Today's winning organizations are the ones that can handle the paradox and tensions of both pulls. These are the firms that analyze the optimum organizational solution in each particular circumstance, without prejudice for one type of organization over another. The result is, almost invariably, a messy mixture of decentralized units sharing cost-effective centralized resources.[25]

 OB IN ACTION

Delta and GE Are a Study in Contrasts

Centralization Helps Delta Air Lines Weather Recessions:

Recession veterans like Delta CEO [Ronald W.] Allen insist that you must have a system that allows you to start cutting costs the moment a downturn hits. At Delta, managers work without an annual budget. Every expenditure over $5,000—jet fuel excepted—must be approved by top management. Every Monday morning Allen and his top aides pore over a list of 40 or so expenditures. If times get tough they can immediately knock out a request for replacing an old Xerox machine or painting a terminal.

The process sounds cumbersome, but it forces every manager in the field to think hard about what's really necessary before kicking a request up to the CEO.

Decentralization Helps CEO Jack Welch Revitalize Newly Acquired Businesses. . .

Once the boss is in place, it is his job to "develop a vision" for the business—Welch's words—and oversee a change in culture to accomplish it. That often means flattening organizational levels, removing bureaucratic barriers, and giving individual employees more responsibility. The idea is to create an environment in which employees' efforts determine whether their careers flourish or perish. There is more opportunity to fail. On the other hand, the gates are open for fast promotion and big pay—as long as you're the GE type.

Sources: Excerpted from Brian Dumaine, "How to Manage in a Recession," *Fortune,* November 5, 1990, p. 72; and Russell Mitchell, "When Jack Welch Takes Over: A Guide For the Newly Acquired," *Business Week,* December 14, 1987, p. 95.

Relevant Research Findings   When they classified a sample of actual companies as either mechanistic or organic, Burns and Stalker discovered one type was not superior to the other. Each type had its appropriate place, depending on the environment. When the environment was relatively *stable and certain,* the successful organizations tended to be *mechanistic. Organic* organizations tended to be the successful ones when the environment was *unstable and uncertain.*[26]

In a more recent study of 103 department managers from eight manufacturing firms and two aerospace organizations, managerial skill was found to have a greater impact on a global measure of department effectiveness in organic departments than in mechanistic departments. This led the researchers to recommend the following contingencies for management staffing and training:

> If we have two units, one organic and one mechanistic, and two potential applicants differing in overall managerial ability, we might want to assign the more competent to the organic unit since in that situation there are few structural aids available to the manager in performing required responsibilities. It is also possible that managerial training is especially needed by managers being groomed to take over units that are more organic in structure.[27]

Another interesting finding comes from a study of 42 voluntary church organizations. As the organizations became more mechanistic (more bureaucratic) the intrinsic motivation of their members decreased. Mechanistic organizations apparently undermined the volunteers' sense of freedom and self-determination. Additionally, the researchers believe their findings help explain why bureaucracy tends to feed on itself: "A mechanistic organizational structure may breed the need for a more extremely mechanistic system because of the reduction in intrinsically motivated behavior."[28] Thus, bureaucracy begets greater bureaucracy.

Most recently, field research in two factories, one mechanistic and the other organic, found expected communication patterns. Command-and-control (downward) communication characterized the mechanistic factory. Consultative or participative (two-way) communication prevailed in the organic factory.[29]

Both Mechanistic and Organic Structures Are Needed   Although achievement-oriented students of OB typically express a distaste for mechanistic organizations, not all organizations or subunits can or should be organic. For example, as mentioned earlier, McDonald's could not achieve its admired quality and service standards without extremely mechanistic restaurant operations. Imagine the food and service you would get if McDonald's employees used their own favorite ways of doing things and worked at their own pace! On the other hand, mechanistic structure alienates some employees because it erodes their sense of self-control.

THREE IMPORTANT CONTINGENCY VARIABLES: TECHNOLOGY, SIZE, AND STRATEGIC CHOICE

Both contingency theories just discussed have one important thing in common. Each is based on an "environmental imperative," meaning the environment is said to be the primary determinant of effective organizational structure. Other organization theorists disagree. They contend that factors such as the organization's core technology, size, and corporate strategy hold the key to organizational structure. This section examines the significance of these three additional contingency variables.

The Impact of Technology on Structure

Joan Woodward proposed a *technological imperative* in 1965 after studying 100 small manufacturing firms in southern England. She found distinctly different structural patterns for effective and ineffective companies based on technologies of low, medium, or high *complexity*. Effective organizations with either low- or high-complexity technology tended to have an organic structure. Effective organizations based on a technology of medium complexity tended to have a mechanistic structure. Woodward concluded that technology was the overriding determinant of organizational structure.[30]

Since Woodward's landmark work, many studies of the relationship between technology and structure have been conducted. Unfortunately, disagreement and confusion have prevailed. For example, a comprehensive review of 50 studies conducted between 1965 and 1980 found six technology concepts and 140 technology-structure relationships.[31] A statistical analysis of those studies prompted the following conclusions:

* The more the technology requires *interdependence* between individuals and/or groups, the greater the need for integration (coordination).
* "As technology moves from routine to nonroutine, subunits adopt less formalized and [less] centralized structures."[32]

Additional insights can be expected in this area as researchers coordinate their definitions of technology and refine their methodologies.[33]

Organizational Size and Performance

Size is an important structural variable subject to two schools of thought. According to the first school, economists have long extolled the virtues of economies of scale. This approach, often called the "bigger is better" model, assumes the per-unit cost of production decreases as the organization grows. In effect, bigger is said to be more efficient. For example, on an annual basis, General Motors supposedly can produce its 100,000th car less expensively than its 10th car.

The second school of thought pivots on the law of diminishing returns. Called the "small is beautiful" model,[34] this approach contends that oversized organizations and subunits tend to be plagued by costly behavioral problems. Large and impersonal organizations are said to breed apathy and alienation, with resulting problems such as turnover and absenteeism. Two strong advocates of this second approach are the authors of the best-selling *In Search of Excellence:*

In the excellent companies, small *in almost every case* is beautiful. The small facility turns out to be the most efficient; its turned-on, motivated, highly productive worker, in communication (and competition) with his peers, outproduces the worker in the big facilities time and again. It holds for plants, for project teams, for divisions—for the entire company.[35]

Recent research suggests that when designing their organizations, managers should follow a middle ground between "bigger is better" and "small is beautiful" because both models have been oversold. Indeed, a newer perspective says *complexity*, not size, is the central issue.[36]

Research Insights   Researchers measure the size of organizations and organizational subunits in different ways. Some focus on financial indicators such as total sales or total asset value. Others look at the number of employees, transactions (such as the number of students in a school district), or capacity (such as the number of beds in a hospital). A meta-analysis[37] of 31 studies conducted between 1931 and 1985 that related organizational size to performance found:

- Larger organizations (in terms of assets) tended to be more productive (in terms of sales and profits).
- There were "no positive relationships between organizational size and efficiency, suggesting the absence of net economy of scale effects."[38]
- There were zero to slightly negative relationships between *subunit* size and productivity and efficiency.
- A more recent study examined the relationship between organizational size and employee turnover over a period of 65 months. Turnover was unrelated to organizational size.[39]

Striving for Small Units in Big Organizations   In summary, bigger is not necessarily better and small is not necessarily beautiful. Hard-and-fast numbers regarding exactly how big is too big or too small are difficult to come by. Management consultants offer some rough estimates (see Table 18–2). Until

---

• **TABLE 18-2**   Organizational Size: Management Consultants Address the Question of "How Big Is Too Big?"

> Peter F. Drucker, well-known management consultant:
>
> > The real growth and innovation in this country has been in medium-size companies that employ between 200 and 4,000 workers. If you are in a small company, you are running all out. You have neither the time nor the energy to devote to anything but yesterday's crisis.
> >
> > A medium-sized company has the resources to devote to new products and markets, and it's still small enough to be flexible and move fast. And these companies now have what they once lacked—they've learned how to manage.
>
> Thomas J. Peters and Robert H. Waterman, Jr., best-selling authors and management consultants:
>
> > A rule of thumb starts to emerge. We find that the lion's share of the top performers keep their division size between $50 and $100 million, with a maximum of 1,000 or so employees each. Moreover, they grant their divisions extraordinary independence—and give them the functions and resources to exploit.

Source: Excerpted from John A. Byrne, "Advice from the Dr. Spock of Business," *Business Week*, September 28, 1987, p. 61; and Thomas J. Peters and Robert H. Waterman, Jr., *In Search of Excellence* (New York: Harper & Row, 1982), pp. 272–73.

better evidence is available, the best that managers can do is monitor the productivity and efficiency of divisions, departments, and profit centers. Unwieldy and overly complex units need to be promptly broken into ones of more manageable size. The trick is to *create smallness within bigness*.[40] For example, the health care products giant, Johnson & Johnson, has more than 166 divisions.[41] Microsoft Corp., the world's largest developer of PC software, has kept the entrepreneurial spirit alive among its 5,200 employees by creating a dozen different business units. Some of these units have as few as 30 individuals. As mentioned in the opening case in Chapter 14, this is how Chairman Bill Gates keeps his decentralized operations focused:

> Each group is in charge of a particular type of software, and each knows exactly how it stacks up against its competitors by every conceivable measure, from the technical sophistication of a program to the amount of labor that went into building it. Business unit managers—known inevitably as BUMs—study the products of competitors along with any financial and productivity information their rivals make public. If the Microsoft unit doesn't outperform its competitors, the unit hears about it—often from Gates, who is known to do the same homework himself.[42]

Strategic Choice and Organizational Structure

In 1972, British sociologist John Child rejected the environmental imperative approach to organizational structure. He proposed a *strategic choice* model based on behavioral rather than rational economic principles.[43] Child believed structure resulted from a political process involving organizational power holders. According to the strategic choice model that has evolved from Child's work,[44] an organization's structure is determined largely by a dominant coalition of top-management strategists.

A Strategic Choice Model As Figure 18–4 illustrates, specific strategic choices or decisions reflect how the dominant coalition perceives environmental constraints and the organization's objectives. These strategic choices are tempered by the decision makers' personal beliefs, attitudes, and values. For example, Sam Bronfman, longtime head of Seagram, had a personal distaste for vodka and kept Seagram from seriously pursuing the vodka market. By the 1980s, when vodka had become the top-selling liquor in the United States, Seagram was lagging.[45] Directing our attention once again to Figure 18–4, the organization is structured to accommodate its mix of strategies. Ultimately, corrective action is taken if organizational effectiveness criteria are not met.

Research and Practical Lessons In a study of 97 small and mid-size companies in Quebec, Canada, strategy and organizational structure were found to be highly interdependent. Strategy influenced structure and structure influenced strategy. This was particularly true for larger, more innovative, and more successful firms.[46]

Strategic choice theory and research teaches managers at least two practical lessons. First, the environment is just one of many codeterminants of structure. Second, like any other administrative process, organization design is subject to the byplays of interpersonal power and politics.

• **Figure 18-4**   The Relationship between Strategic Choice and Organizational Structure

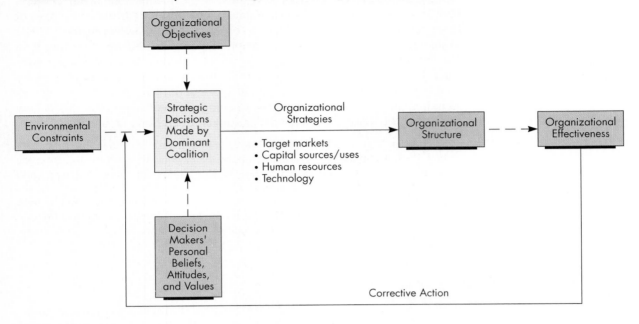

• Alternative Organization Design Configurations: Mintzberg's Typology

Henry Mintzberg, whose work on managerial roles was discussed in Chapter 1, believes most organizations fall into five natural structure–situation configurations. He urges managers not to make the common mistake of haphazardly mixing and matching design components, based on whim, convenience, or fashion. According to Mintzberg:

> Spans of control, degrees of job enlargement, forms of decentralization, planning systems, and matrix structure should not be picked and chosen at random. Rather, they should be selected according to internally consistent groupings. And these groupings should be consistent with the situation of the organization—its age and size, the conditions of the industry in which it operates, and its production technology. In essence, my argument is that—like all phenomena from atoms to stars—the characteristics of organizations fall into natural clusters, or *configurations*. When these configurations are mismatched—when the wrong ones are put together—the organization does not function effectively, does not achieve a natural harmony. If managers are to design effective organizations, they need to pay attention to the fit.[47]

Mintzberg's instructive typology includes the *simple structure*, the *machine bureaucracy*, the *professional bureaucracy*, the *divisionalized form*, and *adhocracy*. Each has its own distinct pattern of coordination, structural elements, and situational elements (see Table 18–3).

• TABLE 18-3   Selected Characteristics of Mintzberg's Five Organization Design Configurations

	Simple Structure	Machine Bureaucracy	Professional Bureaucracy	Divisionalized Form	Adhocracy
Key means of coordination	Direct supervision	Standardization of work	Standardization of skills	Standardization of outputs	Mutual adjustment
Structural elements					
Specialization of jobs	Little specialization	Much horizontal and vertical specialization	Much horizontal specialization	Some horizontal and vertical specialization (between divisions and headquarters)	Much horizontal specialization
Formalization of behavior— bureaucratic/ organic	Little formal-ization— organic	Little formal-ization— bureaucratic	Much formal-ization— bureaucratic	Much formal-ization (within divisions)— bureaucratic	Little formaliza-tion—organic
Decentralization	Centralization	Limited horizontal decentralization	Horizontal and vertical decentralization	Limited vertical decentralization	Selective decentralization
Situational elements					
Age and size	Typically young and small	Typically old and large	Varies	Typically old and very large	Typically young (operating adhocracy)
Technical system	Simple, not regulating	Regulating but not automated, not very complex	Not regulating or complex	Divisible, otherwise like machine bureaucracy	Very complex, often automated (in administra-tive adhocracy), not regulating or complex (in operating adhocracy)
Environment	Simple and dynamic; sometimes hostile	Simple and stable	Complex and stable	Relatively simple and stable; diversified markets (esp. products and services)	Complex and dynamic; some-times disparate (in administra-tive adhocracy)
Power	Chief executive con-trol; often owner managed; not fashionable	Technocratic and external control; not fashionable	Professional oper-ator control; fashionable	Middle-line con-trol; fashionable (esp. in industry)	Expert control; very fashionable

Simple Structure

This configuration is found typically in small entrepreneurial companies. Nearly all organizations start as simple structures. Simple structure organi-zations are organic because standardization, formalization, and admin-istrative layers are minimal. Operations are flexible and adaptive because top managers/owners directly supervise operating personnel.

Machine Bureaucracy

An offshoot of the Industrial Revolution, machine bureaucracies are built around narrowly defined, repetitive, low-skill jobs. Communication and

authority flow through the formal chain of command. Machine bureaucracies are highly mechanistic. Decision making is centralized. There is an
obsession with control to eliminate uncertainty and to contain inevitable
alienation and conflict. This configuration is found in large mass production
companies in the automobile industry, for example. Mass service organizations such as McDonald's are machine bureaucracies, as are most large
government agencies. Employee alienation, lack of flexibility, and poor
adaptability are overriding problems for machine bureaucracies. Nonetheless, according to Mintzberg, "machine bureaucracy remains indispens-
able—and probably the most prevalent of the five configurations today."[48]

Professional Bureaucracy

The distinguishing difference between machine bureaucracy and professional bureaucracy is the means of coordination or control. Machine
bureaucracies rely on standardized tasks for coordination. Professional bureaucracies rely on highly trained professionals to exercise *self-control*.
College professors, accountants, lawyers, and hospital physicians prefer to
work independently in decentralized organizations. Thus, universities, accounting and law firms, and hospitals tend to be configured as professional
bureaucracies. While skilled professionals enjoy the characteristic autonomy and democracy of professional bureaucracies, this configuration is not
very adaptable. Professional bureaucracies are most effective in a stable or
static environment.

Divisionalized Form

"Divisionalization refers to a structure of semiautonomous market-based
units."[49] Typically, a headquarters unit has loose administrative control
over several machine bureaucracies. For example, before its mid-1980s
reorganization, General Motors grew into a world leader by having its
Chevrolet, Buick, Pontiac, Oldsmobile, and Cadillac divisions compete with
each other as if they were independent companies.

Although this configuration appears to be highly decentralized, the opposite is generally true. Division heads often exercise highly centralized
control over their respective units. Headquarters maintains overall control
through financial and performance reporting mechanisms, thus ensuring that
the divisions' outputs are standardized. Other divisional affairs are constrained by headquarters policies and directives. For instance, "Dana
Corp., an automotive-parts maker in Toledo, Ohio, gives its divisions broad
latitude on such matters as hiring and firing, though within limits specified
by the company."[50] Divisionalization enables machine bureaucracies to be
more adaptable. Divisions can be added or expanded and sold or cut back as
business conditions dictate.

Adhocracy

Mintzberg borrowed the term **adhocracy** from Alvin Toffler's book *Future
Shock* to describe highly organic structures based on temporary project
teams. Organizations such as NASA, Boeing Company, and Intel rely on

flexible adhocracy to remain innovative and responsive to fast-changing conditions. According to Mintzberg:

> Of all the configurations, adhocracy shows the least reverence for the classical principles of management, especially unity of command. The regulated system does not matter much either. In this configuration, information and decision processes flow flexibly and informally, wherever they must, to promote innovation. And that means overriding the chain of authority if need be.[51]

The most widely known and used form of adhocracy is the matrix organization.[52]

Matrix Organization   A **matrix organization** is a project-oriented approach to organization design that combines vertical and horizontal authority. It often is referred to simply as project management. Notice the gridlike pattern in Figure 18–5. In flagrant violation of the traditional unity of command principle (each employee should report to only one boss), the functional specialists in Figure 18–5 have two bosses. Each functional manager is responsible for general administrative duties such as hiring, training, per-

---

• **FIGURE 18–5**   A Matrix Organization

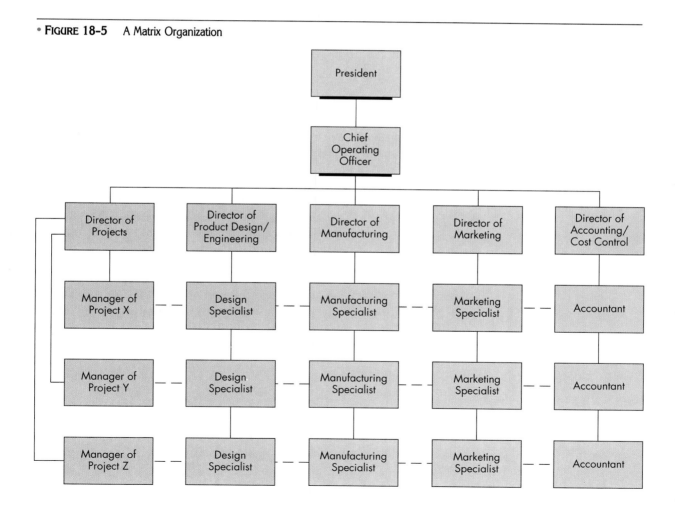

formance appraisal, and project assignments. Meanwhile, the project managers have temporary authority over varying numbers of functional specialists, depending on project requirements. For example, the manager of project X may need the services of three design specialists early in the project, one during the manufacturing phase, and none when the product goes to market.

Matrix Advantages and Disadvantages   Proponents of matrix organizations list among its advantages flexibility, enhanced coordination, better communication, and improved motivation and commitment. Detractors point to power and authority struggles, increased conflict, slow decision making, and the expense of double management.[53] A field study of the implementation of a matrix structure in the engineering division of an aircraft manufacturer uncovered the following consequences:

* A greater *quantity* of communication.
* Lower *quality* communication.
* A negative impact on work attitudes and coordination.[54]

As with each of the other structural configurations, matrix organization is not a cure-all. It needs to fit the circumstances (see the lower-right portion of Table 18–3) and be refined as structural problems arise.[55]

• SUMMARY OF KEY CONCEPTS

A. The three stages of the organizational life cycle are inception, high growth, and maturity. Decline is an ever-present threat during the organizational life cycle, with complacency during periods of success particularly troublesome. Research shows that managerial priorities and effectiveness criteria shift during the organizational life cycle. Thus, managers need to adjust and adapt from one stage to the next.

B. The contingency approach to organization design calls for fitting the organization to the demands of the situation. Environmental uncertainty can be assessed in terms of various combinations of two dimensions: (1) simple or complex and (2) static or dynamic. Harvard researchers Lawrence and Lorsch found that successful organizations achieved a proper balance between the two opposing structural forces of differentiation and integration. Differentiation forces the organization apart. Through a variety of mechanisms—including hierarchy, rules, teams, and liaisons—integration draws the organization together.

C. British researchers Burns and Stalker found that mechanistic (bureaucratic, centralized) organizations tended to be effective in stable situations. In unstable situations, organic (flexible, decentralized) organizations were more effective. These findings underscored the need for a contingency approach to organization design.

D. Technology, organization and subunit size, and strategic choice are important contingency design variables. Regarding the optimum size for organizations, the challenge for today's managers is to achieve smallness within bigness. The strategic choice model emphasizes how environmental and personal factors affect the dominant coalition, which in turn formulates strategies that shape the organization's structure.

E. Henry Mintzberg contends that organizations naturally fall into five structure–situation configurations. They are: simple structure, machine bureaucracy, professional bureaucracy, divisionalized form, and adhocracy. Machine bureaucracies are both the most mechanistic and most common configuration today. Adhocracies, typically in the form of matrix organizations, are the most organic configuration.

• KEY TERMS

contingency approach to
  organization design
differentiation
integration
mechanistic organizations

organic organizations
centralized decision making
decentralized decision making
adhocracy
matrix organization

• DISCUSSION QUESTIONS

1. Why is it instructive to view organizations from a life cycle perspective?

2. Which phase of the organizational life cycle—inception, high-growth, maturity—do you think would be the most difficult for management?

3. How does decline relate to organizational life cycles?

4. Why is it important to focus on the role of complacency in organizational decline?

5. In a nutshell, what does contingency organization design entail?

6. What evidence of integration can you find in your present (or last) place of employment?

7. What is wrong with an organization having too much differentiation and too little integration?

8. If organic organizations are popular with most employees, why can't all organizations be structured in an organic fashion?

9. How can you tell if an organization (or subunit) is too big?

10. Why would early management writers who promoted the military/mechanical model of organizations probably dislike the matrix configuration?

BACK TO THE OPENING CASE

Now that you have read Chapter 18, you should be able to answer the following questions about the W. L. Gore case:

1. Why is Gore a prime example of an organic organization? How can this structure enhance the firm's effectiveness?
2. Would you like to work at W. L. Gore? Why or why not?
3. What problems could arise with W. L. Gore's "lattice" system of organization?
4. Do you think W. L. Gore has an effective strategy for dealing with excessive size? Explain.

• EXERCISE 18

Objectives

1. To get out into the field and talk to a practicing manager about organizational structure.
2. To increase your understanding of the important distinction between mechanistic and organic organizations.
3. To broaden your knowledge of contingency design, in terms of organization-environment fit.

Introduction

A good way to test the validity of what you have just read about organizational design is to interview a practicing manager. (Note: If you are a manager, simply complete the questionnaire yourself.)

Instructions

Your objective is to interview a manager about aspects of organizational structure, environmental uncertainty, and organizational effectiveness. A *manager* is defined as anyone who supervises other people in an organizational setting. The organization may be small or large and for-profit or not-for-profit. Higher-level managers are preferred, but middle managers and first-line supervisors are acceptable. If you interview a lower-level manager, be sure to remind him or her that you want a description of the overall organization, not just an isolated subunit. Your interview will center on the adaptation of Figure 18–3, as discussed below.

When conducting your interview, be sure to explain to the manager what you are trying to accomplish. But assure the manager that his or her name will not be mentioned in class discussion or any written projects. Try to keep side notes during the interview for later reference.

Questionnaire

The following questionnaire, adapted from Figure 18–3, will help you determine if the manager's organization is relatively mechanistic or relatively organic in structure. Note: For items 1 and 2 on the following questionnaire, have the manager respond in terms of the average nonmanagerial employee. (Circle one number for each item.)

Characteristic

1. Task definition and knowledge required — Narrow; technical — 1—2—3—4—5—6—7 — Broad; general
2. Linkage between individual's contribution and organization's purpose — Vague or indirect — 1—2—3—4—5—6—7 — Clear or direct
3. Task flexibility — Rigid; routine — 1—2—3—4—5—6—7 — Flexible; varied
4. Specification of techniques, obligations, and rights — Specific — 1—2—3—4—5—6—7 — General
5. Degree of hierarchical control — High — 1—2—3—4—5—6—7 — Low (self-control emphasized)
6. Primary communication pattern — Top-down — 1—2—3—4—5—6—7 — Lateral (between peers)
7. Primary decision-making style — Authoritarian — 1—2—3—4—5—6—7 — Democratic; participative
8. Emphasis on obedience and loyalty — High — 1—2—3—4—5—6—7 — Low

Total score = _____

Additional question about the organization's environment:

This organization faces an environment that is (circle one number):

Stable and certain 1—2—3—4—5—6—7 —8—9—10 Unstable and uncertain

Additional questions about the organization's effectiveness:

a. Profitability (if a profit-seeking business):
Low 1—2—3—4—5— 6—7—8—9—10 High
b. Degree of organizational goal accomplishment:
Low 1—2—3—4—5— 6—7—8—9—10 High
c. Customer or client satisfaction:
Low 1—2—3—4—5— 6—7—8—9—10 High
d. Employee satisfaction:
Low 1—2—3—4—5— 6—7—8—9—10 High

Total effectiveness score = _____
(Add responses from above)

Questions for Consideration/Class Discussion

1. Using the following norms, was the manager's organization relatively mechanistic or organic?
   8–24 = Relatively mechanistic
   25–39 = Mixed
   40–56 = Relatively organic

2. In terms of Burns and Stalker's contingency theory, does the manager's organization seem to fit its environment? Explain.

3. Does the organization's degree of effectiveness reflect how well it fits its environment? Explain.

• NOTES

[1] Robert W. Keidel, "Triangular Design: A New Organizational Geometry," *Academy of Management Executive,* November 1990, p. 35.

[2] Robert E. Quinn and Kim Cameron, "Organizational Life Cycles and Shifting Criteria of Effectiveness: Some Preliminary Evidence," *Management Science,* January 1983, p. 40.

[3] Ten organizational life cycle models are reviewed in Ibid., pp. 34–41. Also see, for example, Robert K. Kazanjian and Robert Drazin, "A Stage-Contingent Model of Design and Growth for Technology-Based New Ventures," *Journal of Business Venturing,* 1990, pp. 137–50; and Robert Drazin and Robert K. Kazanjian, "A Reanalysis of Miller and Friesen's Life Cycle Data," *Strategic Management Journal,* May–June 1990, pp. 319–25.

[4] Richard Brandt, "Don Kingsborough's Latest World of Wonder," *Business Week,* June 11, 1990, p. 23.

[5] Richard A. Cosier and Dan R. Dalton, "Search for Excellence, Learn from Japan— Are These Panaceas or Problems?" *Business Horizons,* November–December 1986, p. 67.

[6] Robert A. Mamis and Steven Pearlstein, " '1–2–3' Creator Mitch Kapor," *Inc.,* January 1987, p. 31. (Kapor retained a seat on Lotus's board of directors and 1.6 million shares of the firm's stock.)

[7] See "The Disenchantment of the Middle Class," *Business Week,* April 25, 1983, p. 86.

[8] Peter Lorange and Robert T. Nelson, "How to Recognize—and Avoid—Organizational Decline," *Sloan Management Review,* Spring 1987, p. 47.

[9] Excerpted from Ibid., pp. 43–45.

[10] For details, see Kim S. Cameron, Myung U. Kim, and David A. Whetten, "Organizational Effects of Decline and Turbulence," *Administrative Science Quarterly,* June 1987, pp. 222–40.

[11] Twelve dysfunctional consequences of decline are discussed and empirically tested in Kim S. Cameron, David A. Whetten, and Myung U. Kim, "Organizational Dysfunctions of Decline," *Academy of Management Journal,* March 1987, pp. 126–38.

[12] Additional scholarly treatment of organizational decline can be found in Robert I. Sutton and Thomas D'Aunno, "Decreasing Organizational Size: Untangling the Effects of Money and People," *Academy of Management Review,* April 1989, pp. 194–212; and Robert I. Sutton, "Organizational Decline Processes: A Social Psychological Perspective," in *Research in Organizational Behavior,* Vol. 12, eds. Barry M. Staw and L. L. Cummings (Greenwich, Conn.: JAI Press, 1990), pp. 205–54.

[13] Based on Ken G. Smith, Terence R. Mitchell, and Charles E. Summer, "Top Level Management Priorities in Different Stages of the Organizational Life Cycle," *Academy of Management Journal,* December 1985, pp. 799–820.

[14] Additional details may be found in Quinn and Cameron, "Organizational Life Cycles and Shifting Criteria of Effectiveness: Some Preliminary Evidence," pp. 33–51.

[15] For an instructive conceptual model of the relationship between organizational politics, strategy, and organizational life cycles, see Barbara Gray and Sonny S. Ariss, "Politics and Strategic Change across Organizational Life Cycles," *Academy of Management Review,* October 1985, pp. 707–23. Practical advice regarding the organizational life cycle can be found in Jim Mayers, "How to Withstand a Merger," *Management Review,* October 1986, pp. 39–42; and Bruce G. Posner and Bo Burlingham, "Getting to Prime," *Inc.,* January 1991, pp. 27–33.

[16] See Robert O. Metzger, "Organizational Life Cycles in Banking," *Group & Organization Studies,* December 1989, pp. 389–98.

[17] An interesting distinction between three types of environmental uncertainty can be found in Frances J. Milliken, "Three Types of Perceived Uncertainty about the Environment: State, Effect, and Response Uncertainty," *Academy of Management Review,* January 1987, pp. 133–43.

[18] Robert Duncan, "What Is the Right Organization Structure?" *Organizational Dynamics,* Winter 1979, p. 63.

[19] Ibid.

[20] See Thomas Moore, "He Put the Kick Back into Coke," *Fortune,* October 26, 1987, pp. 46–56; and Pete Engardio, "In Asia, The Sweet Taste of Success," *Business Week,* November 26, 1990, p. 96.

[21] Paul R. Lawrence and Jay W. Lorsch, *Organization and Environment* (Homewood, Ill: Richard D. Irwin, 1967), p. 157.

[22] Pooled, sequential, and reciprocal integration are discussed in Jay W. Lorsch, "Organization Design: A Situational Perspective," *Organizational Dynamics,* Autumn 1977, pp. 2–14.

[23] See Russell Mitchell, "Masters of Innovation," *Business Week,* April 10, 1989, pp. 58–63; and Brian Dumaine, "Ability to Innovate," *Fortune,* January 29, 1990, pp. 43, 46.

[24] Kathleen Deveny, "Bag Those Fries, Squirt That Ketchup, Fry That Fish," *Business Week,* October 13, 1986, p. 86.

[25] Paul Kaestle, "A New Rationale for Organizational Structure," *Planning Review,* July–August 1990, p. 22.

[26] Details of this study can be found in Tom Burns and G. M. Stalker, *The Management of Innovation* (London: Tavistock, 1961).

[27] Dennis J. Gillen and Stephen J. Carroll, "Relationship of Managerial Ability to Unit Effectiveness in More Organic versus More Mechanistic Departments," *Journal of Management Studies,* November 1985, pp. 674–75.

[28] J. Daniel Sherman and Howard L. Smith, "The Influence of Organizational Structure on Intrinsic versus Extrinsic Motivation," *Academy of Management Journal,* December 1984, p. 883.

[29] See John A. Courtright, Gail T. Fairhurst, and L. Edna Rogers, "Interaction Patterns in Organic and Mechanistic Systems," *Academy of Management Journal,* December 1989, pp. 773–802.

[30] See Joan Woodward, *Industrial Organization: Theory and Practice* (London: Oxford University Press, 1965); and Paul D. Collins and Frank Hull, "Technology and Span of Control: Woodward Revisited," *Journal of Management Studies,* March 1986, pp. 143–64.

[31] See Louis W. Fry, "Technology-Structure Research: Three Critical Issues," *Academy of Management Journal,* September 1982, pp. 532–52.

[32] Ibid., p. 548.

[33] For example, see Judith W. Alexander and Barbara Mark, "Technology and Structure of Nursing Organizations," *Nursing & Health Care,* April 1990, pp. 194–99.

[34] The phrase "small is beautiful" was coined by the late British economist E. F. Schumacher. See E. F. Schumacher, *Small Is Beautiful: Economics as If People Mattered* (New York: Harper & Row, 1973).

[35] Thomas J. Peters and Robert H. Waterman, Jr., *In Search of Excellence* (New York: Harper & Row, 1982), p. 321.

[36] See, for example, John A. Byrne, "Is Your Company Too Big?" *Business Week,* March 27, 1989, pp. 84–94.

[37] Richard Z. Gooding and John A. Wagner III, "A Meta-Analytic Review of the Relationship between Size and Performance: The Productivity and Efficiency of Organizations and Their Subunits," *Administrative Science Quarterly,* December 1985, pp. 462–81.

[38] Ibid., p. 477.

[39] Results are presented in Philip G. Benson, Terry L. Dickinson, and Charles O. Neidt, "The Relationship between Organizational Size and Turnover: A Longitudinal Investigation," *Human Relations,* January 1987, pp. 15–30. Also see Masoud Yasai-Ardekani, "Effects of Environmental Scarcity and Munificence on the Relationship of Context to Organizational Structure," *Academy of Management Journal,* March 1989, pp. 131–56.

[40] See Vijay Sathe, "Fostering Entrepreneurship in the Large, Diversified Firm," *Organizational Dynamics,* Summer 1989, pp. 20–32.

[41] Data from Christopher Power, "At Johnson & Johnson, A Mistake Can Be a Badge of Honor," *Business Week,* September 26, 1988, pp. 126–28.

[42] Brenton Schlender, "How Bill Gates Keeps the Magic Going," *Fortune,* June 18, 1990, p. 84.

[43] See John Child, "Organizational Structure, Environment and Performance: The Role of Strategic Choice," *Sociology,* January 1972, pp. 1–22.

[44] See Jay Galbraith, *Organization Design* (Reading, Mass.: Addison-Wesley Publishing, 1977); John R. Montanari, "Managerial Discretion: An Expanded Model of Organization Choice," *Academy of Management Review,* April 1978, pp. 231–41; and H. Randolph Bobbitt, Jr., and Jeffrey D. Ford, "Decision-Maker Choice as a Determinant of Organizational Structure," *Academy of Management Review,* January 1980, pp. 13–23.

[45] Example drawn from "What Edgar Bronfman Wants at Seagram," *Business Week,* April 27, 1981, pp. 135–42.

[46] Details may be found in Danny Miller, "Strategy Making and Structure: Analysis and Implications for Performance," *Academy of Management Journal,* March 1987, pp. 7–32. Also see James B. Thomas and Reuben R. McDaniel, Jr., "Interpreting Strategic Issues: Effects of Strategy and the Information-Processing Structure of Top Management Teams," *Academy of Management Journal,* June 1990, pp. 286–306. Contrary evidence is presented in Mohammad Ibrahim Ahmad At-Twaijri and John R. Montanari, "The Impact of Context and Choice on the Boundary-Spanning Process: An Empirical Extension," *Human Relations,* December 1987, pp. 783–98.

[47] Henry Mintzberg, "Organization Design: Fashion or Fit?" *Harvard Business Review,* January–February 1981, pp. 103–4.

48 Ibid., p. 109.

49 Ibid., p. 110.

50 Amanda Bennett, "Airline's Ills Point Out Weaknesses of Unorthodox Management Style," *The Wall Street Journal,* August 11, 1986, p. 15.

51 Henry Mintzberg, *Structure in Fives: Designing Effective Organizations* (Englewood Cliffs, N.J.: Prentice-Hall, 1983), p. 255; see also, Henry Mintzberg, "The Effective Organization: Forces and Forms," *Sloan Management Review,* Winter 1991, pp. 54–67.

52 For an informative update, see Christopher A. Bartlett and Sumantra Ghoshal, "Matrix Management: Not a Structure, A Frame of Mind," *Harvard Business Review,* July–August 1990, pp. 138–45.

53 An excellent analysis of matrix organization may be found in Erik W. Larson and David H. Gobeli, "Matrix Management: Contradictions and Insights," *California Management Review,* Summer 1987, pp. 126–38.

54 See William F. Joyce, "Matrix Organization: A Social Experiment," *Academy of Management Journal,* September 1986, pp. 536–61.

55 Problems with Texas Instruments' widely acclaimed matrix structure are discussed in "Texas Instruments Cleans Up Its Act," *Business Week,* September 19, 1983, pp. 56–64.

International OB and Organizational Cultures

When you finish studying the material in this chapter, you should be able to:

- Explain how societal culture and organizational culture combine to influence on-the-job behavior.
- Distinguish between high-context and low-context cultures.

- Discuss each of the following relative to cross-cultural awareness: time, interpersonal space, language, and religion.
- Explain the practical lessons from the Hofstede and Bond cross-cultural studies.
- Define the term *organizational culture*.

- Describe four functions of organizational culture and explain how culture can become a competitive advantage.
- Describe the HOME model for developing an organization's culture.

OPENING CASE 19

Can Mazda Make It in Michigan?

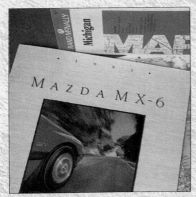

Sharon Hoogstraten

Mazda Motor Corp.'s sprawling assembly plant . . . [in Flat Rock, Michigan] was supposed to show the world that Japanese management and experienced U.S. auto workers from the heart of union country could be a profitable mix.

But 2½ years after Mazda began building cars just 15 miles south of Detroit, the mix is turning sour.

Four top U.S. managers have quit the company since 1988, and now Japanese executives have taken the senior posts that Americans once held. The company is on its fourth director of labor relations since hiring began in 1986. Unionized workers are boycotting Mazda's suggestion box, a cornerstone of Japanese-style management.

What's more, union leaders here curry favor among rank-and-file workers by taking pot-shots at Japanese managers. Mazda executives, in turn, grouse about the

Americans' poor work attendance. Overall, industry experts say, Mazda's relations with its American workers, both blue- and white-collar, are worse than at any of the seven other Japanese-owned or operated U.S. auto plants.

As more Japanese companies set up shop in the United States, relations between Japanese bosses and American workers are shaping up to be a workplace issue of the 1990s. Most Japanese companies are loath to acknowledge any problems. But experts say Mazda isn't the only one having trouble.

"What's happening in Flat Rock isn't unique, it's just that the union situation makes problems there public," says Robert Cole, a University of Michigan professor who studies Japanese companies in the United States. "Americans feel as if they're left out of the information network" in many Japanese-run operations, he adds, and American managers "feel that the top spots are blocked." Increasingly, as at Mazda, the results are high turnover among American executives, and resentment among blue-collar workers.

This isn't how Mazda officials envisioned it would be in 1984. That's when they bowed to pressure from Ford Motor Co., which owns 25 percent of Mazda, and declared they would become the first—and so far only—Japanese auto maker to build cars in Michigan.

UAW leaders wanted smooth labor relations at Mazda. That, they reasoned, would give them "a chance to be more successful in organizing the other Japanese plants" in the United States, says William Judson, the top UAW official at the Flat Rock plant before he was ousted in an election last year.

But UAW higher-ups lost control of events at Flat Rock. They got blind-sided when hard-line activists unseated local leaders, such as Mr. Judson, who espoused a more cooperative line. Now, the trouble at Mazda is bolstering the resolve of other Japanese auto makers to fight the union.

"In my opinion, the work ethic is stronger down here" without a union, says Jerry Benefield, plant manager of Nissan Motor Co.'s assembly plant in Smyrna, Tenn. In a bitter campaign, Nissan rebuffed a UAW organizing drive at Smyrna last year. So far, the UAW has organized only those Japanese plants where the company agreed to the idea before operations began.

Mazda did just that, but tried to weed out any rabble-rousers when it screened 100,000 candidates for plant jobs. The company got a work force more educated and nearly a generation younger than the old-line UAW workers at most Big Three plants. But it didn't keep out people like Mildred Willis, a dedicated labor activist whose father founded a chapter of

OPENING CASE 19

(concluded)

the plumbers union.

Ms. Willis, an outspoken 32-year-old, shares with older UAW members a distaste for things Japanese. She drives a Chevrolet, not a Mazda. And as a representative for Mazda's night-shift workers, she's quick to criticize the Japanese managers.

"I think they need to listen a little bit more," she says. "I like to see that an employee's word is being taken." Ms. Willis is now a thorn in Mazda's side, distributing anti-management leaflets at the plant gate and fighting to allow workers to get treatment for sore elbows and other minor injuries on company time. . . .

Underlying the tension over specific issues are deeper cultural divides. Even before Flat Rock opened, Mazda executives wondered aloud if U.S. workers could hustle the way Japanese workers do. Then came Osamu Nobuto, former chief of Mazda's U.S. operations. Unusually blunt for a Japanese executive, Mr. Nobuto publicly lambasted U.S. workers for lacking dedication.

"Mr. Nobuto didn't understand us and we didn't understand him," says Greg Drudi, the top UAW official in the plant.

Mr. Uchida, who recently succeeded Mr. Nobuto, says he won't be so outspoken. He's quick to say that Mazda cars built at Flat Rock are just as good as those built in Japan. (Independent experts also give Flat Rock high marks for quality.)

Swearing by Kaizen

But Mr. Uchida's arrival hasn't changed the *kaizen*, or continuous improvement, management philosophy that Mr. Nobuto put in place. In practice, kaizen translates into a never-ending push to cut the number of worker-hours spent building each car, reduce assembly defects, and simplify factory processes. Mazda swears by kaizen. Mazda's U.S. workers swear at it. To some union members, kaizen is only a Japanese word for the old Detroit practice of speeding up the assembly line.

Mazda and its union also are scuffling over charges that the company is being unreasonable about absenteeism, sick leave, and worker compensation requests. . . .

Last fall, Mazda's top ranking U.S. executives tried applying their own ideas to fix the absenteeism problem. Their plan: boost the annual bonus for perfect attendance to $1,500 from $500. In return, the company got a union concession making it easier to fire workers who were absent more than 15 days.

Abrupt Resignations

But the day after the union approved the agreement, the two senior U.S. managers who negotiated the deal abruptly resigned. A Mazda spokesman said the Americans quit because their Japanese superiors weren't happy with the negotiations.

The incident illustrates how little latitude Mazda's U.S. managers have to make their own decisions, says Robert Fucini, who has co-written a book on the plant. Each morning, for instance, U.S. managers at Mazda get a "grocery list" from their Japanese "adviser" that tells them just what they are supposed to do that day.

Mr. Uchida concedes that Mazda's practice of making decisions by consensus often gives the appearance of keeping authority away from its U.S. executives. But despite such problems, he insists that Flat Rock will be a success. "I don't think there's anything that has hurt the future of our company," he says.

Does that mean Mazda would build cars in Michigan if it could start all over again? Mr. Uchida just breaks into a broad grin and laughs.

For Discussion

What is the central problem in this case?

• Additional discussion questions linking this case with the following material appear at the end of this chapter.

Globalization of the economy challenges virtually all managers to become more internationally aware and adept. Those adventurous enough to accept a foreign assignment will experience the international arena firsthand. Even managers who stay behind will not escape the global economy. They, too, will be thrust into the international arena as they deal increasingly with foreign suppliers, customers, and co-workers.

A case in point is the strategic direction American Airlines' chief executive officer, Robert Crandall, has set for the 1990s:

> By the year 2000, Crandall aims to generate about 30 percent of American's revenues from foreign routes, up from virtually nothing ten years ago. To reach that ambitious target, he has committed $11 billion—more than half American's capital spending budget—to expanding and upgrading his international operations over the next five years.[1]

To achieve Crandall's bet-the-company strategy, American's managers and employees in both its foreign and U.S. operations, including its Texas headquarters, are sharpening their international competitiveness. Foreign language skills and cross-cultural awareness are being stressed as never before. The airline's menus are being reformulated to international tastes. Service standards are being honed to international standards. Foreign business deals are being negotiated worldwide. The organization's culture is being reshaped to accommodate a multicultural work force. Thanks to its global strategy, American Airlines is evolving into a whole new company, one that will be comfortable competing anywhere on the planet.

If you have not done so already, the time to begin preparing to work in the global economy with its rich mix of cultures is now! Accordingly, the purpose of this chapter is to help you take a step in that direction by exploring the impact of culture on work behavior in today's increasingly internationalized organizations. Societal and organizational cultures are covered together in this chapter because they have a common conceptual heritage—cultural anthropology. Separating these two intertwined cultural domains would be unrealistic and inadequate in today's international workplace. We begin with a model showing how societal culture and organizational culture combine to influence work behavior, followed by a fundamental cultural distinction. Next we examine key dimensions of international OB with the goal of enhancing cross-cultural awareness. Practical lessons from cross-cultural management research are then reviewed. Attention subsequently turns to understanding and managing organizational cultures.

• CULTURE AND ORGANIZATIONAL BEHAVIOR

How would you, as a manager, interpret the following situations?

> An Asian executive for a multinational company, transferred from Taiwan to the Midwest, appears aloof and autocratic to his peers.
> A West Coast bank embarks on a "friendly teller" campaign, but its Filipino female tellers won't cooperate.

> A white manager criticizes a black male employee's work. Instead of getting an explanation, the manager is met with silence and a firm stare.[2]

If you attribute the behavior in these situations to personalities, three descriptions come to mind: arrogant, unfriendly, and hostile. These are reasonable conclusions. Unfortunately, they are probably wrong, being based more on prejudice and stereotypes than on actual fact. However, if you attribute the behavioral outcomes to *cultural* differences, you stand a better chance of making the following more valid interpretations: "As it turns out, Asian culture encourages a more distant managing style, Filipinos associate overly friendly behavior in women with prostitution, and blacks as a group act more deliberately, studying visual cues, than most white men."[3] One cannot afford to overlook relevant cultural contexts when trying to understand and manage organizational behavior.

Culture Defined

While noting that cultures exist in social units of all sizes (from civilizations to countries to ethnic groups to organizations to work groups), Edgar Schein defined **culture** as:

> A pattern of basic assumptions—invented, discovered, or developed by a given group as it learns to cope with its problems of external adaptation and internal integration—that has worked well enough to be considered valid and, therefore, to be taught to new members as the correct way to perceive, think, and feel in relation to those problems.[4]

The word *taught* needs to be interpreted carefully because it implies formal education or training. While cultural lessons may indeed be taught in schools, religious settings, and on the job, formal inculcation is secondary. Most cultural lessons are learned by observing and imitating role models as they go about their daily affairs or as observed in the media.

Culture Is a Subtle but Pervasive Force

Culture generally remains below the threshold of conscious awareness because it involves *taken-for-granted assumptions* about how one should perceive, think, act, and feel. Cultural anthropologist Edward T. Hall put it this way:

> Since much of culture operates outside our awareness, frequently we don't even know what we know. We pick . . . [expectations and assumptions] up in the cradle. We unconsciously learn what to notice and what not to notice, how to divide time and space, how to walk and talk and use our bodies, how to behave as men or women, how to relate to other people, how to handle responsibility, whether experience is seen as whole or fragmented. This applies to all people. The Chinese or the Japanese or the Arabs are as unaware of their assumptions as we are of our own. We each assume that they're part of human nature. What we think of as "mind" is really internalized culture.[5]

In sum, it has been said: "you are your culture, and your culture is you."

A Model of Societal and Organizational Cultures

As illustrated in Figure 19–1, culture influences organizational behavior in two ways. Employees bring their societal culture to work with them in the form of customs and language. Organizational culture, a by-product of societal culture, in turn affects the individual's values/ethics, attitudes, assumptions, and expectations.[6] The term *societal* culture is used here instead of national culture because the boundaries of many of today's nation-states were not drawn along cultural lines. The Soviet Union, prior to its recent fragmentation, included 15 republics and more than 100 ethnic nationalities, many with their own distinct language.[7] Meanwhile, English-speaking Canadians in Vancouver are culturally closer to Americans in Seattle than to their French-speaking countrymen in Quebec. Societal culture is shaped by the various environmental factors listed in the left-hand side of Figure 19–1.

Once inside the organization's sphere of influence, the individual is further affected by the *organization's* culture. Mixing of societal and organizational cultures can produce interesting dynamics in multinational companies. For example, with French and American employees working side by side at General Electric's medical imaging production facility in Waukesha, Wisconsin, unit head Claude Benchimol has witnessed some culture shock:

> The French are surprised the American parking lots empty out as early as 5 P.M.; the Americans are surprised the French don't start work at 8 A.M. Benchimol feels the French are more talkative and candid. Americans have more of a sense of hierarchy and are less likely to criticize. But they may be growing closer to the French. Says Benchimol: "It's taken a year to get across the idea that we are all entitled to say what we don't like to become more productive and work better."[8]

Same company, same company culture, yet GE's French and American co-workers have different attitudes about time, hierarchy, and communication. They are the products of different societal cultures. When managing people at work, the individual's societal culture, the organizational culture, and any interaction between the two need to be taken into consideration. Otherwise, mistaken performance attributions will be a serious problem.

• **FIGURE 19-1**   Cultural Influences on Organizational Behavior

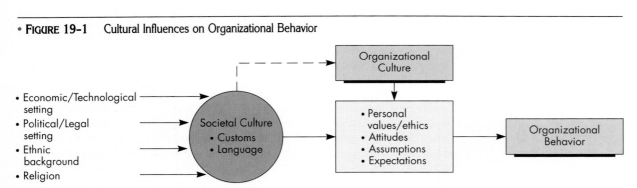

Source: Adapted in part from Betty Jane Punnett and Sirinimal Withane, "Hofstede's Value Survey Module: To Embrace or Abandon?" in *Advances in International Comparative Management*, Vol. 5, ed. S. Benjamin Prasad (Greenwich, Conn.: JAI Press, 1990), pp. 69–89,

High-Context and Low-Context Societal Cultures

Cultural anthropologists believe interesting and valuable lessons can be learned by comparing one culture with another. Many models have been proposed for distinguishing among the world's rich variety of cultures. One general distinction contrasts high-context and low-context cultures[9] (see Figure 19–2). Managers in multicultural settings need to know the difference, if they are to communicate and interact effectively.

Reading between the Lines in High-Context Cultures   People from **high-context cultures** rely heavily on situational cues for meaning when perceiving and communicating with another person. Nonverbal cues such as one's official position or status convey messages more powerfully than do spoken words. Thus, we come to better understand the ritual of exchanging *and reading* business cards in Japan (see International OB). Japanese culture is relatively high-context. One's business card, listing employer and official position, conveys vital silent messages to members of Japan's homogeneous society. An intercultural communications authority explains:

> Nearly all communication in Japan takes place within an elaborate and vertically organized social structure. Everyone has a distinct place within this framework. Rarely do people converse without knowing, or determining, who is above and who is below them. Associates are always older or younger, male or female, subordinate or superior. And these distinctions all carry implications for the form of address, choice of words, physical distance, and demeanor. As a result, conversation tends to reflect this formal hierarchy.[10]

Verbal and written communication in high-context cultures such as China, Korea, and Japan are secondary to taken-for-granted cultural assumptions about other people.

Reading the Fine Print in Low-Context Cultures   In **low-context cultures**, written and spoken words carry the burden of shared meaning. True, people in low-

• **FIGURE 19-2**   A Continuum of High-Context and Low-Context Cultures

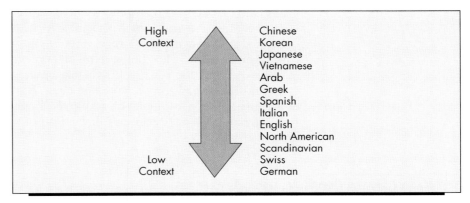

Source: Ronald E. Dulek, John S. Fielden, and John S. Hill, "International Communication: An Executive Primer," *Business Horizons*, January–February 1991, p. 21 as based on Edward T. Hall, *Beyond Culture* (Garden City, N.Y.: Anchor Press/Doubleday, 1976), and "How Cultures Collide," *Psychology Today*, July 1976, pp. 66–74, 97.

INTERNATIONAL OB

The Art of Exchanging Business Cards in Japan

The exchange of business cards in Japan is an absolutely essential ritual, so you must go prepared with several hundred cards, preferably printed on one side in English and on the other in Japanese.

Do not underestimate the social requirement for exchanging your card with *everybody* that you meet. This includes offering and receiving one card for every person in the room, even if there are twenty people at the meeting on both sides!

An American negotiator once exchanged 112 business cards at the start of a session. It took fifteen minutes to complete the ritual, and he knew that there was no way honor and mutual respect could be satisfied until he had been around the entire room to each person to exchange a bow and a card. He also made sure that he looked carefully at the cards he was offered, even though many of them were in Japanese without English translations.

Source: Gavin Kennedy, *Doing Business Abroad* (New York: Simon & Schuster, 1985), p. 77. Used with permission.

context cultures read nonverbal messages from body language, dress, status, and belongings. However, they tend to double-check their perceptions and assumptions verbally. To do so in China or Japan would be to gravely insult the other person, thus causing them to *lose face* (see International OB). Their positions on the continuum in Figure 19–2 indicate the German preoccupation with written rules for even the finest details of behavior and the American preoccupation with precise legal documents. In high-context cultures, agreements tend to be made on the basis of someone's word or a handshake, after a rather prolonged trust-building period. European-Americans, who have been taught from birth not to take anything for granted, see the handshake as a prelude to demanding a signature on a detailed, lawyer-approved, iron-clad contract.

Implications for a Diverse Work Force   High- and low-context cultural differences can be found in countries with heterogeneous populations such as the United States, Australia, and Canada. African-Americans, Asian-Americans, and Native-Americans tend to be higher-context than Americans of European descent. This helps explain our earlier example of the white manager's frustration with the black employee's nonverbal response. Culture dictates how people communicate. The white manager's ignorance of (or insensitivity to) the black employee's cultural context blocked effective communication. (Recall our discussion of managing diversity in Chapter 2.)

• TOWARD GREATER CROSS-CULTURAL AWARENESS

Aside from being high- or low-context, cultures stand apart in other ways as well. Let us briefly review the following basic factors that vary from culture to culture: time, interpersonal space, language, and religion.[11] This list is intended to be indicative rather than exhaustive. Separately or together

International OB

Saving Face in Asia

Pride and dignity are important to all human beings, but nowhere in the world are they so culturally protected as in Asia. To speak or act in a way that causes an Asian person to "lose face" is tantamount to physical assault in the West. Asians go to great extremes to save their own face *and* everyone else's. This causes problems for the Westerner, who may not get a straight answer to a straightforward question. . . .

Americans pride themselves on their frankness and honesty. Asians also are honest people, but honesty is mediated by the demands of face. For this reason, "frankness" in Asia is almost always rudeness.

The most important goal in the Orient is to keep a smooth surface on the sea of life. Appearance is more important than truth. The person who forces bare truth at the expense of appearance is the outcast and the troublemaker. Appearance is all, because face is involved. Everyone in Asia understands this, and Westerners must also understand this if successful business relationships are to be established in the Orient. Truth may be discussed in private, but the public surface must be smooth. . . .

A rule that should be burned into your consciousness is this: Compliment, but never criticize, even if asked for criticism. . . .

Not putting people "on the spot" is very important. . . .

If you ask a question in Asia and don't receive an answer, don't push it. It is probably a matter of face. Give it time. Ask again later in a different way and, preferably, in private. Face is less paramount if other people are not present.

Face need not always work against the American, who can use it in negotiations. The statement "I would lose face if I accepted those terms" is a more effective bargaining tool than all the facts and figures even the most sophisticated computer can generate.

Source: Excerpted from John A. Reeder, "When West Meets East: Cultural Aspects of Doing Business in Asia," *Business Horizons*, January–February 1987, pp. 69–74. Copyright 1987 by the Foundation for the School of Business at Indiana University. Used with permission.

these factors can foster huge cross-cultural gaps. Effective multicultural management often depends on whether or not these gaps can be bridged.

A qualification needs to be offered at this juncture. It is important to view all of the cultural differences in this chapter and elsewhere as *tendencies* and *patterns,* rather than as absolutes. As soon as one falls into the trap of assuming *all* Germans are this, *all* British are that, and so on, potentially instructive generalizations become mindless stereotypes. Well-founded cultural generalizations are fundamental to successfully doing business in other cultures. But one needs to be constantly alert to *individuals* who are exceptions to the local cultural rule. For instance, it is possible to encounter talkative and aggressive Japanese and quiet and deferential Americans who simply do not fit their respective cultural molds.

Cultural Perceptions of Time

In North American and Northern European cultures, time seems to be a simple matter. It is linear, relentlessly marching forward, never backward, in standardized chunks. To the American who received a watch for his or her third birthday, time is like money. It is spent, saved, or wasted. Americans are taught to show up 10 minutes early for appointments. When working across cultures, however, time becomes a very complex matter.[12] Imagine a New Yorker's chagrin when left in a waiting room for 45 minutes, only to find a Latin American government official dealing with three other people at once. The North American resents the lack of prompt and undivided attention. The Latin American official resents the North American's impatience and apparent self-centeredness. This vicious cycle of resentment can be explained by the distinction between **monochronic time** and **polychronic time.**

> The former is revealed in the ordered, precise, schedule-driven, use of public time that typifies and even caricatures efficient Northern Europeans and North Americans. The latter is seen in the multiple and cyclical activities and concurrent involvement with different people in Mediterranean, Latin American, and especially Arab cultures.[13]

Low-context cultures such as that of the United States tend to run on monochronic time while high-context cultures such as that of Mexico tend to run on polychronic time. People in polychronic cultures view time as flexible, fluid, and multidimensional.

• Time clocks have been a longstanding tradition in monochronic cultures, but they can cause discomfort in polychronic cultures. *(Murray Alcosser/The Image Bank)*

The Swiss have made an exact science of monochronic time. Many a visitor has been a minute late for a Swiss train, only to see its taillights leaving the station. Time is more elastic in polychronic cultures. During the Islamic holy month of Ramadan in Middle Eastern nations, for example, the faithful fast during daylight hours and the general pace of things markedly slows. Managers need to reset their mental clocks when doing business across cultures.

Interpersonal Space

As discussed relative to nonverbal communication in Chapter 12, anthropologist Edward T. Hall noticed a connection between culture and preferred interpersonal distance. People from high-context cultures were observed standing close when talking to someone. Low-context cultures appeared to dictate a greater amount of interpersonal space. Hall applied the term **proxemics** to the study of cultural expectations about interpersonal space.[14] As mentioned in Chapter 12, he specified four interpersonal distance zones. Some call them space bubbles. Once again, they are *intimate* distance, *personal* distance, *social* distance, and *public* distance. Ranges for the four interpersonal distance zones are illustrated in Figure 19–3, along with selected cultural differences.

North American business conversations normally are conducted at about a 3-to-4-foot range, the personal zone in Figure 19–3. A range of approximately one foot is common in Latin American and Asian cultures, uncomfortably close for Northern Europeans and North Americans. Arabs like to get even closer. Mismatches in culturally dictated interpersonal space zones can prove very distracting for the unprepared. Hall explains:

• **FIGURE 19–3**   Interpersonal Distance Zones for Business Conversations Vary from Culture to Culture

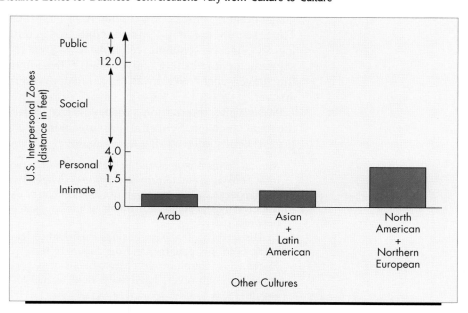

Arabs tend to get very close and breathe on you. It's part of the high sensory involvement of a high-context culture. . . .

The American on the receiving end can't identify all the sources of his discomfort but feels that the Arab is pushy. The Arab comes close, the American backs up. The Arab follows, because he can only interact at certain distances. Once the American learns that Arabs handle space differently and that breathing on people is a form of communication, the situation can sometimes be redefined so the American relaxes.[15]

Asian and Middle-Eastern hosts grow weary of having to seemingly chase their low-context guests around at social gatherings to maintain what they feel is proper conversational range. Backing up all evening to keep conversational partners at a proper distance is an awkward experience as well. Awareness of cultural differences, along with skillful accommodation, are essential to productive intercultural dealings.

Language

More than 3,000 different languages are spoken worldwide. What is the connection between these languages and information processing and behavior? There is an ongoing debate among anthropologists concerning the extent to which language influences perception and behavior. On one side of the argument, the *relativists* claim each language fosters unique perceptions. On the other side, *universalists* state that all languages share common elements and thus foster common thought processes and perceptions. A recent study involving subjects from eight countries attempted to resolve this debate. Subjects from the United States, Britain, Italy, Greece, Yugoslavia, Pakistan, Hong Kong, and Vietnam were shown 15 flash cards, each printed with three pairs of words. Language experts certified the various translations as accurate. The idea was to see if adults from different cultures, speaking different languages, would perceive the same semantic elements in the paired words. Illustrative semantic elements, or basic language building blocks, are: opposite = alive/dead; similar = furniture/bed. The researchers found "considerable cross-cultural agreement on the meaning and use of semantic relations."[16] Greatest agreement was found for semantic opposites (e.g., alive/dead). These findings tip the scale in favor of the universalists. We await additional research evidence for a definitive answer.

Meanwhile, international managers say there is no substitute for knowing the local language. Scott Latham, president of a U.S.–Japan trade consulting firm, recently offered this assessment:

Mutual cultural understanding between the United States and Japan is crucial to better business and improved relations between the two countries. Unfortunately, the Japanese for the most part are miles ahead of us Americans in this department, a factor that accounts for much of the current economic and political tension between us.

Historically, Japanese businessmen had to learn English in order to develop markets in this country, and the Japanese have spent years living in the United States, and learning our customs, business regulations and way of life. We Americans, however, have been slow to make the same effort to learn about Japan.[17]

INTERNATIONAL OB

Which English? Australian, British, or American?

Ben Lochtenberg, the new chairman of ICI Americas Inc., is an Australian who also has worked for ICI in Britain and Canada. He quickly learned that a common language is no insurance against cultural shocks. When he went to England, he couldn't get any respect with his direct Australian manner, so he learned the oblique ways of the English. For example, he says, if an English boss reacts to a pet project by saying, "Perhaps you ought to think about this a little more," what he really means is "You must be mad. Forget it." In the United States, Lochtenberg had to unlearn the lesson. He told a manager, "Perhaps you ought to think about this a little more." The manager took him literally. Asked why he had gone ahead, the man replied, "Well, I thought about it, like you said, and the idea got better."

Source: Excerpted from Jeremy Main, "How to Go Global—and Why," *Fortune,* August 28, 1989, p. 72.

For those Americans who claim English has become the universal language of business, there is still no getting around the need for cross-cultural familiarity (see International OB).

Religion

Religious beliefs and practices can have a profound effect on cross-cultural relations. A comprehensive treatment of different religions is beyond the scope of our present discussion. However, we can examine the relationship between religious affiliation and work-related values. A study of 484 international students at a Midwestern U.S. university uncovered wide variability. The following list gives the most important work-related value for each of five religious affiliations:

Catholic—Consideration ("Concern that employees be taken seriously, be kept informed, and that their judgments be used.")

Protestant—Employer effectiveness ("Desire to work for a company that is efficient, successful and a technological leader.")

Buddhist—Social responsibility ("Concern that the employer be a responsible part of society.")

Muslim—Continuity ("Desire for stable environment, job longevity, reduction of uncertainty.")

No religious preference—Professional challenge ("Concern with having a job that provides learning opportunities and opportunities to use skills well.")[18]

Thus, there was virtually *no agreement* across religions about the primary work value. This led the researchers to conclude: "Employers might be wise to consider the impact that religious differences (and more broadly, cultural factors) appear to have on the values of employee groups."[19] Of course, in the United States and other selected countries, equal employment opportunity laws forbid managers from basing employment-related decisions on an applicant's religious preference.

• PRACTICAL INSIGHTS FROM CROSS-CULTURAL MANAGEMENT RESEARCH

Nancy Adler, an international OB specialist at Canada's McGill University, has offered the following introductory definition. **"Cross-cultural management** studies the behavior of people in organizations around the world and trains people to work in organizations with employee and client populations from several cultures."[20] Inherent in this definition are three steps: (1) understand cultural differences; (2) identify culturally appropriate management practices; and (3) teach cross-cultural management lessons. The cross-cultural studies discussed in this section contribute to all three.

The Hofstede-Bond Stream of Research

Instructive insights surfaced in the mid-1980s when the results of two very different cross-cultural management studies were merged. The first study was conducted under the guidance of Dutch researcher Geert Hofstede. Canadian Michael Harris Bond, at the Chinese University of Hong Kong, was a key researcher in the second study. What follows is a brief overview of each study, a discussion of the combined results, and a summary of important practical implications.

The Two Studies   Hofstede's study is a classic in the annals of cross-cultural management research.[21] He drew his data for that study from a collection of 116,000 attitude surveys administered to IBM employees worldwide between 1967 and 1973. Respondents to the attitude survey, that also asked questions on cultural values and beliefs, included IBM employees from 72 countries. Fifty-three cultures eventually were analyzed and contrasted according to four cultural dimensions. Hofstede's data base was unique, not only because of its large size, but also because it allowed him to isolate cultural effects. If his subjects had not performed *similar jobs* in *different countries* for the *same company,* no such control would have been possible. Cross-cultural comparisons were made along the first four dimensions listed in Table 19–1, power distance, individualism–collectivism,[22] masculinity–femininity, and uncertainty avoidance.

Bond's study was much smaller, involving a survey of 100 (50 percent women) students from 22 countries and 5 continents. The survey instrument was the Chinese Value Survey (CVS), based on the Rokeach Value Survey discussed in Chapter 3.[23] The CVS also tapped four cultural dimensions. Three corresponded to Hofstede's first three in Table 19–1. Hofstede's fourth cultural dimension, uncertainty avoidance, was not measured by the CVS. Instead, Bond's study isolated the fifth cultural dimension in Table 19–1. It was labeled *Confucian dynamism* to reflect how strongly a person believes in the ethical principles evident in the teachings of the Chinese philosopher Confucius (551–479 B.C.). Importantly, one may embrace Confucian values without knowing a thing about Confucius. The label is simply a

• **TABLE 19-1**   Key Cultural Dimensions in the Hofstede–Bond Studies

Power distance: How much do people expect *inequality* in social institutions (e.g., family, work organizations, government)?
Individualism-Collectivism: How loose or tight is the bond between individuals and societal groups?
Masculinity–Femininity: To what extent do people embrace *competitive* masculine traits or *nurturing* feminine traits?
Uncertainty avoidance: To what extent do people seek to avoid *unstructured* situations through laws, rules, and procedures?
Confucian dynamism: To what extent do people perceive the importance of the values of persistence, status, thrift, and feeling shame and the *unimportance* of the values of personal stability, face saving, respect for tradition, and reciprocation of favors and gifts?

Source: Adapted from discussion in Geert Hofstede and Michael Harris Bond, "The Confucius Connection: From Cultural Roots to Economic Growth," *Organizational Dynamics*, Spring 1988, pp. 4–21.

• **TABLE 19-2**   Countries Scoring the Highest in the Hofstede–Bond Studies

High Power Distance	High Individualism	High Masculinity	High Uncertainty Avoidance	High Confucian Dynamism
Philippines	U.S.	Japan	Japan	Hong Kong
India	Australia		Korea	Taiwan
Singapore	Great Britain		Brazil	Japan
Brazil	Netherlands		Pakistan	Korea
Hong Kong	Canada		Taiwan	
	New Zealand			
	Sweden			
	Germany*			

* Former West Germany.
Source: Adapted from Exhibit 2 in Geert Hofstede and Michael Harris Bond, "The Confucius Connection: From Cultural Roots to Economic Growth," *Organizational Dynamics*, Spring 1988, pp. 12–13.

convenient way of organizing a particular set of values. Westerners may see the values in Confucian dynamism (defined in Table 19–1) as contradictory. *But that is precisely the point.* An individual's Confucian dynamism score reveals how he or she balances life's basic contradictions.

East Meets West   By merging the two studies, a serious flaw in each was corrected. Namely, Hofstede's study had an inherent Anglo-European bias and Bond's study had a built-in Asian bias. How would cultures compare if viewed through the overlapping lenses of the two studies? Hofstede and Bond were able to answer that question because 18 countries in Bond's study overlapped the 53 countries in Hofstede's sample.[24] Table 19–2 lists the countries scoring highest on each of the five cultural dimensions. (Countries earning between 67 and 100 points on a 0–100 relative ranking scale qualified as "high" for Table 19–2.) The United States scored the highest in individualism, moderate in power distance, masculinity, and uncertainty avoidance, and low in Confucian dynamism.

Practical Lessons   Individually, and together, the Hofstede and Bond studies yielded the following useful lessons for international managers:

1. Due to varying cultural values, management theories and practices need to be adapted to the local culture. This is particularly true for made-in-America management theories (e.g., McClelland's, Maslow's, Herzberg's, and Vroom's) and Japanese management practices.

2. High Confucian dynamism was the only one of the five cultural dimensions to correlate positively with national economic growth. (Notice how the four Asian countries listed under high Confucian dynamism in Table 19–2 have been the world's economic growth leaders over the last 25 years.) This correlation does not bode well for countries scoring lowest on this dimension: Pakistan, Philippines, Canada, Great Britain, and the United States.

3. Industrious cultural values are a necessary but insufficient condition for economic growth. Markets and a supportive political climate also are required to create the right mix. (Thus, Hong Kong's economic success may be at risk because of the pending 1997 takeover by China.)

4. Cultural arrogance is a luxury individuals and nations can no longer afford in a global economy.

A Contingency Model for Cross-Cultural Leadership

If a manager has a favorite leadership style in his or her own culture, will that style be equally appropriate in another culture? According to a recently proposed model that built upon Hofstede's work, the answer is "not necessarily."[25] Four path–goal leadership styles—directive, supportive, participative, and achievement—were matched with variations of three of Hofstede's cultural dimensions. The dimensions used were power distance, individualism–collectivism, and uncertainty avoidance. (Recall our discussion in Chapter 14 of the path–goal theory of leadership.)

By combining this model with Hofstede's and Bond's findings, we derived the useful contingency model for cross-cultural leadership in Table 19–3. Participative leadership turned out to be culturally appropriate for all 18 countries. Importantly, this does *not* mean that the participative style is necessarily the *best* style of leadership in cross-cultural management. It simply has broad applicability. Also of note, with the exception of France, the directive style appears to be culturally *inappropriate* in North America, Northern Europe, Australia, and New Zealand. Some locations, such as Hong Kong and the Philippines, require great leadership versatility. Leadership needs to be matched to the prevailing cultural climate.

Interpersonal Conflict-Handling Styles

In a cross-cultural study of Jordanian, Turkish, and U.S. managers, the collaborative (problem-solving) style of handling interpersonal *conflict* emerged as the preferred option in all three cultures. Beyond that there was general disagreement about which backup styles were most appropriate.[26] One practical lesson from this study is: even when we find commonalities

• **TABLE 19-3** A Contingency Model for Cross-Cultural Leadership

Country	Most Culturally Appropriate Leadership Behaviors			
	Directive	**Supportive**	**Participative**	**Achievement**
Australia		X	X	X
Brazil	X		X	
Canada		X	X	X
France	X		X	
Germany*		X	X	X
Great Britain		X	X	X
Hong Kong	X	X	X	X
India	X		X	X
Italy	X	X	X	
Japan	X	X	X	
Korea	X	X	X	
Netherlands		X	X	X
New Zealand			X	X
Pakistan	X	X	X	
Philippines	X	X	X	X
Sweden			X	X
Taiwan	X	X	X	
United States		X	X	X

* Former West Germany.

Sources: Adapted in part from Carl A. Rodrigues, "The Situation and National Culture as Contingencies for Leadership Behavior: Two Conceptual Models," in *Advances in International Comparative Management*, Vol. 5, ed. S. Benjamin Prasad (Greenwich, Conn.: JAI Press, 1990), pp. 51–68; and Geert Hofstede and Michael Harris Bond, "The Confucius Connection: From Cultural Roots to Economic Growth," *Organizational Dynamics*, Spring 1988, pp. 4–21.

across cultures, care needs to be taken not to gloss over underlying differences.

We now shift our cultural focus to the organizational level. Like societal cultures, organizational cultures have a powerful impact on how we think and act.

• UNDERSTANDING ORGANIZATIONAL CULTURES

Much has been written and said about organizational, or corporate, cultures in recent years. The results of this activity can be arranged on a continuum of academic rigor. At the low end of the continuum are simplistic typologies and exaggerated claims about the benefits of imitating Japanese-style corporate cultures. Here the term *corporate culture* is little more than a pop psychology buzzword. At the other end of the continuum is a growing body of theory and research with valuable insights but plagued by definitional and measurement inconsistencies. By systematically sifting this diverse collection of material, we find that an understanding of organizational culture is central to learning how to manage people at work in both domestic and international operations.

What Is Organizational Culture?

Organizational culture is the social glue that binds members of the organization together through shared values, symbolic devices, and social ideals.[27] An organization's culture may be strong or weak, depending on variables such as cohesiveness, value consensus, and individual commitment to collective goals. Contrary to what one might suspect, a strong culture is not necessarily a good thing.[28] The nature of the culture's central values is more important than its strength.[29] For example, a strong but change-resistant culture may be worse, from the standpoint of profitability and competitiveness, than a weak but innovative culture. Thus, when evaluating an organization's culture, we need to consider the strategic appropriateness of its central values as well as its strength.

Manifestations of Organizational Culture

When is an organization's culture most apparent? According to one observer, cultural assumptions assert themselves through socialization of new employees, subculture clashes, and top management behavior.[30] Consider these three situations, for example: A newcomer who shows up late for an important meeting is told a story about someone who was fired for repeated tardiness. Conflict between product design engineers who emphasize a product's function and marketing specialists who demand a more stylish product reveals an underlying clash of subculture values. Top managers, through the behavior they model and the administrative and reward systems they create, prompt a significant improvement in the quality of a company's products.

A Model for Interpreting Organizational Culture A useful model for observing and interpreting organizational culture was developed by a Harvard researcher (see Figure 19–4). Four general manifestations or evidence of organizational culture in his model are: shared things (objects), shared sayings (talk), shared doings (behavior), and shared feelings (emotion). One can begin collecting cultural information, within the organization, by asking, observing, reading, and feeling. However, a more detailed analysis is required to capture the essence of an organization's culture. We need to supplement the foregoing model with a more extensive list of cultural manifestations.

A Closer Look Organizational culture expresses itself in a rich variety of ways. For example, a comprehensive list of cultural manifestations and definitions is presented in Table 19–4. We now see why Schein has called organizational culture "a deep phenomenon."[31] Missing from the list in Table 19–4 are values and organizational heroes, both worthy of mention. The instrumental and terminal values discussed in Chapter 3 become culturally embedded through group or organizational consensus. Apple Computer, for example, published a detailed list of nine "Apple Values" identified a few years ago by a task force of employees. Among those Apple values, imparted during the socialization process for new employees, are empathy

• **FIGURE 19-4**   A Model for Observing and Interpreting General Manifestations of Organizational Culture

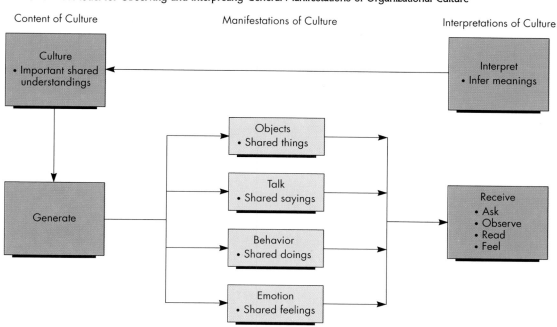

Source: Excerpted, by permission of the publisher, from "Implications of Corporate Culture: A Manager's Guide to Action," by Vijay Sathe, from *Organizational Dynamics*, Autumn 1983, © 1983 American Management Association, New York. All rights reserved.

for customers/users, positive social contribution, team spirit, and good management. Johnson & Johnson also has formally documented its cherished corporate values and ideals, as conceived over four decades ago by the founder's son. The resulting Credo has helped J&J become a role model for corporate ethics (see A Matter of Ethics).

Organizational Heroes   Heroes are those individuals who personify the organization's highest ideals. At IBM, for example, corporate heroes primarily are marketing representatives from the computer giant's 10,000-person sales force.

"Reps" are first among equals in IBM. Every man who ever ran the company rose through their ranks, beginning with [IBM's founder] Thomas Watson, Sr. They are the main reason for the company's tight hold on the computer market. IBM treats them accordingly, motivating this army of politely aggressive blue suits with tons of cash [some make over $100,000 a year], intense peer pressure and enough rah-rah rallies to rival a college fraternity. The rewards begin in IBM's 250 U.S. sales branches, where size is limited to 100 or 200 people to instill a small-team spirit.

Each January, branches stage glitzy "kickoff" meetings replete with slogans, skits and mascots. Monthly meetings often close with a dramatic tale about an unnamed rep; finally, the person is named and comes forward to accept an award amid crackling applause. "It takes your breath away, it really does," says Diana Ingram, a Chicago rep who has received four awards in less than four years at IBM.[32]

• **TABLE 19-4**   Specific Manifestations of Organizational Culture

Rite	A relatively elaborate, dramatic planned set of activities that combines various forms of cultural expressions and that often has both practical and expressive consequences.
Ritual	A standardized, detailed set of techniques and behaviors that manages anxieties but seldom produces intended, practical consequences of any importance.
Myth	A dramatic narrative of imagined events, usually used to explain origins or transformations of something. Also, an unquestioned belief about the practical benefits of certain techniques and behaviors that is not supported by demonstrated facts.
Saga	A historical narrative of some wonderful event that has a historical basis but has been embellished with fictional details.
Story	A narrative based on true events—often a combination of truth and fiction.
Folktale	A completely fictional narrative.
Symbol	Any object, act, event, quality, or relation that serves as a vehicle for conveying meaning, usually by representing another thing.
Language	A particular manner in which members of a group use vocal sounds and written signs to convey meanings to each other.
Gesture	Movements of parts of the body used to express meanings.
Physical setting	Those things that physically surround people and provide them with immediate sensory stimuli as they carry out culturally expressive activities.
Artifact	Material objects manufactured by people to facilitate culturally expressive activities.

Source: Excerpted, by permission of the publisher, from "How an Organization's Rites Reveal Its Culture," by Janice M. Beyer and Harrison M. Trice, from *Organizational Dynamics*, Spring 1987, © 1987 American Management Association, New York. All rights reserved.

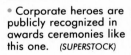

• Corporate heroes are publicly recognized in awards ceremonies like this one.   *(SUPERSTOCK)*

A MATTER OF ETHICS

Johnson & Johnson's Corporate Values Point the Way

CEO Ralph Larsen likes to tell the troops at Johnson & Johnson about his time as a trainee in one of the company's baby-shampoo factories. One morning he attended a meeting where managers argued over whether to ship a large batch of shampoo that was safe but didn't meet J&J's "no tears" standard. The decision: Take the loss.

That kind of dedication to customer and community service hasn't kept Wall Street from weeping with joy: Over the past year J&J's stock has risen nearly 40 percent. And it *has* won the medical products company top honors for community and environmental responsibility in this year's survey. [*Fortune*'s annual "Most Admired" survey.] Says Larsen, who became chief last April: "If we keep trying to do what's right, at the end of the day we believe the marketplace will reward us."

The key to understanding J&J's unusual corporate culture is the Credo, a 44-year-old, 309-word statement created by Robert Wood Johnson, son of the founder. The Credo stresses honesty, integrity, and putting people before profits—phrases common to most such documents. What's unusual is the amount of energy J&J's high executives devote to ensuring that employees live by those words. Every few years, in a kind of conference of bishops, the company gathers senior managers to debate the Credo's contents, a process meant to keep its ideals fresh. On his globe-trotting tours Larsen never fails to mention the document. "I tell employees they have to be prepared to take the short hit," he says. "In the end, they'll prosper."

As an example, Larsen cites the tragic Tylenol case in which eight people died from swallowing poisoned capsules. Although J&J believed someone altered the pill in the stores, not the factory, it recalled all its product and quickly lost $240 million in earnings. That swift action persuaded consumers to stay loyal, and today Tylenol remains the nation's leading brand of painkiller.

Source: Excerpted from Brian Dumaine, "Corporate Citizenship," *Fortune*, January 29, 1990, pp. 50, 54. © 1990 The Time Inc. Magazine Company. All rights reserved.

By setting sales quotas so about 80 percent of the marketing representatives meet or exceed them, IBM ensures it will not run out of heroes. At Sikorsky Aircraft, an innovation-driven company, the heroes are inventors. Sikorsky employees who have been awarded a patent wear special name tags emblazoned with a U.S. Patent Office logo.[33]

When management makes heroes of outstanding employees, the message is clear: "Look at these people. Be like them. It pays." Often-repeated stories and legends of company heroes deepen the culture.

Four Functions of Organizational Culture

As illustrated in Figure 19–5, an organization's culture fulfills four functions.[34] To help bring these four functions to life, let us consider how each of them has taken shape at United Parcel Service (UPS), the company with the

• **FIGURE 19–5**   Four Functions of Organizational Culture

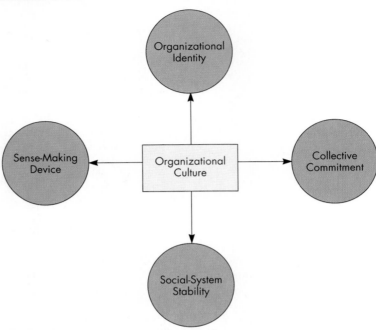

Source: Adapted from discussion in Linda Smircich, "Concepts of Culture and Organizational Analysis," *Administrative Science Quarterly,* September 1983, pp. 339–58.

familiar brown delivery vans. UPS is a particularly instructive example because it is the most profitable company in its industry and has a very strong and distinctive culture.

1. *Gives members an organizational identity:* According to *Fortune* magazine: "What makes UPS stand out is its ability to attract, develop, and keep talented people. Top managers, most of whom have come up through the ranks, instill a spirit of winning so pervasive that people who fail are ranked as least best, not losers. Workers, in turn, have almost a Japanese-like identification with the company."[35]

2. *Facilitates collective commitment:* UPS managers own almost all of the firm's stock. Many managers who began their careers with UPS as drivers and clerks have retired as multimillionaires. Compensation throughout the company is high by industry standards, with delivery truck drivers averaging $16 per hour. Middle managers receive generous stock bonuses and dividend checks.

3. *Promotes social system stability:* UPS is known for its strict standards and tight controls. For instance, employees must meet grooming standards and task performance is specified down to the finest detail. "Longtime UPSers—most of the work force due to a 4 percent turnover rate—talk about their company's 'mystique,' an aura that generates an unusual mixture of passionate commitment to hard work and a strong identification with the company."[36]

4. *Shapes behavior by helping members make sense of their surroundings:* UPS recruits primarily from its 40,000-person part-time work force of

college students. Only the most promising are offered full-time positions. Even those with college degrees start at bottom-rung jobs to learn the basics of the business.

This example shows why the term *social glue* is indeed appropriate in reference to organizational culture.

Research on Organizational Cultures

Because the concept of organizational culture is a relatively recent addition to OB, the research base is incomplete. Studies to date are characterized by inconsistent definitions and varied methodologies. Quantitative treatments are rare since there is no agreement on how to measure cultural variables. Anecdotal accounts, in the form of practical examples drawn from interviews, are the norm. As a matter of convenience, we will review two streams of organizational culture research in this section. One stream has been reported in best-selling books and the other in research journal articles.

Anecdotal Evidence from Best-Selling Books about Organizational Culture   Initial widespread interest in organizational cultures was stirred by William Ouchi's 1981 best-seller, *Theory Z: How American Business Can Meet the Japanese Challenge*. Interviews with representatives from 20 large American corporations doing business in both the United States and Japan led Ouchi to formulate his Theory Z model. Ouchi applied the Theory Z label[37] to a few highly successful American organizations—including IBM, Eli Lilly, Intel, Eastman Kodak, and Hewlett-Packard—that exhibited Japanese-like qualities. Primary among those qualities was a participative, consensual decision-making style (see Figure 19–6). Ouchi found the internal cultures of these hybrid companies so consistent that he called them *clans*.

Ouchi noted, however, that clannish Theory Z organizations can become socially inbred to the point of rejecting unfamiliar ideas and people. Theory Z characteristics, when taken to extreme, can stifle creativity and foster unintentional sexism and racism. For instance, Ouchi described top management in one Theory Z company as "wholesome, disciplined, hard-working, and honest, but unremittingly white, male, and middle class."[38] From a research standpoint, Ouchi's two main contributions were: (1) focusing attention on internal culture as a key determinant of organizational effectiveness and (2) developing an instructive typology of organizations based in part on cultural variables.

Close on the heels of Ouchi's book came two 1982 best-sellers: Deal and Kennedy's *Corporate Cultures: The Rites and Rituals of Corporate Life*[39] and Peters and Waterman's *In Search of Excellence*.[40] Both books drew upon interviews and the authors' consulting experience. Each team of authors relied on abundant anecdotal evidence to make the point that successful companies tend to have strong cultures. For example, Peters and Waterman observed:

> Without exception, the dominance and coherence of culture proved to be an essential quality of the excellent companies. Moreover, the stronger the culture and the more it was directed toward the marketplace, the less need was there for policy manuals, organization charts, or detailed procedures and rules. In these

• **Figure 19–6**   Ouchi's Theory Z Model of Organization

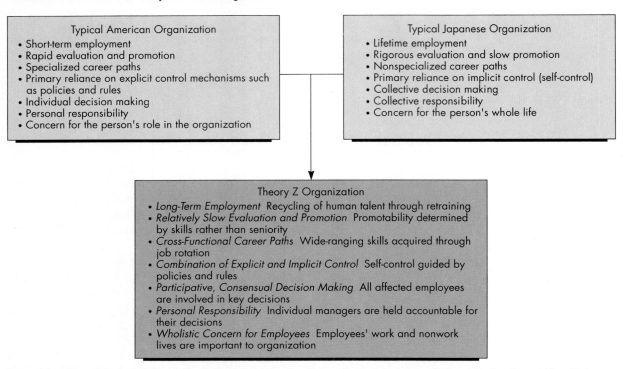

Source: Adapted from discussion in William G. Ouchi, *Theory Z: How American Business Can Meet the Japanese Challenge* (Reading, Mass.: Addison-Wesley Publishing, 1981).

companies, people way down the line know what they are supposed to do in most situations because the handful of guiding values is crystal clear.[41]

These best-sellers generated excitement about cultural factors such as heroes and stories. But they failed to break new ground in the measurement and evaluation of organizational cultures.[42] Their main contribution was the vivid portrayal of the rich cultural texture of today's organizations.

Evidence from Research Articles   Three very different studies yielded the following insights:

- A survey of 1,498 American managers (13 percent female) suggested that greater congruence between individual and organizational values can enhance personal fulfillment and organizational effectiveness.[43]

- According to a case study of a merger between two banks, the blending of different but functional organizational cultures can cause major difficulties. Poor communication, resistance to change, and even sabotage were observed before, during, and after the merger.[44]

- Seventy-five interviews with human resource executives from 14 large U.S. companies revealed two distinct reward systems: hierarchy-based and performance-based. Companies with hierarchy-based reward systems were found to have cultures characterized as clans (following Ouchi's use of the term). On the other hand, organizations with performance-based reward systems tended to have "market" cultures. In a market culture, the individual-organization relationship is driven by a negotiated contract rather than mutual loyalty, as in a clannish organization. While noting that the different reward systems and cultures are not necessarily good or bad, the researchers emphasized the importance of reward systems in shaping organizational cultures.

> Reward systems express and reinforce the values and norms that comprise corporate culture. A careful consideration of reward system design can help decision makers successfully modify the organization's culture. Reward systems are, in effect, powerful mechanisms that can be used by managers to communicate desired attitudes and behaviors to organization members. We believe that, over time, cultures are amenable to change through the clear communication of performance criteria and the consistent application of rewards.[45]

• DEVELOPING ORGANIZATIONAL CULTURES

Imagine yourself in the position of a manager at Atari a few years ago when the following conditions prevailed:

> A marketing manager who worked at Atari before it got new management recalls: "You can't imagine how much time and energy around here went into politics. You had to determine who was on first base this month in order to figure out how to obtain what you needed in order to get the job done. There were no rules. There were no clear values. Two of the men at the top stood for diametrically opposite things. Your bosses were constantly changing. All this meant that you never had time to develop a routine way for getting things done at the interface between your job and the next guy's. Without rules for working with one another, a lot of people got hurt, got burned out, and were never taught the 'Atari way' of doing things because there wasn't an Atari way."[46]

Atari's new management turned the company around. But what could you, as a manager at Atari, have done to develop the company's culture? This section suggests some workable answers by discussing how culture can become a competitive advantage and introducing a practical model for developing an organization's culture.

Organizational Culture as a Competitive Advantage

It is possible for the four cultural functions listed in Figure 19–5 to be so well fulfilled that they give the organization a competitive advantage. One scholar cited three criteria of an organizational culture capable of providing a sustained competitive advantage. The culture must be *valuable, rare,* and *impossible to imitate.*[47] While many organizations achieve valuable and rare cultures, it requires great diligence to build one that is impossible to imitate. Of course, from a competitive standpoint, *impossible* does not necessarily mean physically impossible; it can mean doing more than others are *willing* to do.

A prime example of building a culture around things that competitors are unwilling to do is Stew Leonard's, the world's largest dairy store, in Norwalk, Connecticut. Picture a single 100,000-square-foot store with 100,000 customers which sells $100 million worth of groceries annually! That's Stew Leonard's. At the front door of the store is a huge 3-ton rock with the following inscription:

OUR POLICY

Rule 1—The customer is always right!
Rule 2—If the customer is ever wrong, reread Rule 1.[48]

To casual observers, it is just a big rock with an interesting inscription. To Stew Leonard's employees, however, it is a tangible symbol of a deep-seated commitment to serving customers better than anyone else. Supporting that symbol are a rigorous hiring program and a promote-from-within policy ensuring that outstanding people are hired and retained. Stew Leonard's competitors could put all kinds of inscribed boulders in front of their stores, but they would have great difficulty imitating the cultural commitment to excellent day-to-day customer service. Stew Leonard's culture gives the company a competitive advantage.

A Practical Model for Developing an Organization's Culture

Judging from the foregoing discussion, imitation of another organization's culture is unsatisfactory. (Careful study of successful organizations' cultures and skillful *adaptation,* on the other hand, is a good idea.) This is true not only from a competitive standpoint but also because management has imperfect control over culture. According to Schein, every culture is unique because:

> The culture that eventually evolves in a particular organization is . . . a complex outcome of external pressures, internal potentials, responses to critical events, and, probably, to some unknown degree, chance factors that could not be predicted from a knowledge of either the environment or the members.[49]

The best alternative for management is to influence and develop the organization's unique culture as it evolves naturally. The model in Figure 19–7 is a practical road map for this endeavor.

Because the authors of this model view a strong organizational culture as being analogous to a well-functioning family, the word HOME is a particularly appropriate acronym.[50] H stands for *history,* O stands for *oneness,* M stands for *membership,* and E stands for *exchange.* Each of these intervening conditions can foster the desired outcome, a cohesive organizational culture, if management makes a concerted and coordinated effort to implement the methods listed in Figure 19–7. Regarding company history, John Thorbeck, chief executive officer of Geo. E. Keith, a shoe company in Bridgewater, Massachusetts, recently offered the following caution:

> Of course, corporate history is tricky. As an external, cosmetic reference, history is just hype. History can also be a form of escape, a way of turning your back on the present by invoking a comfortable past and clinging to it. But as a statement of company values, of a company's inherent way of doing things, history can be powerful.[51]

Also, as discussed in Chapter 13, reward systems (in the M portion of the model) are a potent cultural force subject to managerial control.

• FIGURE 19-7   How to Develop an Organization's Culture

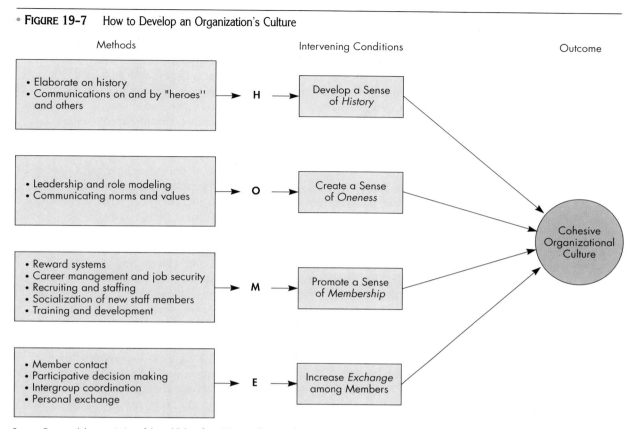

Source: Excerpted, by permission of the publisher, from "How to Grow an Organizational Culture," by Warren Gross and Shula Shichman, from *Personnel*, September 1987, © 1987 *American Management Association*, New York. All rights reserved.

• SUMMARY OF KEY CONCEPTS

A. All managers, both domestic and international, are being increasingly affected by the globalized economy. Greater cultural awareness and sensitivity are a must. Societal and organizational cultures involve taken-for-granted assumptions about how people should perceive, think, act, and feel. Organizational behavior is the product of interacting societal and organizationl cultures.

B. People from high-context cultures place heavy emphasis on nonverbal cues when communicating. People from low-context cultures infer relatively less from situational cues and extract more meaning from spoken and written words.

C. While being wary of overgeneralizing about cultural differences, it is possible to distinguish cultures on the basis of time, interpersonal space, language, and religion. Those on monochronic time see time as a limited resource, divided into fixed increments. Polychronic-based cultures view time in multiple and cyclical ways. Polychronic people tend to view monochronic people as being impatient and in too much of a hurry.

D. Anthropologist Edward Hall coined the term *proxemics* to refer to the study of cultural expectations about interpersonal space. Asians and Latin Americans like to stand close (6 inches-to-1 foot) during business conversations, while North Americans and Northern Europeans prefer a larger (3-to-4 feet) interpersonal distance. Conflicting expectations about proper interpersonal distance can create awkward cross-cultural situations. Recent research uncovered a high degree of agreement about semantic elements across eight cultures. Another study found no agreement about the primary work value across five different religious preference groups.

E. According to the Hofstede–Bond cross-cultural management studies, caution needs to be exercised when transplanting management theories and practices from one culture to another. Also, Confucian dynamism was the only one of five cultural dimensions in the Hofstede–Bond studies to correlate positively with national economic growth. Another cross-cultural management study suggests the need to vary leadership styles from one culture to another. The participative style turned out to be the only leadership style applicable in all 18 countries studied. Yet another cross-cultural management study of Jordanian, Turkish, and U.S. managers found a common preference for the collaborative problem-solving conflict-handling style. But backup styles varied.

F. Organizational culture is the social glue that binds organizational members together through shared values, symbolic devices, and social ideals. Most of the assumptions underlying an organization's culture are taken for granted. A culture's central values are more important than its strength.

G. General manifestations of an organization's culture are shared objects, talk, behavior, and emotion. Specific manifestations of culture include rituals, legends, stories, values, and heroes. Four functions of organization culture are organizational identity, collective commitment, social system stability, and sense-making device. Ouchi's Theory Z, which described a hybrid type of American company with Japanese-like qualities, prompted much early managerial interest in organizational cultures.

H. An organization's culture can become a competitive advantage if it is valuable, rare, and impossible to imitate. Given that successful organizations evolve their own unique cultures, passive imitation needs to be replaced by active development. The HOME model—history, oneness, membership, exchange—can help.

• KEY TERMS

culture	polychronic time
high-context cultures	proxemics
low-context cultures	cross-cultural management
monochronic time	organizational culture

• DISCUSSION QUESTIONS

1. What are your expectations about being affected by the global economy?

2. Regarding your cultural awareness, how would you describe the prevailing culture in your country to a stranger from another land?

3. What is your personal experience with cross-cultural dealings? What lessons have you learned?

4. Why are people from high-context cultures such as China and Japan likely to be misunderstood by low-context Westerners?

5. Are you relatively monochronic or polychronic? What difficulties do you encounter because of this cultural tendency?

6. Based on your personal experience with one or more of the countries listed in Table 19–3, do you agree or disagree with the leadership profiles? Explain.

7. How would you respond to someone who made the following statement? ''Organizational cultures are not important, as far as managers are concerned.''

8. What taken-for-granted assumptions do you have about the organization where you presently work or go to school? How did you learn those assumptions?

9. Can you think of any organizational heroes who have influenced your work behavior? Describe them and explain how they affected your behavior.

10. Why is it inappropriate for a manager to read a book like Peters and Waterman's best-seller, *In Search of Excellence,* and attempt to imitate the culture of an excellent company such as IBM?

BACK TO THE OPENING CASE

Now that you have read Chapter 19, you should be able to answer the following questions about the Mazda case:

1. What would you like to tell Mazda's Japanese managers about managing Americans?

2. What would you like to tell Mazda's American employees about working for Japanese managers?

3. How is it possible that Mazda's Japanese managers could view *kaizen* (the Japanese word for continuous improvement) positively while the company's American employees consider it a serious threat? How could this misperception be corrected?

4. How could Mazda improve the organizational culture in its Flat Rock, Michigan, facility with the HOME model?

• EXERCISE 19

Objectives

1. To increase your cross-cultural awareness.
2. To see how your own work goals compare internationally.

Introduction

This exercise is a variation of the one at the end of Chapter 5. Only this time, you will be asked to rank your work goals and then compare the results internationally with samples from the United States, Britain, Germany, and Japan. The idea is to see what people from different countries and cultures want from the work place.

Instructions

Below is a list of 11 goals potentially attainable in the work place. In terms of your own personal preferences, rank the goals from 1 to 11 (1 = Most important; 11 = Least important). After you have ranked all 11 work goals, compare your list with the national samples under the heading *Survey Results*. These national samples represent cross sections of employees from all levels and all major occupational groups. (Please complete your ranking now, before looking at the national samples.)

How important are the following in your work life?

Rank	Work Goals
_____	A lot of opportunity to *learn* new things
_____	Good *interpersonal relations* (supervisors, co-workers)
_____	Good opportunity for upgrading or *promotion*
_____	*Convenient work hours*
_____	A lot of *variety*
_____	*Interesting* work (work that you really like)
_____	Good *job security*
_____	A good *match* between your job requirements and your abilities and experience
_____	Good *pay*
_____	Good physical working *conditions* (such as light, temperature, cleanliness, low noise level)
_____	A lot of *autonomy* (you decide how to do your work)[52]

Questions for Consideration/Class Discussion

1. Which national profile of work goals most closely matches your own? Is this what you expected, or not?
2. Are you surprised by any of the rankings in the four national samples? Explain.
3. What sorts of motivational/leadership adjustments would a manager have to make when moving among the four countries?

Survey Results[53]

Ranking of Work Goals by Country
(1 = Most important; 11 = Least important)

Work Goals	United States	Britain	Germany*	Japan
Interesting work	1	1	3	2
Pay	2	2	1	5
Job security	3	3	2	4
Match between person and job	4	6	5	1
Opportunity to learn	5	8	9	7
Variety	6	7	6†	9
Interpersonal relations	7	4	4	6
Autonomy	8	10	8	3
Convenient work hours	9	5	6†	8
Opportunity for promotion	10	11	10	11
Working conditions	11	9	11	10

* Former West Germany.
† Tie.

• NOTES

[1] Kenneth Labich, "American Takes on the World," *Fortune*, September 24, 1990, p. 41.

[2] Marcus Mabry, "Pin a Label on a Manager—and Watch What Happens," *Newsweek*, May 14, 1990, p. 43.

[3] Ibid.

[4] Edgar H. Schien, *Organizational Culture and Leadership* (San Francisco: Jossey-Bass, 1985), p. 9.

[5] "How Cultures Collide," *Psychology Today*, July 1976, p. 69.

[6] See Mark Mendenhall, "A Painless Approach to Integrating 'International' into OB, HRM, and Management Courses," *Organizational Behavior Teaching Review*, no. 3 (1988–89), pp. 23–37.

[7] See C. L. Sharma, "Ethnicity, National Integration, and Education in the Union of Soviet Socialist Republics," *The Journal of East and West Studies*, October 1989, pp. 75–93; and Rose Brady and Peter Galuszka, "Shattered Dreams," *Business Week*, February 11, 1991, pp. 38–42.

[8] Jeremy Main, "How to Go Global—and Why," *Fortune*, August 28, 1989, p. 73.

[9] See "How Cultures Collide," pp. 66–74, 97.

[10] Dean C. Barnlund, "Public and Private Self in Communicating with Japan," *Business Horizons*, March–April 1989, p. 38.

[11] This list is based on Edward T. Hall, "The Silent Language in Overseas Business," *Harvard Business Review*, May–June 1960, pp. 87–96; and Rose Knotts, "Cross-Cultural Management: Transformations and Adaptations," *Business Horizons*, January–February 1989, pp. 29–33.

[12] For a comprehensive treatment of time, see Joseph E. McGrath and Janice R. Kelly, *Time and Human Interaction: Toward a Social Psychology of Time* (New York: The Guilford Press, 1986).

[13] Robert W. Moore, "Time, Culture, and Comparative Management: A Review and Future Direction," in *Advances in International Comparative Management*, Vol. 5, ed. S. Benjamin Prasad (Greenwich, Conn.: JAI Press, 1990), pp. 7–8.

14 See Edward T. Hall, *The Hidden Dimension* (Garden City, N.Y.: Doubleday, 1966).

15 "How Cultures Collide," p. 72.

16 Douglas Raybeck and Douglas Herrmann, "A Cross-Cultural Examination of Semantic Relations," *Journal of Cross-Cultural Psychology*, December 1990, p. 470.

17 "Do Cultural Differences Affect U.S.–Japan Business Relations?" *Economic World*, June 1990, p. 11.

18 Results adapted from and value definitions quoted from Scott R. Safranski and Ik-Whan Kwon, "Religious Groups and Management Value Systems," in *Advances in International Comparative Management*, Vol. 3, eds. Richard N. Farner and Elton G. McGoun (Greenwich, Conn.: JAI Press, 1988), pp. 171–83.

19 Ibid., p. 180.

20 Nancy J. Adler, *International Dimensions of Organizational Behavior*, 2nd ed. (Boston: PWS-Kent, 1991), p. 10.

21 For complete details, see Geert Hofstede, *Culture's Consequences: International Differences in Work-Related Values*, abridged edition (Newbury Park, Calif.: Sage Publications, 1984); and Geert Hofstede, "The Interaction between National and Organizational Value Systems," *Journal of Management Studies*, July 1985, pp. 347–57. Also see Viv J. Shackleton and Abbas H. Ali, "Work-Related Values of Managers: A Test of the Hofstede Model," *Journal of Cross-Cultural Psychology*, March 1990, pp. 109–18.

22 For recent research evidence on this key cultural variable, see C. Harry Hui and Marcelo J. Villareal, "Individualism–Collectivism and Psychological Needs: Their Relationships in Two Cultures," *Journal of Cross-Cultural Psychology*, September 1989, pp. 310–23; and Shalom H. Schwartz, "Individualism–Collectivism: Critique and Proposed Refinements," *Journal of Cross-Cultural Psychology*, June 1990, pp. 139–57.

23 See Geert Hofstede and Michael H. Bond, "Hofstede's Culture Dimensions: An Independent Validation Using Rokeach's Value Survey," *Journal of Cross-Cultural Psychology*, December 1984, pp. 417–33.

24 For complete details, see Geert Hofstede and Michael Harris Bond, "The Confucius Connection: From Cultural Roots to Economic Growth," *Organizational Dynamics*, Spring 1988, pp. 4–21.

25 See Carl A. Rodrigues, "The Situation and National Culture as Contingencies for Leadership Behavior: Two Conceptual Models," in *Advances in International Comparative Management*, Vol. 5, ed. S. Benjamin Prasad (Greenwich, Conn.: JAI Press, 1990), pp. 51–68.

26 See M. Kamil Kozan, "Cultural Influences on Styles of Handling Interpersonal Conflicts: Comparisons among Jordanian, Turkish, and U.S. Managers," *Human Relations*, September 1989, pp. 787–99.

27 Adapted from Linda Smircich, "Concepts of Culture and Organizational Analysis," *Administrative Science Quarterly*, September 1983, pp. 339–58. Also see Edgar H. Schein, "Organizational Culture," *American Psychologist*, February 1990, pp. 109–19.

28 See Guy S. Saffold III, "Culture Traits, Strength, and Organizational Performance: Moving beyond 'Strong' Culture," *Academy of Management Review*, October 1988, pp. 546–58.

29 A good discussion of organizational value systems can be found in Yoash Wiener, "Forms of Value Systems: A Focus on Organizational Effectiveness and Cultural Change and Maintenance," *Academy of Management Review*, October 1988, pp. 534–45.

[30] Based on Alan L. Wilkins, "The Culture Audit: A Tool for Understanding Organizations," *Organizational Dynamics,* Autumn 1983, pp. 24–38.

[31] Edgar H. Schein, "What You Need to Know about Organizational Culture," *Training and Development Journal,* January 1986, p. 30.

[32] Dennis Kneale, "Working at IBM: Intense Loyalty in a Rigid Culture," *The Wall Street Journal,* April 7, 1986, p. 21. Also see Ron Zemke, "Storytelling: Back to a Basic," *Training,* March 1990, pp. 44–50.

[33] See Allan Halcrow, "A Symbolic Gesture at Sikorsky," *Personnel Journal,* March 1986, p. 11.

[34] Adapted from Smircich, "Concepts of Culture and Organizational Analysis."

[35] Kenneth Labich, "Big Changes at Big Brown," *Fortune,* January 18, 1988, p. 56.

[36] Ibid., p. 58. Also see Todd Vogel, "Hello, I Must Be Going: On the Road with UPS," *Business Week,* June 4, 1990, p. 82.

[37] For an instructive discussion of alternative Theory Z models, see David M. Hunt and Donald S. Bolon, "A Review of Five Versions of Theory Z: Does Z Have a Future?" in *Advances in International Comparative Management,* Vol. 4, ed. S. Benjamin Prasad (Greenwich, Conn.: JAI Press, 1989), pp. 201–20.

[38] William G. Ouchi, *Theory Z: How American Business Can Meet the Japanese Challenge* (Reading, Mass.: Addison-Wesley Publishing, 1981), p. 91.

[39] See Terrence E. Deal and Allan A. Kennedy, *Corporate Cultures: The Rites and Rituals of Corporate Life* (Reading, Mass.: Addison-Wesley Publishing, 1982).

[40] See Thomas J. Peters and Robert H. Waterman, Jr., *In Search of Excellence* (New York: Harper & Row, 1982).

[41] Ibid., pp. 75–76.

[42] Critical reviews of these two popular books can be found in William I. Gorden, "Corporate Cultures," *Academy of Management Reviw,* April 1984, pp. 365–66; and Daniel T. Carroll, "A Disappointing Search for Excellence," *Harvard Business Review,* November–December 1983, pp. 78–88.

[43] Details may be found in Barry Z. Posner, James M. Kouzes, and Warren H. Schmidt, "Shared Values Make a Difference: An Empirical Test of Corporate Culture," *Human Resources Management,* Fall 1985, pp. 293–309.

[44] See Anthony F. Buono, James L. Bowditch, and John W. Lewis III, "When Cultures Collide: The Anatomy of a Merger," *Human Relations,* May 1985, pp. 477–500. Fears about incompatible cultures in the proposed AT&T–NCR merger are discussed in Laurent Belsie, "AT&T Going for Miracle Merger," *The Christian Science Monitor,* December 10, 1990, p. 8; and John W. Verity, "If AT&T Walks In, Will NCR's Talent Walk Out?" *Business Week,* December 17, 1990, p. 26.

[45] Jeffrey Kerr and John W. Slocum, Jr., "Managing Corporate Culture through Reward Systems," *Academy of Management Executive,* May 1987, p. 106.

[46] Richard Pascal, "Fitting New Employees into the Company Culture," *Fortune,* May 28, 1984, p. 40.

[47] Drawn from discussion in Jay B. Barney, "Organizational Culture: Can It Be a Source of Sustained Competitive Advantage?" *Academy of Management Review,* July 1986, pp. 656–65.

[48] Stew Leonard, "Love That Customer!" *Management Review,* October 1987, p. 36.

[49] Schein, *Organizational Culture and Leadership,* pp. 83–84.

[50] See Warren Gross and Shula Schichman, "How to Grow an Organizational Culture," *Personnel,* September 1987, pp. 52–56. An alternative perspective is presented in Thomas H. Fitzgerald, "Can Change in Organizationl Culture Really Be Managed?" *Organizational Dynamics,* Autumn 1988, pp. 5–15.

⁵¹ John Thorbeck, ''The Turnaround Value of Values,'' *Harvard Business Review,* January–February 1991, p. 58. The role of history in organizational culture is discussed in Alan L. Wilkins and Nigel J. Bristow, ''For Successful Organizational Culture, Honor Your Past,'' *Academy of Management Executive,* August 1987, pp. 221–29.

⁵² This list of work goals is quoted from Itzhak Harpaz, ''The Importance of Work Goals: An International Perspective,'' *Journal of International Business Studies,* First Quarter 1990, p. 79.

⁵³ Adapted from a seven-country summary in Ibid., Table 2, p. 81.

Changing and Developing Organizations

LEARNING OBJECTIVES

When you finish studying the material in this chapter, you should be able to:

- Discuss the external and internal forces that create the need for organizational change.
- List at least five reasons why employees resist change.
- Contrast Lewin's change model with a systems model of change.

- Explain how the two main modes of Nutt's transactional model of change interact.
- Describe the identifying characteristics of organization development (OD).

- Demonstrate your familiarity with organizational diagnosis.
- Distinguish between human-process and technostructural approaches to OD.
- Discuss four specific techniques for conducting OD.

Organizational Change Meant Life or Death to Will-Burt Co.

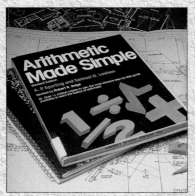

Sharon Hoogstraten

It's no fun being up against the wall, which is where Harry Featherstone found himself in the autumn of 1985. He had recently taken command of The Will-Burt Co., a troubled manufacturing outfit in Orrville, Ohio. The company's troubles began with a product liability lawsuit.

The lawsuit centered on a scaffold that collapsed in Miami in 1980, killing one person and crippling another. The scaffold maker declared bankruptcy. But Will-Burt, which had produced one of the parts, was sued under the principle of joint and several liability. Its insurer settled out of court in 1984, paying $6.2 million. A year later it canceled the company's coverage.

Amid the legal proceedings, Will-Burt's chief executive dropped dead of a heart attack. And with other lawsuits pending, the family that owned the company, fearful of losing everything, decided to sell or liquidate Will-Burt.

"We could have liquidated, but I didn't want to tell 350 people and their families that the business was closing," he recalls. "We thought of merging, but who wants a company burdened with all that litigation?" . . .

Finally Featherstone's lawyer proposed that he do a leveraged buyout and place Will-Burt into an employee stock ownership plan [ESOP]. This made sense in a rather elegant way. "My attorney told me that if we got ourselves highly leveraged, we wouldn't make much money, but neither would we be a deep-pocket target for some liability lawyer," Featherstone says. "Lawyers love rich companies, and we wouldn't be one." And so on December 30, 1985—the deadline set by the owners to avoid liquidation—

Featherstone completed a frantic two-month negotiation with an Ohio bank. He borrowed $3.2 million to buy 97 percent of Will-Burt stock, all he could get hold of. . . .

The company was in dismal shape. It had $20 million in sales, but profitability ranged from 1 percent to 5 percent over the past few years. Product quality was such that workers spent nearly 25,000 hours a year redoing faulty parts. Its wage rate was $2 below the area's average, and turnover often topped 30 percent. The pension plan was so bad that a 35-year veteran could expect to retire with $80 to $120 a month. . . .

And now, on top of everything else, Will-Burt had the ESOP . . . loan to repay—at a first-year cost of a cool $1 million and a second-year tab of almost $900,000. That weighed heavily on Featherstone. "This company had never even made $1 million a year," he says. "So I had quite a task." . . .

Featherstone's first steps, imperative though they were, won him few friends. He stopped making parts for ladders, scaffolds, and aircraft—anything that could create liability problems—and

---

T he only certainty in modern organizational life is constant change. This statement may be a well-worn cliche, but it remains a fact of life. Consider the tidal wave of mergers and work force reductions that occurred over the past decade. In 1984, for example, there were 2,543 corporate mergers and acquisitions in the United States worth a combined value of $122 billion. The number rose to 3,701 in 1987 with a total value of $165.5 billion. Down in the trenches, mergers affected over 15 million employees from 1985–88.[1] A less publicized fact, however, is that an estimated 75 to 95 percent of corporate

(continued)

shut down some plants in the process. That forced him to let go of 80 people, factory and office workers alike. If morale was low before, this stomped it to the ground. . . .

But making money would be even harder now. The plant closings backed sales down from $20 million to $15 million and eliminated some high-margin items. To curb costs, Featherstone brought in "the toughest controller I could find, somebody who would say no even to me." He slashed capital outlays, cutting machinery purchases from $1 million a year to $50,000. . . .

But the controversy attending those early moves was nothing compared with the conflicts that erupted over the ESOP itself. Companies converting to ESOPs often spend months preparing employees for the change. But in Featherstone's scramble to do the leveraged buyout, he had told the employees very little about what was going on. "We all heard the word ESOP, but nobody knew what it was all about," Cecil Martin recalls. "We all said, ESOP? What's an ESOP? They got some pamphlets out to us and said we'd

all own a piece of the place. But a lot of people had trouble grasping the concept." . . .

The rumor mill kicked into overdrive. Will-Burt had never been unionized, but that didn't matter. There was labor–management animosity, and the workers harbored suspicions about Featherstone's motives. "There were lots of misconceptions," recalls welder Russ White. "Some guys said it was Harry's way to get control of the company for his own private gain." Others thought it was some kind of trick, a ruse, so that if the company fell apart, then they, the new owners, could be blamed.

But gradually the fog cleared. "As we had more meetings and got information, we learned that the ESOP was under strict government guidelines," says Martin. "We learned it wasn't just for Harry but all of us. That made everybody feel a little better. We also liked the fact that it might stave off some lawsuits." . . .

That wasn't all. In late 1986, after countless meetings, the workers began to understand that they did, in fact, own the company. And as owners, they

wanted benefits—namely, some fat raises. . . . But money wasn't all they wanted. "When people hear employee-owned, they think, hey, I'm a boss now," says Larry Murgatroyd, a gear machinist. "That means control." They wanted to elect the board of directors and the president and call the shots on all major decisions.

This wasn't everyone, but enough to make life miserable for the beleaguered Featherstone. "I tried to explain that this was a business, not Athenian democracy," he recalls. "You can't have 300 people making decisions—it would be anarchy. . . ."

Will-Burt needed some edge, Featherstone knew, something to set it apart.

He decided to shoot for perfect quality and perfect on-time delivery. Perfect quality meant manufacturing parts exactly to blueprint—zero defects. That sounded good. But pulling it off, Featherstone knew, would require the dedication and participation of each and every worker. Ownership alone would not generate the kind of commitment he needed. No, the employees would have to be given a more sharply defined

mergers were disappointments for those involved. Observers attributed this poor showing partly to management's inability to handle large-scale change.[2]

Work force reductions have become a common occurrence in organizations throughout the 1980s and early 1990s. For example, 10.8 million people in the United States were involuntarily unemployed in the years 1981 to 1988. A more recent survey of American Management Association members indicated that about one third reduced their work force in 1989 and more than 20 percent expected additional cutbacks in 1990.[3] Unfortunately, work

OPENING CASE 20

(continued)

role in the running of the business—more power to make their own decisions. They'd have to work harder and smarter.

His work force, though, was hardly eager to pioneer new-fangled techniques. Its overall education level was somewhere around the 10th grade. There were fourth-generation welders. Many workers were high-school dropouts, and more than a few were illiterate. "I think we had four degrees in the company at that time," Featherstone recalls, "and I had two of them." If Featherstone needed a work force that would move mountains—and he did now—he was starting with little muscle.

"I had been a troubleshooter all my life," he says. "I had spent a lot of time in Japan with Ford and was really interested in how the Japanese did things. I studied them and decided that their success hinged on education, training, and their emphasis on business. . . ."

For openers, Featherstone focused on math. "Our people work from blueprints, and to

make sense of them you have to know some math," he says. "I started out on a voluntary basis, on company time, and it just didn't work. You take someone who's been out of school for 20 years and put him back in a classroom atmosphere, and he hates it. Here's a teacher saying, 'Go home tonight and figure out the cosine of this tangent,' and the guy says, 'You've got to be out of your mind! I volunteered for this?' We started out with 25 people and ended up with 3. It was bad."

So Featherstone made the training mandatory, still on company time. He began with basic blueprint reading for all production workers—it remained voluntary for office workers—taught by a local high-school teacher for an hour or two a week. There were tests and homework. From there he moved into advanced blueprint reading, and for this he enlisted the continuing education staff of the University of Akron. . . .

Featherstone himself caught some flak. "When I made it mandatory, some people got mad at me, called me dictatorial," he

says. "I even got hate mail." But the price was worth paying. Almost immediately, product quality picked up and the number of rejects dropped. "Now I knew why we were getting hammered," he says. "It turned out we had guys running machines who couldn't read a scale, let alone a blueprint. And they worked with blueprints all day long." . . .

Something had to change. In 1987 Featherstone decided to put the floor workers on salary. He totaled up each one's base compensation and overtime pay and divided that by 40, effectively raising wages by up to $3.50 an hour for a standard week, which didn't include overtime. That made Will-Burt competitive. Turnover dropped to single-digit numbers. Featherstone cashed in some insurance policies, enabling him to increase pensions nearly tenfold. He started a 401(k) retirement plan and installed a disability program that provided full pay for up to six months. A new policy awarding two extra floating holidays for perfect attendance over a year cut daily absenteeism from 8

force reductions will continue to be a fact of life in the 1990s as organizations restructure and adopt advanced technology aimed at enhancing their ability to compete in global markets.

Present and future managers are clearly challenged to either prepare for change and manage it or be bowled over by it. According to a pair of consulting psychologists:

Today's business environment produces change in the workplace more suddenly and frequently than ever before. Mergers, acquisitions, hostile takeovers, deregulation, new technology, and organizations going through cycles of centralization and decentralization are all factors that contribute to a growing climate of

OPENING CASE 20

(concluded)

percent to 2 percent.

And Featherstone pressed on with education, relying heavily on a University of Akron industrial training specialist named Hank Jeanneret. He sent his floor workers through a rigorous course on geometric tolerancing, a three-dimensional view of blueprints. Then came basic high-school mathematics—fractions, decimals, a touch of algebra. . . .

Finally, Featherstone introduced statistical process control, which entails measuring and tracking parts through a manufacturing process. By examining random parts, for instance, one can spot deviations and trends that might signal problems with machinery or tooling. "I said we had to do this or we wouldn't have a company," he recalls. "The people we sell to were preaching quality and beating on us to provide better products."

But Will-Burt was looking better all the time. In December 1987 . . . [another] product liability suit was dismissed. By 1988 the company once again could obtain full-coverage liability insurance. Banks suddenly agreed to lend the company money. . . .

On-time delivery was running at 98 percent for months on end. Product quality was surging dramatically. In 1986, for example, the part rejection rate stood at 35 percent. By late 1988 it fell below 10 percent. Time spent reworking faulty parts dropped from 2,000 hours a month to 400, even though Will-Burt was doing far more high-precision work than ever. That slashed annual reject reworking costs from $800,000 to less than $180,000. . . .

To get the employees even more involved in decision making, this year [1990] Featherstone launched a two-year cross-training program he calls the "Mini M.B.A." The University of Akron's Jeanneret is leading the instruction, which embraces everything from accounting to inventory control. . . .

What astounded Featherstone was the turnout. He expected 15 people. Instead, 54 signed up. They are welders, machinists, metal punchers. By and large, they are the younger workers, the ones betting their future on Will-Burt. "It's remarkable," he says. "Four years ago I couldn't get 10 people to stick with basic blueprint reading on a voluntary basis, and they see blueprints every day. Now, I've got 25 percent of the factory guys taking these classes on their own time. And they're pretty much the same people. It's a long process to teach people what ownership is all about, but education is really working."

For Discussion

What was the most important contribution to successful change at Will-Burt?

• Additional discussion questions linking this case with the following material appear at the end of this chapter.

Source: Excerpted from Jay Finegan, "The Education of Harry Featherstone," *Inc.*, July 1990, pp. 57–66. Reprinted with permission, *Inc.* Magazine. Copyright © 1990 by Goldhirsh Group, Inc. 38 Commercial Wharf, Boston, MA 02110.

uncertainty. Jobs, health, even marriages can be placed at risk, jeopardizing productivity and profitability. Now, more than ever, organizations must find ways to manage and master change.[4]

This final chapter explores the complex process of organizational change and how it can be managed through a collection of techniques called organization development. Specifically, we discuss the forces that create the need for organization change, resistance to change, models of planned change, organization development, and conclude by reviewing a model of organization development that can be used to help managers facilitate and manage planned change.

• FORCES FOR CHANGE

Organizational survival depends on the ability to effectively respond to change. For example, a company is hard pressed to stay in business if it does not design and sell products that satisfy changing customer preferences and market conditions. How do organizations know when they should change? What cues should an organization look for? Although there are no clear-cut answers to these questions, the ''cues'' which signal the need for change are found by monitoring the forces for change.

Organizations encounter many different forces for change. These forces come from external sources outside the organization and from internal sources. This section examines the forces that create the need for change. Awareness of these forces can help managers determine when they should consider implementing an organizational change. The external and internal forces for change are presented in Figure 20–1.

• FIGURE 20–1   The External and Internal Forces for Change

External Forces

Demographic Characteristics
• Age
• Education
• Skill-level
• Gender
• Immigration

Technological Advancements
• Manufacturing automation
• Office automation

Market Changes
• Mergers and acquisitions
• Domestic and international competition
• Recession

Social and Political Pressures
• War
• Values
• Leadership

Internal Forces

Human Resource Problems/Prospects
• Unmet needs
• Job dissatisfaction
• Absenteeism and turnover
• Productivity
• Participation/Suggestions

Managerial Behavior/Decisions
• Conflict
• Leadership
• Reward systems
• Structural reorganization

The Need for Change

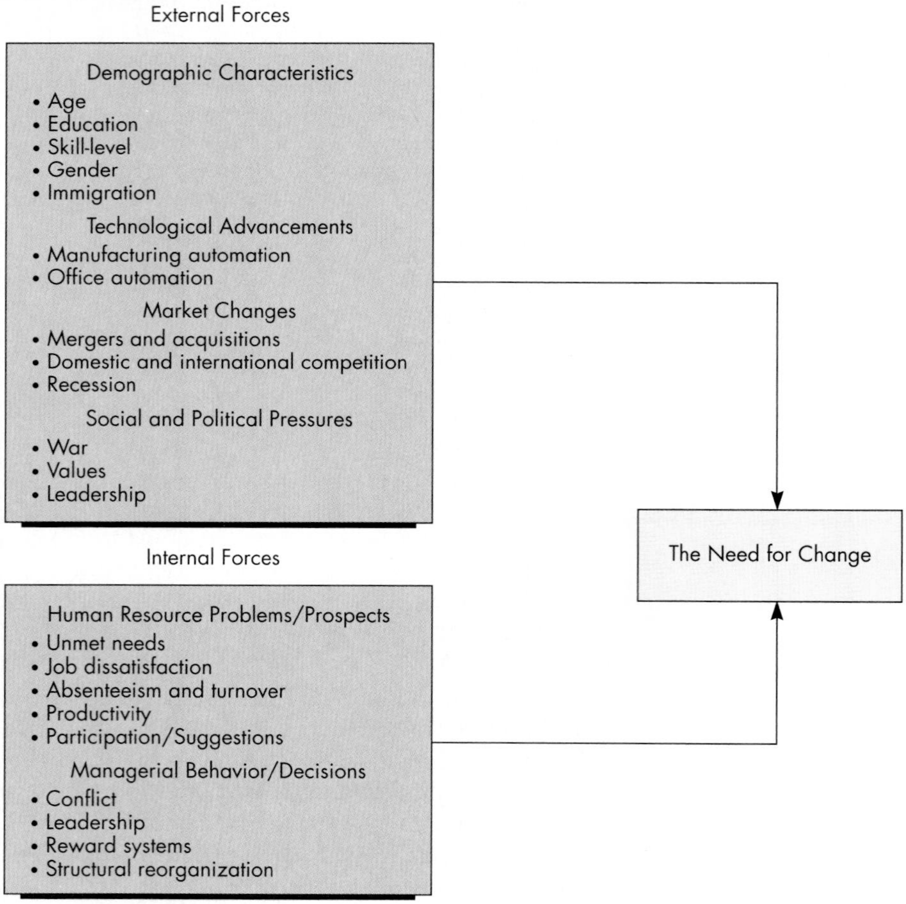

External Forces

External forces for change originate outside the organization. Because these forces have global effects, they may cause an organization to question the essence of what business it is in and the process by which products and services are produced. There are four key external forces for change: demographic characteristics, technological advancements, market changes, and social and political pressures. Each is now discussed.

Demographic Characteristics   Chapter 2 provided a detailed discussion of the demographic changes occurring in the U.S. work force. Let us briefly review the trends:

- The work force is aging.
- Education and skill levels of the work force do not match organizational needs.
- Women and minorities will make up the majority of new entrants into the work force.
- There is a shortage of entry-level workers. The supply of workers is being increased through both increased immigration to the United States and employment of retirees.[5]

As discussed in Chapter 2, new managerial paradigms and practices are being used to respond to these changes. Chapters 11 and 17 further identified new forms of organizational structure that may help manage these changes.

Technological Advancements   Both manufacturing and service organizations are increasingly using technology as a means to improve productivity and market competitiveness. Manufacturing companies, for instance, have automated their operations with robotics, computerized numerical control (CNC), which is used for metal cutting operations, and computer-aided design (CAD). CAD is a computerized process of drafting and designing engineering drawings of products. Companies have just begun to work on computer-integrated manufacturing (CIM). This highly technical process attempts to integrate product design with production planning, control, and operations. Interestingly, the United States is not the world leader in factory automation. Japan and Asia accounted for 42 percent of the world market in 1990. In 1988, for example, Japan had 50,000 robots at work while the U.S. had 28,000.[6]

In contrast to these manufacturing technologies, the service sector of the U.S. economy is using office automation. **Office automation** consists of a host of computerized technologies that are used to obtain, store, analyze, retrieve, and communicate information. Wal-Mart, for example, spent $500 million from 1985 thru 1990 for such technology. Part of this automation includes a computer system that links the company with its suppliers, thereby enabling Wal-Mart to lower its inventory costs and increase efficiency.[7] Overall, experts estimated that between 40–50 percent of the work force used computer equipment to perform their jobs in 1990. Simply pur-

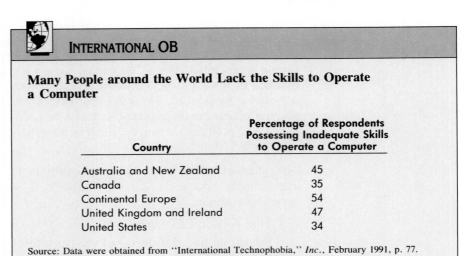

INTERNATIONAL OB

Many People around the World Lack the Skills to Operate a Computer

Country	Percentage of Respondents Possessing Inadequate Skills to Operate a Computer
Australia and New Zealand	45
Canada	35
Continental Europe	54
United Kingdom and Ireland	47
United States	34

Source: Data were obtained from "International Technophobia," *Inc.*, February 1991, p. 77.

chasing and implementing these types of technologies does not guarantee positive results, however.

Failure rates are estimated at 50–75 percent for implementing manufacturing automation and around 40 percent for office automation. These failure rates are attributed to poor management, failure to accommodate human resource considerations such as training and resistance to change, and organizational structures that are inconsistent with the technology.[8] For example, a recent survey of 1,344 people from around the world indicated that many employees lacked the necessary skills to operate a computer (see International OB). Training is a necessary component for successfully implementing any type of technological innovation.

Market Changes   As previously discussed, mergers and corporate failures were frequent occurrences over the last decade. Organizations also must adjust to changing customer preferences. Consumers increasingly are demanding quality products at bargain rates. Consider how Apple is responding to this external force by revamping its legendary Macintosh product line (see OB in Action). Time will tell whether Apple's new strategy is successful.

The emergence of a global economy is forcing U.S. companies to change the way they do business. The gap left by the United States' decreasing share of the global economy has been filled by countries like Germany and Japan. The U.S. steel, automobile, consumer electronics, computer, and memory chip industries, for example, have felt the sting of international competition. International competition is expected to heat up even more in the future.

Recessionary periods are another powerful external force for change. They necessitate reducing costs, increasing productivity, and redesigning jobs. Successful companies such as Corning, for instance, also monitor the marketplace in order to change their operations before a recession actually hits.

Corning has told its salespeople to look for recessionary signs: A slight drop in orders, a customer or supplier who suddenly starts haggling over prices, even

OB IN ACTION

Apple Responds to Market Changes

Later this month [October 1990] Apple will revamp its popular Macintosh product line, rolling out three new systems priced to undercut similarly equipped IBM compatibles. One of the new machines, a budget model retailing for less than $1,000, made it from drawing board to factory in under nine months, half the usual development time. Another, outfitted with a full-color monitor, will sell for under $2,500, half the price of current color Macs. . . .

Hawking Macs at low prices represents a screeching U-turn in Apple's strategy. Since 1986, in an attempt to shed the company's hobbyist image and tap into the lucrative market for office computers, Sculley had focused on building ever more powerful—and expensive—Macs. . . .

But last winter the strategy ran out of gas. Unit sales of Macs started to slip, and Apple's worldwide market share declined from 9.5 percent in 1988 to 7.3 percent. . . . The company's problem: a dramatic change in the PC industry.

Source: Brenton R. Schlender, "Yet Another Strategy for Apple," *Fortune*, October 22, 1990, p. 81. © 1990 The Time Inc. Magazine Company. All rights reserved..

• When its market share slipped because of global competition, Apple began selling its computers at a lower price in new target markets.   *(Courtesy of Apple Computer.)*

something as seemingly innocuous as a customer's office in need of a new paint job.

The company is also using what has become a common manufacturing tool—the just-in-time, or JIT, system of managing inventory—to provide an early warning of recession and to lessen the threat it could pose. With JIT, customers order parts from Corning only as needed, and the company, thanks to an electronic ordering system, can supply them in a few days rather than the months it took under the old system. This allows Corning to track swings in demand much more closely. When Corning sees customers starting to pull back, it knows it's time to cut production and avoid a nasty buildup of inventory.[9]

Corning's proactive approach enabled it to cut costs without layoffs during the 1990–1991 recession.

Social and Political Pressures   These forces are created by social and political events. Personal values, which were discussed in Chapter 3, affect employees' needs, priorities, and motivation. Managers thus may need to adjust their managerial style or approach to fit changing employee values. Political events can create substantial change. For example, the 1991 war in the Persian Gulf resulted in some employees leaving work to go to the Middle East. These employees had to be temporarily replaced. The war also affected the sale of various products. Whereas sales of army fatigues increased, sales related to the travel industry decreased. Although it is difficult for organizations to predict changes in political forces, many organizations hire lobbyists and consultants to help them detect and respond to social and political changes.

Internal Forces

Internal forces for change come from inside the organization. These forces may be subtle, such as low morale, or can manifest in outward signs, such as low productivity and conflict. Internal forces for change come from both human resource problems and managerial behavior/decisions.

Human Resource Problems/Prospects   These problems stem from employee perceptions about how they are treated at work and the match between individual and organizational needs and desires. Chapter 5 highlighted the relationship between an employee's unmet needs and job dissatisfaction. Dissatisfaction is a symptom of an underlying employee problem that should be addressed. Unusual or high levels of absenteeism and turnover also represent forces for change. Organizations might respond to these problems by using the various approaches to job design discussed in Chapter 5, by implementing realistic job previews, which were discussed in Chapter 8, by reducing employees' role conflict, overload, and ambiguity (recall our discussion in Chapter 8), and by removing the different stressors discussed in Chapter 16. Prospects for positive change stem from employee participation and suggestions and continuity input.

Managerial Behavior/Decisions   Excessive interpersonal conflict between managers and their subordinates is a sign that change is needed. Both the manager and the employee may need interpersonal skills training, or the two individuals may simply need to be separated. For example, one of the parties might be transferred to a new department. Inappropriate leader behaviors such as inadequate direction or support may result in human resource problems requiring change. As discussed in Chapter 14, leadership training is one potential solution for this problem. Inequitable reward systems— recall our discussion in Chapters 6 and 13—and the type of structural reorganizations discussed in Chapter 17 are additional forces for change.

• UNDERSTANDING AND MANAGING RESISTANCE TO CHANGE

We are all creatures of habit. It generally is difficult for people to try new ways of doing things. It is precisely because of this basic human characteristic that most employees do not have enthusiasm for change in the workplace. Rare is the manager who does not have several stories about carefully cultivated changes that died on the vine because of resistance to change (see OB in Action). This section examines why employees resist change, relevant research, and practical ways of dealing with the problem.

Why People Resist Changes in the Workplace

No matter how technically or administratively perfect a proposed change may be, *people* will make or break it. **Resistance to change** is an emotional/behavioral response to real or imagined threats to an established work routine. Resistance can take many forms (see Table 20–1). This list reveals that resistance ranges from vocal opposition to foot-dragging and lack of cooperation. (Extreme resistance may even involve sabotage.) It is important for managers to learn to recognize the manifestations of resistance both in themselves and in others if they want to be more effective in creating and supporting change. For example, managers can use the list in Table 20–1 to prepare answers and tactics to combat the various forms of resistance.

Now that we have examined the manifestations of resistance to change, let us consider the reasons why employees resist change in the first place. Eight leading reasons are:[10]

1. *Surprise and fear of the unknown.* When innovative or radically different changes are introduced without warning, affected employees become fearful of the implications. Grapevine rumors fill the void created by a lack of official announcements. Harvard's Rosabeth Moss Kanter recommends

---

 OB IN ACTION

Resistance to Change in Action

A large multinational corporation in Orange County, California, decided to invest $1 million in office automation, furnishing each of their key executives with personal computers accessing mainframe information. The planning was centrally focused on the technical aspects of implementation and hardly considered the human factor. In addition, it happened at a time of severe cost-cutting, leading many to view the project as being excessively expensive and unnecessary.

The end result of a year-long effort was that less than 20 percent of the executives were using their computers, although the system was technically fully functional. The company finally abandoned the project, removing the computer networks and writing off the project as a loss.

Source: Irv Gamal and C. Woody McLaughlin, "Organizationl Change: Blessing or Burden?" *Personnel Administrator*, August 1989, p. 95.

• **TABLE 20-1**   Common Forms of Resistance to Change

1. An individual directly attacks the new idea or suggestion.
2. An individual quickly asks a lot of questions, some of which may be irrelevant to the change.
3. An individual plays the silent role and says nothing.
4. An individual appears troubled and unable to decide about the proposed change.
5. An individual quickly intellectualizes the discussion and then analyzes why the current approach is the best way to go.
6. An individual insists that the change is not fair to everyone.
7. An individual drums up past negative results from proposed changes, even if they aren't relevant.
8. An individual minimizes the need for change.
9. An individual is very agreeable but expresses regrettable criticism. "What a great idea, however . . ."
10. An individual suggests a "quick-fix" solution that really does not amount to any real change.

Source: Adapted from discussion in John A. Keeler, "Overcoming Resistance to Change," *Fueloil & Oil Heat*, November 1989, p. 35.

appointing a transition manager charged with keeping all relevant parties adequately informed.[11]

2. *Climate of mistrust.* Trust, as discussed in Chapter 11, involves reciprocal faith in others' intentions and behavior. Mutual mistrust can doom to failure an otherwise well-conceived change. Mistrust encourages secrecy, which begets deeper mistrust. Managers who trust their employees make the change process an open, honest, and participative affair. Employees who in turn trust management are more willing to expend extra effort and take chances with something different.

3. *Fear of failure.* Intimidating changes on the job can cause employees to doubt their capabilities. Self-doubt erodes self-confidence and cripples personal growth and development.

4. *Loss of status and/or job security.* Administrative and technological changes that threaten to alter power bases or eliminate jobs generally trigger strong resistance. For example, participative management programs often run into stubborn resistance from middle managers and supervisors who fear a loss of status.

5. *Peer pressure.* Someone who is not directly affected by a change may actively resist it to protect the interest of his or her friends and co-workers.

6. *Disruption of cultural traditions and/or group relationships.* Whenever individuals are transferred, promoted, or reassigned, cultural and group dynamics are thrown into disequilibrium.

7. *Personality conflicts.* Just as a friend can get away with telling us something we would resent hearing from an adversary, the personalities of change agents can breed resistance.

8. *Lack of tact and/or poor timing.* Undue resistance can occur because changes are introduced in an insensitive manner or at an awkward time. One

of J. C. Penney Company's nine principles of managing change advises: "Determine if there is a 'natural' point in time to end the old and begin the new."[12]

Research on Resistance to Change

The classic study of resistance to change was reported in 1948 by Lester Coch and John R. P. French. They observed the introduction of a new work procedure in a garment factory. The change was introduced in three different ways to separate groups of workers. In the "no participation" group, the garment makers were simply told about the new procedure. Members of a second group, called the "representative" group, were introduced to the change by a trained co-worker. Employees in the "total participation" group learned of the new work procedure through a graphic presentation of its cost-saving potential. Mixed results were recorded for the representative group. The no participation and total participation groups, meanwhile, went in opposite directions. Output dropped sharply for the no participation group, while grievances and turnover climbed. After a small dip in performance, the total participation group achieved record-high output levels while experiencing no turnover.[13] Since the Coch and French study, participation has been the recommended approach for overcoming resistance to change.

Two studies of attitudes toward computers have implications for those concerned with resistance to change. Computers are an appropriate subject matter because they are a significant and common technological change encumbered by a great deal of resistance.

1. A survey of 284 nonmanagerial office personnel (43 percent male) employed by three California manufacturers examined preconditions for willingness to use computers. Regarding the use of computers, female employees tended to have more experience, stronger favorable attitudes, and fewer negative attitudes than their male counterparts. There were no significant relationships between education, age, or tenure and positive or negative attitudes toward computers. Employees who actually used computers in their work had more positive attitudes toward computers than co-workers who had little or no experience with computers. Those reporting high job involvement had significantly fewer concerns about working with computers than co-workers with low job involvement. These results suggest that hands-on experience with computers, whether through training or on-the-job practice, can foster positive attitudes toward working with computers.[14]

2. A pair of studies relying on university psychology students as subjects revealed a significant positive correlation between personal efficacy and the use of a number of advanced technology products. People with high personal efficacy scores believe they can handle nonsocial situations such as solving puzzles and building things. The researchers concluded that "only through changes in perceived efficacy does experience with computer technology lead to a higher likelihood of technology adoption."[15] A practical implication springing from this study involves the need to accompany computer skills training with self-efficacy development. For example, computer train-

ees could be exposed to persuasive evidence about the many *personal* benefits of learning how to use computers. (Recall our discussion of self-efficacy in Chapter 3.)

Alternative Strategies for Overcoming Resistance to Change

Before recommending specific approaches to overcome resistance, there are key conclusions that should be kept in mind. First, organizational change is less successful when top management fails to keep employees informed about the process of change.[16] Second, employees' perceptions or interpretations of a change significantly affect resistance.[17] Employees are less likely to resist when they perceive that the benefits of a change overshadow the personal costs. At a minimum then, managers are advised to (1) provide as much information as possible to employees about the change, (2) inform employees about the reasons/rationale for the change, (3) conduct meetings to address employees' questions regarding the change, and (4) provide employees the opportunity to discuss how the proposed change might affect them.[18] These recommendations underscore the importance of communicating with employees throughout the process of change.

In addition to communication, employee participation in the change process is another generic approach for reducing resistance. Organizational change experts have nonetheless criticized the tendency to treat participation as a cure-all for resistance to change. They prefer a contingency approach because resistance can take many forms and, furthermore, because situational factors vary (see Table 20–2). Participation + Involvement does have its place, but it takes time that is not always available. Similarly, as indicated in Table 20–2, each of the other five methods has its situational niche, advantages, and drawbacks. In short, there is no universal strategy for overcoming resistance to change. Managers need a complete repertoire of change strategies.[19]

• When employees are resistant to change, managers are advised to use a persuasive approach to bring about acceptance of, for example, a new policy. (Howard Grey/Tony Stone Worldwide.)

• **TABLE 20-2**   Six Strategies for Overcoming Resistance to Change

Approach	Commonly Used in Situations	Advantages	Drawbacks
Education + Communication	Where there is a lack of information or inaccurate information and analysis.	Once persuaded, people will often help with the implementation of the change.	Can be very time-consuming if lots of people are involved.
Participation + Involvement	Where the initiators do not have all the information they need to design the change, and where others have considerable power to resist.	People who participate will be committed to implementing change, and any relevant information they have will be integrated into the change plan.	Can be very time-consuming if participators design an inappropriate change.
Facilitation + Support	Where people are resisting because of adjustment problems.	No other approach works as well with adjustment problems.	Can be time-consuming, expensive, and still fail.
Negotiation + Agreement	Where someone or some group will clearly lose out in a change, and where that group has considerable power to resist.	Sometimes it is a relatively easy way to avoid major resistance.	Can be too expensive in many cases if it alerts others to negotiate for compliance.
Manipulation + Co-optation	Where other tactics will not work, or are too expensive.	It can be a relatively quick and inexpensive solution to resistance problems.	Can lead to future problems if people feel manipulated.
Explicit + Implicit coercion	Where speed is essential, and the change initiators possess considerable power.	It is speedy, and can overcome any kind of resistance.	Can be risky if it leaves people mad at the initiators.

Source: Reprinted by permission of the *Harvard Business Review*. An exhibit from "Choosing Strategies for Change" by John P. Kotter and Leonard A. Schlesinger (March/April 1979). Copyright © 1979 by the President and Fellows of Harvard College; all rights reserved.

• MODELS AND DYNAMICS OF PLANNED CHANGE

American managers are criticized for emphasizing short-term, quick-fix solutions to organizational problems. When applied to organizational change, this approach is doomed from the start. Quick-fix solutions do not really solve underlying problems and they have little staying power.[20] Researchers and managers alike thus have tried to identify effective ways to manage the change process. This section sheds light on their insights. After discussing different types of organizational changes, we review Lewin's change model, a systems model of change, and a transactional model of change that highlights the mechanics of planned change.

Types of Change

A useful three-way typology of change is displayed in Figure 20-2.[21] This typology is generic because it relates to all sorts of change, including both administrative and technological changes. Adaptive change is lowest in

• **FIGURE 20-2**   A Generic Typology of Organizational Change

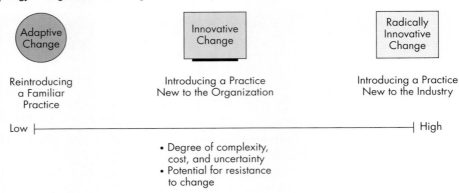

complexity, cost, and uncertainty.[22] It involves reimplementation of a change in the same organizational unit at a later time or imitation of a similar change by a different unit. For example, an adaptive change for a department store would be to rely on 12-hour days during the annual inventory week. The store's accounting department could imitate the same change in work hours during tax preparation time. Adaptive changes are not particularly threatening to employees because they are familiar.

Innovative changes fall midway on the continuum of complexity, cost, and uncertainty. An experiment with flextime, as discussed in Chapter 2, by a farm supply warehouse company qualifies as an innovative change if other firms in the industry already use it. Unfamilarity, and hence greater uncertainty, make fear of change a problem with innovative changes.

At the high end of the continuum of complexity, cost, and uncertainty are radically innovative changes. Changes of this sort are the most difficult to implement and tend to be the most threatening to managerial confidence and employee job security. They can tear the fabric of an organization's culture. For example, organized labor was very resentful when robots were introduced in the automobile industry. Resistance to change tends to increase as changes go from adaptive, to innovative, to radically innovative.

Lewin's Change Model

Most theories of organizational change originated from the landmark work of social psychologist Kurt Lewin. Lewin developed a three-stage model of planned change which explained how to initiate, manage, and stabilize the change process.[23] The three stages are unfreezing, changing, and refreezing. Before reviewing each stage, it is important to highlight the assumptions that underlie this model:[24]

1. The change process involves learning something new, as well as discontinuing current attitudes, behaviors, or organizational practices.

2. Change will not occur unless there is motivation to change. This is often the most difficult part of the change process.

3. People are the hub of all organizational changes. Any change, whether in terms of structure, group process, reward systems, or job design, requires individuals to change.
4. Resistance to change is found even when the goals of change are highly desirable.
5. Effective change requires reinforcing new behaviors, attitudes, and organizational practices.

Let us now consider the three stages of change.

Unfreezing   The focus of this stage is to create the motivation to change. In so doing, individuals are encouraged to replace old behaviors and attitudes with those desired by management. Managers can begin the unfreezing process by disconfirming the usefulness or appropriateness of employees' present behaviors or attitudes. In other words, employees need to become dissatisfied with the old way of doing things. Managers also need to devise ways to reduce the barriers to change during this stage.

Changing   Because change involves learning, this stage entails providing employees with new information, new behavioral models, or new ways of looking at things. The purpose is to help employees learn new concepts or points of view. Role models, mentors, experts, and training are useful mechanisms to facilitate change.

Refreezing   Change is stabilized during refreezing by helping employees integrate the changed behavior or attitude into their normal way of doing things. This is accomplished by first giving employees the chance to exhibit the new behaviors or attitudes. Once exhibited, positive reinforcement is used to reinforce the desired change (recall our discussion in Chapter 7). Additional coaching and modeling also are used at this point to reinforce the stability of the change.[25]

A Systems Model of Change

A systems approach takes a "big picture" perspective of organizational change. It is based on the notion that any change, no matter how large or small, has a cascading impact throughout an organization. For example, promoting an individual to a new work group affects the group dynamics in both the old and new groups. Similarly, creating project or work teams may necessitate the need to revamp compensation practices. These examples illustrate that change creates additional change. Today's solutions are tomorrow's problems. A systems model of change offers managers a framework to understand the broad complexities of organizational change.[26] The three main components of a systems model are inputs, target elements of change, and outputs (see Figure 20–3).

Inputs   All organizational changes should be consistent with an organization's strategic mission and resulting strategic plan. A **strategic mission**

• **FIGURE 20-3**   A Systems Model of Change

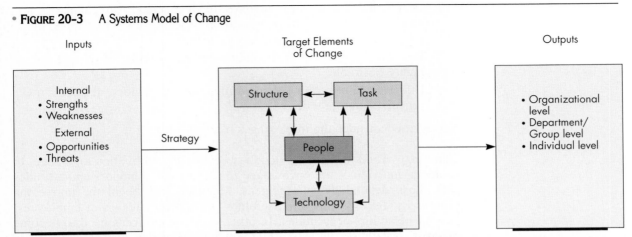

Sources: Adapted from Paul Dainty and Andrew Kakabadse, "Organizational Change: A Strategy for Successful Implementation," *Journal of Business and Psychology*, Summer 1990, pp. 463–81; and David A. Nadler and Michael L. Tushman, "Organizational Frame Bending: Principles for Managing Reorientation," *Academy of Management Executive*, August 1989, pp. 194–203.

statement describes an organization's ultimate purpose. It broadly establishes what an organization intends to do, for whom, and under what philosophical premises. A Matter of Ethics presents the managerial premises by which VLSI Technology, Inc., conducts business (see A Matter of Ethics).

A **strategic plan** outlines an organization's long-term direction and actions necessary to achieve planned results.[27] Strategic plans are based on considering an organization's strengths and weakness relative to its environmental opportunities and threats. This comparison results in developing an organizational strategy to attain desired outputs such as profits, customer satisfaction, adequate return on investment, and acceptable levels of turnover and employee commitment (see Figure 20–3). In summary, organizations tend to commit resources to counterproductive or conflicting activities when organizational changes are not consistent with its strategic plan.

Target Elements of Change   Target elements of change represent the components of an organization that may be changed. As shown in Figure 20–3, change can be directed at realigning organizational structure, tasks, technology, or people.[28] The choice is based on the strategy being pursued or the problem at hand. For example, if lack of cooperation or teamwork is causing low productivity, change might be geared toward people or tasks. Moreover, the double-headed arrows among the target elements of change indicate that a change in one organizational component affects the others. Consider how United Parcel Service's decision to invest $1.4 billion in computerization in order to compete with Federal Express must be interfaced with other target elements of change (see OB in Action). As previously discussed, change begets change. Finally, Figure 20–3 underscores the assumption that people are the hub of all change. Change will not succeed unless individuals embrace it in one way or another.

A MATTER OF ETHICS

VLSI Technology, Inc., Runs Its Business in a Positive, Proactive, and Ethical Manner

- **People are our greatest asset and the strength of our company:** We must provide a challenging, satisfying environment based on mutual respect and teamwork, where all employees have the opportunity to learn and contribute to their maximum potential.
- **Quality is essential to our long-term success:** We must supply leadership-quality products and services to achieve customer satisfaction.
- **Continuous improvement is fundamental to accomplishing our mission:** We are committed to continually improving our products, services and competitive position to achieve long-term success.
- **Teamwork is the way we operate:** Teamwork among our employees, as well as with our customers and our vendors, is a critical part of our success.
- **Integrity, trust, loyalty and open communication are our way of life:** We will practice these fundamental values in our relationships with customers, fellow employees, stockholders, vendors, and communities.
- **Leadership:** We are committed to being a leader and long-term success in our chosen businesses.

Source: VLSI 1991 Annual Report, p. 9.

OB IN ACTION

UPS Finds that Technological Change Affects Other Target Elements of Change

The huge $1.4 billion budget for computerization has spawned a system aimed at tracking a package from door to door. . . .

While the system is designed to leapfrog Federal's [Federal Express] in terms of capability and quickness, however, it won't be put to full use for three years. For one thing, "they've got to get their people comfortable with the technology," says Federal Express Senior Vice President Ron J. Ponder. Then there are the thousands of outsiders brought in to implement the system. They have to get used to UPS's quirks. New hires are told bluntly of rules barring coffee at desks, and beards. And they're expected to join the team for good. . . .

International expansion is also a strain. . . . "You can't impose the UPS culture on people outside the U.S. You have to let them assimilate at their own pace," says Donald W. Layden, senior vice president.

Source: Todd Vogel and Chuck Hawkins, "Can UPS Deliver The Goods in a New World?" *Business Week,* June 4, 1990, pp. 81–82.

Outputs   Output represents the desired end-result of a change. Once again, this end-result should be consistent with an organization's strategic plan. Figure 20–3 indicates that change may be directed at the organizational level, department/group level, or individual level. Change efforts are more complicated and difficult to manage when they are targeted at the organizational level. This occurs because organizational-level changes are more likely to affect multiple target elements of change shown in the model.

A Transactional Model of Planned Change

Some changes are forced upon the organization by unforeseen circumstances. Examples include wildcat strikes, accidents, and death of a key executive. Other changes, including strategic shifts, reorganizations, personnel changes, or adoption of new technology, are purposefully implemented by management. Contingency plans and crisis management teams help managers deal with unintentional change.[29] A systematic and planned approach is needed for the intentional variety. Our focus in this section is on the general concept of planned change.

Paul Nutt, a well-known OB researcher, has developed a dynamic and realistic model of planned organizational change (see Figure 20–4). It is labeled a *transactional model* because it describes the interactions among the five stages of planned change. The five stages of change are formulation, concept development, detailing, evaluation, and installation. Let us explore the primary components of this model.

Decision and Developmental Modes   Nutt's model makes an important distinction between the decision-making and developmental portions of the change process. Within the circle, in the decision mode portion of the model, is the manager who has formal authority and ultimate responsibility for the proposed change. As we know from previous chapters, however, organizational problem solving, creativity, and decision making generally are *group* activities. This is where the developmental mode enters the picture. Committees and project teams normally are responsible for assisting line managers as they translate a change from an idea into an accomplished fact. The decision-making manager may or may not play a full role in the developmental team. Regardless, as indicated by the arrows in Figure 20–4, critical transactions occur between the manager and developmental team during each stage.

A Series of Transactions   Each set of transactions brings the proposed change closer to reality. The manager can contribute to the change process by specifying needs in stage I and premises (assumptions about how to proceed) in stage II. He or she can further assist the developmental team by pointing out misconceptions in stage III and specifying criteria for weighing options in stage IV. Before installation of the change, in stage V, the manager needs to do some administrative housekeeping. Skilled people, resources, incentives, and delegation mechanisms must be in place. For its part, the committee or project team defines problems and suggests objectives. It also recommends options and tentative plans, considers costs and benefits, and

• **FIGURE 20–4**   Nutt's Transactional Model of Planned Organizational Change

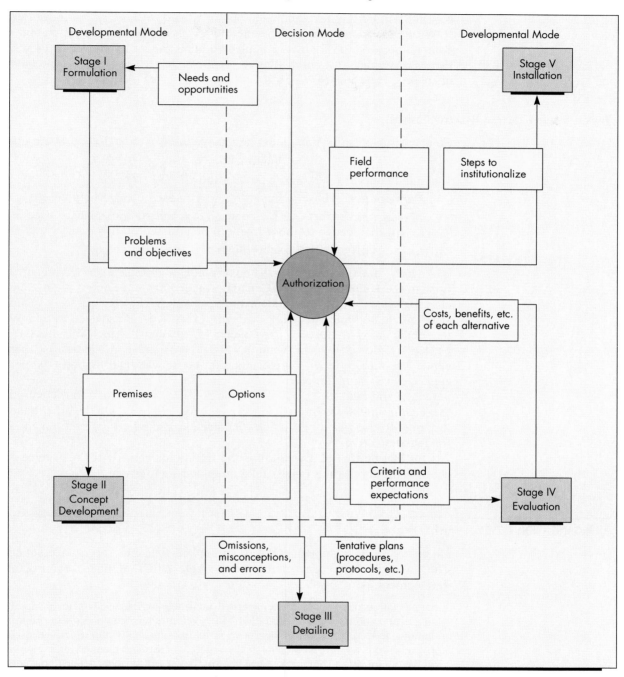

Source: Paul C. Nutt, "Tactics of Implementation," *Academy of Management Journal*, June 1986, p. 235. Used with permission.

gathers feedback information once the change has been installed.[30] Of course, the greater the degree of participative management, the greater the contribution by the developmental team.

Within the framework of this general process of planned change one (or a combination) of the following implementation tactics is employed. These tactics determine how much relative say the manager and support team have in shaping the change.

Implementation Tactics: Research Insights

Four basic tactics for implementing change are:[31]

- *Intervention*. Key executives establish a rationale for the change, build support for it, and influence the change process.
- *Participation*. Those affected by the proposed change help design it.
- *Persuasion*. Experts such as consultants and staff specialists attempt to sell the change to those likely to be affected by it.[32]
- *Edict*. Managers direct subordinates to adopt the change.

A study of major changes in 91 government and private service organizations in the United States and Canada provided evidence about the use and effectiveness of these four implementation tactics. The changes were reconstructed via multiple interviews with key executives. Persuasion turned out to be the *most frequently used* tactic (42 percent). Edict was next (23 percent), followed by intervention (19 percent) and participation (17 percent). The *most effective* implementation tactic was intervention (100 percent success rate), followed by participation (84 percent), persuasion (73 percent), and edict (43 percent). Ironically, intervention and participation, the *least frequently used* tactics, were the *most effective*. On the other hand, the most frequently used tactics—persuasion and edict—turned out to be the least effective.[33]

Considering that participation is the traditional remedy for resistance to change, these research results take on added significance.

• ORGANIZATION DEVELOPMENT

Organization development (OD) is an applied field of study and practice. The authors of a recent review of the field of OD defined **organization development** as follows:

> Organization development is concerned with helping managers plan change in organizing and managing people that will develop requisite commitment, coordination, and competence. Its purpose is to enhance both the effectiveness of organizations and the well-being of their members through planned interventions in the organization's human processes, structures, and systems, using knowledge of behavioral science and its intervention methods.[34]

As you can see from this definition, OD provides managers with the tools and techniques needed to manage organizational change.

In this section, we briefly review the history of organization development and discuss its identifying characteristics.

History of Organization Development

Organization development is a branch of applied behavioral science that has a short but colorful history. Its roots trace back to the mid-1940s and such practices as laboratory training (also known as T-groups and sensitivity training) and survey feedback.[35] T-groups originally were used to develop self-awareness and interpersonal skills in structured laboratory settings.[36] Later, the practice was extended to the workplace, with enhancements such as flip-chart data collection and feedback. But abuses by inadequately trained facilitators caused T-groups to fall out of favor. Survey feedback, meanwhile, was developed by Rensis Likert (father of the five-point Likert scale commonly found on questionnaires) and his University of Michigan colleagues. They discovered that a positive climate for change could be created by having employees complete an attitude survey and then discuss the cumulative results. Unlike T-groups, survey feedback is alive and well today.

The field of OD has continued to grow since these mixed beginnings. Managers now have a wide variety of OD techniques to choose from. For example, an encyclopedia of organizational change methods identified over 375 separate techniques.[37] We review some of the more popular techniques in the next section of this chapter. Moreover, consultants and researchers expanded the role of OD by using it as a technique to develop, guide, and implement an organization's strategic planning process.[38] OD also has been used to execute the type of transformational leadership discussed in Chapter 14.[39] Given these trends, and the external and internal forces for change discussed at the beginning of this chapter, we expect organization development to play an increasing role in promoting organizational effectiveness in the future. Let us now consider the unique characteristics of OD.

Identifying Characteristics of Organization Development

The sheer diversity of practitioners and techniques wearing the label *OD* makes its precise definition difficult. Lack of a unifying theory does not help. Consequently, a better understanding of OD can be achieved by considering its four identifying characteristics.

OD Involves Profound Change   Change agents using OD generally desire deep and long-lasting improvement. OD consultant Warner Burke, for example, who strives for fundamental *cultural* change, wrote: "By fundamental change, as opposed to fixing a problem or improving a procedure, I mean that some significant aspect of an organization's culture will never be the same."[40]

OD Is Value-Loaded   Owing to the fact that OD is rooted partially in humanistic psychology, many OD consultants carry certain values or biases into the client organization. They prefer cooperation over conflict, self-control over institutional control, and democratic and participative management over autocratic management. Not surprisingly, these values are not eagerly embraced by managers with a Theory X view of employees. (Recall the discussion of McGregor's Theories X and Y in Chapter 1.) As a case in point, researchers demonstrated that OD is more likely to fail when an OD consultant and top management have inconsistent values.[41]

OD Is a Diagnosis/Prescription Cycle   OD theorists and practitioners have long adhered to a medical model of organizations. Like medical doctors, internal and external OD consultants approach the ''sick'' organization, ''diagnose'' its ills, ''prescribe'' and implement an intervention, and ''monitor'' progress (see Figure 20–5). This model is discussed in the next section.

OD Is Process-Oriented   Ideally, OD consultants focus on the form and not the content of behavioral and administrative dealings. For example, product design engineers and market researchers might be coached on how to communicate more effectively with one another without the consultant knowing the technical details of their conversations. In addition to communication, OD specialists focus on other processes, including problem solving, decision making, conflict handling, trust, power sharing, and career development.

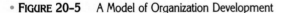

• A MODEL OF ORGANIZATION DEVELOPMENT

Figure 20–5 reveals that organization development is a three-step process. OD begins by conducting an organizational diagnosis. An appropriate intervention then is prescribed and implemented. As with any organizational change, the final step of monitoring progress and taking corrective action is used to keep the intervention on track. After taking a closer look at each of these steps, this last section discusses OD research and practical implications.

• **FIGURE 20-5**   A Model of Organization Development

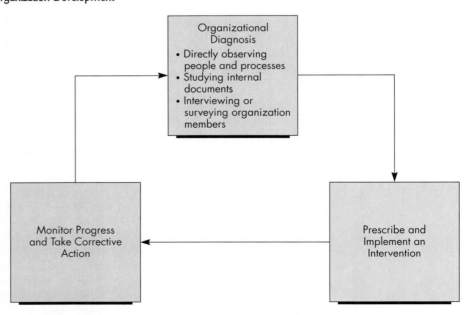

Organizational Diagnosis

There are two purposes of an organizational diagnosis. The first is to proactively identify future changes that are needed to help an organization meet its strategic goals. A needs analysis is the typical method used for this diagnosis. **Needs analysis** consists of figuring out the type of skills or competencies that employees must possess for the organization to accomplish its goals (see OB in Action). Surveys and interviews are frequently used for this purpose. Training programs and management development ultimately are used as the vehicle to help employees acquire the relevant skills or competencies.

The second purpose of organizational diagnosis is to identify past or current organizational problems that inhibit the diagnostic framework for conducting such an analysis (see Figure 20–6). Although the framework in Figure 20–6 does not provide an exhaustive list of places to look for organizational problems, it helps managers begin the process of OD. There are six organizational areas in which to look for problems: purpose, structure, rewards, support systems, relationships, and leadership.[42]

Purpose Organizational problems frequently start with a lack of direction from the top. Lack of direction leads to the poor allocation of resources and confusion about what people should be doing. It is important for top management to establish what business the organization is in. As found by the authors of the best-selling book *In Search of Excellence,* successful com-

---

OB IN ACTION

Corning Identified the Critical Skills and Competencies Needed by Employees

"We plan to have our Level One course—on fundamental skills and fundamental knowledge that make the biggest difference to people—early in their careers—things like formal presentation, project-management skills," explains Mr. O'Brien [Corning's director of education and training].

Competencies play an important role in the Corning strategy. With the assistance of consultant Steve Schoonver, Corning defined the key competencies for a manager at various stages of his or her career. Leadership competencies include empowering, networking, and accurate self-assessment; operational competencies include "visioning" and quality orientation.

Knowing what a company wants or needs in terms of these competencies is strategically shrewd, says Mr. O'Brien. "We put a greater than 50 percent weight on competencies that we don't have but wish we had right now," he says. "Another emphasis, based on where we want to go, is on competencies that are not terribly significant today but are getting increasingly more important."

Source: Joseph F. McKenna, "Looking for—and Building—a Few Good Heroes," *Industry Week,* October 15, 1990, p. 18. Reprinted with permission. Copyright, Penton Publishing, Inc., Cleveland, Ohio.

• **FIGURE 20-6**   A Framework for Diagnosing Organizational Problems

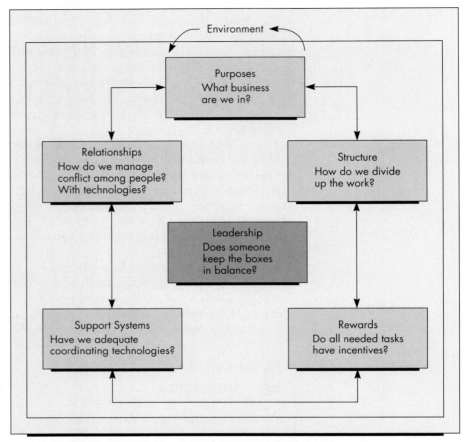

Source: Marvin R. Weisbord, "Organizationl Diagnosis: Six Places to Look for Trouble with or without a Theory," *Group and Organization Studies*, December 1976, p. 432. Copyright © 1976 by *Group and Organization Studies*. Reprinted by permission of Sage Publications, Inc.

panies identify their business mission and then focus on providing quality products or services to accomplish that mission.[43] OD is used to keep organizations on track.

Structure   Organizationl structure, which was discussed in Chapter 17, reflects the reporting relationships within an organization. This structure should support or reinforce the accomplishment of strategic goals. For example, a flatter structure is more appropriate for an organization operating in a highly volatile industry because it facilitates faster communication across organizational levels. In contrast, a centralized structure helps to reduce the duplication of effort that commonly exists in decentralized organizations.

Rewards   Employees exhibit behaviors that get rewarded (recall our discussions in Chapters 6, 7 and 13). Organizations need to design reward systems that reinforce desired results. Unfortunately, organizations frequently reward the wrong behaviors. For example, group incentives should be used instead of individual rewards when productivity is highly dependent on

OB IN ACTION

A Computerized Cost-Accounting System Provides Managerial Support at Re:Member Data

John Davis—colleagues call him J.D.—runs the department known as conversions and training. Once a sale is made, his people convert the customer's data base to the new system, then train the customer's employees.

Until 1989, when Re:Member bought it, J.D.'s office was owned by a big Minneapolis firm, which seemed to delight in keeping him in the dark. He'd learn about a new job when it landed on his desk, deadline attached. He never knew which prospects were being courted or what the salesperson was promising them or how many jobs he and his colleagues would be faced with in the next month or three. Nor did he know how much money his department made or lost or indeed how the office itself was doing.

All this ignorance was costly. On one memorable job, the salesman had told the customer, sure, our system can handle all your forms. He had neglected to find out—or maybe to mention—that the customer had some 120 separate forms, each one requiring custom programming from J.D.'s department. The conversion took several months longer than expected.

When Re:Member came in, J.D. was made a vice president and thereby had access to all the information he needed. But the frustrating experience of working in the dark stuck with him. What would happen, J.D. wondered, if every employee knew as much as I know now—about upcoming jobs, about how our department's doing, even about how much they themselves contribute to the business? Dave Becker, owner of the newly consolidated $6-million company, was already preparing to discuss his five-year business plan with his employees and had no objection if J.D. wanted to do a little information sharing of his own. So J.D. developed a plan.

Step one was to develop a detailed cost-accounting system. The company had always billed customers a per-diem fee for conversions and training, but to J.D.'s knowledge his former bosses had never tried to monitor costs. Under the new system, each employee would keep a record of time spent on each job, materials costs, travel and entertainment, and so on.

Step two: J.D. had the computer track each employee's time, daily billing, salary costs, and expenses. Not so unusual; just good management.

Source: John Case, "The Open-Book Managers," *Inc.*, September 1990, p. 105. Reprinted with permission. Copyright © 1990 by Goldhirsh Group, Inc. 38 Commercial Wharf, Boston, MA 02110.

teamwork.[44] Organizational problems can be reduced by having managers identify and reward appropriate behaviors and results.

Support Systems   **Support systems** represent the tools, techniques, and processes that organizations use to achieve efficiency and effectiveness. For example, John Davis, vice president at Re:Member Data, a company that sells data processing systems to credit unions, implemented a computerized cost-accounting system to help reduce costs and increase productivity (see OB in Action). Other examples include a good phone system and a computerized project control system. Project control systems help managers and project teams complete projects on time.

Relationships   This diagnostic area focuses on the quality of interpersonal relationships among individuals and groups. It is important for organizations to foster constructive conflict while also removing any dysfunctional conflict. Conflict was discussed in Chapter 10.

Leadership   Successful change is unlikely without effective leadership. First off, someone is needed to champion the change effort in order to overcome the forces of resistance to change. Secondly, someone must coordinate and manage the change and development process.

Prescribe and Implement an Intervention

OD interventions involve different methods of introducing planned change. There are two dominant strategies for implementing OD: the human-process approach and the technostructural approach.[45] Although these strategies have a different focus, they are not mutually exclusive. They can and should be used together.

The human-process approach focuses on identifying and correcting problems within interpersonal, group, and intergroup processes. Three frequently used interventions are role analysis, survey research and feedback, and team building. The technostructural approach assumes that organizational problems revolve around issues associated with the match between technology and organizational structure. Common interventions involve work restructuring, compensation systems, structural change, and implementing new information technology.

Although there are many different types of OD interventions that qualify as either human-process or technostructural strategies, our focus here is on four widely used interventions. Our discussion is intended to be an illustrative rather than exhaustive exposure to OD offerings.

Role Analysis   The **role analysis technique** strives to enhance cooperation among work-group members by getting them to discuss their mutual expectations.[46] Ambiguity and misconceptions about one's own role and the roles of one's co-workers are targeted. Role analysis is typically facilitated by a consultant in a workshop setting. Each team member writes his or her role expectations on a flip-chart for discussion by the entire work group. This can be time-consuming, but the investment of time can pay off in better communication, less conflict, and improved performance.

Survey Research and Feedback   As mentioned earlier, a stimulus for improvement can be generated by surveying employees and then feeding back the results of the survey. This widely used practice is called **survey research and feedback.** To prevent defensiveness or embarrassment, only cumulative, anonymous data are shared with respondents. Future behavior is influenced through the feedback mechanisms discussed in Chapter 13. While warning against information overload, feedback expert David Nadler recommends that feedback data be relevant, understandable, illustrative of real problems, valid and accurate, and controllable by those involved.[47]

Team Building   *Team building*, which was discussed in Chapter 11, is a catchall term for a whole host of techniques aimed at improving the functioning of work groups. It is extensively used as an OD intervention. Moreover, a survey of human resource managers from 179 Fortune 500 companies indicated that team building is effective at improving interpersonal processes.[48]

Work Restructuring   As discussed in Chapter 5, work restructuring or job design is based on the notion that employee motivation is increased by giving employees the opportunity to experience increased meaningfulness of work, responsibility for work outcomes, and feedback. Moreover, research indicates that job design should be implemented from a sociotechnical perspective.

The sociotechnical model is based on a stream of research conducted during the 1950s by the Tavistock Institute in London. Among other issues, this research focused on the relationships among technological changes, social processes, and productivity. For example, one study examined productivity changes associated with implementing an assembly-line method in a coal mine. The change was unsuccessful because management failed to recognize the social importance the miners attached to working in small, autonomous groups.[49] Findings such as these led researchers to conclude that work environments represent an intertwined combination of technology (physical plant and equipment) and social system. The Tavistock researchers also concluded that these two subsystems influenced and shaped each other. Generalizing from these basic conclusions, the thrust of the **sociotechnical model** involves considering:

> The relationships both between people and technology and between the organization and its environments to suggest changes in work arrangements designed to improve the fit among the needs of individuals, groups, and technological processes in the pursuit of organizational goals.[50]

So, the sociotechnical model is a dynamic approach that incorporates components of both the human-process and technostructural strategies for organization development. This model added two significant contributions to the field of OD in addition to uncovering the critical interaction between people and technology. First, it led to increased use of participative management in a variety of organizations. Second, it fostered the increased use of self-managed work groups (discussed in Chapter 11).[51]

Monitor Progress and Take Corrective Action

Evaluation and feedback is the final step of OD. Evaluation is needed to determine if expected results are being achieved. Interviews, surveys, and performance indices are frequently used to evaluate the effectiveness of an organizational change. Finally, feedback provides the mechanism to reinforce and adjust the planned change effort.

OD Research and Practical Implications

Research on OD effectiveness has been hampered by a number of problems. For example, consultants' clients want concrete action for their expenditures of time and money, not experimental setups complete with control groups.[52] However, a recent meta-analysis of 126 studies involving OD-related interventions produced the following insights:

- Multifaceted interventions using more than one OD technique were more effective in changing job satisfaction and work attitudes than interventions that relied on only one human-process or technostructural approach.
- Team building was the most effective technique for modifying job satisfaction and work attitudes.
- OD had a greater effect on changing work attitudes than it did on job satisfaction.

The researchers concluded that there is not one change technique that is universally effective.[53] The choice of the best OD intervention is determined by using the systems model of change to diagnose the organizational context in which change is being considered.

One practical implication derived from this research is that a contingency approach to OD is required. Until researchers are able to more precisely specify the situational appropriateness of the various OD interventions, managers are advised to rely on multifaceted interventions. As indicated elsewhere in this book, goal setting, feedback, modeling, training, participation, and challenging job design have good track records relative to improving performance and satisfaction. OD's unique contribution to effective management can be to combine as many of these potent tactics as possible into well-integrated programs for planned and systematic change.

• SUMMARY OF KEY CONCEPTS

A. Organizations encounter both external and internal forces for change. There are four key external forces for change: demographic characteristics, technological advancements, market changes, and social and political pressures. Internal forces for change come from both human resource problems and managerial behavior/decisions.

B. Resistance to change is an emotional/behavioral response to real or imagined threats to an established work routine. Eight reasons employees resist change are: (1) surprise and fear of the unknown, (2) climate of mistrust, (3) fear of failure, (4) loss of status and/or job security, (5) peer pressure, (6) disruption of cultural traditions and/or group relationships, (7) personality conflicts, and (8) lack of tact and/or poor timing. Because of the classic Coch and French study of change in a garment factory, participation has long been considered the best tool for overcoming resistance to change.

C. Alternative strategies for overcoming resistance to change are education + communication, participation + involvement, facilitation + support, negotiation + agreement, manipulation + co-optation, and explicit + implicit coercion. Each has its situational appropriateness and advantages and drawbacks.

D. Three types of change are adaptive, innovative, and radically innovative. They are listed in increasing order of complexity, cost, uncertainty. Most theories of organizational change originated from Lewin's change model. Lewin proposed that the three stages of change were *unfreezing,* which entails creating the motivation to change, *changing,* and stabilizing change through *refreezing.*

E. A systems model of change takes a big picture perspective of change. It focuses on the interaction among the key components of change. The three main components of change are inputs, target elements of change, and outputs. Nutt's transactional model of planned organizational change demonstrates the interdependence of two modes, the decision-making manager and the developmental team. Research indicates that the two least-used change implementation tactics, intervention and participation, tend to be the most effective.

F. Modern organization development (OD) grew out of laboratory training and survey feedback. Today OD is used to help organizations develop, guide, and implement the strategic planning process. The identifying characteristics of OD are that it: (1) involves profound change; (2) is value-loaded; (3) is a diagnosis/prescription cycle; and (4) is process-oriented.

G. The three stages of organization development are: make a diagnosis, prescribe and implement an intervention, and monitor progress and take corrective action. Organizational diagnosis entails looking for problems in six organizational areas: purpose, structure, rewards, support systems, relationships, and leadership.

H. There are two dominant strategies for implementing OD: the human-process approach and the technostructural approach. The human-process approach focuses on identifying and correcting problems within interpersonal, group, and intergroup processes. The technostructural approach assumes that organizational problems revolve around issues associated with the match between technology and organizational structure. Managers are encouraged to use the two strategies jointly when implementing planned change via interventions such as role analysis, survey research and feedback, team building, and work restructuring.

• KEY TERMS

external forces for change	organization development
office automation	needs analysis
internal forces for change	support systems
resistance to change	role analysis technique
strategic mission statement	survey research and feedback
strategic plan	sociotechnical model

• DISCUSSION QUESTIONS

1. Which of the external forces for change do you believe will prompt the greatest change during the 1990s?
2. Have you worked in an organization where internal forces created change? Describe the situation and the resulting change.

3. Have you ever resisted a change at work? Explain the circumstances and your thinking at the time.
4. Which source of resistance to change do you think is the most common? Which is the most difficult for management to deal with?
5. How would you respond to a manager who made the following statement: "Unfreezing is not important, employees will follow my directives?"
6. What are some useful methods that can be used to refreeze an organizational change?
7. Have you ever observed the systems model of change in action? Explain what occurred.
8. Why is organizational diagnosis a critical step in organization development (OD)?
9. What distinguishes human-process and technostructural approaches to OD?
10. What would you say to a manager who insists that team building, for example, is the best overall OD technique?

BACK TO THE OPENING CASE

Now that you have read Chapter 20, you should be able to answer the following questions about the Will-Burt case:

1. What were the external and internal forces for change?
2. Which of the eight reasons for resistance to change affected Harry Featherstone's attempt to radically change Will-Burt?
3. Using the framework for diagnosing organizational problems (see Figure 20–6) what problems were evident at Will-Burt?
4. What were the two best and two worst things that Mr. Featherstone did during the change process? Discuss your rationale.

• EXERCISE 20

Objectives

1. To help you understand the diagnosis step of OD.
2. To give you a practical diagnostic tool to assess organizational areas in need of OD.

Introduction

Diagnosis is the first step of OD. It is used to identify past or current organizational problems that inhibit organizational effectiveness. As was indicated in Figure 20–6, there are six organizational areas in which to look for problems: purpose, structure, rewards, support systems, relationships, and leadership. In this exercise, you will be asked to complete a brief survey assessing these six areas of an organization.

Instructions

If you currently have a full-time or part-time job, think of your organization and describe it by circling an appropriate response for each of the following 12 statements. If you are not currently employed, describe the last organization you worked for. If you have never worked, use your current university or school as your frame of reference. Compute a total score for each diagnostic area.

After completing the survey, think of an "ideal" organization: An organization that you believe would be most effective. How do you believe this organization would stand in terms of the six diagnostic areas? We would like you to assess this organization with the same diagnostic survey. You may want to use a different color pen to highlight the difference between your two sets of evaluations.

Organizational Diagnostic Survey

Purpose	Strongly Disagree	Disagree	Neutral	Agree	Strongly Agree
1. I am familiar with the organization's strategic mission statement.	1	2	3	4	5
2. I am aware of the organization's strategic goals.	1	2	3	4	5
Total Purpose Score = _____					

Structure

	Strongly Disagree	Disagree	Neutral	Agree	Strongly Agree
3. The organizational structure facilitates goal accomplishment.	1	2	3	4	5
4. The organizational structure helps the company make better decisions.	1	2	3	4	5
Total Structure Score = _____					

Rewards

	Strongly Disagree	Disagree	Neutral	Agree	Strongly Agree
5. I believe there is a relationship between my annual pay increase and my annual performance review.	1	2	3	4	5
6. This organization rewards the behaviors/performance that are critical for organizational success.	1	2	3	4	5
Total Rewards Score = _____					

Support Systems

	Strongly Disagree	Disagree	Neutral	Agree	Strongly Agree
7. I understand my job duties and responsibilities.	1	2	3	4	5
8. I have all the tools and resources I need to do my job.	1	2	3	4	5
Total Support Systems Score = _____					

Organizational Diagnostic Survey (concluded)

Relationships	Strongly Disagree	Disagree	Neutral	Agree	Strongly Agree
9. There is a sense of team spirit in my department.	1	2	3	4	5
10. Interpersonal and group conflict are handled in a positive manner.	1	2	3	4	5
Total Relationships Score = _____					

Leadership

	Strongly Disagree	Disagree	Neutral	Agree	Strongly Agree
11. This organization is well managed.	1	2	3	4	5
12. This organization inspires the very best in me in the way of job performance.	1	2	3	4	5
Total Leadership Score = _____					

Questions for Consideration/Class Discussion

1. Based on your evaluation of your current organization, which diagnostic area(s) is most in need of change?
2. Based on a comparison of your current and ideal organizations, which diagnostic area(s) is most in need of change? If your answer is different from the first question, explain the difference.
3. What sort of OD intervention would be appropriate for your work group or organization? Give details.

• NOTES

[1] The magnitude of mergers and acquisitions is discussed by Jeanette A. Davy, Angelo J. Kinicki, John Kilroy, and Christine L. Scheck, "After the Merger: Dealing with People's Uncertainty," *Training and Development Journal,* November 1988, pp. 57–61.

[2] The failure of mergers is discussed by Richard McKnight and Marilyn Thompson, "Navigating Organizational Change," *Training and Development Journal,* December 1990, pp. 46–49.

[3] See Ronald D. Elliott, "The Challenge of Managing Change," *Personnel Journal,* March 1990, pp. 40–49; and James Fraze, "Displaced Workers: The Okies of the 80s," *Personnel Administrator,* January 1988, pp. 42–51.

[4] Cynthia D. Scott and Dennis T. Jaffe, "Survive and Thrive in Times of Change," *Training and Development Journal,* April 1988, p. 25.

[5] For a thorough review of demographic statistics, see Lynn R. Offermann and Marilyn K. Gowing, "Organizations of the Future: Changes and Challenges," *American Psychologist,* February 1990, pp. 95–108.

[6] See Janet Turnage, "The Challenge of New Workplace Technology for Psychology," *American Psychologist,* February 1990, pp. 171–78.

[7] See Alison L. Sprout, "America's Most Admired Corporations," *Fortune,* February 11, 1991, p. 57.

[8] Turnage, "The Challenge of New Workplace Technology."

9 Brian Dumaine, "How to Manage in a Recession," *Fortune,* November 5, 1990, p. 60.

10 Adapted in part from Joseph Stanislao and Bettie C. Stanislao, "Dealing with Resistance to Change," *Business Horizons,* July–August 1983, pp. 74–78.

11 See Rosabeth Moss Kanter, "Managing Traumatic Change: Avoiding the 'Unlucky 13,'" *Management Review,* May 1987, pp. 23–24.

12 Alan Ofner, "Managing Change," *Personnel Administrator,* September 1984, p. 20.

13 See Lester Coch and John R. P. French, Jr., "Overcoming Resistance to Change," *Human Relations,* 1948, pp. 512–32.

14 Complete details may be found in Anat Rafaeli, "Employee Attitudes toward Working with Computers," *Journal of Occupational Behavior,* April 1986, pp. 89–106.

15 Thomas Hill, Nancy D. Smith, and Millard F. Mann, "Role of Efficacy Expectations in Predicting the Decision to Use Advanced Technologies: The Case of Computers," *Journal of Applied Psychology,* May 1987, p. 313.

16 See Karen N. Gaertner, "Winning and Losing: Understanding Managers' Reactions to Strategic Change," *Human Relations,* June 1989, pp. 527–46; and Marcia Kleiman, "Ease the Stress of Change," *Personnel Journal,* September 1989, pp. 106–12.

17 The impact of employee perceptions on planned change is discussed by Connie J. G. Gersick, "Revolutionary Change Theories: A Multilevel Exploration of the Punctuated Equilibrium Paradigm," *Academy of Management Review,* January 1991, pp. 10–36; and Lynn A. Isabella, "Evolving Interpretations as a Change Unfolds: How Managers Construe Key Organizational Events," *Academy of Management Journal,* March 1990, pp. 7–41.

18 These recommendations were based on Sharon L. Baker, "Managing Resistance to Change," *Library Trends,* Summer 1989, pp. 53–61.

19 Excellent advice on how to reduce the resistance to change can be found in John Lawrie, "The ABCs of Change Management," *Training and Developmental Journal,* March 1990, pp. 87–89; and Richard McKnight and Marilyn Thompson, "Navigating Organizational Change," *Training and Development Journal,* December 1990, pp. 46–49.

20 See Ralph H. Kilmann, *Managing Beyond the Quick Fix* (San Francisco, Calif.: Jossey-Bass, 1989).

21 This three-way typology of change is adapted from discussion in Paul C. Nutt, "Tactics of Implementation," *Academy of Management Journal,* June 1986, pp. 230–61.

22 These variables come from Manuel London and John Paul MacDuffe, "Technological Innovations: Case Examples and Guidelines," *Personnel,* November 1987, pp. 26–38.

23 For a thorough discussion of the model, see Kurt Lewin, *Field Theory in Social Science* (New York: Harper & Row, 1951).

24 These assumptions are discussed in Edgar H. Schein, *Organizational Psychology,* 3rd ed. (Englewood Cliffs, N.J.: Prentice-Hall, 1980).

25 For examples of how Lewin's model was used to create change in a railroad company and a police department, see Paul E. O'Neill, "Transforming Managers for Organizational Change," *Training and Development Journal,* July 1990, pp. 87–90; and Keith M. Rippy, "The Ins and Outs of Implementing Change," *The Police Chief,* April 1990, pp. 136–40. Also see Leonard D. Goodstein and W. Warner Burke, "Creating Successful Organization Change," *Organizational Dynamics,* Spring 1991, pp. 4–17.

26 Systems models of change are discussed by Ralph H. Kilmann, "A Completely Integrated Program for Creating and Maintaining Organizational Success," *Organizational Dynamics,* Summer 1989, pp. 5–19; and David A. Nadler and Michael L. Tushman, "Organizational Frame Bending: Principles for Managing Reorientation," *Academy of Management Executive,* August 1989, pp. 194–204.

27 The process of strategic planning is thoroughly discussed by Patrick J. Below, George L. Morrisey, and Betty L. Acomb, *The Executive Guide to Strategic Planning* (San Francisco, Calif.: Jossey-Bass, 1989).

28 A thorough discussion of the target elements of change can be found in Paul Dainty, "Organizational Change: A Strategy For Successful Implementation," *Journal of Business and Psychology,* Summer 1990, pp. 463–81; and Harold J. Leavitt, "Applied Organization Change in Industry: Structural, Technical and Human Approaches," in *New Perspectives in Organizational Research,* eds. W. W. Cooper, Harold J. Leavitt, M. W. Shelly (New York: John Wiley, 1964), pp. 55–71.

29 See, for example, Dale D. McConkey, "Planning for Uncertainty," *Business Horizons,* January–February 1987, pp. 40–45; and Ian I. Mitroff, Paul Shrivastava, and Firdaus E. Udwadia, "Effective Crisis Management," *The Academy of Management Executive,* November 1987, pp. 283–92.

30 For excellent reading on large-scale organizational change, see Gary D. Scudder, Roger G. Schroeder, Andrew H. Van de Ven, Gary R. Seiler, and Robert M. Wiseman, "Managing Complex Innovations: The Case of Defense Contracting," in *Research on the Management of Innovation: The Minnesota Studies,* eds. Andrew H. Van de Ven, H. Angle, and M. S. Poole (New York: Ballinger, 1989); and Gloria Barczak, Charles Smith, and David Wilemon, "Managing Large-Scale Organizational Change," *Organizational Dynamics,* Autumn 1987, pp. 22–35.

31 Adapted from Nutt, "Tactics of Implementation," p. 242.

32 For a thorough discussion of the importance of persuasion in implementing technological change, see Jane M. Howell and Christopher A. Higgins, "Champions of Change: Identifying, Understanding, and Supporting Champions of Technological Innovations," *Organizational Dynamics,* Summer 1990, pp. 40–55.

33 See Nutt, "Tactics of Implementation," pp. 242, 252.

34 Michael Beer and Elise Walton, "Developing the Competitive Organization: Interventions and Strategies," *American Psychologist,* February 1990, p. 154.

35 An historical overview of the field of OD can be found in Richard W. Woodman, "Organizational Change and Development: New Arenas for Inquiry and Action," *Journal of Management,* June 1989, pp. 205–28.

36 A more recent perspective is discussed by Robert Kaplan, "Is Openness Passé?" *Human Relations,* March 1986, pp. 229–43.

37 See Andrzej Huczynski, *Encyclopedia of Organizational Change Methods* (Brookfield, VT.: Gower Publishing, 1987).

38 For a discussion and example of how OD can be used within the strategic planning process, see Chet Borucki and John Sollazzo, "Restructuring within GE to Facilitate Strategic Change: A Self-Design Process Approach," *Journal of Organizational Change Management,* no. 1, 1990, pp. 15–31.

39 An interesting example is provided by Frances R. Westley, "The Eye of the Needle: Cultural and Personal Transformation in a Traditional Organization," *Human Relations,* March 1990, pp. 273–93.

40 W. Warner Burke, *Organization Development: A Normative View* (Reading, Mass.: Addison-Wesley Publishing, 1987), p. 9.

41 See, for example, Kevin C. Wooten and Louis P. White, "Toward a Theory of Change Role Efficacy," *Human Relations,* August 1989, pp. 651–69.

[42] A thorough discussion of organizational diagnosis is provided by Marvin R. Weisbord, "Organizational Diagnosis: Six Places to Look for Trouble with or without a Theory," *Group and Organization Studies,* December 1976, pp. 430–47.

[43] See Thomas J. Peters and Robert H. Waterman, Jr., *In Search of Excellence: Lessons From America's Best-Run Companies* (New York: Warner Books, 1982).

[44] See Luis R. Gomez-Mejia, David B. Balkin, and George T. Milkovich, "Rethinking Rewards for Technical Employees," *Organizational Dynamics,* Spring 1990, pp. 62–75.

[45] This framework was developed and discussed by Michael Beer and Elise Walton, "Developing the Competitive Organization: Interventions and Strategies," *American Psychologist,* February 1990, pp. 154–61.

[46] Role analysis is discussed in detail in Wendell L. French and Cecil H. Bell, Jr., *Organization Development* (Englewood Cliffs, N.J.: Prentice-Hall, 1984).

[47] See David A. Nadler, *Feedback and Organization Development: Using Data-Based Methods* (Reading, Mass.: Addison-Wesley Publishing, 1977), pp. 147–48.

[48] Data from Eric Stephan, Gordon E. Mills, R. Wayne Pace, and Lenny Ralphs, "HRD in the Fortune 500: A Survey," *Training and Development Journal,* January 1988, pp. 26–32.

[49] Results are found in E. Trist and K. Bamforth, "Social and Psychological Consequences of the Long-Wall Method of Coal-Getting," *Human Relations,* February 1951, pp. 3–38.

[50] William A. Pasmore, "Overcoming the Roadblocks in Work-Restructuring Efforts," *Organizational Dynamics,* Spring 1982, p. 55.

[51] Recent applications of the sociotechnical model can be found in Toby D. Wall, Martin Corbett, Robin Martin, Chris W. Clegg, and Paul R. Jackson, "Advanced Manufacturing Technology, Work Design, and Performance: A Change Study," *Journal of Applied Psychology,* December 1990, pp. 691–97; and Kenyon B. De Greene, "Rigidity and Fragility of Large Sociotechnical Systems: Advanced Information Technology, the Dominant Coalition, and Paradigm Shift at the End of the 20th Century," *Behavioral Science,* January 1991, pp. 64–79.

[52] The problems associated with evaluating the effectiveness of organizational change are thoroughly discussed by Robert T. Golembiewski, *Ironies in Organizational Development* (New Brunswick, N.J.: Transaction Publishers, 1990).

[53] Results from the meta-analysis can be found in George A. Neuman, Jack E. Edwards, and Nambury S. Raju, "Organizational Development Interventions: A Meta-Analysis of Their Effects on Satisfaction and Other Attitudes," *Personnel Psychology,* Autumn 1989, pp. 461–90.

Advanced Learning Module

Research Methods in Organizational Behavior

A s a future manager, you probably will be involved in developing and/or implementing programs for solving managerial problems. You also may be asked to assess recommendations derived from in-house research reports or judge the usefulness of management consulting proposals. These tasks might entail reading and evaluating research findings presented both in scientific and professional journal articles. Thus, it is important for managers to have a basic working knowledge of the research process. Moreover, such knowledge can help you critically evaluate research information encountered daily in newspaper, magazine, and television reports. Consider, for example, the issue of whether to wear rear-seat lap belts while riding in an automobile.

A recent study conducted by the National Transportation Safety Board (NTSB) concluded, "Instead of protecting people, rear-seat lap belts can cause serious or fatal internal injuries in the event of a head-on crash."[1] Despite previous recommendations to wear seat belts, do you now believe rear-seat lap belts are dangerous? To answer this question adequately, one needs to know more about how the NTSB's study was conducted and what has been found in related studies. Before providing you with this information, however, this advanced learning module presents a foundation for understanding the research process. Our purpose is not to make you a research scientist. The purpose is to make you a better consumer of research information, such as that provided by the NTSB.

• THE RESEARCH PROCESS

Research on organizational behavior is based on the scientific method. The *scientific method* is a formal process of using systematically gathered data to test hypotheses or to explain natural phenomena. To gain a better understanding of how to evaluate this process, we discuss a model of how research is conducted, explore how researchers measure organizationally relevant variables, highlight three ways to evaluate research methods, and provide a framework for evaluating research conclusions. We also discuss how to read a research article. Finally, we return to the NTSB study and evaluate its conclusions on the basis of lessons from this advanced learning module.

A Model of the Research Process

A flowchart of the research process is presented in Figure A–1. Organizational research is conducted to solve problems. The problem may be one of current interest to an organization, such as absenteeism or low motivation, or may be derived from published research studies. In either case, properly identifying and attempting to solve the problem necessitates a familiarity with previous research on the topic. This familiarity contributes background knowledge and insights for formulating a hypothesis to solve the problem. Students who have written formal library-research papers are well-acquainted with this type of *secondary* research.

According to a respected researcher: "A *hypothesis* is a conjectural statement of the relation between two or more variables. Hypotheses are always in declarative form, and they relate, either generally or specifically, variables to variables."[2] Regarding the problem of absenteeism, for instance, a manager might want to test the following hypothesis: "Hourly employees who are dissatisfied with their pay are absent more often than those who are satisfied." Hypothesis in hand, a researcher is prepared to design a study to test it.

There are two important, interrelated components to designing a study. The first consists of deciding how to measure independent and dependent variables. An *independent variable* is a variable that is hypothesized to affect or cause a certain state of events. For example, a recent study demonstrated that losing one's job led to lower self-esteem and greater depression.[3] In this case, losing one's job, the independent variable, produced lower levels of self-esteem and higher levels of depression. A *dependent variable* is the variable being explained or predicted. Returning to the example, self-esteem and depression were the dependent variables (the variables being explained). In an everyday example, those who eat less (independent variable) are likely to lose weight (dependent variable). The second component of designing a study is to determine which research method to use (recall the discussion in Chapter 1). Criteria for evaluating the appropriateness of different research methods are discussed in a later section.

• **FIGURE A-1**   Model of the Research Process

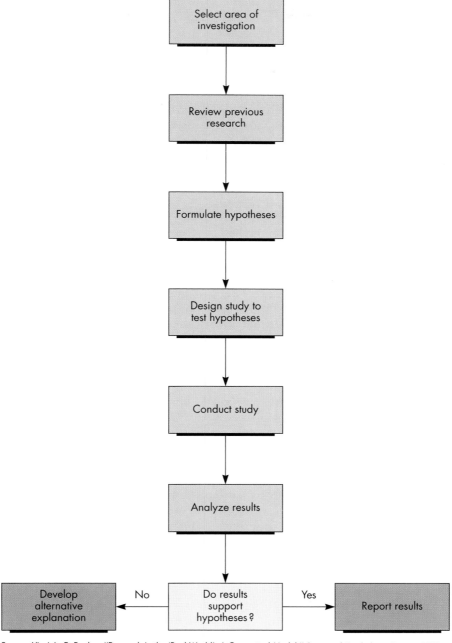

Source: Virginia R. Boehm, "Research in the 'Real World': A Conceptual Model," *Personnel Psychology*, Autumn 1980, p. 496.

After a study is designed and completed, data are analyzed to determine whether the hypothesis is supported. Researchers look for alternative explanations of results when a hypothesis is not supported.

Measurement and Data Collection

"In its broadest sense, measurement is the assignment of numerals to objects or events according to rules."[4] Organizational researchers measure variables. Job satisfaction, turnover, performance, and perceived stress are variables typically measured in OB research. Valid measurement is one of the most critical components of any research study because research findings are open to conflicting interpretations when variables are poorly measured.[5] Poor measurement reduces the confidence one has in applying research findings. Four techniques are frequently used to collect data: (1) direct observation, (2) questionnaires, (3) interviews, and (4) indirect methods.

Observation   This technique consists of recording the number of times a prespecified behavior is exhibited. For example, psychologist Judith Komaki developed and validated an observational categorization of supervisory behavior. She then used the instrument to identify behavior differences between effective and ineffective managers from a large medical insurance firm. Managerial effectiveness was based on superior ratings. Results indicated that effective managers spent more time monitoring their employees' performance than did ineffective managers. Komaki recently applied the same instrument to examine the performance of sailboat captains competing in a race. Similar to the managerial study, skippers finished higher in the overall race standings when they monitored and rewarded their crews.[6] There are few "valid" observational schemes for use in OB research outside of Komaki's taxonomy.

Questionnaires   Questionnaires ask respondents for their opinions or feelings about work-related issues. They generally contain previously developed and validated instruments and are self-administered. Given their impersonal nature, poorly designed questionnaires are susceptible to rater bias. Nevertheless, a well-developed survey can be an accurate and economical way to collect large quantities of data.

Interviews   Interviews rely on either face-to-face or telephone interactions to ask respondents questions of interest. In a *structured* interview, interviewees are asked the same questions in the same order. *Unstructured* interviews do not require interviewers to use the same questions or format. Unstructured interviews are more spontaneous. Structured interviews are the better of the two because they permit consistent comparisons among people.[7] Accordingly, human resource management experts strongly recommend structured interviews during the hiring process to permit candidate-to-candidate comparisons.

Indirect Methods   These techniques obtain data without any direct contact with respondents. This approach may entail observing someone without his or her knowledge. Other examples include searching existing records, such as personnel files, for data on variables such as absenteeism, turnover, and output. This method reduces rater error and generally is used in combination with one of the previously discussed techniques.

Evaluating Research Methods

All research methods can be evaluated from three perspectives: (1) generalizability, (2) precision in control and measurement, and (3) realism of the context.[8] *Generalizability,* which also is referred to as external validity, reflects the extent to which results from one study are generalizable to other individuals, groups, or situations. *Precision in control and measurement* pertains to the level of accuracy in manipulating or measuring variables. A *realistic context* is one that naturally exists for the individuals participating in the research study. In other words, realism implies that the context is not an artificial situation contrived for purposes of conducting the study. Table A-1 presents an evaluation of the five most frequently used research methods, in terms of these three perspectives.

In summary, there is not one best research method. Choosing a method depends on the purpose of the specific study.[9] For example, if high control is necessary, as in testing for potential radiation leaks in pipes that will be used at a nuclear power plant, a laboratory experiment is appropriate (see Table A-1). In contrast, sample surveys would be useful if a company wanted to know the generalizable impact of a television commercial for light beer.

Evaluating Research Conclusions

There are several issues to consider when evaluating the quality of a research study. The first is whether results from the specific study are consistent with those from past research. If not, it is helpful to determine why discrepancies exist. For instance, it is insightful to compare the samples, research methods, measurement of variables, statistical analyses, and general research procedures across the discrepant studies. Extreme differences suggest that future research may be needed to reconcile the inconsistent results. In the meantime, however, we need to be cautious in applying

• TABLE A-1 Assessment of Frequently Used Research Methods

Method	Generalizability	Precision in Control and Measurement	Realistic Context
Case study	Low	Low	High
Sample survey	High	Low	Low
Field study	Moderate	Moderate	High
Laboratory experiment	Low	High	Low
Field experiment	Moderate	Moderate	Moderate

Source: Adapted in part from Joseph E. McGrath, Joanne Martin, and Richard A. Kulka, *Judgment Calls in Research* (Beverly Hills, Calif.: Sage Publications, 1982).

research findings from one study that are inconsistent with those from a larger number of studies.

The type of research method used is the second consideration. Does the method have generalizability (see Table A–1)? If not, check the characteristics of the sample. If the sample's characteristics are different from the characteristics of your work group, conclusions may not be relevant for your organization. Sample characteristics are very important in evaluating results from both field studies and experiments.

The level of precision in control and measurement is the third factor to consider. It is important to determine whether valid measures were used in the study. This can be done by reading the original study and examining descriptions of how variables were measured. Variables have questionable validity when they are measured with one-item scales or "ad-hoc" instruments developed by the authors. In contrast, standardized scales tend to be more valid because they typically are developed and validated in previous research studies. We have more confidence in results when they are based on analyses using standardized scales. As a general rule, validity in measurement begets confidence in applying research findings.

Finally, it is helpful to brainstorm alternative explanations for the research results. This helps to identify potential problems within research procedures.

• READING A SCIENTIFIC JOURNAL ARTICLE

Research is published in scientific journals and professional magazines. *Journal of Applied Psychology* and *Academy of Management Journal* are examples of scientific journals reporting OB research. *Management Review* and *HRMagazine* are professional magazines that sometimes report research findings in general terms. Table A–2 contains a list of 54 highly regarded management journals and magazines. You may find this list to be a useful source of information when writing term papers.

Scientific journal articles report results from empirical research studies, overall reviews of research on a specific topic, and theoretical articles. To help you obtain relevant information from scientific articles, let us consider the content and structure of these three types of articles.[10]

Empirical Research Studies

Reports of these studies contain summaries of original research. They typically comprise four distinct sections consistent with the logical steps of the research process model shown in Figure A–1. These sections are:

- *Introduction:* This section identifies the problem being investigated and the purpose of the study. Previous research pertaining to the problem is reviewed and sometimes critiqued.
- *Method:* This section discusses the method used to conduct the study. Characteristics of the sample or subjects, procedures followed, materials used, measurement of variables, and analytic procedures typically are discussed.

• **TABLE A-2**   A List of Highly Regarded Management Journals and Magazines

1. *Administrative Science Quarterly*	28. *Journal of Organizational Behavior Management*
2. *Journal of Applied Psychology*	29. *Organizational Dynamics*
3. *Organizational Behavior and Human Decision Processes*	30. *Monthly Labor Review*
4. *Academy of Management Journal*	31. *Columbia Journal of World Business*
5. *Psychological Bulletin*	32. *Journal of Business Research*
6. *Industrial and Labor Relations Review*	33. *Group and Organizational Studies*
7. *Journal of Personality and Social Psychology*	34. *Human Resource Planning*
8. *Academy of Management Review*	35. *Journal of Management Studies*
9. *Industrial Relations*	36. *Administration and Society*
10. *Journal of Labor Economics*	37. *Negotiation Journal*
11. *Personnel Psychology*	38. *Arbitration Journal*
12. *American Psychologist*	39. *Compensation and Benefits Review*
13. *Journal of Labor Research*	40. *Journal of Collective Negotiations in the Public Sector*
14. *Journal of Vocational Behavior*	41. *Public Personnel Management*
15. *Journal of Applied Behavioral Science*	42. *Organizational Behavior Teaching Review**
16. *Occupational Psychology*	43. *Review of Business and Economic Research*
17. *Sloan Management Review*	44. *Personnel Journal*
18. *Journal of Conflict Resolution*	45. *Journal of Small Business Management*
19. *Human Relations*	46. *SAM Advanced Management Journal*
20. *Journal of Human Resources*	47. *Business Horizons*
21. *Labor Law Journal*	48. *Business and Public Affairs*
22. *Harvard Business Review*	49. *Personnel Administrator†*
23. *Social Forces*	50. *Mid-Atlantic Journal of Business*
24. *Journal of Management*	51. *Training and Development Journal*
25. *California Management Review*	52. *Akron Business & Economic Review*
26. *Journal of Occupational Behavior*	53. *Southwest Journal of Business and Economics*
27. *Public Administration Quarterly*	54. *North Carolina Review of Business and Economics*

* Now titled *Journal of Management Education.*
† Now titled *HRMagazine.*

Source: Marian M. Extejt and Jonathan E. Smith, "The Behavioral Sciences and Management: An Evaluation of Relevant Journals," *Journal of Management,* September 1990, p. 545.

- *Results:* A detailed description of the documented results is presented.
- *Discussion:* This section provides an interpretation, discussion, and implications of results.

Review Articles

These articles "are critical evaluations of material that has already been published. By organizing, integrating, and evaluating previously published material, the author of a review article considers the progress of current research toward clarifying a problem."[11] Although the structure of these articles is not as clear-cut as reports of empirical studies, the general format is:

- A statement of the problem.
- A summary or review of previous research that attempts to provide

the reader with the state of current knowledge about the problem (meta-analysis frequently is used to summarize past research).
- Identification of shortcomings, limitations, and inconsistencies in past research.
- Recommendations for future research to solve the problem.

Theoretical Articles

These articles draw on past research to propose revisions to existing theoretical models or to develop new theories and models. The structure is similar to that of review articles.

• BACK TO THE NTSB STUDY

This module was introduced with a National Transportation Safety Board study that suggested it is not safe to wear rear-seat lap belts while riding in an automobile. Given what we have just discussed, take a few minutes now to jot down any potential explanations for why the NTSB findings conflict with past research supporting the positive benefits of rear-seat lap belts. Now compare your thoughts with an evaluation presented in the *University of California, Berkeley Wellness Letter*.

> Critics claim that the NTSB study paints a misleadingly scary picture by focusing on 26 unrepresentative accidents, all unusually serious and all but one frontal. The National Highway Traffic Safety Administration has strongly disputed the board's findings, citing five earlier studies of thousands of crashes showing that safety belts—including lap belts—are instrumental in preventing death and injury. And a new study of 37,000 crashes in North Carolina shows that rear-seat lap belts reduce the incidence of serious injury and death by about 40 percent. . . .
>
> In the meantime, most evidence indicates that you should continue to use rear-seat lap belts. You can minimize the risk of injury by wearing them as low across the hips as possible and keeping them tight.[12]

The NTSB findings were based on a set of unrepresentative serious frontal accidents. In other words, the NTSB's sample was not reflective of the typical automobile accident. Thus, the generalizability of the NTSB results is very limited.

• NOTES

[1] "Buckle Up in the Rear Seat?" *University of California, Berkeley Wellness Letter,* August 1987, p. 1.

[2] Fred N. Kerlinger, *Foundations of Behavioral Research* (New York: Holt, Rinehart & Winston, 1973), p. 18. (Emphasis added.)

[3] See Anthony H. Winefield and Marika Tiggemann, "Employment Status and Psychological Well-Being: A Longitudinal Study," *Journal of Applied Psychology,* August 1990, pp. 455–59.

[4] S. S. Stevens, "Mathematics, Measurement, and Psychophysics," in *Handbook of Experimental Psychology,* ed. S. S. Stevens (New York: John Wiley & Sons, 1951), p. 1.

[5] A thorough discussion of the importance of measurement is provided by Donald P. Schwab, ''Construct Validity in Organizational Behavior,'' in *Research in Organizational Behavior,* eds. Barry M. Staw and Larry L. Cummings (Greenwich, Conn.: JAI Press, 1980), pp. 3–43.

[6] See Judith L. Komaki, ''Toward Effective Supervision: An Operant Analysis and Comparison of Managers at Work,'' *Journal of Applied Psychology,* May 1986, pp. 270–79. Results from the sailing study can be found in Judith L. Komaki, Mitzi L. Desselles, and Eric D. Bowman, ''Definitely Not a Breeze: Extending an Operant Model of Effective Supervision to Teams,'' *Journal of Applied Psychology,* June 1989, pp. 522–29.

[7] Advantages and disadvantages of different interviews are discussed by Richard D. Arvey and Robert H. Faley, *Fairness in Selecting Employees,* 2nd ed. (Reading, Mass.: Addison-Wesley Publishing, 1988).

[8] A complete discussion of research methods is provided by Thomas D. Cook and Donald T. Campbell, *Quasi-Experimentation: Design & Analysis Issues for Field Settings* (Chicago: Rand McNally, 1979).

[9] Ibid.

[10] This discussion is based on material presented in the *Publication Manual of the American Psychological Association,* 3rd ed. (Washington, D.C.: American Psychological Association, 1983).

[11] Ibid., p. 21.

[12] ''Buckle Up in the Rear Seat?''

B

Advanced Learning Module

Personality Testing: Some Words of Caution for Managers

echniques for measuring personality vary widely. Inferences about personality typically are drawn from one or more of three sources. Those sources are adjective checklists (e.g., *thrifty, lenient, individualistic*), self-report inventories (e.g., the Minnesota Multiphasic Personality Inventory), and projective tests (e.g., interpretations of Rorschach inkblots and pictures). Although numerous personality traits have been isolated over the years, the so-called big five are agreeableness, conscientiousness, emotional stability, extroversion, and openness to experience. In a recent meta-analysis of 162 samples involving 23,994 people from many occupations, only one of the big five—conscientiousness—consistently predicted relevant job performance criteria across all occupations. The performance criteria included job and training proficiency and personnel data such as tenure, salary level, and turnover. Results were mixed for the other four traits.[1]

Controversy continues to swirl around all kinds of personality testing. Some companies, such as Intel Corporation, reject the idea of personality testing altogether; others rely on it to varying extents. Legitimate complaints involve claims of racial and ethnic bias, scoring problems, and outdated norms.[2] Within the workplace, questions concerning if and how to use personality tests are being influenced by changing times.

The following tips can help managers avoid abuses and costly discrimination lawsuits when using personality testing for employment-related decisions:

- Rely on reputable, licensed psychologists for selecting and overseeing the administration, scoring, and interpretation of personality tests.
- Do not rely on homemade personality theories or tests. Managers, like anyone else, tend to formulate their own cause-and-effect beliefs about personality traits and behavior. These beliefs are referred to as **implicit personality theories.** Unfortunately, implicit personality theories all too often are a vehicle for prejudice and bigotry. For example, it is often said that people with red hair have hot tempers. When making employment-related decisions profoundly affecting the quality of people's lives, managers need to question and discipline their implicit personality theories to weed out such unfounded prejudices and stereotypes.
- Do not make employment-related decisions strictly on the basis of personality test results. Supplement any personality test data with information from reference checks, personal interviews, ability tests, and job performance records.
- Avoid hiring people on the basis of specified personality profiles. As a case in point, there is no distinct "managerial personality." One recent study found the combination of mental ability and personality to be responsible for only 21 percent of the variation in managerial success.[3] However, personality profiles can be helpful in identifying training and development needs (see, for example, Table B–1).
- Regularly assess any possible adverse impact on women and minorities.
- Be wary of slickly packaged gimmicks claiming to accurately assess personalities. A prime example is *graphology*, whereby handwriting "experts" infer personality traits and aptitudes from samples of one's penmanship. This European transplant has enjoyed zealous growth in the United States, with over 1,000 corporate users by the late 1980s.[4]

• **TABLE B-1**   Do the Heads of Large and Small Businesses Have Different Personality Traits?

It takes a certain something to head a company, but apparently that something differs sharply depending on whether the executive runs a start-up or a giant corporation.

London House, a psychological research firm, administered tests to 70 chief executives—half of them at Fortune 500 companies and half of them from the 500 list of *Inc.*, a magazine for entrepreneurs. The tests measured drive and creativity along with the ability to reason and handle stress. The results: Members of the two groups showed very different personality traits.

The Inc. 500 executives were far more able to work under pressure than their big-company counterparts. They were more satisfied with doing a job for its own sake, but suffered more from feelings of inadequacy. Fortune 500 executives, on the other hand, demonstrated a strong drive to climb up through an organization and an instinct for leadership.

The standout skill of Fortune chiefs was their ability to communicate. On a vocabulary test with words such as jejune, obstreperous and abstemious, they scored better than 90% of a control group of corporate executives.

In contrast, the Inc. executives "were pretty poor in communications," says Donald Moretti, director of testing systems at London House, which is based in Park Ridge, Ill. The Inc. executives' strong suit: Creativity, an area in which the Fortune executives didn't shine at all.

Source: Jolie Solomon, "Managing: Corporate Heads Show Split in Personalities," *The Wall Street Journal,* August 17, 1989, p. B1.

But judging from recent research evidence, graphology is an inappropriate hiring tool and probably an open invitation to discrimination lawsuits. In a meta–analysis of 17 studies, 63 graphologists did a slightly *worse* job of predicting future performance than did a control group of 51 nongraphologists. Indeed, psychologists with no graphology experience consistently outperformed the graphologists.[5]

• Finally, no personality testing is better than haphazard or invalid testing.

• NOTES

[1] For complete details, see Murray R. Barrick and Michael K. Mount, "The Big Five Personality Dimensions and Job Performance: A Meta-Analysis," *Personnel Psychology,* Spring 1991, pp. 1–26.

[2] For example, see John G. Nicholls, Barbara G. Licht, and Ruth A. Pearl, "Some Dangers of Using Personality Questionnaires to Study Personality," *Psychological Bulletin,* November 1982, pp. 572–80; Richard I. Lanyon, "Personality Assessment," in *Annual Review of Psychology,* eds. Mark R. Rosenzweig and Lyman W. Porter (Palo Alto, Calif.: Annual Reviews Inc., 1984), Vol. 35, pp. 667–701; "A Test by Any Other Name," *Personnel Management,* March 1989, pp. 47–51; and Robert T. Carter and Jane L. Swanson, "The Validity of the Strong Interest Inventory with Black Americans: A Review of the Literature," *Journal of Vocational Behavior,* April 1990, pp. 195–209. Criticisms of personality testing are answered in Robert Hogan and Robert A. Nicholson, "The Meaning of Personality Test Scores," *American Psychologist,* August 1988, pp. 621–26.

[3] For details, see Jeffery S. Schippmann and Erich P. Prien, "An Assessment of the Contributions of General Mental Ability and Personality Characteristics to Managerial Success, *Journal of Business and Psychology,* Summer 1989, pp. 423–37.

[4] See M. Susan Taylor and Kathryn K. Sackheim, "Graphology," *Personnel Administrator,* May 1988, pp. 71–76.

[5] Data from Efrat Neter and Gershon Ben-Shakhar, "The Predictive Validity of Graphological Inferences: A Meta-Analytic Approach," *Personality and Individual Differences,* no. 7, 1989, pp. 737–45.

Glossary

ability A durable characteristic responsible for a person's optimum performance on mental and physical tasks. (Ch. 3)

adhocracy Fluid networks of individuals used to perform tasks of temporary importance. (Ch. 18)

aggressive style Self-enhancing method of expression that tends to take advantage of others. (Ch. 12)

aided-analytic A decision-making strategy in which technology is used to analyze and evaluate alternatives. (Ch. 15)

Asch effect The distortion of individual judgment by group opposition. (Ch. 9)

assertive style Self-enhancing method of communication which does not violate basic human rights of dignity and respect. (Ch. 12)

attention The process of becoming consciously aware of something or someone. (Ch. 4)

attitude A learned response pattern that is consistent with respect to a given object or situation. (Ch. 3)

authority The right to seek compliance. (Ch. 10)

barriers to communication Personal and environmental characteristics that interfere with the transmission or reception of a message. (Ch. 12)

baseline data Measurement of preintervention behaviors observed without the target person's knowledge. (Ch. 7)

behavior chart Graphing technique showing both preintervention and postintervention behavior data. (Ch. 7)

behavior modeling A learning process by which one observes and imitates the actions of others. (Ch. 8)

behavior modification Managing environmental cues and consequences to strengthen or weaken specific behaviors. (Ch. 7)

behavioral contingencies The concept that if a certain antecedent is present it will lead to a certain behavior that in turn leads to a specific consequence. (Ch. 7)

behavioral learning theory Theory of how behavior is developed through personal interaction with the environment. (Ch. 7)

behavioral self-management The process of changing one's own behavior by managing cues, cognitions, and consequences. (Ch. 7)

behaviorally anchored rating scales (BARS) A graphical performance rating technique with a continuum of specific behaviors. (Ch. 13)

behaviorism A philosophy of human behavior that focuses on actions instead of mental processes. (Ch. 7)

bounded rationality The idea that decision makers are restricted by a variety of constraints when solving problems. (Ch. 15)

brainstorming The generation of multiple ideas and alternatives for solving problems. (Ch. 15)

buffers Resources or administrative changes that alleviate the causes of burnout. (Ch. 16)

bureaucracy Max Weber's concept of the ideally efficient organization. (Ch. 17)

burnout The absence of the desire to perform effectively caused by long-term emotional exhaustion and negative attitudes. (Ch. 16)

cafeteria benefit plans Employees determine the make-up of their individual benefit packages. (Ch. 2)

career The pattern of work-related experiences that spans a person's life. (Ch. 8)

career anchor The self-image an individual develops around his/her work that both propels and restrains work-related decisions. (Ch. 8)

career appraisal Obtaining and using work-related feedback from work and nonwork sources. (Ch. 8)

career exploration Obtaining career-related information about oneself and the environment. (Ch. 8)

career management The ongoing process of gathering information, setting and refining goals, and assessing work-related progress and satisfaction. (Ch. 8)

career plateauing   The point in a career at which future promotion seems improbable. (Ch. 2)

career stages   Common work experiences encountered at similar points in careers regardless of occupation or organization. (Ch. 8)

case study   A thorough investigation of a single entity. (Ch. 1)

causal attributions   Suspected causes of behavior. (Ch. 4)

centralized decision making   Key decisions are made only by top management. (Ch. 18)

classical conditioning   A basic form of learning involving reflex training. (Ch. 7)

clique   Friendship-based, informal cluster of network members. (Ch. 9)

closed system   A self-sufficient entity with no dependence on the environment. (Ch. 17)

coalition   An informal group whose specific purpose is the active pursuit of a single goal. (Ch. 10)

coercive power   The ability to achieve compliance to the extent that a manager can threaten punishment. (Ch. 10)

cognitions   One's knowledge, beliefs, or opinions about oneself and one's surroundings. (Ch. 3)

cognitive categories   Perceptual grouping of objects based on their equivalencies. (Ch. 4)

cognitive style   The pairing of perception and judgment tendencies a person uses to evaluate information. (Ch. 3)

cohesiveness   The process by which group unity (a "we" feeling) transcends individual interests. (Ch. 11)

collaboration   A dimension of cooperation that occurs when group members share responsibility for work outcomes. (Ch. 11)

communication   The exchange of information and the perception of meaning between a sender and a receiver. (Ch. 12)

communication competence   A performance-based index reflecting a person's proficiency in using language in the social context. (Ch. 12)

communication distortion   Deliberate modification of a message. (Ch. 12)

compressed workweek   Working approximately 40 hours in less than five days. (Ch. 2)

conflict   Universal term covering all types of antagonistic interactions. (Ch. 10)

consensus   The outcome of group decision making that occurs when all agree to support the group's chosen course of action. (Ch. 15)

consideration   A leadership behavior that creates mutual respect by focusing on group members' needs and desires. (Ch. 14)

contingency approach   Use of different management techniques dependent on the situation and environment. (Ch. 1)

contingency approach to organization design   The process of organization design that takes into consideration both the organization's needs and the effects of the environment. (Ch. 18)

contingency factors   Situational characteristics that make one leadership style more effective than another. (Ch. 14)

continuous reinforcement   The strengthening of a behavior by reinforcing every instance of that behavior. (Ch. 7)

coordination   A dimension of cooperation that occurs when subtasks are assigned sequentially to group members. (Ch. 11)

coping   The process of managing extraordinary demands made on a person. (Ch. 16)

core job dimensions   Common characteristics found to some degree in all positions. (Ch. 5)

creativity   The development of anything new and currently non-existent. (Ch. 15)

critical incidents   Examples of good or bad performance noted at the time of their occurrence. (Ch. 13)

cross-cultural management   The ability to know and direct the behaviors of people from diverse cultural backgrounds in order to achieve an organizational goal. (Ch. 19)

cross-functionalism   Combining specialists from different areas to form a management team. (Ch. 11)

culture   A pattern of basic assumptions proved valid over time and taught to new group members as correct reactions to certain problems and opportunities. (Ch. 19)

decentralized decision making   Key decisions are made by middle and lower-level management. (Ch. 18)

decision making   Identifying and choosing alternative solutions that lead to a desired end. (Ch. 15)

delegation   The process of assigning decision-making power to subordinates. (Ch. 10)

Delphi technique   A group process which anonymously generates ideas or judgments, typically from questionnaires, rather than face-to-face. (Ch. 15)

descriptive relevance   The extent to which applied research translates to real-life situations. (Ch. 1)

devil's advocacy   A conflict stimulation technique that involves assigning someone the role of the "naysayer." (Ch. 10)

dialectic method   A programmed conflict technique that involves managers structuring debate by use of opposing viewpoints. (Ch. 10)

differentiation   Division of labor by technical specialization. (Ch. 18)

dysfunctional conflict   Antagonistic interaction that works against the organization's goals or performance. (Ch. 10)

employee assistance programs   Company-sponsored programs of treatment for any employee problem that affects job performance. (Ch. 16)

employee substance abuse   Any time the use of drugs or alcohol is used to the extent that it alters a person's job performance. (Ch. 16)

equity theory   A model of motivation explaining how people try for fairness and justice in exchanges and relationships. (Ch. 6)

escalation of commitment   The tendency to adhere to an ineffective course of action even though it is unlikely to reverse a poor situation. (Ch. 15)

ethics   The study of moral issues and the propriety of choices made. (Ch. 3)

expectancy   A person's belief that a given amount of effort will yield a given level of performance. (Ch. 6)

expectancy theory   The idea that people are motivated to behave in ways that will generate desired, anticipated outcomes. (Ch. 6)

experienced meaningfulness   The extent to which an individual perceives his/her work as being worthwhile or important. (Ch. 5)

experienced responsibility   The extent to which an individual believes he/she is personally accountable for the outcomes of his/her job. (Ch. 5)

expert power   The ability to achieve compliance through the use of valued knowledge or information. (Ch. 10)

external factors   Elements or traits of the environment that are construed as causes for behavior. (Ch. 4)

external forces for change   Factors outside the organization that dictate a need for change. (Ch. 20)

external locus of control   A dimension of personality in which people tend to believe that their behavior is caused by forces outside their control. (Ch. 3)

extinction   The process of weakening a behavior by not reinforcing it in any manner. (Ch. 7)

extrinsic rewards   Rewards or positive outcomes, that come from the environment. (Ch. 13)

feedback   Objective information given to a worker regarding his/her job performance. (Ch. 13)

field study   Probing individual and group processes in real-life situations. (Ch. 1)

fight-or-flight response   A physiological response to stress that triggers hormonal changes that mobilize the body to meet extraordinary demands. (Ch. 16)

 itime   Job scheduling method whereby employees determine their own starting and finishing time within a given period. (Ch. 2)

formal group   Two or more people specifically organized to assist an organization in achieving its goals. (Ch. 9)

functional analysis   When a person-environment situation is reduced to behavioral contingencies. (Ch. 7)

functional conflict   Antagonistic interaction that works to support the organization's goals or performance. (Ch. 10)

functional social support   Mechanism that buffers the effects of stress in specific situations. (Ch. 16)

fundamental attribution bias   Tendency to believe that another person's behavior is caused by his/her internal factors rather than environmental factors. (Ch. 4)

gainsharing   Productivity measurement and calculation of a bonus designed to give workers a mutual share in any organizational productivity increase. (Ch. 13)

garbage can model   A model that purports that decision making occurs within a complex, sometimes haphazard, interaction of independent factors, including problems, solutions, participants, and choice opportunities. (Ch. 15)

global social support   The composite amount of support available through esteem support, informational support, social companionship, and instrumental support avenues. (Ch. 16)

goal   The purpose or target of an action. (Ch. 6)

goal commitment   The degree to which an individual is personally pledged to meeting an organizational goal. (Ch. 6)

goal difficulty   The amount of effort needed to meet a goal. (Ch. 6)

goal relevance   The extent to which applied research focuses on outcomes managers perceive as important. (Ch. 1)

goal specificity   The degree to which a goal may be measured. (Ch. 6)

group   Two or more freely interacting individuals who share norms, goals, and an identity. (Ch. 9)

groupthink   A deterioration of decision-making processes as a result of the overwhelming desire for group unanimity. (Ch. 9)

hardiness   A collection of personality characteristics that neutralizes occupational stress by transforming negative stressors into positive challenges. (Ch. 16)

hedonism   A behavorial principle that states that people are motivated to seek pleasure and to avoid pain. (Ch. 5)

hierarchical communication   Exchanges of information and influence between organizational members, at least one of whom holds a position of authority within the organization. (Ch. 12)

high-context cultures   A cultural tendency to rely heavily on situational cues for perception and communication. (Ch. 19)

holistic wellness approach   Encompasses nutritional awareness, stress reduction and relaxation, physical fitness, and environmental sensitivity to achieve lifestyle balance and harmony while promoting personal responsibility for one's health. (Ch. 16)

horizontal differentiation   A structural variable denoting the number of job categories represented in a work group. (Ch. 9)

hygiene factors   Elements in the work context or environment, such as company policy and coworkers, which are related to job dissatisfaction. (Ch. 5)

informal group   Two or more people united primarily for friendship. (Ch. 9)

information richness   Potential message-carrying capacity of data. (Ch. 12)

ingroup exchange   A type of leader-member interaction characterized by a leader-member partnership of mutual respect, influence, trust and a sense of common fates. (Ch. 14)

initiating structure   A leadership behavior that organizes and defines group member activities to maximize output. (Ch. 14)

instrumental cohesiveness   Sense of group unity that occurs when group members feel mutual dependency is necessary for achievement of group goals. (Ch. 11)

instrumental values   Different means or behaviors by which desired end-states are achieved. (Ch. 3)

instrumentality   Belief that a desired outcome is contingent on a certain level of performance. (Ch. 6)

integration   Specialists cooperating to achieve a specific organizational goal. (Ch. 18)

intelligence   A person's capability to think and reason constructively. (Ch. 3)

interaction involvement   The extent to which a person consciously involves himself/herself in ongoing conversation. (Ch. 12)

intermittent reinforcement   The strengthening of a behavior with a positive consequence or reward for some but not all instances of that behavior. (Ch. 7)

internal factors   Elements or traits within a person that are construed as causes for behavior. (Ch. 4)

internal forces for change   Factors within an organization that dictate a need for change. (Ch. 20)

internal locus of control   A dimension of personality in which people tend to believe that they control the events that affect their behavior. (Ch. 3)

internal motivation   The predisposition to perform a task because of the positive feelings aroused by doing well. (Ch. 5)

intrinsic rewards   Rewards, or positive motivators, that come from within the worker. (Ch. 13)

job design   Alteration of tasks or groups of tasks with the intent of improving the quality of employee job experience and productivity. (Ch. 5)

job enlargement   Varying a person's work by combining specialized tasks of comparable difficulty. (Ch. 5)

job rotation   Moving employees from one specialized task to another. (Ch. 5)

job satisfaction   The contentment, or lack of it, a person feels about his/her work. (Ch. 2)

job sharing   Two employees, each working part-time, performing a full-time job. (Ch. 2)

knowledge of results   The extent to which an individual is knowledgeable about the effectiveness of his/her work. (Ch. 5)

laboratory study   Probing individual and group processes in a contrived environment. (Ch. 1)

law of effect   Thorndike's concept that favorable consequences will cause repetition of certain actions, while unfavorable consequences will cause the extinction of certain actions. (Ch. 7)

leader trait   A physical or psychological characteristic that can be used to differentiate leaders from followers. (Ch. 14)

leader-member relations   Reflects the extent to which a leader has the support, loyalty, and trust of the work group. (Ch. 14)

leadership   A social influence process in which one person seeks the voluntary participation of others in order to reach organizational objectives. (Ch. 14)

leadership grid   A matrix formed by the intersection of the "concern for production" and "concern for people" dimensions of leadership behavior. (Ch. 14)

learned helplessness   The perception that one has no control over a situation or environment. (Ch. 3)

legitimate power   The ability to achieve compliance through use of a manager's formal position within the organization. (Ch. 10)

liaison individuals   Persons who consistently communicate grapevine or informal information. (Ch. 12)

line managers   People with decision-making authority. (Ch. 17)

listening   Actively interpreting verbal messages. (Ch. 12)

listening with understanding   Empathetic reception of a message. (Ch. 12)

low-context cultures   A cultural tendency to rely heavily on the literal spoken and written word for perception and communication. (Ch. 19)

maintenance roles   A category of functional roles that allows a group to develop constructive interpersonal relationships. (Ch. 9)

management   Working with and through others to efficiently achieve organizational goals. (Ch. 1)

matrix organization   An approach to organization design that combines vertical and horizontal authority to accomplish some specific task or project. (Ch. 18)

mechanistic organizations   Tightly managed units with

strict rules, narrowly defined tasks, and top-down communication. (Ch. 18)

mentoring Forming and maintaining a developmental relationship between a senior and a junior person within an organization. (Ch. 8)

met expectations The difference between what a person anticipates getting from a job, and what he/she actually receives. (Ch. 5)

meta-analysis A statistical pooling method that yields general conclusions or patterns about given variables, even when many different studies are used. (Ch. 1)

monochronic time The rigid adherence to ordered, precise interpretation of public time. (Ch. 19)

motivating potential score Index representing the extent to which job characteristics generate a predisposition to perform a task because of the positive feelings of doing a job well. (Ch. 5)

motivation Psychological processes that stimulate direction and persistence of voluntary goal-directed actions. (Ch. 5)

motivation to manage The strength of personal traits positively correlated with rapid, upward career movement and managerial effectiveness. (Ch. 1)

motivators Job factors related to the content of the task that can cause a person to move from a state of no satisfaction to satisfaction. (Ch. 5)

mutuality of interest Win-win situations in which cooperating with potential adversaries serves one's self-interest. (Ch. 10)

natural rewards Reinforcing consequences resulting from everyday personal interactions. (Ch. 7)

need for achievement To increase self-regard, rival and surpass others, excel one's self in any task. (Ch. 5)

need for affiliation Preference for excelling at maintaining social relationships and being well liked. (Ch. 5)

need for power One's desire for influence and control of others. (Ch. 5)

needs Physiological or psychological deficiencies that arouse behavior. (Ch. 5)

needs analysis Determining the skills and capabilities employees must possess in order for an organization to meet its goals. (Ch. 20)

negative inequity Occurs when a person perceives that a relevant co-worker is enjoying greater outcomes for similar, or smaller, inputs. (Ch. 6)

negative reinforcement The process of strengthening a behavior by contingently withdrawing or terminating a negative situation. (Ch. 7)

noise Anything that interferes with the transmission or reception of a message. (Ch. 12)

nominal group technique Group decision making procedure that aids in evaluating and selecting solutions. (Ch. 15)

nonanalytic Using a predetermined, simplified rule to make a decision. (Ch. 15)

nonassertive style Timid and self-denying method of communication. (Ch. 12)

nonprogrammed decisions Novel and unstructured decisions that require unique solutions. (Ch. 15)

nonverbal communication Any message, sent or received, by a method other than spoken or written word(s). (Ch. 12)

norm A shared attitude, opinion, action or feeling that directs the behavior of two or more people. (Ch. 8)

office automation The computerized technology that is used to obtain, store, analyze, retrieve, and communicate information. (Ch. 20)

open system An entity that must constantly interact with the environment to function and survive. (Ch. 17)

operant behavior Behavior learned through contingent cues and consequences. (Ch. 7)

optimizing Solving problems by implementing the best possible solution. (Ch. 15)

organic organizations Flexible and fluid networks of individuals who freely interact to perform a variety of tasks. (Ch. 18)

organization System of consciously coordinated activities of two or more people. (Ch. 17)

organization chart Graphic representation of formal authority and task assignments. (Ch. 17)

organization development Process whereby managers plan administrative and leadership changes designed to motivate commitment, coordination, and competence among workers. (Ch. 20)

organizational behavior A research and application-oriented interdisciplinary field devoted to understanding and managing people at work. (Ch. 1)

organizational culture The consensus of shared values, symbolic devices, and social ideals that binds members of an organization together. (Ch. 19)

organizational politics Manipulative acts of influence designed to improve or protect the self-interest of individuals or groups. (Ch. 10)

organizational socialization The process by which an individual learns the norms, values, and behaviors required for him/her to acceptably function in an organization. (Ch. 8)

organization-based self-esteem (OBSE) A concept of one's own self-worth as it pertains to the organization. (Ch. 3)

outgroup exchange A type of leader-member interaction characterized by a leader-member relationship without mutual trust, influence, and respect. (Ch. 14)

participative management A process whereby employees have an active role in direction and change of the organization. (Ch. 15)

part-time work Working less than the amount of hours considered to be normal full-time employment. (Ch. 2)

pay for performance Monetary rewards that are tied, at least in part, to results or accomplishments. (Ch. 13)

perception A mental and cognitive process that enables people to interpret and understand their surroundings. (Ch. 4)

perceptual model of communication A depiction of information processing in which receivers create meaning in their own minds. (Ch. 12)

performance appraisal A manager's evaluation of a worker's traits, behaviors, and/or accomplishments. (Ch. 13)

persistence The effort given to a task over a period of time. (Ch. 6)

personality That combination of physical and emotional traits that give a person his/her identity. (Ch. 3)

personalized power The ability to achieve compliance while giving major emphasis to self-aggrandizement. (Ch. 10)

polychronic time The flexible interpretation of time involving multiple, cyclical, and concurrent activities. (Ch. 19)

position power A dimension of situational control concerned with the degree to which the leader has formal authority to reward, punish, or in some other way obtain compliance of the group. (Ch. 14)

positive inequity Is experienced when an individual perceives that he/she is enjoying greater outcomes for similar, or smaller, inputs than a relevant co-worker. (Ch. 6)

positive reinforcement The process of strengthening a behavior by consistently presenting a favorable consequence or reward. (Ch. 7)

problem Occurs when an actual situation is different from a desired one. (Ch. 15)

process-style Listeners who want extensive background information, including relevant importance of an issue, before entering a comprehensive discussion. (Ch. 12)

profit sharing Individual employees are given a portion of the economic profits of the business. (Ch. 13)

programmed conflict The encouragement of antagonistic interactions involving honest and constructive disagreement. (Ch. 10)

programmed decisions Repetitive and routine decisions that are made by some prescribed procedure within an organization. (Ch. 15)

proxemics The study of interpersonal space within the context of cultural expectations. (Ch. 19)

psychological contract Reciprocal formal and informal expectations between the employer and the employee. (Ch. 8)

Punishment The process of weakening a behavior by consistently presenting an unfavorable consequence. (Ch. 7)

quality circles Small groups of volunteers whose main purpose is to analyze problems and to recommend changes to enhance productivity, quality, and cost reduction. (Ch. 11)

rational model A four-step model for decision making that involves identifying the problem, generating alternative solutions, and implementing and evaluating a selected solution. (Ch. 15)

readiness The degree to which a group member has the ability and desire to complete a task. (Ch. 14)

realistic job preview Giving recruits a practical, no-nonsense idea of job expectations. (Ch. 8)

reality shock The upset of the expected order of things that occurs to a newcomer anytime he/she enters a new organization. (Ch. 8)

reasons-style Listeners who first want to know the rationale of a communication message. (Ch. 12)

reciprocity The widely held belief that one should be paid back for one's actions. (Ch. 10)

referent power A manager's ability to achieve compliance through use of his/her own personality or charisma. (Ch. 10)

relationship-oriented style A leadership method in which the leader seems to be primarily interested in the success of interpersonal relationships. (Ch. 14)

relaxation response The physiological and psychological opposite of the fight-or-flight response. (Ch. 16)

resistance to change An emotional or behavioral response to real or imagined threats to the work routine. (Ch. 20)

respondent behavior Unlearned or reflexive reactions to stimuli. (Ch. 7)

results-style Listeners who first want to know the end-product of the communication message. (Ch. 12)

reward equity norm system by which rewards are commensurate with contribution. (Ch. 13)

reward power The ability to achieve compliance to the extent that a manager can promise or grant tangible rewards. (Ch. 10)

role ambiguity Occurs when an individual is not provided with clear expectations of his/her role. (Ch. 8)

role analysis technique An intervention method which endeavors to enhance cooperation among group members by discussion of their mutual expectations. (Ch. 20)

role conflict Is experienced by the focal person when different members of the role set hold different expectations of him/her. (Ch. 8)

role overload Occurs when the total of the role

sender's expectations exceeds an individual's capabilities. (Ch. 8)

roles   Sets of expected behaviors. (Ch. 8)

sample survey   A small number from the given population respond to questionnaires. (Ch. 1)

satisficing   Choosing a solution which is not necessarily the best, but simply good enough. (Ch. 15)

scenario technique   A speculative forecasting tool used to identify future states given certain environmental conditions. (Ch. 15)

schema   A mental picture of a particular event or type of stimulus. (Ch. 4)

scientific management   That sort of administration that guides business affairs through systematic observation, experiment and reasoning. (Ch. 1)

self-concept   A person's perception of himself/herself—physically, socially, and spiritually. (Ch. 3)

self-efficacy   A dimension of self-esteem encompassing one's belief in his/her chances of successfully achieving a certain goal. (Ch. 3)

self-esteem   A concept of one's own self-worth based on thorough self-evaluation. (Ch. 3)

self-fulfilling prophecy   One's beliefs or expectations determine behavior and, therefore, cause the realization of expectations. (Ch. 4)

self-managed team   Groups of workers who are given administrative authority over their task areas. (Ch. 11)

self-management leadership   The process of training others to lead themselves. (Ch. 11)

self-serving bias   One's tendency to take more credit for success than for failure. (Ch. 4)

self-talk   Self-evaluating thoughts expressed privately. (Ch. 7)

sex-role stereotype   Belief that differing attributes and abilities make men and women particularly suited to different roles. (Ch. 4)

shaping   Selective reinforcement of behaviors as they approach closer and closer approximations to the target behavior. (Ch. 7)

situational theories   A class of leadership theories that proposes that the effectiveness of a leadership style depends on the specific situation at hand. (Ch. 14)

skill   The ability to physically accomplish a specified task. (Ch. 3)

social facilitation   The theory that the performance of some tasks can be either aided or hindered through the mere presence of other people. (Ch. 9)

social information-processing model of job design   A model proposing that informal cues provided by other people affect one's perceptions of job characteristics. (Ch. 5)

social learning   The process of acquiring behavior through reciprocal interaction of one's cognitions, behavior, and environment. (Ch. 7)

social loafing   The tendency for individual effort to decline as group-size increases. (Ch. 9)

social network analysis   A sociological technique for graphing and categorizing social transactions to identify meaningful patterns. (Ch. 9)

social power   The ability to combine human, informational and material resources to reach a goal. (Ch. 10)

social support   The amount of perceived helpfulness gained from informal relationships. (Ch. 16)

socialized power   The ability to achieve compliance while showing concern for others. (Ch. 10)

sociotechnical model   An OD intervention model that purports that work environments represent an interwoven combination of technology and social systems, both internal and external to the organization. (Ch. 20)

socio-emotional cohesiveness   Sense of group unity that occurs when individuals derive emotional satisfaction from group participation. (Ch. 11)

span of control   Number of people reporting directly to a given manager. (Ch. 17)

spillover model   A theory that proposes that job and life satisfaction/dissatisfaction constantly impact each other. (Ch. 2)

staff personnel   People doing background research and providing technical expertise and recommendations to line managers. (Ch. 17)

stakeholder audit   Systematic identification of all constituencies significantly impacted by the organization's performance. (Ch. 17)

stereotypes   Largely oversimplified beliefs or expectations about groups of people. (Ch. 4)

strategic mission statement   A formal description of an organization's ultimate purpose. (Ch. 20)

strategic plan   The outline of an organization's direction and actions necessary to achieve long-term goals/results. (Ch. 20)

stress   An adaptive response to any external action, situation, or event that places special physical or psychological demands on a person. (Ch. 16)

stressful life events   Nonwork-related changes that disrupt a person's lifestyle or social relationships. (Ch. 16)

stressors   Environmental factors that force either a physical or a psychological adaptive response. (Ch. 16)

substitutes for hierarchy   A contingency approach to management in which situational factors such as work design, financial data, and emergent leadership can reduce or eliminate the need for constant direct supervision (Ch. 17)

support systems   Processes, techniques, and tools that organizations use to achieve efficiency and effectiveness. (Ch. 20)

survey research and feedback An intervention method that endeavors to promote improvement through the collection of anonymous surveys and return of data. (Ch. 20)

synergy The whole is greater than the sum of its parts (e.g., peanut butter and chocolate taste better together than they do separately). (Ch. 9)

task roles A category of functional roles that helps a group to define, clarify, and pursue a common goal. (Ch. 9)

task structure A dimension of situational control concerned with the amount of structure contained within tasks performed by the work group. (Ch. 14)

task-oriented style A leadership method in which the leader seems to be primarily interested in successfully completing tasks. (Ch. 14)

team A formally organized group of individuals charged with a specific function and who must depend on each other to achieve their goals. (Ch. 11)

team building A generic term encompassing the many techniques used to improve internal functioning of work groups. (Ch. 11)

team viability Team members' satisfaction and continued willingness to contribute. (Ch. 11)

telecommuting Receiving and sending work from a home computer to an office computer by using a modem. (Ch. 2)

terminal values The lifetime or endstate goals a person is striving to achieve. (Ch. 3)

theory An effective explanation as to why something happens or is true. (Ch. 1)

Theory Y A positive set of assumptions about human nature used by progressive managers with regard to perception of employees. (Ch. 1)

transactional leadership Focuses on the quality of interactions between managers and employees. (Ch. 14)

transformational leadership Occurs when leaders motivate employees to place organizational or group progress above personal interest. (Ch. 14)

trust Mutual faith in the intentions and behaviors of others. (Ch. 11)

unaided-analytic Decision making style in which no technology is used to analyze and evaluate alternatives. (Ch. 15)

underemployment Refers to a person being placed in a job requiring less than his/her full potentials determined by his/her education, training, or skills. (Ch. 2)

unity of command principle Hierarchical control mechanism whereby each employee reports to only one manager. (Ch. 17)

valence The value, either positive or negative, which a person places on outcomes. (Ch. 6)

value The belief that one mode of conduct or state of existence is preferable to another. (Ch. 3)

value attainment A model of job satisfaction that proposes results from a job allowing fulfillment of a person's important work values. (Ch. 5)

value system The organization and relative importance of preferable modes of conduct or states of existence. (Ch. 3)

vertical differentiation A structural variable denoting the number of hierarchical levels represented in a work group. (Ch. 9)

vertical dyad linkage (VDL) model A model of leadership theory that proposes that leaders develop unique relationships with each group member. (Ch. 14)

whistle blowing The reporting of questionable behavior or unethical conduct to higher management or outside agencies. (Ch. 3)

work ethic The extent to which an individual believes that hard work is the key to success and happiness. (Ch. 2)

work force demographics Statistical profiles of the characteristics and composition of the adult working population. (Ch. 2)

NAME INDEX

L

S

Z

SUBJECT INDEX